ADDITIONAL FEATURES

Chapter Outlines & Summaries provide a thorough review of each chapter.

Learning Objectives in the form of short-answer questions help you focus on the important topics in each chapter.

Quizzes with multiple choice and essay questions allow you to test your comprehension of each chapter and synthesize and apply the concepts you have learned. (Instructors must register in order for their students to be able to take the quizzes.)

Flashcards help you quickly learn and review all the important terminology introduced in each chapter.

In addition, the website includes a set of **Web Links** for each chapter, as well as a complete **Glossary**.

WEB ACTIVITIES

The following activities are available on the site.
Page numbers indicate where in the textbook each is referenced.

Discovering Human Sexuality
THIRD EDITION

Discovering Human Sexuality

THIRD EDITION

Simon LeVay
WEST HOLLYWOOD, CALIFORNIA

Janice Baldwin
UNIVERSITY OF CALIFORNIA
SANTA BARBARA

John Baldwin
UNIVERSITY OF CALIFORNIA
SANTA BARBARA

Sinauer Associates, Inc. • Publishers
Sunderland, Massachusetts U.S.A.

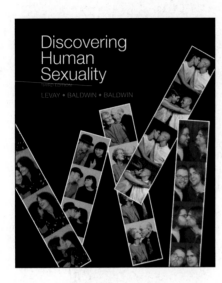

Discovering Human Sexuality, Third Edition
Copyright © 2015 by Sinauer Associates, Inc.

For information or to order, address:
Sinauer Associates
P.O. Box 407
Sunderland, MA 01375 USA
Fax: 413-549-1118
E-mail: publish@sinauer.com
Internet: www.sinauer.com

Library of Congress Cataloging-in-Publication Data

LeVay, Simon.
Discovering human sexuality / Simon LeVay, West Hollywood, CA, Janice Baldwin, University of California, Santa Barbara, John Baldwin, University of California, Santa Barbara. -- Third edition.
    pages cm
ISBN 978-1-60535-275-6 (alk. paper)
1. Sex (Psychology) 2. Sex (Biology) 3. Sex--Social aspects. I. Baldwin, Janice I. II. Baldwin, John D., 1941- III. Title.
 BF692.L47 2015
 306.7--dc23
                                        2014044757

Printed in the USA
5 4 3 2 1

About the Authors

Simon LeVay, PhD is a British-born neuroscientist turned writer and teacher. He has served on the faculties of Harvard Medical School and the Salk Institute for Biological Studies and has taught at Harvard; the University of California, San Diego; and Stanford University. He is best known for a 1991 study that described a difference in brain structure between heterosexual and homosexual men; this study helped spark a wealth of new research on the biology of sexual orientation. LeVay is the author or coauthor of 11 books, the most recent of which is a historical novel, *The Donation of Constantine* (Lambourn, 2013).

Janice Baldwin, PhD and **John Baldwin, PhD** are sociologists at the University of California, Santa Barbara. They have been collaborators in numerous studies and coauthored many articles in the areas of play, creativity, sexuality, and sex education, as well as the textbook *Behavior Principles in Everyday Life* (Prentice Hall). John Baldwin's latest book is *Ending the Science Wars* (Paradigm, 2008). The Baldwins coteach an undergraduate human sexuality course that is regularly voted best course at UCSB. They also teach an advanced seminar course on the same topic. Their students run a sex-ed website, SexInfoOnline (www.SexInfoOnline.com).

Brief Contents

Contents

Chapter 3 Men's Bodies 61

Chapter 4 Sex, Gender, and Transgender 87

Chapter 5 Attraction, Arousal, and Response 123

Chapter 6 Sexual Behavior 155

Chapter 9   Contraception and Abortion 265

Chapter 10 Sexuality across the Life Span: From Birth to Adolescence 305

Chapter 11 Sexuality across the Life Span: Adulthood 335

Chapter 12   Sexual Orientation 365

Chapter 13 Atypical Sexuality 401

Chapter 14 Sexual Disorders 431

Chapter 15   Sexually Transmitted Infections   461

Chapter 16 Sexual Assault, Harassment, and Partner Violence 493

Chapter 17 Sex as a Commodity 523

Preface

This past year was tough, making the switch to LeVay et al., but I'm glad I did it. Discovering Human Sexuality *is unique in both approach and content. The authors have a point of view, but still provide balanced coverage of controversial issues. The boxes are wonderful. One of the things I like about it is the inclusion of historical and cross-cultural detail in the boxes. It's a very readable and beautiful book. The illustrations and diagrams are excellent—the best of any text I have ever used.*

Josephine Caldwell-Ryan
Southern Methodist University

Discovering Human Sexuality, Third Edition, is the continuation of a textbook that originated in 2003 with the publication of *Human Sexuality* by Simon LeVay and Sharon Valente. Since then, the book has gone through several changes of authorship, format, and title. One consistency, however, has been the identity of the lead author. Another has been the book's high academic and pedagogical standards, which have earned it a prominent place in the market and broad praise from reviewers and users, including the kind words cited above.

The Second Edition of *Human Sexuality* appeared in 2006 with the same two authors. For the 2009 edition, however, Janice Baldwin replaced Sharon Valente. Also, we decided to produce two distinct versions of the book. One of them—*Human Sexuality*, Third Edition—continued the approach pioneered in the earlier editions. The other, which we titled *Discovering Human Sexuality*, was a somewhat shorter and more accessible version that demanded less prior knowledge on the part of the students, especially in the area of biology. John Baldwin joined LeVay and Janice Baldwin as third author of this version. In 2012 we continued with the same two versions (*Human Sexuality*, Fourth Edition, and *Discovering Human Sexuality*, Second Edition).

For the current edition we have decided to merge the two versions into one, which we have titled *Discovering Human Sexuality*, Third Edition. It was a difficult decision to make because both versions had been successful in the marketplace and each served a somewhat different need. However, the workload involved in producing two different textbooks at the same time was excessive. In addition, we realized that we could incorporate the best features of *Human Sexuality* into *Discovering Human Sexuality* by judicious changes to the text and by the addition of two appendices containing more advanced "optional" material.

Features of *Discovering Human Sexuality,* Third Edition

Important features of *Discovering Human Sexuality* distinguish our book from competing texts:

EVIDENCE-BASED APPROACH   We believe that human sexuality is an academic subject like any other, meaning that it should be grounded in reason. Throughout the book, we have sought to present statements that are supported by data, ideas that are tested or testable, and recommendations that are based on research. There are many unanswered questions in sexuality, of course—questions about how abnormal modes of sexual expression (paraphilic disorders) develop, for example, and how best to treat them. In dealing with these controversies, an evidence-based approach demands a nondogmatic style and a willingness to admit that not everything is known. Some students may feel challenged to enter the field of sex research themselves in order to help fill those gaps in our understanding.

Some human sexuality texts contain a great deal of advice to students, especially in the area of relationships. Much of this advice has no objective basis and seems designed more to transmit the authors' values than to foster an authentic learning experience. In *Discovering Human Sexuality*, we keep the total quantity of advice down and try to ensure that the advice we do give has been "field-tested." Even in such an elementary matter as how to put on a condom, many texts include useless steps, such as squeezing the tip of the condom to leave space for the ejaculate. Doing so serves no purpose—the man who could burst a condom with his ejaculate has yet to be born—and neither the World Health Organization nor the leading U.S. experts believe that it should be part of the instructions for condom use. It has become an element in the folklore that gets perpetuated by textbooks—though not by this one.

Literature citations are, of course, an important element of an evidence-based book. We have been surprised by how cavalierly some competing books deal with this issue—quite commonly, citations in the text are not matched by any corresponding entries in the bibliography. In *Discovering Human Sexuality* we have made every effort to ensure that references are fully documented. Another common practice that we consider unacademic is referring to original research studies by citing magazine or newspaper articles that mention them, rather than the journal articles in which the research was presented. Our policy has been to cite original sources wherever possible, and to use magazine and newspaper references for the kinds of topics they excel at, such as news stories, cultural trends, and the like.

EMPHASIS ON DIVERSITY Today's college students come from a wide range of backgrounds, and in their adult lives they will have to deal with people very different from themselves. Our text presents this diversity in a detailed and nonjudgmental fashion. For example, with regard to sexual orientation, we go far beyond "gay," "bisexual," and "straight": We talk about the ever-changing history of the butch-femme dichotomy in lesbian culture, women whose self-identity is too fluid for one-word labels, gay men who are "bears" or "bear cubs" or into the leather scene, what it's like to be gay and Asian-American or Native American, how the gay experience differs for different generations of Americans and for gay people around the world, and so on. Similarly, we take pains to discuss racial, ethnic, and religious diversity, as they affect sexuality, and of course diversity in the actual modes of sexual behavior—including some of the more unusual forms of sexual expression such as "adult babies" and men whose partners are (literally) dolls.

PRESENTATION STYLE Simon LeVay, Janice Baldwin, and John Baldwin are all experienced authors of college textbooks. In creating *Discovering Human Sexuality*, we have pooled our writing skills to ensure that the text is fully accessible, engaging, and relevant to students of diverse backgrounds. The result of these combined efforts is, we believe, the most readable and student-friendly human sexuality text on the market.

ART PROGRAM Another way that we have striven to maintain both comprehensibility and interest is through the illustrations. One might think that it would be a simple matter to illustrate a book on human sexuality, but in reality it is a significant challenge. Illustrating some of the concepts discussed in this book, especially in its more biologically oriented sections, requires a great deal of thought and design skill. Our publisher, Sinauer Associates, is an industry leader in the use of art as a pedagogical medium. Thanks to our publisher's efforts, many complex topics, such as the regulation of the menstrual cycle, have been given a visual representation that gracefully parallels and clarifies the accompanying text. Nearly every two-page spread in the book offers one or more illustrations—photographs, drawings, diagrams, graphs, or charts—relevant to the text on that spread. Besides their informative value, illustrations offer important visual relief. Some of our competitors' texts contain sequences of

up to ten pages without a single illustration—a definite challenge to the average student's attention span.

BOXES The 76 boxes are an important feature of the book. The boxes are organized into eight themes: Controversies; Biology of Sex; Cultural Diversity; Research Highlights; Sexual Health; Sex in History; Personal Points of View; and Society, Values, and the Law. Within each theme, the subjects range from the serious to the lighthearted, but they all attempt to broaden the reader's horizons with a more in-depth look at specific questions than is possible within the main text: What exactly does "losing one's virginity" mean to today's teenagers, behaviorally and emotionally? Is there more than one kind of female ejaculation? What's it like to be a rubber fetishist? Why do some Amazonian peoples believe that a child can have several fathers? In tackling these and many other questions, the boxes provide breaks from the steady flow of the text and allow students to consider specific issues in a more relaxed and informal way.

Other aids to learning and revision include key terms (indicated by boldfaced type and defined in a running glossary), FAQs (frequently asked questions), discussion questions, chapter summaries, Web resources, and recommended reading materials.

Discovering Human Sexuality's student companion website (sites.sinauer.com/discoveringhumansexuality3e) is an invaluable learning aid. This site parallels the text with a thorough set of study questions, animations, activities, Web topics, quizzes, and other resources. Website activities are linked to the text and are referenced in maroon type in the printed text. In addition, a complete set of instructor supplements is available to qualified adopters of the textbook. See the section on Media and Supplements for details on the full range of material that accompanies *Discovering Human Sexuality*.

The Third Edition

The following are examples of the many changes that we have made for the Third Edition:

- Chapter 1, "Sexuality: Pathways to Understanding," has been thoroughly rewritten. It now pays less attention to the history of sex research and more to the diversity of methods that are used to study sexuality. We discuss a specific example of the use of each methodological approach.

- We have added discussions of many topics that were not covered, or only briefly covered, in earlier editions. These topics include group sex (Chapter 6); data-mining studies based on OkCupid and other websites (Chapters 5, 12, and elsewhere); the influence of physical attractiveness on men's and women's satisfaction with their long-term relationships (Chapter 5); the new definitions of paraphilias and paraphilic disorders in *DSM-5* and the controversy surrounding them (Chapter 13); the current debate on how to respond vigorously and yet fairly to allegations of campus rape (Chapter 16); and the personalities and attitudes of men who use prostitutes (Chapter 17). We have also deleted numerous passages that seemed less interesting or instructive than they were a few years ago.

- We have added 19 new boxes on a wide range of topics, including "Foot Orgasms," "Pain-free Childbirth," "Feticide," "Why Gay Genes?" "STIs and the Law," and "What's It Like to Be a Porn Star?"

- We have of course taken the opportunity to update the book with the latest research, surveys, statistics, laws, medical advances, contraceptive techniques, and cultural happenings.

- The two appendices cover material that was not included in *Discovering Human Sexuality*, Second Edition. We present this material in the form of appendices so that instructors may include it or not as suits the purposes of their classes and the interests and backgrounds of their students. Appendix A is an abbreviated and updated version of the chapter "Sex and Evolution" from *Human Sexuality*, Fourth Edition. It tackles important questions that are addressed in few other undergraduate human sexuality textbooks, such as: What is the adaptive value of sexual reproduction? How does sexual selection work? What are the benefits and costs of male and female promiscuity? and What is the basis of incest avoidance? Appendix B lays out more detail on the role of the nervous system in sexual behavior and physiology than is presented in the main text, including, for example, the anatomy and functional role of the autonomic nervous system in genital responses.

Acknowledgments

Producing a modern college textbook such as this one requires the combined efforts of a much larger team of professionals than the three of us who are privileged to have our names on the front cover. The staff members of Sinauer Associates have produced, with great efficiency and good humor, a textbook of outstanding visual quality and educational value. Those with whom we have had the most enduring contacts are editor Sydney Carroll, production editor Martha Lorantos, and photo researcher David

McIntyre, but many others labored behind the scenes to ensure the book's high quality and timely production. We are especially grateful for the production oversight of Janice Holabird and Christopher Small, and for the creative cover design by Joan Gemme. We also thank Lou Doucette for her skillful copyediting; Jason Dirks, Carolyn Mailler, Mara Silver, Suzanne Carter, Ann Chiara, Thomas Friedmann, and Nate Nolet for their work on the media and supplements package; Marie Scavotto, Nancy Asai, and Susan McGlew for their effective work promoting the book; Johanna Walkowicz for obtaining outside reviews; and Penny Grant for sending us our checks on time!

Reviewers

We acknowledge with gratitude the extensive and constructive comments made by the people who reviewed chapters of *Discovering Human Sexuality* for the new edition. These reviewers are listed below. Helpful comments have also come from the Baldwins' students at the University of California, Santa Barbara.

Ernest Abel, *Wayne State University*
Amy Beeman, *San Diego Mesa College*
Kimberly Blackwell, *Hampton University*
Elizabeth Calamidas, *Richard Stockton College*
Michael Clayton, *Youngstown State University*
Karen Gee, *Mission College*
Samantha Gibeau, *Lane Community College*
John Hallock, *Pima Community College*
Julie Harris, *East Carolina University*
Lynda Hoggan, *Mt. San Antonio College*
Nathan Iverson, *California State Polytechnic University, Pomona*
Jason Lavender, *North Dakota State University*
Janet Lever, *California State University, Los Angeles*
Vicki Lucey, *Modesto Junior College*
Stephanie Marin, *California State Polytechnic University, Pomona*
Wanda C. McCarthy, *University of Cincinnati Clermont College*
Heather Meggers, *Birmingham Southern College*
Tami James Moore, *University of Nebraska at Kearney*
Peggy Oberstaller, *Lane Community College*
Carolyn Peterson, *University of Cincinnati*
Jason Rothman, *California State Polytechnic University, Pomona*
Justine Shuey, *Montgomery County Community College*
Peter Sparks, *Oregon State University–Cascades*
Paul Vasey, *University of Lethbridge*
James Vaughn, *University of Science and Arts of Oklahoma*

Media and Supplements

to accompany *Discovering Human Sexuality*, Third Edition

For the Student

Companion Website

sites.sinauer.com/discoveringhumansexuality3e

The *Discovering Human Sexuality*, Third Edition Companion Website includes a robust set of study and review aids—all available at no cost to the student. This online companion to the textbook takes the place of a printed study guide and includes the following resources:

- *Chapter Outlines*: Complete outlines of each chapter provide an overview of the chapter and include links to the relevant Study Questions for each section.

- *Chapter Summaries*: A thorough review of each chapter's content.

- *Learning Objectives*: The objectives help focus the student on the important concepts and topics in each chapter; each is referenced to specific textbook headings and pages.

- *Activities*: For selected chapters, animations, dynamic illustrations, and labeling exercises help the student learn and understand complex concepts and anatomical (and other) terms.

- *Study Questions*: An extensive set of interactive self-study questions covers the full range of content in every chapter.

- *Flashcards*: Students can quiz themselves on all the important terms from each chapter, or they can browse the list of terms as a review.

- *Web Links*: A set of online sites and resources relevant to each chapter.

- *Glossary*: A complete online version of the book's glossary.

- *Online Quizzes*: Two sets of questions are available for each chapter, for instructors to assign or make available to students as review exercises (instructor registration required):
  - Multiple-Choice Quizzes test student comprehension of the material covered in each chapter.
  - Essay Questions challenge students to synthesize and apply what they have learned.

For the Instructor

(available to qualified adopters)

Instructor's Resource Library

The *Discovering Human Sexuality*, Third Edition Instructor's Resource Library (IRL) contains a wealth of resources for use in course planning, lecture development, and assessment. Contents include:

- *Textbook Figures & Tables*: All of the textbook's figures (both line art and photographs) are provided as JPEG files at two sizes: high-resolution (excellent for use in PowerPoint) and low-resolution (ideal for web pages and other uses). All the artwork has been reformatted and optimized for exceptional image quality when projected in class.

- *PowerPoint Resources*: Two ready-to-use presentations are provided for each chapter:
  - A lecture presentation that includes text covering the entire chapter, with selected figures.
  - A figures presentation that includes all the figures and tables from the chapter.

- *Instructor's Manual*: The Instructor's Manual provides instructors with a variety of resources to aid in planning their course and developing their lectures. For each chapter, the manual includes a chapter overview, a chapter outline, the complete chapter summary, class discussion questions, teaching resources, and suggested readings.

- *Media Guide*: The Media Guide includes extensive lists of suggested video segments (and full-length titles) that are ideal for use as lecture starters or other in-class activities. Video suggestions (with links and sources) are provided for topics across all chapters, and suggested discussion questions are also included.

- *Test Bank*: The Test Bank consists of a broad range of questions covering all the key facts and concepts in each chapter. Each chapter includes multiple-choice, fill-in-the-blank, and, new for the Third Edition, short answer questions. Also included are all of the Companion Website quizzes (multiple-choice and essay), the textbook end-of-chapter questions, and the Media Guide discussion questions. All questions are keyed to Bloom's Taxonomy and referenced to specific textbook sections.

- *Computerized Test Bank*: The entire test bank is provided in Blackboard's Diploma software. Diploma makes it easy to assemble quizzes and exams from any combination of publisher-provided questions and instructor-created questions. In addition, quizzes and exams can be exported to many different course management systems, such as Blackboard and Moodle.

Online Quizzing

The *Discovering Human Sexuality* Companion Website features pre-built chapter quizzes (see above) that report into an online gradebook. Adopting instructors have access to these quizzes and can choose to either assign them or let students use them for review. (Instructors must register in order for their students to be able to take the quizzes.) Instructors also have the ability to add their own questions and create their own quizzes.

Value Options

eBOOK

Discovering Human Sexuality, Third Edition is available as an eBook, in several different formats. The eBook can be purchased as either a 180-day rental or a permanent (non-expiring) subscription. All major mobile devices are supported. For details on the eBook platforms offered, please visit www.sinauer.com/ebooks.

Looseleaf Textbook (ISBN 978-1-60535-379-1)

Discovering Human Sexuality is available in a three-hole punched, looseleaf format. Students can take just the sections they need to class and can easily integrate instructor material with the text.

Discovering Human Sexuality

THIRD EDITION

Chapter 1

Sexuality is a fundamental aspect of human nature.

Sexuality: Pathways to Understanding

Sexuality is a central and all-pervasive theme of human existence. At its best, sexuality charges our lives with energy, excitement, and love. It offers a deep sense of connectedness, capable of spanning and healing social divisions. It creates family, the primary unit of society and the cradle of future generations.

At its worst, sexuality brings prejudice, anguish, violence, and disease.

To begin our exploration of this powerful and mysterious force, we first ask what the terms "sex" and "sexuality" mean and why sexuality is a topic worth studying. We go on to review some of the ways in which human sexuality has changed between the origin of our species and the present day. Our purpose is to make clear that, even though there may be some eternal truths about sexuality, it is not static: It changes slowly as a result of evolutionary forces, and much faster under the influence of culture. We then go on to describe the variety of methods by which sexuality can be studied, methods that will be applied repeatedly throughout the remainder of the book.

To do it justice, we must approach human sexuality with open minds, with respect for diversity, and with all the modes of inquiry that have been used to illuminate human nature. Approached in this way, the topic is not just another step in your college career: It is a personal voyage of discovery that will help you to enjoy the best that sexuality has to offer, and to avoid the worst.

Sexuality Is a Broader Concept than Sex

The term **sex** has two meanings. First, it means the distinction between female and male—a distinction that, as we'll see in later chapters, is not as clear-cut as you might imagine. Second, it means engaging in sexual behaviors. These behaviors may be very obviously sexual because they are marked by genital phenomena such as vaginal lubrication, penile or clitoral erection, orgasm, and so on. But they also include behaviors that do not directly involve the genitals, such as courtship, as well as behaviors such as kissing that may or may not be sexual depending on context.

The term **sexuality** includes sex but also goes beyond it to encompass the entire realm of human experience that is more or less closely connected with sex. It means, for example, our gendered traits—the psychological traits that differ, to a greater or lesser extent, between women and men. It means our sexual and romantic attractions and relationships—who we find attractive or fall in love with, and how we establish, maintain, or dissolve sexual partnerships. It means becoming a parent (or preventing that from happening). It also includes the two-way relationship between our personal sexual identities and behaviors and social structures such as the law, religion, medicine, and politics.

Studying Sexuality Has Practical Benefits

There are many possible reasons why you have chosen to take a course in human sexuality. Maybe you're simply curious about a topic that is often treated with embarrassment, evasion, or flippancy. Maybe you are looking for ways to improve your own sex life, or you think you have sexual problems that need to be solved. Maybe you are planning a career that requires an understanding of human sexuality.

Regardless of your specific motives, many practical benefits are to be gained from taking this course and reading this textbook. Here are some examples:

- Improving your understanding of the structure and function of your genitals and those of your partners will help you give and receive more pleasure from sex.

- Learning more about how people communicate on sexual topics will increase your chances of forming and maintaining satisfying relationships and avoiding abusive ones.

- Learning about sexual diversity will encourage you to be more understanding of unusual sexual desires and behaviors—whether in others or in yourself.

- Educating yourself about contraception and sexually transmitted infections will lessen the chance that your sexual behavior may end up harming you or your partners.

- Becoming knowledgeable about sex will be an asset to you in your future career—most especially if you enter the medical or helping fields, but also in any career that brings you into contact with other people.

- Educating yourself about sex will enable you to educate others—including your friends and your own children, if you plan to have them.

- By learning to think critically about research, you will become a more discriminating consumer of media reports and advertising relating to sexuality.

sex A person's identity as female or male, or sexual behavior.

sexuality The feelings, behaviors, and identities associated with sex.

Sexuality Has Changed over Time

Most—but not all—women and men experience sexual desire and engage in sexual relationships at some point in their lives. This has likely been true across the course of human history and prehistory, and it is true around the world today. But the ways in which these desires and relationships express themselves have been extraordinarily varied. Here we sketch some of the changes that have occurred over time.

Sexuality has been influenced by evolution

Humans evolved from the common ancestors of humans and nonhuman primates, who lived about 7 million years ago. You might think that we could get some idea of early human sexuality by studying the sexual behavior of our closest relatives, the great apes (chimpanzees, bonobos, gorillas, and orangutans), on the assumption that these animals have changed less over time than we have.

It turns out, however, that there is a great deal of sexual diversity even among these closely related species. Among chimpanzees, for example, most sexual behavior is between males and females and has the potential to lead to pregnancy. Among bonobos, which look very similar to chimpanzees, sexual contact between individuals of the same sex is common. The function of such behavior is clearly not reproductive; rather, it serves the purposes of conflict resolution and alliance formation (Parish & de Waal, 2000). Among orangutans coercive sex—analogous to rape in humans—is common (Knott et al., 2010), but that's not true for bonobos. Some of these species differences are described in Appendix A.

Male primates, such as these golden snub-nosed monkeys, often fight over access to females.

One general characteristic of sexual behavior among our primate relatives is that more of it takes place than is strictly necessary for reproductive purposes—sometimes a great deal more. Another is that individuals *compete* for sex partners: Males often compete for access to the most fertile females, while females often compete for the attention of high-ranking males. You don't have to be a sex researcher to know that these kinds of competition are prevalent in our own species today. It's likely that competition for partners has characterized sexuality throughout human history and prehistory, and that this competition has driven the evolution of sex differences in appearance and behavior.

Early in the evolution of our species, humans probably lacked understanding of the connection between **coitus** (penile-vaginal intercourse) and reproduction. Of course, they acted *as if* they understood, just as our primate relatives do, but their sexual behavior was actually driven by instincts that required little conscious awareness. Even today, there are human cultures where people are unaware of biological facts that seem obvious to us, such as the fact that a child has just one father, or that pregnancy and childbirth result from a single act of coitus (**Box 1.1**).

Over the course of human history the trend toward an increasingly conscious understanding of how sex "works" has influenced human sexuality in directions that seem counterintuitive in evolutionary terms. For example, the knowledge that the deposition of semen (the male ejaculate) in the vagina is what causes pregnancy led to the introduction of contraceptive practices. These included withdrawal of the penis prior to ejaculation—a practice known already in Old Testament times—and the use of various kinds of barriers placed in the vagina. Similarly, methods intended to interrupt an established pregnancy—by use of certain herbs or poisons, or by black magic—were widely used in the Middle Ages, with varying success. As methods for contraception and abortion have improved over the centuries, so has it become increasingly possible to enjoy the pleasures of sex without its natural consequences. This has undoubtedly increased people's—especially women's—willingness to engage in sex both within and outside of established relationships.

Society has changed sexuality

Human sexuality has been greatly influenced by the development of social controls. The transition from a hunter-gatherer lifestyle to one of settled agriculture took place

coitus Penile-vaginal intercourse.

Box 1.1 Cultural Diversity

Meet My Dads

No matter how many men a woman has sex with, any child she bears has only a single biological father—the man whose sperm fertilized the woman's ovum. In most cultures around the world, people accept this reality of single paternity. Yet anthropologists have discovered an exception among many of the indigenous tribal societies of lowland South America (Amazonia and nearby areas). Here people believe that a man's semen remains in the woman's body indefinitely after sexual intercourse, so if several different men have sex with her before she becomes pregnant, then all of them contribute to the making of her child (Beckerman & Valentine, 2002).

This belief is called **partible paternity** ("divisible fatherhood"). By studying language relationships among the societies where partible paternity is found, anthropologist Robert Walker of the University of Missouri and his colleagues have traced it back to the distant past, probably to the time when the lowlands were first settled and the settlers spoke a common language (Walker et al., 2010).

What benefit does the concept of partible paternity confer? Anthropologists such as William Crocker of the Smithsonian Institution have found that the societies that believe in partible paternity engage in distinctive sexual practices (Crocker & Crocker, 2003). They may participate in rituals in which women engage in sex sequentially with multiple men. And unlike in other cultures, where men typically guard their wives from sexual contact with other males, men in these Amazonian tribes may freely offer their wives to male relatives as well as to powerful men who are actual or potential allies.

Partible paternity, and the practices associated with them, benefit women's efforts to raise children. That's because the multiple "fathers" of a given child may give gifts in exchange for sex, may support or protect the child, or may at least refrain from killing the child. (The killing of infants and children by men has traditionally been a significant cause of mortality in Amazonian cultures.)

What about the men? On the face of it, the notion of partible paternity seems to disadvantage them, because they may

This Araweté woman of Brazil may believe that two or more men fathered her son.

end up supporting children who are not biologically theirs. On the other hand, they are "hedging their reproductive bets" by spreading their semen widely. This may be of particular value to high-status men, who gain disproportionate access to other men's wives, thanks to partible paternity. In addition, partible paternity gives men some assurance that their biological children will have male support in the event of their own premature death, something that's all too common in Amazonia.

This still leaves unanswered the question of why partible paternity is common in lowland South America but rare elsewhere. The answer may be related to the importance of kinship and alliances in those societies, combined with a general absence of material wealth. In such circumstances paternity may be used as a unit of wealth that can be traded, as it were, in social networks.

partible paternity   The belief that two or more men may be fathers of the same child.

in the Middle East roughly 10,000 years ago. This transition led eventually to the formation of city-states, which required governments and the regulation of social behavior. Nudity was restricted, in part with the aim of reducing sexual arousal, preventing the sight of sexual arousal in others, and eliminating sexual conflicts. (Some present-day hunter-gatherer cultures still permit nudity.) Marriage was formalized, and nonmarital sex was discouraged to a greater or lesser degree.

Organized religion played a role in these changes (Endsjo, 2011). Although religious teachings have varied greatly, they have often fostered procreative **heterosexual** sex within marriage while labeling other forms of sexual expression as sinful. This was particularly true for the Christian religion: For most of the two millennia since its foundation, Christian teachings forbade all nonmarital sex, **homosexual** sex, masturbation, contraception, abortion, and polygamy. Even marital sex was restricted to coitus in certain positions, and it was forbidden on certain days of the week and during Lent (Ranke-Heinemann, 1990). Priests were commonly barred from marriage or any kind of sexual activity. This changed to some extent after the Reformation, when western Christianity splintered into numerous denominations, some of which have become much more liberal in the area of sexual ethics compared with the Catholic Church.

Figure 1.1   The *Kama Sutra* describes a wide variety of sexual positions.

The development of large-scale societies led to the emergence of class structures, with the rich and powerful at the top and the impoverished masses at the bottom. What class you belonged to greatly influenced your sex life. Take India: The *Kama Sutra*, compiled around the 2nd century, describes innumerable ways for men to obtain sexual pleasure and to give sexual pleasure to women (Vatsyayana, 1991) (**Figure 1.1**). It also describes sex between women and between men. But the *Kama Sutra* was written for and about the idle rich. (What to do between breakfast and lunch? Teach your parrot to talk.) If the sex lives of low-caste Indians were anything like they are today, they involved hasty, fully-clothed couplings with the minimum of pleasure or romance (Nath & Nayar, 1997).

Another way that class influenced sexuality had to do with **polygamy**. The majority of human cultures have permitted men to have more than one wife, but it was largely rich and powerful men who did so, because they had sufficient means—King Solomon is said to have had a thousand wives. Polygamy reduced the numbers of available women and thus made it harder for poor men to afford even one wife. What's more, polygamy is connected with the idea that women are men's property— if a rich man has many cattle, why shouldn't he have many wives? By banning polygamy, the Christian religion promoted a somewhat more gender-equitable society.*

Across history, large numbers of men have been deprived of a sex life altogether by being **castrated**—that is, by having their testicles removed, and sometimes the penis also. Such men were called **eunuchs**. Castration was carried out as a punishment among criminals or prisoners of war, or (if done before puberty) to produce asexual male slaves who could serve certain roles such as court attendants, harem guards, dancers, or singers. Some eunuchs achieved powerful positions in imperial courts across Asia. In India, some men were (and still are) voluntarily castrated as an initiation into the **transgender** religious caste known as *hijras*, who are described further in Chapter 4 (Nanda, 1998).

heterosexuality   Sexual attraction to, or behavior with, persons of the opposite sex.

homosexuality   Sexual attraction to, or behavior with, persons of the same sex.

polygamy   Having more than one spouse at the same time, as a social institution.

castration   Removal of the testicles or testicles and penis.

eunuch   A man who has been castrated.

transgender (or trans)   Identifying with the other sex or rejecting gender norms.

---

* In early Islam, polygamy helped provide for the many women whose husbands died in warfare.

Figure 1.2 Declining birthrates
This graph shows the average number of children born to American women between 1800 and 2010. The data for white and African-American women are plotted separately.

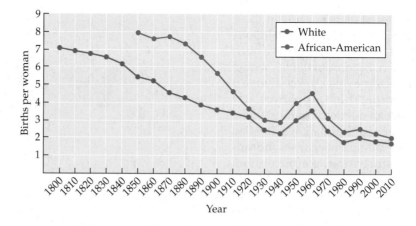

In general, castration has served the interests of noncastrated men, especially powerful men, and it therefore represents another way in which class and sexuality interact. Today, castration by surgery or "chemical castration" by drugs is performed voluntarily on some men with prostate cancer in an effort to prolong their lives—perhaps a quarter of a million American men are in this situation (Wassersug et al., 2014).

Another important effect of cultural change has involved sexually transmitted infections. When people lived in small groups and stayed in a restricted area, they tended to reach a biological accommodation with the infectious agents (bacteria and viruses) present in that population, such that their effects were not especially severe. Increases in population density and long-distance travel changed this picture: The organism that causes syphilis, for example, was present in the native populations of the Americas long before the arrival of Columbus and other explorers, but when these men returned to Europe, bringing the organism with them, it unleashed a devastating epidemic (Rothschild et al., 2000). Potentially fatal diseases such as syphilis and (more recently) AIDS made sex itself seem frightening and sinful.

Marriage has been transformed

Yet another important change has been the radical decline in birth rates that has taken place in most countries, starting in the late 18th century. Over this period the number of children born to the average American woman has fallen from 7 or 8 to about 2 (**Figure 1.2**). Today, there are plenty of women or couples who choose to have no children at all—something that used to be quite unusual, except for women in religious orders. This decline has not been accompanied by any decline in people's interest in sex. Thus the idea has gained currency that sex has a legitimate emotional or recreational function, beyond the production of children.

The institution of marriage has changed over time (Abbott, 2011). In many traditional societies marriage signified the transfer of ownership of a woman from her father to her husband; marriages were negotiated and often involved large bridal payments. People fell in love, but they were lucky if they married the people they fell in love with. In Europe and America, even as late as the 19th century, a suitor was expected to ask the girl's father for permission to propose to her, and if permission was refused—because the young man had insufficient means, for example—the young couple's only recourse might be to run away (elope) and marry at some distant location.

A woman was expected to be a virgin when she married, but a man could be forgiven or even admired for "sowing his wild oats." (This was an example of the **double standard**, by which males and females were, and still may be, held to different moral codes.) The husband's and wife's roles in marriage were also quite distinct:

double standard The idea that acceptable behavior is different for men than for women.

Figure 1.3   Supreme Court justice Clarence Thomas and his wife Virginia are one of the many couples who have benefited from the court's 1967 ruling that there is a constitutional right to marry across racial lines.

The husband was the breadwinner, the wife the homemaker and child rearer, perhaps with the help of servants.

Before the 20th century, marriage was for life: Divorce was quite uncommon and was only permitted in cases of proven adultery. Divorce laws were greatly liberalized over the course of the 20th century, and now nearly half of all U.S. marriages end in divorce rather than death (Wilcox & Marquardt, 2011). What's more, it's now widely accepted that women are sexually active before marriage, and that couples may live together (**cohabit**) before marriage or without marrying at all. And the birth of children outside of marriage, once a shocking secret, is now more or less routine: Over 40% of all U.S. births are now to unmarried women, who may be single or cohabiting with a man or with a woman (Martin et al., 2013).

Up until the mid-20th century the vast majority of Americans considered interracial marriage to be sinful, and such marriages were illegal in many states. Attitudes changed gradually after World War II, and in 1967 the U.S. Supreme Court established a constitutional right to marry across racial lines (**Figure 1.3**). Currently we are witnessing a similar trend with regard to same-sex marriage, but gay couples who marry today are joining an institution that has lost a great deal of its former significance.

Sex has become a topic of social discourse

The 20th century saw a dramatic increase in people's willingness to talk about sex. At the beginning of the century Victorian prudery still ruled: Most people could talk about sex only obliquely, if at all. Then came a series of outspoken researchers and activists whose work turned sex into a hot topic of conversation. Here are a few of them:

- Havelock Ellis (1859–1939) was an English physician who described unusual kinds of sexual expression (which had previously been called "perversions") in a sympathetic rather than a condemnatory way.

- Sigmund Freud (1856–1939) was an Austrian neurologist and founder of psychoanalysis. He proposed that our lives are governed by a roiling unconscious world of sexual drives and conflicts (**Box 1.2**).

- Margaret Sanger (1879–1966), an American social activist, campaigned tirelessly and effectively for women's right to learn about and practice contraception.

- Alfred Kinsey (1894–1956) was an Indiana University biologist whose pioneering sex surveys (the "Kinsey Reports") caused a sensation when they were published in 1948 and 1953 (**Figure 1.4**).

- Margaret Mead (1901–1978) was an American cultural anthropologist who described the sexually uninhibited lifestyles of some Pacific Islanders.

- William Masters (1915–2001) and Virginia Johnson (1925–2013), of Washington University in St. Louis, pioneered the physiological study of sexual responses in healthy people and in those with sexual disorders.

cohabitation   A live-in sexual relationship between individuals who are not married to each other.

Figure 1.4   Let's talk about sex. Sex researcher Alfred Kinsey (far right) lectures at the University of California in 1949.

School sex education, which is now mandated in 22 U.S. states (National Conference of State Legislatures, 2014) and throughout Canada, has also promoted discussion and awareness of sexual issues. Even today, though, many Americans find it difficult or inappropriate to talk about sex, and in some more-conservative cultures it may be completely off-limits.

Social movements have affected sexuality

Political and social movements have impacted sexuality in America and elsewhere. In the 1970s and 1980s the women's movement asserted women's right to control their own bodies (through contraception and abortion, for example), to be free of sexual coercion, and to seek pleasure in sexual relationships. The idea gained ground that men shared responsibility for ensuring that their female partners experienced pleasure, including orgasm, during sex.

The gay liberation movement led to the increasing acceptance of homosexuality, which led in turn to the enactment of anti-discrimination laws, starting in the 1980s, and the nationwide legalization of gay sex by a 2003 ruling of the U.S. Supreme Court. Advocates have campaigned for recognition and social acceptance of many other facets of sexuality: bisexuality, asexuality, transgender identity, intersexuality, plural marriage (polygamy), polyamory, sadomasochism, fetishes, pedophilia, pornography, and prostitution. (If some of these terms are unfamiliar to you, don't worry: We will be covering them all in later chapters.) Although these efforts have met with widely varying success—and rightly so, you may think—what they have done is change the conversation: Sexual expression, it's now increasingly agreed, should be legally restricted only when it makes rational sense to do so, not simply when it runs afoul of tradition, prejudice, or good taste.

Of course, sexuality doesn't just change over time; it also varies widely from place to place around the present-day world, and among individuals within the same population. We will focus primarily on North America, the region where this text is used, but from time to time we will make trips overseas to look at examples of global diversity in sexual behavior and ideas about sexuality.

FAQ

What was the "sexual revolution" of the 1960s?

It was a youth-led movement for greater sexual freedom and individuality, driven by rebellion against the more orthodox World War II generation and fueled by feminism, the contraceptive pill, rock and roll, and drugs. An enduring consequence was the greater acceptance of sex outside of marriage.

Box 1.2 Controversies

Freud and Hirschfeld: Contrasting Theories on Sexual Orientation

About a century ago, two European doctors proposed radically different theories to account for why some people are sexually attracted predominantly to members of the other sex while others are attracted to members of the same sex or to both sexes—a characteristic we now call sexual orientation. In Vienna, Sigmund Freud (**Figure A**) developed a theory that was based on the concept of an unconscious mind, whose operations could supposedly be probed by psychoanalytic techniques such as free association, the interpretation of dreams, and slips of the tongue. The unconscious mind, though hidden from view and free from moral restraints, nevertheless resembled the conscious mind in many respects—both were capable of rational thought, planning, memory, and emotion.

In Freud's conception, the unconscious mind was more broadly focused in its sexual desires than was the conscious mind. This was particularly true during early childhood, which he believed included autoerotic and homosexual phases as well as incestuous desires directed toward one or the other parent. Freud thought that the "normal" progression to adult heterosexuality could be derailed in various ways, often involving unconscious emotional processes such as a hostile, too-close, or jealous relationship with a parent or sibling. These phenomena could lead to what Freud called **perversions**, that is, mental states in which adult sexual desires were directed toward atypical targets, such as people of the same sex (homosexuality), inanimate objects (fetishism), and so on. Or they could lead to **neuroses**, in which the sexual element was supposedly repressed from consciousness altogether and reemerged in the form of nonsexual traits and disorders, such as obsessive-compulsive behaviors, depression, or "hysteria."

In Berlin, Magnus Hirschfeld (**Figure B**) took a quite different view. Hirschfeld proposed the existence of two neural centers in the brain that were responsible for sexual attraction to men and to women, respectively. He suggested that during early fetal life all humans possessed both centers, but later one center grew and dominated, while the other regressed. In men, of course, it was usually the center for attraction to women that persisted, while in women it was the center for attraction to men. Only in the minority of homosexual individuals did development take the opposite course. Hirschfeld believed that sex hormones (then understood in only a very rudimentary way) channeled development in one direction or another, and that people also had a genetic predisposition to same-sex or opposite-sex attraction.

In many ways, the views of Freud and Hirschfeld represented opposite approaches to understanding the mind and sexuality. Freud tried to understand the mind in terms of processes that, though hidden, were inherently *mental*—unconscious thoughts. And he believed interpersonal relationships held the key to sexual orientation and other aspects of adult sexuality.

(A) Sigmund Freud (1856–1939)

(B) Magnus Hirschfeld (1868–1935)

To Freud, getting to your adult sexuality was a long, sometimes chaotic drama in which the unconscious mind took the leading role. Hirschfeld, on the other hand, tried to reduce the mind to relatively simple *nonmental* phenomena such as the growth and activity of nerve cells, hormone secretion, and information encoded in the genes. In Hirschfeld's view, these phenomena controlled sexual development in a manner that was largely independent of family relationships and other aspects of life experience. To Hirschfeld, getting to your adult sexuality was a process that unfolded mechanistically without your active participation—it simply happened to you.

Freud's theories came to dominate most people's ideas about the mind and sexuality through the early and middle part of the 20th century, while Hirschfeld's theories languished in obscurity. Toward the end of the century, however, a noticeable shift of views occurred. To some people, Freud's theories began to seem capricious, poorly substantiated, or inspired by prejudice (against women especially). Meanwhile, scientific advances tended to bolster a biological view of sexuality. Studies in animals showed that prenatal hormone levels do indeed influence sexual behavior in adulthood, and family studies supported the idea that genes do have some influence on sexual orientation in humans.

Probably the dominant view at present is that both approaches offer potential insights into human sexuality. There must be some biological underpinnings to our thoughts and behaviors, and exploring these underpinnings is likely to tell us a lot about why people differ from one another sexually. On the other hand, it seems likely that some aspects of human sexuality need to be studied at the level of thoughts—in other words, by a cognitive approach. Thus, even if neither Freud's nor Hirschfeld's theories turn out to be entirely correct, they may both have contributed useful styles of thinking to the discussion.

perversion An obsolete term for atypical sexual desire or behavior, viewed as a mental disorder.

neuroses Mental disorders such as depression that, in Freudian theory, are strategies for coping with repressed sexual conflicts.

Sexuality Can Be Studied with a Wide Variety of Methods

Investigators trained in many different disciplines make contributions to our understanding of human sexuality. We could fill a whole book with an account of the methods that are being used to study the topic. Here, we pick out some of the key areas and highlight certain research studies that illustrate the methods that are available.

Biomedical research focuses on the underlying mechanisms of sex

Biomedical research is the approach that has the greatest practical impact on people's sex lives. Here are a few examples:

- Hormone-based contraception and abortion
- Drug treatments for reproductive cancers
- Drug treatments for erectile disorder, premature ejaculation, and low male sex drive (with research into drug treatments for female sexual disorders being, so far, less successful)
- Methods to prevent, cure, or effectively treat sexually transmitted infections, including AIDS
- Technologies to treat infertility in women and men
- Improvements in the safety of pregnancy and childbirth

Biomedical researchers often turn to nonhuman animals to deepen their understanding of human nature, including human sexuality. Animal research involves studying the structure, function, and development of bodily systems that are involved in sex and reproduction. Most of the advances listed above were made possible by research using laboratory animals. In addition, researchers study the sexual *behavior* of animals, both in the laboratory and in the wild. Although this book is titled *Discovering Human Sexuality*, we make no apology for including a great deal of information about, or derived from, nonhuman species.

Still, the introduction of modern imaging technologies has enabled the direct study in humans of topics that earlier could only be studied in animals. This is particularly true for brain function, which can now be studied with a variety of imaging techniques (**Figure 1.5**). In addition, the decipherment of the human genome is enabling all kinds of advances, such as the ability to ascertain the sex of a fetus and to diagnose certain fetal abnormalities on the basis of a simple blood sample drawn from the mother. And as we'll discuss in Chapter 12, current research is attempting to home in on genes that influence such important traits as a person's **sexual orientation**.

One study that exemplifies the biomedical approach to sexuality was conducted by one of this textbook's authors (Simon LeVay) about 25 years ago (LeVay, 1991). Basing his research on earlier work on laboratory animals, LeVay hypothesized that there might be structural differences between the brains of gay (homosexual) and straight (heterosexual) people. By examining the brains of deceased individuals, he found that a part of the brain involved in sexual behavior (a small region within a part of the brain known as the hypothalamus) was larger in straight men than in gay men. Other researchers extended this line of work to living people by the use of imaging techniques, and it's now known that there are several differences in brain organization, not only between gay and straight men, but also between lesbian and straight women, as we'll discuss in Chapter 12. Collectively, these studies helped shift our conception of homosexuality (and heterosexuality) from something that is learned or culturally imposed to something more akin to an inborn trait.

sexual orientation The direction of an individual's sexual feelings: sexual attraction toward persons of the opposite sex (heterosexual), the same sex (homosexual), or both sexes (bisexual).

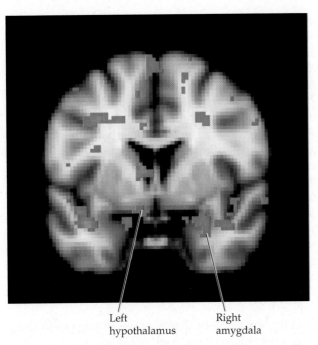

Left   Right
hypothalamus   amygdala

Figure 1.5   Sex on the brain This shows (in red) the average pattern of activity in the brains of ten women while they were experiencing orgasm, using a technique called functional magnetic resonance imaging (fMRI). Activity immediately prior to orgasm has been digitally subtracted from the image, so the image shows activity related specifically to orgasm and not to general sexual arousal. Several parts of the brain are active during orgasm, but two areas of particular interest are the amygdala and hypothalamus, both of which play important roles in the regulation of sexual feelings and behaviors. (Image courtesy of Nan Wise and Barry Komisaruk, Rutgers University.)

Psychology includes diverse approaches to sexuality

Psychology, the study of mental processes and behavior, has splintered into numerous overlapping subdisciplines, each of which tends to use distinct methods. The branch of psychology most significant to the study of sexuality is **social psychology**—the study of how we think about, influence, and relate to other people. Social psychologists concern themselves with all kinds of sexual matters, such as sexual attraction and relationships, violence between intimate partners, and anti-gay prejudice.

Here's one example of how social psychologists tackle an important question relating to sexuality. Researchers at UCLA, led by Neil Malamuth, have been interested in the question of whether portrayals of sexual violence in the media and pornography make men more accepting of such violence, as has been asserted by many **feminists**. Out of a group of male college students, half were randomly assigned to watch movies that portrayed sexual violence against women—specifically, movies in which a woman was raped but subsequently fell in love with her rapist. The other students (the **control group**) watched movies that contained no sexual violence. A few days later the students were given a sexual attitudes questionnaire. The results supported the feminist contention: Male students who watched sexually violent movies expressed significantly more accepting attitudes toward sexual violence than the men in the control group. This and other studies have convinced the UCLA researchers that exposure to images of sexual violence really does predispose some men to commit sexual assaults against women (Malamuth et al., 2000; Hald et al., 2010).

psychology   The study of mental processes and behavior.

social psychology   The study of one's relationship to others.

feminism   The movement to secure equality for women; the study of social and psychological issues from women's perspectives.

control group   A group of subjects included in a study for comparison purposes.

cognitive psychology The study of the information-processing systems of the mind.

evolutionary psychology The study of the influence of evolution on mental processes or behavior.

cultural anthropology The study of cultural variations across the human race.

Cognitive psychology is the study of internal mental processes. As an example, there's a well-known stereotype that gay men are "like women" and lesbians are "like men." How true is this? To find out, cognitive psychologists have conducted many studies comparing a variety of mental traits, skills, and attitudes in gay and straight people. Researchers at the University of Haifa, in Israel, for instance, picked empathy, which is the ability to detect and feel the emotions of other people. This trait is typically better developed in women than in men. Consistent with the stereotype, the researchers found that gay men scored higher on tests of empathy than straight men, whereas lesbians scored lower than straight women (Perry et al., 2013). Still, looking at the entire body of research in this field, gay people show a patchwork of gender-typical and gender-atypical traits, and what's true on average is not necessarily true about individuals (LeVay, 2011). We review this topic further in Chapter 12.

Evolutionary psychology seeks to explain how evolution has molded our genetic endowment to favor certain patterns of sexual feelings and behaviors. One idea in evolutionary psychology is that because reproduction is so much more demanding for females than for males, genes have evolved that cause females to be very picky in their choice of sex partners. As a result, other genes have evolved that cause males to engage in competitive and risky sexual displays—displays that are intended to influence females' choices.

It's well established that men are more likely than women to engage in risky behaviors, but it's not clear whether the risks we take in everyday life—such as when we cross a busy street—are actually sexual displays. To help answer this question, an international group of evolutionary psychologists descended on Britain's University of Liverpool (Pawlowski et al., 2008). They stationed themselves near the campus's busiest crosswalk, and over a period of 3 months they observed how 1000 men and women crossed the street (**Figure 1.6**). Specifically, they noted how much risk the students took in crossing (i.e., whether they crossed when vehicles were approaching) and who else was present when each person crossed. As might have been expected, the researchers found that men took more risks than women. The interesting finding, though, was that the presence of women nearby significantly *increased* the likelihood that a man would attempt a risky crossing, whereas the presence of men nearby did not influence his decision one way or another. Women, on the other hand, paid little or no attention to who was present, regardless of their sex, when they decided whether to cross. The researchers concluded that even a mundane act such as crossing a street can be motivated in part by the urge to engage in sexual displays—but only for men in the presence of women. Women do engage in sexual displays—when they flirt, for example—but these displays don't commonly take the form of risk-taking behavior.

Another area of psychology is concerned with ethnic and cultural diversity in sexual attitudes, behavior, and relationships. This kind of research, which is conducted primarily by **cultural anthropologists**, involves fieldwork of the kind pioneered by Margaret Mead and others. An example is the research into the concept of partible paternity in Amazonia that was discussed in Box 1.1. Another example closer to home concerns the Native American tradition of "two-spirit" people—individuals who incorporate both a male and a female identity and who are accorded a special role in their communities. These people have been studied in detail by anthropolo-

Figure 1.6 Looking for love? Crossing the street in front of traffic can be a form of sexual display, according to research at the University of Liverpool.

gist Walter Williams, who spent a great deal of time living among Native Americans (Williams, 1986). The study of two-spirit people challenges assumptions about **gender** that are prevalent in most Western societies (Sheppard & Mayo, 2013).

Sociologists focus on the connection between sex and society

Sociology is the scientific study of society. Sociologists make a unique contribution to the study of human sexuality by linking the sexual behaviors and attitudes of individuals to larger social structures. Sociologists examine how sexual expression varies with age, race, national origin, religious and political beliefs, place of residence, educational level, and so on. Such studies are often carried out by means of sex surveys.

We already briefly mentioned the surveys conducted by Alfred Kinsey in the mid-20th century. With the onset of the AIDS epidemic around 1980, the need for detailed information about sexual practices and attitudes spurred a host of new sex surveys. Most notable among the surveys was one conducted by sociologists at the University of Chicago and elsewhere—the **National Health and Social Life Survey** (**NHSLS**) (Laumann et al., 1994). A comparable British survey—the **National Survey of Sexual Attitudes and Lifestyles** (**NSSAL**)—was published in the same year (Wellings et al., 1994) and has been repeated twice, most recently in 2013 (Mercer et al., 2013). Besides being more up-to-date than the Kinsey surveys, the NHSLS and NSSAL were technically superior in a number of respects, especially in their use of modern random-sampling methods and advanced techniques of statistical analysis, made possible by computers.

One interesting finding of the NHSLS concerned masturbation. This practice is often thought of as something a person does as a substitute for "real" sex when partners are unavailable. No doubt this is sometimes the case, but the survey findings indicate that people usually masturbate *in addition to* engaging in partnered sex, not as a substitute for it. In fact, women with partners masturbate more than women without them, according to the survey.

In 2010, researchers at the Center for Sexual Health Promotion at Indiana University published findings from a new **National Survey of Sexual Health and Behavior** (**NSSHB**) (Reece et al., 2010b). This survey obtained responses from nearly 6000 Americans age 14 to 94. Among the findings was a gender gap in the experience of heterosexual sex: More men than women experienced orgasm during their most recent act of penile-vaginal intercourse, whereas more women than men experienced pain.

Another valuable source of information is the **General Social Survey** (**GSS**), which is run by sociologists at the University of Chicago. The GSS has been asking Americans pretty much the same questions at 1- or 2-year intervals since 1972. Using the GSS survey data it is possible to find out how people's attitudes toward, say, sex between unmarried couples, has changed over time.

From time to time throughout this book, we cite findings from these and other surveys. We also occasionally refer to magazine-sponsored surveys, which tend to cover intimate topics that the official surveys ignore. In 2012, for example, *Esquire* magazine commissioned a national random-sample survey that came up with all kinds of interesting information about current U.S. sex practices—such as that heterosexual men's favorite sexual position is the "cowgirl" (the woman straddling the man and facing forward) (Esquire, 2012).

Sex surveys are plagued with a variety of problems. It is often difficult to obtain truly representative samples of respondents. In addition, respondents may be reluctant to divulge details of their sex lives, especially if the information could be regarded as shameful. Kinsey tried to overcome this problem by the use of leading questions ("When did you first . . . ?" rather than "Have you ever . . . ?"). In more recent surveys researchers have attempted to reduce the embarrassment factor by

gender   The collection of psychological traits that differ between males and females.

sociology   The scientific study of society.

National Health and Social Life Survey (NHSLS)   A national survey of sexual behavior, relationships, and attitudes in the United States, conducted in the early 1990s.

National Survey of Sexual Attitudes and Lifestyles (NSSAL)   A periodic British survey of sexual behavior, relationships, and attitudes, most recently conducted in 2013.

National Survey of Sexual Health and Behavior (NSSHB)   A national survey of sexual behavior in the United States, based at Indiana University and published in 2010.

General Social Survey (GSS)   A long-running periodic survey of the U.S. population run by the National Opinion Research Center.

Participants in sex surveys give more honest responses when they can do so without the presence of investigators.

allowing interviewees to type their responses directly into a computer.

Random-sample surveys, even very large ones, are likely to encompass very few if any individuals who belong to "minorities within minorities," such as Asian-American lesbians. Yet it is often these neglected groups about whom information is most needed. What's more, when only a small percentage of the subjects belong to a certain group, their truthful responses may be swamped by frivolous responses from others. This apparently happened with a survey of U.S. adolescents called the National Longitudinal Study of Adolescent Health, or AddHealth: In this survey an improbably large number of students described themselves as gay, and they sometimes added other unlikely facts such as having artificial limbs or numerous children. The deception came to light in a repeat survey carried out on the same individuals when they were adults: By then the artificial limbs, the children, and the homosexuality had largely vanished (Savin-Williams & Joyner, 2013).

Sociologists are also interested in the mechanisms by which social structures (ranging from the family to the mass media) mold individual feelings and behaviors. One influential idea is that society gives us "scripts"—ways of presenting ourselves to others as we deal with social interactions. We can select from many different scripts and ad-lib on them too. This idea has been referred to as **script theory** (Reiss, 1986; Simon & Gagnon, 1986; Frith, 2009).

Here's an example of the application of script theory to a sexual topic: Angela Bartoli and Diane Clark of Shippensburg University studied the dating scripts typically used by college students. They found that men's scripts were far more likely to involve an expectation of sex, whereas women's scripts typically included a responsibility for setting limits on sexual interactions (Bartoli & Clark, 2006). This is, of course, consistent with traditional views about men's and women's roles in sexual negotiations. Bartoli and Clark's finding suggest that several decades of "women's lib" did not change this dynamic in any significant way.

Sociologists may also engage in **ethnographic** fieldwork, immersing themselves in their subjects' lives in the same way that cultural anthropologists do. For example, Staci Newmahr, then a graduate student in sociology at the State University of New York (SUNY) at Buffalo, wanted to explore the lives and motivations of people who engaged in BDSM activities (Newmahr, 2011). ("BDSM" means the infliction or receipt of pain, humiliation, and the like as a sexual or recreational outlet.) To do so, Newmahr joined a BDSM club and submitted to treatments that you might consider extreme, or at least well beyond the usual requirements for a PhD. We report on some of her findings in Chapter 13.

The economic approach weighs costs and benefits

How much is sex "worth?" Sometimes, as in the case of prostitution, the answer to this question can be expressed in dollar terms. But even when money doesn't change hands, people calculate—consciously or unconsciously—the costs and benefits of sexual encounters and sexual relationships (Baumeister & Vohs, 2004). The cost may be counted not in money but in time lost from studies or career, or in the effect of a damaged reputation that lowers a person's future value in the sexual marketplace. The benefit may not be sexual pleasure, but a secure relationship. Researchers willing to take a hard-nosed economic approach to these issues help us understand how much more there is to human sexuality than simple romance or "the joy of sex."

script theory   The analysis of sexual and other behaviors as the enactment of socially instilled roles.

ethnography   The study of a cultural group, often by means of extended individual fieldwork.

As an example of this approach, let's take a look at a study that focused on how the sex ratio (the ratio of males to females in a given population) influences sexual negotiations. A basic tenet of economic theory is that the value of scarce resources tends to rise, so if one sex is in a minority, members of that sex gain leverage in the heterosexual marketplace. Because males are typically more interested in uncommitted sex than are women, it might be expected that casual sex would be more common in populations with an excess of females and less common where males are in the majority. Psychologist Nigel Barber tested this prediction by obtaining data on sex ratios and teen birthrates (a proxy indicator of uncommitted sex) in 185 countries (Barber, 2000). Sure enough, teen births were highest in countries with an excess of females, and the association was not a weak one: Nearly 40% of the variability in teen birthrates between countries could be explained by their sex ratios. In later chapters we'll see how sex ratios impact the sex lives of Americans.

It's worth emphasizing that individual researchers often cross the boundaries between the various disciplines just described, or collaborate with researchers from other backgrounds. Psychologists and neuroscientists often work together, for example. This kind of boundary crossing has greatly enhanced researchers' ability to understand the roots of sexual behavior and sexual diversity.

As we have seen, women and men in a variety of academic disciplines and walks of life have made important contributions to our understanding of human sexuality. Increasingly, however, there is a perception that sex research, or **sexology**, is an academic discipline in its own right. This discipline is an unusual one in that it demands training that crosses most of the traditionally established intellectual boundaries.

A variety of factors make sex research especially challenging:

Prostitution is not the only sphere in which people calculate the value of sex and sexual relationships.

- It can be difficult to obtain appropriate subjects to study. It's easy enough to corral a classful of human sexuality students, but how representative are these of the general citizenry, let alone humanity as a whole?

- It can be difficult to phrase survey questions in ways that encourage honest responses and that don't bias responses to conform to researchers' preconceptions.

- It can be difficult to extrapolate from animal research to human subjects.

- It can be difficult to obtain funding for research: Conservative politicians have taken to vetting grant applications, looking for proposals that they can ridicule or defund. On the other hand, the epidemics of AIDS, herpes, and other sexually transmitted infections have led to the investment of a great deal of public and private funds into sex-related research topics.

Numerous organizations at local, international, and global levels now foster sex research. In the United States, the Society for the Scientific Study of Sexuality (SSSS, or "Quad-S") publishes the *Journal of Sex Research* and other periodicals. The American Association of Sexuality Educators Counselors and Therapists (AASECT) and the Society for Sex Therapy and Research (SSTAR) certify educational programs in sex education and therapy. There are also institutes devoted to research or training in issues of sexuality, such as the Kinsey Institute (which is affiliated with Indiana University), and special-purpose organizations such as the Guttmacher Institute (which focuses on family planning issues).

At an international level, two organizations stand out. The International Academy of Sex Research publishes the *Archives of Sexual Behavior.* The World Association for Sexual Health, which represents sex-research and sexual-health organizations from

sexology   The scientific study of sex and sexual disorders.

53 countries, issued a universal Declaration of Sexual Rights in 1997, and it has been updated since that time. The 2014 declaration (in abridged form) is as follows:

- *The right to equality and non-discrimination*
- *The right to life, liberty, and security of the person*
- *The right to autonomy and bodily integrity*
- *The right to be free from torture and cruel, inhuman, or degrading treatment or punishment*
- *The right to be free from all forms of violence and coercion*
- *The right to privacy*
- *The right to the highest attainable standard of health, including sexual health; with the possibility of pleasurable, satisfying, and safe sexual experiences*
- *The right to enjoy the benefits of scientific progress and its application*
- *The right to information*
- *The right to education and the right to comprehensive sexuality education*
- *The right to enter, form, and dissolve marriage and other similar types of relationships based on equality and full and free consent*
- *The right to decide whether to have children, the number and spacing of children, and to have the information and the means to do so*
- *The right to the freedom of thought, opinion, and expression*
- *The right to freedom of association and peaceful assembly*
- *The right to participation in public and political life*
- *The right to access to justice, remedies, and redress*

Go to the
**Discovering
Human Sexuality**
Companion Website at
**sites.sinauer.com/
discoveringhumansexuality3e**
for activities, study questions,
quizzes, and other study aids.

Summary

- Sexuality has changed over time, under the influence of evolution and culture. Certain modes of sexual behavior, such as competition for sex partners, were inherited from our nonhuman ancestors. The increasing conscious understanding of the connection between sex and reproduction led to the development of efforts to interrupt the connection—by contraception and abortion.

- The establishment of large-scale societies and governments led to the regulation of sexuality. Marriage in particular has undergone many changes, from a contract arranged by men to a more voluntary and egalitarian arrangement that benefits both partners. The banning of polygamy by the early Christian church laid the groundwork for greater equality in marriage. Organized religion has often established moral codes that restrict sexual expression, especially nonreproductive behaviors such as sex between same-sex partners.

- The steep reduction in the birthrate in many countries over the last two centuries has also allowed women to take a role in marriage that goes beyond incessant pregnancy and child rearing. Marriage itself has lost some of its significance in Western societies as nonmarital cohabitation and child rearing, and at-will divorce, have become increasingly common and accepted.

- Sexuality can be studied with a wide variety of approaches. The biomedical approach has been based primarily on studies in nonhuman animals, but recent advances, such as brain-scanning technology and the decoding of the human genome, allow for more direct study of sexual processes in humans.

- The psychological approach falls into several subdisciplines. Social psychology concerns itself with the diverse ways in which sex influences interpersonal relations. Cognitive psychology is focused on the mental processes, such as sexual arousal, that underlie sexual expression. Evolutionary psychology is devoted to understanding how evolutionary forces have molded our sex lives. Cultural anthropology investigates the influence of ethnic and cultural diversity on sexual expression.

- Sociologists are concerned with the interactions between the sexuality of individuals and larger demographic groupings. Sex surveys are an important tool in this approach. An example of a theoretical social-science approach is sexual script theory: the notion that, as a result of constant interaction with others, people learn to play certain sexual roles. Sociologists also do ethnographic fieldwork in the environments where sexual transactions take place.

- The economic approach to sexuality asks how the perceived costs and benefits of interactions within a sexual marketplace influence people's sexual decision making.

- Sexology, or sex research, is gradually asserting itself as an independent and multidisciplinary field of study. National and international organizations, conferences, and journals are devoted to the subject. The World Association for Sexual Health has issued a universal Declaration of Sexual Rights.

Discussion Questions

1. Do you think that the sexual behavior of nonhuman animals has anything to teach us about what is morally acceptable in human sexual behavior?

2. How much does marriage or the prospect of marriage matter to you? Do you think men and women differ in how they view marriage?

3. What course of education would you recommend to someone who plans a career in sex research?

4. To what extent do you think that your religious upbringing and beliefs—or the lack of them—affect your current or future sexual and marital choices? If you're not comfortable with this question, discuss how you believe college students should interpret the teachings of their religious leaders when making sexual decisions.

5. After reading the basics of the World Association for Sexual Health's Declaration of Sexual Rights, do you agree with everything in it? Do you think the declaration fails to address any important topics? How would the principles laid out in the declaration bear on topics where there are marked differences between cultures, such as polygamy, female circumcision, prostitution, and homosexuality?

6. According to its mission statement, the Sexuality Information and Education Council of the United States (SIECUS) "advocates the right of individuals to make responsible sexual choices." Should people also have the right to make *irresponsible* sexual choices? Where would you draw the line and on what grounds?

Web Resources

American Association of Sex Educators Counselors and Therapists (AASECT) **www.aasect.org**

Archive for Sexology—English-language site at the University of Berlin **www2.hu-berlin.de/sexology**

Guttmacher Institute **www.guttmacher.org**

International Academy of Sex Research (IASR) **www.iasr.org**

Kinsey Institute for Research in Sex, Gender, and Reproduction **www.kinseyinstitute.org**

Sex Information and Education Council of Canada (SIECCAN) **www.sieccan.org**

Sexuality Information and Education Council of the United States (SIECUS) **www.siecus.org**

Society for Sex Therapy and Research (SSTAR) **www.sstarnet.org**

Society for the Scientific Study of Sexuality (SSSS) **www.sexscience.org**

Statistics Canada **www.statcan.gc.ca**

World Association for Sexual Health (WAS) **www.worldsexology.org**

Recommended Reading

Ellis, H. (1900). *Studies in the psychology of sex*. Davis.

Freud, S. (1905/1975). *Three essays on the theory of sexuality*. Basic.

Kinsey, A. C., Pomeroy, W. B. & Martin, C. E. (1948). *Sexual behavior in the human male*. Saunders.

Kinsey, A. C., Pomeroy, W. B., Martin, C. E. & Gebhard, P. H. (1953). *Sexual behavior in the human female*. Saunders.

Krafft-Ebing, R. v. (1886/1999). *Psychopathia sexualis, with special reference to contrary sexual instinct: A clinical-forensic study*. Bloat.

Masters, W. H. & Johnson, V. E. (1966). *Human sexual response*. Little, Brown.

Masters, W. H. & Johnson, V. E. (1970). *Human sexual inadequacy*. Little, Brown.

Mead, M. (1928). *Coming of age in Samoa: A psychological study of primitive youth for Western civilization*. Morrow.

(The books listed above are historically important works but don't necessarily represent current thinking.)

Dabhoiwala, F. (2012). *The origins of sex: A history of the first sexual revolution*. Oxford University Press.

Michael, R. T., Gagnon, J. H., Laumann, E. O. & Kolata, G. (1994). *Sex in America: A definitive survey*. Little, Brown.

Roach, M. (2008). *Bonk: The curious coupling of science and sex*. Norton.

Tolman, D.L. & Diamond, L.M. (Eds.) (2013). *APA handbook of sexuality and psychology*, Vols. 1 and 2. American Psychological Association.

Chapter 2

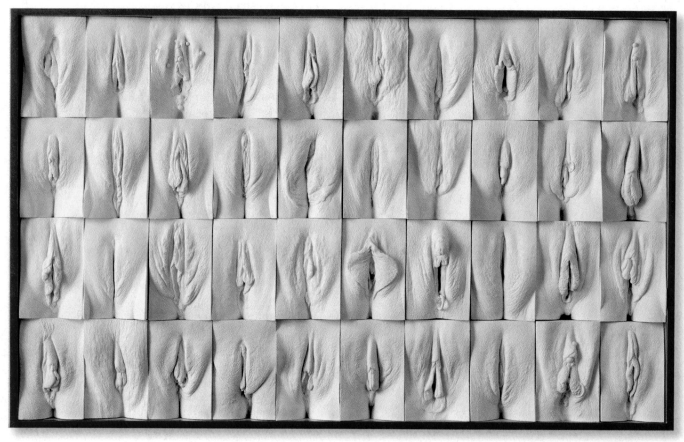

Diversity in women's vulvas. These life casts are among 400 that constitute *The Great Wall of Vagina*, by British artist Jamie McCartney.

Women's Bodies

Women and men are different, both in their bodies—the subject of this and the following chapters—and in their minds. Indeed, bodily differences, especially in the external genitals, are commonly used to decide whether a person is male or female. Yet many similarities and parallels exist between the bodies and minds of men and women—they are only variations on a common theme, after all. And there is considerable anatomical diversity within the categories of male and female. In fact, some babies are born with bodies that are not easy to categorize as either male or female, as we'll discuss in Chapter 4.

By presenting women's bodies first, we intentionally distance ourselves from the traditional perspective, which discussed women's sex organs in terms of their equivalence to, or difference from, the sex organs of men. Neither men nor women are the "original" sex from which the other was molded: Women and men coevolved over millions of years from females and males of our ancestral species.

Figure 2.1 **The vulva,** or female external genitalia. (A) Vulva with labia drawn apart to show the vestibule, urethral opening, and vaginal opening. The perineum and anus are not part of the vulva. (B) The inner labia are quite variable in shape and color from woman to woman. (See **Web Activity 2.1: The Vulva.**)

(A)

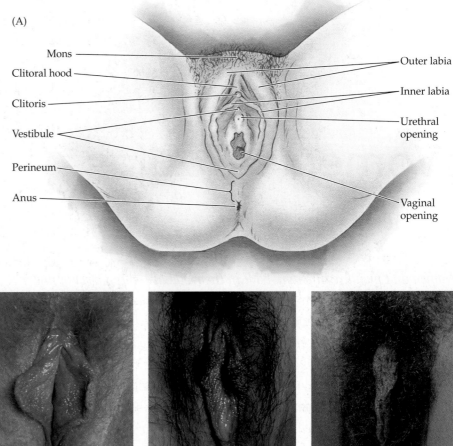

Mons
Clitoral hood
Clitoris
Vestibule
Perineum
Anus

Outer labia
Inner labia
Urethral opening
Vaginal opening

(B)

 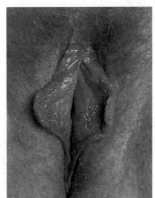 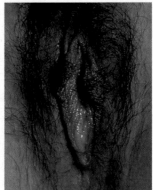 

external genitalia The sexual structures on the outside of the body.

vulva The female external genitalia.

mons (or mons veneris) The frontmost component of the vulva: a mound of fatty tissue covering the pubic bone.

pubic hair Hair that appears on portions of the external genitalia in both sexes at puberty.

A Woman's Vulva Includes Her Mons, Labia, Vaginal Opening, and Clitoris

Many girls and women have little understanding of their sexual anatomy, in part because the female **external genitalia** are not as prominent as those of men. In addition, girls often learn that it's not "nice" to inquire or talk about these body parts, or even to take a close look at them. Vague phrases such as "down there" may substitute for specific terms. Plenty of adult women—and men—do not know what the word "vagina" means and could not make a reasonable sketch of a woman's genital anatomy. Thus, the "naming of parts" and the description of their layout is the crucial first stage of education in sexuality (**Figure 2.1**).

The word **vulva** is a scientific term that refers to the entire external genital area in a woman. The appearance of the vulva varies from woman to woman, a fact illustrated clearly in Figure 2.1B and in the body casts of 40 women pictured at the beginning of this chapter.

The **mons** is a pad of fatty tissue covered by skin and **pubic hair**. It lies immediately in front of the pubic bone. The mons is erotically sensitive, and it may serve as a cushion for the woman's pubic area during sex. The hair helps vaporize odors that arise in specialized sweat glands, similar to those in the armpits, and these odors may act as pheromones (chemical attractants). The mons with its pubic hair may also be a visual trigger for sexual arousal in a woman's partner, since it is the most easily visible portion of the vulva.

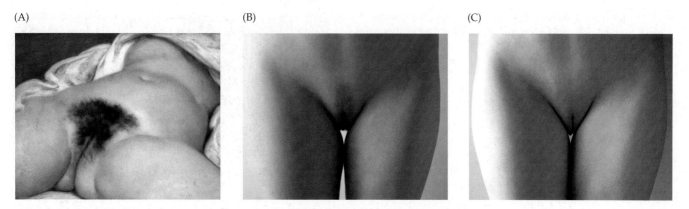

Figure 2.2 Pubic hair—love it or loathe it? (A) Gustave Courbet's 1866 painting *The Origin of the World* put natural pubic hair front and center. (B) A Brazilian wax removes all pubic hair except a narrow strip. (C) Complete removal of pubic hair.

In spite of these possible functions for pubic hair, many women remove some or all of the hair by shaving, waxing, or other methods (**Figure 2.2**). Artistically expressive women may "vajazzle" the shaven area with sequins or crystals. Pubic hair removal is much more common among young women than among older women, according to a 2010 study by researchers at the Indiana University (**Figure 2.3**). However, the *New York Times* reports that some women are going back to the natural look, led by Hollywood actresses who either announced that they gave up hair removal or showed off their pubic hair in nude scenes (Meltzer, 2014). Many cultures (such as that of Japan) have viewed abundant pubic hair as highly erotic.

The **labia** (Latin for "lips") are two pairs of skin folds that extend down from the mons on either side of the vulva. The **outer labia**, or **labia majora**, are padded with fatty tissue and are hairy on the surfaces nearest to the thighs. The skin of the outer labia is often darker than the skin elsewhere, and it is erotically sensitive, especially on the inner, hairless sides of the labia.

The **inner labia**, or **labia minora**, are two thin folds of hairless skin that lie between the two outer labia. In some women the inner labia are only visible after parting the outer labia; in other women they protrude to variable degrees (see Figure 2.1B). The inner labia meet at the back of the vulva, and also at the front, where they form the **clitoral hood**. The left and right inner labia generally touch each other in the midline when the woman is not aroused, and the area encircled by the labia is called the **vestibule**.

labia Two pairs of skin folds that form the sides of the vulva.

outer labia (or labia majora) Fleshy skin folds, partially covered in pubic hair, that extend from the mons.

inner labia (or labia minora) Thin, hairless folds of skin located between the outer labia and immediately flanking the vestibule.

clitoral hood A loose fold of skin that covers the clitoris.

vestibule The potential space between the left and right inner labia.

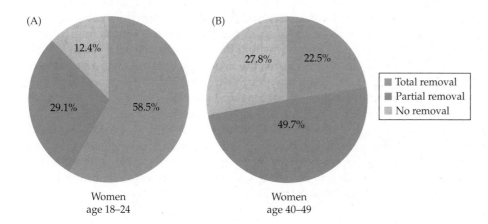

Figure 2.3 Removal of pubic hair These charts compare hair removal practices in (A) young and (B) middle-aged women, based on a nonrandom survey of 2451 sexually active women. "Total removal" means that women were completely hairless at least once in the prior month. (After Herbenick et al., 2010d.)

Figure 2.4 A woman's vulva before and after surgical reduction of the inner labia (Courtesy of Dr. Robert H. Stubbs.)

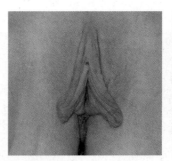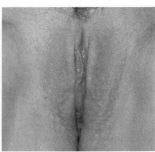

The inner labia are amply supplied with glands, blood vessels, and nerve endings and are very erotically sensitive. The appearance of the inner labia varies greatly from woman to woman. In some women they are virtually absent and are represented merely by slight ridges on the inner sides of the outer labia. In other women they extend well beyond the outer labia. In some cultures the inner labia are not left in their natural state, but are stretched, from childhood onward, with the aim of making the vulva more attractive. A small labia-stretching culture exists in the United States, too. Conversely, some women with naturally prominent or asymmetrical labia have them surgically reduced (**Figure 2.4**). During sexual arousal the inner labia swell and darken as they fill with blood, a process called **vasocongestion**.

When people use the word "labia" without any qualifier, they usually mean the inner labia.

There is more to the clitoris than meets the eye

Within the vestibule are three important structures: the clitoris, the urethral opening, and the vaginal opening. The **clitoris** is a complex organ, only a portion of which is visible. The external portion is the clitoral **glans**, a small but highly sensitive knob of tissue positioned at the front of the vestibule. It is about the size of a pearl and, like a pearl, its size can vary. It is covered, or partly covered, by the clitoral hood but can be made visible by gently retracting the hood. The shaft of the clitoris, which is about 1 inch (2 to 3 cm) long, runs upward from the glans, under the hood. Although the shaft cannot be seen directly, it can be felt, and its outline may be visible through the skin of the hood. Both the shaft and the glans are erectile; that is, they are capable of becoming larger and firmer during sexual arousal. The erectile tissue within the clitoral shaft consists of two **corpora cavernosa** ("cavernous bodies") that lie side by side. The erectile tissue within the glans consists of a single **corpus spongiosum** ("spongy body").

Ointment-like secretions from the underside of the clitoral hood lubricate the motion of the hood over the clitoris, but when these secretions dry and mix with dead cells and bacteria, they form a pasty material called **smegma**, which can collect under the hood. Smegma may be removed, or prevented from accumulating, by pulling the clitoral hood back and gently washing the area with soap and warm water.

Two internal extensions of the clitoris, the **crura**, diverge backward and downward from the clitoral shaft, giving the entire clitoris a wishbone structure (**Figure 2.5**). The crura are about 3 inches (7 cm) long and partially enwrap the urethra. Yet another pair of structures, the **vestibular bulbs**, are closely associated with the clitoris (O'Connell et al., 1998). They are curved masses of erectile tissue consisting of the same corpus spongiosum material that forms the clitoral glans. They surround the vestibule and underlie the inner labia. Like the crura, the vestibular bulbs are considered to be internal portions of the clitoris. Erection of the vestibular bulbs during sexual arousal helps to lengthen and stiffen the vagina.

vasocongestion The swelling of tissue caused by an influx of blood.

clitoris The erectile organ in females, whose external portion is located at the junction of the inner labia, just in front of the vestibule.

glans The terminal knob of the clitoris or penis.

corpus cavernosum (pl., corpora cavernosa) Either of two elongated erectile structures within the clitoris or penis that also extend backward into the pelvic floor.

corpus spongiosum A single midline erectile structure. In both sexes, it fills the glans.

smegma A whitish, greasy secretion that builds up under the hood of the clitoris or the foreskin of the penis.

crura (sing. crus) The two internal extensions of the corpora cavernosa of the clitoris or penis.

vestibular bulbs Erectile structures beneath the inner labia, on either side of the vestibule.

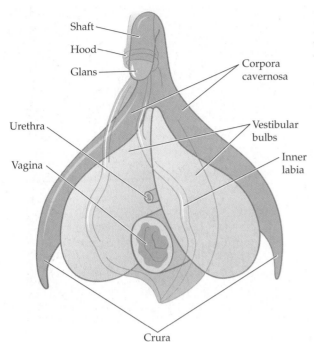

Shaft

Hood

Glans

Urethra

Vagina

Corpora cavernosa

Vestibular bulbs

Inner labia

Crura

Figure 2.5 Structure of the clitoris The inner labia are shown as if transparent. Both the clitoral glans and the vestibular bulbs are composed of corpus spongiosum tissue.

The clitoris, especially the glans, is richly supplied with sensory nerve fibers whose function is to produce sexual arousal. Indeed, the only certain function of the clitoris is sexual pleasure, and its stimulation is the most reliable way for most women to experience orgasm. The clitoris is so sensitive that many women prefer diffuse or indirect stimulation rather than direct touching of the clitoris itself.

During sexual arousal, the clitoris swells and becomes erect: The shaft of the clitoris becomes firmer and more easily felt, but the glans remains soft. This is because a layer of tough connective tissue surrounds the shaft, restricting its expansion, whereas the glans is free to expand. The mechanism of erection is described in more detail in connection with the penis (see Chapter 3), where it has been studied in detail. The process of erection involves not just the shaft and glans, but also the deeper clitoral structures—the crura and vestibular bulbs (Suh et al., 2004). Typically, the glans of the clitoris is visible in the nonaroused state, but it may disappear under the clitoral hood during erection or with increasing sexual arousal, so sexual stimulation of the clitoris may occur through the hood rather than directly on the clitoral glans itself. Still, there's quite a bit of variation from woman to woman in terms of her clitoral anatomy and what kind of clitoral stimulation she finds arousing. The clitoris is more erotically sensitive in the erect than in the flaccid state.

Not all women know that they have a clitoris or understand its function. Discussion of the clitoris can easily get skipped over in sex education classes, and plenty of women have never had a sex-ed class anyway. If they were discouraged, as girls, from exploring their bodies, and their partners have no particular interest in their sexual fulfillment, the structure may remain undiscovered.

On the other hand, in many societies or parts of societies, the clitoris gets quite a bit of attention. Piercing—usually of the clitoral hood but sometimes of the labia—is becoming an increasingly popular form of self-expression in the United States. It may be done for adornment, to enhance sexual stimulation, or even as a spiritual act. As with any genital piercing, scrupulous hygiene is required during the procedure as well as during the several-week healing period, in order to prevent infection and other potential complications (Dalke et al., 2013).

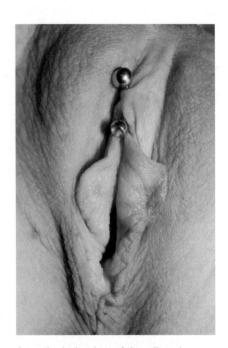

A vertical piercing of the clitoral hood—the most popular genital piercing in women.

Box 2.1 Society, Values, and the Law

Female Genital Cutting

I was frozen with fear . . . I peered between my legs and saw the gypsy woman getting ready . . . I expected a big knife, but instead, out of the bag she pulled a tiny cotton sack. She reached inside with her long fingers, and fished out a broken razor blade . . . I saw dried blood on the jagged edge of the blade. She spat on it and wiped it against her dress. While she was scrubbing, my world went dark as my mother tied a scarf around my eyes as a blindfold. The next thing I felt was my flesh, my genitals, being cut away. (Dirie, 1998)

Like Waris Dirie, author of the foregoing account, an estimated 80 to 120 million women worldwide have been subjected to some form of cutting of their external genitals during childhood or puberty. The various procedures are referred to collectively as **female circumcision**, female genital cutting, or female genital mutilation. The practice is prevalent in 29 countries, most of them in Africa. Eighty percent or more of the women in Djibouti, Egypt, Eritrea, Ethiopia, Gambia, Sierra Leone, Somalia, and Sudan are believed to have been circumcised. Female genital cutting is also practiced in the Middle East, Indonesia, and elsewhere (World Health Organization, 2010). It is particularly associated with Islamic cultures, and although female circumcision is not prescribed in the Quran, it is referred to favorably in later Islamic texts and is often perceived to have religious significance.

There are three principal types of female genital cutting. In the least invasive version, known as **sunnah**, the clitoral hood is incised or removed. This procedure is roughly analogous to male circumcision as we know it in the United States (see Box 3.1). In practice, however, some part of the clitoris itself is often removed during sunnah circumcision.

In the second procedure, known as **clitoridectomy** or excision, the entire clitoral glans and shaft may be removed, along with the hood and sometimes nearby portions of the inner labia. The procedure varies according to local custom.

The third procedure, known as **infibulation**, is the most invasive. It is widely practiced in the Sudan and Somalia. (Waris Dirie is Somali.) The procedure includes clitoridectomy but goes beyond it to include removal of the entire inner labia and the inner parts of the outer labia. The cut or abraded edges of the

Waris Dirie from Somalia lifts up her World Social Award during the Women's World Awards gala in Hamburg, Germany. Dirie has campaigned against the practice of female genital cutting.

two outer labia are then stitched together to cover the vestibule. Only a small opening is left for the passage of urine and menstrual blood. When the woman first has coitus, the opening has to be enlarged—by forceful penetration with the penis or other object, or by cutting.

Female genital cutting is generally performed by traditional practitioners who lack medical training. It is often done with crude instruments and without anesthesia or attention to sanitary conditions, so there is a risk of potentially fatal complications, including hemorrhage and infection. There has been a recent trend toward the "medicalization" of the procedure—that is, its performance by trained medical personnel. This trend could reduce the rate of complications. The trend is controversial, however, since it may be seen as legitimizing the practice.

The long-term effects of female genital cutting are also controversial. In some cases, especially with infibulation, the procedure can cause serious problems with urination, menstruation, intercourse, childbirth, and fertility. But some studies have suggested that the harmful effects of the less-invasive forms of the practice have been exaggerated (Shell-Duncan & Hernlund, 2000).

Female circumcision, also known as female genital cutting, is a traditional but highly controversial practice in some cultures. Cutting or removal of the external parts of the clitoris is a central element in female circumcision (**Box 2.1**).

Female genital cutting may be done simply because it is a tradition in a given culture. A woman who retains her clitoris may be considered ritually unclean or dangerous to the health of a man who has sex with her. However, there may be a second purpose to the procedure: the reduction of female sexual activity, especially before or outside of marriage. This reduction is achieved either by decreasing the pleasure of sexual acts (especially by removal of the clitoris) or by making them painful or physically impossible (as with infibulation). In many cultures in which female genital cutting is practiced, a woman who has not undergone the procedure is not marriageable—which often means that she is condemned to a life of poverty.

In the United States, female circumcision has been illegal since 1996. Significant numbers of immigrant women have been subjected to circumcision in their countries of birth, however, so Western medical professionals need to be aware of the phenomenon. Some circumcision of the daughters of immigrants does occur in the United States, but the prevalence of this illegal activity is hard to estimate. In 2010 the American Academy of Pediatrics (AAP) floated the idea of legalizing the least invasive form of female genital cutting, in which the operator makes a nick or small cut in the clitoral hood. The suggestion met with a firestorm of opposition, and the AAP eventually withdrew it (Shweder, 2013).

The practice of female circumcision has been strongly condemned by many Americans on several grounds: that it is harmful and dangerous; that it interferes with women's right to self-expression, especially in the sexual domain; that it subjugates women's interests to the purported interests of men; and that it makes irreversible decisions for children before they are able to make those decisions for themselves.

In 2005 the African Union's Protocol on the Rights of Women in Africa was ratified: It requires all 53 member states to prohibit female circumcision. This is a promising step, but its effect is uncertain. In Egypt, for example, female circumcision has been illegal since 2007, but this has not led to any appreciable decrease in the practice. In fact, the 2011 overthrow of President Hosni Mubarak, whose wife was an ardent opponent of female circumcision, has been followed by an increase in its popularity (Sharma, 2011).

Although campaigning against female circumcision may seem like an entirely praiseworthy activity, it does potentially conflict with another value, namely, respect for cultural diver-

sity and autonomy. While *we* may be tempted to use words such as "mutilation" to describe female circumcision, women in the countries concerned have mostly positive views about the practice, and many girls *want* to have it done as a token of their womanhood and their membership in their culture. "Why should I avoid the exercise when my mother and grandmother went through it?" said one 19-year-old Ugandan woman a year after that country banned the practice (Magga, 2010).

It may be that the greatest progress will come from the work of activist organizations within the cultures concerned. Such organizations now exist in many countries. One possible avenue for change is the institution of "ritual without cutting," in which the traditional rites are preserved but the actual circumcision is omitted. The poster shown here was created by a Gambian organization dedicated to ending female genital mutilation and replacing the rite with one that does not involve cutting.

Waris Dirie now runs the Desert Flower Foundation, which campaigns against genital cutting and supports girls and women who have undergone cutting.

female circumcision Any of several forms of ritual cutting or excision of parts of the female genitalia.

sunnah Female genital cutting limited to incision or removal of the clitoral hood.

clitoridectomy Removal of the entire external portion of the clitoris (glans, shaft, and hood).

infibulation The most invasive form of female genital cutting; involves removal of the clitoris, inner labia, and parts of the outer labia, plus the sewing together of the outer labia over the vestibule.

The appearance of the vaginal opening is variable

The vaginal opening, or **introitus**, occupies the rear portion of the vestibule. In newborn girls, the vaginal opening is usually covered by a membranous fold of skin,

introitus The entrance to the vagina, usually covered early in life by the hymen.

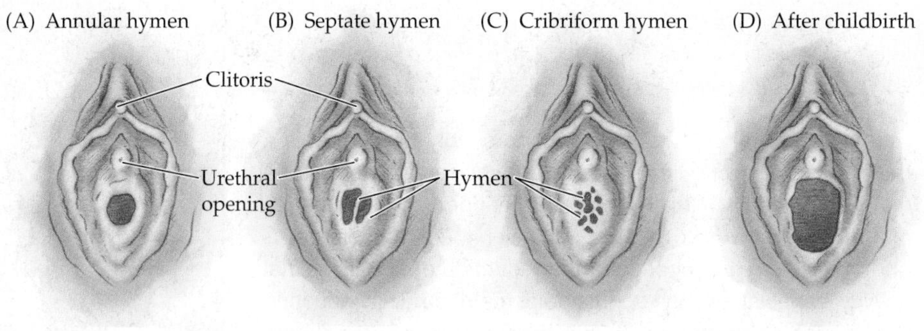

(A) Annular hymen   (B) Septate hymen   (C) Cribriform hymen   (D) After childbirth

Figure 2.6 The hymen is highly variable in structure. Most commonly it is annular (A); that is, it has a round central opening that is large enough for passage of the menstrual flow and insertion of a tampon, but usually not large enough for coitus. (B) The opening may be crossed by a band of tissue (septate hymen) or (C) by several bands that leave numerous small openings (cribriform hymen). If the openings are very small, or are absent entirely (imperforate hymen), the outflow of vaginal secretions and menstrual fluids may be blocked. First intercourse often tears the hymen but leaves it partially intact. (D) Vaginal childbirth removes all but small remnants of the structure. Familiarity with variations in hymen structure is important for professionals who evaluate female sexual assault victims.

the **hymen**. The hymen has one or several openings that allow for menstrual flow after a girl begins to menstruate, and for the insertion of tampons (**Figure 2.6**). In a rare condition called **imperforate hymen**, this structure completely closes the vaginal opening (Adams Hillard, 2003). Imperforate hymen is often first diagnosed at puberty because it causes a blockage of menstrual discharge; it is treated surgically to create an opening through which the menstrual discharge can flow.

The hymen may tear or stretch when a woman first has sexual intercourse, which may lead to some pain and bleeding. This phenomenon has led to the traditional notion that the state of a woman's hymen indicates whether or not she has ever engaged in coitus—that is, whether she is a virgin in one meaning of the term (see Chapter 10). One can certainly debate whether a woman's virginity—or lack of it—should be a matter of concern to anyone besides the woman herself. In any case, the state of her hymen is not a reliable indicator of virginity. In some women the hymen undergoes changes at puberty that allow for intercourse without any tearing. Some women may have widened the opening during tampon use or athletic activities, or they may have deliberately stretched the opening with the intention of facilitating first intercourse.

In many Middle Eastern countries it is traditional for a bride's mother or other relative to display the bloodstained sheets from a window after the bride's wedding night, thereby proving to the community that the marriage was consummated and that the bride was indeed a virgin. Of course there may be no stain, for any number of reasons—the bride was not a virgin; she was a virgin but didn't have an intact hymen; the couple achieved coitus without tearing of the hymen or without sufficient bleeding to stain the sheets; or they didn't engage in coitus because the man ejaculated prematurely or because one or both parties were too anxious, too tired, or otherwise unable to perform the act. To guard against any of these possibilities, the mother may bring a vial of chicken blood with her.

In some Westernized regions of the Middle East, this ritual has become a lighthearted tradition. In more conservative communities, however, proof of a bride's virginity is still so important that a woman who lacks an intact hymen may undergo an operation to reconstruct one before she marries (Bentlage & Eich, 2007).

The opening of the **urethra** is located between the vaginal opening and the clitoris. Given that the main function of the urethra is to pass urine, you might not consider

hymen   A membrane, usually perforated or incomplete, that covers the opening of the vagina. It may be torn by first coitus or by other means.

imperforate hymen   A hymen that completely closes the introitus.

urethra   The canal that conveys urine from the bladder to the urethral opening.

it a sexual structure, but some women do ejaculate from it during sexual climax, as we'll see shortly.

The **perineum** is the erotically sensitive area between the vaginal opening and the anus (or, in males, between the scrotum and the anus). Intestinal bacteria can be spread rather easily from the anus across the perineum to the vagina or urethra, which may cause a genital or urinary infection. For this reason, women are advised to wipe themselves in a backward, not a forward, direction after using the toilet.

Important structures underlie the vulva. We have already described the deep extensions of the clitoris. They are associated with various **pelvic floor muscles**, especially the **pubococcygeus muscle** (see **Web Activity 2.2: Internal Anatomy of the Vulva**). The steady contraction of these muscles stiffens the walls of the vagina during sex, thus increasing sexual sensations for both participants. These muscles, which contract more strongly at orgasm, increase pleasure, prevent urinary and fecal leakage, and possibly help to keep semen in the vagina. Exercises to increase the tone of the pubococcygeus muscle and other muscles of the pelvic floor (Kegel exercises) have been recommended for the treatment of sexual disorders as well as to prevent the involuntary leakage of urine or feces (incontinence). Kegel exercises are described in Chapter 14.

The Vagina Is the Outermost Portion of the Female Reproductive Tract

As shown in **Figure 2.7**, the female **reproductive tract**, when viewed from the front, takes the shape of a capital letter T. The stem of the T is formed by the vagina, the cervix, and the body of the uterus. The two horizontal arms of the T are formed by the oviducts, also called fallopian tubes, whose ends are adjacent to the two ovaries. The reproductive tract serves the purpose of transport of the female's eggs (ova) and the male's sperm, as well as fertilization, pregnancy, and passage of the fetus during childbirth.

In a woman who is not sexually excited, the **vagina** is a collapsed tube that runs about 3 to 4 inches (8 to 10 cm) upward and backward from the vaginal opening. Penetration of the vagina by the penis constitutes **coitus** or **sexual intercourse**. The vagina plays a role in sperm transport and (along with the cervix) forms the **birth canal** through which a fetus reaches the outside world.

The vaginal wall is highly elastic and consists of three layers: a thin cellular lining, or **mucosa**; an intermediate muscular layer; and an outermost tough, elastic layer. The mucosa can be seen by parting the inner labia. When a woman is in a nonaroused state, it is pink in color. The vaginal wall has a series of folds that run around the circumference of the vagina.

The outer third of the vagina, near the vaginal opening, has a structure different from that of the internal portion (see Chapter 4). It is tighter, more muscular, and also more richly innervated than the deeper portion. Thus, most of the sensation during coitus—for both partners—derives from contact between the penis and this outer portion of the vagina.

The vagina is normally inhabited by large numbers of "friendly" bacteria that convert sugars to lactic acid. This bacterial activity usually makes the surface of the vagina mildly acidic (pH 4.0 to 5.0), and this helps to prevent the growth of harmful bacteria. The vagina also normally contains a variety of fungal organisms, especially *Candida albicans*. It sometimes happens that the fungal organisms overgrow, causing inflammation of the vaginal walls, itching, and possibly a thick white discharge. This condition is called **candidiasis**, vaginal thrush, or (in popular language) a "yeast infection." The condition is diagnosed by microscopic examination of the discharge and is treated with antifungal medications. Some of these medications are available without a prescription. It is better to get a medical diagnosis, however, at least for the

perineum   The region of skin between the anus and the vulva or scrotum.

pelvic floor muscles   A muscular sling that underlies and supports the pelvic organs.

pubococcygeus muscle   A muscle of the pelvic floor that runs from the pubic bone to the coccyx (tailbone). In women it forms a sling around the vagina.

reproductive tract   The internal anatomical structures in either sex that form the pathway taken by ova, sperm, or the conceptus.

vagina   A muscular tube extending 3 to 4 inches (8 to 10 cm) from the vestibule to the uterine cervix.

coitus   Penetration of the vagina by the penis.

sexual intercourse   Sexual contact, usually understood to involve coitus.

birth canal   The canal formed by the uterus, cervix, and vagina, through which the fetus passes during the birth process.

mucosa   A surface layer of cells that is lubricated by the secretions of mucous glands.

candidiasis   A fungal infection of the vagina. Also called thrush or a yeast infection.

Figure 2.7 The female reproductive tract (See **Web Activity 2.3: The Female Reproductive Tract, Part 1** and **Web Activity 2.4: The Female Reproductive Tract, Part 2**.)

(A) **Midline view**

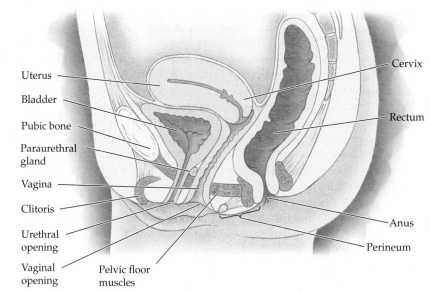

Uterus

Bladder

Pubic bone

Paraurethral gland

Vagina

Clitoris

Urethral opening

Vaginal opening

Pelvic floor muscles

Cervix

Rectum

Anus

Perineum

(B) **Frontal view**

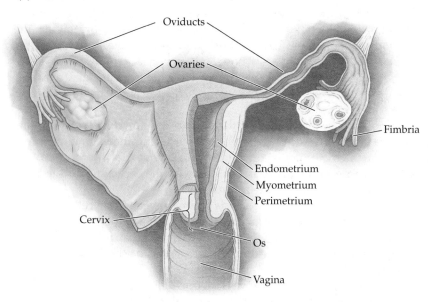

Oviducts

Ovaries

Fimbria

Endometrium

Myometrium

Perimetrium

Cervix

Os

Vagina

douche To rinse the vagina out with a fluid; the fluid so used.

first episode, because women sometimes use over-the-counter medications for inappropriate conditions, a practice that can lead to the development of drug-resistant infections (Centers for Disease Control, 2004). Though unpleasant, vaginal candidiasis does not have serious health consequences. Persistent candidiasis can, however, be a sign of an underlying problem with the immune system.

One of the factors that can predispose women to candidiasis is frequent **douching**—the rinsing of the vagina with a stream of water or other liquid as a "cleansing" or deodorizing procedure. Gynecologists discourage douching, because the vagina is usually a self-cleansing organ. A clear, odorless vaginal discharge is normal and does not require douching or any other treatment. Depending on the time of the menstrual cycle, the normal vaginal discharge may take on a whitish or yellowish appearance.

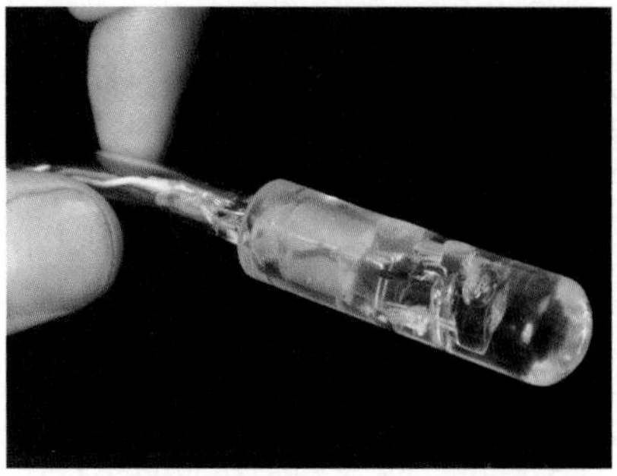

Figure 2.8 **A photocell** is used to measure female sexual arousal. It is placed against the vaginal wall and tracks the change in color as the tissues become engorged with blood.

If the discharge develops an unusual appearance or odor, however, this may be a sign of a sexually transmitted infection or of bacterial vaginosis. These conditions and their treatment are discussed in Chapter 15.

The vagina undergoes changes during arousal

Like the inner labia, the walls of the vagina swell because of vasocongestion during sexual arousal. As a result, their color changes from pink to purple—the color of venous blood. One way that sex researchers monitor physiological arousal in women is to place a photocell in the vagina to track this color change (**Figure 2.8**). Vasocongestion of the vagina and inner labia, combined with the contraction of musculature in the vaginal walls and erection of the vestibular bulbs, cause the vagina to wrap more tightly around the penis during sexual intercourse than would otherwise be the case, which in turn increases sexual stimulation for both partners. For the woman, vasocongestion of the inner labia facilitates motion of the clitoral hood and thus increases stimulation of the clitoris, the structure that is usually most erotically sensitive.

Another response of the vagina to arousal is **lubrication**. This involves a diffuse seepage of watery fluid through all parts of the vaginal mucosa. The fluid is made slippery by the addition of mucus secreted by glands in the cervix. Lubrication serves two functions. First, the lubricant has a near-neutral pH (neither acid nor alkaline), which offers a more sperm-friendly environment than the acidic pH of the nonaroused vagina. Thus, lubrication favors sperm survival and transport. Second, lubrication makes coitus and other stimulation of the vulva easier and more pleasurable for both partners. This natural lubrication can be supplemented with the use of water-based "personal lubricants" if necessary.

lubrication The natural appearance of slippery secretions in the vagina during sexual arousal, or the use of artificial lubricants to facilitate sexual activity.

Gräfenberg spot (G-spot) A possible area of increased erotic sensitivity on or deep within the front wall of the vagina.

paraurethral glands Glands situated next to the female urethra, thought to be equivalent to the prostate gland in males. Also known as Skene's glands.

The G-spot is a controversial erogenous zone

Perhaps the most famous and controversial feature of the vagina is the **Gräfenberg spot**, or **G-spot**, named for the sexologist Ernst Gräfenberg, who described it in the early 1950s. Only a minority of women say they have a G-spot, but for those who do, it is an area of heightened sensitivity on the front wall of the vagina, about 1 to 2 inches (3 to 5 cm) from the vaginal entrance (**Figure 2.9**). Deep pressure at this location can first trigger the desire to urinate, but continued stimulation is sexually arousing and is said to trigger an orgasm that is different in quality from an orgasm caused by stimulation of the clitoris (Ladas et al., 2004).

What is the structural basis of the G-spot, if it exists? One candidate is a set of **paraurethral glands**, which are located between the front wall of the vagina and the urethra (see Figure 2.7A). Their ducts open into the urethra. The female paraurethral glands and the male prostate gland are thought to develop from the same embryonic precursors (Zaviacic & Whipple, 1993). The paraure-

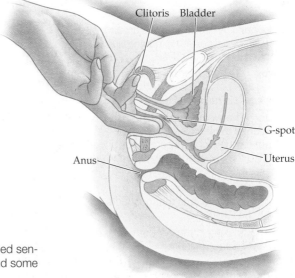

Figure 2.9 **Finding the G-spot** The G-spot is said to be an area of heightened sensitivity on the front wall of the vagina. Not all women say they have a G-spot, and some sexologists question its existence altogether.

FAQ

What is "G-spot amplification"?

It's a procedure, such as the injection of collagen into the supposed region of a woman's G-spot, that is claimed to amplify its function. The procedure hasn't been shown to be effective or safe, and the American College of Obstetricians and Gynecologists strongly discourages it.

thral glands could be the G-spot because, in some women, orgasms triggered by stimulation of this area are accompanied by ejaculation of fluid from the glands (see Chapter 5). Nevertheless, there has as yet been no clear identification of the G-spot with any anatomical structure (Kilchevsky et al., 2012; Hines & Kilchevsky, 2014).

Experts disagree vigorously about the existence or identity of the G-spot (Jannini et al., 2010). Some claim that every woman has a G-spot and that those who are unaware of its existence can be helped to identify it (Ladas et al., 2004). Others assert that the G-spot is a complete myth (Puppo, 2012). Debate about the G-spot is related to a controversy about vaginal versus clitoral orgasms, which we will consider in Chapter 5.

The Anus Can Also Be a Sex Organ

Both heterosexual and homosexual couples may engage in penetration or manual or oral stimulation of the **anus**—anal sex (see Chapter 6), so the anus needs to be described along with the more obviously sexual structures. The anal orifice is located at the back of the perineum (see Figure 2.7A). It is kept tightly closed most of the time by contraction of the external and internal anal **sphincter** muscles. You can feel these sphincters by inserting your finger a short way into the anus. The external sphincter is under conscious control—you can squeeze down on your finger or release the tension at will. The internal sphincter is not ordinarily under voluntary control; thus, it can cause problems during anal penetration. With experience a person can learn to relax this sphincter too.

Beyond the sphincters lies the **rectum**, the lowermost portion of the gastrointestinal tract. It is usually empty of feces except immediately before a bowel movement. The rectum is a much larger space than the anus, so most of the sensation generated during anal sex (for both partners) derives from penetration of the anus itself (which is both relatively tight and richly innervated), rather than from penetration of the rectum. In women, the structure in front of the rectum is the vagina. Stimulation of this and other nearby structures during anal sex may also contribute to sexual arousal.

The anus and rectum are lined by mucosa, but unlike the vaginal walls, this surface does not provide significant amounts of lubrication. Thus, most people who engage in anal sex use some type of lubricant. Other health concerns regarding anal sex are discussed in Chapter 6. Although we are postponing discussion of sexually transmitted infections (STIs) to Chapter 15, it's worth mentioning now that condoms offer significant protection from STIs during anal sex, just as they do during vaginal sex.

The Uterus Serves a Double Duty

The **uterus** or womb—the inward continuation of the female reproductive tract beyond the vagina—is a hollow organ that lies within the pelvic cavity (the portion of the abdominal cavity that is surrounded by the bones of the pelvis). In a nonpregnant woman the uterus is about the shape and size of a small upside-down pear (see Figure 2.7). The narrow part, the **cervix**, protrudes into the deep end of the vagina. A woman can feel her own cervix by inserting one or two fingers deeply into the vagina until she touches something that feels like the tip of her nose. She can see her cervix with the help of a mirror, a flashlight, and a speculum (an instrument that holds open the walls of the vagina; **Box 2.2**).

A constricted opening—the **os**—connects the vagina to a short canal that runs through the cervix. The cervical canal contains numerous glands that secrete **mucus**. The consistency and amount of this mucus change with the menstrual cycle, and this is why women experience changes in their vaginal discharge around the cycle.

anus   The opening from which feces are released.

sphincter   A circular muscle around a tube or orifice whose contraction closes the tube or orifice.

rectum   The final, straight portion of the large bowel. It connects to the exterior via the anus.

uterus   The womb; a pear-shaped region of the female reproductive tract through which sperm pass and where the conceptus implants and develops.

cervix   The lowermost, narrow portion of the uterus that connects with the vagina.

os   The opening in the cervix that connects the vagina with the cervical canal.

mucus   A thick or slippery secretion.

Box 2.2 Sexual Health

Genital Self-Examination

If you're a woman and you've never really taken a close look at your genital area, now may be a good time to do so.

Genital self-examination has several potential benefits. If you are reluctant or embarrassed to pay attention to your sexual anatomy, doing so in connection with this course may help you overcome these inhibitions and become more comfortable with your body. Are there aspects of the way it looks that seem to you especially attractive, unattractive, or unusual, and if so, why? Vulvas differ greatly from woman to woman, especially in the distribution of pubic hair, the size and visibility of the clitoris, and the shape and color of the inner labia, but your anatomy is no more or less "normal" than any other woman's. Finally, by becoming familiar with your vulva, you can more easily recognize any changes that may call for medical attention.

To get a good look at your vulva, you should use a hand mirror and possibly a flashlight (see Figure). Look while in a variety of postures and from a variety of angles. Be sure you can recognize the parts that are described in the text. Also, explore them with your fingers: What do they feel like to your fingers, and what do your fingers feel like to them? Use your fingers to gently draw back the clitoral hood and to separate the labia, thus getting a view of the vestibule. If you become sexually aroused in the course of examining yourself, notice how the appearance of your vulva changes.

If you are curious to see the inside of your vagina and your cervix, you will need a flashlight and a vaginal speculum. This is a two-armed, "duck-billed" device made of plastic that holds the walls of the vagina apart. (A speculum can be obtained through women's health organizations. They come in three sizes; a small is probably right unless you have reason to think you need a larger one.) First, wash the speculum and practice opening, locking, and unlocking it. Then lubricate the speculum with a water-based lubricant (or just water). With your knees

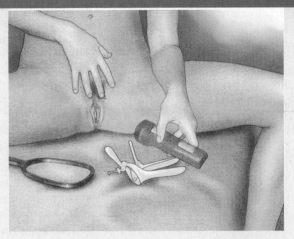

Genital self-examination. The white instrument is a speculum.

apart, use the fingers of one hand to separate your labia. With the other hand, hold the speculum, with handle up and the twin arms closed, and slide it gently into your vagina. Any discomfort should be a signal to pause and relax, and if comfortable insertion isn't possible, you should stop. Once the speculum is fully in place, gently open and lock the arms, so that you now have both hands free to hold the mirror and flashlight. By shining the flashlight onto the mirror, you should be able to see your cervix, which looks like a rounded knob with a central hole or slit (the os). The appearance of the cervix varies around the menstrual cycle (due to changes in the cervical mucus) and from woman to woman. Some women may see fluid-filled sacs on the cervix protruding through the os; these are usually harmless. To remove the speculum, first unlock and close the arms, then gently withdraw it. You should carefully wash the speculum with soap and water, rinse it, and put it away in a clean place. Self-examination with a speculum helps a woman get to know her own body, but it isn't a practical way to diagnose medical problems or a substitute for regular professional checkups.

Near the time of ovulation its consistency is optimal for passage of sperm through the cervix.

The cervical canal opens into the cavity of the uterus proper. The wall of the uterus has three layers: an inner lining (**endometrium**), a muscular wall (**myometrium**), and a thin, outer covering (**perimetrium**) that separates the uterus from the pelvic cavity, as shown in Figure 2.7B.

The endometrium must switch between two reproductive functions—the transport of sperm up the reproductive tract toward the site of fertilization, and the implantation and nourishment of an embryo. Because each of these two functions requires a very different organization, the structure of the endometrium changes

endometrium   The internal lining of the uterus.

myometrium   The muscular layers of the wall of the uterus.

perimetrium   The outer covering of the uterus.

menstruation The breakdown of the endometrium at approximately monthly intervals, with consequent loss of tissue and blood from the vagina.

Pap test The microscopic examination of a sample of cells taken from the cervix or (less commonly) the anus.

pelvic examination A visual and digital examination of the vulva and pelvic organs.

FAQ

I've had the HPV vaccine. Do I still need Pap tests?

Yes, HPV vaccines don't protect against all the types of HPV that cause cervical cancer.

---

over the menstrual cycle. A visible sign of this reorganization is **menstruation**—the shedding of part of the endometrial lining and its discharge, along with some blood, through the cervix and vagina.

The myometrium is composed primarily of muscles that are not under voluntary control. Involuntary contractions of the myometrium during labor play a vital role in delivery of the fetus. Myometrial contractions (often perceived as menstrual cramps) are also thought to aid in the shedding and expulsion of the endometrial lining at menstruation.

Cancer can affect the cervix or the endometrium

Cancer of the cervix (cervical cancer) strikes about 13,000 American women annually and causes about 4400 deaths. The main factor predisposing women to cervical cancer is infection with human papillomavirus (HPV), a virus that is sexually transmitted (see Chapter 15). Less important risk factors include chlamydia infection (Koskela et al., 2000), smoking, and immune system dysfunction.

The death rate from cervical cancer has dropped by about 75% since the 1950s. Much of this reduction can be attributed to the use of regular **Pap tests**—named for the pathologist George Papanicolaou (1883–1962), who developed the test. A Pap test is generally done as part of a **pelvic examination**. The American Cancer Society (ACS) recommends that women have Pap tests every 3 years between ages 21 and 30, every 5 years between ages 30 and 65, and no screening thereafter if previous tests have been negative (Saslow et al., 2012). There are more details about this in Chapter 15.

In a pelvic exam, the gynecologist or other health care provider first inspects the vulva for external problems and then uses a speculum to hold the walls of the vagina apart so that the vagina and cervix can be visually inspected for lesions, inflammation, or a discharge. For the Pap test, a specially shaped wooden or plastic spatula is inserted while the speculum is in place, and a sample of cells and mucus is wiped from the cervix (**Figure 2.10**). To get a sample from the cervical canal, a small brush may be inserted into the cervical os.

The sample of cells and mucus taken from the cervix is spread on a slide and examined under a microscope. If the cells show precancerous changes, the health

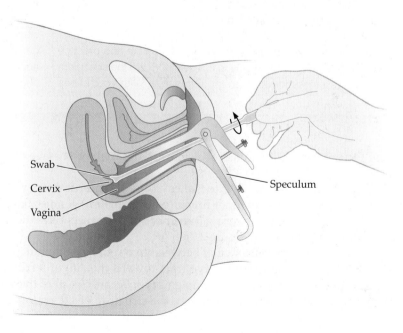

Figure 2.10 **The Pap test** A sample of cells is taken from the cervix. (See **Web Activity 2.5: The Pap Test**.)

care provider may proceed to a more-detailed examination of the cervix using an operating microscope. This procedure is called **colposcopy**. During the colposcopy, the provider may take biopsies or destroy precancerous lesions by freezing or other methods. Follow-up examinations are required to ensure that the lesions have not recurred.

A second sample may be taken at the same time to test for the presence of HPV—specifically, types of HPV that can cause cervical cancer (see Chapter 15). HPV testing is recommended for women age 30 and older (Centers for Disease Control, 2014j).

If a precancerous lesion escapes detection (most likely because the woman has not had a Pap test for several years, or has never had one), it may progress to true invasive cervical cancer. Symptoms of cervical cancer may include an abnormal, sometimes bloodstained vaginal discharge, pain during intercourse, or bleeding during intercourse. Of course, these symptoms are not specific to cervical cancer, but a woman who experiences them should see a doctor right away to ensure that if cancer is present, it is detected as soon as possible.

Endometrial cancer (often called uterine cancer) is three times more common than cervical cancer but causes only 50% more deaths. In other words, the survival rate is better for endometrial cancer: 90% of women diagnosed with early-stage endometrial cancer are still alive 5 years later (American Cancer Society, 2013c). A diagnosis is usually made on the basis of cells or tissue removed from the uterus.

Except for the earliest-stage cervical cancers, cancers affecting the uterus are usually treated by removal of the entire organ (**hysterectomy**). Sometimes other pelvic organs, such as the oviducts and ovaries, also have to be removed, depending on how advanced the disease is. Chemotherapy, radiation therapy, or a combination of both is commonly added to improve the woman's chances of survival.

A full pelvic exam traditionally includes a "bimanual exam," in which the health care provider inserts a gloved finger into the vagina and presses down on the abdomen with the other hand. This allows the provider to feel the various pelvic organs. Because there are many false-positive findings that lead to unnecessary operations, increasing numbers of experts now believe that bimanual exams should be limited to women who have symptoms suggestive of a pelvic disorder (Brody, 2013).

Other uterine conditions include fibroids, endometriosis, abnormal bleeding, and prolapse

Several noncancerous conditions are much more common than uterine cancer:

- **Fibroids** are noncancerous tumors of smooth muscle that grow within or outside the uterus (**Figure 2.11**). They are very common: 20% to 25% of women develop them, usually after the age of 30 but before menopause. They are often asymptomatic, but they can cause pain and abnormal bleeding. When fibroids do cause symptoms, they can be removed surgically or destroyed by blockage of the arteries that supply them with blood. If the woman does not want to have children in the future, hysterectomy is an option.

- **Endometriosis** is the growth of endometrial tissue at abnormal locations within the pelvic cavity, such as on the oviducts, the ovaries, or the outside of the uterus. These patches of endometrial tissue are most likely derived from cells in the menstrual discharge that pass backward up the oviducts into the pelvic cavity, but other theories of causation have also been proposed. The most common symptom of endometriosis is pelvic pain; this pain may be worse before or during the

colposcopy The examination of the cervix with the aid of an operating microscope.

endometrial cancer Cancer of the endometrium of the uterus.

hysterectomy Surgical removal of the uterus.

fibroid A noncancerous tumor arising from muscle cells of the uterus.

endometriosis The growth of endometrial tissue at abnormal locations such as the oviducts.

Figure 2.11 Fibroids are noncancerous tumors of the uterus. They may be located on the endometrium (A), within the myometrium (B), or near the outer surface of the uterus (C). Sometimes they are attached to the inner or outer surface of the uterus by stalks (D).

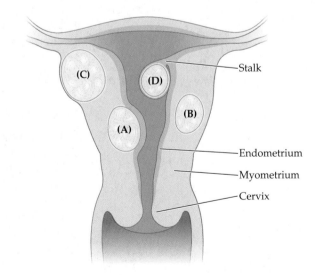

prolapse The slipping out of place of an organ, such as the uterus.

oviduct Either of two bilateral tubes that lead from the uterus toward the ovaries, the usual site of fertilization. Also called a fallopian tube.

cilia Microscopic, hairlike extensions of cells, often capable of coordinated beating motions.

menstrual period, or at the time of ovulation, or it may be ongoing. Endometriosis can cause infertility. There is no simple cure for the condition: Pain medications are helpful, as are oral contraceptives. Sometimes the patches of endometrial tissue can be removed surgically.

- Abnormal endometrial bleeding can be caused by some of the conditions we have already discussed, but it can also occur for a variety of other reasons, or for no apparent reason at all. It can be treated with certain oral contraceptives, by surgery, or (if very persistent) by hysterectomy.

- **Prolapse** is a downward sagging of the uterus into the vagina. It is caused by weakening of the ligaments that support the uterus and of the muscles of the pelvic floor. The condition is seen most often in elderly women who have had at least one child, because both aging and childbirth weaken the structures that support the uterus. Obesity and smoking are also risk factors. Uterine prolapse may be treated by a variety of surgical techniques or by insertion of a plastic ring that keeps the uterus in place. Kegel exercises help to prevent uterine prolapse.

Should hysterectomy be so common?

About 430,000 hysterectomies are performed in the United States annually (Wright et al., 2013b), and 1 in 3 women has had a hysterectomy by the age of 60. The associated costs exceed $5 billion annually. Medical research indicates that many hysterectomies are unneeded.

In a premenopausal woman hysterectomy puts an end to menstruation and renders the woman infertile, but the operation does not have any hormonal effects unless it is accompanied by removal of the ovaries. Hysterectomy should not interfere with a woman's enjoyment of sex or her ability to engage in coitus or experience orgasm. In some cases the cervix can be left intact, making it even less likely that there will be any impairment of the woman's sexual pleasure. In this case, however, she will need to continue having regular Pap tests.

One study found that most women who have had a hysterectomy derive more pleasure from sex after the operation (Roovers et al., 2003). Women who undergo hysterectomy also report an improved general quality of life, and these improvements are greater than in women treated for the same conditions by nonsurgical means (Showstack et al., 2006).

Even so, the chances that a woman will undergo a hysterectomy are influenced by factors such as her race and the region of the country where she lives. This suggests that some hysterectomies are unnecessary. Women with noncancerous disorders of the uterus should be aware of the increasing range of options for treatment. Inpatient hysterectomy rates in the United States declined by 36% between 2002 and 2010 (Wright et al., 2013b).

The Oviducts Are the Site of Fertilization

At the upper end of the uterus, the reproductive tract divides into two symmetrical branches, the **oviducts** (see Figure 2.7B), also called fallopian tubes or simply "tubes." Each oviduct is about 4 inches (10 cm) long and forms a pathway between the uterus and the left or right ovary. Fertilization of an ovum by a sperm takes place in the outer third of an oviduct.

The interior surface of the oviducts is lined with **cilia**, microscopic hairlike structures that wave in a coordinated fashion toward the uterus. Sperm moving from the uterus toward the ovary have to swim against the current set up by the beating cilia,

FAQ

If hysterectomies are unnecessary why are they done?

Some *are* necessary. Some are not strictly necessary but do relieve pain or bleeding. Some are done because women are unaware of alternative treatments or their doctors are not trained to provide them..

rather like salmon swimming upstream, but this current is too slow to offer a serious impediment to healthy, fast-moving sperm.

The portion of each oviduct near the uterus is relatively narrow, but it widens somewhat as it nears the ovary. The oviduct ends in a flared opening with a fringe composed of fingerlike extensions. This fringe is known as a **fimbria**. Each fimbria lies near, but is not actually fused with, the ovary on that side of the body. Like the rest of the two oviducts, the left and right fimbrias are lined with cilia that help draw the ovum into the oviduct.

A continuous pathway extends from the outside of a woman's body, up her reproductive tract, and into the pelvic cavity. The body has many mechanisms to prevent disease-causing organisms from migrating up this pathway: For example, the presence of mucus in the cervix acts like a plug, hindering the passage of microorganisms. In some circumstances, however, sexually transmitted organisms can travel part or all of the way up the pathway, causing inflammation in the reproductive tract or even within the pelvic cavity. This kind of infection is known as **pelvic inflammatory disease** (**PID**).

The Ovaries Produce Ova and Sex Hormones

The **ovaries**—a woman's **gonads**—are paired organs located on either side of the uterus. They are egg-shaped structures measuring about 1 to 1.5 inches (3 cm) long. A woman's ovaries and a man's testicles are about the same size and shape.

Under the microscope, an adult woman's ovary can be seen to contain a large number of **follicles** at various stages of development (**Figure 2.12**). Each follicle consists of an **ovum**, or egg cell, surrounded by fluids and supporting cells.

The ovaries have two distinct functions. The first is to release ova in a process called **ovulation**. A newborn female has about a million undeveloped ova in each ovary, but these numbers decline throughout life. By puberty a woman has about 200,000 ova in each ovary. During her reproductive life she typically releases only one mature ovum per menstrual cycle. Thus, only a tiny fraction of a woman's ova are actually ovulated during her lifetime. Much greater numbers of ova die and are reabsorbed by the body.

fimbria   The fringe at the end of the oviduct, composed of fingerlike extensions.

pelvic inflammatory disease (PID)   An infection of the female reproductive tract, often caused by sexually transmitted organisms.

ovary   The female gonad; the organ that produces ova and secretes sex hormones.

gonad   An organ that produces ova or sperm and secretes sex hormones.

follicle   A fluid-filled sac that contains an egg (ovum), with its supporting cells, within the ovary.

ovum (pl. ova)   A female gamete, or egg.

ovulation   Release of an ovum from an ovary.

(A)

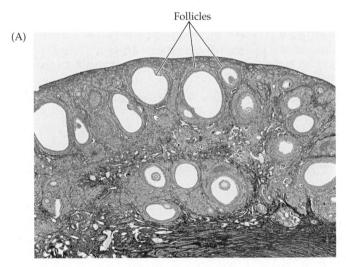

(B)

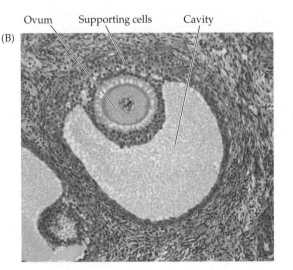

Figure 2.12 Microscopic structure of the ovary (A) Ovarian follicles. Low-power view of an ovary, showing a number of follicles. (B) Higher-power view of a single follicle, showing the central cavity and the ovum surrounded by supporting cells.

Box 2.3 Biology of Sex

The Feedback Loop that Controls Female Hormone Production

Ovulation and hormone secretion are regulated by a three-segment control loop that involves the passage of hormones between the brain, the **pituitary gland**, and the ovaries (see figure). First, a small region at the base of the brain named the **hypothalamus** secretes **gonadotropin-releasing hormone (GnRH)** into local vessels that carry it to the nearby pituitary gland. There it activates cells that manufacture and secrete two more hormones, **follicle-stimulating hormone (FSH)** and **luteinizing hormone (LH)**. Because these two hormones act on the gonads (in women, the ovaries), they are named **gonadotropins**, meaning gonad-influencing substances. Second, these two hormones enter the general blood circulation and reach their targets, the ovaries. FSH, as its name suggests, stimulates the development of ovarian follicles to the point that they are capable of ovulation. LH triggers ovulation itself, and it also causes the release of sex steroids by the ovaries. In the third segment of the loop, ovarian hormones pass via the general circulation system to the hypothalamus and pituitary gland, where they influence the release of GnRH, FSH, and LH. This feedback influence is inhibitory at low estrogen levels but switches to stimulation at high levels. As described later in the chapter, the switch occurs late in the preovulatory phase of the menstrual cycle and is a key trigger for ovulation.

pituitary gland   A gland under the control of and situated below the hypothalamus; its anterior lobe secretes gonadotropins and other hormones.

hypothalamus   A small region at the base of the brain; it contains cells involved in sexual responses and other basic functions.

gonadotropin-releasing hormone (GnRH)   A hormone secreted by the hypothalamus that stimulates the release of gonadotropins from the anterior pituitary gland.

follicle-stimulating hormone (FSH)   One of the two major gonadotropins secreted by the pituitary gland; it promotes maturation of ova (or sperm in males).

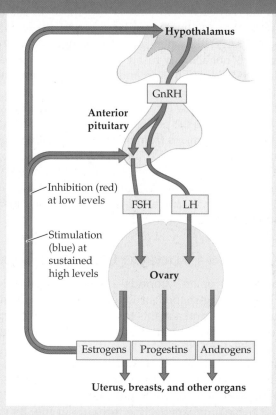

The hypothalamus in the brain sends signals to the pituitary gland. In response to these, the pituitary releases FSH and LH that affect the ovaries. At different times in the menstrual cycle, the ovaries produce various mixes of estrogens, progestins, and androgens. These affect the uterus, breasts, and other organs differently across the cycle. (See **Web Activity 2.6: Ovarian and Uterine Cycles**.)

luteinizing hormone (LH)   One of the two major gonadotropins secreted by the pituitary gland; it triggers ovulation and promotes the secretion of sex steroids by the ovaries (or testicles).

gonadotropins   Hormones that regulate the function of the gonads.

sex steroid   Any of the steroid hormones that are active in sexual and reproductive processes.

The second function of the ovaries is the production and secretion of sex hormones (**Table 2.1**). These sex hormones regulate the monthly menstrual cycle (**Box 2.3**). The ovarian hormones are mostly **sex steroids**, which are fatty molecules derived from

TABLE 2.1
Principal Sex Hormones and Their Actions

Class/subclass of hormone	Name	Site of production	Main targets	Main hormonal actions
SEX STEROIDS				
Estrogens	Estradiol	Gonads	Widespread in body and brain	Feminizes body at puberty; contributes to menstrual cycle; increases density of bone; ends growth of limb bones at puberty; feedback inhibition of gonadotropins; maintains sex drive (?)
Androgens	Testosterone	Gonads, adrenal cortex	Widespread in body and brain	Masculinizes body and brain during fetal development and at puberty; anabolic effects; maintains sex drive; feedback inhibition of gonadotropins
	5α-Dihydro-testosterone (DHT)	External genitalia, prostate gland, skin (converted from testosterone)	External genitalia, prostate gland, skin	Development and maintenance of male external genitalia and prostate gland; adult male patterns of hair distribution
Progestins	Progesterone	Ovary (corpus luteum), placenta	Uterus	Contributes to menstrual cycle; maintains pregnancy
PROTEINS/PEPTIDES				
Releasing hormones	Gonadotropin-releasing hormone (GnRH)	Hypothalamus	Anterior lobe of pituitary gland	Causes release of gonadotropins
	Follicle-stimulating hormone (FSH)	Anterior lobe of pituitary gland	Gonads	Stimulates maturation of ovarian follicles; stimulates spermatogenesis
Gonadotropins	Luteinizing hormone (LH)	Anterior lobe of pituitary gland	Gonads	Stimulates secretion of gonadal steroids; stimulates ovulation
	Human chorionic gonadotropin (hCG)	Conceptus	Ovary	Maintains corpus luteum
	Prolactin	Anterior lobe of pituitary gland	Breast	Prepares breast for lactation
	Growth hormone	Anterior lobe of pituitary gland	Widespread in body	Stimulates growth spurt at puberty
Other	Inhibin	Gonads	Anterior lobe of pituitary gland	Feedback inhibition of gonadotropin secretion
	Oxytocin	Hypothalamus (transported to posterior pituitary for secretion)	Breast, uterus	Milk letdown; uterine contractions during labor; role in orgasm (?); other nonreproductive functions
	Anti-Müllerian hormone (AMH)	Developing testes	Müllerian duct	Causes regression of Müllerian duct during male fetal development

estrogens Any of a class of steroids—the most important being estradiol—that promote the development of female secondary sexual characteristics at puberty and that have many other functions in both sexes.

estradiol The principal estrogen, secreted by ovarian follicles.

progestins Any of a class of steroids, the most important being progesterone, that cause the endometrium to proliferate and help maintain pregnancy.

progesterone A steroid hormone secreted by the ovary and the placenta; it is necessary for the establishment and maintenance of pregnancy.

androgens Any of a class of steroids—the most important being testosterone—that promote male sexual development and that have a variety of other functions in both sexes.

testosterone The principal androgen, synthesized in the testicles and, in lesser amounts, in the ovaries and adrenal glands.

menarche (Pronunciations vary; MEN-ar-kee is most common.) The onset of menstruation at puberty.

ovarian cysts Cysts within the ovary that can arise from a number of different causes.

polycystic ovary syndrome (PCOS) A condition marked by excessive secretion of androgens by the ovaries.

FAQ

Can a woman menstruate during pregnancy?

No, but many women experience some light vaginal bleeding early in pregnancy—for example, as the conceptus implants in the uterus. Major bleeding, bleeding accompanied by pain, or any bleeding after the first trimester are reasons to see your doctor promptly.

cholesterol. The sex steroids come in three classes: **estrogens** (of which the main representative is **estradiol**), **progestins** (main representative: **progesterone**), and **androgens** (main representative: **testosterone**).

Both the female gonads (ovaries) and the male gonads (testicles) make all three classes of sex steroids, but in differing amounts. The ovaries secrete relatively *large* quantities of estrogens and progestins, which are therefore sometimes thought of as "female hormones." The ovaries secrete relatively *small* quantities of androgens, but these small amounts are supplemented by androgens from another source, the adrenal glands, which lie on top of the kidneys.

Several medical conditions can affect the ovaries. The most significant is ovarian cancer, which is not a particularly common form of cancer: It strikes about 22,000 American women annually. Risk factors for ovarian cancer include older age (the median age at diagnosis is 65), a family history of the disease, possession of cancer-promoting genes, early onset of menstruation (**menarche**), late menopause, not having children, obesity, and prolonged hormone replacement therapy. The use of oral contraceptives for more than 5 years *decreases* the risk of ovarian cancer by about 60%.

Early ovarian cancer is usually asymptomatic, and no screening tests have been shown to reduce mortality in average-risk women. Women with a family history of ovarian cancer can be tested for the possession of cancer-causing genes—damaged versions of *BRCA1* and *BRCA2*—which are the same genes that cause breast cancer, discussed later in the chapter. Typically, ovarian cancer makes itself known by abdominal swelling, a constant feeling of a need to urinate or defecate, digestive problems, or pain in the pelvis, back, or leg. The accuracy of diagnosis can be improved by measuring blood levels of a marker known as CA-125 (Gordon, 2008). Treatment typically involves surgery to remove as much of the tumor as possible, as well as chemotherapy. Often the cancer has spread beyond the ovary by the time of diagnosis; thus, the survival rate is low: Only about 1 in 2 women survives for 5 years.

Another condition affecting the ovaries is the presence of **ovarian cysts** (fluid-filled sacs). These may be discovered when they cause pain, or they may be diagnosed during a pelvic exam. In women of reproductive age, the cysts are usually normal ovarian follicles that have not yet ovulated or that have grown larger than usual. These usually regress without treatment. Nevertheless, cysts can also be a sign of cancer, especially when found in prepubescent girls or in postmenopausal women.

Polycystic ovary syndrome (**PCOS**) is a common but poorly understood condition in which the ovaries secrete high levels of androgens. The condition may cause irregular menstruation, infertility, and a male-like pattern of facial and body hair. Ovarian cysts are often, but not always, present. PCOS is not curable, but most of the symptoms can be controlled with contraceptive pills or other drugs.

Menstruation Is a Biological Process with Cultural and Practical Aspects

The menstrual cycle has one obvious external sign: menstruation, also known as menses, a menstrual period, or simply a period. This is the vaginal discharge of endometrial tissue and blood that women experience at approximately monthly intervals during their fertile years. It is brought about by a complex internal mechanism that involves the ovaries, the brain, the pituitary gland, and the uterus.

The length of the menstrual cycle varies greatly among women and can also vary from one cycle to the next in the same woman. Most women have cycles lasting between 24 and 32 days, but cycles as short as 20 days or as long as 36 days are not unusual or unhealthy. Cycle length tends to be irregular for several years after the cycles first begin at puberty. Health care providers should ask teenage girls about their menstrual cycles, both in order to provide information and reassurance, and to identify problems needing medical attention (American Academy of Pediatrics, 2006). Cycles are also irregular at the approach of menopause. Menstrual cycles cease during pregnancy and, to a less predictable degree, during the time when a mother is breast-feeding her infant. It has been claimed that the menstrual cycles of women who live together tend to synchronize, but some researchers have contested the reality of this phenomenon (**Box 2.4**).

Box 2.4 Controversies

Menstrual Synchrony: Reality or Myth?

Do women who live together get their periods at the same time? Anecdotal accounts have long suggested that they do, but scientific evidence was lacking until 1970. In that year Martha McClintock, then a student at Wellesley College, decided to investigate the matter. Her results ignited a scientific controversy that still rages.

McClintock kept records of the menstrual periods of the students in her dormitory. She reported that, over the course of a semester, the periods of women who spent a lot of time together occurred closer and closer in time. Her analysis (McClintock, 1971) appeared to give "menstrual synchrony" scientific grounding.

Out of sync Martha McClintock (left) says menstrual synchrony exists; Beverly Strassmann (right) is skeptical.

What's more, her findings resonated with the spirit of 1970s feminism. Here was a biological expression of solidarity among women—a sisterhood that men knew nothing about and could never join. Before long, menstrual synchrony became common knowledge—something that most people had heard about and probably believed.

Yet the existence of menstrual synchrony remains highly controversial. Although some studies seem to support McClintock's claims, at least in part (Weller et al., 1995; Weller & Weller, 1997), other researchers have failed to detect synchrony, even in circumstances very similar to those of McClintock's original study, or have found methodological problems in the studies that do claim to find synchrony (Arden & Dye, 1998; Yang & Schank, 2006). Two groups of researchers failed to find any menstrual synchrony between cohabiting lesbian couples, who one might imagine would be the *most* likely to synchronize (Trevathan et al., 1993; Weller & Weller, 1998). And recent studies have failed to observe menstrual synchrony among nonhuman primates (Furtbauer et al., 2011; Setchell et al., 2011).

One of the most vocal critics of McClintock's work is anthropologist Beverly Strassmann (Strassmann, 1997, 1999). Strassmann studied the Dogon, a traditional West African people who have the custom of sending menstruating women to a "menstrual hut" (see Box 2.5). Because of this practice, it was easy for Strassmann to keep track of the menstrual periods of all the women in the community. She never observed synchronization of cycles, even between women who were sisters or close friends.

McClintock herself remains adamant that the phenomenon of menstrual synchrony exists, and she claims to have discovered its mechanism—pheromones released by women that supposedly affect the timing of menstruation in other women who receive these chemical signals (McClintock, 1999). Still, McClintock is willing to admit that the phenomenon may be a lot more complicated than she originally thought. Sometimes women synchronize, she says, sometimes they *de*synchronize, and sometimes they just remain random.

An even older and more popular belief is that women's menstrual cycles are synchronized to the phases of the moon. A group of Greek researchers went to the trouble of testing this idea; they found no evidence to support it (Ilias et al., 2013).

menstrual phase The days of the menstrual cycle on which menstrual bleeding occurs.

preovulatory phase The phase of the menstrual cycle during which follicles are developing in the ovaries.

follicular phase An alternative term for preovulatory phase.

postovulatory phase The phase of the menstrual cycle between ovulation and the beginning of menstruation.

luteal phase An alternative term for postovulatory phase.

corpus luteum A secretory structure in the ovary derived from an ovarian follicle after ovulation.

A woman's menstrual period lasts somewhere between 2 and 6 days (most commonly 4 to 5 days) and involves a total loss of 1 to 2 fluid ounces (30 to 60 mL) of blood, plus other fluids and endometrial tissue, amounting to a total volume of 2 to 7 fluid ounces (60 to 210 mL) discharged through the vagina.

The menstrual cycle has three phases

Although menstruation, or the **menstrual phase**, is the obvious outward sign of the menstrual cycle, the cycle's most significant internal event is ovulation, which involves the release of an ovum from one or the other ovary about midway between one menstrual period and the next. Some women feel abdominal pain at the time of ovulation and may even be able to tell from the location of the pain whether the ovum was released from the left or right ovary.

The portion of the menstrual cycle between menstruation and ovulation is called the **preovulatory** or **follicular phase** because it is marked by the maturation of follicles in the ovaries. The portion of the cycle between ovulation and menstruation is called the **postovulatory** or **luteal phase** because it is marked by the presence of a **corpus luteum**—a hormone-secreting structure formed from the single follicle that ruptured at ovulation.

A typical 28-day cycle is divided up roughly as follows: The menstrual phase occupies days 1 through 5, the preovulatory phase occupies days 6 through 14, and the postovulatory phase occupies days 15 through 28 (**Figure 2.13**). Of these three phases, the postovulatory phase is the most constant: It usually lasts 14 days, give or take 2 days. Most of the variation in total cycle length is accounted for by variation in the menstrual and preovulatory phases (see **Web Activity 2.6: Ovarian and Uterine Cycles**).

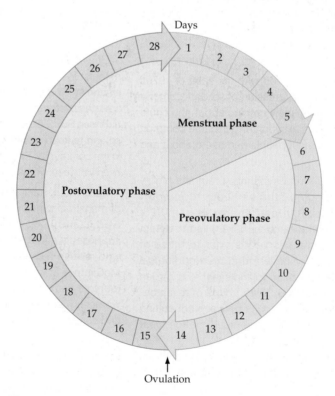

Figure 2.13 A 28-day menstrual cycle When cycles are markedly longer or shorter than 28 days, it is because of differences in the lengths of the menstrual and/or preovulatory phases; the postovulatory phase is nearly always close to 14 days long, as shown here.

The cycle is driven by hormonal changes

During the menstrual phase, much of the inner lining of the uterus—the endometrium—sloughs off, thus beginning the process of preparing the uterus for the development of a fresh endometrium whose properties facilitate the transport of sperm. The sloughing-off process is triggered primarily by a drop in the circulating level of the hormone progesterone. Blood levels of estrogens also drop at this time. These and other processes are represented diagrammatically in **Figure 2.14**.

High FSH levels at the start of the preovulatory phase promote the development of about 15 to 20 immature follicles in the ovaries. These follicles secrete estrogens and androgens, so the levels of these sex steroids in the bloodstream gradually rise during the preovulatory phase. The estrogens cause the endometrium in the uterus to thicken. In the latter part of the preovulatory phase, the cervix secretes a type of mucus that permits the passage of sperm, greatly increasing the chances of fertilization. By this time all but one of the 15 to 20 immature follicles in both ovaries have died, and the remaining one (which can be in either the left or right ovary) grows larger.

Toward the end of the preovulatory phase—about 36 hours before ovulation—estrogen levels rise high enough that their feedback influence on the hypothalamus switches from inhibition to stimulation (see Box 2.3), triggering a surge in the secretion of GnRH, LH, and FSH (see Figure 2.14). This surge drives the final development of the one remaining follicle, which expands to a diameter of about 1 inch (25 mm). The follicle creates a bulge on the wall of the ovary. At the moment of ovulation, the bulge breaks, releasing the ovum and its halo of supporting cells. The fimbria of the oviduct on that side actively reaches out and catches the ovum, and the waving of cilia propels it into the oviduct. The moment of ovulation has been captured on video—see Web Resources at the end of this chapter.

If sperm are present in the oviduct, one of them may fertilize the ovum. Otherwise, the ovum simply dies after about 24 hours in the oviduct. The woman's body has no immediate way of "knowing" if fertilization has occurred. Therefore, for about 2 weeks after ovulation, the uterus changes its structure to prepare for a possible pregnancy, regardless of whether fertilization has occurred or not. This process is guided by the hormones secreted from the remnants of the ruptured follicle, which transforms itself into a secretory structure, the corpus luteum. The predominant hormone secreted by the corpus luteum is progesterone, along with some estrogens. Progesterone stimulates the endometrium to thicken even further and become richly supplied with blood vessels. In this state it is capable of supporting an embryo. Progesterone also causes the cervical

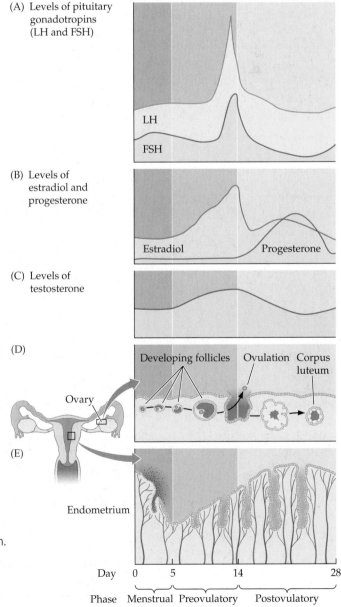

Figure 2.14   Main processes of the menstrual cycle (A–C) Changes in the circulating levels of the major hormones involved in the cycle. (D) The development of an ovarian follicle, the release of the ovum at ovulation, and the conversion of the follicle to a corpus luteum. (E) The breakdown of the endometrium during the menstrual phase, followed by its regrowth during the preovulatory and early postovulatory phases. (See **Web Activity 2.6: Ovarian and Uterine Cycles** and **Web Activity 2.7: Main Processes of the Menstrual Cycle**.)

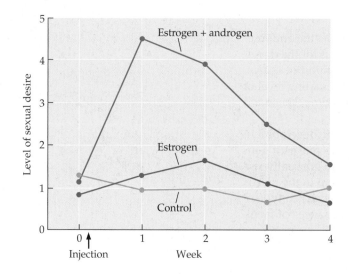

Figure 2.15　**Evidence that androgens contribute to female sexual desire**　Women whose ovaries had been removed were given injections of estrogens alone, estrogens plus androgens, or no injections (control). Only the combined estrogen-androgen injections caused a significant increase in the women's subjectively assessed sexual desire. (After Sherwin & Gelfand, 1987.)

mucus to change its properties, such that sperm cannot easily travel through it.

If fertilization does not occur, the corpus luteum eventually begins to degenerate; hence the hormones it produced in the second half of the menstrual cycle drop to lower levels. As the endometrium loses its hormonal support, it begins to break down. The resulting flow of blood and endometrial tissue marks the beginning of the next menstrual period and a new cycle. (See **Web Activity 2.8 The Reproductive Years**.)

Does the menstrual cycle influence sexuality?

If women's sexual behavior had reproduction as its sole goal, women would engage in coitus only on the day of ovulation and the five preceding days, because the great majority of pregnancies result from having sex on one of those days. In actuality, women are capable of desiring, initiating, and engaging in sex at any time of the menstrual cycle, as well as during pregnancy and after menopause, when fertilization is not possible. That's because, in humans, sex has functions not directly connected with reproduction, such as building interpersonal bonds based on sexual pleasure (Abramson & Pinkerton, 2002), and women's sexuality is not strictly regulated by the hormonal fluctuations of the menstrual cycle.

Still, women's sexual feelings and behaviors are not completely constant around the menstrual cycle. Some studies show that women are more interested in sex and more sexually active during the six fertile days than on the other days of the cycle (Tarin & Gomez-Piquer, 2002; Wilcox et al., 2004). Other studies report a secondary peak in activity during the premenstrual period.

The high levels of circulating estrogens and androgens before and at the time of ovulation facilitate the increased interest in sex. Women's sexual desire is influenced significantly by androgens, as was shown in a study of women whose ovaries and uterus had been removed some years previously (Sherwin & Gelfand, 1987). In this study, one group received no hormone replacement therapy, a second group received monthly injections of estradiol, and a third group received monthly injections of estradiol plus an androgen (**Figure 2.15**). The women who had received estradiol plus an androgen experienced greatly increased levels of desire, fantasies, and arousal compared with the other groups, especially in the period immediately after receiving the androgen.

Women who have had both their ovaries and their adrenal glands removed, thus eliminating both of their bodies' sources of androgens, experience an even more profound decrease in sexual interest. Again, the administration of estrogen plus androgen can restore their sexual interest.

Attitudes toward menstruation vary

Beyond the basic biology, menstruation has important psychological, cultural, and practical aspects. Most women can remember their first menstrual period more clearly than any other. The event, which heralds their passage into womanhood, is celebrated

Box 2.5 Society, Values, and the Law

Attitudes toward Menstruation

Across many cultures and historical periods, men have often viewed menstruating woman with distaste, fear, or moral concern. The Roman naturalist Pliny the Elder declared that menstrual blood was a dangerous poison. If a man had sex with a menstruating woman, Pliny wrote, he risked serious harm or even death—especially if the sex act coincided with a total solar eclipse!

According to Judeo-Christian scripture, a menstruating woman is unclean, as is any person who touches her bedding (Leviticus 15:19–21). In the Orthodox Judaic tradition of *niddut*, a woman must sleep apart from her husband for several days during and after her period and must undergo a ritual cleansing bath (*mikvah*) before returning to him. The Christian theologian St. Augustine taught that sex with a menstruating woman was sinful. The Quran likewise prohibits sex with a menstruating woman and (in some interpretations) prohibits a menstruating woman from praying, fasting, or entering a mosque.

Some cultures have even required women to sleep away from the household altogether during their periods. For example, among the Dogon, a traditional cliff-dwelling people in Mali, Africa, menstruating women have to sleep in a "menstrual hut" for about 5 nights (see photo). During that time they may work in the fields but may not sleep with or cook for their husbands. The taboo is imposed by the Dogon men, and its ultimate motive is that it gives men precise information about the timing of women's menstruation (Strassmann, 1992, 1996). Why is this information important? In a culture such as that of the Dogon, women experience menstrual cycles (and therefore are able to become pregnant) only for very short stretches of time; the rest of the time they are either pregnant or they are intensively breast-feeding their babies, a practice that suppresses the menstrual cycle. Knowledge of the occurrence of menstruation helps a man identify the limited time during which a woman can become pregnant, and this in turn helps him avoid being deceived into raising another man's child.

A Dogon menstrual hut. (Photo © Beverly I. Strassmann.)

In contemporary Western culture, attitudes toward menstruation vary, but the belief that women should avoid vaginal intercourse during their periods is still widespread. A sizable majority (70% to 80%) of men and women do in fact avoid this practice (Barnhart et al., 1995; Tanfer & Aral, 1996). Among some women, this avoidance is bolstered by the idea that sex during menstruation endangers their own health.

Other men and women may avoid sex during menstruation out of distaste for the practice, for religious reasons, or because the woman has symptoms associated with menstruation that make her uninterested in sex. A further possible reason may be the low testosterone levels at the menstrual phase of a woman's cycle, which may reduce her interest in sex.

Still, about 20% of women in the United States do engage in vaginal sex during menstruation, according to surveys conducted in the 1990s (Barnhart et al., 1995; Tanfer & Aral, 1996). Unscientific polls suggest that this percentage may have increased in recent years. Some women use a diaphragm (see Chapter 9) or menstrual cup to block the menstrual discharge during sex. Others may simply place a dark-colored towel over their sheets to prevent staining, or have sex in the shower. Alternatively, many couples engage in forms of lovemaking during menstruation that do not involve coitus.

with special rituals in many cultures. Yet negative attitudes and beliefs about menstruation are also common around the world, especially among men (**Box 2.5**).

Contemporary American women have very divergent attitudes toward menstruation. In 1999, Brazilian gynecologist Elsimar Coutinho published his book *Is Menstruation Obsolete?* in which he suggested ways that women could abolish the entire phenomenon. Some women saw his message as a godsend, but others saw it as the ultimate sexist assault—the "perfecting" of women's bodies by making them more like men's. The debate has continued and has intensified with the Federal Drug

Administration (FDA) approval of contraceptive regimes that reduce the frequency of a woman's periods or eliminate them completely (see Chapter 9).

A long-running international debate on the question "Would you stop menstruating if you could?" has enlivened the web pages of the Museum of Menstruation—over a thousand women have voiced their opinions (see Web Resources at the end of this chapter). Here are some contributions posted in 2013:

> *Yes. I'm a 28-year old woman and would love to stop. I've had erratic periods since I started in my mid-teens and have developed severe headaches and panic attacks before having mine along with my periods getting gradually more painful and heavy. I also don't intend on having children either and thus, making this useless. While I have been put on the pill to help with some of these issues and it has been helping, I want it to be gone for good.*

> *No—I would not stop if I had the choice! I would go on forever. I can't imagine what my life will be like when I have gone through the menopause—how will I know where I am? The bleeding has brought me to bed sometimes, and is inconvenient in terms of normal everyday society, but I don't look upon this as bad, it's a gift. Everything is made more amazing by my bleeding cycle—it's brought to life.*

> *I already did. I am 32 years old and it has been 10 years since my last period. I take Depo-Provera shots every 3 months and this was the best decision I have ever made in my life. And as far as I am concerned I am going like that until real menopause.*

In recent years "yes" answers have come to predominate, perhaps on account of women's increasing awareness of methods to suppress menstruation with hormonal contraceptives. In a recent survey, 17% of female university students said that they used these methods to skip or delay their periods (Lakehomer et al., 2013). As far as is known, abolishing menstruation has no harmful effects on the body, as we'll discuss further in Chapter 9.

Women use pads, tampons, or cups during menstruation

Most American women who menstruate use sanitary napkins ("pads"), panty liners, or tampons in order to absorb their menstrual flow (**Figure 2.16**). Pads and panty liners are worn on the outside of the body—the main difference between them is that panty liners are thinner and usable only for very light flow. Tampons—absorbent plugs, about 1.5 inches (3 to 4 cm) long, made of cotton or synthetic fiber—are placed

(A)

(B)

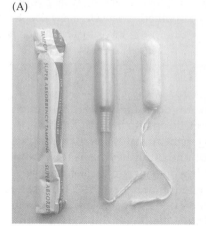
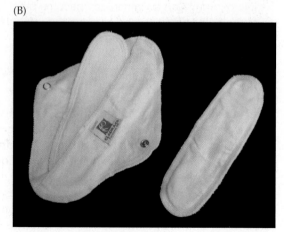

Figure 2.16 Tampons and menstrual pads (A) Tampons come in varying absorbencies and are available with or without applicators. (B) Most menstrual pads are disposable, but these are washable and made of cotton cloth.

(A)   (B)

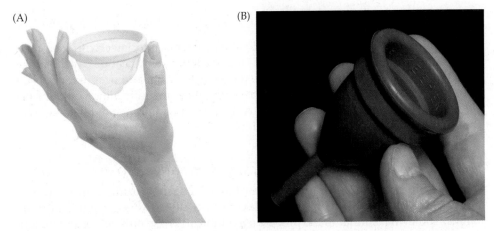

Figure 2.17   Menstrual cups block menstrual flow. (A) The Instead cup is disposable. (B) The Keeper cup lasts for years.

inside the vagina, sometimes with the help of a plastic or cardboard applicator. They have an attached string that hangs outside the body to facilitate removal. About 70% of women in the United States and Canada who are menstruating use tampons (Parsonnet et al., 2005).

Although tampons are very convenient—even allowing such activities as swimming during a woman's period—their use has been linked to a rare but dangerous condition known as **menstrual toxic shock syndrome** (Mayo Clinic, 2014c). This condition, caused by certain strains of the bacterium *Staphylococcus aureus*, is marked by high fever, vomiting, diarrhea, rash, and other symptoms, and it is fatal in close to 10% of affected women. Any woman who develops a high fever (102°F, or 38.9°C) while using a tampon should remove the tampon and seek medical attention immediately.

Nevertheless, toxic shock syndrome is hardly a reason not to use tampons: Many millions of women in the United States use them, and only a very few cases of menstrual toxic shock syndrome are reported per year. Tampons range in absorbency from less than 0.2 ounces (5 g) ("low absorbency") to 0.6 ounces (18 g) or more ("highest absorbency"). To reduce the risk of toxic shock syndrome, a woman who uses tampons is advised to use the least absorbent tampon compatible with satisfactory function. Tampons should be changed after 4 to 8 hours of use. If the tampon is not saturated after that time (i.e., it still has white cotton showing), she should switch to a less absorbent tampon. It's a good idea to have varying grades of tampons available to deal with the varying flow over the course of the period, because the flow usually lessens toward the end of the period. The FDA recommends that women use a pad rather than a tampon for some portion of their menstrual period (Office on Women's Health, 2009).

Menstrual cups (Figure 2.17) are an alternative to pads and tampons. They are worn inside the vagina and dam the menstrual flow rather than absorbing it. Menstrual cups have to be emptied and replaced two or three times a day. The three most widely available brands are called the Keeper, the DivaCup, and the Instead Softcup. The Keeper, as its name suggests, is a reusable device—it is made of latex—and it is therefore cheaper over time (and more environmentally friendly) than tampons or pads. It is placed just a little way into the vagina, so coitus is not possible while wearing it. Another version of the Keeper, called the Moon Cup, is made of silicone. The DivaCup resembles the Moon Cup and is also reusable. The Instead cup, made of soft thermoplastic, is for one-time use only. It is placed deep within the vagina against the cervix, so it permits coitus while it is worn. (It does not function as a contraceptive, however.)

menstrual toxic shock syndrome A rare but life-threatening illness caused by a staphylococcal infection and associated with tampon use.

menstrual cup A cup placed within the vagina that collects the menstrual flow.

Menstrual Problems Are Common but Treatable

menstrual cramps   Sharp pelvic pains that may accompany or precede menstruation.

dysmenorrhea   Menstrual pain severe enough to interfere with a woman's activities.

primary dysmenorrhea   Painful menstruation that begins at puberty and has no clear cause.

secondary dysmenorrhea   Painful menstruation that begins during adult life, usually as a consequence of a pelvic disorder.

Many women experience some kinds of health problems associated with their menstrual cycles. These may include painful menstruation, physical or psychological effects in the days before the onset of the menstrual period, and irregular or absent menstrual cycles. For most women menstrual problems are quite minor, but for some they are very disruptive or impair fertility. Luckily, a wide range of effective treatments are available for menstrual conditions.

Menstrual pain may or may not reflect underlying pelvic disease

The sloughing off and discharging of endometrial tissue during menstruation is aided by contractions of the muscular layer of the uterus (the myometrium) in a manner somewhat similar to the process of childbirth. These muscle contractions are the cause of the **menstrual cramps** experienced by some women during or shortly before their periods. There can also be persistent, aching pain within the pelvis or in the lower back. The pain may be accompanied by nausea or headaches. Menstrual pain is called **dysmenorrhea** when it is severe enough to limit a woman's activities. Dysmenorrhea is very common, and a family history of the disorder greatly increases a woman's chances of suffering from it (Ju et al., 2014).

There are two kinds of dysmenorrhea:

- **Primary dysmenorrhea** is disabling menstrual pain that is not associated with any diagnosable pelvic condition. It begins at menarche and is especially common among young women who have not had children. Primary dysmenorrhea can be alleviated with heat (e.g., warm showers, or heating pads on the lower abdomen), calcium supplements, plentiful fluid intake, or nonsteroidal anti-inflammatory drugs such as ibuprofen. Exercise and a high-fiber diet are also thought to be helpful. Another strategy is the use of oral contraceptives: The menstrual period experienced during the "off days" of an oral contraceptive regime is often lighter and less painful than a natural menstrual period. And as mentioned earlier, certain types of hormonal contraception make a woman's periods less frequent or abolish them altogether. Thus, hormonal contraceptives are an option for the treatment of dysmenorrhea even in women who do not need them for contraceptive purposes.

- **Secondary dysmenorrhea** is menstrual pain caused by a pelvic disorder. In an affected woman, it usually begins not at menarche but at some point during her reproductive life. Among the possible causes are endometriosis, pelvic inflammatory disease, uterine fibroids, and ovarian cysts. Intrauterine devices (IUDs; see Chapter 9) and even tampons can sometimes cause menstrual pain. Secondary dysmenorrhea may respond to the same treatments listed above for primary dysmenorrhea. If possible, however, the underlying condition should be corrected. Menstrual pain associated with IUD use tends to diminish over time.

The main points to know about disabling menstrual pain are that it should be medically investigated to rule out underlying conditions and that effective treatment options are available.

The premenstrual syndrome has physical and psychological aspects

It is common for women to experience some form of physical discomfort or negative mood change in the 1 or 2 weeks *before* their period. If the problems go away soon

Premenstrual syndrome is often portrayed as something worse than it is.

after the onset of menstruation but recur over several menstrual cycles and are severe enough to interfere with daily living, the condition is called **premenstrual syndrome** (**PMS**) (Yonkers et al., 2008). If the psychological symptoms are severe enough to interfere with relationships—including difficult-to-control anger, for example—they may be diagnosed as a psychiatric condition, **premenstrual dysphoric disorder** (Epperson et al., 2012).

Six core symptoms are most useful in defining PMS and distinguishing it from other problems (Freeman et al., 2011):

- Anxiety/tension
- Mood swings
- Aches
- Altered appetite or food cravings
- Cramps
- Decreased interest in activities

Other symptoms that may occur include breast tenderness, diarrhea or constipation, and "bloating" (the sense of being overloaded with fluid).

The prevalence of PMS is hard to estimate because the severity of the condition varies so greatly. The majority of women experience at least one symptom, but only 3% to 10% of women are severely enough affected to warrant a diagnosis of PMS (Kessel, 2000; Tschudin et al., 2010). The reason that women differ in the extent to which they experience PMS is not so much that their sex hormone levels differ as that their bodies respond to sex hormones in different ways (Schmidt et al., 1998).

Treatments for mild or moderate PMS include lifestyle changes such as regular exercise, quitting smoking, reducing intake of alcohol, getting sufficient sleep, and managing stress. Women who get a lot of calcium and vitamin A in their diet are much less likely than other women to experience PMS (Bertone-Johnson et al., 2005). Calcium supplements provide some relief, but even better results have been obtained with the antidepressant fluoxetine (Prozac and generics) (Yonkers et al., 2013). Several studies have reported that PMS symptoms are alleviated by combination-type oral contraceptives (see Chapter 9) when taken on a continuous basis (Freeman et al., 2012).

PMS is rarely the monster that it is portrayed to be in popular literature. The great majority of women experience few or mild PMS symptoms, and for those who do experience severe symptoms, effective treatments are available. PMS doesn't disqualify the women who suffer from it from any field of human activity—and dismissing any woman's bad mood or unfriendly behavior with "She's PMS-ing" is ignorant and sexist.

Menstruation stops during pregnancy—and for many other reasons

Most women will notice at some point or another that their menstrual periods have stopped (**amenorrhea**) or have become irregular. The most common reasons for amenorrhea are entirely natural and normal ones: The woman is pregnant, is breastfeeding her baby, or has reached menopause. Irregular periods are also common for some time after the onset of menstruation and during the climacteric—the months or years preceding menopause. But many other factors can interfere with menstruation:

- *Some hormonal contraceptives.* It may take months for menstruation to return after the contraceptive is discontinued.
- *Drugs.* Common culprits include steroids, antidepressants, and some cancer drugs.
- *Stress.* This could be caused by physical illness, depression, or social problems.

premenstrual syndrome (PMS) A collection of physical and/or psychological symptoms that may start a few days before the menstrual period begins and continue into the period.

premenstrual dysphoric disorder PMS-associated mood changes that are severe enough to interfere with relationships

amenorrhea Absence of menstruation.

primary amenorrhea The failure to begin menstruating at puberty.

mammary glands The milk-producing glands within the breasts.

secondary sexual characteristics Anatomical characteristics, such as breasts and facial hair, that generally differ between the sexes but are not used to define an individual's sex.

- *Loss of weight for any reason.* This includes anorexia nervosa, severe dieting, and extreme athletic exercise. A woman is at risk of amenorrhea if her body fat drops below 15% to 17% of total weight.
- *Medical conditions.* These include thyroid dysfunction and pituitary tumors.

A girl also may not begin menstruating at puberty (**primary amenorrhea**). This may be due to one of the factors listed above. Alternatively, puberty itself may be delayed for a variety of reasons, or the girl may have a disorder of sex development (see Chapter 4) that makes menstruation impossible.

Unless it is caused by a congenital anomaly, amenorrhea can nearly always be corrected by lifestyle changes or treatment of the underlying condition. Amenorrhea is not harmful in itself—scientists have not identified any health benefit of menstrual bleeding—but the underlying condition may be harmful, and failure to menstruate may cause psychological distress. In addition, a woman is usually unable to become pregnant during the time she is not experiencing menstrual periods. That is not a sure thing, however; a woman who is breast-feeding, for example, may become pregnant before her menstrual periods return.

The reverse condition, excessively heavy menstrual bleeding, affects about 10% of all women. Causes are numerous, the most common being hormonal imbalance and fibroids. Treatment is with drugs such as ibuprofen or hormonal contraceptives, or surgical treatment of the fibroids. Repeated heavy bleeding predisposes a woman to iron-deficiency anemia, so iron supplements are usually recommended.

Sex steroids affect systems in women besides the reproductive tract

Although the main function of sex hormones in women is to regulate the functional state of the uterus and other parts of the reproductive tract during the menstrual cycle, they do have other significant effects:

- Estrogens are responsible for most of the anatomical changes that occur in a girl's body at puberty. Androgens, however, are responsible for the development of armpit and pubic hair.
- Estrogens maintain bone density, protecting a woman from osteoporosis. They also protect against blood clotting, including the clots that cause heart attacks.
- Progesterone acts on neural centers that control body temperature. Thus, a woman's body temperature rises at least 0.4°F (0.22°C) after ovulation, when progesterone levels rise.
- Progesterone also influences mood: It is an anxiety-reducing agent. Thus, the fall in progesterone levels toward the end of the postovulatory phase of the menstrual cycle can cause or contribute to an increase in anxiety and irritability at that time.
- Both estrogens and androgens act on many regions of the brain to influence women's sexual feelings and behaviors.

The Breasts Have Both Erotic and Reproductive Significance

The breasts (or **mammary glands**) are considered **secondary sexual characteristics**, meaning that they are not components of the genitals but do differ between the sexes. Although both men and women have nipples and some men have a certain amount of breast tissue, breasts of significant size are generally a feature unique to

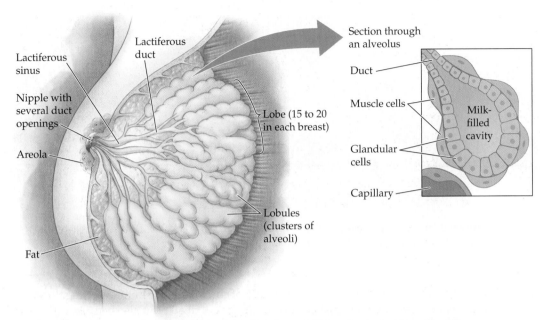

Figure 2.18 Internal structure of the lactating breast When the breast is not lactating, the alveoli regress to a less-developed state. (See **Web Activity 2.9: Internal Structure of the Lactating Breast**.)

women's anatomy. Occasionally, women or men may have extra nipples or even extra breasts, usually located somewhere along the line between the armpit and the groin.

The breast tissue lies between the skin and the muscles of the chest wall; some breast tissue extends up toward the armpits. Each breast consists of about 15 to 20 **lobes** that are separated from one another by fibrous and fatty tissue (**Figure 2.18**). The functional units of the breast are microscopic sacs called **alveoli**: Each alveolus is lined by glandular cells that secrete milk into its central cavity. Milk leaving the alveolus travels down the ducts that connect at the nipple. When the baby suckles at the nipple, the stimulation causes "milk letdown."

Each nipple is situated at the tip of the breast in the center of a circular patch of darker skin known as an **areola**. The nipples are capable of erection in response to sexual arousal, tactile stimulation, or cold. Many women have sparse hair around the areola. As with all secondary sexual characteristics, breasts vary considerably among individuals (**Figure 2.19**), and there may also be a size difference between the left and right breasts. Variation in breast size is due largely to differences in the amount of fatty tissue in the breast; women with small breasts have adequate glandular tissue to breast-feed an infant.

Breasts are of great erotic significance to many people. For women, tactile or oral stimulation of the breasts (especially the nipples) in the appropriate circumstances is sexually arousing. The appearance or feel of the breasts is also an important erotic stimulus to women's sex partners, especially in contemporary Western culture. Probably for this reason, some women are unhappy with their breasts; they may seek to alter their appearance by wearing bras that enhance the appearance of their breasts or by plastic surgery.

Breast cancer mortality can be reduced

About 230,000 women and 2000 men are diagnosed with invasive breast cancer in the United States each year, and about 40,000 women and 400 men die of the disease (Siegel et al., 2014). Based on current incidence rates, about 1 in 8 American women will

lobe A subdivision of a gland or other organ.

alveolus (pl. alveoli) Microscopic cavity, such as one of those in the breast where milk is produced.

areola The circular patch of darker skin that surrounds the nipple.

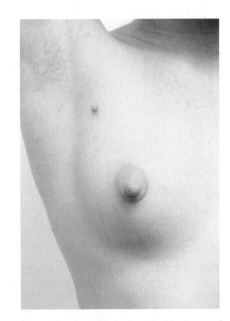

A small extra nipple located between the normal nipple and the armpit.

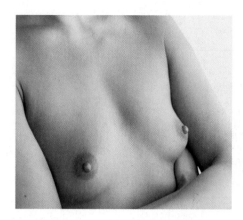 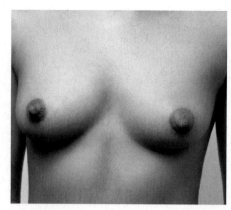 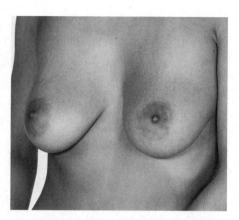

Figure 2.19 Breasts vary greatly in appearance. There may also be some difference in size between a woman's left and right breast.

mastectomy Surgical removal of a breast.

be diagnosed with (but not necessarily die of) breast cancer in her lifetime. Women may fear breast cancer not just because of the risk of death, but also because one treatment for the disease—surgical removal of the affected breast (**mastectomy**)—may damage a woman's self-image and affect her sex life.

We don't wish to downplay the seriousness of breast cancer, but it is worth pointing out that, contrary to many women's belief, breast cancer is far from being the leading cause of death for women (**Figure 2.20**). Heart disease kills far more women than do all cancers combined. In fact, breast cancer is not even the leading cause of *cancer* deaths among women: Lung cancer kills more women in the United States than does breast cancer. Still, breast cancer is a leading cause of death among middle-aged women.

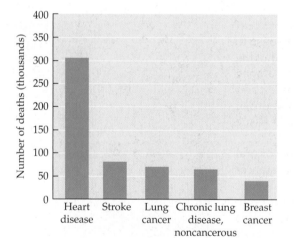

Figure 2.20 Breast cancer is not the leading cause of death among U.S. women. The graph shows the most common causes of death among women in the United States and the number of women who die annually from each of them. (After Centers for Disease Control, 2010b.)

Many factors affect the risk of breast cancer

A number of known factors can increase or decrease the chances that a woman will develop breast cancer:

- *Genes.* A woman who has one first-degree relative (mother, sister, or daughter) with breast cancer faces twice the risk of getting the disease as a woman who does not. Having two first-degree relatives with breast cancer multiplies her risk fivefold. Certain genes normally protect against breast cancer and other cancers; the most important of these genes are *BRCA1* and *BRCA2*. Women who inherit damaged (mutated) versions of these genes have up to an 80% risk of developing breast cancer during their lifetime, as well as a heightened risk of developing ovarian cancer (King et al., 2003). Tests for the presence of these genes are available. Mutations in these genes account for only about 10% of all breast cancers, however; in fact, most breast cancers occur in women with no family history of the disease.

- *Age.* Breast cancer is primarily a disease of older women: About 85% of newly diagnosed cases are in women over 50.

- *Reproductive history.* Women who had early menarche (before age 12) or late menopause (after age 55), who have had no children, or who had their first child after age 30 have a modestly increased risk of developing breast cancer. Prolonged breast-feeding may offer some reduction in risk.

- *Alcohol.* Women who consume two to five alcoholic drinks per day have about a 1.5-fold increase in risk of developing breast cancer compared with women who consume fewer than two drinks per day. It is the quantity of alcohol consumed, not the type of drink, that matters (Science Daily, 2007).

- *Obesity.* Women who are obese—especially those who become obese during adulthood and those whose body fat is concentrated at the waist—face an increased risk of developing breast cancer. Some studies suggest that a high-fat diet is a risk factor independent of obesity, but this is uncertain.

- *Breast size.* A large-scale prospective study of physically active women found a strong association between large breast size and breast cancer: Women who wore a C-cup bra had a fourfold greater likelihood of developing breast cancer during the 11-year study, as compared with women who wore an A-cup bra. This association was independent of obesity (Williams, 2013).

- *Breast density.* Women whose breasts appear dense on mammograms—that is, they consist largely of breast tissue with little fat—are at increased risk of cancer. High breast density also makes it more difficult to spot early cancers on mammograms.

- *Exercise.* Women who exercise several hours a week (and who don't have a family history of breast cancer) reduce their risk of developing breast cancer almost by half (Carpenter et al., 2003). This benefit may result from the estrogen-lowering effect of exercise.

- *Medical history.* A history of breast cancer, even when successfully treated, raises the risk of a second, independent cancer in the same or the other breast. A history of high-dose radiation treatment that includes the breast raises the risk of breast cancer. (The X-ray doses associated with mammography are believed to be insignificant in this respect.)

- *Hormones.* The use of oral contraceptives by young women (ages 20 to 34) is associated with a slightly increased risk of breast cancer (Hunter et al., 2010). (Bear in mind, though, that breast cancer is very uncommon in this age bracket whether or not oral contraceptives are used.) The increase in risk disappears by 10 years after cessation of contraceptive use (Collaborative Group on Hormonal Factors in Breast Cancer, 1996). There is little or no risk for older women who use oral contraceptives (Marchbanks et al., 2002). Postmenopausal hormone treatment raises the risk of breast cancer slightly.

Opportunities for breast cancer prevention include lifestyle changes—mainly weight control, exercise, and restriction of alcohol intake. Health care practitioners recommend these changes because they provide other, additional health benefits besides reducing breast cancer risk. Some studies have reported that regular aspirin use is associated with a modest reduction in breast cancer incidence, but a randomized controlled trial of aspirin failed to show a benefit (Luo et al., 2012).

Women who are at especially high risk have the option of taking drugs that lower estrogen levels (anastrozole) or that block the effects of estrogen on breast tissue (tamoxifen or raloxifene) (National Cancer Institute, 2010; Cuzick et al., 2013). These drugs provide partial protection against breast cancer but may have significant side effects.

Actress Angelina Jolie elected to have a double mastectomy on account of her high risk of breast cancer. Here, she is speaking at the Global Summit to End Sexual Violence in Conflict, which took place in London in June of 2014.

FAQ

How big must a breast lump be to be detectable by mammogram or by self-examination?

The typical lump detected by mammogram is 0.2 inch (5 mm) in diameter; by self-exam it is 0.8 inch (2 cm). It is possible to detect smaller lumps with either technique, depending on the examiner's experience, the position and density of the lump, and the general texture of the breast.

mammography Radiographic inspection of the breasts.

Removal of both breasts (double mastectomy) is an effective but drastic preventive measure that is seldom chosen except by women at very high risk. One such woman was actress Angelina Jolie, who faced an 87% risk of breast cancer on account of her carrying a mutated *BRCA1* gene and a family history of the disease. She had her breasts removed in 2013, at the age of 37, followed by breast reconstruction. Her willingness to speak out about this (Jolie, 2013) drew wide attention to the issue, but only a very small percentage of all breast cancers occur in women carrying *BRCA1* or *BRCA2* mutations.

In general, because of the limited preventive strategies that are currently available, the emphasis is on early diagnosis and treatment rather than on prevention.

Early detection is important

For many years, the ACS urged women to regularly examine their own breasts for lumps. According to the results of two very large prospective studies, however, women who are taught breast self-examination (BSE) undergo twice as many breast biopsies as other women, but they are just as likely to die of breast cancer (Kosters & Goetzsche, 2008). This is probably because the lumps discovered by self-examination, if cancerous, are often too far advanced to be curable. The ACS now states that "it is acceptable for women to choose not to do BSE or to do BSE occasionally" (American Cancer Society, 2013b).

Breast self-exams remain an option, and instructions on how to perform them are presented in **Box 2.6**. Women who choose not to perform self-exams should remain aware of their breasts and promptly report any changes to their doctor. Periodic breast exams by a clinician, combined with mammography, are more useful than self-examination.

Mammography is a breast cancer screening technique that uses low-dose X-rays to image the soft tissues of the breast (**Figure 2.21**). During a mammogram, each

(A)

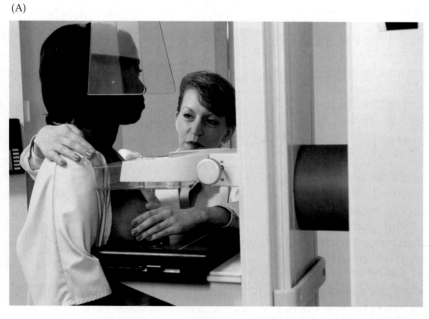

(B)

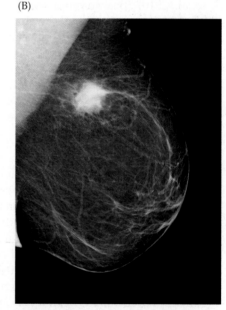

Figure 2.21 Mammography (A) A low-dose X-ray image is taken while the breast is compressed between two plates. (B) This breast lump, visualized as a white patch on the mammogram, is a "ductal carcinoma in situ," the earliest detectable stage and the easiest form of breast cancer to cure.

Box 2.6 Sexual Health

Breast Self-Examination

The best time for breast self-examination (BSE) is about a week after your menstrual period ends, when your breasts are not tender or swollen. If your periods are irregular or you are not menstruating, do BSE on the same day every month.

- Lie down with a pillow under your right shoulder and place your right arm behind your head (**Figure A**).

- Use the finger pads of the three middle fingers on your left hand to examine your right breast.

- Feel with dime-sized circular motions, and with three different pressures: light pressure to feel the tissue near the surface, medium pressure for deeper tissue, and firm pressure to feel the deepest tissue. Feel for lumps; a firm ridge in the lower curve of the breast is normal.

- Examine the breast in a regular, up-and-down pattern as shown in **Figure B**, making sure you go up as far as the collar bone and down far enough that you feel only the ribs. Then use your right hand to examine your left breast. Remember how your breasts feel from month to month.

- Then, while standing or sitting, raise your right arm slightly and use your left hand to examine your right underarm, and vice versa for the left underarm (**Figure C**).

- Finally, stand in front of a mirror with both hands pressing firmly down on your hips. (This contracts the chest muscles and makes the breast tissue more prominent.) Look for any changes in the size, shape, color, dimpling, or texture of the nipples or breast skin, or any abnormal discharge.

If you find any changes, see your doctor right away.

Source: American Cancer Society, 2013b.

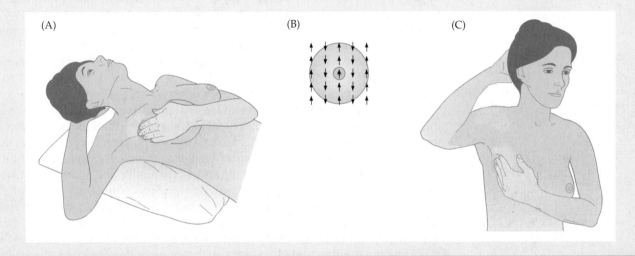

(A) (B) (C)

breast is compressed between two plastic plates to spread out the breast tissue and make interpretation of the X-ray image easier. The procedure can be uncomfortable, but it is very brief.

There has been some disagreement about the appropriate guidelines concerning mammographic screening. According to a federally supported panel of preventive-medicine experts, average-risk women should undergo mammography every 2 years beginning at age 50 (United States Preventive Services Taskforce, 2009). The ACS and the American Congress of Obstetricians and Gynecologists (ACOG), on the other hand, recommend annual mammograms beginning at age 40 (American Cancer Society, 2010; American College of Obstetricians and Gynecologists, 2011).

The reason for the disagreement has to do with the difficulty of weighing the positive and negative effects of screening programs. The most important negative effect is that about 70,000 U.S. women are diagnosed and treated annually for early-

prosthesis An artificial replacement for a body part.

stage breast cancers that would never have caused symptoms in the women's lifetime. Breast cancer screening programs have had at best only a small impact on U.S. death rates from breast cancer (Bleyer & Welch, 2012). A recent randomized study that followed 90,000 Canadian women for 25 years found that women screened by mammography and breast examination were just as likely to die of breast cancer as women screened by breast examination alone, and they were more likely to suffer unnecessary treatments (Miller et al., 2014). This finding is, to a degree, good news: It means that treatment of the larger lumps detected by manual examination is now as effective as treatment of the very small lumps that are only detectable by mammography. The findings of the Canadian study may lead to a revision of the current screening guidelines (Kolata, 2014).

Treatment depends on the diagnostic findings and the woman's choice

If definitive tests show that the lump *is* cancerous, the woman and her doctors must decide on the best course of treatment, based on the diagnostic findings, the woman's age and other circumstances, and the woman's own wishes. Surgical options range from removal of the cancerous lump itself plus some surrounding healthy tissue (lumpectomy) to removal of the entire breast, chest wall musculature, and regional lymph nodes (radical mastectomy), with a number of options in between. Most women with early breast cancer do as well with lumpectomy plus radiation therapy as they do with removal of the entire breast. Radical mastectomy has therefore become a much less common operation than it was in the past.

The majority of women diagnosed with invasive breast cancer undergo some kind of surgical treatment. There are several other forms of treatment, including hormone-blocking therapy with drugs, such as tamoxifen or letrozole, and immunotherapy with the drug Herceptin.

If a woman's breast must be removed, she has several options. She can accept her body's new appearance. She can use an external **prosthesis** to conceal the absence of the breast. She can also have reconstructive surgery, which can be done either at the time of the mastectomy or at a later date (American Cancer Society, 2014c). Reconstructive surgery is not perfect: Even when it is done well, it leaves scars, numbness, and a lack of erogenous sensation in the area of the nipple. Still, many women experience a great deal of psychological benefit from the procedure.

One type of reconstructive surgery involves the insertion of an implant filled with silicone gel or sterilized saltwater (saline). This is a safe procedure that does not affect the chances that the cancer will recur. Any type of breast implant can lead to problems at later times, such as a gradual change in the implant's shape, but the chances that an implant will cause any serious long-term medical condition are close to zero. Earlier fears about implants causing autoimmune diseases have turned out to be unwarranted.

Most women with breast cancer return to an active sex life

Breast cancer and its treatment can affect a woman's sexuality in a number of ways (Sheppard, 2008). First, the grief and fear triggered by a cancer diagnosis are likely to put sexual feelings out of mind, at least for a while. Second, the side effects of cancer treatment may be so exhausting as to interfere with sexual feelings and activities. Third, some treatments may have hormonal or other effects that decrease physiological arousal or interest in sex. Fourth, women who have been through breast cancer treatment, especially if they have had a mastectomy, may fear that they are no longer attractive to their current sex partners, or to potential partners.

Health care providers who encourage women with breast cancer to discuss these issues are already helping to resolve them. Even in the days when radical mastectomy was the standard treatment for breast cancer, most women reported no change in key aspects of their sexuality, such as frequency of sex and overall sexual satisfaction (Morris et al., 1977). Today, women treated for early-stage breast cancer report emotional well-being and sexual satisfaction (American Cancer Society, 2014d). Of 800 women with breast cancer who were interviewed or quoted in one book (most of whom had surgical treatment), the great majority spoke positively about their lives, including their sex lives (Peltason, 2008).

Go to the **Discovering Human Sexuality** Companion Website at **sites.sinauer.com/ discoveringhumansexuality3e** for activities, study questions, quizzes, and other study aids.

Summary

- A woman's vulva (external genitalia) consists of the mons, clitoris, outer and inner labia (labia majora and minora), and vaginal opening.

- A woman's clitoris is a complex erectile organ, only a portion of which (the glans) is visible externally. Stimulation of the clitoris is a major source of sexual arousal in women.

- The outer labia are two fat-padded folds of skin that form the sides of the vulva. The inner labia are two thinner, erotically sensitive folds of skin that enclose the vestibule—they fuse together at the front to form the hood of the clitoris. The vestibule is the space that encloses the entrance to the vagina and the opening of the urethra.

- The female reproductive tract includes the vagina, cervix, uterus, and oviducts. At birth, the infant's vagina is partially covered by a membrane (the hymen), which may be torn at first intercourse or earlier. The inner surface of the vagina is mildly acidic. Frequent douching can disturb the microbial balance, leading to a fungal infection and other problems. The walls of the outer portion of the vagina are more muscular and more sensitive than the deeper portion. The G-spot is said to be a site of heightened erotic sensitivity on the front wall of the vagina, but its existence is a matter of controversy.

- The portion of the uterus that connects with the vagina is the cervix, which can be seen by inspection with a vaginal speculum or felt by inserting a finger into the back of the vagina. The main cause of cervical cancer is human papillomavirus (HPV), which is a sexually transmitted infection. Early detection of cancer by means of regular Pap tests has greatly reduced mortality from the disease.

- The uterus serves as a pathway for sperm transport and also for implantation and development of the embryo. Medical conditions affecting the body of the uterus include fibroids, endometrial cancer, abnormal bleeding, uterine prolapse, and endometriosis. Hysterectomies (surgical removal of the uterus) may be done more frequently than necessary.

- The oviducts bring an ovum and sperm together for fertilization, and they transport the resulting conceptus to the uterus. The ovaries are the female gonads; they produce ova and sex hormones. Ovulation is the release of an ovum from an ovary. The ovum enters the oviduct where, if sperm are present, it may be fertilized.

- Steroid sex hormones fall into three classes—estrogens, androgens, and progestins—and are secreted by the gonads (ovaries or testicles). Protein and peptide sex hormones include two gonadotropins—luteinizing hormone (LH) and follicle-stimulating hormone (FSH)—that are secreted by the pituitary gland, as well as gonadotropin-releasing hormone (GnRH), which is secreted by the hypothalamus.

- Menstruation—the sloughing off of the uterine lining (endometrium)—is the outward manifestation of the menstrual cycle. A complete cycle usually lasts between 24 and 32 days.

- The menstrual cycle has three phases: the menstrual phase, the preovulatory phase, and the postovulatory phase. The cycle is regulated by hormonal interactions between the hypothalamus, the pituitary gland, and the ovaries.

- Women may use tampons, pads, or menstrual cups to absorb or block the menstrual flow. Some women experience pain during menstruation, or symptoms such as bloating and irritability during the days before menstruation, but many women do not think of their menstrual period as burdensome.

- Women may experience painful periods (dysmenorrhea), a variety of physical and psychological symptoms prior to menstruation (premenstrual syndrome), absence of menstrual periods (amenorrhea), or excessively heavy menstrual bleeding. There are many causes for these conditions, but effective treatments are usually available.

(continued)

Summary (continued)

- Besides regulating the menstrual cycle, sex hormones have other functions: They are responsible for the anatomical changes in a girl's body at puberty, they maintain bone density, and they affect brain organization and function—thus influencing a woman's sexual feelings and behaviors in a fashion that varies with the phase of her menstrual cycle.

- A woman's secondary sexual characteristics include her breasts, which combine sexual functions (being a potential source of sexual arousal to her and her partner) with a reproductive function (lactation).

- Breast cancer is the second most common cancer affecting women; risk factors include a family history of the disease, age, childlessness, alcohol use, and obesity. It can be detected early by mammography. Most breast lumps are not cancerous. Early-stage cancers can be treated without removal of the entire breast. Some breast cancer treatments, especially chemotherapy and mastectomy, may challenge women's sexual self-image or sexual function, but most women who undergo breast cancer treatments resume sexually active relationships.

Discussion Questions

1. Do you think that genital cutting (circumcision) of girls, in countries where it is a traditional practice, should be permitted or banned? What role do you think the United States should take in this matter?

2. Historically, the clitoris has been largely ignored, and even today it may be neglected in sex education classes. What do you think is the reason for this?

3. Women may change the appearance of their vulva by hair removal, labial surgery, piercing, tattooing, and so on. What is your opinion of these practices?

4. Make a list of anything you have heard about menstruation. Identify the myths and falsehoods. Compare and contrast these misconceptions with the material in the text and, if you choose, with your own experience or observations.

5. If you're a woman, how would you respond to this question: "Would you stop menstruating if you could?" If you're a man, what's your opinion on the matter?

6. Does sexual intercourse during menstruation strike you as appealing or not? Why?

7. What was your reaction to reading about all the gynecological disorders described in this chapter? If you're a woman, did you feel hypochondriacal ("I probably have several of them right now"), bored ("I knew everything about them already"), or empowered ("I've learned things that will help me avoid or deal with them")? If you're a man, did you find it interesting and useful to learn about women's bodies and their disorders, or not? Your instructor and the authors of this book welcome feedback from students.

Web Resources

American Cancer Society (ACS) www.cancer.org
AnatomyZone www.anatomyzone.com/tutorials/reproductive/introduction-to-female-reproductive-anatomy
Endometriosis Association www.endometriosisassn.org
Gray, H. Anatomy of the Human Body www.bartleby.com/107
Human ovulation captured on video www.newscientist.com/article/dn14155-human-ovulation-captured-on-video.html
King, M. W. The Medical Biochemistry Page themedicalbiochemistrypage.org
Miller, L. (University of Washington) (site devoted to menstrual suppression) www.noperiod.com
Museum of Menstruation www.mum.org
National Breast Cancer Coalition www.breastcancerdeadline2020.org
National Cancer Institute www.cancer.gov
National Cervical Cancer Coalition www.nccc-online.org
National Uterine Fibroids Association www.nuff.org
National Women's Health Information Center www.innovations.ahrq.gov
National Women's Health Network nwhn.org
Ovarian Cancer National Alliance www.ovariancancer.org
Tostan (Senegal-based organization opposed to female circumcision) www.tostan.org
University of Delaware histology site (female reproductive system) www.udel.edu/Biology/Wags/histpage/colorpage/cfr/cfr.htm

Recommended Reading

Abusharaf, R. M. (Ed.). (2007). *Female circumcision: Multicultural perspectives.* University of Pennsylvania Press.

American Cancer Society. (2005). *A breast cancer journey: Your personal guidebook* (2nd ed.). American Cancer Society.

Angier, N. (1999). *Woman: An intimate geography.* Houghton Mifflin.

Boston Women's Health Book Collective. (2011). *Our bodies, ourselves: A new edition for a new era* (rev. ed.). Touchstone.

Dirie, W. & Miller, C. (1998). *Desert flower: The extraordinary journey of a desert nomad.* William Morrow.

Ensler, E. (2007). *The vagina monologues.* Villard.

Herbenick, D. & Schick, V. (2011). *Read my lips: A complete guide to the vagina and vulva.* Rowman & Littlefield.

Johnson, M. A. (2013). *Essential reproduction* (7th ed.). Blackwell.

Komisaruk, B. R., Beyer-Flores, C. & Whipple, B. (2006). *The science of orgasm.* Johns Hopkins University Press.

Lightfoot-Klein, H. (2007). *Children's genitals under the knife: Social imperatives, secrecy, and shame.* BookSurge.

Love, S. M. & Lindsey, K. (2010). *Dr. Susan Love's breast book* (5th ed.). Da Capo Lifelong Books.

Nelson, R. J. (2011). *An introduction to behavioral endocrinology* (4th ed.). Sinauer.

Northrup, C. (2010). *Women's bodies, women's wisdom: Creating physical and emotional health and healing* (rev. ed.). Bantam.

Peltason, R. (2008). *I am not my breast cancer: Women talk openly about love and sex, hair loss and weight gain, mothers and daughters, and being a woman with breast cancer.* William Morrow.

Stein, E. & Kim, S. (2009). *Flow: The cultural story of menstruation.* St. Martin's Griffin.

Chapter 3

Penises come in many shapes and sizes, as suggested by these stone and wooden penises at a shrine in Thailand.

Men's Bodies

Biologically speaking, men's only reproductive function is to make and deliver sperm. Everything else—ovulation, fertilization, pregnancy, childbirth, and lactation—is the responsibility of women. Accordingly, the reproductive anatomy of men is much simpler than that of women. What's more, many of men's sex organs are visible on the outside of their bodies, so they are relatively familiar in appearance. For that very reason, however, they can also be the cause of considerable anxiety: Many men are concerned—often needlessly—about whether their genitals look or perform "right." One of the purposes of this chapter is to normalize the diversity in the structure and function of men's genitals.

Perhaps because of the social emphasis on male sexuality as performance, there has been more research into the function of male genitals than female genitals, particularly with regard to erection. We therefore take the opportunity in this chapter to discuss the behind-the-scenes biological control systems that orchestrate male genital functions, while bearing in mind there are likely to be close parallels between these systems in women and men.

(A)

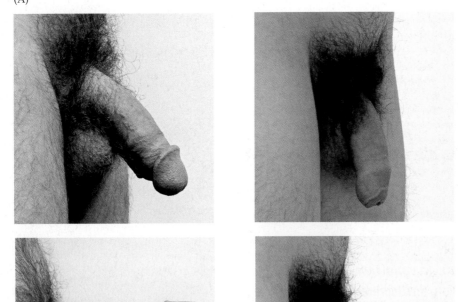
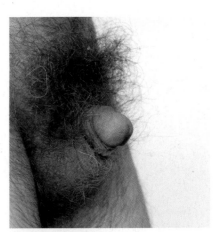
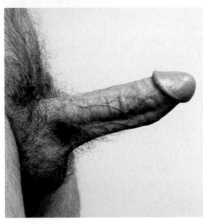
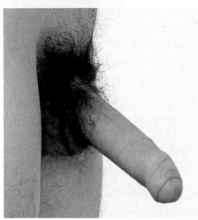
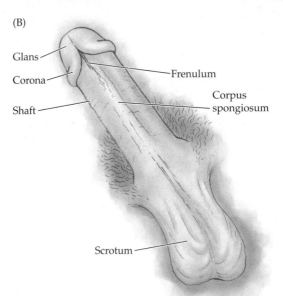

Figure 3.1 The male external genitalia (A) Three penises in the flaccid (above) and erect (below) states. The middle example is an uncircumcised penis; the other two are circumcised. (B) Drawing of an erect circumcised penis seen from below, showing the glans, corona, and frenulum—the most erotically sensitive portions of the penis. (See **Web Activity 3.1: The Male External Genitalia**.)

(B)

Glans

Corona

Shaft

Frenulum

Corpus spongiosum

Scrotum

The Male External Genitalia Are the Penis and Scrotum

The penis and the scrotum are the parts of the male reproductive system that can be seen from the outside (**Figure 3.1**). The testicles, or "balls," are indirectly visible as the twin bulges that give the scrotum its shape, but they are part of the internal male reproductive system.

Although men don't usually have the prominent pubic fat pad (the mons) seen in women, they do have a similar distribution of pubic hair. The hair may extend upward toward the navel or merge with the general body hair. Sparse hair usually covers the scrotum.

The penis combines erotic, reproductive, and urinary functions

Developmentally, the **penis** is equivalent to the clitoris.* In a functional sense, however, the penis corresponds to the clitoris, urethra, and vagina all rolled into one, because it is involved in sexual arousal, excretion of urine, and the delivery of sperm. It's no wonder men focus so much attention on the penis and are so gravely concerned when it fails to perform as expected.

The penis in its natural (i.e., uncircumcised) condition has three visible portions: a shaft, a head (or glans), and a foreskin. The **foreskin** (or **prepuce**) is a loose, tubular fold of skin that partially or completely covers the glans. In some males—during childhood especially—the foreskin extends well beyond the tip of the glans and urine passes through it as if through an extension of the urethra. In adult males, but not necessarily during childhood, the foreskin can readily be pulled back to expose the glans.

Male **circumcision** is the surgical removal of the foreskin, or part of it, exposing all or part of the glans. It may be performed at any age, but most circumcisions in the United States are done soon after birth. With babies, the 5- to 10-minute procedure is facilitated by the use of a clamp or other device such as the PlastiBell (**Figure 3.2**). The

* This equivalence is not precise, as is explained further in Chapter 4.

penis The erectile, erotically sensitive genital organ in males.

foreskin (or prepuce) The loose skin that partially or completely covers the glans in males who have not been circumcised.

circumcision The removal of the male foreskin. In women, an alternative term for genital cutting.

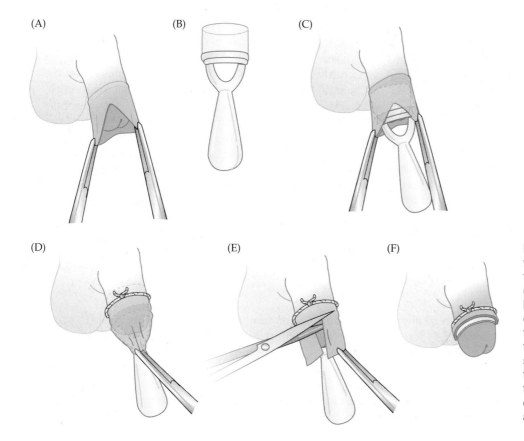

Figure 3.2 Neonatal circumcision with use of the PlastiBell (A) The foreskin is separated from the glans. (B) The PlastiBell is a clear plastic collar attached to a handle. (C) The collar of the PlastiBell is inserted between the foreskin and the glans. (D) A string is tightened around the base of the foreskin to prevent bleeding. (E) The excess foreskin is cut away. (F) The handle of the PlastiBell is broken off. The remainder of the PlastiBell falls off the penis after a few days.

Box 3.1 Controversies

Male Circumcision

Circumcision offers some significant benefits but also carries slight risks. One important benefit is a tenfold or greater reduction in the incidence of urinary tract infections in infancy (McNeil, 2007). In adulthood, circumcised men enjoy *partial* protection from infection with several sexually transmitted viruses, including those that cause AIDS, herpes, and cervical and anal cancer (Auvert et al., 2005; Gray et al., 2007; Tobian et al., 2009). (In the case of cervical and anal cancer, the benefit is to the man's sex partners.) Circumcised men also enjoy a 15% lower risk of prostate cancer, probably on account of the lower incidence of sexually transmitted infections (Wright et al., 2012).

Besides its medical benefits, circumcision facilitates hygiene. In uncircumcised men, a cheesy substance called **smegma** builds up under the foreskin and can develop a rancid smell and taste—something that a man's sex partner may find unpleasant, especially when performing oral sex. This problem can easily be avoided, however, if a man washes under his foreskin whenever he takes a bath or shower.

The risks of circumcision include hemorrhage, infection, and—extremely rarely—damage to the penis. No deaths from conventional circumcision have been reported in the United States in recent times. Several infants circumcised during an Orthodox Jewish ritual that involves mouth-to-penis contact ("oral suction") have died of herpes infections (Robbins, 2012). In South Africa, unsanitary circumcision by traditional practitioners results in dozens of deaths and penile mutilations every year (Smith, 2014). Some opponents of circumcision have suggested that the operation reduces the erotic sensitivity of the penis. However, one large random-sample study found that circumcision is associated with a slightly *lower* incidence of sexual disorders, especially erectile dysfunction (Laumann et al., 1997). In trials of adult circumcision conducted in Africa, the volunteers not only experienced an approximately 60% reduction in HIV infection rates (Rosario et al., 2013) but also expressed a high degree of satisfaction with the results of the procedure. The men's wives were twice as likely to say they enjoyed sex as compared with the wives of uncircumcised men (Shacham et al., 2013).

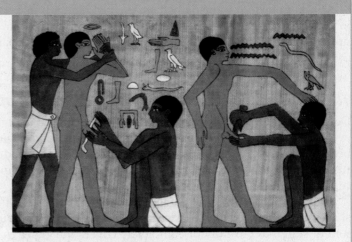

Egyptian circumcision, ca. 2300 BCE. The hieroglyphs on the left read "Hold him so that he doesn't fall" and "It is for your benefit." This is a modern painting based on a stone relief.

In a 2012 policy statement, the American Academy of Pediatrics (AAP) declared "that the health benefits of newborn male circumcision outweigh the risks and that the procedure's benefits justify access to this procedure for families who choose it" (AAP Task Force on Circumcision, 2012). The American College of Obstetricians and Gynecologists endorsed the AAP's statement (American Academy of Pediatrics, 2010). The CDC released draft guidelines in 2014 that recommend circumcision at any time of life as a means to reduce the risk of acquiring HIV and other STIs during coitus, but cautioned that a similar benefit with regard to anal sex has not been proven (Centers for Disease Control, 2014e).The Canadian Paediatric Society has opposed routine circumcision, but it is expected to issue new, more neutral guidelines shortly (Kirkey, 2013). Many European pediatricians remain opposed to routine circumcision: They are skeptical of the procedure's claimed health benefits and believe that circumcision can wait until a boy is old enough to make the decision for himself (Frisch et al., 2013). The "genital equity" argument also carries some weight: This holds that opponents of female genital cutting should oppose male genital cutting too (Shweder, 2013).

smegma   A whitish, greasy secretion that builds up under the foreskin of the penis or the clitoral hood.

clinician typically uses a nerve block or another form of local anesthesia to provide pain relief. When circumcision is performed in adulthood, stitches are necessary, and the man needs to refrain from sex, including masturbation, for about 4 to 6 weeks. A nonsurgical device known as PrePex has been approved for adult circumcision by the World Health Organization (McNeil, 2013b). It is expected to be widely used in Africa, where adult circumcision has been encouraged as a means to reduce transmission of HIV (see Chapter 15).

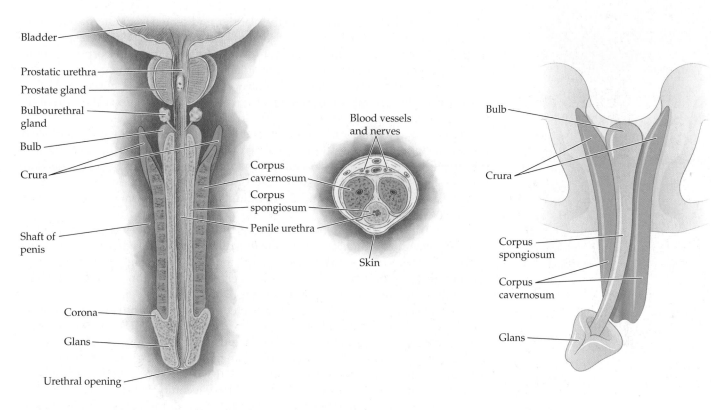

Bladder

Prostatic urethra

Prostate gland

Bulbourethral gland

Bulb

Crura

Shaft of penis

Corona

Glans

Urethral opening

Blood vessels and nerves

Corpus cavernosum

Corpus spongiosum

Penile urethra

Skin

Bulb

Crura

Corpus spongiosum

Corpus cavernosum

Glans

Figure 3.3 Internal structure of the erect penis and the urethra Note that the corpus spongiosum surrounds the penile urethra and expands at the tip of the penis to form the glans. Because it lacks a tough capsule, the corpus spongiosum is less rigid than the corpora cavernosa when the penis is erect. (See **Web Activity 3.2: Internal Structure of the Erect Penis and the Urethra**.)

Worldwide, about 30% of all men are circumcised (UNAIDS, 2007). In the United States, the figure for 2010 was 58%; the circumcision rate has probably declined somewhat since then, but definitive numbers are lacking (Rabin, 2010). Circumcision is most popular among whites, less popular among African-Americans, and least popular among Hispanics and Asian-Americans (Centers for Disease Control, 2010c).

Circumcision is an ancient practice that is religiously prescribed for Muslims and Jews. It has also been practiced as a nonreligious tradition in many cultures. There is some controversy over whether circumcision of male infants should be recommended or discouraged (**Box 3.1**).

The shaft of the penis contains three erectile structures (**Figure 3.3**): two **corpora cavernosa**, which lie side by side and account for the bulk of the penis's erectile capacity, and a single **corpus spongiosum**, which runs along the middle of the undersurface of the penis. The corpus spongiosum extends from the shaft into the **glans**, where it balloons out and fills the entire volume of the glans. Both the corpora cavernosa and the corpus spongiosum extend backward into the body under the pubic bone, forming the root of the penis, which is about 2 inches (5 cm) long.

At the inner end of the root of the penis, the corpus spongiosum expands into a rounded mass of erectile tissue known as the **penile bulb**. The two corpora cavernosa diverge, forming two **crura** similar to those of a woman's clitoris. As in women, there are several muscles in the pelvic floor that play an important role in the sexual response. These pelvic floor muscles assist with erection of the penis, ejaculation, and orgasm.

corpus cavernosum (pl. corpora cavernosa) Either of two elongated erectile structures within the penis or clitoris, which also extend backward into the pelvic floor.

corpus spongiosum A single midline erectile structure. In both sexes it fills the glans; in males it extends backward along the underside of the penis, surrounding the urethra.

glans The terminal knob of the penis or clitoris.

penile bulb An expansion of the corpus spongiosum at the root of the penis.

crus (pl. crura) Internal extensions of the corpora cavernosa of the clitoris or penis.

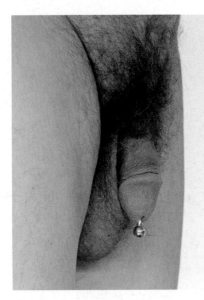

A "Prince Albert" piercing enters the glans through or near the frenulum and exits via the urethra.

FAQ

Is there such a thing as fracture of the penis?

Yes. Unlike many other primates, human males lack a penile bone that might break, but the term "fracture of the penis" refers to a tear in the capsule of a corpus cavernosum. This can happen when a man's erect penis collides very forcefully with his partner's body. There will be a cracking noise, severe pain, and a large bruise. The man should go to an emergency room: Surgical repair is usually necessary to prevent long-term damage.

corona   The rim of the glans of the penis.

frenulum   A strip of loose skin on the underside of the penis, running between the glans and the shaft.

balanitis   Inflammation of the glans of the penis.

phimosis   A tightening of the foreskin, preventing its retraction from the glans.

paraphimosis   Entrapment of the retracted foreskin behind the corona.

Peyronie's disease   Pathological curvature of the penis.

The urethra discharges urine from the bladder, and semen from internal reproductive glands (see *The Testicles Produce Sperm and Sex Hormones*). Within the penis, the urethra runs close to the underside, entirely contained within the corpus spongiosum, and emerges at or near the tip of the glans as a slit-like opening.

The shaft of the penis contains other structures, most notably nerves and blood vessels that play an important role in sexual arousal and erection. The skin of the penis is hairless and only loosely attached to the underlying tissue.

The glans has a rim, or **corona**, that encircles the penis. On the undersurface of the penis, the corona comes closer to the tip of the glans than on its upper surface. In this area lies a loose strip of skin named the **frenulum** that runs between the glans and the shaft (see Figure 3.1B). Although stimulation anywhere on the penis can be sexually arousing, the corona and the frenulum are usually the most erotically sensitive regions.

The size of the penis—in both the flaccid and erect states—varies considerably among men. A nonpornographic website illustrates some of this diversity and shows the process of erection (see Web Resources at the end of this chapter). Some men are concerned about the size or shape of their penis, but these dimensions rarely have any significant effect on sexual performance (**Box 3.2**).

Men have been piercing their penises for tens of thousands of years: The practice is depicted in Paleolithic (Old Stone Age) art (Angulo et al., 2011). Men considering a penis piercing should carefully review the potential problems, which can include scarring, damage to erectile tissue, nerve damage, interference with urination, and serious infections such as hepatitis and HIV (Grossman, 2008). Selection of an experienced practitioner who uses scrupulous sanitary techniques is paramount.

Considering the demands that may be placed on it, the penis is a remarkably sturdy organ. Aside from erectile disorder (see Chapter 14) and sexually transmitted infections (see Chapter 15), the penis is subject to only a few medical problems that occur with any frequency:

- **Balanitis** is inflammation of the glans, caused by infection and/or poor hygiene. It is quite common in uncircumcised men. Treatment involves regular cleansing and antibiotics as appropriate.

- **Phimosis** is the inability to retract the foreskin far enough to expose the glans. This is the normal condition in male babies, and it persists in many boys into the teen years. There is no need to treat it unless the flow of urine is affected. Phimosis may also develop as a new condition in adults, especially in association with balanitis, in which case surgical treatment may be required.

- **Paraphimosis** is the entrapment of a retracted foreskin behind the corona of the glans. It can occur as a result of efforts to retract a phimotic foreskin. Paraphimosis is an emergency condition because it can lead to tissue death of the glans. It can usually be reversed without circumcision, but later circumcision is recommended to prevent recurrence.

- **Peyronie's disease** is an unnatural curvature of the erect penis caused by scar formation in the corpora cavernosa—possibly as a late consequence of trauma. (Many men have some natural curvature in their penis.) Peyronie's disease can cause pain or even prevent penetrative sex. Surgical treatments are available.

Penile cancer is rare: It strikes about 1200 men in the United States per year and causes about 300 deaths. Infection with certain types of human papillomavirus (HPV—see Chapter 15) is an important factor predisposing men to penile cancer. Detected early, penile cancer can be treated by fairly minor surgical procedures. If the cancer has invaded the deep structures of the penis, however, part or all of the organ

Box 3.2 Research Highlights

How Big Should a Penis Be?

Many men fear that they are under-endowed—specifically, that their penis is too small to arouse or physically satisfy their partners or that its small size will provoke ridicule from their peers (Wylie & Eardley, 2007). But because penises—especially erect ones—are rarely seen, it's possible that men develop erroneous ideas about the average or most desirable size of the penis. These ideas could come from watching pornography, for example.

Let's take a look at some objective data: Researchers at Indiana University obtained the self-measured dimensions of the erect penises of 1661 sexually active men (Herbenick et al., 2014). (The men were asked to give the measurements so that they could be given custom-sized condoms, which makes it likely that they reported the measurements accurately.) Penile length (measured along the underside) ranged from 1.6 inches (4 cm) to 10.2 inches (26 cm) and averaged 5.6 inches (14.2 cm). Penile circumference ranged from 1.2 inches (3 cm) to 7.5 inches (19 cm) with an average of 4.8 inches (12.2 cm). These dimensions did not differ significantly with age, race/ethnicity, or sexual orientation, but the low number of subjects in some categories meant that small differences, such as have been reported in some previous studies, may have been missed.

In a large Internet survey, researchers at California State University, Los Angeles, and at University of California, Los Angeles (UCLA) found that only 55% of heterosexual men were satisfied with the size of their penis, but 84% of straight women were satisfied with the size of their partner's penis, and only 14% wanted it larger (Lever et al., 2006). Thus, unless a lot of men with small penises are lacking partners altogether, many heterosexual men may be suffering needless anxiety about the size of their penis.

There exists a small industry devoted to the surgical augmentation of the penis. The penis may be lengthened by cutting the suspensory ligament (see figure), followed by many weeks of traction (hanging weights from the penis). This procedure extends the apparent length of the penis by 0.5 to 1.0 inch (1 to 2 cm) (Li et al., 2006; Vardi et al., 2008). The procedure only lengthens the flaccid penis, however; the erect penis length is not affected. There are also more complex procedures involving tissue grafts (Austoni et al., 2002). Numerous self-help methods have been recommended, such as jelqing (repeated squeezing

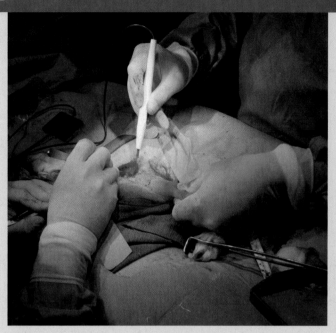

Lengthening of the penis by cutting of the suspensory ligament.

of the penis in a motion from the base to the corona), but there is no objective evidence that any of these methods work, and some may cause damage to the penis.

The girth of the penis can be increased by fat injections (Panfilov, 2006) or by transplanting slabs of fatty tissue from the buttocks to under the skin of the penis. The procedure leaves visible scars, and the penis often comes to look lumpy or otherwise abnormal over time.

The incidence of complications from penile augmentation surgery is very high (Vardi et al., 2008), and the American Urological Association states that the surgery "has not been shown to be safe or efficacious" (American Urological Association, 2013). Although some surgeons report high rates of patient satisfaction, most studies find that men who undergo the surgery are, on average, dissatisfied with the outcome and do not experience improved sex lives afterward (Wessells et al., 1996; Klein, 1999; Li et al., 2006). Men who are obsessively concerned about the size of their penis can be helped by reassurance or psychotherapy (Wylie & Eardley, 2007).

may have to be amputated. It may surprise you to learn that many men who have had their penis removed develop the ability to experience orgasm through stimulation of nearby areas of skin.

Very rarely boys are born with two penises (**Box 3.3**). Other congenital disorders are discussed in Chapter 4.

Box 3.3 Biology of Sex

Diphallia

"Diphallia" means having two penises. This is the normal condition for snakes and lizards, as well as for some invertebrates, and it also occurs in humans, but very seldom—about once in every 5 million male births. Of the 30 or so individuals known to have been born with diphallia in the United States, the great majority have other congenital malformations such as a double bladder or a urethra that opens in the wrong place (hypospadias—see Chapter 4) (Kundal et al., 2013; Tirtayasa et al., 2013). One of the two penises is often small and nonfunctional, and this one may be surgically removed during infancy. It may be that diphallia comes about because of a problem with the molecular signals that define the midline of the body during fetal development.

Extremely rarely, both penises are of equal length and fully functional for urination and sex, without any accompanying malformations. One such instance came to light in 2014, when a man with the username DoubleDickDude went public on Reddit's "Ask Me Anything" (AMA) pages (Anonymous, 2014b). Besides having two normally functioning penises, DoubleDickDude is bisexual and has had sex with both men and women, sometimes in three-ways that involve simultaneous oral sex from both partners. Men, he says, are much more enthusiastic about interacting with his penises than women.

Out of the 9000+ questions and answers posted on Reddit, here are three:

How do women react when they find out?

"For the most part, girls were nervous and some changed their mind at the last minute. Dudes NEVER change their mind, they always want it even if they're freaked out a little."

DoubleDickDude's genitals. Neither penis is circumcised. Photograph published with permission.

Did you ever consider a career in porn?

"Yes, but I decided against it. . . . The only reason I let photos out is because I thought people might like to know that at least one guy with two normal dicks exists. All the others are pretty scary-looking and I feel for them."

What's the best thing about having two penises?

"Having two cocks... It's great—no complaints."

A corresponding condition sometimes occurs in women: In this case the woman's vagina has a septum (tissue wall) that divides it into a left and right passageway, each of which leads into a separate uterus. The condition may require surgery, but it is usually compatible with pregnancy.

Penile Erection Involves Nerves, Blood, and Chemistry

Erection of the penis can occur in response to local stimulation of the genital region, especially of the penis itself. Alternatively, it may occur in response to higher-level inputs, such as erotic thoughts or sensations (sights, odors, and so on) that are analyzed by the brain.

With regard to local stimulation, the penis (as well as the clitoris) possesses a unique class of sensory nerve endings termed **genital end-bulbs** (Halata & Munger, 1986) (**Figure 3.4**). In these structures, the nerve fibers form tangled knots in the deeper part of the skin. The highest density of genital end-bulbs occurs around the corona of the glans and in the frenulum—the zones generally considered to be the most erotically sensitive regions. It is believed that genital end-bulbs are specialized to detect the tactile stimulation that occurs during sexual behavior.

genital end-bulbs Specialized nerve endings found in the genital area that probably detect the tactile stimulation associated with sexual activity.

Figure 3.4 Sensory innervation of the penis A bundle of nerve fibers (circled) approaches the skin surface and forms a dense knot of terminal branches—a genital end-bulb. (From Halata & Munger, 1986; courtesy of Z. Halata and K. Baumann, University of Hamburg.)

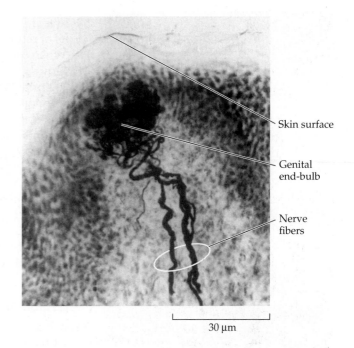

Skin surface

Genital end-bulb

Nerve fibers

30 μm

Of course, a man's penis and woman's clitoris are not their only erogenous zones: A wide zone of genital skin, as well as the anus and the nipples, are erotically sensitive in both sexes, though to a varying degree from person to person. Using brain imaging techniques, researchers at Rutgers University found that nipple stimulation activates two zones in the cerebral cortex: the zone devoted to the nipples themselves and also the zone devoted to the genitals (Komisaruk et al., 2011). In other words, it's as if the brain is capable of interpreting nipple stimulation as arising in the genitals.

Local stimulation of the genital receptors triggers a spinal reflex: That is, nerves carry the information to the spinal cord, which then sends a return signal to the penis that triggers erection. Thus, local stimulation can cause an erection even after a spinal injury that completely separates the spinal cord from the brain. The nerves that regulate penile erection are part of the **autonomic nervous system** (see Appendix B).

If the stimulation originates in the brain, specific neural pathways transmit the information to the spinal cord and then to the penis. This kind of erection cannot occur after an injury that completely severs the spinal cord.

The nerves that innervate the erectile tissue and control the process of erection are not under voluntary control. A man cannot, therefore, develop or lose an erection by a simple act of will.

autonomic nervous system The portion of the nervous system that controls smooth muscles and glands without our conscious involvement.

sinusoid A vascular space, such as within erectile tissue, capable of being expanded by filling with blood.

nitric oxide A dissolved gas that functions as a neurotransmitter in erectile tissue.

Erection is filling of the penis with blood

Now let's take a look at the erectile tissue itself (**Figure 3.5**). We will focus on the two corpora cavernosa of the penis, which have received the most study. The tissue within the corpora cavernosa is like a sponge: It contains numerous collapsible spaces named **sinusoids**. These spaces are part of the circulatory system; that is, blood enters them from arteries and exits by way of veins. When the penis is in a flaccid state, the arteries are in a constricted state, so little blood can flow into the sinusoids. Erection occurs when neural signals cause the arteries of the penis to expand and the veins to contract, resulting in expansion of the corpora cavernosa. As sexual climax approaches, vasocongestion causes further swelling of the penis, especially the glans, and the pooling of blood within the glans turns it a purplish color.

A neurotransmitter, or neural-signaling molecule, called **nitric oxide** is involved in the triggering of an erection. As we'll describe in Chapter

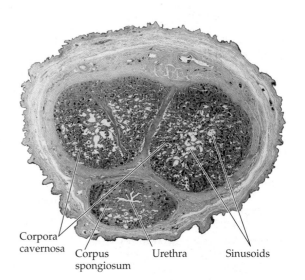

Figure 3.5 The mechanism of penile (or clitoral) erection Cross section of the penis, showing the appearance of erectile tissue (in the flaccid state) within the corpora cavernosa. The small white collapsible spaces (sinusoids) fill with blood, causing an erection. (See **Web Activity 3.3: The Mechanism of Erection**.)

Corpora cavernosa

Corpus spongiosum

Urethra

Sinusoids

Figure 3.6 **Priapism** is named for the Greco-Roman fertility god Priapus, who was always portrayed with an erection. In this wall painting from Pompeii, Priapus weighs his penis against a bag of gold (visible under the damaged area of the painting). This is an allusion to the wealth of the family that commissioned the painting. For mere mortals, an erection that won't go down calls for prompt medical attention.

priapism A persistent penile erection in the absence of sexual arousal.

nocturnal orgasm Orgasm during sleep.

nocturnal emission Ejaculation during sleep.

scrotum The sac behind the penis that contains the testicles.

testicle (or testis; pl. testes) The male gonad: one of the two glands within the scrotum that produce sperm and secrete sex hormones.

14, Viagra and other drugs that help produce erections do so by increasing the level of nitric oxide in the erectile tissue.

When complete erection occurs, no additional blood can enter the corpora cavernosa, so blood flow ceases. An erection that won't go down—a condition called **priapism**—will starve the erectile tissue of oxygen and cause damage if it is prolonged for more than a few hours (**Figure 3.6**).

The ability of the corpora cavernosa to expand is limited by the tough connective tissue capsules that enclose them. This resistance to expansion causes the rigidity of the erect penis. Although both the corpora cavernosa and the corpus spongiosum expand during erection, the corpus spongiosum does not contribute as much to the erect penis's stiffness. The difference in rigidity can be appreciated by feeling an erect penis: The corpus spongiosum, which forms the ridge along the underside of the penis and also occupies the entire glans, is much softer to the touch than the rest of the organ. If the corpus spongiosum were as rigid as the rest of the penis during erection, the urethra would be compressed and ejaculation might be impossible.

Muscles are also involved in erection

Pelvic floor muscles, including the pubococcygeus muscle, also contribute to erection. If a man's penis is erect but hanging down from the body, a light touch on a sensitive area of the penis, or even on nearby skin, will cause the penis to lift up and project forward or upward. At the same time, the glans of the penis will become more swollen. It is also possible for a man to produce the same reaction voluntarily, without any physical stimulation, by contracting the pelvic floor muscles, which pull on and squeeze the corpora cavernosa and corpus spongiosum in the root of the penis. In spite of the participation of these muscles, we emphasize that the main process of penile erection, described above, is not under voluntary control.

Erections occur during sleep

Although we usually think of erections as resulting from sexual arousal or behavior, they also occur spontaneously during sleep. They accompany the rapid eye movement (REM) phase of sleep, during which vivid dreams are experienced (**Figure 3.7**). The dreams may be erotic in nature and may culminate in **nocturnal orgasms** (also called **nocturnal emissions** or "wet dreams"), but erections accompany all REM phases, whatever their dream content. Kinsey reported that 4 out of 5 men experience nocturnal emissions at some time in their lives, most commonly in their teen years (Kinsey et al., 1948).

The function of nocturnal erections is not certain, but it is suspected that they serve to oxygenate the erectile tissue and to prevent fibrosis (scarring) and loss of elasticity. Nocturnal genital arousal is common in women as well as men, and one study reported that about 1 in 5 young women experienced orgasms during sleep (Henton, 1976).

The scrotum regulates the temperature of the testicles

The **scrotum** or scrotal sac (**Figure 3.8**) is a loose bag of skin that hangs down behind the penis and contains the two **testicles** or **testes**.* In adult men the scrotum is lightly covered with hair, and it possesses numerous sweat glands that help to regu-

---

*Although the terms "testicle" and "testis" denote the same thing, "testicle" is used when referring to the anatomical structure, whereas "testis" is used when referring to its function or early development.

Figure 3.7 Penile erections accompany REM sleep. The graph shows an entire night's sleep (9 hours) for a healthy young man. The upper trace indicates the stages of sleep as determined by electroencephalography (EEG): Stage I is light sleep, stage II is intermediate-level sleep, and stages III and IV are both deep sleep. The five REM episodes, shown here as being stage I, are actually a distinct kind of sleep characterized by rapid eye movements. The lower trace shows changes in penile circumference (3.0 cm = maximal erection). Note that the erections occur during the REM episodes. (Data from Brain Information Service, UCLA, School of Medicine.)

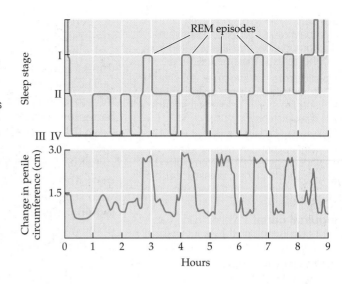

late the temperature of the scrotal contents. Stimulation of the scrotal skin is sexually arousing in most men, though not to the same degree as in the most sensitive areas of the penis. Underneath the scrotal skin lies a sheetlike smooth muscle. Contraction of this muscle in response to cold (and also during sexual arousal—especially near orgasm) causes the scrotal skin to wrinkle and appear thicker. This makes the skin a more effective insulator and also brings the testicles closer to the body, warming them.

The Testicles Produce Sperm and Sex Hormones

The testicles, or male gonads, have two functions that are analogous to those of the ovaries (female gonads): They produce **sperm** (or **spermatozoa**) and secrete sex hormones. Men do not become pregnant, and they lack any structures equivalent to the uterus or oviducts. However, men do need to create and store large numbers

sperm (or spermatozoon; pl. spermatozoa) The male gamete, produced in the testicles.

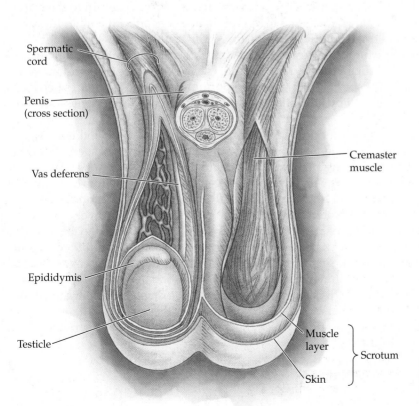

Figure 3.8 The scrotum and its internal structure (See **Web Activity 3.4: The Scrotum and Its Contents**.)

semen   The fluid, containing sperm and a variety of chemical compounds, that is ejaculated from the penis at male sexual climax.

epididymis   A structure, attached to each testicle, where sperm mature and are stored before entering the vas deferens.

spermatic cord   Either of two bilateral bundles of structures, including the vas deferens, blood vessels, and the cremaster muscle, that pass through the inguinal canal to a testicle.

inguinal canal   A short canal passing through the abdominal wall in the region of the groin in males.

cremaster muscle   A sheetlike muscle that wraps around the spermatic cord and the testicle.

vas deferens (pl. vasa deferentia)   Either of the two bilateral ducts that convey sperm from the epididymis to the ejaculatory duct.

seminiferous tubules   Convoluted microscopic tubes within the testicle; the site of sperm production.

spermatogenesis   The production of sperm.

interstitial cells   Cells located between the seminiferous tubules in the testicle that secrete hormones.

FAQ

Lance Armstrong had testicular cancer—was that caused by his doping?

Some of the drugs he took, such as human growth hormone, can promote cancer growth, but there is no particular reason to make a causal connection in Armstrong's case: He was in the age range where testicular cancer is not rare.

of sperm, mix them with other secretions, and deliver the resulting **semen** to the urethral opening for ejaculation. These functions require a number of structures, including several specialized glands and assorted pieces of tubing to connect everything together.

The testicles are twin egg-shaped structures that can easily be seen or felt within the scrotal sac. The testicles are not completely symmetrical: One (usually the left) hangs lower, and one (usually the right) is slightly larger. Each testicle weighs about 0.4 to 0.5 ounces (11 to 14 g) and lies within a protective capsule. Above and behind each testicle is an **epididymis**, through which sperm pass after leaving the testicle.

Before considering the structure of the testicle, let's take a look at the **spermatic cord**. This cord is the testicle's lifeline—a bundle of structures that connect the testicle with several crucial organs inside the body. The spermatic cord runs through the **inguinal canal**—a 1.5-inch (4 cm) tunnel through the abdominal wall in the region of the groin.

A layer of muscle tissue known as the **cremaster muscle** wraps the spermatic cord and forms a sling around the testicle. The cremaster contracts automatically in response to cold, pulling the testicle toward the body, and thus helps to regulate the temperature of the testicle.

Within the spermatic cord runs the **vas deferens**, the tube that carries mature sperm away from the epididymis. In addition, the spermatic cord contains arteries, veins, and nerves that supply the testicle. The arteries and veins run close to each other, an arrangement that facilitates the transfer of heat from the arterial to the venous circulation. This helps keep the temperature of the testicle below the temperature of the remainder of the body.

With all these temperature-regulating elements, it should be no surprise to learn that the testicles require a specific temperature range for the production of sperm, which is 7°F to 12°F (4°C to 7°C) below core body temperature. Warming the testicles to core body temperature for prolonged periods decreases a man's sperm count and reduces fertility, probably by shortening the lifespan of sperm stored in the epididymis (Bedford, 1991). The sperm count recovers after the testicles return to their preferred temperature range. Increased temperature does not affect the other function of the testicles—hormone production—to any significant extent.

The internal structure of the testicle (**Figure 3.9**) is dominated by the **seminiferous tubules**, a set of about a thousand fine, highly convoluted tubes. The seminiferous tubules are the site of sperm production, or **spermatogenesis**. The spaces between the tubules are occupied by **interstitial cells**, which secrete sex hormones—mainly testosterone (see below).

Each sperm cell is the product of a 64-day process of cell division and maturation that begins within a seminiferous tubule. Of course, huge numbers of sperm develop simultaneously. The average man produces about 150 million sperm per day—day after day for several decades. A man's sperm are genetically different from one another, because they carry different selections of genes from the man's mother and father.

After leaving the seminiferous tubules, the immature sperm travel to the epididymis. The epididymis has the shape of the letter C and is attached to the top and back surface of the testicle. It contains a single extremely convoluted tubule. Sperm spend about a week traversing this tubule, during which time they become about a hundredfold more concentrated. They also mature functionally, gaining the capacity for forward motion. Still, this swimming motion is sluggish and does not contribute to the sperm's movement along the male reproductive tract.

A number of medical conditions can affect the testicles. The most serious is testicular cancer (**Box 3.4**).

(A)

(B)

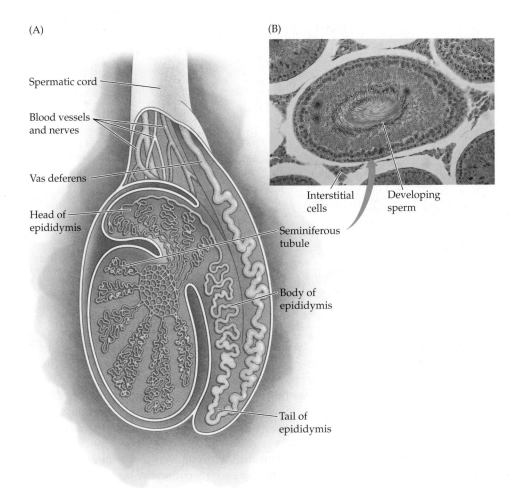

Spermatic cord

Blood vessels
and nerves

Vas deferens

Head of
epididymis

Seminiferous
tubule

Body of
epididymis

Tail of
epididymis

Interstitial
cells

Developing
sperm

**Figure 3.9   Internal structure of the
testicle and epididymis** (A) Diagram
of the sperm-forming pathway. Sperm
initially develop in the seminiferous
tubules of the testicle; they then pass
to the epididymis, where they mature
further and are stored, before moving
through the vas deferens to the urethra. (B) Cross section of a seminiferous
tubule. The sperm develop while their
heads are embedded in the cells lining
the tubule; their tails fill the lumen (central canal) of the tubule. The cells scattered between the tubules (interstitial
cells) secrete sex hormones. (See **Web
Activity 3.5: Internal Structure of the
Testicle and Epididymis.**)

Other glands contribute secretions to the semen

The sperm pass from the epididymis into the vas deferens. Each vas deferens passes
up through the spermatic cord into the abdomen, past the bladder, and down toward
the prostate gland (**Figure 3.10**). The vasa deferentia are not only transport routes
but also storage reservoirs for mature sperm, which have been concentrated by the
epididymis into a paste-like mass. Further progress of the sperm occurs not by fluid
flow or by their own motility, but by muscular contractions of the walls of the vasa
deferentia. These contractions occur just before ejaculation.

The **seminal vesicles** are two small glands that lie behind the bladder. Their name
is misleading: They are not storage areas for semen, but rather glands that add their
secretions to the semen. The ducts of the left and right seminal vesicles join the left
and right vasa deferentia, and the combined ducts are thereafter named the **ejaculatory ducts**. The left and right ejaculatory ducts join the urethra as it passes through
the prostate gland. From that junction on, the function of the urethra is to pass urine
or semen as needed. The **prostate gland** lies in the midline immediately below the
bladder. It completely surrounds the urethra as it exits the bladder. The normal prostate is slightly larger than a walnut. The secretion of the prostate is a cloudy, alkaline
fluid; at ejaculation, this fluid is pumped into the urethra by the contraction of muscle
fibers within the gland.

seminal vesicles   Two glands
situated to either side of the
prostate; their secretions are a
component of semen.

ejaculatory duct   Either of the
two bilateral ducts formed by the
junction of the vas deferens and
the duct of the seminal vesicle. The
ejaculatory ducts empty into the
urethra within the prostate.

prostate gland   A single gland
located at the base of the bladder
that surrounds the urethra; its
secretions are a component of
semen.

Figure 3.10 The male reproductive tract Note how the prostate gland surrounds the urethra as it exits the bladder. Enlargement of the prostate can interfere with urination. (See **Web Activity 3.6: The Male Reproductive Tract**.)

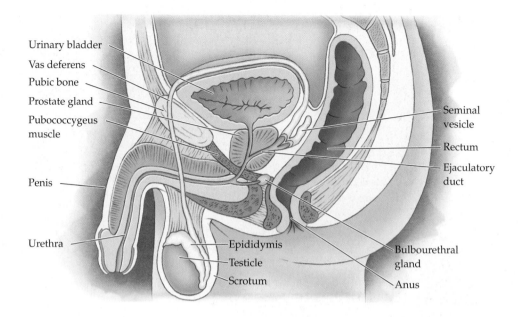

Urinary bladder
Vas deferens
Pubic bone
Prostate gland
Pubococcygeus muscle
Penis
Urethra
Epididymis
Testicle
Scrotum
Seminal vesicle
Rectum
Ejaculatory duct
Bulbourethral gland
Anus

bulbourethral glands (or Cowper's glands) Two small glands near the root of the penis whose secretions ("pre-cum") may appear at the urethral opening during sexual arousal prior to ejaculation.

Because the prostate gland is out of sight and because the role of its secretions (see below) is not widely known, it comes to most men's attention only when it malfunctions, which it does all too commonly, especially in old age (**Box 3.5**).

The last glands that need to be mentioned are the **bulbourethral glands (or Cowper's glands)**. These two pea-sized glands lie below the prostate gland, and their secretion—a clear, alkaline, mucous fluid—is expelled into the urethra. In many men, secretion from the bulbourethral glands begins early during sexual arousal and can be seen as a drop or two of slippery liquid that appears at the urethral opening sometime between erection and ejaculation; hence its colloquial name, "pre-cum." During coitus, the alkaline bulbourethral and prostatic secretions may help neutralize the acidic environments within the man's urethra and the woman's vagina, thus increasing the viability of the sperm.

Bulbourethral secretions do not contain sperm. Nevertheless, they can become mixed with sperm remaining in the urethra from a previous ejaculation. This happens chiefly when a man has sex for a second time without urinating between times. In those circumstances, remnants of the first ejaculate that have remained behind in the urethra get mixed in with the bulbourethral secretions from the second episode. In this case the man might unwittingly impregnate his partner during this second episode, even if he doesn't ejaculate or delays putting on a condom until just before ejaculating. "Pre-cum" can also contain disease organisms and can therefore be responsible for the spread of sexually transmitted infections.

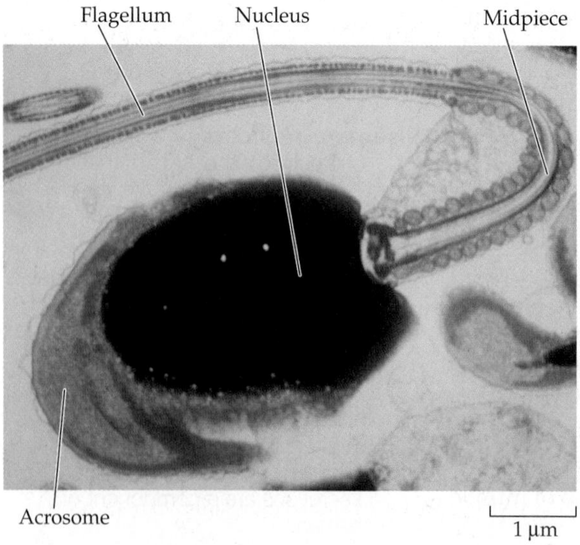

What is semen?

Semen, or seminal fluid ("cum" in colloquial English), is the thick, cloudy, off-white liquid that is ejaculated from the male urethra at sexual climax.

The volume of a single ejaculate usually ranges between 2 and 5 mL (up to 1 teaspoon). The most important component of semen is, of course, the sperm (**Figure 3.11**). Each milliliter of semen contains 50 to 150 million sperm, and a normal ejaculate contains between 100 and 700 million sperm.

Flagellum   Nucleus   Midpiece

Acrosome

1 μm

Figure 3.11 Human sperm Electron micrographic view of a single sperm, showing the acrosome, nucleus, midpiece, and flagellum (tail).

Box 3.4 Sexual Health

Disorders of the Testicles

About 8800 cases of testicular cancer are diagnosed in the United States annually, but less than 400 men die of the disease (American Cancer Society, 2014b). In other words, it is usually a curable condition. It most commonly strikes men in their 20s or 30s. Risk factors include a history of undescended testicles, other developmental abnormalities of the testicles, and Klinefelter syndrome (see Chapter 4).

Testicular cancer is usually diagnosed when the individual or his health care provider notices a lump or an increase in size in one testicle. There may also be a sudden accumulation of fluid in the scrotum, pain in the testicle, or an ache or heaviness in the lower abdomen, groin, or scrotum. A provisional diagnosis is made by means of an ultrasound scan; the definitive diagnosis is made by removing the entire affected testicle through an incision in the groin and examining it microscopically.

By itself, the removal of one testicle is of no great consequence, since the remaining testicle can compensate. Unfortunately, further treatments—lymph node dissection, radiation, or chemotherapy—may be necessary, and these have the potential to interfere with erectile function and sperm production. Men with testicular cancer who may want to father children in the future have the option of depositing semen samples in a sperm bank before treatment.

Other noncancerous conditions can affect the testicles and nearby structures:

- **Orchitis** is an inflammation and swelling of a testicle, caused by infection with a variety of organisms, some of which may be sexually transmitted.

- **Epididymitis** is an inflammation of the epididymis, caused by trauma or by infection with *E. coli* or any of a number of sexually transmitted organisms.

- A **varicocele** is an enlargement of the veins that drain the testicles, causing the spermatic cord to feel lumpy. It can be surgically corrected.

- A **hydrocele** is a collection of fluid in the membrane-lined space surrounding one testicle. It can be drained or surgically corrected.

- **Testicular torsion** is a twisting of a testicle and its spermatic cord, which cuts off the testicle's blood supply.

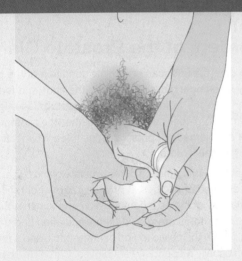

Testicular self-examination.

Torsion causes sudden and severe pain; it must be treated within a few hours or the affected testicle may die from the lack of blood.

Regular testicular self-examination (see figure) is recommended for men at increased risk of testicular cancer. There are no objective data about its value for men of average risk, but the exam is simple enough and might be lifesaving.

To do the exam, choose a warm location such as the shower, so that the scrotal sac is relaxed. Roll each testicle in turn between thumb and fingers. The surface of the testicle is usually fairly smooth, and the epididymis can be felt as a soft, elongated structure behind and above each testicle. One testicle is normally slightly larger than the other, but it is a matter of concern if one testicle has enlarged since the last time you examined it. Also feel for any lumps, rounded or irregular masses, changes in the consistency of a testicle, or tender areas. None of these signs are definitive indicators of cancer, but they merit a visit to your doctor.

orchitis   Inflammation of a testicle.

epididymitis   Inflammation of the epididymis.

varicocele   Enlargement of the veins that drain the testicle.

hydrocele   A collection of fluid around a testicle.

testicular torsion   Twisting of a testicle that cuts off its blood supply.

Each sperm (or spermatozoon) has the familiar tadpole-like structure: a head, containing the cell's nucleus with its all-important DNA packed into a dense inert mass; and a motile tail, or **flagellum**, which propels the spermatozoon forward. When we

flagellum   A whiplike cellular structure, such as the tail of a sperm.

Box 3.5 Sexual Health

Disorders of the Prostate Gland

A health care provider can check the condition of the prostate gland by inserting a gloved finger into the anus and feeling the gland through the front surface of the rectum (see figure). In this way, the provider can assess whether the prostate gland is tender or enlarged or contains lumps. (See **Web Activity 3.7: Anatomy of the Prostate.**)

Prostatitis—inflammation of the prostate gland—is a disorder that affects men of all ages. It may be acute or chronic. Acute prostatitis may occur as a complication of a urinary tract infection. The symptoms are pain during ejaculation and urination, ongoing pain in the pelvic region or lower back, and a fever. The condition usually responds to antibiotics. Chronic prostatitis, or **chronic pelvic pain syndrome**, is a puzzling and difficult-to-treat condition whose symptoms resemble acute prostatitis but can last for months or years (Pontari & Giusto, 2013).

Benign prostatic hyperplasia, or "enlarged prostate," is a common disorder of older men. The prostate gland continues to grow slowly throughout adult life, and its growth may eventually constrict the urethra where it passes through the gland. More than half of all men in their 60s and beyond experience chronic urinary problems—weak urine flow, urgency and frequency of urination, and leakage—as a result of this condition. It may be alleviated with drugs, but surgery is sometimes needed.

Prostate cancer is the most common nonskin cancer among American men: Nearly 240,000 cases are diagnosed yearly. Though 1 in 6 men will be diagnosed with prostate cancer in his lifetime, only about 1 in 8 men diagnosed with the condition will die of it (American Cancer Society, 2013a). Risk factors include age (the average age at diagnosis is 70), a family history of the disease, African-American race, and obesity. The early symptoms of prostate cancer may include problems with urination, blood in the urine or semen, or pain in the lower back or hips. Prostate cancer may also be detected by a routine digital rectal exam or by the presence of abnormally high levels of a prostate-derived protein, **prostate-specific antigen (PSA)**, in the blood. Routine PSA screening is controversial because of its potential to lead to unnecessary surgery; asymptomatic men who are over 50 and who have a life expectancy of at least 10 years should consider screening in discussion with their doctors (National Cancer Institute, 2008).

The treatment of prostate cancer commonly involves **radical prostatectomy**, which means surgical removal of the entire gland and nearby lymph nodes. Radiation therapy can be administered either as an alternative to surgery or as a supplemental treatment. Testosterone-blocking drugs may also be

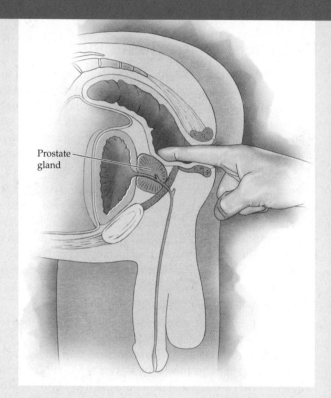

A digital rectal exam allows the clinician to palpate (feel with the finger) the prostate gland.

used. If the cancer is growing slowly, doctors may recommend no treatment but frequent monitoring ("watchful waiting").

The sexual side effects of treatments for prostate cancer may be very significant. Radical prostatectomy puts a permanent end to ejaculation. It is also likely to cause erectile dysfunction because the nerves that supply the erectile tissue run through the prostate gland. Some surgical procedures are specifically designed to leave the nerves in place, but nerve-sparing surgery is no guarantee that normal erectile function will be preserved.

prostatitis Inflammation of the prostate gland; may be acute or chronic.

chronic pelvic pain syndrome An alternative, more-inclusive term for chronic prostatitis.

benign prostatic hyperplasia Noncancerous enlargement of the prostate gland.

prostate cancer Cancer of the prostate gland.

prostate-specific antigen (PSA) An enzyme secreted by the prostate gland; its presence at high levels in the blood is suggestive of, but not diagnostic of, prostate cancer.

radical prostatectomy Surgical removal of the entire prostate gland and local lymph nodes.

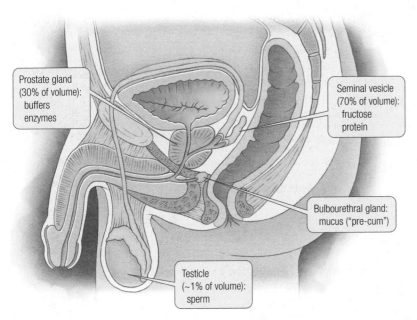

acrosome A structure capping
the head of a sperm that contains
enzymes necessary for fertilization.

midpiece The portion of the tail
of a sperm closest to the head,
containing mitochondria.

Figure 3.12 Glandular contributions to semen Sperm make up less than 1% of the volume of semen; the rest comes from various glands.

look a little more closely, two other structures become apparent. Capping the nucleus is an **acrosome**, which contains a complex suite of receptors and enzymes that are necessary for successful fertilization of an ovum. The part of the tail nearest to the head is slightly thicker than the remainder of the tail and is called the **midpiece**. This section contains mitochondria tightly wound around the tail in a spiral manner. These mitochondria supply chemical energy for propulsion of the sperm.

In spite of the importance of the sperm, they occupy an insignificant proportion (around 1%) of the volume of the semen (**Figure 3.12**). The remainder is a mixture of the secretions of the seminal vesicles (about 70% of the total volume) and the prostate gland (about 30%), plus small contributions from the epididymis and the bulbourethral glands. Among the non-cellular components of semen are proteins, enzymes, antioxidants, water, and salts, plus the following:

- The sugar fructose is an energy source for the sperm.

- Buffers keep the pH of the semen slightly alkaline (between about 7.2 and 7.8). These buffers protect the sperm from the acidic environment encountered if they are deposited in the vagina.

- In men infected with a disease-causing virus such as hepatitis B virus or human immunodeficiency virus (HIV) (see Chapter 15), these viruses may be present at high concentrations in semen.

Ejaculation Requires Coordination of Muscles and Glands

Ejaculation is the forceful ejection of semen from the urethral opening. It is a complex process that requires careful coordination of glands and muscles. Luckily, the spinal cord takes care of most of the details.

Immediately prior to ejaculation, the various components of the semen are expelled from their reservoirs—the left and right vasa deferentia, the prostate gland, and the

(A) Seminal emission

Bladder

Vas deferens

Seminal vesicle

Prostate gland

Posterior urethra

Anus

During emission, the vasa deferentia, the seminal vesicles, and the prostate gland all contract, loading their fluid contents into the posterior portion of the urethra.

(B) Ejaculation

Penile urethra

During ejaculation, the urethra and the muscles of the pelvic floor contract, ejecting semen out through the urethral opening.

Pelvic floor muscles

The urethral sphincter (not shown) at the bladder exit remains closed throughout, which prevents urine from entering the urethra and semen from backing up into the bladder.

Figure 3.13 Seminal emission and ejaculation

emission The loading of the constituents of semen into the posterior portion of the urethra immediately before ejaculation.

testosterone The principal androgen, synthesized in the testes and, in lesser amounts, in the ovaries and adrenal glands.

seminal vesicles—into the urethra (**Figure 3.13A**). This process is called **emission**; it lasts 2 to 3 seconds and can be felt as a pulsing or flowing sensation at the root of the penis. Once emission begins, the man has the sense that ejaculation is inevitable, although some men are able to halt the process even at this late stage. In that case, the semen simply flows out of the urethral opening, rather than being forcefully ejaculated.

Ejaculation itself (**Figure 3.13B**) is caused by a series of rhythmical contractions of the muscular walls of the urethra and the pelvic floor muscles. These contractions, which occur at a rate of about one every 0.8 seconds, can be seen in electrical recordings from the muscles involved (**Figure 3.14**). The muscles forcefully squeeze the semen-filled urethra, especially in the region between the prostate gland and the root of the penis. The entire sequence lasts about 10 to 15 seconds.

The urethral sphincter at the outflow of the bladder is usually closed, and it constricts even more tightly at ejaculation in order to prevent the pressurized semen from flowing backward into the bladder (Bohlen et al., 2000). Thus, with nowhere else to go, the semen is expelled from the urethral opening in a series of spurts of decreasing force. If the man ejaculates into free space, the semen may be propelled some distance from the body, but this projectile ability is quite variable from person to person and declines with age. If he ejaculates within a woman's vagina, the semen may be propelled against the cervix, but not into the cervical canal.

Orgasm refers to all the events at sexual climax, including the physiological processes just described as well as the intense psychological experiences that accompany them. We will discuss orgasm in both sexes in Chapter 5, where we present a comprehensive picture of the sexual response cycle.

The testicles secrete sex hormones

Like women's ovaries, men's testicles manufacture and secrete three kinds of sex steroids: androgens (chiefly **testosterone**), estrogens (chiefly estradiol), and progestins (chiefly progesterone). These hormones are synthesized by the interstitial cells (see Figure 3.9).

Although all three classes of hormones are present in both sexes, their actual levels in the blood differ considerably. In men, testosterone levels are roughly

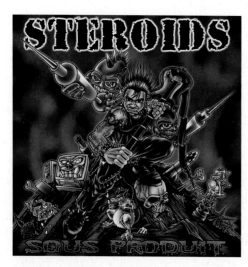

Album cover by a French punk-hardcore band illustrates the popular image of sex steroids.

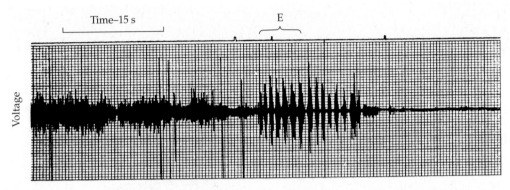

Figure 3.14 Muscle contractions recorded in a male subject during orgasm This recording was obtained from an electrode placed in a pelvic floor muscle. The subject was masturbating to orgasm. Seven spurts of ejaculation (E) occurred in synchrony with the first seven contractions of the muscle. (Courtesy of Roy Levin.)

10 times higher than they are in women, while the concentrations of estradiol and progesterone are roughly 10 times *lower*. (These are approximations because hormone levels in women vary greatly around the menstrual cycle.) Circulating testosterone has a half-life of less than an hour. The main functions of these sex hormones in men are as follows:

ANDROGENS Before birth, testosterone drives development of the fetus—especially the fetal genitalia—in the male direction. Testosterone is also responsible for most of the changes associated with male puberty and for maintenance of these characteristics thereafter. Testosterone acts on the brain in fetal and adult life, promoting the establishment and expression of male-typical gendered traits. It is the chief hormone responsible for the maintenance of the sex drive in men. Testosterone does not regulate sexuality on a minute-to-minute or hour-to-hour basis. Rather, it influences some fairly durable features of brain organization.

Testosterone is an anabolic hormone—it promotes the buildup of tissue, especially muscle, and it increases the oxygen-carrying capacity of the blood. The anabolic effects of testosterone and related androgens are the reason that athletes of both sexes may use them to promote tissue growth, including muscle development. Such use is generally banned, and it carries significant health risks (**Box 3.6**).

To exert some of its effects, testosterone has to be converted to the more potent androgen **5α-dihydrotestosterone** (**DHT**) in the target tissues. This is true for genital tissues and the skin, but not the brain. Drugs that block this conversion are used to treat enlargement of the prostate. Androgens such as testosterone and DHT strongly influence the distribution of head, body, and pubic hair in both sexes.

ESTROGENS As in women, estrogens help maintain bone density in men, and they also terminate the growth of the limb bones after puberty. (Men who are genetically insensitive to estrogens continue to grow after the end of puberty, reaching 7 feet [2.1 m] or more in height.) In addition, estrogens are required for male fertility: They promote the maturation and concentration of sperm in the epididymis.

PROGESTINS The only clearly established function for progestins in men is as metabolic precursors for androgens and estrogens. When given as drugs, however, progestins lower men's sex drive, suggesting that natural progestins may have a hormonal effect on the brain that counteracts the effect of androgens.

5α-dihydrotestosterone (DHT)
An androgen derived from testosterone that plays an important role in the development of the male external genitalia.

Box 3.6 Biology of Sex

Designer Steroids

Athletes have used steroids for decades. Androgens such as testosterone have anabolic effects: They increase muscle bulk and strength—an obvious benefit in most sports. Even though most professional sports organizations forbid their use, illicit use still occurs, and not all androgens are banned in all sports.

Perhaps the most systematic abuse of androgens occurred in the former East Germany, where thousands of athletes of both sexes (including minors) were given testosterone and other drugs as part of a government-sanctioned program (Dennis & Grix, 2012). Since then, sophisticated testing methods have made it difficult for athletes to use testosterone without detection: Cyclist Floyd Landis, for example, had his 2006 Tour de France victory revoked when a urine sample taken during the race was found to contain testosterone of plant origin. The widespread use of such tests has motivated a search for synthetic drugs that have anabolic effects but are not picked up in standard urine or blood tests—the so-called **designer steroids**.

A notorious example is the drug tetrahydrogestrinone, or THG (Catlin et al., 2004). This drug was unknown to science until it showed up in a syringe that was sent to the U.S. Anti-Doping Agency in 2003. Scientists from UCLA developed a screening test to detect THG, and application of this test to previously taken urine samples identified several prominent U.S. track-and-field athletes as users of this steroid. These included Kelli White, the 2003 world champion in the 100 m and 200 m competitions. She was stripped of her titles and banned from competition for 2 years (Associated Press, 2004). Four members of the Oakland Raiders football team also tested positive for THG (Gay, 2004).

Sprinter Marion Jones was also identified as a THG user. She pleaded guilty to lying to federal investigators, and her gold medals from the 2000 Olympics (as well as those of her relay teammates) were forfeited (Associated Press, 2007). She was sentenced to 6 months of imprisonment.

In 2008 Olympic cyclist Tammy Thomas (see figure) was convicted of lying to a grand jury about drug use: Prosecutors alleged that Thomas experienced abnormal growth of her

According to U.S. prosecutors, illegal use of a designer steroid altered the head and body of the female Olympic cyclist Tammy Thomas.

skull, hands, and feet, deepening of her voice, and growth of a full beard necessitating shaving as a result of taking a different designer steroid, norbolethone (Associated Press, 2008). Thomas was banned from competition for life. Yet another designer steroid, metonolone, was allegedly used by Alex Rodriguez when he played baseball for the Texas Rangers (Schmidt, 2009). Rodriguez later received a one-season suspension for other drug violations.

The use of steroids by athletes is a bad idea not only because it is cheating but also because it can cause significant ill effects. These include sterility, liver disease, unhealthy changes in blood lipids, and violent behavior (Beaver et al., 2008). In women it can cause excess hair growth, acne, voice changes, and reproductive problems (Franke & Berendonk, 1997).

designer steroids Synthetic steroids intended to evade detection in drug tests.

As you can see, it is an oversimplification to think of androgens as "male" hormones and estrogens and progestins as "female" hormones. All three classes of hormones have functions in both sexes.

The brain and pituitary gland regulate hormone levels

As with women's ovaries, men's testicles are linked with the hypothalamus and pituitary gland by a hormonal control loop (**Figure 3.15**). The same hormonal messengers—gonadotropin-releasing hormone (GnRH), follicle-stimulating hormone (FSH), and luteinizing hormone (LH)—play similar roles in the two sexes. GnRH, secreted by the hypothalamus, stimulates the secretion of FSH and LH by the pituitary gland. FSH stimulates spermatogenesis in the testicles, and LH stimulates the synthesis and secretion of sex hormones. The androgens in turn exert a negative feedback effect, damping the secretion of the hormones from the hypothalamus and pituitary.

Men's bodies do not experience any monthly hormonal cycle equivalent to that in women, but the levels of testosterone in the blood do peak every 3 hours or so and are higher between midnight and noon than between noon and midnight. The function of these short-term oscillations, if any, is not known—they do not correlate with variations in sexual feelings or behavior.

Because the brain is involved in the regulation of testicular function, life experiences can affect a man's testosterone levels. Entering into a steady romantic relationship or marriage, for example, lowers a man's testosterone level by about 20%, and separation raises it again (Burnham et al., 2003).

Nudity Is Culturally Regulated

In this and the previous chapter we have discussed men and women's bodies, including their genitals, almost as if they were open for public display. In reality they are not, for the most part. Women's and men's genitals are often referred to as "private parts," highlighting the fact that cultural factors prohibit or limit their exposure.

In societies in which women wear clothing of any kind, they are required to cover the vulva while in public. Even in societies in which women traditionally went without clothing, as among the Kwoma people of New Guinea, men were required to look aside when approached by a woman (Ford & Beach, 1951). Men are usually required to cover their genitals, too, but there are exceptions.

The sight of a woman's vulva is sexually arousing to heterosexual men, as has been shown by controlled experiments conducted in strip clubs (Linz et al., 2000).* Thus, social prohibitions against female nudity have the effect of reducing men's arousal, especially in public. Prohibitions against male nudity may have a similar effect on heterosexual women, even if they are not as "visual" as men when it comes to sexual arousal (see Chapter 5). It therefore seems likely that the prohibition of public nudity reduces sexual arousal, sexual coercion, and disputes over potential sex partners—thus facilitating general social cooperation.

Social rules about exposure of the body are indicators of general attitudes toward sexuality. In ancient Greece, male athletes competed without clothing,† and the nude or near-nude body was celebrated in art and sculpture (**Figure 3.16A**). In early Christian art, however, clothing served to desexualize the body—or indeed, to de-emphasize the body as a whole—as part of an emphasis on humanity's spiritual nature (**Figure 3.16B**).

The 19th century was another period when Europeans went to extraordinary lengths to conceal the body. When bathing at the beach, for example, people wore garments so all-covering as to hamper their ability to swim. These practices were part of a general belief that sexual arousal was dangerous to health, morals, and social order.

---

* In the study, researchers from the University of California, Santa Barbara, arranged for exotic dancers to expose themselves, fully naked or with genitals covered, to customers. In questionnaires filled out immediately after the show, the customers exposed to the fully naked dancers reported greater erotic arousal. The study was done in response to a Supreme Court ruling that stated that banning nude dancing did not violate the dancers' First Amendment right to free expression because the "messages" received by the customers were the same whether the dancers were clothed or naked.

† Exposure of the penile glans was considered offensive, so athletes often tied off their foreskins to prevent this from happening.

FAQ

I'm a young guy, but I'm not that interested in sex. Is my testosterone level low?

There are many possible reasons for a low sex drive, ranging from psychological or social factors to hormonal problems. See a sympathetic doctor. A testosterone test can be done, and if your testosterone levels are low, the reason can be investigated and perhaps corrected. In the unlikely case that you need a supplement, your doctor can prescribe testosterone skin patches.

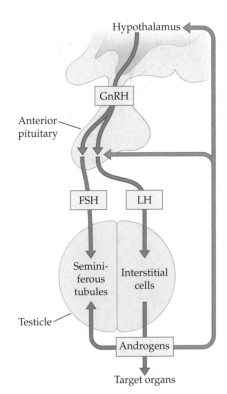

Figure 3.15 A feedback loop controls male hormone levels. Stimulatory influences are shown in blue, inhibitory influences in red.

(A)

(B)

Figure 3.16 Religious attitudes toward the body (A) Classical Greek sculpture celebrated the beauty of nude or near-nude individuals, including gods, as shown here in this statue of Poseidon, god of the sea. (B) In early Christian times, religious figures (except for Jesus on the cross) were shrouded in all-concealing clothing, as in this 8th-century Byzantine mosaic from Ravenna, Italy.

sexting Sending sexually explicit text or images via mobile phone.

In the contemporary United States, attitudes toward nudity are divided. On the one hand, traditional social norms still rule. The "wardrobe malfunction" that exposed Janet Jackson's breast for half a second at the 2004 Super Bowl triggered over half a million complaints. Nonpornographic websites—even sites that display a lot of skin like theCHIVE.com—stop short of showing women's nipples or vulvas. Streakers are arrested. And even a man showing up shirtless at a college lecture would probably be met with negative reactions, if only from the professor.

On the other hand, a more permissive culture has developed in semiprivate settings, especially among young people. The sending of sexually explicit "selfies" by mobile phone (**sexting**) is a fairly common practice among high school students (Strassberg et al., 2013), though one that can have legal ramifications. Pornography—increasingly viewed by couples or groups—has desensitized many people to naked bodies. Nudity is common in certain environments such as private pools and hot tubs, as well as at "clothing optional" hotels, cruises, and beaches. Women may breast-feed their babies in public—a practice protected by state and federal laws and even encouraged by Pope Francis (Davies, 2014). And alcohol may facilitate the shedding of clothes in some social situations.

Nowhere is the collision between these two cultures more evident than in San Francisco. That city has seen more than its share of nudity over the years, starting with the hippie years of the 1970s. Nude or near-nude people have been common sights in parades, runs, bicycle rides, and street fairs, as well as in public spaces in general. In part this may reflect the fact that 60% of Californians claim not to be offended by public nudity (Naturist Education Foundation, 2009). Nevertheless, public opposition to nudity was strong enough that in 2012 the city enacted a ban

Figure 3.17 Nude activist Gypsy Taub is arrested during a 2013 protest against San Francisco's nudity ban.

on nudity in most public spaces (Wollan, 2012). The ban has triggered nude demonstrations and protest marches, mostly in the Castro District (NBC Bay Area, 2014) **(Figure 3.17)**.

> Go to the
> **Discovering**
> **Human Sexuality**
> Companion Website at
> **sites.sinauer.com/**
> **discoveringhumansexuality3e**
> for activities, study questions,
> quizzes, and other study aids.

Summary

- The male external genitalia comprise the penis and the scrotum. A man's penis contains three erectile structures and encloses the urethra. Its erotic sensitivity is highest on the glans and frenulum. The foreskin, which covers the glans, is removed in the operation of circumcision. Circumcision offers some health advantages, but the prevalence of circumcision in the United States is decreasing.

- Health problems affecting the penis include inflammation of the glans (balanitis), inability to retract the foreskin (phimosis), entrapment of the foreskin behind the glans (paraphimosis), pathological curvature of the penis (Peyronie's disease), and penile cancer.

- Penile and clitoral erection involve the filling of vascular spaces (sinusoids) with blood, under the control of the autonomic nervous system. The neurotransmitter nitric oxide plays a key role in this process.

- The scrotum contains the testicles and has muscular and vascular mechanisms for maintaining them below the regular body temperature.

- A man's internal reproductive structures include six paired structures—the left and right testicle, epididymis, vas deferens, seminal vesicle, ejaculatory duct, and bulbourethral gland—as well as two unpaired midline structures, the prostate gland and urethra.

- The testicles contain seminiferous tubules, in which sperm are produced. Between the seminiferous tubules lie interstitial cells, which secrete sex steroids. The most important health problem affecting the testicles is testicular cancer. This can affect young men, but it is one of the most curable cancers.

- The epididymis is the location where sperm mature and become more concentrated. The vas deferens stores sperm and transports them to the urethra. Sperm constitute only about 1% of the volume of the ejaculate.

- The prostate gland and seminal vesicles add the noncellular portion of semen, which consists of proteins, enzymes, antioxidants, water, salts, fructose, and buffers. The bulbourethral glands produce a slippery secretion ("pre-cum") that may be discharged from the urethra in small amounts before ejaculation.

- The prostate gland can be affected by inflammation (prostatitis), age-related enlargement (benign prostatic hyperplasia), and prostate cancer. It is possible to screen for prostate cancer by regular digital rectal examination and by a blood test (PSA test). The treatments for prostate cancer often have a serious impact on a man's sex life, and the question of whether and how to treat early-stage prostate cancer is controversial.

(continued)

Chapter 4

Heterosexual couple? No—a single model photographed in both female and male gender roles. From the series Alone Time, by J. J. Levine.

Sex, Gender, and Transgender

In this chapter we discuss how men and women differ from each other. First we describe the origins of the physical differences that have been the topics of previous chapters: differences in the structures and functions of the genitals, reproductive tract, and other parts of the male and female bodies. We then turn to mental and behavioral differences between men and women—differences that are collectively referred to as "gender." We summarize what is known about gender differences, with special emphasis on those that involve sexuality.

Gender differences, like physical sex differences, are influenced by biological processes, such as the differing hormonal environments that males and females experience before birth. They are also affected by the way our parents treat us in infancy and childhood, by social pressures, and by our own efforts to make sense of the world. In other words, gender differences result from a delicate interplay of nature and nurture. The quest to understand this web of causation is not merely of theoretical interest. It is also deeply relevant to social policy, affecting how we educate our children, how we treat wrongdoers, and how we develop a more just society.

Figure 4.1 Human chromosomes
Women and men have different sex chromosomes: Women have two X chromosomes, men have one X and one Y (as shown here at the lower right). The other 22 pairs of chromosomes are the same in women and men.

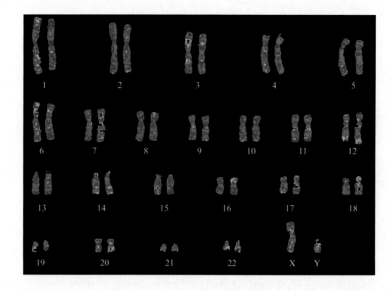

Genes and Hormones Guide Sex Development

Sex chromosomes and genes are the primary arbiters of sex. Recall that every individual (with rare exceptions) possesses a pair of sex chromosomes in every cell nucleus in her or his body. One of these chromosomes is inherited from the person's mother, via her ovum, and is always a large **X chromosome**. The other is inherited from the person's father, via his sperm, and is either an X chromosome or a much smaller **Y chromosome**. An embryo that possesses two Xs develops as a female; an embryo with one X and one Y develops as a male (**Figure 4.1**). Thus, the father's genetic contribution to the embryo determines its sex.

A sex-determining gene called **SRY**, located on the Y chromosome, is the initial switch whose presence directs sexual development along a male pathway, and whose absence allows development to follow a female pathway. Many more genes, linked together in complex networks, are required for the formation of the gonads—the ovaries in females or the testes in males (Quinn & Koopman, 2012). (Recall from Chapter 3 that the term "testes" is used when referring to the function or early development of the testicles.)

Female and male reproductive tracts develop from different precursors

For the first several weeks of development there is no visible difference between female and male embryos. At about 6 weeks after conception, early in the development of the gonads, two pairs of ducts run from the gonads to the outside of the embryonic body at the future site of the external genitalia (**Figure 4.2**). One pair, the **Müllerian ducts**, are the precursors of the female reproductive tract. The other pair, the **Wolffian ducts**, are the precursors of the male reproductive tract.

Notice that embryos of *both* sexes begin with a pair of *both* kinds of ducts. Female development involves eliminating the Wolffian ducts and promoting the development of the Müllerian ducts, while male development involves eliminating the Müllerian ducts and promoting the development of the Wolffian ducts.

Male embryos eliminate the Müllerian ducts by means of **anti-Müllerian hormone (AMH)**. This hormone, secreted by the developing testes, diffuses to the nearby Müllerian ducts and causes them to degenerate. Beginning at about 3 months after conception, the testes secrete testosterone. This hormone diffuses down the Wolffian ducts, triggering each one to develop into an epididymis, vas deferens, and seminal vesicle. Testosterone also promotes development of the prostate gland, although this gland is not derived from the Wolffian ducts.

---

sex chromosome Either of a pair of chromosomes (X or Y) that differ between the sexes.

X chromosome A sex chromosome that is present in two copies in females and one copy in males.

Y chromosome A sex chromosome that is only present in males.

SRY A gene located on the Y chromosome (*Sex-determining Region of the Y chromosome*) that causes the embryo to develop as a male.

Müllerian duct Either of two bilateral ducts in the embryo that give rise to the female reproductive tract.

Wolffian duct Either of two bilateral ducts in the embryo that give rise to the male reproductive tract.

anti-Müllerian hormone (AMH) A hormone secreted by the testes that prevents the development of the female reproductive tract.

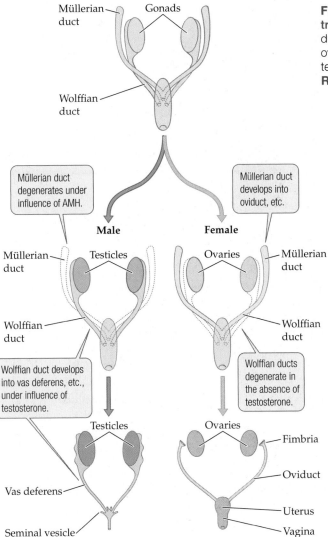

Figure 4.2 Development of the male and female reproductive tracts from different precursor structures—the Wolffian and Müllerian ducts, shown at the top. (The male and female gonads [testes and ovaries] have a common origin and do not belong to either duct system.) (See **Web Activity 4.1: Development of the Male and Female Reproductive Tracts.**)

In female embryos, the absence of testosterone causes the Wolffian ducts to degenerate. The absence of AMH allows the Müllerian ducts to persist and to develop into the oviducts, uterus, and deeper part of the vagina. Although the development of the female reproductive tract is the "default" pathway, in the sense that it goes forward in the absence of hormonal instructions to the contrary, it is an active process that is guided by many genes in the developing tract.

Female and male external genitalia develop from the same precursors

The external genitalia of both females and males develop from the same early tissues. As shown in **Figure 4.3**, at about 4 weeks postconception the embryo's anogenital region consists of a slit known as the **cloaca**. The cloaca is closed by a membrane. It is flanked by two **urethral folds**, and to the side of each urethral fold is a raised region named the **genital swelling**. At the front end of the cloaca is a small midline protuberance called the **genital tubercle**. By 2 weeks later, the urethral folds have fused with each other near their posterior (rear) end. The portion behind the fusion point, called the **anal fold**, eventually becomes the anus. The region of the fusion

cloaca The common exit of the gastrointestinal and urogenital systems; in humans it is present only in embryonic life.

urethral folds Folds of ectodermal tissue in the embryo that give rise to the inner labia (in females) or the shaft of the penis (in males).

genital swelling Regions of the genitalia in the embryo that give rise to the outer labia (in females) or the scrotum (in males).

genital tubercle A midline swelling in front of the cloaca, which gives rise to the glans of the clitoris (in females) or penis (in males).

anal fold The posterior portion of the urethral fold, which gives rise to the anus.

Figure 4.3 **Development of the male and female external genitalia** from common precursor structures, shown at the top. In males, the urethral folds fuse at the midline to form the penile shaft and enclose the urethra. In females, they remain separate, forming the inner labia.

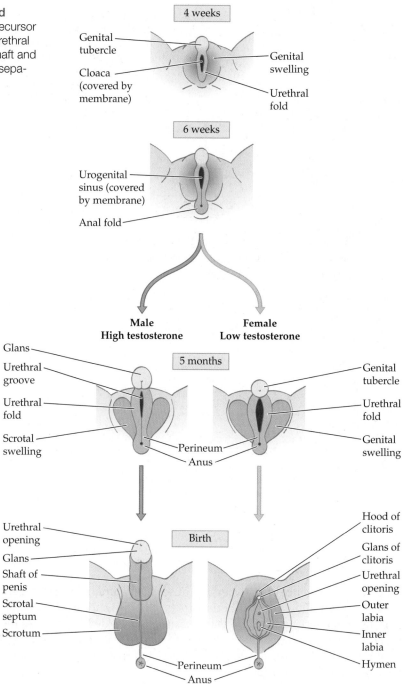

itself becomes the perineum. (Even in adults, the line of fusion is visible as a midline ridge or scar, which can be seen most easily with the help of a hand mirror.)

During the fetal period, the region in front of the fusion point, which includes the opening of the **urogenital sinus**, gives rise to the external genital structures in both sexes. As with the internal reproductive tracts, the female external genitalia develop by default, that is, in the absence of hormonal or other external signals. The genital swellings develop into the outer labia. The urethral folds develop into the inner labia, the outer one-third or so of the vagina, and the crura (deep erectile structures) of the clitoris (see Chapter 2). The genital tubercle develops into the glans of the clitoris. Remnants of the cloacal membrane persist as the hymen.

urogenital sinus The common opening of the urinary and genital systems in the embryo.

The vagina, therefore, develops from two different sets of tissues. The outer portion of the vagina, which develops from the urethral folds, is more muscular and more richly innervated than the inner portion, which develops from the Müllerian ducts.

In male fetuses, the presence of circulating testosterone, secreted by the testes, is required for the normal development of the genitalia. The urethral folds fuse at the midline, forming the shaft of the penis and enclosing the urethra. If this midline fusion is incomplete, a condition called **hypospadias** results, in which the urethra opens on the underside of the penis or behind the penis (Mayo Clinic, 2014a). The genital swellings also fuse at the midline, forming the scrotum. The genital tubercle expands to form the glans of the penis. The prostate gland develops—as the homologous paraurethral glands in females probably do—from tissue beneath the urethral folds.

Thus, the same embryonic structures that become the outer labia in females become the scrotum in males. The structures that become the inner labia in females become the shaft of the penis in males. The structure that becomes the glans of the clitoris becomes the glans of the penis in males.

Why isn't female development driven by secretion of estrogens from fetal ovaries in the same way that male development is activated by testosterone from fetal tissues? The answer is probably that fetuses of *both* sexes are exposed to estrogens coming from the mother's body. Thus, estrogens would not be an effective signal for guiding fetal development in one sex only.

hypospadias An abnormal location of the male urethral opening on the underside of the penis or elsewhere.

The gonads descend during development

In fetuses of both sexes, the gonads (ovaries and testes) begin their development in an area near the kidneys and later move downward. By about 10 weeks postconception they are positioned near the top of the pelvis. In females, the ovaries remain in this position for the remainder of fetal life, but after birth they gradually descend in the pelvis and end up on either side of the uterus.

In males the testes, which may now be called testicles, move even greater distances (**Figure 4.4**). At 6 to 7 months postconception they descend into the pelvis, and shortly before birth they move down into the scrotum. As each testicle enters the scrotum, it draws various structures with it, including the vas deferens, blood vessels, and nerves—which make up the spermatic cord. The connection between the pelvic cavity and the testicles is usually sealed off after the testicles descend.

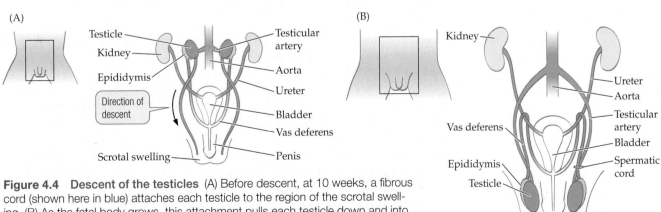

Figure 4.4   Descent of the testicles (A) Before descent, at 10 weeks, a fibrous cord (shown here in blue) attaches each testicle to the region of the scrotal swelling. (B) As the fetal body grows, this attachment pulls each testicle down and into the scrotum. Note how the vas deferens (green) and the testicular artery (red) are pulled after the testicle and the vas deferens comes to loop over the ureter (the tube, shown here in orange, that carries urine from the kidney to the bladder).

My son's testicles did descend, but they're not there anymore. What happened?

The testicles of male infants and toddlers may spend quite a bit of time pulled upward and out of sight by the cremaster muscle. That's not a matter of concern so long as they did complete their original descent.

In 2% to 5% of full-term newborn boys, one or both testicles have not yet arrived in the scrotum. In many of these boys, the tardy testicles will arrive within a few weeks after birth, but if they are still no-shows when a boy reaches 3 months of age, the condition is considered abnormal and is termed **cryptorchidism** or simply undescended testicles (Urology Care Foundation, 2014). About 1% to 2% of boys have this condition. Usually, the missing testicles have been held up somewhere along the path of their fetal descent—most commonly in the groin. Cryptorchidism is associated with lowered fertility and with an increased risk of testicular cancer after puberty. Undescended testicles can often be surgically moved into the scrotum; this procedure is best done before 2 years of age. Correction of cryptorchidism improves the prospects for fertility but does not eliminate the increased risk of cancer. Once they are in the scrotum, however, the testicles can be monitored by regular self-examination, thus increasing the likelihood that any developing cancer would be detected at an early stage. Both testicles are at increased risk of cancer even if only one of them is undescended.

Puberty is sexual maturation

Most prenatal sex development occurs during weeks 8 through 24 of fetal life, when testosterone levels are high in male fetuses. A second surge in testosterone production (to adult levels) occurs in boys for the first 6 months of postnatal life: Further maturation of the male genitals occurs during this half-year period (Wilson & Davies, 2007). After that, sex hormone levels decrease, and they remain low in both sexes until **puberty**, the transition to sexual maturity.

At the onset of puberty both testicles and ovaries begin secreting sex hormones at levels sufficient to initiate reproductive maturity, and the bodies and brains of girls and boys begin to transform into those of women and men. Because of the great impact of this transformation on psychosexual development, we postpone most of our discussion of puberty to Chapter 10.

The brain also differentiates sexually

Although the basic organization of the brain is very similar in men and women, early hormonal influences do produce some sex differences in brain structure, function, and chemistry (Cahill, 2014). Here are some examples:

- Men's brains are about 10% larger, on average, than those of women. This overall size difference is roughly proportional to the overall difference in body size between the sexes, however, and is unlikely to have any functional significance.

- Certain regions within the cerebral cortex are larger in one sex or the other (Ruigrok et al., 2013) (**Figure 4.5**). Connections also differ: Connections between the left and right sides of the brain are stronger in women than men, whereas connections within each side of the brain are stronger in men than women (Ingalhalikar et al., 2014). These structural differences may contribute to mental differences between women and men, as discussed later in this chapter.

- In both sexes, a paired brain structure called the amygdala is involved in the processing of emotionally laden experiences, but women rely more strongly on the left amygdala for this task, whereas men rely more strongly on the right amygdala (Canli et al., 2002; Schneider et al., 2011).

- Men's brains produce serotonin—a neurotransmitter involved in the regulation of mood—at a rate 52% higher than women's brains (Nishizawa et al., 1997). In the case of another neurotransmitter, dopamine, it's the other

cryptorchidism   Failure of one or both testicles to descend into the scrotum by 3 months of postnatal age.

puberty   The transition to sexual maturity.

Top view   Bottom view   Midline view

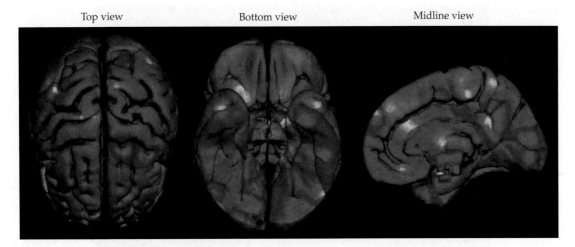

Figure 4.5   Sex differences in the cerebral cortex Regions that are larger in women are shown in red; those that are larger in men are shown in blue. Note that the sex differences are not the same in the left and right hemispheres. These images are based on a meta-analysis of numerous quantitative brain-imaging studies. (From Ruigrok et al., 2013.)

way around (Cosgrove et al., 2007). Such differences offer a potential explanation for differences in the prevalence of certain mental disorders in the two sexes, such as the greater prevalence of depression among women and the greater prevalence of alcoholism in men (Hall & Steiner, 2013).

The difference in circulating androgen levels in the two sexes (higher levels in males than in females) is the main driver of sexual differentiation in the brain, as it is in the rest of the body (Swaab & Garcia-Falgueras, 2009). The brain also "knows" its own intrinsic sex, however, in that the nucleus of each brain cell carries the sex chromosomes corresponding to that individual's sex—XX or XY. This intrinsic brain sex also has some effect on brain development, and the details of this process are the subject of current research interest (McCarthy & Arnold, 2011).

Sex Development May Go Awry

Given the complexity of the genetic and hormonal cascade that guides sex development, it is perhaps surprising how regularly it leads to the "normal" end product—a healthy, fertile woman or man. Yet deviations from stereotypical female or male development do sometimes occur. Some of these are harmless variations, but others have significant implications for health or fertility and are therefore called **disorders of sex development** (Ono & Harley, 2013). The following are some examples of these disorders.

Chromosomal anomalies affect growth and fertility

The standard sets of sex chromosomes are XX (female) and XY (male). Other combinations are possible. They can arise during cell divisions in the production of ova or sperm, or during the first cell division after fertilization. Embryos with abnormal numbers of sex chromosomes are very common, but the great majority die early in development. Among those that survive, the following are the most common anomalies:

- **Klinefelter syndrome**. About 1 in 1000 live-born babies possesses one or more extra X chromosomes (XXY or XXXY). These individuals are male because they possess a Y chromosome with its *SRY* gene, which masculin-

FAQ

Will a man with Klinefelter syndrome pass it on to his children?

No. He will need medical assistance to become a father, but any children he does have will almost certainly be normal girls or boys.

disorders of sex development
Medical conditions producing anomalous sexual differentiation or intersexuality.

Klinefelter syndrome   A collection of traits caused by the possession of one or more extra X chromosomes in a male (XXY, XXXY).

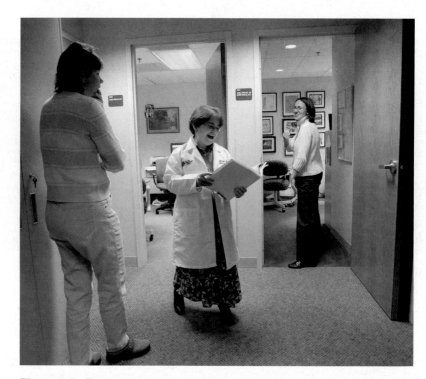

Figure 4.6 Turner syndrome Dr. Catherine Ward-Melver is a geneticist at Children's Hospital in Akron, Ohio, and president of the Turner Syndrome Society. Her short stature (4 feet 8 inches, or 1.42 m) is a feature of Turner syndrome.

izes their bodies. As children they may have slow motor development and delayed speech. Puberty may be delayed or absent. Men with Klinefelter syndrome commonly have low testosterone levels, a small penis and testicles, sparse body and facial hair, and some breast development. They are also generally taller than average. They have a low sperm count and are usually infertile. It is often stated that men with Klinefelter syndrome are not especially likely to be gay or bisexual, but the limited available evidence suggests that they are (Schiavi et al., 1988). In one informal survey of 63 adult men with Klinefelter syndrome, more than half identified as gay or bisexual (Bucar, 2014). This topic deserves further study.

- **Turner syndrome.** About 1 in 4000 live-born children has one X chromosome and no Y chromosome (XO). They are girls, since they lack the Y chromosome and its *SRY* gene. These girls tend to be short, with a characteristic broad chest and neck. They lack normal ovaries, and without medical assistance they do not enter puberty and are infertile. They may suffer from some cognitive deficits but they are not intellectually disabled (Ross et al., 2000): Women with Turner syndrome have excelled in a variety of careers (**Figure 4.6**). Many women with Turner syndrome are actually "mosaics," meaning that their bodies are composed of both XO and normal XX cells; these women have a milder form of the syndrome (Hook & Warburton, 2014).

- **XYY syndrome.** About 1 in 1500 babies possesses one X chromosome and two Y chromosomes. They are male, but they may have genital anomalies and low fertility. The cerebral cortex develops in an atypical fashion, intelligence tends to be low, and autism-related symptoms are common (Bryant et al., 2012; Lepage et al., 2014). Perhaps for these reasons, XYY men are

Turner syndrome A collection of traits caused by the possession of one X and no Y chromosome.

XYY syndrome A collection of traits caused by the possession, in a male, of an extra Y chromosome.

overrepresented among convicted criminals, especially among those convicted of sexual offences (Briken et al., 2006; Stochholm et al., 2012). Most XYY men are not criminals, however, and the once-prevalent notion that the XYY syndrome causes a kind of extreme masculinity is incorrect.

- **Triple-X syndrome**. About 1 in 2000 newborns possesses three X chromosomes (XXX). These babies are girls. They develop mild cognitive deficits and their fertility is low, but many XXX females go undiagnosed.

Although these chromosomal anomalies cannot be corrected, hormonal and other medical treatments, as well as counseling, can often help a great deal. Some of these individuals can become parents with the help of assisted reproductive technologies (see Chapter 8).

The gonads or genitals may be sexually ambiguous

Some disorders of sex development cause the gonads or the genitals to end up in a state that is intermediate between male and female forms or has some features of both. Persons affected by such conditions may be referred to as (or describe themselves as) **intersex**. Here are some examples:

- **Gonadal intersexuality**. In this rare condition, which has traditionally been called true hermaphroditism, the person possesses both ovarian and testicular tissue—either on different sides of the body or in gonads that contain mixtures of the two tissues. The cause is not usually known, but chromosomal anomalies may be to blame. The appearance of the external genitalia varies, but most persons with this condition look like women and identify as such. They are usually infertile.

- **Androgen insensitivity syndrome** (**AIS**). This is a genetic condition in XY individuals in which androgen receptors are defective or absent. AIS embryos develop as female because the body fails to respond to the testosterone secreted by the testicles. People with AIS lack the reproductive tract of either sex: They possess a shallow, blind-ending vagina, and they are infertile. Persons with complete AIS look like and identify as women, but people with partial androgen insensitivity have a more variable appearance and self-identification.

- **Congenital adrenal hyperplasia** (**CAH**). In this genetic condition, the fetus's adrenal glands secrete abnormally large amounts of androgens during the latter part of fetal life. In XX fetuses, which otherwise would develop into typical girls, the condition causes a partial masculinization of the genitals: The clitoris is often enlarged, for example, and the labia may be partially fused in the midline (**Figure 4.7**). Most of these children are raised as girls, but some children with very marked masculinization are raised as boys.

For many children with ambiguous genitalia, the cause is not known. Whatever the cause, however, treatment of these children raises a host of difficult ethical questions. Should the genitals be surgically altered early in life to "normalize" them, with the hope of sparing the child or the child's family from embarrassment?

triple-X syndrome   A collection of traits caused by the possession, in a female, of three X chromosomes rather than two.

intersex   Having a biologically ambiguous or intermediate sex.

gonadal intersexuality   The possession of both testicular and ovarian tissue in the same individual.

androgen insensitivity syndrome (AIS)   The congenital absence of a functional androgen receptor, making the body unable to respond to androgens.

congenital adrenal hyperplasia (CAH)   A congenital defect of hormonal metabolism in the adrenal gland, causing the gland to secrete excessive levels of androgens.

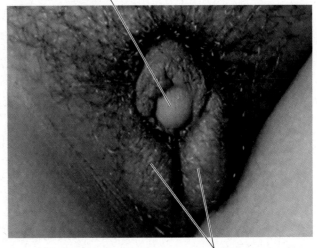

Enlarged clitoris

Fused labia

Figure 4.7   Partial masculinization of genitalia in a girl with congenital adrenal hyperplasia.

Box 4.1   Personal Points of View

My Life with Androgen Insensitivity Syndrome

Katie Baratz Dalke graduated from the Perelman School of Medicine at the University of Pennsylvania in 2011; she is now a psychiatrist practicing in Philadelphia. She is also a board member of Advocates for Informed Choice, which supports the civil rights of children born with variations of sexual anatomy. Baratz Dalke wrote the following essay for this textbook.

Katie Baratz Dalke.

By all accounts, I was a perfectly healthy and normal baby girl, thriving under the love and attention of my family and constantly seeking opportunities to sing, dance, and try on my mother's dresses and jewelry—the more sparkles, the better!

My family's world changed forever when I was 6. That year, I collapsed in the shower with a painful lump in my groin. Convinced I had a hernia, my parents, both doctors, took me to the hospital. But when surgeons operated, they found a testicle that had started descending. Tests soon showed that instead of the typical XX chromosomes found in girls, I had the XY chromosomal complement of boys.

The doctor told my stunned parents that I had complete androgen insensitivity syndrome. He assured them that I would grow up normally, fall in love, and have a family through adoption, but they shouldn't tell me that I had XY chromosomes and testicles.

My parents did decide to tell me, but gradually. As a young girl, they showed me an anatomy book and told me that the uterus was the nest inside a woman where the baby grew. I didn't have one, but I could adopt a baby that would grow in my heart and be part of my family. I learned about periods and knew I wouldn't get them. Although I was sad that I wouldn't be able to become pregnant and felt different from my girl friends, I thought that was it—until I turned 16.

That year, my sister came home from school with a biology project. Everyone in her class was assigned a condition to research, and she randomly drew AIS. "Mom and Dad, it sounds a lot like Katie," she said at dinner one night. "And there's a woman with Mom's name on the support group website." My parents looked at each other. They'd wanted to wait until I was 18, but there was no going back now. They told me and my brother and sister everything. My dad finished up by saying, "You're still our girl."

I was devastated and angry, feeling betrayed by my parents and my own body. Looking back, I know those emotions came from a fear of what was wrong with me, plus the eternal conflict of adolescence: someone else deciding what's best for you.

High school was grim. I went through puberty very late, and was taller and thinner than most of the boys all the way through senior year. I had horrible insomnia and tons of anxiety that sometimes veered into depression. I felt as if all of my girl friends were living a life I couldn't access, one marked by the common experiences of periods, dating, and an effortless transition to womanhood. I, on the other hand, had to take estrogen pills to develop a womanly figure, and I had to use a vaginal dilator for 30 minutes a day so that I could comfortably have sex.

College was better. In my senior year, I met Sam, a runner and English major with a romantic streak. We started talking, and before I knew it, he was courting me with chocolate-covered strawberries and Marilyn Monroe movies. Shortly after we began dating, I knew that it was time to tell him about my AIS. He listened patiently and assured me that nothing about my genes or gonads changed the way he felt about me.

Four years later, we were married on an unseasonably warm New Year's Eve, surrounded by our friends, family, and yes, lots of sparkles. We are beginning our lives together and planning to adopt our children, although I still feel pangs of sadness when I think about how much I'd like to be able to have children biologically.

I'm also really involved in the AIS community. It feels incredible to help others with the pain I went through—it was only after finding the AIS Support Group, the summer before college, that I realized AIS could be part of my life without dominating it, and that the loneliness I'd felt abated.

What should the child be told, and as which gender should the child be raised? Partly in response to activism by people with intersex conditions, there has been a movement away from early surgery, unless it is medically essential. The idea is to postpone irreversible decisions until affected children are able to make known their own gender identity and participate in the decision-making process. The secrecy and denial that often surrounds these cases is harmful to children's psychological development and self-acceptance, according to the testimony of intersex people (**Box 4.1**).

Gender Is a Central Aspect of Personhood

The word **gender**, as used in this book, means the entire collection of mental and behavioral traits that, to a greater or lesser degree, differ between females and males. Thus, gender consists of all those things that make females and males different, aside from the primary and secondary sex traits.*

Some traits are "highly gendered": That is, they are markedly different between females and males. An example is a person's subjective sense of femaleness or maleness, a trait called **gender identity**. The great majority of females have a secure identity as females, and the great majority of males have a secure identity as males. Transexual and transgender people are important exceptions—but they form a very small percentage of the population.

An example of a trait that is highly gendered, but less so than gender identity, is that of **sexual orientation**—the direction of an individual's sexual attractions. Most men are predominantly attracted to women, and most women are predominantly attracted to men, but several percent of the population do not fit this pattern.

Verbal fluency is a trait that is much more weakly gendered than gender identity. On average, girls outperform boys on tests of this cognitive skill, but it takes the testing of large numbers of children, and the application of statistical tests to the results, to demonstrate the difference.

In our discussion of gender, we first review the aspects of mental life that are known to be gendered to a greater or lesser degree, without regard to causation. We then discuss theories about how gender differences arise.

Gender identity might not match anatomical sex

In its simplest conception, a person's gender identity is his or her response to the question "Do you feel as if you are a woman or a man?" More than 99% of people give an answer that is consistent with their genital anatomy, but a few individuals give a discordant answer: anatomical women who say they feel like men and anatomical men who say they feel like women, as well as others for whom neither "female" nor "male" satisfactorily describes how they think about themselves. The existence of these transgender persons, discussed in greater detail later in the chapter, makes us realize that there must be something more to gender identity than simply reporting on one's genitals. Gender identity is a central and stable aspect of who we are—our personhood. The way we express gender identity in gendered behavior—everything from what clothes we wear and how we walk and talk, to what sex we claim to be—is called our **gender role**.

Although self-identified transgender persons are uncommon, research indicates that gender identity may have a more blurred distribution in the general population than is captured by a simple "male/female" dichotomy. If, for example, people are asked to rate their own "masculinity/femininity" on a scale in comparison with other persons of the same sex, responses are quite variable, and men's and women's

gender The collection of psychological traits that differ between males and females.

gender identity A person's subjective sense of being male or female.

sexual orientation The direction of an individual's sexual feelings; sexual attraction toward persons of the other sex (heterosexual), the same sex (homosexual), or both sexes (bisexual).

gender role The expression of gender identity in social behavior.

---

* Elsewhere you may encounter other definitions of "gender": It may be used simply to denote a person's sex, or it may refer to the socially constructed aspects of sexual identity.

Figure 4.8 Mental rotation task
From the four images at right, the subject is asked to select the two objects that could be rotated in space to match the object shown at left. Men generally outperform women in this kind of task.

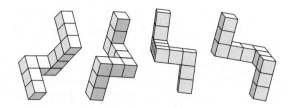

responses overlap (Lippa, 2008). In fact, if you tried to guess people's sex based on where they place themselves on such a scale, you would be wrong about one time in four. We will revisit the spectrum of subjective masculinity/femininity when we discuss the topic of sexual orientation (see Chapter 12).

Women and men differ in a variety of cognitive and personality traits

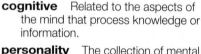

cognitive Related to the aspects of the mind that process knowledge or information.

personality The collection of mental and behavioral traits, especially those related to emotions and attitudes, which characterizes an individual.

Some sex differences are seen in aspects of mental life having to do with perception, motor performance, reasoning, judgments, knowledge, and memory—collectively referred to as **cognitive** traits (Miller & Halpern, 2014). For example, men as a group outperform women in some visuospatial skills, such as the ability to mentally rotate three-dimensional objects (**Figure 4.8**). This difference might contribute to the predominance of males in certain fields such as engineering (Voyer, 2011). Women outperform men on tasks involving fine finger movement, some verbal tasks, and some memory tasks such as face recognition. Interestingly, the female superiority in face recognition may not reflect any difference in the ability to maintain a face in memory, but rather, a more detailed inspection of faces in the first place (**Figure 4.9**) (Kimura, 1999; Rahman et al., 2003a; Heisz et al., 2013).

The cognitive sex differences just described are moderate to large in size,* but they are smaller than obvious physical differences between the sexes, such as the difference in average height. Many other cognitive traits show small differences between the sexes.

Other sex differences have to do with feelings, attitudes, goals, interests, values, and behaviors (including sexual behavior)—traits that loosely cluster under the term **personality**. Notable among these traits is aggressiveness: Males score higher than women on written tests of aggressiveness, show more verbal and physical aggression in real-life situations, and are more likely to commit violent crimes, both in the United States and across most cultures (Archer, 2004). Women are more likely to express aggression through indirect, nonphysical means, such as malicious gossip (Hess & Hagen, 2006).

Another personality difference has to do with interests, and this is one of the strongest gender differences, statistically speaking: Women's interests are more people related and empathetic, whereas men's interests are more thing related (Baron-Cohen, 2003; Lippa, 2005). Again, this difference might incline women and men toward different occupations, but it is difficult to disentangle such internal influences from the effects of social expectations and discrimination, which certainly exist.

Turkish soccer fans clash with riot police in Istanbul in 2013.

---

* For statistics buffs, they show effect sizes (*d*) of about 0.5–1.0.

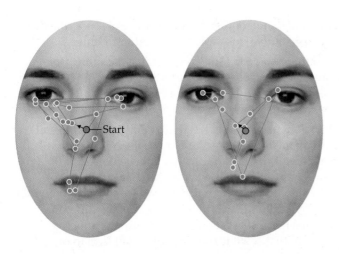

Figure 4.9 Female superiority in face recognition may reflect the fact that women inspect faces more carefully. Here a woman's (left) and a man's (right) gazes are tracked as they look at a face for 5 seconds: The woman makes many more eye movements (23 vs. 14), thus generating a more vivid mental picture of the face. (From Heisz et al., 2013.)

One cross-cultural study, based on data from 23,000 men and women in 26 cultures, found robust cross-cultural gender differences in six personality factors: Men scored higher in factors of "assertiveness" and "openness to ideas," while women scored higher in "agreeableness," "warmth," "openness to feelings," and "neuroticism" (Costa et al., 2001).

There are Many Sex Differences in Sexuality

More directly relevant to the overall subject of this book are sex differences related to sexuality. Here we summarize the most important of these differences:

- Men have a stronger *sex drive* than women—they think more often about sex, have more frequent and more intense sexual fantasies, want more frequent sex, are more likely to initiate sex, make more sacrifices for sex, and are less willing to forgo sex (Baumeister et al., 2001; Sine, 2014) (see Chapter 5).

- Men and women have marked differences in their attitudes toward *casual or uncommitted sex*, a personality dimension known as **sociosexuality**. Men express far more permissive attitudes than women regarding casual sexual encounters, are more desirous of engaging in such encounters, and make more attempts to do so. This is true not just in the United States, but also in over 50 nations where men and women have been surveyed, and this sex difference has been fairly constant over time (Lippa, 2009; Sprecher et al., 2013). Asked in a U.S. random-sample survey how they would feel after a one-night stand, men were more than three times as likely as women to say they would feel "satisfied," while women were more than twice as likely as men to say they would feel "regret" or "shame" (Esquire, 2007). The topic of how men and women view casual sex is covered in more detail in Chapters 7 and 11.

- Women and men tend to *seek different things* in their sex partners. Women are typically attracted to older partners, men to younger ones. Women are more concerned than men with their partners' status or wealth; men are more concerned than women with their partners' physical attractiveness. These differences exist across cultures—in Chinese college students just as much as in American students, for example (Toro-Morn & Sprecher, 2003). Of course, there are any number of exceptions to these generalizations— men who adore powerful older women, for example, and women who are

sociosexuality Interest in casual or uncommitted sex.

double standard The application of different moral standards to the behavior of males and females.

drawn to penniless but handsome youths. But in a statistical sense, the differences hold up very consistently. This topic is covered in Chapter 5.

- Men are more interested in *visual sexual stimuli* generally, including pornography, and are more sexually aroused by such stimuli, than are women (Janssen et al., 2003). Not surprisingly, most pornography is oriented toward consumption by men, as is discussed in Chapter 17.

- Women and men both experience *jealousy*, but they tend to experience different kinds of jealousy (Buss, 2013). Women are more likely than men to experience emotional jealousy—that is, to fear that their male partner may commit himself emotionally to a different woman. Men, in contrast, are more likely than women to experience sexual jealousy—to fear that their female partner is being physically unfaithful to them. This sex difference decreases with age, perhaps because women's decreasing reproductive potential makes it less likely that sex with a third party will lead to pregnancy (IJzerman et al., 2014). The role of jealousy in sexual relationships is discussed in Chapter 7.

- There are differences in the *sexual orientations* of men and women. First, obviously, there is the fact that most women are sexually attracted to men, whereas most men are sexually attracted to women. Beyond that, the distribution of non-heterosexual orientations differs between the sexes: The majority of non-heterosexual men are homosexual (gay), whereas the majority of non-heterosexual women are bisexual. These and other sex differences in the realm of sexual orientation are taken up in Chapter 12.

- Men are much more likely than women to desire and engage in *unusual forms of sexual expression*, such as fetishisms. Men are also more likely to engage in rape, child molestation, and other forms of *sexual coercion* (see Chapter 16).

- Men are much more likely than women to *pay for sex*, and more women than men receive money for sex (see Chapter 17).

- The *sexual response cycles* of women and men differ (see Chapter 5). Men are aroused and reach orgasm faster than women. Many women but few men experience multiple orgasms within one cycle of sexual arousal. Women are more likely than men to say that they can experience sex as satisfying even without reaching orgasm.

- Males *masturbate* more than females, beginning at puberty (Gerressu et al., 2008) (see Chapter 10). Males also report more frequent sexual intercourse, a younger age at first intercourse, and a larger number of total sex partners than do females, but these apparent differences result at least in part from men's tendency to exaggerate their sexual activities and women's tendency to minimize them (Alexander & Fisher, 2003; Fisher, 2013). This relates to the sexual **double standard**, by which the sexual exploits of men are admired but those of women are stigmatized (see Chapter 11).

- Men's *reproductive capacity* declines gradually over time but extends into old age, whereas women's reproductive capacity ceases more abruptly at menopause. Nevertheless, women's sexual desires and behaviors may continue long after menopause (see Chapter 11).

- Reproduction is more of a "gamble" for men than for women: Some men have large numbers of children and other men have none, whereas women are more likely to have some moderate number of children. This difference in reproductive variance encourages *sexual risk taking* by men. This topic is discussed further below and in Appendix A.

- Sexual behavior has more direct potential *consequences* for women—in terms of pregnancy and motherhood—than it does for men, and sexually transmitted infections have a much higher risk of impairing fertility in women than in men (see Chapter 15). So, quite aside from the double standard, the choice to engage or not engage in sexual contacts may be perceived as a more serious or fraught decision for women than for men.

stereotype A common opinion about a class of people that is false or overgeneralized.

Stated in this brief fashion, some of the statements listed above may strike you as more akin to **stereotypes** (opinions about classes of people that are based on overgeneralization or prejudice) than to well-documented facts. As generalizations about average differences between women and men they are valid, but there are also many important exceptions and nuances that we cannot touch on here. We urge you to withhold judgment until we have the opportunity to discuss all these topics in greater detail. We should also emphasize that documenting the existence of sex differences says nothing about the morality of women's or men's sexual behavior, nor whether differences that exist today are permanent and immutable.

With regard to all these sex differences in cognition, personality, and sexuality, there is still controversy about their reality, magnitude, and meaning. Psychologist Janet Hyde and others have argued that sex differences, if they exist at all, are so small, and show so much overlap between men and women, that they are irrelevant in any practical context (Hyde, 2005; Jordan-Young, 2011). Others say that Hyde ignores some large and well-replicated sex differences, both in mental traits and in brain organization, and that even the overlapping traits become far more distinct when measured collectively (multivariate analysis) (Lippa, 2006; Del Giudice et al., 2012; Cahill, 2014).

Many gender differences arise early in life

Boys and girls show quite marked differences in behavior from a young age. Even before birth, male fetuses are more active than females, and this difference in activity level increases during childhood (Campbell & Eaton, 1999). Sex differences in toy preferences are detectable as early as 3 months of age (Alexander et al., 2009) and are well established by the first birthday (Servin et al., 1999): Boys prefer toy vehicles, toy weapons, balls, and construction toys, while girls prefer dolls and toy kitchen implements (Berenbaum & Snyder, 1995; Alexander & Saenz, 2012) (**Figure 4.10**). Boys engage in more competitive, strenuous, and rough-and-tumble play and

Figure 4.10 Toy preference test A child is placed within a circle of toys, and his or her play behavior is videotaped. Later, observers measure the amount of time the child spends playing with toys generally preferred by girls and those generally preferred by boys. Figure 4.12 shows examples of data from this kind of study.

aggression than do girls, who engage in more conversation and socializing (Maccoby, 1998; Holmes, 2012). By 4 years of age most boys prefer to play with boys, and most girls with girls. This segregation by sex is universal across cultures and is most marked when adults are not present (Fabes et al., 2003). At the same age, girls' and boys' play is governed by different moral rules: Girls appeal to social conventions ("The teacher will be angry if we don't play nicely"), while boys are more likely to refer to principles of justice ("Hands off the car, it's mine!") (Tulviste & Koor, 2005).

Biological Factors Influence Gender

So far, we have attempted to describe gender differences without drawing any conclusions about how these differences arise. We now turn to the topic of causes. Researchers have taken a wide variety of approaches to this topic and have viewed gender through the lenses of several different disciplines. We begin by discussing the biological approach.

Evolutionary forces act differently on females and males

The field of evolutionary psychology investigates how gender characteristics have been molded by a long period of human and prehuman evolution. During this period, the struggle to survive and reproduce has favored the spread of genes that predispose their owners to certain sex-specific traits and behavior patterns. Here are three examples of how evolutionary psychology attempts to explain aspects of women's and men's sexual strategies (Buss, 2011).

Hadza boy practicing archery, Tanzania.

INTEREST IN CASUAL SEX   Men's greater interest in casual sex can be explained in terms of evolutionary processes. The cost of fathering a child—when stripped to its biological essentials—is minimal. In theory, therefore, a man can have hundreds of offspring if he impregnates many different women and walks away from each. Women, however, have to invest so much time and resources into pregnancy and child care that they are very limited in the total number of offspring they are able to have. Therefore, it's argued, genes evolved that promote men's interest in casual sex and women's choosiness about whom they mate with.

JEALOUSY   Women have always been certain of the identity of their children: Any child to whom a woman gave birth was necessarily her genetic offspring. A man, however, could not be certain which children were his: Even in a supposedly monogamous relationship, there was always the risk that his partner might have sex with someone else and that he might end up helping to rear a child that was not genetically his own. According to David Buss, this difference between the sexes, persisting over countless generations, led to the spread of genes promoting the different styles of jealousy in women and men described above. Men's sexual jealousy served to reduce the likelihood of rearing children that were not theirs; women's emotional jealousy served to reduce the likelihood that their male partners would abandon them and leave them without resources to rear their children (Buss, 2013).

Mayan mother teaches daughter to weave, Guatemala.

COGNITIVE   Evolutionary psychologists believe that cognitive differences between the sexes have arisen because of a long-standing division of labor between women and men. Because of their greater physical strength, it is argued, men have always taken a leading role in hunting, warfare, and exploration; women, because of their biologically mandated role in pregnancy and breast-feeding, have taken a leading role in activities near the homesite. Over many generations, such a division of labor might well have favored the spread of genes for different cognitive skills in the two

Box 4.2 Biology of Sex

Gendered Play in Primates

If girls' and boys' toy preferences are influenced by internal bio-logical factors, rather than resulting solely from parental encour-agement, then we might expect to see similar preferences among our primate relatives. To test this idea, developmental psychologists Gerianne Alexander (of Texas A & M University) and Melissa Hines presented male and female vervet monkeys with the same kinds of toys that they had previously used to test children's toy preferences (Alexander & Hines, 2002). The mon-keys' preferences were uncannily similar to those of humans: Male monkeys played more with model cars and balls, for exam-ple, and female monkeys played more with dolls (**Figures A** and **B**). Similar results have been obtained more recently with rhesus monkeys (Hassett et al., 2008).

(A) (B)

Monkeys show humanlike toy preferences.   (A) A female vervet monkey plays with a doll. (B) A male monkey plays with a toy car. (From Alexander & Hines, 2002.)

Since the monkeys had not seen the test items previously, they could hardly have learned to prefer some toys to others. Probably, some internal process of brain differentiation influ-ences toy preferences in both human and nonhuman primates. It's not that there's an innate representation of the concept "car" or of any other toys in the brain, of course. Rather, children and monkeys choose toys that facilitate the behaviors they like to engage in, such as active movement in the case of males.

What about primates in the wild, where toy cars and dolls are not available? Sonja Kahlenberg of Bates College and Richard Wrangham of Harvard University observed the behavior of juve-nile chimpanzees in Kibale National Park in Uganda (Kahlenberg & Wrangham, 2010). They found that juvenile females often car-ried sticks around, and they appeared to care for the sticks as girls care for dolls, holding them close to their bodies, cradling them, or taking them into their nests to sleep. These juvenile females could not have learned this behavior by imitating their mothers, because the mothers never carried sticks. Juvenile males carried sticks much less often than females, and when they did do so, they used them as weapons or for some other purpose. Because of the similarity of this sex difference in chim-panzees and humans, the researchers suggested that it existed in the common ancestors of the two species, who lived about 6 million years ago, long before socialization became an important influence on behavioral development.

sexes, such as the greater throwing and navigating skills of men and the greater hand and finger dexterity of women.

To the extent that these evolutionary theories—about interest in casual sex, jeal-ousy, and cognitive skills—are correct, one might expect that nonhuman species (especially those closely related to us) would exhibit some of the same gender-dif-ferentiated traits that humans do, even without the benefit of human culture. Experi-ments and field observations show that they do (see **Box 4.2**).

Experiments demonstrate a role for sex hormones

Earlier in this chapter we mentioned the structural and functional differences between the brains of women and men. These differences result, at least in part, from differences in circulating levels of sex hormones during fetal life, at puberty, and during adult life. So, do hormones contribute to the psychological differences between the sexes?

Experiments in animals certainly suggest so. Biologists have altered the hormonal environments of fetal rats and monkeys—by adding testosterone to a female fetus, for example, or by blocking the action of a male fetus's own testosterone. In postnatal

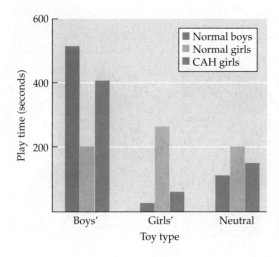

Figure 4.11 Hormones and play Exposure to androgens during fetal life influences choice of toys during childhood. Normal boys, normal girls, and girls with congenital adrenal hyperplasia (CAH) were observed while playing with toys. The toys available included those generally preferred by boys (e.g., trucks) and those generally preferred by girls (e.g., dolls), as well as gender-neutral toys. The toy preferences of the CAH girls were more like those of boys than like those of non-CAH girls. (After Berenbaum & Snyder, 1995.)

Figure 4.12 Finger length ratio and gender The 2D:4D ratio is the length of the index finger divided by the length of the ring finger. The ratio is typically lower in men than women, but it also varies with gender characteristics within each sex. (D = digit.)

life the treated females behave in many ways like males, and vice versa (Goy et al., 1988; Arnold, 2009).

Although it would obviously be unethical to conduct such experiments in humans, biologists can take advantage of "experiments of nature" in which a similar situation has occurred spontaneously (Hines, 2011). One example is the condition of congenital adrenal hyperplasia. As mentioned earlier in this chapter, girls with CAH are exposed to abnormally high levels of testosterone-like hormones (androgens) that are secreted by their adrenal glands during part of their fetal life. Psychologists have found that some, but not all, of the behavioral traits of these girls are shifted in the masculine direction. The CAH girls engage in more rough-and-tumble play than other girls, for example, and they prefer "boys' toys" to "girls' toys" (**Figure 4.11**). The differences persist into adult life, affecting such things as spatial skills, hobby interests, and career choices (Puts et al., 2008; Beltz et al., 2011; Berenbaum et al., 2012), as well as sexual orientation (see Chapter 12). These observations indicate that the high androgen levels experienced by female CAH fetuses influence their gender characteristics after birth.

But do these results say anything about typical children? To address this question, researchers have estimated testosterone levels in healthy fetuses—by measuring levels of the hormone in the amniotic fluid or in their mothers' blood (Hines, 2006; Knickmeyer & Baron-Cohen, 2006). The children born of those pregnancies were studied at various ages after birth. It turned out that fetal testosterone levels predicted a variety of gender characteristics in these children, even within a single sex. The lower a girl's testosterone levels prenatally, for example, the more strongly she would prefer "girls' toys" over "boys' toys" when she was 3 years old.

It's difficult to study adults with the same methodology, because of the long time interval involved. To get around this problem, biologists have looked for anatomical markers in adults that may reflect their degree of testosterone exposure prenatally. One marker that has attracted a great deal of attention is the ratio of the length of the index finger (second digit, or 2D) to the length of the ring finger (fourth digit, or 4D)—the so-called 2D:4D ratio (Manning et al., 2014) (**Figure 4.12**). Men typically have a lower 2D:4D ratio than women, and several lines of evidence suggest that this difference is caused in part by the higher testosterone levels that males typically experience during fetal life (Berenbaum et al., 2009; Breedlove, 2010). Researchers have found that the 2D:4D ratio correlates with many gendered characteristics, even within one sex. A Canadian group, for example, reported that men with lower (more male-typical) ratios are more aggressive than men with higher ratios (Bailey & Hurd, 2005).

These kinds of findings suggest a relationship—presumably a causal one—between the brain's exposure to androgens before birth and a variety of gendered characteristics in childhood and adult life. None of the biological findings allow the conclusion that prenatal hormones *determine* a person's gender characteristics, however. They suggest an *influence*—an influence that may be quite strong for some characteristics and quite weak, or totally absent, for others. Thus, there is plenty of room for other factors to play a role. These may include nonhormonal biological processes, such as aspects of brain development that are controlled directly by genes (Ngun et al., 2011), as well as a variety of social and learning factors that we will discuss next.

Life Experiences Influence Gender

Newborn girls and boys enter a world that imposes gender on them from the very beginning (**Figure 4.13**). Psychologists have discerned a variety of ways in which interactions among individuals, their families, and society help create and strengthen gendered traits.

Gender is molded by socialization

The earliest social influences on a child's gender come from the family. Children are exposed to myriad inputs from their parents and siblings that could influence gendered attitudes and behaviors. Parents may influence children's gender by the way they dress them; by the way they decorate their rooms; by the toys they provide; by the way they attend to, reward, or punish their children's behavior; and by the activities that they initiate with them. Some parents take great

Figure 4.13 Babies enter a gendered world. Eva and Nicholas have been dressed in the pink and blue outfits that our culture deems appropriate for infant girls and boys, respectively.

pains to encourage gender conformity by these various methods, while others take a more lenient stance. Even if they do not set out to influence a child's gender, parents and siblings may do so simply by virtue of acting as role models.

OBSERVING SOCIALIZATION Here's just one example of a study in which the influence of family members (older siblings, in this case) on children's gender was demonstrated and measured (Rust et al., 2000). A British group of psychologists examined the gender-related behaviors and interests of over 5000 3-year-old children; the researchers reduced the data for each child to a single measure of masculinity/ femininity. Some of the children had older siblings. Those who had older siblings of the same sex were significantly more gender typical than were children who had no siblings (singletons) (**Figure 4.14**). Conversely, children who had older siblings of the other sex were less gender typical than the singletons. These data indicate that the presence of same- or opposite-sex siblings does influence a child's gender characteristics to an appreciable degree. The influence was modest in size, however,

(A)

(B)

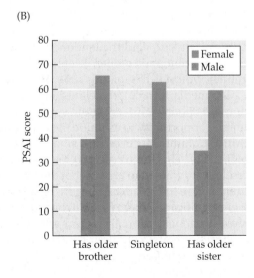

Figure 4.14 Influence of siblings on gender (A) Older siblings act as gender role models. (B) The Pre-School Activities Inventory (PSAI) score is a measure of gender-typical activities and interests in which male-typical traits score higher and female-typical traits score lower. This figure shows the PSAI score for 5542 British 3-year-olds, broken down according to whether they are singletons or have older brothers or sisters. The children's gender traits are slightly shifted in the direction of the sex of the older sibling. (After Rust et al., 2000.)

as can be seen in the figure: A child's own sex was a much stronger predictor of her or his gender-related traits than was the sex of the older siblings. Girls with older brothers, for example, were far more feminine than any boys, even boys with older sisters.

Parents are presumably in a stronger position than siblings to influence children's gender characteristics. This influence was illustrated in a study by researchers at Johns Hopkins University (Pappas et al., 2008). They reported on 40 individuals who, as a result of a variety of intersex conditions, were born with ambiguous genitalia. Although the genitalia of all the children had roughly the same anatomical appearance, those individuals whose parents raised them as boys became increasingly masculine through adolescence and adulthood, whereas those who were raised as girls became increasingly feminine.

REWARDS AND PUNISHMENTS   Studies such as the ones just described indicate that social interactions influence gender but don't pinpoint the exact mechanisms. One possible influence is the way family members use rewards, punishments, or withdrawal of rewards with any given child. Under these circumstances children learn from trial and error, often discovering how their behaviors lead to rewards or avoid punishments. In one study focusing on these learning processes, psychologist Robert Fagot and his colleagues studied interactions between parents and their 18-month-old infants and then followed the infants for about a year afterward. They found that the infants whose parents reacted to their behavior in the traditional fashion (rewarding or approving of gender-typical behavior and punishing or disapproving of gender-atypical behavior) learned to make gender distinctions earlier than other infants and exhibited more traditional gender-specific behavior (Fagot et al., 1992). Studies of this kind support the notion that gender-related traits are influenced by rewards and punishments.

IMITATION   Gender-typical behavior is also influenced by a child's observing and imitating the behavior of parents or older siblings, and not just by reward and punishment (Bussey & Bandura, 1984; Grace et al., 2008). A child might first imitate both parents but be rewarded most for observing and imitating the same-sex parent. In one study, Walter Mischel tracked the eye movements of children while they were watching films featuring male and female characters. In accordance with the theory of observational learning, the children attended more to the same-sex characters in the films than they did to the characters of the other sex. Such behavior could easily lead children to become better acquainted with, and imitate, the behaviors typical of their own sex. And the tendency of children to play with other children of their own sex, mentioned earlier, offers another way in which they can observe and learn gender-typical behavior, this time from their peers (Paechter & Clark, 2007).

The media, particularly television, offer much for children to imitate in the gender domain (**Figure 4.15**). A classic study conducted in the 1970s took advantage of a unique opportunity to examine the effects of the media. A group at the University of British Columbia focused on a small Canadian town, fictitiously named Notel (Kimball, 1986). This town received television broadcasts for the first time in 1974. The researchers wanted to know what the effect of television would be on the town's children. Before the broadcasts began, Notel's children had gender-related attitudes that were significantly more flexible than those of children in two comparable towns that already had television. By 2 years after the beginning of television transmissions, the attitudes of Notel's children had become much more stereotypical and comparable to those of children in the other towns. The girls had particularly marked changes in their attitudes toward peer relationships, while the boys showed marked changes concerning future occupations—both in the direction of greater gender rigidity. All in all, the Notel study demonstrated a powerful effect of television in promoting ste-

FAQ

Can I raise my child "gender free"?

Not unless you're willing to refer to your child as "it." But you can avoid imposing your gender expectations on him or her.

Figure 4.15   The media influence gender. Because overweight women, such as the character played here by Mo'Nique, are often portrayed as losers in love, girls may learn to imitate thin actors. This image is a scene from her 2005 movie *Domino*.

reotypical gender attitudes. Of course, it's possible that television promotes more flexible attitudes to gender today than it did in the 1970s, but some more recent studies suggest that television and other media have been slow to move beyond traditional gender stereotypes (Collins, 2011).

LANGUAGE   The language we speak is another cultural influence on gender, but one that we're barely aware of. Children acquire a knowledge of their own sex by 2 to 3 years of age, but this age actually varies according to the language environment that children are exposed to. Children in Hebrew-speaking households, for example, know their own sex about a year earlier than children in Finnish-speaking households. That's because Hebrew grammar emphasizes gender: Even the Hebrew word for "you" varies according to whether one is addressing a male or a female. Finnish grammar, on the other hand, doesn't specify gender at all. English falls in between, and correspondingly, children in English-speaking households learn their sex at an intermediate age (Guiora et al., 1982; Boroditsky, 2011).

GENDER LEARNING FROM ADVICE   Language also facilitates the learning of gender roles by means of verbally communicated advice (Baldwin & Baldwin, 2001). When a boy gets hurt and begins to cry, his older brother or father may state the rule "Big boys don't cry." The message is very clear, though the boy may need several months of additional learning before he can control his tears in a broad range of situations. Many girls learn that they are allowed to cry, and they may even get extra attention (a social reward) when they cry. Thus, social advice helps children learn that crying is much more acceptable for females than males. Swearing provides an opposite example: In many households, teenage girls are told more firmly than teenage boys that they should not swear.

Gender advice is communicated not just by family members but also from many other social sources. As an example, Kathleen Denny, a graduate student in sociology at the University of Maryland, compared the messages conveyed by the U.S. Girl Scouts and Boy Scouts handbooks (Denny, 2011). There were consistent differences. The girls' book placed more emphasis on group activities, artistic expression, and unstructured inquiry ("Take turns holding different colors up to your face [to] decide which colors look best on each of you"), whereas the boys' book placed more emphasis on science, learning facts from books, and solo activities ("Draw a floor plan of your home"). The girls' book encouraged aspiration and effort ("I will do my best to be…"), whereas the boys' book encouraged self-assuredness ("A Boy Scout is…"). Scouting manuals provide just one example of the countless different messages conveyed to girls and boys, and each individual is influenced by a unique subset of all these types of advice.

Advice-based gender learning is often backed up by the promise of rewards or the threat of punishments—or reinforced by the social aura of respected role models. The key feature of this form of learning, however, is that advice allows for the acquisition of general concepts that children can apply to a broad range of circumstances, includ-

sexual script A socially negotiated role that guides sexual behavior.

ing those that they have not previously encountered. In that way, advice contributes to the creation of durable attitudes and opinions about gender that may be passed down from generation to generation.

The weight of evidence supports the belief that socialization powerfully influences gender development. But, as with the biological approach, socialization can't explain everything. For one thing, some children are remarkably resistant to gender socialization. For example, children who become gay or transgender often violate some or many gender norms in rather dramatic ways, yet there is no evidence that these children are encouraged or trained to become gender rebels. And some children who are born as one sex but reared as the other may fiercely oppose this kind of reassignment, as if they somehow know which sex they ought to be (**Box 4.3**). It therefore seems unlikely that a complete account of gender development can be made in terms of either socialization or biology, and in fact few if any present-day workers in the field would make such a claim.

Cognitive developmental models emphasize thought processes

Cognitive psychologists believe that studying gender development requires getting inside children's minds to see how they think about gender. Children actively seek to make sense of the social world in which they live, and in the process they gradually develop a gender identity and acquire gender stereotypes (Martin & Ruble, 2010).

One example of a cognitive developmental model is the **sexual script** theory of John Gagnon and William Simon (Simon & Gagnon, 1986). As the word "script" suggests, this theory asserts that sexual behavior is a form of role-playing, influenced by scripts that we have learned. People are especially reliant on sexual scripts when interacting with prospective partners that they don't know very well. As we'll describe in more detail in Chapter 7, first encounters between heterosexual men and women have traditionally been organized according to gendered scripts governing such matters as what it means to invite someone out for a drink, who pays, and how the man and woman negotiate any sexual interactions.

Scripts can change over time under the influence of culture. Early in the 20th century, for example, oral-genital contact was a form of sex that men largely received from prostitutes and in transient relationships. Now, however, it has become a common and acceptable sexual practice between young adults who are hooking up or dating, and both males and females give oral sex to their partners (Reece et al., 2010b). Thus, men and women today follow different scripts about oral sex than their grandparents did.

Scripts, according to Gagnon and Simon, influence not only sexual dealings among people, but also the psychosexual development of individuals. They noted that post-pubertal boys masturbate a great deal more than do girls, as we mentioned above, whereas girls' early sexual experiences tend to be with partners. As a consequence, script theory suggests, the meaning of sex for males becomes embedded in the notion of the male's own sexual pleasure, whereas for females it becomes embedded in the notion of relationships.

Sexual scripts are relevant to the important social issues such as sexual coercion. In one longitudinal study of high school students, for example, male students who endorsed a script in which men were expected to take sexual risks were more likely to engage in aggressive sexual behavior, and female students were more likely to experience sexual victimization (Krahe et al., 2007).

Gender Development Is Interactive

Gender researchers, like researchers in most other areas, tend to invest themselves in certain approaches to their subject, perhaps due to the training they have received.

Box 4.3 Personal Points of View

The Boy Who Was Raised as a Girl

Bruce and Brian Reimer were monozygotic ("identical") twins born in Winnipeg, Canada, in 1965. When the twins were 7 months old, they developed phimosis, a common condition in which the foreskin of the penis becomes constricted (see Chapter 3). The parents were advised to have the twins circumcised, but during Bruce's operation, an accident led to the complete destruction of his penis.

The parents were understandably devastated and at a loss as to what to do. Eventually they brought Bruce to sexologist John Money at the Johns Hopkins School of Medicine. Money believed that children developed a male or female gender identity according to whether they were reared as girls or boys. Since it would not be possible to refashion a normal penis, Money recommended that Bruce be surgically transformed into, and reared as, a girl. He told the parents that as long as they treated the child as a girl, she would become a feminine, heterosexual woman.

The parents followed Money's advice. They immediately changed Bruce's name to Brenda and dressed and treated her as a girl. When Brenda was 2 years old, her sex reassignment was completed: Her testicles were removed, and a rudimentary vagina was constructed from the scrotal skin. Her parents dedicated themselves to rearing Brenda and Brian as sister and brother. Money saw the parents and the twins from time to time and advised the parents on the appropriate ways to treat Brenda that would best encourage her femininity.

As the years went by, Money reported in detail on the case in lectures, papers, and books. He claimed that Brenda was developing as a normal girl, apart from a certain tomboyishness. While Brian copied his father, Brenda copied her mother, wrote Money (and colleague Anke Ehrhardt) in a 1971 book: "Regarding domestic activities, such as work in the kitchen and house traditionally seen as part of the female's role, the mother reported that her daughter copies her in trying to help her tidying and cleaning up the kitchen, while the boy could not care less about it" (Money & Ehrhardt, 1971). Brenda chose dolls as presents, Money wrote, while Brian chose model cars. The case became widely cited, both in the popular press and in academic circles, as evidence for the malleability of gender.

Eventually, Money reported that he had lost contact with the Reimer family. It took detective work by University of Hawaii sexologist Milton Diamond (Diamond & Sigmundson, 1997), and later by journalist John Colapinto (Colapinto, 2000), to discover

David Reimer (1965–2004).

what had happened to Brenda. It seems that she was never successfully socialized into a feminine gender identity in the way that Money had claimed. Rather, she rebelled against it at every stage. Although a female puberty was induced by means of treatment with estrogen, Brenda loathed her developing breasts. By the age of 15 she had changed her name to David and was dressing as a boy. David had a double mastectomy, testosterone treatments, and a phalloplasty (reconstruction of a penis). He was always sexually attracted to women, and he eventually married, engaged in coitus with the aid of a prosthesis, and adopted children.

Sadly, David killed himself in 2004 at the age of 38. The exact reason for his suicide is not known, but possible causes include the breakup of his marriage, financial difficulties, the earlier death of his twin brother Brian, and of course his traumatic childhood (Chalmers, 2004).

The case of Bruce, then Brenda, then David Reimer suggests a conclusion different from the one drawn by John Money: Prenatal development seems to strongly influence gender identity and sexual orientation even when rearing conditions, genital anatomy, and pubertal hormones all conspire to produce the opposite result. This conclusion has been reinforced by the study of genetically male children with a condition in which the external genitalia fail to develop. Although surgically reconstructed as girls and reared as such, all are male-shifted in their gender characteristics, and nearly half of them insist they are boys or men (Reiner, 2004). "It's been a monstrous failure, this idea that you can convert a child's sex by making over the genitals in the sex you've chosen," said the author of that study. "If we as physicians or scientists want to know about a person's sexual identity, we have to ask them" (Dreifus, 2005).

transgender (or trans) Having a gender identity that is not fully congruent with one's birth sex.

cisgender Having a conventional gender—masculine if anatomically male, feminine if anatomically female. "Cis" is the opposite of "trans."

transexual (or transsexual) A person who identifies with the other sex and who seeks to transition to the other sex by means of hormone treatment and sex-reassignment surgery.

Some are interested in biological theories, some in socialization, and so on. Yet it is unlikely that something as complex as human gender could be fully explained by any single approach. It's more probable that nature and nurture interact in the development of gender-related traits.

Take, for example, a childhood trait such as toy preference. The observations of atypical toy preference in CAH girls strongly suggest that prenatal hormone exposure contributes to the gender difference in this trait. However, many parents themselves encourage gender-specific play, for example by giving children toys preferred by girls or by boys. Such encouragement does in fact strengthen children's preference for gender-specific toys (Wong et al., 2013). Thus, it seems that there is an additive effect of biological predisposition and socialization on the development of toy preference.

Another complicating factor is that the influence of socialization is not unidirectional; it can pull people in opposite directions at the same time. Concerning the male disposition to commit sexual violence, for example, some social forces strongly encourage such violence and others strongly discourage it (**Figure 4.16**). Given all these complexities, it will remain for future generations of researchers to fully tease out the web of causation that establishes gender.

Transgender People Cross Society's Deepest Divide

The term **transgender**, often shortened to **trans**, is used in a broad way to encompass all individuals whose gender identity does not fully correspond with their biological sex: They may identify fully with the other sex, or they may reject a simple male/female dichotomy. Transgender is sometimes contrasted with **cisgender**, which refers to the conventionally gendered majority of women and men. About 0.3% of the population—3 in 1000 people—are transgender, according to one review of several studies (Gates, 2011). The true figure could be higher if, as seems likely, some transgender people are uncomfortable talking about it.

The term **transexual** is generally used for the subset of transgender individuals who seek to change their body into that of the other sex by medical means (i.e., hormone treatment and in many cases sex-reassignment surgery). This transition may be in either direction. Persons who transition from male to female are referred to as transexual women or trans women, while those who transition from female to male are referred to as transexual men or trans men. *In other words, the gendered terms "man" and "woman" refer to the sex the person identifies as or wants to become, not the anatomical sex in which they were born.* Some people who are transexual by our definition prefer to use the term transgender. Transgender and transexual people have existed in most—perhaps all—human societies (**Box 4.4**). We focus first on transexual men and women, and then take a look at the broader population of transgender people.

(A)

(B)

Figure 4.16 Social influences work in contradictory ways. (A) Video games may encourage sexual violence. In *Grand Theft Auto: Vice City*, a man has sex with a prostitute and then beats her to death to get his money back. (B) The criminal justice system may restrain sexual violence: Few want to join the 65,000 rapists who are serving long prison sentences.

Box 4.4 Cultural Diversity

Trans Men and Women in Cross-Cultural Perspective

Transgender men and women have probably existed in all human societies. In many societies, they have been given special names and accorded a special status—often, a spiritual or sacred one. Throughout Polynesia, for example, there existed a class of transgender individuals known as **mahus**. *Mahus* were born male but dressed in female (or a mixture of female and male) attire, engaged in women's activities, and had sex with conventional men. *Mahus* was attached to the village headman's household and performed sacred dances. They were traditionally accorded high status, and families encouraged or even trained one of their sons to become a *mahu*. From time to time, a European explorer or trader took a fancy to a *mahu* and brought her to his ship for sex, only to be shocked by the discovery of her male anatomy.

There still exists a comparable group of trans women in northern India and Pakistan. Known as **hijras**, they cut off their genitals and work as religious dancers or as prostitutes serving men. Thailand has an especially large and visible community of trans women, who are known as **kathoey** (see figure). Some have undergone sex reassignment. *Kathoey* are well accepted in the entertainment field and in some jobs typically held by women, but they face discrimination in "male" occupations.

In several native cultures of North America, rituals conducted at or before puberty gave a boy the option to choose between the status of a conventional male and that of a **two-spirit** (male-female) **person**, or *berdache* (Williams, 1986). Among the Tohono O'odham Indians of the Sonoran Desert, for example, a boy who preferred female pursuits was tested by being placed within a brushwood enclosure, along with a man's bow and arrows and a woman's basket. The enclosure was then set on fire. If, in escaping the flames, the boy took with him the bow and arrows, he became a conventional man, but if he took the basket, he became a *berdache*. The *berdaches* wore special clothes fashioned from male and female attire, practiced mostly female occupations, and engaged in sexual relationships with conventional men. They were often shamans (healers who derived their curative powers from their knowledge of the spirit world), chanters, dancers, or mediators.

Trans men have also been described in many societies. According to legend, female warriors known as Amazons battled the Greeks during the Trojan War. In the 16th century an explorer described female warriors among the Tupinamba Indians of northeastern Brazil (de Magalhaes, 1576/1922):

Members of the Thai ladyboy (transgender) band Venus Flytrap.

There are some Indian women who determine to remain chaste: they have no commerce with men in any manner, nor would they consent to it even if refusal meant death. They give up all the duties of women and imitate men, and follow men's pursuits as if they were not women. They wear the hair cut in the same way as the men, and go to war with bows and arrows and pursue game, always in company with men; each has a woman to serve her, to whom she says she is married, and they treat each other and speak with each other as man and wife.

The Amazon River was named after these women.

Westernization has led to considerable suffering for transgender persons in traditional societies. Under British influence, the once-honored *hijras* of India came to be despised. Spanish conquistadores killed many of the trans people they encountered in Central America. In Colorado in 2001, a self-described two-spirit Navajo youth, Fred Martinez, Jr., was beaten to death by an 18-year-old white man, who boasted to friends that he had "beat up a fag" (Quittner, 2001).

mahu   A man who took a female gender role in Polynesian society and performed ritual dances.

hijra   A member of a class of male-to-female transexuals in northern India and Pakistan.

kathoey   Trans women in Thailand.

two-spirit person   In Native American cultures, a person with the spirit of both a man and a woman; a transgender person. Also called *berdache*.

gender dysphoria The unhappiness caused by discordance between a person's anatomical sex and gender identity.

transvestism Wearing clothes of the other sex for purposes of sexual arousal. Sometimes applied to cross-dressing for any reason.

autogynephilia A form of male-to-female transexuality characterized by a man's sexual arousal at the thought of being or becoming a woman.

natal Describing a person's condition at birth.

Transexual individuals are of more than one kind

Imagine yourself waking up one morning in a body of the other sex. Very likely you would be shocked and would move heaven and earth to get back into your "right" body. That is the kind of mental experience transexual people deal with on a daily basis, unless and until they undergo sex-reassignment procedures and transition to the other sex. The unhappiness caused by discordance between **natal** anatomical sex and gender identity is called **gender dysphoria**. This is a diagnostic category in the American Psychiatric Association's *Diagnostic and Statistical Manual of Mental Disorders* (*DSM-5*), but it could also be viewed as a healthy reaction to the difficult situation in which transexual individuals find themselves.

Most transexual men share a similar life history. Even as very young girls they say they are boys or insist that they want to become boys, and they try to express their masculine identity in their clothing, hairstyles, friendships, activities, and career plans. Of course, this usually puts them on a collision course with the gender expectations of family, peers, and the world at large. As they enter puberty, they resent the developing signs of womanhood and may seek to hide them by, for example, binding their breasts. In adulthood they seem quite masculine in many respects, and they are usually sexually attracted to women, but they do not identify as homosexual or lesbian. Rather, they identify as heterosexual men. The well-known expression "man trapped in a woman's body" describes them fairly aptly.

Transexual women, on the other hand, fall into two contrasting types with different life histories. The first kind, who we may call "classical" transexual women, are pretty much the converse of the transexual men just described. As young boys they say that they are girls or insist that they want to become girls, and they try to dress as girls and to play with girls. They dislike the man's body that puberty gives them and may try to pass (be identified by others) as women. Feminine mannerisms, gait, and conversational style seem to come naturally to them. They are usually sexually attracted to men, but they identify as heterosexual women, not as gay men. They are "women trapped in men's bodies." M-to-F transexuals of this type often seek sex reassignment in their teen years or young adulthood—as soon as they are legally allowed to do so or as soon as they can raise the money to pay for it.*

Another kind of transexual woman, however, is much less well known to the general public (Lawrence, 2011). During childhood, these boys are only mildly gender nonconformist, or not at all. When they grow up, they are usually sexually attracted to women, so they are heterosexual with respect to their birth sex. However, their interest in women takes an unusual course, being colored with fetishistic elements. In particular, they are erotically aroused by wearing women's clothes—a trait known as heterosexual **transvestism**. Eventually, this kind of ideation may progress to the point that they are aroused by the idea, not merely of being in women's clothes, but of being in a woman's *body* and possessing female genitals. In other words, their desire to become a woman is fueled by the sex drive and by the desire to incorporate the object of their attractions into themselves, rather than by having a female gender identity. Feminine mannerisms, gait, and conversational style do not necessarily come naturally to these transexual women, and so they may take lessons on how to act like a woman. They tend to seek sex reassignment later in life, often after they have been heterosexually married and fathered children.

A Canadian sexologist, Ray Blanchard, gave this second developmental pathway the name **autogynephilia**, meaning "being attracted to oneself as a woman" (Blanchard, 2005). Some sex researchers believe that most M-to-F transexuals who are sexually attracted to women are autogynephilic (Bailey, 2003). Others don't find

* The Affordable Care Act ("Obamacare") does not explicitly guarantee insurance coverage of medical costs for transitioning, but it does improve the likelihood of coverage by removing the exclusion for "preexisting conditions."

a close correlation between a trans woman's sexual orientation and whether or not she displays characteristics of autogynephilia (Veale et al., 2008). Among transexual women themselves, some have strongly opposed the concept of autogynephilia (James, 2004). Others have embraced the concept and added important details to its theoretical underpinnings (Lawrence, 2013).

The cause or causes of transexuality are not well understood. Because, as discussed earlier, gender is influenced by biological factors such as prenatal hormones, many researchers suspect that such factors also lie behind transexuality. Consistent with this idea, there have been reports of differences in genes (Hare et al., 2009), brain structure (Garcia-Falgueras & Swaab, 2008; Rametti et al., 2011a,b), and finger length ratios (Schneider et al., 2006) between transgender persons and conventionally gendered persons of the same natal sex. Twin studies also suggest that genes influence transexuality (Diamond, 2013; Segal & Diamond, 2014). The rarity of transexual individuals, their life histories (which may include hormone treatments), and the autogynephilic/non-gynephilic distinction all complicate the search for a biological explanation for transexuality.

Changing sex is a multistage process

No form of psychiatric treatment can bring a transexual person's gender identity into concordance with his or her natal sex. In fact, any attempt to do so would be experienced as a violation of personhood. Therefore, doctors and therapists have followed a different strategy, helping transexual people to achieve their dream of changing their anatomical sex and their social gender role (**Figure 4.17**). Transexual people call this process **transitioning**, and it may take several years to complete.

From the perspective of the professionals who help people transition, the process has four major elements (World Professional Association for Transgender Health, 2008). The first element is psychological and physical evaluation. This may include psychotherapy, with the goal of probing the client's history, mental health, motivation, and education about the sex-reassignment process and the inevitable limitations of the results.

The second element is known as the **real-life experience**. For this, the client lives and interacts with others as a member of the other sex for a period of time—usually 1 to 2 years, but sometimes less. The idea is to ensure that the client can function well in the desired gender role.

transitioning   Changing one's physical sex and social gender.

real-life experience   A period of living in the role of the other sex as a prelude to sex reassignment.

Figure 4.17   Chastity Bono (left), transitioned to Chaz Bono (right) between 2008 and 2010.

sex-reassignment surgery
Surgery to change a person's genitals or other sexual characteristics.

The third element is hormone treatment to initiate the process of bodily change. Transexual women are treated with estrogens, often in combination with androgen-blocking drugs. The effects of this treatment include changes in body fat distribution to a more female pattern, a decrease in the frequency of erections, and possibly a cessation of ejaculations. The breasts may enlarge, sometimes to a degree that makes later breast augmentation surgery unnecessary. Estrogens do not abolish facial hair or reverse baldness, however. Transexual women often have to undergo a lengthy process of beard removal by electrolysis or laser treatment.

Transexual men are given androgens, which cause a beard to grow, though sometimes only a very thin one. The voice deepens, and the body fat distribution changes in a male direction. Because hormones do not remodel the skeleton, however, the general body shape may remain similar to that of the person's original sex.

Ideally, the real-life experience precedes the hormone treatment, because not all the effects of hormone treatment can be reversed if the person decides not to go ahead with the transition. In practice, however, hormone treatment is often started early because it may be difficult to undertake the real-life experience without such treatment.

The fourth element of transitioning is **sex-reassignment surgery** (Wroblewski et al., 2013). An estimated 1000 male-to-female surgeries are performed in the U.S. every year (Conway, 2013), as well as a smaller but uncertain number of female to male surgeries.

For a transexual woman, the key procedures are removal of the penis and testicles; construction of a vagina, labia, and clitoris (**Figure 4.18**); and augmentation of the breasts. The vagina may be constructed from the inverted skin of the penis, or a graft of intestinal tissue. Recently, tissue engineers have succeeded in constructing vaginas in the laboratory, using cells from the intended recipient; so far, these have been implanted only into girls who were born without vaginas (Raya-Rivera et al., 2014), but the technology might be used in sex-reassignment surgery in the future. Other procedures that may be performed include surgery on the vocal cords (to raise the pitch of the voice), liposuction to the waist, reduction of the Adam's apple, and various procedures to feminize the appearance of the face.

For a transexual man, surgery can include removal of the breasts, ovaries, oviducts, uterus, and vagina. (The breasts may be removed before the real-life experience if they are large enough to make passing as a man impossible.) In addition, a scrotum and penis may be constructed (i.e., scrotoplasty and phalloplasty).

Construction of a penis that looks natural, contains a functioning urethra, and can be made to have an erection (with the aid of a pump-and-reservoir system or some kind of stiffening device; see Chapter 14) is a very costly multistage process, and the results are far from ideal. Frequently, the new urethra develops narrowings (strictures) or unwanted openings to the outside (fistulas), which necessitate further surgery. Urinary tract infections can occur. Furthermore, there is major scarring in the body region that is used as the source of graft tissue. Because of the expense and the imperfect results, many transexual men forgo a phalloplasty. In some clients, the clitoris can be enlarged by hormonal treatment and surgery to produce a small penis. This procedure

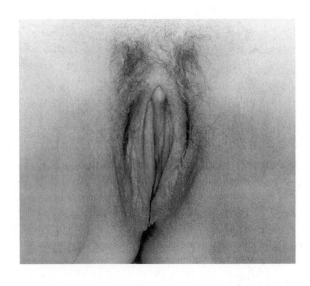

Figure 4.18 The vulva after sex-reassignment surgery The clitoris is constructed from the top surface of the penis with its nerve supply intact and may therefore be capable of triggering orgasm. The clitoris and adjacent labial tissue are covered with mucosa derived from the penile urethra, giving them a pink color. The remainder of the penile skin, including the glans, is inverted to form the vagina. Often, additional skin must be grafted from other areas to make the vagina deep enough for coitus. (Courtesy of Eugene A. Schrang, MD.)

Figure 4.19 **Transformation of the clitoris into a small penis** by hormone treatment and surgery (metoidioplasty). This procedure is simpler, less invasive, and a less expensive alternative to the construction of a large penis usable for penetrative sex (phalloplasty). This F-to-M transexual also had a scrotum constructed from labial skin, with saline-filled implants to simulate testicles.

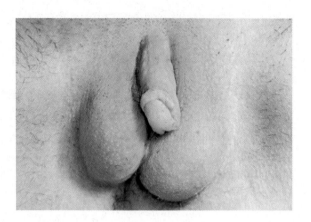

is called **metoidioplasty** (**Figure 4.19**) (Perovic & Djordjevic, 2003). This is not generally usable for coitus, but it may be capable of erection and orgasm, and the procedure may also be psychologically and socially beneficial in confirming a male identity. Even with this simpler procedure, however, complications requiring further surgery are common.

People who have transitioned from one sex to the other have to make many practical decisions (e.g., whether to be open about the sex change or to conceal their past), and they face all kinds of personal and social challenges. Even getting an amended birth certificate may be a struggle. Establishing sexual and affectional relationships is often difficult.

Transexual people who can pass as members of their new sex have to deal with the problem of whether and when to let their prospective partners know about their history. When a heterosexual man finds out that his female partner was born a male, he may refuse to accept the reality of the sex change and may therefore reject the woman and possibly even assault her. Luckily, there are also people who are willing to accept transexuals as truly belonging to the sex with which they identify, or who are even specifically attracted to transexual individuals. Some transexual men and women remain in relationships that existed prior to their transition.

Not all transexual people who wish to change sex do so via the "official" route just described. Some pursue another strategy: They learn about sex reassignment through peer networks, obtain hormones on the black market, and, when they feel they are ready for surgery, go straight to a private surgeon. Of course, such self-medication carries significant risks.

The long-term outcome of sex-reassignment surgery is fairly good, with the majority of individuals reporting an improved quality of life (Murad et al., 2010). However, some studies have reported that a significant proportion of people who have transitioned are depressed or regret having undergone the transition, and attempted and completed suicides are more common among postoperative transexuals than among non-transexuals (Dhejne et al., 2011). Better patient selection, preoperative counseling, and postoperative support would no doubt improve these outcomes.

Among the factors that correlate with long-term satisfaction are young age at reassignment, good general psychological health, a body build that permits passing as the other sex, good family and social support, and the success of the surgical procedure itself. Sexual orientation and whether or not a person is autogynephilic do not seem to be useful predictors of the success of a trans person's sex reassignment and should not therefore be used as criteria for accepting or rejecting a person for medical assistance with the process (Lawrence, 2003).

Because age at treatment seems to be so important, some centers are now treating children at or before puberty. Often these children are treated with a drug, leuprolide (Lupron), that blocks the onset of puberty; this prevents the appearance of difficult-to-reverse secondary sexual characteristics such as beards, and it gives the children time to make a more mature decision about whether to transition (**Box 4.5**).

Some transgender people do not want surgery

Transexuality forms just the visible tip of an iceberg of transgender identity: Much larger numbers of transgender women and men do not fully identify with their birth

metoidioplasty Surgical construction of a small penis from a clitoris.

Box 4.5 Controversies

How Should We Treat Gender-Dysphoric Children?

In the past, children—boys especially—who acted in a gender-nonconformist fashion or who expressed a wish to be the other sex suffered taunting and isolation at the hands of their peers and were subjected to persistent and sometimes traumatizing efforts by parents and therapists to "normalize" their behavior.

In more recent times some parents have taken the opposite tack, respecting and even celebrating gender variance in their children. In addition, there has been a move, especially in Europe, to facilitate sex reassignment at increasingly early ages. Because puberty produces undesired changes in gender-dysphoric children—changes such as the appearance of beards or breasts that may be difficult to reverse at a later time—some of these children are being given drugs that postpone the onset of puberty. Then, when the child is considered old enough to make a mature decision, hormonal and surgical procedures may be instituted to induce a puberty of the kind appropriate to the child's self-declared gender (de Vries et al., 2011).

This was the path chosen by the parents of Nicole Maines, a New England child who was born one of two monozygotic (so-called identical) twin boys, but who always identified as a girl. They helped her legally change her name from Wyatt to Nicole when she was in 5th grade. At the age of 11 she was started on puberty-blocking drugs. When the twins were 14, her brother was halfway through a typical male puberty, but Nicole was 5 inches shorter than him and quite different in facial appearance and manner. At the age of 16 (see figure), Nicole won a many-year legal battle to use the girls' bathroom at school—a battle that went all the way to the Maine Supreme Court (Jeltsen, 2014).

This kind of approach could certainly ease the psychological path to sex transition for children who are destined to become transexual adults, but not all experts believe that it is the best strategy. The reason is that, as many studies have shown, the majority of gender-dysphoric children lose their gender dysphoria as they transition through puberty, even without any treatment (Drummond et al., 2008; Wallien & Cohen-Kettenis, 2008). They may well become gay adults (see Chapter 12), but only a minority maintain their desire to change sex. It would seem counterproductive to support and facilitate a child's cross-gender identity, and to take medical steps toward a sex change, if that child would eventually have become perfectly happy with

Monozygotic ("identical") twins Jonas and Nicole Maines photographed in 2013 at age 16. Nicole was born male.

his or her birth sex. Thus, Kenneth Zucker, who directs a gender-identity clinic at Toronto's Centre for Addiction and Mental Health, believes that it is better to encourage gender-dysphoric children to accept their birth sex and not to look forward to an eventual transition (Zucker, 2005).

This controversy could be resolved if it were possible to identify the "persisters"—those children who will remain gender dysphoric after puberty and who therefore might truly benefit from support in their cross-gender identity and from an early sex change. To some extent, this may be possible. According to a longitudinal study by a Dutch research group, the persisters are the most radically gender-dysphoric children—the ones who truly believe that they *are* the other sex, rather than merely *wanting to be* the other sex (Steensma et al., 2013a). Whether this distinction is clear enough to justify selection of children for early treatment, however, is an unresolved issue. Perhaps the wisest course at present is for parents to love and support their gender-nonconformist children and for schools to protect them from bullying, but not to positively encourage or facilitate the children's desire to change sex until such time as this desire seems permanent.

Nicole Maines is certainly a persister. Now nearly 17, she is likely to undergo sex-reassignment surgery soon. However, she rejects the either-or concept of gender. "There's an infinite amount of space on the gender spectrum," she tweeted recently. "Being trans doesn't mean that you have to be feminine or masculine."

sex but do not seek to physically transition to the other sex. They may not see any contradiction between living as a woman while possessing the genitals of a man, or vice versa. They may not have the money, they may be put off by the less than ideal results, or they may be perfectly satisfied with cross-dressing and passing as a person of the other sex. This choice also gives them the option of switching between male and female roles, or adopting an identity that defies the stereotypes for both male and female gender roles. They may even get satisfaction from not passing—from being recognizable as a "gender outlaw" or "genderqueer" rather than trying to deceive everyone. They may position themselves as "beyond the binary" of the two sexes or even deny that the two sexes exist as objective categories of human beings (Fausto-Sterling, 2000). The term "trans*" (where the asterisk is a wild card representing any number of suffixes) is sometimes used to refer to the broad spectrum of nonstandard gender identities.

The traditional view of transexuality is *medical*: Transexual people have a "disorder" that needs to be "treated" in order to make them "well." Most transexual people accept this medical model, if somewhat reluctantly, because it's a precondition to getting any kind of financial coverage and other accommodations relating to their transition. But among trans men and women who don't want sex-reassignment surgery, many see the medical model as outdated and even demeaning. They may believe that it is *society* that has a "problem" with gender-variant people, and it is society that needs to be "treated."

Certainly, many Americans have an aversion to transgender people, who are victimized by abuse and hate crimes at a much higher rate than are lesbians and gay men. Could it be that the desire to change one's genital anatomy represents the internalization of these hostile attitudes? Kate Bornstein (**Figure 4.20**), a gender theorist who is herself a postoperative M-to-F transexual, put it this way:

> *People think that they have to hate their genitals in order to be transsexual. Well, some transsexuals do hate their genitals, and they act to change them. But I think that transsexuals do not "naturally" hate their birth-given genitals—I've not seen any evidence of that. We don't hate any part of our bodies that we weren't taught to hate. We're taught to hate parts of our bodies that aren't "natural"—like a penis on a woman or a vagina on a man. (Bornstein, 1994)*

Figure 4.20   Kate Bornstein, a trans woman, believes that social pressures force people into impossible-to-live-up-to gender categories.

To some extent Bornstein's point of view is supported by anthropological research. In the native culture of Samoa, for example, transgender persons (called *fa'afafine*) rarely desire sex reassignment, because it is socially acceptable to possess a penis and yet live in a gender role that is not male (Vasey & Bartlett, 2007).

This is how one 18-year-old transexual man, who has had a mastectomy but no genital surgery, put it: "Some transmen want to be seen as men—they want to be accepted as born men. I want to be accepted as a transman—my brain is not gendered. There's this crazy gender binary that's built into all of life, that there are just two genders that are acceptable. I don't want to have to fit into that" (Quart, 2008).

Depending on what changes trans people have made to their bodies, they may still be able to fulfill some of the physiological functions of their natal sex. Thomas Beatie is a trans man who underwent double mastectomy in 2002 and is legally male; he entered a heterosexual marriage in 2003. Beatie attracted a great deal of media attention in 2008 when he became pregnant by artificial insemination. His first pregnancy was not successful, but he later gave birth to three children. In 2012 he had a metoidioplasty. In the same year he and his wife began divorce proceeding, but the process was interrupted by a Superior Court judge in their state (Arizona), who questioned whether Beatie was legally male. (Arizona didn't grant same-sex divorces at the time.) Eventually, in 2014, a higher court ruled that Beatie was legally male and allowed the divorce to proceed. Trans men who have not had mastectomies may be able to breastfeed infants (La Leche League, 2014).

Trans people struggle for awareness and acceptance

Transgender adults have had a difficult struggle to gain recognition as a group distinct from lesbians and gay men. Of course, the introduction of sex-reassignment surgery in the 1960s, with all the attendant publicity, did educate the public about the phenomenon of transexuality, but it also prompted most people to accept the medical model of transexuality, which, according to some gender theorists, was an attempt to erase trans people by hiding them in their newly assigned sexes (Bettcher, 2014).

One factor that has hampered the advancement of trans people is that they are relatively few in number. Thus, their political activism has generally taken place under the umbrella of the much larger gay rights movement. In fact, transgender persons participated in the "Stonewall Rebellion"—the 1969 riot in New York that was a key event in the modern gay rights movement (see Chapter 12).

Still, like bisexuals, trans people have fought to clarify their separate identity. In gay rights and gay pride marches and parades, trans people form their own contingents, and these events now usually carry names such as "March for Lesbian, Gay, Bisexual, and Transgender Equality." Transgender role models are beginning to appear, such as Victoria Kolakowski of California, who was elected as the nation's first transgender trial judge in 2010 (Sheridan, 2010). In academe, transgender professors, such as neuroscientist Ben Barres and ecologist Joan Roughgarden of Stanford University, offer role models for trans students.

Legal protections for transgender people lag behind those for gays and lesbians, even though the transgender population is at greater risk of violence and discrimination. Only 16 states have hate crime laws that cover transgender identity. However, the 2009 federal Hate Crimes Prevention Act does authorize federal prosecution of hate crimes based on gender identity, wherever they may occur.

An example of **transphobic** violence occurred in New York in 2013. Islan Nettles, a 21-year-old African-American who had recently identified as a trans woman, was walking on the street when she was approached by a young man who allegedly made a sexually suggestive remark to her. After realizing that she was transgender, he beat her senseless, and she died in the hospital a few days later. (Charges were dropped against one suspect, and the case remains open.) A recurrent theme in such crimes is

transphobia Hatred of transgender people.

(A)

(B)

Figure 4.21   Transgender teen Gwen Araujo of Newark, California (A), was beaten to death by four men who realized that she was anatomically male immediately after having sex with her. All four, three of whom are shown in (B), were convicted of murder or manslaughter.

Go to the
**Discovering
Human Sexuality**
Companion Website at
**sites.sinauer.com/
discoveringhumansexuality3e**
for activities, study questions,
quizzes, and other study aids.

that a heterosexual man becomes violent when he realizes that the object of his desire is not a biological woman; this suggests that the fear of being considered homosexual might underlie this kind of attack (**Figure 4.21**).

Growing up trans can be a very stressful experience, especially when there is a lack of family or community support. Attempted and completed suicides are common. A tragic example occurred in late 2014 when 17-year-old Leelah (born Joshua) Alcorn of Ohio threw herself under a freeway truck; in a note she blamed her death in part on her parents' refusal to accept her trans identity. Even so, that same year saw a great increase in public interest in, and support for, trans people, and there is reason to expect that their lives will become far more rewarding in the future—both to themselves and to the communities with whom they share their lives.

Summary

• Sex is usually determined by the sex chromosomes: The XX pattern causes female development, and the XY pattern causes male development. The key player in male development is the gene *SRY*, on the Y chromosome, which induces the embryo's genital ridges to become testes. In the absence of *SRY*, other genes induce the genital ridges to become ovaries.

• The male and female internal reproductive tracts develop from different precursors—the Wolffian and Müllerian ducts. In XY embryos, the testes secrete anti-Müllerian hormone (AMH), which causes the Müllerian ducts to regress, and androgens, which cause the Wolffian ducts to develop further and produce the male internal anatomy. In XY embryos lacking functional androgen receptors (a condition called androgen insensitivity syndrome), neither the male nor the female reproductive

tract develops. In XX embryos (normal females), the lack of AMH allows the Müllerian ducts to develop further, and the lack of androgens allows the Wolffian ducts to regress, producing the female internal anatomy.

• The external genitalia of the two sexes develop from common precursors. The urethral folds give rise to the inner labia in females and to the shaft of the penis in males. The genital swellings give rise to the outer labia in females and the scrotum in males. The genital tubercle forms the external portion of the clitoris in females and the glans of the penis in males. Male-typical development of the external genitalia requires the presence of testosterone and its conversion to 5α-dihydrotestosterone (DHT). In female fetuses that are exposed to high levels of androgens (as in congenital adrenal hyperplasia), the external genitalia are partially masculinized.

(continued)

Summary (continued)

- Male and female brains differ in structure, chemistry, and function. Some sexual differentiation of the brain occurs prenatally—high levels of androgens drive male-typical brain development, and low levels permit female-typical development. At puberty and thereafter, estrogens become important in establishing and maintaining female-typical body structure and function and also influence the brain.

- Disorders of sex development include chromosomal anomalies such as Klinefelter syndrome (XXY or XXXY) and Turner syndrome (XO), as well as genetic conditions that affect sex hormone production (e.g., congenital adrenal hyperplasia) or the body's sensitivity to sex hormones (e.g., androgen insensitivity syndrome). The proper treatment of children with ambiguous genitalia is a subject of controversy.

- Gender is the entire collection of mental traits that differ between women and men. Gender identity is a person's core sense of being a woman or a man. Gender role is the social expression of gender identity.

- On average, women outperform men in fine movements, verbal fluency, and some aspects of memory. Men outperform women in some cognitive traits, such as visuospatial skills. Personality differences include greater aggressiveness in men.

- In the area of sexuality, men and women differ in the strength of sex drive, interest in casual sex, interest in visual sexual stimuli, styles of jealousy, sexual orientation, interest in unusual forms of sexual expression, likelihood of engaging in coercive sex, sexual risk taking, willingness to pay for sex, frequency of masturbation, sexual response cycles, and the duration of reproductive capacity over the lifespan. Gender differences show considerable overlap between the sexes, and their significance is debated.

- Many gender differences arise early in life. Boys are typically more active and aggressive; girls are more interested in socializing. Boys and girls prefer different toys, and both prefer to associate with children of their same sex. Sex-specific interaction styles develop within these same-sex groups. Differences in other cognitive traits emerge gradually during childhood.

- Biological factors influence gender. These include genes that have evolved to help men and women improve their reproductive success. A role for sex hormones, especially during prenatal life, is illustrated by experiments on animals, by observation of humans affected by endrocrinological disorders, and by the study of anatomical markers (such as finger length ratios) that are correlated with gender traits.

- Socialization influences gender. This can happen through the innumerable rewards and punishments that children receive from parents and others. Imitation is also an important mediator of gender learning.

- A variety of cognitive developmental models stress the importance of children's thought processes in the development of gender. The understanding of gender develops sequentially in young children. In sexual script theory, gender learning involves the social negotiation of roles, such as those to be played by the man and woman in heterosexual relationships.

- Transgender people are those whose gender identity does not match their biological sex. Transexuals are transgender people who seek to change their anatomical sex: They may transition from male to female (M-to-F transexuals, or transexual women) or from female to male (F-to-M transexuals, or transexual men). The change may involve hormone treatment and sex-reassignment surgery, or just hormone treatment. All transexual women and some transexual men have a childhood history of strong gender nonconformity. They dislike the bodily changes induced by puberty and may attempt to conceal them. They are usually homosexual in the sense that they are sexually attracted to persons of the same birth sex as themselves. They usually do not identify as gay, however, but rather as heterosexual individuals of the sex with which they identify. Some transexual women are sexually attracted to women: Some or most of these individuals have a different developmental history, in which their desire to change sex develops out of a wish to incorporate the sex characteristics of their preferred sexual partners (women) into their own bodies (autogynephilia).

- Sex reassignment is a multistage process involving living for some period in the identity of the other sex, followed by hormonal treatments and, sometimes, sex-reassignment surgery. Genitals can be transformed into those of the other sex, but the procedure is expensive and, particularly in the case of F-to-M reassignment, yields imperfect results. Not all people who transition undergo genital surgery. Many transexual women and men are satisfied with the results of sex reassignment and are able to surmount the social and sexual challenges of post-transition life.

- Other transgender people do not seek sex reassignment for a variety of reasons. They may not fully identify with either sex. Some believe that sex reassignment would be unnecessary if society could be persuaded to abandon its obsession with the binary nature of gender. All transgender people face discrimination and the risk of violence, and many states fail to offer them specific protections.

Discussion Questions

1. Imagine that you have just become the proud parent of a newborn baby, but the nurse-midwife or pediatrician tells you that the baby has sexually ambiguous genitalia. Do you think this child would be stigmatized and disadvantaged? How? Consider what you would do and why.

2. If you or your partner was pregnant and learned that you would have a baby with Turner or Klinefelter syndrome, what would you decide to do about it? What would be the disadvantages of such abnormalities for your child? Argue the reasons for your choice.

3. Do you think that this chapter presents a balanced account of psychological differences between the sexes, and of research into the origins of these differences? If not, why? Did anything you read surprise you or cause you to reconsider your beliefs in this area?

4. How would you react if your young daughter insisted she was a boy and asked to go to school in boys' clothes? Would you mention the possibility that she might eventually be helped to change sex?

Web Resources

Accord Alliance (concerned with disorders of sex development / intersexuality) www.accordalliance.org

Androgen Insensitivity Syndrome Support Group www.aissg.org

Bodies Like Ours (support and information for people with atypical genitals) www.bodieslikeours.org/forums

CARES Foundation (congenital adrenal hyperplasia education and support) www.caresfoundation.org

Gender Inn (a bibliographic source for books, articles, and websites concerning gender) tinyurl.com/y73pk25

Klinefelter Syndrome Information and Support www.klinefeltersyndrome.org

National Center for Transgender Equality www.transequality.org

National Institute of Child Health and Human Development—Turner Syndrome turners.nichd.nih.gov

National Public Radio: Two families grapple with sons' gender preferences (radio program that describes two opposing therapeutic strategies for helping gender-dysphoric children) tinyurl.com/lxvdc5a

Turner Syndrome Society of the United States www.turnersyndrome.org

World Professional Association for Transgender Health www.wpath.org

Recommended Reading

Bailey, J. M. (2003). *The man who would be queen: The science of gender-bending and transsexualism*. Joseph Henry.

Baron-Cohen, S. (2004). *The essential difference: Male and female brains and the truth about autism*. Basic Books.

Beltz, A. M., Blakemore, J. E. O. & Berenbaum, S. A. (2013). Sex differences in brain and behavioral development. In: Rubenstein, J. & Rakic, P. (Eds.), *Neural circuit development and function in the brain* (Vol. 3 of *Comprehensive developmental neuroscience*). Academic.

Bertelloni, S. & Hiort, O. (Eds.). (2010). *New concepts for disorders of sex development*. Karger.

Bornstein, K. & Bergman, S. B. (2010). *Gender outlaws: The next generation*. Seal.

Colapinto, J. (2000). *As nature made him: The boy who was raised as a girl*. HarperCollins.

de Haan, M. & Johnson, M. H. (Eds.). (2003). *The cognitive neuroscience of development*. Psychology.

Drescher, J. & Byne, W. (Eds.). (2012). *Treating transgender children and adolescents: An interdisciplinary discussion*. Routledge.

Erickson-Schroth, L. (2014). *Trans bodies, trans selves: A resource for the transgender community*. Oxford University Press.

Eugenides, J. (2002). *Middlesex*. Farrar, Straus and Giroux. (Pulitzer Prize–winning novel about a person with 5α-reductase deficiency.)

Fausto-Sterling, A. (2000). *Sexing the body: Gender politics and the construction of sexuality*. Basic Books.

Fine, C. (2011). *Delusion of gender: How our minds, society, and neurosexism create difference*. Norton. (An anti-biological take on gender.)

Lippa, R. A. (2005). *Gender, nature, and nurture* (2nd ed.). Erlbaum.

Maccoby, E. (1998). *The two sexes: Growing up apart, coming together*. Harvard University Press.

Mayor, A. (2014). *The Amazons: Lives and legends of warrior women across the ancient world*. Princeton.

Nanda, S. (1999). *Gender diversity: Crosscultural variations*. Waveland.

Pfaff, D. (2010). *Man and woman: An inside story*. Oxford University Press.

Sax, L. (2005). *Why gender matters: What parents and teachers need to know about the emerging science of sex differences*. Doubleday.

Chapter 5

Psyche, a beautiful princess, wins the heart of Cupid, the god of desire and attraction, in this 18th century statue by Antonio Canova.

Attraction, Arousal, and Response

In sex, one thing leads to another. To be more specific, a predictable sequence of mental and bodily processes characterizes sexual interactions. In this chapter we present these stages as follows: Sexual attraction to a potential sex partner, psychological sexual arousal, and the physiological changes in the genitals—the sexual response cycle—that precede and accompany sexual behavior. This sequence is not universal. Sometimes people engage in sex without prior attraction or arousal, for example, and only become aroused as a consequence of their behavior. But the three sequential stages provide a useful story line or framework for discussing the key processes underlying sexuality.

To describe the basic structure of this sexual story line, we must postpone consideration of many issues that relate to it in important ways: how we negotiate sexual interactions, how we enter into sexual relationships, what specific forms of sexual contact we engage in, and how the aging process influences our sexual psychology and performance. What is left, however, is the central core of sex: wanting it, and getting it.

Figure 5.1 Human faces offer astonishing diversity, and no two people would place them in the same order of attractiveness. Yet there do seem to be some universals that affect people's judgment.

Sexual Attraction: It Takes Two

Sexual attraction is an erotically charged orientation toward a specific other person. The attraction may be calm and controlled ("He is a really charming guy"), or it may be madly impetuous ("If I don't have sex with her in the next 5 minutes, there is no God"). It may be felt at first meeting, or it may build over time. The attraction may be mutual, or it may be one-way. It may be accompanied by feelings of love and commitment, or not.

Sexual attraction is different from simple *liking*. In fact, we may be sexually attracted to people we dislike or to people we don't know well enough to like or dislike. Sexual attraction is also different from the judgment that a person is attractive. A heterosexual woman might judge that another woman is attractive, for example, but not be sexually attracted to her. Sexual attraction is also different from mate choice: We may choose to cohabit with someone, marry someone, or even have sex with someone for entirely nonsexual reasons. And sexual attraction is different, at least in part, from romantic love.

Because sexual attraction involves two people, we may approach it in two ways. First, we may ask, what causes a person to be attractive? Second, we may ask, what causes a person to experience attraction? Both questions are important, but we begin with the former. We are asking, essentially, what is beauty?

Beauty is not entirely in the eye of the beholder

If we define beauty as the attributes that combine to make a person sexually attractive, then beauty can include many things, ranging from physical traits such as appearance, voice quality, and odor to nonphysical attributes such as personality, behavior, and social circumstances. These nonphysical attributes are decisive in the long run, but our looks are usually the first cues to attractiveness that are available to others. We therefore consider physical appearance before other aspects of beauty (**Figure 5.1**).

The saying "Beauty lies in the eye of the beholder" suggests that everything is subjective or idiosyncratic—that no objective characteristics make a person more or less attractive to others. In fact, however, psychologists have found a considerable degree of consensus on the topic of beauty. They have identified certain characteristics that influence the perceived attractiveness of faces and other physical features, no matter who is doing the judging.

Figure 5.2   The face that changes sex Seven frames from a movie of a face that gradually morphs from hypermasculine (left) through androgynous (center) to hyperfeminine (right). (From Johnston et al., 2001.)

MASCULINITY–FEMININITY   The faces of women and men differ in consistent ways that allow one to judge a person's sex, with fair accuracy, from facial appearance alone—even without obvious clues such as beards or hairstyles. Women typically have fuller lips and larger eyes than men, for example, while men have wider jaws and noses and larger chins. These sex differences are small during childhood but increase greatly at puberty under the influence of sex hormones. They are therefore indicators of reproductive maturity and fertility, so that we would logically expect them to influence judgments of attractiveness. The differences are most obvious in computer-generated images derived from large numbers of actual women's and men's faces (**Figure 5.2**).

When viewers are asked to adjust the masculinity–femininity of a computer-generated female face to make it look most attractive, they do indeed move the image in the direction of the "hyperfeminine" face. This is true regardless of whether the viewer is male or female and regardless of whether the images are derived from the faces of European, African, or Asian women (Little et al., 2011). It's no wonder, then, that women who want to look attractive use cosmetics in ways that increase their apparent femininity and exaggerate their differences from male faces.

With men's faces, it's more complicated. Extremely masculine faces, such as the leftmost image in Figure 5.2, may be very attractive, but they may also be judged as cold or unkind, which reduces their attractiveness (Perrett et al., 1998). Thus, studies in which viewers are asked to adjust the masculinity–femininity of a computer-generated male face have yielded inconsistent results (Johnston et al., 2001; Perrett, 2010), and the overall relevance of this dimension of male attractiveness is probably not great. One consistent finding, however, is that women's attraction to masculine-looking faces varies around their menstrual cycle; we will discuss this finding later.

Figure 5.3   Babyfacedness increases attractiveness. A face generated by computer-averaging the faces of 64 adult women (A) and the same face morphed 30% of the distance to an averaged face of young children (B). The image in B was preferred by most viewers. (C) Supermodel Gemma Ward has babyfaced features. (A and B courtesy of Martin Gruendl.)

BABYFACEDNESS   We just mentioned that traits indicative of passage through puberty increase the attractiveness of women's faces. Thus, you wouldn't expect that making an adult woman's face more like a young child's would increase her attractiveness, but that is exactly what a research group at the University of Regensburg, in Germany, has reported (Braun et al., 2001). The researchers first quantified the facial proportions of children: They computer-averaged images of the faces of a number of actual 4- to 6-year-old children and then measured the layout of facial features on this averaged image. Then they generated an image of an adult woman's face by averaging images of the faces of 64 actual women (**Figure 5.3A**). This adult face was judged as quite attractive, but its

(A)   (B)   (C)

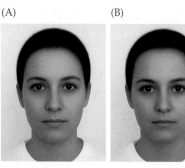

0%   30%
Babyfacedness (percentage)

(A) (B)

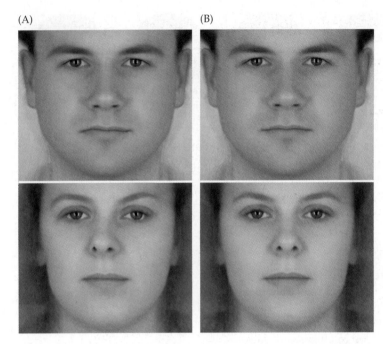

Figure 5.4 Symmetry increases attractiveness. (A) Naturally asymmetrical male and female faces. (B) The same faces manipulated to make them symmetrical. Most viewers rate the symmetrical faces as more attractive, even though they are not generally aware that symmetry is being adjusted. (From Perrett et al., 1999.)

attractiveness increased as it was progressively morphed toward the standard childlike face. In the example shown in the figure, viewers found that a 30% admixture of "babyfacedness" produced the most attractive face (**Figure 5.3B**). Well-known supermodels often have "babyfaced" features (**Figure 5.3C**). It may be that these features are attractive because they evoke the positive feelings that most people have toward young children.

SYMMETRY Animals look for symmetry in their mates. So do humans, both in industrialized countries and in hunter-gatherer societies (Little et al., 2007). The more symmetrical a person's face, the more attractive, sexy, and healthy that person seems to others (Fink et al., 2006; Perrett, 2010) (**Figure 5.4**). Symmetry raises the attractiveness of the remainder of the body, too (Brown et al., 2008). This preference for symmetrical features is not present in young children but develops between 5 and 9 years of age (Vingilis-Jaremko & Maurer, 2013).

Evolutionary psychologists have proposed a reason to explain why symmetrical features are more attractive than asymmetrical ones (Little et al., 2011). Because a single genetic program guides the development of the left and right sides of the body, asymmetrical features may develop if the person's genetic make-up is less robust or if the genetic program is derailed in some way, such as by an infection. Some studies do report that people with asymmetrical features are more likely to suffer from a variety of disorders, but others have failed to observe such an association, especially with regard to the slight asymmetries that are commonly present in the general population (Pound et al., 2014).

Thus, it is plausible that evolution has given us the ability to detect marked asymmetries on account of a connection to ill-health, but the influence of common, slight asymmetries on attractiveness may have some other cause. Asymmetrical structures require greater perceptual work to process and encode into memory, and it could be this extra work that makes them less attractive (Ryan, 1998). This could also explain why we find symmetry attractive in nonliving things, such as snowflakes.

Culture influences the attractiveness of bodies

Men's and women's bodies are more distinct than are men's and women's faces. Like facial attractiveness, bodily attractiveness is often a matter of being near one or the other extreme of the masculine–feminine continuum. Thus, body parts that differ relatively little between the sexes, such as the hands and feet, also contribute relatively little to judgments of attractiveness. In general, then, it is likely that the attractiveness of a body signals information about its sexual differentiation under the influence of sex hormones, and hence about its fertility, strength, health, and other traits important for reproduction. Nevertheless, criteria for bodily beauty are not nearly as universal as one might imagine.

Slimness–fatness is an important dimension influencing judgments of attractiveness, especially when women's attractiveness is being judged (by women or by men). This dimension is usually expressed as the body mass index (BMI—calculators can be found online.) The "healthy" BMI range has been defined as 18.5 to 25, but the median BMI in the contemporary United States is near the top of this range (about

24.5 for women in their 20s), so by this standard nearly half of U.S. women in this age range are over-weight (BMI of 25 to 30) or obese (BMI > 30).

In a number of studies, male and female rat-ers have been asked to judge the attractiveness of women varying in BMI. (They are shown photos of bodies only, without the faces.) Subjects in the United States and other Western countries prefer women with BMIs around 18 to 22, that is, well below average and near the low end of the normal range. On the basis of these findings, one might be tempted to conclude that slimness is universally preferred, but this is not the case. For one thing, during certain periods in Western history, such as the 17th century, fatness was considered much more attractive than it is now.

Cross-cultural studies have also demonstrated quite diverse preferences. One revealing study was done by a British–South African group of research-ers (Tovee et al., 2006). They confirmed that white Britons prefer women with BMIs around 20 and that attractiveness falls off steadily both below and above that value (**Figure 5.5**). But when judging the same images, rural Zulus in South Africa gave high ratings to women with BMIs of 20 and above, with no suggestion of a falloff in attractiveness up to a BMI of at least 40. Only on the lower side of 20 was there a rapid reduction in attractiveness.

The researchers added a third group of subjects, namely South African Zulus who had migrated to the United Kingdom within the previous 18 months. As shown in the figure, these subjects quickly changed their preferences, exhibiting much the same dislike of fuller-bodied women as is typical of native Britons. In other words, this study suggested that BMI preferences, at least over the upper part of the range, are influenced by socialization.

It may be that the low attractiveness ratings for very underweight women *are* universal, however. This would make sense in evolutionary terms, because severely underweight women are unlikely to be fertile.

Ample-bodied women were admired in 17th-century Europe, as illustrated in this painting, *The Judgment of Paris* by Peter Paul Rubens.

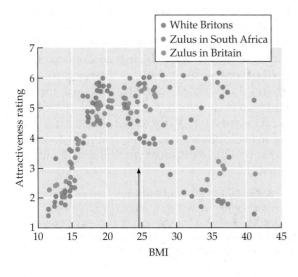

Figure 5.5   Body mass index and beauty This fig-ure plots the BMI and beauty of 50 women (each dot within a category represents one woman) as rated by three mixed-sex groups of raters: white Britons (red), Zulus in South Africa (blue), and Zulus within 18 months of migrating to Britain (green). After migrating to Britain, the Zulus' preferences shifted toward the typical West-ern pattern: Their attraction to large-bodied women decreased. The vertical arrow shows the median BMI for U.S. women in their 20s. (After Tovee et al., 2006.)

waist-to-hip ratio (WHR)
The ratio of the circumference of the body at the waist to the circumference at the hip.

Another measure related to BMI is the **waist-to-hip ratio** (**WHR**), which is the circumference of the body at the waist divided by the circumference at the hip. It could be thought of as a simple estimator of curvaceousness. Women with a WHR of about 0.7 are judged more attractive than women with lower or higher WHRs, whereas the most attractive WHR in men is about 0.9 (Singh, 2002; Dixson et al., 2011) (**Figure 5.6**). In other words, a more hourglass-like form is preferred in women and a more tubular form is preferred in men.

Female breasts are obviously sexually attractive to many men, and eye-tracking studies have shown that men spend a disproportionate amount of time looking at the breast region of female figures, whether they are clothed or unclothed (Suschinsky et al., 2007; Dixson et al., 2011). According to a large online survey by researchers at UCLA and California State University, Los Angeles, most women are dissatisfied with their own breasts (too small, large, pendulous, or asymmetrical), but most heterosexually partnered men are satisfied with their partners' breasts (Frederick et al., 2008). This is an example of a general tendency for people to underrate their own attractiveness—something that causes a great deal of needless anxiety.

As with body mass index, culture has a considerable influence on the assessment of attractiveness of female breasts. Some human cultures place little emphasis on them as sexually attractive features and do not require women to cover them. This is the case in the traditional culture of Mali (in West Africa), for example (Dettwyler, 1994). In non-Western cultures that do consider the breasts sexually attractive, the preferred appearance may range from small and upright to long and pendulous (Ford & Beach, 1951).

People generally find faces of individuals from their own ethnic group more attractive than faces from other groups—a finding that almost certainly reflects an influence of familiarity and culture. However, individuals in different cultures rely on similar cues to attractiveness. Furthermore, people make consistent judgments of faces from other cultures. The way that Caucasians rank the attractiveness of Japanese faces, for example, is similar to the way that Japanese rank those same faces (Perrett et al., 1994). In other words, the judgment of beauty depends on a blend of cultural and universal factors.

From the general appearance of a person's face and body, we can assess their age, which is an important criterion for attractiveness in women, at least according to men. When judging women solely by physical appearance, straight men find women most attractive in their late teen years and decreasingly so thereafter (Buss, 2011). This makes sense in evolutionary terms because young women are most fertile and have the most years ahead to nurture

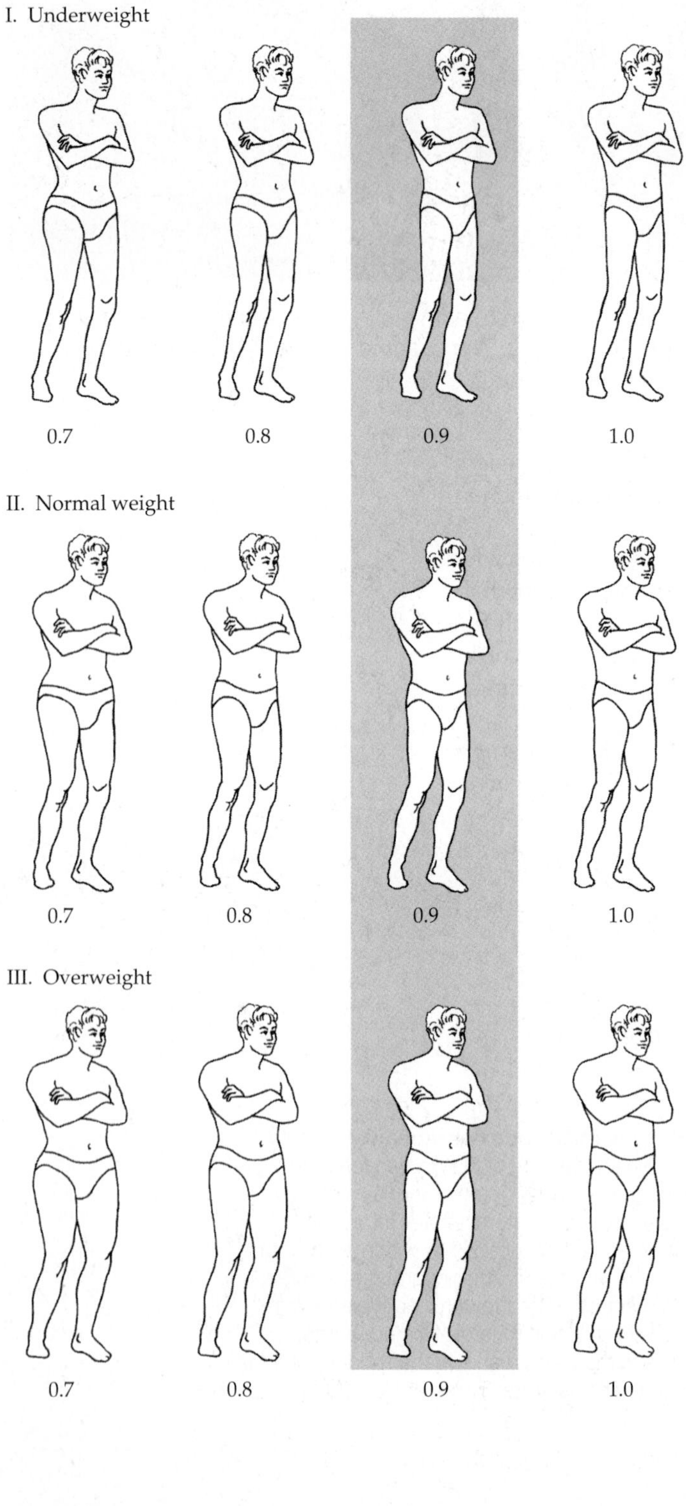

I. Underweight

0.7   0.8   0.9   1.0

II. Normal weight

0.7   0.8   0.9   1.0

III. Overweight

0.7   0.8   0.9   1.0

Figure 5.6   Waist-to-hip ratio and attractiveness Women are most attracted to men with a waist-to-hip ratio (WHR) of 0.9 (shaded row); this is true whether men are underweight (row I), normal weight (row II), or overweight (row III). Men are most attracted to women with a WHR of about 0.7.

Figure 5.7   Improving on nature Once flat-chested, singer and television personality Katie Price (a.k.a. Jordan) shows off some major enhancements.

children. Straight women's judgments of men's physical attractiveness do not vary nearly so much with the men's age, but young women generally prefer men who are somewhat older than themselves. The age preferences of gay people are similar to those of their heterosexual peers (Silverthorne & Quinsey, 2000).

A striking real-world illustration of the sex difference in age preference comes from an analysis of messaging behavior on the OkCupid dating website (Rudder, 2010): In their early 20s, men typically message women who are about 2 years younger than themselves, whereas women in that age group tend to message men who are about 2 years older than themselves. In the older age ranges the 2-year age difference increases for men (they seek women who are more than 2 years younger than themselves), whereas it decreases and eventually disappears for women (they message men who are about the same age as themselves).

The cosmetic enhancements that people use to increase their own attractiveness often involve the exaggeration of sexually differentiated traits. Breast augmentation is a well-known example in Western society (**Figure 5.7**).

Very little research has been done into the physical features that non-heterosexual women and men use to judge attractiveness. It would be interesting, for example, to know whether bisexual people use a single set of criteria to rate the physical attractiveness of potential partners regardless of their sex, or whether they use completely distinct sets of criteria when assessing men and when assessing women. We suspect that the latter alternative is closer to the truth, but we're not aware of any quantitative studies bearing on the question. Another question deserving of study is whether one can classify gay or lesbian people into distinct subtypes based on the criteria they use for attractiveness.

It's worth stressing that the process of judging visual attractiveness is a largely *unconscious* process. When men are asked to choose the more attractive of two women's faces, for example, and then asked why they found that face more attractive, they will give detailed, persuasive reasons for their choice, as if they had carefully thought the matter through before choosing. But if they are deceived into thinking that the face they *rejected* was the one they chose, they will usually fail to notice the deception and will give equally detailed and persuasive reasons why *that* face was the more attractive one (Johansson et al., 2005). This phenomenon has been called "choice blindness." It's as if consciousness simply provides a plausible explanation for choices that are made at a much deeper level of the mind.

Attractiveness involves senses besides vision

Although we tend to rely on our eyes in assessing the physical attractiveness of potential partners, especially in the first moments of meeting them, other senses also play a role. If that were not true, blind people could not experience sexual attraction, but they do. Here's how one blind person expressed it on an online bulletin board: "If anything I think being blind has made me kinkier and more intense as you touch a lot more. Being blind, I would have to say sex is better and deeper, feeling your way around a body you get to know everywhere."

 Besides touch, hearing and smell may also be important. Men's voices generally have deeper pitch than those of women, reflecting the sexual differentiation of the larynx at puberty. Women find men with deep voices more attractive than those with higher-pitched voices, and in hunter-gatherer societies fertile women bestow their favors more readily on deep-voiced men (Apicella et al., 2007). Men, on the other hand, prefer women's voices that have higher pitch than average (Feinberg et al.,

2008). These are further examples of sexually differentiated traits being particularly important criteria for physical attractiveness.

Everyone knows that body odor can have a strong influence on a person's attractiveness. Some researchers, however, have gone further, claiming that specific sex pheromones in women and men influence sexual arousal through unconscious olfactory mechanisms. This topic is highly controversial (**Box 5.1**).

To summarize the research on physical attractiveness, we can say that there are some respects in which beauty is not in the eye of the beholder but, rather, reflects objective, universal attributes of men and women. The attributes that make for attractiveness give some indication of a person's health, strength, fertility, or genetic fitness. How significant these traits are in the modern world may vary a great deal: Physical strength is obviously not as important as it was hundreds or thousands of years ago, for example, so finding bulging pecs attractive could be thought of as a pointless holdover from earlier times.

Yet attractiveness is also associated with traits that are still of great importance in our contemporary world, which may mean that attending to physical attractiveness is about more than simply appreciating eye candy. There is a robust association—in both women and men—between attractiveness and several measures of physical and mental health (Nedelec & Beaver, 2014). And according to two very large longitudinal studies, attractiveness is associated with an approximately 10-point advantage in IQ (Kanazawa, 2011). Still, let's keep this in proportion: One can probably assess a person's intelligence far more reliably in other ways, such as by having a conversation.

Behavior and personality influence sexual attractiveness

All this talk of physical beauty can have a downside because it can provoke anxiety among people who think that their faces or bodies fall short of the standards necessary to attract a desirable partner. Yet this kind of anxiety is seldom justified. For one thing, as already mentioned, people tend to underestimate their own physical attractiveness. For another, they can improve their attractiveness by means of all the technologies—from cosmetics to plastic surgery—that human ingenuity has devised. And most important, they can influence their attractiveness through their behavior.

In fact, we may speak of a behavioral or psychological beauty that can be independent of physical beauty. Behavior and personality tend to influence attractiveness more slowly than appearance does, because they are not so immediately apparent. But even in a still photograph, behavior matters: Smiling faces are judged to be more attractive than those with neutral expressions, at least when the faces are looking directly at the observer (Jones et al., 2006).

Another simple behavior affecting attractiveness is gait (manner of walking or running). Because they have wider hips, women rotate and tilt their hips more than men when walking, and they also take shorter strides. Wearing high heels forces women to exaggerate or "hyperfeminize" these behavioral traits. Psychologists at the University of Portsmouth, in England, created "point-light displays" of women walking—that is, computer screen displays that showed only the positions of LED lights attached to the women's joints. The displays created from women walking in high heels were judged by both women and men to be much more attractive than those from the same women in flat shoes (Morris et al., 2013).

Presumably, sexual attractiveness influences the desirability of partners for casual encounters or dating relationships more than it does for longer-term, live-in relationships such as marriage, because long-term relationships involve so much more than sex. To get some insight into the spectrum of traits that influence sexual attractiveness, therefore, we do best to look at studies that have questioned men and women about the traits they would value in a casual or short-term sex partner, or that study interactions in social situations such as parties. Most such studies report that physical appearance

---

FAQ

I'm stepping out to snare a man. Any tips from psychology?

Wear red. This boosts a woman's attractiveness by 1.25 points on a 7-point scale, compared with any other color of clothing (Elliott & Niesta, 2008).

Box 5.1 Controversies

Sex Pheromones

"BE IRRESISTIBLE" yell the online ads. Whether you're a man or a woman and whether you're straight, gay, or transgender, there's a pheromone product custom-designed for you. But what's in those pricey little bottles, and do they work?

Sex pheromones are substances released by an animal that influence the sexual behavior or physiological state of other individuals of the same species. They were first identified in insects, in which they function as powerful come-hither signals, luring prospective mates from blocks away. Many nonhuman mammals also release sex pheromones (Liberles, 2014). And many mammals possess a special sense organ within the nose, the **vomeronasal organ** (**VNO**), which is specialized for the detection of pheromones. The receptor cells in the VNO possess a suite of receptor molecules not found in the regular olfactory mucosa, and nerves run from this organ to parts of the brain that are known to be involved in sexual behavior. When a rodent's VNO is blocked, its sex life is seriously disrupted. And when male mice are genetically modified to lack a key protein in the VNO, they fail to distinguish males from females and engage in sexual behavior with both (Stowers et al., 2002).

In the 1990s researchers at the University of Utah claimed to have identified a VNO in humans, and to have isolated two pheromones that activated it—one in men and one in women (Monti-Bloch et al., 1998). These substances became the active ingredients in the Erox Corporation's Realm perfumes. Other companies quickly jumped in with their own pheromone products.

Unfortunately, it turns out that the human VNO, if it exists at all, is nonfunctional, contains no receptors, and is not connected to the brain. The genes encoding the VNO receptor molecules are mutated and silent. In other words, the human VNO is at most a useless vestige of a system that used to be functional in our distant nonhuman ancestors (Trotier, 2011).

All is not lost for pheromone believers, however. In rodents, some pheromone effects are mediated by the regular olfactory organ rather than by the VNO (Liberles, 2014). It has been suggested that this might be the case in humans too. There have been reports that certain human-derived compounds are capable of influencing mood—enhancing a sense of well-being, for example. These substances include androstadienone (AND), a steroid derivative found in men's armpit sweat, and estratetraenol (EST), found in women's urine.

A Swedish research group exposed male and female volunteers to air containing one or the other of these compounds while the volunteers' brain activity was imaged with a PET scanner. Brain activity evoked by the two substances was sex specific: For example, AND evoked activity in the anterior

Pharmaceutical company technicians examine flasks containing substances thought to be sex pheromones.

hypothalamus in women but not men, whereas with EST it was the reverse. Even more intriguingly, Savic's group reported that when gay men or women were exposed to these compounds, their patterns of brain activity were similar to those of heterosexual persons of the other sex: The anterior hypothalamus of gay men lit up in response to AND, for example, like that of straight women (Savic et al., 2005).

In a more recent study, a Chinese research group had volunteers watch computer-generated displays of walking figures whose sex was ambiguous (Zhou et al., 2014). When heterosexual female subjects (and gay male subjects) were subconsciously exposed to AND, they were biased toward judging the figures to be men; when heterosexual male subjects were subconsciously exposed to EST, they were biased toward judging the figures to be women. (Bisexual and lesbian women showed less clear effects.)

These and other studies suggest that sex-specific volatile substances do affect brain function and perception, and do so differently in heterosexual men and women, and in straight and gay people. Still, there is reason for caution in interpreting such findings in terms of pheromones. For one thing, both these studies used very high concentrations of AND and EST—higher than are likely be experienced in real life (Marazziti et al., 2011). Also no one as yet has observed in humans the kinds of automatic sexual responses that are triggered by pheromones in some nonhuman species. The question of whether true human sex pheromones exist remains largely unanswered.

sex pheromones   Chemical signals released by an animal that influence the sexual behavior or physiological state of other individuals of the same species.

vomeronasal organ (VNO)   A special sense organ within the nose that many mammals possess, which is specialized for the detection of pheromones.

is the most important criterion used by both men and women in judging attractiveness and initiating contacts (Hatfield et al., 2012), but many personality traits are also highly rated, including trustworthiness, warmth, and a sense of humor (Regan et al., 2000). These are traits that are likely to be important in any relationship. It may be that even when people are "hooking up," they are still unconsciously evaluating the person they are hooking up with as a potential long-term partner (Sprecher & Regan, 2002). In any event, general likability traits seem to intensify sexual attraction.

To fully understand behavioral beauty, it is necessary to go beyond surveys and use tests that are closer to real-life situations. Both women and men say that they value a sense of humor in their sex partners, for example, but what do they actually mean by that? To find out, one group of psychologists presented subjects with photos of people along with humorous or nonhumorous statements that those people had supposedly written. For women subjects, the humorous statements increased the attractiveness of the people in the photos, as expected. For men, however, the humor had no such effect (Bressler & Balshine, 2006).

Why then do men say that they value a sense of humor in their partners? A follow-up study revealed the reason (Bressler et al., 2006). Male subjects find their partners sexually attractive when they respond with laughter to the *subjects'* jokes, not when they make their own jokes. Subjects labeled their partners' appreciation of their wit a "sense of humor." In a potentially sexual situation, laughter often signals sexual receptivity; thus, when men say they find a "sense of humor" attractive, they might simply mean that they are glad when a sexual situation shows signs of moving toward actual sex. Nevertheless, humorous interactions between potential sex partners are an indication that they are interested in a relationship beyond a sexual encounter (Li et al., 2009).

In one study, men and women were asked to list desirable characteristics in romantic partners and then were invited to a speed-dating event (an event in which people meet a large number of potential partners in a sequence of brief one-on-one conversations). The people who the subjects chose for future dating were not those whose characteristics matched the subjects' previously stated preferences (Eastwick & Finkel, 2008). For example, a woman who rated high earnings as the most important criterion for selecting a romantic partner actually chose the lowest earner of the men she talked with at the event. Thus, people might not have a clear idea of what they are looking for in a sex partner until they actually meet someone who appeals to them—another example of the limited role of conscious processes in sexual attraction. What people think they want does not necessarily predict what they actually choose.

At speed-dating events, people's choices may not be based on conscious criteria.

It has been reported over and over again that men are more interested than women in the physical attractiveness of their prospective sex partners, whereas women are more interested than men in their partners' wealth, social status, or intelligence (Shackelford et al., 2005; Li et al., 2011). Regarding physical attractiveness, an informative study was conducted by Andrea Meltzer of Southern Methodist University and several colleagues (Meltzer et al., 2014). Meltzer's group recruited newlywed heterosexual couples, took photographs of both partners, and had their facial attractiveness rated by a panel of judges. Then all the subjects rated their satisfaction with their marriages, and they did so again every 6 months for 4 years. The husbands who had more attractive wives were more satisfied with their marriages, and this was true both initially and throughout the 4-year follow-up. The wives' satisfaction with their marriages, on the other hand, bore no relationship to their husbands' attractiveness at any time. (Intriguingly, the wives' satisfaction did correlate with *their own* attractiveness—why do you think this might be?) The researchers repeated the study at three other locations in the United States, with the same results. Thus, regardless of whether we think this is right or fair, physical attractiveness does predict marital satisfaction over the long term, but it's only the women's attractiveness that matters.

Familiarity may increase or decrease attraction

How attractive we find people (and things in general) is strongly influenced by our prior experience, but this influence can work in either direction, making people and things more attractive or less attractive. In general, mere exposure to any stimulus— whether it be the music of a particular composer or a particular kind of food—makes us like that stimulus better when we encounter it again, even if we don't remember having experienced it before. The same is true of faces: The mere fact of having seen a face before makes us judge it as more attractive than if we are seeing it for the first time (Peskin & Newell, 2004).

One face we see a lot of is our own, so are we especially attracted to our own face or to faces like our own? That's a tricky question to answer. For one thing, most of us are heterosexual, so our faces are the wrong sex—for *sexual* attraction, at least. Also, recognizing one's own face carries a lot of cognitive baggage—thoughts that could interfere with judgments of attractiveness. A Scottish research group got around these problems in an ingenious way: They took photographs of their subjects, then changed the subjects' apparent sex by computer-morphing techniques (Penton-Voak et al., 1999). The subjects did not recognize themselves in their morphed "twins"; nevertheless, they found their "twins" more attractive than the "twins" of other subjects. This could be taken as support for the idea that familiarity contributes to attractiveness.

The influence of familiarity also helps explain an intriguing observation, which is that composite faces generated by averaging a considerable number of individual faces are rated as more attractive than any of the individuals that contributed to the composite (Langlois & Roggman, 1990; Perrett, 2010) (**Figure 5.8**). This seems an improbable finding, because the phrase "average looking" is hardly a compliment. However, the attractiveness of such composites derives in large part from the fact

(A)   (B)

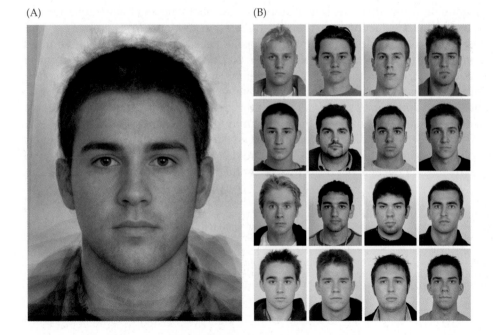

Figure 5.8 Attractiveness of computer-averaged faces The composite face (A) is rated more attractive than any of the 16 individual faces (B) from which it was derived. (Images supplied by faceresearch.org.)

Figure 5.9   A penile strain gauge The loop of rubber tubing contains mercury, whose electrical resistance increases as the loop is stretched by the erection of the penis.

that they emphasize features common to many faces, and are therefore very familiar. Indeed, if you look at the composite face in Figure 5.8 for long enough, the individual faces that contributed to the composite may begin to look more and more unusual.

In general, the more a couple interact with each other, the more they find each other attractive (Reis et al., 2011). In some circumstances, however, familiarity can *reduce* attractiveness. For example, being close to another child (such as a sibling) during early childhood makes it unlikely that one will find that person sexually attractive in adult life (De Smet et al., 2014). This seems to be an evolved mechanism whose adaptive value is that it reduces the likelihood of incestuous matings. Olfaction may be involved in this process, because opposite-sex siblings develop an aversion to the scent of each other's bodies (Weisfeld et al., 2003).

According to researchers at the University of Stirling, in Scotland, familiarity can affect attractiveness in opposite ways in women and men (Little et al., 2013). They had subjects assess the attractiveness and "sexiness" of an opposite-sex face at two different times. For women, the face was judged more attractive and sexier at the second viewing, an observation that is consistent with the generally positive effect of familiarity on attractiveness. But for men, the face was judged *less* attractive and *less* sexy at the second viewing. The researchers suggested that the men's liking for familiarity was overriden by their preference for sexual novelty and multiple partners.

In this connection, it's well known from animal experiments that males who have just mated will mate again more promptly if presented with a novel female. This is called the **Coolidge effect**.* There has never been a full-scale test of the Coolidge effect in humans, but here's something close: Researchers at the University of North Dakota (Plaud et al., 1997) recruited male psychology students for a study that involved listening to erotic tapes narrated by a female student. (As if further incentive were needed, the students received $20 and research credit.) The students' sexual arousal—monitored by a strain gauge placed around the penis (**Figure 5.9**)—declined if the same tapes were repeated, but their arousal remained high if new tapes were played. This negative effect of familiarity, known as **habituation**, lasted for several weeks at least. Unfortunately, we're not aware of a comparable study of female students.

Habituation also affects real sexual relationships: Both men and women derive less and less sexual satisfaction from their steady relationships as the duration of the relationship increases, and this effect is relationship specific; that is, it is not accounted for simply by the aging process (Klusmann, 2002). It's likely, however, that couples can counteract this habituation to some extent by introducing forms of novelty other than novel partners. These could include novel sex positions, novel practices such as bondage and dominance, sex in novel locations, and so on. In addition, other forms of satisfaction, such as emotional satisfaction, may counterbalance sexual habituation.

Although we don't discuss falling in love until Chapter 10, we should mention the obvious, which is that falling in love vastly increases the physical and behavioral attractiveness of the beloved. Physical flaws and distracting tics may suddenly seem

Coolidge effect   The revival of sexual arousal caused by the presence of a novel partner.

habituation   A psychological or physiological process that reduces a person's response to a stimulus or drug after repeated or prolonged exposure.

---

*This calls for a brief digression to explain how the phenomenon of arousal by a novel sex partner came to be associated with the name of Calvin Coolidge—yes, the 29th president of the United States. According to legend, President and Mrs. Coolidge were once touring a farm. Soon after their arrival they were taken off on separate tours. When Mrs. Coolidge passed the chicken pens, she paused to ask the man in charge if the rooster copulated more than once each day. "Dozens of times," was the response. "Please tell that to the President," Mrs. Coolidge requested. When the President passed the pens and was told about the roosters, he asked, "Same hen each time?" "Oh no, a different hen each time." "Please tell that to Mrs. Coolidge," said the President.

like special features that make the person unique—for as long as love lasts, at least. In this situation, beauty may truly lie in the eye of the beholder.

Perceived attractiveness varies around the menstrual cycle

Another way in which attractiveness is affected by factors intrinsic to the viewer has to do with the menstrual cycle. Two research groups have found that women prefer men with somewhat more masculine faces near the time of ovulation, when they are most likely to conceive, and prefer less masculine faces at other times (Penton-Voak & Perrett, 2000; Johnston et al., 2001). Similarly, women prefer deep-voiced men near the time of ovulation but not at other times (Hodges-Simeon et al., 2010).

These changes in women's perception of male attractiveness around the menstrual cycle have a tempting explanation in terms of evolutionary psychology: Women may be attracted to masculine-looking men during their fertile period because such men are most likely to possess genes conferring health and strength. During the rest of their cycle they may be drawn to other males, such as their regular partner (who, by the law of supply and demand, is not likely to be the most genetically favored male out there).

Women's sexual attractiveness to men also varies around the menstrual cycle: They are most attractive during the "fertile window" leading up to ovulation, when their estrogen levels are high, and less attractive after ovulation, when progesterone levels are high (Puts et al., 2013). The increased attractiveness during the fertile window is due to subtle changes in facial appearance, voice quality, and gait (Guéguen, 2012). Female lap dancers in gentlemen's clubs receive much higher tips near the time of ovulation than at any other time in their cycle (Miller et al., 2007) (**Figure 5.10**). Women also pay more attention to grooming, makeup, and clothing during their fertile window (Haselton et al., 2007). However, compared with the females of many other mammalian species, who may be totally unattractive and unreceptive to males outside of their fertile windows, the changes around women's menstrual cycles are relatively subtle.

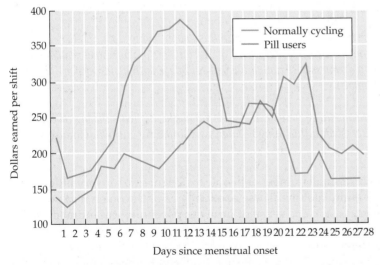

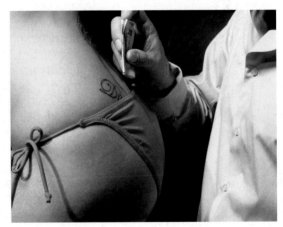

Figure 5.10 Lap dancers' earnings around the menstrual cycle. In normally cycling women, there is a broad peak in earnings between about 9 and 14 days after the onset of menstruation. This peak corresponds approximately to the fertile window leading up to ovulation. In women taking contraceptive pills, which often prevent ovulation, this peak is lower and occurs at a different time. (After Miller et al., 2007.)

Judgments of attractiveness change as people get to know each other

We have discussed evidence that there is some consensus in the way that attractiveness is judged: Certain individuals are judged to be very attractive by most people, and other individuals are judged to be less so. If that were the whole story, the most attractive people would use their looks and personalities to pair off with other very attractive people, and the rest of us would have to make do with less attractive mates. There would be a sorting out of the population into desirable couples, less desirable couples, and downright undesirable couples. But that's not how it works out, because consensus judgments give way to more person-specific judgments as people become more familiar with each other.

Psychologists Paul Eastwick and Lucy Hunt, of the University of Texas at Austin, have documented this process in a variety of ways (Eastwick & Hunt, 2014). In one study, they asked heterosexual students, at the beginning of the semester, to rate the opposite-sex students in the class on such variables as attractiveness, warmth, and potential for success. At this time, when the students had known each other only briefly, there was a considerable measure of agreement about the relative desirability of different students. Eastwick and Hunt repeated the survey at the end of the semester, by which time the students had had the opportunity to get to know each other much better. By this time, the consensus had largely broken down: There was very little correlation between the ratings made by different students. In fact, similar findings emerged from a variety of experiments: The more people knew each other, the more person-specific judgments dominated consensus judgments—with regard to not just physical attractiveness but a broad spectrum of personality traits. Thus, to the extent that intimate relationships develop between people who already know each other, people are not competing for the "hottest" partners so much as they are searching for their own individual soul mates.

Asexual women and men do not experience sexual attraction

All this talk of sexual attraction probably resonates with experiences you have had in your own life. But what do you make of these comments?

> I've never in my life had a dream or a sexual fantasy about being with another woman. So I can pretty much say that I have no lesbian sort of tendencies whatsoever. But I've never had a dream or a sexual fantasy about being with a man either—that I can ever, ever remember.

> I didn't find the act something I enjoyed. I guess I thought, "What's the big whoop? Why are they so interested in this thing?" I don't get anything out of it. (Prause & Graham, 2007)

For reasons unknown, a small number of people experience no (or very little) sexual attraction over their entire lifetime. These **asexual** men and women may still experience romantic attraction in the sense of desiring psychological intimacy with a specific partner, but they do not desire to express that intimacy in physical sex.

Asexuality is different from a conscious decision not to engage in sexual relationships (sexual abstinence). Nor does it stem from conditions such as autism that impair general social interactions, from a morbid fear of sex, from repressed homosexuality, or from problems in sexual performance such as erectile disorder. In fact, self-identified asexual men masturbate at about the same frequency as sexual men (Brotto et al., 2010). This suggests that the difference between asexual and sexual men lies not in the pleasure that genital stimulation and orgasm can provide, but in the

asexual Describes a person who does not experience sexual attraction.

Figure 5.11   Asexual pride Asexual women and men believe that asexuality is an alternative sexual orientation comparable to being lesbian, gay, etc. Hence the acronym LGBTA is sometimes used.

interpersonal aspect of sexual desire. There are some indications that asexuality may have a biological basis (Yule et al., 2014).

Self-identified asexual women and men say that their lack of sexual motivation has both positive and negative effects on their lives (Prause & Graham, 2007). On the plus side, they have more free time and are spared the complications of negotiating sexual relationships, sexually transmitted diseases, and unwanted pregnancies. On the negative side, they may worry about what is wrong with them, and they may have difficulty maintaining close relationships while rebuffing sexual advances. In fact, asexual people often do enter into sexual relationships, not for the sex but for the relationship. Some individuals do not usually experience sexual attraction, but may do so toward persons with whom they have established a romantic relationship. Such individuals are called **demisexual**.

The Asexual Visibility and Education Network (AVEN—see Web Resources at the end of this chapter) works to promote understanding and dispel myths about asexuality. AVEN promotes the recognition of asexuality as a legitimate sexual orientation (**Figure 5.11**).

This mention of "sexual orientation" reminds us that a person's sexual orientation, defined as the predisposition to experience sexual attraction to one sex or the other, or to both or neither, is the most dramatic example of an internal trait influencing sexual attraction. Because of its personal and social significance, however, we dedicate an entire chapter to it (see Chapter 12).

demisexual Experiencing sexual attraction only in the context of a strong emotional bond.

Sexual Arousal Has Multiple Roots

Sexual arousal is an acute psychological state of excitement marked by sexual feelings, attractions, or desires. In addition, it is a physiological state marked by changes in the genitalia. Psychological and physiological arousal usually go together, but not always. Sexual arousal may be triggered by external events, such as the appearance of a sexually attractive person, or by some particular aspect of that person, such as their sexually suggestive behavior or their nudity. However, arousal may come entirely from within, apparently triggered by nothing (this phenomenon is called spontaneous sexual arousal).

Fantasy is a common mode of sexual arousal

fantasy An imagined experience, sexual or otherwise.

Sexual **fantasy**—imagined sexual experiences during waking hours—is a route by which internal mental processes promote sexual arousal. The great majority of men and women engage in sexual fantasy, and people who place a positive value on fantasy are more sexually assertive—in terms of asking for sex, requesting contraceptive use, and refusing unwanted sex—than those who feel bad about such fantasies (Santos-Iglesias et al., 2013). Men engage in sexual fantasies more than women, but women increase the frequency of their sexual fantasies near the time of ovulation (Dawson et al., 2012). Fantasies may occur during regular activities, or they may accompany masturbation or partnered sex. The content of sexual fantasies varies a great deal, but common scenarios involve the kinds of behaviors people actually engage in or would like to engage in.

In your fantasies you can have sexual experiences that might not be advisable in real life.

Women's rape fantasies are a notable exception to this generalization: Something like half of all women experience erotic fantasies of being physically coerced into sex, something they would do anything to avoid in real life (Bivona & Critelli, 2009). Here is one woman's account of a rape fantasy:

This friend of mine comes over and immediately shoves me against the wall, pinning my hands over my head and kisses me passionately. I tell him to stop, that it's wrong and we can't do this. He says he doesn't care; he cannot wait another minute. His motivation is satisfying his own sexual hunger. While my hands are still pinned over my head he uses his other hand to tear off my clothes, not caring if they rip. We're both naked and he kisses me all over my body. I am begging him to stop, telling him it's wrong and that we can get caught any minute. He picks me up and screws me against the wall. At first it hurts but it feels so good that I can't help but enjoy it. When we're done he leaves because he knows my boyfriend is going to be over soon. I am torn between the pleasure and knowing that it's morally wrong. (Bivona & Critelli, 2009)

Several explanations for prevalence of rape fantasies have been proposed:

- By fantasizing that they have no choice in the matter, women avoid feeling guilty about the fantasy.
- Rape fantasies are really fantasies of sexual power: The woman is so irresistible that men cast aside their inhibitions against sexual violence.
- Rape fantasies are simply part of a general openness to a variety of sexual experiences.

According to a study by Jenny Bivona and colleagues at the University of North Texas, women who experience rape fantasies are relatively high in self-esteem, have more frequent sexual fantasies and a wider variety of fantasies, and have generally more positive attitudes toward sex than women who do not have rape fantasies (Bivona et al., 2012). Their findings suggest that rape fantasies are part of a general openness to experience, rather than fantasies of power or strategies to avoid guilt (**Figure 5.12**).

Another counterintuitive finding is that many women and men who identify as heterosexual have experienced homosexual fantasies (Joyal et al., 2014). Again, this may be part of a general openness to experience rather than a sign that these individuals are really bisexual or gay.

FAQ

How come I'm sexually aroused when I don't want to be?

Sexual arousal is not under conscious control, and it's common and harmless for arousal to occur in circumstances that seem inappropriate. Rarely, arousal may be so persistent as to constitute a disorder (see Chapter 14).

Figure 5.12   Rape fantasy This is *Pan and Selene* by the German artist Hans von Aachen (ca. 1605). Because the god Pan was part goat, there is a hint of bestiality as well as rape. Selene's ambivalence is suggested by the contrasting gestures of her left and right hands.

Arousal occurs in response to a partner

Being with an actual or potential sex partner in real life is a potent trigger to arousal, especially if that person is judged sexually attractive. In such a situation, both women and men are aroused by looking at the partner's face, but men also find looking at their partner's genital area arousing, as we mentioned in our discussion of nudity in Chapter 3. Men are more likely than women to report that they are highly aroused by watching their partner undress (Laumann et al., 1994). Even in totally nonsexual situations, in fact, men tend to look at people's crotches, but women don't (**Figure 5.13**).

Men

Women

Figure 5.13   Men look at crotches; women don't. These images were obtained by tracking the gaze of a large number of men and women while they viewed a photograph of baseball Hall of Famer George Brett. (Images courtesy of Kara Pernice, from Nielsen & Pernice, 2008.)

(A)

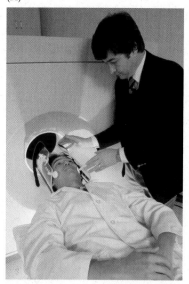

(B)

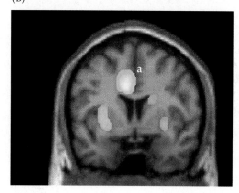

Figure 5.14   **The brain and sexual arousal** (A) Person undergoing a PET scan. The standing man is Michael Phelps, coinventor of the PET technology. (B) Brain activity specific to sexual arousal in men. This image shows the difference between scans taken during states with sexual arousal or without sexually arousal. The anterior cingulate area of the left hemisphere (a) is one of the most active regions during sexual arousal. The other active regions visible in this slice are components of the basal ganglia. (B courtesy of Jérôme Redouté.)

Arousal increases as flirting or other forms of sexual negotiation proceed (see Chapter 7). It increases even further as actual sexual contact is initiated, because sensory signals from the genitals and other body regions feed into the brain circuits that mediate arousal.

In order to identify the brain regions that are involved in sexual arousal, researchers have shown erotic film clips to subjects who are undergoing functional brain imaging (Stoleru et al., 2012). Among the brain regions that light up under these conditions is a region of the cerebral cortex named the anterior cingulate cortex (**Figure 5.14**). This region also lights up when people who are in love simply view a photo of their beloved (Bartels & Zeki, 2004) and when people are given euphoria-inducing drugs such as cocaine. Thus, it seems to be involved in the processing of "happy" states.

For reasons that are not well understood, sexual arousal appears to operate in a more specific manner in men than in women. Most men are aroused (psychologically and genitally) by erotic images that are appropriate to their sexual orientation; that is, straight men are aroused by images of women, and gay men are aroused by images of men. Most women, on the other hand, are aroused about equally by erotic images of women and men, although bisexual and lesbian women usually experience more arousal to images of women than of men (Chivers et al., 2007; Suschinsky et al., 2009; Chivers et al., 2010). Another study tracked the gaze of men and women while they were watching erotic heterosexual videos: The men looked mostly at the women, whereas the women looked about equally at the men and the women (Lykins et al., 2008). It may be that these differences reflect a greater fluidity of sexual orientation in women than in men—a topic we will discuss in Chapter 12.

Hormones influence sexual arousability

Do biological factors influence sexual arousal? The first thing one thinks of in this context is testosterone. A popular misconception is that this hormone influences sexual arousal—particularly in men—on a minute-by-minute or hour-by-hour basis. A man who is feeling "horny" (that is, who is experiencing an unfocused sense of sexual arousal and is motivated to find some way of satisfying it) might comment that he "can feel the testosterone flowing," or the like.

In reality, testosterone does not seem to have any short-term influence on the sexual feelings or behavior of either men or women. There is, however, an effect in the reverse direction: Sexual ideation and behavior increase testosterone levels in both sexes (Goldey & van Anders, 2011, 2012).

Testosterone does have a longer-term influence on our capacity to experience sexual arousal. The clearest connection between testosterone levels and sexual arousability is found in boys at around the time of puberty. Boys experience a great increase in sexual feelings and behaviors at the time of the puberty-associated rise in testosterone levels. Even more direct evidence comes from the study of boys with delayed puberty, who receive testosterone as part of their treatment. A group of such boys agreed to participate in a study in which their testosterone treatments were alternated with placebo treatments in a double-blind experimental design (that is, neither the patients nor their doctors knew who was receiving the real hormone). The researchers then studied the boys' sexual ideation and behavior over a period of 21 months. The boys thought more about sex and engaged in more sexual touching and "necking" during treatment with testosterone than with the placebo (Finkelstein et al., 1998). Still, the researchers concluded that social factors must also play a significant role in determining when adolescent boys begin to engage in sexual behavior (see Chapter 10).

Testosterone levels do influence sexual arousability in adult men; in fact, men who have a profound reduction in testosterone levels for any reason (**hypogonadal** men) suffer a gradual decline in sexual desire and activity, and this decline can be reversed by testosterone replacement therapy (Khera et al., 2011; Miner et al., 2013). Most young and middle-aged men seem to have levels of testosterone that are well above the "ceiling" for its effect on arousability, however. In other words, variation in the testosterone levels among these healthy men does not account for variation in their sexual feelings and behavior—or it does so to only a small degree. Testosterone is one of many substances used as **aphrodisiacs (Box 5.2)**, but it's doubtful that testosterone enhances sexual desire or performance in healthy men.

The situation in women is more complex because at least two groups of hormones are involved—androgens (including testosterone) and estrogens—and their levels vary around the menstrual cycle. Testosterone levels in women are quite low compared with those in men—roughly 10 to 20 times lower—so it is less likely that these levels are at a ceiling. In other words, there may be more potential for changes in testosterone levels to modulate sexual arousability in women than in men. In general, it appears that testosterone is more important than estrogens in influencing female sexual arousability, both in adolescent girls and in adult women, and it contributes to changes in women's sex drive and sexual activity at different times in the menstrual cycle (Caruso et al., 2014). Estrogens may have important indirect effects on sex, however: A reduction in estrogen levels, such as the decline that occurs at menopause, may lead to vaginal dryness and hence to painful intercourse, which in turn may cause a decline of interest in sex.

Conditioning may influence arousal

Classical, or **Pavlovian**, **conditioning** is the name given to a form of associative learning first studied by the Russian physiologist Ivan Pavlov in the early 20th century. Pavlov observed that dogs salivate automatically when they smell food (which is an "unconditioned stimulus," that is, one that naturally triggers a response). Pavlov began to ring a bell just before a dog was given food. Over time, the dog began to salivate at the sound of the bell alone—which had become a "conditioned stimulus" due to its repeated association with food.

Classical conditioning influences sexual arousal. For example, a research group based in the Netherlands conducted an experiment on women that was somewhat analogous to Pavlov's experiments on dogs (Both et al., 2008). In this case the unconditioned stimulus (analogous to food for a dog) was the application of a vibrator to the clitoris, which typically elicits sexual arousal. In conjunction with the vibratory stimulus, the women were shown a test photo of a heterosexual couple engaging in sex. (The photo was presented subliminally—that is, it was shown too briefly for the women to be conscious of it.) As a control, a different photo of heterosexual sex was shown while the vibrator was turned off. Later the test photo, unaccompanied by the vibrator, elicited more genital blood flow than did the control photo, suggesting that the association of the test photo with the vibrator turned the test photo into a conditioned stimulus.

In this study the conditioned stimulus (the photo of heterosexual sex that accompanied the genital stimulation) was in itself potentially arousing sexually; the effect of the conditioning was simply to make it more so. By extension, it's conceivable that the same process could explain how a person becomes sexually aroused by an

hypogonadal Producing insufficient levels of sex hormones.

aphrodisiac A substance believed to improve sexual performance, enhance sexual pleasure, or stimulate desire or love.

classical (or Pavlovian) conditioning A form of behavioral learning in which a novel stimulus is tied to a preexisting reflex.

Box 5.2 Biology of Sex

Aphrodisiacs and Drugs

Aphrodisiacs—named for the Greek goddess of love, Aphrodite—are substances intended to improve one's own sexual desire, sexual performance, or sexual pleasure or to cause someone else to respond to one's advances or to fall in love. In the last case, they may be called "love potions."

Traditionally, the belief that certain substances are aphrodisiacs has been based on magical thinking, especially the "law of similarity," which holds that "like produces like" (Frazer, 1922). Thus, aphrodisiacs have been derived from things that resemble penises (e.g., rhinoceros horns) or vulvas (e.g., oysters, see figure) or from sex organs or secondary sexual structures of animals, such as bull's testicles, the bacula (penis bones) of harp seals, and deer velvet (the skin covering the growing antlers of male deer). It's not likely that any of these substances work, unless simply by the power of suggestion.

Eastern medical practitioners have long claimed that ginseng root is useful in the treatment of sexual disorders. Controlled scientific studies have lent some support to this belief: Ginseng facilitates sexual behavior in male rats (Murphy et al., 1998), and studies report that it alleviates erectile disorder in some men (de Andrade et al., 2007) and improves sexual function in some menopausal women (Oh et al., 2010). Botanicals such as ginseng are poorly regulated and are not necessarily safe simply because they are natural products.

Another class of substances that is sometimes used as aphrodisiacs is recreational drugs. Here the issue is not so much whether they work—they often do—but their safety. The following are some examples:

- Amyl nitrite ("poppers") and related drugs such as butyl nitrite, which are administered by inhalation, produce a brief rush, during which time sexual feelings are enhanced and the pleasurable sensations of orgasm are intensified. It is dangerous to use these drugs in combination with Viagra or related drugs, since a life-threatening drop in blood pressure can result. Even used alone, they can have serious harmful effects in people with cardiovascular or breathing problems.

- Marijuana has different effects in different people. In some it induces relaxation that makes sex more enjoyable. In

Oysters' reputation as aphrodisiacs probably results from their slight resemblance to vulvas.

others it increases anxiety. In chronic users it may cause difficulty in experiencing orgasm (Johnson et al., 2004).

- Methamphetamine ("meth") is said to intensify the pleasure of sexual experiences. It is a highly addictive drug, however. With repeated use, it damages the brain's dopamine system. It eventually may make orgasm unattainable even with the help of the drug.

- Cocaine in moderate doses can enhance sexual sensations but in high doses or with chronic use can cause erectile difficulties as well as the inability to achieve orgasm.

- MDMA (Ecstasy) is a serotonin-related drug that can increase sexual arousal. With repeated use it can damage the brain's serotonin system. It can cause psychological problems such as depression and anxiety that persist after drug use ceases.

- Heroin and other opiates, when injected intravenously, produce a rush that users often describe as resembling orgasm, but these dangerous drugs lower the sex drive and impair sexual performance.

- Alcohol is a central nervous system depressant that can facilitate sexual expression by removing inhibitions. In large amounts it can impair sexual performance.

A safety issue that applies to the use of all recreational drugs in a sexual context is that they may impair judgment, thus promoting unsafe sex, sexual victimization (whether the drug is taken by the perpetrator or the victim), or sexual encounters that are later regretted.

object—such as a shoe—that originally was not sexually arousing at all. What it might take would be for the person to repeatedly use or fantasize about the object while masturbating or having sex. We will discuss this issue when we cover unusual forms of sexual expression, such as fetishism, in Chapter 13.

Sexual Arousal Follows a Response Cycle

In Chapters 2 and 3 we described some of the genital phenomena that accompany sexual arousal in women and men. We now attempt to tie these phenomena together into a coherent sequence or process—the **sexual response cycle**. This cycle goes forward in a fairly similar way regardless of how arousal occurs (e.g., through part-nered sex or by solitary masturbation).

The best-known description of the overall response cycle is the one developed by Masters and Johnson (introduced in Chapter 1), in which they divided the process into four phases: excitement, plateau, orgasm, and resolution.

In the excitement phase, genital responses begin

The **excitement phase** is just what it sounds like: the period during which sexual arousal begins. In women it is marked by swelling and opening up of the inner labia, vaginal lubrication, a deepening in the color of the inner labia and the vaginal walls (caused by **vasocongestion**), erection of the clitoris and nipples, swelling of the breasts, and an increase in heart rate and blood pressure (**Figure 5.15**). The uterus elevates within the pelvis; this is known as the "tenting effect."

sexual response cycle   The sequence of physiological processes that accompany sexual behavior.

excitement phase   The beginning phase of the sexual response cycle.

vasocongestion   Tissue swelling caused by increased filling of local blood vessels.

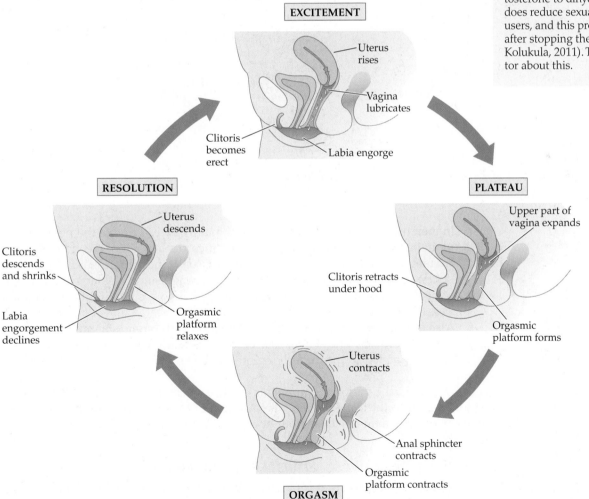

Figure 5.15   **Genital changes in women** during the sexual response cycle.

Figure 5.16 Genital changes in men during the sexual response cycle.

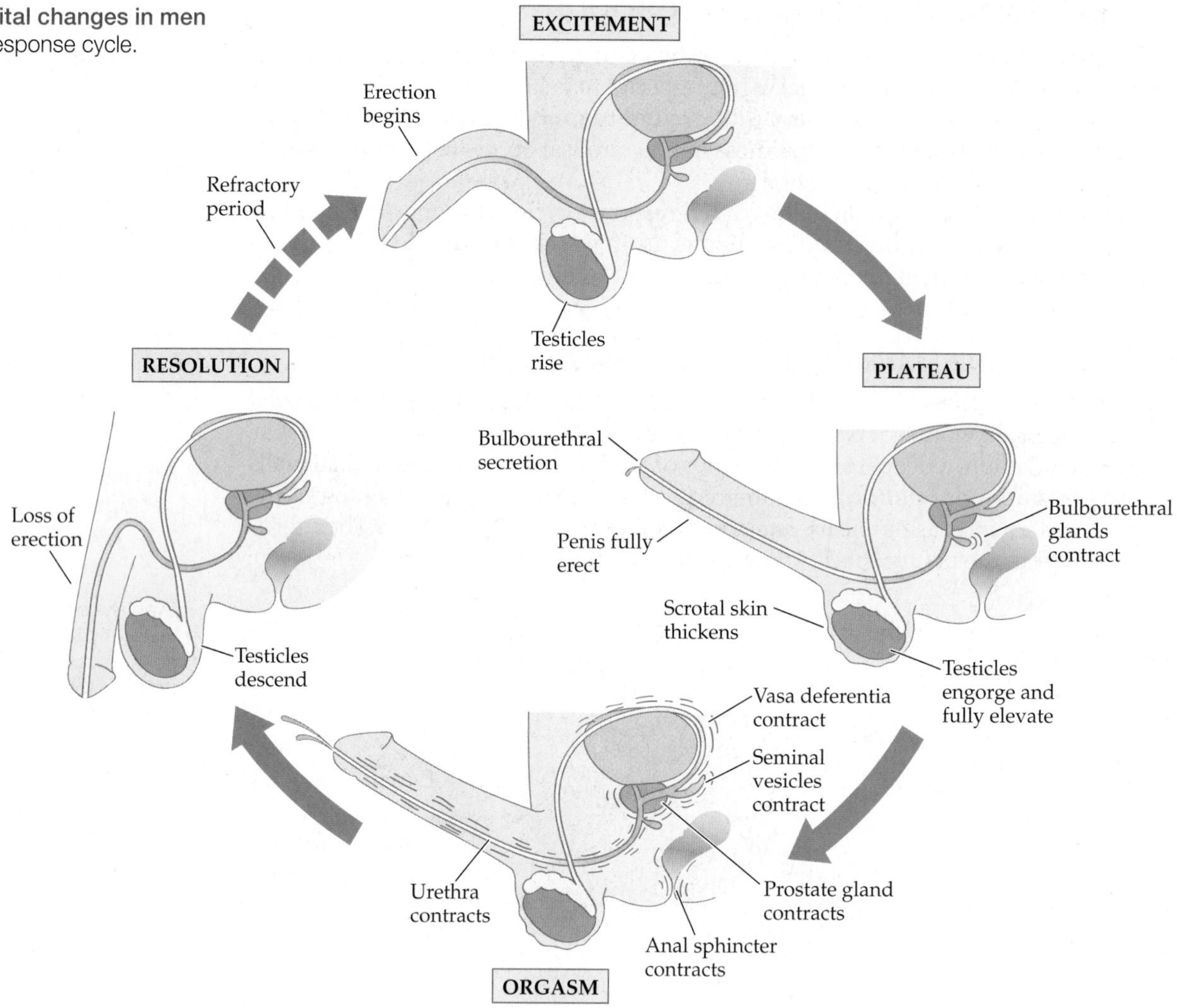

In men the excitement phase is marked mainly by erection of the penis (**Figure 5.16**). In healthy and highly aroused young men the process of erection takes less than a minute—perhaps as little as 10 seconds. Usually the corpora cavernosa become erect first, followed more slowly by the corpus spongiosum. In older men, men who have health problems affecting erection, or men who are not highly aroused, the process of penile erection may take many minutes.

Also during the excitement phase, contraction of the cremaster muscle begins to elevate the testicles. The skin of the scrotum becomes firmer and more wrinkled, due to contraction of the underlying muscle layer. The nipples may also become erect.

Of course, the various components of the excitement phase don't always occur together or to the same degree. The duration of the excitement phase also varies, from less than a minute to an hour or more.

In the plateau phase, arousal is maintained

plateau phase The phase of the sexual response cycle during which arousal is maintained at a high level.

The **plateau phase** is a state of high arousal that may be maintained for some time, from several minutes to several hours (in the case of extended lovemaking). Among men, there is considerable variability in how long a man is able (or wishes) to remain in the plateau phase before reaching orgasm. In women, physiological events that occur during the plateau phase include the thickening and tightening of the outer third of the vagina and the surrounding muscles of the pelvic floor. This causes the outer part of the vaginal canal to narrow, so (if coitus is occurring) it grips the penis more tightly. This tense outer region of the vagina and surrounding tissues is called the **orgasmic platform**. The inner part of the vagina, in contrast, tends to balloon out and lengthen, so it does not grip the penis at all tightly during coitus.

During the plateau phase, the glans of the clitoris usually disappears under its hood. The breasts may swell further, and the areolae may become engorged and swollen, making the nipples appear less prominent than before. In some women, the breasts or other parts of the body may take on a flushed appearance. Heart rate and blood pressure increase further, accompanied by a general increase in muscle tension (**myotonia**) throughout the body.

In men, secretions from the bulbourethral glands ("pre-cum") may appear at the urethral opening during the plateau phase. The erection of the penis becomes stronger and is less readily lost. The testicles elevate farther. According to Masters and Johnson, the testicles also swell by a variable amount (Masters & Johnson, 1966). Heart rate and respiration rate increase, accompanied by a general increase in muscle tension.

The term "plateau," which means a flat region in a graph, suggests a steady state in which not much is changing, physiologically speaking. This may be misleading, however. Sometimes a person will pass rapidly from excitement through plateau to orgasm. (This might be because the person deliberately tries to reach orgasm quickly, or because he or she has difficulty in delaying orgasm.) In such cases the plateau phase may be a brief period of rapidly increasing arousal that is difficult to distinguish from the excitement phase. If the plateau phase is maintained for an extended time, however, there are likely to be periodic increases and decreases in arousal depending on the stimulation the person is experiencing, distraction, fatigue, and other factors. Thus, the plateau phase is more of a general concept than a definable episode within each and every sexual experience.

Orgasm is the climax of sexual arousal

Orgasm is the subjective experience of intense pleasure and release at sexual climax, as well as the accompanying physiological processes. As previously discussed in Chapter 3, it is very similar in women and men. Orgasm is usually felt as a brief series of muscle contractions in the genital area, but the sensation often radiates out to involve other parts of the body. Respiration rate, heart rate, and blood pressure all reach peak levels during orgasm. Muscle contractions may occur anywhere in the body. In men orgasm is accompanied by two genital events described in Chapter 3: emission, in which the various components that make up semen are released into the urethra, and ejaculation, in which the semen is forcefully expelled from the urethral opening. Some women also ejaculate during orgasm (**Box 5.3**).

Orgasm may be experienced as a brief period of altered consciousness or as a loss of control. The person experiencing orgasm may groan or shout involuntarily. Orgasm is usually felt as a release of sexual tension, followed by calm. What about the actual sensation of orgasm in women and men—is it the same? In a much-cited study conducted in the 1970s, researchers collected descriptions of orgasm written by women and men. Experts who read these descriptions were unable to tell which had been written by women and which by men (Vance & Wagner, 1976). This suggests that there is little if any difference in the experience of orgasm in the two sexes.

orgasmic platform The outer portion of the vagina and surrounding tissues, which thickens and tenses during sexual arousal.

myotonia A general increase in muscle tension.

orgasm The intense, pleasurable sensations at sexual climax, and the physiological processes that accompany them.

Box 5.3 Biology of Sex

Female Ejaculation

You might think that ejaculation would be a purely male experience, but some women say that they experience a discharge of some type of fluid from the urethra at sexual climax (Darling et al., 1990). The discharge seems to be of two kinds. In one kind, a small amount (a few drops to a teaspoonful or so) of a milky or pearly fluid is discharged, usually without great force. In another kind, a larger quantity of clear fluid is discharged, sometimes with sufficient force to project the fluid away from the woman's body ("squirting"). For the most part, different women report experiencing the two different kinds of discharge.

The low-volume, milky discharge appears to be a secretion from the paraurethral glands. As described in Chapter 2, these small glands, which are probably equivalent to the much larger prostate gland in men, lie just in front of the front wall of the vagina, in close proximity to the urethra, but are highly variable in size and position (Wimpissinger et al., 2009). Some researchers believe that they are the anatomical basis for the G-spot. The ducts of these glands open into the urethra about 1 inch (2 cm) back from the urethral opening. Consistent with this interpretation, the low-volume discharge contains an enzyme characteristic of secretions from the male prostate gland (Belzer et al., 1984). The functional role of this kind of discharge in women, if any, is unknown. Because the male ejaculate consists in part of prostatic secretions, the paraurethral ejaculation in women is a partial parallel to male ejaculation—minus the sperm, of course.

The high-volume, clear discharge has been much more controversial, with some sexologists doubting the reality of the phenomenon or interpreting it as urine. To solve the riddle, sexologist Gary Schubach recruited volunteers who stated that they experienced large-volume discharges (Schubach, 2001). Schubach observed that these women did indeed expel large volumes—3 ounces (100 mL) or more—of watery fluid from the urethra at orgasm.

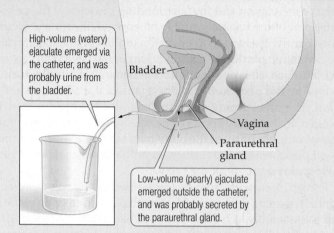

High-volume (watery) ejaculate emerged via the catheter, and was probably urine from the bladder.

Bladder

Vagina

Paraurethral gland

Low-volume (pearly) ejaculate emerged outside the catheter, and was probably secreted by the paraurethral gland.

Gary Schubach's experiment to determine the origin of fluids ejaculated by women. A catheter was inserted through the urethra into the bladder, and the women masturbated to orgasm.

To investigate the origin of this fluid, Schubach passed a fine rubber tube (catheter) through the urethra of some of the women, past the ducts of the paraurethral glands and into the bladder (see figure). The women then masturbated (or were stimulated by their partners) to orgasm. The idea was that if the fluid was urine, it should exit the urethra via the inside of the catheter, but if it was a secretion from the paraurethral glands or other nearby glands, it should exit the urethra *outside* the catheter. In all cases, the high-volume fluid expelled at orgasm exited via the inside of the catheter. Schubach's conclusion: High-volume female "ejaculation" involves the expulsion of urine from the bladder. However, this discharge may be experienced as sexual in nature. Some of the women also released the low-volume, opalescent discharge, and this fluid emerged outside the catheter, consistent with an origin in the paraurethral glands.

Both types of discharge may legitimately be referred to as "female ejaculation," but only the low-volume, milky discharge has anything in common with male ejaculation.

Masters and Johnson, as well as more recent sex researchers, have investigated the physiological basis of the muscle contractions experienced during orgasm. (We described some of the research, on men, in Chapter 3). In women, the spasms derive from intense contractions of the pubococcygeus muscle and nearby pelvic floor muscles, which cause tightening of the outer portion of the vagina. The anal sphincters, the uterus, and even the oviducts may also undergo contractions. The contractions occur about once per 0.8 second, and a total of about eight or ten occur in a typical orgasm. This would give a total duration of about 10 seconds, but researchers using a different method (blood flow in the vaginal wall) came up with a longer estimate (20 seconds), which corresponds more closely to the average duration of orgasm as indicated by women in a laboratory setting (26 seconds) (Levin & Wagner, 1985).

There has long been debate about whether women experience different kinds of orgasms depending on what parts of their genitals are stimulated. According to Masters and Johnson, the key physiological sign of orgasm in women—rhythmic contractions of the muscles around the outer part of the vagina—are the same no matter how orgasm is triggered and are probably the result of direct or indirect stimulation of the clitoris (Masters & Johnson, 1966). Masters and Johnson placed relatively little emphasis on erotic sensitivity within the vagina itself.

A different view has been put forward by Barry Komisaruk and Beverly Whipple (of Rutgers University) and several colleagues (Ladas et al., 2004; Komisaruk et al., 2006). According to studies by this group, stimulation of the clitoris and stimulation of the anterior wall of the vagina (a region thought to include the G-spot—see Figure 2.9 in Chapter 2) give rise to two different orgasmic sensations. Clitoral orgasms, they say, involve sensations more or less restricted to the area of the clitoris itself, whereas vaginal orgasms are described as involving the entire body. Yet a third kind of sensation is said to be elicited by direct stimulation of the cervix. The differences arise, according to these authors, because these three regions are connected to the brain via different neural pathways.

The idea that clitoral and vaginal stimulation lead to different kinds of orgasm has received some support from a recent ultrasound study. A French-Italian research group placed ultrasound probes in three women's vaginas and then asked the women to masturbate to orgasm by stimulation of either the clitoris or the vagina (Buisson & Jannini, 2013). Orgasms induced by clitoral stimulation were accompanied by increases in blood flow within the external portion of the clitoris only, whereas orgasms induced by vaginal stimulation were accompanied by movement and blood-flow increases throughout the deep portions of the clitoris and neighboring tissues.

Another research group found that women reported different kinds of orgasms but said that the location stimulated (clitoris versus vagina) is not as relevant as psychological factors and relationship quality (King et al., 2011; King & Belsky, 2012). All in all, there is a need for more research to clarify the nature and basis of different orgasmic experiences in women.

Although orgasms are usually triggered by genital stimulation, the site of stimulation or the site where the orgasm is experienced may sometimes be located far from the genital area (**Box 5.4**). Some women and an occasional man say that they can reach orgasm from nipple stimulation alone (Anonymous, 2014a).

Brain imaging suggests where orgasm may be experienced

The subjective experience of orgasm must result from some kind of activity in the brain, but where in the brain does that activity occur? To study this question in men, a Dutch group (Holstege et al., 2003) used a functional brain-imaging technique (PET scanning). The researchers took scans in two conditions: when the subject was being manually stimulated by his female partner but was not experiencing orgasm, and in the same situation when he was experiencing orgasm (**Figure 5.17**). One scan was then digitally subtracted from the other to show the pattern of activity that was specifically associated with orgasm. The researchers found that the most active region was a zone in the midline of the brain including part of the thalamus and nearby structures. Interestingly, this same region has been shown to be active during a heroin rush. It contains many neurons that use dopamine as a neurotransmitter; dopamine is believed to be involved in brain processes that have to do with pleasure and reward. Activity in the cerebral cortex—seat of our intellectual lives—decreases greatly during orgasm. This may reflect a switching off of cognitive or behavioral processes that would otherwise inhibit orgasm.

More recently, the Dutch group extended their observations to women: Again, there was activation of dopamine-related systems and a general drop in activity

Box 5.4 Biology of Sex

Foot Orgasms

Two clinical case histories illustrate that orgasms may be stimulated or experienced far from the genitals, especially when there has been neurological damage. In the first case, psychologist V. S. Ramachandran of the University of California, San Diego, interviewed a man whose foot had been amputated some time previously (Ramachandran & Blakeslee, 1999). "I actually experience my orgasm in my [missing] foot," he told Ramachandran, "and therefore it's much bigger than it used to be, because it's no longer confined to my genitals."

Ramachandran noted that the area of the brain's cerebral cortex that maps the foot lies next to the area that maps the genitals. It's known that when a part of the body is missing, the region of the cerebral cortex that maps the missing body part may be commandeered by neighboring cortical areas. Thus it seems that genital inputs to the cerebral cortex invaded the empty representation of this man's amputated foot, leading to misinterpretation of the location of his orgasms.

In the second case, a woman who had suffered neurological damage during an intensive care emergency later complained

Feet may be especially sexy because they are located next to the genitals in the brain's map of the body.

that stimulation of her left foot (in nonsexual contexts) triggered unwanted orgasmic sensations (Waldinger et al., 2013). In the clinic, electrical stimulation applied to her foot triggered an instant orgasmic sensation that spread from her foot to her genital area. Conversely, electrical stimulation of the left side of her vagina triggered an orgasmic sensation that spread to her left foot. The researchers speculated that the original neurological damage was followed by regeneration of sensory nerves to the wrong body regions. The unwanted orgasmic sensations were eliminated by surgical destruction of sensory nerves that innervate both a portion of the left foot and the left side of the genital area.

Feet can be highly erogenous zones even in healthy people, and erotic fixations (fetishisms) that focus on body parts involve the feet much more commonly than any other regions (see Chapter 13). It may be that the ready sexualization of the feet has something to do with the neighboring representation of feet and genitals in the cerebral cortex.

---

in the cerebral cortex (Georgiadis et al., 2006). The Rutgers University group has also observed activation of dopamine-related systems during orgasm in women. In particular, they saw heightened activity in the **nucleus accumbens**. Portions of the nucleus accumbens appear to serve as a final common pathway for reward and pleasure: The evidence for this is that, given the opportunity, animals will electrically stimulate their own nucleus accumbens in preference to any real-world reward such as food or sex. Thus, the activation of this region during orgasm may help explain why the experience of orgasm is intensely pleasurable.

In both men and women, orgasm is accompanied by the surge-like release of the hormone **oxytocin** from the pituitary gland (Carmichael et al., 1994). Oxytocin contributes to the contraction of smooth (involuntary) muscles such as those in the wall of the uterus and in breast tissue. (It plays an important role in childbirth and breastfeeding, and possibly also in the formation of durable sexual relationships, as we'll see in Chapter 7.) Its release during orgasm may contribute to the contractions that accompany orgasm. In addition, however, oxytocin released during orgasm probably acts directly on the brain, helping generate the pleasurable sensations of orgasm. If the release of oxytocin is blocked, the physiological events of orgasm occur more or less normally, but the pleasurable quality of the orgasm is greatly reduced (Murphy et al., 1990). Administration of oxytocin may help some individuals experience orgasm who otherwise would have difficulty doing so (Ishak et al., 2008).

nucleus accumbens A nucleus within the basal ganglia that is part of the brain's reward system.

oxytocin A hormone secreted by the pituitary gland that stimulates uterine contractions and the secretion of milk.

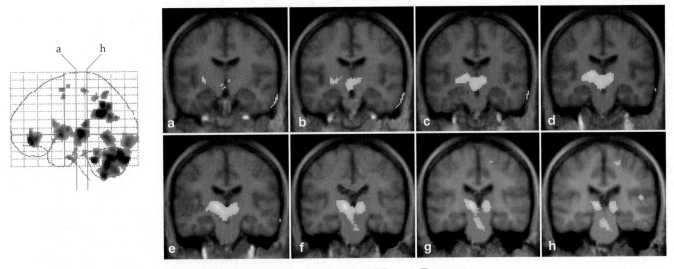

Figure 5.17 **Brain activity during orgasm** in a man, as revealed in a PET scan. The most active areas (yellow) involve subcortical structures such as the thalamus.

In the resolution phase, arousal subsides

The **resolution phase** is the period during which the physiological signs of arousal reverse themselves. In women, clitoral erection, vasocongestion, and lubrication subside, the vaginal and pelvic floor muscles relax, and the breasts lose their swollen appearance. In men, the penis loses its erection and the testicles descend within the scrotum. In both sexes, heart rate and blood pressure return to normal levels. Psychological arousal usually subsides too, and there is often a sense of relaxed contentment. Full resolution typically takes about 15 minutes, but resolution is slower if an orgasm has not occurred.

resolution phase The phase of the sexual response cycle during which physiological arousal subsides.

The phases may be linked in different ways

Although the excitement, plateau, orgasm, and resolution phases are the building blocks of the sexual response cycle, individual cycles may be assembled in a variety of ways (**Figure 5.18**). In one type of cycle (shown in green in the figure), the person

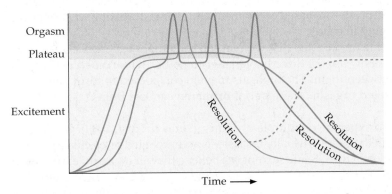

Figure 5.18 **Patterns of sexual response** In the pattern shown in green, a single orgasm is experienced before loss of arousal (resolution), but a new cycle of arousal (dashed line) may begin after resolution. In the pattern shown in blue, the person passes through excitement to the plateau phase and then experiences more than one orgasm, returning to the plateau phase between orgasms. In the pattern shown in red, the person experiences the plateau phase but no orgasm.

passes sequentially through the four phases in the sequence just described—excitement, plateau, orgasm, and resolution. This might be called the "standard version" of the response cycle.

A second type of cycle (shown in red in the figure) skips the orgasm phase: The person passes from excitement to the plateau phase, and then directly to the resolution phase. We have become socialized to think of this as a sign of something wrong or missing: We might say that the person "failed to achieve" orgasm. Still, the fact is that it is a common type of cycle. Women may describe it as a fully satisfying sexual experience—in fact some women never experience orgasm but nevertheless express satisfaction with their sex lives. Alternatively, they may feel frustrated, especially if the lack of orgasm results from the cessation of stimulation by their partners after their own orgasms.

Men are less likely than women to be satisfied with a sexual experience that doesn't include orgasm—only 34% of men, compared with 50% of women, believe that sex without orgasm can be satisfying, according to a large British survey (Wellings et al., 1994). Besides the loss of the pleasure and release associated with orgasm, men sometimes experience testicular pain ("blue balls"), which is likely due to vasocongestion and anoxia (Chalett & Nerenberg, 2000). Men sometimes plead "blue balls" as a way to pressure their partner into continuing a sexual encounter. That's hardly a compelling argument, because in that situation the condition—if real—could easily be relieved by masturbation. A comparable condition has been described in women, and it has been called "blue vulva" by Columbia University's Go Ask Alice advice website (Columbia Health, 2013).

Some people experience multiple orgasms

A third type of cycle involves **multiple orgasms** (the blue line in Figure 5.18). A multiple orgasm means a sequence of at least two orgasms, between which the person descends only to the plateau phase of genital arousal (Amberson & Hoon, 1985). It does not refer to having an orgasm, losing one's arousal completely, and then quickly entering another arousal cycle that culminates in a second orgasm.

Multiple orgasms are far more common in women than in men. One survey of college-educated U.S. nurses found that about 43% of them usually experienced multiple orgasms (Darling et al., 1991). No doubt many more women could experience multiple orgasms if they wanted to or if they had the cooperation of their partners. However, women are not necessarily more satisfied with multiple orgasms than with a single orgasm, as many men would imagine. Reports of large numbers of multiple orgasms—up to 50 or so—are based on women who are masturbating with vibrators, rather than engaging in coitus.

Masters and Johnson reported that women can sometimes experience a sequence of orgasms that follow almost directly one after the other with no descent into the plateau phase between them. The orgasms may be considered to form one single, unusually prolonged orgasm. These **serial orgasms** can last from 20 seconds to a minute or so.

A few men also experience multiple orgasms (Dunn & Trost, 1989). Commonly, only one orgasm in the series—usually the last—is accompanied by ejaculation, while the previous ones are "dry." Some sexologists believe that all men can learn to have multiple orgasms. For those who wish to try, instructions are available online (Silverberg, 2008). The key, it is said, is learning to separate orgasm from ejaculation by stopping stimulation just short of ejaculation.

A small number of men, however, are naturally capable of experiencing multiple ejaculatory orgasms. One such man was observed in the lab while he experienced six orgasms over the course of 36 minutes, without any loss of erection between orgasms.

multiple orgasms Two or more orgasms, between which the person descends only to the plateau level of arousal.

serial orgasms Two or more orgasms with no more than a few seconds between them.

Each of the six events was accompanied by ejaculation, intense psychological arousal, and all the other manifestations of orgasm (Whipple et al., 1998).

refractory period In males, a period of reduced or absent sexual arousability after orgasm.

Men experience a refractory period

In spite of the unusual case just described, most men experience a period of time after orgasm during which further sexual stimulation does not lead to renewed erection or a second orgasm. According to Masters and Johnson, this **refractory period** lasts between 30 and 90 minutes. The length of the period varies greatly with age, however, being negligible in some boys around the age of puberty but extending over a day or more in some older men. While the early part of the refractory period may be absolute—that is, the man cannot be physiologically aroused by any means—it may be followed by a relative refractory period during which the man can be aroused by stronger than usual stimuli, such as a novel sex partner. This is probably related to the Coolidge effect, described earlier.

The Masters and Johnson cycle may be incomplete

Masters and Johnson's four-stage model of the sexual response is primarily a description of physiological processes—effects that one can observe or measure during sexual behavior, such as erection or changes in blood pressure. Since Masters and Johnson's time, researchers have made efforts to place the physiological response cycle into a larger psychological context.

One important issue is this: Do the physiological markers of sexual arousal—erection, vasocongestion, lubrication, and so forth—correspond to *psychological* or *subjective* arousal, meaning the person's sense of being sexually excited? There appears to be a difference between men and women in this respect. A man's psychological arousal is usually closely tied to his genital arousal—his mind and his penis are one, so to speak. Women, however, do *not* always feel sexually excited when their genitals are showing every sign of arousal (Suschinsky et al., 2009). It may be that a woman's genital arousal is less obvious to her than is penile erection to a man, or women may be socialized to ignore the messages from their genitals. But the reason for this potential disconnect between physiological and psychological arousal in women remains mysterious and deserves further study. For one thing, it may affect whether drugs that increase genital arousal offer any psychological benefit for women with sexual disorders.

Another issue is this: Where does sexual *desire* fit into the overall response cycle? According to Helen Singer Kaplan, sexual desire is the psychological state that precedes and leads to physiological arousal (Kaplan, 1979). This makes intuitive sense: We want to engage in sex, so we do things that cause our genitals to become aroused. But here again, there may be a difference between men and women. For men, Kaplan's model is widely accepted. In the case of women, however, several researchers have moved away from Kaplan's model (Basson, 2000, 2001). Psychiatrist Rosemary Basson proposes that many women, especially those in established relationships, are not motivated to engage in sexual behavior by what we would usually think of as sexual *desire*—"horniness," "sex hunger," "the urge to merge," or whatever you want to call it. Rather, they have an *interest* in sex that flows from a wish for intimacy with the partner or from an expectation of benefits that may flow from a sexual interaction. This interest is responsive, cognitive, or even intellectual in quality, rather than being the expression of a biological drive. Once physical interactions begin, however, and the physiological processes of sexual arousal are triggered, genital sensations provide a feedback stimulus that reinforces sexual interest and gives it more the quality of true sexual desire, so a self-reinforcing cycle is set up. Again, this model has implications for the treatment of sexual disorders in women (see Chapter 14).

Go to the
**Discovering
Human Sexuality**
Companion Website at
**sites.sinauer.com/
discoveringhumansexuality3e**
for activities, study questions,
quizzes, and other study aids.

In fact, a survey by Cindy Meston and David Buss identified no fewer than 237 distinct reasons why people have sex, many of them having nothing to do with sexual attraction, desire, or arousal (Meston & Buss, 2007). These included such reasons as "I wanted to get back at my partner for cheating on me," "I wanted to get closer to God," and "I wanted the person to feel good about himself/herself." Evidently the motivations for engaging in sex can be complex and diverse and can't be encompassed by any single model.

Summary

- Sexual attraction is a response to another person that is influenced by objective attributes of that person, as well as by both durable and varying characteristics of the person experiencing the attraction.

- The "masculinity" and "femininity" of faces is an important part of their attractiveness. In women, most people find very feminine faces the most attractive. Women's judgments of the attractiveness of male faces vary around the menstrual cycle.

- Another attribute that increases a person's attractiveness is facial and bodily symmetry. One reason we may find symmetry attractive is because it indicates that a person had a healthy physical development.

- One important factor influencing the attractiveness of bodies is the body mass index (BMI). For cultural reasons, lower BMIs are preferred in Western cultures than in some non-Western cultures. The waist-to-hip ratio considered most attractive in women is lower than that in men.

- Youthful appearance—another cue to fertility—is an important criterion of physical attractiveness in women, but less so in men.

- Attractiveness is strongly enhanced by general "likability" traits such as trustworthiness, warmth, and a sense of humor. When people are given the opportunity to select partners from a large group, however, they don't generally choose the partners who correspond most closely to their stated preferences. This suggests that some aspects of attraction operate below the level of conscious thought.

- Other factors modulating sexual attraction include familiarity and, in women, the phase of the menstrual cycle.

- Some individuals are asexual: They never experience sexual attraction, but they often value close relationships and they may engage in sex in order to satisfy their partners.

- Sexual arousal may be triggered internally or by external factors. Internal processes include erotic dreams and sexual fantasies. Fantasies are a healthy part of most people's sex lives.

- Testosterone plays an important role in conferring the capacity for sexual arousal in males, especially at puberty. Testosterone does not play a minute-by-minute role in sexual arousal, however. Both testosterone and estrogens may contribute to sexual arousability in women; testosterone is probably the more important of the two.

- Classical conditioning may increase the sexual arousal that individuals learn to associate with people, body parts, and other things that have been linked with sexual behavior in the past.

- The sexual response cycle has four phases: excitement, plateau, orgasm, and resolution.

- The subjective experience of orgasm is similar in women and men. Many women but few men experience multiple orgasms in a single cycle. Sometimes a response cycle does not include orgasm. A cycle without orgasm may be perceived as sexually satisfying, or it may leave the person dissatisfied and in discomfort from vasocongestion that is slow to resolve.

- After orgasm, men but not women experience a refractory period during which they cannot enter a new cycle. The length of the refractory period increases with age but can be shortened by situational factors such as exposure to a novel partner.

Discussion Questions

1. Cultural influences shape sexual arousal and attractiveness. Identify the culture of your ancestors, and identify the attributes that your culture finds sexually attractive (e.g., are thin women or those with "curves" and "meat on their bones" more attractive?).

2. Consider your reactions as you walk around campus or other areas and see people holding hands, kissing, lying on the grass in a passionate embrace, or almost having intercourse. What are your reactions to seeing such behavior? How does your reaction differ depending on whether it is an opposite-sex or same-sex couple? Do you think we should have rules or limits on the extent of public displays of affection or arousal?

3. Should sexual partners discuss what is arousing for each person? What are the costs and benefits of this type of communication? What are your attitudes toward talking with an intimate partner about what is arousing and what is not? Imagine for a moment that your partner had a fascination with your feet and wanted to kiss and touch them. How would your attitudes encourage or discourage this discussion?

4. As a class, make a list of words or phrases (e.g., common expressions, slang, words in other languages) that are used for (1) a woman who has sex with numerous partners, (2) a woman who doesn't engage in partnered sex at all, (3) a man who has sex with numerous partners, and (4) a man who doesn't engage in partnered sex. After the list is complete, discuss the attitudes and values it illustrates about men's and women's sexuality. Do you think that a double standard exists?

Web Resources

Asexuality Visibility and Education Network (AVEN) **www.asexuality.org**
Beautycheck (study of attractiveness, using digitally manipulated faces) **tinyurl.com/rd92**
Face Research (an interactive site at the University of Glasgow) **www.faceresearch.org/**

Recommended Reading

Bogaert, A. F. (2012). *Understanding asexuality.* Rowman & Littlefield.

Buss, D. (1994). *The evolution of desire: Strategies of human mating.* Basic Books.

Komisaruk, B. R., Beyer-Flores, C. & Whipple, B. (2006). *The science of orgasm.* Johns Hopkins University Press.

Meston, C. M. & Buss, D. M. (2009). *Why women have sex: The psychology of sex in women's own voices.* Times Books.

Perrett, D. (2010). *In your face: The new science of human attraction.* Palgrave Macmillan.

Portner, M. (2009). The orgasmic mind. *Scientific American Mind, 20,* 26–31.

Rutter, C. (2014). *Dataclysm: Who we are when we think no one's looking.* Crown. (Insights from social media about sexuality and many other topics.)

Swami, V. & Furnham, A. (2007). *The psychology of physical attraction.* Routledge.

Thornhill, R. & Gangestad, S. W. (2004). The evolution of human attractiveness and attraction. In: Moya, A. and Font, E. (Eds.). *Evolution: From molecules to ecosystems.* Oxford University Press.

Chapter 6

Scenes from the *Kama Sutra*, an ancient Indian sex manual, in the Juna Mahal fort, Dungarpur, India.

Sexual Behavior

Which human activities do you consider sexual? Which of these, if any, do you engage in or find enjoyable? Which do you consider morally acceptable, and which strike you as repugnant? Probably no two people would give precisely the same answers to these questions. In this chapter, we survey common forms of sexual behavior, with a central emphasis on sexual practices in the contemporary United States and other Westernized countries. We will defer a discussion of atypical sexual practices to Chapter 13.

Everyone has to make important decisions about their sex life. Questions arise, such as: Do I want to have sex at all, and if so, under what circumstances and in what kind of a relationship? Do I want to have children, and if not, how should I prevent pregnancy? How can I best reduce the likelihood of acquiring or transmitting diseases in the course of sexual encounters? We will discuss these important topics in later chapters. For the moment, we deal with sexual behavior itself.

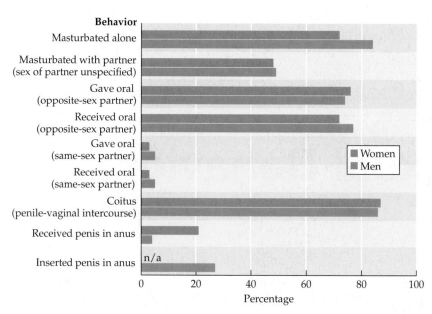

Figure 6.1 Overview of sexual behavior The bar graph shows the percentages of 334 U.S. men and 383 U.S. women, age 25 to 29, who said they had engaged in the specified behavior at least once in the previous 12 months. (Data from Herbenick et al., 2010c.)

People Derive Pleasure from Diverse Sexual Behaviors

Sexual behaviors can be very diverse, but certain behaviors are the mainstay of sex for most Americans. The National Survey of Sexual Health and Behavior (NSSHB) asked nearly 6000 Americans whether they had engaged in masturbation, oral sex, coitus (penile-vaginal sex), or anal sex within the previous 12 months (Herbenick et al., 2010b). **Figure 6.1** shows the findings for men and women age 25 to 29—the age range in which partnered sexual activity is most frequent. (The data for a wider range of ages are presented in Chapter 11.) Masturbation, oral sex, and coitus are all very common activities—large majorities of all men and women engage in them. Anal sex is less common but far from rare. Most partnered sex is heterosexual—the low figures for homosexual behaviors reflect, very roughly, the percentage of the population that is gay, lesbian, or bisexual. Regardless of the kind of sex and whether it is homosexual or heterosexual, sex with a partner makes people happy during the sex act itself and also boosts their ongoing level of happiness (**Box 6.1**).

Masturbation Is a Very Common Form of Sexual Expression

We have already discussed one way in which people can arouse themselves sexually: through sexual fantasy (see Chapter 5). Because it doesn't involve *doing* anything in the external world, fantasy is not classified as a behavior. But people also have the capacity to arouse themselves sexually through physical stimulation of their own bodies—**masturbation**, a term that has countless slang equivalents, ranging from the delicate ("self-pleasuring") to the colorful ("muffin buffin'") or the onomatopoeic ("fapping").

The term "masturbation" can be used to indicate any kind of manual stimulation of the genitals, including those of a partner. Commonly, though, the term refers to

masturbation Sexual self-stimulation. Sometimes also used to refer to manual stimulation of another person's genitalia.

Box 6.1 Research Highlights

Sex and Happiness

We concluded the previous chapter by mentioning that people engage in sex for a wide variety of reasons. Nevertheless pleasure—whether the physical pleasure of sex itself or the emotional pleasure of sexual intimacy—is likely to be the main sexual motivator for most people. To see how pleasurable sex generally is, let's look at two studies that used different approaches to the question.

In a study by Matthew Killingsworth and Daniel Gilbert of Harvard University (Killingsworth & Gilbert, 2010), over 2000 men and women agreed to be called at random times by an automated iPhone application that asked them what they were doing at the time and how happy they were (see figure). Although the subjects spent only a tiny fraction of their time "making love," they were far happier while doing so than at any other time—in spite of the aggravation of being interrupted by an automated phone call! The subjects were also least likely to be distracted—to be thinking about something other than the matter at hand—while they were making love. The researchers have established that letting your mind wander from what you are doing is associated with a decrease in happiness, so this focus on sexual activities probably contributes to the pleasure of sex.

In the other study, David Blanchflower of Dartmouth College and Andrew Oswald of the University of Warwick, in England, analyzed data from the General Social Survey (Blanchflower & Oswald, 2004). Among many other questions, this annual survey asks randomly selected respondents to rate their overall happiness. The survey also asks respondents to provide information about their frequency of sex and the number of their sex partners during the previous 12 months.

The researchers found that increasing frequency of sex was strongly correlated with increasing happiness: Having partnered sex four or more times per week increased happiness by about half as much as being married did. (Being married is one of the

People are happiest making love. This graph shows the happiness (on a subjective 0–100 scale) of 2250 subjects contacted at random times during their waking hours by an automated iPhone application. The amount of time spent on each activity is indicated by the size of the circles. (After Killingsworth & Gilbert, 2010.)

strongest demographic predictors of happiness.) It made no difference whether the sex was with same- or opposite-sex partners. In terms of numbers of partners, the happiest number was 1, and engaging in extramarital sex, or paying for sex, decreased happiness. In other words, having frequent sex doesn't just cause happiness during the sexual act but is also associated with an increase in a person's ongoing level of happiness. Nevertheless, the data suggest that sex needs to take place within a monogamous relationship for it to provide the greatest overall level of happiness.

autoerotic (self-arousing) behavior, whether by use of the hand or by other means such as vibrators or pillows, and we use it in that sense here. Masturbation may be performed while alone, in the presence of a partner, or even in a group. An example of the last is the "circle jerk" practiced by some teenage boys.

Masturbation may be combined with other sexual activities: For example, a woman may manually stimulate her own clitoris while engaging in coitus with her male partner, or a man may masturbate while being anally penetrated by another man. Mostly, though, people connect the notion of masturbation with solo sex, and this is probably what people are thinking of when they answer survey questions on the topic.

autoerotic Providing sexual stimulation to oneself or being aroused sexually by oneself.

Unsweetened cornflakes were introduced at the Battle Creek Sanitarium in Michigan by anti-masturbation crusader John Harvey Kellogg. His brother Will added sugar to the flakes and successfully marketed them as a breakfast cereal.

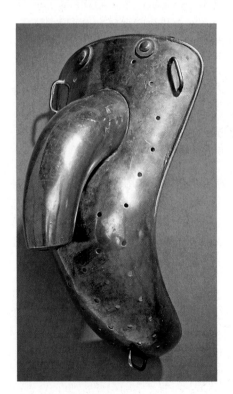

Negative attitudes toward masturbation are still prevalent

Masturbation is a normal, common, and healthy sexual behavior. It's not always perceived that way, however. In Victorian times (the 19th century), masturbation was considered disgusting, sinful, and unhealthy and was referred to with morally loaded terms such as "self-pollution." According to many authorities of the time, the practice led to "masturbatory insanity" or to "degeneracy," a condition of physical, mental, and moral decay that affected not just the masturbator, but also any offspring that he or she might have.

The connection between masturbation and insanity may have come about because religious proscriptions against masturbation influenced medical thinking. It's also possible that doctors were only able to observe masturbation in people whose social inhibitions had been broken down by mental illness (Hare, 1962).

Considerable efforts were made to discourage masturbation. It was believed that the consumption of rich or highly flavored foods provoked masturbation and that bland foods discouraged it. Two bland foods that are still popular today—the graham cracker and Kellogg's Corn Flakes—were specifically introduced with the hope of reducing the prevalence of masturbation and sexual arousal. (Sylvester Graham was a minister and moral campaigner; John Harvey Kellogg was a medical doctor.)

Nineteenth-century health manuals recommended a variety of methods for discouraging masturbation, and one could even purchase mechanical devices that made masturbation physically impossible (**Figure 6.2**). These devices were mostly used on children and patients in mental hospitals who masturbated compulsively and openly. Similar devices are still for sale today, but they are now used as bondage toys more than as aids to abstinence.

Mark Twain poked fun at Victorian attitudes toward masturbation in a speech that he delivered to a private gathering in 1879. "The signs of excessive indulgence in this destructive pastime are easily detectable," he declared. "They are these: a disposition to eat, to drink, to smoke, to meet together convivially, to laugh, to joke and tell indelicate stories—and mainly, a yearning to paint pictures" (Twain, 1879).

Few people are campaigning against the evils of masturbation in the United States today, but children may still absorb negative attitudes about it from their parents and peers. Furthermore, the Catholic Church and various other religions still teach that masturbation is sinful. Another reason for masturbation's bad reputation is the belief that it is an activity practiced only by people who cannot get access to "real" sex. Thus, several factors combine to make people feel bad about masturbation. In the National Health and Social Life Survey (NHSLS) mentioned in Chapter 1, about half of all the respondents who stated that they masturbated also stated that they felt guilty after they did so. The youngest age group interviewed (18 to 24 years) reported the highest levels of guilt; it is very possible that those under 18 are even more likely to feel guilty about masturbating.

Several demographic factors influence masturbation

Although most people masturbate at least occasionally, the likelihood that people masturbate varies with a number of demographic factors, according to data from the NHSLS and NSSHB surveys:

Figure 6.2 Emission Impossible This is a late-19th-century device intended to prevent male masturbation. The metal shield would have been attached to the body with a lockable harness. (From the collection of the Science Museum, London.)

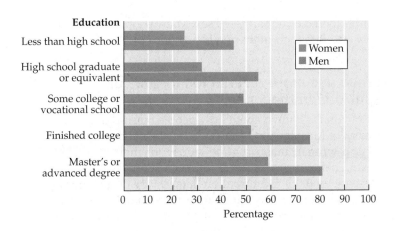

Figure 6.3 Educational level and masturbation This bar graph shows the percentages of U.S. women and men who reported having masturbated at least once in the previous 12 months, broken down by educational level. (Data from NHSLS.)

- People over 50 (women especially) masturbate less than those in younger age groups.
- African-Americans masturbate less than other ethnicities.
- The more educated a person, the more likely it is that he or she masturbates (**Figure 6.3**).
- Women (but not men) who have a religious affiliation—especially as fundamentalist Protestant—masturbate less than women who have no religious affiliation.
- People who lack a regular sex partner masturbate slightly more than people who have a partner (**Figure 6.4**).

All these data need to be viewed with some caution: It's possible that the differences in the reported prevalence of masturbation reflect, to some degree, differences in the respondents' willingness to admit to engaging in a stigmatized behavior.

Men experience orgasm during masturbation more frequently than women do. In the NHSLS study, 82% of the men but only 61% of the women stated that they always or usually had an orgasm when masturbating. This sex difference is not unique to masturbation: Women are less likely than men to have an orgasm during sex with a partner, too. In fact, the average woman is more likely to experience orgasm when masturbating than when engaged in sex with a partner (Hite, 2003).

Asked *why* they masturbated, the men and women in the NHSLS survey gave similar answers: They did it to relieve sexual tension, for the physical pleasure, and/or because a partner was not available. Some women masturbate to relieve menstrual pain (Ellison, 2000) or migraine headaches (Evans & Couch, 2001; Akkus, 2011).

The survey data lend only limited support to the notion that lack of a sex partner is the major reason for masturbation. Men and women without partners do masturbate more than those who have partners, but the difference is not great: Most people masturbate at least occasionally even if they do have a partner. Thus, it doesn't seem that people have a certain fixed endowment of sexual need that they can allot to

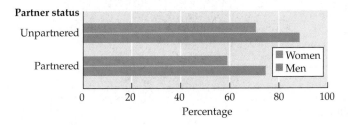

Figure 6.4 Partner status and masturbation This bar graph shows the percentages of women and men age 25 to 29 who reported having masturbated at least once in the previous 90 days, broken down into those who have regular sex partners and those who do not. (Data from NSSHB.)

either partnered or unpartnered sex. Many people who masturbate simply add it to their other sexual activities.

Women use more diverse techniques of masturbation than men

Most of what is known about how people masturbate comes from the work of Masters and Johnson, who observed several hundred men and women masturbating as part of their overall studies of sexual behavior (Masters & Johnson, 1966). Women use quite diverse methods of masturbation (**Figure 6.5**). One common technique involves manually stimulating the area of the clitoris with a circular or to-and-fro motion of the fingers. Alternatively, pulling on the inner labia causes the clitoral hood to move back and forth on the clitoral glans, thus stimulating the clitoris indirectly. (For many women, the clitoral glans is too sensitive for direct stimulation.) Another way of stimulating the clitoris is for a woman to cross her legs and squeeze them together rhythmically. Yet another technique is to rub or press the genital area against some object, such as a bed or pillow. Women sometimes use electric vibrators, either directly on the genitalia, or attached to the back of the hand to give the fingers an extra vibratory motion.

Figure 6.5   Female masturbation

Many men imagine that women masturbate by thrusting their fingers or an object deeply into the vagina, thus simulating coitus. Some women do this, but it is quite a bit less common than clitoral stimulation. Some women can give themselves a different kind of orgasm by stimulation of the region of the vagina thought to include the G-spot.

While manually stimulating the genitals, many women stimulate the nipples or breasts with their free hand. In fact, some women can bring themselves to orgasm by breast stimulation alone. A small number of women can experience orgasm by fantasy alone, without any kind of physical stimulation of the body. One such woman is pop singer Lady Gaga, according to her own statements (Brennan, 2010). These mentally induced orgasms are physiologically identical to those produced by physical stimulation (Whipple et al., 1992).

Men's techniques of masturbation tend to be less varied than women's (**Figure 6.6**). The usual method is to grasp the shaft of the erect penis with one hand and move the hand rhythmically up and down, thus stimulating the most sensitive areas

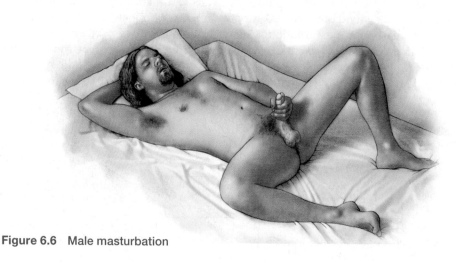

Figure 6.6   Male masturbation

of the penis: the glans, corona, and frenulum. The penis does not produce a significant amount of lubrication (and neither does the hand, of course). For that reason, some men like to use saliva, oil, soapsuds, or a water- or oil-based sexual lubricant—whatever feels good and does not irritate the penis. Because their foreskin glides freely over the glans, men who are uncircumcised have less need for a lubricant.

Alternative methods of masturbation include lying in contact with an object such as a pillow or the edge of a bed and thrusting against it. Some men like to stimulate the nipples or anus with their free hand while masturbating with the other, but few can reach orgasm without direct stimulation of the penis.

Most men take about 2 to 3 minutes from the beginning of masturbation to reach the point of orgasm, compared with about 4 minutes for women, though these data are old and need to be replicated (Kinsey et al., 1948, 1953). Some men and women like to draw out the experience over a period of many minutes, perhaps approaching orgasm several times and then easing off before finally climaxing; others like to reach orgasm as quickly as possible.

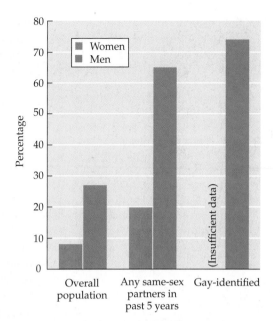

Figure 6.7   Masturbation and sexual orientation Homosexual behavior or identity is associated with a high frequency of masturbation. These histograms show the percentages of women and men who masturbate at least once per week. (Data from NHSLS.)

Gay people masturbate more than heterosexuals

Intuitively, one might imagine that gay men and lesbians would enjoy masturbation more than heterosexual men and women and might masturbate more frequently. Gay people's own bodies, after all, are of the sex that they find sexually attractive, so autoerotic behavior might be more arousing for them than for straight people. According to the NHSLS data, gays and lesbians (or people with recent homosexual experience) do masturbate far more frequently than do heterosexual men and women (**Figure 6.7**), and the same finding was reported in a British survey (Gerressu et al., 2008).

The difference was further confirmed in a survey of male German college students: Gay students not only masturbated more frequently (regardless of whether they were partnered or not), but they also derived greater pleasure from masturbation (Schmidt, 2000). Furthermore, gay male students were far more likely than straight male students to masturbate in front of a mirror—48% of gay students had done so in the previous 12 months, versus only 18% of straight students (G. Schmidt, personal communication). Comparable data for women are not available.

These findings suggest that gay people's relatively greater interest in masturbation may result from a greater erotic response to their own bodies. (Other explanations are possible, such as that the high rates of masturbation result from a generally stronger sex drive in gay people.) This is not meant to imply that gay people are, in general, erotically focused on themselves. Both lesbians and gay men are as "other directed" in their sex lives as heterosexual men and women (see Chapter 12).

Different cultures have different attitudes toward masturbation

In the *International Encyclopedia of Sexuality*, which is a compilation of reports by sex researchers from about 50 countries (Francouer & Noonan, 2004), masturbation is most commonly presented as something practiced by children or adolescents; adults seldom masturbate, it is said, and they often consider the practice shameful, ridiculous, or unhealthy. Nevertheless, many of the researchers stress the difficulty of finding out the true frequencies of masturbation. In addition, most of the countries represented in the encyclopedia are either Western or have been strongly influenced by Western ideas about sex.

What about truly non-Western people? Some cultures have taboos against male masturbation on account of beliefs about semen: that it is contaminating or, conversely, that it is so valuable that its loss will cause ill health or even death. Nevertheless, there are examples of more positive attitudes. Hortense Powdermaker, an American anthropologist who spent a decade living in a Melanesian village in New Ireland (part of Papua New Guinea) during the 1920s, wrote as follows:

> *A woman will masturbate if she is sexually excited and there is no man to satisfy her. A couple may be having intercourse in the same house, or near enough for her to see them, and she may thus become aroused. She then sits down and bends her right leg so that her heel presses against her genitalia. Even young girls of about six years may do this quite casually as they sit on the ground. The women and men talk about it freely, and there is no shame attached to it. It is a customary position for women to take, and they learn it in childhood. They never use their hands for manipulation [of their genitals]. (Powdermaker, 1933, cited in Ford & Beach, 1951)*

In Chapter 4 we mentioned Gagnon and Simon's idea that the high rate of masturbation by pubertal boys plays a role in focusing male sexuality on the physical pleasures of sex. Conversely, it has been suggested that the relatively low frequency of masturbation by girls might hinder their development of the ability to experience sexual pleasure and orgasm in partnered sex. Some therapies aimed at overcoming sexual problems in women, especially the inability to experience orgasm, therefore involve instruction in masturbation (see Chapter 14).

There has been speculation about the possible evolutionary significance of masturbation. One idea, for example, is that male masturbation increases fertility by getting rid of sperm that have passed their "use-by" date. This idea has some support from observations in Japanese macaque monkeys (Thomsen, 2000). Males of this species ejaculate about once a day, either by coitus or (failing that) by masturbation. In this species, sperm quality begins to deteriorate 15 to 20 hours after the previous ejaculation, so if a female partner is not available, masturbation keeps sperm quality high. There is some limited evidence that frequent ejaculation improves sperm quality in humans too, but it also decreases the total number of sperm in the ejaculate (Green, 2009), and the net effect on fertility is unknown. Evolutionary explanations for female masturbation are even more speculative. It should be borne in mind that many behaviors have no adaptive significance in themselves but are mere by-products of selection for other traits (such as, in this case, the highly rewarding nature of sexual stimulation, and especially orgasm).

The Kiss Represents True Love— Sometimes

To anyone familiar with the poetry and music that depicts the kisses of dying lovers—Shakespeare's Romeo and Juliet and Wagner's Tristan and Isolde, among many others—or who remembers the great screen kisses of Clark Gable and Vivien Leigh (in *Gone with the Wind*) or of Heath Ledger and Jake Gyllenhaal (in *Brokeback Mountain*), to name just a few, the kiss signifies one thing and one thing only: a passionate love that transcends life itself.

In reality, of course, kisses come in many different degrees and flavors, from the no-contact air-kiss and the perfunctory cheek peck to the wildest oral adventures that tongue, lips, and teeth are capable of. A kiss may mean nothing, it may be a way of saying that "real sex" is on the way, or it may solemnify the union of two souls "till death do us part."

Classic kiss—Clark Gable and Vivien Leigh in *Gone with the Wind* (1939).

Surprisingly, kissing is not as ubiquitous a custom as many Westerners might imagine. Anthropologists Clellan Ford and Frank Beach listed eight non-Western societies in which kissing of any kind was unknown (Ford & Beach, 1951). One of these societies was that of the Thonga, who live in the southern lowlands of Mozambique. "When the Thonga first saw Europeans kissing," wrote Ford and Beach, "they laughed, expressing this sentiment: 'Look at them—they eat each other's saliva and dirt.'"

Even in the United States, attitudes toward kissing vary. In the Kinsey studies of the 1940s, well-educated men and women were much more likely than less-educated people to report engaging in **deep kissing** ("French kissing")—another example of the association between education and more liberal attitudes toward sexual practices. It is likely that deep kissing has become more broadly accepted today than it was in Kinsey's time, although concern about HIV/AIDS and other sexually transmitted infections may discourage deep kissing in a casual context—even though it is very rare for HIV to be transmitted by any kind of kissing.

Mouth-to-mouth kissing between two straight men used to be a rarity, because doing so would have stigmatized the men as gay. Now that anti-gay attitudes are fading, however, it is becoming increasingly common for young men to kiss each other as an expression of nonsexual intimacy, especially in Britain (Anderson et al., 2012). Similarly, mouth-to-mouth kissing between straight women has become widespread, popularized in part by a much-publicized kiss between Madonna and Britney Spears at the 2003 MTV Video Music Awards.

Men and women view the purpose of kissing differently. Men (more specifically, male college students) see kissing primarily as a stepping-stone to "real" sex; women, on the other hand, use it to evaluate a person's suitability as a mate or to assess the status of an established relationship (Hughes et al., 2007; Wlodarski & Dunbar, 2014). Of course, mouths can roam farther than a partner's mouth. In the heat of passion, almost every body part may be licked, sucked, chewed on, or bitten. Breasts are a perennial favorite. Oral-genital contacts are discussed below. Even the sucking of toes ("shrimping") can be highly arousing to both partners.

Sexual Touching Takes Many Forms

Simple touching of another person's body can be a powerfully intimate and sexual act. "Necking," "petting," and "heavy petting" are terms traditionally used to describe some of this behavior: **Necking** means kissing and touching confined to the head and neck; **petting** (now a rather old-fashioned term) means touching naked skin below the neck—usually excluding the breasts or genitalia; **heavy petting** includes touching the breasts or genitals. If two persons manually stimulate each other's genitals, the behavior may be termed **mutual masturbation**.

Fondling is a broader term that can indicate any of these behaviors. **Outercourse** is another term used to describe noncoital or nonpenetrative sexual contact, especially when it is practiced as a way to avoid pregnancy.

General body-to-body contact, accompanied by rubbing or thrusting motions of the pelvis that stimulate the clitoris or penis, is a common part of sexual activity for many people. When two women engage in this behavior, rubbing their vulvas against each other's bodies with pelvic thrusting motions, it is called **tribadism** (**Figure 6.8**). Another way for two women to bring their vulvas together is by "scissoring," that is, by spreading their legs and engaging each other like two open pairs of scissors.

People may engage in these behaviors as **foreplay** (behavior designed to increase pleasure and arousal prior to some "main event," such as coitus) or as **afterplay**. But quite commonly, nonpenetrative contacts *are* the main event. Although our culture often depicts coitus as the one essential element of "real" sex (Sanders & Reinisch, 1999), plenty of people derive equal or greater satisfaction from other forms of love-

deep kissing   Kissing, with entry of the tongue into the partner's mouth.

necking   Kissing or caressing of the head and neck.

petting   Sexually touching the partner's body (often taken to exclude the breasts or genitalia).

heavy petting   Sexually touching the partner's genitalia or breasts.

mutual masturbation   Reciprocal, simultaneous manual stimulation of a partner's genitals.

fondling   Any kind of sexual touching of the partner's body.

outercourse   Sexual activities other than coitus, promoted as a means for preventing unwanted pregnancy and reducing the risk of STI transmission.

tribadism   Sexual behavior between two women, who lie front to front and stimulate each other's vulvas with thrusting motions.

foreplay   Sexual behavior engaged in during the early part of a sexual encounter, with the aim of increasing sexual arousal.

afterplay   Sexual behavior engaged in after coitus or orgasm, or at the end of a sexual encounter.

Figure 6.8 Tribadism

making. They may engage in noncoital sex for the sake of variety, to avoid pregnancy, because coitus is painful or the man has erectile disorder (see Chapter 14), or for the simple pleasure of it. Same-sex couples can't engage in coitus, obviously, but that doesn't limit their sexual satisfaction.

Oral Sex Is Increasingly Popular

fellatio Sexual contact between the mouth of one person and the penis of another.

Oral sex has become an increasingly prevalent activity among younger people over the last few decades, both in the United States and elsewhere. Thus, paradoxically, younger people are more likely than older people to have engaged in oral sex at some point during their lifetime. In the British National Survey of Sexual Attitudes and Lifestyles (NSSAL) study, for example, only 50% of women in the 45 to 59 age bracket said that they had ever participated in any kind of oral sex, but 83% of women in the 25 to 34 age bracket had done so. The corresponding figures for men were 62% and 88%. In the NSSHB survey, about 60% of both men and women in the 25 to 29 age bracket had given oral sex to an opposite-sex partner within the previous 90 days, and a similar percentage had received it.

Oral-genital contacts are of three main kinds: mouth-penis contact (fellatio, also known as a "blow job," "sucking off," "going down on," or "giving head"), mouth-vulva contact (cunnilingus, "eating," or "going down on"), and mouth-anus contact (anilingus or analingus, also known as "rimming").

Fellatio is oral stimulation of the penis

Fellatio, like most sex, is a pretty simple matter (**Figure 6.9A**). One person (the "insertee") takes the insertor's penis into her or his mouth, and usually runs the lips rhythmically up and down the shaft of the penis, keeping them fairly tight to provide optimal stimulation. The insertee may also use the tongue to stimulate the most sensitive portions of the penis: the corona and frenulum.

The "insertor" often wants his penis to go deeper and deeper into his partner's mouth as he becomes increasingly aroused, but this may cause gagging, depending on the length of the man's penis and his partner's experience. As with every aspect of two-person sex, good communication is key. The focus on gagging in many porn videos suggests that gagging itself can be eroticized, but this is more likely to be true for the insertor than the insertee.

Fellatio can be continued to the point that the insertor ejaculates. Here again, however, communication is important. Some people don't like the experience of receiving the ejaculate in the mouth or have concerns about disease transmission. As to swallowing the ejaculate, the perennial question is: How many calories does it contain? The answer: an insignificant amount—less than 5 calories.

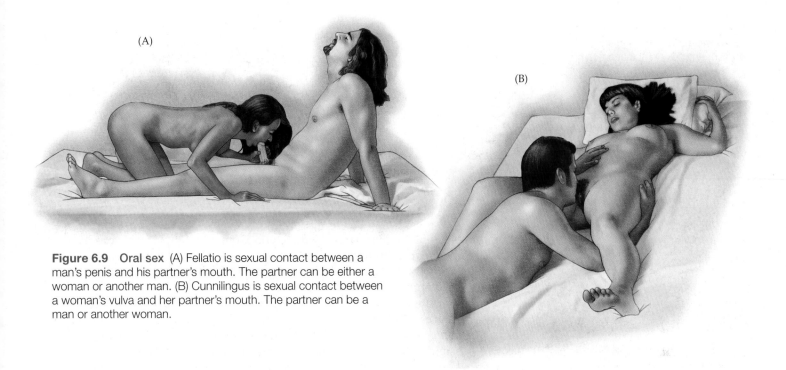

Figure 6.9 Oral sex (A) Fellatio is sexual contact between a man's penis and his partner's mouth. The partner can be either a woman or another man. (B) Cunnilingus is sexual contact between a woman's vulva and her partner's mouth. The partner can be a man or another woman.

In heterosexual contexts, men typically enjoy fellatio more than women do (**Figure 6.10**). Thus, it seems that women engage in fellatio to give their male partners pleasure more than as a directly pleasurable experience for themselves. The NHSLS study also found cultural differences: For example, more-educated people tended to enjoy it more than less-educated people.

In a variation on fellatio commonly known as "tea-bagging," the man squats astride his partner's head and repeatedly dips his scrotum into her or his mouth, as if dunking a tea bag in a cup of hot water.

Not a great deal is known about fellatio in non-Western cultures. One well-studied exception is the Sambia, a small tribal community in New Guinea (Herdt, 2005). Ritualized fellatio is practiced between older and younger Sambia youths; it is believed to confer the physical and spiritual attributes of manhood on the younger boys (the insertees). Besides its ritual significance, this activity provides a sexual outlet for the older youths, who have no access to women, because they are sequestered in all-male groups.

Cunnilingus is oral stimulation of the vulva

In **cunnilingus** (**Figure 6.9B**), a woman's partner explores her vulva with tongue and lips. The tongue provides very effective sexual stimulation for many women because it is soft, wet, warm, and highly mobile. Thus, it is much easier to stimulate the clitoris and inner labia in an uninhibited way with the tongue than with, say, the fingers, which may provide too-harsh stimulation to the most sensitive areas, such as the glans of the clitoris. For some women, cunnilingus is the only way by which they regularly achieve orgasm (Hite, 2003).

Considering that men enjoy fellatio more than women, you might expect that women would enjoy cunnilingus more than men. In the NHSLS study, however, slightly more men than women said that they found cunnilingus "very appealing" (see Figure 6.10). It may be that some women's unease with cunnilingus is based on a sense that their genitals are not very attractive and that their partners are only

cunnilingus Sexual contact between the tongue or mouth of one person and the vulva of another.

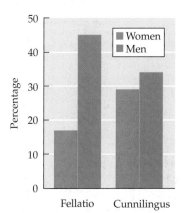

Figure 6.10 Popularity of oral sex The graph shows the percentages of men and women who find fellatio and cunnilingus "very appealing." (Data from NHSLS.)

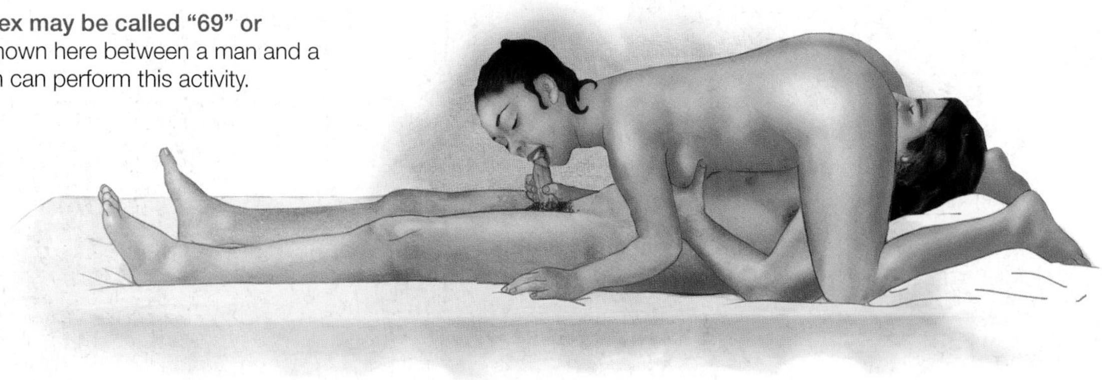

Figure 6.11 Mutual oral sex may be called "69" or "soixante-neuf." Though shown here between a man and a woman, any sex combination can perform this activity.

doing it to please them. But in reality men (and women) who perform cunnilingus do mostly find it enjoyable and sexually arousing. Oftentimes women become more comfortable in their own skins as they get older, and are therefore more able to enjoy their partners' attention to their erogenous zones.

If a couple arrange themselves in a mutual head-to-genital position, they can perform oral sex on each other simultaneously (**Figure 6.11**). This practice is often called "69" or "*soixante-neuf*" (French for "69"). While sixty-nining can be very exciting, it has two possible drawbacks. The first is that each partner may be distracted from enjoying what is going on at one location by the need to attend to the other location. Also, when fellatio is performed in the 69 position, the tongue of the insertee is located on the upper, less sensitive surface of the penis and cannot easily reach the area of the frenulum.

There is little information about the prevalence of **anilingus** (mouth-anus contact). This practice can be very arousing because the skin around the anus is erotically sensitive. Sometimes anilingus is performed as a prelude to anal penetration. Many people avoid anilingus, however, because of negative associations with defecation or because of health concerns. These concerns are to some extent justified by the risk of transmitting disease agents, such as the virus that causes hepatitis A (see Chapter 15).

Oral-genital contacts are common among nonhuman animals. Among bats, for example, such contacts precede and facilitate copulation (Tan et al., 2009; Maruthupandian & Marimuthu, 2013). Many animals (and a few male humans) are able to orally stimulate their own genitals. Certain male ground squirrels, for example, fellate themselves to ejaculation after copulating with females; this behavior may reduce the risk of acquiring sexually transmitted infections (Waterman, 2010).

FAQ

I've heard that blowing into a woman's vagina is dangerous. Is it?

Blowing into a pregnant woman's vagina as if trying to inflate a balloon may indeed cause an air embolism (blockage of arteries with air) that can be fatal. Whether this can happen in a nonpregnant woman is unclear—we suggest you avoid vigorous blowing.

Most Heterosexual Sex Includes Coitus

Penetration of the vagina by the penis is called **coitus** (**Figure 6.12**), or "fucking," in blunt English. (The phrase "sexual intercourse" is usually taken to mean coitus, but it is a less well-defined term that could include other activities.) Coitus is central to many people's sex lives. Ninety-five percent of sexual encounters between opposite-sex adults include coitus, according to the NHSLS study, and it is usually the final behavior in an encounter.

Coitus can be performed in many different positions

Perhaps the most striking thing about human coitus, compared with coitus in animals, is the wide variety of positions that a couple may adopt to perform it. Among animals, only our closest primate relatives exhibit any significant degree of variety in this regard: Bonobos, for example, engage in both front-to-front and rear-entry

anilingus Sexual contact between the mouth or tongue of one person and the anus of another.

coitus Penetration of the vagina by the penis.

Figure 6.12   **Coitus** as envisaged by Leonardo da Vinci (ca. 1492). The copulating couple (with the woman only partially shown on the left) are represented as if they had been sliced down the middle.

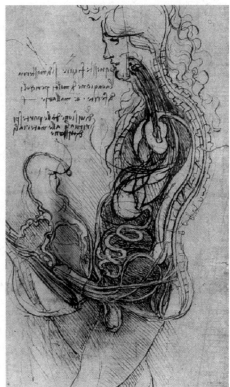

coitus. But humans can and do attempt an almost unlimited number of different positions.

If people explore the various coital positions, they will discover that each provides a somewhat different physical and emotional experience, and certain ones are preferable in some particular situations. Some positions, for example, allow the man to make thrusting motions of his pelvis but restrict the woman's mobility. Some allow the reverse, while others allow both partners some degree of freedom. Thus, there may be positions that are appropriate when one or the other partner is in an active, take-control mood or, conversely, desires to play a passive role. In some positions, the hands of one or both partners are free to explore and stimulate erogenous zones; in others, the arms and hands may be occupied in supporting the weight of the body. Some positions require strenuous exertion and cannot be maintained for long periods of time, while others are more relaxed and may be suitable for couples who want to engage in prolonged, leisurely sex, or for obese or frail people. Yet others may be suitable if the woman is advanced in pregnancy. Some positions allow for eye contact between the man and the woman; this may be crucial for a head-over-heels-in-love couple, but less so for other couples. Some positions provide more erotic stimulation to the man, and others provide more stimulation to the woman; such considerations may be relevant if the couple is trying to reach orgasm simultaneously. Some positions provide the woman with more clitoral stimulation, and some stimulate the area of the G-spot, which may affect the quality of the woman's orgasm or whether she experiences one at all. In short, there seems to be every reason for couples to experiment and to communicate, not just for variety's sake, but in order to suit their sexual activities to their needs.

The man-above position is a traditional favorite

In spite of the advantages of experimentation, Americans tend to stick to one tried-and-true position for coitus, in which the woman lies on her back with her legs parted and the man places himself above her, supporting his upper body with his hands or elbows (**Figure 6.13**). This man-above position is also referred to derisively as the "missionary position," a phrase apparently invented by Alfred Kinsey (Priest, 2001). At the time of his surveys in the 1940s, Kinsey estimated that 75% of Americans had never tried any other position for coitus.

Figure 6.13   **The man-above position for coitus** is also called the "missionary position."

With coitus in the man-above position, one partner guides the man's penis into the woman's vagina. If the woman does this, it may give her a sense of control that otherwise is lacking in the man-above position. Because the man is above, he has to do most of the "work" of coitus (i.e., the pelvic thrusting); the woman's freedom of movement is restricted by the man's body, especially if he is much larger than she is. This position has the advantage of allowing eye contact during sex but the disadvantage that the man's hands are not free to roam over the woman's body.

Simple variations on the man-above position include the woman's achieving more hip flexion by curling her legs around the man's back or even draping them over his shoulders. Such positions allow the man's penis to extend more deeply into the vagina than when the woman's legs are straight or only slightly bent at the knees.

The man-above position generally provides good erotic stimulation for the man—sometimes too good, if he tends to ejaculate more rapidly than he or his partner would like. For the woman, it is more variable. Some women are well stimulated by coitus in this position; for others, there is insufficient stimulation, especially of the G-spot, since the penis is directed toward the rear wall of the vagina (**Box 6.2**).

The women's movement encouraged alternative positions

Since Kinsey's time, the sexual revolution and the women's movement have spurred Americans to try positions other than the man-above position. The connection between the women's movement and changes in coital position was well illustrated in 1975, when students at Smith College celebrated their school's centennial with T-shirts proclaiming "A Century of Women on Top."

One alternative is the woman-above position (**Figure 6.14**). In this position the man lies on his back, and the woman either lies on top of him in a face-to-face arrangement (which allows full body contact) or sits upright. The woman-above position gives the woman greater control, since she generates much of the thrusting motion. In general, the woman-above position may give the man somewhat less erotic stimulation than the man-above position, and the woman may receive somewhat more stimulation. (This may be helpful if the man tends to reach orgasm more rapidly than the woman does, which is common.) Furthermore, especially when the woman adopts a sitting

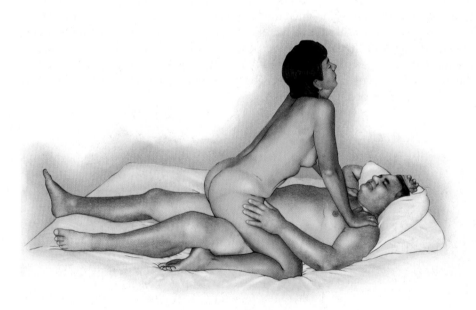

Figure 6.14 The woman-above position for coitus In this position, the woman is more in control and does most of the thrusting. The man may receive less stimulation, which can be a good thing if he tends to reach orgasm prematurely.

Box 6.2 Research Highlights

Progress in Coitus Research

In Figure 6.12 we show Leonardo da Vinci's anatomical drawing of a couple engaged in coitus. Of course, Leonardo didn't really cut people in half in the way that he depicted it—he just imagined it—and as a result, the anatomical details are highly suspect. Leonardo showed the man's penis sticking straight out from his body like a flagstaff. He also had some odd ideas about internal anatomy. If you look back to the drawing, you'll see that there's a tube running from the woman's uterus to her breast, which has no basis in reality. The scientific value of Leonardo's study, however, lay not so much in its veracity, or lack thereof, as in its implied message: that sex was a suitable subject for study.

Half a millennium later, gynecologist Willibrord Schultz and his colleagues at the University of Groningen hospital, in Holland, decided to check on Leonardo's conception of coitus by means of magnetic resonance imaging (MRI) (Schultz et al., 1999). It wasn't easy. First, there was the question of space. If you have ever been inside an MRI machine, you'll know that it's a tight fit: The tube you lie in is only 20 inches (51 cm) in diameter. Imagine having someone else in there with you, and then going through the contortions required even for missionary-position sex. The researchers had to select smallish volunteers, and in fact, the first couple that succeeded in achieving penetration in the MRI machine was a pair of amateur acrobats.

The researchers had an even more serious problem, however: The male volunteers' penises did not stand up well to the study's high-stress conditions. It took nearly a minute to acquire a single MRI image at that time, and the men just couldn't keep their penises stationary and erect inside the women's vaginas for that long. (Ongoing stimulation is usually required for men to maintain erection.)

Five years after the start of the study, however, two unexpected breakthroughs occurred. The researchers obtained a new MRI machine that could generate an image in a mere 12 seconds, and sildenafil (Viagra) came onto the market (see Chapter 14). By swallowing a pill an hour before entering the machine, the men were able to maintain an erection as long as necessary. At last the researchers obtained sharp pictures of a man's fully erect penis deep within a woman's vagina (see figure).

In these pictures, the penis is not straight, as depicted by Leonardo, but bent upward, with the hinge point near the abdomen. Thus, the entire penis (including the root of the penis within the man's body) has the shape of a boomerang.

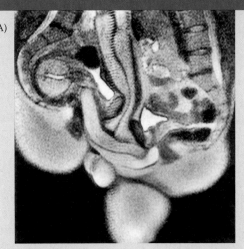

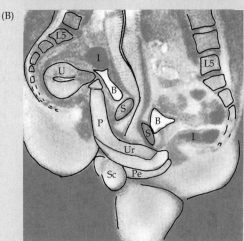

(A) MRI image of a woman (left) and man (right) engaged in coitus. (B) Explanatory drawing. (P = penis; Ur = urethra; Pe = perineum; U = uterus; B = bladder; I = intestine; L5 = fifth lumbar vertebra; Sc = scrotum; S = pubic symphysis; From Schultz et al., 1999.)

In the images, the sensitive lower surface of the penis presses against the back wall of the woman's vagina, an arrangement that may be highly stimulating to the man. Yet the penis makes little contact with the front wall of the vagina, which is the location of the controversial G-spot. (The particular women who participated in the study said they did not have G-spots.) These findings support the notion that positions other than the missionary position would provide better stimulation to the female partner, especially if she desires stimulation of the G-spot.

Figure 6.15   The side-by-side position for coitus Because both partners are lying directly on a flat surface, it is a less tiring position and thus can be sustained for longer periods of time.

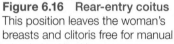

FAQ

What is "varting"?

It's the noisy expulsion of air from the vagina—similar to farting, but without the fire hazard.

Figure 6.16   Rear-entry coitus This position leaves the woman's breasts and clitoris free for manual stimulation by either partner.

position, it is relatively easy for her or the man to manually caress her breasts or her clitoris, thus increasing her erotic stimulation further. In a variation of the woman-above position, the woman sits upright but faces away from the man. This "reverse cowgirl" position allows for deep penetration, but it doesn't allow for eye contact. Perhaps for that reason, it is not popular: Only about 1 in 50 Americans chose it as a favorite in an *Esquire/Marie Claire* magazine survey (Esquire, 2007).

Another alternative is the side-by-side position (**Figure 6.15**), in which the woman and the man face each other, but each lies with one side directly on the bed. Coitus in this position tends to be relatively relaxed, since neither partner's thrusting is aided by gravity, and penetration tends to be shallow. This may be desirable if the intention is to prolong the sexual encounter or if health concerns restrict one or both partners' ability to expend energy. One problem with side-by-side coitus, however, is that limbs tend to get trapped under bodies and may go numb in the middle of the action. In addition, the penis rather easily becomes dislodged from the vagina, and reinsertion can be awkward in the side-by-side position. An arm around the waist of the woman can decrease the likelihood of the penis slipping out of the vagina.

In rear-entry coitus (**Figure 6.16**), the man faces the woman's back. There are a number of ways of accomplishing rear-entry coitus: The couple may lie side by side with the woman turned away from the man; or the woman may lie prone or in a crouched position, or stand and lean over some object. Because the penis enters the vagina from the rear, it comes into strongest contact with the vagina's front wall (for potential G-spot stimulation), and penetration tends to be fairly shallow. There are rear-entry positions that give deep penetration, however, such as when the woman is crouching on her knees, with her chest down.

As indicated by its slang name, "doggy style," rear-entry coitus is a reminder of our kinship with the animal world (**Box 6.3**). It has a number of potential advantages and disadvantages. The man may find contact with the woman's back and buttocks arousing, and the fact that the woman's front is free makes it easy for either partner to stimulate her breasts and clitoris during coitus. Rear-entry coitus in the side-by-side ("spooning") position may be the most comfortable position for a woman in the later stages of pregnancy, but nonpregnant people can enjoy this position

Box 6.3 Research Highlights

Sex and the Seasons

Many nonhuman animals show marked variations in sexual behavior around the year—breeding and nonbreeding seasons—which are driven by changes in day length, temperature, and other seasonal factors. The key control element is gonadotropin releasing hormone (GnRH—see Chapters 2 and 3). The release of GnRH by the hypothalamus, in response to these external signs, promotes the release of LH and FSH from the pituitary gland, which in turn kick-start the ovarian cycle in female animals and increase spermatogenesis and testosterone secretion in males.

Humans can of course mate and produce offspring at any time of year. Nevertheless there are seasonal variations. In most parts of the world, conceptions peak at times of moderate temperatures and 12-hour daylight, that is, at the spring and fall equinoxes, according to a German research group (Roenneberg & Aschoff, 1990a,b). The authors of that study concluded that either sexual activity or women's chances of conceiving are indeed influenced by the seasons, at least when humans live closer to nature.

These spring and fall peaks are not seen in the United States, perhaps because Americans spend most of their time indoors and therefore have little exposure to seasonal signals. Yet there is evidence for variations in the frequency of sexual behavior around the year in the United States. Using Google Trends, Patrick and Charlotte Markey of Villanova University determined the week-by-week frequency of Google searches for a variety of terms related to prostitution, pornography, and mate seeking: They found that these searches (unlike searches for non-sex-related terms) peaked twice in each year, once in early summer and again in winter (Markey & Markey, 2013) (see figure). These two peaks probably correspond to peaks in actual sexual behavior, because they are matched by peaks in condom sales, HIV tests, and STI diagnoses (Wellings et al., 1999). (The STI diagnoses lag by a few weeks, as might be expected.)

It's possible that the two peaks are driven by social factors such as vacation time (in summer) and the alcohol-fueled party season (in December). Only the December peak in sexual activity results in a peak in births, which in the United States is in late summer (ABC News, 2005). We could guess at a reason—that alcohol causes people to be less cautious with regard to contraception.

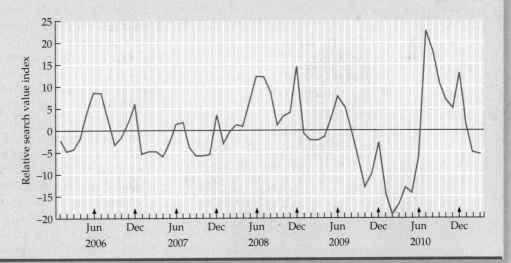

Sex and the seasons This graph plots the frequency of Google searches related to pornography over a 5-year period. The "relative search value index" is a measure of how searches for porn-related terms vary relative to all Google searches. There are two peaks per year, one in June and one in December. The large swings in 2009 and 2010 may reflect economic factors (recession and recovery). (After Markey & Markey, 2013.)

too. In rear-entry coitus, the angle of penetration of the vagina is ideal for women who like stimulation of the G-spot, but there is no direct stimulation of the clitoris. Another possible disadvantage is that eye contact is limited.

In some cultures, heterosexual couples favor coital positions that are uncommon in the United States. In some Pacific Islands cultures, for example, a position called *haku noho* is popular: The man squats in front of the woman, and she places her legs across his thighs, whereupon he pulls her up toward himself and they embrace in a front-to-front fashion (Dixson, 2009).

anal sex Penetration of the anus by the penis, or any sexual behavior involving the anus.

sphincter A circular muscle around a tube or orifice whose contraction closes it.

rectum The final, straight portion of the large bowel. It connects to the exterior via the anus.

Figure 6.17 Anal penetration may be performed by a man on a woman or on another man (as shown here).

There are plenty of other coital positions as well as variations on the ones already described. One adventurous couple took up a challenge from *Cosmopolitan* magazine to work their way through all 77 positions described in *The Cosmo Kama Sutra* in 77 days. They succeeded with a day to spare, while blogging an amusing and instructive commentary (Anonymous, 2014c).

Anal Sex May Be a Part of Either Heterosexual or Male Homosexual Behavior

By **anal sex** (Figure 6.17), we mean penetration of the anus by the penis ("butt fucking"). Anal sex should be distinguished from rear-entry coitus, in which the penis penetrates the vagina from behind. Until 2003, anal sex was illegal in some states.

Although anal sex is often thought of in connection with sex between men, it is not rare in heterosexual sex: In the NSSHB study, about 13% of adult women had engaged in receptive heterosexual anal sex within the past year, whereas only 3.6% of men had engaged in receptive homosexual anal sex. Given that gay men constituted only about 4% of the sample, however, these data do suggest that gay male couples are far more likely to engage in anal sex than are straight couples, which makes sense as gay couples have fewer orifices to choose from.

Heterosexual couples may engage in anal sex in order to avoid pregnancy, to avoid "having sex" in the narrow sense of the phrase, because the greater tightness of the anus (compared with the vagina) may be stimulating to the man, because anal stimulation is arousing to the woman, or simply for the sake of variety.

The mechanics of anal sex deserve some discussion. The anus is normally kept closed by the sustained contraction of two **sphincter** muscles, the external and internal sphincters (see Chapter 2), and the internal sphincter may go into an even stronger contraction as the penis begins to make entry. Anxiety on the part of the insertee may also promote contractions of the sphincter. For anal penetration to take place without causing discomfort to the insertee, it is usually necessary for the insertor to start very slowly, or to hold a finger or the tip of the penis against the orifice for 15 to 30 seconds or until the sphincter relaxes. People who have some experience with receptive anal sex learn how to relax the sphincter during penetration and tend to enjoy the experience more than first-timers.

Because the anus has no natural lubrication, it is usually necessary to employ a lubricant during anal sex. This lubricant should be water or silicone based if, as we recommend, a condom is used. (If a condom is not used, the insertor should urinate soon after withdrawal in order to clear any fecal particles from his urethra.) It has been reported that lubricants containing the spermicide nonoxynol-9 damage the rectal tissue (Phillips et al., 2004), so neither these lubricants nor condoms coated with them should be used for anal sex.

As it passes through the anal orifice, the penis enters the **rectum**, the lowermost portion of the intestinal tract. Repeated thrusting is likely to bring the insertor to orgasm by direct stimulation of the penis. The insertee is stimulated by friction against the anal skin and possibly by the massage of deep structures (especially the prostate gland, if the insertee is male). Only a minority of insertees can be brought to orgasm by anal sex alone, but they may reach orgasm if they accompany the anal penetration with genital stimulation.

There are three general positions that couples can adopt for anal sex. In one, the insertor approaches the insertee from the

SEXUAL BEHAVIOR   **173**

rear; the insertee may be standing or lying prone, but is usually most comfortable with hips flexed. This can be accomplished by lying on one side with knees up, by leaning over an object such as a bed, or by adopting a crouching posture. In a second position, the insertee lies on her or his back, with legs raised and perhaps draped over the shoulders of the insertor, who approaches from the front. In a third approach, the insertor lies on his back and the insertee sits atop him, facing forward or backward. In this case, the insertee must do most of the thrusting.

The anus can also be penetrated with objects other than the penis, such as a dildo, a finger, or even the entire hand and forearm ("fisting"). Some objects may go into the rectum more easily than they come out, however, triggering an embarrassing trip to the emergency room and, conceivably, surgery to remove the foreign body (Clarke et al., 2005). The medical literature records the extraction of all kinds of objects from the rectum—usually of men—including plastic and glass bottles, cucumbers, carrots and other root vegetables, tools, cigar containers, a curtain rod, and even a baseball. The insertion of any large, hard, or sharp object into the rectum (or for that matter into the vagina) risks causing a dangerous perforation of the wall of the organ, but nonforcible penetration by the penis does not harm the anus or rectum, even when practiced repeatedly over many years (Chun et al., 1997). Regarding fisting, this practice does not usually cause harm, but there are some reports of bowel perforations, which can be life-threatening if the person is too embarrassed or too drug-impaired to seek immediate medical care (Cohen et al., 2004). Other health concerns related to anal sex are mentioned in Chapter 15.

Men and Women May Have Different Preferences for Sexual Encounters

People vary considerably in their preferred scenarios for a sexual encounter. Coitus is the preferred culmination of a sexual encounter for most heterosexual people. Some like to precede coitus with extended foreplay, while others like to engage in coitus as soon as both the man and woman are physiologically aroused (i.e., erect and lubricating, respectively).

It is widely believed that women are more interested in extended foreplay than are men, who tend to be more focused on coitus. A Canadian survey of couples in long-term heterosexual relationships casts some doubt on this assumption, however (Miller & Byers, 2004). Both the women and the men in the study believed that women prefer longer foreplay, but their own preferences didn't bear this out: The "ideal duration" of foreplay, as stated by the women and the men, was nearly the same (an average duration of 18.9 and 18.1 minutes, respectively). Interestingly, the couples' *actual* duration of foreplay (about 11 to 13 minutes) fell well short of this ideal.

Men usually lose their erection soon after ejaculating, and often their psychological arousal with it. Thus, a man who wishes his female partner to feel sexually fulfilled by an encounter may want to delay his own orgasm until his partner is satisfied, whether that satisfaction means orgasm, more than one orgasm, or a certain length or intensity of non-orgasmic sex. A man can delay his ejaculation by any of a number of methods, such as thrusting slowly or using sexual positions that stimulate him less strongly. He can also use techniques taught by therapists specifically to treat **premature ejaculation** (see Chapter 14). Another possibility is not to resist the tendency to ejaculate early but to learn to value and enjoy sexual interactions *after* ejaculation (afterplay), including activities, such as oral or manual sex, that can bring his partner to orgasm even though he himself no longer has an erection.

That women often prefer sex on a more relaxed schedule than men is made obvious when two women get together. According to a nonrandom survey by *The Advocate*, a gay and lesbian magazine, 96% of lesbians spend more than 15 minutes on a lovemaking session, and 39% spend more than an hour (Lever, 1995). Besides taking longer

FAQ

Can sex trigger a heart attack?

Yes, but the risk is low and primarily affects people with preexisting heart conditions who don't get regular exercise (Dahabreh & Paulus, 2011).

premature ejaculation   Ejaculation before the man wishes, often immediately on commencement of coitus. Also called rapid ejaculation.

Figure 6.18 **Vibrators** are electrically powered sexual stimulators. The "rabbit vibrator" (center rear) is designed to stimulate a woman's vagina and clitoris simultaneously. (Photo courtesy of Oh My Sensuality, www.ohmysensuality.com.)

vibrator An electrically powered vibrating device used to provide sexual stimulation.

than a typical heterosexual encounter, sexual encounters between women are marked by a greater variety of behaviors and by an emphasis on general body contact in addition to specific genital contacts (Hite, 2003).

While on the topic of same-sex encounters, it's worth pointing out that same-sex couples have one advantage over opposite-sex couples: They are interacting with partners whose basic anatomy, physiology, and psychology are quite familiar to them even before their first sexual experience. Furthermore, people's upbringing often allows them to communicate more effectively with people of their own sex than with people of the other sex. Thus, gay and lesbian couples may find it easier to express their sexual desires and needs. This very familiarity may also create problems, however, by lessening the sense of mystery and tension that energizes heterosexual relationships (LeVay, 2006).

Sex Toys Are Used to Enhance Sexual Pleasure

Innumerable natural and artificial objects have been recruited for sexual use at one time or another. Some are widely used, while others serve minority sexual interests or fetishisms or are designed to alleviate sexual disorders.

Vibrators, sometimes referred to as "personal massagers," are electrically (usually battery) powered devices (**Figure 6.18**). Their function is exactly what their name implies: to provide vibratory stimulation. Typically, a vibrator consists of a handle and a vibrating head, whose shape may be designed to stimulate a specific target: clitoris, vagina, the entire vulva, penis, or anus. The more expensive vibrators offer extra options, such as a greater range of speeds, and may be more durable.

Vibrators are very popular among women: about half of all women age 18 to 60 have used them, according to a survey by the Center for Sexual Health Promotion at Indiana University (Herbenick et al., 2009). Usage is highest among non-heterosexual women: About 70% of lesbians and 80% of bisexual women have used them, according to the same survey.

Vibrators are most often thought of as an aid to women when masturbating, and indeed, they are commonly used for that purpose. Many women need prolonged, continuous clitoral stimulation to reach orgasm, and a vibrator may be the most effective way to provide it.

Women may also use a vibrator during sex with a partner. A woman engaged in coitus or oral sex, for example, may simultaneously stimulate her clitoris with a vibrator. If her partner is a man, he may be unfamiliar with vibrators, or he may believe that a woman who uses one is telling him that he is an inadequate lover. (In reality, many women are not brought to orgasm by vaginal penetration alone, no matter who is doing the penetrating.) Most women who use vibrators are comfortable using them in partnered sex, and those who do so have a generally high level of sexual function (Herbenick et al., 2010a). Men may also use vibrators. About 40% of heterosexual men have used them, usually in the context of sex with a woman (Reece et al., 2010a). There are also vibrators specifically designed for stimulation of the penis—these may have a vibrating sleeve or ring. Alternatively, a vibrator may be used to stimulate the scrotum, perineum, or anus while the penis is stimulated by masturbation or partnered sex.

Figure 6.19 Dildos are designed for penetration of the vagina or anus. (Photo courtesy of Oh My Sensuality, www.ohmysensuality.com.)

Dildos are sex toys designed for penetration of the vagina or anus. They are not electrically powered; in fact, they predate the discovery of electricity by thousands of years. They may be realistic imitations of a penis (sometimes complete with scrotum), but they also come in a wide variety of other shapes and sizes, some designed to stimulate the clitoris at the same time the shaft of the dildo penetrates the vagina (**Figure 6.19**). The back end of the dildo may be flared to prevent its getting lost in the rectum, in which case it may be called a "butt plug." Alternatively, it may be double-ended, allowing two people to use the same dildo simultaneously.

Another kind of dildo is made to fit into a strap that a woman can wear around her hips or around one thigh (**Figure 6.20**). Strap-on dildos are mainly designed for sex between women (though many lesbians never use any kind of dildo). These devices also have a long history: Women of the Azande people of eastern Sudan traditionally used a banana, manioc, or sweet potato tied around the waist to engage in vaginal penetration with female partners (Ford & Beach, 1951). Heterosexual couples can also employ strap-on dildos: A man who is temporarily or permanently unable to achieve an erection may use one instead of his own penis, or a woman can use one to anally penetrate a man (Queen, 1998).

Dildos are made from a range of materials, but silicone rubber is generally preferred for its flexibility, smooth surface, and ease of cleaning. Dildos usually have to be used with a lubricant, not just for anal penetration but for vaginal penetration as well. They need to be used gently and with respect for anatomy—that is, they should be moved in the natural direction of the vagina or rectum. It is also best to use small sizes, at least to begin with. (Some health issues connected with the use of sex toys are discussed in Chapter 15.)

Humans are not the only species to use dildos. Orangutans, for example, have been observed to use twigs or vines for vaginal penetration (Rijksen, 1978). There are plenty of sex toys besides vibrators and dildos:

dildo A sex toy, often shaped like a penis, used to penetrate the vagina or anus.

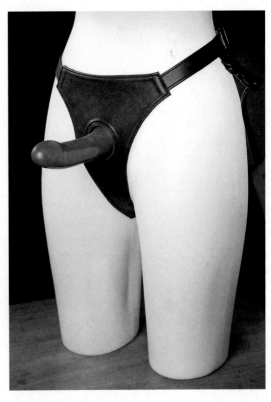

Figure 6.20 A strap-on dildo (Photo courtesy of Oh My Sensuality, www.ohmysensuality.com.)

Figure 6.21 Anal beads The beads shown here are made of a single piece of silicone, making them easier to keep clean than beads on a cord.

- *Anal beads* are a set of silicone or plastic beads on a string that are inserted into the anus and then pulled out slowly, often at the same time as orgasm (**Figure 6.21**). The passage of the beads through the anus can be highly arousing. They are used by both men and women, and in both solo and partnered sex.

- *Cock rings* (made of rigid or elastic materials) are placed around the base of the penis (or the penis and scrotum). They enhance erections, or extend them after ejaculation, by restricting the outflow of blood from the penis. They are especially useful for men with erectile disorder. Cock rings should be worn only for the duration of the sexual activity; prolonged use can damage the erectile tissues of the penis.

- Unpowered *masturbatory sleeves* are basically the inverse of dildos, for use by men (**Figure 6.22**). Some have orifices that are designed to resemble the vulva, the mouth, or the anus, and they all have an inner sleeve with a flesh-like feel.

- *Erotic dolls* are popular with some men. They may be simple blow-up dolls, or they may be very realistic, custom-made dolls that weigh as much as a real person and possess internal skeletons and joints that allow for lifelike positioning (**Figure 6.23**). A standard female doll of this kind costs about $6000, but the price quickly escalates with options such as alternative faces, clothes, or a removable penis to turn her into a "shemale."

sex play A variety of playful activities that add pleasure to sexual interactions.

For most people, sex toys are used in **sex play**—a catchall phrase for activities that add spice and variety to sex. Besides sex toys, sex play can include such things as the use of ice, oil, food, feathers, pillow fights, erotic biting, bondage and other role-playing fantasies, massage, fully clothed sex, striptease, sex with masks or blindfolds, use of mirrors, or sex in unusual locations. Sex play can incorporate penetrative sex or be a prelude or alternative to it. All that's required is a belief that sex should be fun,

Figure 6.22 Masturbatory sleeves have openings for the user to insert his penis. These Fleshlight sleeves are intended to resemble the vulva, mouth, or anus.

Figure 6.23   An erotic doll

as well as an active imagination—and even the latter isn't strictly necessary, given the number of books that offer advice in this area (see Recommended Reading at the end of this chapter).

All sex toys are capable of transmitting infections, so any toy that is to be used by more than one person should be scrupulously cleaned after use. Even after cleaning, agents that can carry sexually transmitted infections (STIs) such as human papillomavirus can sometimes be detected on the surfaces of sex toys (Anderson et al., 2014), so it's not a good idea for sex toys to be shared among multiple users.

It's worth stressing that sex is about much more than the mechanical issues that we've been discussing in the previous pages. For a discussion of what really makes for "great sex," see **Box 6.4**.

Sex May Be in Groups

Most of what we have described so far involves interactions between just two people, but in reality there's no limit to the number of persons who can participate in a single sexual encounter. Group sex may involve three or more people who are in a stable polyamorous relationship (see Chapter 11), or it may be a casual coming-together of strangers (a three-way, four-way, etc.) in a swingers' club, bathhouse, or outdoor "cruising" area.

The practical details of group-sex encounters vary widely. Among the possibilities are the following:

- All the participants take turns to have sex with one target individual.
- Two people simultaneously penetrate or orally stimulate a third person.
- One person penetrates another while simultaneously being penetrated by a third person.

FAQ

Why do I feel sad after sex?

If you're a woman, you're not alone—1 in 10 women has experienced the post-sex blues within the last month, according to one survey (Bird et al., 2011). The reason isn't known, unfortunately.

Box 6.4 Personal Points of View

What Is "Great Sex"?

Popular books and magazines tend to stress performance, technique, and novelty as the main elements of sexual satisfaction. But Peggy Kleinplatz, a sex therapist and professor at the University of Ottawa, wanted to find out what really made for "great sex" (Kleinplatz et al., 2009). So she and her colleagues recruited a diverse group of 64 subjects: sex therapists, members of sexual minorities, and older people, all of whom claimed to have experienced "great sex" or were currently experiencing it. (Curiously, they did not recruit any young, straight, non-professional subjects.) On the basis of extended interviews the researchers identified eight major components of "great sex" that were mentioned by most subjects:

1. **Being present and focused**: "The difference is when I can really just let go and completely focus and be in the moment and not have that, you know, running commentary going through my head about anything else."

2. **Connection**: "A melding, blurring of identity boundaries so that one feels like you were literally feeling with the other and the distinction between what the other person feels and what you feel seems almost irrelevant."

3. **Intimacy**: "Being loved and wanted, accepted and cherished." "Trust that this partner, whom you trust, will take care of you just as you are taking care of him."

4. **Communication—verbal and nonverbal**: "Being able to listen, to recognize, what, when, even if you're not told, that one kind of touch elicits a certain response in your partner and another does not."

5. **Authenticity, transparency**: "Getting to the point where I am completely stripped bare emotionally, physically, you know, spiritually."

6. **Transcendence, bliss**: "An experience of floating in the universe of light and stars and music and sublime peace."

7. **Exploration, risk taking**: "Where can we take each other? Where can we go?" "An opportunity for creativity." "If you're not having fun, it's not great."

Great sex is about more than technique.

8. **Vulnerability**: "It's saying I'm going to jump off this cliff where I'm going to, you know, be naked and be vulnerable and give myself to somebody else and take them in and I hope I feel good after I do that."

Some subjects also mentioned the importance of intense physical sensations, such as those of orgasm, or of intense attraction to the other person. ("Oh, my god! If I go another minute without my hands on you, I'll die.")

Based on their analysis of the interviews, the researchers concluded that performance and technique were of secondary importance to most people who experienced "great sex." Indeed, some had great sex in spite of significant sexual disorders. Rather, what mattered was something much more personal. "Being comfortable in one's own skin is the foundation for being authentically present and involved in the moment," Kleinplatz writes. "It is also a prerequisite for revealing oneself and taking a leap of faith with a lover."

- A number of people arrange themselves in a circle so that each can orally stimulate the next ("daisy-chaining").
- A large number of people engage in more or less random couplings (an orgy).
- Multiple couples engage in monogamous sex in a common space ("same-room sex").

The participants in group sex may be all of the same sex (usually gay men) or both sexes. If the latter, the individual contacts may be all heterosexual or a mix of oppo-

Figure 6.24 Orgy in stone This and many other erotic sculptures decorate the 1000-year-old Khajuraho temples in the Indian state of Madhya Pradesh.

site-sex and same-sex contacts. Sometimes there are participants who don't have any physical contact with others but whose arousal comes from watching the proceedings. (In that sense, viewing porn videos could be thought of as a form of group sex.)

Although group sex is sometimes viewed as sordid or sinful, it has often been portrayed in art, including religious art (**Figure 6.24**). It is also commonly observed among nonhuman animals. Bonobos, for example, are especially fond of group encounters. Some snakes form "mating balls" in which dozens of males attempt to penetrate a single female, but only a few succeed. Threesomes, in which one male penetrates a female while being penetrated by a second male, have been observed in many mammalian species: Whether such couplings are simply mistakes, or whether they have some adaptive significance, is not known.

Sexual Behavior and Attitudes Vary among Cultures

American culture seems to be in a state of transition with regard to the discussion of sexual practices. On the one hand, one can visit online websites, see video clips, or purchase books that cover not only mainstream sex, but any number of minority interests, from fisting to sex with animals. On the other hand, sex education in schools is still a very controversial topic, reflecting a conflict between traditional negative attitudes toward sex and an increasing desire for openness and realism, especially in the areas of contraception, disease prevention, masturbation, and homosexuality.

The Kama Sutra *is the classic work on how to make love*

Because attitudes in the United States have been changing so rapidly over the past few decades, open discussion of sexual behavior seems like a modern American phenomenon. In reality, however, some other societies have been more open in the way they deal with sexuality than we are. Nothing illustrates this better than the *Kama Sutra* of Vatsyayana, which was written in India no later than the 5th century.

Kama Sutra means "love guide." In Hindu teaching, *kama* ("love") is one of the four goals of life. Unlike the selfless love that is celebrated in Judeo-Christian tradition, however, *kama* includes a hefty dose of erotic pleasure, and this is a central topic of Vatsyayana's book.

Indicative of Vatsyayana's approach, he begins the chapter on sexual intercourse with a discussion of genital size. Unlike current textbooks such as this one, which tend to downplay the significance of size variations, Vatsyayana considers it a major problem if a man and woman's genitals are mismatched—particularly if the man is a "hare" (i.e., has a small penis) and the woman is a "female elephant" (i.e., has a large, deep vagina).

In such a case, Vatsyayana recommends penis enlargement, which is to be accomplished by repeated application of the bristles of certain tree-living insects, followed by rubbing the penis with oil for 10 nights and sleeping with the penis hanging down through a hole in the bed. ("He should take away all the pain from the swelling by using cool concoctions.") If this does not provide the woman with satisfaction, the man can use metal or ivory sleeves studded with "pleasure bumps" on the outside. They fit over the penis in a modular fashion, increasing its girth and length as much as desired. (Rather similar devices, made of plastic or silicone rubber, can be bought in sex toy shops today—they are called cock sleeves.) In an extreme case, says Vatsyayana, the man should forget about his penis altogether and simply tie the tubular stalk of a bottle gourd around his waist with string—another variation on the strap-on dildo.

The *Kama Sutra* is best known for its detailed description of coital positions, which include all the ones we have discussed plus more exotic ones that "require practice" (see the photograph that opens this chapter). There are also several chapters on foreplay, with detailed instructions for embracing, kissing, touching, slapping, scratching with the nails, and biting. Every kind of foreplay escalates by precise gradations, to slowly increase the degree of passion. Thus, if a man gives a woman a "line of points" (a mark caused by a nip by several teeth), she should respond with a "broken cloud" (a circular arrangement of marks caused by biting down on a large chunk of skin). He, in turn, may respond with the "biting of the boar," and so on.

Vatsyayana covers fellatio in considerable detail and cunnilingus briefly, but he barely mentions anal sex. (According to Indian tradition, the Muslims introduced anal sex in the 11th century.) Vatsyayana describes sex between women, but he sees it as a choice of last resort (e.g., among the women of the king's harem when no man can be smuggled in). Sex between men is chiefly a matter of eunuchs (castrated men) performing fellatio on other men in connection with bodily services such as massage. There is no notion of homosexuality as a stable orientation, but other sources show that both male and female homosexuality were known in ancient India (Vanita, 2001).

Vatsyayana is far more mindful of women's interests than are other ancient texts on sexuality, such as Ovid's *Art of Love* (a poem from the decadent period of Roman literature, which is basically a man's guide to seduction). Many of Vatsyayana's observations on how men and women interact seem right on target today. But his understanding of women's bodies is rudimentary: He seems not to know of the clitoris, for example.

Whether the open and positive attitude toward sex seen in the *Kama Sutra* was generally typical of Vatsyayana's time is difficult to know. For one thing, the book was written for and about the wealthy classes. The sex lives of the great majority of Indian people in the 5th century are lost to history, but they are unlikely to have been as rich and varied as described in the *Kama Sutra*. Today, the sex lives of poor Indians leave a lot to be desired. This is how two Indian sexologists summarized their survey of Dalit (lowest-caste) women living in cities:

Most of these women portrayed their experience with sexual intercourse as a furtive act in a cramped and crowded room, lasting barely a few minutes and with a marked absence of physical or emotional caressing. It was a duty, an experience to be submitted to, often from a fear of beating. None of the women removed their clothes during intercourse since it is considered shameful to do so. (Nath & Nayar, 1997)

India is of course not the only country where women's sexual interests may be subordinated to those of men. In southern Africa, many men's preference for "dry sex"—sex in which astringent substances have been placed in the woman's vagina to dry up her secretions—reduces women's sexual pleasure and threatens their health.

The Aka emphasize the importance of frequent sex

As an example of a contemporary non-Western culture, we'll take a look at sex among the Aka, a hunter-gatherer people who live in the rain forest of the Congo Basin (**Figure 6.25**). Aka culture is remarkably egalitarian: They have no dominant leaders, and men and women share their responsibilities, including hunting and child care.

Anthropologists Barry and Bonnie Hewlett, of Washington State University, have spent many years studying the Aka and have interviewed numerous men and women (in their native language) concerning their sex lives (Hewlett & Hewlett, 2010). One of their most striking findings concerns the frequency of sex. Married Aka couples have sex on about three nights every week, and on each of these nights they engage in coitus an average of three times, resting or sleeping between episodes. Men experience orgasm on every occasion, while women do so at least once on every night when they engage in coitus.

While this frequency of sex might not be unusual for American newlyweds, the Aka continue to have sex at roughly the same frequency throughout their fertile years. "I am now doing it five times a night to search for a child," one Aka man told the Hewletts. "If I do not do it five times my wife will not be happy because she wants children quickly." To facilitate this level of performance, Aka men use a sexual stimulant that they obtain by chewing the bark of a certain tree. (This stimulant may be yohimbine, a drug that is sometimes used in the United States for treatment of erectile disorder.)

The Aka men and women told the Hewletts that sex was "hard work"—work that was motivated by the need to produce numerous children in a culture where infant and child mortality is high. Although frequent sex does (within limits) increase the likelihood of pregnancy, the Aka also subscribe to a belief that makes it particularly important to have sex as often as possible. They believe that fetuses require repeated infusions of a man's semen in order to grow, an idea called **seminal nurture**. There is some kinship between seminal nurture and partible paternity, discussed in Chapter 1 (see Box 1.1, page 6): Central to both ideas is the belief that several or many coital acts—not just one—contribute to the making of a baby.

Consistent with their emphasis on the reproductive function of sex, none of the male or female interviewees had engaged in masturbation or homosexual behavior, or had even heard of these practices. The Hewletts cite the difficulties faced by an anthropologist who tried to obtain semen samples from another rain forest people: "It was very difficult to explain to men how to self-stimulate. . . . Despite explicit and lengthy instructions three of four semen samples came to him mixed with vaginal secretions." Although further research might identify some Aka individuals who do practice these behaviors, the Hewlett's observations challenge the notion that non-reproductive sexual behaviors are a human universal.

Many Disabled People Have Active Sex Lives

So far in this chapter, we have discussed sexual behavior as if everyone who wanted to engage in it was fully able-bodied and healthy. That's not the case, of course. Many people have disabilities or illnesses that present challenges to sexual expression. Here

Figure 6.25 An Aka mother and her children According to Aka beliefs, the birth of a child results from multiple acts of coitus.

seminal nurture The belief that fetuses require repeated infusions of semen to grow.

Box 6.5 Personal Points of View

On Seeing a Sex Surrogate

Mark O'Brien was a Berkeley-based writer who, as a consequence of childhood polio, had to spend most of his life inside an iron lung (a kind of mechanical respirator), as shown in the figure. In a 1990 article for *The Sun* magazine, O'Brien described his efforts to achieve sexual fulfillment with the help of a sex surrogate, Cheryl Cohen-Greene. The following is a condensed version of the article, which is available in full on the Web (O'Brien, 1990).

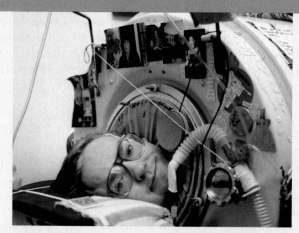

Mark O'Brian (1949–1999)

When March 17 arrived, I felt unbearably nervous. Vera, one of my morning attendants, dressed me, put me in my wheelchair, and pushed me to Marie's cottage. Once inside, Vera put a sheet I had brought with me on the double bed. Then she lowered me onto it. The bed was close to the floor, unlike my iron lung. Since it's difficult for me to turn my head to the left, Vera pushed me over to the left side of the bed, so that Cheryl could lay next to me and I could still see her. Then Vera put the hose of my portable respirator near my mouth, in case I needed air. I thought it likely because I'd never been outside the iron lung for an hour without using the portable respirator. I was all set.

Oh God, would she ever come? Perhaps she had found out what an ugly, deformed creep I am and was breaking the appointment.

A knock on the door. Cheryl had arrived. I turned my head as far to my left as I could. She greeted me, smiling, and walked to where I could see her better. She doesn't hate me yet, I thought. Marie went out the door with Vera, saying that she would return at 1. Cheryl and I were alone. "Your fee's on top of the dresser," I said, unable to think of anything else to say. She put the cash into her wallet, and thanked me.

She wore a black pantsuit, and her dark brown hair was tied behind her head. She had clear skin and large brown eyes and she seemed tall and strong, but then I'm 4' 7" and weigh sixty pounds. As we talked, I decided that she was definitely attractive. Was she checking out my looks? I was too scared to want to know.

Talking helped me to relax. I began to tell her about my life, my family, my fear of sexuality. I could see that she was accepting me and treating me with respect. I liked her, so when she asked me if I would feel comfortable letting her undress me, I said, "Sure." I was bluffing, attempting to hide my fear.

My heart pounded—not with lust, but with pure terror—as she kneeled on the bed and started to unbutton my red shirt. She had trouble undressing me; I felt awkward and wondered if she would change her mind and leave once she

saw me naked. She didn't. After she took my clothes off, she got out of bed and undressed quickly. I looked at her full, pale breasts, but was too shy to gaze between her legs.

Whenever I had been naked before—always in front of nurses, doctors, and attendants—I'd pretend I wasn't naked. Now that I was in bed with another naked person, I didn't need to pretend: I was undressed, she was undressed, and it seemed normal. How startling!

She explained about the body awareness exercises: first, she would run her hand over me, and I could kiss her wherever I wished. I told her I wished that I could caress her, too, but she assured me I could excite her with my mouth and tongue. She rubbed scented oil on her hands, then slowly moved her palms in circles over my chest and arms. I asked her if I could kiss one of her breasts. She sidled up to me so that I could kiss her left breast. So soft.

I was getting aroused. Her hand moved in its slow circles lower and lower as she continued to talk in her reassuring way and I continued my chattering. She lightly touched my cock—as though she liked it, as though it was fine that I was aroused. No one had ever touched me that way, or praised me for my sexuality. Too soon, I came.

After that, we talked a while. I asked Cheryl whether she thought I deserved to be loved sexually. She said she was sure of it. I nearly cried. She didn't hate me. She didn't consider me repulsive.

She got out of bed, went into the bathroom, and dressed. By then it was nearly 1. The door opened. It was Marie and Dixie. They asked me about the experience. I told them it had changed my life. I felt victorious, cleansed, and relieved.

Mark O'Brien's article formed the basis of the 2012 film *The Sessions*, in which John Hawkes played O'Brien and Helen Hunt played Cohen-Greene.

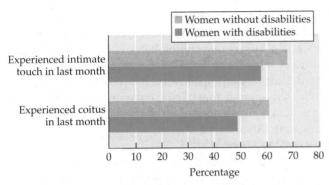

Figure 6.26 Disabilities have only a moderate effect on women's sexual activity. (Data from Nosek et al., 1997.)

we briefly focus on three kinds of disabilities—one that raises questions of choice and competency (intellectual disability) and two that may directly affect sexual behavior (spinal cord injuries and arthritis).

Probably the main thing to understand about disabilities is that they do not generally interfere with sexual desire or they do so only indirectly, in the sense that disabled people may internalize other people's stereotypes of them. Even severely disabled men and women are likely to experience sexual attraction, to fall in love, to desire intimacy, and to make great efforts to consummate those feelings (**Box 6.5**). There is every reason to respect and facilitate loving, nonabusive sexual expression by disabled people. Unfortunately, health care professionals who deal with disabled people often fail to bring up issues of sexual function with them, perhaps out of embarrassment or fear that they will not be able to offer useful advice.

In one large-scale national study of women with and without disabilities, the disabled women were only moderately less sexually active than the nondisabled women (Nosek et al., 1997) (**Figure 6.26**). The differences that did exist were primarily a consequence of the fact that the women with disabilities were less likely to be in a marriage or cohabitation.

Many intellectually disabled people are competent to make sexual choices

In most modern societies, people with mild or moderate intellectual disabilities often participate in community life and may live in independent or semi-independent settings. There has been an increasing acknowledgment that most intellectually disabled people have sexual feelings—only some profoundly disabled people seem to lack them. Like anyone else, intellectually disabled people may belong to sexual minorities, such as being gay or lesbian, though this is a possibility that is often ignored by caregivers and others (Noonan & Taylor Gomez, 2010).

Intellectually disabled people have the same constitutional right as other people (under the right to privacy) to make informed choices about sexual activity, to the extent that they are capable of doing so. They also have a right to protection from sexual exploitation, however. Balancing these rights can be difficult.

In general, it is illegal, as well as reprehensible, for anyone to have sexual contact with an intellectually disabled person if that person lacks the mental capacity to give informed consent. Mental capacity means knowledge about sex, the intelligence to understand the risks and benefits of sexual activity (including an awareness of the social and moral nature of sexual relations), and the ability to make a decision free of coercion (Lyden, 2007).

quadriplegia Paralysis affecting almost the entire body below the neck.

paraplegia Paralysis affecting the lower half of the body.

No one can give consent on behalf of the disabled person. Thus, if psychiatrists or others judge a person to be incapable of giving consent, caregivers have a responsibility to protect that person from all sexual contact with others, because such contact would be sexual assault or statutory rape. Institutional staff may realize that an intellectually disabled person of borderline mental capacity has the wish to engage in sex, and they may therefore be motivated to judge that person competent. The downside of doing this is that if the judgment of competence holds up, the disabled person may be sexually exploited by others, with little recourse.

Luckily, many intellectually disabled people are well within the bounds of competence and chiefly need education in such matters as potential sexual behaviors, appropriate partners, privacy, sexual exploitation, STIs, pregnancy prevention, and the like (Lumley & Scotti, 2001). The Arc, a national organization of and for the intellectually disabled, asserts the right of these people not only to engage in sexual relationships, but also to marry and have children and, if they do have children, to receive assistance in raising them.

Spinal cord injuries present a major challenge to sexual expression

Each year there are about 10,000 spinal cord injuries in the United States that result in significant and permanent neurological deficits. The majority of victims are young or middle-aged men (**Figure 6.27**). Most of these injuries result from motor vehicle accidents, violence, sports accidents, or falls. A complete injury at the cervical (neck) level results in almost total loss of movement and sensation below the neck (**quadriplegia**), while injuries at lower levels usually affect the legs and the lower portion of the trunk, including the genitals (**paraplegia**).

One option adopted by many men and women with spinal cord injuries is to make increased use of parts of the body whose movement and sensation are unimpaired. In quadriplegics that may mean primarily the mouth, while for paraplegics it may include the hands and breasts. Many people with spinal cord injuries report that the erotic sensitivity of their unaffected body regions increases over time, so much so that the person may experience orgasm, or highly pleasant sensations comparable to orgasm, from sexual use of those regions. In some cases the sensations may be experienced as if they were coming from the genitalia ("phantom orgasm").

A man with a spinal cord injury may or may not be able to have an erection. If the injury is to the lowest portion of the spinal cord, the man is unlikely to be able to have an erection under any circumstances, because the neural mechanisms that activate erection are located there. If the injury is high in the spinal cord, he probably will be able to have erections in response to sensory stimulation of the genitalia, because the entire reflex loop from the genitalia to the spinal cord and back is intact. In fact, the loss of inhibitory influences from the brain may cause reflex erections to be stronger and more frequent than usual (Elliott, 2009). However, if the spinal injury is complete, the man will not feel any sensations from his penis, erect or not. Nor will he have erections in response to erotic sights or fantasies ("psy-

Figure 6.27 Paraplegia typically strikes young men. Sexual expression is still possible but requires adaptability.

chogenic erections"), because the long pathways between the brain and the lower spinal cord have been interrupted.

Viagra and similar drugs have proved helpful for men with spinal cord injuries who have difficulty obtaining or maintaining an erection, but only if at least a partial erection can be obtained without the drug (Schmid et al., 2000).

Ejaculation may be possible for men with lower-level injuries, especially if there is not a complete transection of the spinal cord, but a complete upper-level injury generally makes ejaculation impossible because it cuts off signals from the brain centers that are involved in triggering this process. (The brain's involvement in ejaculation is discussed in Appendix B.) Even if ejaculation is possible, it is not likely to be accompanied by the normal subjective sensations of orgasm. Ejaculation may occur retrogradely (into the bladder) because of the failure of the sphincter at the upper end of the urethra to close.

Men with spinal cord injuries who wish to engage in coitus are usually capable of doing so. If the man is paraplegic, he can take the man-on-top position. He may have to push his flaccid penis into the woman's vagina by hand (the "stuffing" technique); the woman can help this process by actively contracting the muscles of the vaginal walls. The man's penis may then become erect as a result of reflex action as the woman performs thrusting motions. If the man is quadriplegic, the woman does best to kneel astride him and place his penis in her vagina; again, the penis may become erect in response to this stimulation. An additional complication is urinary incontinence. If a urinary catheter is in place, it can be kept in place with the aid of a condom or tape; this, then, will necessitate the use of a lubricant.

Women with spinal cord injuries have deficits roughly comparable to men's: Besides the loss of movement and sensation (depending on the level and severity of the injury), women may lose vaginal lubrication (necessitating use of a lubricant). With lower-level injuries, engorgement of the vulvar tissues may be lost as well. Coitus is possible in several positions, however, including the man-on-top position, or side by side with either front or rear entry.

In one laboratory-based study (Sipski et al., 2001), somewhat fewer than half of the women with spinal cord injuries were able to reach orgasm, compared with 100% of uninjured women. Ability to reach orgasm was lowest with complete injuries affecting the lowest region of the spinal cord. Among women who did reach orgasm, the time required to do so was longer than among the uninjured women, but the orgasms themselves were similar in quality.

The usual explanation for how women with spinal-cord injuries can experience orgasm is that the cord has not been completely severed. Some women with *complete* transection of the cord still report experiencing orgasm in some circumstances, however, especially in response to deep stimulation of the vagina or cervix. It is thought that this is made possible by sensory signals carried in the vagus nerve (one of the cranial nerves), which has sensory branches that innervate the abdomen and pelvis, bypassing the spinal cord altogether (Komisaruk et al., 2004). Paraplegic and quadriplegic women can sustain a pregnancy and deliver a baby vaginally, although they are at a somewhat increased risk of complications or premature birth. Contraception presents some special problems for women with spinal cord injuries: These women may have a higher-than-normal risk of blood clots when using hormonal contraceptives, and the lack of feeling in the pelvis means that problems with intrauterine devices may go undetected. Condoms, or sterilization of either partner, are safe options.

If you are an able-bodied and sexually active young person, you might be wondering whether sexual interactions are really worth it for spinal-cord-injured men and women or their partners. The answer, however, is often a resounding "yes"—

whether in terms of physical pleasure, intimacy between partners, or the psychological reward of accomplishing such a basic human activity in the face of a major challenge.

Arthritis is the number one disability affecting sex

Some disabilities interfere with sexual expression by limiting movement. In this connection, people generally think first of spinal cord injuries, but numerically, the leading villain is arthritis. This collection of conditions (chiefly osteoarthritis, rheumatoid arthritis, and systemic lupus erythematosus) affects an estimated 22% of American adults; women and the elderly are disproportionately affected.

If arthritis affects the large joints, such as the hips, it may impair the postures or body movements (such as pelvic thrusting) involved in partnered sex. If it involves the small joints of the hands, it may interfere with masturbation, sensual touching, and tasks requiring dexterity, such as putting on a condom or inserting a diaphragm.

A certain degree of planning can make lovemaking a much more positive experience for people with arthritis. Sex can be timed for a part of the day when the person's arthritis is least bothersome, or medications can be timed to be maximally effective during sex. It may be helpful to precede sexual intercourse with a warm shower, gentle massage, or use of a vibrator to assist arousal.

What about positions for coitus? If the woman has arthritis that affects her hips (one of the most common conditions), the man-above (missionary) position may not be suitable. It may help to modify the man-above position so that the woman keeps her thighs together and the man places his legs on the outside of hers. Alternatively, the rear-entry position is often suitable, either with both man and woman lying on their sides, or with both man and woman standing and the woman leaning over and supporting herself on something. If the man's knees or hips are affected, the woman-above position may be the best. If coitus is too painful on a particular occasion, oral or manual stimulation, or use of a vibrator, may be a fine alternative. Each couple can experiment to find what works for them.

Go to the **Discovering Human Sexuality** Companion Website at **sites.sinauer.com/discoveringhumansexuality3e** for activities, study questions, quizzes, and other study aids.

Summary

- Historically, attitudes toward masturbation or autoerotic behavior have been quite negative. These attitudes derive from moral teachings, from the notion that masturbation is unhealthy, and from a sense that people who masturbate are those who can't find a sex partner. Even today, many people feel guilty about masturbating.

- Masturbation is a common sexual behavior. Factors associated with higher rates of masturbation include a younger age and a higher educational level. Factors associated with lower rates of masturbation include having a regular sex partner, being more religious, and being African-American. Gay people masturbate more than heterosexuals and derive more enjoyment from it.

Masturbation does not seem to be simply a substitute for sex with partners.

- Men tend to use a single technique for masturbation—direct manual stroking of the penis—whereas women use a greater variety of techniques, such as manual stimulation of the clitoris, labia, or vagina, or rubbing of the vulva against objects. Men experience orgasm during masturbation more frequently than do women.

- Kissing is an important form of sexual expression in the United States, where it often has strong romantic significance, but it is not practiced in all human cultures.

- Sexual touching includes a variety of behaviors short of penetrative sex. It may be a prelude to penetrative sexual interaction (foreplay), or it may form the entire sexual encounter, especially among adolescents.

- Oral sex means contact between the mouth and the penis (fellatio), the vulva (cunnilingus), or the anus (anilingus). Oral sex has become increasingly popular among younger people in the United States and Britain, where 80% to 90% of young people have engaged in it. Like many noncoital sexual behaviors, it is more common among well-educated people.

- About half of U.S. men, but fewer women, find fellatio very appealing. Men and women enjoy cunnilingus about equally; approximately one-third of the U.S. population find it very appealing. Oral sex may be performed mutually in a head-to-genital arrangement; this position is called 69, or *soixante-neuf*.

- Most adult heterosexual couples engage in coitus as the culmination of a sexual encounter. The most popular and traditional position for coitus in the United States is the man-above position ("missionary position"), which requires the man to do most of the pelvic thrusting. The rise of feminism in the 1970s encouraged the exploration of other positions, such as the woman-above position and rear-entry coitus. Each position may have particular advantages and disadvantages for certain couples or in certain situations.

- Anal sex (penetration of the anus by the penis) is practiced in both male-male and female-male encounters. Anal sex can be performed in a variety of positions and does not damage the anus or rectum when performed in a nonforcible manner.

- Some couples like to make coitus almost the entirety of a sexual encounter, while others include much foreplay and afterplay, or even dispense with coitus altogether. Women generally take longer to reach orgasm than do men, so men might have to learn to postpone orgasm in heterosexual encounters when the man and woman wish to experience orgasm at close to the same time.

- Vibrators are electrically powered devices that deliver erotically arousing vibratory stimulation. Men or women may use them, but they are particularly associated with use for masturbation by women and to help women reach orgasm in partnered sex. Dildos are unpowered, sometimes penis-shaped objects used for vaginal or anal penetration, in either partnered or solo sex. Other sex toys include anal beads, cock rings, masturbatory sleeves, and erotic dolls.

- Group sex can take many forms, involving interactions within polyamorous relationships as well as between strangers. Group contacts can be gang bangs, orgies, "same-room sex," and other combinations.

- Different cultures vary greatly in the openness with which they discuss sexual behavior. One classic how-to manual on sexual behavior is the *Kama Sutra* (from India, 5th century or earlier). This book demonstrates that explicit discussion of sex is not the sole prerogative of modern Western society. Contemporary India, however, has attitudes toward sex that are less positive than those described in the *Kama Sutra*.

- Among the Aka, an African hunter-gatherer people, couples have sex at high frequencies throughout their fertile years. This practice is connected with the belief that multiple acts of coitus are required to nurture a fetus.

- Most intellectually disabled people experience the same sexual feelings and desires as everyone else. They have a right to make informed choices about sexual behavior if they are capable of doing so. Facilitating the exercise of this right must be balanced against the need to protect intellectually disabled people from sexual exploitation. With appropriate education, many intellectually disabled people can enjoy active sex lives, and some become parents and raise children.

- Spinal cord injuries can cause a near-complete loss of movement and sensation in the body below the neck (quadriplegia) or in the lower half of the body (paraplegia). Although conscious sensations from the genitalia are often lost, reflex penile erection and vaginal lubrication and engorgement may be preserved, depending on the level of the injury and whether the spinal cord has been completely severed. Most people with spinal cord injuries can engage in coitus if they desire it, and women with spinal cord injuries can sustain pregnancy and deliver a baby vaginally.

- Some disabilities interfere with sexual behavior by limiting movement or making movement painful. Arthritis is the leading culprit in this respect, with 15% of the U.S. population affected. Nevertheless, people with arthritis can usually engage in pleasurable and rewarding sex by advance preparation and by choosing positions for sex that put the least stress on affected joints.

Discussion Questions

1. Why do you think a higher educational level is associated with a greater prevalence of masturbation (see Figure 6.3)? How could researchers determine the actual reason? Do you think that teaching about masturbation would help reduce unwanted pregnancies and sexually transmitted infections?

2. Do you think that people in general should not engage in some of the sexual behaviors described in this chapter? Is your view based on your moral beliefs, on practical (e.g., health) considerations, or some other reason?

3. Consider your attitudes and beliefs about whether the government should regulate the kinds of sex acts that American adults engage in. Are there any sex acts that should be prohibited? Imagine that you are testifying before a Senate committee, and argue what should or should not be permitted or prohibited. How might the Supreme Court rule on the decision you make?

4. Do you think that it's possible to have "great sex" with a complete stranger? How do your views on this jibe with Peggy Kleinplatz's eight components of "great sex" described in Box 6.4?

5. You have a friend whose arthritis makes sexual intercourse very uncomfortable. He fears he may have to give up sex because he can't find a comfortable position. What changes might you suggest to help him find a more comfortable approach?

Web Resources

Dr. Ruth Westheimer's sex advice www.drruth.com
NERVE (an online magazine devoted to sex and culture) www.nerve.com
Society for Human Sexuality www.sexuality.org
The Lover's Guide www.loversguide.com

Recommended Reading

Comfort, A. (2009). *The joy of sex: The timeless guide to lovemaking* (rev. ed.). Crown.

Cosmopolitan. (2007). *Cosmo's steamy sex games: All sorts of naughty ways to have fun with your lover.* Hearst.

Dale, L. (Ed.). (2003). *The complete illustrated Kama Sutra.* Inner Traditions.

Dodson, B. (1987). *Sex for one: The joy of self-loving.* Harmony.

Frank, K. (2013). *Plays well in groups: A journey through the world of group sex.* Rowman & Littlefield.

Joannides, P. (2012). *Guide to getting it on!* (7th ed.). Goofy Foot.

Katz, S. (2014). *Lesbian sex positions: 100 passionate positions from intimate and sensual to wild and naughty.* Amorata.

Kaufman, M., Silverberg, C. & Odette, F. (2007). *The ultimate guide to sex and disability: For all of us who live with disabilities, chronic pain, and illness* (2nd ed.). Cleis.

Schwartz, P. and Lever, J. (2012). *Getaway guide to the great sex weekend.* Worldwide Romance.

Silverstein, C. & Picano, F. (2003). *The joy of gay sex* (3rd ed.). William Morrow. (Gay male sex only.)

Sipski, M. L. & Alexander, C. J. (Eds.). (1997). *Sexual function in people with disability and chronic illness: A health professional's guide.* Aspen.

Stengers, J. & Van Neck, A. (2001). *Masturbation: The history of a great terror* (K. A. Hoffmann, Trans.). Palgrave.

Vatsyayana. (1991). *The Kama Sutra of Vatsyayana* (R. F. Burton, Trans.). Arkana.

Chapter 7

Sexual relationships are not just about sex.

Sexual Relationships

In previous chapters we discussed sexual attraction, sexual arousal, and sexual behavior. Now we step back and take a look at the interpersonal frameworks within which partnered sex may occur—in other words, sexual relationships.

Of course, we have to interpret the word "relationship" broadly if we are to encompass the full expression of human sexuality. In common discourse, a "one-night stand"—or an even briefer sexual encounter between strangers—may not constitute a relationship, but for our purposes it does. So does a partnership that lasts a lifetime. So do sexual encounters that involve coercion or payment, although we defer discussion of these two topics to Chapters 16 and 17. What interests us here is the dynamic that brings people together as potential sex partners and keeps them together for minutes, days, or decades.

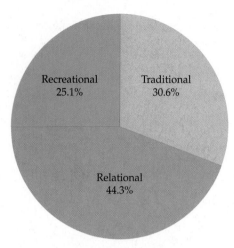

Figure 7.1 Moral perspectives on sexuality Americans can be grouped into three perspectives reflecting different ideas about the purpose of sex. (Data from NHSLS.)

Sexual Relationships Are Motivated by Many Factors

What propels people into sexual relationships? According to the contemporary Western ideal, there are two leading factors: physical attraction and romantic love. Certainly, these powerful forces inspire many sexual encounters and lasting relationships. But they may be mingled with, or entirely replaced by, a wide variety of other motives. These include the desire for status, security, or profit; the desire to conform or to follow moral beliefs—or, conversely, to rebel; the desire to arouse jealousy; and finally, of course, the desire to have children. Most sexual relationships are probably fueled by some combination of these forces. (See **Web Activity 7.1: Definitions of Sexual Relationships.**)

Sexual relationships involve more than just two people: They are played out in a larger social, economic, and moral context. Let's begin with the last of these and consider how moral attitudes influence sexuality.

Moral Judgments about Sex Depend on Its Context

In a series of studies begun in the 1960s, sociologist Ira Reiss showed that people judge the morality of heterosexual behavior by the relationship within which it occurs: The more affectionate, intimate, or committed the relationship, the more likely people are to consider sexual acts morally acceptable (Reiss & Miller, 1979). Some non-heterosexual behaviors, however, may be judged without regard to the relationship within which they occur. At one time, interracial relationships were also widely stigmatized, or even illegal (**Box 7.1**).

How committed does a heterosexual relationship need to be for sex to be morally acceptable? People's views on this question are influenced by their beliefs about the purpose of sex and can be grouped into three perspectives (DeLamater, 1987):

- *Traditional perspective.* The main purpose of sex is procreation; nonmarital sex and sex acts that cannot lead to pregnancy are morally suspect.

- *Relational perspective.* An important purpose of sex is cementing relationships. Sex between unmarried people is morally acceptable if the relationship is a committed one, but extramarital or casual sex is not acceptable.

- *Recreational perspective.* The main purpose of sex is to give pleasure. Most kinds of consensual sex are morally acceptable.

Looking at the U.S. population as a whole, the relational perspective is by far the most common, followed by the traditional perspective. Only about 25% of the population subscribe to the recreational perspective (**Figure 7.1**).

Demographic factors affect sexual attitudes

Surveys such as the National Health and Social Life Survey (NHSLS) and the General Social Survey (GSS—a project of the National Opinion Research Center at the University of Chicago) have found that basic demographic facts about a person, such as sex, age, educational level, region of residence, race/ethnicity, and religion, predict that individual's attitudes on sexual issues (**Figure 7.2**):

- *Sex.* Women are more likely than men to have a traditional perspective, disapproving of casual, nonmarital, and extramarital sex.

- *Age.* Older people are more likely than younger people to have a traditional perspective.

- *Education.* Increasing educational level is associated with relatively permissive attitudes.

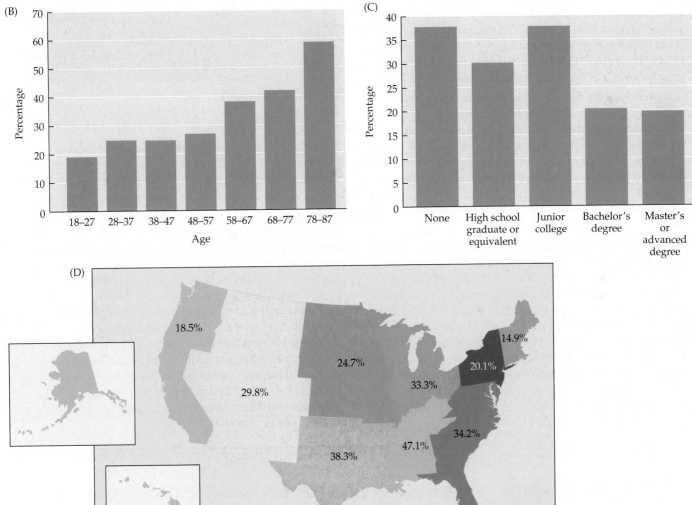
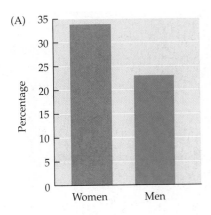

Figure 7.2   Is premarital sex wrong? These four figures show the percentage of respondents who believe that premarital sex is "always wrong" or "almost always wrong," based on their sex (A), age (B), education level (C), and geographic region (D). (Data from the 2010 General Social Survey.)

- *Region.* People living in the Northeast or on the West Coast of the United States are less likely to have a traditional perspective on sex, and more likely to have a recreational perspective, than are people in other regions. Residents of the southern states tend to be more traditional than other easterners.

Box 7.1 Society, Values, and the Law

Who May Marry?

Early in the morning of July 11, 1958, Richard Loving and his wife Mildred were asleep at their home in Central Point, Virginia, when three policemen burst into their bedroom. "Who is this woman you're sleeping with?" they demanded of Richard. Mildred replied, "I'm his wife," and Richard pointed to the marriage certificate hanging on their bedroom wall. "That's no good here," responded the sheriff, and he arrested both of them.

The Lovings (see figure) were an interracial couple (Richard was white; Mildred was African-American). They had married out of state and returned to Virginia to live. They were convicted of violating Virginia's 1924 Racial Integrity Act, which made marriage between a white person and a nonwhite person a felony.

In his sentencing opinion, the judge in the *Loving* case wrote as follows: "Almighty God created the races white, black, yellow, malay, and red, and he placed them on separate continents. The fact that he separated the races shows he did not intend for the races to mix." Although this makes the statute appear to be based on (misguided) moral grounds, historians and jurists believe that it was motivated by white supremacist thinking, because it did not ban marriage between nonwhite persons of different races.

The Lovings were sentenced to a year in prison, but the sentence was suspended provided that they left the state and did not return for 25 years. They moved to Washington, DC, where they appealed the case. In its 1967 *Loving v. Virginia* decision, the U.S. Supreme Court struck down the Virginia statute and affirmed the right to marry across racial lines. The justices based their ruling on the due process and equal protection clauses of the Constitution. These have been interpreted to grant a fundamental right to marry that cannot be denied to certain couples on account of a mere perception of immorality. Some state supreme courts (beginning with California, in a 1948 case titled *Perez v. Sharp*) had reached the same conclusion before the *Loving* decision.

Mildred and Richard Loving

Among the many beneficiaries of *Loving* are the current U.S. Supreme Court justice Clarence Thomas and his wife, an interracial couple who live in the same state where Mildred and Richard Loving were convicted a half century ago.

Although the constitutional battle over interracial marriage has been resolved, the legal principles that were debated then have been brought back into focus by the current debate over same-sex marriage. In 2008, when the California Supreme Court heard arguments on the gay marriage issue, proponents of such marriage successfully argued that the court's 1948 *Perez* ruling set a precedent that was equally applicable to same-sex couples. And in 2013, when the U.S. Supreme Court struck down the Defense of Marriage Act (which banned federal recognition of same-sex marriage), it cited the *Loving* case in support of its decision. (Same-sex marriage is covered in Chapter 12.) Richard Loving died in 1975, Mildred in 2008. In her last public statement before her death, Mildred Loving spoke out in favor of gay couples' right to marry (Martin, 2008).

FAQ

I'm Catholic and the Church says it's sinful to use contraception—what should I do?

Most U.S. Catholics don't follow the Church's teachings on this topic, but if you wish to do so, we describe options in Chapter 9.

- *Race/ethnicity.* Race or ethnicity is not strongly predictive of sexual attitudes, but African-Americans and Hispanics tend to be less approving of homosexuality and abortion than are whites.
- *Religion.* Conservative Protestants, such as Baptists, tend to have a traditional perspective, while people with no religious affiliation tend to have a recreational perspective. Catholics and mainstream Protestants hold a wide range of attitudes, but most have a relational perspective.

Although survey data imply that people's demographic characteristics can predict, to a considerable extent, their sexual attitudes, we don't mean to downplay the individual aspects of moral reasoning. All kinds of life experiences—an unwanted preg-

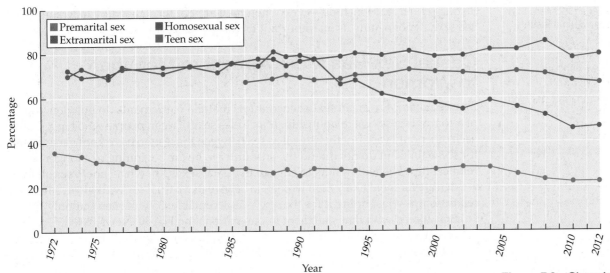

Figure 7.3 Changing attitudes This graph shows changes in the percentage of the U.S. population who considered premarital sex, extramarital sex, gay sex, and teen sex "always wrong," from 1972 through 2012. The question about teen sex (which was first asked in 1986) specified 14- to 16-year-olds. (Data from the General Social Survey.)

nancy, having a daughter or son come out as gay, and so on—may cause people to reconsider their attitudes on sexual issues.

Americans' Attitudes Have Changed over Time

While on the topic of changing attitudes, let's take a look at how Americans' moral stances on sexual topics have changed over the last few decades. The GSS has asked Americans a standard set of questions on a variety of topics since the early 1970s (National Opinion Research Center, 2013) (**Figure 7.3**). The GSS has found a decline in the percentage of the population who consider sex before marriage "always wrong" and a corresponding rise in the percentage who consider it "not wrong at all." When interviewees have been asked specifically about sex between 14- to 16-year-olds, however—a question that was first asked in 1986—opinions have been far more negative and have not changed significantly over the period during which the question has been asked.

With regard to extramarital sex, public opinion has actually become more negative. Between 1973 and 2012, the percentage of people who believed that extramarital sex is "always wrong" increased from 70% to 80%.

With regard to gay sex, opinion has changed in a more complicated way. During the 1980s, when public concern about AIDS was at its height and the disease was largely blamed on gay men, disapproval of gay sex increased to the point that nearly 80% of Americans thought it is "always wrong." Since the early 1990s, however, there has been a very marked liberalizing trend. By 2012 less than half the U.S. population (46%) believed that gay sex is always wrong.

In spite of the diversity of attitudes toward the morality of sex, it's worth emphasizing a belief that represents a common moral ground for many people—the idea that it's not the sex act itself, but its context, that has moral significance. In particular, sexual behavior that may endanger established relationships is very broadly disapproved of. Whereas only about 1 in 5 Americans thinks that *non*marital sex is always wrong, 4 in 5 think that *extra*marital sex is always wrong. The British National Survey of Sexual Attitudes and Lifestyles (NSSAL) study came up with very similar findings but, in addition, found that cohabiting and even *non*-cohabiting sexual relationships were viewed as morally protected, albeit not to the same degree that marriages are: Most of the interviewees felt that people in such relationships should not engage in sex outside the relationship. Evidently, most people place a high moral value on

casual sex Sexual encounters that do not take place within a lasting sexual relationship.

sociosexuality Interest or engagement in sex without commitment.

hooking up Uncommitted sex with an acquaintance.

lasting sexual relationships—even when they are not formalized by marriage—and see sexual monogamy as an important factor in preserving them.

Casual Sex Has More Appeal to Men than to Women

By **casual sex**, we mean sexual encounters that the participants do not view as part of a committed sexual relationship. It includes sex between people who have known each other only very briefly, as well as sex between those who have known each other for some time but do not intend the encounter to be the beginning of a longer sexual relationship. The willingness to engage in casual sex is known as **sociosexuality**.

Men are far more likely than women to believe that casual sex without an emotional relationship—"just doing it for the sex"—is acceptable; 35% of men but only 15% of women agreed with that statement in one national poll (ABC News, 2004). Does this difference in moral stance translate into differences in behavior? In a classic study, psychologists Russell Clark and Elaine Hatfield performed a "real-life test" of this question (Clark & Hatfield, 1989, 2003). They recruited attractive male and female college students as confederates and had them approach unwitting students of the other sex somewhere on a U.S. college campus (**Figure 7.4**). They were told to say "I have been noticing you around campus and I find you to be very attractive." Then they asked one of three questions: "Would you go out with me tonight?" "Would you come over to my apartment tonight?" or "Would you go to bed with me tonight?"

The male and female "targets" of these requests were about equally willing to go out with the confederate—about half assented to this request. When the request was phrased in ways that referred more explicitly to the desire for casual sex, however, women's responses rapidly fell off—in fact, not a single woman agreed to go to bed with the male confederate, and the women often lent emphasis to the rejection with comments such as "What's wrong with you, creep, leave me alone!" Men's responses, however, became more positive as the proposal became more explicit: 69% of the men agreed to go to the female confederate's apartment, and 75% agreed to go to bed with her, sometimes adding a comment such as "Why do we have to wait until tonight?" In other words, reducing a casual date to its sexual essentials robbed the date of all its appeal to women, but actually *enhanced* its appeal to men! When you consider that some of the men must have been in ongoing relationships, some must have been gay, and some must have been otherwise engaged that evening, a 75% acceptance rate to having sex is fairly astonishing.

More recent experiments of the same kind have largely replicated Clark and Hatfield's findings (British Broadcasting Corporation, 2002; Voracek et al., 2005). Nevertheless, there have been critical voices. It's been suggested, for example, that the artificial setup of the Clark-Hatfield experiments, combined with the sexual "double standard," caused women and men to evaluate the proposers in very different ways: Women, perhaps, judged the male proposers to be socially and sexually inept, whereas men judged the female proposers to be experienced and skillful lovers (Conley et al., 2012). What do you think?

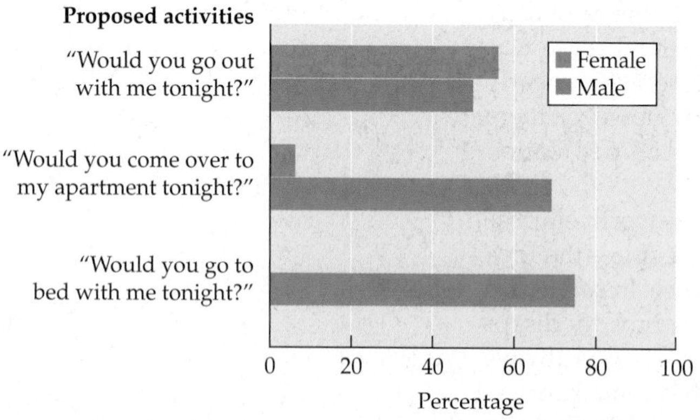

Hooking up—the new norm?

Although women may be as averse to sex with total strangers as they ever were, some young heterosexual women are becoming more open to engaging in casual, uncommitted sex with acquaintances—sometimes including people they have met that same evening, and sometimes involving other women rather

Figure 7.4 **Sex differences in willingness to engage in casual sex** The figure shows the percentage of female and male college students who agreed to three activities proposed by an attractive but unfamiliar student of the other sex. (Data from Clark & Hatfield, 1989.)

Box 7.2 Society, Values, and the Law

Straight Women, Gay Sex

Pop singer Katy Perry rose to fame in 2008 with the song "I Kissed a Girl," whose lyrics included the following lines: "I kissed a girl, just to try it. I hope my boyfriend don't mind it. It felt so wrong, it felt so right. Don't mean I'm in love tonight." With these words Perry put her seal of approval on a form of behavior that has been rapidly gaining popularity, or at least public attention: sexual intimacy between young women who are not lesbians. The practitioners may describe themselves as **heteroflexible**, "gayish," or (in the case of college students) "4-year queer" or "BUG" ("bisexual until graduation"). In the 2012 British NSSAL nearly 1 in 5 young women said that they had had sex with another woman (K. R. Mitchell et al., 2013).

Katy Perry is straight but she "kissed a girl"—Miley Cyrus, in fact.

There is a long tradition of romantic, physically intimate friendships between teenage girls or young women who later become pillars of heterosexual society (Faderman, 1981; Vicinus, 1989). What distinguishes the current trend is that the behavior is overt rather than hidden, and that much of it is quite casual. In fact, part of the purpose of these "lesbian" interactions may be a heterosexual one—to arouse the interest of males. "It's very common to see girls making out at parties," a male Rutgers student told the *Star-Ledger* of New Jersey. "I think it's an attention-getting thing; they only do it in front of guys." A 22-year-old woman said, "The waitresses where I work are doing it right in front of the cooks. They're doing it for attention" (O'Crowley, 2004).

Other young women engage in sexual interactions with women for reasons that have nothing to do with attracting men or with establishing a lesbian identity. It may be a matter of experimentation, the desire to give physical expression to a close friendship, the pressure to follow a trend, or a preference for the safety and mutual understanding of a same-sex relationship. Here's one student's (abbreviated) account:

I had small crushes on women before, but nothing beyond the realm of my imagination had happened—until I met Amy. Our attraction was, at first, that of two best friends destined to keep in touch for life. But by the end of one listless summer an undeniable sexual heat had developed between us. One night, we got drunk on cheap swill and did the deed. Embarrassed, we giggled over our small feat for weeks. It was the first and last time we'd make love. But, hot damn, it was amazing!

I had other encounters with women, but none quite matched the heady rush that followed the first. I quickly became disenchanted with the notion of, well, going down. How could men manage this for minutes on end? And the soft, sweet feminine touch was no match for the firm, male thrust. There was no getting around it: I was straight. (Anonymous, 1999)

The prevalence of heteroflexible behavior by women is consistent with other lines of evidence suggesting that sexual orientation is more fluid in women than in men. We discuss this issue, in Chapter 12.

heteroflexible   Mostly straight but having some interest in same-sex contacts or relationships.

---

than men (**Box 7.2**). This practice is often called **hooking up** (Garcia et al., 2012). An alleged "hookup culture," especially on college campuses, has attracted intense (and perhaps prurient) interest from the media and social scientists: Just one newspaper, the *New York Times*, mentioned hookups in over 200 articles between 2010 and 2014, and over 2000 research studies dealt with or touched on the topic over the same period, according to a Google Scholar search.

Hookups may involve anything from kissing to coitus, are typically unplanned, and arise when young people hang out, party together, and the like. When a hookup is between friends and is arranged by phone or text message, it may be referred to as a "booty call" (Jonason et al., 2010). Booty calls involve a little more romance than the average hookup, but they still don't carry any implication of a long-term sexual relationship. Two persons who are not a "couple" but engage in occasional booty calls may be described as "friends with benefits."

Hookups often arise out of small social gatherings.

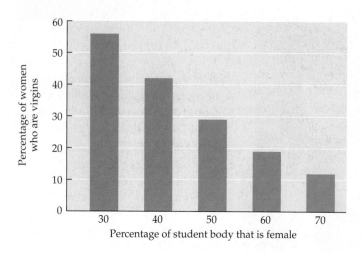

Figure 7.5 The sex ratio influences sexual behavior. The bar graph shows how the likelihood that a college woman is still a virgin varies according to the percentage of female students at her campus. These data are for women with current boyfriends. (Data from the College Women's Survey, cited in Regnerus & Uecker, 2011.)

Hookups are much more common on college campuses than they were a decade or two ago (Bogle, 2008; Claxton & van Dulmen, 2013), but the notion that college life is now dominated by a hookup culture is wrong. According to the 2011 Online College Social Life Survey (an online survey conducted out of Stanford University, which gathered data from over 24,000 students at 22 institutions), the total number of hookups reported by college students only averaged about two (Tafoya, 2012). One in three students say they've never hooked up, and 24% of college students say they are still virgins—compared with only 10% of similar-age Americans who are not in college (Regnerus & Uecker, 2011). (Some of these "virgins" may have engaged in noncoital hookups.) Many college students are more concerned with getting a degree than with getting laid, and many others are in steady relationships that largely exclude casual sex with third parties.

Still, it's worth asking why uncommitted sex is more common and more accepted on campuses today than it was a generation ago. Many reasons have been proposed: These include a postponement of the age of marriage among today's college students, the enforcement of sexual norms by peer groups and popular culture rather than by parents or institutions, and misperceptions of peer behavior (Stinson, 2010). Many students prefer hookups to a "relationship" because relationships take too much time away from study. They are also aware that relationships seldom survive graduation because of the enforced mobility of young professionals (Taylor, 2013).

Economic theory offers another possible answer. As we discussed in Chapter 1, a person's willingness to engage in sex is a resource whose value varies with scarcity. A generation and more ago, women were in the minority on campus, and they were therefore able to set rules that restricted sex to emotionally committed relationships. Now men are in the minority on many campuses, and they can find various women to approach if the first one turns them down. If a woman wants to be in the party scene, she may feel that she cannot afford to be too prudish. Is this the reason for an increase in the kind of uncommitted sex that men typically favor?

To answer this question, Mark Regnerus and Jeremy Uecker mined data from the College Women's Survey, which covered colleges with widely varying proportions of women and men (Regnerus & Uecker, 2011). On campuses where women were in a small minority, these women were quite likely to still be virgins, even if they had boyfriends. It was as if they could say to their partners, "I'd rather not have sex yet, and if you don't like that, there are plenty of other guys I can choose from." As the proportion of women on campus increased, however, the likelihood that they were virgins decreased steeply, as if the boyfriends could now say, "Give me sex, or some other woman will" (**Figure 7.5**). Thus, the general shortage of men on today's campuses does seem to make it easier for men to demand and receive sex.

Hookups can be pleasurable or abusive

How do hookups feel to the participants? To some extent, hookups represent the ancient battle of the sexes writ large: men trying to get sex with little commitment and women trying to get a relationship. Here are two comments, obtained in the course of a qualitative study by Elizabeth Paul and Kristen Hayes of the College of New Jersey (Paul & Hayes, 2002):

Man: "She was weird and said some things that you just don't say during a hookup. She wanted to talk about how we felt about each other. Then halfway through she changed her mind about hooking up. It was too late."

Woman: "I tried to talk with him about slowing down and that was seen as abnormal by the guy. I felt dirty, sad, and mad. He didn't respect my requests. He used me for his own physical pleasure. I was mad at myself and lied to my friends and said that we didn't have sex."

Comments such as these portray hookups as little different from date rape (see Chapter 16). But quite often, both men and women enjoy hookups and have no regrets. Here's one 19-year-old woman's take on them, from the same study:

It puts me in a good mood, just all those, like chemical, science-y things that happen [in the brain during sex]. Just like, I mean, I feel great afterwards. Maybe it's just because the people I have been with make me feel really good, but I always feel good and energized.

In 2010 a 22-year-old female Duke University student put together an illustrated, 42-page PowerPoint presentation—a mock research thesis—that described and rated her encounters with 13 male student athletes in terms such as these:

We ended up in the first long seat of [his] red SUV, where we talked for a little longer before commencing the data collection process. After the most violent, aggressive, steamy research I have ever conducted, we separated, leaving behind a vehicle with windows fogged with passion. (Jezebel, 2010)

Her "dissertation" went viral, triggering more embarrassment for a campus already struggling to rid itself of a reputation for sexual excess (Seelye & Robbins, 2010). Yet there are many other women who enjoy hookups and have no qualms about providing (anonymous) accounts of them online, as for example on The Casual Sex Project (Vrangalova, 2014).

Almost all of this Duke student's encounters were lubricated by alcohol, and there's nothing unusual about that. According to a study by sociologists at Ohio University (Vander Ven & Beck, 2009), alcohol is widely used on campus, both as a chemical tool to lower sexual inhibitions and as a rhetorical device to justify sexual encounters after the fact: "We were so wasted that we just went crazy." These findings have been widely replicated, even at more conservative schools such as Loyola Marymount University (LaBrie et al., 2014).

Men typically derive more sexual pleasure from heterosexual hookups than women. Women are less likely to experience orgasm—only about 1 in 10 women do so during a first-time hookup, according to a large online survey of college students (Armstrong et al., 2009). This may be because of anxiety or guilt about the hookup,

Alcohol fuels many hookups.

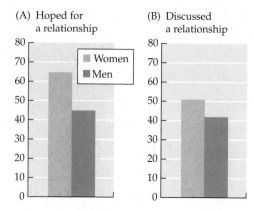

Figure 7.6 Hookups and hope The percentage of men and women who hoped that their hookup would lead to a relationship (A) or who brought up this possibility with their hookup partner (B). (Data from Owen & Fincham, 2011.)

but in addition, men typically pay little attention to women's sexual pleasure during casual encounters. For example, the same survey revealed that men were far more likely than women to receive oral sex.

Although hookups are widely perceived as the ultimate in sex without commitment, many hookup participants do hope that the hookup will lead to something more durable, and they may bring up this possibility with their partners, as with the example cited earlier (Owen & Fincham, 2011). This is more commonly true for women than for men, but even among men, about half do have hopes for a relationship (**Figure 7.6**).

Hookups can have positive or negative consequences

For the most part, these hopes are not fulfilled. According to some critics of the hookup culture, the resulting disillusionment causes emotional damage for hookup participants, especially for women, and makes it more difficult for them to enter into stable relationships (Stepp, 2007). "No condom will protect her from the heartache and confusion that may result," warned a UCLA psychiatrist (Grossman, 2007).

Many studies have looked at the actual consequences of hookups, and the findings are mixed. Using data from the National Longitudinal Study of Adolescent Health, developmental psychologists at Ohio State University reported that young people who engage in casual sex are more likely to suffer from mental health problems such as suicidal ideation *before* they become sexually active, and are even more likely to do so afterwards (Sandberg-Thoma & Kamp Dush, 2014). This suggests that mental health problems can both lead to and result from casual sexual encounters. Surveys of students and others find that both women and men quite commonly regret their hookups (Garcia et al., 2012).

Yet, on the whole, hookups engender more positive than negative feelings in both women and men (Garcia & Reiber, 2008; Lewis et al., 2012). One study of over 1000 young Minnesotans found that the status of their most recent sex partner (i.e., casual versus committed) did not affect their mental health one way or another (Eisenberg et al., 2009). Some hookups do lead to longer-term relationships. And even those hookups that are regretted have potential value: They may be part of the learning curve that leads young people to a better understanding of their sexual and relationship aims and how to fulfill them.

How do students feel about those of their peers who do engage in frequent hookups—who actually live the "hookup culture" stereotype? Given the traditional double standard, we might expect to find widespread disapproval of women who have frequent hookups, but not of men who behave in the same way. The reality is quite different. In the 2011 Online College Social Life Survey, most students made no distinction between the sexes: Either they said that they would lose respect for both men and women who had frequent hookups, or they said that they would not lose respect for either sex. Only small numbers of students judged one sex differently from the other, and within this minority the number who judged *men* more harshly was about the same as the number who judged women more harshly (Allison & Risman, 2013). These findings suggest that traditional sexist attitudes on U.S. campuses have largely given way to egalitarian attitudes, at least with regard to casual sex. Of course, people's real-life behavior does not always correspond to how they respond to surveys.

Casual sex is more accepted in the gay male community

Casual sex has long been more prevalent among gay men—especially among gay men without steady partners—than in the heterosexual population. In the NHSLS study, men who identified as homosexual or bisexual reported an average of 3.1 sex partners in the previous 12 months, compared with 1.8 partners for heterosexual men. A more recent large-scale survey of college students found an even greater difference: Gay male students reported more than twice the number of partners as straight male students, and male students who identified as bisexual also had high numbers of partners (Oswalt & Wyatt, 2013). (Not all these sexual encounters were casual ones, presumably.) Interestingly, the highest number of partners (7.6 in the previous 12 months) was reported by men who said that they were "unsure" what their sexual orientation was; apparently these men were making a serious effort to find out.

Explanations for the greater prevalence of casual sex among gay men may include the following:

- Gay men are not restrained by women's reluctance to engage in casual sex.

- Pregnancy is not an issue.

- Gay men, who may already be stigmatized by society for their sexual orientation, are less likely to pay attention to public opinion on the topic of casual sex.

In addition to gay bars, which are an important feature of gay male life in most U.S. cities, other institutions offer the opportunity for sexual encounters on an even more casual or totally anonymous basis. These include encounters at bathhouses, gymnasia, outdoor **cruising** areas, and sex parties (Solomon et al., 2011), as well as encounters facilitated by GPS-based mobile apps such as Grindr (Landovitz et al., 2013).

Although engaging in casual sex carries little stigma in gay male communities, not all gay men approve of the practice or engage in it. Some limit their sexual activity because of the risk of acquiring AIDS or other diseases. Some believe that casual sex gives the gay community a bad name. And, most important, many gay men are involved in monogamous relationships and have no desire to engage in casual sex— or they feel that doing so would endanger their relationship.

There do exist bars and other locations where lesbians can meet, and one can find "W4W" sections on hookup websites such as BestCasualSex.com. Still, very little research has been done on casual sex between women. The NSSAL survey identified 175 women who had had at least one sexual encounter with another woman. Of these women, only one had had more than 10 female partners in her lifetime. Although the nature of the encounters was not investigated, the low numbers suggest that casual sex between women is uncommon. Even if their numbers are low, however, there clearly is a lively minority of lesbians who thrive on open relationships, polyamory, and casual sex (Munson & Stelbourn, 2013).

Negotiating sex involves flirting

Getting from a regular social encounter to a sexual one involves a set of reciprocal communications known as flirting. This term is rapidly losing ground to colloquialisms like "hitting on," especially when referring to flirting behavior by men, but we'll stick with the traditional term for one more edition of this textbook.

Austrian ethologist Irenäus Eibl-Eibesfeldt spent years observing flirting behavior on several continents as well as on Pacific islands (Eibl-Eibesfeldt, 2007). To capture unselfconscious behaviors, he used a film camera that shot at right angles to the direction it appeared to be aimed at. Eibl-Eibesfeldt found a remarkable consistency in flirting behaviors across cultures: Almost everywhere, for example, a woman who is interested in a man would smile, arch her brows, look down and to the side, and then put her hands near her mouth and laugh. When both persons were attracted to each other, they would move closer, make slight touching movements, nod in agreement, and gaze into each other's eyes. These findings suggested that nature has equipped us with a standard set of flirting behaviors. Nevertheless, more recent

cruising Looking for casual sex partners in public spaces.

Box 7.3 Research Highlights

Flirting Styles

Steve Carter, research director at the matchmaking website eHarmony.com, got together with Jeffrey Hall of the University of Kansas and two other researchers to investigate whether there are distinct styles of flirting (Hall et al., 2010). They recruited several thousand women and men who responded to about 50 Likert-style questions ("strongly disagree" to "strongly agree") relating to flirting. The respondents completed a five-factor personality inventory (which scores extraversion, agreeableness, openness, conscientiousness, and neuroticism), and they provided information about their sexual orientation.

The researchers first eliminated all non-heterosexual respondents—either for the sake of uniformity or because of eHarmony's long-standing anti-gay policies. The data from the remaining respondents was subjected to a rigorous statistical analysis, which provided evidence for five distinct flirting styles:

- *Traditional flirters* believe in following time-honored flirting scripts. For example, they usually agree with statements like "Men should pursue women, not the other way around." In terms of personality, these individuals are low on openness (such as interest in new experiences).

- *Physical flirters* are comfortable expressing their sexual interest in their behavior; they agree with statements like "I have no problem letting others know that I am interested in them." These individuals have extraverted, open personalities.

- *Polite flirters* have a somewhat reserved flirting style: They don't want to appear needy, and as a result their flirtatious behavior is not always recognized as such by the "flirtee." They agree with statements like "People should be cautious when letting someone know they are interested." They have agreeable, conscientious personalities.

- *Playful flirters* see "having a good time" as the main point of flirting. They agree with statements like "Flirting is just for fun—people don't need to be so serious." They may flirt with people they are not actually interested in. They have extraverted personalities but are low on conscientiousness. Men are more likely to be playful

Sincere flirting has the best chance of leading to a lasting relationship.

flirters than women, and they desire rather superficial sexual relationships.

- *Sincere flirters* want to establish an emotional, intimate connection with the flirtee, and they use self-disclosure as a means to that end. They agree with statements like "I really enjoy learning about another person's interests." Sincere flirters are high on extraversion, openness, agreeableness, and conscientiousness, and low on neuroticism.

Regarding the success of these various styles, the researchers reported that traditional and polite flirters are relatively unsuccessful, while the other three styles are relatively successful. As might be expected, the playful and physical flirters were relatively successful at rapidly establishing a physical, sexually charged connection, but one which might not have much emotional depth; the sincere flirters took longer to establish a relationship, but it was emotionally deeper and less closely tied to physical attraction.

If you sometimes flirt, what's your flirting style? Do you think that an insincere person can successfully fake a sincere flirting style? And is there any reason to question whether people's actual flirting behavior corresponds to the information in their survey responses?

work indicates that there are variations on the basic pattern that amount to distinct "flirting styles" (**Box 7.3**).

In spite of these stereotyped signals, humans don't seem to be terribly good at telling whether the person they are interacting with is flirting or not. Researchers at Stanford University developed a computer program that analyzed 4-minute conversations between partners at speed-dating events (Ranganath et al., 2009). After each session the participants were asked whether they had been flirting and whether they thought their partner had been flirting. Although the program analyzed only the audio component of the conversation, and not the facial expressions and gestures of the subjects, it far outperformed the subjects themselves in telling whether their partners were flirting. Besides relying on behaviors noted by Eibl-Eibesfeldt, such as laughter, the program also relied on voice quality and choice of words. For example, men who were flirting used a higher-pitched but quieter voice, and used "you" and "we" more than men who were not flirting.

The reason that the participants were not very good at judging their partners' flirtatiousness was that they were insufficiently objective: They tended to believe that their partners were being flirtatious when they themselves were being flirtatious, and only then. The self-referential nature of these judgments may be the cause of many misunderstandings in the real world.

In spite of these potential misreadings, flirtatious behavior does markedly influence interactions between strangers. A woman of average looks who acts flirtatiously is far more likely to be approached by a man than is a highly attractive woman who doesn't flirt (Moore, 2010). And flirtatious behavior can be used for purposes other than acquiring sex partners: In one survey of college students from the 1980s, most respondents believed that students—especially female ones—could raise their grades by flirting with instructors, and many said that they had engaged in such behavior (Rowland et al., 1982). Do you think that such behavior continues today? And would it be more or less successful than in the past?

Non-Cohabiting Relationships Are Often Short-Lived

One step up the relationship hierarchy from hookups are sexual relationships between people who are not married or living together, but who nevertheless feel some commitment to each other. These have traditionally been called dating relationships. This term is still in use, but it doesn't necessarily mean that the couples go on traditional "dates." Other possible terms include "partners," "boy- or girlfriends," "seeing each other," "an item," and "Facebook official," but we'll use the term **non-cohabiting relationship** because whether two people live together usually says a lot about how committed the relationship is.

Because of all the attention that has been paid to the hookup culture, it's easy to get the impression that non-cohabiting relationships are disappearing, but that's not the case. Certainly there are young people who purposefully select hookups over steady relationships, as mentioned earlier, but there are also many women and men, of all ages, who want a relationship with some degree of commitment but don't want to (or can't) move in together. **Figure 7.7** gives some sense of the numbers: By age 20 a very substantial number of young people describe themselves as "in a relationship," and by age 24 their numbers match those who describe themselves as "single." (The data in the figure do not distinguish between cohabiting and non-cohabiting relationships, but for people in their early 20s most of these relationships are likely to be non-cohabitating.)

The traditional date followed a formalized script: The sharply dressed young man showed up at the young woman's doorstep, he drove her to a restaurant for dinner, and then to a movie where fondling might occur, possibly followed by more serious sex in the car or at someone's home. In this script it was the man's role to take all initiatives (and to pay for the outing), while the woman's role was to decide how far things could go.

Comical though this script may seem now, the fact is that very large numbers of your parents' marriages grew out of this kind of dating relationship. Even the notori-

non-cohabiting relationship An ongoing sexual relationship between two people who do not live together.

Traditionally scripted dates are less common than in the past.

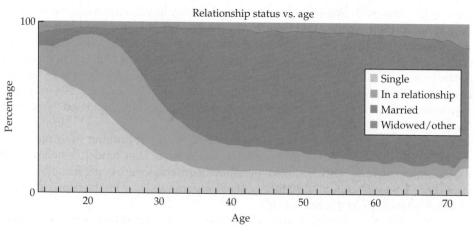

Figure 7.7 **Relationship status of U.S. Facebook users** as a function of age. Where categories correspond, the self-described Facebook data track U.S. Census data quite closely, but there are some distortions: The percentage of young teens who are married is probably lower than shown here, and the percentage of over-70s who are widowed is probably higher than shown here. (After Wolfram, 2013.)

interpersonal scripts Patterns of behavior that develop between couples.

ous "blind date" has been a fruitful source of lasting relationships, as some not-too-serious data mining on our part revealed (**Figure 7.8**).

Some aspects of the gendered scripts that govern non-cohabiting relationships have been surprisingly resistant to change over the last decade or two, in spite of the much more equal positions of women and men than in the past (Eaton & Rose, 2011; Emmers-Sommer, 2014). This is particularly true for the couple's early meetings, when they don't know each other very well. For example, if one person (usually the man) pays for most of the expenses, such as for meals or transportation, an unspoken script may give him the feeling that he's entitled to sex. If the other person (usually the woman) doesn't want this to happen, she is well advised to insist on paying her share of the expenses. As a non-cohabiting relationship progresses, these kinds of social scripts give way to **interpersonal scripts**—sets of rules and expectations that are generated by the couple themselves.

Sometimes a relationship of this kind leads to cohabitation or marriage. Sometimes it is a brief romance that breaks up when the pair find themselves incompatible, find better partners, or get separated by external circumstances such as the end of a school year. Sometimes it is a durable relationship between two people who for some reason don't want to or are unable to live together. Although we think of non-cohabiting relationships as being the hallmark of the teenage years or young adulthood, plenty of older people—unmarried, divorced, or widowed—also engage in them.

Do relationships that begin with hookups, or with sex very early in the relationship, fare worse than more traditional relationships in which sex is postponed until the couple know each other better? Sociologist Anthony Paik of the University of Iowa surveyed 642 individuals in relationships, half of whom started off with sex while the other half delayed sex until later in the relationship (Paik, 2010). The delayers were indeed more satisfied with their relationships, on average, compared with those who "got physical" early on. Paik interpreted this finding as a selection effect, however, rather than a result of the early sex itself. In other words, people who began with sex

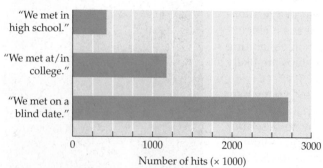

Figure 7.8 **Fate brought us together.** This bar graph shows the number of Google hits for the stated phrases (all in quotation marks), as of April 2014. Random sampling of entries suggest that most refer to marriages or relationships that are still ongoing.

were those who were less interested in a stable relationship in the first place. For someone seeking a committed relationship, Paik concludes, waiting helps weed out potential partners who are mostly focused on instant sexual gratification.

Some men and women who are in non-cohabiting relationships engage in sex outside the relationship (extra-pair sex), but more commonly these relationships are expected to be sexually exclusive, even though the two people do not live together. A person who engages in a series of sexually exclusive relationships with different people over a period of time is said to be practicing **serial monogamy**—a very common lifestyle, especially among adolescents and young adults.

Same-sex relationships have their own scripts

Same-sex non-cohabiting relationships have not been the subject of a great deal of study, but it's worth raising a few points. First, in many environments (such as high school, college, or work) there is a presumption of heterosexuality. Thus, for a same-sex relationship to get going, there has to be an initial recognition or mutual disclosure that the two people are open to such a relationship. This disclosure, once achieved, may promote a more rapid development of the relationship than would be typical for an opposite-sex couple. Conversely, some same-sex couples may have difficulty achieving intimacy because of inculcated negative feelings about homosexuality (internalized homophobia: see Chapter 12).

For women especially, sexual exploration and the development of a homosexual or bisexual identity may occur in the context of a preexisting and intense same-sex friendship (Peplau et al., 1999). In such cases, the two people may essentially be in love before the question of sexual attraction and sexual behavior comes into play at all. Sexual relationships arising in this situation have a very different meaning than those between most heterosexual or male-male couples, in which the two people are typically not very emotionally intimate on their first date but may be very conscious of sexual attraction and the possibility of sexual behavior.

The cultural scripts that regulate heterosexual relationships—especially those related to gender roles—may be less relevant in the gay and lesbian communities. Still, certain expectations apply, such as the idea that a person who provides resources is accruing a degree of sexual entitlement. Within some gay subcultures, such as the gay leather or BDSM communities (see Chapter 13), an explicit negotiation of the kind of sexual role-playing that the two men will engage in is likely (Townsend, 2007).

Non-cohabiting relationships may evolve rapidly

Non-cohabiting relationships are often very dynamic—they are processes, rather than states of being. The process may be one of growing self-disclosure and love, leading to cohabitation or marriage (Sprecher & Hendrick, 2004). Alternatively, there may be a gradual realization by one or both partners that "this was not meant to be," with a resulting breakup.

Often this dynamic process is viewed as taking place entirely within the relationship—in other words, as an exploration of mutual attraction and compatibility. But it may be affected by a larger sexual marketplace in which both persons consciously or unconsciously assess whether they have struck an equitable deal, given their own sense of self-worth and the range of other individuals in the marketplace (Hatfield & Rapson, 2011). If either partner believes that he or she can do better, that partner will feel less commitment to the relationship, and the chances of a breakup increase.

We will postpone our discussion of more-lasting sexual relationships (cohabitations and marriages) to Chapter 11, where we will also discuss sexual relationships that involve more than two people (polyamory and polygamy). Instead, we now turn our attention to the emotional underpinnings of sexual relationships.

serial monogamy Engagement in a series of monogamous relationships.

Love Cements Many Sexual Relationships

Love, in some form or another, is the glue that holds couples in long-term sexual relationships. Celebrated for centuries in poetry and art, love has recently come under the scrutiny of psychologists and even brain scientists, though no consensus has been reached on what exactly love is, or what causes it.

There are different kinds of love

Within the context of sexual relationships, different aspects of love are apparent. Most striking is that the quality of love tends to change over the duration of a relationship, starting with passion and developing over time into a calmer but deeper bond (Hatfield & Rapson, 1993). The early kind of love is called romantic love, passionate love, or limerence and, popularly, "falling in love" or "being head over heels in love." The later kind of love is called companionate, realistic, or mature love.

Here's how one teenager explained the difference (Montgomery & Sorell, 1998): "Being in love with someone and loving someone are two different things; when you're *in love* with someone, you think they're just wonderful and everything they do is perfect and they have no faults. When you *love* someone you know about their faults and you realize that they may not be exactly as you want them to be, but you love them in spite of it."

The capacity for passionate love seems to exist in most or all human cultures (Jankowiak & Fischer, 1992; Hatfield & Rapson, 2005). In one interview with an anthropologist, a woman of the hunter-gatherer !Kung people of the Kalahari Desert of southern Africa drew a distinction between a husband and a lover. A relationship with a husband is "rich, warm and secure," she said, while that with a lover is "passionate and exciting, although often fleeting and undependable." She added that "when two people come together their hearts are on fire and their passion is very great. After a while, the fire cools and that's how it stays" (Shostak, 2000).

Pre-Colombian lovers. Ceramic sculpture from the Olmec culture, Mexico.

Being in love may be the justification for marriage or sex

"Love and marriage," crooned Frank Sinatra in 1955, "go together like a horse and carriage." Yet as recently as the 1960s, only 30% of U.S. women said that being in love was a necessary condition for marriage. By the 1990s, American sentiments better matched the song lyric, with less than 4% saying they would marry someone they didn't love. But compare this with 50% of Indians and Pakistanis—in whose countries arranged marriages are still common (Hatfield et al., 2007).

Falling in love also seems to give people permission—women especially—to engage in sexual intercourse for the first time. In the NSSAL study, 58% of women mentioned "being in love" as a reason they first had intercourse. Only 30% of men mentioned this factor, however; a much more frequently cited reason for men was "I was curious about what it would be like"—not a particularly romantic motive.

Liking and reciprocal attraction precede falling in love

What actually causes Alice to fall in love with Bob?* In surveys that ask Alice what led up to her falling in love with Bob, Alice typically mentions that she already liked Bob, that she perceived that Bob liked her, that she found Bob's personality and appearance attractive, that she and Bob had a lot of similarities, and so on (Pines, 2005).

In a study that asked students in the United States and China about their love experiences, there were some differences. For example, U.S. students mentioned

---

* "Alice" and "Bob" are standard placeholders in communications science; they represent all couples, including same-sex couples.

physical appearance more than Chinese students did, whereas Chinese students mentioned personality and social factors more than U.S. students did (Riela et al., 2010). Thus cultural factors do have some influence on the process of falling in love—in this case the differences between a more individualistic society (United States) and a more group-oriented society (China).

Still, people may not be conscious of, or able to articulate, the actual factors that caused them to fall in love. (Recall the speed-dating experiments mentioned in Chapter 5, in which subjects chose partners who didn't resemble their verbally expressed ideals.) One factor rarely mentioned in surveys is the act of having sex, but coitus and orgasm can cause a person to fall in love with their sex partner, or at least facilitate it. This may be due to the neurochemical events associated with orgasm, including the activation of dopamine, oxytocin, and vasopressin systems (Young & Wang, 2004).

Is it possible to fall in love "at first sight"? About half of the U.S. population thinks it is; in fact, 44% of men and 36% of women say that it has happened to them (Gallup, 2001). Since there is no objective test for "being in love," it is hard to confirm or refute their claims. But the fact that so many people say they have experienced love at first sight highlights the fact that familiarity is not a necessary ingredient for romantic love.

Researchers are probing the biological basis of love

Some research has aimed at finding a biological basis for love. One interesting line of animal research focuses on voles (Nair & Young, 2006) (**Figure 7.9**): Closely related species of these small mammals differ in their sexual and social behaviors. Prairie voles form lifelong pair-bonds that are established at first mating, whereas mountain voles and meadow voles are sexually promiscuous and do not form pair-bonds. Detailed examination of the brain and endocrine system suggest that pair-bonding in prairie voles is mediated by several hormones or neurotransmitters, including oxytocin and vasopressin (McGraw & Young, 2010). A research group at Emory University facilitated pair-bond formation in the promiscuous species of voles by injecting these hormones directly into the voles' brains or by injecting a gene that caused the voles' brains to produce more receptors for these hormones (Lim et al., 2004).

A similar mechanism plays a role in pair-bond formation in songbirds (Klatt & Goodson, 2013). In humans, blood levels of both oxytocin and vasopressin rise dur-

FAQ

I've fallen in love with two different people—can that be?

Most experts say "no." Perhaps one of your "loves" is more of a close attachment than a passionate love.

(A)

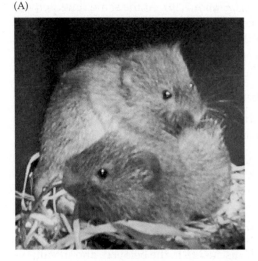

(B)

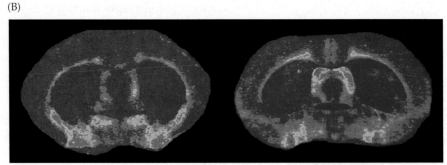

Figure 7.9 Prairie home companions (A) After mating, male and female prairie voles stay together in monogamous relationships until one of them dies. This behavior contrasts with that of the closely related mountain vole, which does not form pair-bonds. (B) Receptors for the hormone vasopressin (indicated here by red, orange, and yellow) are distributed differently in the brains of the monogamous prairie vole (left) and the promiscuous mountain vole (right). This difference probably contributes to the behavioral differences between the two species. (Courtesy of Zuoxin Wang and Thomas Curtis.)

(A)   (B)   (C)

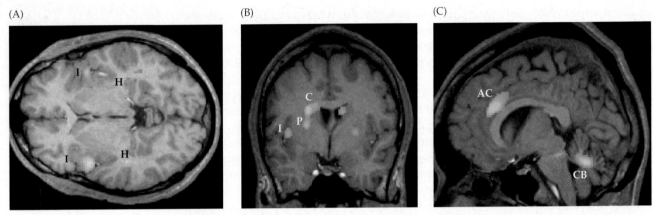

Figure 7.10 The brain in love These functional brain scans show (in orange and yellow) the brain regions that are more active while the subject is viewing a photograph of his or her beloved than when the subject is viewing photos of a nonromantic friend. (A) A horizontal slice, showing activity in an infolded region of the cerebral cortex named the insula (I), most strongly in the left hemisphere (bottom), and in the hippocampus (H). (B) A frontal slice, showing activity in the insula and also in the left caudate (C) and putamen (P), structures that are heavily innervated by the dopamine system. (C) Near-midline slice, showing activity in the anterior cingulate cortex (AC) and cerebellum (CB). (After Bartels & Zeki, 2000.)

passion The overwhelming feeling of attraction typical of the early stage of a loving relationship.

intimacy The sense of connectedness in an established relationship.

ing the intense early phase of romantic love, but whether these hormones are part of the mechanism by which humans fall in love is not yet known (Zeki, 2007).

Another way researchers have probed the biology of love is by using brain-imaging technology. When people who have recently fallen in love are shown photographs of their partners, regions of the brain that use the neurotransmitter dopamine become active (Fisher et al., 2006). The activity patterns are quite similar to those generated by the euphoria-inducing drug cocaine, which operates on the dopamine system. In one study, the activity in certain brain regions correlated with the quality of the person's relationship 18 months *after* the scan (Xu et al., 2011). Thus it might eventually be possible to provide an in-love person with some objective indication of whether his or her beloved is a "keeper" or not.

By a year or so after a person has fallen in love, viewing a photo of one's partner elicits more-complex patterns of brain activity, including not just the dopamine circuitry but also several regions of the cerebral cortex known to be involved in erotic arousal and pleasure (Bartels & Zeki, 2000) (**Figure 7.10**). At the same time, activity in brain regions involved in the experience of negative emotion such as sadness and fear is partially suppressed. In other words, thinking about or seeing one's beloved alters brain activity in a rather global and positive fashion.

One theory proposes that love has three components

Psychologist Robert Sternberg, now at Cornell University, proposed that love consists of three elements that can be represented as the three corners of a triangle (Sternberg, 1986) (**Figure 7.11**):

- **Passion** is the motivational component. It is strongest in the initial heat of romantic love. It is the "urge to merge," in both the physical and psychological senses.

- **Intimacy** is the emotional component. It refers to the feelings of closeness and connectedness in a relationship. It is expressed in the desire to promote the well-being of the beloved, in self-disclosure to the beloved, and in valuing the beloved in one's life

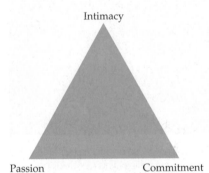

Figure 7.11 Sternberg's love triangle Robert Sternberg proposed that love consists of three elements—passion, intimacy, and commitment—that can be represented as a triangle.

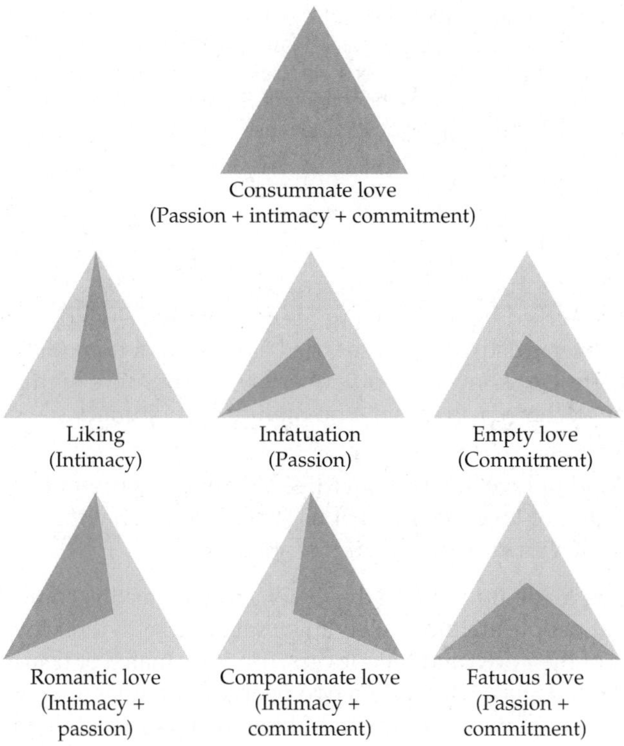

Figure 7.12 **Sternberg's seven types of love** are made up of different proportions of passion, intimacy, and commitment. In the figure, intimacy is at the top vertex of each triangle, passion is at the left, and commitment is at the right as is also shown in Figure 7.11. (See **Web Activity 7.2: Sternberg's Seven Types of Love**.)

- **Commitment** is the cognitive component. It refers, in the short term, to the decision to love the other person. In the longer term, it refers to the commitment to maintain the loving relationship—as expressed in the marriage vows, for example. It is the element over which one has the greatest conscious control.

Just as the three primary colors can be combined in different proportions to create a variety of hues, the three elements of Sternberg's love triangle can be combined in different ways, producing different kinds of love, which can be represented by triangles of differing shapes (**Figure 7.12**). Sternberg names these kinds of love as follows:

- *Liking* is the kind of love in which intimacy is high but passion and commitment are low. It corresponds to what we usually call friendship.

- *Infatuation* is the kind of love in which passion is high but intimacy and commitment are low. It corresponds to "love at first sight," when one loves a person without knowing them well or thinking much about the matter.

- *Empty love* is the kind of love in which commitment is high, but passion and intimacy are low. It could be the final, stagnant stage of a romantic relationship in which passion and emotional involvement have waned, but there is still a conscious commitment to keeping the relationship going. But it could also be the first stage of an arranged marriage, sometimes leading to more complete love.

- *Romantic love* is the kind of love in which both intimacy and passion are high, but commitment is low. Sternberg mentions the love of Romeo and Juliet as an example. (But if you know the play, you might question whether they were low in commitment.)

- *Companionate love* is the kind of love in which intimacy and commitment are high, but passion is low. It frequently occurs in marriages and cohabitations after physical attraction has abated.

commitment The cognitive component of love: the decision to maintain a relationship.

Matching   Mismatched

Figure 7.13 **Couples may have matching or mismatched** love triangles. Each member of the couple on the left (represented by blue and purple) has a triangle approximating Sternberg's "infatuation." In the couple on the right, one member's triangle corresponds to "infatuation" and the other member's to "companionate love." According to Sternberg, the couple on the left are more likely to be satisfied with their relationship because there is more overlap between their triangles.

- *Fatuous love* is the kind of love in which passion and commitment are high, but intimacy is low. According to Sternberg, it is seen in whirlwind romances in which two lovers rush off to get married and set up a home together without ever getting to know each other very well. These are high-risk relationships, although there is always the possibility that intimacy will develop.

- *Consummate love* is the kind of love in which all three elements are present in full. It represents the kind of love that most of us strive for and, having achieved, try to maintain—with variable degrees of success.

Besides asserting that love is made up of these three elements in various combinations, Sternberg claimed that people are most likely to be satisfied with their love relationships when the shapes of their own and their lovers' triangles match or nearly match (Sternberg & Barnes, 1985) (**Figure 7.13**). When two people's triangles are mismatched, as when one partner is high on commitment but low on passion while the other partner is the reverse, both partners are likely to be dissatisfied.

Sternberg's original theory was qualitative in nature. Since then, Sternberg and other researchers have confirmed its basic validity, in both heterosexual and homosexual relationships, by employing factor analysis: this is a statistical procedure to identify key variables within data sets (Lemieux & Hale, 1999; Bauermeister et al., 2011). One finding to emerge from these analyses is that there are sex differences in the love triangles of women and men: While women and men score about equally on the passion component, women typically score higher than men on both intimacy and commitment (Lemieux & Hale, 2000). There are also age differences: For example, older people tend to score higher on commitment than younger people (Sumter et al., 2013). Thus sex and age differences between partners may contribute to the development of mismatched love triangles.

In spite of efforts to dissect it, each individual's experience of love is unique and personal. We create our own narratives and images of love that reflect not only our individual personalities and experiences but also our exposure to popular culture (**Box 7.4**).

Unrequited Love Is Painful for Both Parties

The ultimate in mismatched love triangles is unreciprocated love, or **unrequited love**, in which one person's affection for another is not returned. Unrequited love may take several forms, according to a study by Robert Bringle and colleagues at Appalachian State University (Bringle et al., 2013):

- A **crush** on someone who is distant and unobtainable, such as a rock star
- A secret crush on a friend or acquaintance
- The actual pursuit of a love object who does not reciprocate
- The longing for a past lover

These ill-starred relationships are common: In Bringle's survey of high school students and young adults, episodes of unrequited love were 4 times more common than episodes of reciprocated love.

This late-19th-century Japanese woodblock print, *Reflected Moonlight*, depicts Lady Ariko, a poet of the medieval Heian court, with her lute, preparing to drown herself because of her unrequited love for a lord. Lady Ariko's poem, which appears at the top right of the print, expresses the anguish of the rejected lover: "How hopeless it is / It would be better for me to sink beneath the waves / Perhaps there I could see my man from Moon Capital."

unrequited love Love that is not reciprocated.

crush A short-lived, intense, unreciprocated love, often experienced during adolescence.

Box 7.4 Personal Points of View

Love Stories

Wes and Gina have been going out for six months, and there are times when Wes thinks that Gina sees the two of them as being involved in a competition rather than a relationship. She is determined to be the best at everything—not just at racquetball and other naturally competitive ventures, but at things as seemingly uncompetitive as taking down phone messages. Wes sees Gina as someone who could turn this seemingly mindless task into a challenge of who can take down the better, more comprehensive messages. Gina also turns the romantic aspects of their relationship into a competition. One of her favorite things to do is to play a kissing game with Wes; the two of them sit so that there are just a few inches between their lips, and the winner is the one who resists the temptation to kiss the other the longest. Gina has never lost this game, as Wes always succumbs to his desire to kiss her; after all, he knows that if he does not kiss her, they will sit there all day, because Gina would never give Wes the satisfaction of winning. (Sternberg, 1998)

To Cornell psychologist Robert Sternberg—the creator of the love triangle theory—intimate relationships tend to follow certain well-worn story lines. Gina, for example, is following the "game story," in which the relationship is seen as a zero-sum game—one in which there is a winner and a loser.

Sternberg describes 26 different kinds of stories. Here are some more examples (because these stories should apply equally to same-sex and opposite-sex relationships, we've switched a couple of genders):

- *The fantasy story*. Alexis thinks that Cory, an office coworker, may be the knight in shining armor who will romance and care for her for the rest of their days (see figure).

- *The addiction story*. Kevin has a neurotic need for Tyler and is preoccupied with the fear of losing him.

- *The religion story*. Brenda believes that God brought Timothy to her so that they can imitate God's love in their mutual relationship.

- *The teacher-student story*. Alicia expects Jessica to be the dutiful recipient of her lectures about life and what really makes people tick.

- *The business story*. Although well-off, Kathy focuses more on the economic security of her marriage to Warren than on fostering passion or romance.

- *The war story*. Bob sees his relationship with Dierdre as a series of disputes to be fought over.

The fantasy story.

These love stories are not factual descriptions of relationships but, rather, subjective interpretations of them. A story is not necessarily good or bad; its quality depends in part on whether the other person's story fits in with it. If Jessica is comfortable playing the "student" role to Alicia's "teacher," for example, the relationship may thrive. If Dierdre, like Bob, subscribes to a war story, the battles may go on for years without harm. Thus, relationships that seem (to outsiders) to be doomed to failure may last, while others that seem ideal may quickly end.

Where do these love stories come from? In part, they reflect an interaction between individuals and society, especially popular culture. Books and movies tell the same love stories over and over again. Wes and Gina's "game story," for example, is the theme of the movie *Who's Afraid of Virginia Woolf?* in which Richard Burton and Elizabeth Taylor engaged in an elaborate and increasingly bitter game of make-believe.

A person may go through several relationships while enacting the same story, and each relationship may fail in the same way. "Will he never learn?" think his friends. On the other hand, people are capable of changing their love stories over time—perhaps with the help of insights developed in the course of therapy. "That love is a story closes off no options to us," concludes Sternberg. "Instead, it makes us aware of the infinite options we can create as we write the stories of our lives and loves."

suitor A person who is seeking to establish a romantic relationship with another.

obsessive relational intrusion Obsessive pursuit of a person by a rejected lover.

stalking Obsessive pursuit of a previous, current, or desired sex partner in such a way as to put that person in a state of fear.

For the **suitor**, rejection hurts, of course. How literally this is true was illustrated in a brain-imaging study (Kross et al., 2011): The same brain regions became active when recently rejected lovers thought about their rejection as when a painfully hot stimulus was applied to their arms. Persons who have relatively low self-esteem to begin with may be the ones who are most traumatized by a rejection, whereas persons with high self-esteem may bounce back quickly (Waller & MacDonald, 2010).

The rejected suitor often feels "abandonment anger" without actually falling out of love. The blend of anger and continuing love may seem like a contradiction, but it is a common experience (Ellis & Malamuth, 2000). "You can be terribly angry at a rejecting sweetheart but still very much in love," writes Helen Fisher. "In fact, the opposite of love is not hate but indifference" (Fisher, 2006).

The suitor does at least have a "script" to follow. The role of the unrequited lover is familiar to everyone; it is celebrated in one popular song after another. It is a dramatic role with its prescribed times for grief, anger, acceptance, and moving on.

Unrequited love can be thought of as part of the matching process by which people find long-term mates, and in that sense it can have a positive value. In fact, most people can handle a few experiences with unrequited love and emerge unscathed, perhaps stronger for the experience. For a minority, however, especially those with controlling or manipulative personalities or poor communication skills, it may be difficult to take "no" for a final answer, and a single-minded pursuit of the desired person may ensue (Sinclair & Frieze, 2001). This pattern, termed **obsessive relational intrusion**, is one in which the suitor cannot stop obsessing over the desired relationship, perhaps spending hours each day locked in thoughts and feelings about the unreciprocated love. In rare cases this may eventually lead to the criminal behavior known as **stalking** (see Chapter 16).

The rejector may experience guilt

The person who is the target of unrequited love may not even be aware of the situation—in the case of a secret crush, for example. But a person who is aware of being the object of someone's love and doesn't love in return (a "rejector") is likely to feel guilty. According to research by psychologist Roy Baumeister and colleagues at Florida State University, these guilty feelings may take several forms: guilt at having led the suitor on, even if unintentionally or to a small degree; guilt at not returning the suitor's affection—a violation of the social norm of reciprocity; and guilt at inflicting humiliation on the suitor by expressing that the love is not returned (Baumeister and Dhavale, 2001).

Furthermore, the rejector's role is largely "unscripted": There are few social models for how a rejector is supposed to behave or feel. Thus, the rejector may end up failing to communicate the rejection clearly to the suitor, perhaps representing it as a matter of unfortunate circumstances that might conceivably be overcome in the future. ("I'm really too busy to be thinking about relationships right now.")

By analyzing numerous accounts of unrequited love told from the perspective of both suitors and rejectors, Baumeister's group found systematic biases in the way the episodes were recalled (**Figure 7.14**). Suitors were much more likely than rejectors to recall that the rejector initially reciprocated the suitor's advances and that the rejector led the suitor on. Rejectors, however, were more likely than suitors to recall that the rejector gave the suitor an explicit rejection and that the suitor persisted unreasonably in spite of the rejection. The researchers interpreted these biases as representing efforts by suitors to rebuild their self-esteem and by rejectors to justify themselves and reduce their feelings of guilt.

Figure 7.14 Unhappy memories When college students were asked to recall their experiences of unrequited love—both experiences in which they were rejected and experiences in which they did the rejecting—the two kinds of narratives differed markedly. The figure shows the percentage of "suitor" and "rejector" narratives that included the six listed assertions. (Data from Baumeister et al., 1993.)

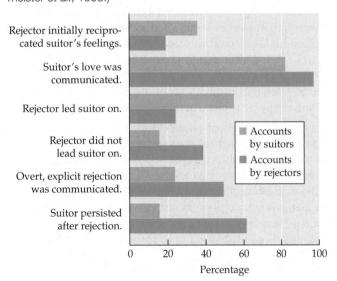

Life Experiences Mold Our Sexual Relationships

Our relationships are often shaped by life experiences that are not under our control. Here we briefly consider two such factors: our early relationship with our parents, and the social group in which we live.

Relationship styles are influenced by childhood attachments

According to research based on **attachment theory**, parenting styles profoundly affect the child's developing personality (Bowlby, 1988; Fraley, 2010). If parents—the mother, especially—respond sensitively to the young child's needs, the child becomes securely attached; that is, the child will become confident in the parent's love, will respond positively to the parent, and will seek contact with her or him but will not be unduly disturbed by brief separations. On the other hand, if the parent is rejecting or emotionally distant, the child may avoid intimate interactions with the parent. If the parent is inconsistent or unresponsive, the child may become anxious or ambivalent, often becoming extremely upset when separated from the parent. In avoidant as well as anxious-ambivalent parent-child relationships, the child ends up with insecure attachments, which are much less fulfilling than the secure attachments we described first. Although usually described in terms of these three categories, actual individual attachment styles usually comprise some mixture of the three attachment types.

According to attachment theory, people who were securely attached as children have a basic self-confidence and trust that allows them to enter into intimate relationships with relative ease during adolescence and adulthood. People who were avoidant as children may be uncomfortable with adult intimacy and may strike potential romantic partners as cold. People who were anxious or ambivalent as children may have an unrealistic fear of being deserted, and this may cause them to seek an emotional "merger" that actually has the opposite effect—driving the partner away.

To some extent, this relationship between childhood and adult attachment styles has been verified in retrospective and longitudinal studies (Hazan & Shaver, 1987; Simpson et al., 2007). Nevertheless, the relationship is not especially strong—people's attachment styles can change over the course of their lives (Fraley, 2010). This may be because people continuously update their attachment styles based on their cumulative interpersonal experiences. Thus attachment theory does not condemn anyone to lifelong failure in love. Rather, it provides insights that can help individuals surmount problems derived from childhood attachment difficulties (Wallin, 2007).

Couples in relationships resemble each other

One striking fact about couples is how similar the two individuals commonly are to each other. According to the NHSLS, couples resemble each other—far more than would be expected by chance—in race or ethnicity, religion, age, educational level, and socioeconomic status. This is true not just for married and cohabiting couples, but for couples in short-term partnerships as well (Black & Lichter, 2004). The resemblance also extends to physical attributes such as height (Courtiol et al., 2010) and facial appearance (Nojo et al., 2012). The tendency of sexually partnered couples to resemble each other is called **homogamy**. (Some scholars reserve this term for married couples.)

To some degree, homogamy results from the fact that people tend to find mates within their own social groups, who are likely to be of the same race, age, religion, and so on. This observation shows that sexual relationships are embedded in larger social

attachment theory   The idea that relationship styles are influenced by the quality of the early parent-child bond.

homogamy   The tendency of sexually partnered couples, or married couples, to resemble each other in a variety of respects.

Couples may resemble each other.

structures, but it doesn't say whether homogamy has any *effect* on relationships, either for good or for bad.

There is some evidence, however, that homogamy does contribute to the success and stability of heterosexual relationships. Longitudinal studies have found that couples who resemble each other in a variety of respects are more likely to stay together, and express greater satisfaction with their relationships at later times in the relationship, than couples who are less alike. The most robust correlation seems to be with age: Couples in which the man is much older or younger than the woman experience at least twice the risk of breakup, compared with couples that are close in age (Kippen et al., 2009).

Similarity between partners may strengthen relationships because companionate love—the hallmark of long-term relationships—is exactly that: a companionship. Like friends, partners who are similar to each other tend to have shared interests and attitudes. Thus, they communicate approval to each other, bolster each other's self-esteem, and help stabilize each other's personalities. In addition, a couple's two birth families are more likely to interact socially and to actively support the couple's relationship if the two partners are similar to each other—in race and religion, for example. Homogamy exists in same-sex couples too, but it is significantly less marked, especially in the case of male couples (Schwartz & Graf, 2009). In other words, gay male couples differ from each other more than straight couples do—except in their sex, of course. Can you think of reasons why this might be the case?

Communication Is a Key Factor in the Success of Relationships

Another important factor influencing the success of relationships is communication (Guerrero et al., 2013). In fact, many therapists name communication problems as the number one reason for dissatisfaction in marriages and other long-term relationships (Markman et al., 2010). According to several longitudinal studies, couples who communicate well before or at the time of marriage are likely to be satisfied with their relationships when interviewed several years later. Couples who communicate poorly early on (even though they may be just as happy at that stage) are likely to be dissatisfied with their marriage later. And couples who communicate via aggression are likely to be separated or divorced a few years later. These correlations are strong enough that researchers can predict with 65% to 90% accuracy the state of a marriage 5 years down the road, simply on the basis of communication styles at the outset (Markman, 1981; Rogge & Bradbury, 1999).

Further bolstering the importance of communication in relationships are studies that demonstrate the benefit of interventions to improve communication skills. Such programs, known collectively as marriage and relationship education (MRE), have quite a good track record: Typically, couples who participate in these programs do communicate better, describe their relationships as happier, and are substantially less likely to break up, compared with couples who don't enroll in such programs (Carroll & Doherty, 2003; Blanchard et al., 2009). Unfortunately, most studies follow couples for only a few years, and they tend not to focus on racial minorities, economically disadvantaged groups, unmarried couples, or same-sex couples—groups in which breakups may be especially common.

Communication may be inhibited by upbringing or by the gender barrier

Communication is a skill that affects many aspects of a relationship. We focus here first on communication in the area of sexuality itself—which is, after all, the topic of this book—and then take a look at more general aspects of communication between intimate partners.

Many couples are reluctant to communicate at all about sexual issues. This reluctance results in part from a tradition of silence about sexual matters that is instilled in young children. Parents tend not to discuss sexual function or genital anatomy with their children, nor do they typically disclose much about their own sex lives or sexual problems. Children quickly learn that sex is a taboo subject. The result is a sense of shame that may profoundly inhibit communication in adulthood.

In heterosexual relationships, the gender barrier may compound communication problems. Boys and young men tend to talk about sexual matters among themselves, as do girls and young women, but they tend to do it in quite different ways, leading almost to separate languages. Young men, for example, may be perfectly comfortable using words such as "dick" and "pussy" among themselves, but the same words may seem vulgar when used with a female

What went wrong? Many couples find it difficult to discuss sexual problems, because they have been socialized to discuss sex only in same-sex groups.

partner. So men are obligated to use words such as "penis" and "vagina," which may put them in an uncomfortable, almost clinical mindset. When this language difficulty is combined with limited knowledge about the other sex's anatomy and physiology, communication may be severely inhibited. Similarly, girls and young women may discuss sexual and relationship issues at great length among themselves, but they may be quite unprepared to bring up these same issues with men. Additionally, cultural factors inhibit communication in certain groups. Asian-Americans, for example—especially Asian-American women—may find it a very foreign concept to discuss sex or relationship problems, whether with family or a partner (Ayuda, 2011).

Relationship and marriage education teaches communication skills

MRE programs, such as the Prevention and Relationship Enhancement Program developed by Howard Markman and his colleagues at the University of Denver, teach basic communication skills that are often as relevant to work and general social life as they are to sexual relationships (PREP Inc., 2011). At the core of all communication, for example, is one person saying something and the other person listening and responding. In premarital counseling programs, couples may first practice this interaction in a formalized manner. The couple may be seated facing and looking directly at each other, perhaps touching each other. One partner ("Pat") holds a speaker's token such as a floor tile (representing "the floor") and makes a statement such as "Kim, I find myself feeling hurt when you just breeze in and start chatting with the kids as if I'm not there." Pat then yields the "floor" to Kim, who replies in a fashion that paraphrases what Pat has just said, such as "You mean, I seem to just take you for granted?" The floor tile changes hands again, and Pat clarifies the initial statement: "Not all the time, just when the kids are around." Another tile change, and Kim gives a response representing a proposed resolution: "You may be right, Pat—sorry! I can understand how you must feel. However much I love the kids, you're the number one person in my life, and I want to make sure you know it." And so on.

Contrived though such "active-listening" exercises may seem, they teach two important points: the right of one partner to make a clear statement of a potential problem without interruption, and the obligation of the other to provide some feedback—to acknowledge understanding the statement and to process it in a way that will bring the interaction to a satisfactory close. In other words, "uh-huh" might not be a fruitful response to each and every one of your partner's utterances. It's not expected that couples will continue to pass floor tiles to and fro for the rest of their lives, but the hope is that the notion of ordered, reciprocal communication will persist.

Active-listening exercises do run the risk of turning sexual relationships into therapy sessions. Partners are not therapists—outsiders whose role is simply to empathize—but players *within* the drama. Thus, it doesn't necessarily help to tell your partner how much you understand their point of view unless that understanding is accompanied by action and resolution.

Let's make up an illustrative example. You buy a giant flat-screen TV, but your partner is distressed about the unplanned hit to your budget, and she gets angry with you. It wouldn't help much for you to say "I hear what you're saying, I can understand that you're angry that I spent so much money without consulting you." That hasn't put your finances back in order. What actions would show genuine empathy? Returning the TV? Being frugal until you've made up the cost of the TV? Consulting with her before every significant purchase in the future? Any or all of these practical responses would stand a better chance of resolving the conflict than apologizing or "understanding."

How couples deal with conflict affects the stability of their relationship

Conflicts are inevitable in all but the briefest relationships, but how conflicts are handled is a good indicator of the likelihood that a relationship will last. John Gottman and his colleagues at the University of Washington have carried out numerous longitudinal studies of conflict styles in marriage. Typically, the researchers videotape interactions between partners early in their relationship and analyze and quantify the conversations, facial gestures, and body movements—since words alone do not capture the breadth of signals people exchange. Then the researchers follow the relationship for a period of years, evaluating the outcomes.

One of the key findings is that the expression of anger is not necessarily a bad thing (Gottman & Krokoff, 1989). Disagreement and anger cause unhappiness at the time they are expressed, but they open up topics for communication—which may not happen much among couples who use other conflict management styles, such as withdrawal, defensiveness, criticism, or contempt.

Getting angry does not necessarily threaten the stability of a relationship, but negative interactions must be countered by more-numerous positive ones.

That doesn't mean that couples should just lay into each other with anger—far from it. The University of Washington researchers have found that when conflicts do occur in stable marriages, communications between the partners feature at least 5 times as many positive interactions as negative ones. Thus, couples who freely express anger during conflict have to balance it out with a high ratio of positive statements and actions if they are to prevent their relationships from dropping below the 5 to 1 ratio. People who get into prolonged fights have to spend hours of "repair work" with positive talk and actions to prevent the anger from harming their relationships. Even more important is attending to the ways that conversations *begin*: People who initiate interactions with "positive start-ups" ("I love the way your body smells. Sometimes I wonder whether you could enhance it by taking a shower occasionally.") are less likely to have later marital break-ups than those who use "negative start-ups" ("You stink.").

Gottman's group claimed to predict, with 92.7% accuracy,* whether a couple would divorce or not in the following 4 years, simply on the strength of their positive interactions during repair conversations (Gottman & Levenson, 1999). Thus, the old advice to "kiss and make up"—and to find a resolution to the problem that triggered the conflict—seems to be right on the mark. Developing the art of positive start-ups puts the frosting on the cake. There are few if any differences between same-sex and opposite-sex relationships regarding these interaction dynamics (Gottman et al., 2003).

In troubled heterosexual marriages and other relationships, a common problem emerges when the woman makes some demand for change in the relationship and the man responds by stonewalling, meaning that he is verbally silent and shows little facial or gestural expression, even though he may be in some turmoil internally. This pattern of demand and withdrawal—which has its origin in gender differences in emotional expressiveness—precludes any possibility of resolution and is therefore quite predictive of an eventual breakup. Nevertheless, making a couple aware of the demand-withdrawal problem—along with alternative strategies for conflict resolution and positive repair conversations—can help them improve their communication skills.

Therapy based on insights of this kind is known as **behavioral couples therapy (BCT)**. This form of therapy is quite successful in helping rescue troubled relationships, no matter what problems couples have. The BCT therapist introduces the couple to simple behavioral exercises, such as practicing the activity called Catch Your Partner Doing Something Nice, which helps increase the ratio of positivity to negativity in a relationship. The therapist also brings social-learning and cognitive principles to bear on the problems faced by the couple.

Gottman has published research on the importance of trust in intimate relationships (see Recommended Reading at the end of this chapter). He stresses that trust is based on *behavior* more than on thoughts or words alone. Do each partner's *actions* show "I am here for you" and "You can count on me"? These trust-inspiring actions are especially important when times get tough: If each partner's actions show genuine concern for the other, even when problems arise, both of them will come to realize that they have a truly trusting relationship.

Trust does not emerge instantly between two people, which can make it hard for individuals in new relationships to be certain whether they are on the road to developing real mutual trust. But the more often the behavior of each partner demonstrates a sincere concern for the other, the sooner the pair will develop a strong emotional bond, which is the basis of intimate trust—and a loving sexual connection.

Although writers such as Gottman often frame their discussion in terms of heterosexual marriage, the principles they put forward are applicable to any relationship that a couple values and wishes to sustain. In fact, even the less durable relationships that are common in the college years are opportunities for exploring and learning skills for building good relationships.

All couples experience some problems in relationships. Repairing them is crucial. Couples are most likely to survive for the long haul if they can fix the things that go wrong. The sooner and more effectively two people can show that they sincerely want to repair any problems that occur, the more likely they are to nurture their trust and love.

behavioral couples therapy (BCT) Therapy focused on improving styles of communication between partners in relationships.

---

* Gottman's claim of high predictive accuracy may be somewhat misleading, as it is based mainly on the large numbers of couples predicted to stay together who did stay together. In many of his studies, the majority of the couples that were predicted to divorce did not in fact do so.

jealousy Fear that a partner may be sexually or emotionally unfaithful.

sexual jealousy Fear that one's partner is engaging in sexual contacts with another person.

emotional jealousy Fear that one's partner is becoming emotionally committed to another person.

Love, Jealousy, and Infidelity Are Intertwined

Jealousy is the unpleasant feeling caused by suspicions of—or the discovery of—one's partner's infidelity.* Infidelity, in this context, could mean anything from an actual sexual contact or relationship with a third party to a mere indication of interest in someone else—as evidenced by looking at, flirting with, or spending time with that person. At any one time, about 1 in 10 college students is experiencing jealousy, according to an Italian study (Marazziti et al., 2003).

Jealousy can be an acute sensation—the instant stab of jealousy that we may feel when our beloved shows attention to a potential rival. This feeling probably involves a physiological stress response. Alternatively, it can be a gnawing, suspicious frame of mind that takes over a jealous person and colors interactions with his or her partner.

We can break down jealousy into two kinds. The first, **sexual jealousy**, is a fear that one's partner is engaging or seeking to engage in sex with another person. The second, **emotional jealousy**, is a fear that one's partner is committing himself or herself to another person and might therefore abandon the relationship. Men and women can experience both kinds of jealousy, but men typically experience sexual jealousy more strongly than women, and women typically experience emotional jealousy more strongly than men. This sex difference exists across many or all cultures (Buss, 2011).

Have you ever checked out a romantic partner's activities on Facebook? That's known as "interpersonal electronic surveillance," or colloquially, "creeping." Most young people have engaged in it at one time or another, the most common motivation being jealousy (Stern & Willis, 2007). "Facebook jealousy" in particular has been the subject of considerable research. The more time romantically involved people spend on Facebook, the more likely they are to experience jealousy, especially of the emotional kind (Muise et al., 2009). Facebook makes it easy—perhaps too easy—for users to monitor the activities of their partners: who they are friending, who they are close to in photos, or how they describe their relationship status. Ambiguous information in these postings then incites further vigilance, and this feedback loop can sometimes lead all the way to cyberstalking (see Chapter 16). People with anxious attachment styles are particularly prone to this kind of escalation (Marshall et al., 2013).

Jealousy can help maintain relationships that are threatened by third parties.

Jealousy can have a positive function

Evolutionary psychologists see the capacity for jealousy as a hardwired adaptation to certain inescapable facts about reproduction. First, female mammals make a much greater biological contribution to reproduction than do males, but in some species, such as ours, this imbalance may be countered by the extra resources (e.g., food and protection) that males contribute. Second, females can be certain that any offspring they bear are their own; males, however, cannot be certain that they fathered their mates' offspring. Thus, during human evolution, the major reproductive risk for a woman was that a man would take up with another mate, leaving her with insufficient resources to rear her children alone. The major reproductive risk for a man, however, was that he would unwittingly devote a great deal of time and

---

* Jealousy is different from *envy*—the distress caused by another person's possession of something that one lacks.

effort to helping rear children who were actually fathered by another man. According to David Buss of the University of Texas, these differences in risks explain why men and women tend to experience different kinds of jealousy—greater sexual jealousy in men and greater emotional jealousy in women (Buss, 2000, 2011).

This evolutionary interpretation gains further support from studies that focus on same-sex cheating (Confer & Cloud, 2011). Men are far less disturbed by the idea that their female partner is having sex with another woman than by the idea that she is cheating with a man—presumably because same-sex infidelity cannot lead to the birth of children that he might mistakenly rear as his own. Conversely, women are, if anything, even *more* disturbed by the idea of their male partner cheating with another man than with a woman—perhaps because the implication of homosexuality is seen as carrying an even greater risk of permanent abandonment.

Jealousy often arises when people in relationships receive sexual advances from outsiders. These "mate-poaching" efforts seem to be universal across human cultures (Schmitt, 2004). In addition, people in relationships may themselves be tempted to cheat on their partners because love—the main glue of relationships—is not always strong enough by itself to preserve monogamy. That's where jealousy attempts to take over the job. And that's where jealousy can have a positive value for the person who experiences it, painful though it is. Jealousy is part of the mechanism that detects and gives salience to cheating by a partner, and then motivates action to prevent or end it.

Because our capacity for jealousy has evolved, it is "built in"; thus, it is not always a rational process. A husband doesn't say to himself, "Oh, my wife's on the pill, so I'm not worried if she sleeps around." Evolution knows nothing about pills: It simply provides everyone with an emotional mechanism that has been effective in the past for protecting people's reproductive interests.

Jealousy is neither a good thing nor a bad thing, but rather a psychological response that can have both positive and negative consequences. The negative consequences can be truly horrendous: About 13% of all homicides are spousal murders, most of them triggered by jealousy. Battered women who seek refuge in shelters are commonly there because of spousal jealousy. And many more relationships are poisoned by less extreme expressions of the same emotion.

Several therapists have described useful techniques for distinguishing healthy jealousy, which can help strengthen and maintain loving relationships, from jealousy that is merely destructive, as well as techniques for overcoming the latter kind (Barker, 1987; Dryden, 1999). Self-destructive jealousy, aggressive jealousy, or jealousy that is based on persistent false beliefs about the partner (**delusional jealousy**) obviously merits therapeutic intervention. Still, one way to deal with jealousy is to act on it, specifically by making oneself more physically attractive to one's partner or by going out of one's way to demonstrate love and commitment. "Men who are successful at keeping their partners often step up their displays of love when threatened with a possible partner defection," writes Buss. "Men who fail in these displays tend to be losers in love" (Buss, 2000).

Extra-Pair Relationships Have Many Styles and Motivations

As we've just discussed, the capacity for jealousy exists because people who are in coupled relationships, whether dating, cohabiting, or married, may also engage in sexual relationships outside their ongoing partnership. We now turn our attention to the forms and motivations of such **extra-pair relationships**. ("Extramarital relationships" is a better-known phrase, but it is inappropriate here because we are not focusing exclusively on married couples.)

About the only thing that all extra-pair relationships have in common is that, as mentioned earlier in this chapter, they tend to incur societal disapproval. Either

FAQ

My boyfriend is constantly accusing me of seeing someone else behind his back, even though I'm not. What should I do?

Delusional jealousy is a serious disorder that can lead to violence or stalking. Your boyfriend needs to be assessed and perhaps treated by a mental health professional. If he refuses, you should consider whether it's worth staying in the relationship.

delusional jealousy Persistent false belief that one's partner is involved with another person.

extra-pair relationship A sexual relationship in which at least one of the partners is already married to or partnered with someone else.

social monogamy   The formation of pair-bonds, or marriages between two persons, that may or may not be sexually exclusive.

sexual monogamy   The formation of pair-bonds or marriages that are sexually exclusive.

monogamy or serial monogamy is considered the ideal, and anything else is stigmatized, though to varying degrees depending on circumstances. Even fantasies about sex with a person outside the partnership are widely considered a form of infidelity, in spite of the fact that most men and about half of women experience such fantasies (Yarab et al., 1998).

If we discount fantasies, we are still left with a broad range of behaviors that fall into the category of extra-pair relationships. These behaviors include casual flirting, fondling, genital contact and coitus, and falling in love. Extra-pair relationships may be single encounters, brief "flings," longer "affairs," or a succession of such relationships with a variety of different partners. They may take place with or without the knowledge or acquiescence of the person's regular partner, who may be a spouse, cohabiting partner, or girlfriend or boyfriend. They may take place in real life or on the Internet (**Box 7.5**).

Personal and evolutionary factors influence infidelity

Why do some women and men in our society engage in extra-pair relationships while others do not? Many factors come into play here. Many people refrain from engaging in extra-pair relationships because of moral beliefs, concern for their partners' feelings, or fear of the consequences. Conversely, lack of physical satisfaction, communication, or love in the primary relationship, or prolonged absence of the primary partner, can drive some people into affairs. So can the sense that one is not getting what one deserves in the primary relationship because one's partner is perceived as less attractive or desirable than oneself. So can the sheer excitement of having a new partner or of falling in love all over again. People may also cultivate secondary relationships to provoke a jealous response on the part of the primary partner, to "get even" with the primary partner if that partner is already having an affair with someone else, or to precipitate an end to the primary relationship. Finally, gay people who are heterosexually married may find their only sexual satisfaction in secondary relationships.

People who are in the early stages of a relationship may also cultivate a relationship with a "back burner" partner. This strategy could be either a form of insurance in case the main relationship doesn't work out or simply a means to increase sexual enjoyment or attention. According to a survey of college undergraduates by Jayson Dibble and Michelle Drouin of Hope University, many students (men especially) cultivate back burners, keeping in touch with them by text, Facebook, and the like (Dibble & Drouin, 2014). Surprisingly, students who said that they were in committed relationships were just as likely to have back-burners as those who were not, suggesting that "commitment" at the college level isn't expected to be forever.

Besides the potential threat posed by back burners, people in long-lasting relationships are exposed to another danger, related to the transition from romantic to companionate love. This transition reopens the possibility of finding new romantic love—but with a different person. It's the stuff of soap operas, but it's often the stuff of real life, too: A man or woman may be deeply attached to his or her regular partner but may also be head over heels in love with someone else.

That infidelity has evolutionary roots is suggested by the fact that promiscuity is common among nonhuman animals, including many species that form pair-bonds (**socially monogamous** species). Male animals probably engage in extra-pair sex because it is a relatively inexpensive way to have more offspring, whereas females are more likely to do so to acquire the resources provided by the extra-pair male or to give her offspring better genes than those provided by her regular mate. Nevertheless, some animals are **sexually monogamous**—they never engage in extra-pair sex even though they are capable of doing so: Female hamadryas baboons, for example, never mate with any reproductive-age male other than the dominant male in their

Box 7.5 Society, Values, and the Law

We Just Clicked

When John Goydan of Bridgewater, New Jersey, filed for divorce from his wife Diane and sought custody of their two young children, his legal papers contained dozens of emails, some of them sexually explicit, that Diane had exchanged with a man who called himself "The Weasel." Diane and The Weasel never met, but to John their online romance amounted to adultery. Similarly, "Nadja" considered that her attorney husband "Steve" had cheated on her when their children found erotic correspondence between him and a woman named "Galaxy Queen" on the family computer—even though Steve and Galaxy Queen had confined their romance to the Internet (Associated Press, 1996).

What drives people to commit Internet infidelity? For the most part, it's the same reasons that have driven people to cheat on their partners since time immemorial. But the Internet offers special incentives—what has been called the "triple-A engine" of accessibility, affordability, and anonymity (Cooper, 2002). Anonymity, in this context, includes selective disclosure and deception: in other words, a level of control over how the other person perceives you that would never be achievable in the real world. And of course it means safety—no hard-to-explain hickeys, no mysterious phone hang-ups, and no sexually transmitted infections. A secure password covers everything.

Diane and Steve's escapades took place in the 1990s, when text emails were about the only option for cyberlovers. Now the profusion of microphones, webcams, video chat–oriented websites, and Web-enabled sex toys allow for the exchange of everything but pheromones. In one study, 8% of partnered respondents said that they had engaged in cybersex with someone other than their partner (Fricker & Moore, 2008).

Partnered individuals who engage in cybersex with third parties may deny that this constitutes "cheating." ("How can you call it cheating—I've never met her/him—it's not real!") But people who discover that their partners are engaging in cybersex—whether by being directly told about it, by finding evidence of it on a computer, or by walking in on a cybersex session—do usually consider it cheating, according to one survey (Schneider et al., 2012). In fact, even viewing pornography without the involvement of any third party is often considered cheating too. Most of the survey respondents said that their partners' online activities had caused them stress and led them to think of themselves as trauma victims, and that it led to a worsening or termination of the relationship. "Now I feel unattractive, ugly, wondering what's wrong with me," wrote one respondent. "I can't sleep or concentrate. I'm missing out on life's happiness, worried, scared all the time."

No doubt there are some people who are able to see their partners' cybersex as "not real" and simply let it go or turn a blind eye to it. Others may be happy to join in on the online activities. But for the majority, cheating online is the same thing as cheating in the real world, and just as painful.

---

group, so if that male happens to be sterile, none of the females in that group will produce any offspring (Birkhead, 2000).

Evolutionary psychologists argue that similar forces influence human behavior. Steve Gangestad and Randy Thornhill, for example, believe that when women have sex outside of their marriages or regular partnerships, they are unconsciously shopping for better genes. This is suggested by the fact that women are more likely to engage in extra-pair sex during the phase of their menstrual cycles during which they are most likely to conceive (Gangestad & Thornhill, 1997).

In addition to these apparent evolutionary forces, we should bear in mind the obvious social factors that influence women and men in different ways when it comes to extra-pair relationships. A man's infidelities tend to be viewed more leniently than those of a woman, and a man often has greater ability to devote time and resources to

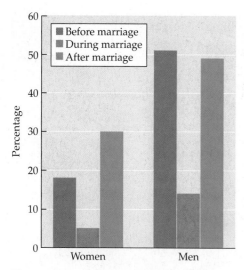

Figure 7.15 **Marriage is an interlude of monogamy** according to NHSLS data. The graph shows the percentage of women and men born between 1943 and 1952 who said they had more than one new sex partner before, during, or after their first marriage.

Go to the
**Discovering
Human Sexuality**
Companion Website at
**sites.sinauer.com/
discoveringhumansexuality3e**
for activities, study questions,
quizzes, and other study aids.

an outside relationship than a woman does, especially if the woman is pregnant or the couple already has children.

Extra-pair relationships are uncommon

Americans don't cheat on their spouses or regular partners very often (**Figure 7.15**). In the NHSLS study, conducted in 1992, most of the interviewees reported that they had been completely monogamous over the entire duration of a marriage or cohabitation, whereas many of these same people had multiple partners *before* and *after* those long-term relationships. The same thing continues to be true today: In the GSS data for 2010, only 20% of ever-married men and 14% of women said that they had sex with a person other than their spouse while they were married.

It's possible, of course, that survey respondents are less than honest about their extramarital relationships. One study found that married women were much more likely to admit to a recent extramarital relationship when entering their responses into a computer than when they were questioned in a face-to-face interview, as was done in the NHSLS study (Whisman & Snyder, 2007). Even among the women who entered data into the computer, however, only 6% said that they had engaged in a recent extramarital relationship.

The low prevalence of extra-pair sex may surprise some readers, for several reasons. As we've discussed, plenty of factors cause marital problems and increase people's motivation to look for other partners. Viagra and improved health care would seem to make infidelity an increasingly available option for older people. And role models for infidelity are in the news every day. So what stops people from straying? Most likely, it is the fact that 4 out of 5 Americans believe that doing so is morally wrong (see Figure 7.3) and the fact that they value the stability of their long-term relationships more highly than the immediate rewards of infidelity.

Couples therapists often have to deal with issues of infidelity (Hertlein & Weeks, 2007). These therapists are very familiar with the pain, confusion, and anger that infidelity can cause. Therapeutic goals include apology, forgiveness, improvement of communication, and setting of new ground rules. If the couple cannot recommit to each other, a therapist may guide them to an amicable separation.

Summary

- People enter into sexual relationships for a variety of reasons: sexual attraction and love; the desire for status, security, or profit; the desire to conform or to rebel; and the desire to have children.

- People tend to judge the morality of sexual behavior by its context, being more approving of sex in committed relationships than of casual or extramarital sex. Beliefs about the morality of sex are tied to beliefs about its purpose. Americans can be grouped into several clusters with characteristic attitudes on sexual matters; to a considerable degree, a particular person's beliefs can be predicted by demographic characteristics such as age, sex, religion, and educational level. Americans have become far more accepting of sex between unmarried individuals

and homosexual sex over the past several decades, but disapproval of extramarital and teen sex remains high.

- Casual sex is more appealing to men than to women. In the college environment, "hooking up" (uncommitted sex between acquaintances) is an increasingly common practice. But the prevalence of casual sex in the college environment is lower than most students believe. Alcohol is an important factor in facilitating hookups. Some participants in hookups—women more than men—later regret them and possibly suffer mental health consequences, but many others enjoy hookups and have no regrets. Casual sex is more accepted and more prevalent in the gay male community than among heterosexuals or lesbians.

- Flirting behaviors by both sexes are quite stereotyped across cultures, but flirting styles vary with personality. Largely unconscious signals, such as prolonged eye contact, communicate a person's desire to escalate an encounter or, conversely, to terminate it.

- Committed but non-cohabiting relationships (traditionally called dating relationships) tend to be fluid and short-lived, leading either to a live-in relationship or to separation. Those relationships that include sex very early tend to be shorter than those in which sex is postponed, but this is probably a selection effect, not an effect of the sex itself.

- Romantic love exists in most or all cultures. Mutual liking, physical attraction, and other factors promote falling in love. Romantic love appears to be mediated by specific hormones and neurotransmitters and by activity patterns within regions of the brain that process pleasurable sensations.

- Sternberg's theory of love proposes that love consists of three elements—passion, intimacy, and commitment—whose relative contributions may be represented by a triangle. The shape of a person's "love triangle" changes over the course of a relationship. A couple are most likely to be satisfied with their relationship when their triangles match.

- Unrequited love is painful to both suitors and rejectors: to suitors because it denies them their love object and diminishes their self-esteem, and to rejectors because it causes them guilt.

- According to attachment theory, young children's relationships with their parents establish patterns that are repeated in romantic relationships during adulthood.

- Partners in relationships tend to resemble each other in a variety of respects. This homogamy contributes to satisfaction in relationships.

- A couple's communication style predicts their satisfaction with their relationship, and its durability. Couples may have difficulty communicating about sexual matters for a variety of reasons, such as a culture of sexual shame. Some premarital counseling programs teach communication skills.

- The way couples deal with conflict is strongly predictive of how long the relationships will last. Optimal strategies involve not avoiding anger, but rather solving the problems that cause anger and developing numerous positive interactions. Couples do best when hostile interactions are followed with positive "repair" conversations. Couples therapy may focus on altering behavior or on unearthing hidden emotional problems.

- Jealousy, though a painful experience, has a positive function in protecting relationships against infidelity and in testing the strength of love bonds. Sex differences in jealousy—sexual jealousy in men and emotional jealousy in women—may reflect the different reproductive interests that men and women have had over the course of human evolution. Some forms of jealousy are damaging and merit treatment, but well-grounded jealousy can spur constructive efforts to improve the relationship, if those involved have learned to respond effectively to problematic situations.

- Many circumstantial factors influence whether people in long-term partnerships engage in sexual relationships outside those partnerships. National surveys suggest that most married Americans are in fact monogamous for most or the entirety of their marriage.

Discussion Questions

1. Compare and contrast your beliefs about what is right or wrong in the sexual domain with your peers' and your parents' beliefs (e.g., consider extramarital sex, premarital sex, casual sex, promiscuity, age of consent, homosexual behavior, contraception, abortion, and divorce). Identify the moral perspective (see Figure 7.1) that best describes your beliefs. Discuss how your attitudes have or have not changed over time.

2. If you have had an experience with a relationship breakup, describe your reactions to that breakup, how it felt, and what you learned. If you have not had a breakup or don't wish to discuss it, imagine the circumstances that would distress you enough to lead to a breakup.

3. Discuss what is important to you about communication and conflict negotiation in a relationship. Are you reluctant to discuss sexual issues? Why? Consider your ability to communicate in light of those factors discussed in the text that hinder communication.

4. Discuss your experiences with jealousy, and compare them with those of your peers.

5. What basis do you think is most effective for selecting a marriage partner—arranged marriage, falling in love, or something else? Why?

Web Resources

American College Health Association www.acha.org

Beliefnet: Relationships (interfaith site with considerable discussion of sexual and relationship issues) www.beliefnet.com/Love-Family/Relationships/index.aspx

Go Ask Alice: Relationships (from Columbia University's Health Services) goaskalice.columbia.edu/relationships

Gottman Institute www.gottman.com

Perel, E. TED Talks: The secret to desire in a long-term relationship tinyurl.com/b7flgz3

SexInfo Online: Love & Relationships (from the University of California, Santa Barbara) www.soc.ucsb.edu/sexinfo/category#love_and_relationships

Recommended Reading

Bogle, K. A. (2008). *Hooking up: Sex, dating, and relationships on campus*. NYU Press.

Browning, D. (2009). *Sex, marriage, and family in world religions*. Columbia University Press.

Buss, D. M. (2000). *The dangerous passion: Why jealousy is as necessary as love and sex*. Free Press.

Fisher, H. (2014). *Anatomy of love: A natural history of mating, marriage, and why we stray* (updated ed.). Norton.

Gottman, J. M. (2011). *The science of trust: Emotional attunement for couples*. Norton.

Guerrero, L. K., Andersen, P. A. & Afifi, W. A. (2013). *Close encounters: Communication in relationships* (4th ed.). Sage.

Hojatt, M. & Cramer, D. (2013). *Positive psychology of love*. Oxford.

Markman, H. J., Stanley, S. M. & Blumberg, S. L. (2010). *Fighting for your marriage* (3rd ed.). Jossey-Bass.

Pierce, C. & Morgan, E. T. (2008). *Finding the doorbell: Sexual satisfaction for the long haul*. Nomad.

Regnerus, M. & Uecker, J. (2011). *Premarital sex in America: How young Americans meet, mate, and think about marrying*. Oxford University Press.

Sternberg, R. J. & Weis, K. (Eds.). (2006). *The new psychology of love*. Yale University Press.

Young, L. & Alexander, B. (2012). *The chemistry between us: Love, sex, and the science of attraction*. Current Hardcover.

Chapter 8

Pregnancy is often something for a woman to celebrate.

Fertility, Pregnancy, and Childbirth

In earlier chapters we described the production and release of gametes (sperm and ova), the site where they meet (one of the woman's oviducts), and the process by which the resulting embryo differentiates as male or female. We now take a broader look at pregnancy and childbirth from the perspectives of both the conceptus and its parents. In this chapter we assume that couples want to become parents—and parents of healthy children. We will see how a couple can optimize their chances of achieving this goal and how medical science has improved their odds of doing so. In Chapter 9 we will take the opposite tack, looking at strategies to prevent pregnancy and childbirth.

Pregnancy and Childbirth Raise Major Health Concerns

In the past, pregnancy and childbirth were events to which women looked forward with a mixture of joy and terror. Joy, because producing and rearing children defined much of a woman's existence. And terror, not just because of the pain of childbirth, but because of the grave risk that pregnancy would end in the death of mother, baby, or both.

Before the advent of modern medicine, no amount of wealth or power could avert the tragic risks of reproduction. Remember England's King Henry VIII (1491–1547) and his six wives? Yes, he had a couple of them beheaded, but two of the remaining four—Jane Seymour and Kathryn Parr—died in or soon after childbirth. Of these six women's 11 children, most died in infancy, and only 3 reached adulthood. Memorials to the millions of women who have died in childbirth are everywhere, from India's fabled Taj Mahal to a humble stone in the pioneers' graveyard at Coloma, California, that records the death of 32-year-old Hannah Seater and her newborn son in 1852.

Today the prospects for pregnant women and their fetuses are far brighter than in the past. If we exclude pregnancies that are terminated by induced abortion, 80% of all established pregnancies in the United States culminate in the delivery of a live child. Once a child is born, it has a better than 99% chance of surviving through infancy. And less than 2 per 10,000 pregnancies now lead to the death of the mother (National Vital Statistics Reports, 2012; Centers for Disease Control, 2013g). (Some key facts concerning U.S. birthrates are listed in **Box 8.1**.)

Still, there is always room for improvement, especially because the statistics for some U.S. minorities are much worse than those for the general population. And parents want not just a live child, but also one who is in the best possible shape to face the rigors of life "on the outside." To achieve this goal, it helps for prospective parents to learn as much as possible about pregnancy, childbirth, and the factors that promote or compromise the health of the mother and her fetus.

Pregnancy Is Confirmed by Hormonal Tests

Fertilization takes place in an oviduct. There, a sperm that has ascended the female reproductive tract from the vagina enters an ovum that was released from an ovary at the time of ovulation. The fertilized ovum is commonly called an embryo.* The embryo begins migrating down the oviduct toward the uterus, a journey of a few days. Meanwhile, the lining of the uterus is being put into readiness to receive an embryo. This process is initiated by progesterone secreted by the ovary (specifically, by the corpus luteum) during the postovulatory phase of the woman's menstrual cycle.

All being well, the embryo burrows into the endometrium—a process called **implantation**—and begins to secrete a hormone known as human chorionic gonadotropin (hCG). This hormone prevents the next menstruation from occurring, and a missed menstrual period is the usual way that a woman learns that she is pregnant.

Many embryos fail to implant. In such cases the embryo simply disintegrates and its remains are washed out of the woman's body during her next menstrual period. The woman has no way of knowing that an embryo has existed. Thus, doctors say that pregnancy is "established" only after successful implantation, not at fertilization.

The absence of a menstrual period at the expected time is not a totally reliable indicator of pregnancy. Many women have irregular periods anyway, and even a woman whose menstrual cycle is normally very regular can experience a missed or delayed period due to illness, stress, or some other reason. Conversely, some "spot-

implantation The attachment of the embryo to the endometrium.

---

* Strictly speaking, it is a conceptus: It does not become an embryo until 2 weeks after conception, when the nonembryonic tissues, such as the fetal membranes and placenta, have separated from the cells that will give rise to the fetus.

Box 8.1 Research Highlights

Birth Facts

In the United States, birthrates are declining. In 2012, the general fertility rate reached an all-time low of 63 births per 1000 women age 15–44. The statistically average woman now has 1.9 children, below the level required to keep the population level stable in the absence of immigration (about 2.1 children), and far below historic levels (see figure). Here are some more specific statistics:

- The birthrate for teenagers (age 15 to 19) is falling especially rapidly. In 2012 it reached an all-time low of 29 births per 1000, representing a 6% decline from the previous year and a 67% drop from 1960.

- The birthrates for women over 30 and over 40 are increasing at a rate of about 1% per year. Social factors and improved fertility treatments are probably responsible.

- 41% of births are to unmarried mothers—more than double the rate in 1980.

- The percentage of all births that are twin births is holding steady at about 3%, but the numbers of triplets and higher multiples is declining rapidly and is now less than two-thirds of the peak rate reached in 1998. This drop is probably due to changes to IVF procedures (implantation of fewer embryos).

Average number of children born over a woman's lifetime in the United States, from 1850 to 1990. The 1950–1960 peak is the post-World War II baby boom. (After National Bureau of Economic Research, 2006 and National Vital Statistics Reports, 2013)

- 33% of all babies are delivered by cesarean section.

- Less than 1% of all babies are born at home.

Sources: Centers for Disease Control, 2012b, 2013a.

---

ting" (light bleeding) can occur even when a woman is pregnant. Other symptoms may help to confirm the pregnancy, including breast tenderness, fatigue, and nausea (the beginning of the "morning sickness" that can plague some women during the first 3 months of pregnancy—see below). Pregnancy tests are designed to test for the presence of hCG in the mother's blood or urine. The most sensitive (and expensive) laboratory tests can detect hCG in the mother's blood almost immediately after implantation—several days *before* a woman would notice a missed period. To get a laboratory test, a woman must see a health care provider.

Another option is to purchase a home pregnancy test kit (**Figure 8.1**). These products are convenient and inexpensive—about 20 million are sold in the United States every year. Various brands are available, ranging in price from about $7 to $17. They show the result by the presence or absence of a colored line on the test strip, or by a digital readout. Unfortunately, home pregnancy tests are not nearly as reliable as laboratory tests. Most of the products claim "99% accuracy," but only the First Response test met that level of accuracy in studies by Laurence Cole of the University of Kansas (Cole, 2011, 2012). Furthermore, even the First Response test only achieved that accuracy on the day of the missed period; at 4 days prior to the missed period, it detected pregnancy only about half the time, and other products performed much less well than that. Thus it is very important to follow up an early negative result with a second test a few days later.

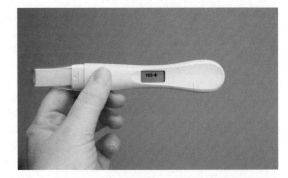

Figure 8.1 Home pregnancy test The user holds one end of the test stick in her urine stream for a few seconds (or dips it in a collected urine sample). This is a digital test. (See **Web Activity 8.1: How a Home Pregnancy Test Works.**)

ultrasound scan   An imaging procedure that depends on the reflection of ultrasonic waves from density boundaries within the body. Also called ultrasonographic scan.

subfertility   Difficulty in establishing a pregnancy; arbitrarily defined as the absence of pregnancy after a couple has had frequent unprotected sex for 12 months.

infertility   Inability (of a man, woman, or couple) to achieve pregnancy.

artificial insemination   An assisted reproduction technique that involves the placement of semen in the vagina or uterus with the aid of a syringe or small tube.

Definitive clinical evidence of pregnancy can be obtained at 5 to 6 weeks by means of an **ultrasound scan**. This can determine whether one or more embryos are present, and by 2 to 3 weeks later it can detect the fetal heartbeat.

Infertility Can Result from a Problem in the Woman or in the Man

For a fertile young couple who are having sex several times a week without any form of contraception, there is about a 20% chance of pregnancy per month. This translates into a 93% chance within the first year. If a woman does not become pregnant after a year of unprotected sex, the couple is described as **subfertile**. This doesn't mean that there is no further chance of pregnancy, but rather that an investigation to find out why pregnancy has not occurred is warranted.

Subfertility and **infertility** (total inability to achieve pregnancy or to carry a pregnancy through to live childbirth) are surprisingly common. About 12% of women age 25 to 44, or their partners, have sought medical services regarding infertility (Centers for Disease Control, 2014k). The most common reason is to get advice or treatment to prevent miscarriage. Fertility problems are about equally likely to be caused by a disorder on the man's side or the woman's side. In about one-third of cases, there are problems on both sides or the cause can't be identified (Office on Women's Health, 2013b).

A variety of factors can reduce sperm counts

The most common cause for difficulty in getting pregnant is that the man is producing insufficient or poor-quality sperm. Sperm-related problems are the cause of about 25% of all couples' difficulties in achieving pregnancy. The usual rule of thumb is that a man is likely to be subfertile (i.e., have difficulty becoming a father) if he has fewer than 20 million sperm per milliliter of semen or if the fraction of his sperm that move normally is less than 50%. Sperm abnormalities (**Figure 8.2**) can also impair fertility, but only if the percentage of abnormal sperm is very high—above about 90% (Guzick et al., 2001).

What causes insufficient or defective sperm? There are many possible causes. Undescended testicles, sex chromosome anomalies, infections that cause blockage of the reproductive tract, and intensive chemotherapy can all cause irreversible reduction or failure of spermatogenesis. Heating of the testes, as can occur with too-tight clothing, causes a lowered sperm count that is usually reversible. A lack of exercise and a sedentary lifestyle are associated with low sperm counts: In a recent study from the Harvard School of Public Health, men who engaged in moderate-to-vigorous exercise for 15 or more hours per week had sperm counts 73% higher than men who exercised for less than 5 hours per week (Gaskins et al., 2013).

Environmental toxins can lower sperm counts, and they are suspected of having contributed to a general reduction in sperm counts in the population of the United States and other countries over the last several decades (**Box 8.2**). Finally, normal aging is associated with a gradual decrease in the volume of a man's ejaculate, as well as an increase in the numbers of sperm that are misshapen, move poorly, or contain damaged DNA. Couples in which the man is over 45 take 5 times longer to achieve pregnancy than couples in which the man is under 25, even after controlling for the woman's age (Robaire et al., 2007; Schmid et al., 2007).

In cases of problems with sperm quality, a couple can take various steps to achieve pregnancy. If sperm numbers are too low, semen can be collected over a period of time and frozen. Then the entire collected amount can be placed in the woman's vagina or directly into her uterus at a time coinciding with ovulation. This procedure is called **artificial insemination**. If the sperm come from

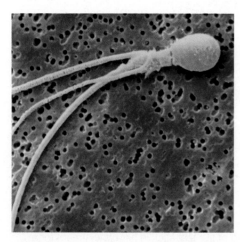

Figure 8.2 Abnormal (multi-tailed) sperm

Box 8.2 Controversies

Declining Sperm Counts?

In 1992 a Danish research group published some disturbing news about male fertility (Carlsen et al., 1992). According to their meta-analysis of about 60 prior studies that employed standardized sperm-counting techniques (Figure A), average sperm counts in several Western countries dropped by nearly one-half between 1940 and 1990—from 113 million to 66 million sperm per milliliter (mL) of semen. This drop was accompanied by a drop in ejaculate volume (from 3.4 mL to 2.75 mL) and by an increase in the prevalence of certain male reproductive disorders, such as undescended testicles (cryptorchidism) and testicular cancer.

The Danish findings have been contested. In 1999, for example, a group at Columbia University in New York argued that the apparent fall in sperm counts in the United States was an illusion caused by variations in where the sampling was done (Saidi et al., 1999). Specifically, many of the early U.S. studies were done in New York City, where (according to the New York researchers, at least) sperm counts are higher than in the rest of the country. The later studies were done in other cities, such as Los Angeles, where sperm counts are said to be much lower.

This conclusion was challenged in turn: A French group found that sperm counts measured at a single sperm bank in Paris declined markedly between 1973 and 1992, belying the geographic explanation (Auger et al., 1995). Another Danish study reported that the median sperm count in unselected young Danish men had fallen to 41 million sperm per mL (Andersen et al., 2000). This level is already in a "gray zone" within which fertility may be affected. And in a very large French study, it was reported that sperm counts fell from 74 to 50 million sperm per mL between 1989 and 2005 (Rolland et al., 2013) (Figure B).

Most experts now believe that the decline in sperm counts is real, so attention is shifting to the question of causation. One trivial explanation—more frequent ejaculation—has been ruled out by studies that control for the length of abstinence prior to specimen donation. Lifestyle changes such as the increased popularity of tight-fitting pants and underwear, which keep the testes too warm, or an increasingly sedentary lifestyle, may be contributing factors.

Most attention, however, has been focused on the possibility that the decline is caused by environmental pollutants, especially by "endocrine disruptors"—agricultural pesticides and other industrial chemicals that mimic or antagonize sex hormones. Agricultural workers do suffer a decline in sperm counts that is related to their degree of pesticide exposure (Abell et al., 2000),

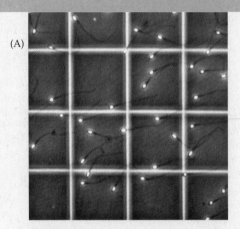

(A)

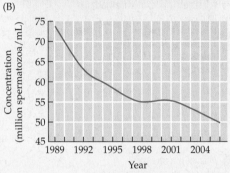

(B)

(A) Sperm are counted in a precisely calibrated chamber.
(B) Estimated sperm counts for a 35-year-old man in France from 1989 to 2006. (After Rolland et al., 2013.)

and men exposed to phthalates (industrial plasticizers) have less motile sperm and are less fertile than other men (Jurewicz et al., 2013; Buck Louis et al., 2014). Other factors may also play a role, however: Mothers who are obese or who smoke or drink during pregnancy or who bottle-feed rather than breast-feed their babies may have sons with smaller testicles in childhood and/or reduced sperm counts in adulthood (Sharpe, 2012). Untangling the roles of these various factors will be a challenging task.

As yet, average sperm counts are mostly above the level that leads to subfertility, but of course it's in the nature of an average for many individuals to fall below it. What's more, low sperm counts are becoming more problematic as women are seeking to have children at older ages than in the past: A sperm count that is perfectly adequate to fertilize a 25-year-old woman may be much less so for a woman whose "clock is ticking" (Sharpe, 2012). All in all, it is likely that declining sperm counts will accelerate the decline in birthrates that is causing problems for many countries—a decline that up until now has been caused largely by social factors.

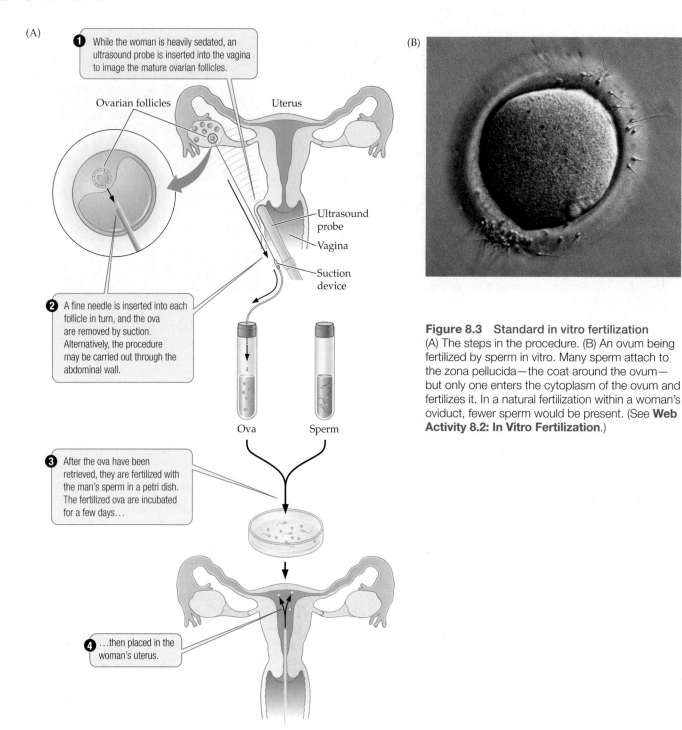

(A)

① While the woman is heavily sedated, an ultrasound probe is inserted into the vagina to image the mature ovarian follicles.

Ovarian follicles

Uterus

Ultrasound probe

Vagina

Suction device

② A fine needle is inserted into each follicle in turn, and the ova are removed by suction. Alternatively, the procedure may be carried out through the abdominal wall.

Ova

Sperm

③ After the ova have been retrieved, they are fertilized with the man's sperm in a petri dish. The fertilized ova are incubated for a few days...

④ ...then placed in the woman's uterus.

(B)

Figure 8.3 Standard in vitro fertilization (A) The steps in the procedure. (B) An ovum being fertilized by sperm in vitro. Many sperm attach to the zona pellucida—the coat around the ovum— but only one enters the cytoplasm of the ovum and fertilizes it. In a natural fertilization within a woman's oviduct, fewer sperm would be present. (See **Web Activity 8.2: In Vitro Fertilization**.)

the woman's partner, the technique is usually called "artificial insemination by husband," or AIH (although the man could actually be the woman's unmarried partner). Men with normal sperm counts may also store their own sperm for future AIH use.

In vitro fertilization can circumvent many sperm problems

Some sperm quality problems may require the use of **in vitro fertilization** (**IVF**). "In vitro" means "in glass," but it's actually in a plastic petri dish. In the standard IVF procedure (**Figure 8.3**), the woman is given hormones to promote the development

in vitro fertilization (IVF) Any of a variety of assisted reproduction techniques in which fertilization takes place outside the body.

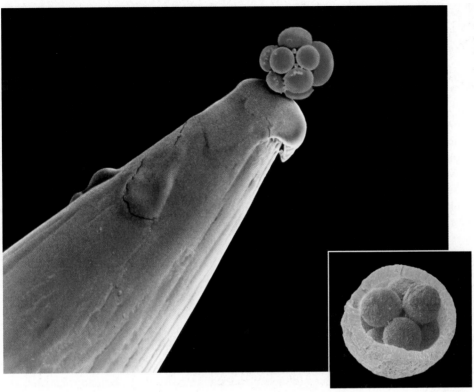

Figure 8.4 **A human embryo (more accurately called a conceptus),** perched on the tip of a pin. The embryo consists of about 10 cells and is 3–4 days old. The zona pellucida has been removed. The inset shows an embryo with the zona pellucida still partially intact.

50 µm

of a group of follicles on a precisely timed schedule. When the follicles are nearly ready to ovulate, a fine needle is passed into each follicle under ultrasound control, and the ovum is aspirated (removed by suction). As many as two dozen ova can be harvested in a single procedure. The collected ova are placed in a petri dish, and the man's sperm are then added. This procedure costs about $12,000 for a single cycle.

If the man's sperm are not capable of performing even this simplified fertilization task, further variations on IVF are available. The most popular is **intracytoplasmic sperm injection (ICSI)**, in which a single sperm is injected directly into the ovum by means of a very fine pipette. In fact, even a man who produces no mature sperm at all may be able to father a child: Precursor cells can be used instead. These are harvested by needle aspiration of one of the man's testicles.

Regardless of the exact IVF procedure used, the artificially fertilized ova are usually kept in tissue culture for several days, during which time they divide several times (**Figure 8.4**). It is possible at this stage to remove a cell from each embryo without harming it, which allows the chromosomal or genetic makeup of the removed cell to then be studied. This **preimplantation genetic screening (PGS)** is useful if one of the parents carries a disease-causing gene and the couple wants to ensure that their child does not inherit it (Harper & Sengupta, 2012). It is not useful for screening out embryos with an abnormal complement of chromosomes (**aneuploidy**), because the removed cell may not be representative of all the cells in the embryo (Harper et al., 2010). PGS technology, which is rapidly advancing, presents significant ethical issues (Hens et al., 2013) (**Box 8.3**).

A number of embryos are then placed in the woman's uterus simultaneously, in order to maximize the chance that at least one of them will implant and become a fetus. If several implant, the woman is offered the opportunity to have the number reduced by selective abortion (often called "fetal reduction"), but this practice can present risks to the remaining fetuses, and it may also cause psychological problems

intracytoplasmic sperm injection (ICSI) Fertilization of an ovum by injection of a single sperm into it.

preimplantation genetic screening (PGS) Testing of in vitro fertilization embryos for genetic defects prior to implantation.

aneuploidy A nonstandard set of chromosomes, as in Down syndrome or Klinefelter syndrome

Box 8.3 Society, Values, and the Law

Choosing Children's Sex

As they plan for pregnancy, some couples would prefer their child to be of a particular sex, either male or female. At times their preference has a specific medical reason. In particular, if the child is at risk of inheriting a genetic disorder that crops up predominantly in one sex, the couple may want a child of the other sex. This usually means a girl, because most sex-linked disorders affect boys. More commonly, couples want a child of a particular sex for some social reason. For example, they may have one or more children of one sex and now want to "balance" the family with a child of the other sex.

In many cultures boys are commonly preferred over girls. Boys are wanted because they will help with farmwork, because they will bring money into the family, or because their children will carry on the family name. Girls are less desired in some cultures because marrying them off requires hefty bridal payments or because they may be essentially lost to their birth family after marriage and therefore will not support the parents in their old age.

The figure shows people's preference for a boy or a girl in several countries. Interviewees were asked, "Suppose you could only have one child. Would you prefer that it be a boy or a girl?" The numbers for each country don't add up to 100% because some interviewees had no preference (Gallup, 1997).

In the past, there have been many suggestions about how to have a child of a particular sex. It was thought, for example, that the timing of intercourse with respect to the date of ovulation might have an influence, but that turns out not to be the case (Wilcox et al., 1995). Only one technique has actually worked: killing or abandoning newborn children of the unwanted sex. Female infanticide still persists to some extent in India and China. One 28-year-old Indian woman, who had poisoned her second daughter by feeding her oleander sap, justified her action as follows: "A daughter is always liabilities. How can I bring up a second? Instead of her suffering the way I do, I thought it was better to get rid of her" (Dahlburg, 1994).

The introduction of obstetric ultrasound has provided a simple and inexpensive means to visualize a fetus's genitals and hence to determine its sex. This can be done as early as 12 to 14 weeks of pregnancy. As a consequence, the practice of aborting female fetuses has become prevalent in some countries, especially India and China, and the sex ratio of newborn children is becoming markedly skewed toward males. In China, for example, about 119 boys are born for every 100 girls (People's

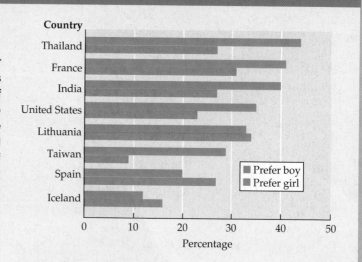

Daily Online, 2010). In both China and India sex-selective abortion is now illegal, but the practice continues.

Considerable efforts have been devoted to developing techniques for selecting a child's sex before pregnancy is established. Because X chromosomes are larger than Y chromosomes, X-bearing sperm contain slightly more total DNA than Y-bearing sperm. A technique called flow cytometry can sense this difference and thus sort out the two kinds of sperm, but not with 100% accuracy. The developers of this technology, which they call MicroSort, claim a 93% success rate in producing girls and an 82% success rate in producing boys (MicroSort, 2012). MicroSort is not currently available in the United States, but it is in Mexico and some other countries. Some U.S. clinics offer to bias the sex ratio by centrifuging the sperm, but this technique is far less reliable than flow cytometry. The most reliable method of selecting a child's sex is by preimplantation genetic screening. Several embryos are produced by in vitro fertilization, a single cell is removed from each embryo for sex determination, and only embryos of the preferred sex are implanted in the woman's uterus. Although this is mostly done to avoid sex-linked diseases, some fertility clinics also offer the service for the purpose of "family balancing."

As with so many issues in the area of reproductive technology, the possibility of selecting children's sex triggers strong reactions. Some say that the practice is morally offensive or will have bad social consequences, such as a skewed sex ratio. Others say that it is a good idea because children will be more like what their parents want and therefore more loved. Some say the practice should be banned; others believe it should be left up to the mother, or to both parents, to decide. What's your opinion?

for some women. Most of the high-number multiple births that have attracted headlines over the past few years involve mothers who have undergone IVF or other assisted reproduction procedures (see below) and have declined abortion. High-number multiple pregnancies are associated with all kinds of serious risks to the fetuses and the mother. According to professional guidelines, healthy young women should receive either one or two embryos on their first IVF attempt (American Society for Reproductive Medicine, 2013).

A more common problem, however, is not multiple but zero pregnancies: In 2012, only 29% of all IVF attempts in the United States succeeded. Couples may have to repeat the procedure several times, at mounting expense and with no guarantee of ultimate success. The prospects are particularly poor for women over age 40 who use their own ova.

Still, over 65,000 babies are born in the United States every year by IVF and related methods (collectively known as **assisted reproductive technologies [ART]**). These represent over 1% of all U.S. births (Centers for Disease Control, 2014c). An estimated 5 million IVF babies have been born worldwide (NBC News, 2013). When you consider the amount of joy this has brought to infertile couples, the inventor of the technology—English physiologist Robert Edwards—richly deserved his 2010 Nobel Prize.

There do remain questions about the safety of assisted reproductive technology. ART pregnancies are high-risk pregnancies, and babies conceived through ART face a greater likelihood of health problems than naturally conceived babies. This has partly to do with the health issues in the parents that caused the infertility in the first place, but ART also introduces its own risks, especially because of the higher incidence of multiple births (Zollner & Dietl, 2012). ART doesn't yet imitate nature closely enough.

Sperm can be donated

Sometimes the male partner is completely sterile or the couple does not want to use his sperm, as, for example, when he carries a gene for a serious disorder. In such cases, a woman can use **artificial insemination by donor (AID)**. In this procedure, sperm from a third party are placed in the woman's vagina or uterus.

Sperm banks provide suitable semen at a cost of $200 per vial and up. Sperm donors are usually college students who are paid a small fee—typically $50 to $100—to donate semen (by masturbation). The donors are screened for heritable medical problems (in themselves or their families) and for infections such as HIV that might be transmitted to the recipient woman. Information about a potential donor's physical appearance, field of study or work, and other interests is usually available to potential recipients. Donors can be either totally anonymous or "open-ID," meaning that a child resulting from the donation may contact the donor once he or she has reached the age of 18.

There are also free donors who can be contacted via the Internet, either directly or via a website such as KnownDonorRegistry.com. Besides the financial savings, which can be considerable if it takes the woman many donations to become pregnant, she and the donor get to meet in person if they so wish. Usually the donor gives the woman a vial and she then inseminates herself with a needleless syringe or by using an Instead menstrual cup (see Chapter 2). (There is also the option of doing it the old-fashioned way.) If they don't want to meet, the donor ships the sperm in a cryo-protected, frozen state. Although the donor provides the same kind of information that is available from a sperm bank, there may be a greater risk that the information is inaccurate or incomplete in important ways, or that problems will arise with any legal agreement they make. On the other hand, some argue that private donation is safer because the woman can check documents herself rather than relying on a sperm bank to do so.

assisted reproductive technology (ART)   In vitro fertilization and related technologies.

artificial insemination by donor (AID)   Artificial insemination using sperm from a man who is not the woman's partner.

sperm bank   A facility that collects, stores, and provides semen for artificial insemination.

**pelvic inflammatory disease
(PID)** An infection of the female
reproductive tract, often caused by
sexually transmitted organisms.

surrogate mother A woman who
carries a pregnancy on behalf of
another woman or couple.

A potential problem with both avenues for sperm donation is that two children fathered by the same donor with different women, when they become adult, may unwittingly commit incest and therefore produce offspring with an increased risk of inherited disorders (Mroz, 2011). For that reason some countries (but not the United States) set legal limits on the number of different women to whom a man may make donations—usually in the range of six to ten women—and many American sperm banks set similar limits.

Women who use sperm donors on account of fertility problems are outnumbered by women who do so for other reasons, such as that they are single or are partnered with another woman.

Abnormalities of the female reproductive tract may reduce fertility

The second most common group of conditions affecting fertility are abnormalities of the woman's reproductive tract. Such conditions are responsible for about 20% of infertility cases. The most common site of abnormalities is the oviducts. They can become scarred, obstructed, or denuded of cilia as a consequence of **pelvic inflammatory disease** (**PID**)—a general term for infections of the uterus or oviducts, usually caused by sexually transmitted organisms, such as chlamydia or gonorrhea (see Chapter 15). In such cases it is possible to bypass the oviducts by performing IVF and placing the resulting embryos directly into the uterus. Uterine fibroids and endometriosis can also reduce fertility, which can sometimes be restored by surgery.

Failure to ovulate can be dealt with by drugs or by egg donation

Another 20% or so of infertility cases are caused by problems with ovulation. We mentioned the failure to begin menstrual cycles at puberty—primary amenorrhea—in Chapter 2. A postpubertal (but premenopausal) woman may also stop cycling or cycle irregularly. These conditions can be caused by weight loss, athletic training, stress, certain drugs, a pituitary tumor, or reduced ovarian function. Sometimes, failure to ovulate can occur in a woman who is experiencing normal menstrual periods. Most ovulatory problems can be reversed by lifestyle changes, drug treatment, or psychotherapy (if the cause is an eating disorder, for example).

If the woman's own ova cannot be used, she can obtain them from donors (Borini et al., 2011). Obtaining ova from female donors is more complex and expensive than sperm donation, however, because the donor must undergo hormone treatment followed by surgical aspiration of the ova from the ovaries, as described earlier for IVF (see Figure 8.3). The donors—who are often college students—are typically paid a few thousand dollars. For both sperm and ova donations, there is a market for donors who are perceived to have desirable traits, and higher fees may be paid in such cases, especially for ova.

Surrogate mothers bear children for others

If the woman cannot sustain a pregnancy at all—say, because her uterus is malformed or has been removed or because her general medical condition makes pregnancy inadvisable—an option is to use a **surrogate mother**. Gay male couples who wish to have children may also make use of this option, as may single men, whether gay or straight (ABC News, 2012).

In traditional surrogacy the surrogate agrees to be artificially inseminated with semen from the man, and she then carries any resulting fetus or fetuses to term. If the woman who cannot sustain a pregnancy can nevertheless produce ova, those ova can be fertilized with the man's sperm by IVF and then implanted in the surrogate.

Either way, after childbirth the surrogate gives the child up for adoption by the couple. The surrogate is usually paid about $20,000 to $25,000, plus expenses—and the total cost to the couple is often $60,000 or more. Because the legal status of surrogacy varies greatly from state to state, most surrogacies are arranged in states such as California and Florida, where surrogacy contracts are fully recognized. Even in those states, however, surrogacy agencies are poorly regulated, and several agencies have been involved in scams or scandals (Lewin, 2014).

Some critics have questioned the ethics of a couple's use of another woman's body to carry their child, especially in cases where the surrogacy involves "reproductive tourism" to developing countries (Deonandan et al., 2012). Yet there is also an altruistic aspect to surrogacy for some women: "Being a surrogate is like giving an organ transplant to someone, only before you die," one woman told a *Newsweek* magazine reporter, "and you actually get to see their joy" (Ali & Kelley, 2008).

Adoption is limited by the supply of healthy infants

Adoption is a low-tech but often very successful way for infertile couples to have children. The main problem with adoption from the perspective of would-be parents is a severe shortage of the preferred adoptees—that is, healthy infants of the same race or ethnicity as themselves. Excluding adoptions between relatives, the number of adoptions in the United States has decreased greatly over the last few decades and is now only about 50,000 per year (Children's Bureau, 2013). The main reason for the decline is the greater willingness of unmarried mothers to keep their babies, but legalized abortion and better access to contraception may also play a role. Older or special-needs children (i.e., children with disabilities or other medical or psychological problems) are much more readily available, as are sets of siblings who want to be adopted together.

Adopting from overseas is an alternative, though usually an arduous and expensive one. The numbers of overseas adoptions dropped from 23,000 to 7000 between 2004 and 2013, in part because of the 2008 Hague Convention, which set tight rules for intercountry adoptions, and also because the Chinese and Russian governments have restricted adoptions from their countries (CNN World, 2013). Many celebrities, such as Madonna, and Angelina Jolie and Brad Pitt, have adopted children from overseas, but the most famous of these was the African-American (later French) singer-dancer Josephine Baker (1906–1975), who adopted a "Rainbow Tribe" of 12 orphans from every corner of the world. She did this as part of her campaign against racism in the United States.

Some states ban joint adoptions or second-parent adoptions by gay people (Lifelong Adoptions, 2014), and even in states where there are no legal restrictions on gay adoption, private agencies may have policies that exclude or disfavor them. Single men find it particularly difficult to adopt children, regardless of their sexual orientation.

Fertility declines with age

A major factor affecting fertility is age—both of the woman and the man. You might imagine that couples stay completely fertile until the woman's menopause, whereupon fertility drops to zero. In reality, fertility drops off steadily beginning in young adulthood, as shown in **Figure 8.5**. Already by their mid-30s about 1 in 4 couples is infertile. This decline in fertility has several causes, including more frequent failures to ovulate, decreasing sperm counts and sperm quality, and an increased likelihood of spontaneous abortion early in pregnancy. This is an issue for women who wish to postpone motherhood on account of their careers, or for other reasons. One strategy to cope with this

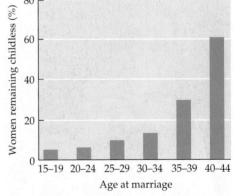

Figure 8.5   Age and infertility The graph shows the percentage of women, grouped by age at marriage, who remain childless after a first marriage in spite of continued efforts to produce a child. Note that the likelihood of infertility rises rapidly in the mid-30s. (After Johnson, 2007.)

(A)

(B)

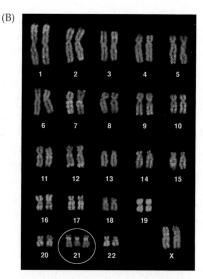

Figure 8.6 Down syndrome (A) A child with Down syndrome; the syndrome is marked by a characteristic facial appearance and sometimes by other physical anomalies. (B) Chromosome set of a person with Down syndrome, showing the three copies (circled) of chromosome 21.

Down syndrome A collection of birth defects caused by the presence of an extra copy of chromosome 21.

problem is for the woman to have some of her eggs frozen early in adulthood for use at a later time. Some companies are starting to pay for this procedure for their employees (Bennett, 2014).

Children who are born to older parents, especially older mothers, also stand a greater risk of having chromosomal abnormalities. One of these causes **Down syndrome**, when there is an extra copy of chromosome 21 (i.e., three copies instead of two). Down syndrome usually includes mild or moderate intellectual disability and a characteristic facial appearance (**Figure 8.6**). It affects 1 in 2000 births at a maternal age of 20, 1 in 900 at age 30, 1 in 100 at age 40, and 1 in 10 at age 49 (National Down Syndrome Society, 2012). Because the great majority of babies are born to younger women, however, 4 out of 5 children with Down syndrome are born to women *under* 35. For that reason, current guidelines call for all pregnant women to be offered screening for Down syndrome, regardless of their age (American Congress of Obstetricians and Gynecologists, 2007).

Increasing paternal age also raises the chances that a child will suffer from physical malformations, mental conditions such as autism or schizophrenia (Hultman et al., 2011; Miller et al., 2011), and poor academic performance (D'Onofrio et al., 2014). The harmful effect of paternal age results from the fact that sperm precursor cells are constantly dividing to produce new sperm. Thus, an older man's sperm are the product of a greater total number of cell divisions, and each round of DNA replication carries some small risk of introducing a harmful mutation. In addition, chronic exposure to toxins such as solvents or tobacco smoke increases the likelihood that a man's children will have developmental problems (Cordier, 2008). Nevertheless, most children of older fathers are healthy.

A postmenopausal woman can become pregnant with the aid of reproductive technology: Donated ova can be fertilized in vitro (usually with her husband's sperm) and the embryos placed in her uterus. The pregnancy must be supported with hormone treatments. The oldest woman to have become a mother by this procedure is Rajo Devi Lohan of India, who gave birth to a daughter, Naveen, at a reported age of 70. Within 18 months, she was reported to be near death, but she recovered, and 5 years later both she and her daughter were thriving. "The only reason I am still alive in spite of my illness is Naveen," Rajo told the

Rajo Devi Lohan with her daughter Naveen. She is the oldest woman ever to have given birth.

Daily Mail. "She is a gift to me from God, and until I get her married I cannot afford to die" (Mail Online, 2013).

Do you think it is right or sensible for a 70-year-old woman to have a baby? What about in a country like India, where many women consider it a disgrace to die childless?

Many Embryos Do Not Survive

Nature has not completely mastered the intricate task of creating a normal embryo. Some large fraction—perhaps more than 50%—of all human embryos are genetically abnormal and have little or no chance of giving rise to a viable child. Most of these abnormalities cause defects at the very earliest stages of development. If the ovum is fertilized by two sperm rather than one, for example, the resulting embryo will have three sets of chromosomes rather than the normal two. In some cases, environmental factors such as alcohol consumption, general anesthesia, or X-ray exposure at around the time of ovulation may trigger chromosomal abnormalities.

The great majority of abnormal conceptuses are lost at some point in their development. Many fail to implant, and the mothers are never aware of their existence. Others implant briefly, causing a transient release of hCG and a slight prolongation of the postovulatory phase, but then die, so menstruation ensues. Of pregnancies that proceed far enough to be detected clinically, about 20% are subsequently lost by spontaneous abortion, usually during the first 3 months. At least half of those have chromosomal abnormalities. In fetuses that make it to term, only 1 in 200 has a chromosomal abnormality.

Rh factor incompatibility can threaten second pregnancies

One major cause of fetal loss is blood group incompatibility, especially when the fetus possesses the blood group antigen known as **Rh factor** and the mother does not (American College of Obstetricians and Gynecologists, 2013). Rh factor is a molecular label on the surface of red blood cells. In cases of Rh incompatibility the fetus will have inherited the factor from its father. The combination of Rh-negative mother and Rh-positive father is common—it is the case for about 10% of all couples in the United States—but only a minority of their pregnancies are marked by problems. These problems arise when the mother develops antibodies against Rh and those antibodies cross the **placenta** and attack the fetus. This does not happen routinely, because the fetus is immunologically isolated from the mother. Nevertheless, the mother may develop anti-Rh antibodies at childbirth if the fetus bleeds into the maternal circulation during delivery. These antibodies develop too late to affect that child, but they may attack a subsequent fetus, destroying its red blood cells and rendering it severely anemic. Such an attack can kill the fetus or newborn child, or it can leave the child intellectually disabled.

Luckily, the initial immune response to a mother's first Rh-positive fetus can be blocked by the administration of an antibody that binds to Rh and hides it from the mother's immune system. If severe anemia does occur in a subsequent pregnancy, the fetus or the newborn child may have to receive a blood transfusion.

Ectopic pregnancy can endanger the mother's life

Another serious condition that causes fetal loss is **ectopic pregnancy**, which is implantation of the fetus at a location other than the uterus (Mayo Clinic, 2014d) **(Figure 8.7)**. This happens in about 1% to 2 % of all pregnancies. The most common site of ectopic pregnancy is the oviduct (in which case it is called a "tubal

Rh factor   An antigen on the surface of red blood cells that, when present in a fetus but not in its mother, may trigger an immune response by the mother, resulting in life-threatening anemia of the fetus or newborn.

placenta   The vascular organ, formed during pregnancy, that allows for the supply of oxygen and nutrients to the fetus and the removal of waste products.

ectopic pregnancy   Implantation and resulting pregnancy at any site other than the uterus.

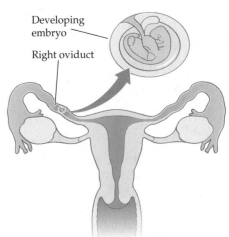

Developing embryo

Right oviduct

Figure 8.7 Ectopic pregnancy can occur in the oviduct (as shown here), on the ovary or cervix, or elsewhere.

pregnancy"), but other possible sites include the cervix, the ovary, and elsewhere within the abdominal cavity.

Ectopic pregnancies can be caused by congenital malformations of the oviducts or uterus, by damage to the oviducts resulting from PID or appendicitis, or by treatment with certain sex steroids and contraceptives that interfere with the normal movement of the embryo into the uterus. Ectopic pregnancies may occur without any of these predisposing factors, however. The rate of ectopic pregnancy is increasing, and the main culprit is the increasing prevalence of PID due to chlamydia infections (see Chapter 15).

Ectopic pregnancy commonly leads to early spontaneous abortion. Alternatively, as the embryo grows, it may cause internal hemorrhage or rupture of an oviduct, both of which are emergencies that threaten the mother's life. Recognition of the condition is hampered by the fact that the woman may not know she is pregnant—the symptoms can appear within 3 weeks of the beginning of pregnancy. Therefore, if a woman of childbearing age has engaged in coitus recently and experiences unexplained abdominal or shoulder pain, pain on defecation or urination, abnormal vaginal bleeding, or signs of shock, she should see a doctor without delay.

Pregnancy Is Conventionally Divided into Three Trimesters

gestational age A fetus's age timed from the onset of the mother's last menstrual period.

Naegele's rule A traditional rule for the calculation of a pregnant woman's due date: 9 calendar months plus 1 week after the onset of the last menstrual period.

trimester One of three 3-month divisions of pregnancy.

Let's return to the happier topic of normal pregnancy. First of all, how long does a normal pregnancy last? Logically, we would time pregnancy from fertilization, or perhaps from implantation, but neither of these events can be used for timing because they don't usually make themselves known to the mother. The only relevant date that the mother is likely to remember is the onset of her last menstrual period, which occurs about 2 weeks before fertilization. Thus, pregnancy is conventionally timed from that date, and a fetus is said to have a **gestational age**, which is calculated based on the number of weeks that have elapsed since the onset of the woman's last menstrual period—even though the embryo didn't actually exist for the first 2 weeks of that time.*

Traditionally, a woman's "due date" is calculated as 280 days, or 40 weeks, from the onset of her last menstrual period. This is the so-called **Naegele's rule,** named for the 19th-century German obstetrician who introduced it. Of course few births occur exactly on the due date: a "term" pregnancy is taken to mean any pregnancy lasting at least 260 days (37 weeks) and no more than 294 days (42 weeks). Many women believe, mistakenly, that 37 weeks is an optimal, full-term pregnancy (Goldenberg et al., 2009), and nearly 4% of mothers choose to have an induced early-term delivery (at 37 or 38 weeks) for no medical reason, even though such deliveries are associated with an increased risk of harm to the baby (Fleischman et al., 2010; Kozhimannil et al., 2014). Unless there is a medical reason, mothers and their doctors should allow pregnancies to continue until at least 39 weeks.

In the context of prenatal care, pregnancy is usually divided into three **trimesters**, each 3 months long. These time periods do not correspond to any particular biologically significant milestones but are simply convenient ways to refer to early, middle, and late pregnancy. The growth and appearance of the fetus over the first half of pregnancy is shown in **Figure 8.8**.

The First Trimester Is a Period of Major Changes

The first trimester is in many ways the most significant period of pregnancy. During this time the embryo implants in the uterine wall and sets up a system of hormonal

---

* Some sources use "gestational age" to mean age timed from the date of fertilization. The usage we adopt is the one recommended by the American Academy of Pediatrics.

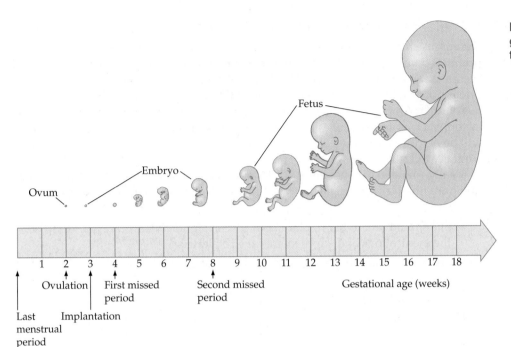

Figure 8.8 Embryonic and fetal growth and changes in appearance through the 18th week of pregnancy.

Fetus

Embryo

Ovum

| 1 | 2 | 3 | 4 | 5 | 6 | 7 | 8 | 9 | 10 | 11 | 12 | 13 | 14 | 15 | 16 | 17 | 18 |

Ovulation   First missed period   Second missed period   Gestational age (weeks)

Last menstrual period   Implantation

and metabolic communication with the mother. The implanted embryo secretes hCG, which prevents the corpus luteum from regressing and therefore keeps progesterone levels high. Later, the embryo and placenta themselves secrete estrogens and progesterone. These hormones enter the mother's circulation, eventually rising to levels not experienced at any other time of her life. Their main role is to sustain the endometrium, but they also prepare the uterine musculature for childbirth and the breasts for lactation.

During the first 8 weeks of gestational age (which is the 6 weeks after fertilization), the embryo develops from a tiny, featureless disk of cells into a miniature human being with all its organ systems present. It is now referred to as a fetus. By the end of the first trimester the fetus is about 4 inches (10 cm) in its longest dimension (crown-rump length) and weighs about 2 ounces (50 g). The external genitalia have differentiated as male or female, and most of the fetus's organ systems are functioning at some primitive level.

The first trimester is an important period for the mother as well. She typically learns that she is pregnant, a piece of news that may bring delight or anxiety. She may have to decide, perhaps in discussions with her partner, whether to continue the pregnancy. Assuming that she goes ahead with it, she is likely to experience some of the early symptoms of pregnancy, especially breast tenderness and morning sickness.

Breast tenderness is a sign that the breasts are preparing for nursing (breast-feeding) the infant, even though it will be months before they can actually function. Morning sickness affects about half of all pregnant women, but it varies in degree, from mild nausea upon awakening to persistent and even life-threatening vomiting. It is often associated with aversions to certain foods, especially strong-tasting foods and animal products (meats, eggs, and fish). Eating bland foods tends to alleviate the condition, which usually disappears by the end of the first trimester.

Other symptoms experienced by many women during the first trimester include frequent urination, tiredness, sleeping difficulties, backaches, mood swings, and, sometimes, depression. The woman's male partner may develop analogous symptoms and may even gain weight faster than the pregnant woman. The phenomenon of pregnancy-like symptoms in men is known as **couvade**. The average woman gains only about 2 to 4 pounds (1 to 2 kg) during the first trimester.

FAQ

I'm pregnant, but I'm still having my periods. What's up?

If you're pregnant, the bleeding is not your normal menstrual period. Minor bleeding commonly occurs around the time of implantation. If you're bleeding at later times, consult your doctor promptly; it could be something harmless, but it could also signal a serious problem such as an ectopic pregnancy or a miscarriage.

couvade Pregnancy-like symptoms in the male partner of a pregnant woman.

prenatal care Medical care and counseling provided to pregnant women.

preconception care Medical care and counseling provided to women before they become pregnant.

rubella German measles, a viral infection that can cause developmental defects in fetuses whose mothers contract the disease during pregnancy.

Prenatal care provides health screening, education, and support

Numerous studies have shown that almost every aspect of pregnancy benefits from **prenatal care**. It decreases the likelihood of maternal, fetal, or neonatal death; fetal prematurity; and low birth weight (Van Dijk et al., 2011). Unfortunately, prenatal care is not as widely utilized in the United States as it is in European countries. The reasons that American women receive inadequate care have to do with psychosocial factors, such as ambivalence about the pregnancy or not believing that prenatal care will be helpful, more than a lack of access to such care (A. A. Johnson et al., 2007; Sunil et al., 2010).

Ideally, prenatal care begins at least 3 months *before* pregnancy. This **preconception care** involves several steps a woman should take (Centers for Disease Control, 2013f):

- She should talk to her doctor about preconception health care and discuss the medications and supplements she is taking.
- She should take 400 micrograms of folic acid daily to reduce the risk of birth defects.
- If she drinks alcohol, smokes, or uses street drugs, she should stop.
- Any medical conditions (e.g., diabetes or obesity) should be under control, and vaccinations, especially for **rubella**, should be up to date.
- An HIV test should be done.
- She should reach and maintain a healthy weight.
- She should avoid exposure to toxic or infectious substances at work and at home.

It's important to take care of these issues before pregnancy, not only because they may take time to deal with, but also because some of them are relevant to the very earliest weeks of development, when a woman may not know that she is pregnant at all. Therefore, if there is a chance that she will become pregnant, she should act as if she *is* pregnant.

The first health care visit after conception typically takes place soon after the first missed period. At this point the health care provider takes a history and does a general examination, a Pap smear, a cervical culture (to test for gonorrhea and other conditions), a rubella test (if not done previously), and a test for blood type and Rh factor. A clinical pregnancy test may be done, even if the woman has already done a home pregnancy test. The provider advises the woman on nutrition and related matters, answers her questions, and helps her make informed decisions about how to manage her pregnancy and childbirth.

On one or more occasions during the first trimester, the provider conducts a pelvic exam (see Chapter 2). In addition to the pelvic exam, many providers perform an ultrasound exam at some point during the first trimester, especially if there is some indication of a problem. This exam permits determination of fetal age, the number of fetuses, and the presence of any abnormality such as ectopic pregnancy. It is not usually possible to discern the fetus's sex by ultrasound during the first trimester.

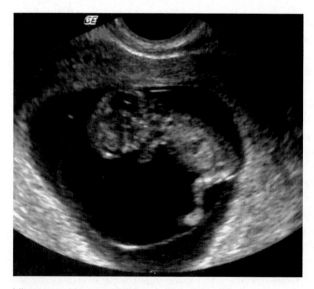

Ultrasound image of a fetus after 10 weeks.

Adequate nutrition is vital to a successful pregnancy

An expectant mother needs an extra 250 to 300 calories per day in addition to what she needs to support herself. At term (just before childbirth), a woman typically weighs 20 to 35 pounds (9 to 15 kg) above her prepregnancy weight; this includes the weight of the

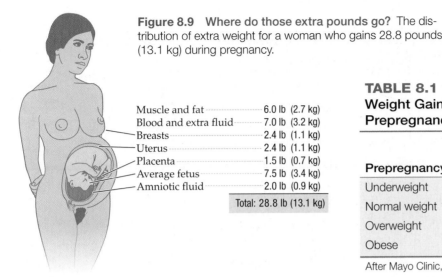

Figure 8.9 Where do those extra pounds go? The distribution of extra weight for a woman who gains 28.8 pounds (13.1 kg) during pregnancy.

Muscle and fat — 6.0 lb (2.7 kg)
Blood and extra fluid — 7.0 lb (3.2 kg)
Breasts — 2.4 lb (1.1 kg)
Uterus — 2.4 lb (1.1 kg)
Placenta — 1.5 lb (0.7 kg)
Average fetus — 7.5 lb (3.4 kg)
Amniotic fluid — 2.0 lb (0.9 kg)

Total: 28.8 lb (13.1 kg)

TABLE 8.1
Weight Gain Recommendations According to Prepregnancy Weight

Prepregnancy weight	BMI	Recommended weight gain at term, in pounds (kg)
Underweight	<18.5	28–40 (13–18)
Normal weight	18.6–24.9	25–35 (11–16)
Overweight	25.0–29.9	15–25 (7–11)
Obese	>30.0	11–20 (5–9)

After Mayo Clinic, 2014f.

fetus, placenta, and amniotic fluid, as well as her own increased fat deposits, enlarged breasts, and increased volume of blood and tissue fluids (**Figure 8.9**). If a woman is already eating healthily, she doesn't need to make significant changes in her diet, but she should be sure that she's taking in adequate amounts of folic acid, calcium, and iron.

Women who begin pregnancy with a normal weight are most likely to give birth to healthy children. Underweight women risk producing underweight children, who are more likely to suffer from a variety of medical problems. Women who are overweight or obese face an increased risk of certain serious disorders during pregnancy, including diabetes and hypertension. These women are advised to gain less weight during pregnancy than women of normal weight (**Table 8.1**). The guidelines for women carrying twins recommend higher weights than those listed in the table (Mayo Clinic, 2014e).

fetal alcohol syndrome A collection of physical and behavioral symptoms in a child who was exposed to high levels of alcohol as a fetus.

Tobacco, alcohol, drugs, and radiation can harm the fetus

A pregnant woman needs to avoid a number of agents that can harm the fetus (**Table 8.2**). Alcohol and tobacco head this list. Alcohol consumption increases the likelihood of spontaneous abortion, infant mortality, and birth defects, and it is associated with a specific cluster of symptoms known as **fetal alcohol syndrome** (Centers for Disease Control, 2014f). Children with this syndrome (**Figure 8.10**) are small and have a characteristic facial appearance (but diagnosis should be left to experts). They also suffer from cognitive and behavioral problems that persist into adulthood (Freunscht & Feldmann, 2011). Binge drinking is particularly dangerous; the evidence regarding moderate drinking (2 drinks per day) is conflicting, but some large-scale longitudinal studies have reported an increased likelihood of spontaneous abortion as well as a measurable reduction in children's intelligence (Streissguth et al., 1990; Andersen et al., 2012). Caffeine can also be harmful: A daily intake of 200 milligrams or more (the amount in a 12-ounce serving of coffee) doubles the risk of miscarriage, and higher amounts early in pregnancy can raise the risk as much as fivefold (Weng et al., 2008; Greenwood et al., 2010).

Figure 8.10 A girl with fetal alcohol syndrome Typical facial features include short eye slits, a flat mid-face, a short nose, an indistinct groove between nose and lip, a thin upper lip, and a small chin.

TABLE 8.2

Examples of Substances, Infections, and Physical Agents That Can Harm the Developing Fetus

Agent	Possible consequences
Drugs	
Alcohol	Fetal alcohol syndrome
Tobacco	Spontaneous abortion; premature birth; low birth weight; addiction of newborn; sudden infant death
Isotretinoin (Accutane)	Heart, brain malformations; intellectual disability
Thalidomide	Limb defects; deafness; blindness
Vitamins A and D (in excessive amounts)	Fetal malformations
Androgens, estrogens	Abnormalities of external genitalia and reproductive tract, especially in females
Diethylstilbestrol (DES)	Reproductive cancers (females); reduced fertility (males)
Aspirin (late in pregnancy)	Interference with blood clotting, potentially causing hemorrhage in mother, fetus, or newborn
Acetaminophen (Tylenol)	Possible modestly increased risk of ADHD-like behaviors[a]
Street drugs (heroin, methamphetamine, cocaine)	Spontaneous abortion; low birth weight; respiratory depression of newborn; addiction of newborn
Marijuana	Possible impairment of neuronal survival in fetal brain[b]
Infections	
Rubella	Damage to ears, eyes, heart
Genital herpes	Spontaneous abortion; premature birth; birth defects
HIV	AIDS in infancy/childhood
Chlamydia	Premature birth; neonatal eye infection
Physical agents	
X-rays	Increased risk of childhood cancer
Nuclear radiation	Increased risk of childhood cancer
Cosmic radiation (from high-altitude flight, for air crew or very frequent flyers)	Possible increased risk of childhood cancer
High body temperature (over 100.4°F, or 38°C) in early pregnancy (from fever, excessive exercise, saunas, hot tubs)	A variety of birth defects

[a] *Source*: Liew et al., 2014.
[b] *Source*: Downer & Campbell, 2010.

Smoking is one of the most harmful practices a pregnant woman can engage in (Centers for Disease Control, 2014p). It is associated with an increased likelihood of spontaneous abortion, premature birth, low birth weight, congenital malformations, and sudden infant death syndrome. Localities that enact bans on smoking in workplaces and public spaces experience a significant drop in the incidence of preterm births (Been et al., 2014).

Many drugs—including prescription, over-the-counter, and street drugs—can harm the fetus. A particularly dangerous drug is isotretinoin (Accutane and its generic equivalents), which is used for the treatment of severe acne. Isotretinoin causes fetal malformations. Because teenage girls have high rates of both acne and unintended pregnancy, the possibility of disaster is real, despite educational programs and stringent prescribing requirements (American Academy of Dermatology, 2014).

Addictive drugs such as cocaine, heroin, and methamphetamine slow fetal development, raise the risk of miscarriage and premature birth, and cause the baby to be born in an addicted state. A pregnant woman, or one who may become pregnant, should also discuss with her doctor all prescription drugs she is taking; often, drugs that are harmful to the fetus or whose safety has not been established can be replaced with safer ones.

Vitamin A, though essential for normal fetal development, can cause malformations in excessive doses. Of particular concern is "preformed vitamin A," which is present in liver and eggs and is often added to breakfast cereals, nonfat milk, and other foodstuffs (check the ingredients list for "retinyl palmitate," "vitamin A palmitate," or similar compounds). Pregnant women should limit their intake of these substances to no more than 100% of the recommended daily allowance.

Another agent that can harm the fetus is radiation. X-rays, especially CAT scans, should be avoided during pregnancy if possible, although the medical benefits of the X-ray may outweigh the risks in some cases.

The Second Trimester Is the Easiest

The second trimester begins at 13 weeks of gestational age. Most women experience the second trimester as a period of calm and well-being. Morning sickness and most of the other unpleasant symptoms of early pregnancy usually disappear, and this may allow for an increased interest in, and enjoyment of, sex. Only the need for frequent urination persists and, in fact, may become worse as the enlarging uterus presses on the bladder. Signs of pregnancy become obvious: The abdomen swells, stretch marks may begin to appear, and the breasts may release small amounts of colostrum, the special kind of milk that nourishes newborn infants.

Around the middle of the second trimester the mother will begin to feel the fetus's movements. This event, known as **quickening**, has always had great psychological significance—it is a major step in the mother's bonding with her child. In early Christian doctrine, quickening was thought to be the time the soul entered into the fetus, so abortion before quickening was not necessarily a sin. The beginning of fetal movement does not mean that the fetus is now a conscious being, however: The cerebral cortex, which is probably the main locus of consciousness, is still at an extremely rudimentary stage of development at the time of quickening.

Tests can detect fetal abnormalities

At prenatal care visits during the second trimester, the health care provider monitors the fetus's growth and well-being. In addition, tests may be done to check for congenital disorders. These tests may include ultrasound scans, amniocentesis, and chorionic villus sampling. These procedures can also be used to determine the fetus's sex (see Box 8.3).

An ultrasound scan done at the beginning of the second trimester or slightly earlier can reveal evidence suggestive of congenital abnormalities, including Down syndrome. When the ultrasound is combined with biochemical tests, about 90% of fetuses with Down syndrome can be identified.

If there are reasons to be concerned about fetal abnormalities, such as advanced maternal age or a history of abnormalities in previous pregnancies, more-invasive tests may be recommended. In **amniocentesis (Figure 8.11A)**, the doctor first determines the precise position of the uterus and the fetus with an ultrasound scan and then passes a thin needle through the front wall of the abdomen into the amniotic sac in which the fetus is floating, avoiding the fetus itself. A sample of the amniotic fluid, containing some free-floating cells derived from the fetus or its membranes, is withdrawn. The information gained through amniocentesis allows for the identification of chromosomal and genetic abnormalities as well as **spina bifida** (incomplete

quickening The onset of movements by the fetus that can be felt by the mother.

amniocentesis The sampling of the amniotic fluid for purposes of prenatal diagnosis.

spina bifida A congenital malformation caused by incomplete closure of the neural tube.

(A) Amniocentesis

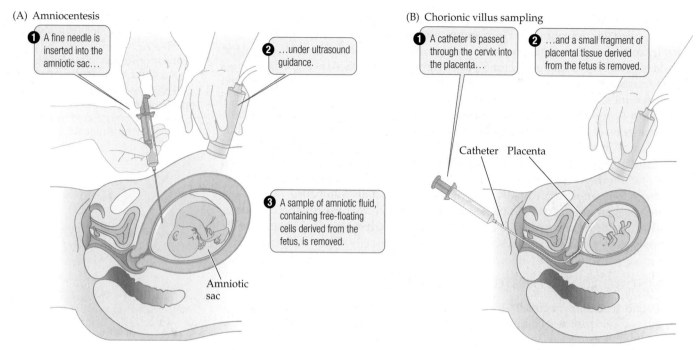

Figure 8.11   Screening for congenital disorders

development of the spine and spinal cord). Amniocentesis is usually done at about 15 to 18 weeks of pregnancy, but it is sometimes done as early as 11 weeks. The procedure carries a slight risk (less than 1 in 1000) of causing a miscarriage (Eddleman et al., 2006).

An alternative to amniocentesis is **chorionic villus sampling** (**Figure 8.11B**). In this procedure, a catheter is passed through the cervix, and a sample of tissue is taken from the placenta. (Chorionic villi are the highly branched tissue projections from the placenta that serve to increase the area of contact with the mother's blood.) The procedure may also be done with a needle inserted through the abdominal wall. Chorionic villus sampling is usually done at 10 to 12 weeks of pregnancy. Although it has the advantage of producing results earlier than amniocentesis, chorionic villus sampling identifies only chromosomal and genetic abnormalities, not spina bifida, and the risk of harm to the fetus, though still low, is slightly higher than with amniocentesis.

In the great majority of cases, the outcome of these tests is reassurance that the baby is probably healthy. Unfortunately, a few women do receive the devastating news that the fetus has a serious genetic abnormality. In some cases, such as congenital adrenal hyperplasia, it may be possible to prevent harm to the fetus by drug treatment during pregnancy, although this strategy is controversial (Dreger et al., 2012). If not, the majority of women choose to abort the fetus. (Women who are opposed to abortion under any circumstances tend not to seek prenatal testing in the first place.) The earlier diagnosis offered by chorionic villus sampling (compared with amniocentesis) usually makes the decision to have an abortion psychologically easier and medically safer.

In 2011, a Hong Kong–based research group showed that it is possible to isolate and sequence the tiny amounts of fetal DNA that leak into the mother's circulation (Chiu et al., 2011). This **cell-free fetal DNA analysis** allows for the diagnosis of Down syndrome and other aneuploidies, and for that reason fewer amniocenteses and chorionic villus samplings are being done than in the past. It is still unclear whether this method can be used to routinely screen fetuses for single-gene disorders such as cystic fibrosis (Bianchi & Wilkins-Haug, 2014).

chorionic villus sampling   The sampling of tissue from the placenta for purposes of prenatal diagnosis.

cell-free fetal DNA analysis   The diagnosis of fetal disorders by sequencing fetal DNA that leaks into the maternal circulation.

Sex during pregnancy is healthy

As the second trimester rolls on, the mother will have switched to looser clothing to accommodate her expanding belly, but otherwise the progress of her pregnancy at this time is fairly uneventful. One topic that couples often think about as the mother grows larger is sex: Is it a good idea in the latter half of pregnancy? In particular, can it harm the fetus? The answer is that in a normal pregnancy, the fetus is well protected from almost anything the couple might do during sex, and coitus does not cause miscarriage or bring on labor, even when practiced close to the due date (Sayle et al., 2001; Jones et al., 2011). The only sex practice known to be dangerous during pregnancy is blowing air into the vagina, which can cause a fatal air embolism (blockage of blood vessels by air bubbles). Anal sex is also discouraged on account of the risk of transferring fecal bacteria to the vagina.

About the only other way that sex can harm the fetus is if the mother acquires a sexually transmitted infection (STI) from her partner. Such diseases can be transmitted to the fetus during pregnancy or as the fetus passes through the birth canal. Organisms that cause only mild or moderate problems for adults can be catastrophic for fetuses or newborns. Thus, pregnant women who are sexually active should be extra vigilant concerning the possibility of acquiring an STI, and they should abstain from vaginal sex if either partner has an active herpes outbreak. Condoms are recommended for coitus.

The foregoing applies to *normal* pregnancies. The following medical conditions may make coitus unwise, especially toward the end of pregnancy:

- Threatened miscarriage or premature birth
- Unexplained vaginal bleeding
- Leakage of amniotic fluid
- **Placenta previa**, a condition in which the placenta covers the cervix
- **Incompetent cervix**, in which the cervix opens too early

The woman's health care provider can advise her about whether or when she should refrain from coitus.

Sex during pregnancy may require some modifications to a couple's usual practices (Nagrath & Singh, 2012). As the woman's belly swells, the man-on-top position for coitus becomes awkward, but there are strategies to make it more practical. For example, placing a couple of pillows under the woman's buttocks will cause her belly to tilt away from the man. Or he can kneel between her legs, again with her buttocks raised on pillows.

The woman-on-top position is also suitable, especially if the woman sits straight up (facing either forward or backward) to allow more space for her belly. Rear-entry coitus becomes the most practical approach as pregnancy goes on: This may be done doggy style, standing, side by side, or sitting (**Figure 8.12**). Some women, especially those with G-spots, find rear-entry coitus very stimulating; for others, simultaneous stimulation of the clitoris by hand or with a vibrator is useful. Side-by-side rear-entry coitus is perhaps the least stressful position during late pregnancy, but it also tends to be the least stimulating because movement is limited.

Of course, coitus is not the only option: Straight people could take their cue from lesbian couples, who enjoy a wide variety of noncoital interactions (see Chapter 6). Psychological factors are even more important: Couples who take a recreational or relational view of sex are more likely to enjoy sex during pregnancy than those whose attitudes to sex are closely tied to procreation.

placenta previa   An abnormally low position of the placenta, such that it partially or completely covers the internal opening of the cervix.

incompetent cervix   A weakening and partial opening of the cervix caused by a previous traumatic delivery, surgery, or other factors.

Figure 8.12   Sex during the later stages of pregnancy may be facilitated by a willingness to try new positions or sexual activities other than coitus.

Moderate exercise during pregnancy is beneficial

Another issue that concerns some women is exercise. Traditionally, pregnant women were thought of as fragile creatures that needed to be spared any kind of exertion.

It's now clear that, except in the case of certain problem pregnancies, exercise has a positive value in maintaining the woman's health and sense of well-being. It is especially useful in counteracting backache, constipation, mood swings, and sleeplessness.

The American College of Obstetricians and Gynecologists (ACOG) recommends that pregnant women engage in moderate, low-impact forms of exercise such as brisk walking and swimming. ACOG adds two caveats: First, after 20 weeks of pregnancy a woman should avoid doing exercises that involve lying on her back, and second, she should avoid exercises that significantly raise her body temperature, especially during the first trimester or when she has a fever already. Paula Radcliffe, world record holder in the marathon, delivered a healthy daughter after training up until the day before she went into labor (Kolata, 2007).

The Third Trimester Is a Time of Preparation

The third trimester begins at 27 weeks of gestational age. At this time, the fetus already weighs about 2 pounds (900 g) and has a decent chance of surviving if born prematurely, although its survival would entail weeks of intensive neonatal care and a six-figure hospital bill. During the third trimester, the fetus increases rapidly in weight; at the time of fastest growth, which is around 33 weeks, the fetus is gaining about 2 ounces (50 g) every day. By the time of birth it has reached a weight of about 7.1 pounds (3.2 kg).

During the third trimester, the fetus performs many of the behaviors that it will need to survive outside its mother, including breathing motions. The mother, and possibly her partner, may be awakened frequently at night by its vigorous movements. The mother's uterus also undergoes occasional, irregularly spaced contractions. These **Braxton Hicks contractions** (or "false labor") are normal and do not endanger the fetus. Only if the contractions come at regular intervals and become gradually more frequent, stronger, and longer lasting need a woman be concerned that true labor is beginning.

Women's experience of the third trimester varies greatly. Some women sail through it serenely, while others are overwhelmed by physical problems (backache, urinary frequency, fatigue, or sleeplessness) or by anxiety about childbirth and motherhood. Couples may find themselves bonding more closely than at any previous time in their relationship, or there may be increasing tension. Depression is not uncommon at this time, particularly among women who do not have a partner.

It is important for caregivers to identify and treat pregnant women who are depressed, not only for the mother's sake, but also because prenatal depression is associated with an increased risk that the baby will be born prematurely or with low birth weight (Grote et al., 2010). There is some evidence that depression or anxiety in a pregnant woman can affect the development of certain regions in the fetus's brain; one of these regions is the amygdala, which helps regulate emotional states (Rifkin-Graboi et al., 2013). This could represent a mechanism for the nongenetic transmission of mood disorders from mother to child (National Scientific Council on the Developing Child, 2009).

Braxton Hicks contractions
Irregular uterine contractions that occur during the third trimester of pregnancy. Also called false labor.

A hospital is the best location for childbirth if complications are foreseen

On a more positive note, the third trimester is a time of preparation for birth. By this time, the mother will probably have decided where to have her baby. If it is her first baby, she and her partner should be taking classes in preparation for the birth.

Concerning where to have the baby, there are three choices: at home, in a hospital, or (in some areas) in a stand-alone facility known as a **birthing center**. Most births in the United States take place in hospitals. The great advantage of a hospital is the immediate availability of obstetricians (physicians who specialize in childbirth) and equipment. The disadvantage is that a hospital can be a relatively impersonal and sometimes intimidating environment, and the mother may feel that less attention is paid to her wishes for the birth process than if she were in her own home.

A birthing center (if one is available) offers a compromise between hospital and home. Most birthing centers are staffed by midwives rather than by physicians. These midwives (especially certified nurse-midwives) are highly trained and experienced in their field. Birthing centers are not as well equipped as hospitals, however, and centers that are staffed only by midwives will not be able to provide certain forms of anesthesia, such as epidurals (see below). It will be necessary to move the mother to a hospital if serious complications arise. For that reason, a birthing center that is part of a hospital complex may be preferable to one that is some distance away.

The most important consideration influencing the choice of location should be the estimated likelihood of complications. The health care provider will advise the mother to have her child in a hospital if labor begins prematurely, if the fetus is not optimally positioned for birth, if there is more than one fetus, if the mother's pelvis is unusually narrow, or if there exist any other medical conditions that increase the risk of complications.

In a 2011 position paper, ACOG (which represents hospital-based physicians) recommended against planned home birth, citing studies reporting a two- to threefold greater risk of neonatal death for planned home births, compared with planned births in hospitals or birthing centers—even though planned home births tend to be the lower-risk ones (American Congress of Obstetricians and Gynecologists, 2011). The American Academy of Pediatrics concurs in this view (American Academy of Pediatrics, 2013). Many home births, especially those of first-time mothers, end up with a transfer to a hospital in any case.

Organizations representing midwives, on the other hand, have presented evidence that they think demonstrates the safety of home birth for most women (Cheyney et al., 2014). Regardless of this controversy, only about 1 in 75 American women choose home birth (National Center for Health Statistics, 2014b); this is an enormous change since the early 20th century, when almost all babies were born at home.

Childbirth classes prepare parents for birth

Many different kinds of childbirth classes are available to parents. Nearly all provide general education about pregnancy, childbirth, and infant care and encourage breast-feeding. Some of the classes incorporate the ideas of the French pio-

birthing center A facility specializing in childbirth care.

Childbirth classes help expectant mothers and their partners prepare for the physical and psychological demands of labor.

neer in "prepared childbirth," Fernand Lamaze. Reacting against the use of general anesthetics during labor, which was widespread in the 1950s and 1960s, Lamaze asserted that women could experience a pain-free childbirth without anesthetics. The **Lamaze method** has undergone considerable revision in recent years, however (Lamaze International, 2014). It now incorporates the concept that pain plays an important role in labor, helping the mother to act in ways that protect the baby and herself. Women are taught techniques of "active relaxation" that help them to stay focused and to participate fully in the birth process, rather than simply averting their minds from it.

Lamaze teachers do not oppose anesthesia during labor if it seems necessary, and a fair proportion of women who take Lamaze classes do receive some kind of anesthesia. Another type of childbirth preparation, the **Bradley method**, stresses "natural" childbirth and places a lot of weight on the role of the woman's partner as "birth coach" (AAHCC, 2014). Although developed by a physician, it is more anti-medical in flavor than the Lamaze method, and women who take classes based on the Bradley method are less likely to accept anesthesia or other medical interventions during labor than are women who take Lamaze classes.

Most hospital-based childbirth classes do not closely follow either the Lamaze or the Bradley model but are based on the experience of the people teaching them. They tend to be eclectic, practically oriented, and responsive to the parents' needs, rather than being based on some overarching theory of childbirth management.

One form of childbirth that has gained some popularity recently is water birth. The mother (often with her partner and midwife) sits in a pool or tub of warm water during delivery, and the baby is born underwater. (The baby does not take its first breath until it is brought above the water's surface.) The advantage of this style of childbirth is said to be its gentleness. Some hospitals and birthing centers have birthing tubs available, or they can be rented. Water births are generally safe and may reduce the need for anesthesia and other interventions (Burns et al., 2012).

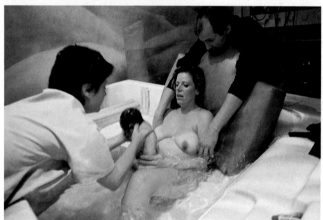

A water birth.

During the final few weeks of pregnancy, it is useful for women to practice **perineal massage**. This involves manual stretching of the perineum, the region of skin between the vulva and the anus. Perineal massage has been shown to reduce the likelihood of perineal tears (or the necessity for episiotomy—see page 254) during labor, especially for women expecting their first child (Cochrane Collaboration, 2009). Instructions on how to perform perineal massage are available online (American College of Nurse-Midwives, 2005).

Lamaze method A method of childbirth instruction that focuses on techniques of relaxation and other natural means of pain reduction.

Bradley method A method of childbirth instruction that stresses the partner's role as birth coach and that seeks to avoid medical interventions.

perineal massage Manual stretching of the perineum in preparation for childbirth.

pulmonary surfactant A compound produced in the fetal lung that reduces surface tension and thus facilitates inflation of the lungs with air at birth.

The fetus also makes preparations for birth

While the parents are preparing themselves for childbirth, so is the fetus. Although the fetus's growth rate slows dramatically after 33 weeks, its organ systems undergo rapid maturation. Much of this preparation for birth is orchestrated by increasing amounts of corticosteroids secreted by the fetus's adrenal glands during the third trimester. Among their effects are important changes in the lungs: These include the production of **pulmonary surfactant**, a detergent-like compound that facilitates opening of the respiratory spaces within the lung when the child draws its first breath (Jobe et al., 2012). Corticosteroids also instruct the fetus's liver to manufacture

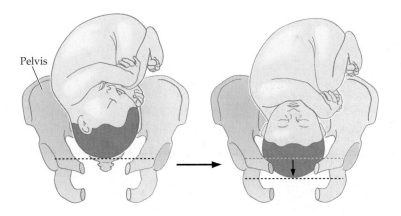

Figure 8.13 **Engagement** is the sinking of the fetus's head deep into the mother's pelvis.

Pelvis

glycogen that will be used to supply the brain's critical glucose needs before, during, and just after birth. Rising corticosteroid levels before birth also affect blood production, switching the hemoglobin in red blood cells to a different form that is better suited to an air-breathing lifestyle. Corticosteroids may be administered to women who are at risk of preterm delivery, for the purpose of accelerating the fetus's preparation for birth.

Labor Has Three Stages

The process of childbirth is referred to scientifically as **parturition**, and more commonly as **labor**. During most of pregnancy, labor is prevented by the inability of the uterine musculature to contract in an organized manner, as well as by the cervix, whose thick wall contains a dense network of connective tissue that resists expansion. Thus, the Braxton Hicks contractions, described earlier, put some downward pressure on the fetus, but this pressure is easily resisted by the cervix, so the fetus does not move into the birth canal.

Before labor begins, the fetus changes its position in the uterus, as its head sinks deep into the pelvis against the cervix (**Figure 8.13**). The mother often notices this event, called **engagement** (or "lightening"), when a bit of extra space opens up between her breasts and her swollen belly. In first pregnancies, engagement may occur a week or more before birth; in later pregnancies, it occurs shortly before or during labor.

Labor itself takes place in three stages: The first stage consists of the uterine contractions that open the cervix. The second stage is the actual delivery of the baby. The third stage is the period from the delivery of the baby to the delivery of the placenta.

The first stage of labor is marked by uterine contractions and cervical dilation

Labor may be heralded by the discharge of the mucous plug that seals off the cervix during pregnancy. The plug may be tinged red with blood, and this event is therefore traditionally called the "bloody show." The amniotic sac may also rupture early in labor, or it may be ruptured by a health care provider. The rupture produces a gush or leakage of amniotic fluid from the vagina ("water breaking"). In other cases the sac does not rupture until later in labor.

The first stage of labor can last anywhere from a couple of hours to more than 24 hours. The two main processes that permit childbirth are the strong, coordinated **contractions** of the uterus and the elimination of much of the connective tissue (**softening** or ripening) of the cervix (**Figure 8.14**).

glycogen   A polymer of glucose used for energy storage.

parturition   Delivery of offspring; childbirth.

labor   The process of childbirth.

engagement   The sinking of a fetus's head into a lower position in the pelvis in preparation for birth. Also called lightening.

contraction   In childbirth, a periodic coordinated tightening of the uterine musculature, felt as a cramp.

softening   The elimination of connective tissue from the cervix, allowing it to thin out and dilate during labor. Also called ripening.

birth canal   The canal formed by the uterus, cervix, and vagina, through which the fetus passes during the birth process.

effacement   Thinning of the cervix in preparation for childbirth.

dilation   In childbirth, the expansion of the cervical canal. Also called dilatation.

transition   The final phase of dilation of the cervix during labor.

epidural anesthesia   Anesthesia administered just outside the membrane that surrounds the spinal cord.

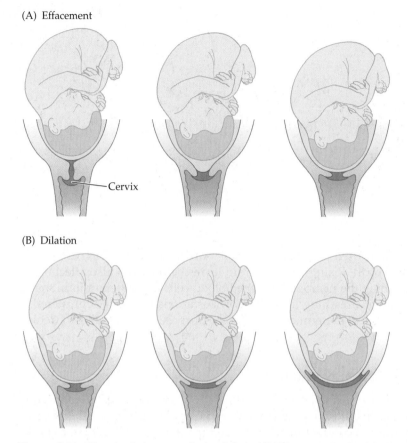

(A) Effacement

Cervix

(B) Dilation

Figure 8.14   Cervical changes during labor (A) Effacement is the thinning of the cervix. (B) Dilation is the opening of the cervix, from fully closed to a width of 4 inches (10 cm).

The effect of the uterine contractions is not yet to move the fetus downward, but to pull the cervix upward so that the vagina and cervix together form a single, continuous **birth canal**. Early in labor, the contractions are fairly mild and spaced 15 to 20 minutes apart. Later, they become more intense and closely spaced—about every 3 minutes.

The softening of the cervix allows thinning out (**effacement**) of the cervix and the gradually opening up (**dilation** or dilatation) of the cervical canal for passage of the fetal head. When this opening process is complete, the canal measures 4 inches (10 cm) in diameter.

The last part of the first phase of labor, when the cervix dilates from 3 to 4 inches (8 to 10 cm), is sometimes called the **transition**; it is a short period of very intense and frequent contractions. The transition is the part of labor that is most likely to be painful and exhausting, and it is here that the woman can most usefully apply what she has learned in her prenatal classes: relaxing rather than resisting the contractions, and directing her attention to forms of natural pain relief that many women find to be useful. These include such seemingly simple activities as walking, pelvic rocking, showering, soaking in a hot tub, sitting on a "birth ball," doing breathing exercises, and using guided imagery.

Some women go through labor with little or no pain (**Box 8.4**). But for those who *are* experiencing significant pain, several different forms of anesthesia are available. The most widely used is **epidural anesthesia**, which involves the infusion of a morphine-like drug or local anesthetic (or combination of both) into the back, just

FAQ

I have a tattoo on my lower back—will that stop me from getting an epidural?

Only if the tattoo reads "No epidurals."

Box 8.4 Personal Points of View

Pain-free Childbirth

This account was provided to us by psychologist Vicki Lucey, who teaches human sexuality at Las Positas College in Livermore, California.

Women often hear the stories of painful childbirth, which lead us to believe that pain is inevitable. But that wasn't my experience. No two birth stories are the same, but I did learn some things that will help you and your partner look forward to childbirth rather than dread it. Here is what I know:

- *Learn all you can during pregnancy.* Ask other women what they might have done differently and take the classes offered at the hospital. My doctor recommended the hospital class, which included one hour of preparation/talk/circle time with other women and one hour of yoga. I got a wealth of information about labor and delivery. The class allowed me to understand the process of childbirth, without judgment, without fear. And talking with other women really helped ease any anxiety that I had.

- *Be your own advocate.* Ask what a typical birth is like with your doctor or at your hospital. My hospital used midwives more than doctors. The only reason I would see a doctor while in labor was if there were problems. I had to ask what they meant by "problems" and why they used midwives. The answers I got helped ease my fears. Be flexible, but if there are some things that are not negotiable, don't negotiate. Case in point: I am more comfortable with my bra on. They told me I'd have to take it off, and when I said no, they were adamant. When I pushed the issue and asked why, they said, "If you need an emergency cesarean, we'll have to cut it off." I said, "Fine, cut it off if you need to, but I want to be comfortable." I kept my bra on through my whole labor.

- *Find what works for you.* I was uncomfortable, so I spent my entire labor on my knees, leaning over the back of the bed. I was in the zone; this allowed me to tune the chaos out that was happening around me. There were people coming and going, staff prodding me, so I just found a position that worked for me. Each time I had a contraction, I moaned! Like the low guttural moan a dog would emit when in danger. Yes, it sounds ridiculous, but it's what worked for me. Of course, it took walking around for a few hours, lying on my side, and rocking on an exercise ball to figure out that those activities, while helpful for a lot of women, were not working for me.

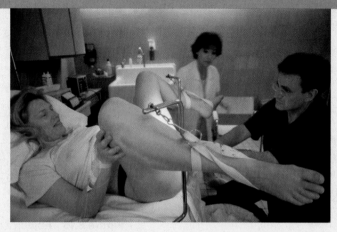

A woman giving birth: It doesn't have to hurt.

- *Keep in mind that pain is perceptual.* When I tell women my birth story, they don't believe me when I say it was not painful. I had no pain medicine, only Pitocin to help my contractions along. When they ask, "How were you not in pain," it's not an easy answer. To a certain degree, pain is in the mind. What is painful to one woman is more painful to another woman and less painful to yet another woman. How we label pain may have an effect on how we view our own labor and childbirth. The moaning and guttural vibrations that came with the moaning helped ease my contractions. Yes, they were uncomfortable, but I can't say they were painful. As my daughter emerged, the perineum stretched—a lot! But again, the labels I use for pain are different. I felt a strong burning sensation as my perineum tore. For me, this worked—using different words for what I was feeling. My labor was uncomfortable and it included that burning sensation, but it was *not* painful.

- *Honor your journey to motherhood for what it is.* Find the resources that you think will be helpful and get as much information as you can, and above all be flexible! And please, honor each woman's journey; we don't need to judge each other, we are in this together. Lean on each other; let's not one-up one another with our horror stories of childbirth. And if you have a positive story, share it! There are a lot of good stories out there. Is it possible to have a pain-free childbirth without drugs? All I know is that it was possible for me. Fear is what causes pain, so try everything you can to reduce your fear. It certainly couldn't hurt—no pun intended!

(A)

(B)

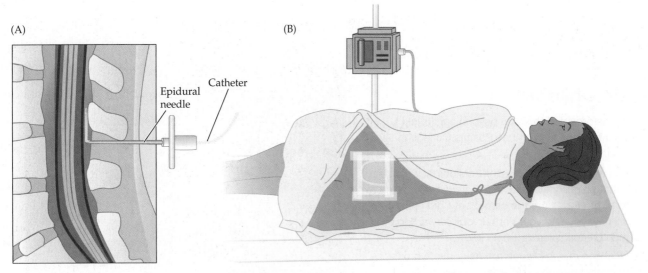

Figure 8.15 **Epidural anesthesia** (A) A catheter is guided into the epidural space through a needle, which is then removed. (B) The anesthetic is infused continuously or as needed.

crowning The appearance of the fetal scalp at the vaginal opening.

episiotomy A cut extending the opening of the vagina backward into the perineum, performed by an obstetrician with the intention of facilitating childbirth or reducing the risk of a perineal tear.

outside the membrane that wraps the spinal cord (**Figure 8.15**). More than half of all women who give birth in hospitals receive epidural anesthesia (American Pregnancy Association, 2014). Done properly, this technique provides satisfactory pain relief with minimal impairment of the mother's ability to move and participate in the birth process. Still, no single method is appropriate for all situations or is entirely free of risk. Pregnant women do well to discuss the issue of anesthesia and develop a birth plan ahead of time with their health care provider.

The second stage is the delivery of the baby

The second stage of labor is the actual passage of the fetus through the birth canal. Although the delivery of the fetus can be accomplished purely by uterine contractions, women usually feel an urge to push, or "bear down." Bearing down—voluntary contraction of the muscles of the abdominal wall and the diaphragm—assists the process by adding to the pressure produced by the uterine contractions.

The second stage of labor is quite variable in duration: It may last just a few minutes, or it may take several hours. It is usually lengthier and more stressful for a woman's first delivery than for subsequent deliveries.

In 2010 a German research group succeeded for the first time in imaging the passage of a fetus through the birth canal (**Figure 8.16**). What this image vividly illustrates is the large size of the fetus's brain in relation to the space through which it must pass.

Toward the end of the second stage, the baby's head begins appearing (**crowning**) at the vaginal opening. At this point, if it seems likely that the delivery of the head will tear the vaginal wall, the provider may make an incision in the perineum to extend the vaginal opening a short distance backward, toward the anus. This procedure, called an **episiotomy**, is done under local anesthesia.

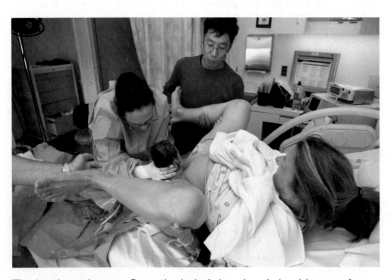

The hard part is over. Once the baby's head and shoulders are free, the rest of its body emerges easily.

Figure 8.16   **A fetus passing through the birth canal,** as seen in an MRI image. Note the large size of the fetal brain (outlined in red) in relation to the canal through which it must pass. A research team at Berlin's Charité Hospital developed a special open-field MRI machine to allow women to give birth inside it while receiving all normal medical support. (From Bamberg et al., 2011.)

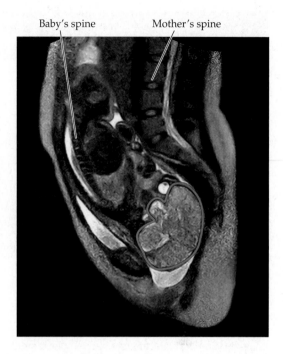

Baby's spine   Mother's spine

The thinking behind doing an episiotomy is that, if the vaginal wall is likely to tear anyway, it is better to make a clean incision that can be neatly sewn up afterward. Still, many people feel that episiotomies are done too often, mostly to hurry delivery along, even though speedy delivery does not convey any particular medical benefit. In fact, episiotomy increases the chances that a woman will subsequently experience pain during coitus (Ejegard et al., 2008).

In the past, episiotomies have been performed in the majority of deliveries, but hospital policies that restrict the use of the procedure are associated with better outcomes (Carroli & Mignini, 2009). In the United States less than 10% of women now receive episiotomies. Still, the procedure may have to be done if delivery must be hurried due to fetal distress.

The newborn child adapts quickly

Once the fetus's head and shoulders have exited the birth canal, the rest of the body follows fairly readily. The compression of the fetus's chest as it passes through the canal effectively "squeegees" the fluid out of its lungs, thus preparing them for their first breath. With the passage of the entire body through the canal, the second stage of labor is complete.

At this point, the newborn is still attached to the placenta by the umbilical cord, so the infant is still getting oxygen from the mother's lungs. Very shortly after birth, however, the baby takes its first breath, probably in response to cold and tactile stimulation. Then, in a beautifully orchestrated feat of physiology, the infant's circulatory system reorganizes itself: The fetal system, which largely bypasses the lungs, is replaced by the circulatory pattern seen after birth, in which the lungs receive all the blood from the right side of the heart.

The cessation of pulsation in the umbilical blood vessels can be readily seen. At this point, the cord is clamped and cut (sometimes by the mother's partner), and the baby is finally a free-living individual. The mother is often given the chance to hold and perhaps breast-feed her baby, at least for a short while. In many hospitals the mother has the option of keeping the infant with her, unless the baby has some health problem that necessitates a trip to the nursery.

The third stage is the expulsion of the placenta

The third stage of labor consists of further uterine contractions that separate the placenta from the uterine wall and expel it (along with the other fetal membranes) through the birth canal. This usually takes about 30 minutes, but it can range from a few minutes to an hour or more. The expelled placenta is called the **afterbirth**.

The fetal blood in the afterbirth and the umbilical cord can be donated to a public cord blood bank; it contains stem cells that are of potential use in the treatment of leukemia and related diseases. Storing the blood in a private bank for the baby's own future use is a growing trend, but it doesn't make a whole lot of sense, given the low chance that the baby will ever need it. What's more, a person requiring a stem cell transplant is not likely to benefit from his or her own stem cells, because those cells will possess the same defect that caused the person's disease (Memorial Sloan Kettering Cancer Center, 2013).

afterbirth   The placenta, whose delivery constitutes the final stage of labor.

Box 8.5 Sexual Health

Cesarean Section

A cesarean section, or C-section, involves the delivery of a baby through a surgical incision in the front of the mother's abdomen and uterus (**Figure A**). The procedure is so named because Julius Caesar was supposedly born by this method. (We know that he wasn't, because his mother was alive during his childhood; no mothers survived C-section before the Renaissance period.)

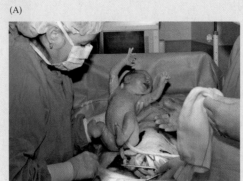 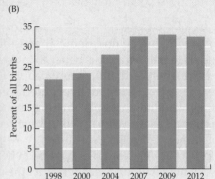

(A) A baby being delivered by cesarean section. (B) C-section rates in the United States since 1998. (After National Vital Statistics Reports, 2010, 2013.)

In the United States today, 1 in 3 hospital births is by C-section (National Vital Statistics Reports, 2013). This is a huge increase from a generation ago, but the rate has remained stable at about 33% since 2008 (**Figure B**). The Canadian rate is somewhat lower, at about 26%.

Cesarean sections are done when vaginal delivery is deemed inadvisable for a variety of medical reasons: if the mother's pelvis is too narrow for the size of the fetus, when labor does not progress after a prolonged period and the mother or fetus is becoming exhausted, or when certain complications occur during labor. A C-section may also be performed if the fetus's position is unfavorable for birth—that is, it is in some orientation other than head down and cannot be manipulated into the head-down position—or the placenta is blocking the baby's passage into the birth canal. Another medical indication for a C-section may be to avoid exposing the baby to an infection present in the birth canal, such as herpes. For unknown reasons, women in whom labor is induced with drugs—an increasingly common practice—are twice as likely to end up having a C-section as women who are allowed to go into labor on their own schedule (Zhang et al., 2010).

Still, as many as 18% of C-sections are performed simply because the mother requests the procedure: sometimes because she fears a painful childbirth (Wax et al., 2004), but sometimes because she believes that a vaginal delivery will impair her sex life afterward, or even sometimes because she doesn't want to devote time to attending childbirth classes. What's more, some doctors also favor C-sections for nonmedical reasons: These procedures are much less likely than vaginal deliveries to lead to malpractice suits, and preplanned C-sections are easier to fit into a doctor's schedule than unpredictable natural births (Kotz, 2008).

Emergency C-section may well save the life of mother or child, but any C-section is major surgery and should not be done without good reason. A review of 79 studies, including randomized trials, indicated that elective C-sections present significantly more risks to mother and child than natural childbirth (Belizan et al., 2007).

The World Health Organization believes that governments should try to keep national C-section rates no higher than 5% to 10% of all births. Some physicians have questioned the rationale for this policy and have argued that higher rates, perhaps even the current U.S. rate of 33%, offer a better policy goal (Tuteur, 2009).

The process of labor can be shortened, or eliminated entirely, by delivering the baby through **cesarean section** (**C-section**), but the popularity of this practice raises serious concerns (**Box 8.5**).

Premature or delayed birth is hazardous

cesarean section (C-section)
The delivery of a baby through an incision in the abdominal wall and the uterus.

Labor is considered premature if it occurs more than 3 weeks before the mother's due date. In most cases of premature labor the cause is not known, but predisposing factors include multiple fetuses, teen pregnancy, the mother's use of tobacco or drugs, malnutrition, and a variety of illnesses during pregnancy.

Premature labor can sometimes be halted with the use of drugs; if not, it leads to **premature birth (or preterm birth)**. This happens in about 10% of all pregnancies in the United States. The earliest time at which a preemie has a reasonable chance of viability (with intensive care) is about 24 weeks of gestational age, making the baby 16 weeks premature. At 23 weeks of gestation about 25% of preemies survive; at 22 weeks, survival is rare (Manktelow et al., 2013).

Premature birth is dangerous to the baby's health: About 75% of all neonatal deaths (aside from those associated with congenital defects) strike the 10% of babies who are born prematurely. Most babies born before 28 weeks experience complications affecting the eyes, brain, lungs, or intestines (Kluger, 2014). Preterm babies, especially those who are small for their gestational age or who are born very prematurely, have a higher likelihood of suffering long-lasting physical and behavioral disabilities, dying during childhood, or (if female) giving birth to premature babies themselves, compared with babies delivered at term (López Bernal & TambyRaja, 2000; Swamy et al., 2008). Even so, the majority of preemies do fine and, though small at birth, eventually catch up with their peers.

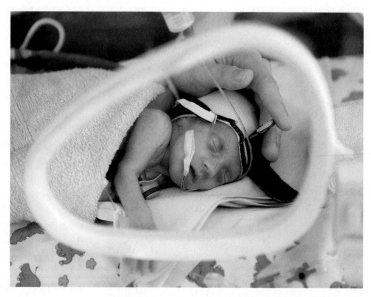

Premature infants have a good chance of surviving, but they require intensive care and may end up with some kind of disability.

Labor that occurs more than 3 weeks past term is considered **delayed labor**: About 10% of babies are born at least this late. Like premature labor, delayed labor has risks. The fetus may grow too large to pass through the birth canal, and in a minority of cases the placenta may cease to adequately nourish the fetus, so it is born too small for its gestational age. Post-term babies are about 3 times more likely to die neonatally than are babies born at term. To avoid these ill effects, drugs such as oxytocin and prostaglandins may be used for **induced labor**. This practice itself carries some risk, but it does at least allow for the date of delivery to be planned ahead of time.

The Period after Birth Places Many Demands on Parents

The weeks after birth are called the **postpartum period**. Although there can be medical problems for the mother during this period, including serious ones such as infections acquired during the birth process, its main feature is physical recovery from the stresses of pregnancy and childbirth. A vaginal discharge continues for a few days after parturition and is then replaced by small volumes of a dark, bloody discharge known as **lochia**; this ceases after a few weeks, but spotty bleeding may continue for 6 to 8 weeks. The uterus gradually shrinks back to its original dimensions, episiotomy or C-section incisions heal, and the mother's levels of estrogens and progesterone, which dropped precipitously at delivery, eventually return to more normal levels.

Psychologically, the postpartum period is a highly variable experience. On the plus side, the mother has the relief of putting pregnancy behind her and the joy of a new baby. Over the first few days after childbirth, these positive feelings tend to dominate. After that, however, the mother faces a great deal of stress. She finds herself back home and devoting a great deal of time and effort to looking after her infant, yet she still needs quite a bit of "mothering" herself. In this situation, the degree of support she receives from her partner or others makes an enormous difference to her psychological well-being.

premature birth (or preterm birth) Birth that occurs more than 3 weeks before a woman's due date.

delayed labor Labor that occurs more than 3 weeks after a woman's due date.

induced labor Labor induced artificially by drugs.

postpartum period The period after birth.

lochia A bloody vaginal discharge that may continue for a few weeks after childbirth.

In her 2005 book, *Down Came the Rain*, actress/model Brooke Shields described how she battled depression after the birth of her daughter Rowan Francis.

postpartum depression
Depression in a mother during the postpartum phase.

postpartum depressive psychosis Postpartum depression accompanied by seriously disordered thinking.

FAQ

I'm just getting back into sex after having my baby, but milk leaks out when I orgasm.

That's normal: The oxytocin surge at orgasm is triggering milk letdown. Try some strategically placed towels, or nurse your baby just before sex.

Postpartum depression may be accompanied by disordered thinking

Many women experience variable moods after childbirth, including periods of sadness and crying ("baby blues"). In about 1 in 7 women this sadness is sufficiently intense and sustained to be diagnosed as **postpartum depression**, a condition that often includes thoughts of self-harm (Wisner et al., 2013). This susceptibility to depression peaks in the period between 10 and 20 days after the birth, when mothers are 7 times more likely to experience depression or other mental disorders requiring hospitalization than are mothers of older children (Munk-Olsen et al., 2006). Depression can linger for several months after the birth, however.

In a small minority of women, postpartum depression is accompanied by a serious disruption of thinking: This is called **postpartum depressive psychosis**, or simply **postpartum psychosis**. On rare occasions, this disorder can lead to infanticide or suicide. In a 2001 case Andrea Yates, a Houston woman with a prior history of postpartum depressive psychosis, drowned her 6-month-old daughter as well as her four older children. After two trials Yates was found not guilty by reason of insanity; she is now confined in a state mental hospital.

Psychosocial factors often play a role in postpartum depression. Single mothers are more likely to experience depression than mothers who have partners (Wisner et al., 2013). In China, where boys are strongly preferred over girls, women who give birth to girls are nearly 3 times more likely to experience postpartum depression than those who give birth to boys (Xie et al., 2007).

Biological factors have not been identified with certainty, but the hormonal and metabolic changes at parturition, especially the severe drop in estrogen levels, are good candidates. Estrogen treatments can alleviate some cases of postpartum depression and psychosis, and a pregnant woman's likelihood of experiencing postpartum depression can be predicted on the basis of her sensitivity to estrogen (Mehta et al., 2014). Nevertheless, postpartum depression is quite commonly a continuation of depression experienced during pregnancy, when estrogen levels are high.

As with depression in general, SSRI-type antidepressants, such as sertraline (Zoloft), have been shown in well-controlled trials to alleviate the symptoms of postpartum depression (Hantsoo et al., 2014). Various forms of psychotherapy are also helpful (O'Hara & McCabe, 2013).

Childbirth and parenthood affect sexuality

The postpartum period is one of low or absent sexual activity, especially coitus, for most women. There are plenty of reasons for this: They are exhausted from the travails of pregnancy and childbirth, they are preoccupied with maternal responsibilities, and the vulva takes time to recover from the stresses of parturition, especially if there has been an episiotomy or a spontaneous tear that had to be sewn up. In addition, low postpartum estrogen levels tend to decrease vaginal lubrication, making coitus uncomfortable. Obstetricians often recommend that women wait about 6 weeks before resuming coitus, and most women do wait about that long or a little longer (Byrd et al., 1998). But after an uncomplicated delivery with no tearing or episiotomy, a woman can safely resume coitus at 3 weeks, if comfort allows. Contraception is necessary even that soon after childbirth.

Some women may be concerned that pregnancy and parturition have reduced their attractiveness (perhaps on account of weight gain or stretch marks) or their ability to enjoy coitus and satisfy their partner (perhaps because of stretching of the vagina). These fears are ill founded. Weight gain can be reversed, and it may not reduce attractiveness even if it isn't. Stretch marks fade. The vagina tightens. (This process can be aided by Kegel exercises; see Chapter 14.)

Although nearly all couples resume sex within a few months after childbirth, the transition to parenthood has profound and often negative effects on their relationship and their sexuality. These effects have been studied most carefully for married couples. For the average couple, marital conflicts increase about ninefold after the birth of the first child, the perceived quality of the marriage drops precipitously, husband and wife adopt more stereotypical gender roles, the husband withdraws into work, and the frequency of marital conversations and sex goes into a steep decline (Gottman & Notarius, 2000).

Of course, not every couple is the "average" couple: Some marriages and cohabitations blossom—especially those in which the baby was truly wanted by both partners (Council on Contemporary Families, 2009). In addition, awareness of how conflicts evolve in the triangular relationship between a baby and its two parents—as studied by family therapy pioneer Murray Bowen, for example (Gilbert, 2006)—can help couples "survive" parenthood.

Breast-Feeding Is the Preferred Method of Nourishing the Infant

Breast-feeding—the trait that links humans with all other mammals—represents many things: a beautifully orchestrated physiological process, a wellspring of intimacy between mother and child, and a source of physical and psychological health for both. In addition, it is a focus of controversy—between those who promote the virtues of breast-feeding and those who see it as something that technology and the demands of modern society have rendered obsolete or excessively burdensome.

Breast-feeding cements the bond between mother and infant.

Lactation is orchestrated by hormones

As described earlier, the breasts are ready to **lactate** (produce milk) by about the fourth month of pregnancy. The main hormone that promotes lactation—**prolactin**—is secreted in ever greater amounts as pregnancy proceeds. Once estrogen and progesterone levels drop, as they do at childbirth, prolactin triggers copious lactation, so the milk glands in the breasts become distended with milk.

While prolactin promotes lactation, oxytocin is responsible for the release of milk from the breast tissue into the milk ducts and nipples. The baby's sucking on the nipples triggers oxytocin release and the **milk letdown reflex**. Interestingly, this reflex is readily "conditioned": After a mother has nursed for some time, simply the sound of her baby crying or the mother's actions in preparing to nurse may trigger the milk letdown reflex. Suckling also promotes the continued secretion of prolactin after birth. Thus, if the mother does not breast-feed her infant, prolactin secretion declines, and the breasts gradually cease to produce milk.

The content of breast milk changes over time

For the first few days after birth, the material secreted by the breasts is not mature milk, but a thick, yellowish special milk called **colostrum**. This material is lower in fat and sugar than mature milk but richer in proteins, especially antibodies. These protect the infant against a wide variety of infectious organisms and other antigens to which the mother has been exposed at some point in her life. Because colostrum is low in calories and is produced in limited amounts, a breast-feeding baby may lose

lactation   The production of milk in the mammary glands.

prolactin   A protein hormone, secreted by the anterior lobe of the pituitary gland, that promotes breast development, among other effects.

milk letdown reflex   The ejection of milk into the milk ducts in response to suckling. Also called milk ejection reflex.

colostrum   The milk produced during the first few days after birth; it is relatively low in fat but rich in immunoglobulins.

TABLE 8.3
Main Constituents of Mature Human Milk

Water	Approximately 90%
Sugar (lactose)	Approximately 7%
Fat	3%–6%
Proteins	0.8%–0.9%
Amino acids	Includes all essential amino acids
Vitamins	Includes A, B1, B2, B12, C, D, E, K
Energy content	Approximately 19 calories per fluid ounce (650 calories per liter)

wet nurse   A woman who breast-feeds someone else's infant.

infant formula   Manufactured breast milk substitute.

In many non-Western cultures, the contraceptive effect of prolonged breast-feeding plays an important role in the spacing of a woman's children.

up to 10% of its birth weight while waiting for the mature milk to come in. This is completely normal.

Over the first 2 weeks after birth, the breast secretions gradually become mature milk (**Table 8.3**) and increase greatly in volume. By 3 weeks after birth, a breast-fed baby is drinking a little over 2 pints (1 L) of milk per day, which provides about 700 calories of energy. Most of that energy comes from the fat content of the milk. Of the proteins in milk, some are digested to provide amino acids for protein synthesis, while others resist digestion and serve as enzymes, antibodies, growth factors, and the like (Lönnerdal, 2003).

Infant formula is an alternative to breast milk

Over most of human history, mothers had little choice but to breast-feed their babies. (Unmodified cow's milk is not a satisfactory substitute for human milk, at least for young infants.) If women could not breast-feed or did not wish to do so, they would sometimes have their baby breast-fed by another woman who had milk to spare—perhaps because she had lost her own baby. Such women were called **wet nurses**. In the 20th century, the industrial production of **infant formula** began, and breast-feeding largely gave way to bottle-feeding in Western countries. Most formula is based on cows' milk that has been modified to make it more digestible; soy-based formula is recommended only for infants who cannot digest cows' milk.

In the 1950s only about 1 in 5 American women breast-fed their infants, but beginning in the 1970s the numbers began to rise. This shift was propelled by medical research, which demonstrated that breast-feeding has specific health benefits, and by the women's movement, which rejected the image of breast-feeding as demeaning. Breast-feeding became a cause, spearheaded by La Leche League International. Currently, about 75% of American mothers breast-feed their babies initially, but that figure drops to 34% at 6 months and 22% at 1 year (U.S. Public Health Service, 2011).

Breast-feeding has many advantages and some drawbacks

Breast-feeding, compared with bottle-feeding, has many advantages:

- *Health benefits for the baby.* Breast-fed babies are less likely to develop infectious illnesses such as pneumonia, botulism, bronchitis, bacterial meningitis, staphylococcal infections, influenza, ear infections, rubella, and diarrhea, and they are also less prone to asthma. These benefits are experienced mainly during the period of breast-feeding; the long-term physical health of breast-fed and bottle-fed infants is about the same. But there do seem to be long-lasting cognitive benefits: In one randomized trial, prolonged, exclusive breast-feeding was associated with a higher IQ and better academic performance at the age of 6 (Kramer et al., 2008).

- *Health benefits for the mother.* By stimulating the release of oxytocin, breast-feeding helps shrink the uterus to its prepregnancy size and reduces postpartum bleeding. It also helps the mother shed the excess weight she gained during pregnancy. (Breast-feeding is nature's own liposuction.) It may also reduce her risk of ovarian cancer and early (premenopausal) breast cancer.

- *Psychological benefits to the mother and infant.* Breast-feeding helps establish a close bond between mother and child. Breast-feeding is usually pleasurable and relaxing for the mother.

- *Convenience and expense.* Breast-feeding is much less expensive than bottle-feeding, even considering the extra food the mother must consume to support it. Breast-feeding is more convenient than bottle-feeding in the sense that no preparations are required: The breast milk is always there, perfectly prepared, at the right temperature, and sterile.

- *Contraceptive effect.* In some non-Western cultures women nurse their children for several years after birth, and intensive nursing is associated with a reduction in fertility. Most American women do not nurse so intensively and stand a good chance of becoming pregnant even if they continue to nurse.

Breast-feeding also has several potential disadvantages:

- *Health problems for the mother.* Women who breast-feed sometimes develop inflamed nipples, which make nursing painful, or their breasts become uncomfortably engorged with milk. About 20% of women develop an inflammation or infection of the breast (**mastitis**), often as a consequence of cracked nipples or a blocked milk duct. These conditions can be easily treated, however.

- *Health problems for the baby.* The infant can acquire some infections, including HIV and hepatitis, from the mother via her milk. Many drugs (including contraceptives) can pass from the mother to the child via milk and may harm the child. A mother who is taking medication and plans to breast-feed should discuss all drugs with her physician.

- *Inconvenience.* Although breast milk comes already prepared and warmed, the process of feeding it to the baby takes considerable time—several hours each day. It can be a real challenge for women to balance breast-feeding with workplace demands. One option is for the mother to remove milk with a breast pump and refrigerate it so that a caretaker—or perhaps the mother's partner—can rewarm it later and feed it to the baby by bottle.

Numerous organizations would like to see more women breast-feed their babies. Still, if a woman cannot do so for one reason or another, she should not feel that she has failed her child. Formula-fed infants can thrive as well as breast-fed ones.

If a mother does breast-feed her infant, when should she stop? The American Academy of Pediatrics has recommended that babies be exclusively breast-fed for 6 months, with continued partial breast-feeding for 1 year or more (American Academy of Pediatrics, 2012).

mastitis   Inflammation of the breast.

Go to the
**Discovering
Human Sexuality**
Companion Website at
**sites.sinauer.com/
discoveringhumansexuality3e**
for activities, study questions,
quizzes, and other study aids.

Summary

- The onset of pregnancy is marked by a missed menstrual period and other symptoms. It can be confirmed by urine or blood tests that detect the human chorionic gonadotropin hormone (hCG) secreted by the implanted embryo.

- Infertility or subfertility can be caused by problems in the man or in the woman. If this condition results from low sperm count or sperm quality, in vitro fertilization (IVF) may still make pregnancy possible. An alternative is artificial insemination with donated sperm.

- Abnormalities of the female reproductive tract, resulting from sexually transmitted infections or other causes, can reduce fertility. The oviducts are the most common site of such problems. These abnormalities can sometimes be corrected surgically. Alternatively, embryos produced by IVF can be placed directly into the uterus.

(continued)

Summary (continued)

- Problems with ovulation can often be treated with drugs. An alternative is the use of donated eggs.

- If a woman cannot sustain pregnancy at all, surrogate motherhood and adoption are possible options.

- Fertility declines steadily with age in both sexes. Age also raises the likelihood of fetal abnormalities such as Down syndrome.

- Many embryos do not survive. Many of those that fail to implant or that die early in pregnancy are abnormal. Other conditions, such as Rh factor incompatibility or ectopic pregnancy, can cause fetal loss or harm the fetus or the mother.

- Pregnancy lasts about 9 months and is conventionally divided into three trimesters. The first trimester may be marked by symptoms such as morning sickness. It is a critical period of fetal development during which the main body plan is laid out and organ systems develop. This process can be impaired by maternal infection or poor nutrition or by use of alcohol, tobacco, or a variety of drugs. Prenatal care offers important benefits, but many women do not receive such care in early pregnancy.

- The second trimester is usually easiest for the mother. The fetus can be screened for congenital abnormalities, and its sex can be determined at this time. Moderate exercise benefits the mother. The frequency of sexual activity tends to decline during pregnancy, but for most women there is no health reason for abstaining from coitus.

- In the third trimester both the parents and the fetus make preparations for birth. Childbirth classes teach strategies to facilitate delivery and to minimize pain.

- Labor has three stages. In the first stage, uterine contractions and cervical softening prepare the birth canal for the passage of the fetus. In the second stage, the fetus passes through the canal and is "delivered." Rapid physiological changes adapt the infant to an air-breathing existence. In the third stage, the placenta (afterbirth) and fetal membranes are expelled.

- Difficult births may necessitate surgical widening of the vaginal opening (episiotomy) or delivery via an abdominal incision (cesarean section). In the United States, episiotomy is performed much less often than in the past, but 1 in 3 women deliver by C-section. Various forms of anesthesia are available if labor is excessively painful. Methods of pain relief that do not rely on medications are also available.

- Premature and delayed labor are associated with increased risks of harm to the fetus.

- The postpartum period, after birth, is a time of recovery for the mother but is marked by depression with disordered thinking in a few women.

- The birth of a child, especially a first one, can bring great happiness, but it also causes major stresses. Marital satisfaction tends to decline after the transition to parenthood, and the frequency of sexual activity decreases.

- Hormones prepare the mother's breasts for lactation and mediate the release of milk during breast-feeding. The content of milk changes during the weeks after childbirth. Breast-feeding has significant advantages over formula-feeding, but formula-fed infants can thrive too.

Discussion Questions

1. Imagine that for some reason you or your partner were not able to become pregnant by sexual intercourse. Discuss your preference for some alternative method of becoming parents (e.g., adoption, assisted reproductive technology, or surrogate motherhood). Discuss what the pros and cons of each solution would be for you.

2. Do you think that IVF clinics should help postmenopausal women who want to become pregnant, regardless of their age?

3. Imagine that you or your partner were pregnant and learned that the fetus had a genetic defect such as Down syndrome. Discuss the costs and benefits of the options available to you (e.g., abortion, delivering the child and putting it up for adoption, or keeping and raising the child) and the rationale behind each one.

4. Do you think that the capability to select a child's sex prenatally is a good thing or a bad thing, and why? Do you think the practice should be permitted, discouraged, restricted, or banned?

5. Imagine that you are, or your partner is, happily pregnant and expecting a normal delivery. Would you elect to deliver the child at home, in a hospital, or in a birthing center? Would you prefer a medical doctor or a certified nurse-midwife to deliver your baby? Why?

6. Your baby is born and is healthy. Discuss the pros and cons of breast-feeding versus bottle-feeding. Which would you select? How long do you think breast-feeding should continue? Give your reasons.

7. What reasons can you list for having *no* children, or just one child?

Web Resources

American College (also Congress) of Obstetricians and Gynecologists **www.acog.org**

American Society for Reproductive Medicine **www.asrm.org**

National Down Syndrome Society **www.ndss.org**

Society for Assisted Reproductive Technology **www.sart.org**

Recommended Reading

Cunningham, F., Leveno, K., Bloom, S., Spong, C. Y., Dashe, J. Hauth, J. C., et al. (Eds.). (2014). *Williams obstetrics* (24th ed.). McGraw-Hill.

King, T. L., Brucker, M. C., Kriebs, J. M., & Fahey, J. O. (2013). *Varney's midwifery* (5th ed.). Jones & Bartlett.

La Leche League International. (2010). *The womanly art of breastfeeding* (8th ed.). Ballantine.

Mayo Clinic. (2011). *Guide to a healthy pregnancy*. Good Books.

Weschler, T. (2006). *Taking charge of your fertility* (10th ed.) HarperCollins.

Chapter 9

Getting creative with condoms, with designer creations for a fashion show in Malaysia.

Contraception and Abortion

The previous chapter treated pregnancy as a natural consequence of vaginal intercourse. Most men and women, however, experience substantial periods of life during which they want to engage in sexual relationships but do not want to produce children. Human ingenuity has come up with a wide variety of methods for preventing pregnancies and— if necessary—ending them. These methods, often referred to collectively as family planning, are the topic of this chapter.

Birth Control Has a Long History

Figure 9.1 Safety check Nineteenth-century users tested condoms by blowing into them before use.

In the ancient world, "birth control" was accomplished largely through the neglect, abandonment, or outright killing of unwanted babies. (The skeletons of scores of newborn babies have been found under the ruins of Roman-era brothels in England and Israel.) In medieval times, herbal preparations were used to induce abortions. Various forms of contraception were also used, though probably with limited success. These methods involved placing some substance, such as olive oil or a vinegar-soaked sponge, in the vagina before sex or douching with wine or vinegar afterward. The withdrawal method of contraception has been known for millennia and is mentioned in the biblical story of Onan, who "spilled his seed upon the ground" to avoid impregnating his deceased brother's wife.

Male condoms—sheaths placed over the penis—also have a long history. The 18th-century Italian adventurer and ladies' man Giacomo Casanova popularized their use, both as contraceptives and to prevent the transmission of disease. Most early condoms were made from animal intestines, and they were so expensive that they had to be used repeatedly. Thus they had to be tested by inflating them with air before each use (**Figure 9.1**). Mass-produced vulcanized-rubber condoms (hence "rubbers") became available at the end of the 19th century, followed by latex condoms in the 1930s.

Diaphragms—barriers that cover the cervix—were originally natural objects, such as squeezed half-lemons. (Besides acting as a barrier, the lemon's acidity had some spermicidal action.) A reasonably effective artificial diaphragm was invented in the 1880s. Diaphragms were the main form of contraception used by women until the 1960s. In the 1920s Ernst Gräfenberg (of "G-spot" fame) developed an effective intrauterine device (IUD).

Scientific discoveries about the endocrinological basis of the menstrual cycle led to the introduction of oral contraceptives ("the Pill") for women in the 1960s. Oral contraceptives, which consist of drugs related to sex hormones, were so effective that they almost eliminated the fear of unwanted pregnancy for many women and thus helped spur the "sexual revolution" of that time. Most recent developments in contraceptive technology employ sex steroids or related compounds.

Feminists led the campaign to legalize contraception

The history of contraception in the United States is not merely a story of technological advances, however, but also one of profound social conflict. At least until the end of the 19th century, contraception was viewed by many as morally offensive because it subverted what was thought to be the natural or divinely intended function of sex: procreation. Indeed, that is still the official position of the Roman Catholic Church today, though this position is currently under review. Early proponents of contraception were harassed, fined, or jailed.

Margaret Sanger (1879–1966) and other early feminists led the struggle to legalize contraception in the 20th century (**Box 9.1**). The birth control movement did not achieve definitive success until the 1960s and 1970s, when two decisions of the U.S. Supreme Court (*Griswold v. Connecticut*, 1965, and *Eisenstadt v. Baird*, 1972) overthrew laws that banned the use or distribution of contraceptives. These rulings were based on a constitutional right of privacy and in fact helped establish that right.

Box 9.1 Sex in History

Margaret Sanger and the Birth Control Movement

Margaret Higgins Sanger was born in Corning, New York, in 1879. Her mother, Anne Higgins, died at age 50 after bearing 11 children, and Sanger attributed her early death to the burden of too-frequent pregnancies. Sanger trained as a nurse and in 1902 married an architect. The couple had three children and then moved to New York City. Working as a visiting nurse on the Lower East Side, Sanger came to realize that unrestricted births were putting a crushing economic and health burden on working-class women. Their all-too-frequent response to this burden—illegal or self-induced abortion—was killing many of them. In 1914 Sanger began publishing a radical feminist monthly called *The Woman Rebel*, which included appeals for the right to practice birth control. Sanger was indicted under the Comstock Laws, which forbade the dissemination of information about contraception. She jumped bail and spent a year in Europe. While there, she visited a birth control clinic in Holland, where women were being fitted with a new type of diaphragm, and she later imported this diaphragm into the United States.

Sanger returned to the United States in 1915 to face the charges against her, hoping to make her trial into a showcase for the birth control cause. The charges were dropped, however, because of widespread public sympathy for Sanger—especially because her only daughter had died that same year. She therefore went on a national lecture tour to promote birth control and was arrested in several cities.

In October of 1916 Sanger opened the country's first birth control clinic, the Brownsville Clinic in Brooklyn, New York. The police closed it down after just 9 days of operation. Sanger was arrested and, because she refused to pay a fine, spent 30 days in prison. While in prison she taught contraceptive methods to other inmates.

The Brownsville affair drew widespread sympathy and financial support to her cause. Although she lost the appeal of her conviction, the appellate court did rule that physicians could provide contraceptive information for medical reasons. This ruling allowed Sanger's group to open a doctor-staffed birth control clinic, and others followed. In 1917 Sanger began publication of a monthly, the *Birth Control Review*, and in 1921 she founded the American Birth Control League, forerunner of the Planned Parenthood Federation.

Filipinos demonstrating in support of 2010 legislation to fund birth control education. The Philippines have a population of 100 million in a land area similar to that of Arizona (population 6.4 million).

Sanger was always trying to find improved birth control techniques. After sex steroids were synthesized, she arranged for funding to support research into hormone-based contraceptives—research that paid off in 1960 when the Food and Drug Administration approved the first contraceptive pill.

Sanger died in 1965, just a few months after the U.S. Supreme Court, in *Griswold v. Connecticut*, declared that married couples had a constitutional right to use birth control.

Although contraception is now widely accepted in the United States, even by American Catholics, some other countries are still wrestling with the issue. The Philippines, for example, is a country where explosive population growth is stymieing attempts to eliminate poverty, but the Roman Catholic Church (to which most Filipinos belong) has long prevented the government from initiating any contraception programs (see figure). Finally, in 2012, President Benigno Aquino signed into law the Responsible Parenthood and Reproductive Health Act, which allows for government assistance with contraception and also mandates sex-education classes in state schools. Members of the Roman Catholic Church challenged the law, but in 2014 it was upheld by the Supreme Court of the Philippines. As in the United States, most Filipino Catholics reject their church's teaching that contraception is sinful (The Economist, 2014a).

Following these decisions, federal and state governments began supporting family planning initiatives—for example, through the Medicaid program. The AIDS epidemic, which began around 1980, boosted the social approval of one form of

Total = 6.4 million

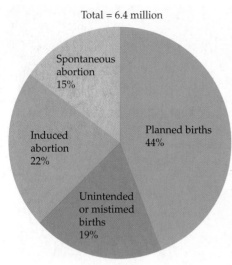

Spontaneous abortion 15%

Induced abortion 22%

Planned births 44%

Unintended or mistimed births 19%

Figure 9.2 **Fewer than half of all U.S. pregnancies** lead to the birth of a planned child. This chart shows the outcome of the 6.4 million pregnancies that are established in the United States per year. (Data from Guttmacher Institute, 2014a.)

contraception—condoms—because it offered protection against the transmission of HIV. But contraception remains controversial in some quarters even today, especially with regard to its use by teens. Much of this debate centers on whether schools should provide information about contraception and access to contraceptives. Because of this controversy, the U.S. government has been much less active in the field of contraception services, education, and research than have governments in many other industrialized countries. Thus, much of the burden of education and service provision has fallen on nongovernmental organizations such as Planned Parenthood.

Contraception has not yet solved the problem of unintended pregnancy

Currently, 90% of American women age 15 to 45 who are sexually active and fertile but do not want to become pregnant are using some contraceptive technique. On the basis of this high rate of contraceptive usage, you might imagine that the great majority of pregnancies would be planned and would lead to the birth of wanted babies. In reality, about one-half of all U.S. pregnancies are unintended; of those unintended pregnancies nearly half end in induced abortion, and only about one-fourth in live births (Finer & Zolna, 2014) (**Figure 9.2**). More than 3 million unwanted pregnancies occur in the United States each year. Among these, half result from not using any method of contraception, while the other half result from failure of a method that *was* used, though perhaps not properly (Finer & Henshaw, 2006).

The new federal health care law ("Obamacare") has made contraception more affordable for many Americans, both by extending medical insurance to more people and by requiring that insurance policies cover contraceptive drugs and devices without co-pays or deductibles. Thus, if costs have caused people to forgo contraception, we may expect a decline in the rate of unintended pregnancies in the near future.

Ideally, couples who engage in sex will cooperate to ensure that pregnancy doesn't occur, but a self-reliant method, or one that is evident in use, may allay concerns about a partner's reliability.

Different users have different contraceptive needs

A wide variety of contraceptive methods are available, each of which has certain features that make it more or less attractive for particular users. Contraceptive options in Canada are quite similar to those in the United States (SexualityandU, 2012). Here are the main issues that people who are choosing a contraceptive technique should consider:

- *How reliable is the method?* With some methods, such as oral contraceptives, less than 1% of users will become pregnant in a single year, provided they practice the method properly. This percentage is called the **perfect-use failure rate** of the method. All humans are fallible, however; a woman might forget to take the pills for a day or two, for example, or a man's

perfect-use failure rate The percentage of women using a contraceptive technique correctly who will become pregnant in the course of one year.

TABLE 9.1
Usage and Failure Rates of the Most Common Contraceptive Techniques

Method	Usage (percentage of all contraceptive users who use this method)[a]	Failure rate (percentage of women using this method who become pregnant in 1 year)	
		With perfect use	With typical use
Physical methods			
Male condom	16.3	2.0	15.0
Female condom	—	5.0	21.0
Diaphragm	—	6.0	16.0
Cervical cap[b]	—	18.0	24.0
IUD	5.6		
Paragard (Copper-T)		0.6	0.8
Mirena		0.2	0.2
Spermicides			
Sponge[b]	—	9.0	16.0
Other	—	18.0	29.0
Hormone-based methods			
Pills (all types)	28.0	0.3	8.0
Injection (Depo-Provera)	3.2	0.3	3.8
Implant (Nexplanon)	1.1	0.05	0.05
Patch[c]	—	0.3	8.0
Vaginal ring[c]	2.2	0.3	8.0
Behavioral methods[d]			
Fertility awareness	1.1	1.0–9.0	25.0
Withdrawal	5.2	4.0	27.0
Sterilization			
Male	9.9	0.1	0.1
Female	27.1	0.5	0.5

After Centers for Disease Control, 2010d; Hatcher et al., 2011.
[a]Where not listed, usage is small or unknown.
[b]For these methods, failure rates are higher for women who have already had a child.
[c]Typical-use failure rates for the patch and the NuvaRing are estimates.
[d]Failure rates for behavioral methods are estimates.

fingernail might tear a condom while he is putting it on. Thus, the **typical-use failure rates** of contraceptive methods tend to be higher—about 8% for pills. Only a few methods have typical-use failure rates below 1%; these are methods that you can basically forget about once you have taken the initial steps. We summarize information about usage and reliability of the most common methods of contraception in **Table 9.1**.

- *How safe is it for me?* We describe any risks associated with the various methods listed in this chapter. Individual users may have risk factors that make specific methods inadvisable for them.

typical-use failure rate The percentage of women using a contraceptive technique with a typical degree of care who will become pregnant in the course of one year.

male condom   A sheath placed over the penis as a contraceptive and/or to prevent disease transmission.

barrier method   Any contraceptive technique in which a physical barrier, such as a condom or diaphragm, prevents sperm from reaching the ovum.

- *Do I need the method to be reversible?* For most young people the answer is "yes," but for older adults who are certain they don't want more children, irreversible methods (sterilization) may be preferable.
- *Do I need STI protection?* The protection against sexually transmitted infections offered by condoms is an important added advantage, especially for women and men who are not in long-term monogamous relationships. Of course, condoms can be added to methods that don't offer STI protection, such as pills.
- *How easy is the method for me to use?* Some methods, such as condoms, require some time and attention before or during every sexual encounter. Some methods require taking pills on a rather precise schedule. Some require regular visits to a health care provider. How burdensome these requirements are depends on your individual circumstances and personality.
- *How much will it cost?* Some methods require substantial up-front expenditure; some require continual purchases over time; and some are free, or nearly so. However, the mandated coverage of contraceptive services and prescriptions under Obamacare has greatly reduced the cost of contraception for many users.
- *Will I be in control?* For some users, it may be important to be in charge of the contraception method, rather than leaving the responsibility to partners who might not be reliable.

Physical Methods Block Sperm Transport

We begin with reversible physical methods, some of which have a long history of safe and successful use.

Male condoms are reliable when properly used

The **male condom** (**Figure 9.3**) is a disposable sheath that is placed over the penis before coitus. It works simply by preventing semen from entering the vagina; thus, it is described as a **barrier method** of contraception. Some condoms come precoated with the spermicide nonoxynol-9, which kills sperm chemically. The amount of spermicide on coated condoms is probably not enough to be effective in the event that the condom breaks, however, and the presence of the spermicide shortens the shelf life of the condom and increases its cost. In addition, as discussed later in this chapter, the frequent use of spermicides can cause health problems for the woman. For all these reasons, spermicide-coated condoms are not recommended.

Most condoms are made of latex. Others are made of polyisoprene, polyurethane, or animal intestinal tissue. Latex condoms are the cheapest: They cost less than $0.50 apiece when bought in multipacks, and several programs distribute them free. When used properly (**Figure 9.4**), condoms are an effective contraceptive, and they also provide substantial protection against transmission of STIs, including HIV. Latex condoms should be used in conjunction with water-based or silicone lubricants only. Oils, fats, lotions, petroleum

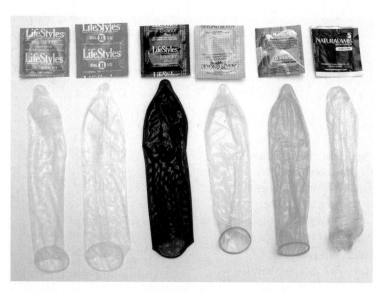

Figure 9.3   **Male condoms** come in a variety of types, sizes, and even flavors.

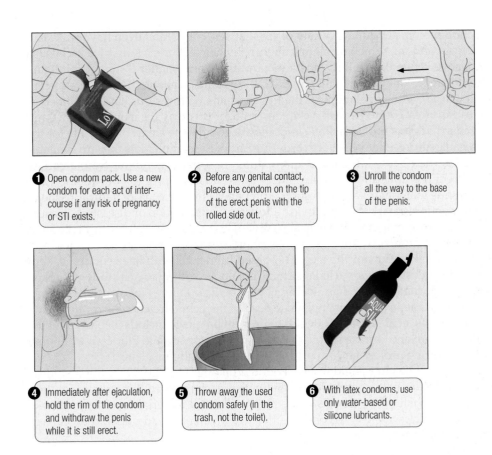

Figure 9.4   How to use a condom These are the instructions recommended by an expert committee of the World Health Organization. (After Warner & Steiner, 2007.)

❶ Open condom pack. Use a new condom for each act of intercourse if any risk of pregnancy or STI exists.

❷ Before any genital contact, place the condom on the tip of the erect penis with the rolled side out.

❸ Unroll the condom all the way to the base of the penis.

❹ Immediately after ejaculation, hold the rim of the condom and withdraw the penis while it is still erect.

❺ Throw away the used condom safely (in the trash, not the toilet).

❻ With latex condoms, use only water-based or silicone lubricants.

jellies, and any lubricants containing those substances will weaken the latex and may cause the condom to break.

Some men and women are allergic to latex. Another potential disadvantage of latex condoms is that they may lessen the sensations of coitus, especially for the man. As many as 33% of young men experience erection difficulties when using a condom, either because of the lessened sensation or because of the tightness of the condom, and this is a common reason why men don't use condoms consistently (Graham et al., 2006). To counter this problem, the British company Futura has developed a new latex condom, currently known as CSD500, which contains an erection-inducing vasodilator drug, glyceryl trinitrate. It is sometimes referred to as the "Viagra condom," but it does not contain Viagra (sildenafil) or any other drug of that class. The CSD500 condom is already on sale in some countries and may be available in the United States by the time you read this.

Polyisoprene condoms are stretchy like latex and therefore fit snugly. Some people find that they provide a better sensation than latex condoms, and they smell better. They are suitable for people (men or their partners) who are sensitive to latex.

Polyurethane condoms are much less stretchy than latex condoms: Thus, if the right size is chosen, it will fit well without the tight feeling of a latex condom, but if it is too large, it may easily slip off. Both polyisoprene and polyurethane condoms are effective contraceptives and cannot be penetrated by any STI-causing agents so long as they remain intact. They can be used with water-, silicone-, or oil-based lubricants. Many condoms come already lubricated with a silicone-based lubricant.

Natural-tissue "lambskin" condoms are also effective contraceptives, but they are known to be *ineffective* in preventing the transmission of HIV and other viral STIs. That's because they have pores large enough to permit the passage of viruses. Thus, they should be used only if STIs are not a concern.

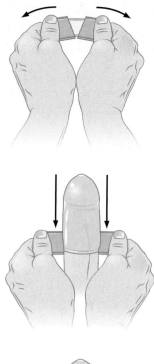

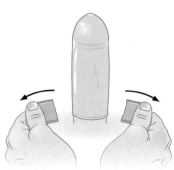

Figure 9.5 The Rapidom, one of the winners of the Gates Foundation's "better condom" competition The package breaks into two tabs with which the user can pull the condom onto his penis in a single stroke.

Condoms come in quite a variety of sizes, styles, colors, and even flavors. A standard-size condom, which measures about 7 inches (180 mm) long by 2 inches (51 mm) across when flat, will fit most men, but there are smaller ("snugger fit") and larger ("large," "magnum," "magnum XL") condoms available. There are also condoms whose width is greater near the tip, condoms with various kinds of ribbed or bumpy surfaces, condoms with a skin desensitizer (to delay the man's orgasm), and condoms that glow in the dark. If condoms are going to be a part of your life for the foreseeable future, it may be worth ordering one of the sampler kits that are available on the Internet. These kits contain many different types of condoms from a variety of different manufacturers. (Testing them all could add spice to your relationship and provide material for an interesting term paper.) Just be wary of natural-tissue or novelty condoms that may not provide adequate contraception or disease protection.

Condoms do sometimes break or slip off (Coyle et al., 2012). Usually this is because of some kind of misuse, such as the use of old or inappropriately sized condoms, insufficient lubrication, or the use of oil-based lubricants with latex condoms. Very infrequently, even properly used condoms break. According to one study of broken condoms returned to their manufacturer, most of these failures involve "blunt puncture," in which repeated thrusting by the head of the penis stretches the condom until it breaks (White et al., 2008). Strategies to prevent breakage include inspection of the condom before and during sex, use of plenty of water-soluble lubricant, changing condoms during prolonged coitus, or using thicker condoms.

In 2013 the Bill and Melinda Gates Foundation offered $100,000 for the best ideas on how to build a better condom. Eleven finalists each received this amount for their ideas, which included condoms made from advanced materials such as graphene and nanoparticles, as well as condoms that are much easier to put on than current versions (**Figure 9.5**).

Advantages of the male condom:

- It is cheap and readily accessible.
- It is reliable when properly used.
- It offers significant protection against STIs and thus helps protect fertility.
- It lacks the possible side effects of hormone-based contraceptives.
- Its use is fully and immediately reversible.

Disadvantages of the male condom:

- Putting on a condom can interrupt lovemaking.
- The man must withdraw promptly after ejaculating.
- Condoms reduce the pleasure of sex for most users.
- Reliability is less than ideal in typical use, mostly due to failure to use condoms consistently.

Because condoms have drawbacks, there is considerable research into other potential methods of male contraception (**Box 9.2**).

Female condoms are relatively intrusive

The **female condom** is made of nitrile rubber (synthetic latex). (A natural latex version is in development.) It resembles a large male condom, but it is stiffened by rings at each end (**Figure 9.6**). The ring at the closed end lies loose inside the condom; it fits around the cervix rather like a diaphragm (see below). The ring at the open end is attached to the condom; it is large because it is intended to stay outside the body. Thus, the condom covers the entirety of the vagina and adjacent parts of the vulva. The condom comes with lubricant on the inside, and additional lubricant for the outside is supplied with the condom.

female condom A nitrile rubber pouch inserted into the vagina as a contraceptive and/or to prevent disease transmission.

Box 9.2 Research Highlights

Male Contraceptives of the Future?

Imagine never having to use a condom again. Many research groups are trying to make that dream a reality—by developing alternative, more acceptable forms of male contraception. Here's a sampler of the technologies that are being explored:

Heat. Sperm production is greatly impaired at elevated temperatures. Devices called suspensories hold the testicles in the inguinal canal, thus keeping them at body heat. Other methods involve the application of external heat. (Neither of these methods should be tried at home—there is a risk of long-term harm.)

Intra-vas devices (IVDs). These are plugs that are placed inside the vasa deferentia, blocking the flow of sperm (see figure). Alternatively, the vas deferens can be blocked with an injected gel. To restore fertility, a second injection flushes out the gel.

Androgens. Testosterone and other androgens exert a feedback inhibition on the production of the gonadotropic hormones, which in turn causes a reduction in sperm counts (see Figure 3.15, page 81). Drugs with androgenic activity might be delivered by depot injection.

"Dry orgasm" pills. Several drugs have been developed that disrupt the action of smooth muscle within the vas deferens or the urethra. These drugs can prevent sperm from being mixed into the semen or cause the semen to be ejaculated backward into the bladder.

Immunology. Some men are infertile because they possess antibodies directed against their own sperm. It is possible to trick the immune systems of healthy men into developing antibodies against sperm or other elements of the male reproductive system.

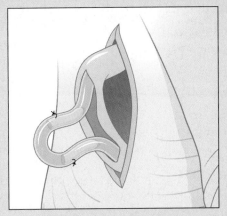

Intra-vas plugs block sperm transport along the vasa deferentia. This procedure, which is still in development, can be more easily reversed than a vasectomy.

Retinoic acid blockers. Retinoic acid, a metabolite of vitamin A, is required for spermatogenesis. Drugs that prevent the attachment of retinoic acid to its receptors in the testicles have been shown to block sperm production in a reversible fashion in laboratory animals.

Adjudin. This drug blocks spermatogenesis. Researchers at the Population Council have attached the drug to follicle-stimulating hormone (FSH), thus ensuring that it is delivered to FSH's target cells in the testicles.

It's uncertain whether any of these methods will make it through clinical trials into general use. A website provides up-to-date and accurate information about this entire field (International Male Contraception Coalition, 2014).

Advantages of the female condom:

- The female condom is the only contraceptive controlled by the woman that probably offers substantial protection from STIs, including HIV.
- It can be inserted ahead of time, thus avoiding any interruption of lovemaking.
- It does not require the man to maintain an erection during use, and it does not constrict the man's penis.
- Its use is easily and immediately reversible.
- It can be used for anal sex if the inner ring is removed.

Figure 9.6   The female condom is made of nitrile (synthetic latex). It is an effective contraceptive, but it is less popular in the United States than in some other countries.

diaphragm A barrier placed over the cervix as a contraceptive.

Disadvantages of the female condom:

- The female condom tends to be less appealing to men than to women; part of the reason for this is that some men consider the protruding free end unaesthetic.

- There is the possibility that the man will unwittingly insert his penis into the vagina outside of the condom

- Sometimes the entire condom may be drawn into the vagina during coitus. To prevent this, it may be necessary to hold the outer ring of the condom.

- Male and female condoms should not be used simultaneously because the friction between them may pull one of them out of place.

The female condom has not gained wide acceptance in the United States, but some couples may find that it works well for them. Larger numbers of female condoms are distributed in developing countries, where there is a greater need for women to control their own contraception (Kremer, 2013).

Diaphragms and cervical caps are inconvenient but have few side effects

The **diaphragm** (**Figure 9.7**) used to be a very popular form of contraception prior to the development of oral contraceptives, but it is now used by fewer than 1 in 50 American women. It is a dome-shaped piece of silicone or latex that is stiffened by a springlike strip around its perimeter. It fits against the walls of the vagina, covering the cervix. It works by preventing sperm from entering the cervix. However, sperm can migrate around the edges of the diaphragm, and it must therefore be used in conjunction with a spermicidal cream or jelly, which is placed inside the dome of the diaphragm and around the rim. Latex diaphragms, like latex condoms, are damaged by oil-based lubricants.

The diaphragm should be left in place for at least 6 hours after sex, but no more than 24 hours in total. For repeated sex while the diaphragm is still in place, more spermicide should be placed in the vagina without dislodging the diaphragm.

Advantages of the diaphragm:

- It is somewhat less intrusive than condoms because it can be inserted ahead of time and does not usually affect sensation during sex.

- Long-term use of the diaphragm is associated with a lowered risk of cervical cancer, probably because the diaphragm offers some protection against infection of the cervix with human papillomavirus, the virus that causes cervical cancer.

Disadvantages of the diaphragm:

- It is inconvenient, both because of the necessity for professional fitting and the need for insertion, removal, and cleaning.

- It can occasionally get dislodged during coitus.

- The diaphragm's failure rate is significantly greater than that of hormone-based methods and slightly greater than that of condoms. The failure rate is even higher for women who have previously given birth.

- It provides much less disease protection than condoms.

- The spermicide may cause irritation, which may increase the risk of STI transmission.

- Some women find that they develop urinary tract infections with diaphragm use.

Figure 9.7 Diaphragms have lost popularity in the United States but are still widely used elsewhere.

Variations on the diaphragm include the **cervical cap**, a smaller device that holds onto the cervix like a suction cup, and the **FemCap**, which has a raised brim that lies against the wall of the vagina, as well as a strap for easier removal.

In general, diaphragms and cervical caps may be acceptable options for women who need to be in charge of their own contraception but cannot or do not want to use hormone-based methods.

Spermicides are not very reliable when used alone

Some women use **spermicides** as their sole method of contraception. Spermicides are sperm-killing chemicals, usually nonoxynol-9, that destroy sperm with a detergent-like action that disrupts their cell membranes. Spermicides come in the form of contraceptive foams, jellies, creams, suppositories ("inserts"), sponges, or dissolvable films (**Figure 9.8**). They are placed deep in the vagina no more than 2 hours ahead of time (and preferably much closer to the time of coitus). Suppositories and some other spermicides need time to dissolve, so they should be inserted at least 10 minutes before coitus. (Follow the instructions carefully that come with the product.) All spermicides must be left in place for at least 6 hours afterward in order to complete the killing of sperm; therefore, the woman should not rinse out her vagina during this time. (Nor does she need to do so after that time has elapsed.) If a woman has coitus again during this 6-hour period, she must insert more spermicide before each act.

One spermicide contraceptive, the Today sponge, sits against the cervix like a diaphragm and thus presents a partial physical barrier in addition to releasing spermicide. It is said to be effective for multiple acts of intercourse over 24 hours.

Advantages of spermicides:

- They are readily available without a prescription.
- They are inexpensive.
- They have few side effects, except in the case of allergic reactions and irritation, which is mostly associated with frequent use.

Disadvantages of spermicides:

- Spermicides can hardly be recommended as the sole means of contraception because their failure rate is quite high—about 25% for the foams and

cervical cap   A small rubber or plastic cap that adheres by suction to the cervix, used as a contraceptive.

FemCap   A type of cervical cap that has a raised brim.

spermicide   A chemical that kills sperm, available as a contraceptive in a variety of forms, such as foams, creams, and suppositories.

FAQ

I'm sensitive to nonoxynol-9. Are there alternatives?

You may be able to find spermicides containing octoxynol-9. In Canada and Europe, spermicides containing benzalkonium chloride are available.

(A)
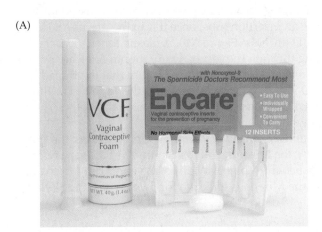

(B)
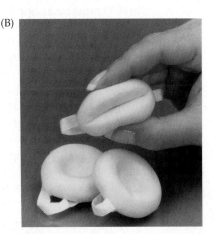

Figure 9.8 Spermicides come in a variety of forms. (A) Vaginal contraceptive foam, Encare inserts, and (B) the Today sponge contain the spermicide nonoxynol-9. (B courtesy of Allendale Pharmaceuticals, Inc.)

(A)

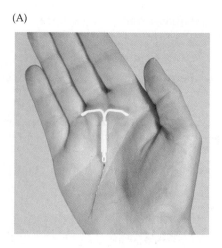

(B)

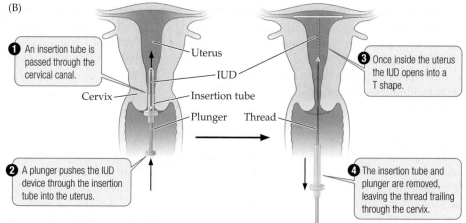

Figure 9.9 **IUD insertion** (A) The Mirena IUD. (B) Insertion of the Paragard IUD. The Mirena is inserted in a similar way.

possibly higher for the suppositories. They are better suited for use in combination with barrier methods. The Today sponge may be a little better, with a reported 16% failure rate in typical use.

• Spermicides, used alone, offer no significant protection against several sexually transmitted infections, including gonorrhea, chlamydia, and HIV. In fact, frequent use of spermicides (more than twice a day) can cause genital irritation or lesions, thus increasing the likelihood of acquiring or transmitting HIV and other infections (Planned Parenthood, 2014c).

Intrauterine devices require little attention

Intrauterine devices (**IUDs**), also called intrauterine contraceptives (IUCs), are plastic objects, often in the shape of a T, that are placed in the uterus. Their mechanism of action is not fully understood. They probably work by causing a low-grade inflammation of the uterus that interferes with sperm transport (Hatcher et al., 2011). Some IUDs also release progestins; we will discuss the contraceptive action of progestins in the section on hormone-based contraceptives below.

An IUD must be inserted by a trained health care professional. It is passed through the cervix while folded up inside an insertion tube; once it is in the uterus, the insertion tube is removed, and the IUD unfolds (**Figure 9.9**). A plastic thread, attached to the bottom of the T, is left trailing through the cervix. Every month after her period, the woman or her partner must feel inside the vagina to be sure that the thread is in place and that no part of the IUD itself has moved down into the vagina. The thread also helps in the removal of the IUD, which is done by a professional. (Women should never attempt to remove their own IUDs.)

Currently, only three models of IUDs are available in the United States: the **Paragard** (also called the "Copper-T"), the **Mirena**, and the **Skyla**. The Paragard releases small amounts of copper; it can be left in place for up to 12 years. The Mirena and Skyla IUDs release a progestin; the Mirena is effective for 5 years and the Skyla for 3 years.

Advantages of the IUD:

• All three IUDs are highly effective; in fact, they are nearly as effective as female sterilization.

---

intrauterine device (IUD)
A device placed in the uterus as a contraceptive. Also called intrauterine contraceptive (IUC).

Paragard A copper-containing IUD.

Mirena A hormone-releasing IUD that is effective for 5 years.

Skyla A hormone-releasing IUD that is effective for 3 years.

- Once inserted, IUDs are convenient and nonintrusive, requiring only the monthly thread check.
- With the Mirena and Skyla, menstrual cramping and bleeding may be reduced and sometimes abolished altogether.
- IUD contraception is reversible immediately on removal of the device.
- For reasons that are not well understood, IUDs offer significant protection against endometrial cancer (Hubacher & Grimes, 2002).

Disadvantages of the IUD:

- The one-time costs are fairly high—$500 to $1000—but they are covered by health insurance. There are no subsequent costs, unless condoms are added for disease prevention.
- Some cramping and irregular bleeding may occur, but these symptoms usually go away after a short period of use. With the Paragard, menstrual flows may increase and remain high as long as the device is in place.
- The progestin-releasing IUDs can have side effects such as nausea, headache, and breast tenderness. Most users experience no side effects, or side effects that are too mild to motivate users to have the IUDs removed (Hardeman & Weiss, 2014).
- IUDs offer no protection against STIs.
- IUDs do not prevent ectopic pregnancies as effectively as they prevent normal (intrauterine) pregnancies. Therefore, in the unlikely event that an IUD user becomes pregnant, the risk of the pregnancy being ectopic is increased (Sivalingam et al., 2011).

In the past there has been concern that IUDs might increase the risk of pelvic inflammatory disease (PID) and thus might endanger a woman's future fertility. Recent research, however, has been very reassuring: Aside from a small transient risk of infection associated with the actual insertion of the IUD, there is no increased risk of PID in IUD users (Hatcher et al., 2011). The American College of Obstetrics and Gynecology (ACOG) now considers IUDs appropriate for all healthy women, including adolescents, and the American Academy of Pediatrics also recommends IUDs (or Nexplanon—see page 285) for use by adolescents (American Academy of Pediatrics, 2014). Women who currently have an STI or PID should not receive an IUD, however.

Fewer than 1% of American women use IUDs, but they are much more popular in other nations: An estimated 85 million women use IUDs worldwide, and the great majority are very satisfied with them. Women who have had children and are thinking about sterilization may want to consider an IUD: It is reversible, less invasive, less expensive, and nearly as effective. IUDs may also be a suitable way to extend the intervals between pregnancies. Even young women who have not had children may want to consider an IUD, especially if STIs are not an issue or if it is used as a backup in combination with condoms. In short, the IUD is a form of contraception that deserves to be much more popular in the United States than it currently is—especially for women whose STI risk is low because they are in a monogamous relationship.

Hormone-Based Methods Are Easy to Use

Several different hormone-based contraceptive methods are available. They differ in the kinds and amounts of hormones they contain as well as in their form of delivery. Because oral contraceptives (pills) are so popular—they are the choice of more than 1 in 4 women who use any kind of contraception—and because they come in a number of significantly different formulations, we will devote most of our attention to them.

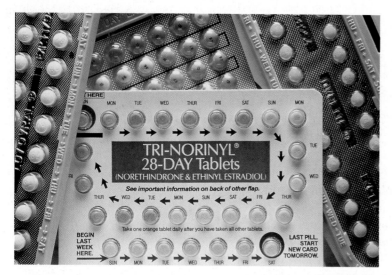

Figure 9.10 A variety of combination-type contraceptive pills in 28-day dispensers. Note the orange dummy pills, seen at the bottom of the photograph, for the 7 no-drug days.

FAQ

Is it safe to take St. John's wort while on the contraceptive pill?

No. St. John's wort, an unregulated medicinal herb used to treat depression, accelerates the breakdown of the pill's ingredients in the body and may therefore raise the likelihood of pregnancy.

constant-dose combination pill
An oral contraceptive regimen in which all pills (except any dummy pills) contain the same drug dosage.

triphasic combination pill An oral contraceptive regimen that varies the doses of estrogens and progestins around the menstrual cycle.

Contraceptive pills (**Figure 9.10**) contain either a combination of two hormones—an estrogen and a progestin—or just one hormone, a progestin. Both hormones are synthetic. Synthetic steroids are used because they are broken down in the body much more slowly than the natural hormones, so the pills need be taken only once a day. Nearly 4 in 10 of all U.S. undergraduate college women use contraceptive pills.

Combination pills offer health benefits

The most commonly used type of contraceptive pill is the **constant-dose** (or "monophasic") **combination pill**. Such pills, of which there are many different brands as well as generic versions, usually contain between 20 and 50 micrograms (mcg) of estrogen and between 0.1 and 1.0 milligrams (mg) of progestin. (Part of the reason for the varying progestin doses is that progestins vary in potency: 0.1 mg of one may be the equivalent of 1.0 mg of another.) Typically, a woman takes one pill a day for 21 days, followed by no pills, or inactive "dummy" pills, for 7 days. Some formulations that contain very low doses of hormones shorten the drug-free interval to 4 or even 2 days.

Another kind of combination pill is the **triphasic** (or "multiphasic") **combination pill** (examples are Ortho-Novum 7/7/7, and Tri-Norinyl). In these pills, the amounts and ratios of estrogen and progestin vary around the cycle, the idea being to minimize the total doses of hormones and decrease side effects. As with most constant-dose pills, triphasic regimens involve a 7-day drug-free interval. Triphasic pills are more expensive than constant-dose pills, but they have not been shown to be more effective or safer (Van Vliet et al., 2011).

One site of action of combination pills is the brain—specifically, the hypothalamic-pituitary control system, whose function is altered in ways that prevent ovulation. The other site is the cervix: The hormones in combination pills cause the cervix to secrete thick mucus that prevents sperm from entering the uterus.

Combination pills also cause development of the endometrium as would happen naturally during the postovulatory phase of the menstrual cycle. During the drug-free portion of the cycle, therefore, the endometrium breaks down and bleeding occurs. This bleeding simulates a natural menstrual period, although the menstrual flow may be less than a woman normally experiences.

Ovarian follicles develop during the drug-free interval, just as they do during the early days of a normal menstrual cycle. A woman is just as well protected from pregnancy during the drug-free days as during the rest of the cycle, because the further development of these follicles is suppressed as soon as the next cycle of pills begins. If a woman forgets to begin the next cycle of pills, however, the developing follicles can proceed to ovulation within a couple of days or so, potentially leading to pregnancy. Thus, if she is in doubt about the number of drug-free days that have elapsed, a woman does better to restart the cycle of pill-taking too early rather than too late.

Many physicians prefer to prescribe pills containing as little estrogen as possible (i.e., 20 mcg or thereabouts) because it is primarily the estrogen in combination pills that is responsible for the health risks associated with these products (see disadvantages below). Low-estrogen combination pills are as effective in preventing pregnancy as are higher-estrogen products. They do not always regulate the woman's menstrual cycle as effectively, however, and this can be a reason why some women discontinue low-estrogen combination pills.

Advantages of combination pills:

- With perfect use, combination pills are extremely reliable: Less than 1% of women who use these pills correctly will become pregnant per year. Unfortunately, it is easy to forget a pill or two. Thus, the typical-use failure rate is about 8%—significantly better than that for condoms or behavioral methods, but significantly worse than the rate for sterilization or the IUD. Remember, though, that a woman doesn't have to be "typical": She can come close to "perfection" by planning her pill-taking schedule carefully or by adding condoms to the mix.

- They are convenient and neither interfere with the spontaneity of sex nor diminish the sensations of coitus.

- They are easily reversible. Fertility should return to normal levels by 3 months after stopping the combination pill. (If the woman doesn't wish to become pregnant, she should use an alternative contraceptive technique immediately after stopping the pills.)

- They have very significant health benefits quite aside from the avoidance of pregnancy (which is a health benefit in itself). Use of combination pills for 10 years is associated with an 80% reduction in the risk of both ovarian and endometrial cancers, and this reduced risk persists for at least 20 years after stopping pill usage. Many women experience lighter menstrual flows and diminished or absent menstrual cramps, premenstrual symptoms,* and mid-cycle pain when on the pills. Pill usage also reduces the prevalence or severity of iron-deficiency anemia, endometriosis, ovarian cysts, acne, hirsutism (excessive facial and body hair), and noncancerous conditions of the breast. The health benefits of contraceptive pills can be so great, for many women, that some experts recommend their use even by women who don't need contraception.

As a 37-year-old smoker, this woman faces a heightened risk of experiencing serious side effects if she uses combination-type contraceptive pills.

Disadvantages of combination pills:

- They offer no protection against STIs, including HIV. (However, condoms can be added for disease protection.)

- The woman needs to remember to take the pills regularly each day.

- The method is not evident to the woman's partner unless he is present every day when she takes a pill. Thus, he has no objective assurance that the woman is employing effective contraception.

- The combination pill can have side effects. Frequently reported side effects include nausea, breast pain, increased breast size, irregular bleeding, abdominal pain, back pain, decreased vaginal lubrication, weight gain, blotchy discoloration of the skin, emotional lability (e.g., crying for little reason) or depression, and decreased or increased interest in sex. Nevertheless, controlled trials have found no increase in these problems in women using combination pills as compared with non-users (Grimes & Schulz, 2011). Regarding weight gain, a large longitudinal study conducted in Sweden found that women using the combination pill did gain weight over time, but no faster than women who did not use the pills (Lindh et al., 2011).

- Among the less common but more serious side effects are hypertension (increased blood pressure) and disorders of blood clotting, which can cause

---

* One combination pill, Yaz, is specifically FDA-approved for treatment of premenstrual symptoms, especially psychological ones. Yaz was tested against a placebo, however, and not against other combination pills, so it may not in fact be superior to other pills when used for this purpose. Yaz may be more likely to cause blood clots than other contraceptive pills (Gronich et al., 2011), and it has been the subject of much litigation.

FAQ

I threw up—did I lose the pill I took?

Episodes of vomiting or diarrhea may interfere with absorption of the pill. Abstain from coitus or use alternative protection until you've taken active pills for 7 days after you've returned to normal digestive health. With progestin-only pills, abstain or use alternative protection for 48 hours, while continuing to take pills as usual.

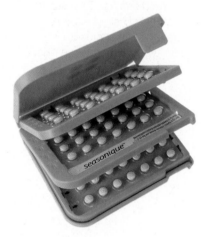

Seasonique contraceptive pills come in a 3-month pack. The seven yellow pills contain a low dose of estrogen only, allowing for a menstrual period during that week.

FAQ

I'm overweight—will contraceptive pills work for me?

Yes—excess weight has little if any effect on the pill's efficacy (Trussell et al., 2009).

Seasonale An extended-use contraceptive pill.

Seasonique An extended-use contraceptive pill.

Lybrel A contraceptive pill designed for complete elimination of menstrual periods.

extended-use regimen A regimen of contraceptive pills that allows for fewer or no menstrual periods.

heart attacks, strokes, and other ill effects. Although these complications are rare, they can be fatal. The risk for women over 35 who smoke is particularly high, and such women are usually advised not to use combination pills.

- Early formulations of the Pill, which included high doses of estrogens, moderately increased the risk of breast cancer. Current formulations have little or no effect on breast cancer risk (Marchbanks et al., 2012).

- Among women who use oral contraceptives for more than 2 years, the risk of glaucoma—a serious eye disorder—is twice the risk for non-users (American Academy of Ophthalmology, 2013). It is not certain that contraceptive pills actually cause glaucoma, but women who are or have been on the pills for extended periods should have periodic eye exams.

- Because the hormones can reach the baby via breast milk, nursing mothers should not use combination pills.

It's important for a user of combination pills to know what to do if she inadvertently misses taking a pill (Hatcher et al., 2011). If she has delayed taking a pill by less than 12 hours, she should simply take the missed pill immediately and then take the next pill at the normal time (even if that means taking two pills on one day). If she has delayed by more than 12 hours, she should do the same thing; in addition, however, she should use other protection or abstain from coitus until she has taken an active pill every day for 7 consecutive days. Furthermore, if she has had unprotected coitus during the week leading up to the day she realizes she's missed a dose, she should use emergency contraception (see page 289).

Continuous use of combination pills eliminates menstrual periods

The standard combination-pill regimen calls for a 7-day drug-free interval every month, which allows for withdrawal bleeding akin to a menstrual period. The only known function of a menstrual period, however, is to prepare the woman's uterus to receive and transport sperm. If pregnancy is not desired, menstrual periods offer no known health benefit and in fact present health concerns such as menstrual pain, premenstrual symptoms, and iron-deficiency anemia in some women.

A variation on the combination pill, **Seasonale**, was approved in 2003. A woman takes this pill continuously for 12 weeks, followed by a 7-day drug-free interval, and so on. Thus, she experiences 4 menstrual periods per year instead of 13. A slightly different version, **Seasonique**, contains the same drugs except that the pills taken during the 7-day interval contain a low dose of estrogen rather than being completely inert. Yet another recently introduced pill, **Lybrel** (Anya in Canada and Britain), contains the same drug combination as Seasonale or Seasonique, but at lower doses. Lybrel is packaged for continuous year-round use with no drug-free intervals at all. The approval of these drugs by the Federal Drug Administration (FDA) signaled the agency's understanding that menstrual suppression is not harmful in healthy women.

The main advantage of these **extended-use regimens** is the reduction in the number of menstrual periods, which should be a major benefit to women who have menstrual problems. On the other hand, there are potential disadvantages. For one thing, Seasonale, Seasonique, and Lybrel are expensive, especially for women who don't have medical insurance. With the advice of her doctor, a woman may be able to get the same benefit from an appropriate regimen of much cheaper, generic contraceptive pills.

More significantly, irregular spotting or breakthrough bleeding is common, especially in the early months of use, and can sometimes be quite severe. Also, a woman's total number of days of exposure to estrogen is greater than with conventional combination pills because of the reduced number (or total lack of) drug-free days. However, there is no clear evidence for differences—in health risks, health benefits, or contraceptive reliability—between extended-use and conventional combination pills.

progestin-only pill An oral contraceptive that contains progestin but no estrogen. Also called the "mini-pill."

Progestin-only pills have fewer side effects

The **progestin-only pill** contains a very low dose of a progestin and no estrogen. A brand called Ortho Micronor, for example, contains just 0.35 mg of the progestin norethindrone. Compare that with the 1.0 mg of norethindrone, plus an estrogen, in the combination pill Ortho-Novum 1/35 and its generic equivalents. How can a pill that contains so much less of an active ingredient have a reliable contraceptive effect? And if it does, why don't the combination pills go out of business? The answer is that the progestin-only pill works differently from the combination pill, requires greater care in use, and has some unique side effects.

The progestin-only pill does not reliably shut down ovulation, although it does do so in some women. It works mainly through its effect on the cervical mucus, making it thick and hostile to sperm transport. It may also make the endometrium resistant to implantation. These actions do not require such high levels of progestin as those needed to prevent ovulation, and they do not require the presence of estrogens.

The effects of each progestin-only pill last a very short time—barely 24 hours. Therefore, a woman who uses this method of contraception must be very careful not to miss taking the pills at the proper time. (If she does miss a dose by more than 3 hours, she should abstain from coitus or use alternative protection for 48 hours, while continuing to take her pills at the normal times. If she has had unprotected sex during the time she missed one or more pills, she should use emergency contraception—see page 289.) There is no 7-day drug holiday every month, as with the combination pill: The progestin-only pill must be taken every single day for as long as this method is used.

With perfect use, the progestin-only pill is just as reliable as the combination pill. There is a widespread assumption that it is less reliable in typical use because of the requirement for accurately timed dosing, but this has not been documented in clinical trials (Raymond, 2007).

Many of the advantages and disadvantages of progestin-only pills are similar to those of combination pills. Here we compare the two kinds of pills.

Advantages of progestin-only pills:

- Progestin-only pills lack the estrogenic side effects of combination pills (although weight gain can still be a problem). They are a good alternative for women who experience serious side effects with the combination pill or who fall into risk groups for whom the combination pill is contraindicated.

- Mothers who are breast-feeding their infants can use progestin-only pills, beginning 6 weeks after birth.

Disadvantage of progestin-only pills:

- Unlike the combination pill, the progestin-only pill tends to disrupt women's menstrual cycles. In fact, irregular bleeding and spotting are reasons some women discontinue this form of contraception. This effect is highly variable from woman to woman, however, and does not have major health consequences so long as total blood loss is not increased. Plenty of women continue to have regular menstrual cycles while using progestin-only pills—presumably, these are women in whom the pills do not suppress ovulation.

Given the wide variety of contraceptive pills available—with more coming on the market all the time—a woman who is considering this form of contraception should

---

FAQ

Can I get pregnant during my period?

The chances are low but increase somewhat toward the end of the period, especially if you have long periods or short or irregular cycles. Also, women sometimes experience light bleeding ("spotting") at midcycle. If you mistake this for your menstrual period and have unprotected sex, you could very easily become pregnant.

Depo-Provera An injectable form of medroxyprogesterone acetate, used as a contraceptive in women or to decrease the sex drive in male sex offenders.

Depo-SubQ Provera A form of Depo-Provera designed for subcutaneous injection.

consult with a knowledgeable professional who can recommend a pill suited to her needs and who can suggest appropriate changes if side effects crop up. Because a woman may take birth control pills for years, it is important that she keep herself well informed to ensure that she is taking the one best suited to her.

Hormones Can Be Administered by Non-Oral Routes

We now shift our attention to hormone-based contraceptives that are administered by some route other than by mouth. The methods we consider depend entirely on the slow release of hormones from some kind of "depot"—a reservoir that is inside or outside of the woman's body. The general advantage of non-oral over oral contraceptives is that they don't require taking a pill every day. Most women on contraceptive pills forget to take one from time to time, and this fact makes non-oral hormonal contraceptives more reliable in typical use.

A general disadvantage of the non-oral methods is that they have been in use for a much shorter time than pills, so their reliability and possible long-term effects (whether beneficial or harmful) have not been as thoroughly researched. It's reassuring that the hormones used are generally similar to those in contraceptive pills, but non-oral administration does introduce some functional differences. For example, the rate of drug delivery is usually more constant than with a once-a-day pill, and the drug does not pass through the liver before reaching the rest of the body, as happens with pills. These differences could affect the cumulative drug load experienced by hormone-sensitive tissues.

Depo-Provera lasts three months

The contraceptive **Depo-Provera** is administered by intramuscular injection or (in a different formulation called **Depo-SubQ Provera**) by subcutaneous injection (Goldberg & Grimes, 2007). Depo-Provera is a slow-release (depot) form of a progestin, medroyxprogesterone acetate (**Figure 9.11**). A single Depo-Provera injection provides contraception for 3 months. The subcutaneous formulation can be self-injected.

Depo-Provera is usually administered within a few days of the onset of menstruation to ensure that the woman is not pregnant. Repeat injections should not be delayed more than 2 weeks beyond the 3-month approved period, or pregnancy may occur.

Initially, a woman who uses Depo-Provera may experience irregular bleeding. After a year of use, however, at least 50% of women experience complete cessation of menstruation. Some women consider this a worrisome side effect, while others consider it a convenience.

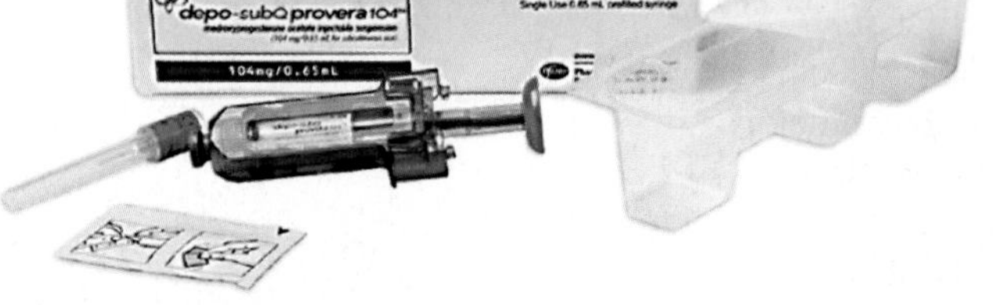

Figure 9.11 Depo-Provera is an injectable progestin that provides 3 months of contraceptive protection. This is the version for subcutaneous injection.

Advantages of Depo-Provera:

- With a typical-use failure rate of 3%, Depo-Provera is more reliable than contraceptive pills. Failures are almost always caused by neglecting to get injections on time—something that a conscientious woman should be able to avoid.

- It doesn't require the user to do anything aside from getting the injections. Teenagers can easily conceal their use of Depo-Provera from their parents, if that is necessary.

- As with progestin-only pills, the lack of an estrogen component may make it safer for some women.

- The eventual cessation of menstrual periods may appeal to women with menstrual problems.

Disadvantages of Depo-Provera:

- Depo-Provera offers no protection against STIs.

- Irregular, sometimes prolonged bleeding is a common problem, especially in the early months of use. Approximately 20% to 25% of women discontinue Depo-Provera during the first year for this reason. Less common side effects can include decreased sex drive, depression, liver damage, acne, and hair loss.

- Some women experience weight gain while on Depo-Provera: Adolescents and young women who are already overweight are particularly likely to do so (Burke, 2011).

- Once injected, Depo-Provera cannot be removed, so if side effects occur, it may take 3 months for them to go away.

- Although Depo-Provera is a fully reversible contraceptive, it may take as long as a year for a woman to return to full fertility after discontinuing the injections.

- Some women experience a loss of bone density while on Depo-Provera, which could increase their chances of experiencing bone fractures later in life. Because of this risk, the FDA issued a "black box warning" (a safety alert with extra emphasis) that advises against the use of Depo-Provera for more than about 2 years unless other birth control methods are inadequate (FDA, 2009). Women who are taking Depo-Provera should be sure they get adequate calcium in their diet, or they should take calcium supplements.

Ortho Evra A contraceptive patch.

Transdermal patches last a week

Transdermal patches look like large, square Band-Aids, but they contain a hormonal contraceptive that diffuses slowly into the body through the skin. The only transdermal contraceptive patch currently available in the United States is **Ortho Evra** (**Figure 9.12**). In Canada a similar patch is named the Evra patch.

Ortho Evra contains an estrogen and a progestin, so it's equivalent to a combination-type oral contraceptive. The woman has many choices as to where to place the patch, but she should not place it on a breast, and she should select a new location each time (to reduce the likelihood of skin reactions).

Each patch is left on for 1 week. The woman uses three in a row and then goes for a week without a patch, resulting in a 4-week cycle, just as with the combination pill. She will probably have (or begin) a period during the patch-free week. She should apply a new patch after the 1-week gap, even if her period hasn't yet stopped.

Generally, the advantages and disadvantages of Ortho Evra are similar to those of combination-type contraceptive pills, but there are a few differences:

Advantages of Ortho Evra (compared with combination pills):

- It requires fewer actions on the part of the user, and compliance is better.

- It is more evident in use and thus offers more assurance to the woman's partner that effective contraception is being used.

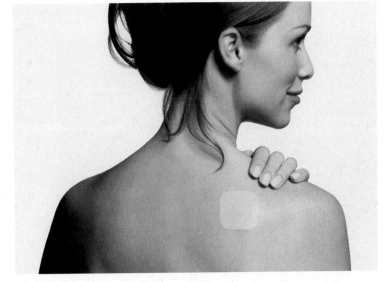

Figure 9.12 The Ortho Evra patch releases an estrogen-progestin combination that is absorbed through the skin.

NuvaRing A contraceptive ring placed in the vagina.

Disadvantages of Ortho Evra (compared with combination pills):

- There may be local skin reactions, which, if severe, could necessitate discontinuance.
- The patch may become loose or fall off, though this is uncommon.
- As with the combination pill, Ortho Evra is not advised for women over 35 who smoke.
- For women who weigh more than about 200 pounds (90 kg), the patch might not deliver enough hormones for reliable contraception. (This may be a particular concern when using the Canadian Evra patch, which contains 20% less estrogen than the U.S. version.)
- The risk of serious side effects, such as heart attacks, may be higher with the patch than with pills. At least a few deaths—and perhaps as many as 50—have been attributed to use of the patch, and sales fell by 80% after the FDA warned the public of the potential risk. A more recent study suggests that the increased risk is restricted to older women using the patch (Jick et al., 2010).
- Preliminary studies suggest that the Ortho Evra patch prevents the normal addition of bone mass in young women, possibly predisposing them to bone fractures in later life (Harel et al., 2010).

Vaginal rings last three weeks

Contraceptive hormones can be absorbed by the vagina, and the **NuvaRing** (**Figure 9.13**) takes advantage of this phenomenon. It is a flexible ring, about 2.1 inches (54 mm) in diameter, and it is placed deep within the vagina. (Its exact placement doesn't matter.) Like the combination pill and the Ortho Evra patch, it releases a combination of an estrogen and a progestin. The ring is kept in place for 3 weeks and then removed. There is then a week's break to allow for a menstrual period, and then a new ring is inserted.

As with the Ortho Evra patch, the hormones released by the NuvaRing spread through the whole body. Thus, the side effects of the NuvaRing are probably similar to those of combination pills and the Ortho Evra patch. These effects include an increased risk of blood clots.

Advantages of the NuvaRing (compared with Ortho Evra):

- The woman has to take fewer actions per month (two versus four), which may improve compliance.
  - There are no skin reactions.
  - Estrogen exposure is lower.
  - The ring is not visible.

Disadvantages of the NuvaRing (compared with Ortho Evra):

- The ring may occasionally slip out. (If it does, it should be washed in cool water and replaced.)
- It can cause vaginal irritation or a discharge.
- Some women or their partners report feeling the NuvaRing during coitus. However, the ring can be taken out beforehand; if so, it should be replaced within 3 hours.
- The NuvaRing must be protected from heat prior to use.

A new vaginal ring, developed by the Population Council, is usable for 12 months on a 3-weeks-on, 1-week-off basis. If the FDA approves the new ring, it will be marketed by Actavis.

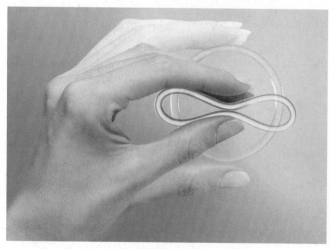

Figure 9.13 **The NuvaRing** is a flexible hormone-releasing ring that is placed in the vagina.

Implants are extremely reliable

Contraceptive implants are small rods containing contraceptive hormones that are implanted under the skin. They are as reliable as sterilization, even in typical use, but are fully reversible. The only implant currently available in the United States is **Nexplanon**. This is a flexible, matchstick-sized rod, which releases a progestin. A health care provider inserts the rod under the skin of the woman's upper arm—the procedure takes about 1 minute. The implant provides protection against pregnancy for at least 3 years.

> **Advantages of Nexplanon (compared with Ortho Evra or NuvaRing):**
>
> - It requires no action on the part of the user beyond the insertion and removal by a health care provider.
> - Because the user does not have to do anything, it is probably more reliable. It may be the most reliable of any hormonal contraceptive technique in typical use.
>
> **Disadvantages of Nexplanon (compared with Ortho Evra or NuvaRing):**
>
> - Initial expenses are higher—$400 to $800 for the exam, the Nexplanon, and the insertion. Removal costs about $100.
> - Because it contains a progestin only, irregular bleeding is common. Up to 30% of women have the implant removed by 2 years after implantation, often because of bleeding.
> - The reliability of Nexplanon in women weighing over 220 pounds (100 kg) is uncertain.

The Nexplanon contraceptive implant is barely visible under the skin of this woman's upper arm. In some women, it is not visible at all.

contraceptive implant A device implanted in the body that slowly releases a hormonal contraceptive.

Nexplanon An implanted hormonal contraceptive.

fertility awareness methods Contraceptive techniques that rely on avoiding coitus during the woman's fertile window. Also called rhythm methods or periodic abstinence methods.

Behavioral Methods Can Be Demanding

For couples who do not want to use "artificial" contraception of any kind for moral or other reasons, there are contraceptive options that depend simply on the manner or timing of sexual encounters. Although these options are considered by some to be more "natural" than other forms of contraception, and although they are inexpensive and free of the side effects of other methods, they make such demands on their users that their reliability in typical use is well below that of the best artificial methods.

In fertility awareness methods, couples avoid coitus during the fertile window

Nearly all pregnancies result from coitus during the fertile window, which is the 6-day period leading up to and including the day of ovulation. Therefore, a woman who avoids coitus during the fertile window will greatly decrease the likelihood of pregnancy (Jennings & Arevalo, 2007). **Fertility awareness methods** of contraception, sometimes called "rhythm methods" or "periodic abstinence methods," depend on knowing the time of the fertile window (**Figure 9.14**). Because this time cannot be known precisely, the woman has to be abstinent for more than 6 days, but the

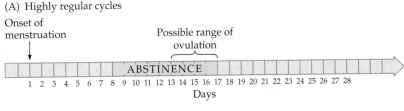

(A) Highly regular cycles

Onset of menstruation

Possible range of ovulation

ABSTINENCE

1 2 3 4 5 6 7 8 9 10 11 12 13 14 15 16 17 18 19 20 21 22 23 24 25 26 27 28

Days

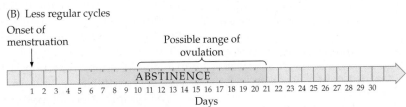

(B) Less regular cycles

Onset of menstruation

Possible range of ovulation

ABSTINENCE

1 2 3 4 5 6 7 8 9 10 11 12 13 14 15 16 17 18 19 20 21 22 23 24 25 26 27 28 29 30

Days

Figure 9.14 Timing methods make different demands on women, depending on the regularity of their cycles. (A) A woman who cycles quite regularly needs to abstain from unprotected sex for only about 9 days per month. (B) A woman who cycles irregularly may have to abstain for 16 days or more because of greater uncertainty as to when ovulation will occur.

Figure 9.15 CycleBeads may help women apply the standard days method of contraception. (Photo courtesy of Cycle Technologies, Inc.)

standard days method
A simplified fertility awareness calendar method of contraception usable by women with regular cycles.

calendar rhythm method
A fertility awareness method of contraception that takes account of variability in the length of a woman's menstrual cycles.

cervical mucus method A fertility awareness method of contraception that depends on observing changes in the cervical mucus.

sympto-thermal method
A fertility awareness method of contraception that depends on the measurement of basal body temperature and the testing of cervical mucus.

required length of abstinence varies from method to method and from woman to woman.

The **standard days method** is the simplest fertility awareness method: It is usable by women who have regular menstrual cycles lasting between 26 and 32 days. (About 3 out of 4 women meet this criterion.) Counting the first day of menstruation as day 1, the couple simply abstains from coitus on days 8 to 19 or uses condoms on those days.

Some women use CycleBeads, a set of color-coded beads (**Figure 9.15**) to help them keep track of the days on which they may and may not have unprotected sex: The woman pushes a rubber ring from bead to bead each day, and the color of the current bead tells her whether coitus is safe or not. Unfortunately, if a woman forgets to move the ring or moves it more than once in a day, she has no way of telling that she has made a mistake. Marking days on a calendar is better in that respect. Several smart-phone applications help women track their menstrual cycles and fertile days.

Some idea of the limitations of the standard days method comes from a prospective study of 221 healthy women that identified the dates of their ovulations precisely using hormonal tests on their urine (Wilcox et al., 2000). From these data the researchers calculated that the women stood at least a 10% chance of being within their fertile window for no less than 15 days of each cycle (days 6 to 21). In other words, the average woman using this method has to avoid unprotected coitus on about half of all days.

With the **calendar rhythm method**, the woman first keeps track of the length of her menstrual cycles over 6 to 12 cycles and notes the length of the shortest and longest cycles. She subtracts 18 from the number of days in her shortest cycle to identify the first no-sex day in her cycle, and she subtracts 11 from the number of days in her longest cycle to identify the last no-sex day in her cycle. So, for example, if her shortest cycle is 24 days and her longest cycle is 34 days, then she must abstain from unprotected sex from day 6 (24 minus 18) to day 23 (34 minus 11) of her cycle. This method is usable by women with cycles that are too irregular for the standard days method, but it rules out a large number of days. For these reasons it is not widely used or recommended.

Using the **cervical mucus method**, the woman monitors changes in her cervical mucus around the menstrual cycle. In the simplest version of the method, called the TwoDay method, the woman does not concern herself with what the mucus is like but simply notes each day whether she has *any* secretions. She asks herself two questions: "Do I have any secretions today?" and "Did I have any secretions yesterday?" If the answer to *both* questions is no, the chances of becoming pregnant are low. If the answer to *either* question is yes, the chances of becoming pregnant are high. The TwoDay method has been validated in large-scale studies; when it is used correctly, fewer than 4 out of 100 women will become pregnant per year (Institute for Reproductive Health, 2008), but typical-use failure rates are higher. Other methods, which involve checking the consistency of the mucus, are also available (Planned Parenthood, 2014a). These methods may allow for a few more safe days per cycle.

The **sympto-thermal method** combines awareness of cervical secretions with the monitoring of body temperature: The woman measures her basal body temperature every day with a digital thermometer before getting up. She stops having unprotected sex on the first day of cervical secretions. Her temperature drops slightly on the day of ovulation and then rises abruptly by at least 0.4°F (0.22°C) on the day after ovulation. Couples can resume unprotected sex 2 days (or, to be extra safe, 3 days) after the rise in temperature.* For both the cervical mucus and the sympto-thermal methods, the woman needs to have at least one detailed consultation with a family planning provider; otherwise she is likely to make mistakes while she is familiarizing herself with the techniques.

Advantages of fertility awareness methods:

- They are inexpensive or free.
- They are usable by people who consider other forms of contraception unacceptable.
- They avoid the side effects and health risks of other forms of contraception.
- They are completely and immediately reversible.

Disadvantages of fertility awareness methods:

- They are considerably less reliable than some other methods (see Table 9.1). This is a particular problem because users of these methods are often opposed to the use of abortion as a backup measure in the event pregnancy occurs. However, a couple who use a fertility awareness method to have children less frequently rather than to avoid pregnancy altogether might find the method perfectly adequate.
- They require a great deal of abstention from coitus. Of course, the couple could use an alternative form of contraception, such as condoms, during the fertile period.
- The more accurate fertility awareness methods (i.e., cervical mucus and sympto-thermal methods) are quite demanding of time and attention.
- With the calendar rhythm method, a woman needs to keep track of her cycles for at least 6 months before even beginning to use the method.
- There is no protection from STIs, including HIV, if condoms are not used.

The withdrawal method is simple but challenging

In the **withdrawal method** of contraception (also called "coitus interruptus"), the man simply removes his penis from the woman's vagina before he ejaculates. It sounds simple and foolproof, but estimates of its failure rate with typical use range from 18% to 27% per year (Kowal, 2007; Kost et al., 2008).

One reason for failure of the method is that some sperm may be present in the pre-ejaculatory fluid, or "pre-cum." Normally, this fluid contains no sperm, but it could contain some if the man ejaculated earlier, did not urinate afterward, and is now having sex for a second time. These sperm can be cleared out by urinating and wiping off the tip of the penis before the second episode.

If this were the only way in which the method could fail, it would probably be one of the most reliable forms of contraception. A more common reason for failure, however, is that the man doesn't pull out soon enough or far enough. He simply gets carried away, or he doesn't get sufficient warning of the impending ejaculation. In the process of withdrawal he may spill semen on the labia, from where some hardy sperm may make it all the way into the woman's reproductive tract.

Advantages of the withdrawal method:

- It requires no advance preparation.
- It is free and always available.

withdrawal method A method of contraception in which the man withdraws his penis from the vagina prior to ejaculation.

---

* An ovum survives for no more than 24 hours after ovulation. The 2- to 3-day wait is necessary because of uncertainty in the temperature determination and also because of the slight chance that a second ovulation might occur up to 24 hours after the first.

- It enables the man to take responsibility for contraception.
- It can be combined with condom use for extra protection.
- There are no medical side effects or health risks.

Disadvantages of the withdrawal method:

- Reliability is only moderate. It is not recommended for men who ejaculate prematurely or have difficulty telling when they are going to ejaculate, or for teenagers.
- It provides little or no disease protection.

Although we are not enthusiastic about the withdrawal method, given the availability of better contraceptive options, the method has been of great importance in global terms. It has played a key role in the "demographic transition"—the dramatic decline in family size that accompanies modernization. Thanks to the withdrawal method, countries such as Turkey have undergone demographic transition without the widespread adoption of medical contraceptive techniques (Ciftcioglu & Erci, 2009).

Noncoital sex is an excellent form of contraception for responsible couples who communicate well.

Noncoital sex can be used as a means of avoiding pregnancy

Knowing that only penile-vaginal intercourse can lead to pregnancy, many couples engage in other forms of sexual activity, including everything from kissing and fondling to body-on-body contact, hand stimulation of the genitals, and oral and anal sex. Sometimes these alternative forms of sex are promoted as a way to avoid pregnancy; in that context, they may be referred to as **outercourse**—the opposite of intercourse. (Some people exclude any form of penetrative sex from the definition of "outercourse.")

Advantages of noncoital sex:

- It is completely reliable if adhered to. (Semen must not be deposited near the vaginal opening, however, or transferred to the vagina after ejaculation by manual or body contact.)
- It is free and requires no preparation.
- It has none of the side effects that may be associated with other forms of contraception.
- For teens who have not yet engaged in coitus, it may be valued as a way to preserve "vaginal virginity."
- There is some STI protection, depending on what kinds of noncoital activities are engaged in. (Anal sex is at least as risky as coitus, and more so in the case of HIV.)

Disadvantages of noncoital sex:

- It misses out on what many heterosexual men and women consider the most pleasurable and intimate kind of sex.
- Some people may find it difficult to refrain from coitus once noncoital sex is under way, and if coitus does happen, contraception may not be available.

outercourse Sexual activities other than coitus, promoted as a means for preventing unwanted pregnancy and reducing the risk of STI transmission.

The main keys to successful outercourse are to decide what kinds of sex you will and will not engage in, discuss this with your partner *before* any sexual behavior begins, and have condoms ready in case plans change.

There Are Contraceptive Options after Unprotected Coitus

You got carried away. He said he was going to pull out. She said she was on the pill. The condom broke. The diaphragm slipped. Who cares how it happened? It's 11:00 PM, ovulation is tomorrow, and a few million sperm are racing toward the cervical canal. Your whole life—as a parent—is passing before your eyes. What next?

A woman's first impulse is to rinse out the contents of her vagina—preferably with something that will kill sperm. Coca-Cola is said to be the traditional favorite of teens.* Some women use water, a commercial douche, or spermicidal foam.

None of these methods is recommended as a regular form of postcoital contraception. Even the spermicidal foam, which is probably the best of the options just mentioned, is a highly unreliable way to prevent pregnancy when applied after coitus, because some sperm are likely to have gotten beyond the reach of the spermicide before it is ever placed in the vagina. For that reason, it would be best for a woman in this situation to assume that sperm have made it into her cervix. She now has two effective options to prevent pregnancy: taking pills, or having an IUD inserted.

The pill method is called **emergency contraception**. Two kinds of pills are available for this use. The first kind contains 1.5 mg of the progestin levonorgestrel.† Brand names are **Plan B One-Step** (Figure 9.16), **Next Choice One Dose**, and the generics My Way and Take Action. The main way by which levonorgestrel works is by preventing ovulation. It reduces the likelihood of pregnancy by 60% to 90% when taken up to 3 days after sex, and there is a weaker effect for 2 days after that. These pills can be bought by anyone, and they are usually found with other family planning products at drug stores. They do not cause the abortion of an already established pregnancy.

The other type of pill (brand name **ella**) contains a progesterone-blocking drug called ulipristal. It remains fully effective for up to 5 days after sex (Fine et al., 2010). Although the main action of ella is to block ovulation, the high efficacy at 5 days suggests that ella may also prevent implantation. (The reason for thinking this is that, by 5 days after sex, ovulation and fertilization will have already occurred in most cases.) A prescription for ella is required, whatever the woman's age, and it is considerably more expensive than the levonorgestrel pills—about $60 including an online prescription.

The efficacy of all these emergency contraceptive pills is reduced in overweight or obese women. The levonorgestrel pills appear to lose their efficacy at a BMI of about 26, while ella retains some efficacy up to a BMI of about 35‡ (Office of Population Research, 2014). Heavier women should not try to compensate by taking higher doses unless this is recommended by new guidelines.

Given that Plan B One-Step and the other versions of levonorgestrel can be bought by anyone without a prescription, it may make sense for sexually active women to buy a dose ahead of need. That way it can be taken quickly after unprotected sex, when it is most likely to be effective. Generic versions can be bought online for about $20.

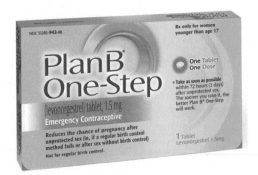

Figure 9.16   Plan B One-Step is a progestin, levonorgestrel, specifically packaged for use as an emergency contraceptive.

FAQ

Can I use my regular contraceptive pills for emergency contraception?

Yes—Planned Parenthood's website has a list of pills with dosages and recommendations for how to take them.

FAQ

I don't have sex very often. Could I just rely on emergency contraception?

It is not recommended. Emergency contraceptive pills are considerably less reliable than other methods of hormonal contraception and can be more expensive.

emergency contraception
Use of high-dose contraceptives to prevent pregnancy after unprotected sex.

Plan B One-Step   A progestin used for emergency contraception.

Next Choice One-Dose   A progestin used for emergency contraception.

ella   A form of emergency contraception that is effective for 5 days after sex.

---

* The 2008 Ig Nobel Prize—an award honoring comical science—was bestowed on two groups who studied whether Coca-Cola is an effective spermicide. One group found that it is, the other found that it isn't. One thing's for sure: It leaves a sticky mess.

† Note that this is a far higher dose of levonorgestrel than the *microgram* amounts that are contained in some regular contraceptive pills.

‡ For a 5 foot 5 inch (1.63 m) woman, a BMI of 26 corresponds to a weight of 152 pounds (69 kg), and a BMI of 35 corresponds to a weight of 204 pounds (92.5 kg).

A completely different strategy to prevent implantation is to have an IUD inserted. The Paragard IUD is used for this purpose. Of course, this is a much more expensive and inconvenient option than taking pills. However, it is nearly 100% reliable—only ten failures have ever been reported. The IUD can be inserted up to 5 days after coitus, or even later so long as it is not more than 5 days after ovulation. (With a 10-day wait, it may work by inducing an early abortion.) Furthermore, the IUD can be left in place, in which case it will provide very reliable contraception for up to 12 years. Alternatively, it can be removed as soon as the woman has had her next menstrual period. The Paragard IUD is not affected by a woman's body weight, so it is a good option for heavier women.

Sterilization Is Highly Reliable

Sterilization is a surgical procedure that puts an end to fertility. Various procedures have this effect. Here we focus on surgical procedures that are used to terminate fertility *electively* in otherwise healthy men and women: vasectomy in men and tubal sterilization in women. Both methods work by preventing sperm from reaching ova.

Sterilization is a serious issue for any individual or couple. Although, as we'll see below, sterilization procedures can be successfully reversed in some cases, there is no guarantee of success, so people who choose sterilization should be clear in their minds that they want to lose their fertility permanently. People select sterilization under a number of circumstances:

- They simply don't want children and are certain they will never change their minds. (However, health care providers may be reluctant to sterilize healthy young men or women who don't have children.)
- They have had enough children and are confident that they will want no more, even if they remarry or their children die.
- A medical condition makes pregnancy a serious health hazard.
- They have a significant likelihood of passing on a serious congenital disorder.

The majority of people who choose sterilization are married couples with children. Among heterosexual couples in the United States who use contraception, about 27% rely on female sterilization, and 9% rely on male sterilization (Bartz & Greenberg, 2008). One in six American men over age 35 has had a vasectomy.

Vasectomy is a brief outpatient procedure

Vasectomy is a very simple and safe procedure that is usually done under local anesthesia (**Figure 9.17**). The physician locates the vas deferens inside the scrotal sac, makes a small incision, and cuts out a short segment of it. The free ends are tied, cauterized, or sealed with clips to prevent them from rejoining. The incision is then closed with a couple of stitches, and the procedure is repeated on the other side. In an alternative "no scalpel" procedure, the scrotal skin is pierced with sharp-tipped forceps. Because the incision is so small, it needs no stitches and heals faster. (See Web Resources for a full-length video of the procedure.) With either method the man can go home directly after the procedure.

The man should refrain from strenuous exercise for a couple of days after surgery. He can usually resume sexual activity in about a week. He is not yet sterile, however, because sperm remain in the portion of each vas deferens above the cut, so he must continue to use another contraceptive method such as condoms. It takes about 15 to 20 ejaculations, over a period of about 3 months, to get rid of these sperm. The man's semen must be checked microscopically for absence of sperm before he can engage in unprotected coitus.

sterilization A surgical procedure to eliminate fertility in either sex.

vasectomy A male sterilization technique that involves cutting or tying off the vas deferens from each testicle.

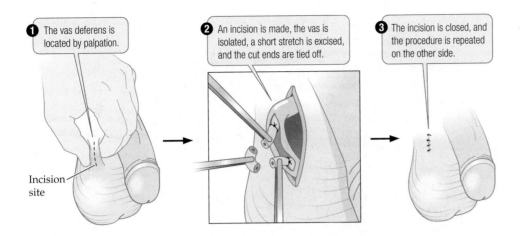

❶ The vas deferens is located by palpation.

❷ An incision is made, the vas is isolated, a short stretch is excised, and the cut ends are tied off.

❸ The incision is closed, and the procedure is repeated on the other side.

Incision site

Figure 9.17   Vasectomy is a relatively simple procedure that can be performed under local anesthesia. (See **Web Activity 9.1: Vasectomy.**)

Complications of the procedure can include bleeding, infection, and—in about 18% of cases—the appearance of lumps formed by leaked sperm. These usually clear up by themselves, but they can be treated surgically if necessary.

Vasectomy costs between $250 and $1000 for the complete treatment—that is, the medical exam, the procedure, the follow-up, and the semen exam. (Some insurance plans may cover vasectomy, but they are not required to do so under Obamacare.) Vasectomy is extremely reliable; early failure can result if the man resumes unprotected sex too soon, and late failure can result from surgical errors, spontaneous reconnection of a vas deferens, or other unusual causes.

About the only way that vasectomy can harm a man's sex life is if he feels psychologically damaged by the procedure. For most men, it's quite the opposite: They and their partners are able to enjoy sex more because they no longer have to worry about contraception or pregnancy. The procedure has no effect on sexual desire, the ability to perform, testosterone levels, or secondary sexual characteristics. Because sperm form such a small component of semen, there is no noticeable reduction in the volume of the ejaculate.

Of course, there are men who for one reason or another end up wanting the procedure reversed. In an operation called **vasovasostomy**, the surgeon, using an operating microscope, locates the two cut ends of each vas and sews them together. The procedure is expensive, however, and has no more than about a 50% chance of success. Quite aside from the difficulty of getting a functional reconnection, the man may have formed antibodies against his own sperm, which interfere with sperm production.

Some men deposit a sperm sample in a sperm bank prior to the vasectomy procedure, with the hope that they can become fathers via artificial insemination in case they change their minds. There is no assurance that this will be possible, however, as there will be only a limited amount available.

Advantages of vasectomy:

- It is almost 100% reliable.
- Once accomplished, it is totally convenient and free.
- Vasectomy is cheaper and safer than tubal sterilization (a sterilization technique performed on women).

Disadvantages of vasectomy:

- Vasectomy is not reliably reversible. Attempts at reversal are very expensive.
- The up-front expenses are considerable if they are not covered by insurance.
- There is no STI protection.

vasovasostomy   Surgery to reverse a vasectomy.

Figure 9.18   Tubal sterilization
(A) Laparoscopic procedure for tubal
ligation. (B) A portion of the oviduct
may be excised and the ends tied off,
as shown here, or the oviduct may be
closed off by cauterization or the application of clips. (See **Web Activity 9.2:
Tubal Sterilization**.)

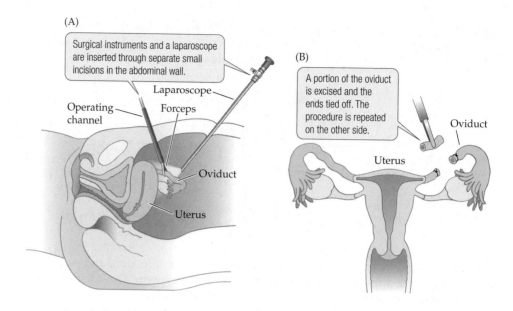

Tubal sterilization is more invasive and expensive

Female sterilization (**tubal sterilization**) is quite analogous to male sterilization: The
oviducts are tied and cut (**tubal ligation**), cauterized, or closed off with clips or other
devices (**Figure 9.18**). The result is that ova and sperm cannot meet. Tubal sterilization
is a more invasive procedure than vasectomy, however, since it involves entering the
abdominal cavity. Many sterilizations are done after childbirth or after an abortion,
while the woman is in a surgical setting. (She has to give consent for the procedure.)
Female sterilization costs from $1500 to $2500, or up to $6000 if the procedure requires
hospitalization, but it is covered by medical insurance.

There are two main procedures for tubal sterilization, called laparoscopy and mini-
laparotomy. These procedures differ not so much in what is done to the oviducts,
but in the surgical approach. In a **laparoscopy**, no extended incision is made in the
abdominal wall. Instead, a viewing instrument (laparoscope) is inserted through
one tiny incision, and an instrument to clamp or cut the oviducts is inserted through
another. Sometimes the two instruments are combined into one, and only a single
incision is made. The laparoscopic procedure is less stressful than mini-laparotomy,
requires no stitches afterward, and can be done under either local or general anesthesia. Often, the woman can go home the same day.

In a **mini-laparotomy** or "mini-lap," a small scalpel incision about 1 inch (2.5 cm)
long is made somewhere between the navel and the mons pubis. The oviducts are
located and pulled to the incision, where they are tied and cut, or closed with clips,
and then allowed to slip back into their normal position. The incision is then sewn
up. Recovery takes a few days.

Tubal sterilization, like any internal surgery, can occasionally cause hemorrhage or
infection. General anesthesia, if used, also carries some risk. These or other complications occur in 1% to 4% of cases, but they can usually be dealt with effectively. In the
United States there are one to four deaths for every 100,000 tubal sterilizations. In
general, one can say that tubal sterilization is a very safe procedure, but not quite as
safe as vasectomy. In some cases, tubal sterilization can be reversed by microsurgical
techniques, but the operation is very expensive, and success is quite unpredictable.

Like vasectomy, tubal sterilization has no effect on other aspects of sexual functioning. Menstrual cycles usually continue as before, and a woman's interest in sex
and her physiological reactions during sex are undiminished. She may enjoy sex
more because she is no longer concerned about pregnancy.

tubal sterilization   Any procedure
that prevents sperm transport in the
oviducts.

tubal ligation   A procedure in which
the oviducts are blocked by tying
them off.

laparoscopy   Abdominal surgery,
such as tubal sterilization,
performed through a small incision
with the aid of a laparoscope (a
fiber-optic viewing instrument).

mini-laparotomy   Abdominal
surgery, such as tubal sterilization,
performed through a short incision.

The advantages and disadvantages of tubal sterilization are very similar to those of vasectomy, but there are a few important differences between the two.

Advantages of tubal sterilization (compared with vasectomy):

- The woman is sterile regardless of who she has sex with.
- For unknown reasons, tubal sterilization is associated with a 39% decrease in a woman's risk of ovarian cancer, and the risk of endometrial cancer is also reduced (Pollack et al., 2007).

Disadvantages of tubal sterilization (compared with vasectomy):

- Tubal sterilization is more invasive and therefore slightly riskier.
- It is more expensive.
- Recovery is longer (but shorter than with most other surgeries).

A newer method of tubal sterilization is called **Essure**. In this method, the provider passes a tube through the cervix to access the oviducts. (Because no skin incision is involved, this method may be referred to as "nonsurgical"; however, it is certainly an invasive procedure.) Small metal coils are then inserted into the oviducts: These coils do not effectively block the oviducts by themselves, but they provoke a tissue reaction that does gradually block them. It takes about 3 months after the procedure for the blockage to be complete, and an X-ray procedure must be performed to check that this has happened. Thus, unlike the situation with traditional tubal ligation, the woman must refrain from unprotected sex for about 3 months after the procedure. The Essure procedure can be performed in a doctor's office without general anesthesia.

Disabled Persons Have Special Contraceptive Needs

Many men and women with physical and mental disabilities are sexually active, but they may face special problems related to contraception (Kaplan, 2006). If they have a movement disorder, arthritis, multiple sclerosis, or a spinal cord injury, they may not be able to put on a condom, insert a diaphragm, or check an IUD. Oral contraceptives are not advisable for women with reduced mobility, because they may raise the risk of blood clots. IUDs are not advisable if the woman does not have normal sensation in the pelvic area. If the disabled person has a nondisabled partner, the couple may agree to leave contraception to that partner. That may not be an option if the disabled person is not in a steady relationship, however.

Contraception is a particularly important issue for intellectually disabled female adolescents and young women, who face a heightened risk of sexual abuse and who may not be able to comply with the usual contraceptive regimes. Careful counseling, repeated over time and tailored to the particular young woman's needs, is often required. Progestin hormone injection methods may be particularly useful for these women; the reduction in menstrual periods associated with these contraceptives may be an advantage in itself. Still, the ethical requirement for informed consent applies to intellectually disabled persons just as it does to other people.

Several Safe Abortion Procedures Are Available

An **induced abortion** is the intentional termination of a pregnancy. In this chapter we use the term "abortion" to refer exclusively to induced abortions rather than spontaneous abortions (miscarriages) (**Box 9.3**).

An abortion may be induced in order to safeguard the mother's health (**therapeutic abortion**) or because the woman chooses not to carry the fetus to term (**elective abortion**). An elective abortion may be performed because the pregnancy was

Essure A method of tubal sterilization that blocks the oviducts by use of metal coils.

induced abortion An abortion performed intentionally by medical or surgical means.

therapeutic abortion An abortion performed to safeguard a woman's life or health.

elective abortion An abortion performed in circumstances when the woman's health is not at risk.

Box 9.3 Society, Values, and the Law

Abortion in the United States: Key Statistics

- Twenty-one percent of all established pregnancies in the United States (aside from those that end in miscarriage) are terminated by abortion. There were 1.02 million abortions performed in 2011, a 13% drop from 2008. The rate has been dropping steadily over the last 30 years. Assuming the continuation of current rates, about 1 in 3 American women will have an abortion by the age of 45.

- Most abortions are done for social, not medical, reasons (see table).

- Young, single women are the major recipients of abortion. Eighteen percent of all abortions are performed on teenagers.

- Minority women are disproportionately represented among women who have abortions.

- About half of all women who have abortions were using some kind of contraceptive technique (though probably not perfectly) when they became pregnant.

- Thirty-three percent of all abortions are performed within the first 6 weeks of pregnancy, and 89% within the first 12 weeks.

- Fewer than 3 in 1000 legal abortions result in a complication requiring hospitalization. Legal abortion performed by 8 weeks of pregnancy has a 1 in 1,000,000 chance of causing the mother's death. Abortion performed at or after 21 weeks has a 1 in 11,000 chance of causing the mother's death.

- Abortion is legal in all U.S. states, but 27 states have at least 4 major restrictions on abortion. These include laws targeted at abortion clinics, intended to force them out of operation.

Most Important Reason Given for Abortion

Reason given	Percentage of women
Not ready for a(nother) child; timing is wrong	25
Can't afford a baby now	23
Have completed my childbearing; have other people depending on me; children are grown	19
Don't want to be a single mother; am having relationship problems	8
Don't feel mature enough to raise a(nother) child; feel too young	7
Would interfere with education or career plans	4
Physical problem with my health	4
Possible problems affecting the health of the fetus	3
Was a victim of rape	<0.5
Husband or partner wants me to have an abortion	<0.5
Parents want me to have an abortion	<0.5
Don't want people to know I had sex or got pregnant	<0.5
Other	6
Total	100

After Finer et al., 2005; Guttmacher Institute, 2014a.

not wanted (e.g., contraception failed or was not used, or the pregnancy resulted from rape) or because the fetus is known or suspected to suffer from some defect or disease. In some countries, but not in the United States, abortions are commonly performed because the child is of the nonpreferred sex—usually female. India and China are most frequently mentioned in this regard.

The moral status of abortion, and the degree to which governments should restrict or regulate the practice, are highly contentious issues in contemporary society. In this chapter, we first describe the technology of abortion and then discuss the social conflicts that surround it.

Abortions can be performed either by physically removing the fetus and its membranes from the uterus (**surgical abortion**) or by administering drugs that cause the

surgical abortion An abortion induced by a surgical procedure.

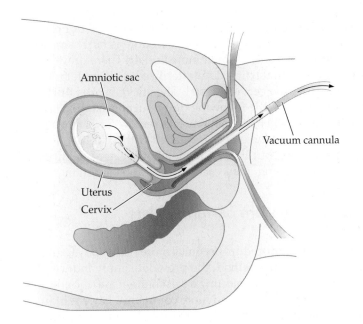

Figure 9.19 **Vacuum aspiration** is the abortion procedure most commonly used in the first trimester.

death and expulsion of the fetus in a manner that resembles a miscarriage (**medical abortion**). In the United States, surgical abortions are more common than medical abortions, but 1 in 4 abortions performed by 9 weeks of age are medical (American College of Obstetricians and Gynecologists, 2014).

Vacuum aspiration is the standard first-trimester surgical method

Surgical abortions are carried out in different ways depending on the age of the embryo or fetus. During the first trimester, most surgical abortions are performed by **vacuum aspiration** (**Figure 9.19**). This procedure—which accounts for the majority of all abortions in the United States—is done on an outpatient basis with local anesthesia or sedation.

The health care provider first dilates the cervix by passing a series of metal rods of increasing diameter through the cervical canal. Once the cervix has been dilated, the provider passes a cannula (tube) into the uterus. The other end of the cannula is connected to a pump that applies suction. (With very early abortions, suction may be applied by hand, using a syringe.) The suction breaks up the embryo or fetus and its membranes and removes them from the uterus. This process takes less than 5 minutes. The extracted tissue is examined to ensure that the abortion is complete. The provider may insert a curette (a metal loop) to clean the walls of the uterus of any remaining tissue.

The woman remains in the clinic or doctor's office for an hour or so before being allowed to go home. She may experience some bleeding and cramping over the following week or two. The woman should refrain from coitus for 2 weeks to allow the cervix to close fully. Complications are rare but can include heavy bleeding, infection, or perforation of the uterus.

Dilation and evacuation is used early in the second trimester

Vacuum aspiration abortions can be performed up to about 14 weeks of pregnancy, but the majority of second-trimester abortions are performed using a different procedure, called **dilation and evacuation** (**D&E**). Most D&Es are done in the period from 13 to 16 weeks, but they are sometimes done up to 20 weeks or even later.

medical abortion An abortion induced with drugs. Also called medication abortion.

vacuum aspiration An abortion procedure in which the conceptus is destroyed and removed by suction.

dilation and evacuation (D&E) A procedure involving the opening of the cervix and the scraping out of the contents of the uterus with a curette (spoonlike instrument). D&E may be done as an abortion procedure or for other purposes.

saline-induced abortion An abortion induced by use of a strong salt solution.

hysterotomy An abortion performed via a surgical incision in the abdominal wall and the uterus.

mifepristone An anti-progesterone drug used to induce abortion. Also known as RU-486.

D&Es are usually performed under general anesthesia in a hospital but may be performed with sedation in an outpatient setting. The procedure is fairly similar to vacuum aspiration, but the cervix has to be dilated more widely. Therefore, a 2-day procedure is commonly employed. On the first day, a sterilized stick made from the seaweed *Laminaria* is inserted into the cervical canal. The stick absorbs fluid and expands, gently opening the cervix. On the following day, a suction cannula is used to remove fluid and some tissue, and then the remainder is removed with forceps or other instruments. Finally, the lining of the uterus is cleaned with a curette.

The D&E is a very safe procedure, but it has a somewhat greater likelihood of complications, such as excessive bleeding, than vacuum aspiration abortion.

Induced labor and hysterotomy are performed late in the second trimester

Late in the second trimester, the D&E procedure becomes more risky, and alternative surgical techniques may be used. In one method, the provider simply induces premature labor. This may be accomplished by injecting a salt solution into the amniotic sac (**saline-induced abortion**). Alternatively, and more commonly, labor is induced by administration of a prostaglandin. The drug is either injected into the amniotic sac or administered by means of a vaginal suppository. Contractions usually begin within an hour or so, and the fetus is expelled within 48 hours.

If the woman's health is such that labor seems risky, the fetus may be removed by means of a surgical incision in the abdomen and the uterus (**hysterotomy**). Neither induced labor nor hysterotomy is performed very frequently—each of them accounts for less than 1% of all abortions in the United States, and some states impose legal restrictions on these procedures.

Medical abortions are two-step procedures

Medical abortions can be performed anytime up to 7 to 9 weeks after the start of the last menstrual period. The drug most commonly used is **mifepristone** (trade name Mifeprex; also known as RU-486). Mifepristone blocks progestin receptors—the cellular molecules that recognize and respond to progesterone and similar hormones. Recall that progesterone, secreted by the corpus luteum and later by the placenta, is required to keep the uterus in a state capable of sustaining pregnancy (**Figure 9.20**). In the presence of mifepristone, the progestin receptors do not "see" progesterone, so

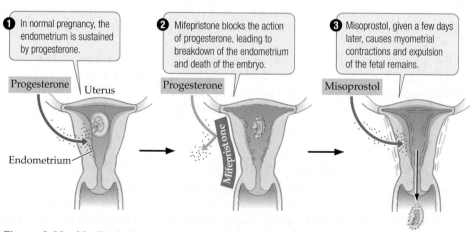

Figure 9.20 Medical abortion with mifepristone and misoprostol.

it is as if progesterone is absent. The endometrium begins to break down and ceases to support the fetus, which consequently detaches from the endometrium and dies.

In about 5% of women the remains of the fetus and its membranes are expelled by spontaneous uterine contractions. In most cases, however, it is necessary to give a second drug, the prostaglandin **misoprostol**, to induce contractions. Misoprostol should be taken orally and not, as was earlier recommended by some clinics, by being inserted in the vagina. (Use of this latter route has been tentatively linked with fatal infections in a few women.) The misoprostol is usually taken 2 or more days after the mifepristone. Bleeding begins within 24 hours of taking misoprostol, and the entire abortion process takes no more than a few days. A follow-up visit to the clinic is necessary to ensure that the abortion is complete.

Under a number of circumstances, women should not use mifepristone, or they must take special steps to allow them to use the drug safely. For that reason, a woman should not attempt to acquire the drug through any means that does not include proper medical assessment. If she cannot take mifepristone, she may still be able to have a medical abortion by use of a different drug, **methotrexate**. This drug, which is usually given by injection, kills rapidly dividing cells, and thus it has a direct toxic effect on the fetus. It must be followed by misoprostol to induce contractions. The abortion process takes longer with methotrexate than with mifepristone (American College of Obstetricians and Gynecologists, 2014).

There is a small difference in reliability between the two methods: Mifepristone works in about 96% of cases, and methotrexate works in 90% of cases. If either procedure should fail, the woman should have a surgical abortion because the fetus may well have been seriously damaged.

Advantages of medical abortion (compared with surgical abortion):

- It requires no invasive surgical procedure.
- It can be performed earlier than surgical abortion—as soon as pregnancy is confirmed.
- The abortion may seem more like a natural miscarriage.

Disadvantages of medical abortion (compared with surgical abortion):

- Medical abortions take longer. A surgical abortion is over within minutes, whereas a medical abortion typically takes a few days and requires a total of two or three visits to the provider.
- Medical abortions cannot be performed after 7 to 9 weeks from the beginning of the last menstrual period.
- Medical abortions generally cost $100 to $300 more than surgical abortions.
- For anyone who is trying to conceal the abortion, having the abortion at home may be a disadvantage.
- Another disadvantage of having the abortion at home is the possibility of seeing the fetal remains, which may disturb some women.

Abortions do not cause long-lasting ill effects

Neither medical nor early surgical abortion impairs a woman's fertility (Paul & Stewart, 2007) or causes any problems during subsequent pregnancies (Virk et al., 2007). There may be some increased risk of spontaneous abortion during pregnancies subsequent to a second-trimester D&E abortion.

Immediately after an abortion, a woman may feel sadness, stress, relief, or some other emotion. There has been a controversy over the question of whether abortion causes any harmful long-term psychological effects. Based on the best evidence, the answer to this question is "no." We discuss the issue in more detail in **Box 9.4**.

misoprostol A prostaglandin used in medical abortions.

methotrexate A drug used in some medical abortions.

Box 9.4 Controversies

Does Abortion Traumatize Women?

Pro-life activists have frequently claimed that a woman who chooses to terminate her pregnancy can expect to suffer serious and long-lasting psychological harm. These consequences, it's alleged, include regret, guilt, anger, insomnia, depression, anxiety, emotional withdrawal, drug dependence, and intrusive thoughts about the "missing child" (Rue, 1997; Coleman et al., 2009). This constellation of symptoms has been given the name "post-abortion syndrome."

Does the "post-abortion syndrome" really exist? Julia Steinberg of the University of California, San Francisco, and Lawrence Finer of the Guttmacher Institute examined data from the National Comorbidity Survey, which is a large-scale field survey of mental health in the United States (Steinberg & Finer, 2011). Women in this study who had had an abortion were indeed more likely to suffer psychological problems, compared with women who had never had an abortion. However, this association resulted from the fact that certain influences—such as a history of abuse or mental illness—predisposed women both to having an abortion and to suffering mental illness after the abortion. There was a correlation, in other words, but not a causation: Having an abortion did not in itself increase the likelihood of psychological problems.

Another study, conducted in Denmark (where researchers can access centralized health records for the entire population), found that women who had an abortion were much more likely to have psychological problems *before* the abortion than were women who carried a pregnancy to term. The women who had an abortion experienced no significant increase in psychological problems after the abortion. The women who delivered their babies, on the other hand, *did* experience an increase in psychological problems after the birth of their child, perhaps caused by postpartum depression (see Chapter 8) or by the stresses of child-rearing (Munk-Olsen et al., 2011). These findings again

According to abortion-rights opponents, many women feel long-term guilt and other psychological symptoms after undergoing an abortion, but research does not bear this out.

indicate that the higher rate of psychological problems after abortion is simply a continuation of a history of psychological problems from earlier in the women's lives, not an effect of the abortion itself. Another study focused on American teenagers also failed to find any effect of abortion on the prevalence of depression or low self-esteem (Warren et al., 2010).

All in all, the only reasonable conclusion from the numerous studies on the "post-abortion syndrome" is that the syndrome does not exist, yet even as a fiction it has had significant effects on the law and public policy (Kelly, 2014). In at least 20 U.S. states, abortion providers are legally required to provide a consultation in which they inform patients of possible psychological responses to abortion. In 7 of these states, this information covers only the purported negative psychological effects, such as those included in the "post-abortion syndrome." Thus, women in these states are being needlessly exposed to messages that may cause them anxiety.

Americans Are Divided on Abortion, but Most Favor Restricted Availability

pro-life Opposed to abortion; believing that abortion should be illegal under most or all circumstances.

pro-choice Believing that abortion should be legal under some or all circumstances.

In its landmark 1973 decision in *Roe v. Wade*, the U.S. Supreme Court ruled that states could not enact outright bans on abortions performed before the age of fetal viability, which was taken to mean before the end of the second trimester of pregnancy. Since that time, Americans have remained divided on the issue of abortion.

The abortion debate is often portrayed as if there are simply two opposing camps: **pro-life**, meaning people who believe that elective abortion is always wrong and that it should be a criminal offense, and **pro-choice**, meaning people who believe that

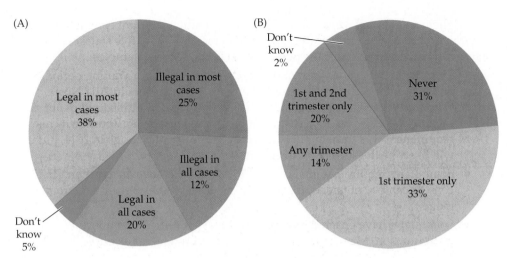

(A)

Legal in most cases 38%

Illegal in most cases 25%

Illegal in all cases 12%

Legal in all cases 20%

Don't know 5%

(B)

Don't know 2%

1st and 2nd trimester only 20%

Any trimester 14%

Never 31%

1st trimester only 33%

Figure 9.21   Americans' views on abortion are not as simple as "pro-life versus pro-choice." (A) Only minorities of Americans have extreme opinions in response to the question "Under what circumstances should abortion be legal?" (B) Abortion is considered more acceptable when it is done early: The graph shows the percentage of Americans who believe abortion should be permitted during different time intervals within pregnancy. (Data from PollingReport.com, 2014.)

women should be allowed to make all abortion decisions for themselves. When Americans are asked "Do you consider yourself pro-life or pro-choice?" most will identify themselves as one or the other, with roughly the same number of people taking each point of view. In a 2013 Gallup poll, for example, 45% of Americans identified as pro-choice and 48% as pro-life (PollingReport.com, 2014). This represents a slight shift toward the pro-life position over the past decade.

When polls give interviewees a wider range of choices, however, it becomes apparent that the interviewees' views are not strictly polarized. Relatively few people favor either complete legality or a complete ban (**Figure 9.21A**). One of the issues that most strongly influences people's opinions is the timing of abortion: Many people believe that abortion should be permissible in the first trimester, but far fewer believe that it should be permissible in the second or third trimester (**Figure 9.21B**). In this respect, Americans tend toward a more conservative position than was spelled out in *Roe v. Wade*, which made abortion legal in both the first and second trimesters.

Furthermore, while 60% of Americans think that the *Roe v. Wade* decision was a good thing, this does not mean that they agree with the core of the decision, which was that a woman has a right to an early abortion for any reason. Americans generally are in favor of the notion that a woman should be able to have an abortion if her life is at risk, if the fetus is likely to have a congenital disorder, or if the pregnancy resulted from rape. In contrast, they are *not* in favor of the idea that a woman should be allowed to have an abortion for a reason of mere convenience—such as the fact that having the baby would interfere with her career. Seventy percent of Americans believe that abortion under these circumstances should be illegal, contrary to the *Roe v. Wade* ruling.

How do views on abortion vary with major demographic variables? Women and men do not differ significantly in their representation in the pro-choice and pro-life camps (Gallup, 2011). The main variables that do correlate with abortion views are religious beliefs, political affiliation, educational level, and age. People with strong religious beliefs or who are Republicans are more likely to have restrictive views on abortion, while Democrats, people who are more highly educated, and younger people are more likely to have permissive views (ReligiousTolerance.org, 2005).

The abortion debate is often portrayed as a conflict between extreme pro-life and pro-choice activists, but many Americans hold intermediate positions.

The availability of abortion is decreasing

Because the *Roe v. Wade* decision affirmed a woman's constitutional right to have an abortion, anti-abortion activists have generally focused their efforts on restricting this right in a variety of ways, rather than on eliminating the right completely. These efforts have been quite successful, especially in more conservative states where pro-lifers constitute a majority of the population. Here are some examples:

- Many states have enacted mandatory 24-hour or 72-hour waiting periods and mandatory counseling about alternatives to abortion. In 2011 North Carolina enacted a requirement that a woman view an ultrasound of her fetus and listen to the fetal heartbeat before undergoing an abortion. (This requirement was thrown out by a federal appeals court judge in 2014, but it will likely be the subject of further litigation.)

- Some states require parental consent for a minor to have an abortion. (If consent can't be obtained, the minor can generally seek permission from a judge.)

- Some states have enacted measures that make it difficult for abortion clinics to function. Mississippi, Texas, and North Dakota, for example, have required that abortion providers have admitting privileges at a nearby hospital; Mississippi's law was ruled unconstitutional by a federal appeals court in 2014.

- Many states limit the use of public funds to provide abortion services. States are only required to fund abortions when pregnancy results from incest or rape, or when the mother's life is in danger, and many states deny funding for abortions in any other circumstances, even for indigent women.

- Some states have attempted to lower the fetal age limit for abortion, which the U.S. Supreme Court has set at the age of viability outside the womb. In 2013 Arkansas set its limit at 12 weeks, which is 10 weeks earlier than the earliest age of viability. In the same year, North Dakota banned abortion after the fetal heartbeat is detectable, which could be as early as 6 weeks, and it banned abortion done because of Down syndrome or other genetic defects in the fetus.

- Fetal homicide laws have been expanded or reinterpreted by some states to include self-induced abortions (**Box 9.5**).

Some of these restrictions clearly violate the *Roe v. Wade* ruling. They may have been enacted simply for political advantage, but in some cases the hope is probably that they will give the Supreme Court the opportunity to reverse *Roe v. Wade*. Whether the Court is disposed to do so is uncertain.

Besides using the political process, anti-abortion activists have put abortion providers in a state of fear by threatening or harassing them, and some extremists within the movement have actually murdered abortion providers (**Figure 9.22**). Many providers have ceased to perform abortions for this reason.

Another strategy used by anti-abortion activists has involved the establishment of deceptive "crisis pregnancy centers." These facilities advertise in a fashion suggesting that they provide abortion services, but once a woman arrives at the center, she is exposed to misinformation and shaming, which is intended to

Figure 9.22 Anti-abortion extremism In 1994 Paul Hill shot and killed an abortion provider and a clinic security guard. Hill was sentenced to death and was executed in 2003. These pro-life activists were expressing their support for Hill at the time of his execution.

Box 9.5 Society, Values, and the Law

Feticide

In 2013 a 33-year-old Indiana woman, Purvi Patel, showed up at a hospital emergency room complaining of bleeding from her vagina. She said that she had delivered a fetus that she believed to be dead, and that she disposed of it in a dumpster, where the fetus was eventually found. According to court papers, investigators found text messages on her mobile phone referring to drugs that she allegedly took to cause an abortion. In August 2014 Patel was charged with "feticide," defined as the intentional killing of a fetus. This crime carries a penalty of up to 20 years' imprisonment under Indiana law (Pilkington, 2014).

Most states have feticide laws, although the details vary from state to state. The laws were originally aimed at providers of illegal abortions, but later came to be used against people (usually the male partners of pregnant women) who caused the death of a fetus in the course of an assault or murder. In the majority of states that have feticide laws, they apply to embryos or fetuses of any gestational age.

More recently, feticide laws have been modified or reinterpreted so that they can be directed against pregnant women themselves, if they cause the death of their fetus by some means other than legal abortion. For example, one Indiana woman, Bei Bei Shuai (see figure), was charged with feticide after her fetus died when she tried to commit suicide by swallowing rat poison. In the case of Purvi Patel, the fetus seems to have already been viable at the time of its death, in which case Patel's right to

Bei Bei Shuai was charged with feticide because her fetus died during a suicide attempt.

induce an abortion was not constitutionally protected under *Roe v. Wade.*

The feticide charge against Shuai was ultimately dropped as part of a plea deal, and the same thing may happen with Patel. Nevertheless, many women have been convicted of feticide, usually in circumstances where they intentionally or recklessly caused a **stillbirth**. A South Carolina woman, Regina McKnight, smoked crack cocaine while pregnant, and the fetus was subsequently stillborn: McKnight was convicted of feticide and sentenced to a 12-year prison term. After 8 years in prison the state supreme court overturned her conviction, ruling that there was insufficient evidence of a connection between her drug use and the death of her fetus (Greene, 2008).

The broader purpose of feticide laws has been to establish the principle that fetuses are persons with rights distinct from those of their mothers. Although these laws are not usually applicable in the context of legal abortions, they create a paradoxical situation in which an embryo or fetus of a certain age may have full rights of personhood (in the case of an assault on a pregnant woman, for example) but no rights at all in the case of a legal abortion. Thus feticide laws tend to foster the belief that legal abortion may also be a violation of the fetus's rights. This may have been the intention of legislators who created these laws and prosecutors who make use of them.

stillbirth The delivery of a dead fetus late in pregnancy.

change her mind about having an abortion (Planned Parenthood, 2014b). These centers may be located in the same building or even on the same floor as real abortion clinics, and they may use deceptive names such as "PP Inc."

The result of these combined activities has been to greatly reduce the availability of legal abortion in the United States: Many women live 100 miles or more from the nearest provider. If it should happen that the Supreme Court does overthrow *Roe v. Wade*, the situation will likely revert to that existing before that ruling was made: In other words, there will be a major increase in illegal abortions, which used to take the lives of many women and impair the health or fertility of many more.

Go to the
**Discovering
Human Sexuality**
Companion Website at
**sites.sinauer.com/
discoveringhumansexuality3e**
for activities, study questions,
quizzes, and other study aids.

One thing that most pro-life and pro-choice activists agree on is that contraception is preferable to abortion. Improved access to contraceptive services, better education in contraceptive methods, development of new methods, and changes in religious attitudes toward contraception all have the potential to greatly reduce the number of abortions performed in the United States.

Summary

- Although various forms of contraception have been known since ancient times, moral repugnance, restrictive laws, and lack of knowledge prevented effective contraception in the United States until the 20th century. Margaret Sanger led the struggle to legalize contraception, to educate the public about contraceptive methods, and to introduce improved methods. Contraception was not fully legalized in the United States until 1972. Even today, about 3 million unintended pregnancies occur in the United States every year, on account of nonuse or failure of contraceptive methods.

- All currently available contraceptive methods have advantages and disadvantages. Different people have different contraceptive needs in terms of reversibility, reliability, cost, and so on, so no one method is best for all users.

- Male condoms (sheaths that cover the penis) require careful use to prevent failure and are somewhat intrusive, but they are cheap and readily accessible and offer significant protection against STIs. They are the only contraception method controlled by the male that is reversible (aside from withdrawal). Female condoms offer similar benefits but are far less popular than male condoms.

- Diaphragms and cervical caps are other barrier methods of contraception. They are used in conjunction with spermicides to prevent the entry of sperm into the cervix. They are less intrusive than condoms, but they provide less pregnancy and disease protection and are fairly inconvenient to use. Spermicides used by themselves are not very reliable, and overuse of spermicides can cause vaginal irritation and raise the risk of STI transmission.

- Intrauterine devices (IUDs) render the uterus hostile to sperm transport. They are very reliable and convenient once inserted. They offer no STI protection.

- Contraceptive pills contain either a combination of estrogen and progestin or progestin only. They work by blocking ovulation and by rendering the uterus hostile to sperm transport. They are fairly convenient once prescribed, nonintrusive, and very reliable if taken regularly. They offer no STI protection. Estrogen-containing pills may have a number of side effects as well as some long-term health risks and benefits. Progestin-only pills often cause irregular bleeding.

- Some contraceptive pills may be taken in an extended fashion that reduces the frequency of menstrual periods or eliminates them entirely.

- Hormone-based contraceptives may also be administered by long-term injections (Depo-Provera), by contraceptive patches (Ortho Evra), by vaginal rings (NuvaRing), or by implants placed under the skin (Nexplanon). These nonpill methods have the advantage of greater reliability than pills in typical use.

- In fertility awareness methods, couples avoid sex near the time of ovulation, which they can determine by a variety of techniques, including simple calendar calculations, body temperature measurements, or examination of cervical mucus.

- In the withdrawal method, the man withdraws his penis prior to ejaculation. Globally, this method has made a major contribution to population control, but many couples find it difficult to practice, especially if the man tends to ejaculate early or without warning.

- Noncoital sex (outercourse) is a reliable form of contraception if adhered to strictly.

- Emergency contraception involves taking a high dose of oral contraceptives within a few days after unprotected sex or failure of a barrier contraceptive. These drugs prevent ovulation. Another postcoital contraceptive technique is the insertion of an IUD.

- Sterilization is the cutting and/or tying off of the vasa deferentia (in men) or the oviducts (in women). The procedure blocks ova or sperm transport and is almost completely reliable in preventing pregnancy. The majority of sterilizations are done in women, but the procedure is simpler, safer, and less expensive in men. Although intended to be permanent, sterilization can be reversed in some cases. Sterilization is generally chosen by couples who have all the children they desire.

- In the United States, about 1 million abortions are performed every year. Most abortions are done in the first trimester of pregnancy by the vacuum aspiration method, in which the cervix is dilated and the contents of the uterus suctioned out under local anesthesia. A slightly more complex procedure, dilation and evacuation (D&E), is used early in the second trimester.

- Early abortions may also be induced with drugs. Medical abortion is a two-step procedure involving the administration of a drug that terminates the pregnancy (usually mifepristone), followed about 2 days later by a second drug (misoprostol) that induces contractions and the expulsion of the fetal remains.

- According to the most recent studies, abortion does not have negative psychological consequences for the mother.

- The moral and legal status of abortion is contentious. The extreme anti-abortion (pro-life) position is that abortion is always wrong and should be illegal, except perhaps when done to save the mother's life. The extreme opposing (pro-choice) view is that a woman should have the right to choose abortion under any circumstances. Most Americans describe themselves as pro-life or pro-choice but actually hold to an intermediate position, believing that abortion should be permitted under certain limited conditions, such as early in pregnancy or when the fetus has a congenital defect.

- The U.S. Supreme Court's 1973 decision in *Roe v. Wade* established a woman's constitutional right to have an abortion for any reason before the age of fetal viability. In recent years, however, pro-life activists have used a variety of strategies to restrict the availability of abortion.

Discussion Questions

1. Your sister or best friend asks you to help her decide which contraceptive method is best for her. She says she could not take pills, use a diaphragm, or use the rhythm method because she is too forgetful. She does not want to have to contemplate an abortion, because it is against her values. Recommend two forms of contraception that would be suitable, and describe the pros and cons of each method. Compare their actions and side effects. Compare their reliability.

2. A teenager tells you that she has no risk of getting pregnant because she can tell when her boyfriend is about to ejaculate by the look on his face, and she makes him pull out. How could you help her understand the risks of this method? What alternative methods would you suggest? Describe how they work and their advantages and disadvantages.

3. What are your own views about abortion? What do the laws say about abortion in your state, and what changes, if any, would you like to make in them?

4. What improvements in contraceptive technology would you most like to see?

Web Resources

Bedsider birth control methods **www.bedsider.org**
California Vasectomy and Reversal Center (vasectomy video) **www.californiavasectomyreversal.com/ vasectomy.html**
Guttmacher Institute **www.guttmacher.org**
International Male Contraception Coalition (covers research on male contraception) **www.malecontraceptives.org**

Ipas (an organization dedicated to the global availability of contraception and safe abortion) **ipas.org**
Marie Stopes International **www.mariestopes.org.uk**
NARAL Pro-Choice America **www.naral.org**
National Abortion Federation **www.prochoice.org**
National Right to Life Committee **www.nrlc.org**
Planned Parenthood Federation of America **www.plannedparenthood.org**

Recommended Reading

Chesler, E. (1992). *Woman of valor: Margaret Sanger and the birth control movement in America*. Simon & Schuster.

George, R. P. & Tollefsen, C. (2008). *Embryo: A defense of human life*. Doubleday. (Makes the case that an embryo is a full human being entitled to legal protection.)

Hatcher, R. A., Trussell, J., Nelson, A. L., Cates, W., Jr., Kowal, D. & Policar, M. S. (2011). *Contraceptive technology* (20th ed.). Ardent Media. (This massive and frequently updated work is the principal reference volume in the field of contraception.)

Sanger, M. (1938/2004). *The autobiography of Margaret Sanger*. Dover.

Solinger, R. (2005). *Pregnancy and power: A short history of reproductive politics in America*. NYU Press.

Wicklund, S. (2007). *This common secret: My journey as an abortion doctor*. Public Affairs.

Zieman, M., & Hatcher, R. (2012). *Managing contraception*. Bridging the Gap Communications. (This inexpensive or free e-book is an easy-to-use reference that emphasizes the "get-it-and-forget-it" methods.)

Chapter 10

In many Latino cultures a girl's transition to sexual maturity is marked by a *quinceañera* celebration.

Sexuality across the Life Span: From Birth to Adolescence

No two lives are alike, yet sexuality does unfold in a somewhat predictable manner across the life span. In fact, a person's age is one of the best predictors of that person's sexual behavior and relationships. Early sex researchers tended to focus on a narrow age range within the total life span—from adolescence to midlife—when sexuality has its greatest social relevance. Yet sexuality is a work that is already in progress at birth and that remains so until death. This chapter focuses on the dynamic changes in sexuality during childhood and adolescence. Chapter 11 focuses on the variations in sexuality during adulthood.

Some Forms of Childhood Sexual Expression Are Common

Studying childhood sexuality is difficult. Adults have very limited memories of their childhood and no recollection at all of their infancy. Infants cannot be interviewed about their sex lives. Older children can be interviewed, but their understanding may be limited, and interviewer suggestions might too easily influence their replies. In addition, parents and society in general may be reluctant to permit questioning of children on sexual matters. Direct observation of children's sexual behavior may be difficult if the behavior is infrequent, and ethical and legal considerations also limit the use of this approach. Thus, observational studies have generally involved asking intermediaries, such as parents or teachers, about sexual behavior they happened to have witnessed among children under their care, rather than direct observation of such behavior by researchers.

Because of these problems, the total number of studies of childhood sexuality has been very limited. Leaving aside the topic of sexual molestation of children by adults, a 2011 review identified just 14 research articles devoted to typical childhood sexuality published within the previous 10 years (de Graaf & Rademakers, 2011), and many of these studies were focused on children's knowledge of or attitudes about sex rather than their actual behavior. Since that time almost nothing has been published on the subject.

Primates display sexual behavior early in life

All of the higher nonhuman primates exhibit a variety of sexual behaviors before puberty. Infant rhesus monkeys, for example, start to engage in presenting and mounting (copulatory behaviors that are typical of adult females and adult males, respectively) pretty much as soon as they begin to wander away from their mothers (Wallen, 2000). These behaviors are not accompanied by actual coitus, however. They seem in part to be play behaviors that serve a rehearsal function, but in addition, they are used as a form of aggression or submission.

In contemporary Western culture, children are insulated from sex

Before the 19th century, families generally slept together, so young children sometimes observed and learned about adult sexual behavior. Also, because farming was the most common occupation, children saw animals mating, becoming pregnant, and giving birth. Climate permitting, young children frequently went naked, so it was easy for them to explore and learn about their own anatomy and that of their siblings.

During the 19th century, however, a belief developed that children needed to be kept in a state of sexual innocence. Despite the changes since then, especially in terms of formalized sex education, children today often experience a "conspiracy of silence" on sexual matters. Many parents, for example, do not permit their children to see them naked or to witness their sexual encounters, in part because some clinicians and therapists have suggested that these experiences are harmful to children and may even represent a form of sexual abuse. Research on this topic has led to reassuring findings, however. In one 18-year longitudinal study—the UCLA Family Lifestyles Project—young children who saw their parents naked or engaging in sex were no more likely to experience psychological problems in later childhood or adolescence than children

Do young children have a sex life? What do you think?

who did not (Okami et al., 1998). In fact, there was a tendency for them to have *fewer* problems—a finding that is in line with another, retrospective study (Lewis & Janda, 1988) (**Figure 10.1**).

Children, especially younger ones, express a lot of curiosity about "where babies come from" and other sexual matters. Some parents are very forthcoming, using these questions as an opportunity to teach their children the basic facts of sexuality in an age-appropriate fashion (**Box 10.1**). But other parents are evasive: They may give fairy-tale explanations, tell their children that they are too young to know such things, or express disapproval of the questions. Thus, many children remain remarkably uninformed about sexual matters. In one survey conducted around 1980, researchers found that North American children lagged far behind children in other Western countries in terms of their sexual knowledge (Goldman & Goldman, 1982). Nine-year-olds, for example, were mostly

Figure 10.1   Nudity allows children to familiarize themselves with anatomical sex differences.

unable to give accurate answers to simple questions such as "How can anyone know whether a newborn baby is a boy or a girl?" Whether such a survey would yield different results today is an open question, but it is unlikely that there have been major advances in this area, given the difficulties facing sex education in many U.S. schools.

Parents also communicate diverse values to their children—values that may be broadly sex-positive, generally sex-negative, or a mixture of the two. As an example of the last, some parents communicate respect for heterosexual relationships and parenting but express disgust for "faggots" and "dykes," thus communicating homophobic attitudes to their children before the children even have a clear grasp of what homosexuality is.

Some children engage in solitary sexual activity

What about children's actual sexual behavior? Newborn babies sometimes have penile erections or vaginal lubrication (Martinson, 1976; Masters et al., 1982). In fact, erections have been detected in male fetuses several weeks before birth, by means of ultrasound imaging. These responses continue to occur throughout infancy and childhood. They are not necessarily brought about by what we would normally consider *sexual* stimuli, however. According to Kinsey's group (Kinsey et al., 1948), penile erections in young boys are triggered by a wide variety of physical stimuli (e.g., the motion of a car or sitting in warm sand) or exciting or fearful events (e.g., playing exciting games or looking over the edge of a building). Thus, it seems that erections in young boys are part of a generalized arousal response. Less is known about these responses in girls at that age.

Infants and young children of both sexes commonly touch their genitals. The great majority of mothers in European countries report having witnessed such behavior, whereas only about half of American mothers say that they have seen genital touching (Friedrich et al., 2000; Larsson et al., 2000). This cross-national difference could be real, but it could also reflect a greater openness of European mothers to the concept of childhood sexuality.

Very young children's tactile exploration may lead to autoerotic behavior.

Of course, simply touching one's genitals may or may not be sexually motivated. By 15 to 19 months of age, however, some girls and boys rhythmically stimulate their genitals by hand or by rubbing their genitals against an object

Box 10.1 Sexual Health

Talking with Children about Sex

Talk early and often. Toddlers should learn the names for their genitals along with other body parts ("These are your toes, and this is your penis"—or "vulva" or "vagina"). Progress from there in an age-appropriate manner through high school. Each stage facilitates later stages: It's a lot easier to talk about a man putting his penis into a woman's vagina if you and the child have already become comfortable with talking about those body parts.

Use teachable moments. Rather than postpone everything to a "big talk about sex"—which may never happen—take advantage of opportunities that arise, such as when the child is undressing, sees a sibling or parent's genitals or nude art (see figure), witnesses sexual intimacy on television or in real life, or sees animals mating or giving birth. Take advantage of a subsequent pregnancy and childbirth, or the puberty of a sibling, to talk about these processes. Above all, respond simply and accurately to the child's questions. If a child asks about the meaning of a word he hears from peers, respond candidly and in a relaxed, nonjudgmental manner. The question "Where do babies come from?" needs to be answered several times over, in increasing detail, beginning with something like "Babies grow in a special place inside the mother" and later explaining about eggs and sperm and how they come together. Respond to things the child has heard or witnessed at school or from friends: If the child announces that "Andy has two mommies," for example, that would be a good opportunity to talk about gay relationships and alternative parenting styles.

Balance negatives with positives. If you see your child masturbating, for example, then (depending on your own beliefs on the topic) you may want to say something like "That feels good, doesn't it? It's fine to do that, but it's best to do it in your bedroom. People like to do that when they're by themselves." When talking about sexual behavior, talk in an age-appropriate way about the physical and emotional pleasure of sexual contact and intimate relationships—including the specific body parts, such as the clitoris, that are involved—as well as the responsibilities and risks that sexual intimacy involves.

Anticipate events. That's especially important for the bodily and psychological changes that accompany puberty. A mother can teach her daughter (or her son, for that matter) about menstruation either in words or with aids such as pictures or her own unused and used tampons. Puberty comes earlier than parents expect, and by the time schools get around to the subject, half the class may have pubic hair. There are dozens of books suitable for kids—check out the Web booksellers' sites under the search term "puberty."

There are many opportunities to teach one's child about sex and reproduction.

Acknowledge diversity. Help your child or teen understand that there is no single "normal" size or shape for genitals or breasts; no single "normal" time for the growth spurt, menarche, a sexual relationship, falling in love, or marriage; and no single "normal" sexual orientation.

Communicate your values. Let your child know your views on when sex is acceptable—whether it should be restricted to marriage or to emotionally committed relationships, or whether it has a place outside of those relationships. If you believe that your teen is ready for some forms of sexual contact, but not for others, say so. Ask for your child's views on these questions, and if you disagree, present the reasons for your point of view rather than simply laying down the law. Explain the core values, such as respect for others, or your religious beliefs that underlie your opinion.

Give practical advice. Bear in mind that most teens become sexually active well before leaving home. Adults can help teens avoid the serious pitfalls of adolescent sexuality without encouraging them to engage in sex. Explain the specific steps they can take to reduce the likelihood of pregnancy and STIs. Remember that, depending on your school's sex-education policy, there may be little or no instruction in contraceptive methods, especially in such practical matters as where to obtain contraceptives. It's unlikely that you'll be able to answer all the spoken or unspoken questions your teen will have about sex, so tell them about teen-oriented sex-education websites such as Teen Wire (www.teenwire.org) and Sex, Etc. (www.sexetc.org).

(Galenson, 1990). Roughly 1 in 5 parents has witnessed such masturbatory behavior in their child before the age of 6: Again, the numbers are higher in some European countries than in the United States (Friedrich et al., 1998; Larsson & Svedin, 2002b).

According to Alfred Kinsey, this masturbatory behavior sometimes climaxes in what looks like an orgasm, even in children just a few months old (Kinsey et al., 1948; Kinsey et al., 1953). There has been very little research in this area since Kinsey's time, but one Chinese study reported on a girl who masturbated to orgasm from about 5 months of age until at least 8 years of age (Zhu et al., 2011a). What was clear from this longitudinal case history was that the rather ambiguous behaviors seen in infancy evolved gradually into a more explicit and purposeful masturbatory style. When she was old enough to be questioned about the behavior, the girl said that she did it for the pleasure it generated.

According to studies that are based on parents' reports, the prevalence of masturbation declines markedly during childhood (Friedrich et al., 1998). In retrospective studies, on the other hand, adolescents recall very little sexual activity in early childhood but a marked increase in sexual interest and behavior as puberty approaches. Among those who recall having masturbated before puberty, for example, the mean age of first masturbation is 8 to 10 years of age (Larsson & Svedin, 2002a).

These conflicting data illustrate the difficulty of conducting research on childhood sexuality. We may guess, however, that the decrease in sexual behavior with age that is reported by parents is only apparent: It could result from the fact that children learn to conceal sexual behavior because they are afraid of being caught and punished (Reynolds et al., 2003). The failure of adolescents or adults to recall masturbation in early childhood could reflect the general impermanence of memory at that age.

Sex with others can occur during childhood

Besides solitary sexual activity, children's sexual behavior may involve others (**Table 10.1**). It is common for young children to show their genitals to adults or to other children and to attempt to view the genitals of others. Such activities begin in the second year of life, and about half of all parents have witnessed it by the time a child reaches the age of 5 or 6. Not only parents, but also preschool staff report seeing this kind of behavior (Davies et al., 2000; Larsson & Svedin, 2002b).

In addition, there may be sexual or quasi-sexual contacts between children. Children often hug and kiss each other. They may also attempt to touch each other's genitals. Sometimes these behaviors are incorporated into games such as "show," "doctor," "house," and the like. In a study carried out at the University of California, Los Angeles, about half the mothers reported that their children had engaged in this type of behavior before the age of 6 (Okami et al., 1997). In a more recent study, on the other hand, less than 2% of the primary caregivers of 2- to 12-year-olds reported having observed such behavior in the previous 6 months (Thigpen, 2009). Why the dramatic difference? A likely cause has to do with the demographics of the subjects: In the first study they were the children of white, average-income California mothers, while in the second study they were the children of African-American, low-income Midwestern mothers. Sociocultural differences of this kind can strongly influence whether caregivers believe that children's sexual behaviors are acceptable, and this in turn influences whether the children will exhibit these behaviors or permit their caregivers to witness them (Thigpen & Fortenberry, 2009).

TABLE 10.1
Children's Sexual Behavior

Behavior	Girls	Boys
Talking about sex	28	30
Looking at pornographic pictures	13	22
Kissing and hugging	44	34
Showing genitals	23	28
Other child touching your genitals	19	17
Touching, exploring genitals of other child	19	17
Inserting objects into other child's vagina or rectum	4	10
Other child inserting objects into your vagina or rectum	2	2
Putting penis in other child's mouth	—	5
Other child putting penis in your mouth	1	2
Vaginal intercourse	1	4
Anal intercourse	0	3

Source: Larsson & Svedin, 2002a.

Note: The table shows the percentage of young adults who recalled having engaged in various voluntary sexual activities with other children when they were 6–10 years of age.

Only very small numbers of children engage in more adultlike sexual behavior, such as coitus (or pretended coitus), oral or anal sex, or insertion of a finger or an object into the vagina or anus (see Table 10.1). At first glance, this might seem surprising, given that coitus-related behaviors (presenting and mounting) are almost universal among the young of nonhuman primates. Bear in mind, however, that children (at least in contemporary American culture) have little opportunity to observe adults engaged in sexual behavior beyond kissing and hugging. Because imitation may play a large role in the learning of interpersonal sexual behavior in childhood, one would not expect to see many children attempting coitus or other forms of penetrative sex.

The data in Table 10.1 refer only to voluntary sexual behavior between children. In one study, 13% of adolescents recalled childhood experiences of being coerced into a sexual contact by another child—the method of coercion being trickery, bribes, threats, or physical force. Eight percent recalled being the perpetrator in such coercive acts (Larsson & Svedin, 2002a).

For the most part, solitary and interpersonal sexual behaviors by children seem to be harmless. Children who engage in sexual play with other children are just as likely to be well-adjusted in the teenage years as children who do not, according to one longitudinal study carried out at UCLA (Okami et al., 1997). When adolescents or young adults are asked to describe how childhood sexual experiences made them feel, most reply with positive descriptors such as "curious," "excited," or "happy," and most say that these experiences were "normal." But a minority report that the experiences made them feel "shamed," "guilty," or "embarrassed." Girls experience more negative feelings than boys, children who are coerced experience more negative feelings than those who participate willingly, and Americans experience more negative feelings than Europeans (Larsson & Svedin, 2002a; Reynolds et al., 2003).

Cultures vary in their attitudes toward childhood sexuality

Children in many non-Western societies engage in sexual behaviors, but societies vary in whether they encourage, tolerate, or suppress them (Frayser, 1994). On the Polynesian island of Mangaia, for example, children traditionally had the opportunity to observe the sexual behaviors of adults and were freely permitted to engage in sex play and masturbation (Marshall, 1971). Similarly, the Chewa people of Malawi encouraged their children to play at being husband and wife in little huts situated away from the village. The Lepcha people of northern India believe that coitus is necessary for girls to mature into women (**Figure 10.2**), and several tribes in New Guinea believe that ingestion of semen (by male-on-male fellatio) is necessary for boys to develop into men (Herdt, 2005).

FAQ

I'm having a hard time teaching my 5-year-old to pee standing up. He's not circumcised, and pee goes everywhere.

Just slightly retracting his foreskin may help him achieve a better stream, but don't force it. If that doesn't help, he may have to continue sitting down for a few years. Plenty of adult men prefer urinating that way.

Figure 10.2 Lepcha

More commonly, however, adults exert some degree of restraint on children's sexual expression. There are usually mild restraints on heterosexual play or masturbation during early childhood, but they may become stronger during later childhood. These restraints are stronger in societies in which sexual restraint is expected of adults; thus, children are essentially being prompted to learn the sexual attitudes they are expected to show in adulthood.

Some Children Have Sexual Contacts with Adults

If only the occasional child had sexual contact with an adult, this topic might be better dealt with in the context of atypical sexuality (see Chapter 13) or sexual assault (see Chapter 16). But in fact these childhood experiences are fairly common. In a large national survey of adults, about 1 in 10 interviewees said that they had experienced at least one sexual contact with an adult during their childhood; of these, 75% were female and 25% were male (Perez-Fuentes et al., 2013). Similar figures have been reported worldwide (Barth et al., 2013). Larger numbers of children have noncontact experiences, such as witnessing a man expose his genitals to them.

We therefore consider it appropriate to discuss adult-child sex in this chapter. We look at the issue only from the point of view of the child, however, focusing particularly on the harm that such contacts may do. The adults who have sexual contact with children are discussed in Chapter 13.

Most adult-child contacts involve older children and are single encounters

According to the National Health and Social Life Survey (NHSLS), most children who have sexual experiences with adults or adolescents have only one such experience—or if they have multiple experiences, they are all with the same partner. For girls, that partner is most often an adult male and less often an adolescent male. For boys, it is most commonly an adolescent female, less often an adolescent male, and even less often an adult male. The data also show that 80% to 90% of adult-child contacts involve the adult touching the genitals of the child. Oral contacts and vaginal or anal penetration are much less common.

How old are children when they have sexual contact with adults or adolescents? The most likely age for a child of either sex to have sexual contact with a male is 7 to 10 years, but about one-third of such contacts occur in the under-7 age bracket. The most likely age for a boy to have contact with a female is 11 to 13 years. The females involved are usually adolescents who are a few years older than the boys.

In most cases, the child knows the adult, who is often a relative or family friend (**Table 10.2**). Girls are more likely to be molested by relatives; boys by family friends. Less than 10% of contacts are with strangers. As the table shows, girls as a group are equally likely to have contacts with fathers and stepfathers, but these figures are misleading, because many more girls live with their fathers than live with stepfathers. Thus a girl who lives with her stepfather is at considerably greater risk of being molested by him than is a girl who lives with her biological father.

Some kinds of adult-child sex are more harmful than others

The effects of adult-child sex on children are controversial. In the minds of most members of the public, politicians, and

TABLE 10.2

Percentage of Adult-Child Sexual Contacts Identified by Relationship and Child's Sex

Relationship of adult to child	Child's sex	
	Girl	Boy
Father	7	1
Stepfather	7	1
Older brother	9	4
Other relative	29	13
Teacher	3	4
Family friend	29	40
Mother's boyfriend	2	1
Older friend of child	1	4
Other person known to child	19	17
Stranger	7	4

Source: National Health and Social Life Survey (Laumann et al., 1994).

Note: The percentages add up to more than 100 because some children had contacts with more than one adult.

jurists—as well as some therapists—such contacts are always extremely harmful to the child. As a result, adults convicted of child molestation are punished more severely than almost any other criminals. Sentences of 60 or more years of imprisonment may be imposed for serious offenses, especially if the person has a prior record.

According to numerous studies, children who have had sexual contacts with adults do indeed experience more harmful consequences than do comparison groups of children who have not had such contacts. The harmful consequences include both short-term effects (e.g., fearfulness, depression, inhibition of emotions, hostility, and antisocial behavior) and long-term effects (e.g., mood disorders, phobias, panic disorders, antisocial personality, suicidality, substance abuse, poor academic performance, premature sexual activity, sexual promiscuity, exposure to sexually transmitted infections, and sexual victimization of others) (Chen et al., 2010; Maniglio, 2013). Personal accounts confirm the traumatic effects that sexual abuse of children can have (Lopez, 2013).

A somewhat different picture emerges, however, when the details of the adult-child contacts are taken into account. The children who are most likely to experience adverse effects are, not surprisingly, those who were physically coerced into a sexual contact (Molnar et al., 2001). Sexual contacts that are repeated over a long period of time, that are with a family member or caregiver, or that involve a very large age difference may also be more likely to cause harm than isolated or nonincestuous contacts or those with a small age difference between the child and the older person. Contacts that involve sexual penetration are more harmful than those that do not (Najman et al., 2005). Girls are also more likely to suffer harm than boys.

Because most adult-child contacts are single events and don't involve physical coercion or penetrative sex, it's possible that most contacts cause little or no harm. According to meta-analyses and original studies by psychologist Bruce Rind of Temple University and his colleagues, most children who experience sexual contacts with adults suffer no long-term adverse consequences, or only mild ones (Rind et al., 1998; Rind, 2001). The Rind studies provoked a great deal of controversy: Some researchers have reached different conclusions (Najman et al., 2005; Najman et al., 2007), while others have confirmed Rind's findings (Ulrich et al., 2005, 2006). (For Rind's defense of his studies see Rind & Tromovitch, 2007.) If Rind's findings were proven to be correct, would you consider it acceptable to legalize some forms of adult-child sex? What other factors might you want to consider before making such a decision?

The issue of adult-child sex and its consequences is greatly complicated by problems of recall. Ideally, children would give reliable testimony about sexual contacts they had recently experienced, and adults would have accurate memories of childhood sexual experiences. Unfortunately, neither is necessarily the case. Children can be induced to believe and report events that didn't happen, and adults can be induced to "recover" supposedly repressed memories of childhood sexual abuse, even when such memories are demonstrably false (**Box 10.2**).

Strategies to prevent adult-child sex are quite effective

Regardless of the answers to those questions, the fact is that some children are indeed traumatized by sexual abuse. These children are at risk of developing **post-traumatic stress disorder** (**PTSD**), just as adult rape victims are (see Chapter 16). One aspect of this disorder is **dissociation**—the tendency to "stand outside" the traumatic experience and to fail to experience the normal emotional responses to it. Another common trait shown by sexually abused children is self-blame. Therapy may be focused on helping the child to experience the missing emotions and to realize that the adult perpetrator was the sole guilty party.

Many schools have programs intended to teach young children how to avoid sexual encounters with adults by learning to distinguish between "good touch" (e.g.,

post-traumatic stress disorder (PTSD) A cluster of physical and psychological symptoms that can affect persons who have experienced severe trauma.

dissociation The distancing of oneself from the emotions evoked by some traumatic experience or memory.

Box 10.2 Society, Values, and the Law

Sex and Suggestibility

In 1984, Peggy McMartin Buckey, along with her son Raymond and four others, faced over 200 counts of child molestation—crimes that were alleged to have taken place at the McMartin Preschool in Manhattan Beach, California (**Figure A**). During their trial—the longest in U.S. history—extraordinary allegations surfaced. These allegations involved not merely sexual abuse of young children, but also underground satanic rituals involving animal sacrifice. After 7 years (including a retrial for Raymond Buckey), all the defendants were acquitted.

The core issue in the trial was the believability of the 349 children who told social workers and investigators that they had experienced, witnessed, or been told about sexual abuse at the school. It became apparent during the trial that many of these children were inculcated by their interviewers with false memories of events that never happened. We may never know whether there was any kernel of truth to the McMartin allegations, but what is certain is that unscrupulous investigators, overzealous prosecutors, and sensation-seeking media blew the case up into a hysterical witch hunt.

The McMartin case was followed by many similar episodes (McRobbie, 2014). In 1992, for example, a Missouri woman who was in therapy with a church counselor "remembered" that she had been repeatedly raped by her father—a minister—between the ages of 7 and 14, that she became pregnant as a result, and that she was forced to perform an abortion on herself with a coat hanger. When her story was publicized, her father had to resign his post as a minister. Before he could be tried, however, a medical examination revealed that the daughter had never been pregnant and, in fact, was still a virgin. The therapist paid $1 million in settlement of the case.

Numerous studies document that memories can be inculcated. The leading figure in this field of research is Elizabeth Loftus (now at the University of California, Irvine), who testified at the McMartin trial and in many similar cases (Loftus & Davis, 2006) (**Figure B**). In her best-known experiment, Loftus instilled in her subjects a false memory of having been lost in a shopping mall as a child, along with various things that happened to the child while lost. Others have instilled "childhood memories" of hospitalization for an ear infection, of the sprinklers going off in a store, of an accident at a wedding reception, and the like. Nothing distinguishes these false memories from real ones—except that they are false.

Several circumstances promote the inculcation of false memories. One is that the initial account comes from a trusted or

(A) Peggy McMartin Buckey and Raymond Buckey.

(B) Elizabeth Loftus.

authoritative person. Another is that the subject is interviewed repeatedly. Oftentimes, details that the subject denies in initial interviews are gradually incorporated into the false memory of the event. Another dangerous but common practice is for interviewers to encourage their subjects to exercise their unfettered imagination. Loftus quotes one therapist as recommending that interviewers tell the client: "Spend time imagining that you were sexually abused, without worrying about accuracy…Who would have been likely perpetrators?" But, as Loftus's research has shown, the mere act of imagining a fictional past event facilitates the process of "remembering" it.

The sexual abuse of children does happen, and when it does it's a tragedy. But there's something about these crimes, or the rumor of them, that has often triggered "moral panics" in which common sense and elementary principles of justice fall by the wayside (Lancaster, 2011).

preadolescence The age range including the beginning of puberty, from approximately age 8 to 12 or 13 years.

patting and hugging) and "bad touch" (e.g., genital fondling). One simple instruction that children often receive is never to allow anyone to touch them on parts of their body that are covered by a bathing suit. Programs of this kind have been quite effective in reducing the incidence of sexual abuse (Davis & Gidycz, 2000). There has been some concern that these programs might inculcate sex-phobic attitudes. A study of college-age women, however, concluded that women who participated in these prevention programs during their childhood were as well adjusted sexually as other women, and were much less likely to have experienced adult-child sexual contact subsequent to the instruction (Gibson & Leitenberg, 2000).

Whatever the reason, child sexual abuse is much less common than it was in the past. Substantiated cases of such abuse dropped by 60% between 1992 and 2010 (Goode, 2012), and there has been a similar decline in online sexual solicitation of children (K. J. Mitchell et al., 2013b).

Preadolescence May Be Marked by an Increase in Sexual Interest

The period between about 8 years and 12 to 13 years of age is often called **preadolescence**, or more familiarly the "tween years." During this period the biological processes of puberty begin. Preadolescence may be marked by some degree of increased sexual feelings and behaviors, but this varies greatly from one individual to another.

In the United States, where many young children receive little or no sex education, the early preadolescent years (say, around age 8 or 9) are the time when most children learn about coitus and other "facts of life." Much information is spread through peer networks, so comical misunderstandings are the rule. For example, children may fail to understand the difference between the anus and the vaginal opening or may think that babies grow in the mother's stomach and emerge via the belly button. Late in elementary school, students usually have one gender-segregated lesson on the basics of puberty. Middle-school students may be exposed to school-based sex-education classes for the first time, but the content and message of these classes varies greatly from school to school.

Preadolescent children segregate by sex

Preadolescent children spend much of their free time in all-male or all-female groups. Obviously, this pattern of socialization minimizes their opportunities for heterosexual interactions. Nevertheless, some older preadolescents do engage in sexual behavior with the other sex. According to the CDC's Youth Risk Behavior Survey, 6% of children under the age of 13 have engaged in sexual intercourse (Centers for Disease Control, 2014q). Black males are especially likely to have done so (**Figure 10.3**). (Because these figures are based on the recollections of high school students, their reliability is uncertain.)

The fact that preadolescent children socialize primarily with peers of the same sex facilitates homosexual behavior. Boys may engage in paired or group masturbation, for example. It's possible that preadolescents who later become homosexual enjoy such behavior more than those who become heterosexual, but the behavior is certainly not predictive of a child's ultimate sexual orientation.

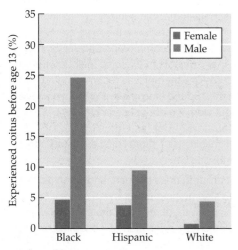

Figure 10.3 Early sexual activity The graph shows the percentages of female and male high school students who say they had sexual intercourse before age 13. (Data from Centers for Disease Control, 2014q.)

Strict gender norms may traumatize children who become gay adults

Actually, preadolescent children who are or will become gay or lesbian tend to distinguish themselves not so much by their sexual behavior, but by gender nonconformity in a variety of nonsexual traits (see Chapter 12). A boy who is or will become gay may be less interested in contact sports than other boys, for example, while a girl who is or will become lesbian may be *more* interested in such sports. Such gender nonconformity may be apparent in earlier childhood, and it may worry parents or teachers, but young children themselves are usually blind to it, so gender-nonconformist children are not seriously disadvantaged within their peer groups.

During the preadolescent years, however, gender norms become much stricter, both within peer groups and with respect to the expectations of adults. The problems are more severe for gender-nonconformist boys than for girls because some degree of masculinity in a girl may actually be an advantage. A degree of athleticism, aggressiveness, or competitiveness may help her gain a leadership position in her peer group, for example. Boys who are unmasculine or who are overtly feminine, however, may find themselves excluded from both their male and female peer groups and may have to content themselves with the company of other misfits at the fringes of childhood society. Furthermore, epithets such as "faggot" and "dyke" are used with increasing frequency in the preadolescent years, and hearing these epithets may begin the internalization of homophobic attitudes by those children. Of course, the degree to which children who will become gay adults experience these problems before adolescence varies greatly, depending on how gender-nonconformist they are as well as on their parents' attitudes, the school they attend, and so on.

Puberty Is a Period of Rapid Maturation

Puberty is the transition to reproductive maturity. It is marked by biological changes that affect the entire body: These include anatomical and physiological maturation of the external and internal genitalia, the development of secondary sexual characteristics such as breasts in girls, a growth spurt, and changes in the brain that affect behavior, especially in the area of sexuality. We first describe all these changes, and then go on to discuss their timing and the mechanisms that bring them about.

Puberty is marked by visible and invisible changes

In girls, the most noticeable change in the external genitalia is the appearance of pubic hair (**Figure 10.4**), but in addition, the outer and inner labia become more prominent, the vagina deepens, and the vaginal wall thickens. Underarm hair appears a little later than pubic hair.

Inside a girl's body, puberty is marked by a spurt of growth in the ovaries, uterus, and oviducts. The oviducts, which before puberty have a somewhat contorted course, become straighter. The cervix begins to produce the characteristic secretions of adult life. In the ovaries, some follicles begin to mature.

Female breasts are important secondary sexual characteristics that develop at puberty. Breast development goes through several stages (**Figure 10.5**). The breasts first emerge as small mounds—the **breast buds**—centered on the nipples. As breast development continues, both the nipple and the surrounding areola come to project forward from the breast, and the areola

puberty The biological transition that confers the capacity to be a parent.

breast bud The first stage of breast development at puberty.

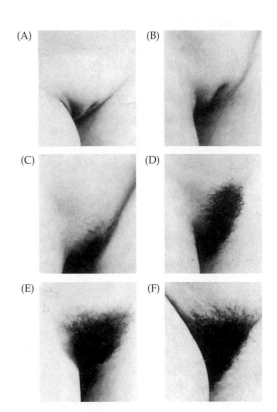

(A) (B) (C) (D) (E) (F)

Figure 10.4 **Typical development of pubic hair in girls at puberty** (A) Prepubescent state: No hair is visible. (B) Sparse, long, downy hair grows along the labia. This stage occurs at about 8.8 years in blacks and 10.5 years in whites, but with considerable variability. (C) Coarser, curly hair grows along the labia. (D) Hair covers the labia. (E) Hair spreads over the mons but not to the adult extent or density. (F) Hair forms an adultlike "inverted triangle" and extends to the inner surface of the thighs; this final pattern varies considerably among women. (From van Wieringen et al., 1971.)

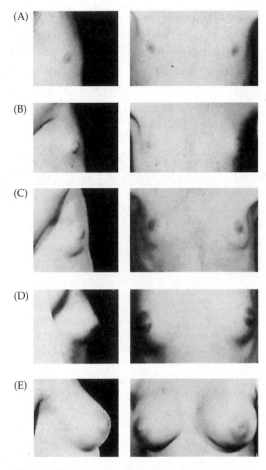

Figure 10.5 Typical development of breasts in girls at puberty, seen in side and frontal views (A) Prepubescent appearance. (B) Breast-bud stage: The nipple, areola, and nearby breast tissue form a small mound at about 8.9 years (for blacks) or 10 years (for whites). (C) Further enlargement of the areola and breast occurs. (D) The nipple and areola project out from the breast. (E) Adultlike stage: The areola is now flush with the breast; only the nipple projects forward. (From van Wieringen et al., 1971.)

enlarges. With the completion of breast development, the areola lies flush with the breast once more, and only the nipple projects.

The onset of menstruation is called **menarche** (pronunciations vary; MEN-ark-ee is the most common). The first menstrual period is often quite slight—perhaps just a single episode of spotting rather than a several-day flow. Even so, menarche is a highly memorable event in most women's lives (**Box 10.3**).

After menarche, menstruation may be irregular for a year or two. Furthermore, the initial menstrual cycles tend not to be accompanied by ovulation. For this reason, a young woman may not be capable of becoming pregnant for up to 2 years after menarche. However, there is much variation in this respect.

For boys, an early sign of puberty is the enlargement of the testicles and scrotum (**Figure 10.6**). The penis grows in length and then in girth, and pubic hair appears. The larynx (voice box) grows and the vocal folds thicken, leading to a deepening of the voice.

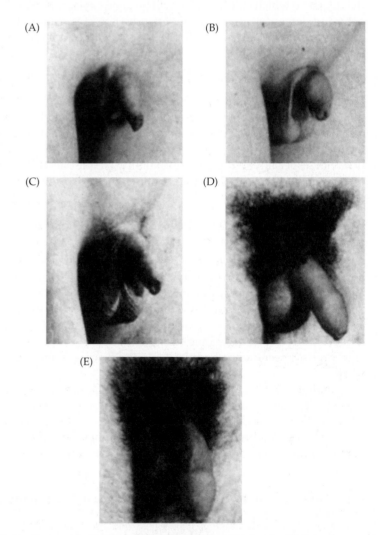

Figure 10.6 Typical development of male external genitalia at puberty (A) Prepubescent appearance. (B) Enlargement of the scrotum and testicles. This stage usually occurs at between 11 and 13 years. (C) Increase in the length of the penis and further enlargement of the scrotum. (D) Increase in the size of the penis, especially the glans, and appearance of pubic hair. (E) Adultlike appearance. (From van Wieringen et al., 1971.)

menarche The onset of menstruation at puberty.

Box 10.3 Personal Points of View

My First Period

Most women recall the circumstances surrounding their first menstrual period. The event is experienced in very different ways by different girls, depending on the culture in which they grow up and how their parents or schools have prepared them for it (see figure). Here are some first-person accounts. The first two are from the website ExperienceProject.com, where girls or women can contribute their recollections. The last two are from a similar site that is no longer online:

I was 11 and my sister was 8. She and I were changing our clothes for bed and she just said "Look—does that mean you're gonna have a baby?" I looked down and saw a big red spot. My mom was working a night shift so I called her, crying. For some reason, I couldn't stop crying. I was so sad. Now, I am happy to see the red spot some months!

I got my first period during the summer between 6th and 7th grade. My friends and I always talked about periods and we were all excited to get them. I was raised where getting your period was a joyous thing. I was at home with my BFF in my bedroom, and I went to the bathroom. I sat down and saw the blood. I jumped up and started screaming until my friend came in, and we jumped for joy. She ran and got my mom and she talked to us about it, and the three of us had a Girls Night Out. It was the best day of my life. The funny thing was that my BFF got her period the next day.

I come from India and my first periods were celebrated in a very grand fashion. In India, particularly southern India, a girl's first menstruation is a matter of great joy to the community. Initially for the first three days she is not allowed to touch anything in the household nor participate in any household chores. After the three days all the women of the

The Dot Girl's First Period Kit was designed and marketed by two sisters who were unprepared for their own menarches. The kit includes 5 menstrual pads with disposal bags, 2 hand wipes, a reusable heating pad, and an answer book/diary.

community are invited to a grand function exclusively for women. Everyone gives her gifts, usually jewelry. From then on she always puts the red spot on her forehead, which signifies womanhood.

I was a few hours late to school, arriving in the middle of music class. All I wanted to do was crawl to my seat and quietly die. I was so sure everyone must know. The guy I had a crush on sat near me in that class. As I reached my seat, he called over to me. God! The last thing I wanted was for him to know! I figured he was going to ask why I'd been late, and what could I say? I'd lie, of course, but I was sure it would show in my face. But he didn't ask that. Instead he said, "Hey, why do you look especially nice today?"

Many boys experience growth of the glandular tissue of the breasts (**gynecomastia**) during the latter part of puberty (**Figure 10.7**). The condition is more obvious among boys who are overweight. The enlarged breasts often disappear without treatment, but while they are present, they may cause embarrassment or distress. Surgical breast reduction or weight loss are options for boys who are self-conscious about the condition.

First ejaculation may occur with masturbation or during sleep (nocturnal emission). Initially, the semen may lack mature sperm; in fact, a male can be infertile for a year or two after his first ejaculation. It's a good idea for parents to mention nocturnal emissions when they are discussing puberty with their sons, because otherwise boys may be surprised and frightened by the experience: Some imagine that it is a medical abnormality or a punishment for masturbation, for example.

The extent of facial and body hair is highly variable among individuals as well as between ethnic groups. One puberty-associated trait that afflicts many teens, espe-

gynecomastia The development of breasts in males.

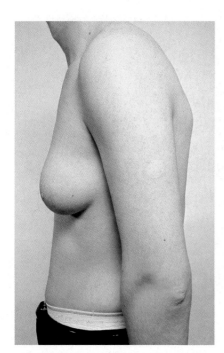

Figure 10.7 Gynecomastia is breast development in a boy.

cially boys, is acne. The key feature of acne is the blockage of oil-producing glands associated with hair follicles—most commonly on the face, neck, or back. The blockage is caused by an excess production of oil and shedding of skin cells within the glands. The blocked glands become a breeding ground for a common skin bacterium, *Propionibacterium acnes*. The blocked gland is called a whitehead if it is below the skin, a blackhead if it reaches the surface, and a pimple or pustule if it becomes inflamed. Severe acne can lead to permanent scarring. The condition can be treated with topical (local) medications containing benzoyl peroxide, salicylic acid, or sulfur. Severe cases may be treated with the oral drug isotretinoin (Accutane), but this drug can have serious side effects, including fetal defects if taken by pregnant women.

One of the most visible processes of puberty is the growth spurt, which takes place over a period of about 5 years. During this time girls gain about 10 inches (25 cm) in height, and boys gain about 11 inches. The spurt in height ends when the **epiphyseal plates**—the cartilaginous growth zones near the ends of the limb bones—cease functioning and turn into bone.

The spurt in height is not the only growth change during puberty. There are changes in skeletal structure, with girls developing wider hips and boys developing wider shoulders. Body composition also changes: By adulthood, men have 50% more bone and muscle mass than women, and women have twice as much body fat as men. Of course, these are statements about averages—there are plenty of muscular women and fat men. Variations in body composition among individuals of both sexes are influenced by many factors, such as genetics, diet, and levels of physical exercise.

During puberty, the brains of boys and girls diverge from each other, in both structure and function (see Figure 4.5, page 93). In one study, scientists at the National Institute of Mental Health (NIMH) repeatedly scanned the brains of about 300 teenagers, using high-resolution magnetic resonance imaging (MRI) (Raznahan et al., 2010, 2014). From these scans they created "movies" that showed how the structure of boys' and girls' brains diverged during adolescence. For example, a region concerned with spatial skills (in which males typically outperform females) ended up thicker in the boys than in the girls, whereas the opposite was seen in a region involved in impulse control (a trait that's better developed in females).

Paralleling these brain changes, there are dramatic psychological developments. Some of these processes—such as an increase in sensation-seeking and risk-taking behaviors—are fairly similar in girls and boys, but others are different. Both girls and boys experience an increase in sexual interest, attraction, and behavior (whether auto-erotic or partnered), but most girls develop attraction to males whereas most boys develop attraction to females, while a minority of girls and boys develop same-sex or bisexual attractions. (We discuss how sexual orientation develops in Chapter 12.) Similarly, both boys and girls become more susceptible to mental disorders as they go through puberty, but the kinds of disorders that strike girls and boys tend to differ: Girls (and adult women) are more liable to anxiety, depression, and eating disorders, whereas boys (and adult men) are more liable to conduct disorders such as antisocial behavior and drug abuse. It is as if the strong emotions that are awakened during puberty are more likely to be internalized in girls, and more likely to be externalized (expressed in behavior) in boys (Eaton et al., 2012).

Puberty occurs earlier in girls than boys

The timing of puberty is quite variable from individual to individual, so during the early teen years children of the same age may have reached very different stages of development (**Figure 10.8**). Nevertheless, the various processes of puberty occur in a fairly predictable sequence. For girls, the earliest events of puberty are the appearance of pubic hair and the breast-bud stage of breast development, which occur at a

epiphyseal plates The growth zones in limb bones, which cease to function after puberty.

median age* of about 9 years of age in black girls and about 10 years of age in white, Hispanic, and Asian girls (Biro et al., 2013). Girls' growth spurt begins about 1 year after the beginning of breast development. Menarche occurs at about 12.2 years in black girls and 12.8 years in other girls. Final height is reached at about 16 years of age.

In boys, the penis and testicles begin to enlarge at the age of about 10 years, pubic hair appears at about 11, the growth spurt begins at about 12, first ejaculation occurs at about 13, and the voice reaches adult pitch at about 15. The growth spurt ends at about 17, but some additional slow growth may occur for 2–3 years after that. As with girls, some of these stages occur 6 months to a year earlier in black boys (Herman-Giddens et al., 2012).

Because the early stages of puberty occur earlier in girls than in boys, boys enjoy a longer prepubertal childhood than girls. One striking result is the difference in the adult height of men and women. Boys have about 2 more years of childhood growth before the growth spurt begins, which gives them an extra 3 inches (7.5 cm) of height. Add the extra inch (2.5 cm) gained over girls during the growth spurt itself, and adult men end up 4 inches (10 cm) taller than women, on average.

Figure 10.8 **The timing of the growth spurt varies.** These girls are all 12 years old.

Over the past century a number of Western countries have experienced a trend toward earlier puberty. In the United States, children are entering puberty 1 to 2 years earlier than they did in the 1970s (Herman-Giddens et al., 2012; Biro et al., 2013). Changes in diet—specifically, the introduction of plentiful, calorie-dense food that allows children to grow faster and put on more fat—is probably the main reason (Biro et al., 2013). Part of the evidence for this is that girls with a high body mass index (BMI) enter puberty earlier than other girls, and the average BMI of prepubertal girls has been rising steadily for many years. Some researchers have also blamed the presence of **endocrine disruptors**—industrial pollutants that mimic the action of sex hormones—in food or in the environment (Fisher & Eugster, 2014).

What drives puberty?

So far, we have simply described the major phenomena associated with puberty. But what triggers and orchestrates these phenomena? Let's start by looking at the proximate (immediate) causes, then track back to the earlier events that get puberty under way (**Figure 10.9**).

The proximate causes of most of the phenomena of puberty are hormones—in particular, *androgens* and *estrogens*, along with growth hormone. Although estrogen effects predominate in girls and androgen effects predominate in boys, both androgens and estrogens are needed in both sexes for normal completion of puberty.

The levels of testosterone and other androgens rise steadily in both sexes during puberty, but they reach much higher final levels in men than in women. Androgens are responsible for muscle development, change of voice, and spermatogenesis (in combination with the gonadotropin follicle-stimulating hormone [FSH]), as well as the appearance of pubic and axillary hair in both sexes. In males, androgens are also responsible for the pubertal development of the external genitalia, prostate,

endocrine disruptors Substances that interfere with development by mimicking sex hormones.

---

* The median age is the age at which half the individuals have reached that stage of development and half have not.

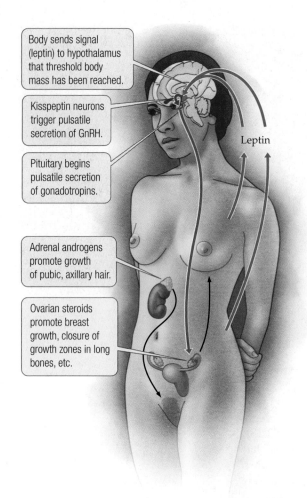

Body sends signal (leptin) to hypothalamus that threshold body mass has been reached.

Kisspeptin neurons trigger pulsatile secretion of GnRH.

Pituitary begins pulsatile secretion of gonadotropins.

Leptin

Adrenal androgens promote growth of pubic, axillary hair.

Ovarian steroids promote breast growth, closure of growth zones in long bones, etc.

Figure 10.9 Hormonal control of puberty This figure shows the chain of events that drive puberty in girls. The regulation of puberty in boys is similar, except that the principal gonadal steroids are androgens, especially testosterone. Signals from body fat may be less important in boys.

seminal vesicles, sebaceous glands, and facial and body hair (and for male-pattern baldness), but full development of these characteristics requires the conversion of testosterone to the more potent androgen 5α-dihydrotestosterone (DHT) in the target tissues (see Chapter 3).

The very high levels of testosterone reached during puberty in boys drive their brain development in a male-typical direction and therefore promote male-typical gender characteristics. Boys who were unmasculine or positively feminine in childhood often become more conventionally masculine during puberty; in fact, boys who say they want to be girls quite commonly change their minds at puberty (see Box 4.5, page 116).

Estrogens (in combination with growth hormone and progesterone) promote development of the breasts. By their actions on the hypothalamus, estrogens and progesterone trigger menarche and are required for the maintenance of menstrual cycles thereafter. These hormones also have more general effects on the brain, affecting mood, memory, and other characteristics. Whether estrogens have a direct effect on women's sexual feelings and behaviors is uncertain (Bancroft & Graham, 2011), but they may do so indirectly by their effects on the genitals (such as increased vaginal lubrication) that make sex more pleasurable. Surprisingly perhaps, testosterone is thought to be a stronger driver of sexual desire in women than estrogen (Davis & Davison, 2012).

In males, estrogens are required for the normal functioning of the epididymis in concentrating sperm and are therefore necessary for male fertility. In both sexes, estrogens are responsible for an increase in bone density at puberty, as well as for the closure of the epiphyseal plates at the end of the pubertal growth spurt. Thus, individuals who cannot manufacture estrogens, or who lack estrogen receptors, keep on growing after the end of puberty and may become exceptionally tall (Sharpe, 1997).

What drives the increase in circulating sex steroids during puberty? The initial rise in androgen levels, which triggers the appearance of pubic and axillary hair in both sexes, is due to an increase in androgen secretion by the adrenal glands. The main increase in sex steroids during puberty, however, is due to an increase in secretion by the gonads. This gonadal secretion is driven by an increase in the release of the *gonadotropins* luteinizing hormone (LH) and FSH.

Gonadotropin secretion is triggered, in turn, by an increase in the secretion of *gonadotropin releasing hormone* (GnRH) by the hypothalamus. This increase is a key event during puberty. The rest of the body seems to be primed from early childhood to heed the call of GnRH; only the lack of GnRH prevents puberty from taking place at 2 or 3 years of age. Thus, we would like to know why GnRH secretion increases when it does, rather than earlier or later.

The body signals its readiness for puberty to the brain

It appears that GnRH secretion increases when the body has reached a certain critical *weight, weight-to-height ratio,* or *body fat ratio* (the proportion of body weight that is fat). The timing of puberty correlates better with body weight than with chronological age. In girls, the pubertal growth spurt begins at an average weight of 66 pounds (30 kg). In boys, puberty is triggered at a higher body weight than in girls: about 121 pounds (55 kg).

Menarche occurs at an average weight of 103 pounds (47 kg). Thus girls who are overweight for their age experience menarche earlier than thin girls, and very thin girls may not experience menarche at all (**primary amenorrhea**). Furthermore, if women lose most of their body fat after puberty—as can happen during famines, as a consequence of eating disorders such as anorexia nervosa, or even as a result of extreme athletic activity—their menstrual cycles may cease (**secondary amenorrhea**).

How might the brain know when the body has reached a certain weight or composition? One key player is **leptin**, a peptide hormone that is secreted by fat cells (Sanchez-Garrido & Tena-Sempere, 2013). In general, leptin levels in the blood provide an indication of how much fat the body has accumulated. It makes sense for a puberty-inducing signal to come from fat cells, especially in girls, because a girl should not become reproductively mature until she has accumulated the energy stores necessary to sustain pregnancy. Supporting the idea that leptin helps trigger puberty is the finding that children suffering from a mutation in the gene for the leptin receptor do not enter puberty (Clement et al., 1998).

Leptin does not directly activate the GnRH-secreting cells of the hypothalamus, however. Rather, leptin, along with other chemical and neural signals, stimulates a group of hypothalamic neurons that manufacture and secrete a signaling molecule named **kisspeptin** (Skorupskaite et al., 2014). Kisspeptin in turn stimulates the GnRH neurons to secrete GnRH, and the rare individuals who lack the receptor for kisspeptin—like those who lack the receptor for leptin—fail to enter puberty.

In summary, puberty is the end result of a long chain of chemical signals: body fat→leptin→kisspeptin→GnRH→gonadotropins→gonadal steroids→target tissues. Why so complicated? Probably because it allows for metabolic and environmental factors to influence the process, including feedback signals from the target tissues and the gonads.

Puberty may come too early or too late

Puberty has generally been diagnosed as **precocious** (or early) if it begins before age 8 in girls or 9 in boys (Carel et al., 2004). Because puberty in the general population has been starting earlier than it used to, especially for girls, there is some question as to whether these criterion ages should be revised downward. After all, about 10% of white and Asian-American girls, 15% of Hispanic girls, and 23% of black girls have some breast development by age 7 (Biro et al., 2010), and so all these girls could be diagnosed with precocious puberty by the criterion just mentioned. Professional guidelines do now revise the cutoff age down to 7 (and to 6 in black girls) (Kaplowitz & Oberfield, 1999; Muir, 2006), but many pediatricians have objected to this revision, arguing that girls who enter puberty between ages 7 and 8 can often benefit from treatment (Sorensen et al., 2012).

There's an interesting philosophical question here: If human action (such as the overfeeding of children) is lowering the general age of puberty, does that change what is "normal" and therefore what should or should not be treated? What do you think?

Precocious puberty causes a child to end up shorter than normal, because some years of prepubertal growth will have been lost. In addition, early sexual maturity may cause psychological and social problems for the child, especially for girls (Dorn, 2007). These girls tend to have low self-esteem on account of the physical differences between them and their peers. They may become targets for sexual advances that they cannot easily repel, and they themselves may develop sexual feelings that they don't know how to cope with.

The earlier children enter puberty, the earlier they are likely to become sexually active. Problems such as early pregnancy, sexually transmitted infections (STIs),

primary amenorrhea The failure to begin menstruating at puberty.

secondary amenorrhea The cessation of menstruation at some time after menarche.

leptin A hormone secreted by fat cells that acts on the hypothalamus.

kisspeptin A signaling molecule in the hypothalamus that promotes the onset of puberty.

precocious puberty Puberty that begins earlier than normal.

delayed puberty Puberty that begins later than normal.

adolescence The period of psychosexual and social maturation that accompanies and follows puberty.

smoking, alcohol and substance abuse, disruptive behavior, truancy, and suicidality are all more common among children who enter puberty early than among those who do so at an average time, although it is not clear whether these outcomes are direct consequences of early puberty.

The cause of precocious puberty cannot usually be determined. However, it can often be treated with a drug, leuprolide (Lupron), which blocks the secretion of the pituitary hormones LH and FSH (see Chapters 2 and 3).* The drug is continued until the child reaches an age or height more appropriate for puberty. (In Chapter 4 we mentioned the use of this drug to delay puberty in children who wish to change their anatomical sex.)

Puberty is considered **delayed** if the early signs of puberty do not appear by age 13 or 14 in girls, or by age 14 in boys. Again, a specific cause cannot usually be identified, although undernourishment or chronic illness may play a role. Puberty does eventually begin in most cases, so patience is often the best treatment. It is sometimes possible to initiate the process with a short course of testosterone (for boys) or estrogens (for girls). Because a delay in puberty allows for more years of childhood growth, persons with delayed puberty are often taller and longer-limbed than those who went through puberty at a typical age.

Adolescence Is a Time of Sexual Exploration

The term **adolescence** is used to mean roughly the teen years (13 to 18, or 13 to 20). The beginning of adolescence may correspond to the biological events of puberty, such as menarche or first ejaculation. The end of adolescence, however, is arbitrary. In fact, the concept of adolescence could be considered a social construction, designed to accommodate the ever-widening gap between the age of reproductive maturity and the age at which society is willing to grant men and women full adult freedoms and responsibilities.

The beginning of adolescence is usually marked by a great increase in a boy's or girl's sexual feelings and often by an increase in sexual behavior as well. This sexual awakening may in part be a response to the obvious bodily changes that accompany puberty. In addition, however, the rising blood levels of sex hormones, especially testosterone, seem to directly activate the brain circuitry that produces sexual feelings and urges in both girls and boys. An adolescent's testosterone level is quite a strong predictor of when she or he will begin to engage in partnered sex (Halpern et al., 1997, 1998).

Many cultures have puberty rites

Puberty, and the consequent increase in sexual feelings and expression, is an important event in a young person's life and has been marked by special coming-of-age ceremonies in many cultures (Ford & Beach, 1951). In girls, puberty includes a dramatic event—menarche—and girls' puberty rites are usually centered on this event. One example is the Western Apaches' Sunrise Ceremony. This 4-day ceremony is a reenactment of the Apache ori-

South African youths participating in initiation rites that include circumcision.

---

* Leuprolide is a GnRH-like peptide and it therefore binds to GnRH receptors on the gonadotropin-secreting cells of the pituitary. These cells are activated only by *pulsatile* GnRH stimulation, however; when leuprolide is *continuously* present, the cells become desensitized and cease to secrete gonadotropins.

gin story, in which Changing Woman had sexual intercourse with the sun, thus bringing forth the Apache hero, Slayer of Monsters. The ceremony, which involves dancing, running to the compass points, and much else, emphasizes the four life goals of physical strength, a good disposition, prosperity, and a healthy old age (Yupanqui, 1999). (Videos of the ceremony can be found online.)

For boys, puberty rites may be simple or complex. On the Truk Islands in the West Pacific, a boy whose pubic hair and facial hair become noticeable simply puts on an adult loincloth and goes to live in the men's quarters. Among the Keraki of New Guinea, however, puberty rites take up to a year. The boys undergoing initiation are gathered in a clearing, where they are shown a sacred musical instrument, the bullroarer, and struck a blow on the back with a heavy banana stalk. There follows a parade and a feast. The boys are confined for nearly a year in a special longhouse, during which time they take the receptive role in anal sex with older males. At the end of this period the boys return home and take on the role of adults. Body modification, including circumcision, is a common feature of male puberty rites around the world (see Chapter 3).

In the West African country of Cameroon, many girls (especially those who enter puberty early) are subjected to a treatment called **breast ironing**. Over a period of weeks or months, their mothers massage or pound their developing breasts with heated wooden pestles or other implements. This painful procedure is intended to delay the outward signs of puberty, thus making the girls less attractive to boys and allowing them to continue school without harassment. The procedure may do permanent damage to the breasts, and there are local and international campaigns to end the practice (Jozwiak, 2014).

In the contemporary United States, puberty rituals may be associated with certain religions and ethnic groups. An example is the Jewish combination of religious instruction and family celebration called **bar mitzvah** for boys and **bat mitzvah** for girls. Hispanics have the ***quinceañera***, a celebration for girls who reach the age of 15 and (traditionally, at least) have maintained their virginity. It incorporates a Catholic mass as well as a traditional *vals* (waltz) danced by the girl and her male escort, along with 14 *damas* and *chambelanes* ("bridesmaids" and their escorts).

breast ironing In Cameroon, a traumatic procedure to delay breast development in girls.

bar mitzvah Jewish coming-of-age ceremony for boys.

bat mitzvah Jewish coming-of-age ceremony for girls.

quinceañera Hispanic coming-of-age ceremony for girls.

There are social influences on teen sexual behavior

Although the physiological processes of puberty play a key role in kick-starting adolescents' sex drive, social influences on teen sexuality also play an important part, especially with regard to sexual behavior with partners. Thus, the overall proportion of the U.S. population who say they first had sex before they were 15 is about 16% (Finer & Philbin, 2013), but it differs greatly among different groups. The percentage is higher among less educated, less religious, and less affluent people (Halpern et al., 2000b; Centers for Disease Control, 2007) (**Figure 10.10**).

To some extent these causes act directly on individuals. For example, individuals from more affluent backgrounds may postpone sexual initiation because they are preoccupied with school and other career-related activities or because they are more alert to the potential

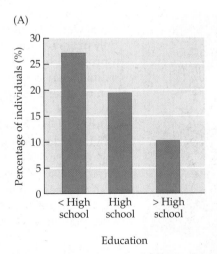
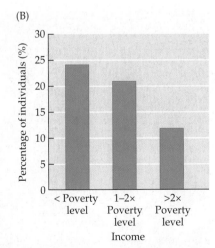

Figure 10.10 Social influences on early sex The graphs show the percentages of individuals who engaged in vaginal, oral, or anal sex before the age of 15, broken down by (A) education and (B) economic status. (After Centers for Disease Control, 2007.)

super peer theory The idea that teens learn from glamorous teen role models in the media.

virginity-pledge programs Programs in which teens take formal pledges not to have sex before marriage.

abstinence-only program A sex-ed program that teaches abstinence and omits mention of safer-sex practices, homosexuality, etc.

comprehensive sex-education programs Sex-ed programs that discuss abstinence as well as safer-sex practices, sexual and gender diversity, etc.

negative consequences of early sexual activity. But there also seems to be an effect based on community norms, because the sexual behavior of individual adolescents is strongly influenced by their perception of peer expectations (Santelli et al., 2004). Thus, adolescents are likely to initiate sexual activity early if their community has a low average income, few college graduates, a high crime rate, or high unemployment. It is likely that such communities offer adolescents few challenging goals and therefore give them little motivation to work hard and avoid risky sexual activities that could derail them from attaining their dreams (Billy et al., 1994).

Another factor associated with the early initiation of sexual activity is having a significantly older boyfriend or girlfriend (VanOss Marin et al., 2000; Halpern et al., 2007). This is hardly surprising, given that older partners are likely to be more sexually experienced and eager to initiate their younger partners.

Television probably promotes early entry into sex by portraying sexual relationships and activities among young people, often in a highly glamorized and unrealistic fashion. According to the American Psychiatric Association, girls are being prematurely sexualized by exposure to inappropriate images and role models in the media and advertising (American Psychiatric Association, 2008). This effect has been interpreted in terms of **super peer theory**, according to which the characters portrayed on TV and the movies act in the same way as a peer group to influence individual behavior, but more powerfully because of their glamor or the attention paid to them (Brown et al., 2005). Thus, if these characters frequently engage in sexual behaviors, a person who's not sexually active may feel compelled to join the perceived majority.

Not all TV shows glamorize sex, of course. MTV's reality show *16 and Pregnant* and its *Teen Mom* spinoffs, for example, highlight the tough situations faced by working-class teen mothers, so they may encourage teens to delay sex or use contraception more effectively. On the other hand, they may actually promote teen pregnancy simply by virtue of the attention paid to the girls or young women in the shows—they're on television, after all. What do you think?

Some cultural forces attempt to dissuade teens from engaging in sexual behavior. In faith-based **virginity-pledge programs**, such as True Love Waits and Silver Ring Thing, teens make a commitment to abstain from sex until marriage, but a large controlled prospective study found that pledge taking had no effect on sexual activity; in fact, most pledge takers later denied ever having taken a pledge (Rosenbaum, 2009).

Abstinence-only sex-ed doesn't work.

School-based sex-education programs that only promote abstinence also have a poor track record (Stanger-Hall & Hall, 2011; Landor & Simons, 2013). In one study mandated by the U.S. Congress, students were randomly assigned to attend or not attend **abstinence-only programs** and then followed up on for several years. Attending a program had no effect on any measure of the teens' subsequent sexual behavior (Trenholm et al., 2007).

Comprehensive sex-education programs, which discuss the risks of sex as well as the means (such as contraception) to mitigate those risks, have had better results: Teens who are exposed to such programs do not engage in more or earlier sex but are more likely to engage in sex in a responsible and safe fashion (Carter, 2012). Under President Obama there was a major shift of federal sex-education funds from abstinence-only to comprehensive programs. Still, only 19 states and the District of Columbia require school sex-ed programs to include a description of contraceptive methods (Guttmacher Institute, 2014c).

Social media have risks and benefits

In recent years a great deal of attention has been paid to the effects of social networking tools on teen sexuality. Through these media teens (and others) engage in "impression management," meaning that they seek to maximize their desirability to potential romantic partners (Alpizar et al., 2012). On Facebook, for example, teens are able to control how they appear to others in ways that are not possible in face-to-face interactions, such as by the choice, manipulation, and frequent changes of their profile photographs (Strano, 2008), and by selective or misleading accounts of their activities and relationships.

Thus, in following their peers on social media, teens can very easily come to believe that they themselves are relatively unattractive, uncomfortable, or unsuccessful in their love lives. This false belief can overwhelm their own behavioral norms and cause them to make themselves more available sexually than they would otherwise. Most research on this topic has been done on college students (Holman & Sillars, 2012; Barriger & Velez-Blasini, 2013), but the phenomenon is likely to be even more pervasive among younger teens because they have less well-established personal norms and are less able to critically evaluate their peers' postings and texts.

Another issue with social media has to do with privacy. Many young people do not understand how difficult it is to restrict the dissemination of information about themselves via social media. Gay or lesbian individuals, for example, may unintentionally out themselves to their parents or others, or they may be outed by third parties such as gay organizations that the individuals join (Fowler, 2012). Similarly, teens may "sext" nude or sexually suggestive photographs of themselves to intimate partners, only to find that these photographs have become much more widely available.

Moreover, it is a federal and state felony to post, send, or receive "lascivious images of the genitals or pubic area" of a person under 18, even if that person is oneself. ("Lascivious" means "intended to arouse sexual desire," so it would not include, for example, the photos of pubertal development that accompany this chapter.) Only a small percentage of teens send or receive these kinds of images (Crimes Against Children Research Center, 2014), and of those who do, an even smaller percentage run into trouble with the law. Still, penalties for these activities can include custodial sentences (Humbach, 2010).

In spite of these negatives, social media can also have positive value, for example in the dissemination of information relating to sexual health (Bull et al., 2012). Moreover, social media and the Internet as a whole can be of great significance to teens who are members of sexual minorities or who have uncommon sexual interests, especially in countries where they face legal or social oppression.

Males masturbate more than females

One of the most common sexual behaviors among adolescents is masturbation. But adolescents often feel guilty about masturbating, believe that the practice is harmful, and taunt others about masturbation as schoolyard insults (Savin-Williams & Diamond, 2004). Thus, adolescents are often reluctant to admit that they masturbate, making the topic difficult to research. In one longitudinal study, for example, only about one-third of 13-year-old boys said that they masturbated, but when these same individuals were reinterviewed in adulthood, more than twice as many said that they had masturbated at that age (Halpern et al., 2000a).

Many studies show that the frequency of masturbation increases during early and mid-teen years and that boys masturbate more frequently than girls. But girls have been catching up: In the mid-20th century only 39% of young women said that they had ever masturbated during childhood or adolescence; by the early 21st century, 84% reported having done so (Bancroft et al., 2003a). Although substantial numbers of both boys and girls begin masturbating before puberty, the onset of masturbation is much more closely synchronized with the onset of puberty in boys than it is in girls (**Figure 10.11**). This suggests a more powerful hormonal influence on masturbation in boys.

Figure 10.11 Masturbation and puberty Female and male college students were asked about the age at which they first masturbated and their age at puberty, defined as menarche (girls) or first ejaculation (boys). The graphs (plotted in number of years before and after puberty) show that the onset of masturbation is not closely tied to puberty in girls (A), but is in boys (B). (Data from Bancroft et al., 2003a.)

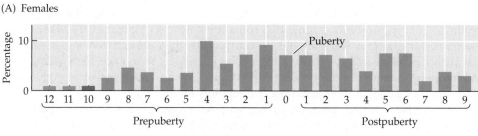

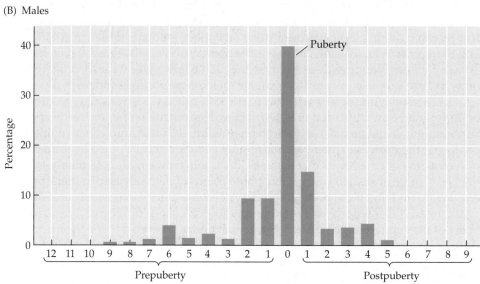

The sexual behavior of American teens has increased and diversified

Cultural changes over the last half century or so have had a tremendous influence on adolescent sexuality in the United States. In the period immediately after World War II, most adolescents' goals were focused on completing schooling, working, marrying, and starting a family. Adolescents dated in the late 1940s, and this behavior was important for their social standing and the development of gender-appropriate roles, but dating at that time generally involved sexual behavior short of coitus. Engaging in coitus and risking pregnancy endangered the social status of unmarried young adult females. The status of males was not endangered in the same way—exemplifying the sexual "double standard"—but males generally found it difficult to persuade females to have intercourse with them, and some turned to prostitutes.

Many social changes since the 1940s have caused teenage sexual activity to increase, especially among girls (**Figure 10.12**). One was the introduction of oral contraceptives in the 1960s. Another was the legalization of abortion in the United States in 1973. Yet another was the introduction of effective treatments for some STIs. These factors reduced the risks of coitus for women, including adolescent women. Another factor was feminism, which encouraged women to attend college, enter the workforce, and postpone marriage. All these changes together made it easier for young women to begin having sex without fears of pregnancy or disease.

Even so, "losing one's virginity" is still a significant event in many women's and men's lives (**Box 10.4**). According to repeated surveys of students at Illinois State University, males report more pleasure than females during their

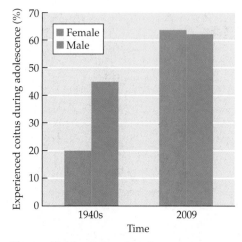

Figure 10.12 Coitus has become more common among teens. The graph shows the percentages of females and of males who experienced coitus during adolescence (by age 18 or 19) in the 1940s and in 2009. The 1940s data refer to coitus by age 19; the 2009 data refer to coitus by grade 12. (After Kinsey et al., 1948, 1953 and Center for Sexual Health Promotion, 2010.)

Box 10.4 Research Highlights

Losing It

What does losing one's virginity mean? Vanderbilt University sociologist Laura Carpenter set out to find the answer to this question by conducting in-depth interviews with 61 young women and men from diverse social backgrounds and sexual identities, most of whom had already lost their virginity (Carpenter, 2005). Comments from four of them appear below:

Kelly: Virginity is supposed to be something special and cherished and wonderful and something to keep and you give to someone who is… don't know if lose is the right word…I'll say you give to someone, whenever you find the right person.

Emma: I just did not want to be a virgin…And looking back, that wasn't particularly intelligent or mature…But at the same time, that was how I viewed it when I was a virgin.

Jason: [Losing one's virginity is] sort of the year zero in between the part of life before sexual activity and then, the one after…the moment between having never had sex and having had it.

Carrie: I think [maintaining one's virginity is] a really great way to honor God, in the sense of knowing that, whatever He has for me is going to be better than the things I can pursue on my own.

Christian reverence for the Virgin Mary helped establish virginity as something sacred. This painting is by Martino Altomonte, 1719.

Traditionally, losing one's virginity meant engaging in penile-vaginal intercourse (coitus) for the first time. But to some of Carpenter's interviewees, losing virginity was more of a mental event than a mechanical one. So, for example, being raped would not cause one to lose virginity. Also, other sexual behaviors, such as oral or anal sex, might count as loss of virginity, especially for gay people.

Carpenter discerned four basic modes of thinking about the loss of virginity:

- *Virginity loss as a gift.* "Gifters" (such as Kelly) believe that virginity is something valuable to be given to a partner in a loving relationship—though not necessarily in a marriage. To gifters, virginity is not really "lost," because it becomes part of the extended self that includes the intimate partner. Although most gifters are female, some are male. Gifters want to lose their virginity to another gifter, but it often doesn't work out that way, due to the shortage of male gifters.

- *Virginity loss as erasing a stigma.* To some young people (such as Emma) virginity is a sign of "irredeemable dorkiness"—a stigma that only becomes more oppressive as the teen years roll by. Losing one's virginity is seen as an end in itself and does not have to happen in the context of a loving relationship. Because the "stigmatized" seize the first opportunity for coitus, they often do not use safer sex practices.

- *Virginity loss as a part of a process.* Some young people see the loss of virginity not as something intrinsically good or bad, but as part of the process of growing up into male or female adulthood. "Processors" (such as Jason) see first coitus as one "stepping-stone" out of many. They typically have sex with partners they are dating. Gay people are disproportionately likely to take this perspective, since they experience virginity loss as intertwined with the process of coming out.

- *Virginity loss as a sacrament.* Some young people (such as Carrie)—mostly evangelical Christians—see abstinence as a form of worship and losing one's virginity (with one's eventual spouse) as a mutual gift to God. These young people typically avoid almost all forms of sexual intimacy before marriage.

Looking back on the encounters that marked their loss of virginity, some of Carpenter's interviewees recalled emotional or physical pleasure, or satisfaction at having accomplished one of life's watershed tasks. But many recalled the event as disappointing, physically painful (women especially), or downright embarrassing. Here's how one young man saw it:

Bill: I was so nervous, it was my first time, and… I didn't want to look foolish… I tried to do what I saw the people do in the porno movies, move my body in a certain way, and do it really fast…She was saying to me "There's another person here, you know." I ejaculated very quickly. I was, like, just interested in getting myself off and didn't even think about her… I felt like I had really fucked this thing up.

Ten years after Carpenter's study, teens experience the same anxieties and conflicts about virginity. The stories of 15 teens and young adults struggling to surrender or hang on to their "v-cards" were told in MTV's 2014 documentary series *Virgin Territory*.

first sexual intercourse, and females report more feelings of guilt. Over the last two decades, however, women's guilty feelings during first intercourse have lessened, and their sense of pleasure has increased (Sprecher, 2014).

All in all, these changes led to a considerable increase in the numbers of sexually experienced adolescents as compared with their numbers 50 or 60 years ago. This increase came to an end around 1990, however: Between 1991 and 2013 the proportion of high school students who had ever had sexual intercourse dropped somewhat—from 54% to 47%—and this drop was particularly marked among the younger students (9th and 10th grades) (Forum on Child and Family Statistics, 2013; Centers for Disease Control, 2014q). What's more, even those teens who engage in coitus don't do so very often: Only 27% of 17-year-old males say that they have done so even once within the previous 90 days (Herbenick et al., 2010b). Among 20-year-olds, about 1 in 4 have never engaged in coitus (Guttmacher Institute, 2014b). What reasons do you think they might give for not having done so?

Noncoital sex is popular among teens

Oral sex is common among U.S. teens; by age 17, 48% of males and 37% of females have engaged in this practice (Centers for Disease Control, 2010e). In part, oral sex may be popular because it is a way to have sex without loss of "vaginal virginity" and without risking pregnancy. About half of all young Americans have oral sex on some occasion prior to their first experience of vaginal intercourse. Nevertheless, engaging in oral sex doesn't seem to be a long-term strategy for avoiding coitus, because the great majority of teens who have engaged in oral sex have engaged in vaginal sex too, according to the National Survey of Family Growth (NSFG) data. This suggests that, for most teens, oral sex is something they add to their sexual repertoire because of the pleasure it brings, not as a substitute for coitus. Anal sex is much less common than oral sex—only about 1 in 10 adolescents has engaged in it—and again, it is practiced mainly by teens who have already begun to experience vaginal intercourse.

There are large racial/ethnic differences in these activities. Black adolescents are more likely to have experienced coitus than similar-age adolescents of other races (**Figure 10.13**), but they are less likely to have engaged in noncoital behaviors, especially cunnilingus. In this, they reflect the attitudes of their elders, because oral sex is much less popular among blacks generally than it is among whites (Laumann & Michael, 2000). Hispanics are more like whites in this respect.

Asian-Americans and Pacific Islanders (AAPI) are a small but very diverse group who often get overlooked in surveys. Far fewer AAPI high school students have ever engaged in coitus than have students of other origins. This could be read as consistent with the stereotype of Asian-Americans as the "model minority." When AAPI teens do finally engage in coitus, however, they are just as likely to do so without protection or while under the influence of alcohol or drugs (Grunbaum et al., 2000), so their "modelness" doesn't necessarily carry over into the details of their sexual activities. Part of the reason for this may be a traditional reluctance of Asian-Americans to discuss sexual matters within their families or with health care providers: Many Asian-American females have never discussed sexual matters with their parents (Meneses et al., 2006). The more acculturated to mainstream U.S. society they are—speak-

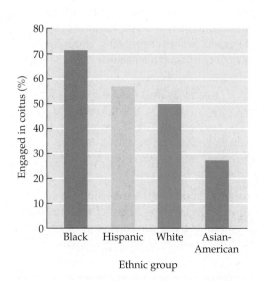

Figure 10.13 Ethnicity and sexual initiation This graph shows the percentages of U.S. 15- to 19-year-olds who have engaged in coitus, by race/ethnicity. More recent surveys report slightly lower percentages but do not include Asian-Americans. (Data from Schuster et al., 1998.)

ing English at home, for example—the more the sexual behavior of Asian-American youths comes to resemble that of other U.S. teens (Tong, 2013).

Teenagers can easily violate age-of-consent laws when they engage in sexual activities, especially if one partner is older than the other. A remarkable example concerned a Georgia youth, Genarlow Wilson, who had oral sex with a willing 15-year-old girl when he was 17. In 2005 Wilson was convicted of aggravated child molestation and sentenced to 10 years of imprisonment. (After he had been behind bars for 2 years, the Supreme Court of Georgia ordered him released; he later graduated with honors from Morehouse College.) Age-of-consent laws are complex and vary from state to state. Detailed information for particular U.S. states and other countries is available online (see Web Resources at the end of this chapter).

Teen Sexuality Is Central to Identity Development

Although public attention focuses mainly on the possible negative consequences of teens' sexual behavior, and on ways to prevent it, we shouldn't ignore the positive role that sexuality plays in the process of growing up. Adolescence involves the development of a sense of self and a social identity independent from one's parents (Erikson, 1968; Steinberg, 2013). Answering questions about one's sexuality figures centrally in this process. Teens must answer many such questions: What is my sexual orientation? What am I looking for in sexual relationships? How attractive am I? Who might I attract as a sexual partner, and what are the best ways for entering into a partnership? How does my sexuality relate to other aspects of my identity, such as my career goals, my ethnic origins, or my religion?

Teen sexual relationships often have a playful quality.

The development of a sense of self is vital to practical sexual concerns. For example, both young women and young men need to be able to refuse unwanted sex, including sex without a condom. In one study of black teenage girls in Birmingham, Alabama, girls with a high evaluation of themselves—including a positive ethnic identity, high self-esteem, and a positive body image—communicated better with their partners concerning condom use and were more likely to refuse unprotected sex than were other girls (Salazar et al., 2004).

Developing a sense of self is not a purely intellectual process—it is not achieved simply by reason or introspection. Rather, it requires social exploration and learning. This exploration takes place chiefly in the milieu in which sexual interactions are likely to arise—namely, in one's peer group. This is not to say that parent-teen interactions are unimportant, however. In the Birmingham study, for example, girls who spoke frequently with their parents about sexual matters were nearly twice as likely to refuse unwanted sex as those who did not (Sionean et al., 2002).

Given all that you may have heard about the harmful consequences of early sexual behavior, it may be surprising to learn that, in a study of seniors in a rural New York high school, those students who became sexually active earlier than average, or who had a higher-than-average number of sex partners, did not report any lesser well-being than those students who became sexually active at an average age or who had not yet become sexually active. In fact, the girls who became sexually active early reported higher levels of well-being than their peers (Vrangalova & Savin-Williams, 2011). If they can avoid STIs and pregnancy, some teens may derive a positive benefit from sex and sexual relationships.

FAQ

If a teen gets pregnant, does her boyfriend have any legal say over whether she has an abortion or not?

No, but his wishes and his commitment to parenthood (or lack of it) often influence her decision.

serial monogamy Involvement in a series of monogamous relationships.

Teen relationships are often short-lived

For some adolescents, sexual exploration involves **serial monogamy**, in which the youth has a series of exclusive non-cohabiting ("dating") relationships (Chapter 7) with girlfriends or boyfriends (or both). Within such serial relationships adolescents can discover what gives them pleasure and how to interact intimately with another person. Typically, the sexual content of these relationships progresses during the adolescent years from kissing and fondling to noncoital orgasmic contacts, and possibly to coitus.

According to some social commentators and newspaper investigations, however, the "hookup culture" has come to the American high school, largely replacing traditional non-cohabiting relationships. As one 17-year-old girl told the *New York Times*, "The couple thing is overrated—it gets too clingy" (Denizet-Lewis, 2004). Another sign of the decline in adolescent non-cohabiting relationships is that teens increasingly attend proms and similar events without specific "dates": They may attend solo or in groups of friends (College Confidential, 2014).

Yet the statistics collected by the CDC offer little support for the notion that casual sex has been on the increase at the high school level. According to their national Youth Risk Behavior Survey, the percentage of high school students who have had four or more sex partners in their lifetime has been *falling* steadily from year to year—from 18.7% in 1991 to 15% in 2013 (Centers for Disease Control, 2014q). And only a small minority of 15- to 17-year-olds (15% of girls and 16% of boys) have had sexual contact with more than one opposite-sex partner within the previous year—"sexual contact" being defined as vaginal, oral, or anal sex. This suggests that if a hookup culture does exist in the adolescent years, it involves only a small minority of young people or doesn't involve penetrative sex.

With the loosening of traditional attitudes over the last few decades has come an increasing interest among adolescents in issues of gender and sexual orientation. Most teens, regardless of their sexual orientation or gender identity, are likely to know something about sexual minorities and the cultures that they have established, and many have openly gay, bisexual, or (less likely) transgender teens in their peer groups. As a result, they are aware of a greater range of sex and relationship options than were their predecessors. The once-rigid categories of "straight" and "gay" have morphed, for some teens, into "mostly straight" and "mostly gay." We will explore this topic further in Chapter 12.

Teen pregnancy is declining but is still too common

Teenage pregnancy is not an inherently bad thing, of course. Evolution has equipped girls with the capacity to have children soon after puberty, and until modern times most did so. In many developing countries females are still expected to marry in their mid-teens and bear children shortly thereafter. What's more, there are some advantages to becoming a mother early. These include a lesser likelihood of fertility problems, a decreased risk of breast cancer later in life, and the ability to look after and enjoy one's children while still in the full vigor of young adulthood. Some U.S. teenagers are able to successfully incorporate pregnancy and motherhood into their lives—with help from their partners, their parents, or social services, as personal accounts testify (Noffsinger, 2014). Those who have difficulty may eventually recover from the disadvantages of early, unassisted motherhood. In fact, the very experience of being a mother helps some previously aimless teenagers focus on their life goals and strive for success (SmithBattle, 2007).

In spite of these positive points, the outcome of pregnancy is not a happy one for many American teenagers (National Campaign to Prevent Teen and

This teenage mother and her child are likely to face economic hardship.

Unplanned Pregnancy, 2014). The majority of teen pregnancies (about 4 out of 5) are unintended, and one-third of all teen pregnancies end in abortion. When unintended pregnancies are allowed to go to term, the children born of them are less likely to be breast-fed and more likely to suffer health problems than other children. If the pregnancy is intended, it may be for less than satisfactory reasons, such as a desire for the self-esteem or social status that is imagined to go with motherhood. Frequently the father is out of the picture before the child's birth or soon thereafter—oftentimes his name does not even appear on the birth certificate. When the father can be identified, he is often significantly older than the mother. Most teen fathers do want to be good fathers, but circumstances often make that role difficult. If the mother and father marry, the likelihood of marital breakdown and divorce is high. Pregnancy and motherhood impair teenagers' opportunities for education and employment, so children of teenage mothers typically grow up in poverty and are more likely than other children to drop out of school.

Perhaps because of increasing awareness of these negatives, the teen birthrate has declined quite dramatically in the United States: The rate dropped by 10% in just one year (2013), and it is now at a record low of 27 births per 1000 females aged 15–19. This is 57% below its 1991 peak (National Vital Statistics Reports, 2014). The decline is due to a decrease in pregnancy rates, not to an increase in abortion. The decline in the pregnancy rate is due mostly (86%) to improved contraceptive use and only to a small degree (14%) to an increase in abstinence among teens (Santelli et al., 2007). In spite of the decline, teen birthrates are far higher in the United States than in many other developed countries, including Canada (National Campaign to Prevent Teen and Unplanned Pregnancy, 2012) (**Figure 10.14**).

Go to the
**Discovering
Human Sexuality**
Companion Website at
**sites.sinauer.com/
discoveringhumansexuality3e**
for activities, study questions,
quizzes, and other study aids.

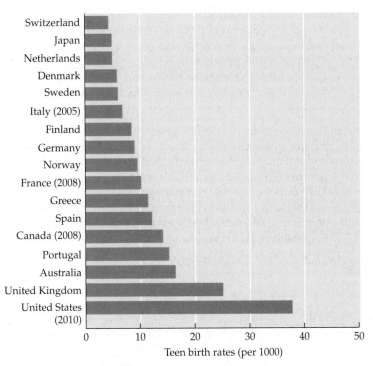

Teen birth rates (per 1000)

Figure 10.14 The United States leads in teen births. This bar graph shows the birthrates per 1000 females age 15–19, for selected countries. Data is for 2009, except where stated otherwise. Since 2009 the U.S. rate has fallen significantly—see text. (After National Campaign to Prevent Teen and Unplanned Pregnancy, 2012.)

Summary

- Basic physiological responses of sexual arousal are seen in infants and young children. They are often triggered by a wide range of stimuli, such as strong emotions of any kind. Masturbation is common in young children, and other sexual behaviors, such as the display of genitals or the inspection of other children's genitals, are also quite prevalent. These behaviors may be incorporated into sexual games such as "doctor." Young children rarely engage in adultlike sexual behavior, however.

- Some non-Western societies tolerate or encourage childhood sexual behavior, while others attempt to restrain it. In the contemporary United States, children are often prevented from engaging in or learning about sexuality.

- Some children, usually older ones, have sexual contacts with adults. These contacts are usually one-time events rather than ongoing relationships. Most adults who have sexual contacts with children are relatives or acquaintances of the child, rather than strangers. Coercive or repeated adult-child sexual contacts can cause long-lasting psychological trauma. Noncoercive, single-event contacts may cause little or no harm.

- In preadolescence, children tend to socialize in same-sex groups and to impose strict gender codes, expecting gender conformity. This practice can be traumatic for gender-nonconformist children. Although segregation by sex limits opportunities for heterosexual encounters, a few children do engage in coitus before the age of 13.

- Puberty is the transition to reproductive maturity. It is marked by development of the genitalia, the appearance of secondary sexual characteristics, a growth spurt, the onset of menstruation in girls and ejaculation in boys, and changes in the brain that lead to sexual behavior and psychological sex differences.

- The onset of puberty is triggered by a complex chain of events: the attainment of a criterion body size or body fat ratio; the communication of this information to the hypothalamus by the hormone leptin; the activity of kisspeptin neurons; the secretion of GnRH; the secretion of LH and FSH by the pituitary; the secretion of sex steroids by the gonads; and the effect of sex steroids on the body and brain.

- Puberty begins at a median age of about 10 (9 years in black children). Children are entering puberty at younger ages than was the case in the past; a likely cause is the faster growth and increasing obesity of contemporary children. Puberty is generally considered precocious (early) if it begins before age 8 in girls or 9 in boys, but some experts believe that the criterion age for girls should be lowered to 7. Puberty is considered delayed if it does not begin by age 13 or 14 in girls or by age 14 in boys.

- Many cultures mark puberty by special celebrations or rites. Examples practiced in the United States are the Jewish bar/bat mitzvah and the Hispanic *quinceañera*.

- Adolescence is usually defined as the teen years. In early adolescence, rising sex hormone levels trigger an increasing interest in sex. Most adolescent males masturbate frequently, but females do so less often.

- Adolescent heterosexual behavior gradually progresses from kissing and fondling to coitus, oral sex, and, sometimes, anal sex. Some characteristics of teen sexual behavior reflect personal and demographic factors such as education and ethnicity. The availability of reliable contraception and modern views of women's roles in society have modified teen sexual behavior over the last several decades. Social media have also affected teens' sexuality, in both negative and positive ways.

- Virginity-pledge programs and abstinence-only sex education have little or no effect on teens' sexual behavior. Comprehensive sex-ed, which includes practical information for those teens who will be sexually active, leads to safer sexual practices and does not increase teens' sexual activity.

- Teen pregnancy has declined over the last two decades, mostly on account of improved use of contraceptives, but it is still much higher in the United States than in Canada or other developed countries. It is also higher among Hispanics and blacks than among whites or Asian-Americans. About 1 in 3 teen pregnancies are terminated by abortion. Teenage mothers and their children face numerous problems, but some thrive.

Discussion Questions

1. What are your attitudes and values about what is normal sexuality during childhood? If you were a parent and found your child engaging in sexual exploration with the child next door, how would you respond?

2. What kind of sex education would you want your child to receive in elementary school, middle school, and high school?

3. Do you recall whether you experienced puberty at the same time as your peers, or earlier or later than most? How did the timing of your puberty affect you, or how were your early- or late-developing peers affected?

4. In high school, were you able to discuss sexual and relationship issues freely with your parents? How might you hope to do a better job if and when you become a parent?

Web Resources

Ages of consent in North America (This article appears to be accurate and up-to-date, but Wikipedia articles can change unpredictably or become outdated.) en.wikipedia.org/wiki/Ages_of_consent_in_North_America

Gay Teens Resources www.gayteensresources.org

National Campaign to Prevent Teen and Unplanned Pregnancy www.thenationalcampaign.org

Sex, Etc. (a website for teens by teens) www.sexetc.org

Sexinfo (University of California, Santa Barbara) www.soc.ucsb.edu/sexinfo

Silver Ring Thing (virginity-pledge program) www.silverringthing.com

Teenwire (Planned Parenthood site) www.plannedparenthood.org/teens

Center for Sexual Health Promotion. National Survey of Sexual Health and Behavior (2010) (includes much information about teen sexuality) www.nationalsexstudy.indiana.edu

Recommended Reading

Bancroft, J. (Ed.). (2003). *Sexual development in childhood*. Indiana University Press.

Carpenter, L. M. (2005). *Virginity lost: An intimate portrait of first sexual experiences*. New York University Press.

Haffner, D. W. (2008). *From diapers to dating: A parent's guide to raising sexually healthy children*. William Morrow.

Levine, J. (2002). *Harmful to minors: The perils of protecting children from sex*. University of Minnesota Press.

Steinberg, L. (2013). *Adolescence* (10th ed.). McGraw-Hill.

Chapter 11

Parenthood is a pleasure and a lot of hard work.

Sexuality across the Life Span: Adulthood

Adulthood is not a fixed state of being, but a story with many episodes. Among them, for most men and women, is finding a true love, then marriage. Yet marriage is changing. For some, wedding vows represent a commitment to sexual loyalty and parenting. For others, marriage is something temporary or unnecessary. Yet regardless of the setting, successful intimate relationships require as much care and nurturing as any children that may be born of them.

Over the course of adult life, a person's sexuality faces many challenges. These include the task of establishing and maintaining durable relationships, and perhaps additional challenges, such as parenthood, separation, menopause, physical decline, and bereavement. As people face these issues, their sexual lives change, but not necessarily for the worse. Sexuality, like life in general, always seems to offer opportunities for growth.

In Young Adulthood, Conflicting Demands Influence Sexual Expression

In Chapter 7 we discussed the kinds of sexual relationships that adults may engage in. We now attempt to describe how those relationships structure individual life courses. We begin with collective data—data that describe generic Americans, with their off-white skin color, predominantly heterosexual orientation, and 1.86 children.

Young adults typically spend several years dating and relating before they move in with a partner.

Most young men and women have only a few sex partners

In 2013, the median age at first marriage in the United States was 29.0 years for men and 26.6 years for women, up from 23 and 21 in 1970 (U.S. Census Bureau, 2014).* Assuming an age of 13 for puberty, men can therefore expect a period of 16 years between puberty and marriage, and women can expect a period of almost 14 years. By many measures, this period includes men's and women's peak sexual years. It includes the years of most frequent sexual behavior (including masturbation), greatest fertility, and greatest physical attractiveness (for females as judged by males, at least—see Chapter 5). Typically, young people spend a portion of this period without a sexual relationship, a portion in one or more noncohabiting ("dating") relationships, and a portion in one or more cohabitations.

Given all one reads and hears about sex among young adults, the actual statistics may be surprising. Between the ages of 20 and 24, only 30% of men and 25% of women report having had more than one opposite-sex sex partner in the previous 12 months, according to data from the 2011 National Survey of Family Growth (NSFG, Centers for Disease Control, 2011b) (Figure 11.1). Some young adults have sexual contact with same-sex partners, of course: In the NSFG survey, 5.6% of men and 15.8% of women reported at least one same-sex partner within the previous year.

About 1 in 8 college undergraduates practices "secondary abstinence," according to one study (Rasberry & Goodson, 2009). Secondary abstinence means actively choosing not to have sex after having had sex at some earlier time. In the study, factors making secondary abstinence more likely were religious beliefs and previous unpleasant sexual experiences. It seems that plenty of college-age women and men are sexually inactive for reasons that have little or nothing to do with partner availability. In a survey of 17,000 college students, over one-third said that they had had no sex partners in the previous 12 months (Oswalt & Wyatt, 2013).

Even by their late 20s about 3% of the population have had no partnered sexual experiences (defined as oral-genital, vaginal, or anal sex) in their lifetime (Haydon et al., 2014). These adult virgins may have chosen not to have sex because of a lack of sexual attraction to anyone (asexuality—see Chapter 5) or for religious reasons. Individuals who enter puberty late are more likely than others to remain sexually inactive, perhaps because they miss out on social learning processes relating to sexuality during their mid-teens.

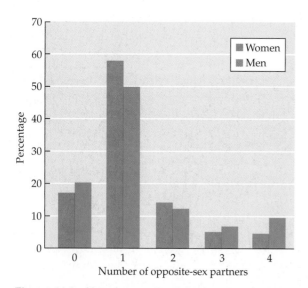

Figure 11.1 Heterosexual activity by young adults This bar graph shows the percentages of women and men age 20 to 24 who reported the stated number of opposite-sex partners within the previous year. (Data from Centers for Disease Control, 2011b.)

---

* The median age at marriage for same-sex couples is probably higher, because many older gay couples are playing catch-up as same-sex marriage is legalized.

Figure 11.2 Cohabitations are on the rise. This graph shows the numbers of unmarried, cohabiting, opposite-sex adult couples in the United States (uncorrected for population growth). (Data from National Marriage Project, 2010 and U.S. Census Bureau, 2010.)

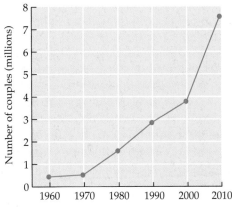

Cohabitation is an increasingly prevalent lifestyle

Most men and women hope to enter into a durable, live-in sexual relationship—a cohabitation or marriage—eventually. Often, a desire for children comes into play here, but even people who don't currently want children commonly want to be part of a long-term, loving relationship.

Cohabitation is the word we use to describe the relationship of a couple—opposite-sex or same-sex—that live together in a sexual relationship without being legally married. Cohabitation has become an increasingly common form of relationship over the past few decades, both in the United States and in other Western countries. As of the most recent U.S. Census, there were about 7.6 million cohabiting opposite-sex couples (**Figure 11.2**), along with about 0.5 million cohabiting same-sex couples (U.S. Census Bureau, 2011b). For nearly all women born before 1940, the first live-in sexual relationship was marriage; now this is true for less than 1 in 4 women (Centers for Disease Control, 2013b). The increase in cohabitation rates has been particularly marked in the six states where heterosexual cohabitation is still technically illegal (**Box 11.1**). Overall, more than 60% of American couples who

cohabitation A live-in sexual relationship between two persons who are not married to each other.

Box 11.1 Society, Values, and the Law

Cohabitation: Laws in Conflict

In February 2004, Deborah Hobbs, a 40-year-old emergency dispatcher in North Carolina (see figure), was fired when her boss, the sheriff of Pender County, found out that she was living with a man to whom she was not married. The sheriff had the law on his side: Cohabitation between unmarried persons has been a crime in North Carolina since 1805. It's a crime that about 144,000 unmarried couples are committing in North Carolina, along with perhaps 3 million couples in the five additional states that have anti-cohabitation laws (Florida, Michigan, Mississippi, Virginia, and West Virginia).

Deborah Hobbs was fired from her job for breaking North Carolina's law against cohabitation, but she went to court to have the law ruled unconstitutional.

Yet these laws are contradicted by other laws in those same states. Florida, for example, has a law that bans discrimination in housing on the basis of whether a couple is married or not. In 2006, the American Civil Liberties Union (ACLU) fought and won a lawsuit on behalf of Hobbs, but the North Carolina law—though declared unconstitutional by a state court—remains on the books. In North Dakota, the conflict between the anti-cohabitation and nondiscrimination statutes led, in 2007, to the repeal of the 118-year-old cohabitation ban.

Nationally, the trend is toward greater legal recognition that cohabiting couples have both rights and obligations. These might include such things as the right to remain in a rent-controlled apartment after the death of an unmarried partner. And when cohabiting couples break up, the law sometimes recognizes implied financial obligations between the partners—obligations that call for "palimony" payments akin to the alimony payments between divorced spouses.

Same-sex couples may be legally recognized in the same way—a fact that first came to public attention in 1981, when Marilyn Barnett brought a suit for palimony (or "galimony," as the newspapers called it) against her former lover, tennis great Billie Jean King. Barnett's case was thrown out, however.

Source: ACLU, 2005.

marry have lived together for some period of time before marrying (National Marriage Project, 2010).

What factors influence the choice of marriage or cohabitation as a first live-in relationship? Factors making marriage more likely include affluence, strong religious convictions, late sexual initiation, and living in a rural area. Factors making cohabitation more likely include economic disadvantage, limited education, and having parents who separated during one's childhood. These same factors increase the chances that the cohabitation will end in a breakup rather than marriage (Laumann et al., 1994; Kroeger & Smock, 2014).

Although so many people now make their first live-in relationship a cohabitation, only a small fraction of the U.S. population (about 7% of men and women age 18 to 59) is cohabiting at any given time. That's because cohabitations typically last only about 2 years, after which couples either marry or split up (Centers for Disease Control, 2013b).

Cohabitation is considerably more popular in Canada than in the United States. Cohabiting couples ("common-law couples" in Canadian terminology) constitute 18% of all Canadian couples, and 35% of all couples in the province of Quebec (Institute of Marriage and Family Canada, 2009).

Cohabitation has diverse meanings

Many cohabiting couples appreciate the informality of their relationship. They may feel less burdened by social expectations and less constrained by traditional roles than if they were married. It may be easier to preserve financial independence, if that is desired. And breaking up, if it comes to that, is less of a public embarrassment. On the downside, cohabiting couples are often denied many rights provided automatically to married couples. Therefore, cohabitation can bring bureaucratic hassles, especially if there are children. People who cohabit have to draw up wills, durable powers of attorney, and other documents if they want their wishes to be respected in case of incapacity or death.

For some couples, cohabitation is a "trial marriage," whose explicit or unstated purpose is to test their compatibility before marrying and having children. But about 20% of women become pregnant during their first cohabitation, and about 40% of cohabiting couples already have children (of one or both partners) living with them (Centers for Disease Control, 2013b; National Marriage Project, 2010). Some cohabitations are lengthy—about 20% last more than 5 years. Some are between old people—widowed or divorced—who see no particular need to marry because they will not have children, or who prefer not to marry in order not to disturb pension or inheritance arrangements. Some are same-sex couples, for whom legal marriage is not yet an option in some states.

For many couples, cohabitation is not perceived as an alternative to marriage but as an alternative to *dating* (Manning & Smock, 2007). In other words, the decision to cohabit may be driven more by economic considerations or convenience than by a deep sense of commitment. "We were paying rent in two places and living in one," a 23-year-old told *USA Today*. "It seemed financially reasonable [to cohabit], and we're pretty compatible" (Jayson, 2005). Given that non-cohabiting relationships tend to be short-lived, we wouldn't necessarily expect couples who cohabit as an alternative to dating to stay in such a cohabitation for long periods of time. And indeed, "serial cohabitation" is an increasingly prevalent lifestyle (Kroeger & Smock, 2014).

For a variety of reasons, couples who are cohabiting are more exposed to jealousy and other stresses than married couples. This has the effect that domestic violence is more common between cohabiting couples than between married couples, and a

Brad Pitt and Angelina Jolie cohabited for 9 years and had several children before marrying in 2014.

cohabiting woman is 9 times more likely than a married woman to be killed by her partner (Shackelford & Mouzos, 2005).

Cohabitation does not harm a subsequent marriage

Many conservative Christians believe that sex outside of marriage is sinful and that it is therefore wrong for a couple to live together before they get married (or without getting married at all). They say that living together before marrying increases the likelihood that a married couple will be unhappy and will eventually divorce, citing studies that they interpret as documenting this so-called "cohabitation effect" (Pennsylvania Catholic Conference, 2009; Baptist Press, 2012).

Several studies conducted in the 1990s and early 2000s did indeed report that couples who cohabited before marriage were more likely to divorce within some stated period than couples who married directly (Lillard et al., 1995; Teachman, 2003). But most of the subjects in those studies got married in the 1970s and 1980s, when cohabitation was far less common than it is today. Those couples who did cohabit tended to be freethinker types who placed little emphasis on the teachings of organized religion. It wasn't their cohabitation that caused them to divorce more readily; it was their preexisting view of marriage as a practical matter rather than a sacrament, along with other demographic characteristics (Woods & Emery, 2002). In other words, the apparent effect of cohabitation was a **selection effect**.

For couples who married recently (since the mid-1990s) there is little difference in divorce rates between cohabitors and "direct marriers" (Manning & Cohen, 2012). That is because as the proportion of couples who cohabit has increased, preexisting differences between them and the direct marriers have lessened. And further, what little "cohabitation effect" remains is the result of an age discrepancy: Couples who cohabit before marriage are necessarily younger when they cohabit than when they marry, and live-in relationships established by younger couples are less stable than those established by couples in their mid-20s or later (Kuperberg, 2014).

If relationships are timed from when couples first move in together, regardless of whether they are in a marriage or a premarital cohabitation, the "cohabitation effect" disappears. Thus, for those who want their live-in relationships to last a long time, the message isn't "Don't cohabit before you marry," but "Don't cohabit *or* marry while you're still in your teens or early 20s."

Marriage Takes Diverse Forms

Most, if not all, human cultures have formalized heterosexual unions in some way, but the manner in which this has been done has varied greatly. In ancient Israel, one way for a couple to wed was simply to let it be known that they had had intercourse. In India, a wedding is an elaborate ceremony that takes up the best part of a week and involves lengthy rituals and enormous expense, particularly on the part of the bride's parents. In the United States, getting married can mean anything from a quick visit to a government office to a multimillion-dollar union of dynasties.

Marriage is not always intended to be permanent. The Shiite branch of Islam, for example, has a temporary marriage known in Arabic as ***mut'a***. The partners specify the terms of this marriage, including its duration, in advance. *Mut'a* may last for as little as 30 minutes if the man and woman want to have just a one-time sexual encounter, or it might last for a year if, for example, a man is living away from home for that period of time and wants a temporary wife for the duration. It is a real marriage in the sense that any offspring of the relationship are legitimate. It is open to unmarried women and to married or unmarried men. In some parts of the Islamic world, however, short-term *mut'a* has become a legal cover for prostitution.

selection effect An effect caused by preexisting differences between subject groups.

mut'a In Shia Islam, a contract to marry for a fixed period of time.

FAQ

When I marry, will whatever I have now become his too?

No—in most states your preexisting assets remain your sole property, so long as you keep them separate from shared assets.

The formalization of sexual unions has social and personal functions

Formalizing sexual unions by marriage has a variety of purposes:

- In some cultures, women are still viewed as men's property; in such cultures, marriage is a contract marking the transfer of a woman from her father to her husband.

- Marriage may bring the couple's extended families together; this was an important function of marriage in traditional societies, in which marriages were often used to end vendettas or to create social alliances.

- To the extent that childbearing is limited to married couples, marriage gives society the power to regulate who may have children (by banning incestuous marriages, for example).

- Marriage creates an environment favorable for child rearing, by identifying two people as responsible for children's rearing and support.

- By publicly identifying two people as a couple, marriage places an obligation on others to respect the sexual exclusivity of their relationship, thus reducing social friction and making paternity more certain.

- By making it difficult for a man and woman to separate, marriage is intended to stabilize their union and ensure that they stay together long enough to rear any children that they may have.

Many societies have permitted polygamy

Nearly all Americans think of a marriage as involving just two people—monogamy—and the law reinforces this attitude: Anyone who marries someone while still married to someone else is committing the crime of **bigamy**. Thus, you might be tempted to think that monogamy is the only legally or culturally recognized form of sexual relationship around the world.

Anthropological studies suggest the reverse: **Polygamy**—having more than one spouse at the same time—is, or has been, commonplace. Out of 853 preindustrial societies analyzed in one survey, 84% permitted men to have more than one female mate (**polygyny**), and in most of these cultures polygynous unions were legally recognized (Fisher, 1989). Today, most Islamic countries permit polygyny, as does India, though only for its Muslim citizens.

The exact arrangements in polygynous societies vary. Often, the initial mate has some kind of official status as "principal wife." In some societies polygynous relationships are permitted but not legally formalized. In such cases, the later mates may be **concubines** whose attachment to the household is impermanent and whose children have no inheritance rights.

Given that most societies have roughly equal numbers of men and women, not every man in a polygynous society can have multiple wives. In fact, most men in such societies have just one wife at best; it is the wealthy and powerful men who have many. The extreme cases were the **harems** associated with Oriental rulers. According to Jewish legend, King Solomon had a harem of a thousand wives, each of whom prepared a banquet every evening in the faint hope that he would dine with her. Harems were traditionally watched over by **eunuchs** (**castrated** men).

Polygyny is connected to the idea that women are men's property: If a rich man has many cattle, why shouldn't he have many wives? Thus, the Christian prohibition of polyg-

---

bigamy   In law, the crime of marrying someone while being already married to another spouse.

polygamy   Marriage to more than one spouse at a time.

polygyny   The marriage or mating of one male with more than one female.

concubine   A woman who cohabits with a man but is not his wife, usually in a polygamous culture.

harem   The quarters for wives and children in a polygamous Muslim household.

eunuch   A man who has been castrated.

castration   Removal of the gonads. (In males, may include removal of the penis.)

FAQ

Can a Muslim man move to the United States with two wives?

Probably yes, if the second wife is able to enter in her own right and the husband does not claim any legal benefits of marriage with respect to her.

Tibetan polyandrous family. Cai Zhuo with her two husbands, who are brothers, and their son.

Box 11.2 Cultural Diversity

Mormon Polygamy

Joseph Smith (1805-1844), the founder of the Mormon faith, secretly married between 30 and 40 women, some of them already married and others as young as 14. His nephew Joseph F. Smith, who became the sixth President of the church, married six women and fathered 43 children (see figure). Many early Mormons believed that polygamy was a necessary path to the highest salvation.

The practice of polgamy drew the Mormons into conflict with the U.S. government, which passed anti-polygamy laws and refused to grant Utah its statehood. In 1890 the Church disavowed polygamy, and when Utah finally became a state in 1896, its constitution banned the practice. Still, the ban was never written into specific statutes.

In spite of the official end of Mormon polygamy (also called "plural marriage"), "Mormon fundamentalists" continue the practice in isolated areas. As many as 30,000 polygamists may be living in Utah and nearby states today. The Church has excommunicated them and opposes their identification as Mormons.

The Mormon polygamists have mostly kept a low profile, but in the late 1990s one of them, Tom Green, went on national television with his five wives. Green was charged with bigamy and, later, with child rape. (Green's first wife gave birth when she was only 13 years old.) He was convicted and served 6 years in prison. Another polygamist leader, Warren Jeffs, controlled a community of several hundred people, many of whom moved to the YFZ ("Yearning for Zion") ranch near Eldorado, Texas. In 2011 he was convicted of aggravated sexual assault against children and sentenced to life imprisonment (Associated Press, 2011a). Seven other men at the ranch had already been convicted on related charges.

The legal campaign against polygamists runs counter to the recent trend toward greater respect for individual freedom in

Early Mormon leader Joseph F. Smith (1838–1918) with some of his wives and children.

sexual arrangements. For that reason, the ACLU of Utah has opposed the bigamy statute that has been used to prosecute some Mormon polygamists. In 2013 a federal district court ruled that plural marriage cannot be criminalized if none of the participants are legally married (Service, 2013).

On the other hand, law enforcement and child welfare officials allege that many social ills are prevalent in some polygamous Mormon communities: They cite incest, physical and sexual abuse of children, poverty, welfare and tax fraud, criminal nonsupport of children, and diminished availability of educational opportunities and health care (Eckholm, 2007).

In addition, polygamy in these communities creates a situation where there are too many young men for the numbers of available women. To solve this problem, many teenage boys have been banished from their communities for seemingly minor violations of church teachings, such as listening to music or talking to girls (Eckholm, 2007). These "lost boys" are ill prepared for life in mainstream America: Their struggles, and efforts to help them, have been the topic of an HBO television series, *Big Love*, and a 2010 documentary film, *Sons of Perdition*.

yny, which distinguishes it from many other religions, such as Islam, can be viewed as an attempt to ensure some equity in marriage. Still, shades of polygyny persist in Western culture: Some wealthy men support mistresses, and a polygynous culture persists among some fundamentalist Mormons (**Box 11.2**).

Societies in which one woman takes more than one husband or mate (**polyandry**) are less common than polgynous societies. In some, resources are so limited that a man cannot maintain a wife and children on his own. That has been true for high-altitude communities in Tibet and other parts of the Himalayas (Samal et al., 1997). In these communities, a woman may be married to two or more brothers. This arrangement prevents the subdivision of scarce arable land and also ensures that any children are genetically related to all husbands. Polyandry may also arise as a response to a shortage of women, according to a study by anthropologists Kathrine

polyandry Marriage or mating of one female with more than one male.

polyamory The formation of non-transient sexual relationships in groups of three or more.

swingers Couples who agree to engage in casual sexual contacts with others.

group marriage Three or more people living together in a marriage-like relationship. Also called *polyfidelity*.

Starkweather and Raymond Hames (Starkweather & Hames, 2012). Those authors identified over 50 societies where polyandry is permitted, so these kinds of marriages are not as rare as commonly believed.

The Human Rights Committee of the United Nations sees polygamy as an affront to the dignity of women and recommends that all nations ban the practice (United Nations Human Rights Committee, 2008).

Polyamory includes a variety of nonmonogamous relationships

Somewhat related to polygamy is **polyamory** (Anapol, 2010). This is a catch-all term for people who openly and intentionally participate in nonmonogamous relationships.

Some polyamorists are **swingers**, or "mate swappers." Swingers are usually couples (married or otherwise) who engage in casual sex with like-minded others, often at sex clubs. Whether they visit these clubs as couples or separately, the main point is that both partners are aware of and happy with what they are doing. Swingers often see their lifestyle as a way of avoiding the desire or necessity for secret extramarital affairs. According to one survey, swingers say that their marriages are happy and that swinging makes a positive contribution to marital stability (Bergstrand & Blevins Williams, 2000). On the negative side, one study conducted in the Netherlands found that a substantial proportion of people seeking treatment for sexually transmitted infections were swingers (Dukers-Muijrers et al., 2010).

Other polyamorists form stable, sexually linked groups of three or more people who usually live together as a family. This phenomenon is called **group marriage**, or polyfidelity. Group marriage has surprisingly deep roots in America. From 1848 to 1881, one group of about 250 people flourished as the Oneida Community in upstate New York. Every man in the community was considered to be married to every woman, and exclusive sexual relationships were forbidden. Excessive pregnancies were prevented by "male continence," which meant that men were expected not to ejaculate during coitus.

Many of the hippie communes of the 1960s and 1970s practiced polyfidelity in one form or another. A notable example was the Kerista Commune located in San Francisco's Haight-Ashbury district. The commune had about 30 members, divided into four clusters of about 8 individuals each. Within each cluster, sleeping partners changed every night, the schedule being arranged by computer. Most of the men underwent vasectomy before joining the group.

While polyamory no longer has the visibility it enjoyed in the 1960s, it is still quite widespread. According to estimates, live-in polyamorous families in the United States number over half a million (Bennett, 2009).

Within group marriages, a variety of sexual relationships can exist (**Figure 11.3**). Also, group marriages can be either closed—that is, the members have no sex with outsiders—or open. Relationships within a group marriage may not all be equivalent: There may be "primary," "secondary," and "tertiary" relationships involving different degrees of commitment. Bisexuality is common in the "poly" community, especially among the women, but it is not universal.

Polyamorists adopt a wide variety of rules or ethical codes to regulate their sexual relations. Although polyamory presents an interesting alternative to standard monogamous relationships, its appeal is limited by the problem of jealousy, which often tears sex-sharing groups apart. Successful polyamorists say that they inten-

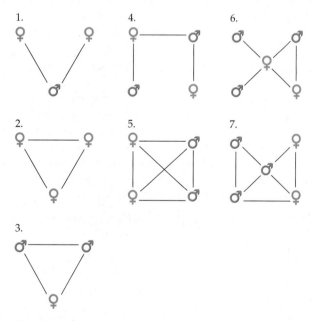

Figure 11.3 Polyamory Polyamorists are small groups of people linked by sexual bonds. "Poly" relationships are highly diverse. They may consist of three (1–3), four (4, 5), five (6, 7), or more persons. All the members of a group may have sexual interactions with one another (2, 3, 5), or they may have sex only in certain combinations (1, 4, 6, 7). The sexual interactions may be all heterosexual (1, 4), all homosexual (2), or both heterosexual and homosexual (3, 5, 6, 7).

tionally cultivate an emotion that is the very opposite of jealousy, namely a pleasure in the knowledge that their partners are enjoying sexual relations with others.

A group of social psychologists at the University of Michigan reviewed all the evidence relating to the advantages and disadvantages of monogamy as compared with other arrangements such as polyamory (Conley et al., 2013). They found no evidence to support the common belief that monogamy is superior to other kinds of sexual or marital arrangements.

companionate marriage   A form of marriage in which the husband and wife are expected to be emotionally intimate and to engage in social activities together.

The Institution of Marriage Is Evolving

To understand the place of cohabitation and marriage in people's lives today, it's important to recall that the Western institution of marriage has changed greatly over the centuries. In ancient Greece, marriage was not companionate—a wife was not expected to be a social partner to her husband but was chiefly there to have children (who were then looked after largely by slaves). **Companionate marriage** had its origins in Roman culture, and it got a boost from the banning of polygamy by the early Christian church. It did not reach its heyday, however, until the 19th and early 20th centuries, when the improved education of women led to their being seen as more desirable companions for men.

Before industrialization and the shift of the population to cities, a married couple typically formed the core of a large extended family that dwelled together under one roof. Although some Americans, especially Hispanics, still maintain that pattern to some degree, the average household size in the United States now numbers fewer than three people; most married couples live alone or accompanied only by their children, and the number of children has fallen dramatically. In 1800, the average American woman had eight live-born children over her lifetime; now she has just under two.

In the 19th century the average age at first marriage was fairly high, especially for men, who couldn't marry until they had the means to support a family (**Figure 11.4**). During the 20th century people married progressively younger, reaching a minimum in the post-World War II years. Since then the age at first marriage has increased steadily and is showing no signs of leveling off.

Companionate marriage had its origins in ancient Rome. This couple is portrayed in a wall painting from the city of Pompeii (79 CE).

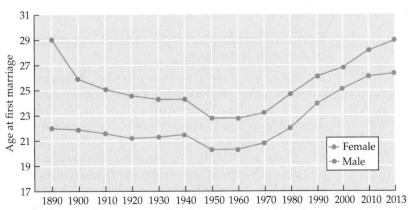

Figure 11.4   Age at first marriage reached a minimum in the post-World War II era and has since climbed back to near (male) or beyond (female) Victorian levels. (Data from U.S. Census Bureau, 2014.)

Box 11.3 Society, Values, and the Law

Extreme Marriages

Traditionally, a couple's wedding vows included the promise to stay together "until death do us part," and nearly everyone did. Divorce gradually became more common in the 19th and early 20th centuries, and the introduction of **no-fault divorce** in the 1970s gave the practice another boost. In a no-fault divorce, either partner may unilaterally end the marriage without having to prove wrongdoing by the other. Currently, about 45% of all American marriages end in divorce. Some wedding ceremonies acknowledge this lowered expectation of permanence by changing the phrase "until death do us part" to "until love's death do us part," or something similar.

Believing that the breakup of marriages is a major cause of personal distress and social harm, some Americans (mostly conservative Protestants) have advocated a return to covenant marriages, in which the couple commit themselves to a lifelong monogamous relationship. A typical covenant marriage includes a vow such as the following: "Believing that marriage is a covenant intended by God to be a lifelong relationship between a man and a woman, we vow to God, each other, our families, and our community to remain steadfast in unconditional love, reconciliation, and sexual purity, while purposefully growing in our covenant marriage relationship."

To give covenant marriages some "teeth," four states (Louisiana, Arizona, Kansas, and Arkansas—see figure) have made these marriages into legal alternatives to conventional marriages. In a legal covenant marriage, the couple is required to undergo premarital counseling. Once married, the couple may not receive a no-fault divorce. Divorce may be legally granted only if one party proves that the other party has committed adultery or a felony or has permanently abandoned the marriage, or if the couple has been separated for 2 years.

So far, covenant marriages have not proved very popular—an estimated 1% to 3% of marrying couples choose the cov-

On Valentine's Day 2005, the then governor of Arkansas, Mike Huckabee, and his wife Janet converted their 30-year marriage to a covenant marriage.

enant option (National Healthy Marriage Resource Center, 2010). According to a study that followed couples in regular and covenant marriages for 7 years, covenant marriages do not improve marital satisfaction, or do so only to a miniscule degree (DeMaris et al., 2012). Couples in covenant marriages do stay married longer, but this could well be a selection effect rather than an effect of the covenant itself.

At the opposite end of the spectrum of formality are "double-proxy marriages"—an institution legalized by the state of Montana and available chiefly in the city of Kalispell. In these marriages the couple is not even present at the ceremony. Instead, a pair of professional "vow takers" stand in for them, promising to love, comfort, honor, and keep each other so long as they both shall live—a promise they renew many times over in the course of an afternoon as various couples' paperwork is pushed in front of them (Barry, 2008).

no-fault divorce Divorce without proof of wrongdoing by either party.

---

prenuptial agreement A contract signed before marriage, spelling out the disposition of wealth in the event of divorce.

postnuptial agreement A financial agreement between spouses.

covenant marriage A form of marriage that requires a stronger vow of commitment than a regular marriage and that makes divorce harder to obtain.

Companionate marriage makes the availability of divorce a necessity

The institution of companionate marriage suffers from various problems. First, companionate marriage demands intimacy and affection, yet not all couples are capable of sustaining these feelings over a lifetime, so companionate marriage has driven demand for access to at-will divorce. Indeed, the divorce rate has skyrocketed since Victorian times (see "Many Factors Bring Relationships to an End" later in this chapter). Yet the availability of divorce makes marriage a less serious commitment in the first place. Essentially, it converts marriage from a permanent status to a contractual relationship. A sign of the increasingly contractual nature of marriage is the appearance of custom-designed legal agreements. These include **prenuptial agreements**, which are used primarily to specify the distribution of wealth in the eventuality of divorce; **postnuptial agreements**, which are similar agreements made after marriage; and **covenant marriages** (**Box 11.3**).

Second, a companionate marriage implies some kind of equivalence between husband and wife. Indeed, past generations would be amazed at the similarity of the roles of men and women in present-day marriages—especially in terms of the distribution of breadwinning, household, and decision-making responsibilities. That's not to say that women earn as much as men (they don't) or that men do an equal share of housework (they don't), but the fact that these activities are shared at all is a major break from the past. This increasing equivalence of women and men has been brought about not only by the education of women and their entry into the labor market, but also by the decline in the number of children produced by women during marriage. This lack of or small number of children minimizes the biologically distinct roles of men and women.

Husbands and wives have become all-purpose companions: They are expected to be romantic partners, friends, economic collaborators, fellow workers in the home, and colleagues in parenting. And they are expected to sustain all these relationships with far less support from relatives or neighbors than was customary a generation or two ago.

It is no small challenge, but for many it works: Statistically speaking, married people are significantly happier than the unmarried (**Figure 11.5**). In fact, a 2007 Gallup poll found that more married people in the lowest income bracket are "very happy" (56%) than are unmarried people in the highest income bracket (50%), suggesting that marriage is more important to personal happiness than wealth. The greatest bliss, however, is being married *and* rich (67%) (Gallup & Newport, 2008).

Marriage is becoming a minority status

So is marriage on the way out? It's certainly on the decline. Currently, less than half (48%) of Americans over age 15 are married, down from 64% in 1970 (National Center for Family and Marriage Research, 2014). Just between the 2000 and 2010 censuses, the marriage rate (marriages per 1000 people per year) fell by 17% (Centers for Disease Control, 2013e).

Of course, these general statistics conceal major demographic variations in marriage rates. The rate has declined most steeply among less-educated people. And black women are far less likely to be married or cohabiting than other groups, so the majority of black children live in households where their fathers are not present (U.S. Census Bureau, 2010) (**Figure 11.6**). The absence of fathers can be traced to low employment and wages for black men, increasing employment for black women, and a history of welfare policies that favor single mothers (Lu et al., 2010). However, among black families living in the suburbs, living arrangements are much more like those of other middle-class Americans. Furthermore, black single-mother families are often strengthened by the presence of other relatives in the household or by strong kinship links outside of it (Taylor, 2010).

Relationship options have diversified

A generation or two ago, couples had two starkly different options: to live together in a legally unrecognized (and sometimes illegal) cohabitation, or to marry. Today, the dividing line between cohabitation and marriage has blurred. Cohabitation has become more like marriage: It has lost much of its stigma (including the stigma of **illegitimacy** directed against the couple's children); also, some of the benefits of marriage have been extended to cohabiting couples by local and state laws, by employers and insurance policies, or by the option to draw up powers of attorney, revocable trusts, and the like. And marriage has become more like cohabitation: Separation and divorce are less stigmatized, couples can file their taxes separately, and same-sex couples can marry in many states.

illegitimacy   An obselete term referring to children born to unmarried parents.

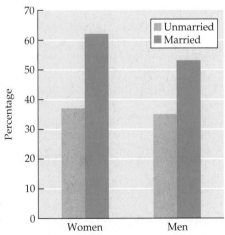

Figure 11.5   Happily married The graph shows the percentage of unmarried women and men and married women and men who call themselves "very happy" (when given the choices of "very happy," "fairly happy," and "not too happy"). (Data from Gallup, 2000.)

(A)

(B)

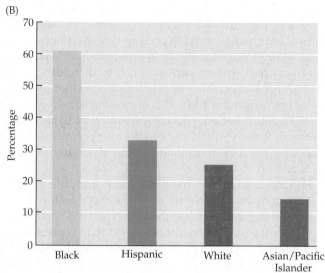

Figure 11.6 Single parenthood (A) Black women are much more likely to be single mothers than are women of other racial or ethnic groups. (B) The graph shows the percentage of children who do not live with both of their parents, by race/ethnicity. Most of these children live with their mother. (Data from U.S. Census Bureau, 2010.)

domestic partnership A legal arrangement that confers some or most of the rights and obligations of marriage.

civil union A legal arrangement that confers most or all of the rights and obligations of marriage except the name.

In addition, a kaleidoscope of intermediate arrangements has come into being under the designations **domestic partnership** and **civil union**. Domestic partnerships offer some or most of the rights of marriage; civil unions offer most or all of the rights of marriage except for the name "marriage." The original impetus to formalize such arrangements came from the gay community, but both arrangements offer advantages to some heterosexual couples also. The specifics vary too greatly from state to state for us to detail them here, but couples who envisage a long-term relationship do well to explore the options.

Marriage is both a civil institution that confers specific legal rights and obligations and also a rite that has religious or moral meanings that vary from couple to couple. Some legal scholars, political philosophers, and ethicists, such as Martha Nussbaum of the University of Chicago—she is all three—have suggested that these two functions could be split: States could confer civil unions only, and other organizations such as churches could issue marriage certificates (Nussbaum, 2010). This might well facilitate the acceptance of same-sex marriage, given that so much of the opposition to same-sex marriage relates to the word "marriage" itself, rather than to the practical rights and obligations associated with it. In your opinion, would such a change be a good idea?

Most Long-Term Couples Are Satisfied with Their Sex Lives

This and the following sections deal mainly with heterosexual married couples, because those are the people on whom most researchers have focused their attention. It's likely, however, that much of what we have to say is relevant to long-term relationships in general, including same-sex relationships.

Marriage has many functions, but this book is about sexuality, so our main concern is with marital sex. Here the picture is somewhat paradoxical: Married (and cohabiting) couples generally seem happier with their sex lives than the frequency of their sexual activities would suggest. According to National Health and Social Life Survey

(NHSLS) data, married women are less likely than dating women to have sex more than twice a week. They are also less adventurous sexually and less likely to experience orgasm. Nevertheless, women's physical satisfaction with sex is much greater in long-term relationships than in short-term relationships, and their emotional satisfaction is higher in marriage than in any other class of relationship. The same is true for men, except that men have a high likelihood of experiencing orgasm regardless of the kind of relationship they are in.

Why would this be? There could be at least two different reasons. These results could be an artifact reflecting different demographic characteristics among the various groups studied. Alternatively, it could be that marriage somehow confers satisfaction—especially emotional satisfaction—on the sexual aspects of relationships. The NHSLS researchers carried out a statistical analysis to resolve this question and came up with the following answer (Waite & Joyner, 2001): For men, demographics are key—when men are matched for other characteristics, they are about equally likely to be satisfied by sex within marital or nonmarital relationships. Women, however, do derive extra emotional satisfaction from sex within a married relationship simply by virtue of that relationship being a marriage. We may speculate that the reason for the extra satisfaction is the high level of commitment and exclusivity represented by the institution of marriage—qualities that are more important to women than to men.

The frequency of sex declines in the course of long-term relationships

Sexual interactions between married partners fall off with increasing duration of marriage and also with age. According to the 2010 National Survey of Sexual Health and Behavior (NSSHB), the proportion of married men and women having sex (coitus) at least once per month decreases from over 3 in 4 in early adulthood to about 1 in 4 after age 70 (**Figure 11.7**).

Several factors probably contribute to this decline in sexual activity. First, there is a loss of sexual interest associated with increasing familiarity between the partners (**habituation**) and the dimming of passionate love. Second, there is a long-lasting decline in sexual interest and frequency of coitus following the birth of children. Finally, a decline in sexual behavior is associated with the process of aging itself, which is accompanied by declining health and fitness and falling levels of sex hormones. As you can see from Figure 11.7, a rapid decrease in sexual activity begins at about age 50, which is about the age of women's menopause (see below).

Innumerable self-help books and magazine articles offer advice to couples on how to keep the sex hot over time. According to New York sex therapist Esther Perel, for example, the secret is to maintain some distance in the relationship—in other words, to resist the all-purpose intimacy that companionate marriage seems to demand (Perel, 2006). Perel believes that a mother's excessive involvement with her children short-circuits the erotic charge between her and her partner.

Another issue has to do with housework. The average heterosexually married man today does far more housework than his

habituation A psychological or physiological process that reduces a person's response to a stimulus or drug after repeated or prolonged exposure.

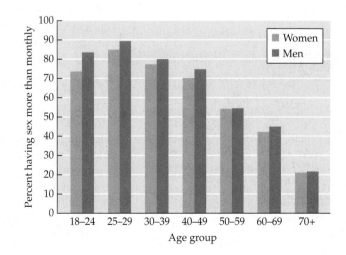

Figure 11.7 **Marital sex** becomes less frequent with increasing age. This bar graph shows the percentage of married women and men having sex more than once per month, for different age ranges. (Data from the 2010 National Survey of Sexual Health and Behavior.)

father or grandfather did, even if he still doesn't take a 50% share. It's widely believed that this makes for a happier and therefore sexier marriage. But the truth turns out to be different, according to a U.S.-Spanish collaboration (Kornrich et al., 2012). This group analyzed data from the U.S. National Survey of Families and Households. The more egalitarian the marriage (in terms of the husband sharing household chores, for example), the *lower* was the frequency of marital sex, according to their analysis. This finding suggests that maintaining some degree of gender difference between spouses may help keep the sexual spark alive in a marriage. "It's the first time in history we are trying this experiment of a sexuality that's rooted in equality and that lasts for decades," Esther Perel told the *New York Times*. "It's a tall order for one person to be your partner in Management Inc., your best friend and passionate lover. There's a certain part of you that with this partner will not be fulfilled. You deal with that loss. It's a paradox to be lived with, not solved" (Gottlieb, 2014).

On a more positive note, sociologists Pepper Schwartz and Janet Lever have conducted numerous studies and surveys of what factors keep sex alive in long-term relationships. In their *Getaway Guide to the Great Sex Weekend* they distill what they've learned into three pieces of advice: First, maintain good sexual communication, which includes building anticipation of sexual encounters; second, be willing to try new things (new locations, new sex toys, new positions) to ward off sexual boredom; and third, take the time to set the right mood for romance.

Marital satisfaction declines during middle age

Marital satisfaction also falls off over time, although to a highly variable degree (Musick & Bumpass, 2006); some couples remain very satisfied with their marriage over a long lifetime. Two life events are particularly likely to trigger a drop in satisfaction. One is the birth of the first child: This seems to be caused by the loss of "quality time" in the relationship, as well as by a perception by both husbands and wives (but particularly by wives) that each is having to shoulder an unfair share of family responsibilities (Lawrence et al., 2008). The other is the entry of the oldest child into adolescence (Cui & Donnellan, 2009): The father and mother often have differences over how to cope with the stresses associated with having an adolescent child.

It has often been said that women are less satisfied with their marriages than men, but a recent meta-analysis found that not to be the case, at least for the general population (Jackson et al., 2014). Wives in marital therapy are indeed less satisfied than husbands, according to the meta-analysis, but this may simply be because unhappy wives bring their spouses into therapy, whereas unhappy husbands don't.

There is of course a great deal of variation among both men and women in how their marital satisfaction changes as the years pass. Interestingly, recent research suggests that people already know at the time they marry—although only unconsciously—how successful their marriage is going to be (**Box 11.4**).

Many Factors Bring Relationships to an End

At the present time, nearly half of all marriages end in separation or divorce, sometimes referred to as "breakups" or "marital disruption." The divorce rate has been climbing steadily since the 1960s, and for persons over 35 the divorce rate has doubled over the last 20 years and is still rising (Kennedy & Ruggles, 2014). For the youngest couples, the divorce rate has leveled off or even fallen slightly. However, this may simply be because economically disadvantaged young people, who are especially divorce prone, are now less able to marry in the first place.

In the preceding section (and in Chapter 7), we discussed some of the family circumstances and psychological factors that seem to promote or prevent the breakup

FAQ

Can divorced Catholics remarry in the church?

Strictly speaking, no—because the Catholic Church doesn't recognize divorce. But they can have their former marriages annulled (declared to have never existed) for a variety of reasons, and then marry in the church.

Box 11.4 Research Highlights

You Know the Future of Your Marriage

When newlywed men or women are asked about their future satisfaction with their marriage, and then followed over a period of years, their answers have virtually no predictive value: People don't seem to have any clue about how their marriage is going to work out (Lavner et al., 2013). But social psychologist James McNulty of Florida State University, Tallahassee, and several colleagues suspected that there might be more to it than that. They devised an experiment to probe beneath the surface of newlyweds' minds (McNulty et al., 2013).

First, the researchers assessed the subjects' conscious feelings toward their spouses by means of a simple questionnaire. Then they sidestepped the subjects' conscious minds by using an **implicit association test**. In the test, subjects were very briefly exposed to photos of their spouses or to various control faces. Immediately thereafter they had to decide as quickly as possible whether a certain emotionally loaded word (e.g., "love" or "sickness") was "good" or "bad." The more positive feelings the subjects had toward their spouses, the more they were biased toward a "good" response, so it took them less time to associate "love" with "good" than to associate "sickness" with "bad"—and vice versa if they had negative feelings. Thus, by calculating the ratio of the "good" to the "bad" response times, the researchers could get an estimate of the subjects' "automatic" feelings about their spouses.

After the subjects did the test, they were followed for 4 years, and every 6 months they were asked how satisfied they were

Young couples want to know the future—but perhaps they know already.

with their marriage. In agreement with previous studies, the subjects' consciously expressed feelings bore no relationship to their later satisfaction (or lack of it) with their marriage. But the "automatic" feelings revealed by the implicit association test did bear a relationship: The more positive these feelings, the less likely the subjects were to experience any decline in marital satisfaction over the follow-up period. Thus it appears that newlyweds do have an implicit knowledge of how their marriage is going to work out, even if they are not conscious of it, or unable or unwilling to express it. It's possible that this kind of approach could be useful in marriage counseling.

implicit association test A psychological test designed to reveal unconscious or unexpressed feelings.

---

of marriages and other long-term relationships. In a broader, demographic sense, the likelihood of marital disruption is linked to four major factors: age at marriage, the passage of time, ethnicity, and educational level.

Marriage during the teen years increases the risk of disruption. If the woman is under 18 at the time of marriage, the chances of breakup within 10 years are double what they are for women over 25 (1 in 2 versus 1 in 4). The reasons for the vulnerability of teen marriages probably include the immaturity of the partners, the economic stresses of early marriage, and the fact that some teen marriages are "shotgun" (forced by pregnancy).

The likelihood of marital disruption is highest during the first few years of marriage, but breakups continue at significant rates thereafter. About 1 in 5 of all first marriages ends within 5 years, and 1 in 3 ends within 10 years. The overall divorce rate—the portion of all marriages that end in divorce or separation—is about 45% (Hurley, 2005).

Race/ethnicity has a significant effect on marital stability. Asian-Americans have the most stable marriages, followed by Hispanics, whites, and then blacks (**Figure 11.8**) (Centers for Disease Control, 2012a).

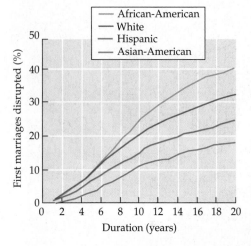

Figure 11.8 **Ethnicity influences the durability of marriage.** The percentage of first marriages that have broken up rises fastest for marriages in which the wife is African-American and slowest for marriages in which the wife is Asian-American. (Data from U.S. Census Bureau, 2001.)

On the positive side, a college education does wonders for marital stability (Centers for Disease Control, 2012a) (**Figure 11.9**): If you graduate from college, your first marriage will have a 75% chance of lasting at least 15 years. Throw in a few other favorable demographics (**Table 11.1**), and your marriage will be virtually divorce-proof.

Dissimilarity between husbands and wives shortens marriages

As indicated above, similarity between partners influences marital stability in the way one might imagine, at least in the early years of marriage, according to NHSLS data. Thus, married couples who have different religions are more likely to break up than are couples who share the same religion. Interracial couples are more likely to break up than same-race couples (Bratter & King, 2008). Large age differences also increase the chances of a breakup.

The reason for these trends is not entirely clear. Besides possible direct effects, such as marital tensions arising from the partners' differences or a lack of shared interests, there are likely to be indirect effects: Couples that differ in religion or ethnicity may be exposed to social prejudice and may be more isolated from their extended families than couples who share the same religion or ethnicity. Thus, their marriages may receive less external support.

When individual divorced people are asked about why their marriages ended, they do not refer to demographic variables, but rather to specific problems in their own marriages (de Graaf & Kalmijn, 2006). These problems include psychological incompatibility, behavioral problems (including drinking and drug use), and abuse.

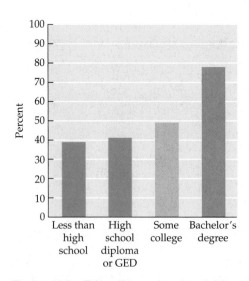

Figure 11.9 **Education makes for stable marriages.** This bar graph shows the percentages of women of different educational levels whose first marriages last at least 20 years. (Data from Centers for Disease Control, 2012a.)

TABLE 11.1
Your Divorce Calculator

Factors[a]	Percent decrease in risk of divorce
Earning over $50,000 annually (vs. under $25,000)	30
Having graduated from college (vs. not completed high school)	25
Having a baby 7 months or more after marriage (vs. before marriage)	24
Marrying at over 25 years of age (vs. at under age 18)	24
Coming from an intact family of origin (vs. having divorced parents)	14
Religious affiliation (vs. having none)	14

Data from National Marriage Project, 2010.

[a]Overall, almost half of U.S. marriages end in divorce, but each of these factors reduces the chances of divorce by the stated percentage. Each figure represents the contribution of the stated factor in isolation from other factors—for example, the effect of graduating from college does not include the effect of the higher income that college graduates typically enjoy.

Infidelity, as you might imagine, is one of the strongest predictors of imminent breakup. Husbands cheat about 3 times more often than wives, but the disruptive effect is the same regardless of the sex of the cheater (DeMaris, 2013).

In non-Western societies, infertility is also a common reason for divorce (Inhorn, 1996). In European history, countless queens have been divorced, banished to nunneries, or executed for their failure to produce a son; no one ever considered the possibility that the fault might lie on the king's side.

Marital Disruption Can Have Negative and Positive Consequences

In the immediate aftermath of a divorce, negative emotions such as anger, guilt, sadness, or fear for the future often predominate. Yet divorce is a mixed bag in terms of its effects on the ex-spouses and any children they may have.

Divorced men and women can suffer psychological, physical, and economic damage

When marriages end, there are all kinds of negative consequences that go far beyond the bitter feelings of the breakup itself (Amato, 2010). Divorced people suffer higher rates of psychological and physical ill health (including higher mortality) than do married people. They are less happy, less sexually active, more socially isolated, and more prone to substance abuse. Divorced women—who usually retain custody of children—generally suffer a severe drop in per capita household income. (Divorced men, on the other hand, may see a rise in per capita household income.) The children of divorced parents experience a heightened risk of depression, behavior problems, low academic performance, substance abuse, criminality, and early sexual activity. Couples who separate without divorcing may suffer similar problems: This is particularly relevant to separated black couples, who tend to remain in that state without divorcing for much longer than do white or Hispanic couples (Centers for Disease Control, 2002).

Of course, not all these ill effects can be blamed on divorce or separation per se: They may well be the ongoing consequences of the kind of marriage that preceded the breakup. People who divorce are generally unhappy in their marriages, and if divorce were not possible, they might become even less happy and might eventually experience impairments in their mental and physical health at least as severe as those that affect divorced men and women. What is really desirable is to increase people's marital satisfaction to the point that they won't want to split up in the first place. We discussed some strategies to accomplish this above and in Chapter 7.

Divorce may be the start of a new life

To some extent, the concept of divorce as an unmitigated evil has arisen from a religious conservative tradition that uses terminology such as "failed marriages" and "broken homes," that refers to the children of divorced parents as "victims," and that sees rising divorce rates as a symptom of society's "moral decay." In reality, marital disruption can also have positive consequences. In fact, if it

Statistically, this interracial couple stands a much higher chance of breaking up than do couples of the same ethnicity. Interracial couples may lack the social supports that help sustain marriage.

Divorce, Vegas style. Former Miss USA Shanna Moakler celebrated her 2006 split from drummer Travis Barker with a party at the Bellagio Hotel, complete with divorce cake.

didn't, it would be hard to explain why divorce is so popular—there are about 1.2 million divorces in the United States annually, compared with about 2.4 million marriages.

The benefits of divorce include escape from an unhappy, possibly abusive relationship and the potential for forming a better one. Divorce is always a challenge, but for some people, women especially, it can be the key that unlocks previously untapped sources of talent, energy, and resolve. For married men and women who are gay or bisexual, divorce may be an opportunity to "come out of the closet" and develop same-sex relationships.

For all these reasons, divorce is sometimes seen as a cause for celebration: an occasion to be marked with a party and perhaps gifts to make up for whatever the ex took with him or her. To satisfy this need, at least one British department store maintains a divorce gift registry (Ling, 2010).

Many divorced people remarry

It's common for divorced men and women to marry again—about half of them are remarried by 5 years after their divorce (U.S. Census Bureau, 2006). But the remarriage rate (the number of previously married people who remarry per year), like the marriage rate, has fallen dramatically in recent years—from 50 per 1000 in 1990 to 29 per 1000 in 2011 (National Center for Family and Marriage Research, 2013). The drop is particularly marked for the younger age groups; for people over 55, many of whom are widowed rather than divorced, the remarriage rate was always very low and has not changed much.

Remarriage brings economic and other benefits, especially to women. It is also associated, not surprisingly, with an increase in sexual activity—clear evidence that the general decline in sexual behavior during marriage is not solely a biological effect of aging.

Unfortunately, children of divorce tend to remain disadvantaged when their mothers remarry: The adverse effects that strike children of divorced parents (see above) also strike stepchildren at about the same frequency (Coleman et al., 2000). Stepchildren are twice as likely to suffer from behavioral problems as are children who live with their biological parents (Bray, 1999; Evenhouse & Reilly, 2004). Nevertheless, the majority of stepchildren do well in school and don't have emotional or behavioral problems (Ganong & Coleman, 2003).

Another downside of remarriage is that later marriages are somewhat less durable than first marriages. For example, a woman 25 years old or older who marries for the first time has a 1 in 4 chance of breaking up within 10 years, but if she has been married previously, she has a 1 in 3 chance of breaking up within the same period. In other words, experience gained from the first marriage doesn't seem to stabilize later marriages. Bear in mind, though, that it's a special subset of people who remarry: namely, those who have already divorced at least once. These people may have personality traits or economic circumstances that reduce marital stability, or they may see less moral or practical value in lasting marriages.

Does marriage have a future?

Marriage is not just a romantic goal: It is also a major engine of wealth creation because a married couple is so much more efficient economically than the same two people living apart. Thus, as marriage becomes increasingly restricted to the wealthier and better-educated sectors of American society, a social and economic problem is created.

If the decline in marriage were simply a matter of cohabiting couples neglecting to visit the marriage registrar's office, as is widely the case in Europe, there would be no harm to anyone except the wedding industry. But in reality, marriage is declining in significant part because it has become an unattainable dream for many poorer Americans. Changes in the labor market—in particular, the less-rewarding employment prospects for people with a high school education or less—greatly limit many young people's ability to marry. Thus, strengthening education and employment opportunities may be an important step toward restoring a central place for marriages—and marriage-equivalent cohabitations—in American society.

Sociologist Andrew Cherlin of Johns Hopkins University has discussed the corrosive effect of economic disadvantage on American marriage (Cherlin, 2009). But in his 2010 book *The Marriage-Go-Round*, Cherlin went beyond an economic analysis to pose this question: Has something fundamentally changed about the American mind-set that makes marriage less attractive in prospect, and a less satisfying experience, than it was a generation or two ago? Why, he asks, do Americans "step on and off the carousel of intimate relationships" at a much faster rate than their European peers—damaging their children's lives in the process?

In answer, Cherlin points to a conflict between two long-prized American ideals: the high valuation of marriage and the equally high valuation of individuality. After the generation that lived through the Great Depression and World War II left the stage, "individuality" morphed into "self-fulfillment" and then "self-gratification," negating the sense of responsibility and teamwork that underlies successful family life.

If correct, this line of thought could actually bode well for the future of marriage. That's because generational shifts come and go. Fifteen years ago a series of polls suggested that teenagers were substantially more committed to the ideals of marriage and monogamy than was a previous generation of teens (Whitehead and Popenoe, 2000). Now these teens are facing marriage choices. How they make these choices will reveal much about marriage's future.

Also, the legalization of same-sex marriage in many states, and the accompanying national debate on the topic, has forced Americans to think about what marriage is and what it's for. Religious conservatives fear that legalizing same-sex marriage damages the sanctity of marriage as a whole, because same-sex marriage lacks scriptural authority (Linderman, 2014). Progressives can point to the finding that overall divorce rates have *fallen* in states that have legalized gay marriage and *risen* in states that have banned it (Silver, 2010). One speculative interpretation of this finding is that heterosexual couples value their own marriages more when they see gay people fighting successfully for the right to join them.

The great majority of today's college students do desire and expect to get married and have children one day. But unlike their parents or grandparents, they also stress the importance of giving themselves time to enjoy life, travel, and take advantage of sexual freedom before the more dutiful burdens of marriage overtake them. To some, marriage is so remote in their minds that they associate it with the end of life. "I don't want to die alone," said one student when asked why he planned to marry. "Just to have a good ending to my life, basically," said another. Some students, though, take a more positive view. One 20-year-old woman said: "[Being 30 and married is] when your life is really gonna kick into gear" (Regnerus & Uecker, 2011)

Menopause Marks Women's Transition to Infertility

Midlife has major effects on the sex lives of both men and women. The effects are more dramatic in women, so we discuss those first.

When women reach their early or mid-40s, they may find that their menstrual periods become less regular. This change marks the onset of a gradual transition to infertility—a phase called the

Menopause is an aspect of aging, but it comes at what we now consider midlife.

climacteric The transition to infertility at the end of a woman's reproductive life, lasting for several years and culminating in menopause.

perimenopause The phase prior to menopause that is marked by irregular menstrual cycles.

menopause The final cessation of menstruation at the end of a woman's reproductive years.

climacteric, or "change of life." The first portion of the climacteric, when a woman misses some menstrual periods but has not stopped menstruating completely, is called **perimenopause**. **Menopause** is the final cessation of menstrual cycles. Because of the irregularity that commonly precedes menopause, a woman can't *know* that her last period was in fact her last until some time afterward. Conventionally, menopause is said to be "confirmed" after 12 months without a period—in the absence of health factors that might be responsible for the amenorrhea.

Among American, Canadian, and European women, menopause occurs at a median age of 51, but with considerable variation: Some women reach menopause in their early 40s, while others continue to menstruate into their late 50s or even early 60s. In South America and Asia, menopause tends to occur earlier—as early as the mid-40s—probably on account of disadvantageous socioeconomic conditions (Palacios et al., 2010).

Women's fertility declines well before menopause, but a woman can't be sure that she's incapable of becoming pregnant until menopause is confirmed. Plenty of women in their 40s think that they are unlikely to conceive, let their guard down with regard to contraception, and then are surprised to find themselves pregnant. Particularly at risk are women who use fertility awareness methods of contraception: That's because the cycles of perimenopausal women are too irregular to allow for reliable timing of ovulation.

Although people often focus on the negative aspect of menopause, namely the loss of fertility, evolutionary biologists look at it in a different way, asking why women have evolved the capacity for many years of active life *after* cessation of reproduction. They suspect that the reason has to do with the resources, such as food and knowledge, that postmenopausal women have been able to provide to their adult children, thus enabling them to be more prolific and successful parents. This is the so-called "grandmother hypothesis" of menopause (Hawkes & Coxworth, 2013). It is supported by data showing that, in premodern times, women who lived for many years after menopause had more surviving grandchildren than those who did not (Lahdenpera et al., 2004).

Menopause may be caused by depletion of ova

A woman's genes influence the age at which she will enter menopause (Stolk et al., 2012). In addition, women who have had fewer pregnancies, who have short cycle lengths, who have had one ovary removed, or who don't use oral contraceptives are all likely to experience menopause earlier than other women. Several lifestyle factors influence age at menopause, sometimes in ways one might not expect: Smoking and being a vegetarian are associated with earlier menopause, whereas engaging in strenuous exercise, having a high body mass index, and drinking alcohol are associated with later menopause (Morris et al., 2012).

It appears that women are born with the capacity for a certain number of ovarian cycles and that the main reason for the transition to infertility may be the depletion of the cells that give rise to ova (Santoro, 2005). By the time of menopause, the ovaries contain very few such cells. Consistent with this view, the secretion of pituitary gonadotropins (FSH and LH) does not decrease at menopause, but rather *increases*—in response to the decline in blood levels of ovarian hormones (Curran, 2011). Surgical removal of the uterus (hysterectomy) in a premenopausal woman puts a stop to menstruation but not to the hormonal processes that underlie the menstrual cycle. If the ovaries are removed, however, menopause occurs immediately.

Women may experience a decline in sexual desire at menopause

Menopausal women often experience a decline in sexual desire and sexual arousal, but only a part of this decline is attributable to the biological processes of menopause. Other

FAQ

My mother thinks she may be entering menopause. Should I buy her one of those menopause test kits?

No—those tests will only give a meaningful result at a point when it is already obvious to your mother that she has reached menopause. A copy of the *Menopause Guidebook* (see Recommended Reading) would be a more useful gift in the same price range.

factors, such as relationship issues, attitudes toward sex and aging, general health, and cultural background have larger effects on sexual desire and sexual function than does menopausal status (Avis et al., 2005; Hayes et al., 2008). Bear in mind that androgens play a significant role in female sexual desire, and although some androgens come from the ovaries, they are also secreted by the adrenal glands. This latter supply continues after menopause and is often sufficient to maintain a high level of sexual interest.

The psychological effects of menopause on sexuality are diverse. For women who believe that the main or only purpose of sex is reproduction, the loss of fertility at menopause may lead to a loss of interest in sex. For the larger number of women who see an emotional or recreational significance in sex, menopause may actually be welcome because it removes the fear of unwanted pregnancy and makes contraception unnecessary. Such women may get increased pleasure from sex for that reason. (The risk of sexually transmitted infections may still make the use of condoms advisable, of course.)

vasomotor control The physiological regulation of peripheral blood flow.

hot flashes (or hot flushes) Episodes of reddening and warmth of the skin associated with menopause.

osteoporosis Reduction in the mineral content of bone, predisposing an individual to fractures.

Decreased hormone levels affect a woman's physiology

The reduction in circulating ovarian hormones, especially estrogens, has direct effects on the body. These effects can include a reduction in vaginal lubrication in response to sexual arousal, a rise in the pH (decrease in acidity) of vaginal fluids, and sometimes a thinning of the walls of the vagina. In some women these changes may lead to painful coitus and vaginal inflammation. However, many perimenopausal and postmenopausal women do not experience these vaginal symptoms (Agency for Healthcare Research and Quality, 2005).

Menopause (and perimenopause) may be accompanied by a variety of other symptoms that can influence sexual expression indirectly. The reduction in estrogen levels often leads to instability in the control of blood vessels (**vasomotor control**), so many menopausal women experience **hot flashes** or **hot flushes** (dilation of blood vessels in the skin that may cause reddening, a sensation of warmth, and perspiration, sometimes followed by a cold chill), as well as night sweats, headaches, tiredness, and heart palpitations (bouts of accelerated or irregular heartbeats). Sleep problems are also common. The extent to which these menopausal symptoms occur and how bothersome women find them is highly variable. Many symptoms disappear within a few years after menopause, even without medical treatment.

Lowered estrogen levels may also have long-term health effects. The most significant of these are a loss of bone density (**osteoporosis**), which carries a risk of fractures and vertebral compression (**Figure 11.10**), and changes in blood lipid (fat) chemistry, which increase the risk of cardiovascular disease. In addition, there are noticeable effects on the skin (loss of thickness, elasticity, hydration, and fat content).

Hormone therapy can reduce menopausal symptoms

Menopausal women have the option of taking sex hormones or other drugs to compensate for the loss of their own ovarian hormones and thus

(A)

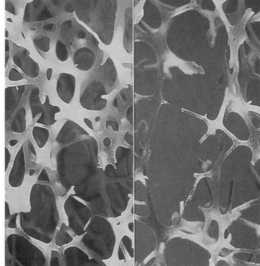

1 mm

(B)

Figure 11.10 Osteoporosis (A) Low estrogen levels after menopause can lead to thinning of the mineral structure of bone. These are scanning electron micrographs of normal bone (left) and osteoporotic bone (right). (B) Osteoporosis can cause spinal fractures resulting in increasingly stooped posture, but exercise, diet, and drugs can help prevent this process.

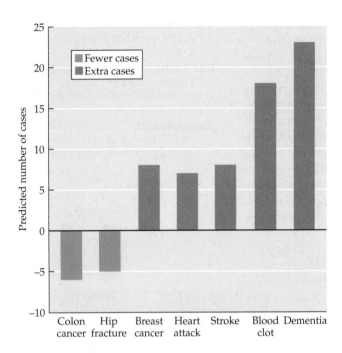

Figure 11.11 **Risks may outweigh benefits** for postmenopausal hormone therapy. This bar graph shows the predicted number of extra cases (red bars) or fewer cases (green bars) of the listed conditions experienced by 10,000 women on long-term combined estrogen/progestin therapy per year. (Data from U.S. Food and Drug Administration, 2009.)

to alleviate the symptoms of menopause. This practice is called **menopausal hormone therapy.** The most common regimen is a combination of estrogens and progestins. The estrogens alleviate symptoms such as hot flushes and vaginal dryness. Progestins are added to protect the woman from one unwanted side effect of the estrogen treatment, which is an increased risk of endometrial cancer. For women who have had a hysterectomy, this risk is not an issue, so the therapy may consist of estrogens alone. For women in whom vaginal symptoms are the main problem, estrogen can be administered directly to the vagina by means of a ring, tablets, or cream. Hormone therapy not only relieves menopausal symptoms, it also improves the general quality of life for women whose menopausal symptoms are severe (Utian & Woods, 2013).

Until about 15 years ago, large numbers of women took hormones for many years or even decades *after* menopause. In the early 2000s, however, large-scale studies reported that this **postmenopausal hormone therapy** significantly increased the risk of cardiovascular disease, breast cancer, and even dementia (Women's Health Initiative, 2002; Shumaker et al., 2003) (**Figure 11.11**). For that reason, the Food and Drug Administration and the National Institutes of Health recommended that hormone therapy generally be restricted to the short-term relief of menopausal symptoms. These recommendations led to a dramatic drop in the use of postmenopausal hormone therapy, which in turn led to a significant drop in the incidence of breast cancer.

More recently, though, professional opinion has changed again: It's now believed that the risks of postmenopausal hormone therapy apply mainly to older women, and that this form of therapy is beneficial and safe for women under 60 who have continuing postmenopausal symptoms (Rozenberg et al., 2013). Of course, it's a fair bet that therapeutic options and recommendations will change several more times before today's female college students reach menopause.

There has been a search for alternative, more "natural" therapies for menopausal symptoms and for long-term postmenopausal use. In particular, there has been interest in **isoflavones**, which are plant-derived molecules with an estrogen-like structure. Unfortunately, carefully controlled studies have found little or no effect of isoflavones in reducing either menopausal symptoms or bone loss (Levis et al., 2011). The practice of yoga does alleviate menopausal symptoms, according to a controlled trial conducted in India (Joshi et al., 2011). In a more general way, lifestyle choices such as exercise (especially weight-bearing exercise such as walking), keeping a healthy weight, not smoking, and eating a healthful, calcium-rich diet are likely to reduce menopausal symptoms and postmenopausal health risks.

The use of testosterone in the treatment of women's sexual disorders is discussed in Chapter 14.

Ethnicity influences the experience of menopause

Women of different ethnic or national backgrounds may experience menopause differently, both in terms of the physical symptoms and in how they react to menopause psychologically (Green et al., 2010; Richard-Davis & Wellons, 2013). White women

menopausal hormone therapy Use of hormones to treat symptoms occurring during or soon after menopause.

postmenopausal hormone therapy Hormone treatment extending for a long time after menopause.

isoflavones Estrogen-like compounds of plant origin.

tend to medicalize menopause, to suffer more psychosomatic symptoms, and to be relatively concerned about a perceived loss of youthfulness and attractiveness. Black and Latina women, especially Latinas from Central America, report more severe physical symptoms associated with menopause, and yet they tend to adopt a more positive, even welcoming view of the event—as a normal life stage that allows them to restructure their priorities, with a greater emphasis on self-fulfillment. Asian-American women experience fewer menopausal symptoms than women in other groups (Im et al., 2010). Regardless of ethnicity, a fear of menopause before the event commonly gives way to a sense of emancipation after it arrives.

andropause In men, the gradual decline of fertility with age; a hypothetical male equivalent of menopause.

Men's Fertility Declines Gradually with Age

Men do not experience a sudden or complete cessation of fertility comparable to menopause. Instead, they experience a gradual reduction in fertility and sexual function with aging, evidenced by declining sperm counts and ejaculate volume, an increased likelihood of erectile disorder (see Chapter 14), and decreased sexual desire and frequency of sex. More general changes associated with aging include loss of muscle bulk and bone density, changes in the skin and hair, and possible cognitive changes such as memory impairment.

Some people refer to this collection of changes as the "male menopause," or **andropause**, but these terms are misleading if they suggest that the changes are sudden or result in a total cessation of reproductive function. Although sperm counts decline, some men in their 80s have fathered children.

Driven in part by pharmaceutical advertising, middle-aged American men are increasingly coming to believe that their decreased libido, declining athletic ability, or general world-weariness are symptoms of a medical condition, "low T," which can and should be corrected with testosterone patches. The reality is different: Testosterone levels do not affect sexual functioning in middle-aged or aging men until they fall below a level that is not commonly encountered (O'Connor et al., 2011). Using an objectively validated definition of "hypogonadism" (free testosterone below the level of 220 picomoles per liter, combined with sexual symptoms), this condition affects only 1 in 1000 men in their 40s, and only 1 in 20 men in their 70s (Wu et al., 2010).

With regard to middle-aged or older men whose testosterone levels do test low, there are conflicting data about the long-term benefits and risks of testosterone supplementation. One trial found that testosterone greatly reduced mortality (Shores et al., 2012), whereas another (on elderly men with limited mobility) had to be stopped early because of a high rate of adverse events among the testosterone-treated subjects (Basaria et al., 2013). An obvious concern for men of any age is that testosterone treatment may increase the risk of developing prostate cancer or accelerate the growth of pre-existing, undiagnosed cancers. It is also likely to worsen benign enlargement of the prostate, a common condition in older men.

The Sex Lives of Old People Have Traditionally Been Ignored

Our knowledge of sexuality in old age is fairly limited. There has been a traditional assumption that old people are asexual, and any indications to the contrary (such as sexual behavior by the residents of nursing homes) have generally been viewed with embarrassment and disapproval. Large national sex surveys, such as the 1994 NHSLS survey and its British equivalent, the 1994 National Survey of Sexual Attitudes and Lifestyles (NSSAL), restricted their samples to people under age 60.

The sexuality of this older couple is important to the well-being of their relationship

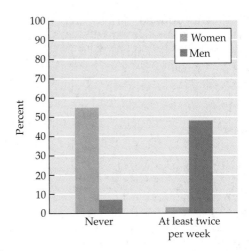

Figure 11.12 **The sex drive in old age** Survey participants over 70 were asked the question "How frequently have you had sexual thoughts, fantasies, or erotic dreams." These bar graphs show the percentages of women and men who never had such thoughts and the percentages who had them at least twice per week. (Data from American Association of Retired Persons, 2010.)

More recently, however, greater attention has been paid to the sexuality of old people. The 2010 NSSHB survey, for example, included individuals as old as 94, and the new version of the British NSSAL, published in 2013, raised the upper age limit to 74. A periodic survey conducted for AARP (American Association of Retired Persons, 2010) pays particular attention to the sexuality of midlife and older Americans.

Looking at the results of the most recent (2009) AARP survey, one of the most striking findings is the difference between older men and older women in how much they think about and value sex. Men typically have a stronger sex drive than women by various measures, as we discussed in Chapter 4, but this sex difference increases greatly as people age. In fact, over half of all women over 70 said that they never had sexual thoughts, fantasies, or erotic dreams, compared with only about 7% of men over 70 (**Figure 11.12**). Correspondingly, 80% of men over 70 said that a sexual relationship was important to their quality of life, whereas only 39% of women said the same thing.

In considering these numbers, it's important to bear in mind that heterosexual women face an increasing shortage of potential sex partners as they age. This is because men die younger than women, tend to marry women who are younger than themselves, and are much more likely than women to be in a same-sex relationship (4 times more likely in the AARP data). Thus, far more older men than older women have regular sex partners (**Figure 11.13**). It's likely that more older women would value and think about sex if sex partners were available. Still, even solo sex shows a major sex difference in the AARP data: Nearly 3 times more men than women masturbated at least once per week.

Among the AARP respondents who did have a sex partner, however, almost equal percentages of women and men said that they were satisfied with their sex lives (56% and 59%, respectively). Being married, being healthy, experiencing little stress, exercising frequently, and of course having frequent sex were all predictors of sexual satisfac-

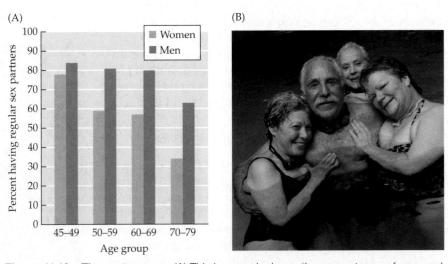

Figure 11.13 **The partner gap** (A) This bar graph shows the percentages of men and women in different age groups who have a regular sex partner. (B) Because of the imbalance between the sexes, a single older man may be a hot property. (A after American Association of Retired Persons, 2010.)

tion. About half of partnered men and women in the 70+ group said that their partners were physically attractive, and two-thirds said that their partners "loved them deeply."

Aging is accompanied by physiological changes in the sexual response

Old people experience changes in the physiological processes underlying sexuality. For men, these changes include the following:

- The penis becomes erect more slowly in response to either tactile or mental stimulation. The erect penis is less hard. Some degree of erectile disorder is reported by about 45% of men over age 65 (Waite et al., 2009).
- Ejaculatory volume is smaller, and the semen is discharged less forcefully. (It may flow out slowly or even be discharged backward into the bladder.)
- The erection is lost more rapidly.
- The refractory period (time before another erection and ejaculation are possible) is longer.

Women may experience the following changes:

- The walls of the vagina become thinner, and the entire vagina may become shorter and narrower. (This condition can be alleviated with local application of estrogens.)
- Vaginal lubrication decreases. Nearly half of women over age 65 report this problem (Waite et al., 2009).
- There are fewer contractions during orgasm.
- There is a more rapid decrease in arousal after orgasm.

Medical conditions, drugs, and social factors can impair the sexuality of older people

Medical conditions that become more common with advancing age can also impair sexual performance. These conditions include arthritis, heart disease, osteoporosis, incontinence, diabetes, chronic obstructive pulmonary disease (emphysema and chronic bronchitis), and obesity. Surgeries such as prostatectomy, mastectomy, and hysterectomy can affect sexual performance, either directly, or indirectly by causing pain or embarrassment.

Older people take more prescription drugs than younger people, and many of these drugs can interfere with sexual performance. Examples include antihypertension drugs, diuretics, tranquilizers and antidepressants, cancer chemotherapy, ulcer medicines, and anticoagulants. (Individual drugs vary, as do patients' responses to them; alternative drugs can often be prescribed that do not impair sexual desire or performance.)

Psychological and social factors that can impair sexual expression in older people include depression, poor self-image, performance anxiety, bereavement, lack of an available partner, and the internalization of the negative expectations of others, especially the older person's children and medical professionals.

For older couples who have difficulty with coitus (because of physiological changes in one or both partners), it might make good sense to practice oral sex instead. However, people in the oldest age groups came of age at a time when oral sex was relatively uncommon and was practiced mainly by the better-educated levels of society. This age cohort did not necessarily join the rush to oral sex in the 1960s; in fact, nearly half of them have never had a single experience of fellatio or cunnilingus, according to NHSLS data, and many of them probably consider these behaviors immoral or unappealing. Obviously, it may be hard for such people to accept or enjoy oral sex now that they are well into their retirement years, even if health care provid-

Box 11.5 Personal Points of View

Seniors on Sex

In 2014 Gloria Steinem, a leader in the 1970s women's liberation movement, reached her 80th birthday. She marked the occasion by speaking positively about her dwindling libido, saying, "The brain cells that used to be obsessed [with sex] are now free for all kinds of great things" (Collins, 2014). Britain's *Guardian* newspaper asked its readers for their reactions, and several hundred British and American women obliged (Spencer, 2014). Their remarks give some idea of the diverse ways in which aging affects women's sex lives. Here are some samples:

> *My lack of sex drive has been enormously liberating. I look back with some regret at the years I wasted on men. I've recently, at age 60, completed a BSc in Computer Science and I now work as a software engineer.*

> *For me, diminished libido is yet another manifestation that my time has passed. Outliving my vitality has not made me feel happy, free, or wise.*

> *I had zero sex drive until my gyno prescribed testosterone cream. It made a huge difference. I recently fell in love with a man who is 73 and I'm having the best sex of my life and am multi-orgasmic for the first time. Hooray senior love.*

> *Far from dwindling, my sex drive has surged since menopause. Sex toys are my best friends.*

This comment comes from a different source:

> *It's just the huge warmth of being with somebody that you've been in bed with for 40-plus years and still feeling that immense rush of joy, that—you know—what a gift! (Kleinplatz et al., 2009)*

And here are some comments from men, culled from a variety of online sources:

> *I started taking a daily drug for erections and it makes me feel like 20 again.*

> *I had a laser treatment for BPH [enlarged prostate]. Since then I have been unable to sustain an erection, nor am I able to ejaculate.*

> *My appetite for sex is about normal. The problem is that my wife no longer feels that way. All the fun and excitement has gone from our sex life.*

> *There's a great beauty in the freedom from necessity. Sex becomes more a matter of choice and is more interesting and intriguing for each partner.*

> *I am experiencing the best sex ever. I can attribute it to the mutual love that I have with my partner. We have sex almost daily.*

If your grandparents are available and agreeable, why not get their perspectives on sex in old age? They may be happy to know that at least one person has an interest in their sex lives.

ers or others suggest it to them. In the AARP survey, less than 1 in 5 respondents said that they engaged in oral sex at all frequently.

Because of the problems just mentioned, about half of all sexually active older people experience at least one bothersome sexual problem (Lindau et al., 2007). We will discuss these problems, and ways to alleviate them, in Chapter 14.

The experience of aging affects people in diverse ways

There is no one way in which old people express their sexuality, or lack of it. The comments of individual women and men show that sex can be frequent or nonexistent, a pain or a joy (**Box 11.5**).

Sex is also not static over the generations, for either young or old people. Even between the 2004 and 2009 AARP surveys, the respondents' frequency of sexual intercourse and satisfaction with their sex lives both dropped by nearly 10%, possibly because worsening economic conditions affected their sexuality. Attitudes change too—either because people change their views or because new cohorts of people are entering the older age brackets. As an example, in the 1999 AARP survey 41% of the respondents said that unmarried people shouldn't have sex; by the time of the 2009 survey, that number had dropped almost by half (22%).

Baby boomers (people born shortly after World War II, who lived through the sexual revolution of the 1960s) are now entering or well into their retirement years. This generation has been much more interested in sexual variety and much less tied to the notion that sex is only for reproduction, as compared with their predecessors. They also have a greater sense of entitlement with regard to personal fulfillment generally. Thus, they will be far less ready to give up sex if physiological or social problems get in their way. The huge demand for Viagra when it came on the market in 1998 was a harbinger of things to come: Both men and women are likely to demand effective medical treatments for age-associated sexual disorders. They will also ensure that sexual expression by old people is recognized and respected, rather than being pushed into the closet.

Go to the **Discovering Human Sexuality** Companion Website at **sites.sinauer.com/ discoveringhumansexuality3e** for activities, study questions, quizzes, and other study aids.

Summary

- Young adults typically spend a few years "hooking up" and/or dating before they enter their first live-in relationship, but the average number of sex partners during this period is quite low. Sexual desires have to compete with other interests, such as the pursuit of education or career advancement.

- For many adults, their first live-in relationship is a non-marital cohabitation. Cohabitation may serve simply as a convenient alternative to dating, or it may represent a committed relationship without the legal trappings of marriage. Cohabitation does not harm a subsequent marriage.

- Marriage has had many different functions and forms. Many past and present human societies have allowed polygamy. In the United States, polyfidelity, Mormon polygamy, and same-sex marriage exemplify nonstandard marital arrangements.

- Western society is moving from a traditional, one-size-fits-all institution of marriage to a greater variety of live-in sexual relationships. Because women have fewer pregnancies than in the past and are more likely to be in the labor market, distinct gender roles in marriage have diminished. People are marrying later and divorcing more readily; marriage may soon become a minority status for American adults. Nevertheless, most people desire to be in some kind of monogamous, long-term relationship.

- Married men and women tend to have less sex than those who are dating or cohabiting, and they are less adventurous sexually, but their physical and emotional satisfaction with their sex lives is high. For women, simply being married makes sex more satisfying. However, marital satisfaction tends to fall off over time.

- One in three marriages breaks up within 10 years. The likelihood of breakup is increased by a number of factors, such as early (teen) marriage, dissimilarity between husband and wife, and low educational level. A college education is associated with marital stability.

- Divorced people experience a variety of physical and psychological ill effects, but many divorced men and women remarry.

- Menopause—the cessation of menstrual cycles—is the culmination of a gradual transition to infertility in women. The hormonal changes of menopause can impair the physiological processes of sexual arousal and may be accompanied by a decline in sexual interest and activity.

- Hormone therapy can alleviate menopausal symptoms. Postmenopausal women over 60 are discouraged from using hormone therapy, because of cardiac and other risks.

- Men experience a gradual decline in fertility, physiological arousal, and sexual interest, rather than a rapid transition to infertility. A few men father children in old age.

- Many people continue to experience sexual desire into old age. The physical expression of this desire may be compromised by declining physiological responsiveness (for example, erectile disorder or loss of vaginal lubrication), by a variety of medical conditions and drugs, or by the lack of a partner. Nevertheless, many older women and men continue to engage in sexual behavior, including masturbation, coitus, and noncoital contacts.

Discussion Questions

1. Describe your ideal marriage partner or cohabiting partner and his or her characteristics (e.g., appearance, personality, and occupation). What circumstances or conflicts (if any) do you think would lead you to consider a separation or divorce (e.g., infidelity, refusal to have children, disease, or cross-dressing)?

2. Why do you think the divorce rate for college graduates is so much lower than it is for people without college degrees?

3. Identify the myths and what you "have heard" about menopause. Contrast these descriptions with the facts. What behaviors are characteristic of menopause? Do men have a "change of life"?

4. Describe the advice you would give to your mother or an older female friend who asks you to explain the pros and cons of menopausal hormone therapy. Do you think the fact that menopause is a natural part of the aging process should discourage women from attempting to counteract its effects with hormone treatment?

5. Think about your grandparents or people who are older than 60. What are your beliefs and thoughts about sex among older people? What do you think are the barriers to enjoying a happy sex life after 60?

Web Resources

Alternatives to Marriage Project www.unmarried.org
Divorcenet www.divorcenet.com
Mayo Clinic. Sexual health and aging: Keep the passion alive www.tinyurl.com/mayosex
National Healthy Marriage Resource Center www.healthymarriageinfo.org
North American Menopause Society www.menopause.org
Parents Without Partners www.parentswithoutpartners.org
Study of Women's Health Across the Nation www.swanstudy.org

Recommended Reading

Anapol, D. (2010). *Polyamory in the 21st century: Love and intimacy with multiple partners.* Rowman & Littlefield.

Bair, D. (2007). *Calling it quits: Late-life divorce and starting over.* Random House.

Bogle, K. A. (2008). *Hooking up: Sex, dating, and relationships on campus.* NYU Press.

Butler, R. N. & Lewis, M. I. (2002). *The new love and sex after 60.* Ballantine.

Cherlin, A. J. (2010). *The marriage-go-round: The state of marriage and the family in America today.* Vintage.

Crowley, C. & Lodge, H. S. (2007). *Younger next year for women.* Workman.

Crowley, C. & Lodge, H. S. (2011). *Younger next year for men.* Workman.

Easton, D. & Hardy, J. W. (2009). *The ethical slut: A practical guide to polyamory, open relationships and other adventures* (2nd ed.). Celestial Arts.

Levine, S. B. (2013). *How we love now: Women talk about intimacy after 50.* Plume.

North American Menopause Society. (2012). *Menopause guidebook* (7th ed.). (Can be ordered at www.menopause.org.)

Northrup, C., Schwartz, P. & Witte, J. (2014). *The normal bar: The surprising secrets of happy couples and what they reveal about creating a new normal in your relationship.* Harmony.

Regnerus, M. & Uecker, J. (2011). *Premarital sex in America: How young Americans meet, mate, and think about marrying.* Oxford University Press.

Schwartz, P. & Lever, J. (2012). *Getaway guide to the great sex weekend.* Worldwide Romance.

Chapter 12

Same-sex marriage is transforming the social role of many gay people.

Sexual Orientation

The direction of our sexual attractions—to the other sex, to our own sex, or to both sexes—has a profound influence on our personal and public lives and on how we are viewed and treated by others. In this chapter we first ask what sexual orientation is and how it develops. We then turn to the social aspects of sexual orientation. Here we largely neglect heterosexuality, because that topic is a leading theme of most other chapters of this book. Instead, we focus on gay people—lesbians and gay men. What is causing their rapid emergence from a history of discrimination and exclusion? How do their life courses differ from those of heterosexual men and women, beginning in childhood? What subcultures exist within the larger gay community? What causes some people to fear or dislike lesbians and gay men, and how can these negative attitudes be changed?

Finally, we take a look at what might be the least well-understood sexual orientation: bisexuality. Bisexual men and women are the subject of considerable scientific and social controversy. Does bisexuality even exist—or are we all bisexual? And by being attracted to both women and men, do bisexual people enjoy the best of all possible worlds—or the worst?

Figure 12.1 Distribution of sexual orientations This bar graph shows the direction of sexual attraction for U.S. men and women age 18–44, based on data from the National Survey of Family Growth. Note the break in the *y*-axis and the change of scaling to allow for clearer representation of the non-heterosexual groups. (Data from Centers for Disease Control, 2011b.)

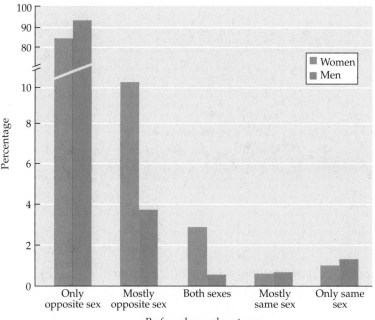

There Is a Spectrum of Sexual Orientations

Sexual orientation is the dimension of personality that describes the balance of our sexual attraction to the two sexes. At either end of this continuum are **heterosexuality** (attraction only to persons of the other sex) and **homosexuality** (attraction only to persons of one's own sex). Between these two endpoints lie degrees of **bisexuality**—sexual attraction to both sexes. The colloquial terms **straight** and **gay** have come to replace the more clinical-sounding words "heterosexual" and "homosexual" in most contexts, and bisexual people may simply call themselves **bi**. The term "gay" can apply to either homosexual men or homosexual women. An alternative term that applies only to homosexual women is **lesbian**. This term comes from the Greek island of Lesbos, home of the ancient poetess Sappho, who wrote passionate love poems to other women.

In his pioneering studies, Alfred Kinsey developed a 7-point scale of sexual orientation that ranged from group 0 (exclusively attracted to the opposite sex) to group 6 (exclusively attracted to the same sex), with the intervening groups defining various degrees of bisexuality. Although well-known to the public, the **Kinsey scale** is less widely used by researchers today than it was in the past, chiefly because it suggests finer gradations of sexual orientation than are usually supported by scientific studies. Instead, modern researchers often use a 5-point scale (**Figure 12.1**).

In terms of numbers, the distribution of sexual orientations is strongly biased toward the heterosexual end of the continuum. In most random-sample surveys, at least 85% to 90% of men and women say that they are attracted sexually only to persons of the other sex, and another several percent say that they are attracted "mostly" to the other sex. At the other end of the spectrum, less than 2% of men and less than 1% of women say that they are attracted only to persons of the same sex as themselves. If one includes in the definition of gay people those who say they are attracted "mostly" to the same sex, their numbers sometimes rise to about 2% to 4% of the population (Centers for Disease Control, 2011b). The true figures may be somewhat higher, given that some respondents may be reluctant to admit to same-sex attraction, but even surveys that have gone to extraordinary lengths to eliminate this problem have not come up with significantly higher numbers (Coffman et al., 2013). When

sexual orientation   The direction of a person's sexual feelings: sexual attraction toward persons of the opposite sex (heterosexual), the same sex (homosexual), or both sexes (bisexual).

heterosexuality   Sexual attraction only (or predominantly) to persons of the other sex.

homosexuality   Sexual attraction only (or predominantly) to persons of one's own sex.

bisexuality   Sexual attraction to persons of both sexes.

straight   Colloquial term for heterosexual.

gay   Colloquial term for homosexual.

bi   Colloquial term for bisexual.

lesbian   Homosexual—applied to women only.

Kinsey scale   A 7-point scale of sexual orientation devised by Alfred Kinsey.

people are asked what they call themselves, the numbers are even more strongly biased toward heterosexuality: In the most recent survey, 97.7% of Americans identified as straight, and only 2.3% identified as gay, lesbian, or bisexual (National Center for Health Statistics, 2014a).

Although the various surveys have come up with somewhat different figures, a common finding is this: More men than women are exclusively homosexual, whereas more women than men are about equally attracted to both sexes. This is true regardless of whether people are asked about their attractions or how they identify themselves. Furthermore, when sexual orientation is assessed by measuring subjects' genital arousal (penile erection or vaginal vasocongestion) while they are viewing erotic images or videos of females or males, the sex difference in sexual orientation is even more pronounced: The great majority of men are aroused much more strongly by one sex than the other, whereas many or most women show nonspecific arousal to both sexes (Chivers et al., 2004). We will return to this issue in the section on bisexuality toward the end of this chapter.

There are many other aspects of sexual attraction that might logically be included within the term "sexual orientation," such as the preferred age or race of one's sex partners. Traditionally, however, the term refers only to the balance of same-sex versus opposite-sex attraction, and that is how we use the term here. Other aspects of sexual attraction are dealt with elsewhere in this book.

Lesbian, gay, and bisexual people are often linked with transgender people under the umbrella term "LGBT," or with an even wider range of identities such as LGBTQQIAP.* Trans people certainly have some overlap and shared concerns with people who are gay, lesbian, or bisexual, as we discuss in this chapter and elsewhere in the textbook. But gender identity is distinct from sexual orientation: Knowing that someone is transgender does not tell us whether they are sexually attracted to males or females or to both sexes. That is why we cover gender identity and transgender people in Chapter 4 rather than here.

gender-variant Atypical in gender characteristics.

Sexual Orientation Is Not an Isolated Trait

Lesbians and gay men have often been thought of as having many characteristics of the other sex. Words such as "effeminate" or "queeny" have been applied to gay men, and "mannish" or "butch" to lesbians, usually with derogatory implications. These are stereotypes—false or overgeneralized beliefs about classes of people.

Some gay people themselves, however, have promoted the idea that they are **gender-variant** (**Figure 12.2**). Others have rejected this notion, asserting that they differ from straight people only in "who we love."

You probably know at least one or two gay people. If you are gay yourself, you may have scores of gay friends and acquaintances. Either way, you can hardly have avoided noticing that lesbians and gay men are a very mixed bunch. Some are entirely conventional in their gender characteristics, some are a trifle nonconformist, and some are flagrant gender rebels. Straight people are not always so "straight-acting," either. But are there gender-related differences between gay and straight people considered as entire groups?

Psychologists have studied this issue by examining gender-related traits in large numbers of gay and straight people. They find that gay people—*on average*—do differ, in a number of gender-related traits, from straight people of the same sex (LeVay, 2011). In fact, these differences are apparent well before people become aware of the direction of their own sexual attractions. During childhood, boys who later become gay men tend to be less focused on typical boys' toys and

Figure 12.2 Novelist Radclyffe Hall (1880–1943) (standing, with her partner Una Troubridge) portrayed lesbians, including herself, as resembling men.

---

* This stands for lesbian, gay, bisexual, trans, queer, questioning, intersex, asexual, and pansexual.

gaydar The ability to recognize gay people on the basis of unconscious behaviors, voice quality, gait, and so on.

boys' activities, to be judged by others as unmasculine or girlish, and to have less stereotypically male career plans. For girls who later become lesbians, the opposite is true: Such girls tend to prefer boys' toys and activities, to be judged by others as unfeminine or boyish, and to have male-typical career plans (Bailey & Zucker, 1995; Steensma et al., 2013b). These conclusions are based on prospective studies of gender-conformist and gender-nonconformist children (**Box 12.1**) and on the recollections of gay and straight adults. In one particularly convincing study, raters watched childhood video clips provided by gay and straight adults (without knowing which was which); they rated the "pre-gay"* children as far more gender-nonconformist than the "pre-straight children" (Rieger et al., 2008). It is not possible to predict with certainty the future sexual orientation of even extremely gender-nonconformist children, but many or most of them—feminine boys especially—do become gay adults.

In adulthood, gay and bisexual men describe themselves as less masculine (on average) than do straight men, and lesbians and bisexual women describe themselves as less feminine than do straight women. Gays and lesbians also tend to be gender-atypical in their choice of occupations and recreational interests. All these differences hold up across several different regions of the world (Lippa, 2008; Ueno et al., 2013).

Gay men are (on average) gender-atypical in some of the sex-differentiated cognitive traits that we discussed in Chapter 4. They are less aggressive than straight men; perform less well on some tasks at which men typically excel, such as targeting accuracy and mental rotation; and perform better on some tasks at which females typically excel, such as verbal fluency (**Figure 12.3**), object-location memory, and face recognition (Brewster et al., 2011). Lesbians also score in gender-atypical fashion in some tests—doing better than heterosexual women in mental rotation and worse in object-location memory, for example.

To some extent, it is possible to identify a person's sexual orientation on the basis of unconscious behaviors such as body motions and voice quality (Pierrehumbert et al., 2004; K. L. Johnson et al., 2007; Rieger et al., 2010). This ability is referred to colloquially as **gaydar**. For the most part, the cues that gaydar relies on are gender-atypical behaviors.

In short, there is a partial correlation between sexual orientation and other aspects of gender, and any theory of sexual orientation needs to explain the existence of this correlation. Gays and lesbians are certainly not transgender, but they are distinctly atypical, on average, in some gender-related traits. These differences between gay and straight people are generally more consistent for men than for women.

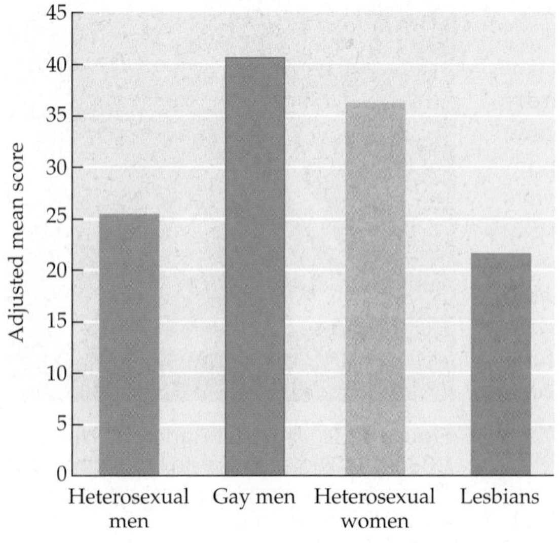

Diverse Theories Attempt to Explain Sexual Orientation

What causes a person to become heterosexual, bisexual, or homosexual? This question has aroused a great deal of interest and controversy

---

* We use the term "pre-gay" in reference to children who later become gay adults, regardless of their childhood identity or characteristics.

Figure 12.3 Gay men and lesbians are sex-atypical in verbal fluency. The bar graph charts the mean scores of heterosexual men, heterosexual women, gay men, and lesbians (60 individuals per group) in tests of the type "In 1 minute, list as many words as you can that have the same meaning as 'dark.'" The scores have been adjusted for age and IQ. The results for gay men are about the same as for heterosexual women, while the results for lesbians are about the same as for heterosexual men. (Data from Rahman et al., 2003b.)

Box 12.1 Research Highlights

Boys Will Be Girls

There has long been "folk wisdom" to the effect that feminine boys have a high chance of becoming gay when they grow up. In the late 1960s, psychiatrist Richard Green of UCLA initiated an ambitious prospective study to test the truth of this notion (Green, 1987). He recruited 66 families in which there was a son (age 4 to 10) who was markedly feminine. These were not just slightly unmasculine boys. Here's an excerpt from one interview Green had with a 5-year-old boy, "Richard," whose parents brought him to Green because of his persistent cross-dressing, role-playing as a girl, and avoidance of male playmates:

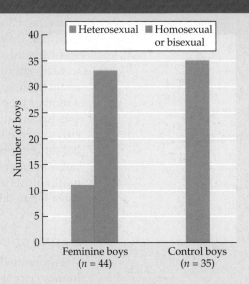

Green: Have you ever wished you'd been born a girl?

Richard: Yes.

Green: Why did you wish that?

Richard: Girls, they don't have to have a penis.

Green: They don't have to have a penis?

Richard: They can have babies. And—because they—it doesn't tickle when you tickle them here.

Green: It doesn't tickle when you tickle them here? Where your penis is?

Richard: Yeah. 'Cause they don't have a penis. I wish I was a girl.

Green: You wish you were a girl?

Richard: You know what? I might be a girl.

Green also recruited 56 boys as matched controls; these boys were chosen without regard to their gender characteristics. He interviewed the boys and their parents repeatedly during the boys' childhood, adolescence, and (in many cases) young adulthood.

The central finding of the study could hardly be more striking. The control boys became, with one slight exception, totally heterosexual (see figure, which includes data only for the boys who could be followed into adolescence or adulthood). Of the feminine boys, the majority became gay or bisexual. Although many of the feminine boys wished they were girls, most of them actually became fairly conventional gay men who were no more obviously feminine than gay men in general; and only one expressed an interest in sex-reassignment surgery.

In spite of the marked difference in outcomes for the two groups, we should make a couple of cautionary points. First, some of the feminine boys were entirely heterosexual at their last interview. In fact, "Richard" was one of these. It's possible that some of these "heterosexual" youths would have come out as gay or bisexual if they had been followed for longer, because it has been common for gay and bisexual men to have a history of claiming to be heterosexual, especially in the era of Green's study (Stokes et al., 1997). However, childhood characteristics are not entirely predictive of adult orientation, even for these extreme gender-nonconformist children. Second, most gay men do not have a history of such radical gender nonconformity during their childhood; in fact, some recall a very conventionally masculine childhood.

Richard Green's 20-year study is now considered a classic in the field of sexology; its findings have been confirmed in a variety of ways by later research.

---

over the years. In popular discourse, the question has often been phrased in such forms as "What makes people gay?"—as if heterosexuality didn't require any explanation. In reality, of course, heterosexuality, homosexuality, and bisexuality all need some kind of explanation.

Most theories of sexual orientation could be described as either psychodynamic or biological. Psychodynamic theories attempt to explain the development of a person's sexual orientation in terms of internal mental processes, especially as they are affected by interaction with others, rewards and punishments, and so on. Examples include psychoanalytic and socialization theories. Biological theories, in contrast, attempt to explain sexual orientation in terms of phenomena such as brain circuitry, hormones, genes, and evolution.

FAQ

Why don't gay people fall in love with themselves?

A mechanism called the Westermarck effect ensures that people don't fall in love with persons they grew up with, such as siblings. Presumably this same effect rules out oneself as a target of romantic love.

Freud proposed psychodynamic models

Throughout most of the 20th century, thinking about sexual orientation centered on the psychoanalytic theories of Sigmund Freud. Freud saw heterosexuality as the "normal" culmination of a complex, multistage process of psychosexual development (Freud, 1905/1975). This process, he believed, included a homosexual phase in early childhood that was later forgotten. The "normal" developmental process could be disrupted by abnormal relationships within the family: These could include a mother who was too "close-binding" or "seductive" toward a child, a father who was too distant or hostile, intense sibling rivalry, or penis envy—the trauma supposedly suffered by a girl when she discovered that she lacked a body part possessed by her father or brother. If these phenomena blocked "normal" development, the child might remain stuck in the early homosexual phase. Freud suggested a variety of other mechanisms by which a person might become homosexual. None of them have been substantiated by scientific research.

Sexual orientation has been attributed to socialization

One potentially very powerful form of socialization consists of sexual interactions. In this vein, it has often been suggested that both male and female homosexuality result from consensual same-sex experiences in boarding schools, from molestation during childhood, from rape during young adulthood, or from other early sexual experiences. Again, though, the evidence does not support such ideas. People who attend single-sex boarding schools do have more homosexual experiences during that time than people who don't attend such schools, but they are no more likely to be gay in adulthood (Wellings et al., 1994). And lesbians are no more likely to have been molested during childhood than are straight women (Dominguez et al., 2002).

Socialization effects could, of course, be much subtler than those just described and could include important cognitive aspects. Women, in particular, whose sexual feelings are more strongly modulated by considerations of love and intimacy than are those of men, may for that reason be more responsive to life events and sexual scripts (see Chapter 1), which might give their sexual orientation greater fluidity than that of men (Peplau & Garnets, 2000; Diamond, 2008b).

In Chapter 4 we described the work of John Money, who proposed that parents guide their children's developing gender and sexual orientation by innumerable rewards and punishments—by operant conditioning, in other words. We described how Bruce Reimer, the boy who was reared as a girl, became Money's poster child for this theory but later became Money's nemesis when he changed his sex back to male and developed a clear heterosexual orientation (see Box 4.3 on page 109). Although it seems likely that parental influence does mold some aspects of children's gender characteristics, there is no positive evidence for an influence on sexual orientation. It is certain, however, that socialization strongly influences how gay people think of themselves and how they live their lives: Some learn to feel guilty about their sexuality and have to fight those feelings in adulthood, while others grow up in families and peer groups that encourage them to feel positive about themselves.

Many desires and behaviors, including sexual ones, are "contagious," meaning that they spread in friendship networks. This is especially true during adolescence, when young people shift their allegiance from family to peer groups. To see if this was true for same-sex attraction, an international group of psychologists, sociologists, and public health specialists examined data from the U.S. National Longitudinal Study of Adolescent Health (Brakefield et al., 2014). In this study nearly 15,000 adolescents were asked about their sexual feelings, desires, and behaviors, and they were also asked to identify their friends. As expected, the researchers found that many phenomena, such as becoming sexually active and desiring to enter into a romantic relationship, were strongly influenced by a teen's friendship networks, but neither

Figure 12.4   The prenatal hormone theory of sexual orientation In its simplest form, this theory proposes that adult sexual orientation depends on the level of androgens to which the brain is exposed during a sensitive period of fetal development. Most males and a few females exceed some threshold of androgen exposure and therefore become attracted to females. Most females and a few males fall below that threshold level and therefore become attracted to males. In the figure, the threshold has been arbitrarily set at a value that would produce more homosexual males than females, corresponding to what has been observed in most studies.

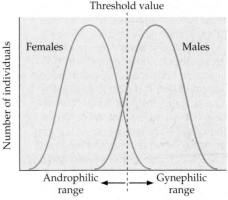

identifying as gay/lesbian nor desiring to enter a same-sex romantic relationship showed any influence of this kind. On the basis of this and other studies, it appears that social factors have little if any influence on sexual orientation, at least during the teen years.

Biological theories focus on prenatal hormones and genes

The leading biological theory of sexual orientation proposes that sexual orientation, like other aspects of gender, reflects the sexual differentiation of the brain under the influence of prenatal sex hormones. In the simplest version of this theory (**Figure 12.4**), everything depends on androgen levels during a sensitive period of prenatal development. Fetuses whose brains are exposed to high levels of androgens during this period (mostly males, but a few females) will be sexually attracted to women (**gynephilic**) in adult life; conversely, fetuses whose brains are exposed to low levels of androgens (mostly females, but some males) will be sexually attracted to men (**androphilic**) in adult life. Alternatively, it might be not the hormone levels themselves but the brain's sensitivity to hormones that differs between "pre-gay" and "pre-straight" fetuses.

The prenatal hormone hypothesis could explain why gay people are, on average, gender-atypical in a variety of traits besides their sexual orientation, as described above. We would just need to suppose that differences in androgen levels during development affect the differentiation, not only of brain circuits that are responsible for sexual orientation, but also of brain circuits that mediate some other gendered traits—specifically, those whose brain circuitry happens to differentiate in the same fetal time period.

The prenatal hormone theory has a solid basis in animal research: The preference of animals such as rats for male or female sex partners can be modified by experimental manipulation of their androgen levels during development (Alexander et al., 2011). Of course, it is not ethically possible to do comparable experiments in humans. As we mentioned in Chapter 4, however, the condition of congenital adrenal hyperplasia (CAH), in which human fetuses are exposed to high levels of androgens regardless of their sex, offers an equivalent "experiment of nature." Women with CAH are more likely to experience same-sex attraction and engage in same-sex relationships than are control groups of women such as their unaffected sisters (Meyer-Bahlburg et al., 2008). This suggests that the findings of the animal studies are relevant to humans too.

Of course, CAH is a rare medical condition. Do the findings in CAH-affected persons say anything about people who don't have such a condition? To study this question, researchers have looked for biological markers related to sexual orientation in the general population. Neuroscientist Simon LeVay (one of the authors of this textbook) focused on the hypothalamus. We already mentioned this brain region in Chapter 2 and Chapter 3 on account of its participation in the regulation of sex hormone levels and the menstrual cycle. From studies in animals, it appears that a region at the front of the hypothalamus known as the **medial preoptic area** is involved in the regulation of sexual behaviors typically shown by males, including the prefer-

gynephilic   Sexually attracted to women.

androphilic   Sexually attracted to men.

medial preoptic area   A region of the hypothalamus involved in the regulation of sexual behaviors typically shown by males.

Figure 12.5 The hypothalamus and male sexual orientation (A) A cell group known as INAH3 lies within the medial preoptic area of the hypothalamus, a region concerned with male-typical sexual behavior. (B) Microscopic view of INAH3 in a man; INAH3 is the oval-shaped cluster of darkly stained cells occupying most of the center of the image—it measures about 0.5 mm across. (C) Two autopsy studies found that INAH3 is smaller in women and gay men than in straight men, but they did not agree on the magnitude of the difference. (Data from LeVay, 1991; Byne et al., 2001.)

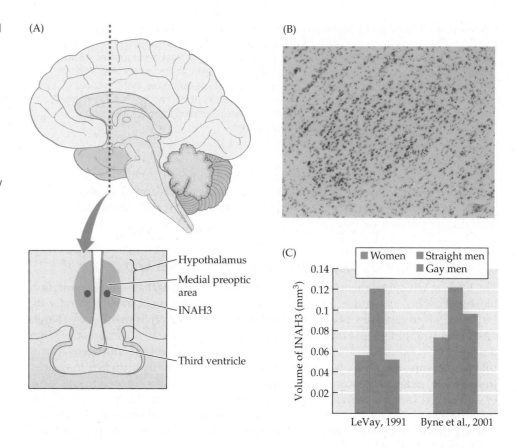

INAH3 Third interstitial nucleus of the anterior hypothalamus—a neuronal cell group in the hypothalamus that differs in size between men and women and between gay and straight men.

ence for female partners (**Figure 12.5**). Within the medial preoptic area is a cell group that is typically larger in males than in females. In humans it has the name **INAH3**. Again, based on animal experiments, it appears that this sex difference results from differences in circulating sex hormone levels during the prenatal period when this region of the brain is developing. LeVay measured the volume of INAH3 in autopsied brains of gay and straight men. He reported that the volume was significantly smaller in the gay men than in the straight men and, in the gay men, not significantly different from the volume found in women (LeVay, 1991). A replication study found a difference of the same kind, though smaller in degree (Byne et al., 2001). A research group at Oregon Health and Science University made similar findings in the brains of sheep—a species in which about 8% of males are naturally homosexual (Roselli & Stormshak, 2009). And a Dutch group found that INAH3 in male-to-female transexual individuals is similar in size to INAH3 in heterosexual women and smaller than in heterosexual men (Garcia-Falgueras & Swaab, 2008).

Functional differences in the hypothalamus between gay people and straight people have also been described. As we already mentioned in Chapter 5 (Box 5.1, page 131), there are differences between heterosexual men and women in how neural activity in the hypothalamus is affected when subjects breathe air containing substances thought to be sex pheromones, but the activity pattern in gay men and lesbians tends to be sex-atypical—for example, neural activity in gay men, but not straight men, is increased by exposure to a pheromone derived from men (Savic et al., 2005; Berglund et al., 2006) (**Figure 12.6**). These findings suggest that functional connections between the olfactory system and the hypothalamus differ between homosexual and heterosexual individuals of the same sex. Whether these differences result from early biological processes of brain development, or from the sexual or social experiences of gay and straight people in adult life, is not known.

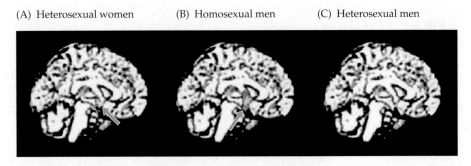

(A) Heterosexual women   (B) Homosexual men   (C) Heterosexual men

Figure 12.6 **Brain function and sexual orientation** The PET scans show the averaged brain activity of (A) heterosexual women, (B) homosexual men, and (C) heterosexual men, elicited when they breathed air containing androstadienone, a volatile compound that is present in men's sweat. There is an active response to the odor in the hypothalamus of heterosexual women and gay men (see arrows) but not in the hypothalamus of heterosexual men. (From Savic et al., 2005.)

A variety of other biological differences between gay and straight people have been reported. These include differences in the relative sizes of the left and right cerebral hemispheres (Savic & Lindstrom, 2008), in the function of the inner ear (McFadden & Pasanen, 1999), in eye-blink reflexes (Rahman et al., 2003c), and even in anatomical features such as the relative lengths of the fingers (Williams et al., 2000; Manning et al., 2007; Hiraishi et al., 2012) and the ratio of arm length to height (Martin & Nguyen, 2004). None of these traits are "diagnostic" of an individual's sexual orientation, but differences emerge when large numbers of gay and straight subjects are compared. In most of these studies, the traits under investigation are reported to be sex-atypical (or intermediate between the sexes) in gay men or lesbians, and such findings have been interpreted as further evidence in support of the prenatal hormone theory. Still, the exact processes by which these traits come to differ between the sexes, let alone how they come to differ between gay and straight people, remain to be nailed down.

Even if correct, the prenatal hormone theory is not an ultimate explanation of sexual orientation, because it does not explain why androgen levels (or sensitivity to androgens) should differ between "pre-gay" and "pre-straight" fetuses. It is possible that a variety of different ultimate causes, including both internal and environmental processes, could affect fetal hormone levels or hormone responsiveness and, hence, ultimately influence sexual orientation.

One possibility is that a fetus's *genes* affect prenatal hormone levels or sensitivity to hormones. Family and twin studies indicate that genes do indeed have a significant influence on sexual orientation. Finding one gay person in a family increases the likelihood of finding others, as if genes running in certain families increase the likelihood of family members being gay. Monozygotic, or "identical," twins—who share the same genes—are much more likely to share the same sexual orientation than are nonidentical twins, whose genes differ (**Figure 12.7**) (Långström et al., 2010). Genetic factors account for as much as half of the overall diversity in men's sexual orientation, according to some studies. Genes have a weaker but still measurable influence on women's sexual orientation. Whether this genetic influence works through the prenatal hormone pathway, however, or through some quite different mechanism, remains to be determined.

Molecular geneticists have identified two regions of the human genome as containing genes that influence men's sexual orientation: one is on the X chromosome and the other is on chromosome 8 (Hamer et

Figure 12.7 **Gay identical twins** Joshua and Jacob Miller of the pop duo Nemesis.

Box 12.2 Research Highlights

Why Gay Genes?

The idea that genes cause people to be sexually attracted to their own sex is puzzling. How could such genes survive in the population if they cause their owners to engage in nonreproductive sex? Many gay people are in fact parents (as discussed in a later section), but they do have fewer children, on average, than their heterosexual peers, so this question is a significant one. Gay genes should die out, but they don't, to judge by the apparent persistence of homosexual behavior since prehistoric times (see figure).

Researchers have put forward a number of ideas to explain this paradox. Most of these ideas relate to gay genes in men, because the genetic influence on sexual orientation is stronger in men than in women.

Most theories involve the supposition that not everyone who possesses a gay gene is actually gay. Let's say, for example, that a man is gay because he has inherited a gene causing him to be sexually attracted to males. This man's female relatives, such as his sisters, have a good chance of inheriting the same gene, because of their genetic relatedness to him. But in these female relatives this gene might also increase their attraction to males, making them "hyperheterosexual," as it were, and causing them to engage in more heterosexual sex and have more children. In this way the man's gay gene could be transmitted to the next generation, albeit not via the gay man's own offspring. This theory has some empirical support, because the female relatives of gay men do in fact have significantly more children than other women, according to several studies (King et al., 2005; Camperio Ciani et al., 2008).

Another idea is that gay males increase their sisters' reproductive success by their behavior: Not being parents themselves, they might be able to devote their resources to their sisters, enabling them to have more children and helping those children survive and reproduce in their turn. Here again then, the man's gay genes are perpetuated via his female relatives, but not because of any direct effect of the genes on those relatives.

Pre-Columbian ceramic vessel from northern Peru showing homosexual fellatio.

Evidence concerning this idea is mixed. In Western countries such as the United States and United Kingdom gay men do not seem to devote more resources to their female relatives than straight men do (Bobrow & Bailey, 2001; Rahman & Hull, 2005). Among the native inhabitants of American Samoa, on the other hand, *fa'afafine* (biological males who assume a "third-gender" role and who are sexually attracted to conventional men—see Chapter 4) do provide substantial support to the children of their female relatives, according to studies by researchers at the University of Lethbridge in Canada, and this support could help explain why some female relatives of *fa'afafine* have higher-than-usual numbers of children (Vasey & VanderLaan, 2009; VanderLaan et al., 2012).

These are only two out of several ideas that have been proposed to explain the persistence of gay genes (LeVay, 2011). If and when specific gay genes are identified and their mode of action understood, it will become easier to select the most plausible theories.

al., 1993; Mustanski et al., 2005; Sanders et al., 2014), but the individual "gay genes" within these regions of the genome have not yet been identified. If and when they are identified, they may help us understand in evolutionary terms why homosexuality exists (**Box 12.2**). Comparable searches for genes influencing women's sexual orientation have not yet been undertaken.

Boys who have older brothers are more likely to grow up gay than boys who don't (Bogaert & Skorska, 2011). Adoption studies indicate that this birth order effect is not caused by the social experience of living with an older brother. Rather, it appears to operate through some biological mechanism whose nature is still a mystery.

The Gay Community Has Struggled for Equal Rights

As with some other minorities, gay people's identity has been powerfully molded by a history of oppression and by the struggle to overcome that oppression. Thus, to understand the gay community today, it is necessary to have some knowledge of its political history, a history that began in Europe rather than in the United States.

The gay rights movement began in Germany

The world's first gay rights organization, the Scientific-Humanitarian Committee, was founded in Berlin in 1897. The main figure behind this group was Magnus Hirschfeld (see Box 1.2 on page 10), a gay Jewish doctor and sexologist who developed a biological theory of sexual orientation and gender (Dose, 2014). For 30 years Hirschfeld led the struggle to have the German sodomy statutes overthrown, but his efforts were ultimately unsuccessful. During the Nazi period several thousand German gay men, and a much smaller number of lesbians, were sent to concentration camps, where most of them died.

The first enduring American gay rights organization, the Mattachine Society, was founded in Los Angeles in 1950, and the first lesbian organization was founded in San Francisco 5 years later. These organizations functioned largely as support groups for gays and lesbians, who were generally reviled at that time. In the mid-1960s, more politically active gay organizations sprang up on the East Coast and began a series of actions, such as picketing the White House to protest the firing of gay federal employees (**Figure 12.8**).

Early on the morning of June 28, 1969, a riot erupted outside the Stonewall Inn, a bar in New York's Greenwich Village that catered to gay men, transvestites, and trans women (Carter, 2004). The rioters were protesting against a police raid—something that gay bars endured frequently in those days. Street demonstrations continued for several nights. These demonstrations were followed by the formation of more-confrontational gay rights organizations. The Stonewall Riots are often viewed as the starting point of the modern gay rights movement.

It may be difficult for you to imagine what life was like for gay people at the time of the Stonewall Riots. Homosexuality was officially listed by the American Psychiatric Association as a mental disorder. Sex between men or between women was illegal in most states, and most Americans thought that gay sex was morally wrong. Gay people had no legal protection from discrimination and were often dismissed from public or private employment on the basis of their sexual orientation. Not a single openly gay person had ever been elected to public office, and there were few if any gay role models in most occupations. Yet many gay people thrived "under the radar," and new gay organizations, such as the Metropolitan Community Church (founded in 1968), gave gays and lesbians opportunities to socialize beyond the bar scene.

The 1970s were a period of rapid change. The first gay rights marches took place in 1970. In 1971, the National Organization for Women (NOW) officially acknowledged the role of lesbians in that organization. In 1973, homosexuality was deleted from the *Diagnostic and Statistical Manual of Mental Disorders* (*DSM*), the American Psychiatric Association's handbook. In 1974, the first openly gay

Figure 12.8   Early gay activists picket the White House in 1965.

Box 12.3 Society, Values, and the Law

Gay Martyrs

Harvey Milk was a city supervisor of San Francisco. In 1977 Milk was the first openly gay man to be elected to city government in the United States (Figure A). During his short tenure as supervisor (1977–1978), Milk helped lead the successful campaign to reject California Proposition 6, which would have forced the state to fire openly gay teachers. He was also instrumental in passing San Francisco's first gay rights ordinance.

On November 27, 1978, shortly after Proposition 6 was rejected, Milk and San Francisco Mayor George Moscone were shot dead in their city hall offices by Dan White, an anti-gay city supervisor. White was convicted of the double murder, but he received an extraordinarily light sentence—fewer than 8 years in prison. After his release he committed suicide. Milk's life has been commemorated in a biography (Shilts, 1982), plays, music, and the 2008 feature film *Milk* starring Sean Penn.

David Kato was a Ugandan gay rights activist and the cofounder of Sexual Minorities Uganda (Figure B). At the age of 38 he came out as gay—he may have been the first person in Uganda to do so. In October 2010 a Ugandan tabloid newspaper published photographs of Kato and other gay Ugandans under the banner "Kill Them." Three months later Kato was beaten to death by a man wielding a hammer. The assailant was convicted of the murder and was sentenced to 30 years' imprisonment. His motives have not been clarified. "David showed tremendous courage in speaking out against hate," stated President Barack Obama. "He was a powerful advocate for fairness and freedom." (White House, 2011)

(A)  (B)

(A) Harvey Milk (1930–1978) (right, with Mayor George Mascone) and (B) David Kato (ca. 1964–2011), seen in the documentary *Call Me Kuchu*.

person won elected office (Massachusetts State Representative Elaine Noble), and others followed (Box 12.3).

During the 1970s, urban gay districts such as San Francisco's Castro Street drew thousands of young gay men from around the country and became the centers of their sexual, social, and political lives. Homosexuality became a topic of considerable public interest, and while many people continued to despise gays and lesbians, others became sympathetic. By 1977, about 40 cities had enacted some kind of anti-discrimination ordinance.

The AIDS epidemic began around 1980, and by the end of the decade the disease had taken the lives of more than 65,000 Americans, of whom the majority were gay or bisexual men (Centers for Disease Control, 1989). The initial public and political response to AIDS was to ignore it or dismiss it as a "gay disease" (Shilts, 1987). In

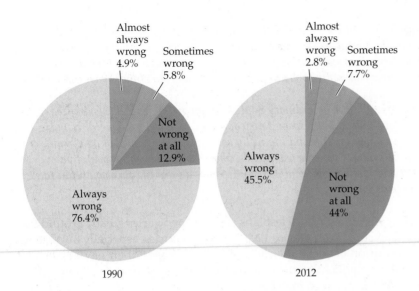

Figure 12.9 Changing views on gay sex These charts show responses of Americans in 1990 and 2012 to the question: "What about sexual relations between two adults of the same sex—Is that always wrong, almost always wrong, sometimes wrong, or not wrong at all?" "Don't knows" have been excluded. (Data from National Opinion Research Center, 2013.)

reaction, countless thousands of gay men were motivated to involve themselves in AIDS activism and gay activism. Lesbians, who during the 1970s had been involved in feminist causes more than in specifically lesbian or gay ones, joined forces with gay men and founded co-gender organizations. Gays and lesbians **came out of the closet** in droves. Americans came to *know* gay people—not just the distant, famous ones, but also family members, neighbors, and coworkers. The percentage of Americans who said that they personally knew someone who was gay rose from 30% in 1983 to 87% in 2013 (Rubin, 2000; Pew Research Center, 2013). It seems likely that this increased familiarity with gay people has been an important factor in changing public attitudes toward them.

All in all, pro-gay attitudes have dramatically increased over the last 25 years, as revealed by opinion polls that asked the same questions in the 1990s and again more recently (**Figure 12.9**). There have also been important judicial and legislative decisions affecting gay people:

- In 2002, the U.S. Supreme Court ruled that state laws banning gay sex were unconstitutional.

- In 2003, the Massachusetts Supreme Court paved the way for gay marriage in that state. By early 2015, about 70% of Americans lived in states where gay marriage was legal. (Future Supreme Court rulings may increase or decrease this number.).

- In 2011, the U.S. Armed Forces accepted openly gay and lesbian recruits into their ranks for the first time.

- By 2014, 22 states and many cities had enacted laws banning discrimination on the basis of sexual orientation, and 18 of these states included gender identity as a protected category (National Gay and Lesbian Task Force, 2014).

Gay rights are a global issue

Here are two shortened but otherwise unedited letters sent to AVERT, an international organization combating AIDS (AVERT, 2014b):

Hi my name is B am 19. I live in Addis Ababa, Ethiopia . . . i am gay i knew that i'm gay befor 8 years when i was in grade 5. I'm ashamed of it and even it is unthinkable to expose that I am gay. I'm always think that i am sinner and God will never give me mercy. Sometimes i think to sucide my self. I'm now university student all my dorm

come out of the closet (or come out) Reveal a previously concealed identity, such as being gay.

mates talk about girls but even i don't have an idea about girls. . . . My gay friends in z campus are dissmissed becaus of they are gay. I can't learn every time i am alone think about my sexual orientation. As ethiopian orthodox church is dominant homosexuality is so punishable abtu 26 yrs in prison that is why am afraid. What can i do?

Hi my name is Jane and I'm an ordinary South African girl. I've recently admitted to myself that I'm a lesbian but it wasn't easy doing so. . . . I feel as though I've made more friends since I've come out and I'm really coming out of my shell at an alarming rate. . . . It helps that I've got a few friends who are also bisexual/lesbian. I've also learnt that love just happens and you start to have a great life once you begin to remain true to yourself.

As these letters suggest, the status of lesbians and gay men varies greatly around the world (TheGuardian.com, 2014) (**Figure 12.10**). Some countries, especially in Western Europe, have a tradition of social tolerance that has allowed their gay citizens to sidestep some of the inequities that their American counterparts have experienced. In France, for example, sex between men has been legal since 1791. Also, the "religious right" is a much less significant political force in most European countries than it is in the United States. Thus, with relatively little effort gay couples in 11 European countries have acquired the full legal rights of marriage. In many European countries anti-gay discrimination and gay bashing are less common than in the United States, and gay culture flourishes. Canada is also more accepting of gay people than the United States, as exemplified by the fact that same-sex marriage has been legal throughout the country since 2005.

South America is a mixed bag in terms of how gay people are seen and treated. Argentina may be the most progressive: Gay sex has been legal there since the 19th century, and gay marriage since 2010. Three other countries have gay marriage (Brazil, French Guiana, and Uruguay). But hate crimes, police harassment, and discrimination against LGBT people are very common throughout the continent.

More than 2.5 billion people live in countries where gay sex is illegal and gay people lack legal protections. These include most countries in Africa (except South Africa), the Middle East (except Israel), and South Asia. Homosexual acts are punishable by the death penalty in Iran and a few other Islamic countries. Police harassment of gay people is common in many countries, including countries where gay sex is ostensibly legal.

Islamic traditions are partially responsible for negative attitudes toward homosexuality: Muhammad is believed to have prescribed the death penalty for sex between men. Nevertheless, Western countries have also played a role. In many countries, such as India, sodomy statutes were originally imposed by European colonialists. More recently, evangelical Christians from the United States have stirred up anti-gay sentiment in sub-Saharan Africa, especially in Uganda (Gettleman, 2010).

In 2011 the United Nations Human Rights Council passed a resolution expressing "grave concern at acts of violence and discrimination, in all regions of the world, committed against individuals because of their sexual orientation and gender identity" (Associated Press, 2011b). Of the 47 nations represented on the council, 19 voted against the resolution: These included Russia, Pakistan, Saudi Arabia, Jordan, Nigeria, and Uganda. Two years later, Russia enacted a law banning "propaganda of nontraditional sexual relations," which potentially criminalized any public manifestation of gay identity or culture. The passage of the law was followed by arrests of gay activists and by a surge in anti-gay violence (Luhn, 2013).

The clampdown on gay people throughout much of the world represents a reaction against an increasing openness and activism by gays and lesbians themselves. What do you foresee as the ultimate outcomes of these conflicts?

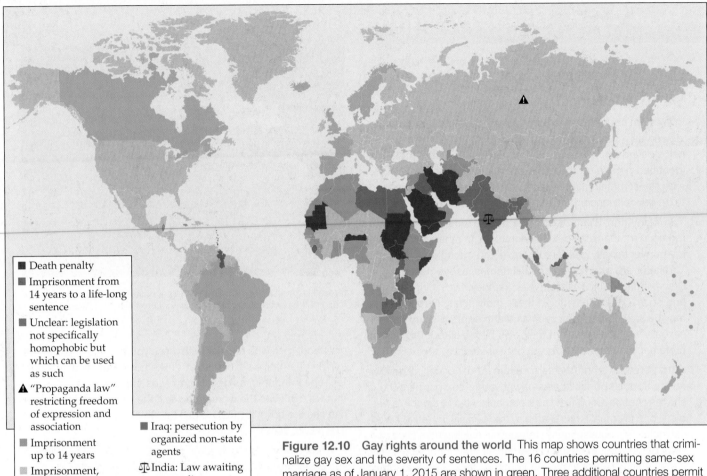

Death penalty

Imprisonment from 14 years to a life-long sentence

Unclear: legislation not specifically homophobic but which can be used as such

▲ "Propaganda law" restricting freedom of expression and association

Imprisonment up to 14 years

Imprisonment, no precise indication of the length/banishment

Iraq: persecution by organized non-state agents

⚖ India: Law awaiting court ruling

Same-sex marriage is legal

Figure 12.10 Gay rights around the world This map shows countries that criminalize gay sex and the severity of sentences. The 16 countries permitting same-sex marriage as of January 1, 2015 are shown in green. Three additional countries permit same-sex marriage in some regions: the United States (36 states and the District of Columbia as of early 2015), Mexico (2 states and Mexico City), and the United Kingdom (England and Wales, and Scotland). (Data from ILGA, 2013 with updates.)

In this section we have made the assumption that homosexuality is the same the world over. That may be true at the basic level of people's sexual attractions to males and females, but sexual orientation is not conceptualized everywhere in the same way. We discuss this issue in **Box 12.4**.

Growing Up Gay Presents Challenges

It's possible that at some future time, people's sexual orientation will be of as little significance as, say, their handedness. For now, however, many gay people have to grow up in a hostile environment, and the experience of this hostility may strongly color their worldviews as adults.

We mentioned above that many gays and lesbians are somewhat gender-nonconformist as children. Of course, there's a lot of variation among individuals. Some pre-gay children act like miniature transexuals and cannot be cajoled or forced by any means to behave like conventional children of their own sex. Others fit easily into the conventional mold. The majority are probably somewhere in the middle—not quite conventional boys and girls but not outrageously unconventional either.

Pre-gay children's positions on this gender continuum strongly affect their growing-up process. Markedly gender-nonconformist children "out" themselves before

Box 12.4 Society, Values, and the Law

Global Perspectives on Sexual Orientation

In Western countries a person's sexual orientation is generally viewed as a fundamental aspect of identity—something that helps define who we are, both to ourselves and others. Having identified people on the basis of their sexual orientation, we may say something about them, such as that gay people tend to be gender-nonconformist.

In many non-Western cultures people's gender identity is more salient than their sexual orientation. In other words, there are conventionally gendered people and transgender people. The latter are often given special names, as we described in Box 4.4 (page 111): *mahus*, *hijras*, *kathoey*, two-spirit persons, and so on. Having identified these individuals, certain things may be said about them, such as that they are likely to partner sexually with individuals of their own birth sex, but this sexual preference is not a core aspect of their identity.

If a person in a non-Western culture is not noticeably gender-nonconformist but still has sex with same-sex partners, he or she may not be recognized as a particular kind of person (a "lesbian" or "gay man"). For example, traditionally in Native American cultures a conventionally masculine man might marry a two-spirit person, but that didn't label him as "gay" or anything else; if they split up and he married someone else, it was assumed that he'd be just as likely to marry a natal woman (Williams, 1986). Similarly, Indian men who have sex with *hijras*, or Hawaiian men who have sex with *mahus*, are not thought to be any different from men who have sex with natal women (see figure).

In cultures where unmarried women are highly sequestered and virtually invisible to unmarried men, those men may have sex with male youths. That was true in ancient Greece, for example, and it was also true in Afghanistan during the period when the Taliban imposed strict Islamic codes of behavior. Here again, it was not generally thought that there was anything spe-

Native Hawaiian *mahu* Kumu Hina and her husband Hema. They are the focus of the documentary film *Kumu Hina* (From Hamer & Wilson, 2014.)

cial about men who had sex with these youths—the youths were just an alternative sexual outlet. "I like boys, but I like girls better," one Kandahar resident told the *Los Angeles Times*. "It's just that we can't see the women to see if they are beautiful. But we can see the boys, and so we can tell which of them is beautiful" (Reynolds, 2002).

What is rarely recognized in many non-Western cultures is a same-sex sexual relationship between two conventionally gendered and similar-aged adults, both of whom identify as gay. Such relationships were more or less unrecognized in Western cultures too, until a century or so ago. Yet this kind of relationship is often conceptualized as the standard form of homosexuality in Western countries today.

It's likely that gay people and gay relationships have existed in most or all cultures, but they were not recognized and named as we recognize and name them now. Homosexuality isn't a modern Western invention, as some theorists have asserted (Halperin, 1990). But the concept may be.

they even enter kindergarten. Parents may already suspect—with good reason—that a child is likely to become gay, and they may do everything in their power to prevent it. A "sissy" boy may quickly become the least favorite child in the family—especially in the eyes of his father. For tomboyish girls, it's less predictable—some such girls thrive.

Initially, a gay child's experiences in school may be unremarkable, but trouble often crops up in the preadolescent years (age 8 through 13). Because children form same-sex social networks at this age and rigorously enforce gender norms, a child who is gender-nonconformist to any extent may be excluded from friendship groups and even verbally abused. This can happen even before the child becomes aware of same-sex attraction—in fact, some of these children don't become gay at all. But it's all the same to their peers. Terms of abuse such as "faggot" and "dyke" are used com-

Box 12.5 Society, Values, and the Law

Gay and Homeless

My father was very abusive, he was an alcoholic, and tell-
ing me "If you ever be homosexual, I'll break your neck." It
scared me, so I was running away. I went back home one
day and he beat me up real bad. My lip was busted, my
eye was black, everything. I knew—at 16—it was over for
staying at home. I told him to his face I hated him. (Bratton,
2014)

About 40% of homeless youth in the United States identify as
gay, lesbian, bisexual, or transgender (Williams Institute, 2012).
The leading reasons for the homelessness of LGBT youth are
as follows:

- Ran away because of family rejection of sexual
  orientation or gender identity (46%)

- Forced out by parents because of sexual orientation or
  gender identity (43%)

- Left because of physical, emotional, or sexual abuse at
  home (32%)

- Aged out of the foster care system (reached the age of 18)
  (17%)

- Left because of financial or emotional neglect from the
  family (14%)

Other reasons include substance abuse, mental illness, and
release from the juvenile justice system.

When it started raining and getting colder, I had to do more
stuff I didn't want to do just to get a place to sleep for a
couple of hours. I've been abused and attacked in the
streets. I remember one night I was trying to sleep in the
piers, but I was just crying and crying all night, wishing God
could just take me out of this. (Siciliano, 2012)

Homeless trans and gay youth at a gathering spot in Chicago.

Homeless gay youths have difficulty finding shelter and may
turn to prostitution to survive. By doing so, they place themselves at risk of violence, sexually transmitted infections, trafficking to distant cities, depression, and suicide. New York's
Ali Forney Center, the nation's largest provider of shelter and
support for homeless LGBT youth, was named for a youth who
was murdered while engaged in survival sex.

Homeless gay youth—who are mostly people of color—represent the invisible underside of a community that people are
more likely to associate with security and affluence (Freakonomics, 2013). Yet many of these youths ultimately rejoin their
families or find a home elsewhere. Even while homeless, some
LGBT youth lead positive and creative lives. For example, they
are major participants in the voguing culture of New York and
other cities.

monly in preadolescent and adolescent school society, and teachers do not always
make serious efforts to stop this abuse.

It's not possible to provide a single image of what it's like to grow up gay. For
some youths, such as those whose first-person narratives are presented in **Box 12.5**,
it can be an unrelenting torment. Some are rejected by their parents or run away
from home, perhaps becoming prostitutes in the nearest big city. Some contemplate
or attempt suicide. It is primarily the gay youths who are obviously gender-nonconformist who experience abuse (Rieger & Savin-Williams, 2012).

In September of 2010, in separate incidents, five gay (or apparently gay) teens—all
of whom had been subjected to some form of bullying or harassment—took their
own lives. While this particular cluster was exceptional, it does appear that gay
teens are at greater risk of suicide than other adolescents (Plöderl et al., 2013). The
much-publicized 2010 suicide cluster triggered a national discussion about how to
stop bullying of both gay and nongay youth.

Figure 12.11 Gay wunderkind Jack Andraka announced that he was gay at the age of 13. Two years later he won Intel's Gordon E. Moore Award for developing an improved blood test for pancreatic cancer. Here he stands after being acknowledged by President Obama at the 2013 White House Science Fair.

Gay adolescents who are relatively conventional in their gender characteristics have the option of passing as straight, and many do. Quite commonly, such teens go into an "overachiever" mode, in which excellence in academics or other fields serves to mask their problematic sexuality. Although this course of action may prevent the kind of harassment that more obviously gay teens experience, it may inflict its own wounds: specifically, anxiety and a hemming in of normal self-expression, which interfere with psychological development and with sexual and social relationships in later life (Pachankis & Hatzenbuehler, 2013).

For increasing numbers of today's adolescents, however, growing up gay can be relatively painless or, indeed, a very positive experience—one in which their identity as gay may take a backseat to a richer kaleidoscope of sexual and social engagement (Savin-Williams, 2005) **(Figure 12.11)**. Circumstances that have made such a difference for today's gay youth include the existence of role models, the frequent discussion of gay issues on youth-oriented television shows and online sites, the presence of support organizations such as Gay-Straight Alliances in some schools, the efforts of some teachers to confront anti-gay attitudes and bullying, and the greater willingness of some parents to accept and love their gay or gender-nonconformist children.

Given the continuing trend toward acceptance and respect for gay people, we may predict that growing up gay will be a more widely positive experience for the next generation of gay youth.

Coming out is a lifelong process

Although there are some analogies between gay people and ethnic minorities, there is one major difference: Ethnic minority children are usually brought up by parents of that same minority, whereas most pre-gay children are brought up by straight parents. Thus, whether or not gay people are "born gay" in a *biological* sense, they are usually "born straight" in a *social* sense: They are born into a predominantly straight culture, and everyone (including probably themselves) expects them to become heterosexual adults. Coming out of the closet, though it may involve a dramatic moment or two, is really a lifelong voyage away from the social expectation of heterosexuality and toward a fully integrated and healthy gay identity (Rosario et al., 2011). That individual voyage repeats, to some extent, the social and political history of gay people as a whole.

The process of coming out has several elements. The first is coming out to oneself; that is, realizing and consciously accepting that one is gay. Although it is only the first step in the process of coming out, it is the hardest step for many gay people, especially those who grow up in a social setting that strongly disapproves of gays and lesbians or whose religion labels homosexual behavior as immoral. Some gay people live in denial for many years, perhaps even for their entire lives.

The National Coming Out Day logo, created by Keith Haring. National Coming Out Day is an opportunity for closeted gays and lesbians to reveal their sexual orientation.

The second element in most gay people's life stories is coming out to others. Of course, that's usually a gradual process: A gay adolescent may come out first to another gay youth, a best friend, a sibling, or a counselor. Parents tend to find out late; gay adolescents fear parental rejection, sometimes with good reason. However, many parents whose initial reaction is negative go through a rapid change of heart after their child comes out, and they may even take an activist role and join a pro-gay organization such as Parents, Families and Friends of Lesbians and Gays (PFLAG). Among minority and immigrant families especially, there is a strong instinct to close ranks around a family member who is perceived to be victimized or stigmatized by society.

The third element of coming out is joining a gay or lesbian community. For some gay men, that means moving to a big city that has a well-developed gay community. An example is West Hollywood, California, an independent city within Los Angeles whose population is about one-third gay men. Lesbians tend to be more scattered, but some smaller cities, such as Northampton, Massachusetts, have become centers of lesbian life. In locations such as West Hollywood and Northampton, gay people can find communities that offer sex partners, acceptance, and a wide range of gay or lesbian cultural institutions.

Moving to a "gay mecca" has lost quite a bit of the significance it once had for young gay people, however. That's because many young lesbians and gay men can now find other gay people, be openly gay, and experience some degree of organized gay life in the communities in which they grew up. In addition, the Internet, with its endless opportunities for gay networking, chat, and cybersex, has delivered the gay community to gay youth in their own homes. Meanwhile, cities known for their nightlife, such as West Hollywood, are being invaded by gay-friendly straight people. Even San Francisco's Castro District, the most famous of all gay meccas, faces an identity crisis as straight people move in and gay bars close or take on a more generic identity (Kane, 2014).

One problem with moving to a gay mecca is that it may also represent a flight from other aspects of a gay person's cultural identity. In becoming openly gay and moving to a gay-friendly community, many young gay people isolate themselves from their ethnic roots, their religion, and their extended families. Thus, an important fourth element of coming out for many gay people is integrating the gay side of their identity with other aspects of who they are. This may involve returning to their roots or participating in organizations that straddle the boundary that they have crossed—for example, gay Catholic groups, gay Asian groups, or gay Deaf groups. Of course few people, straight or gay, achieve fully integrated lives, but efforts to do so represent what has been called "bridging social capital"—the web of relationships and commitments that ties diverse groups together into a larger community (Putnam, 2007).

Lesbians and gay men are well represented in certain occupations

Lesbians and gay men are found in all walks of life. Yet, as we mentioned above, gay people are more likely to violate gender norms in their occupational choices than are heterosexual men and women (Ueno et al., 2013). Concerning the specific occupations that may attract lesbians and gay men, there is relatively little hard information, but a lot of speculation. Lesbians do seem to be overrepresented, and particularly successful, in professional sports such as golf and tennis, but of course only a tiny fraction of all lesbians are in this field.

Gay men seem to be overrepresented and especially successful in the creative arts. In fact, a survey of one group of male creative artists—professional dancers—concluded that one-half or more of the men in this field are gay (Bailey & Oberschneider, 1997). Another set of occupations in which gay men seem to be disproportionately represented are those involving personal service or caring; many are nurses, teachers, flight attendants, or waiters. Occupations that combine artistic creativity and personal service, such as hairstyling, floristry, and interior design, are the most stereotypical of all gay male occupations—these are the occupations in which practitioners are "gay until proven otherwise."

One point of mentioning these apparent occupational preferences is to highlight the fact that gay people are not simply people who get together to have sex, nor are they simply a community united in resistance to oppression. They also, to a degree, share common interests and a common sensibility. If and when gay people are fully accepted by mainstream society, it is not likely that they will be completely assimilated and disappear from view as a distinct group, as has happened to left-handers, for example. More probably, homosexuality will retain a special salience, and gay people will be valued for their unique gifts.

Gay People Who Belong to Minorities Have Special Concerns

As far as is known, roughly similar proportions of different racial or ethnic groups in the United States are gay or lesbian. Nevertheless, the experience of being gay can be different for members of minorities. For one thing, there were until recently few or no role models for gay people within their own minority communities.

That situation is now changing, as increasing numbers of minority public figures have come out as gay (**Figure 12.12**). To mention a few examples: comedian Wanda Sykes, professional footballer Michael Sam, and television news anchor Don Lemon (African-American); singer Ricky Martin, U.S. District Judge Nitza Quiñones, and singer Vicci Martinez (Hispanic); and model Jenny Shimizu, actor George Takei, and gay rights activist Urvashi Vaid (Asian-American).

Nevertheless, many minority gay people have to deal with cultural traditions that make heterosexual marriage into a near-sacred obligation (for oldest sons in many Asian-American cultures, for example) or that place taboos on the discussion of sexual topics in general, especially for women. Thus, acknowledging their own gay identity might, for some minority gay people, come at a cost of distancing themselves from their communities or their cultural roots.

Immigrant families in particular may see their children's homosexuality as a sign that they are losing them to an alien culture, but this reaction can be overcome.

Figure 12.12 Judge Nitza Quiñones and footballer Michael Sam are role models for minority lesbian and gay youth.

Here's how one first-generation Chinese-American woman, who belonged to a support group for Asian-American lesbians and bisexual women, put it:

> [My parents] always had this perception of "Who are these people you always hang out with?"—shadowy people that they didn't know, a bad influence, or whatever. But as soon as they met other Asian [lesbian] women, who spoke the same language as we do at home, it made a really big difference, and now they're meeting other parents, and it's just made a world of difference, because before they felt very isolated. (LeVay & Nonas, 1995)

Members of sexual minorities who are nonwhite may develop their own cultural institutions. A striking historical example is that of the "voguing balls"—elaborate contests in dance, drag, and "realness" that sprang up among gay and transgender African Americans and Hispanics in the 1980s. The lifestyle surrounding these balls constituted a parallel universe that was largely unknown to most Americans until it was made the topic of a notable documentary film, *Paris Is Burning* (1991) (**Figure 12.13**). Although largely wiped out by the AIDS epidemic, the voguing culture made a comeback in the 2000s and has influenced mainstream entertainers such as Lady Gaga.

Figure 12.13 The documentary film *Paris Is Burning* brought voguing to the attention of a wider audience.

Gay Sex Has Its Own Style

With the exception of coitus, most sexual behaviors that male-female couples engage in are also practiced by same-sex couples. It's worth pointing out some differences, however. Most obviously, no one has gay sex in order to procreate, so physical pleasure and emotional intimacy are the principal reasons for engaging in sex.

Among the sexual behaviors practiced by female couples are kissing, fondling, oral or manual breast stimulation, body-to-body rubbing involving the vulva (tribadism), "scissoring," cunnilingus, rimming (anilingus), manual stimulation of the clitoris, penetration of the vagina or anus with a finger or sex toy, and sex play involving elements of bondage/dominance/sadomasochism (BDSM play; see Chapter 13). Among behaviors practiced by male couples are kissing, fondling, nipple stimulation, body-to-body rubbing, penis-to-penis rubbing ("frot"), fellatio, anal penetration with the penis or fingers or sex toys, intercrural (between-the-thighs) intercourse, "tea-bagging" (see Chapter 6), and BDSM play. Many of these behaviors can be either unidirectional or reciprocal (for example, reciprocal fellatio, or "69").

Same-sex couples take their time over sex (Masters & Johnson, 1979). Lesbians may spend a great deal of time on breast and nipple stimulation, for example, before focusing on the genitals and may extend the entire sexual interaction for well over an hour. Gay men often bring each other close to orgasm and then back off, thus prolonging sexual pleasure and causing a more intense orgasm when it finally arrives.

Although nearly all lesbians and many gay men confine their sexual activity to paired encounters in the privacy of their own bedrooms, some gay men have sex in other places, including secluded outdoor spots whose locations become known by word of mouth or via websites like cruisingforsex.com. The gay slang term "cruising," by the way, means looking for casual sex partners in public spaces. To some extent, random cruising has been superseded by the use of gay hookup apps that inform the user about other available men in the vicinity, along with their photos and interests.

Bathhouses are another location for sex between men. Gay bathhouses are facilities in which large numbers of men cruise for partners in cubicles, steam rooms,

bathhouse A facility, usually in the form of a private club, used for casual sex between men.

butch Masculine-acting, often used to describe certain lesbians.

femme Feminine-acting, often used to describe certain lesbians or bisexual women.

or dimly lit open spaces. As with outdoor cruising areas, sex may be in pairs or in groups. Early in the AIDS epidemic, bathhouses were closed down in many cities, but many still operate or have reopened, usually under city regulations that attempt to enforce safe sex practices.

There may be reasons for outdoor and bathhouse sex that are purely practical: Home may be too far away, or the participants may want to hide their sexual orientation or sexual activities from people they live with (parents, wives, or steady boyfriends). In addition, however, men may seek out these locations for the thrill of the hunt, the risk of public exposure, or the chance to have sex with a number of strangers in a short time.

Although gay male culture includes and is fairly accepting of outdoor sex, bathhouses, and group sex, it's worth reemphasizing that large numbers of gay men do not engage in these practices, preferring to live in monogamous relationships that, aside from their same-sex aspect, are indistinguishable from the relationships of most heterosexual Americans. These different lifestyles reflect something of a dichotomy within the gay male community. Conservative gay men, such as political commentator Andrew Sullivan, are anxious to emphasize the normality and conventionality of gay culture, hoping that this will speed the acceptance of gay people by mainstream society (Sullivan, 2014). More radical gay men see their role as breaking down society's traditional taboos concerning sex and restoring its status as a primitive, creative, and even spiritual life force (Conrad, 2014; Radical Faeries, 2014).

There is diversity within the gay community

"One of my moms is kind of like my dad, and my other mom is the girly mom," explained Noah, the 10-year-old son of a lesbian couple, Roxanne and Kelly Prejean (Bagby, 2008). Noah was echoing, on the basis of his own experience, a concept that has enjoyed varying degrees of acceptance within the gay community over the years—the idea that gay people can be divided into subtypes on the basis of gender characteristics, and that gay couples should consist of one gender-conformist and one gender-variant partner.

A generation or two ago, this concept ruled many lesbian communities in the United States (Kennedy & Davis, 1983). The two kinds of lesbians were called **butch** and **femme**: The butch lesbians looked, dressed, and acted like men and took a dominant role in sex, while the femme lesbians were like heterosexual women and took a submissive role in sex. A lesbian couple would consist of a butch-femme pair. Similarly, gay men were thought to be of two kinds, sometimes referred to as "tops" and "bottoms": Tops were defined by a preference for the insertive role in anal intercourse and were relatively masculine and dominant generally, while bottoms preferred the receptive role and were more feminine. With this thinking, lesbian and gay male relationships were "regularized": Although they were same-sex relationships, they mimicked heterosexual relationships in the sense that they were formed by the union of partners, one more masculine and one more feminine.

Since those years there has been a relaxation and splintering of gender norms among both lesbians and gay men. Today's gay and lesbian communities are characterized by a kaleidoscopic variety of "types" and a generally more playful attitude toward gender. Lesbians who identify as butch ("dykes"*) and those who identify as femme still exist, but their behaviors and relationships are no longer regulated by strict cultural codes. No one would be surprised to see two butch or two femme lesbians forming a couple, for example—something that would have been unusual in the 1950s.

---

* Originally a term of abuse directed at lesbians in general, some butch or politically radical lesbians have reclaimed the term "dyke" to identify themselves.

As for tops and bottoms among gay men, these descriptors are still current, but many gay men define themselves as "versatile," meaning that they enjoy both insertive and receptive sex roles (Moskowitz et al., 2008; Moskowitz & Hart, 2011), and plenty of gay couples are not comprised of top-and-bottom pairs.

In addition, the lesbian/straight and gay/straight dichotomies are themselves under siege, especially among women. While many non-heterosexual women remain out-and-out lesbians, others move fluidly between relationships with both men and women (Diamond, 2008b). Some of these women, especially those who describe themselves as femme, may identify as bisexual rather than lesbian (Rosario et al., 2009). But others may reject these kinds of classifications altogether, preferring to define their sexual desires in terms of the specific people they are attracted to, rather than by overall classes of partners. Thus, they challenge the significance of sexual orientation as we currently define it.

There are other subtypes among gay people that form the basis of sexual subcultures. Among gay men there exists an extensive BDSM culture, which overlaps with the "leather community." BDSM practitioners are not necessarily gay, of course, but they are a far more visible and accepted subculture within the gay community than in the heterosexual world. Leather bars are common in gay communities. Gay leather art is widespread. Some lesbians are also involved in leather or BDSM practices. Most gay people think of leather and other BDSM practices as a normal but minority sexual interest.

Another gay subculture is that of **bears** (Wright, 2001; Moskowitz et al., 2013). A stereotypical "bear" is a big, bearded man with plenty of body hair and a noticeable beer gut (**Figure 12.14**). It's not really appearance or body type that defines a bear, however, so much as an attitude: specifically, a rejection of the necessity to conform to the "pretty boy" or "muscle boy" images so popular elsewhere in the gay world, combined with a warm, nonjudgmental personality. Bears generally pair up with other bears fairly like themselves, but older bears may also pair up with younger "bear cubs." There are numerous social organizations for bears in most parts of the United States.

Lesbians don't have such prominent sexual subcultures as gay men, although, as just mentioned, some lesbians are into BDSM practices. Lesbians do have innumerable *social* subcultures, ranging from literary salons to softball leagues to women's music festivals. The latter are Woodstock-like events, but they combine music with art, crafts, discussion groups, and many other activities. The best known of these festivals is held in Michigan in August; it attracts thousands of lesbian, bisexual, and other "woman-identified" women, but trans women have not been welcomed (Michigan Womyn's Music Festival, 2014).

Some gay people are parents

Because sex between two men or two women is nonprocreative, you might think of lesbians and gay men as being childless. That's not always the case, however. About 22% of cohabiting female couples, and 11% of male couples, have their own children living with them; other same-sex couples may have children who have already left home, and single lesbians and gay men may also be parents. An estimated 6 million Americans have at least one parent who is gay, lesbian, bisexual, or transgender (Gates, 2013; U.S. Census Bureau, 2013).

Where do these children come from? Most come from opposite-sex relationships, such as marriages—many lesbians and gay men have been in such relationships before coming out as gay, or are still in them. Increasing numbers of lesbians and gay men, however, are producing and rearing children as gay couples or, less commonly, as single gay people (**Figure 12.15**).

bear In gay slang, a burly gay man with plenty of body hair; more generally, a member of a gay male subculture that rejects many of the prevailing standards of gay male attractiveness and behavior.

Figure 12.14 "Bears" form a well-known subculture within the gay male community.

Figure 12.15 Married with children Canadians Jeff Hall and Emil Florea with their two pairs of twins, who were produced with the help of surrogate mothers.

Gay couples who wish to become parents can avail themselves of most of the reproductive options described in Chapter 8 (Mamo, 2007). A lesbian can simply have sex with a man or use artificial insemination, perhaps utilizing sperm from one of her partner's male relatives or a friend. Gay male couples can employ a surrogate mother, who may be artificially inseminated or made pregnant through in vitro fertilization. They can also adopt a child. Either way, becoming parents is an expensive proposition for most gay male couples.

The ultimate wish of gay would-be parents is probably for both partners to be the true genetic parents of their child. Some gay male couples mix their sperm prior to artificial insemination. This practice randomizes and conceals the identity of the genetic father, but it does not produce a genetically blended embryo, of course, since only one sperm actually fertilizes the ovum. Experiments in laboratory animals have demonstrated that it is possible to create offspring from two female or two male parents (Kawahara et al., 2008; Deng et al., 2011); it's unclear whether this technology will ever be applicable to human same-sex parenting.

The legal status of gay parenting, co-parenting, and adoption is evolving rapidly and varies greatly from state to state. No state has a blanket ban on adoption of a child by a gay person, but some do not allow joint adoption by a gay couple or second-parent adoption by a parent's same-sex partner (Human Rights Campaign, 2014). The American Academy of Pediatrics and the American Psychological Association have put themselves on record as supporting gay adoptions. As gay marriage becomes legal in more states, adoption will become easier. Ironically, adoption from abroad will become more difficult because most of the source countries forbid adoption by gay people, and the fact that someone is gay becomes all too apparent if that person is in a same-sex marriage.

There have been dozens of studies of children brought up by gay (mostly lesbian) parents. Based on a review of these studies, the American Psychological Association, the American Psychiatric Association, and several other professional groups jointly declared that "there is no scientific basis for concluding that gay and lesbian parents are any less fit or capable than heterosexual parents, or that their children are any less psychologically healthy and well adjusted" (Gilfoyle, 2010).

Changing One's Sexual Orientation Is Difficult or Impossible

During the 1950s and 1960s many gay men (and a few lesbians) tried to become straight by psychoanalysis or other forms of psychotherapy. The market for this kind of treatment has dwindled in recent years, but there is still enough demand to keep a small number of therapists in business (NARTH, 2014).

In 2009 an expert panel of the American Psychological Association concluded there is no convincing evidence for success of any conversion treatments and that some evidence indicates that these treatments may be harmful to the persons who undergo them (American Psychological Association, 2011). The harmful effects include depression and thoughts of suicide. More recent studies have supported the panel's conclusions (Dehlin et al., 2014).

The states of California and New Jersey have passed legislation banning the application of conversion treatments to minors, and other states are considering similar legislation. In 2013 a federal appeals court upheld the California law, and in the following year the U.S. Supreme Court declined to hear a challenge to the appeals court decision, thus leaving the state bans in place (Joachim, 2014).

For several decades a Christian group, Exodus International, offered programs that supposedly helped young people overcome homosexual feelings and become "ex-gay." The group disbanded in 2013, and its president apologized for the harm done by his organization to gay people and their parents (Lovett, 2013).

What is difficult or impossible to change is the direction of one's sexual *attractions*—a person's sexual orientation as we define it. People can certainly choose to change their sexual *behavior*, and some gay people do decide to enter heterosexual relationships for moral or practical reasons (Beckstead, 2001). In doing so, however, they risk inflicting long-lasting distress on themselves and their partners.

Homophobia Has Multiple Roots

Antagonistic feelings and behaviors directed toward gay people are common. They range all the way from the simple belief that homosexual behavior is morally wrong—an attitude held by nearly half of all Americans—to the killing of lesbians and gay men by a few hate-filled **gay bashers**.

The use of **implicit association tests** reveals that most people have an unconscious or automatic preference for straight people over gay people (**Figure 12.16**). And in an experimental study, researchers led heterosexual men to believe that a coworker was gay; this caused them to psychologically distance themselves from the coworker, regardless of whether they were overtly prejudiced against gay people or not (Talley & Bettencourt, 2008).

The word **homophobia** literally means "*fear* of homosexuality," but it has come to be used for the entire spectrum of anti-gay attitudes and behaviors, and that is how we use it here. A variety of different factors probably contribute to homophobia, so it may be difficult to unravel the causes of a particular person's anti-gay attitude or to figure out what sparked a particular hate crime.

gay bashing Hate crimes against gay people. Sometimes includes verbal abuse as well as physical violence.

implicit association test A psychological test that is intended to reveal unconscious or unstated preferences.

homophobia Prejudice against homosexuality or gay people.

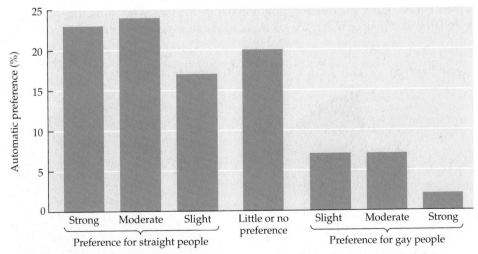

Figure 12.16 Most men and women have an automatic preference for straight people. The bar graph shows data from a Web-based implicit association test taken by about 150,000 subjects. The test uses reaction times to assess the strength of unconscious mental linkages between values (good/bad) and a variable of interest (gay/straight, in this case). (Data from Nosek et al., 2004.)

heterosexism The cultural establishment of heterosexuality as the normal and preferred form of sexual expression.

Related to homophobia is **heterosexism**: This is a social norm by which all people are expected to be heterosexual, or the idea that heterosexuality is intrinsically superior to other forms of sexual expression. Homophobia is a personal attitude; heterosexism is the institutionalized prejudice that allows homophobia to flourish.

The severe effects of homophobia and heterosexism on gay people were demonstrated in a study by social scientist Mark Hatzenbuehler and colleagues at Columbia University (Hatzenbuehler et al., 2014). This group combined regional information on anti-gay prejudice (from the General Social Survey) with mortality statistics (from the CDC's National Death Index); they found that sexual-minority people who lived in areas of high anti-gay prejudice suffered a 12-year reduction in life expectancy, compared with similar people living in low-prejudice areas. The reduction in mortality was due to increased rates of suicide, homicide, and cardiovascular disease. (Why do you think that heart disease would be a contributing factor?)

Researchers have noted a higher rate of alcoholism among gays and lesbians than among straight people (Drabant et al., 2012; Centers for Disease Control, 2013c), and there is evidence that social stigmatization is a large part of the reason (Pachankis et al., 2014). Lesbian, gay, and bisexual individuals are also at increased risk of mental disorders such as depression and anxiety as compared with straight people (King et al., 2008), and again it appears to be stigmatization and social exclusion that are to blame.

Cultural indoctrination transmits homophobia across generations

Some children and adults learn to dislike homosexuality and gay people by receiving anti-gay messages from parents, teachers, peers, religious authorities, political figures, and so on. The messages can be quite vocal and explicit: The Roman Catholic Church, for example, labels homosexuality a moral disorder, calls gay sex sinful, and has actively opposed gay marriage and other gay rights initiatives in the United States and worldwide. Regular participation in organized worship is the strongest demographic predictor that a person will disapprove of gay sex (**Figure 12.17**). Nevertheless, plenty of religious denominations or congregations are gay affirmative, and many religiously observant individuals support gay rights or are openly gay themselves.

Another factor that correlates strongly with people's attitudes toward gay people is their beliefs about the cause of homosexuality. Persons who think that being gay is a choice that people make are far more likely to espouse anti-gay attitudes than

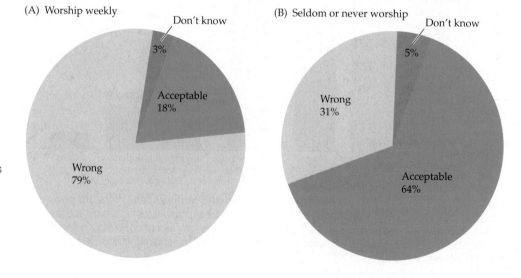

(A) Worship weekly
Don't know
3%
Acceptable
18%
Wrong
79%

(B) Seldom or never worship
Don't know
5%
Wrong
31%
Acceptable
64%

Figure 12.17 Organized religion and anti-gay attitudes These charts show the percentages of Americans who believe that gay sex is morally acceptable or morally wrong among (A) those who worship weekly and (B) those who seldom or never worship. (Data from Gallup, 2006.)

those who think of homosexuality as a trait that people are born with. Why thinking of homosexuality as a choice should predict anti-gay attitudes is somewhat perplexing, but the correlation has held up in many studies and opinion polls (Collier et al., 2014; Overby, 2014). Perhaps disliking people for an inborn trait feels too close to racism. As for gay people themselves, the great majority deny that they chose to be gay (Herek et al., 2010), but some (more lesbians than gay men) do experience their orientation as a choice.

Gays are seen as rule breakers

One motivation for anti-gay prejudice is the sense that gay people break rules—not just society's rules, but what seems to some heterosexual people to be the natural order of things. Gay people break these rules by engaging in gay sex, but, in addition, they may do so by being recognizably gender-nonconformist (Wellman & McCoy, 2014). In fact, the earliest experience of anti-gay prejudice that many pre-gay children experience is really a prejudice against gender transgression. Sometimes this attitude is called **femiphobia** because it is directed most strongly against males who act like females, rather than vice versa. Even some gay men are femiphobic, devaluing other gay men who seem at all feminine, or feeling bad about themselves on account of their perceived femininity (Sanchez & Vilain, 2012). In gay men's personal ads, for example, "masculine" and "straight-acting" are frequently cited as sought-after qualities, while femininity is often dismissed with stock phrases such as "no fats or fems" (Bailey et al., 1997).

People who view lesbians and gay men as transgressors tend to be those who themselves live by very strict rules (Young-Bruehl, 1996). Extending this same line of thought, is it possible that people who hate or actually attack lesbians and gay men are themselves homosexual or bisexual? The thinking behind this idea is that a homophobic attitude is part of a defense mechanism that helps these people control, hide from, or mask their own homosexual urges.

One study did come up with some experimental evidence in support of this hypothesis. Henry Adams and his colleagues at the University of Georgia recruited two groups of self-described "exclusively heterosexual" men: One group consisted of men who scored very high on an index of homophobic attitudes, while the other group scored low (Adams et al., 1996). (The questionnaire used in the study is available online—see Web Resources at the end of this chapter.) The researchers then showed the men videotapes of male-female, female-female, and male-male sex. During the viewing, the men's sexual arousal was monitored by penile plethysmography (measurement of penile erection). When asked, all the men said that only the male-female and female-female tapes aroused them. According to the plethysmographic data, however, the male-male tapes also aroused the homophobic men (but not the nonhomophobic men), though not to the same extent that the heterosexual tapes did (**Figure 12.18**). The researchers concluded that strongly homophobic attitudes are associated with homosexual feelings that the person denies or is unaware of.

From time to time, politicians, preachers, and others who promote an anti-gay agenda are caught in situations that raise questions about their own sexuality. A striking example involved George Rekers, a psychologist and Southern Baptist minister who has devoted much of his career to disparaging homosexuality and supporting efforts to "convert" gay people. (He was a leading member of the National Association for Research and Therapy of Homosexuality [NARTH].) In 2010 Rekers was photographed at Miami International Airport in the company of a male prostitute. Rekers resigned from NARTH but said, "I am not gay and never have been" (Rothaus, 2010). Another example involved evangelical preacher Ted Haggard, founder of the New Life Church in Colorado Springs. Haggard, who is married to a woman and has five children, condemned homosexuality on scriptural grounds

femiphobia Prejudice against femininity, especially in males.

Figure 12.18 Do homophobic men have homosexual urges? These graphs show the penile responses of homophobic and nonhomophobic men, all of whom identified themselves as heterosexual, to videotapes containing heterosexual or homosexual images. Both groups responded to the heterosexual videos, but only the homophobic men responded to the homosexual videos. (After Adams et al., 1996.)

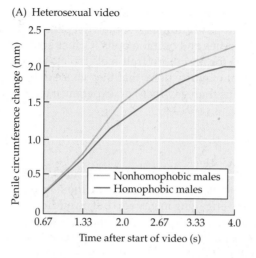

(A) Heterosexual video

— Nonhomophobic males
— Homophobic males

Penile circumference change (mm)

Time after start of video (s)

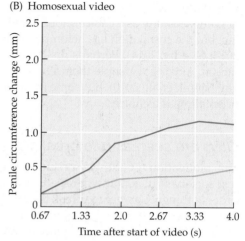

(B) Homosexual video

Penile circumference change (mm)

Time after start of video (s)

and opposed gay marriage. In 2006 a male prostitute alleged that Haggard had paid him for sex on many occasions. In the letter resigning from his ministry, Haggard was a little more forthcoming than Rekers. "There is a part of my life that is so repulsive and dark that I've been warring against it all of my adult life," he wrote (CNN, 2006). Yet another example involved Bishop Eddie Long, pastor of a Georgia megachurch and "one of the most virulently homophobic black leaders" (Southern Poverty Law Center, 2007). In 2010 Long faced four lawsuits from young men who claimed that he used his pastoral office to coerce them into sexual relations. Long promised to fight the accusations but eventually settled the lawsuits on undisclosed terms (Poole & Boone, 2011).

In spite of these laboratory studies and real-life stories, there are likely to be many motivations for homophobic attitudes and actions, some of which have little or nothing to do with the homophobic person's own sexuality.

Overcoming homophobia is a grassroots enterprise

Considerable research has been done on methods to overcome anti-gay attitudes. Because these attitudes have such diverse roots, it is unlikely that any one strategy will be successful by itself.

To some extent, a reduction of homophobia can be engineered through legislation and other public policy measures—by the passage of nondiscrimination and hate crime statutes, for example. Thirty states and the District of Columbia now have hate crime statutes that include sexual orientation, and 14 of these also include gender identity as a protected category (**Figure 12.19**). The U.S. federal hate crime law was expanded to include sexual orientation and gender identity in 2009.

Nevertheless, social science research suggests that people's attitudes toward gays and lesbians, as in other matters, are most readily influenced by interactions with relatives, friends, coworkers, and other people with whom they have personal contact. In one recent study, people who had a brief conversation with an openly gay person on the topic of same-sex marriage were markedly more likely to favor same-sex marriage when interviewed 9 months later, and this change of attitude diffused to other members of the target person's household. Having a similar conversation on the same topic with a straight person caused no lasting change in attitudes (LaCour & Green, 2014).

Recent history supports the same view; for example, as mentioned earlier in the chapter, there has been a large increase over the last two decades in the number of Americans who know a gay person, and there has been a dramatic easing of anti-gay attitudes over the same period.

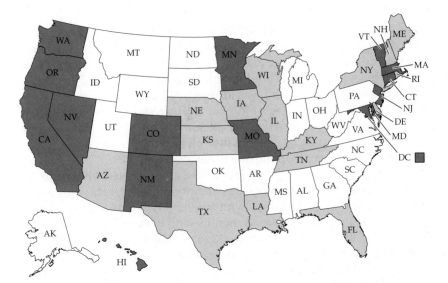

Figure 12.19   Hate crime laws This map shows the states (pink) that have hate crime laws covering sexual orientation and those (red) whose laws cover both sexual orientation and gender identity. Hate crime laws in other states (white) do not cover either of these categories. (Data from National Gay and Lesbian Task Force, 2013.)

This trend has greatly benefited the current generation of gay youth, of course, but it has benefited non-gay youth too—boys and young men especially. Less intimidated by the fear of being labeled gay, they are able to express same-sex intimacy in ways that were off-limits earlier. Researchers have noted increased physical and emotional intimacy among straight youths, and a greater willingness to include gay peers among their intimate friends (McCormack & Anderson, 2014). There has also been a trend toward young people describing themselves as "mostly heterosexual," meaning that they might not be averse to some sexual exploration with a same-sex friend—possibly after a few beers (Savin-Williams et al., 2012).

Bisexual People Are Caught between Two Worlds

"Labels put people in boxes, and those boxes are shaped like coffins." That was how Chirlane McCrae, former lesbian activist and now wife of New York mayor Bill de Blasio, explained her sexual orientation to *Essence* magazine (Villarosa, 2013). McCrae is one of many people who reject the simple heterosexual/homosexual dichotomy. On the other hand, one still hears the mantra "Straight, gay, or lying"—the idea that claiming to be attracted to both sexes is a form of self-delusion or a convenient fiction (Carey, 2005). These opposing points of view have been expressed since ancient times.* What's the truth of the matter?

There is no question—in our minds at least—that bisexuality exists, both in women and in men. But defining and measuring bisexual attraction has been a difficult and controversial enterprise. In this section we first consider some of the research studies that bear on this issue. We then discuss the topic from a social and personal perspective: What is it like not to fit into the either/or model of sexual orientation?

The prevalence of bisexuality depends on definitions

Population-based surveys suggest that bisexuality—when defined as *any* degree of sexual attraction to both men and women—is more prevalent than exclusive homosexuality in both sexes (see Figure 12.1). But the majority of bisexual people defined in this manner are much more attracted to the other sex than to the same sex. If bisexuality is defined as a *roughly equal* attraction to the two sexes, it is far less common, especially in men.

---

* Plato's *Symposium* (ca. 380 BCE) divided humanity into four groups: heterosexual and homosexual men and women. A later Greek poet compared his own sexuality to that of the god Zeus, who had sex with both males and females (Boswell, 1980).

Bisexual punk rocker Billie Joe Armstrong.

Indeed, some sexologists have questioned the notion that true bisexuality exists in men at all—at least at the level of genital arousal. Kurt Freund, a pioneer in the measurement of sexual arousal, studied sexual orientation by measuring men's penile tumescence while they viewed erotic photographs of men and women; he claimed never to have encountered a man who was aroused by both adult men and adult women (Freund, 1974). Michael Bailey's group at Northwestern University specifically advertised for men who identified as "bisexual," but when they showed these men erotic videos featuring men or women, they all showed much greater genital arousal to one sex (usually men) than the other (Rieger et al., 2005).

In a later study, however, Bailey's group recruited a group of men who met much more stringent criteria for bisexuality: Besides identifying as bisexual, they had to have had at least two sexual relationships with men and two with women, as well as a romantic relationship lasting at least 3 months with both a man and a woman (Rosenthal et al., 2011). These men also showed greater genital arousal to videos of one sex than to videos of the other, but their arousal patterns were significantly less biased toward one sex than were the arousal patterns shown by comparison groups of gay or straight men. What's more, they were more aroused by videos of a male and female actor together than were men who identified as heterosexual or homosexual. In other words, one can indeed identify a distinctly bisexual pattern of arousal, but this requires selecting those men whose bisexual identity is most strongly supported by their sex history.

Longitudinal studies indicate that the term "bisexual" is sometimes used as a self-identifier by young men who are on their way to an adult gay identity (Rosario et al., 2006). This conclusion is also supported by the results of data mining by the dating site OkCupid. Among 18-year-old males on the site who identified as "bisexual," only about 1 in 5 sent messages to both men and women; most of the others sent all their messages to men (OKtrends, 2010). Thus, it is possible that some of the "bisexual" men in Bailey's first study fell into that transitional category. Alternatively, they may have been men whose subjective feelings of arousal, or their romantic attractions, were not congruent with their patterns of genital arousal. Looking at all the evidence, it is clear that bisexual men do exist, but they may be outnumbered by other men who identify as bisexual for a short time or for reasons that are not indicative of their sexual attractions or arousal patterns.

No one doubts the reality of bisexuality in women. In fact, at the level of genital arousal, most or all women who identify as heterosexual show bisexual responses: They show genital arousal and report sexual desire to erotic videos of either men or women. Only non-heterosexual (bisexual- or lesbian-identified) women show category-specific arousal and desire: Such women respond to female erotic videos more than to male videos (Dawson & Chivers, 2014). These findings, which are consistent with a body of other evidence, do not disprove the existence of exclusive heterosexuality in women. Rather, they show that, in women, there is not always a straightforward connection between patterns of physiological arousal and those of verbally stated sexual attraction. Most men can figure out their sexual orientation by monitoring their genitals; few women can do so. This is not because women's genital arousal is less obvious than that of men, but because of the loose correlation between genital and subjective arousal in women.

Psychologist Lisa Diamond followed about 80 young non-heterosexual women over a period of 10 years (Diamond, 2008a, b). At the onset of her study, all the women described themselves as "lesbian," "bisexual," or "unlabeled." Over the course of the study many of the women changed their self-descriptions, but there was no overall trend in one direction or another. Rather, the women adopted identities that matched their current relationship patterns. Diamond's work suggested not only that women's sexual orientation is more fluid than men's, but also that there is little distinction between different kinds of non-heterosexual women, such as "lesbian" and "bisexual," when women's lives are viewed over a longer term. For some women, these labels are not as important as the specific individuals to whom they are attracted. Thus Chirlane McCrae, when asked about her attraction to Bill de Blasio, said, "I didn't think: 'Oh, now I'm attracted to men.' I was attracted to Bill."

Another complicating issue is that many self-identified bisexuals are not attracted to men and to women in the same way. For example, a bisexual man may be more emotionally attracted to women but more physically drawn to men (Matteson, 1991). Alternatively, the strength of a person's attraction to one or the other sex might change over the life span. Unidimensional measures of sexual orientation do little justice to these complexities.

Other personality traits that are not directly associated with sexual orientation influence where a man or woman stands on the sexual orientation spectrum. One example is novelty seeking (or its close relative, sensation seeking). This trait is heritable, and it is linked to possession of a particular variant of a dopamine receptor gene. Men who possess this genetic variant are far more likely than other men to have sex with both men and women (Hamer, 2002). Matthew Stief and colleagues at Cornell University found that bisexual individuals score higher than other people in sexual sensation seeking (e.g., "I like to have new and exciting sexual experiences"), sexual curiosity ("If I were invited to an orgy, I would accept"), and sexual arousability ("When a sexually attractive stranger accidentally touches me, I easily become aroused") (Stief et al., 2014). Another study found that among men who identify as bisexual, only those who showed genital arousal to both sexes scored high in sexual curiosity (Rieger et al., 2013). In other words, it's as if there's one developmental process that drives people's main attractions to males or to females, and one or more other personality factors, partly biological in nature, that broaden their sexual horizons, causing them to have sexual interest in persons of their nonpreferred sex.

You might think that when bisexually identified men or women entered committed sexual relationships, they would do so in roughly equal numbers with same-sex and opposite-sex partners. But that's not the case: If one partner in a committed relationship identifies as bisexual, the other partner is nearly always of the opposite sex, according to a large random-sample survey (Herek et al., 2010). Why do you think that this is the case?

The term **pansexuality** (or omnisexuality) overlaps considerably with bisexuality, but it is a broader term, referring to attraction to persons of any sex or gender identity (American Institute of Bisexuality, 2014). People who identify as pansexual often think of themselves as "gender-blind," meaning that a person's sex or gender is simply not a factor influencing their attractiveness. Many bisexually identified people, on the other hand, use different criteria for the attractiveness of men and women or relate sexually to men and women in different ways.

Bisexual comedian Margaret Cho.

Bisexual people face prejudice

Being bisexual has certain advantages: "It doubles your chance of a date on Saturday night," as Woody Allen is reputed to have said. But bisexual men and women are exposed to prejudice and discrimination (**biphobia**). To explore the negative stereotypes associated with bisexual men, Israeli psychologists had a group of subjects evaluate a man on a first date, in one of four scenarios: a bisexual man dating a straight woman, a bisexual man dating a gay man, a straight man dating a straight woman, or a gay man dating a gay man (Zivony & Lobel, 2014). The bisexual men were evaluated as being more confused, untrustworthy, and open to new experiences, and less monogamous and less able to maintain a long-term relationship, as compared with either straight or gay men. Another stereotype about bisexual men is that they are especially likely to spread HIV and other sexually transmitted infections (Spalding & Peplau, 1997).

pansexuality   Sexual attraction to persons of any sex or gender.

biphobia   Prejudice against bisexuals.

bisexual erasure Ignoring or denying the existence of bisexual people.

By calling these beliefs stereotypes, we don't mean that they are necessarily flat-out wrong: We've just mentioned evidence that bisexual people may be relatively open to new sexual experiences, and some young people who identify as bisexual may be, if not "confused," at least in a state of uncertainty about their sexual orientation. But these beliefs are stereotypes when applied indiscriminately against the entire population of bisexual people with the aim of denigrating them.

Anti-bisexual stereotypes are harmful at a personal level, of course, but also at a political level. Here's one example: In opposing legal protection for bisexual people, then U.S. senator Don Nickles said, "Bisexual by definition means promiscuous, having relations with both men and women" (Religious Tolerance.org, 2012). Nickles's comment reflects a general tendency for conservatives to define words like "heterosexual," "homosexual," and "bisexual" in terms of sexual behavior rather than sexual attraction.

Another manifestation of prejudice against bisexual people is when other people deny that they exist or simply ignore them. These attitudes have been called **bisexual erasure**, a phenomenon that has caused bisexual people to be largely invisible (San Francisco Human Rights Commission, 2011). Not only straight people but also gays and lesbians may participate in bisexual erasure, if they assume that everyone who identifies as bisexual is simply a gay person who is halfway out of the closet or someone who just wants attention (Alarie & Gaudet, 2013; Eisner, 2013). This form of prejudice is an aspect of "monosexism"—the belief that everyone is or should be attracted to only one sex.

These negative views about bisexual people are changing, however, especially among the young and well educated. We mentioned earlier that increasing numbers of young people are describing themselves as "mostly heterosexual." Such people are especially likely to reject negative stereotypes about bisexual people, because they have recognized at least a trace of bisexuality in themselves. Another factor promoting acceptance of bisexual people is the emergence of self-identified bisexual role models in some walks of life. Examples include actresses Drew Barrymore and Angelina Jolie, feminist leader Patricia Ireland, choreographer Paul Taylor, and businessman/politician Michael Huffington. Still, bisexual role models (especially male ones) are in short supply outside of the arts and the entertainment industry.

Bisexuals have lagged behind gays and lesbians in developing a community identity. A Bisexual Center was founded in San Francisco in 1976, and various regional bisexual organizations sprang up. Bisexuals formed their own contingents in gay rights marches beginning in the late 1980s, and the 1993 March on Washington for Lesbian, Gay and Bi Equal Rights was the first national event to include "bi" in its name. BiNet, a national-level bisexual organization, was formed in 1990. Several important books by or about bisexuals have appeared since the early 1990s (see Recommended Reading at the end of this chapter).

Bisexuals debate whether they should ally closely with lesbians and gay men, forge an independent social identity, or act as some kind of bridge between heterosexual and homosexual people. The bisexual community is very much a work in progress.

Lesbian, gay, straight, bi, other—more alike than different

This chapter has necessarily emphasized what distinguishes people of different sexual orientations, whether in their biological development, their cognitive and personality traits, their communities, or their life experiences. It's important to know something about these differences, both because they offer a window into an important aspect of human nature, and also because they help us relate to people whose sexual orientations differ from our own.

Still, we wrap up the chapter by emphasizing that nearly all of us experience sexual and romantic attraction in similar ways, regardless of our sexual orientation. Nearly everyone has had or will have the experience of falling in love for the first time, for example, and it feels the same, regardless of who one falls in love with. Here's how an African American rap artist, Frank Ocean, described the experience in a Tumblr post (Ocean, 2012):

"4 summers ago, I met somebody. I was 19 years old. He was too. We spent that summer, and the summer after, together. Everyday almost, And on the days we were together, time would glide. Most of the day I'd see him, and his smile. I'd hear his conversation and his silence. Until it was time to sleep. Sleep I would often share with him. By the time I realized I was in love, it was malignant. It was hopeless. There was no escaping, no negotiating with the feeling. No choice. It was my first love, it changed my life."

Go to the **Discovering Human Sexuality** Companion Website at **sites.sinauer.com/ discoveringhumansexuality3e** for activities, study questions, quizzes, and other study aids.

Summary

- Sexual orientation defines how a person's disposition to experience sexual attraction varies with the sex of potential partners. It can be represented on a 5- or 7-point scale from heterosexual (attracted to people of the opposite sex only), through varying degrees of bisexuality, to homosexual (attracted to people of one's own sex only). A small percentage (2% to 3%) of the population is homosexual. Exclusively homosexual men are more common than exclusively homosexual women. The percentage that is bisexual depends greatly on the definition used but is always higher in women than in men.

- Lesbians and gay men, although very diverse, tend to be sex-atypical in their self-described masculinity or femininity, in cognitive and personality traits, and in occupational interests. This gender nonconformity is evident in children who later become gay adults.

- A variety of theories have been put forward to explain how sexual orientation develops. According to Freudian psychoanalytic theory, heterosexuality emerges from a complex sequence of stages of psychosexual development; the disruption of several of these stages may lead to homosexuality. According to socialization theories, a child's ultimate sexual orientation is molded by innumerable rewards and punishments given by parents and others.

- According to biological theories, sexual orientation is affected by factors such as prenatal hormone levels, which are thought to influence the organization of brain systems responsible for sexual attraction. Genes also influence sexual orientation, especially in men, but the specific genes involved have not yet been identified.

- The modern gay rights movement began in 19th-century Germany and spread to the United States after World War II. A key event was the Stonewall Rebellion, riots in New York City in 1969 that led to the politicization of the gay community. The AIDS epidemic, which began around 1980, devastated gay male communities. It was also the spur to more effective political action and to greater openness on the part of gay people.

- The rapid advances made by lesbians and gay men have made them the focus of a cultural conflict between conservative and progressive forces in American society. The same conflict is playing itself out worldwide; in some countries, gay people have gained greater acceptance than in the United States, while in others gay sex is still a crime.

- Pre-gay children who are markedly gender-nonconformist typically experience taunting, abuse, or efforts to normalize them. For gay people, psychological development is a process of "coming out." This process involves several stages: self-realization and self-acceptance, disclosure to others, joining the gay community, and integrating one's homosexuality with other aspects of one's cultural identity.

- Gay sex and gay relationships are quite similar to their heterosexual counterparts. Gay men tend to be more sexually adventurous and to have more partners than lesbians or heterosexual people, but monogamous gay relationships are also common.

- There is diversity within the gay and lesbian communities. Some lesbians identify as "butch" (more masculine) and some others as "femme" (more feminine). Some gay men have preferred sex roles as "tops" or "bottoms," but many are "versatile." Within the gay male community

(continued)

Summary (continued)

there is a leather/BDSM subculture as well as a "bear" community that rejects the prevalent gay standards of male beauty.

- Many lesbians and some gay men are parents, either from earlier heterosexual relationships or as a result of a variety of reproductive techniques that are open to gay couples. The children of gay parents generally thrive: They may experience some taunting in school, but they are as well adjusted as the children of straight parents.

- Anti-gay attitudes and behaviors (homophobia) have multiple roots. These roots include cultural indoctrination, an image of homosexuality as a transgression of social rules, and a defense mechanism against real or feared personal homosexual tendencies. Overcoming homophobia depends primarily on personal interactions at a grassroots level.

- Bisexual men and women have the advantage of a wider potential range of sexual experience, but they also face social stigma ("biphobia"). They may be mischaracterized as closeted gay people, as oversexed, as spreaders of AIDS, or as inconstant partners. Bisexuals have attempted to forge a social and political identity that is at least partially separate from that of gay people.

Discussion Questions

1. How do your views on homosexuality compare with those of your grandparents, your parents, and your college peers?

2. Take the "gay-straight" implicit association test at tinyurl.com/ml3a79s or the Homophobia Questionnaire at tinyurl.com/jmgq. Do you think that the test reveals anything about your attitude toward gay people?

3. Your friend tells you, "A person can tell if someone is gay without even asking them." Do you agree or disagree with this statement? If you agree, what clues you in to a person's sexual orientation?

4. You are a board member of a local school district. This school district proposes to start a program in which openly gay faculty would provide support, information, and role models for students. Would you support or discourage this program? Give a rationale for your answer. What would the effect of the program be on the students?

5. Imagine that you have always been attracted emotionally and sexually to your own sex and that your family has rather traditional religious and conservative views. Would you tell your family about your attraction? If you were to disclose your sexual orientation to your family, how would you do it? What do you think their response would be?

6. Researchers find more evidence of bisexuality and sexual fluidity among women than among men. Do you think this says something profound about men's and women's sexuality, or does it have more to do with how boys and girls are acculturated to think about sexual attraction and sexual relationships?

7. In 2008 the Ad Council ran a public service announcement featuring actress Hilary Duff, who urged young people not to use the put-down "That's so gay." Do you agree with Duff, or was this an example of unnecessary "political correctness"?

Web Resources

American Civil Liberties Union (ACLU). Lesbian Gay Bisexual & Transgender Project page www.aclu.org/lgbt-rights

American Institute of Bisexuality www.bisexual.org

Asian Pacific Islander Queer Women and Transgender Coalition www.apiqwtc.org

BiNet USA www.binetusa.org

Bisexual Resource Center www.biresource.net

Gay Asian Pacific Support Network (GAPSN) www.gapsn.org

Gay, Lesbian and Straight Education Network (GLSEN) www.glsen.org

Homophobia Questionnaire tinyurl.com/jmgq

Human Rights Campaign (political and educational organization for the gay, lesbian, bisexual, and transgender communities) www.hrc.org

Lambda Legal (the main gay and lesbian legal organization) www.lambdalegal.org

National Center for Lesbian Rights (NCLR) www.nclrights.org

National Gay and Lesbian Task Force (serves the same communities as the Human Rights Campaign, but with an emphasis on grassroots activism) www.thetaskforce.org

Parents, Families and Friends of Lesbians and Gays (PFLAG) www.pflag.org

TheGuardian.com: Lesbian, gay, bisexual and transgender rights around the world tinyurl.com/LGBTglobal

United Lesbians of African Heritage www.uloah.com

Recommended Reading

Bronski, M. (2012). *A queer history of the United States*. Beacon.

Diamond, L. M. (2008). *Sexual fluidity: Understanding women's love and desire*. Harvard University Press.

Garber, M. (2000). *Bisexuality and the eroticism of everyday life*. Routledge.

Herek, G. M. (Ed.). (1998). *Stigma and sexual orientation: Understanding prejudice against lesbians, gay men, and bisexuals*. Sage.

LeVay, S. (2011). *Gay, straight, and the reason why: The science of sexual orientation*. Oxford University Press.

Ochs, R. & Rowley, S. E. (Eds.). (2009). *Getting bi: Voices of bisexuals around the world* (2nd ed.). Bisexual Resource Center.

Owens-Reid, D. & Russo, K. (2014). *This is a book for parents of gay kids: A question and answer guide to everyday life*. Chronicle.

Rust, P. C. R. (Ed.). (2000). *Bisexuality in the United States: A social science reader*. Columbia University Press.

Savin-Williams, R. C. (2001). *Mom, Dad, I'm gay: How families negotiate coming out*. American Psychological Association.

Chapter 13

For some, sexuality is inextricably tied to fetish objects or to behaviors outside the sexual norm.

Atypical Sexuality

Most of us, at one time or another, have experienced an unusual sexual fantasy or have tried out some "kinky" sexual practice. Such thoughts and behaviors may add spice to our sex lives and help maintain our interest in sexual relationships. However, have you ever been sexually aroused by a horse? Have you ever masturbated while holding an item of lingerie? Have you ever enjoyed having your sex partner inflict pain on you during sex? For some people—most of whom are men—such unusual desires take a central place in their sex lives. These desires become problematic only if they cause distress to the people who experience them or if they are acted out in behaviors that harm others or run afoul of the law. In this chapter we describe a variety of atypical sexual desires and behaviors, discuss theories about what causes them, and present treatment options if treatment is called for.

Sexual Variety Is the Spice of Life

fetish Sexual fixation on an inanimate object, material, or part of the body.

partialism A fetishistic attraction to a specific part of the body.

The blows fell rapidly and powerfully on my back and arms. Each one cut into my flesh and burned there, but the pains enraptured me. They came from her whom I adored, and for whom I was ready at any hour to lay down my life.

She stopped. "I am beginning to enjoy it," she said, "but enough for today. I am beginning to feel a demonic curiosity to see how far your strength goes. I take a cruel joy in seeing you tremble and writhe beneath my whip, and in hearing your groans and wails; I want to go on whipping without pity until you beg for mercy, until you lose your senses. You have awakened dangerous elements in my being. But now get up."

I seized her hand to press it to my lips.

"What impudence." She shoved me away with her foot. "Out of my sight, slave!"—Venus in Furs (Sacher-Masoch, 1870/2000)

Does this passage strike you as an example of healthy sexuality? Or was one or both of the participants mentally deranged? Richard von Krafft-Ebing, the 19th-century encyclopedist of sexual "aberrations," was so impressed by Leopold von Sacher-Masoch's autobiographical account that he borrowed the author's name to create the term "masochism," which he saw as a psychiatric disorder.

Today, however, most sex researchers believe that only a small province within the realm of atypical sexuality needs to be cordoned off as "disordered" (**Figure 13.1**). We cover that province later in this chapter. For now, we discuss variant sexual interests and practices—or "kinks" in common parlance—as, at worst, harmless oddities and, at best, creative strategies to enrich sexual experiences and to strengthen relationships.

Most fetishes are related to the body

Most of us find that certain items of clothing or certain perfumes are especially effective in enhancing a partner's sexual attractiveness—and whole industries depend on that fact. For many of us, particular body parts—for example, breasts, penises, buttocks, legs, or feet—carry a special erotic charge. When any such sexual attraction comes to play a central role in a person's sexual life, it is known as a **fetish**. Far more men than women have fetishistic interests, as is true for atypical forms of sexual expression generally. For that reason, we often use male pronouns—for example, "he" or "him" rather than "she" or "her"—to describe individuals in this chapter.

The most common fetishes are associated with the human body (**Figure 13.2**). If the focus is on specific body parts, it is called **partialism**. Alternatively, the arousing stimulus may be something worn on the body, such as women's lingerie or jewelry, or a general feature of the body, such as obesity (eroticized by "fat admirers" or "chubby chasers").

As shown in the figure, a remarkably high proportion of fetishes are directed toward feet and shoes. Why this should be so is something of a mystery. Sigmund Freud proposed that feet are taken as a symbolic representation of the penis. It may also be relevant that feet are often hidden from view, inside shoes or stockings, perhaps giving them a special allure. (Hands, which are much more visible and are frequently touched, are rarely the focus of fetishes.) The frequent eroticization of feet might also have to do with the close proximity of the feet and the genitals in the brain's map of the body, as discussed in

Fetishism is erotic fixation on inanimate objects or, as here, on certain body parts.

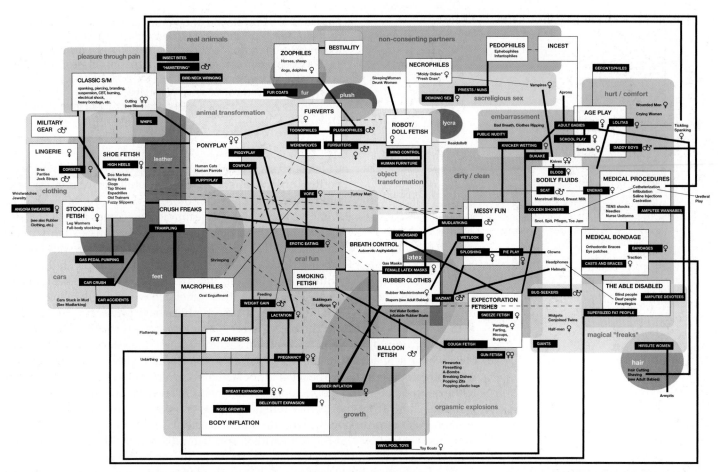

Figure 13.1 A map of "deviant" sexuality by Katharine Gates (see Recommended Reading at the end of this chapter), showing the clustering of traits into conceptual categories, with their links. Only small regions of this map cover forms of sexual expression that are definitely abnormal or illegal (especially the blue section labeled "non-consenting partners"), but other regions may be considered pathological if they cause distress to the people who experience them. This diagram should be viewed as one writer's attempt to organize the diversity of atypical sexual expression, rather than as a definitive or consensus-based analysis. (Diagram Katharine Gates/deviantdesires.com.)

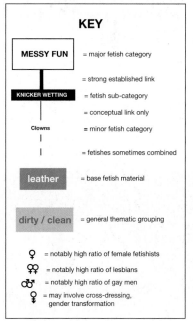

Box 5.4, page 148. Other common body fetishes are for body fluids (e.g., urine), hair, and body modifications (e.g., piercings).

Sometimes, fetishistic desire is directed toward *materials*—such as leather, rubber, silk, or fur—that are arousing regardless of the specific object into which they are fashioned (**media fetishism**). Usually, however, the material is most arousing when it is worn on the body as an item of clothing. Sacher-Masoch was a fur fetishist as well as a masochist.

Besides normal body parts, a few men have a fetishistic attraction to abnormal body parts such as congenital malformations or amputation stumps, while some other men are sexually aroused by the thought of having malformations or amputations themselves, and they may actually seek to have an amputation to satisfy their desire. (There may also be men who seek to have an amputation for nonsexual reasons.) Within the world of amputation fetishism, these two kinds of men are referred to as "devotees" and "wannabes," respectively.

media fetishism Sexual attraction to materials such as rubber or silk. Also called *material fetishism*.

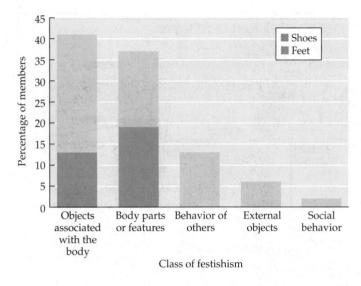

Percentage of members

Shoes
Feet

Objects associated with the body | Body parts or features | Behavior of others | External objects | Social behavior

Class of festishism

Figure 13.2 **Prevalence of different classes of fetishes** based on membership in Yahoo groups devoted to single fetishes. The total number of group members was 136,040, and the bar graph breaks these down according to five classes of fetishes. Note that body parts or objects associated with the body constitute by far the most prevalent kinds of fetishes. Within those two categories, note the high prevalence of foot and shoe fetishes. (Data from Scorolli et al., 2007.)

object fetishism (objectophilia or **objectum sexuality)** Sexual arousal by objects that are not associated with bodies.

Fetishes involving inanimate objects not associated with bodies (**object fetishism**, **objectophilia**, or **objectum sexuality**) are much less common, but they do occur. Most of what we know about object fetishism comes from a website created by and for objectophiles (Objectum-Sexuality Internationale, 2013). Sometimes the love object is a well-known landmark: An American woman, for example, fell in love with the Eiffel Tower, "married" it, and changed her name to La Tour Eiffel (Independent, 2010), and another American woman fell in love with a roller coaster (**Figure 13.3**). The majority of objectophiles have physical sexual contact with their love object or (if the object is very large or far away) with a scale model of it. According to the website, objectum sexuality is not a fetish because the loved objects have sentient spirits that reciprocate the objectophile's love. Even though this is the objectophile's sincere belief, it is not factually correct and therefore not relevant to the question of whether objectophilia is a fetish. One respect in which object fetishism does differ from most other fetishes, however, is that many objectophiles are women. Also according to the website, some objectophiles have Asperger syndrome (now reclassified by *DSM-5* as an autism spectrum disorder), which is marked by difficulty in establishing social relationships with human beings.

That fetishistic interests are common is made obvious by a visit to any sex shop or sex toy website, both of which offer a wide variety of fetish-related objects. Fetish-related videos comprise 25% or more of the output of some large adult video companies. Some smaller companies, such as Kink Video and RedBoard Video of San Francisco, specialize entirely in fetish videos. The term "fetish" is used broadly in the sex industry, however, and may include bondage/dominance and almost any other sexual behavior aside from "vanilla sex" (conventional intercourse).

How does a person express fetishistic sexuality? A foot fetishist may incorporate foot worship into sexual foreplay with his partner. He may spend a lot of time watching foot fetish videos or visiting foot fetish websites. He may belong to groups of people who share the same interest. A lingerie fetishist may spend a lot of time purchasing (or stealing) items of women's underwear and viewing and touching them during solitary masturbation, or he might ask his partner to wear specific items that he finds arousing. He might even wear these items himself (see below).

At what point does someone with fetishistic interests deserve to be called a fetishist? There is no universal agreement about this: Some authorities reserve the term "fetishist" for a person whose interest clearly crosses the line to a

Figure 13.3 **Object fetishist** Amy Wolfe, a church organist from Pennsylvania, fell in love with a roller coaster, rode it over 3000 times, and stated her intention to marry it, even though she also has relationships with spaceship models and a banister railing. In object fetishism, polygamy is legal.

Box 13.1 Personal Points of View

Rubber Fetishism and the Internet

The following is an interview with "Ataraxia," a 59-year-old Pittsburgh man who is a rubber fetishist (or "rubberist") and founder of the International Association of Rubberists and its website, Rubberist.net:

Is rubber fetishism a mental illness?

That's what I thought for the first half of my life. I got out of the Navy because of it. And on the way out their psychiatrists told me, "There's not a whole lot we can do to cure this, so why don't you learn to enjoy it?" That's where I came up with "Ataraxia," which means "peace of mind."

What kinds of problems do fetishists have?

One problem is spousal: With many of them, their wives are either not into it at all, or they barely tolerate it. And then there's the social aspect, where people think that we're kinky and therefore dangerous. We're not: We don't hurt anybody.

What's the purpose of Rubberist.net?

The aim is to help others go through that process I went through. Before the Internet, fetishists might think they were the only one in the world.

What can they find on the site?

Personal stories, as well as practical information, like how to make rubber clothing or where to get it. News, culture, surveys. And a way to meet other rubberists. They can post on a bulletin board or jump into a conversation. About 1000 rubberists visit the site every day.

What kinds of people visit the site?

Ninety percent or more are male. There's some confusion because some are transgendered. True female rubberists are rare. As for sexual orientation, my site tends to be heterosexually oriented, but it includes a lot of material that is not specifically straight or gay. There are plenty of gay rubber sites. Life is easier for gay fetishists—they can find partners without too much trouble.

A man in a latex "vacuum bed" is disciplined by a dominatrix at a rubber fetish event in Hamburg, Germany.

What are the options for straight ones?

They can grin and bear it, or they can reach some sort of compromise, as I did with my wife. Some of the younger women are more open to it.

Is there a connection between rubber and BDSM, like there is between leather and BDSM?

Yes, a large proportion of rubberists are into that—mostly the bondage side of it.

What's the psychology of rubber fetishism?

Mostly it's the sense of encasement. The term is "total enclosure," which means covering every inch of your body with rubber—making two or three layers if you can. It's a combination of the sense of tightness and being shielded from the rest of the world. I think it's a "return to the womb" kind of thing—the warm, moist, enclosing environment, it seems like a womb. It seems to be a phenomenon of the industrialized world. About a third of our members are from England.

mental disorder (see below), but others hold that someone who is strongly invested in fetishism, even if not diagnosable as having a mental disorder, can be called a fetishist. We take the second view—*we use the term "fetishist" without any implication that the person has a disorder*.

The Internet has had a major impact on the lives of fetishists, as it has for all people with minority sexual interests (**Box 13.1**). It has facilitated communication among fetishists, thus bolstering self-acceptance and satisfaction and reducing the

A drag king.

likelihood that fetishists will feel the need to seek psychological help. It has also promoted awareness about fetishism in the general population. Thus, the Internet has played a key role in "normalizing" fetishism and other uncommon forms of sexual expression.

People cross-dress for a variety of reasons

Some people repeatedly or continuously wear the clothes of the other sex. Both men and women may **cross-dress**, and they do so with a wide variety of motives.

PRACTICAL REASONS   There may be entirely nonsexual reasons for cross-dressing. Women have often cross-dressed in order to pass as men and thus obtain male employment or other privileges of masculinity. Male attire may be more practical for many activities. In fact, as women have gained increasing parity with men, traditionally masculine attire, such as blue jeans and T-shirts, have become unisex.

DOING DRAG   Men or women may dress as the other sex for entertainment purposes or to mock stereotypical gender expectations or fashion norms. In this case their clothing, makeup, and hairstyle are likely to be an over-the-top caricature, not a real attempt to replicate the typical dress of the other sex. Many, but not all, **drag** artists are gay men, in which case they are often called "drag queens." Female performers who dress in male attire may be called "drag kings."

TRANSGENDER DRESSING   For transgender people, wearing the clothes of the gender with which they identify is a natural expression of their gender identity. Trans people do not typically wear these clothes for purposes of erotic arousal or as a parody. They are only "cross" dressing with respect to their natal (birth) sex, not their gender identity or (if they have physically transitioned) their current sex. Trans people who reject a gender binary may dress in a manner that expresses this attitude—perhaps in some combination of male-typical and female-typical attire, or in attire that is not conventionally congruent with their physical appearance (e.g., a skirt with a beard).

TRANSVESTIC FETISHISM   Another class of cross-dressers comprises heterosexual individuals (nearly all men) who wear clothes appropriate to the other sex because they find the practice itself sexually arousing. This is therefore a form of fetishism, and its technical name is transvestic fetishism, or simply **transvestism**. (Again, the use of the term "fetishism" here is not intended to brand this form of sexual expression as a mental disorder.) Transvestic fetishism is not especially rare: One random-sample study of the general population of Sweden found that 2.8% of men and 0.4% of women had engaged in at least one episode of transvestic fetishism (Långstrom & Zucker, 2005).

Many heterosexual transvestites keep their cross-dressing secret, for fear of public ridicule or rejection by their partners. Others venture out in public while cross-dressed, and they may be sexually excited by doing so. Many heterosexual transvestites are married; some conceal their cross-dressing from their wives, but others tell their wives or it is discovered by accident. Wives are commonly disturbed by cross-dressing behavior and may worry that her husbands are gay. Some wives come to accept their husbands' cross-dressing, however, and couples may even incorporate it into their sexual activities.

It seems that there is a continuum of traits in which heterosexual men's sexual desires move from their usual target—women—to *representations* of women that can be progressively stripped away, co-opted, and internalized (Blanchard, 1993; Bailey, 2003). The first stage in this continuum is regular fetishism, in which a woman's identity is represented by an object, such as a piece of feminine attire that is separable from the woman and can be completely owned and controlled by the man. In the second stage (transvestic fetishism), the clothing that represents the woman is put on, rather than simply viewed or handled. This practice may progress to fantasies of *being* an alluring woman, including the possession of breasts and female genitalia. In the extreme stage, the man may seek sexual satisfaction in actually transitioning to the female sex (**autogynephilia**—see Chapter 4). Most fetishists do not progress through this series of traits, of course, but autogynephiles often have regular fetishism and transvestic fetishism in their history.

Certainly, not all heterosexual cross-dressers go this route. For others, cross-dressing may lose some of its erotic significance over time and become a matter of gender expression more than sexual expression. Such men may join the Society for the Second Self (more commonly known as Tri-Ess), a support organization that organizes events at which heterosexual cross-dressers can socialize in a safe and accepting atmosphere. Support of this kind is important because heterosexual cross-dressers may encounter a lot of misunderstanding.

The *Femme Mirror* is the magazine of Tri-Ess, an organization for heterosexual cross-dressers.

Some men are aroused by trans women

While on the subject of gender variance, it's worth mentioning that some men have a specific sexual attraction to transgender or transexual women—often to those who look feminine and have breasts but still have male genitals (Blanchard, 1993). In popular speech these men may be called "transfans" or "tranny chasers." The numbers of these men are not small, to judge by the large number of "she-male" websites that cater to their interests, as well as the many streetwalking prostitutes who are recognizably transgender (see Chapter 17). The existence of transfans may enlarge the relationship options for heterosexual trans women, because many conventional heterosexual men are put off by knowing that a woman was a natal male. However, if a transfan is attracted to trans women precisely because they are trans, this may not be a good basis for a relationship with a trans woman who identifies as wholly female.

Sadomasochism involves the infliction or receipt of pain or degradation

In regular discourse, the word **sadist** may be applied to any cruel person, and the word **masochist** to anyone who is a "glutton for punishment." When these terms are used by sexologists, however, they refer to people who are sexually aroused by physical pain or psychological humiliation. Sadists are sexually aroused by inflicting such pain or humiliation on others (or by witnessing the recipient's suffering); masochists are sexually aroused by experiencing pain or submitting to humiliation themselves.

The term "sadism," like "masochism," was coined by Krafft-Ebing from the name of a real person—in this case the Marquis de Sade (1740–1814) (**Figure 13.4**). The two terms are often combined into the single word **sadomasochism (S/M)** because they may coexist in the same person or involve reciprocal interactions between a sadist and a masochist.

Sadomasochism, narrowly defined, involves the infliction, or enjoyment, of physical pain—by such practices as spanking, paddling, whipping, piercing, cutting, branding, nipple clamping, or "cock-and-ball torture." Alternatively (or in addition), the emphasis may be on psychological torture. This may include placing someone in a humiliating position by means of restraints (**bondage**), verbal abuse, or enslavement (**dominance**). The person may be forced to engage in some degrading activity, such as licking his tormentor's boots, verbally acknowledging his enslavement, being

autogynephilia A form of male-to-female transexuality characterized by a man's sexual arousal at the thought of being or becoming a woman.

sadism Sexual arousal by the infliction of pain, bondage, or humiliation on others, or by witnessing the recipient's suffering.

masochism Sexual arousal from being subjected to pain, bondage, or humiliation.

sadomasochism (S/M) The infliction and acceptance of pain or humiliation as a means of sexual arousal.

bondage The use of physical restraint for purposes of sexual arousal.

dominance The use of humiliation or subservience for purposes of sexual arousal.

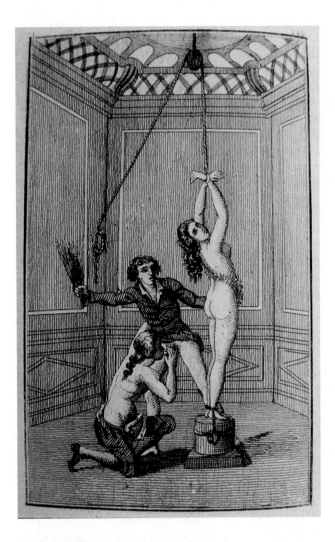

Figure 13.4 Donatien Alphonse François de Sade, better known as the Marquis de Sade, described his own sadistic interests in *The 120 Days of Sodom*, a book that he wrote while imprisoned in the Bastille.

led around on all fours like a dog, or being urinated or defecated on. **Submission** is the key element—it may be experienced as erotic by both the dominant and the submissive partner. Sadomasochistic behavior often includes fetishistic elements such as the wearing of leather, military uniforms, chains, or dog collars.

BDSM is the term generally used for the entire collection of sexual behaviors involving the infliction of, or submission to, pain, humiliation, restraint, and the like. What the letters BDSM originally stood for is lost to history, but bondage, dominance, discipline, submission, sadism, and masochism are commonly mentioned. A Google search under the keyword "BDSM" in 2014 elicited 62 million hits, so BDSM is obviously a topic of widespread interest. Any attempt to label BDSM as "sick" or "disordered" would risk pathologizing a significant fraction of the population.

As with other forms of variant sexual expression, BDSM may be practiced with all degrees of intensity. Most couples probably engage in some slapping, wrestling, or biting from time to time as a way of heightening their sexual arousal. For many people, BDSM represents a fashion statement or a cultural identity, perhaps validated by an occasional visit to a BDSM sex club (**Box 13.2**). Other people may spend a great deal of time pursuing BDSM interests: They may seek out partners at sex clubs or via the Internet, or they may create BDSM "dungeons" in their own homes.

Some individuals are so focused on the infliction or receipt of pain or humiliation that the usual physiological manifestations of sex, such as erection, ejaculation, and orgasm, play little or no role. At some BDSM parties, especially those that are semipublic, penetrative sex and even genital exposure may be banned.

Within the BDSM community, individuals who subject others to pain or humiliation are referred to as "tops" or "doms" (dominants) while those who prefer to be on the receiving end are "bottoms" or "subs" (submissives). In general, it seems that bottoms are quite a bit more common than tops, and appreciable numbers of "bottoms" are female. Good female "tops" are in short supply and are much sought after in heterosexual BDSM communities. For gay men, of course, that's not a problem; in fact there exists a flourishing gay male BDSM subculture. Because female tops are hard to find, some heterosexual male masochists pay for the services of a **dominatrix**—a woman who inflicts pain or humiliation in a BDSM setting. There is a small but flourishing lesbian BDSM community (**Figure 13.5**), as well as communities in which gay and straight men and women mingle freely.

Consent is an important issue in any sexual interaction. It is a particularly tricky issue with BDSM, however, because compulsion or a master-slave relationship is often a part of the sexual activity (or "scene") itself. "Stop, stop!" may mean "More, more!" Establishing consent is an ongoing process. Before the scene, perhaps as a part of flirtation or foreplay, the partners negotiate what will transpire and set limits for behavior. (For example, they may agree that no blood is to be drawn or that condoms are to be used for any sexual penetration.) During the scene, there may be brief interruptions to check that the bottom is still OK with what is going on. In addition, the participants often have prearranged "safe words" or nonverbal signals that cue the top to desist. After the BDSM scene, the partners usually share a period of cud-

submission   Taking the subservient role in BDSM activity.

BDSM   An all-inclusive term for forms of sexual expression that involve inflicting and receiving physical pain, restraint, or humiliation.

dominatrix   A woman who acts the role of the dominant partner in a BDSM setting.

Box 13.2 Personal Points of View

In the Dungeon

In 2002 Staci Newmahr, a sociologist at SUNY Buffalo, undertook an ethnographic study of the heterosexual BDSM scene at a club in a northeastern U.S. city (Newmahr, 2011). That meant getting personally involved:

He began with Florentine—two-handed flogging—which I had never seen him do, and he was quick and light and agile. I really wouldn't have thought that he'd be so dexterous with them. After a few minutes—maybe ten or fifteen, but I'm not the best one to ask—he checked in with me. I said I was fine. I was still facing the cross [an X-shaped frame to which she was tied by her hands and feet].

The next thing I felt was an enormous thud across my back. I turned to look at him. He had taken all nine of his floggers in his hands, and hit me with them in one blow. Trey is over six feet tall and nearly 200 pounds. The floggers alone must have weighed thirty pounds. . . .

At some point, about midway through the scene, Trey switched to a singletail. Each time the whip landed, it burned me—a tiny precise sharp hotness that lasted just a half-second short of unbearable. He threw it fast, slicing my skin with one blow after the other, diagonal down the left shoulder, then the right, then the left—then a shot across the middle of my back. It fucking hurt. . . .

We played for three hours. When our scene ended the dungeon was closing and many of the onlookers had gone to their rooms. The ones that remained approached us to compliment us.

Newmahr found that many or most members of the BDSM club took an "essentialist" view of themselves, thinking of their interest in BDSM as something they were born with. As one practitioner told her:

The interest [in SM] was literally the first thing that I can remember about most of the world. It's why I say it's so deeply ingrained in who I am. It's more today than a sexual orientation, than a gender identity—it's SM. It's really where I identify with; it's that strong.

The members of the club also had an essentialist perspective on the particular role they took in BDSM activities. "My name is Jane," a person might say, "I've been a member for two years, and I'm a submissive." People's roles could change, but that was viewed as something like coming out of the closet. People might be labeled as "a top who can't admit it," or "a submissive and doesn't know it yet." Nevertheless, it's clear that actual BDSM practices rely heavily on socially constructed "scripts" that are derived from literature (e.g., de Sade), modern media, and person-to-person communication.

Although many members of the club viewed BDSM as sexual in nature, overt sexual activity was not a significant part of the club scene. In many gay BDSM clubs, on the other hand, sexual activity may be part of the public scene or something that goes on in more private areas of the club.

---

dling, intimacy, or more conventional sex, during which they may review what has transpired, thus learning for future occasions what is exciting and what should be avoided. These kinds of communications are of particular importance in male-male BDSM scenes, which tend to involve more intense interactions than what typically takes place in male-female or female-female scenes. BDSM scenes that challenge the bottom's tolerance or that approach the boundaries of safety or consent are known as "edge play." Serious injuries and even deaths do sometimes occur during BDSM activities; it's not a good idea to plunge into edge play without first gaining experience from the milder BDSM scenes and learning from skilled practitioners.

On the surface, BDSM activities involve entirely negative feelings such as pain, fear, and anger. Dedicated BDSM practitioners, however, assert the very opposite: that the relationship of power, trust, and dependency that exists between top and bottom represents a condition of heightened intimacy and that a participant in a

BDSM scene may enter an altered state of consciousness that amounts to a spiritual experience.

Adult babies reenact infancy

As may be appreciated from a perusal of Figure 13.1, the range of atypical sexual interests is almost limitless. One example out of many consists of men who derive sexual satisfaction from acting as infants or toddlers. A technical term for this behavior is **infantilism**, but most men in this group don't consider it a disorder or seek professional help, and they simply call themselves **adult babies** (Little AB, 2014).

Adult babies may wear diapers or toddler clothes, sit in baby chairs, drink from baby bottles, sleep in cribs, and talk and act in a baby-like fashion. Sometimes there are BDSM elements: The man may play a role in which returning to babyhood is a punishment to which he is forced to submit. Adult babies are not interested in sexual contacts with actual babies.

If a man's sexual interest is largely focused on the wearing of diapers, he may call himself a "diaper lover." Diaper lovers may masturbate while wearing diapers, or they may act in more authentically baby-like fashion by wetting or soiling the diaper. Some diaper lovers wear diapers under their regular clothes during daily activities, like an adult with incontinence.

As with so many other minority sexual interests, adult babies have been normalized by the Internet. In the past they may have thought they were the only people in the world to have an erotic interest in babyhood, but now many websites and Internet-based groups serve them. On some websites, for example, adult babies can hire "babysitters" who will play that role for an hourly fee, doing such things as pampering, feeding, or disciplining the adult baby, or changing his diapers.

Paraphilic Disorders Cause Distress or Harm Others

So far in this chapter, we have discussed feelings and behaviors that, though uncommon, are generally agreed to lie within the realm of healthy or, at worst, harmless sexual expression. We now turn to sexual desires or behaviors that are problematic enough to be considered disorders.

At this point we need to introduce the terms "paraphilia" and "paraphilic disorder." Until recently, the term "paraphilia" meant any unusual and persistent sexual desire that caused distress to the person experiencing it or that led to behavior that harmed others or involved them without their consent. In other words, a paraphilia was by definition a psychiatric disorder. However, the 5th edition of the American Psychiatric Association's *Diagnostic and Statistical Manual of Mental Disorders* (*DSM-5*), issued in 2013, altered the definition of **paraphilia** to mean "any intense and persistent sexual interest other than sexual interest in genital stimulation or preparatory fondling with phenotypically normal, physically mature, consenting human partners." A great example of committee-speak! The phrase "phenotypically normal" presumably means not being intersex or transgender, having missing limbs, or being anything other than a garden-variety woman or man. So a paraphilia now means basically any uncommon sexual desire or behavior that plays a central role

infantilism Sexual satisfaction from acting as an infant.

adult baby An adult who obtains sexual satisfaction from acting as a baby or toddler.

paraphilia A persistent, intense sexual desire or behavior that is uncommon or unusual.

in a person's sex life (but it doesn't include homosexuality or bisexuality). It's what in common speech is often called a **kink**. On the other hand, **paraphilic disorders** are defined as the subset of paraphilias that justify clinical intervention because they cause distress or impairment to the individual or because they may lead to behaviors that entail the risk of harming others.

What the editors of *DSM-5* tried to achieve by this change was to make a clear distinction between uncommon sexual desires or behaviors in general (paraphilias) and those desires and behaviors that are problematic (paraphilic disorders). Thus what we've described up to this point are paraphilias by the *DSM-5* definition. We did not use the term "paraphilia" earlier in this chapter, however, because in spite of the change in the *DSM*'s definition, the word inevitably retains a medical flavor. We don't wish to perpetuate a tradition of turning certain forms of sexual expression into mental illnesses simply because they are rare or strange-seeming to the average person.

Let's discuss a specific example. We have already described sadism as an unusual form of sexual desire that can be expressed in mutually fulfilling behavior involving consensual partners. According to the *DSM-5*, however, a paraphilic disorder called **sexual sadism disorder** can be diagnosed if both of the following conditions are met:

1. *Over a period of at least 6 months, [the person experiences] recurrent and intense sexual arousal from the physical or psychological suffering of another person, as manifested by fantasies, urges, or behaviors.*

2. *The person has clinically significant distress or impairment in important areas of functioning, or has sought sexual stimulation from behaviors involving the physical or psychological suffering of two or more nonconsenting persons on separate occasions.*

Note that the two alternatives presented within the second condition—distress to the sadist or harm to others—highlight two distinct roles for psychiatrists and other professional therapists: (1) caring for their patients and (2) protecting the general public. Sometimes, as when a child molester confides in a psychiatrist about crimes he has committed or plans to commit, the psychiatrist may be put in a difficult ethical position, in that the principle of doctor-patient confidentiality may conflict with legally mandated reporting requirements. U.S. courts have ruled that health care professionals must inform law enforcement if the public is at risk.

DSM-5 lists nine categories of paraphilic disorders: (1) sexual masochism disorder, (2) sexual sadism disorder, (3) transvestic disorder, (4) fetishistic disorder, (5) exhibitionistic disorder, (6) voyeuristic disorder, (7) frotteuristic disorder, and (8) pedophilic disorder, as well as a catch-all category: paraphilic disorders not otherwise specified.

The first four categories in this list cover forms of sexual expression that we discussed earlier, in the context of normal sexual expression. All that we need say about them here, then, is that they are diagnosable as paraphilic disorders if (and only if) they cause significant distress to the person who experiences them or risk harming other people who are exposed to them. We will focus our attention on the other four specific paraphilic disorders, as well as some that fall into the "not otherwise specified" category. The paraphilic disorders that come to medical or legal attention most often are those that involve victims (**Figure 13.6**).

We can make some generalizations about paraphilic disorders:

- They are often extensions or exaggerations of common sexual desires and behaviors.

- Far more men than women develop them.

kink Colloquial term for an unusual sexual desire or behavior; a paraphilia.

paraphilic disorder A paraphilia that causes distress or harms others.

sexual sadism disorder Sexual arousal by the suffering of others, viewed as a paraphilic disorder.

Figure 13.6 The prevalence of paraphilias among men being evaluated clinically for suspected inappropriate sexual interests. Of course, these behaviors are biased toward those that bring men to medical or legal attention, namely, those that involve victims. "Coprophilia/urophilia" refers to sexual fixation on defecation or urination. No men in this sample had necrophilic interests. (Data from Abel & Osborn, 2000.)

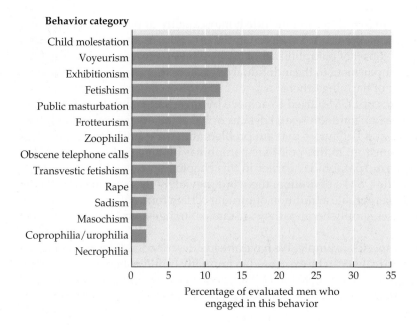

• Paraphilic disorders begin at an early age—usually around the time of puberty or early adolescence—and tend to become more pronounced over time.

• People who start out with one kind of paraphilic disorder may eventually exhibit multiple forms; by the time they come to professional attention, 54% report experiencing more than one disorder, and 18% report four or more (Abel & Osborn, 2000).

• Certain personality traits are common among people with paraphilic disorders: These include a lack of social skills (especially in dealing with women), a sense of inadequacy, depression, and sometimes a sense of rage against women.

• People with paraphilic disorders commonly have cognitive distortions, believing, for example, that their behaviors are sexually exciting or beneficial to the people they target.

Exhibitionists expose themselves to nonconsenting persons

The paraphilic disorder called exhibitionistic disorder, or simply **exhibitionism**, applies to people who are sexually aroused by the act or fantasy of exposing their genitals to unsuspecting strangers. Typically, an exhibitionist (or "flasher") will station himself in some location where women are present but which offers little danger of his being identified or arrested. As a woman approaches, the man will step into her line of sight and open his coat to expose his genitals. Alternatively, he may remove a book or newspaper that conceals them. During this action, the man may fantasize having a sexual interaction with the woman. He may masturbate and ejaculate while doing so; alternatively, he may flee and masturbate later, using his recollection of the event as an arousing stimulus. In legal terms, this behavior is the crime of **indecent exposure**, which commonly leads to mandatory registration as a sex offender.*

exhibitionism Sexual arousal by exposure of the genitals to strangers.

indecent exposure The crime of exposing the genitals or female breasts in public—exact legal definitions vary.

---

* Genital exposure for nonsexual reasons, such as public urination, skinny-dipping, or "streaking" is a minor misdemeanor termed "public lewdness" or something similar. In 2013 a 15-year-old from Huntsville, Alabama, ran naked across his school football field during a game; he is said to have been threatened by school officials with an indecent exposure charge, but he committed suicide before the matter was referred to the district attorney (AL.com, 2013).

Exhibitionism is defined *behaviorally*—by what people do—rather than as a sexual preference. Exhibitionists are no more excited by exposing themselves than by other forms of sexual expression, to judge from studies that measure genital arousal (Marshall & Fernandez, 2003). Rather, exhibitionists often exhibit high rates of many different kinds of sexual behaviors—a trait called hypersexuality (see below) (Murphy & Page, 2008).

An exhibitionist often misinterprets his victim's reactions—whether of shock, fear, or amusement—as a reciprocation of his sexual interest. Because of this cognitive distortion on the exhibitionist's part, the woman's emotional reactions tend to reward him and promote a continuation of his behavior. Women who encounter an exhibitionist do best to stay calm and simply walk away, although there is the option of attempting to have the man arrested if circumstances permit.

Exhibitionism is very common: In one survey of college students, over 40% of women and 12% of men said that they had experienced at least one episode (Clark et al., 2014). Most of the victims had strong emotional reactions to the event: They felt violated, angry, or scared. Less than 1 in 10 of the victims reported the event to the police.

Obscene telephone calling is related to exhibitionism

There is an auditory version of exhibitionism in which the perpetrator derives sexual arousal from making sexually suggestive remarks to a nonconsenting person. This is usually done by telephone, so it is called obscene telephone calling or **telephone scatalogia**. This term does not cover prank phone calls that may have sexual content but are not made for purposes of sexual arousal. Nor does it cover phone sex between willing partners.

The perpetrator (almost always a man) calls a known or unknown victim (usually a woman) and makes sexual suggestions or utters obscenities. Sometimes the caller boasts about his sex organs. Sometimes he makes threats in an attempt to coerce the recipient into a sexual act or a lewd conversation, or he may pose as a sex researcher in order to ask intimate questions as if they form part of a survey. In the latter case he may try to pass as a female.

Improved technology for tracing calls, and the decreasing number of public pay phones, has made obscene telephone calling riskier for the perpetrator than in the past, and the number of such calls may be on the decline. But some women are still plagued by them. Women who staff suicide hotlines and other 24-hour services are particularly likely to be victimized.

Voyeurs are aroused by watching others

Voyeuristic disorder, or simply **voyeurism**, means obtaining sexual arousal from watching unsuspecting people (usually women) while they are undressing, naked, engaged in sexual behavior, or urinating or defecating (Lavin, 2008). Typically, voyeurs ("peepers") carry out their activities in a discreet fashion, such as by peering through a bedroom window from a dark location. Thus, even though they may masturbate while watching, they are usually safe from arrest and may never come to the attention of the women who are being observed. Some voyeurs may use mirrors or camera phones to peer under women's clothing, or look through peepholes into dressing rooms or toilets. A gynecologist at Johns Hopkins Health System photographed the genitals of as many as 8000 women and girls who were his patients, using a secret pen camera; after his activities came to light, he committed suicide, and the hospital agreed to pay $190 million in settlement of the case (CNN, 2014).

Voyeurism is probably even more common than exhibitionism. It could be considered an extension of normal male sexuality, which includes a strong visual com-

telephone scatalogia   Sexual arousal from making obscene telephone calls.

voyeurism   Sexual arousal by watching persons while they are undressing, naked, or engaged in sex.

FAQ

I've been getting obscene telephone calls—what should I do?

Hang up immediately. Use an Anonymous Call Rejection or Privacy Manager option to block the calls, or change your telephone number. Speak with your phone company or college operator—they may put a "trap" on the line, which allows police to identify the source of the call, or they may ask that you dial *57 after the call to have it traced. With cell phones, contact the police first, then contact your phone company's customer service department.

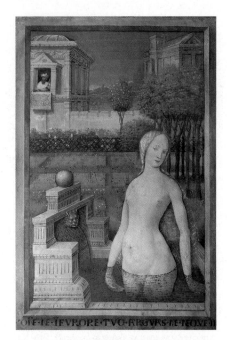

Figure 13.7 Biblical voyeurism King David spying on Bathsheba, from Jean Bourdichon's *The Book of Hours* (ca. 1500).

frotteurism Sexual arousal from touching or rubbing the genitals against strangers without their consent or without their knowledge, as in a crowded public place.

ponent (**Figure 13.7**). Many adolescent or adult males might take advantage of an opportunity to watch women who are undressed or engaged in sexual activity, especially if they can do so "guilt free" because the woman's bedroom is in plain sight from their own window or from the street. About half of all adolescent males report having engaged in such behaviors (McConaghy, 2005). The popularity of pornographic videos reflects a similarly widespread voyeuristic interest. Voyeuristic acts were not crimes in either Canada or the United Kingdom until 2004; they are now misdemeanors. In some U.S. jurisdictions voyeuristic acts remain legal so long as no trespassing, photography, or video recording is involved.

Frotteurism involves surreptitious physical contact

Frotteuristic disorder, or **frotteurism**, means obtaining sexual arousal from physical contact with others—usually women—in public places without their consent and often without their knowledge (Lussier & Piché, 2008) (**Box 13.3**). A frotteur ("groper") seeks out women in places that are sufficiently crowded that physical contact goes unnoticed—subway cars, elevators, crowded bars, sporting events, and the like. He rubs his erect penis, hand, leg, or an object such as a newspaper against the woman's thighs, buttocks, vulva, or breasts. Because he may ejaculate under his clothes during the encounter, the frotteur may wear a plastic bag or condom around his penis to prevent any visible staining of his clothes. If he is arrested, evidence of such precautions may be used to prove his criminal intent. Other frotteurs may expose themselves and ejaculate directly onto their victim's clothing, however.

In the survey of college students mentioned in the section on exhibitionism (Clark et al., 2014), 24% of women and 7% of men reported having been victims of frotteurism. These figures were closely matched by a national survey (Stop Street Harassment, 2014). The true percentages are likely to be higher because people in a crowded environment are not always aware that they are being touched by a frotteur. Besides the victims' immediate emotional responses to the event, more than one-third reported suffering long-term psychological consequences, and many changed their behavior—for example, by monitoring their proximity to others in public spaces. Only about 5% of the victims reported the event to the police.

Again, frotteurism could be viewed as an extension of conventional sexuality; many heterosexual men would like to "cop a feel" of an attractive female stranger with whom they find themselves in close proximity, and some actually indulge this wish. Still, a great deal of the "groping" that is done in public places represents the persistent activity of dedicated frotteurs, rather than the occasional acts of otherwise conventional men.

With all three of these behaviors—exhibitionism, voyeurism, and frotteurism—it is the lack of consent that makes them into disorders (and crimes). There is of course nothing wrong with self-exposure, watching a naked person, or touching him or her sexually, if it is done in a private and consensual situation.

Some Adults Are Sexually Attracted to Children

Few topics in the area of human sexuality arouse such strong feelings, or are the focus of so many news stories, as the topic of sexual contact between adults and children. In Chapter 10 we discussed this issue from the point of view of the children who experience such contacts, and we described the harm that many such children suffer. Here we revisit the issue from the point of view of the adults: people (usually men) who are sexually attracted to children or youths below the legal age of consent, or who actually engage in sexual contact with them.

Box 13.3 Personal Points of View

Frotteurism on Public Transit

The following first-person accounts describe groping incidents on subway trains:

> Once, when I felt a surreptitious hand on my nether parts, and fed up with just silently standing there, I turned and shouted to the man behind me, "Take your hands off me!" The response was: "I don't know what you are talking about. You are making improper accusations." The men around stood silently by, and it was I who was embarrassed. (Katz, 2006)

> A hand went up my skirt and down my panties. I gasped. The nearest woman asked what was wrong. I said, "That guy's got his hand inside me." Just then, the train pulled into 161st Street. The crowd threw the guy out the door, like a watermelon seed. (Randall, 2006)

> A man sat down next to me in the aisle seat, then began worming his fingers under my hip as we sat side by side. I got up immediately, making sure to step on his foot and grind my heel as hard as I could as I passed him. It certainly made me feel good; I can't say the same for the perp. (Andrews, 2002)

> A man on the train . . . tried to rub himself against me. . .. My instinct made me turn around, and I saw this person exposed in front of me, wearing a condom. There are really no proper words to describe the anger and sense of violation that one feels when something like that happens to you. I confronted him, announcing to the subway car at the top of my lungs what he had been doing to me. I also enlisted other passengers to help me detain him . . . all of us taking pictures on our cell phones. "That's it!" I screamed. "You're getting fucking arrested." Upon exiting the train the perpetrator was immediately arrested by transit police. He was later convicted and is now a registered sex offender for life. And he was deported, too." (Briggs, 2014) (A video of part of this incident is at nydn.us/UosOnu.)

In an effort to stop "groping" on public transit, the Massachusetts Bay Transit Authority launched a public safety campaign.

Occasionally, transit officials conduct stings to catch offenders. One sting in New York City netted 13 suspected gropers and flashers (exhibitionists) (Hartocollis, 2006). The associated publicity may have served as a short-term deterrent to potential offenders. Still, sexual offenses in transit systems are a worldwide problem that shows no signs of going away. Some cities, such as Tokyo and Mexico City, have tackled the problem by banning all men from at least one car in every train (see figure).

Pedophilia and child molestation are not synonymous

The terms "pedophilia" and "child molestation" characterize different but overlapping populations of individuals (Camilleri & Quinsey, 2008) (**Figure 13.8**). A **pedophile** is a person—nearly always a man—who has a persistent sexual attraction to prepubescent children, generally defined as children under the age of 11. To meet the definition of pedophilia, a person's sexual attraction to children must be greater than, or equal to, his attraction to adults. In other words, a person who does experience some sexual attraction to prepubescent children, but less than he does to adolescents or adults, is not to be regarded as a pedophile.

pedophile   A person whose sexual feelings are directed mainly toward prepubescent children.

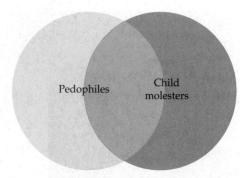

Figure 13.8 Pedophiles and child molesters are distinct but partially overlapping populations.

pedophilic disorder Pedophilia that causes distress or that is expressed in sexual contacts with children.

hebephile An adult whose sexual attraction is directed mainly toward pubescent children.

Pedophilia is a paraphilia, according to *DSM-5*, but it is only a disorder (**pedophilic disorder**) if the person is distressed by his sexual attraction to prepubescent children or if he is at risk of expressing his attraction in actual sexual contacts. Thus it is possible to be a pedophile without having a mental disorder, according to *DSM-5*. Some experts disagree with this idea, but the lead editor of this section of *DSM-5*, Ray Blanchard, has defended it with a rhetorical question: "If you take an individual who has a very strong erotic attraction for children, but who has never acted on it, who never would act on it, who agrees that society's prohibition of adult child sexual interactions should be in place, do you want to say this individual has a mental disorder?" (Stuart, 2013). What's your opinion?

Pedophiles generally become aware of their sexual attraction to children in early adolescence—most commonly at the age of 12 to 14 (**Figure 13.9**). This is about the same time that nonpedophilic men become aware of their sexual attraction to women or to men. Thereafter, pedophilic attraction remains unchanged over the life span.

Some pedophiles actually molest children, but some do not. They may refrain from doing so because they believe it is wrong, are afraid of the consequences, or can obtain sufficient sexual gratification from older partners, from fantasies, or from viewing child pornography. (The last of these is a crime—see Chapter 17.)

Some adults are primarily attracted to children who are going through puberty—pubescent children—roughly in the 11- to 14-year-old range. These adults (**hebephiles**) do not fit the definition of pedophiles given above. Hebephilia is not a diagnostic category in *DSM-5*, although some of the *DSM* editors believed that it should be.

Most pedophiles have a preference for children of a particular sex. Heterosexual pedophiles predominate; they outnumber homosexual pedophiles by a factor of about 2 or 3 to 1 (Blanchard et al., 2000). Because gay men are sometimes accused of being pedophiles, it's worth emphasizing the obvious: Homosexual pedophiles are not the same thing as regular gay men, any more than heterosexual pedophiles are the same thing as regular straight men.

Pedophilia is an exaggeration of a sexual interest that exists fairly widely in the male population. You may be reluctant to believe that many "normal" men are sexually aroused by children, but this has been demonstrated in laboratory studies. Arousal is generally greatest in response to older children, and in response to girls in heterosexual men and to boys in homosexual men (Freund et al., 1989). Quite a few of these adults are only prevented from acting on their attraction to children by fear of punishment: In an online survey conducted by researchers at the University

Figure 13.9 **Age at onset of attraction to children** This bar graph shows the responses of 192 adults (190 males, 2 females) attracted to minors to the question "How old were you when you first had a preferential attraction to boys or girls younger than yourself?" (Data from B4U-ACT, 2011.)

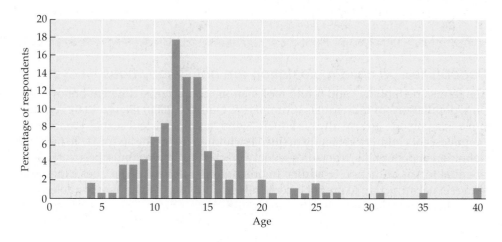

of Colorado, 6% of men, as well as 2% of women, said there was some likelihood that they would have sexual contact with a child if they were guaranteed that they would not be caught (Wurtele et al., 2013).

Child molestation is a behavioral and legal term

A **child molester** (or sexual offender against children) is any adult who has sexual contact with a child—the actual age limit varies between jurisdictions. It is primarily a legal definition. Some child molesters are pedophiles; others molest children for a variety of other reasons, such as the lack of available older partners, the desire to hurt a child's parent (perhaps an ex-girlfriend of the perpetrator), alcohol or drug intoxication, or neurological damage. The majority of child molestation convictions are for nonpenetrative acts, such as touching a child's genitals or buttocks.

Some child molesters have sexual interactions with their own children or step-children (**intrafamilial child molesters**, or incest offenders). Others have interactions with children outside their immediate families (**extrafamilial child molesters**). There are differences between these two types of molesters. Extrafamilial molesters are more likely to engage in penetrative sex with their victims, to injure their victims, to molest boys, to repeat their offenses, and to be exclusive pedophiles (as assessed by penile plethysmography), compared with men who molest their own children (Rice & Harris, 2002; Blanchard et al., 2006).

Female child molesters are uncommon, but they do exist. Cases in which female teachers enter into sexual relationships with male teenage students grab the headlines from time to time. In one much-publicized case, a 34-year-old Seattle teacher, Mary Kay LeTourneau, who was married and the mother of four children, began an affair with a 13-year-old student, Vili Fualaau, and had two children by him. After LeTour-neau served a 7-year prison sentence, she and Fualaau reunited, and in May 2005 they married. The Fualaaus earned a reported $750,000 from the sale of their wedding video to the television show *Entertainment Tonight*. They have remained married.

Vili Fualaau denied that he was a "victim," and that viewpoint is common. When eBaum's World Forum posted photographs of female teachers accused of sexually abusing their underage male students, typical male readers' comments included "Lucky kids," "I'd be the last to press charges," and "Where can I find some of these 'pedophiles'?" (Hayes & Carpenter, 2010).

Priests and others may molest children under their care

Over the last 20 years, an unfolding scandal has involved revelations about Roman Catholic priests, both in the United States and elsewhere, who sexually molested children under their pastoral care. Church authorities relocated many of the offend-ing priests rather than suspending them or reporting them to the police—whereupon some of them reoffended in their new locations. By 2004, over 4000 U.S. priests were reported to have abused as many as 10,000 minors, of whom about 80% were boys. (Many of the reported offenses occurred decades ago.) The resulting legal actions have led to settlements totaling over $3 billion, which have driven numerous U.S. dioceses to seek bankruptcy protection or to sell extensive church-owned lands and properties (BishopAccountability, 2014).

In 2014 the United Nations Committee on the Rights of the Child issued a report that accused the Vatican of failing to protect children, adopting policies that have led to the continuation of abuse, and protecting perpetrators from punishment (Cum-ming-Bruce, 2014). Later in the same year, Pope Francis met with victims of sexual abuse by priests: He expressed his sorrow, asked forgiveness, and promised not to tolerate abusive priests and to discipline bishops who failed to protect minors (Yardley, 2014).

child molester An adult who has sexual contact with a prepubescent child.

intrafamilial child molester A person who has had sexual contact with his own children or stepchildren. Also called *incest offender*.

extrafamilial child molester A person who has had sexual contact with children outside his immediate family.

Catholic priest John Geoghan was known to the archbishop of Boston as a frequent molester of children, but he was shuffled from parish to parish over a period of 30 years, during which time he continued his offenses. In 2002 he was sentenced to a 9-year prison term; in the following year he was murdered by a fellow inmate.

bestiality Obsolete term for sexual contact between a person and an animal.

The fact that Catholic priests are not permitted to marry could be one factor contributing to the high prevalence of abuse. That is, it may make the seminary and the priesthood a desirable option for men who want to avoid marriage because they are not attracted to adult women, or it may make the men more likely to abuse children by denying them a sexual outlet within marriage. In 2014 Pope Francis was reported to have hinted that the rules banning married priests might be changed because priestly celibacy is not a "dogma"—that is, it is not a required article of faith revealed by God (Catholic Online, 2014).

Of course, Catholic priests are not the only people who have violated their fiduciary responsibilities to children. Scout leaders, doctors, teachers, and athletic coaches have from time to time been accused and convicted of molesting minors. A much-publicized 2012 case involved Penn State's assistant football coach Jerry Sandusky, who was convicted on 45 counts of sexually abusing boys. Sandusky was sentenced to 30 to 60 years in prison, and the university's president and two other officials resigned and faced trial for covering up Sandusky's crimes.

Some organizations support "minor-attracted people"

Men who are sexually attracted to underage youths or children risk arrest and lengthy prison sentences if they attempt to satisfy that attraction with physical contacts. Even if they do not make any such attempts, their lives are likely to be stressful and lonely. In one survey, 45% of these men said that they had seriously contemplated suicide, most commonly in their mid- to late-teen years (B4U-ACT, 2011).

One organization that supports these men is the Maryland-based nonprofit B4U-ACT (B4U-ACT, 2014). This is run by a mix of minor-attracted persons and mental health professionals who take a nonjudgmental view of them. Its purpose is to promote mental health services, public understanding, and mutual support for minor-attracted persons and to help them lead fulfilling lives while remaining within the law. Another organization, Virtuous Pedophiles, is a mutual support group for minor-attracted persons who do not want to have sexual contacts with children, because they believe that such contacts are wrong (Virtuous Pedophiles, 2014).

Whatever your views on the morality of sex between adults and minors, it's worth noting that the age of legal consent (the age at which a person is deemed capable of consenting to sexual contact with others) varies significantly from jurisdiction to jurisdiction. In the United States it ranges from 16 to 18, depending on the state. Internationally, the age of legal consent is commonly 14, 15, or 16—Canada raised its age of consent from 14 to 16 in 2008. Thus, there does seem to be room for debate about the age at which youths are capable of giving meaningful consent to sexual activity with adults.

A Variety of Other Paraphilic Disorders Exist

Besides the paraphilic disorders already discussed, there are many others, some specifically listed in *DSM-5* and others not. The following are some examples.

Zoophiles are sexually attracted to animals

Sexual contact between humans and nonhuman animals—a behavior traditionally called **bestiality**—is not particularly rare (Earls & Lalumière, 2009). In the Kinsey studies, about 3.6% of women and 8% of men stated that they had had at

Bestiality as portrayed in a sculpture at Lakshmana Temple, Khajuraho, India.

least one sexual contact with an animal after adolescence. Among men raised on farms, nearly half had had sexual contact with an animal, and about 17% reported a contact leading to orgasm. In such contacts, the man may penetrate the animal vaginally or anally or may induce the animal to fellate him or penetrate him anally.

Most human-animal contacts occur during the preadolescent or adolescent years and constitute only a tiny fraction of the person's total sexual activity. They can hardly be considered signs of a paraphilic disorder. A few people—mostly men—do persist in having sexual contacts with animals throughout their lives, however, largely to the exclusion of human sexual contacts. This condition is called **zoophilia**. In one study, two-thirds of zoophiles (or "zoos") stated that they would rather have sex with an animal than with a human (Williams & Weinberg, 2003). In one case study, a man was found (by penile plethysmography) to be sexually aroused more strongly by horses than by any other species, including humans (Earls & Lalumière, 2002). A first-person account (also written by a horse lover) asserted that zoophilia is a matter of romantic intimacy and not merely physical gratification (Matthews, 1994). This is an almost universal theme in writings by zoophiles, some of whom describe themselves as being "married" to particular animals.

In 2005 a 45-year-old man in Washington state died of a perforated colon after being anally penetrated by a stallion. The man had been one of a group of men who visited a farm to have sex with horses. At the time, Washington had no law banning sex with animals, but it passed one in the aftermath of this case. Five years later another Washington man was found to have kept four stallions and seven large-breed male dogs for sexual purposes. The man had been an outspoken proponent of sex with animals and said that his life partner of 10 years was a horse named Capone. He was sentenced to 3 years of imprisonment, and another man was sentenced to 3 months in jail for having sex with dogs at the same location (Clarridge, 2010).

Although household pets and farm animals are the main objects of zoophilic desire, some zoophiles have been romantically attracted to, and had sex with, more exotic animals such as dolphins (Saincome, 2013). Another variant on zoophilia is **formicophilia**, which means deriving sexual arousal from the movements or bites of ants on or inside the genitals or elsewhere on the body. We know of only one case study, and it is not clear whether this man, who lived in Sri Lanka, had a romantic relationship with a particular ant (Dewaraja & Money, 1986).

Joking aside, do you think that having sex with nonhuman animals should be considered a mental disorder, a crime, both, or neither?

In necrophilia, nonresistance of the partner may be arousing

Necrophilia is a sexual fixation on corpses. It is a rare paraphilic disorder, with probably fewer than 200 cases having been reported in the medical literature. Still, there is enough interest in necrophilia to keep some Internet bulletin boards busy. Necrophiliacs may take positions as mortuary workers or other jobs that give them access to dead bodies. (Of course, the overwhelming majority of mortuary workers are not necrophiliacs.)

Necrophiliacs may view or touch a dead body while masturbating or may actually have penetrative sex with it. Apparently, it is the lack of resistance or rejection by the dead person that is a key motivator for necrophilic behavior (Rosman & Resnick, 1989). In fact, some men are turned on when their (living) sex partners feign unconsciousness, "play dead," or join them in necrophilic fantasies. Such activities may not be entirely harmless, because some men have committed murder to satisfy their necrophilic interests.

Not all states criminalize sex with corpses, and in those that do, the interpretation of the law is often murky, as was highlighted by an unusual case in Wisconsin (**Figure 13.10**). In September 2006, 20-year-old Nick Grunke saw an obituary of a

zoophilia A persistent preference for sexual contacts with animals.

formicophilia Sexual arousal from having ants crawling on the body.

necrophilia A paraphilia involving sexual arousal from viewing or having contact with dead bodies.

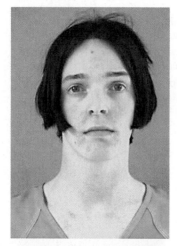

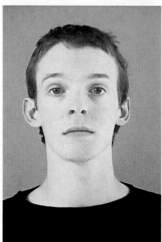

Figure 13.10 Necrophile wannabes (Top to bottom) Nick Grunke, Alex Grunke, and Dustin Radke.

young woman who had died a few days earlier in a motorcycle accident. Grunke was so smitten with the young woman's photograph that he conceived a plan to disinter her body from the local cemetery and have sex with it. Grunke, his twin brother Alex, and a friend drove to the cemetery late at night, after stopping off at a Walmart store to purchase some condoms. Once at the cemetery, the three men dug down to the woman's vault but could not pry it open. Shortly thereafter they were apprehended by the police and charged with attempted third-degree rape. Wisconsin had a statute banning sex with corpses, but Nick Grunke argued that it only applied to cases where the sex act took place in conjunction with a murder. The trial court, and an appeals court, agreed with him. But the prosecutors appealed the case to the Wisconsin Supreme Court, and those justices took a different view. They ruled in 2008 that the statute did cover sex with a dead person who had not been murdered, and they sent the case back to the lower court for further proceedings. These ended in a conviction and a 2-year prison sentence for Nick Grunke, who was also ordered to undergo 5 to 7 years of psychotherapy. All three men had to register as sex offenders. According to the judge, confidential records indicated that Nick Grunke had been the victim of a "horrific crime" when he was a young child (Wiedemann, 2009).

Sexual violence can be paraphilic

Not all violent forms of sexual expression warrant diagnosis as paraphilic disorders. Consensual S/M scenes are not usually an indication of a paraphilic disorder, nor are most cases of rape (though rape is a crime, of course). If a person has a persistent and distressing fixation on sexual violence, however, or commits acts of nonconsensual sexual violence *because the violence itself is sexually arousing*, the person probably has a paraphilic disorder. This condition is not specifically listed in *DSM-5*. There was a proposal to introduce a "paraphilic coercive disorder" in *DSM-5*, but it was rejected. The reason for the rejection was the fear that ordinary rapists would be placed in this category: This could have led to rapists being detained indefinitely after the expiration of their sentences ("civil commitment").

Some of the most notorious serial killers, such as Jack the Ripper, or Jeffrey Dahmer—who killed, dismembered, and ate portions of 17 boys or youths in the Milwaukee area for sexual gratification—clearly had a paraphilic disorder of this kind. (Dahmer was also a necrophiliac.) Paraphilic sexual killers often have a complex mental disorder, including brain damage, psychosis, and a history of severe childhood abuse (Pincus, 2001). These crimes are not impulsive. Typically, they are carefully planned and involve hours or days of torture before the victim is finally killed. The perpetrator often records his crimes on videotape or in diaries.

One sexual serial killer who generated enormous publicity was Gary Ridgway (the "Green River Killer"). In 2003 Ridgway

Gary Ridgway—the Green River serial killer—said that he killed prostitutes because he hated them and because "I thought I could kill as many of them as I wanted without getting caught."

Box 13.4 Research Highlights

Autoerotic Asphyxia

"When you find my body hanging . . . with a tight noose around my neck, do not look for a murderer. I have executed myself. I say execute rather than suicide because I didn't really intend to hang unto death." This cryptic note was found next to the strung-up, half-naked body of a young Canadian man. Indeed, the cause of his death was not murder, nor was it suicide. It was autoerotic asphyxia—a sexually charged near-death experience that went a step too far (Blanchard & Hucker, 1991).

People who practice autoerotic asphyxia (also called hypoxyphilia) do so in order to increase the intensity of orgasm by constricting the flow of blood to the brain during masturbation. The practitioners of this behavior—mostly male—may tighten a belt around their neck or suspend themselves by a noose, often using a closet rail, rafter, or tree. Alternatively, they may put their head in a plastic bag. The cerebral cortex is partially knocked out by the resulting lack of oxygen, and its normal inhibitory influence on lower centers of the brain is removed. This probably results in the same kind of heightened, semiconscious orgasm that some people experience with the use of nitrite inhalers, or "poppers."

At least two prominent individuals have died in circumstances suggestive of auroerotic asphyxia. One was Australian rock star Michael Hutchence (lead singer for INXS), who died in 1997. (His death may have been suicide, however.) The other was American actor David Carradine (see figure): In 2009 he was found hanging naked in a Thai hotel room, with a rope around his neck and genitals (McShane, 2009).

Actor David Carradine is thought to have died by autoerotic asphyxia.

For many practitioners, autoerotic asphyxia is about more than experiencing a supernormal orgasm. To judge by the death scenes of victims, it is often linked with a complex of paraphilic elements, including bondage, punishment, and execution by hanging. The victim's body may be tied up around the ankles and genitals as well as the neck, and sadomasochistic literature or images are often found in the vicinity. Transvestism can also play a role: One victim was found dressed in women's clothes and surrounded by documents containing passages such as "the law of the land for any man dressed as a woman and found guilty is that he be hanged." Another was found hanging in front of a computer that had been playing a "snuff video" (a movie depicting a real or staged murder, perhaps in a pornographic context) (Vennemann & Pollak, 2006). A survey of living practitioners of autoerotic asphyxia confirmed the connection with masochism, transvestic fetishism, and other paraphilic behaviors (Hucker, 2011).

Never experiment with autoerotic asphyxia: It carries a dire risk of accidental death if the practitioner passes out before he has time to release whatever is constricting his neck. (Loss of consciousness occurs just 10 or 11 seconds after complete strangulation.) Over 400 deaths have been reported in the forensic literature (Sauvageau & Racette, 2006; Sauvageau & Geberth, 2009), and the true numbers are probably much higher because many cases are misidentified as suicides. Deaths have occurred even when a second person has been present.

---

pleaded guilty to murdering 48 young women and girls—mostly prostitutes—in the Seattle area over a period of 16 years (Seattle Times, 2004). He killed most of the women by strangling them during sexual encounters. In his confession Ridgway expressed contempt for prostitutes, but this seems to have been merely what permitted him to direct his murderous sexual impulses at them, rather than being the actual motive, which—while obviously pathological—remains obscure. Ridgway escaped the death penalty by agreeing to provide information about his victims and the location of their bodies.

Some masochists inflict pain or suffering on themselves without the aid of a partner. A particularly dangerous form of this behavior is **autoerotic asphyxia**, in which the practitioner partially asphyxiates himself while masturbating. Although this behavior can have the aim of enhancing sexual arousal, it is often connected with BDSM ideation and practices (**Box 13.4**).

autoerotic asphyxia   Self-strangulation for purposes of sexual arousal.

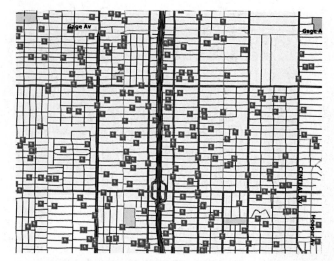

Figure 13.11   Sex offender in your backyard? In densely populated areas, most people have a registered sex offender living within a block or two. This screenshot from the California sex offender registry website shows (in blue squares) the residences of sex offenders in a fairly typical area of Los Angeles.

Sex Offenders Do Not Necessarily Repeat Their Offenses

Sex offenders, especially offenders against children, are widely perceived as incorrigible monsters who will inevitably repeat their offenses if given the chance. This perception has led to draconian measures against convicted sex offenders: very long prison sentences, denial of parole, detention after the completion of sentences, and compulsory drug treatments (see below). Registration of sex offenders' addresses, and access by the public to this information, are mandated in all states (**Figure 13.11**). In some states the police are required to notify the public when a registered sex offender moves into a neighborhood. These requirements are known as "Megan's laws," named for Megan Kanka, a 7-year-old New Jersey girl who was raped and murdered by a known child molester in 1995. The molester had moved onto the Kankas' street without their knowledge.

In reality, the **recidivism** rate for most sex offenders (the probability that they will commit another sex offense) is no more than 7% at 5 years after release (Helmus et al., 2012); this is well below the rates for most non-sexual offenders. Some sex offenders are at higher risk of reoffending—these include men who have already committed more than one offense, whose previous offenses involved violence, or who have antisocial personality disorder. These high-risk offenders have an approximately 22% recidivism rate at 5 years after release, but if they are offense free at 10 years, there is only a small chance that they will offend again (Hanson et al., 2014). In other words, high-risk sex offenders do not remain high risk forever.

There Are Numerous Theories of Paraphilic Disorders

recidivism   The tendency of convicted offenders to reoffend.

Understanding the causes of uncommon sexual desires and behaviors might lead to effective treatment or prevention of those that are unwanted, that is, paraphilic disorders. Yet theories to explain why people develop these desires are very diverse (Laws & O'Donohue, 2008). This may in part reflect the diversity of sexual desires themselves, ranging as they do from minority sexual interests such as fetishism—that only become disorders by virtue of any distress they may cause—to highly abnormal desires that may trigger grave sex crimes.

BIOLOGICAL FACTORS   Kinks and paraphilic disorders sometimes run in families, suggesting the existence of genes predisposing individuals to them (**Figure 13.12**).

Figure 13.12   Familial pedophilia This Canadian family tree has nine male pedophiles (black squares), all attracted to prepubescent girls, in 4 successive generations. The pattern suggests the presence of a gene predisposing to pedophilia that is transmitted directly from father to son. (After Labelle et al., 2012.)

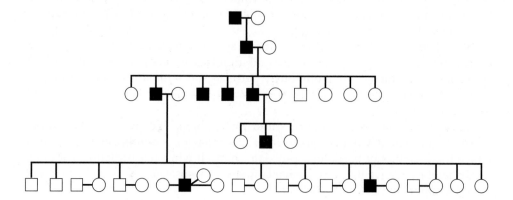

There are also reports of differences in brain structure between pedophiles and nonpedophiles, such as a reduction in the volume of gray matter in the prefrontal cortex (Schiffer et al., 2007; Poeppl et al., 2013). These findings need to be interpreted cautiously, however, because they might relate to personality traits (such as impulsiveness) that would cause a pedophile to act on his attractions, rather than to the attraction itself. (Most studies of this type have been done on men who have actually molested children.)

conditioning The modification of behavior by learning through association and/or reinforcement.

LEARNING PROCESSES In Chapter 5 we discussed research into the classical (Pavlovian) **conditioning** of sexual arousal. Some researchers have reported that it is possible to "sexualize" nonsexual stimuli by this method. In one study, nonparaphilic male volunteers were repeatedly shown images of a piggy bank in conjunction with erotically arousing images. After 3 weeks of exposure to these pairings, the men developed penile arousal responses to the piggy bank alone (Plaud & Martini, 1999) (**Figure 13.13**). Conditioning experiments of this kind have generally yielded weak or inconsistent results, however. This could be because the subjects were adults, whose sexuality may be less malleable than that of young adolescents.

DISORDERS OF COURTSHIP The usual process by which a man acquires a sex partner consists of four stages: (1) location and evaluation of a potential sex partner; (2) initial nontactile interactions, such as smiling, displaying attractive features, and talking

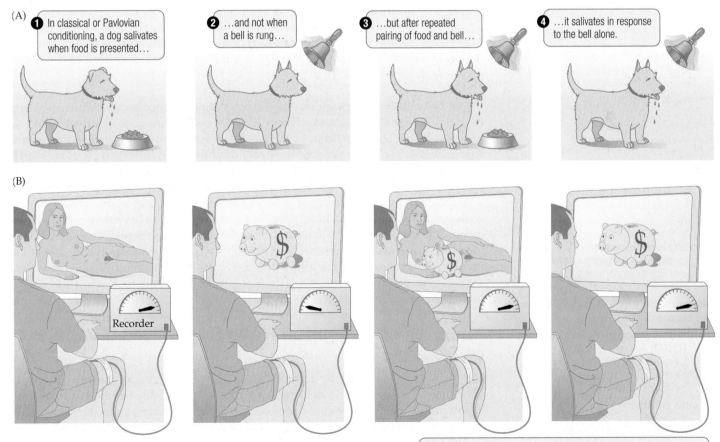

Figure 13.13 **Conditioned arousal** could be a mechanism for the development of fetishisms.

In similar conditioning experiments by Plaud and Martini (1999), men developed sexual arousal to a nonsexual stimulus—a piggy bank.

Figure 13.14 Breaking the cycle Former U.S. senator Scott Brown of Massachusetts was sexually abused as a child. He had some behavior problems as a teenager but did not become a sexual abuser.

with the partner; (3) tactile interactions such as embracing and fondling; and (4) genital sex. Each of these stages has a paraphilic counterpart: (1) voyeurism, (2) exhibitionism and obscene telephone calling, (3) frotteurism, and (4) paraphilic rape. In the 1980s Kurt Freund and colleagues suggested that some higher organizing principle that normally ties the elements of male courtship together into a coherent sequence has been lost in people with paraphilic disorders. This could leave the individual elements in a state of psychic disorder that allows them to be expressed inappropriately (Freund & Blanchard, 1986). Freund gave this concept the name **courtship disorder**.

ESCAPE ROUTE Another idea is that paraphilic disorders are caused by the blockage of normal avenues of sexual expression. If a person can't explore typical sexual relations, he might turn to alternative, atypical ones. What could cause such a blockage? As mentioned above, some studies have reported that men with paraphilic disorders are deficient in social skills and relate poorly to women. Such personality traits might hamper adolescents' attempts to establish conventional sexual relationships and might lead them to explore atypical activities that require few or no social skills.

INFLUENCE OF OTHER TRAITS It is possible that certain personality traits or disorders make the development of paraphilic disorders more likely. These traits could include **hypersexuality** (an excess of sexual desire that shows itself in compulsive masturbation and the devotion of a great deal of time to sexual fantasy, pornography use, and the pursuit of sex partners), **obsessive-compulsive disorder** (**OCD**), attention deficit hyperactivity disorder (ADHD), impulsivity, mood disorders, and alcohol and drug dependency (Kafka, 2008; Laws & O'Donohue, 2008).

CYCLE OF ABUSE Most victims of childhood abuse do not become abusers when they are adults (**Figure 13.14**). Nevertheless, abusers are more likely to have a history of childhood victimization than are other men, according to numerous studies (Seto, 2008). This is called the **cycle of abuse**. The correlation is particularly strong between childhood sexual abuse and adult pedophilia (Nunes et al., 2013). It is not known why some abused children become abusers and others do not, nor why childhood victimization predisposes some individuals to adult abuse.

In summary, researchers have proposed a variety of ideas to explain the development of paraphilic disorders and unusual sexual desires in general. Because no single idea seems adequate, there have been attempts to develop integrative theories that involve interactions among multiple causal factors (Ward & Beech, 2008). However, a comprehensive and persuasive picture of how people come to develop and act on paraphilic desires remains an elusive goal.

Theories of Causation Have Suggested a Variety of Treatments

Most people with paraphilic disorders do not seek treatment of their own accord. They may be pressured into doing so by spouses, or they may be referred to mental health professionals by the courts. For convicted sex offenders, attending some kind of risk-reduction program might be a condition of their sentencing or parole.

The fact that people with paraphilias do not usually initiate their own treatment makes that treatment difficult, both practically and ethically. For example, a person

courtship disorder A paraphilia or cluster of paraphilias seen as a disorder of normal courtship behavior.

hypersexuality Excessive sexual desire or behavior.

obsessive-compulsive disorder (OCD) A mental disorder marked by anxiety, repetitive thoughts or urges, and behaviors that temporarily relieve those urges.

cycle of abuse The cycle in which some abused children grow up to perform similar forms of abuse on others. Also called *victim-perpetrator cycle*.

who is incarcerated may be highly motivated to feign a disappearance of his paraphilic interests. A child molester may learn to control his penile responses during laboratory testing, for example, to make it seem that he is no longer aroused by images of children. Some reports of treatment successes probably result from uncritical acceptance of such "cures."

Conditioning is intended to change sexual desires

If paraphilic disorders result from conditioning or other forms of learning, then it might be possible to treat them by driving the learning process in reverse or by fostering new learning processes that lead to more typical sexual desires or behaviors. Treatments based on these ideas are called **behavior therapy**. One of these techniques is **aversion therapy**. In this approach, aversive (unpleasant) experiences are paired with something that was previously experienced as attractive, in hopes of making it unattractive or even repulsive. If a man is attracted to prepubescent girls, for example, he is shown pictures of girls or told to masturbate to fantasies of girls, but these pleasant experiences are now paired with something unpleasant, such as the smell of ammonia, or disgusting images.

Another technique, **masturbatory reconditioning**, does not rely on aversive stimuli. A man who is sexually excited by prepubescent girls is instructed to masturbate to fantasies of girls, but then to switch his fantasies to focus on adult women just as orgasm is approaching—in order that images of adult females will become positively conditioned by association with the pleasant experience of orgasm. The hope is that, after many repetitions of such experiences over weeks or months, the man will gradually lose his paraphilic interests and develop sexual arousal to more acceptable targets. This kind of "positive control" has largely replaced aversion therapy because it is less likely to instill negative feelings such as guilt or anger.

Cognitive therapy is aimed at preventing repeat offenses

In **cognitive therapy** (which is often combined with the conditioning treatments just described) the aim is to correct the disordered thinking that the man uses to justify or rationalize his behaviors. For example, the man may believe that his behavior is sexually arousing to his victims or benefits them in some way. In that case, therapy will be aimed at helping him realize that his behavior is harmful, rather than helpful, and will attempt to awaken some empathy toward his victims. In fact, empathy training is one of the most commonly used techniques in the treatment of sex offenders (Morin & Levenson, 2008).

Another approach seeks to remove blockages to normal sexual expression. The therapist will attempt to strengthen the man's social skills, self-esteem, assertiveness, and desire for intimacy. The man may be encouraged to practice interactions with women, including such basic matters as how to behave on a date as well as how to deal with conflicts and jealousy.

In yet another approach, called **relapse prevention therapy**, the offender is trained in how to identify the situations that may trigger a repeat offense and how to avoid or cope with those situations. This may include mental tricks, such as "thought stopping," that interrupt obsessive ideation—"I've got to stop thinking about young girls and focus more on my wife"—as well as very practical issues, such as avoiding locations that offer temptations to offend. These programs also encourage the development of peer relationships that can give the offender a sense of purpose and acceptance. Although aimed primarily at sex offenders, relapse prevention therapy can also be used to treat paraphilias that don't involve criminality or victims but do distress the people who experience them.

behavior therapy   Treatment of mental disorders by training of behavior.

aversion therapy   A form of behavior therapy that attempts to eliminate unwanted desires or behaviors by associating them with some unpleasant experience, such as a noxious smell.

masturbatory reconditioning The attempt to change a person's sexual attractions by control of fantasy content during masturbation.

cognitive therapy   Therapy based on changing a person's beliefs and thought processes.

relapse prevention therapy Therapy aimed at training a person to avoid or cope with situations that trigger the undesirable behavior.

Figure 13.15 **Relapse prevention** Social worker Karen Swearingen leads a discussion in an education group for sex offenders at the Circleville Juvenile Correctional Facility in Ohio.

These various forms of therapy are often conducted in small groups (**Figure 13.15**). Group therapy doesn't just save money: Peer interaction is an important therapeutic tool in itself (Levenson & Macgowan, 2004).

The efficacy of psychological treatments is doubtful

Although some of these therapeutic strategies have been employed, alone or in combination, for several decades, there is surprisingly little evidence that they work, whether "working" is taken to mean curing paraphilic disorders or merely stopping criminal recidivism. Certainly, any number of case studies report on the apparent benefits of the various approaches. But the more rigorous the investigation, the less benefit they demonstrate. Probably the most thorough study was the Sexual Offender Treatment and Evaluation Project (SOTEP), funded by the state of California (Marques et al., 2005). The study began in 1985. Sex offenders were randomly assigned either to be treated with a state-of-the-art intervention program that focused on relapse prevention or to receive no treatment. Individual offenders were treated for many years, both during and after incarceration. Follow-ups continued until 2005. The outcome: Offenders who participated in the program were just as likely to reoffend as were offenders who dropped out of the program or never took it.

Considering that many new treatment modalities have been introduced over the last several decades, we might expect treatment outcomes to have improved, but that is not the case: Outcomes of recent studies are no better than those of studies published a generation or more ago (Camilleri & Quinsey, 2008). "We now have a 50-year history of such treatments," wrote two leading experts, "and it is entirely reasonable to ask: What have we got to show for it? The answer, sadly, is very little" (Laws & O'Donohue, 2008). Regarding child molesters, a recent review found only very weak evidence for the effectiveness of any program in reducing recidivism (Langstrom et al., 2013).

That's not to say that psychologists and criminologists have given up hope for effective treatments. One approach focuses on helping the person implement a meaningful plan based on the **Good Lives model** while living in the community (Good Lives Model, 2014). This plan is the collection of skills and knowledge that enable him to attain "primary human goods": life, health, knowledge, excellence in work and play, autonomy, inner peace, friendship, and spirituality. In a related approach, known as **Circles of Support and Accountability** (**COSA**), a group of community volunteers pledges to help a sex offender follow principles similar to those of the Good Lives model. This approach was pioneered in Canada, and it has spread to several U.S. states and to Britain (Circles UK, 2014; Wilson, 2014). It is too early to make any definitive judgment about the effectiveness of these programs; nevertheless, one study reported that a Canadian COSA program reduced sexual reoffending by as much as 83% compared with matched offenders who didn't participate in the program (Wilson et al., 2009).

Drug treatments interact with neurotransmitters or hormones

As an alternative to psychological interventions, or in combination with them, many researchers and clinicians have turned to drug treatments. One class of drugs that has been widely used is that of **selective serotonin reuptake inhibitors** (**SSRIs**),

Good Lives model A form of therapy for sex offenders that focuses on improving the subject's ability to achieve a broad range of life goals.

Circles of Support and Accountability (COSA) A program of community support for released sex offenders.

selective serotonin reuptake inhibitors (SSRIs) A class of drugs, including antidepressants such as Prozac and Lexapro, that depress sexual function.

which are antidepressants like Prozac. These drugs affect the activity of two neurotransmitters, serotonin and dopamine, in the brain. For reasons not well understood, they tend to lower a person's interest in sex. Although this is a bothersome side effect when these drugs are given to treat depression, it is helpful in lowering the sex drive of men with paraphilic disorders. In addition, these drugs tend to relieve obsessive-compulsive conditions, which, as mentioned above, often contribute to paraphilias. SSRIs are used in the treatment of the less severe paraphilic offenders, such as exhibitionists. Although they are widely believed to be helpful, their efficacy has not yet been documented in controlled trials (Thibaut et al., 2010).

A more radical pharmaceutical approach is to interfere with the production or action of testosterone, the principal hormonal driver of male sexuality (**Figure 13.16**). One drug used for this purpose is Depo-Provera. As described in Chapter 9, Depo-Provera is a synthetic injectable progestin that is used as a long-term contraceptive in women. In men Depo-Provera depresses the secretion of GnRH by the hypothalamus, which results in a steep decline in testosterone secretion by the testes (see Chapter 3). The end result is a profound drop in testosterone levels and a concomitant reduction in sexual desires and behaviors. Leuprolide (Lupron), a drug we mentioned in Chapter 10 in connection with the treatment of precocious puberty, produces similar results. Yet another drug, cyproterone acetate, blocks testosterone receptors, thus making the body and brain insensitive to the hormone.

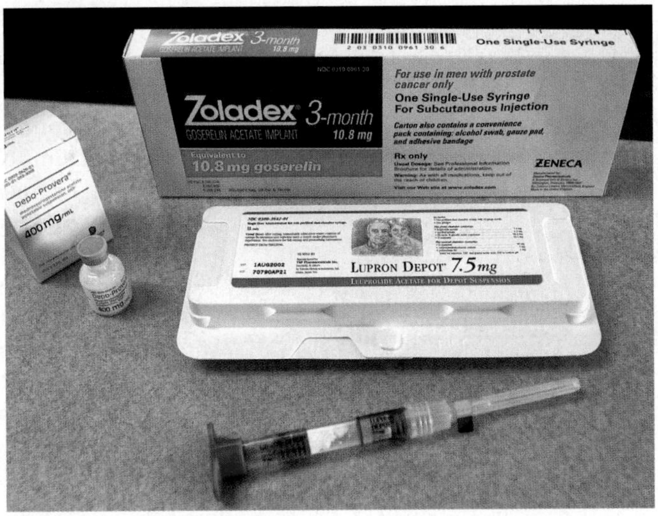

Figure 13.16 Drugs used to treat sex offenders include the injectable progestin Depo-Provera and the GnRH blockers Lupron and Zoladex.

Use of these drugs to prevent the expression of paraphilic behavior—an approach sometimes referred to as "chemical castration"*—is far from ideal. The drugs do not cure paraphilic disorders in the sense of redirecting sex offenders' sexual desires into more acceptable channels; they simply decrease sexual desire and arousal generally. Still, they are often effective in eliminating criminal sexual behavior over periods of many years (Thibaut et al., 2010).

Some states, such as California and Louisiana, have mandated Depo-Provera treatment for serious or recidivist sex offenders. These laws raise ethical and practical problems and are sometimes counterproductive because they may prevent therapists from trying other forms of treatment.

Castration is a treatment of last resort

Surgical castration (removal of the testicles) removes a man's main source of androgens, including testosterone. The surgery is followed by a rapid drop in circulating androgen levels and a slower, somewhat variable decline in sexual desires and behaviors, including physiological responses such as erection and ejaculation (Zverina et al., 1990). Castration may be more effective than other treatments for the prevention of sexual recidivism (Weinberger et al., 2005). A very small number of repeat offenders have opted for castration and have subsequently been released into the community. However, there is a serious question about whether such a choice is truly voluntary if the price of refusal is lifelong detention. This issue, as well as a long history of forced sterilizations in the early 20th-century United States (Dowbiggin, 2003), has made the "voluntary" castration of sex offenders a distasteful notion to many Americans.

---

* We do not particularly like this term because, unlike surgical castration, drug treatment is reversible.

Few "Kinks" Are Disorders

Because the previous few sections have dealt with serious sexual disorders or crimes, we need to reinforce what we said at the beginning of the chapter: Most unconventional or uncommon forms of sexual desire and behavior are neither disorders nor crimes, but simply examples of human diversity. Sex researchers and psychiatrists have tended to medicalize this diversity, for example by giving each uncommon form of sexual expression a Greek-sounding name, akin to a medical diagnosis: podophilia (foot fetishism), katoptronophilia (arousal from sexual activity observed in mirrors), klismaphilia (arousal from the administration of enemas), and so on. These terms are sometimes useful for their specificity, but more commonly they create an unjustified aura of scientific understanding. Even the word "paraphilia" serves little real purpose, now that *DSM-5* has redefined it to mean any uncommon form of sexual expression. The colloquial term "kink" is more readily understood and carries no implication of sickness.

Go to the
**Discovering
Human Sexuality**
Companion Website at
**sites.sinauer.com/
discoveringhumansexuality3e**
for activities, study questions,
quizzes, and other study aids.

Summary

- Most variations in sexual desire and behavior are not mental disorders but represent minority interests or a means of adding excitement to sexual relationships.

- Fetishism is sexual arousal by objects, materials, or body parts. Transvestic fetishists are sexually aroused by cross-dressing, but not all cross-dressers are fetishists—others may cross-dress for practical reasons, for entertainment purposes, or as an expression of a transgender identity.

- Bondage/dominance and sadomasochism (collectively known as BDSM) involve sexual arousal by the infliction or receipt of humiliation, degradation, or physical pain. BDSM practices generally take place in safe, consensual settings.

- The boundary between normal and abnormal sexuality is imprecise and subjective and is defined socially as well as medically. According to the American Psychiatric Association, paraphilias are uncommon sexual desires or behaviors; those paraphilias that cause significant distress, social dysfunction, or harm to others are called paraphilic disorders. Paraphilic behaviors directed at nonconsenting persons are illegal.

- In general, paraphilias are extensions or exaggerations of normal sexual feelings or behaviors. Far more men than women have paraphilias. It is common for a person to develop multiple paraphilias over time. Persons with paraphilic disorders who commit sex offenses may have psychological problems and deficient social skills, and some have suffered child abuse, but others have ordinary personalities and histories.

- Exhibitionists are sexually aroused by exposing their genitals to others (usually women) in public places. Making obscene phone calls is a variation on exhibitionism. Voyeurs spy on women who are undressed or engaged in sex. Frotteurs make body contact with women in crowds.

- Pedophiles are sexually attracted to prepubescent children more than to adults. Pedophiles and child molesters are overlapping but nonidentical groups. Most pedophiles are attracted to children of one sex more than the other. Hebephiles are aroused by pubescent children. Children are sometimes molested by adults with fiduciary responsibilities toward them, such as Catholic priests, teachers, and scout leaders. There are organizations that aim to help minor-attracted adults avoid sexual contacts with children.

- Zoophiles are aroused by sexual contact with animals. Necrophiles are aroused by dead bodies. Autoerotic asphyxia is often combined with BDSM elements; it is a highly dangerous practice.

- Although rape is not in itself a paraphilic disorder, the commission of violent sexual acts is considered paraphilic if the perpetrator experiences the violence itself as sexually arousing. Paraphilic sadism has motivated many notorious serial killers.

- Recidivism—the tendency for criminals to repeat their offenses—is lower among sex offenders than among many other kinds of offenders. Certain factors, such as antisocial personality disorder or a history of violence, are associated with an increased likelihood of recidivism.

- A variety of theories attempt to explain paraphilias. Biological theories attribute paraphilias to neurological or genetic disturbance. Behavioral theories see them as the result of distorted learning processes or as the result of a blockage of normal sexual expression. It has also been suggested that paraphilic disorders result from the disintegration of the normal behavioral sequence of courtship (courtship disorder). In some cases—but not all—the experience of abuse during childhood can be the trigger for the abuse of others in later life.

- The various theories of paraphilia have led to diverse forms of treatment. Behavioral approaches, such as aversion therapy, attempt to help people unlearn their paraphilias and acquire more conventional sexual desires. Psychotherapeutic approaches include cognitive therapy, which attempts to correct paraphilic thinking; social skills training programs, which encourage normal communication with women; and relapse prevention programs, which help sex offenders identify and avoid situations in which they are likely to reoffend. There is little evidence that any of these methods are successful in preventing recidivism.

- Biological approaches to treatment include the use of drugs that reduce testosterone levels or block testosterone's effects, as well as selective serotonin reuptake inhibitors. The drugs appear to be quite effective but can have serious side effects. Castration is an effective but rarely used method of preventing recidivism by men who commit repeated, serious sex crimes.

Discussion Questions

1. Do you think society should place any legal restrictions on the expression of noncoercive sex practices (e.g., those undertaken as a solo activity or with a consenting partner)? Give a rationale for your point of view.

2. People with paraphilias often find it very difficult to give them up. Compare the advantages and disadvantages of various treatments (e.g., psychotherapy, behavior therapy, drug therapy).

3. Strippers may exhibit their genitals. Are they exhibitionists?

4. If you were confronted by an exhibitionist who exposed himself, what would you do? Why?

5. A pedophile who has been arrested for molesting a child argues that he has a sexual compulsion that he cannot resist. Do you think treatment should be legally mandated? Which treatments do you think would be best for him, and why?

6. The Catholic Church has faced an ongoing controversy over reports that priests have had sexual contacts with minors. In several cases the priests received counseling and were moved to another parish, where they repeated their behavior. Take a position on what an institution (e.g., religious or educational) should do about reports of child molestation. Should the institution handle the accusation itself, or should it turn the matter over to the police? If the reports of molestation are accurate, how should the perpetrators be treated? What should be done to prevent further incidents?

7. Imagine that you're a therapist who is counseling a couple. The woman has caught the man cross-dressing. What questions would you ask him to find out what's really going on and whether he has a paraphilia? How would you advise the couple?

8. How would you respond if you learned that a sex offender had moved into your neighborhood? How can public safety be balanced against the right of someone who has "served his time" to get on with his life?

Web Resources

American Professional Society on the Abuse of Children **www.apsac.org**

Association for the Treatment of Sexual Abusers **www.atsa.com**

Tri-Ess (organization for heterosexual cross-dressers) **www.tri-ess.org**

United States Department of Justice. Dru Sjodin National Sex Offender Public Website **www.nsopw.gov**

Recommended Reading

Bering, J. (2013). *Perv: The sexual deviant in all of us*. Scientific American.

De Sade, Marquis. (1966). *The 120 days of Sodom, and other writings* (R. Seaver & A. Wainhouse, Trans.). Grove. (Original work written in 1785 and published in 1904.)

Dekkers, M. (1994). *Dearest pet: On bestiality*. Norton.

Gates, K. (2000). *Deviant desires: Incredibly strange sex*. Juno.

Largier, N. (2007). *In praise of the whip: A cultural history of arousal*. Zone Books.

Laws, D. R. & O'Donohue, W. T. (Eds.). (2008). *Sexual deviance: Theory, assessment, and treatment* (2nd ed.). Guilford.

Newmahr, S. (2011). *Playing on the edge: Sadomasochism, risk, and intimacy*. Indiana University Press.

Ortmann, D. M. & Sprott, R. (2012). *Sexual outsiders: Understanding BDSM sexualities and communities*. Rowman & Littlefield.

Sacher-Masoch, L. v. (2000). *Venus in furs*. Viking Penguin. (Full text available online at www.gutenberg.org/ebooks/6852.) (Original work published in 1870.)

Seto, M.C. (2013). *Internet sex offenders*. American Psychological Association.

Smith, M. (2014). *The erotic doll: A modern fetish*. Yale University Press.

Terry, K. J. (2012). *Sexual offenses and offenders* (2nd ed.). Cengage Learning.

Weiss, M. (2011). *Techniques of pleasure: BDSM and the circuits of sexuality*. Duke University Press.

Chapter 14

In a form of sex therapy known as sensate focus, the partners take turns giving and receiving intimate touch.

Sexual Disorders

We turn now from uncommon forms of sexual expression to common problems that can interfere with any kind of sexual relationship. A number of mental and physical conditions can impair sexual interest or arousal or make sexual interactions painful or unrewarding. Most of these conditions are deficiencies, such as a lack of interest in sex or a difficulty with erection, lubrication, or orgasm. Some, however, represent overexcitable states, such as premature ejaculation and excessive sexual behavior. Either way, these problems are common. For the most part, they are more readily treatable than the paraphilic disorders discussed in Chapter 13. The major factor impeding their successful treatment is people's reluctance to discuss sexual problems openly with their partners or to seek appropriate professional advice and therapy.

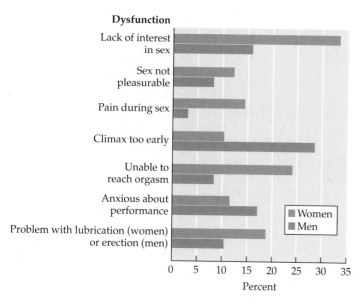

Dysfunction

Lack of interest in sex
Sex not pleasurable
Pain during sex
Climax too early
Unable to reach orgasm
Anxious about performance
Problem with lubrication (women) or erection (men)

■ Women
■ Men

0 5 10 15 20 25 30 35
Percent

Figure 14.1 Sex differences in the prevalence of sexual disorders This bar graph refers only to people age 18–59, the ages that were surveyed. (Data from Laumann et al., 2000.)

Sexual Disorders Are Common

Large numbers of women and men have problems with some aspect of sexual function, according to surveys by sociologist Ed Laumann and his colleagues at the University of Chicago (Laumann et al., 2009). The problems most commonly reported are a lack of interest in sex, a lack of pleasure in sex, pain during sex, problems with erection or lubrication, inability to reach orgasm, climaxing too early, and anxiety about sexual performance. The percentages of the population who acknowledge experiencing these problems range from a low of 3% (men who experience pain during sex) to a high of 30% or 40% (women who lack sexual desire) (Shifren et al., 2008; Laumann et al., 2009).

According to the 5th edition of the *Diagnostic and Statistical Manual of Mental Disorders* (*DSM-5*), a sexual difficulty must occur at least 75% of the time and over a period of at least 6 months to qualify as a "disorder." Of course these criteria are fairly arbitrary. What's important to know is that sexual difficulties can usually be alleviated, by psychological treatment, drug therapy, or some combination of the two (Fruhauf et al., 2013; Schmidt et al., 2014). This chapter can offer only a very brief survey of the field, but excellent books (see Recommended Reading at the end of this chapter) and professional sex therapists are available to help women and men surmount sexual problems and develop (or return to) an active and rewarding sex life.

Men's and women's sexual problems differ

Men and women tend to experience different kinds of sexual problems (**Figure 14.1**). The leading problems for women are a lack of interest in sex, an inability to experience orgasm, problems with physiological arousal (especially vaginal lubrication), and pain during sex. For men, climaxing too early (premature ejaculation) is the leading problem, followed by anxiety about performance and a lack of interest in sex. Studies of people who seek professional help for sexual problems echo this kind of distinction (**Figure 14.2**). This is how Sandra Leiblum (1943–2010), a leading authority on sex therapy, summarized the distinction: "Men are typically motivated to seek treatment for *problems with sexual performance....* In contrast, women often enter treatment expressing *concerns about sexual feelings....*" (Leiblum, 2007).

We should emphasize right away, though, that these stereotypical differences mask a lot of overlap and commonality between the problems encountered by the two sexes. Some performance issues, such as difficulty experiencing orgasm, are quite common among women, and some men are troubled by a lack of interest in sex, especially as they age.

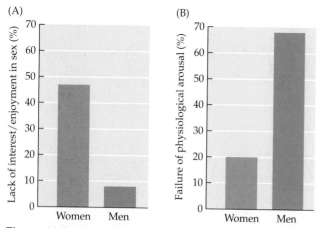

(A)
Lack of interest / enjoyment in sex (%)
70
60
50
40
30
20
10
0
Women Men

(B)
Failure of physiological arousal (%)
70
60
50
40
30
20
10
0
Women Men

Figure 14.2 Sex differences in a clinical population The bar graphs show the percentages of 533 men and 577 women attending a sexual problems clinic who complained of (A) lack of interest/enjoyment in sex and (B) failure of physiological arousal. (Data from Warner & Bancroft, 1987.)

A multidisciplinary approach to treatment is preferred

A person suffering from a sexual disorder may visit a family doctor, a psychotherapist, or some other nonspecialist provider. Sometimes these professionals resolve the problem satisfactorily: For example, a family doctor might write a prescription for a drug that successfully treats a man's erectile disorder, or a therapist might help a person work through relationship difficulties that are interfering with sexual pleasure.

Commonly, though, sexual problems are complex and multifaceted. In this case the person or couple who has the problem may benefit from the combined insights of a group of experts—experts who focus on sexual disorders from different perspectives. Among these experts might be a clinical psychologist or psychotherapist who specializes in sexual problems (often called a **sex therapist**), a physician who treats genital or hormonal disorders, and a physiotherapist who can give instruction on Kegel exercises (described later in the chapter) and other methods of improving genital function. When several such experts work together in a sexual disorders clinic (which may be a freestanding private practice or a department in a hospital or medical school), they are in the best position to identify useful lines of therapy.

Although many different kinds of treatments may be offered to persons with sexual disorders, as described in various sections of this chapter, sex therapists commonly use a standard core of therapeutic techniques as a basis to treat a variety of sexual problems. One example is the set of exercises known as **sensate focus**, described in **Box 14.1**.

In Box 6.5 (page 182) we gave an account of a paralyzed man's session with a sex surrogate. Sex surrogates don't just work with disabled people, however: In collaboration with sex therapists, surrogates can help anyone with sexual difficulties—especially those who currently lack partners. Although sex surrogates are not officially licensed, many are professionally trained and certified (International Professional Surrogates Association, 2014).

Sexual disorders can be primary, secondary, or situational. A **primary disorder** is lifelong. A **secondary disorder** is one that appears after some period of normal function. A **situational disorder** is one that appears in some circumstances but not in others.

Sex therapists may recommend a combination of psychotherapy, sexual exercises, and drugs to alleviate sexual problems. Success is most likely when both partners participate in therapy.

Premature Ejaculation Is Men's Number One Sex Problem

Premature ejaculation (sometimes called rapid or early ejaculation) is ejaculation that occurs before the man wants it to (Jannini et al., 2012). If the man's intention is to engage in coitus, he might ejaculate before he can place his penis in the woman's vagina, at the moment he does so, or quickly thereafter. Some authorities give a particular cutoff time for a definition of premature ejaculation: 1 minute after onset of coitus is a widely used criterion (International Society for Sexual Medicine, 2010). Still, it's really the distress caused by the problem, more than the precise timing, that is relevant. Premature ejaculation must be a persistent problem, not just an occasional phenomenon, to merit a diagnosis.

Many young people (both male and female) think that a healthy man should be able to continue coital thrusting without ejaculation for as long as he wishes, and that any man who cannot do so has a sexual disorder (Wincze, 2009). This is not the case, however: Whether they want to or not, most healthy men will ejaculate after a very few minutes of thrusting: 2 to 8 minutes is the typical range, and 5 minutes is the average (Rowland et al., 2010). This information alone may "cure" quite a few cases of supposed premature ejaculation.

sex therapist   A person who treats sexual disorders, usually by means of psychotherapy and sexual exercises.

sensate focus   A form of sex therapy that involves graduated touching exercises.

primary disorder   A disorder that is not preceded by any period of healthy function.

secondary disorder   A disorder that follows some period of healthy function.

situational disorder   A disorder that appears only in certain circumstances.

premature ejaculation   Ejaculation before the man wishes, often immediately on commencement of coitus. Also called *rapid ejaculation*.

Box 14.1 Sexual Health

Sensate Focus

Sensate focus is a set of touching exercises for couples who want to build closer intimacy and overcome sexual difficulties in their relationship (see figure). As the name implies, these exercises involve focusing on the physical sensations of gently touching and being touched, to the exclusion of other thoughts. The couple could be you and your partner—and that might mean two women, two men, or a woman and a man. For any couple, the procedure is the same (Keesling, 2006; Weiner & Avery-Clark, 2014).

After finding some free time and a quiet place—and turning off your cell phones—you and your partner undress and make yourselves comfortable, perhaps lying face-to-face with partial or full body contact. You may spend the first 5 minutes or so simply focusing on relaxed breathing. Then with your free hand you (the toucher) gently caress a nonerogenous zone of your partner (the "touchee"), such as the back. You can use your bare fingers or, if it feels good, some kind of massage oil. But we're not talking massage here: The motions should be gentle caresses, barely indenting the skin, if at all, and slow, slow, slow. If in doubt, go slower.

Focus your mind on what your fingertips are feeling as your partner's skin drifts slowly by. At first, probably, you will experience intrusive thoughts—sometimes anxious ones, such as "This is weird" or "Am I going at the right speed?"or "Is my partner enjoying this?" or "Is it time to switch roles yet?" These thoughts, and all the other anxieties that may be interfering with your sex life, will gradually recede and disappear as you consciously bring your attention back to the sensations at your fingertips. You are doing this for your own pleasure, not your partner's.

After an agreed-on period of time, such as 10 or 15 minutes, you and your partner exchange roles. As the touchee, your role is not to provide a running commentary. (No "Ahh, that feels good!" or "A little lower down please.") Instead, you just lie there, muscles relaxed, breathing relaxed, and focus on the movement of your partner's fingers and the pleasurable sensations they afford you. Again, in time this consciously willed focus becomes easier to maintain and causes intrusive or anxious thoughts to fade away. It's just two people individually experiencing the pleasure of the moment, but a pleasure that is generated by a shared activity. You may or may not become genitally aroused—it doesn't matter. If you do become genitally aroused, however, don't switch the agenda to regular sex, because that will invite any problems and anxieties that are interfering with your sex life to come flooding back.

In sensate-focus exercises, one partner is pleasured by the other but lets go of any responsibility to reciprocate.

At the end of the session, spend a few minutes discussing what transpired. Tell your partner honestly how you felt, even if it was unpleasurable or created anxiety for you for some or all of the time. Now is the time, if you wish, to tell your partner how his or her touch might be made more pleasurable for you on future occasions.

If you are doing sensate-focus exercises under the guidance of a sex therapist, at your next meeting with the therapist you will discuss what transpired. She or he will probably suggest that you repeat the exercise several times until you and your partner are completely comfortable with it. Then, the therapist will suggest that you graduate to another region of the body. The sessions will be organized in a sequence, beginning with nonerogenous zones (perhaps the head and shoulders, with both partners fully dressed), and progressing to naked caressing of the back, the front, and then the genitals, over a period of a few weeks. The genital sessions may start with manual touch. Later sessions may involve oral sex and/or coitus, or perhaps tribadism or anal sex, depending on what the couple would like to engage in.

Sensate focus is a basic exercise whose purpose is to overcome performance anxiety, "spectatoring," and other distractions that impair many couples' ability to focus on the sheer pleasure of sexual interactions. Depending on the particular difficulty that an individual or a couple is experiencing, more specific exercises are available. If you feel that you could benefit from sensate-focus or other exercises but don't want to consult a therapist, we suggest you read one of the books that covers these topics in detail (see Recommended Reading at the end of this chapter).

There are different kinds of premature ejaculation

Premature ejaculation can be a primary, secondary, or situational disorder. As an example of the last of these, premature ejaculation might occur during partnered sex but not during masturbation. The following two vignettes (Althof, 2007) illustrate some of this diversity:

> *John, a 6-foot-2-inch, well-muscled, 30-year-old, never-married police officer sought consultation because he had developed rapid ejaculation with his new partner of 6 weeks. John prided himself on his masculinity and said that he could not understand why this was happening to him now. There was a bragging quality to John as he detailed his sexual history. . . . The essential question in my mind was what was different now. With some embarrassment John revealed that he was intimidated by Kim. She was a beautiful, successful woman, the CEO for a small corporation, and he felt "dominated" by her. I asked whether he had ever been in a relationship with any other woman where he felt dominated. At first he said no, and then he laughed and recalled that many years ago there was such a woman and yes, he also suffered from rapid ejaculation with her.*

> *Jim, a 58-year-old businessman in his second marriage, typifies men with lifelong rapid ejaculation. He described never being able to last more than 15 seconds with any sexual partner. He had tried masturbating prior to lovemaking and tried to distract himself with nonsexual thoughts. He had read books about premature ejaculation and diligently practiced the exercises, to no avail. This "disability" was a great source of shame for him, and he felt that it had greatly interfered in his relationships prior to marriage and in both of his marriages. His wife, Claire, was supportive and praised Jim for going "all out to please her after his orgasm." They appeared to have a good relationship, and neither partner had significant psychological problems.*

The causes of premature ejaculation are not well understood. The traditional view, espoused by Masters and Johnson, was that it results from learning. They suggested that a man whose early sexual experiences are conducted in haste and anxiety (perhaps in the backseat of a car or in the parents' family room) might become conditioned to reaching orgasm very quickly (Masters & Johnson, 1970). Another hypothesis, based on animal research as well as pharmaceutical studies in humans, is that lifelong premature ejaculation is caused by a dysfunction in certain receptors for the neurotransmitter serotonin (Waldinger, 2004). Psychological theories seem most plausible in cases where premature ejaculation is situational (as with John in the first vignette above), while biological theories may account better for lifelong premature ejaculation that affects a man in all circumstances (as with Jim in the second vignette).

A man who suffers from premature ejaculation may try various kinds of self-devised remedies for his condition. These include masturbating to orgasm prior to partnered sex, distracting himself during sex with irrelevant thoughts (such as doing mental arithmetic or imagining having sex with a person he's not attracted to), or trying to bring his partner as close to orgasm as possible prior to coitus. Such remedies rarely work and, worse, they often prevent the man or his partner from having a rewarding sexual experience. When he finally sees a doctor or therapist, he is often close to despair, and his relationship, if he has one, may be on the rocks.

The clinician's first task is to reassure the man that he is not a sexual failure and that premature ejaculation is a common condition that can usually be successfully treated. The mainstays of treatment are sex therapy and drugs: The combination of both is often the most effective approach (Althof, 2007).

Sex therapy may help men to regulate excitation

stop-start method A sex therapy technique for the treatment of premature ejaculation that involves alternating between stimulating and not stimulating the penis.

One aspect of sex therapy is simply talking through the history of the man's condition and the factors that may exacerbate it. In the first vignette above, for example, it quickly became clear that interpersonal dynamics lay behind John's premature ejaculation—specifically, the power relationship between John and his partners—and this became the focus of discussion. In other cases, it may be useful to concentrate on cognitive distortions. These distortions can range from discounting the positive ("My partner says she is satisfied because she doesn't want to hurt my feelings") to all-or-nothing thinking ("I am a complete failure because I come quickly") or catastrophizing ("If I fail tonight, my girlfriend will dump me") (Althof, 2007).

Sex therapy exercises may be very useful. These often include the same sensate-focus exercises already described. In addition, there are exercises specifically designed for premature ejaculation. One example is the **stop-start method**:

- Initially, the man masturbates alone, bringing himself to a medium level of excitement. (He may be taught to think about sexual arousal on a 10-point scale, 10 being orgasm, and to focus on staying in the 5- to 7-point range.) He learns to recognize what the 8- and 9-point levels feel like and then stops masturbating to avoid such high levels of arousal. This is repeated a few times, until he is finally allowed to masturbate to orgasm. He does these exercises several times a week for several weeks, with the goal of being able to stimulate his penis for 15 minutes without ejaculating.

- In the next stage, the man and his partner are together, in a position such as that shown in **Figure 14.3A**. She (assuming it's a woman) stimulates his penis by hand or orally, but he asks her to stop before he climaxes. Masters and Johnson recommended that the partner firmly pinch or squeeze the man's penis, just below the glans, at the time that stimulation ceases, as a means of reducing his arousal (**Figure 14.3B**). Again, the goal is to be able to experience sexual stimulation for 15 minutes without ejaculation.

- The third stage progresses to coitus. The woman simply places the man's penis in her vagina, and the couple lies still for a prolonged period. The

(A)

(B)

Figure 14.3 Sex therapy exercises for premature ejaculation Position of a couple for "stop-start" exercises directed at premature ejaculation. (A) The man lies on his back with his legs apart. His partner lies to one side and partly astride him, so that she can manually or orally stimulate his genitals. (B) The "squeeze technique" for premature ejaculation. When the man is close to orgasm, he communicates this fact to his partner with a prearranged signal. (Some couples do this with random timing.) The partner then grasps the man's penis with a thumb on the frenulum and squeezes firmly for a few seconds. This diminishes the man's urge to ejaculate and possibly causes a partial loss of his erection.

idea is that the man gets accustomed to the sensations of coitus without being too excited. Then the woman begins to move slowly, but the man tells her to stop whenever he nears orgasm. The woman can apply the squeeze technique in this situation too, as necessary. She can squeeze the base of his penis when it is still partially inserted in her vagina. After several repetitions, the man is allowed to ejaculate. As the exercises proceed, the man should be able to postpone his ejaculation for a longer and longer time.

According to sex therapist Barbara Keesling, the squeeze technique for genital arousal may be counterproductive and difficult to incorporate into real-life lovemaking. Instead, Keesling emphasizes the teaching of relaxation, especially relaxation of the pelvic floor muscles, along with conscious awareness of arousal (Keesling, 2006).

How helpful is sex therapy to men with premature ejaculation? Masters and Johnson claimed success rates of over 90%, even at 5 years after treatment, but more recent studies have come up with far less positive findings: Up to 75% of men or couples experience treatment failure or an initial improvement followed by a relapse (Althof, 2007). Specialists often recommend various methods to prevent relapses, such as repeating the initial exercises periodically and having regular follow-up visits with the therapist.

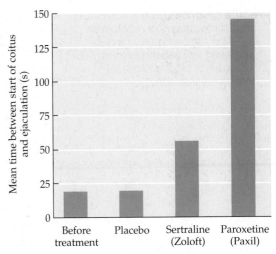

Figure 14.4 Drug treatment for premature ejaculation Effect of 6 weeks of treatment with a placebo or one of two SSRIs. (Data from Waldinger et al., 2001.)

Drug treatment may be effective

The drugs used to treat premature ejaculation are mostly selective serotonin reuptake inhibitors (SSRIs—antidepressants such as Prozac, Paxil, and Zoloft). Of the SSRIs that are currently available in the United States, paroxetine (Paxil) may be the most effective (Waldinger & Olivier, 2004). In one randomized, double-blind study of men with severe premature ejaculation, a 6-week course of Paxil increased the time between commencement of coitus and ejaculation from about 20 seconds to 2.5 minutes (**Figure 14.4**), whereas the placebo had no effect at all.

A new short-acting SSRI, Priligy (dapoxetine), has been developed specifically for treatment of premature ejaculation: It is taken as needed 1 to 2 hours before a sexual encounter. Several double-blind studies have found it to be efficacious and safe, though it does have a range of potential side effects (McMahon et al., 2011). Dapoxetine has been approved for use in several European countries and may be approved in the United States during the lifetime of this book's current edition.

Topical anesthetics, in the form of a cream applied to the penis, can also be used to reduce sensitivity. This method is moderately effective in slowing ejaculation, but unless a condom is used, the anesthetic may also numb the woman's vulva and vagina, impeding her ability to reach orgasm (Rowland et al., 2010).

There Are Multiple Causes for Delayed Ejaculation

Delayed (or absent) **ejaculation** is the opposite of premature ejaculation: The man can reach the point of ejaculation only with difficulty or not at all (Perelman, 2013). Sometimes delayed ejaculation is specific to a certain kind of sexual behavior, such as coitus or partnered sex generally; in other cases the man may not be able to reach orgasm under any circumstances. Either way, it is a fairly uncommon problem: Estimates of its prevalence range from less than 3% to about 8% of the male population (Hartmann & Waldinger, 2007). As with premature ejaculation, delayed ejaculation can be a lifelong problem or it may be acquired at some point in adult life.

The cause or causes of delayed ejaculation are not certain. One idea is that it affects men who have become accustomed since adolescence to frequent, lengthy mastur-

delayed ejaculation Difficulty achieving or inability to achieve orgasm and/or ejaculation. Also called *male orgasmic disorder*.

erectile disorder (ED) A persistent inability to achieve or maintain an erection sufficient to accomplish a desired sexual behavior such as coitus to orgasm. Also called *erectile dysfunction*.

bation using a tight grip and vigorous strokes, or who masturbate by rubbing their penis against bedding or rough surfaces. According to Barbara Keesling, this leaves men insensitive to the more gentle stimulation that is likely to be experienced during coitus (Keesling, 2006). This interpretation is contested by others, who argue that these men masturbate often and vigorously *because* they have such difficulty experiencing orgasm any other way (Hartmann & Waldinger, 2007). Alternatively, too much viewing of pornography could be the cause. It should be possible to correct either of these problems by changing the man's habits. Sometimes stopping masturbation for a few weeks makes it easier for a man to reach orgasm during partnered sex.

Other models suggest that sexual shame, inculcated during upbringing, leads to an inhibition of the orgasmic process, or that the root cause is a lack of sexual desire. In either of these cases, more in-depth psychotherapy would be needed to identify and correct the problem. Delayed ejaculation can also follow some traumatic life event, such as a relationship crisis. Or perhaps the man's thought processes during sex are so distracting or negative that they interfere with sexual arousal.

Delayed ejaculation can have biological causes, such as neurological damage. It can also result from the use of certain drugs, including antihypertensive drugs, major tranquilizers, and antidepressants. If it is caused by drugs, delayed ejaculation can usually be treated by switching to a different drug or by adding a second drug that counteracts this side effect. For example, delayed ejaculation caused by SSRIs is often successfully treated by adding or substituting the non-SSRI antidepressant bupropion (Wellbutrin).

There is no drug treatment for lifelong delayed ejaculation. Sometimes the use of a vibrator and lubricant jelly helps (Wincze, 2009). If the man can reach orgasm through masturbation but not with his partner, he may be encouraged to do exercises in which his partner is gradually incorporated into his masturbatory activities.

A few men have no difficulty reaching orgasm but never ejaculate. This is most likely a neurological problem. Even if the condition cannot be corrected, such men can usually become fathers via medically induced orgasm (using vibratory or electrical stimulation) or by harvesting sperm directly from the testes.

Erectile Disorder Has Many Causes and Treatments

Erectile disorder (**ED**) (also called erectile dysfunction) is a recurrent inability to achieve an adequate penile erection or to maintain it through the course of the desired sexual behavior—if such inability causes distress to the man or difficulty between the man and his partner (Shamloul & Ghanem, 2013). The condition may be partial or complete, and it may be a primary, secondary, or situational disorder. Although ED can certainly occur in young men, it becomes much more common as men age. In fact, it affects about one-half of all men over the age of 60 and the majority of men who are 70 or older. Nevertheless, younger men are more likely to be severely distressed by erectile disorder and are more likely to seek treatment.

Erectile disorder can have physical or psychological causes

A great variety of factors can cause or contribute to ED, ranging from entirely physical factors to entirely psychological ones (Glina et al., 2013). Here are some of the chief villains:

Smoking, alcohol use, and obesity all increase the risk of erectile disorder.

- *Behavioral/lifestyle factors.* These include smoking (which doubles the risk of erectile disorder), chronic alcohol abuse, obesity, and lack of exercise. Extended bicycle riding is also a risk factor on account of potential damage to nerves and blood vessels supplying the penis (Sommer et al., 2010).
- *Medical conditions.* These include diabetes, hypertension, atherosclerosis ("hardening of the arteries"), and prostate surgery.
- *Drugs.* These include certain tranquilizers, diuretics, antidepressants, and some recreational drugs. The drug finasteride (Propecia, used for male pattern hair loss, or Proscar, used for enlarged prostate) is thought to cause erectile dysfunction and loss of libido in some men (Traish et al., 2011).
- *Injuries.* These include spinal cord injury, injury to the nerves and blood vessels that supply the penis, and injury to the penis itself.
- *Psychological factors.* These include performance anxiety, distraction, inadequate stimulation, relationship difficulties, stress, and depression.
- *Developmental issues.* These include childhood trauma, sexual orientation issues, and religious taboos.

Older men are less likely than younger men to achieve erections by purely psychological means, such as by anticipation of a sexual encounter or viewing a naked partner; they are more likely to require direct physical stimulation of the penis.

Often, erectile disorder results from an interplay of physical and psychological factors, which reinforce each other and need to be disentangled (Goldstein, 2000; Rosen, 2007). For example, a middle-aged man may notice on some occasion that his penis doesn't become erect as fast as he expected. This may be part of the normal physiological aging process, compounded by some circumstance such as tiredness or alcohol use. But the next time he has sex, the memory of that event may cause him to fear that he will embarrass himself, that he will fail to satisfy his partner, or that he will cause his partner to think that he has lost interest in her or him. These anxieties may then make his erectile difficulties worse by distracting him from the pleasure of sex, thus triggering a downward spiral of dysfunction.

Simple measures may alleviate the problem

Sometimes the cause of ED can be removed rather simply. If the problem is caused by a prescription drug, for example, it may be possible to substitute another drug that does not have the same side effect. Lifestyle changes such as quitting smoking, reducing alcohol consumption or drug use, losing weight (if the patient is obese), and beginning an exercise program may alleviate erectile difficulties. Regarding bicycling, genital numbness during rides should be a warning to take more frequent breaks, make adjustments to one's position on the bike, or try a different seat (Dettori et al., 2004).

If the man can develop an erection but loses it during sex, he may be able to maintain the erection for a longer period simply by placing a constricting elastic band ("cock ring") around the penis after the erection has developed. (The ring should be taken off as soon as it has served its purpose, to avoid damaging the erectile tissue.)

Psychological treatments may be useful

If a man's erectile difficulties appear to result from psychological or relationship issues, he may seek out a sex therapist. One common objective in sex therapy is to reduce anxiety. This may be accomplished by means of sensate-focus exercises, as described in Box 14.1. These exercises are thought to be useful for less severe cases or early stages of erectile disorder. The particular aim will be to help the man enjoy sensual contacts without worrying about whether he has an erection or not. Another approach is cognitive: Here the aim is to overcome misperceptions, such as the idea that a first-class erection and coitus are the be-all and end-all of sex. When the man realizes that he can fully satisfy his partner by means other than coitus, his anxiety may be reduced to the point that his erectile difficulties also decrease. Simply reassuring men that it is normal for the process of erection to take longer as they age can be very helpful.

Even more important may be efforts to resolve relationship problems. These problems may be of various kinds (Rosen, 2007). The man's self-esteem in the relationship may be traumatized by a loss of status, such as may follow loss of a job or development of an illness. His experience of intimacy may be damaged by an extramarital (or extra-pair) relationship or by the birth of a child. His partner's or his own perceived attractiveness may be diminished by aging, obesity, or alcoholism. The impact of these issues on erectile function may be lessened by bringing them out into the open and trying to resolve them in one-on-one psychotherapy, in couples therapy, or even in group therapy. Sex therapy can be combined with drug treatment.

Viagra and similar drugs have become the leading treatments

The introduction of Viagra (sildenafil)* in 1998 revolutionized the treatment of erectile disorder, allowing many cases to be treated successfully by first-line physicians rather than by specialists or sex therapists. Besides Viagra itself there are now three other drugs in the same class: Levitra (vardenafil), Cialis (tadalafil), and Stendra (avanafil). The efficacy of these drugs in improving the quality of life of men with erectile disorder has been well documented in placebo-controlled trials (Ralph et al., 2007), and the men's partners also experience much more satisfying sex lives as a result (Fisher et al., 2005).

Viagra-type drugs work by increasing the responsiveness of the erectile tissue to nitric oxide, the neurotransmitter that is chiefly responsible for penile erection. At the usual doses, these drugs do not cause erection unless the nerves in the penis are releasing some nitric oxide. What this means is that simply swallowing a Viagra tablet does not produce an erection—there has to be sexual excitation as well. And if the nerves are not active—if they have been destroyed in the course of prostate surgery, for example—then Viagra is unlikely to work, no matter how sexually excited the man may feel.

Viagra and the other drugs must not be taken in conjunction with certain other substances, most especially nitrate- or nitrite-containing drugs (drugs prescribed for heart pain or abused as the inhaled recreational drugs "amyl," "rush," or "poppers"). The reason for this is that combining these drugs can cause a life-threatening drop in blood pressure. Nor should they be taken by people who have the eye disease retinitis pigmentosa.

The ED drugs can cause a variety of undesirable side effects, such as headache, facial flushing, or visual disturbances. Cialis is longer-acting than the other drugs—it works for up to 36 hours, and it is also available in a formulation for daily rather than as-needed use. This appeals to many men because it allows for greater spontaneity in sexual activities. In addition, the daily-use formulation alleviates the symptoms of enlarged prostate, which is common in older men with ED. As a result Cialis has become the market leader among Viagra-type drugs. Still, the long duration of Cialis's action means that side effects may also be prolonged: For some men, the price of a happy 10 minutes may be an hours-long headache. If this is a problem, Stendra may be a better choice—it acts within 15 minutes, has a milder side effect profile than Cialis, and is broken down in the body much more quickly (Wang et al., 2014).

Advertising for Viagra, Levitra, and Cialis links the drugs with relatively young, healthy men.

---

* Generic versions of Viagra are available in most countries (but not the United States) at greatly reduced prices.

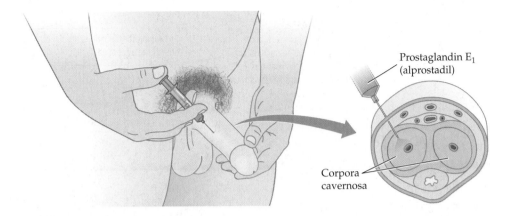

Figure 14.5 Prostaglandin E₁ produces an erection when injected directly into the corpora cavernosa.

Prostaglandin E₁ (alprostadil)

Corpora cavernosa

Do these drugs do anything for men who *don't* have erectile disorder? One study compared the effects of Viagra and an inactive placebo on sexual performance in healthy men (Mondaini et al., 2003). The drug was no different from the placebo in terms of the quality of the men's erections or orgasms, but the men who took Viagra did experience a shorter refractory period after ejaculation before they could develop an erection again. The pornographic video industry is well aware of this effect: Viagra is frequently used by male actors who need to perform several times in the course of a 1-day shoot (Huffstutter & Frammolino, 2001).

Recreational use of drugs like Viagra by young men without erectile dysfunction is fairly common, but we advise against it. In the absence of medical supervision, serious side effects can occur; in addition, recreational users may lose confidence in their ability to perform satisfactorily without the drug (Harte & Meston, 2012).

Some men are not helped by drugs like Viagra, even if their erectile disorder has a clear biological cause. These include men whose penile nerves have been destroyed by prostate surgery, as mentioned above. However, the drug **prostaglandin E₁** produces a very reliable erection in any circumstances, so long as the erectile tissue itself is still intact. This drug has to be delivered locally to the penis, either by self-injection into the corpora cavernosa (**Figure 14.5**) or by means of a soft pellet that is pushed into the urethra.

prostaglandin E₁ A hormone that is injected into the penis to produce an erection.

vacuum constriction system A device for treating erectile disorder that creates a partial vacuum around the penis, thus drawing blood into the erectile tissue.

Erectile disorder can be treated with devices and implants

Nondrug methods can also help men who experience erectile disorder. One such method is a **vacuum constriction system** (**Figure 14.6**), versions of which are made

Figure 14.6 Vacuum constriction systems produce an erection by drawing blood into the penis.

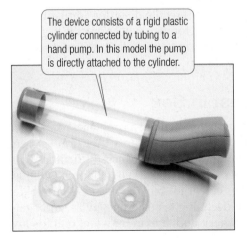

The device consists of a rigid plastic cylinder connected by tubing to a hand pump. In this model the pump is directly attached to the cylinder.

❶ The cylinder, with a constriction band at the lower end, is placed over the flaccid penis.

Constriction band

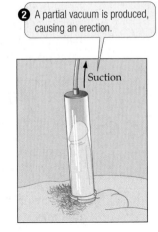

❷ A partial vacuum is produced, causing an erection.

Suction

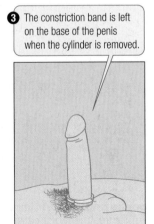

❸ The constriction band is left on the base of the penis when the cylinder is removed.

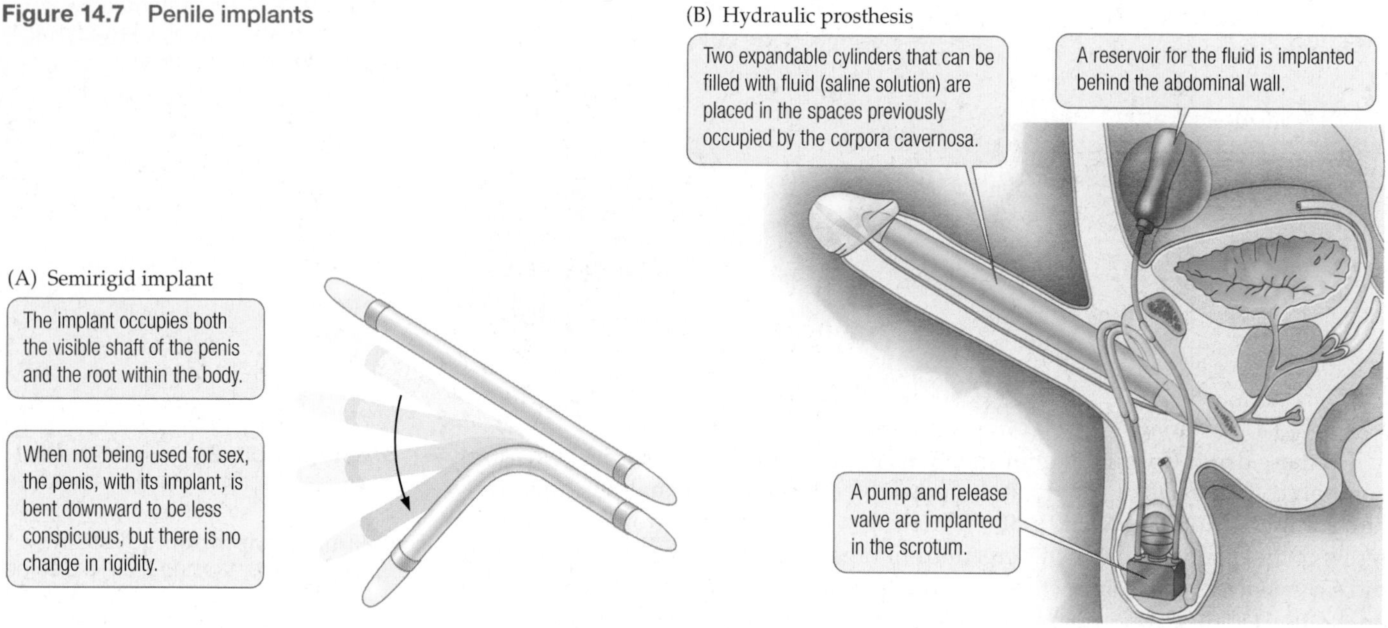

Figure 14.7 Penile implants

(B) Hydraulic prosthesis

Two expandable cylinders that can be filled with fluid (saline solution) are placed in the spaces previously occupied by the corpora cavernosa.

A reservoir for the fluid is implanted behind the abdominal wall.

(A) Semirigid implant

The implant occupies both the visible shaft of the penis and the root within the body.

When not being used for sex, the penis, with its implant, is bent downward to be less conspicuous, but there is no change in rigidity.

A pump and release valve are implanted in the scrotum.

by several manufacturers. (A medical-grade device recommended by a doctor is likely to work better and more safely than one bought in a sex store.) The man lubricates his penis, places a clear plastic cylinder over it, and then produces a partial vacuum inside the tube with the aid of a pump powered by hand or by a battery. The vacuum draws blood into the erectile tissue. Once an erection has been attained, the man slips a constriction band around the base of the penis to maintain the erection after the cylinder is removed, though the presence of the constriction band may interfere with ejaculation.

A more invasive and expensive treatment involves the surgical insertion of a **penile implant** (**Figure 14.7**). One kind of implant is a semirigid plastic rod that keeps the penis permanently stiff enough for coitus. It is relatively easy to have inserted surgically, but the permanent erection may be difficult to conceal and therefore embarrassing in some circumstances. Another kind of implant is hydraulic; it is filled from a reservoir that is implanted under the groin muscles. The pump and valves that control the filling and emptying are placed in the scrotum, where they can be accessed manually through the skin. This kind of implant is costlier and more prone to malfunction, and the erect penis is not usually as long as it was originally. On the positive side, the hydraulic implant is more discreet and produces a more natural-seeming erection than the semirigid implant.

With the advent of effective drug treatments for erectile disorder, implants have lost most of their popularity, but they are still useful for men whose erectile tissue has been damaged by scarring or other processes. Having an implant does not usually interfere with the capacity for orgasm or ejaculation.

Men May Have Little Interest in Sex

If a man is not interested in sex, that may or may not create a problem. Young men who are asexual have little or no desire for partnered sex because they don't experience sexual attraction; they are often fine with that, unless it causes difficulties with relationships because the other person does want to have sex (Chapter 5). Other young men may be too focused on school or career to think about sex. Many older men have little interest in sex on account of declining testosterone levels, and again this may not cause any problems. On the other hand, a man may feel that his low

penile implant An implanted device for treatment of erectile disorder.

sexual desire is causing him to miss out on one of life's major pleasures, or he may be having sex with his regular partner but only out of a desire to satisfy her or him—an obligation that is difficult to fulfill over the long term.

When low sexual desire causes problems of this kind, it is called **hypoactive sexual desire disorder**. Besides asexuality and hormonal factors, a variety of psychological factors can reduce a man's interest in sex. These could include, for example, a lack of attraction to his spouse or regular partner, bereavement, illness, disability, depression, or inculcated sex-negative attitudes. Or he may have no desire for sex because he knows that he is likely to experience erectile difficulties or premature ejaculation.

If psychological factors are at work, psychotherapy, relationship counseling, or behavioral sex therapy may alleviate the problem. Lack of sexual desire caused by low testosterone can be reversed by testosterone supplementation—usually via transdermal patches. This treatment is unlikely to be of use if testosterone is in the normal range, however, which is the case in the great majority of young men. What's more, testosterone supplementation can have a variety of side effects: It may increase the risk of prostate cancer or accelerate the growth of a preexisting cancer, and it is also thought to raise the risk of cardiovascular disease. The notion that testosterone replacement has a broadly beneficial effect on health is incorrect (Emmelot-Vonk et al., 2008, 2011). In fact, testosterone is the main reason why men die earlier than women: In one study based on historical records, castration early in life increased men's life expectancy by 14 to 19 years (Min et al., 2012).

As a means of restoring interest in sex, using testosterone patches has benefits, limitations, and risks.

Sexual Pain Is Uncommon in Men

Pain during coitus is called **dyspareunia**. This is not something that men experience at all frequently, and *DSM-5* does not list pain as a male sexual disorder. Even so, sex can sometimes be painful for men. The pain can result from acute or chronic prostatitis, Peyronie's disease, or phimosis, all of which are described in Chapter 3. In one form of phimosis, movement of the foreskin over the glans is limited by an unusually short frenulum. A man with that condition may be able to avoid pain by using a condom, but a urologist can often resolve the problem with minor surgery or by performing a circumcision. Finally, allergic reactions to latex or soap can cause pain during sex for either men or women.

Female Sexual Arousal Disorder Involves Insufficient Genital Response

In women, the three early processes of physiological arousal are vaginal lubrication, engorgement of the vaginal walls, and clitoral erection. These processes are often accompanied by psychological arousal—the feeling of sexual excitement. The absence or insufficiency of any of these processes can make coitus unpleasurable or downright painful. **Female sexual arousal disorder** is a term used to refer collectively to these problems.

In *DSM-5*, problems with sexual arousal and problems with sexual desire are grouped together under the diagnostic term **sexual interest/arousal disorder**. This makes some sense because a lack of sexual desire and a lack of genital arousal can trigger or exacerbate each other. Nevertheless the two issues are conceptually and practically distinct, so we deal with them separately here. This section is about arousal problems; problems with sexual desire are covered toward the end of the chapter.

Insufficient lubrication during sex is a common complaint, especially after menopause. In postmenopausal women, the condition may well respond to hormone treatment, although such treatment carries risks, as discussed in Chapter 11. Estrogens

hypoactive sexual desire disorder   Low or absent interest in sex, when this condition causes distress.

dyspareunia   Pain during coitus.

female sexual arousal disorder   Lack or insufficiency of physiological sexual arousal in women.

sexual interest/arousal disorder   Lack of interest in sex or insufficient sexual arousal, when it causes distress.

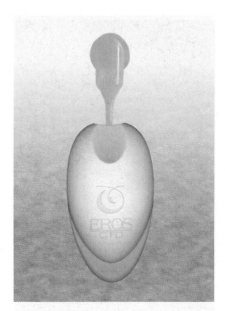

Figure 14.8 **The Eros Clitoral Therapy Device** increases blood flow to the clitoris and the surrounding area by producing a partial vacuum. No constriction band is used.

may be administered orally or directly to the vagina in the form of creams, tablets, or slow-release rings. (Application to the vagina does not eliminate the health risks associated with estrogen treatment, because the hormone spreads into the general circulation.) If poor lubrication is the woman's only problem, hormone treatment may be an "overkill" remedy: Over-the-counter water-based lubricants do a good job, are inexpensive, and have few, if any, side effects. The lubricant may be applied to the woman's vagina, to her partner's penis, or to anything else that is inserted into the vagina.

Because Viagra-type drugs have proved so successful in the treatment of erectile disorder in men, it was hoped that they might prove equally useful in women with sexual arousal disorder. Results so far have been disappointing, however. One large U.S. study found no benefit at all from use of Viagra—it merely caused unpleasant side effects such as headaches (Basson et al., 2002). One subgroup of women is helped by Viagra, however: These are women who experience arousal difficulties as a side effect of antidepressant medications (Nurnberg et al., 2008).

Erectile disorder is usually thought of as an exclusively male problem, but women can experience a lack of clitoral erection. Clitoral erectile disorder can coexist with absence of vaginal engorgement; both can be caused by diseases that compromise the blood vessels supplying the genitals (Goldstein & Berman, 1998). A small pump called the Eros Clitoral Therapy Device has been approved for treatment of this condition (**Figure 14.8**). A soft plastic cup is placed over the clitoris, and a partial vacuum is produced. This increases blood flow into the clitoris and nearby structures. Women who used the device reported moderate benefits in terms of increased sensation, lubrication, and satisfaction with sex (Wilson et al., 2001; Munarriz et al., 2003).

Psychotherapy and sex therapy can play an important role in the treatment of female arousal disorder. We will postpone discussion of this topic until after we have covered other aspects of sexual dysfunction in women.

Some women experience the very opposite of female arousal disorder: They are troubled by frequent, unwanted, or near-continuous physiological arousal, including vasocongestion, tingling, and sensitivity of the genital area. Even orgasms may occur without any obvious trigger. An orgasm may relieve the distressing sensations, but only for a short time.

This condition is called **persistent genital arousal disorder** (Facelle et al., 2013). Another name, "restless genital syndrome," has also been applied to the condition because it is similar (except for location) to the better-known restless legs syndrome. Sometimes the two conditions occur together. It may be caused by problems with the pudendal nerves or their sensory endings in the genitals (Waldinger et al., 2009). Because the physiological arousal is completely disconnected from any subjective sexual arousal or desire, it is extremely distressing. One woman described it as feeling like "hormonal rape." Electrical stimulation of the affected areas has proven helpful in some cases (Bohannon, 2014). Occasional cases have been reported in men (Waldinger et al., 2011; Huffington Post Canada, 2014).

There Are Many Reasons for Sexual Pain in Women

Dyspareunia is far more common among women than among men, and it is especially common among young women. Dyspareunia can severely impact women's sex lives and relationships.

The following are the common causes of dyspareunia:

- Developmental malformations, intersexed conditions, or a persistent unbroken hymen

- Scars from vaginal tearing during labor or from episiotomy, hysterectomy, sexual assault, or female circumcision

persistent genital arousal disorder   Long-lasting physiological arousal in women, unaccompanied by subjective arousal or pleasure.

- Vaginal atrophy (a thinning of the vaginal walls that occurs with aging)
- Acute or chronic infections or inflammation of the vagina, internal reproductive tract, or urinary tract, including several STIs and pelvic inflammatory disease
- **Vulvodynia**—a poorly understood condition in which pain is experienced when the vulva is even lightly touched (called vestibulodynia if the sensitive area is limited to the vestibule) (Basson, 2012)
- Endometriosis (see Chapter 2)
- Allergic reactions to foreign substances, such as latex, spermicides, or soap
- Insufficient genital arousal, especially insufficient vaginal lubrication
- Vaginismus (see below)

The treatment of dyspareunia depends on the diagnosis. Infections may be treatable with antibiotic, antiviral, or antifungal drugs. If the problem is vaginal dryness, a lubricant can be used, or the woman's natural lubrication may be improved by prolonging foreplay or by clitoral stimulation before coitus. Because natural lubrication sometimes decreases during the course of prolonged arousal, it may be useful to add a lubricant during the course of lovemaking. If the dryness is associated with vaginal atrophy, treatment with estrogens (by mouth or by local administration) is an option. If there is a suspected latex allergy, polyurethane condoms can be substituted. Endometriosis can be treated with drugs or with surgery. Psychological problems and relationship difficulties are often associated with dyspareunia, as either a cause or a result of the condition, and it often takes a combination of physical treatments and psychotherapy to work through these issues (**Box 14.2**).

Vaginismus may make intercourse impossible

Some women have no obvious vaginal abnormalities, and yet they cannot experience coitus: Penetration of the vagina by the penis, or by any other object, is impossible on account of some combination of anxiety, pain, and pelvic muscle spasm. This condition has traditionally been known as **vaginismus**. The editors of *DSM-5* took vaginismus and combined it with certain forms of dyspareunia to make a new diagnostic entity, "genito-pelvic pain/penetration disorder." This cumbersome phrase is not likely to come into widespread use, however, and so we stick with "vaginismus."

The usual explanation for why penetration is impossible in vaginismus is that the nearby muscles—either those of the vaginal walls (**Figure 14.9A**) or the entire musculature of the pelvic floor—go into spasm, so the outer third of the vagina is tightly closed. Mental anticipation of pain is thought to be the main reason for the spasm, as if the body were conditioned to protect against penetration. The root cause of vaginismus is not well understood. Some sexologists believe that it is a state of

vulvodynia   Painful sensitivity of the vulva to touch.

vaginismus   Inability to experience coitus due to spasm of the muscles surrounding the outer vagina combined with pain, or fear of pain.

Figure 14.9 Vaginismus (A) The usual explanation of vaginismus is that it is caused by muscular spasm of the vaginal walls (red), preventing coitus. The inner part of the vagina (orange) remains relaxed. (B) In one treatment for vaginismus, the woman uses progressively larger dilators in combination with relaxation exercises.

(A) Vaginismus

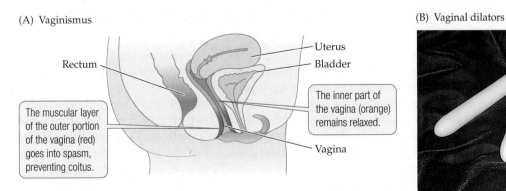

Rectum

Uterus

Bladder

The muscular layer of the outer portion of the vagina (red) goes into spasm, preventing coitus.

The inner part of the vagina (orange) remains relaxed.

Vagina

(B) Vaginal dilators

Box 14.2 Sexual Health

Dyspareunia: A Case History

This is an abridged account of a case history described by Yitzchak Binik and his colleagues at McGill University Health Centre, reproduced by permission (Binik et al., 2007):

Heather and Steven, ages 31 and 35, were referred by their gynecologist with a diagnosis of vulvar vestibulitis syndrome. The gynecologist had also referred them to a physical therapist, and pelvic floor rehabilitation had already begun when the couple came to see us.

Heather and Steven had been married for 5 years and reported a good relationship. Heather was an accountant and Steven was a pharmacist. They planned to have children but wanted to wait until the genital pain problem was resolved. The couple had begun to limit all forms of sexual contact, and both experienced self-doubt, each wondering how they were contributing to the problem.

Their family histories were similar; each had one parent who had been depressive and who was absent for long periods of time from the daily routine of family life. The two had always done well in school, excelled in sports, and had had significant past romantic relationships before meeting one another. They currently lead busy and active lives, with many nights taken up by work or sports.

The genital pain had begun a few years ago but had been bearable until a year previous, when it had worsened following a particularly stressful time in Heather's career. The problem had affected Heather's sexual desire, which fluctuated but had generally decreased. They both believed that intercourse was an important part of sex and felt inadequate for not engaging in it more often.

Initial goals were to explore factors related to Heather's desire fluctuations and to decrease the intensity of her genital pain. Among the first issues worked on was lifting some of the obstacles to having uninterrupted time together and to find ways to connect other than sex. Heather often leaned on Steven for support, and in return Steven tended to over-

protect Heather to the point of neglecting his own needs. We also did some cognitive restructuring to separate sex from intercourse and to reduce catastrophizing about pain. Information was provided about vulvar vestibulitis, and sex education focused on broadening their definition of sex and on decreasing the emphasis they placed on intercourse. Both Steven and Heather were very receptive to these interventions and made significant attempts to integrate new knowledge and behaviors between sessions.

Heather and Steven were seen for a total of 18 sessions. The couple learned to create high-quality moments for intimacy and sex and felt more connected than at the start of therapy. They developed coping strategies, for example, opening up more to each other about their respective difficulties. In doing so, they learned that they could cope with intermittent episodes of pain.

During therapy we learned that both felt unlovable at times and that this drove many of their reactions to each other. Heather improved her management of emotions, and Steven began to concentrate more on his own needs. At the end of therapy, both reported that sexual desire was no longer a major issue and that the pain was negligible.

Both Heather and Steven dealt with their difficult childhoods by placing a high value on creating a healthy marriage; in addition, they were obviously committed to doing whatever work was necessary to ensure this outcome. The fact that they had previously enjoyed pain-free sex may have contributed to Heather's recovery from pain and restoration of her sexual desire. The relationship work that was accomplished during the course of therapy helped Steven become less passive both inside and outside of the bedroom. Finally, the increased emotional intimacy of the couple along with the decreased focus on intercourse may have helped the couple to reinject passion into their sex life.

anxiety about coitus resulting from early traumatic experiences (such as experiencing or witnessing sexual assault) or from the inculcation of very strict or sex-negative attitudes during childhood and adolescence.

A mix of psychotherapy and sex therapy are the currently favored options for treatment of vaginismus. The psychotherapy may be aimed at identifying and overcoming the root cause of the woman's aversion to coitus. The sex therapy may include general exercises such as sensate focus. In fact, the key ingredients of sensate focus—the emphasis on relaxation, focus on the pleasure of gentle touch, and the gradual shift from nonerogenous zones to the vulva, are ideally suited to resolving the crippling anxiety felt by many women with this condition.

One sex therapy exercise specific to vaginismus is the use of **vaginal dilators** (**Figure 14.9B**): Once having mastered the relaxation exercises, the woman inserts the smallest dilator, while continuing to focus on relaxing her pelvic floor muscles. After she becomes comfortable with this dilator, she gradually progresses to the larger-sized dilators. In one study, nearly all the women treated with this form of therapy were able to engage in intercourse after about six sessions (Schnyder et al., 1998).

Success has also been reported with cognitive behavioral therapy, which focuses on working through the negative thoughts and emotions associated with coitus (Engman et al., 2010). Finally, several groups have had success using Botox injections to relax the affected muscles directly (Werner et al., 2014).

Difficulty in Reaching Orgasm Is Common among Women

Some women experience considerable distress in their sex lives on account of a persistent difficulty in reaching orgasm, which is termed **anorgasmia** (or female orgasmic disorder) (Rellini & Clifton, 2011). In the National Health and Social Life Survey (NHSLS) study, 71% of women (compared with only 25% of men) said that they did not always experience orgasm during sex with their regular partner. But plenty of women are satisfied with their sexual relationships in spite of infrequent or absent orgasms, so the percentage who could be said to have anorgasmia as a clinical disorder is lower than these high numbers might suggest (Bancroft et al., 2003b).

Psychotherapy and directed masturbation may be helpful

Anorgasmia can be caused by drugs, especially by antidepressants and antihypertensive drugs. Such cases can usually be treated by adjusting dosage, switching drugs, or adding another drug to counteract the effect. A variety of medical conditions, especially those that cause neurological damage, such as diabetes or multiple sclerosis, can interfere with orgasmic function. So can pelvic surgery, including hysterectomy in some women. The biological changes associated with menopause also can make it difficult for some women to experience orgasm. Finally, it has been reported that the vulvas of anorgasmic women differ anatomically from those of orgasmic women (Oakley et al., 2014). Specifically, the glans of the clitoris is reported to be smaller, and both the glans and shaft of the clitoris are located farther from the vagina (Wallen & Lloyd, 2011; Oakley et al., 2014).

If a woman is anorgasmic for no obvious reason, the clinician or therapist will suggest different strategies depending on the details of the problem. If the woman can experience orgasm with masturbation but not with partnered sex, it may be possible to suggest modifications of partnered sex that will allow orgasm to occur. First, the therapist will reassure the couple that it is common for a woman not to experience orgasm with coitus alone. The couple should be encouraged to add clitoral stimulation—by hand or mouth, or with a vibrator (**Figure 14.10**). This stimulation can be provided by either partner and can take place before, during, after, or instead of coitus. Increasing the duration of sexual activity (for example, by helping a male partner delay his orgasm) or trying different coital positions may also resolve the problem.

One variant on the man-above position, known as the **coital alignment technique** (**CAT**), was specifically developed by sex therapist Edward Eichel and his colleagues with the purpose of helping women experience orgasm during coitus (Eichel et al., 1988; Pierce, 2000). In CAT, the man enters the woman in the man-above position, but then slides a few inches forward over her pelvis so that the upper surface of the base of his penis is pressing against her clitoris. (This is the "riding high" position.) Now, during the inward stroke of coitus, the man's penis moves downward rather than upward, and it glides over the woman's pubic bone and clitoris like a bow over

vaginal dilator   A plastic cylinder used to enlarge the vagina or to counteract vaginismus.

anorgasmia   Difficulty experiencing or inability to experience orgasm. In women, also called *female orgasmic disorder*.

coital alignment technique (CAT)   A variation of the man-above position for coitus that increases clitoral stimulation.

Figure 14.10 Helping a woman experience orgasm during partnered sex If a woman has difficulty experiencing orgasm during coitus, it may be helpful to adopt a position, as here, that allows either partner to provide clitoral stimulation by hand or with a vibrator.

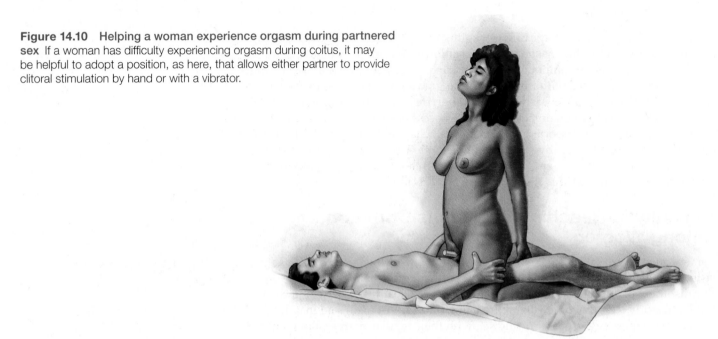

violin strings. By adjusting the upward and downward pressure exerted by each partner during the coital cycle, they turn the coital strokes into a series of gentle collisions between penis and clitoris so that the whole coital motion is more of a vibration than a friction. In Eichel's studies, women were far more likely to experience orgasm during coitus with CAT than with the standard man-above position. Later, Helen Kaplan had 26 sex researchers and their partners tested the technique over a period of 2 weeks, and only one of the couples experienced more female orgasms (Kaplan, 1992). To put a positive spin on this disappointing result, it may be that the women were reliably orgasmic before the study even started: Being a sex researcher has to be good for something, after all.

Encouraging couples to communicate better about their sexual feelings and the sexual activities that are most arousing can be very helpful as well. Men do not automatically know what their female partners find sexually arousing. A man may rush from foreplay to coitus before his partner is sufficiently aroused, in which case coitus may be a turn-off for her, rather than a turn-on. The man may stimulate the woman's nipples or clitoris too strongly—these are tender areas, after all. A postmenopausal woman may take longer to become aroused than she did earlier in her life. All these things can make it difficult for the woman to experience orgasm. In an environment in which the woman feels free to let her partner know whether the things he is doing are working or not, these difficulties can often be resolved.

If the woman does not experience orgasm under any circumstances, a somewhat different strategy is called for. Bear in mind that over half of all women say that they never masturbate (NHSLS data). Thus, if they are open to trying masturbation, they may be easily helped to experience orgasm for the first time. Sex therapy for anorgasmia often includes a program of self-stimulation, in which the woman begins with visual and manual exploration of her naked body and later progresses to genital stimulation. Vibrators are particularly useful in these kinds of exercises. Sometimes this directed masturbation program is accompanied by exercises in the use of fantasy or erotic materials. In addition, the woman may be encouraged to perform **Kegel exercises** (**Box 14.3**), although these are more useful for improving the quality of orgasm than for helping women experience orgasm at all. Sensate-focus exercises with a partner are often added.

Kegel exercises Exercises to strengthen pelvic floor muscles, with the aim of improving sexual function or alleviating urinary leakage.

Box 14.3 Sexual Health

Kegel Exercises

Kegel exercises strengthen the muscles of the pelvic floor. They were developed in the 1950s by Arnold Kegel, a urological surgeon at UCLA, for the purpose of helping women overcome urinary incontinence. The pelvic floor muscles are also involved in sexual functions, however, and women with strong pelvic floor muscles enjoy better sexual function (Martinez et al., 2014). Thus Kegel exercises have also been promoted as a way to improve sexual function, both in women and in men.

The first step in doing Kegel exercises is to identify the muscles that need to be exercised (National Library of Medicine, 2001). The usual recommendation is for the person to begin to urinate, and then to voluntarily interrupt the flow of urine. The muscles that accomplish this are the pubococcygeus muscles (see figure) and possibly other muscles of the pelvic floor. Alternatively, you can place a finger in the vagina (or the anus, if you're a man) and squeeze down on the finger. (You should not assist this effort by clenching your buttock muscles.) Another possibility, if you're a man, is to raise your penis while standing, an action that requires contraction of pelvic floor muscles attached to the root of the penis (see Chapter 3). These muscles participate in erection and ejaculation. At first you will need to have an erection in order to see that you are contracting the right muscles; once you know how to contract them, you can do the exercise with a flaccid penis.

After learning how to contract your pelvic floor muscles, begin a regular program of exercises. Do these exercises without a finger insertion, unless you need to recheck that you are using the right muscles. The routine for each repetition is squeeze-hold-release. At the beginning it may be difficult to hold a contraction for more than a second or so. But with practice you will be able to hold the contraction for several seconds. One recommended routine to aim for is a set of ten 3-second contractions, three times a day. In an alternative routine, which requires less attention to timing and counting of reps, you perform three contrac-

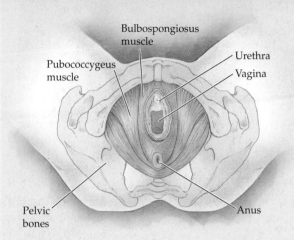

tions, each for the duration of two normal breaths and separated by two normal breaths; this routine is performed four times each day for a total of 12 contractions (Bridgeman & Roberts, 2010). Some guidelines recommend at least 30 10-second contractions per day (Mayo Clinic, 2014b). If you'd like your smartphone to share the experience, there are apps to analyze data transmitted wirelessly from an intravaginal sensor.

There hasn't been much objective research into the effects of Kegel exercises on sexual function. In one early study, healthy women were randomly assigned to practice Kegel exercises or not (Messe & Geer, 1985). At intervals thereafter, the women's capacity for sexual arousal was assessed both subjectively and by measurement of vaginal engorgement. By the end of the first week, the women who exercised experienced significantly greater sexual arousal than the control group.

From the perspective of this book, the main benefit of Kegel exercises is greater genital arousal and more intense and pleasurable orgasms. A side benefit, however, is improved bladder control, which will come in handy later in life, or after pregnancy and childbirth.

As might be expected, directed masturbation programs are most successful at helping women reach orgasm during masturbation. The great majority of women are able to do so by the end of a sex therapy program, but fewer are able to transfer this newfound capacity to partnered sex (Heiman, 2007).

Directed masturbation programs work better for women with primary (lifelong) orgasmic disorder than for women who develop the problem after some years of satisfactory orgasmic functioning (Althof & Schreiner-Engel, 2001). In the latter group of women, the problem usually reflects relationship difficulties, other psychological issues, or medical conditions that are not addressed by masturbation training.

Orgasm—genuine or faked?

Faked orgasms offer a questionable solution

If a woman (or a man) doesn't experience orgasm during an episode of partnered sex and this causes a problem, a possible solution is to fake one. It may not be possible to replicate the vaginal contractions associated with a genuine female orgasm—let alone the ejaculation associated with a male orgasm. Still, the vocalizations and facial expressions can certainly be faked, though with variable effectiveness depending on the person's acting skills.

Faked orgasms are the stuff of lore and legend. To bring some scientific respectability to the topic, psychologists Charlene Muehlenhard and Sheena Shippee surveyed students at the University of Kansas about their experiences with faking orgasm (Muehlenhard & Shippee, 2010). Among the students who had experienced coitus, 67% of the women and 28% of the men said that they had faked orgasm. Most of the fake orgasms occurred during coitus, but some occurred during oral sex, manual stimulation, or phone sex.

There are several reasons for people to fake orgasms (Cooper et al., 2014). They may do so to avoid hurting their partners' feelings, to heighten their own arousal, to cope with their fears of being "abnormal," or simply to bring sex to an end. This last reason is common among women: If a woman does not reach orgasm, her male partner may hold off on his own orgasm indefinitely because he has been taught to follow a "ladies first" script.

In another study, researchers asked 326 college undergraduates whether a man can tell if a woman is faking orgasm (Knox et al., 2008). The male students were much more likely than the female students to believe that men could tell. Presumably that's because if a woman successfully fakes an orgasm, she knows that the man was unable to tell, but the man doesn't. Alternatively, he might know that she faked the orgasm but might say nothing to avoid embarrassing her, in which case she would overestimate his gullibility. More research is needed to tease out these possibilities!

Is faking orgasm wrong? Sex therapist Barbara Keesling draws a moral distinction between deeds and words:

> There's nothing wrong with making a lot of noise during intercourse. If your doing so makes your partner believe you're having an orgasm when you're not, in a sense that's his problem, not yours. It's different if he asks you if you've had an orgasm and you say yes even though you haven't. Now we're into the realm of lying, and that's a problem. (Keesling, 2006)

Regardless of whether you agree with Keesling or not, the deception involved in faked orgasms can create a long-term problem in a relationship, especially if they are frequently repeated. It's difficult for a woman to tell a man that she's unsatisfied by their sexual encounters if, to all appearances, she has been having orgasms on a regular basis. So she may feel obliged to continue with the deception. We therefore suggest that anything beyond an occasional faked orgasm should be a hint that work needs to be done—by the couple—to understand why one partner is remaining unsatisfied, and to find a way to overcome the problem. That, of course, is if the faker is truly unsatisfied by orgasmless sex.

Too Much Interest in Sex Can Cause Problems

We now shift from disorders of sexual performance to disorders characterized by too much or too little sexual desire or sexual behavior. Of course, it is difficult to define what constitutes "too much" or "too little" in the area of sexuality. Still, these conditions can cause serious problems for individuals and relationships, especially when the levels of sexual activity desired by two partners are very different, that is, there is **discrepant sexual desire**.

Excessive sexual desire or behavior is called **hypersexuality**. Some people—males, for the most part—spend several hours each day engaged in masturbation, reading or viewing pornography, participating in sex-related online chat rooms, using commercial phone sex services, seeking casual sex partners in bars, cruising the streets for prostitutes, or having anonymous sex with multiple partners in bathhouses or sex clubs. They often feel that they have lost control of their own behavior. In fact, these activities may so take over their lives as to destroy their careers and marriages and expose them and their partners to HIV and other sexually transmitted infections.

According to some therapists, hypersexuality is a form of addiction (Carnes, 2001; Weiss, 2013). The term **sex addiction** has come into widespread use, driven in part by the media attention paid to celebrity "sex addicts" such as golfer Tiger Woods and actor Charlie Sheen. Certainly the craving for sex can resemble the craving for addictive drugs, especially in terms of its cyclical nature (**Figure 14.11**). On the other hand, the concept of sex addiction has been criticized on several grounds: that excessive sexual behavior lacks the classic signs of addiction such as tolerance (the need to have greater doses over time to produce the same "high") or physical withdrawal symptoms; that it is a way to avoid responsibility for one's actions; that it is the product of a "reverse double standard" (judging male sexual behavior by standards that were traditionally only applied to women); or that it is simply a label assigned to healthy men who happen to have been caught viewing pornography (Levine, 2010; Ley, 2012; Ley et al., 2014).

For these and other reasons, many experts prefer to use the phrase **compulsive sexual behavior** rather than "sex addiction." This designation acknowledges a key attribute of the behavior—namely, that it is experienced as being carried out against a person's will and often in a self-destructive manner. However, this term links excessive sexual behavior with other compulsive behaviors, such as compulsive hand washing or compulsive gambling, rather than with substance addiction. In fact, persons who show those other compulsive behaviors sometimes show compulsive sexual behavior too (Grant et al., 2006).

In some cases compulsive sexual behavior has an obvious pathological cause, as for example when it follows brain injury, dementia, epilepsy, or the use of certain drugs (Kaplan & Krueger, 2010). In most of these conditions the abnormal nature of the person's sexual behavior is clear because it represents a radical departure from behavior prior to the onset of the medical condition. It is as if an "internal censor," which normally limits a person's quest for self-gratification, has been damaged or lost.

Most cases of compulsive sexual behavior do not have an obvious biological cause, however, and some therapists have suggested psychological causes such as childhood sexual abuse or inculcated sexual shame (American Association for Marriage and Family Therapy, 2014). On account of its controversial nature, hypersexuality is not listed as a disorder in *DSM-5*. It has appeared in previous editions, however, and we suspect that it will reappear in some form in the future. Whatever its theoretical basis, for some individuals excessive sexual behavior is a real problem that requires professional help.

Compulsive sexual behavior can often be treated with SSRIs

Psychologists have used a variety of methods to treat hypersexuality or compulsive sexual behavior, with a moderate amount of success. Traditional psychotherapy may be used to explore possible origins for hypersexuality in childhood trauma (Schwartz, 2008). Cognitive behavioral treatments, such as relapse prevention therapy (see Chapter 13), have also proven useful. The sex addiction model has led

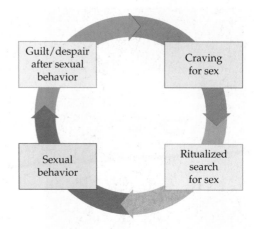

Figure 14.11 Hypersexual behavior often takes the form of a four-stage cycle. (After Carnes, 2001.)

discrepant sexual desire   The situation in which one partner in a relationship has much more interest in sex than the other.

hypersexuality   Excessive sexual desire or behavior.

sex addiction   The idea that a person may be addicted to sexual behavior by a mechanism similar to that of substance addiction.

compulsive sexual behavior   Sexual behavior perceived subjectively as involuntary and diagnosed as a symptom of a compulsive disorder. Also called *obsessive-compulsive sexual disorder*.

Sex addict—or normal guy with deep pockets? According to news stories, golfer Tiger Woods entered rehab for sex addiction in 2010 after admitting to numerous marital infidelities.

to the development of 12-step programs analogous to those available for alcohol addiction. These programs go by names such as Sexaholics Anonymous and Sex Addicts Anonymous.

In addition, drug therapy can be very effective. SSRIs are the drugs most commonly used for this purpose (Kaplan & Krueger, 2010). Indeed, the effectiveness of these antidepressants in the treatment of many cases of hypersexuality could be taken as supportive evidence that these behaviors belong to the family of obsessive-compulsive disorders, since SSRIs are known to be helpful in the treatment of those conditions. In more serious cases of hypersexuality, especially those in which an underlying brain pathology cannot be corrected, it may be necessary to use drugs that lower testosterone levels or that block testosterone's effects.

Lack of Desire for Sex Is Not Necessarily a Problem

We previously discussed the issue of low sexual desire in men. Low or absent desire for sex is much more common in women than in men, but estimates of its prevalence among women vary greatly (from about 3% to 30%) depending on the criteria used (McCabe & Goldhammer, 2013). The proportion of women who are uninterested in sex increases with age. However, many older women who lack interest in sex are not troubled by their lack of interest and should not be considered to have a problem of any kind. Lesbians in long-term relationships are said to be especially likely to lose interest in sex over time (**Box 14.4**).

Problems with sexual desire often come to therapists' attention when one partner in a relationship is more interested in sex than the other (discrepant sexual desire). Because women are more likely than men to experience a lack of interest in sex, it's not uncommon for heterosexual couples to be mismatched in this respect, with the man wanting sex more than the woman. Here's how one 21-year-old woman described the situation (Meston & Buss, 2009):

Having been with my previous boyfriend for three years, our sex life declined due to my disinterest. At times his discontent with the situation was so overwhelming and disruptive to the rest of our lives that I would feign interest and have sex with him just to make him happy, in part because I felt I wasn't holding up my end of the relationship sexually.

Situational factors such as child-rearing responsibilities, which usually affect women more than men, tend to exacerbate this gender-based discrepancy in sexual desire.

Estrogen or androgen treatment may improve sexual desire in women

The diagnosis and treatment of low sexual desire in women is more complex than in men. Traditionally, clinicians assessed women's sexual health by asking how often they engaged in intercourse. The answer to this question can give an erroneous notion of the state of a woman's sexual desire, however. She may be engaging in intercourse in response to sexual advances by her partner but have little or no interest in sex herself. Conversely, she may have a great interest in sex but not be able to gratify that interest because of a lack of partner availability or because of her partner's disinter-

Elite female athletes, especially in sports where extreme leanness is an advantage, may experience a drop in sex hormone levels, which puts them at risk of developing sexual disorders, including a lack of interest in sex.

Box 14.4 Sexual Health

Sexual Minorities and Sexual Disorders

Men and women who belong to sexual minorities face the same kinds of sexual problems and disorders as do heterosexual men and women and benefit from the same kinds of treatments. Yet in certain ways sexual orientation or gender identity is especially relevant in the context of sexual disorders:

- Some gay people are in heterosexual marriages or relationships. The gay partner may have performance difficulties or avoid sex as a result of a lack of sexual attraction, and this in turn is likely to create problems for the straight partner and for the relationship as a whole. Surprisingly, though, many gay people perform quite well in heterosexual relationships.

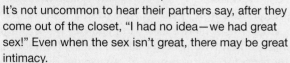

Lesbians, perhaps more than other couples, may lose interest in sex over time.

It's not uncommon to hear their partners say, after they come out of the closet, "I had no idea—we had great sex!" Even when the sex isn't great, there may be great intimacy.

- Lesbian, gay, and bisexual people may have a culturally induced sense of shame or self-hatred about their sexual orientation (internalized homophobia or biphobia). "Gay-affirmative" therapy addresses this issue, not merely by rejecting negative stereotypes, but also by building on the strengths of gay people and gay couples (Pachankis, 2004; Rutter, 2012). These strengths include resilience, a sense of humor, and a sense of equality within a relationship that facilitates communication (Gottman et al., 2003).

- Some gay men have developed an unreasonable fear of sex because of the AIDS epidemic, anxiety about sexual practices in a relationship in which one of the partners is HIV-positive, or feelings of guilt as AIDS "survivors."

- Anal penetration, practiced by some gay men, can present performance difficulties for either the receptive or the insertive partner. Fear of pain may make relaxation of the anal sphincter difficult, and a man with erectile difficulties will have more difficulty with anal penetration than with vaginal penetration. Advice on how to deal with these problems is not always easy to come by (see Chapter 6).

- Transgender and transexual people may have special concerns about sexual practices; they may be dissatisfied with their genitals and not wish to use them in sex, or if they have undergone sex-reassignment surgery, they and their partners will have to deal with the functional limitations of their new genitals—which may include difficulty experiencing orgasm (see Chapter 4).

- Although all couples can lose interest in sex with each other over time, this seems to occur particularly commonly for lesbians (Bigner & Wetchler, 2004; Averett et al., 2012). Still, the sex that lesbian couples do have may be of high "quality": It tends to last longer and to be more varied, it is more likely to include orgasm, and it is less likely to be undertaken in response to a partner's pressure, compared with the sexual experiences of heterosexual women (Nichols & Shernoff, 2007). Lesbian couples who wish to reinject some passion into their relationship can follow the same recommendations that apply to all established couples: Make time for each other, introduce novelty (dates and trips, new sexual positions or sex toys, sex in new locations), express romantic feelings, and resolve conflicts.

Men and women who belong to sexual minorities may fear that they will not receive understanding treatment from heterosexual doctors and therapists and therefore may not seek help with their sexual problems. This fear is often groundless, but some health care professionals do still fail to recognize either the commonalities between the problems of gay and straight people (performance problems, desire problems, relationship problems) or the special concerns of sexual minorities, as listed above. The American Psychological Association's Division 44 consists of over 1500 gay or gay-affirmative members and has published guidelines for psychotherapy with lesbian, gay, and bisexual clients (American Psychological Association, 2004). The Association of Gay and Lesbian Psychiatrists provides referrals (Association of Gay and Lesbian Psychiatrists, 2008). Regional lists of gay health care providers and therapists are available on the Web, but word of mouth is often a more effective way to locate a suitable provider. There are also some transgender sexologists and therapists, such as Dr. Anne Lawrence of Seattle (Lawrence, 2014).

est. To determine whether a particular woman really has a troubling lack of sexual desire requires thoughtful questioning and a sympathetic ear.

Women's sexual desire is supported by two classes of hormones, estrogens and androgens, although there is still considerable uncertainty about their relative roles (Meston & Bradford, 2007). The levels of these hormones drop when levels of body fat are very low (e.g., as a result of demanding athletic regimens, starvation, or eating disorders) as well as after menopause. In these circumstances, sexual desire often declines or disappears. Some women continue to initiate sexual activity long after menopause, however. Their behavior may reflect the importance of a loving relationship and cultural factors in sexual desire, or it may depend on the continuing presence of sex steroids secreted by the adrenal glands.

In premenopausal women who are not menstruating and have low sexual desire (because of low body weight, for example), an interest in sex usually reappears when body weight returns to normal and menstruation resumes. In postmenopausal women with low sexual desire, interest in sex may reappear with hormone therapy (i.e., treatment with either an estrogen or an estrogen plus progestin). The positive effect of hormone treatment on sexual desire is probably twofold: Part of it is due to the direct effect of estrogens on the brain, and part is due to improved physiological arousal (vaginal lubrication, engorgement, and clitoral erection), which makes sex more pleasurable and therefore rekindles an interest in it.

Administration of testosterone (via transdermal patches or implants) has been reported to increase interest in sex in women who are menstruating normally, in women who have low sexual desire as a side effect of treatment with antidepressants, and in women who are menopausal because they have had their ovaries removed (Guay, 2001; Buster et al., 2005; Fooladi et al., 2014). (In the last case, the women also received estrogen therapy.) Nevertheless, the benefits are not great. In the study by John Buster and colleagues, for example, women who used a testosterone patch reported an average of 1.6 satisfying episodes of sexual activity per month, compared with 0.7 episodes in the women who used a placebo patch. The FDA has not approved testosterone in any form for the treatment of any sexual disorder, mostly because of the risk of masculinizing side effects; some other countries have approved a low-dose testosterone patch named Intrinsa.

A drug named flibanserin, which acts on the serotonin system in the brain, has been in clinical trials for several years. So far, its modest beneficial effect along with the existence of potentially worrisome side effects (including daytime somnolence) have caused the FDA to deny approval for the drug. A possibly more effective drug, also in clinical testing, is bremelanotide. This drug activates receptors in the brain for a hormone named melanocortin, one of whose functions is to stimulate skin pigmentation. During research intended to develop a sunless tanning agent, male volunteers who took drugs of this type experienced spontaneous penile erections, and bremelanotide now appears to be an effective treatment both for male erectile disorder and for low sexual desire in women (Portman et al., 2014). Again, the issue of side effects (in this case elevated blood pressure) has slowed progress toward FDA approval. It's possible that neither flibanserin nor bremelanotide will come to market, but they inspire hope that novel and safe drug treatments for female sexual disorders will eventually be found.

Sex therapy may be helpful for low sexual desire in women

Sex therapy is an alternative (or possibly additional) option in the treatment of low sexual desire in women, as it is in men (Meston & Bradford, 2007). As with other sexual problems, sex therapists often use a combination of cognitive and behavioral approaches. The cognitive portion might involve challenging negative beliefs and expectations that interfere with sexual desire (such as the idea that low sexual desire is simply "part of who I am") and helping the woman and her partner improve their communication skills. The behavioral portion will likely include sensate-focus and other exercises that do not make excessive demands on the woman's interest in becoming sexual. Case reports support the usefulness of the sex therapy approach; large-scale outcome studies have not been done.

Another approach that has proven useful in women troubled by low sexual desire is mindfulness-based therapy: Mindfulness is a form of meditation in which a person focuses nonjudgmentally on his or her own mental state in the present moment (Brotto & Basson, 2014).

New views on women's response cycles may influence treatment options

In Chapter 5 we described Rosemary Basson's model of women's sexual arousal, in which sexual desire may be generated or amplified once a woman begins to engage in the physical stimulation of sexual behavior (Basson, 2001, 2007). In other words, a woman may not be conscious of any desire for sex, but she may be willing to engage in sex as an expression of intimacy or to please her partner. Once sexual interactions begin, sexual desire may be awakened in response to her physiological arousal.

Women who have sexual disorders are especially likely to endorse Basson's model (Sand & Fisher, 2007). Here's an example:

> Caroline, age 55 and 6 years postmenopause, was referred because of low sexual desire—for some 8 to 10 years in her estimation, and for some 20 years according to her husband, George. George recalled how Caroline's sexual interest decreased with each of her three pregnancies, recovering only partially in between, and then plummeted some 8 years ago around menopause. There had been minimal sexual activity since that time. . . . After hearing that many women have close to zero spontaneous desire but go ahead anyway and engage in sex, having previously ensured their partner's knowledge and skill in giving them sexual pleasure and satisfaction, Caroline totally changed her situation around between the first and second visit. We had suggested the couple might begin to discuss bringing back into their lives some nonintercourse sexual caressing and some "date like" contexts. However, apparently no discussion occurred—just action. Caroline went ahead and instigated two sexual episodes with her husband, inclusive of intercourse, during the 7 days between the visits. . . . We simply congratulated the couple and were pleased to find that their progress continued when they were seen some 6 months later. This truly appears to be an example of therapy that consisted entirely of giving information. (Basson, 2007)

If desire does follow physiological arousal for some women, then problems with physiological arousal could be an important cause of low sexual desire, and treatments for these problems could help restore missing desire. In addition, recognition of the importance of motivations for sex other than sexual desire itself points to a wider view of sexual disorders and their treatment. Indeed, Basson postulates a "sexual interest disorder" that is much broader than the traditional "hypoactive sexual desire disorder" and that takes account of social and other situational factors.

Not everyone agrees that these issues should be medicalized by labeling them as a new disorder (Tiefer, 2002). Still, there is general agreement that relational and social factors play an important role in women's sexual feelings—probably much more so than for men. Consider the following case history provided by a family physician:

A 32-year-old Salvadoran married woman, a documented immigrant, works 40 hours cleaning houses, looking after her two children and her husband's aging mother, cares for the house, and does all the housework and cooking. She [visits] her family physician with an urgent concern about sex. She reports that for the last few months she has not been interested in having sexual relations, and she worries that her husband will seek sex elsewhere. Family history reveals that her mother died when she was young. She was raised by an older brother in whose home she was a servant. She was never sexually abused but felt neglected and poorly treated by her brother and sister-in-law. She became pregnant on the first episode of intercourse, married promptly, immigrated to the U.S., and never had any further partners. Further inquiry reveals that communication between her and her husband about sex or the relationship is minimal and that he is not affectionate. Nevertheless, she finds him to be a good provider and good father. She has no interest in other partners or in divorce. She reports that although she used to become sexually aroused, she has never had orgasm. She takes oral contraceptives and wonders if they are the cause of her lack of interest. She does not feel depressed, although sometimes she is tired for days on end, but she wonders if her husband could be depressed. (Candib, 2002)

To deal with the issues raised by this kind of account, feminist-oriented psychologists, sex therapists, and social workers have put forward a revised conceptualization of women's sexual problems (Working Group for a New View of Women's Sexual Problems, 2002; Wood et al., 2006). This model categorizes sexual problems under four major headings:

- *Sexual problems due to sociocultural, political, or economic factors.* These include lack of information about sex or lack of access to relevant services, culturally imposed anxiety about one's attractiveness or shame about one's sexual orientation, conflicts between one's own cultural norms and those of the dominant culture, and lack of interest in sex due to family and work obligations.

- *Sexual problems relating to the partner and the relationship.* These include sexual inhibition resulting from relationship conflicts or unequal power, different desires, poor communication, or the partner's health or sexual problems.

- *Sexual problems due to psychological factors.* These include sexual aversion due to past trauma, feelings of attachment or rejection, depression, anxiety, or fear of the consequences of sex or of refusing sex.

- *Sexual problems due to medical factors.* These include painful intercourse or lack of physiological arousal caused by physical issues listed earlier in this chapter.

Women in the real world, such as the woman in the case history above, might well have problems in several of these categories. Viewed in this way, women's sexual problems demand a "biopsychosocial approach" to treatment (Leiblum, 2007), but turning this idea from a catchphrase into an objectively assessable treatment program demands a great deal of further research.

Go to the
**Discovering
Human Sexuality**
Companion Website at
**sites.sinauer.com/
discoveringhumansexuality3e**
for activities, study questions,
quizzes, and other study aids.

Summary

- Sexual disorders are common. Among women, the most frequent problems are a lack of interest in sex, difficulty experiencing orgasm, and a lack of vaginal lubrication. Among men, the most common problems are premature ejaculation, anxiety about performance, and a lack of interest in sex.

- Sexual disorders are clinical problems requiring treatment only if they cause distress. Treatment may involve some combination of drugs, psychotherapy, and sex therapy exercises. Sensate-focus exercises are commonly recommended.

- The causes of premature ejaculation, a very common male sexual disorder, are poorly understood. A man who ejaculates prematurely may be helped by sex therapy exercises in which he learns to maintain himself at a medium level of arousal for extended periods of time. Premature ejaculation can also be treated with selective serotonin reuptake inhibitors (SSRIs).

- Difficulty in reaching ejaculation or orgasm is fairly uncommon in men but may be caused by certain drugs, such as SSRIs. It may be treated by changing or adding drugs or by sensate-focus exercises in which the man and his partner progressively explore each other's bodies while avoiding performance demands.

- Many conditions can lead to problems with penile erection; these include smoking, use of alcohol and certain prescription or recreational drugs, diabetes, cardiovascular disease, spinal cord injury, and prostate surgery. Among psychological factors that may impair erectile function, performance anxiety is probably the most important. Treatment of erectile disorder can include alleviation of the underlying disorder, psychotherapy, or the use of a Viagra-type drug. The nondrug treatments available include vacuum devices and penile implants.

- "Female sexual arousal disorder" refers to difficulties with vaginal lubrication or engorgement or with clitoral erection. Insufficient lubrication is common, especially after menopause; it can be dealt with by the use of lubricants. Hormone replacement often restores physiological arousal in postmenopausal women. Sex therapy exercises may be helpful.

- In women, painful coitus (dyspareunia) can result from a wide variety of biological causes, including insufficient lubrication, infections, allergies, developmental malformations, scars, and vaginal atrophy. It can often be treated by correction of the underlying condition.

- In vaginismus, coitus is impossible because of some combination of pelvic muscle spasm and pain or fear of pain. It is treated by psychotherapy and sex therapy exercises, including the use of vaginal dilators.

- Many women have problems with orgasm. Some have never experienced it, and some do not experience it during partnered sex or during coitus. A biological cause for orgasmic disorder cannot usually be identified. Sex therapy for anorgasmia may include a program of directed masturbation or sensate-focus exercises. A woman may be helped to experience orgasm during partnered sex or coitus by adding effective clitoral stimulation, trying different positions, or extending the duration of the sexual interaction. It may also be helpful to address relationship problems.

- Excessive sexual desire or behavior (hypersexuality) in either sex can be caused by neurological damage, various mental illnesses, or certain drugs. Hypersexuality may include frequently repeated and seemingly involuntary involvement in masturbation, partnered sex, pornography use, telephone sex, and the like. Such behaviors may be classed as compulsive disorders, and like other such disorders, they often respond well to SSRIs. The use of the term "sex addiction" to describe these conditions is controversial.

- Women are more likely than men to experience a lack of interest in sex. Sex hormone levels strongly influence sexual desire. Women who are distressed by a lack of sexual desire may be helped by treatment with estrogens, androgens, or a combination of the two, but androgen treatment can cause unwanted or harmful side effects. Sex therapy may help people with low desire "let go" of thought patterns that interfere with sexual pleasure, such as a perceived obligation to ensure their partner's satisfaction. Lack of sexual desire has to be evaluated in a broad context, which includes not just medical problems but also psychological, relationship, and socioeconomic issues.

Discussion Questions

1. "Many people have sexual disorders but are prevented by embarrassment or ignorance from seeking treatment that could help them." "Many people have unrealistic expectations about sex and therefore demand treatments, such as drugs or psychotherapy, when there's really not much wrong with them." Which of these two statements describes contemporary U.S. society more accurately, in your opinion, and why?

2. A married woman friend complains to you that she cannot reach orgasm during intercourse with her husband. If you were a therapist, what questions would you ask her, and what recommendations would you give her?

3. Do you think faking orgasm is acceptable behavior, and if so, under what circumstances?

4. An older male friend complains that he has been unhappy with his sexual performance and unable to sustain an erection over the past 2 years. How would you advise him about the various treatment options available?

5. Do you think that anxiety about performance, or excessive attention to one's partner's sexual satisfaction, can interfere with one's own sexual pleasure or performance? If so, what steps could be taken to alleviate the problem?

6. Some old people have lost interest in sex but are not bothered by that fact. If they were to take a pill that somehow restored their sex drive, do you think that would improve their lives, or would it simply create extra problems for them?

Web Resources

American Association of Sexuality Educators Counselors and Therapists (AASECT) www.aasect.org
American Board of Sexology
  www.americanboardofsexology.com
National Vulvodynia Association www.nva.org
Society for Sex Therapy and Research www.sstarnet.org

Recommended Reading

Balon, R. & Segraves, R. T. (Eds.). (2009). *Clinical manual of sexual disorders*. American Psychiatric Publishing.

Berman, J., Berman, L. & Bumiller, E. (2005). *For women only: A revolutionary guide to reclaiming your sex life* (rev. ed.). Henry Holt.

Bigner, J. & Wetchler, J. L. (2004). *Relationship therapy with same-sex couples*. Routledge.

Cass, V. (2007). *The elusive orgasm: A woman's guide to why she can't and how she can orgasm*. Da Capo.

Goldstein, A., Pukall, C. & Goldstein, I. (2011). *When sex hurts: A woman's guide to banishing sexual pain*. Da Capo Lifelong Books.

Hall, K. S. K. & Graham, C. A. (Eds.). (2012). *The cultural context of sexual pleasure and problems: Psychotherapy with diverse clients*. Routledge.

Herbenick, D. (2009). *Because it feels good: A woman's guide to sexual pleasure and satisfaction*. Rodale.

Jannini, E. A., McMahon, C. G. & Waldinger, M. D. (Eds.). (2013). *Premature ejaculation: From etiology to diagnosis and treatment*. Springer.

Kaschak, E. & Tiefer, E. (2002). *A new view of women's sexual problems*. Haworth.

Keesling, B. (2006). *Sexual healing: The completest guide to overcoming common sexual problems* (3rd ed.). Hunter House.

Kleinplatz, P. J. (Ed.). (2012). *New directions in sex therapy: Innovations and alternatives* (2nd ed.). Routledge.

Leiblum, S. R. (2010). *Treating sexual desire disorders: A clinical casebook*. Guilford.

Metz, M. E. & McCarthy, B. W. (2004). *Coping with erectile dysfunction: How to regain confidence and enjoy great sex*. New Harbinger.

Metz, M. E. & McCarthy, B. W. (2004). *Coping with premature ejaculation: How to overcome PE, please your partner, and have great sex*. New Harbinger.

Chapter 15

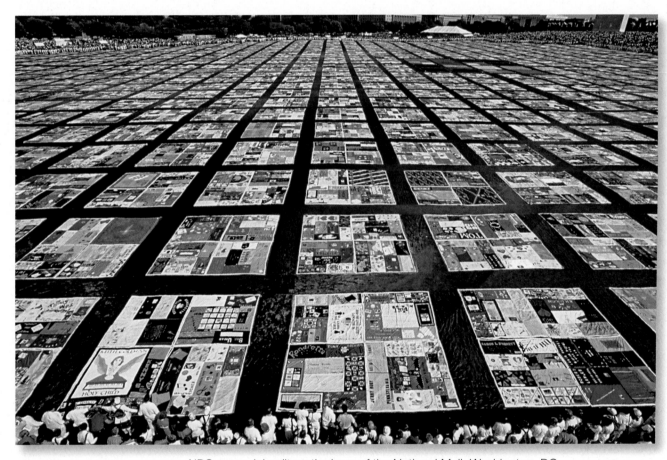

AIDS memorial quilt on the lawn of the National Mall, Washington, DC.

Sexually Transmitted Infections

The sustained physical intimacy of sexual contact offers an ideal opportunity for many disease-causing agents to spread from one person to another. Some of these organisms are highly specialized for transmission by the sexual route, while others can spread either sexually or by alternative means. The existence of sexually transmitted infections (STIs) has always added an element of risk to sex, and it has strongly influenced people's sexual behaviors and attitudes. The AIDS epidemic, which struck the United States in the late 1970s and continues to cause immense human suffering worldwide, is just the most recent example. Medical research has brought spectacular advances in our knowledge of the causes of STIs and in many cases has given us the power to prevent or treat them. Yet there are deep social conflicts about how the battle against STIs should be conducted. These conflicts, rooted in moral differences about the nature and purpose of sexuality, have undercut the effectiveness of public health campaigns aimed at eliminating STIs.

Women and men who educate themselves about STIs can greatly reduce their risk of acquiring one. If they do contract one, they are in a better position to participate in effective treatment and can minimize the risk of passing the infection on to others.

Anti-VD (venereal disease) posters in the mid-20th century often blamed prostitutes and promiscuous women for the spread of syphilis and gonorrhea.

Venereal Diseases Were Seen as Punishment for Sexual License

Until about a generation ago, STIs were called **venereal diseases**, after Venus, the Roman goddess of love. The archetypal venereal disease was **syphilis**, the first European cases of which were described in the mid-1490s, a year or two after Christopher Columbus discovered the New World. It is likely that Columbus or his sailors brought the disease from the Americas, where it had been endemic (Harper et al., 2011). For centuries, syphilis was essentially untreatable; it spread inexorably and returned to America with the colonists. By 1918, an estimated 1 in 22 Americans was infected (Amstey, 1994).

During the 19th century, there was very little sympathy for people with syphilis. They were thought to have brought the disease on themselves by engaging in a sinful behavior. Except for innocent wives infected by their husbands, people with syphilis were denied admission to hospitals for the poor. The facial disfiguration that commonly accompanied late-stage syphilis was taken as proof that the disease was divine retribution for wrongdoing.

Until the mid-20th century, young men commonly used prostitutes as a sexual outlet prior to marriage—a practice that promoted the spread of syphilis and other STIs. Prostitutes were blamed, but of course the men who visited them played an equal role. Military servicemen in particular used prostitutes in huge numbers: During World War I, the British army alone had to hospitalize over 400,000 soldiers for treatment of sexually transmitted diseases (Marshall, 2012).

Men used primitive condoms to protect themselves from syphilis and other diseases. Many other men refrained from sex altogether for fear of infection. Thus, syphilis and other STIs helped make sex seem like something frightening and evil.

Syphilis still exists in America, but in recent years it has become much less common. This has resulted from medical advances, beginning with the discovery of the causative bacterium in 1905 and the introduction of the first effective antibiotic 4 years later. Grassroots activism and public health campaigns have also played an important role, as well as the decline of prostitution as a social institution. Unfortunately, as we'll see, the disease is proving harder to wipe out than was expected just a few years ago.

The history of AIDS has mimicked that of syphilis in many respects: the importation of the disease from another continent (in the case of AIDS, Africa), its rapid spread, the initial lack of any effective treatment, the stigmatization of those who were affected, and the gradually increasing success in combating the epidemic, thanks to medical advances, social activism, and public health campaigns. The main difference is that the process has been compressed into a couple of decades rather than half a millennium. At present, AIDS can only be held at bay, whereas syphilis can now be cured.

STIs Are Still Major Problems in the United States

Here are some basic statistics that give some idea of the magnitude of the STI problem in this country (American Sexual Health Association, 2014):

- Nearly 20 million new infections with STI-causing organisms occur in the United States every year.
- About half of these infections occur in 15- to 24-year-olds.
- The total direct costs of STIs in the United States are about $16 billion annually.
- The United States has the highest incidence rates for curable STIs of any developed country—even higher than many developing countries. The rate

venereal disease Obsolete term for a sexually transmitted infection.

syphilis A sexually transmitted infection caused by a spirochete, *Treponema pallidum*.

TABLE 15.1

Estimated Incidence and Prevalence of Some Important STIs in the United States

STI	Incidence (estimated number of new cases per year)	Prevalence (estimated number of people currently infected)
Trichomoniasis	1 million	3.7 million
Syphilis	15,600	117,000
Gonorrhea	820,000	270,000
Chlamydia	2.9 million	1.6 million
Genital herpes	776,000	24 million[a]
Human papillomavirus (HPV)	14 million	79 million
Hepatitis B	19,000	422,000
HIV[b]	48,000	1.2 million

After Centers for Disease Control, 2013d.
[a]In age range 15–49; total is higher.
[b]HIV infections are not all by sexual contact.

for gonorrhea, for example, is 8 times higher than in Canada and 50 times higher than in Sweden, even though sexual activity patterns are roughly comparable in the three nations.

Some STIs occur much more commonly than others. Furthermore, because some STIs are readily treatable while others persist for a lifetime, there are enormous differences in the numbers of Americans who are carrying the various STIs at any one time (**Table 15.1**).

Some STIs are **reportable diseases**, meaning that medical professionals who encounter cases are required to notify state or federal authorities. The main federally reportable STIs are syphilis, gonorrhea, chlamydia, and HIV/AIDS. In reality, many cases of these diseases go undiagnosed or unreported. The prevalence of STIs that are not reportable, such as herpes and human papillomavirus, is usually estimated on the basis of surveys.

There are very marked differences in the incidence of STIs in different racial/ethnic groups in the United States. These disparities result from a variety of geographic, socioeconomic, and cultural factors (Kraut-Becher et al., 2008). African-Americans in particular experience much higher STI rates than do other groups, especially for gonorrhea, which is 15 times more common among black than among white Americans (Centers for Disease Control, 2014m). The rates for Hispanics and Native Americans are also elevated, though less markedly. Asian-Americans, on the other hand, have lower STI rates than do white Americans.

In this chapter we discuss those STIs that are most commonly encountered in the United States and Canada (**Table 15.2**). We describe them in a sequence based on what causes them, beginning with visible organisms and progressing down the size scale to viruses. To an approximation, this also represents a sequence of increasing seriousness: Insects and mites are an annoyance, but viruses can be killers.

We intend this chapter to be an educational overview of STIs rather than a specific source of medical advice for STI sufferers. That's because, for one thing, we are not medical doctors. For another, the information we provide may not be up to date at the time you read it. Therefore, if you have (or someone you know has) an STI, we urge you (or them) to get medical attention. You may also consult websites that carry up-to-date information on STIs and their treatment, such as the site of the Centers for Disease Control and Prevention (CDC) (see Web Resources at the end of this chapter).

reportable disease A disease, cases of which must by law be reported to health authorities.

TABLE 15.2
Basic STI Facts[a]

STI (causative agent)	Typical symptoms	Diagnostic tests	Treatment
Insects and mites			
Pubic lice	Itching at site of infestation	Visual recognition	Topical insecticide
Scabies (scabies mite)	Itching, rash	Microscopic examination of skin scrapings	Topical insecticide
Protozoa			
Trichomoniasis (*Trichomonas vaginalis*)	Foul-smelling vaginal discharge, vaginal itching	Microscopic examination of discharge	Oral metronidazole (Flagyl)
Bacteria			
Syphilis (*Treponema pallidum*)	Primary: chancre at site of infection Secondary: rash, fever Latent period: none Tertiary: widespread organ damage	Primary: microscopic examination of discharge Secondary: blood test (antibodies to *T. pallidum*)	Penicillin by injection
Gonorrhea (*Neisseria gonorrhoeae*)	Thick, cloudy discharge from urethra, vagina, or anus; may be asymptomatic or cause PID	DNA test on discharge or urine	Oral antibiotics
Chlamydia (*Chlamydia trachomatis*)	Thin discharge from urethra, vagina, or anus; local pain or irritation; often asymptomatic	DNA test on urine or swabs from penis, cervix, etc.	Oral azithromycin
Viruses			
Herpes (herpes simplex virus 1, herpes simplex virus 2)	Recurrent outbreaks of blisters or fissures localized to site of infection; may be painful	DNA tests on swabs from sores, or on blood; or visual recognition	Oral antivirals; not curable
Genital warts (human papillomavirus type 6 or 11)	Painless genital or anal warts	Visual recognition	Destruction of warts by freezing, podophyllin application, laser treatment, or surgical excision
Precancerous changes in cervix or anus (human papillomavirus type 16, 18, or others)	None at early stages	Microscopic examination of sample from cervix or anus (Pap test)	Destruction of abnormal cells by freezing; prophylactic vaccines against HPV types 16 and 18 available
Hepatitis B	Jaundice, fever; recovery common, but may cause chronic hepatitis and liver failure	Blood test (antibodies to virus)	No specific treatment for acute infection; antivirals available for chronic hepatitis
Hepatitis A	Jaundice, nausea, flu-like illness; no progression to chronic hepatitis	Blood test (antibodies to virus)	No specific treatment
HIV/AIDS (human immunodeficiency virus)	Acute flu-like illness; after latent period, opportunistic infections, cancers, wasting	Blood test (antibodies to virus; alternatively, DNA test)	Combination of several oral antiviral drugs; not curable

[a]This table lists only the major STIs and their typical symptoms, most commonly used diagnostic tests, and usual forms of treatment.

What's the difference between a "sexually transmitted infection" and another commonly used phrase, "sexually transmitted disease (STD)"? A sexually transmitted infection occurs when an agent such as a bacterium enters a person's body during a sexual encounter and establishes itself there. A sexually transmitted disease is the harm to a person's health that may be caused by such an infection. Some people who acquire a sexually transmitted infection suffer no health consequences, or do so only a long time after acquiring the infection: Such people are called **asymptomatic carriers**. The importance of asymptomatic carriers is that they can sometimes infect other people, and they themselves may fall ill at a later time.

Lice and Mites Are More of an Annoyance Than a Danger

Two species of lice (head and pubic lice), as well as scabies mites, are specialized for living on or in human skin. Of these, pubic lice and scabies mites are frequently spread by sexual contact and are therefore discussed here. These conditions are usually called "infestations" rather than "infections" or "diseases." They do not usually cause serious harm to the body, but they are very bothersome conditions that, luckily, can be quickly and effectively treated.

Pubic lice itch, and that's all they do

Pubic lice (*Phthirus pubis*) are popularly known as "crabs," but they are insects, not crustaceans (**Figure 15.1**). They are small but visible—a large adult louse may measure about 0.04 inches (1 mm) across and is dark or tan colored, while newly hatched lice are considerably smaller and colorless. Pubic lice are flat, so they can lie very close to the skin; this makes them hard to dislodge. In addition, they grasp two nearby hairs with their clawlike legs, anchoring themselves in place. Once anchored, they burrow their mouthparts into the skin between the hairs and gorge themselves on their host's blood.

Pubic lice are happiest living among pubic hairs because the spacing between hair shafts in that region is optimal for them. They can also spread to other hairy areas of the skin, however, such as the armpits, eyebrows, and the general body surface of hairy people. They can even spread to the scalp, especially around the edges. Still, the scalp is the preferred hunting ground of another louse—the head louse.

Pubic lice lay eggs ("nits"), which they glue onto hairs near the base. Each nit can be seen as a tiny dark lump near the base of a hair. It takes about a week for the nits to hatch and begin the cycle anew. Both the lice and their nits may fall off the body and end up on bedding, underwear, or towels. The lice can survive in these locations for 2 days at the most, but the nits can survive for a week. It is therefore possible to acquire a louse infestation either by direct contact with an infested person or by using that person's bedding, clothing, or towels. Most infestations are probably passed on by direct contact, however. Sleeping with someone is the most favorable situation for transmission.

The "disease" part of a pubic louse infestation is simply the itching that the lice cause—plus any skin damage done by scratching. The amount of blood lost is trivial, and fortunately, pubic lice don't seem to transmit more dangerous disease agents.

Diagnosing pubic lice is a simple matter of looking for the insects in the region of irritated skin, digging one out, and watching it wave its legs. Pubic lice are probably the one STI that you don't need a medical degree to diagnose.

Pubic lice are treated with insecticidal lotions or shampoos. Medications containing permethrin or pyrethrins (for

asymptomatic carrier Someone who is infected with a disease organism but is not experiencing symptoms.

pubic lice Insects (*Phthirus pubis*) that preferentially infest the pubic region.

1 mm

Figure 15.1 Scanning electron micrograph of pubic lice The claws at the ends of the insects' legs are well shaped to clamp onto oval-shaped hair shafts.

Figure 15.2 A scabies mite (left) and a severe case of scabies rash (right).

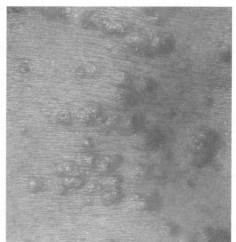

0.2 mm

example, RID) are available over the counter. The lotion should be applied to all hairy areas, left on for the exact period of time specified in the instructions, and then washed off. All clothes, sheets, and towels that might harbor pubic lice must be washed and dried at a high heat setting. (Items that cannot be washed can simply be left in a sealed plastic bag for 2 weeks or dry-cleaned.)

The over-the-counter medications to treat lice infestations do not always work well; if they don't, it may be necessary to see a doctor and get a prescription for a more effective insecticide, lindane. Because this chemical is potentially toxic if misused, it is important to follow instructions carefully. Pregnant or breast-feeding women should not use lindane. Pubic lice and nits may also be removed by close shaving of affected areas. As with any STI, all recent sex partners should be notified.

Scabies may be transmitted sexually or nonsexually

Scabies is an infestation with a parasitic mite, *Sarcoptes scabiei* (**Figure 15.2**). (Mites are not insects but arachnids—the class that includes spiders.) The mites are big enough to see (about 0.02 inches, or 0.5 mm, across), but they are not usually seen because they spend most of their time in tunnels that they dig within the superficial layers of the skin. The tunnels themselves are visible as reddish tracks, spots, or pustules. If the infested person is sensitive to scabies mites, there may also be a generalized rash even in places where no mites are located. Unlike lice, scabies mites do not require hairy skin. In fact, they are commonly found in hairless areas such as the wrists, elbows, knees, penis, breasts, back, or between the fingers.

The female mites live for about 2 months below the skin in their tunnels, laying eggs every few days. The eggs hatch after 3 to 8 days. The young go through a couple of juvenile stages and then return to the skin surface as adults to mate. Impregnated females burrow into the skin again, completing the cycle.

The itching caused by scabies infestations can be severe and may interfere with sleep. Infested people may scratch themselves to the point of causing sores, which can become infected. Scabies spreads from person to person quite easily, so it is common wherever people live in crowded conditions. Sexual contact is just one of many modes of transmission.

Scabies is best diagnosed by a physician, who may examine skin scrapings under a microscope. The recommended treatment is a topical application of permethrin lotion, which is left on for several hours or overnight before being washed off. Because the eggs may not all be killed, a repeat treatment 7 to 10 days later may be

scabies Infestation with a mite (*Sarcoptes scabiei*) that burrows within the skin.

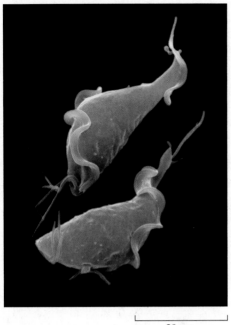

Figure 15.3 **Trichomonas vaginalis,** the single-celled organism that causes trichomoniasis, as seen in a colorized scanning electron micrograph. The bundle of whiplike processes carries receptors that specifically recognize and bind to the cells of the vaginal lining.

20 μm

necessary. As with pubic lice, possibly infested clothes and bedding must be washed and dried on a hot cycle or left unused for 2 weeks.

Trichomoniasis Is Caused by a Protozoan

Trichomoniasis (or **"trich"**) is an infection of the vagina or the male urethra and prostate gland with *Trichomonas vaginalis*. This organism is not a bacterium, but rather a single-celled protozoan with a bundle of whiplike flagella (**Figure 15.3**). In women, trichomoniasis is marked by a foul-smelling, greenish, or frothy discharge from the vagina. There may be vaginal itching and redness, as well as abdominal discomfort or the urge to urinate frequently. Some women, however, are asymptomatic carriers. Women who do have symptoms develop them within 6 months of infection, which usually happens through coitus. The trichomoniasis organism survives poorly outside a human host or even on the outside of the body, so nonsexual transmission is thought to be rare. At any one time, about 3% of reproductive-age women in the United States are infected with trichomoniasis (Sutton et al., 2007), and about one-fourth of all cases of vaginitis (inflammation of the vagina) are caused by this organism.

In men, trichomoniasis infections are usually asymptomatic. Sometimes they are marked by a slight discharge from the urethra, the urge to urinate frequently, and pain during urination.

Trichomoniasis is usually diagnosed by microscopic examination of specimens from the vagina or the urethra. A more sensitive diagnostic method is to culture the organism, that is, to grow it in the laboratory; this process takes a few days and is more expensive.

Trichomoniasis can usually be cured with a single oral dose of metronidazole (Flagyl or its generic equivalents). The infected person's partner should be treated at the same time, whether symptomatic or not; otherwise partners may continue to swap the infection back and forth between them.

trichomoniasis (or "trich") Infection with the protozoan *Trichomonas vaginalis*.

spirochete Any of a class of corkscrew-shaped bacteria, including the agent that causes syphilis.

Bacterial STIs Can Usually Be Treated with Antibiotics

The main sexually transmitted bacterial infections in the United States are syphilis, gonorrhea, and chlamydia. These cause diseases that can be fatal in themselves (syphilis), impair fertility (gonorrhea and chlamydia), or facilitate HIV infection (all three). Treated promptly, however, they can be readily cured, and complications can be avoided.

Syphilis Is Down but Not Out

Syphilis is caused by infection with a corkscrew-shaped bacterium, or **spirochete**, with the name *Treponema pallidum* (**Figure 15.4**). Syphilis is spread by direct contact, nearly always sexually. (It can also spread from mother to fetus.) If not treated, syphilis can last a lifetime and eventually cause death.

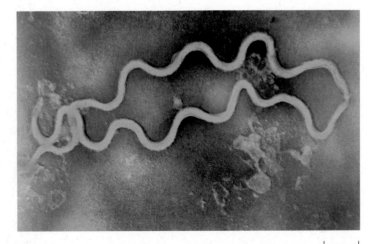

10 μm

Figure 15.4 **Treponema pallidum,** the bacterium that causes syphilis.

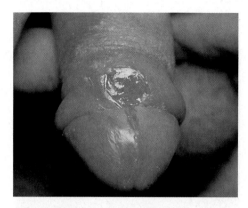

Figure 15.5 Primary syphilitic sore (chancre) on the penis.

chancre A primary sore on the skin or a mucous membrane in a person infected with syphilis. (Pronounced SHANK-er.)

primary syphilis The first phase of syphilis, marked by the occurrence of a chancre.

secondary syphilis The second phase of syphilis, marked by a rash and fever.

latent phase An asymptomatic phase of syphilis or other infectious disease.

tertiary syphilis The third phase of syphilis, marked by multiple organ damage.

Untreated syphilis progresses through three stages

A man or woman can acquire syphilis by sexual contact with a person who is in the primary or secondary stage of the disease or in the first year or so of the latent phase (see below). Most commonly, infection comes from a syphilitic sore, or **chancre** (Figure 15.5), which exudes a fluid containing huge numbers of spirochetes. The chancre is often painless. It may be visible on the penis or labia, or it may be hidden inside the vagina, on the cervix, inside the anus or rectum, or even inside the mouth. Thus, it may or may not be possible to tell whether a sex partner has a chancre.

The spirochetes penetrate the skin and multiply at the site of infection. Between 10 and 90 days (usually about 21 days) after infection, a chancre appears at that same site. This condition is known as **primary syphilis**. The chancre begins as a red bump that then breaks down, becoming a sore or ulcer. The chancre has a hard, rubbery rim and a wet or scabbed-over interior. If left untreated, it will heal by itself within 3 to 6 weeks. Because a chancre is a break in the skin, it greatly facilitates the transmission of an even more serious pathogen, HIV.

Secondary syphilis may begin while the primary chancre is still visible, or it may be delayed for several weeks. The main sign of secondary syphilis is a painless rash, which classically affects the palms of the hands and the soles of the feet but may also occur elsewhere (Figure 15.6). The rash takes the form of red or reddish-brown blotches. It is often accompanied by a fever, swollen lymph nodes, sore throat, and muscle pain. If left untreated, these symptoms generally disappear within a few weeks.

In many individuals, the spirochetes are not eliminated at the end of the second stage but continue to multiply in the body, even though the symptoms are gone. After about a year of this **latent phase**, the person is no longer infectious to sex partners. A pregnant woman can pass the organism to her fetus, however. The fetus may be stillborn, die neonatally, or suffer severe neurological impairment.

During the latent phase, the spirochetes continue to multiply within the body at a slow rate. They may gradually invade the cardiovascular system, the bones, the liver, and the nervous system without initially causing any symptoms.

Eventually—sometimes decades after infection—syphilis may begin to do serious damage. This phase is called **tertiary syphilis**; it occurs in about 15% of untreated individuals. Large ulcers may appear on the skin or internal organs. The disease may attack the heart, the central nervous system, or the skeleton. Tertiary syphilis is now

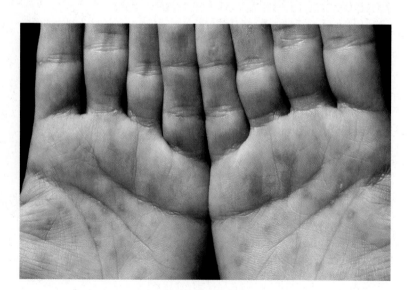

Figure 15.6 Secondary syphilitic rash may appear on the hands, as here, on the soles of the feet, or elsewhere on the body.

thankfully rare, but its very rarity, combined with the variety of sites that may be attacked, can make it difficult for today's physicians to diagnose.

Syphilis has resisted elimination

Syphilis is diagnosed by recognizing the clinical signs and symptoms, by finding spirochetes in the fluid discharge from the primary chancre, or by detecting antibodies to these organisms in the blood. During the first year after infection, a single large injection of penicillin is curative; at later times a more prolonged course of the drug may be required. Having had syphilis in the past does not protect a person from reinfection.

The introduction of effective antibiotic treatment, along with other public health measures, greatly reduced the prevalence of syphilis in the United States from the 1 in 22 rate in 1918, mentioned earlier. In 2000 the rate of new cases was so low (about 2.5 new infections per 100,000 people) that public health officials spoke hopefully of eliminating the disease. By 2013, however, the syphilis rate had rebounded to 5.3 new infections per 100,000 people (Centers for Disease Control, 2014o).

There are really two distinct but interconnected syphilis epidemics in the United States. One is a heterosexual epidemic among black men and women in the southern states. This epidemic has persisted for well over a century (**Box 15.1**). The other is a more recent series of outbreaks among gay and bisexual men in large cities such as Los Angeles, New York, and Atlanta.

Gonorrhea Can Lead to Infertility

Gonorrhea ("the clap," "the drip") is caused by infection with the bacterium *Neisseria gonorrhoeae*. The symptoms of gonorrhea develop quickly—within 2 to 10 days after infection in most people. In women, the initial site of infection is usually the cervix. Symptoms include a yellow or bloody vaginal discharge, bleeding during coitus, and a burning sensation when urinating. Sometimes—perhaps in the majority of cases—the initial infection is asymptomatic. In men, the usual site of infection is the urethra, and the symptoms are a discharge of pus from the urethra (**Figure 15.7**) and pain on urination. Like women, men can be infected with gonorrhea without experiencing symptoms (Mimiaga et al., 2008).

Both men and women can be infected rectally through receptive anal sex. The symptoms of rectal infection include a rectal discharge, anal itching, and, sometimes, painful bowel movements with fresh, bright-red blood on the surface of the feces. In women, a vaginal infection can spread to the rectum. Infections of the mouth or pharynx can occur as a result of oral sex, especially fellatio, with an infected person.

Untreated gonorrhea usually resolves in a few months (Zhu et al., 2011b). Unfortunately, serious complications can occur. In women, a gonorrheal infection can spread into the uterus and oviducts, causing **pelvic inflammatory disease** (**PID**). In some women, PID symptoms are the first symptoms of gonorrhea to be noticed. These symptoms can include abdominal cramps and continuous pain, vaginal bleeding between menstrual periods, vomiting, and fever. PID may cause scarring of the oviducts, resulting in infertility or subfertility and a heightened risk of ectopic pregnancy. In men, the infection can spread to the epididymis (causing pain in the scrotum) or to the prostate gland. **Epididymitis**, like PID, can affect fertility. Other organ systems can be affected in both sexes, and babies can become infected—usually in the eyes—during the birth process. To prevent this, all newborns in the United States are given antibiotic eye drops.

Gonorrhea is usually diagnosed by the detection of the bacterium's DNA in the discharge or in urine. It is also possible to make a diagnosis by culturing the organism from a sample of the discharge.

gonorrhea A sexually transmitted infection caused by the bacterium *Neisseria gonorrhoeae*.

pelvic inflammatory disease (PID) An infection of the female reproductive tract, often caused by sexually transmitted organisms.

epididymitis Inflammation of the epididymis.

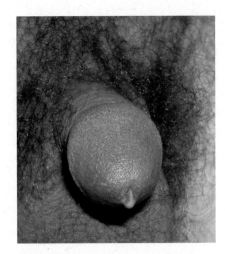

Figure 15.7 Gonorrheal urethritis in men is usually marked by painful urination and a discharge of pus from the urethra.

Box 15.1 Society, Values, and the Law

The Tuskegee Syphilis Study

One of the most shameful episodes in the history of American medicine began in 1932, when Public Health Service researchers initiated a study of the effects of untreated syphilis on several hundred African-American men living near Tuskegee, Alabama (Reverby, 2000) (see figure). The aim of the project was to follow the natural history of the disease, to study whether there were differences between the disease in black and in white people, and to compare symptoms during life with autopsy findings after death. (The study initially had a treatment element, but this was soon abandoned.)

The researchers, some of whom were based at the Tuskegee Institute (now Tuskegee University, a historically black college), recruited black farmers, renters, and laborers who had latent syphilis. That is, they had progressed beyond the first two stages of the disease but had not yet shown systemic symptoms. Most of the subjects thought that they were being treated for their condition, but in reality they only received dubious medications such as "tonics."

The study continued for decades, and 13 research papers described the findings. In 1947, penicillin was recognized as the standard of care for syphilis. In the same year, the Nuremberg Code was promulgated in response to the atrocities committed by doctors in Nazi Germany. The code declared that informed consent must be a condition for participation in medical experiments. Nevertheless, the Tuskegee experiment continued, and the subjects were not told that a simple and effective treatment was now available. In fact, the researchers went to considerable lengths to prevent the subjects from receiving treatment at the hands of other doctors. Thus the moral status of the study changed radically.

The study did not end until 1972, when a CDC researcher who was opposed to the continuation of the study gave an account of it to an Associated Press reporter. The ensuing publicity led to the rapid termination of the project. By that time, however, dozens of the subjects had died of the disease, and 22 wives, 17 children, and 2 grandchildren had contracted it, probably as a result of the nontreatment of the subjects.

In 1974 a lawsuit brought on behalf of the survivors was settled for $10 million. In May 1997, President Clinton, responding to pressure from civil rights activists and the Black Congressional Caucus, formally apologized to the survivors in a White House ceremony. In response, one of the survivors, Herman

Shaw, declared that "it is time to put this horrible nightmare behind us as a nation. We must never allow a tragedy like the Tuskegee study to happen again."

Contrary to widespread belief, no one was deliberately infected with syphilis during the Tuskegee study. Nevertheless, that did happen in the late 1940s in Guatamala. According to historian Susan Reverby of Wellesley College, doctors from the U.S. Public Health Service infected Guatamalan prisoners and mental patients with syphilis without their knowledge or consent (Reverby, 2011). They did this either by exposing them to infected prostitutes (some of whom had syphilitic material placed in their vaginas just before contact with the prisoners) or by inoculating the subjects directly with syphilis-infected tissue. Later the subjects were treated with penicillin to cure any syphilis infection that took hold. The lead doctor on this project was later involved in the Tuskegee study.

These events exemplify a long tradition of abusive medical research on black Americans, prisoners, orphans, asylum inmates, and other disadvantaged groups (Washington, 2007; LeVay, 2008). Research practices have changed greatly since the time of the Tuskegee study. It is unthinkable that such a project could be carried out in the United States today. These historical abuses should remind us of the need for continuing vigilance to ensure the protection of research subjects, but they should not discourage members of any minority from seeking medical care or participating in research. In fact, the participation of minorities (including gays and lesbians as well as racial groups) in research is essential if we are to ensure that medical advances benefit all Americans and harm none.

In 2012 there were about 106 cases of gonorrhea per 100,000 people in the United States (Centers for Disease Control, 2014g). This rate is far below historical levels. Nevertheless, rates remain high in the southeastern United States (**Figure 15.8**).

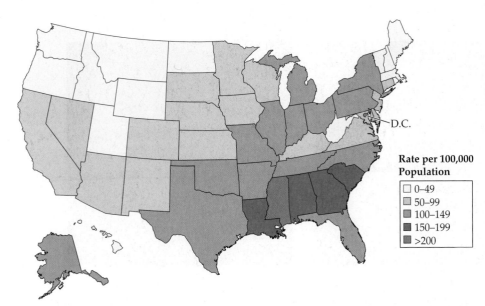

Figure 15.8 Geographic distribution of gonorrhea Gonorrhea is most prevalent in the southeastern United States. The map shows the rate of reported new cases per 100,000 people in 2012. (After Centers for Disease Control, 2014b.)

D.C.

Rate per 100,000 Population

☐ 0–49
☐ 50–99
☐ 100–149
☐ 150–199
☐ >200

At one time, gonorrhea was readily treatable with standard antibiotics such as penicillin and tetracycline. Unfortunately, the bacteria that cause gonorrhea have shown a remarkable ability to develop drug resistance. The CDC now recommends that all cases of this disease be treated with a more advanced antibiotic, ceftriaxone (delivered by injection) in combination with an oral antibiotic, azithromycin. CDC experts predict that gonorrhea will eventually become resistant to this drug regimen too, which will make it very difficult to treat the infection (Centers for Disease Control, 2011c).

It's important for infected people to notify their partners so that they too may be treated before serious complications develop. Women in particular may have few or no symptoms, at least initially, so they may not seek medical treatment unless they know that their sex partner is infected.

Infection with gonorrhea does not trigger a lasting immune response, so a person who has recovered from an infection is not protected from reinfection. Efforts to develop a vaccine against gonorrhea have so far been unsuccessful, but there is reason to believe that this goal is attainable (Jerse et al., 2014).

Chlamydia Causes a Common Infection with Serious Complications

Chlamydia is a relatively newly recognized STI. Reported cases in the United States rose from 17 to 457 per 100,000 people between 1985 and 2012, and chlamydia is now the most common of all reportable infectious diseases: 1.4 million cases were reported in 2012, and many more probably went unreported or undiagnosed (Centers for Disease Control, 2013d). This increase did not represent the explosive spread of a new disease, as with AIDS. Rather, it was due at least in part to increased recognition of a condition that had previously been diagnosed as a nonspecific genital infection.

The causative agent, *Chlamydia trachomatis*, is a bacterium, but an unusual one (**Figure 15.9**): Like viruses, it is active inside cells and exists outside of cells only in the form of inert but highly infectious particles. Besides its role in causing an STI, this bacterium

chlamydia A sexually transmitted infection caused by infection with the bacterium *Chlamydia trachomatis*.

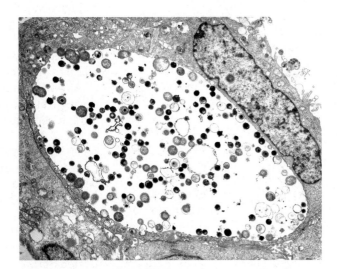

Figure 15.9 Chlamydia This colorized electron micrograph shows a cell that has been infected with chlamydia. The cell's nucleus is at upper right. The chlamydia organisms live within an intracellular vacuole (the white space) where they are protected from immune attack. The larger (red) chlamydia are metabolically active: They secrete chemical signals that take control of the host cell's metabolism, and they also divide. The smaller, dark forms are inert but highly infectious chlamydia that are destined for export.

Figure 15.10 (A) Normal cervix and (B) cervical inflammation caused by chlamydia, as seen on visual examination through the vagina. (Not all healthy cervixes look exactly like the one on the left.)

(A)　(B)

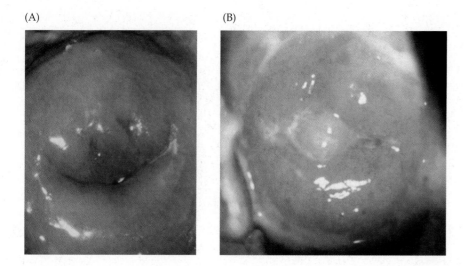

is a leading cause of blindness in tropical countries, where it is transmitted by eye-seeking insects.

In the United States and Canada, chlamydia is usually spread by genital contact. Symptoms appear a few days to 3 weeks after infection. In men, the organism infects the urethra, causing a thin discharge (different from the thick discharge of gonorrhea) and burning pain during urination. As in gonorrhea, the organism can migrate farther up the male reproductive tract and cause epididymitis or prostatitis.

In women, the organism infects the cervix (**Figure 15.10**) or urethra, causing irritation, a thin vaginal discharge, and painful urination. But 75% of infected women (as well as 50% of infected men) experience no symptoms. In both men and women, chlamydia infections can also occur in the rectum and in the mouth or throat if those parts have been involved in sexual contact with an infected partner.

Like gonorrhea, chlamydia can migrate up the female reproductive tract and cause PID (whether the initial infection was symptomatic or not). Up to 40% of women with untreated chlamydia infections develop PID; 20% of these women with PID will become infertile, and 9% of them will have an ectopic pregnancy. About half of all cases of PID are probably caused by chlamydia infections.

As with gonorrhea, chlamydia can spread from an infected woman to her infant during childbirth, causing a serious but treatable eye or respiratory infection. Testing (and, if necessary, treatment) of all pregnant women is recommended.

Chlamydia is usually diagnosed from cell samples obtained from the penis or cervix. (The cervical sampling procedure is different from the Pap test described in Chapter 2.) Chlamydia can also be diagnosed from urine samples. Chlamydia can be cured with a single dose of an antibiotic, usually azithromycin. Unlike with gonorrhea, drug resistance is uncommon, so far at least. Reinfection from an infected partner can easily occur, so it's important that partners be tested and successfully treated before they resume sexual contact.

Chlamydia is common among young, sexually active men and women across the United States. As many as 1 in 10 of all adolescent girls is infected, and the figures for older adolescents in urban areas may be even higher. By age 30, about half of all sexually active women show evidence of current or prior chlamydia infection.

The CDC recommends that all sexually active women under 25 be tested for chlamydia once per year, as well as older women who have had a new sex partner and all pregnant women. Since the test merely involves giving a urine sample—and taking a single dose of an antibiotic if the test is positive for chlamydia—it is a small price to pay for peace of mind.

The Status of Bacterial Vaginosis as an STI Is Uncertain

Bacterial vaginosis is a condition in which the normal vaginal microorganisms—mostly acid-producing bacteria known as lactobacilli—are replaced by a variety of other bacterial species (Centers for Disease Control, 2014d). The vaginal secretions become less acidic (pH rises), the vagina develops a characteristic fishy odor, and there may be itching, pain, and a thin, off-white discharge. Many women who have bacterial vaginosis have no symptoms, however.

Bacterial vaginosis is uncommon in women who have not had sexual intercourse, but it is very common among sexually active women, especially those who have multiple partners. Vaginal douching, which disturbs the bacterial ecosystem within the vagina, increases the likelihood of developing vaginosis (Brotman et al., 2008), as does the insertion of substances such as oils and petroleum jelly (Brown et al., 2013).

While it is clear that engaging in sex increases the likelihood of developing bacterial vaginosis, it is not clear whether sexually transmitted organisms are responsible for the condition. That does seem to be the case for female-to-female sexual contact, however: Lesbians whose partners have bacterial vaginosis are much more likely to have the condition themselves, compared with lesbians whose partners do not have it (Marrazzo et al., 2010). As to the question of heterosexual transmission, at least one of the organisms that characterize bacterial vaginosis, *Gardnerella vaginalis*, can also infect men; such infections may be asymptomatic, or they may be accompanied by urethritis. Nevertheless, the CDC does not recommend routine treatment of males whose partners have been diagnosed with bacterial vaginosis.

In a minority of women, bacterial vaginosis may lead to serious complications, such as pelvic inflammatory disease and (in pregnant women) premature delivery. Having bacterial vaginosis makes it easier for a woman to acquire STIs such as chlamydia, gonorrhea, and HIV. What's more, having bacterial vaginosis greatly increases the risk that an HIV-positive woman will transmit HIV to male sex partners (Cohen et al., 2012).

Bacterial vaginosis can be treated effectively with antibiotics, and it is especially important for pregnant women with the condition to be treated. Relapses can occur; treating the male partners of affected women does not reduce the likelihood of recurrence. This observation suggests that heterosexual transmission is not a likely cause of bacterial vaginosis.

Urethritis Can Be Caused by a Variety of Organisms

Infections of the urethra (**urethritis**) are very common. They are not necessarily caused by sexually transmitted bacteria, but they often are. We already mentioned gonorrhea as a cause of urethritis in men. Urethritis caused by other organisms, especially when it occurs in men, is referred to as **nongonococcal urethritis** (**NGU**). The main agents are chlamydia, discussed above, and a group of organisms called **mycoplasmas**, the smallest cellular organisms known. (Sometimes "NGU" is taken to exclude chlamydia as well as gonorrhea.) Another potential agent is *Gardnerella vaginalis*, also mentioned above.

Urethritis causes pain during urination and, often, a urethral discharge. The infection can spread to the bladder (cystitis) and reproductive tract. If gonorrhea has been ruled out, the doctor may treat the urethritis with antibiotics without attempting to identify the specific organism responsible. As with any STI, partner notification is important.

bacterial vaginosis A condition in which the normal microorganisms of the vagina are replaced by other species, causing discomfort and a foul-smelling discharge.

urethritis Inflammation of the urethra, usually caused by an infection.

nongonococcal urethritis (NGU) Urethritis not caused by gonorrhea.

mycoplasmas A group of very small cellular organisms that may cause urethritis.

FAQ

Will vaginal probiotics cure my bacterial vaginosis?

Not by themselves, but they may help in conjunction with oral antibiotics.

virus An extremely small infectious agent. When not inside a host cell, viruses are metabolically inert but infectious.

molluscum contagiosum A skin condition marked by small raised growths; it is caused by a pox virus.

oral herpes Herpes infection of the mouth, caused by HSV-1 or (less commonly) HSV-2.

genital herpes An infection of the genital area caused by HSV-2 or (less commonly) HSV-1.

Viral STIs Can Be Dangerous and Hard to Treat

Viruses are extremely small infectious particles (10 to 200 nanometers in diameter). When not inside a host cell, viruses are metabolically inert but infectious. A virus's genome consists either of DNA or RNA and is very limited in size: It may possess as few as 10 genes, compared with about 1000 genes for a bacterium. Once inside a host cell, the viral genes take over the cell's metabolic machinery in order to replicate themselves. This replication may occur right away and be followed by the release of new viral particles. Alternatively, the viral genes may persist in the cell in an inactive form for months or years before coming out of hiding and generating new viral particles.

Many viral diseases are self-limiting because they trigger an effective immune response in the infected person. Some viruses have found ways to protect themselves from their host's immune system, however. Viral infections are not treatable with antibiotics. A variety of effective antiviral drugs have been introduced over the last two decades, but these drugs are rarely curative, and they often have serious side effects.

In this section we discuss five viruses or classes of viruses: a pox virus, herpes simplex viruses, human papillomaviruses, hepatitis viruses, and the human immunodeficiency virus. This sequence corresponds approximately to the increasing seriousness of the diseases they cause.

Molluscum Contagiosum Is a Self-Limiting Condition

Molluscum contagiosum is a skin condition caused by a pox virus. It is characterized by small, bump-like growths on the skin up to about the size of a pencil eraser (**Figure 15.11**). Each bump has a central pit or dimple. The virus is transmitted by direct skin-to-skin contact or by contact with infected clothing or towels. In adults the most common affected site is the genital area, in which case sexual transmission is the likely route of infection (Hughes et al., 2013). The condition does not cause any serious health problems, and it usually disappears within a year of its first appearance, but several treatments are available, the most common being removal of the growths by freezing. Because it is so contagious, people with molluscum should take care to prevent others from coming into contact with the growths.

Genital Herpes Is a Lifelong but Not Life-Threatening Infection

The genetic material of herpesviruses is DNA (**Figure 15.12**). Two herpesviruses, herpes simplex 1 and 2 (HSV-1 and HSV-2), may be transmitted sexually. HSV-1 commonly causes **oral herpes**, often in the form of "fever blisters" or "cold sores" on the lips. Oral herpes may be spread by sexual or nonsexual contact. If a person with oral herpes performs oral sex on another person, however, that other person may acquire a genital HSV-1 infection. The proportion of genital herpes infections that are caused by HSV-1 has been increasing in recent years and is estimated to reach 30% to 50% among college students, probably because of the increasing popularity of oral sex (Wald, 2006). The more common cause of **genital herpes**, however, is HSV-2, which is usually transmitted directly from the anogenital area of one person to that of another. Over 24 million Americans are currently infected with this virus.

The initial symptoms of HSV-2 infection usually occur within 2 weeks after exposure, taking the form of an outbreak of sores at the site of infection. This site is most commonly somewhere in the genital or anorectal area or on the surrounding skin,

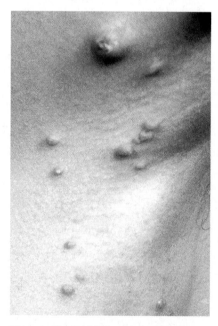

Figure 15.11 Molluscum contagiosum takes the form of small growths on the skin.

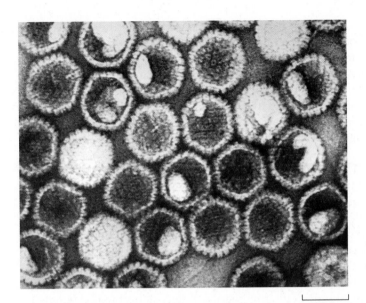

Figure 15.12 **Particles of herpes simplex virus 2 (HSV-2),** the usual causative agent of genital herpes, are shown in an electron micrograph, using negative contrast. Each viral particle measures about 200 nanometers in diameter. The DNA cores are visible as dense, light-colored clumps within some of the particles.

150 nm

but may be elsewhere on the body or around the mouth. The most frequently affected sites are the penis in men and the labia, clitoral hood, or vaginal walls in women.

The outbreak may be preceded by tingling or itching at the site where the outbreak is about to occur. Such anticipatory signs are useful, especially in later outbreaks, because they can warn the person to abstain from sex or use protection (to decrease the likelihood of giving herpes to a sex partner) and to begin taking medication (see below). Shortly after any anticipatory signs, a reddish, slightly elevated spot or cluster of spots appears. A day or so later, the spots turn into blisters (**Figure 15.13**). The blisters then break, leaving sores or ulcers that give rise to a clear discharge. Alternatively, there may be cracks in the skin or mucosa, rather than blisters. The discharge from the blisters or cracks contains immense numbers of viral particles and is highly infectious. After a few more days, the sores crust over, dry up, and gradually heal and disappear.

Herpes outbreaks may be painless or mildly itchy—especially if they occur on a less sensitive patch of skin. In that case, they may not come to the person's attention at all. Alternatively, the outbreaks may be quite painful. If they are in a site that is contacted by urine, the act of urination may be extremely painful.

The first outbreak may be accompanied by fever and swollen lymph nodes or, rarely, by more serious symptoms. Also, the virus can be spread to other parts of the body, including the eyes, by the person's fingers. This can happen only during the initial outbreak.

Recurrent outbreaks are the rule

Unless the immune system is compromised, the primary infection is quickly resolved, and the sores disappear within a couple of weeks. However, some viral particles enter the terminals of sensory nerve fibers in the vicinity of the infection site. They then travel up the

(A)

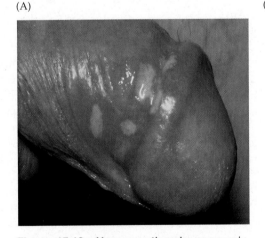

(B)

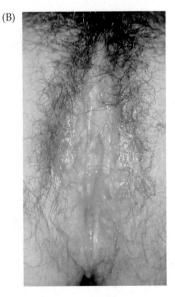

Figure 15.13 **Herpes outbreaks** commonly occur (A) on the shaft of the penis or (B) on the vulva.

nerve fibers to the nerve cell bodies, close to the spinal cord. Once the viral particles have reached the cell bodies, they may remain inert for weeks or months. In this location, they are protected from the host's immune system.

At some point, a new round of viral replication occurs, and the new viral particles travel back down the nerves to the original infection site or nearby, where they cause another outbreak of sores. Because the host's immune system has already been exposed to the virus, the second and later outbreaks are usually less severe than the first, and during these later outbreaks the virus cannot be spread to other parts of the body.

A few people infected with genital herpes caused by HSV-2 may experience only the initial outbreak, but the great majority continue to experience outbreaks indefinitely. Typically, the frequency of outbreaks decreases over time, from a median of six outbreaks in the first year to three outbreaks in the fifth year. When genital herpes is caused by HSV-1, the initial outbreak is more severe, but recurrent outbreaks are much less frequent and commonly cease altogether after a year.

It is widely believed that most HSV-2 infections are asymptomatic, because the majority of people who have been infected (as documented by the presence of antibodies to HSV-2 in their blood) deny any history of herpes outbreaks. However, many of these "asymptomatic" carriers have outbreaks that they haven't noticed because they are painless and in an inconspicuous location (Leone & Corey, 2005). It's not known how many people carry HSV-2 but never have outbreaks. What's important, though, is that many people have HSV-2 but don't know it.

During outbreaks, herpes sufferers can very easily transmit the disease to their sex partners. People with herpes are generally most infectious from the time they experience the first symptoms to the time that all their sores are dry and crusted over. However, HSV-2 can sometimes be detected on the affected area of skin during times when no outbreak is present, as well as in the genital area of individuals who deny having outbreaks (Tronstein et al., 2011). As many as half of all herpes transmissions may occur when no symptoms are present, according to some experts (Mertz, 2008). People with herpes who carefully watch for outbreaks and who abstain from sex while they are present are going a long way toward protecting their partners from infection, but for greater security, condoms should be used at all times. Drugs can also be used to reduce the risk of transmission (see below).

A herpes-infected pregnant woman can transmit the infection to her child during the birth process, and the infection can be fatal to the infant or leave it severely disabled. Mother-to-infant transmission can be prevented by delivering the baby via cesarean section.

FAQ

My herpes seems to come back when I'm stressed out—is there a connection?

There have been conflicting findings on this. A meta-analysis did find a connection between stress and herpes recurrences, but the connection was less strong for genital than for oral herpes (Chida & Mao, 2009).

FAQ

My boyfriend has oral herpes—can he give me genital herpes through oral sex when he's not having an outbreak?

There's little research on this. If it's HSV-1, you may already be infected—most college-age Americans are—in which case you're unlikely to suffer further harm. If he takes acyclovir or valacyclovir continuously, it will lessen the likelihood of your getting infected, whether it's HSV-1 or HSV-2.

Drug treatment can shorten or prevent outbreaks

Genital herpes is sometimes diagnosed simply from the patient's history and from clinical observation of the sores. Herpes is often difficult to recognize, however, and other, more serious diseases can closely mimic herpes. Also, simple inspection cannot distinguish whether herpes was caused by HSV-1 or HSV-2, but the distinction is important because of the difference in the long-term course of the two diseases. For all these reasons, both the CDC and independent experts recommend that the diagnosis be confirmed by laboratory tests on either samples swabbed from the sores or blood samples (Patel et al., 2011; Centers for Disease Control, 2014a).

The mainstays of treatment are acyclovir (Zovirax and generic equivalents) or valacyclovir (Valtrex and generics). Oral tablets are more effective than topical ointments. If a course of oral acyclovir or valacyclovir is begun at the first sign of an outbreak, the outbreak is shortened and may never get to the point of producing a discharge. People who are bothered by frequent or painful outbreaks can take acyclovir or valacyclovir on a continuous basis as a preventive measure. Doing so reduces the frequency of outbreaks or eliminates them entirely, and it also greatly lowers (but doesn't eliminate) the chance that partners will be infected.

Human Papillomaviruses Can Cause Genital Warts—and Cancer

Human papillomaviruses (HPV) are DNA viruses that fall into about 100 different types, out of which over 40 can infect the urogenital tract or the skin near the genitalia (Centers for Disease Control, 2013i). Transmission is usually by sexual contact. Once inside a host cell, the virus can remain in an inactive form; alternatively, it can spur cell division, leading to the appearance of **genital warts** (**Figure 15.14**) or other skin lesions. The types of papillomaviruses that cause common skin warts (such as those on the hands) do not generally infect the genitals.

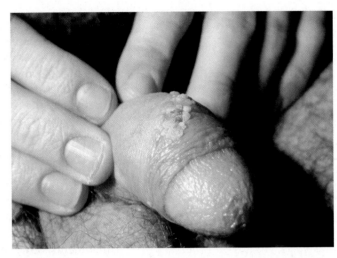

Figure 15.14 Genital warts on the penis Genital warts vary greatly in appearance.

Genital warts usually appear a few months after infection, but many infected people have no warts or other symptoms. The warts are benign (noncancerous) tumors that are typically located at the vaginal opening, within the vagina, on the cervix, on the penis, at or within the anus, or even in the mouth. They can be single soft pink bumps or more elaborate cauliflower-like growths. They are highly infectious, but they are usually painless and do not often cause serious health problems. These raised genital warts are most frequently caused by HPV types 6 and 11, which rarely cause cancer.

More dangerous are HPV types 16 and 18. These are not common causes of raised genital warts. They can cause other kinds of lesions in the genital region, including flat lesions that may be precancerous, but most commonly there are no symptoms. The problem with these HPV types is that, in women, they can eventually promote the development of cervical cancer (**Figure 15.15**). In fact, HPV infection is the principal cause of this disease. A key strategy in preventing the progression from HPV infection to cervical cancer is the Pap test. Most genital warts do *not* contain the types of HPVs that predispose women to cervical cancer.

These same two types of HPVs (16 and 18) can also cause anal cancer; in fact, HPV is thought to be responsible for 9 out of 10 cases of this disease (Centers for Disease Control, 2014i). HPV infection of the anus occurs most readily during unprotected receptive anal sex, but the virus can also spread to the anus from the genital area, according to the American Cancer Society. Anal cancer is not very common: About 4500 women and 2600 men develop the disease in the United States annually, and it causes about 1000 deaths (American Cancer Society, 2014a). Some specialists recommend regular anal Pap tests for at-risk groups, but there is no positive evidence of benefit from such screening.

In addition, HPV infection is an increasingly common cause of cancers of the mouth and throat (Pytynia et al., 2014) and of the vulva. According to a random survey, nearly 7% of U.S. teens and adults carry HPV in their mouths. These infections were acquired through oral sex and possibly also through deep kissing (Gillison et al., 2012). Only a small minority of these infections will progress to oral cancer, however.

Unlike the situation with HSV, the fact that a pregnant woman has been infected with any type of HPV is unlikely to have any adverse effect on her fetus or newborn

human papillomavirus (HPV) Any of a group of viruses that can be sexually transmitted and that cause genital warts or other lesions; some types predispose infected persons to cancer of the cervix or anus.

genital warts Wart-like growths on or near the genitalia or anus, caused by infection with human papillomavirus.

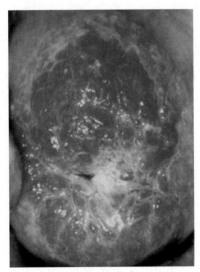

Figure 15.15 Cervical cancer as seen on visual examination through the vagina. Compare with the normal cervix shown in Figure 15.10A. Most cases of cervical cancer are caused by HPV infection.

child. Very rarely, the infant can develop warts in the mouth or respiratory tract; these are treatable, but recurrences can occur.

An estimated 50% to 75% of sexually active men and women acquire an HPV infection at some point in their lives, and HPV is the most common STI in the United States in terms of the number of new infections per year. In one study that followed a large group of HPV-negative female college students, over 60% had acquired an HPV infection by 5 years later (Baseman & Koutsky, 2005). Most infected people eventually clear the virus from their bodies and become noninfectious to others within a couple of years from the initial infection, but an estimated 79 million Americans are currently infected and potentially infectious to others. About 14 million new HPV infections occur annually.

A clinician can remove genital warts by a variety of means, such as by cutting them off, by freezing them with liquid nitrogen, by laser ablation, or by the application of podophyllin or other agents. HPV may not be eliminated from the body by these treatments, however, and the warts sometimes recur.

HPV vaccines are available

Two vaccines, Gardasil and Cervarix, offer protection against infection with some types of HPV (National Cancer Institute, 2011). Gardasil provides complete protection against the two types of HPV (16 and 18) that cause 70% of all cervical cancers, as well as the two types (6 and 11) that cause 90% of genital warts. It is approved for use in females and males age 9 through 26—the CDC-recommended age for vaccination is 11 or 12. Although males cannot develop cervical cancer, the vaccine offers three benefits to them: protection against most genital warts, likely protection against anal and oral cancers caused by HPV, and protection against becoming an HPV carrier who can infect others.

Gardasil is given as three injections over 6 months and costs about $360 for the complete series, but there are various insurance and governmental programs that provide the vaccines at nominal cost. Protection lasts for at least 8 years and probably longer—it is not yet known whether and when booster shots will be necessary.

Cervarix provides protection against the cancer-causing HPV types 16 and 18 only, and it has been approved only for females. It appears to stimulate a stronger protective response to those two types than Gardasil, however (Einstein et al., 2009), which may mean that the protection will last longer. Cervarix is much less widely used than Gardasil.

To be effective against a given HPV type, the vaccines must be administered *before* a person becomes infected by that type. Ideally, therefore, children or adolescents should be vaccinated before they become sexually active. However, even if a person has already acquired an HPV infection, the vaccines will still protect her against the HPV types to which she was not exposed. (Commonly available tests cannot determine which HPV types, if any, a person has been exposed to in the past.)

The Merck corporation (the manufacturer of Gardasil) has developed a new HPV vaccine (V503) against nine HPV types—the four in Gardasil plus five others. It may become available during the lifetime of this edition. This vaccine is expected to prevent 9 out of 10 cases of cervical cancer, compared with 7 out of 10 for Gardasil (Serrano et al., 2012).

The introduction of HPV vaccines is potentially a major advance in the battle against STIs as well as cancer. Unfortunately, only 1 in 3 girls and even fewer boys in the United States receive HPV vaccines. Some parents are reluctant to have their children vaccinated, out of unfounded fears that the vaccines are harmful or that they will encourage unsafe sexual activity (American Council on Science and Health, 2014). Unvaccinated young people jeopardize their own health as well as that of their sex partners.

The most dramatic benefits of HPV vaccination could be in the developing world, where few women undergo regular Pap testing. The manufacturers of the vaccines sell them for less than $5 per dose in the poorest countries (McNeil, 2013a); a child who is vaccinated in the United States is effectively sponsoring the vaccination of girls and boys in the developing world.

Hepatitis Viruses Can Be Sexually Transmitted

Viruses that attack the liver, called **hepatitis viruses**, belong to a number of unrelated types, of which the best known are hepatitis A, B, C, D, and E. The most important of these viruses in terms of sexual transmission is hepatitis B, followed by hepatitis A (Lester & Agarwal, 2011).

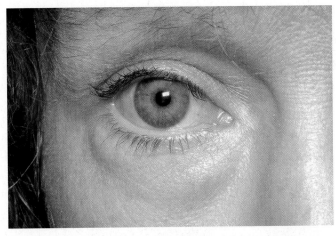

Figure 15.16   Jaundice is a yellowing of the skin and mucous membranes, seen most easily in the whites of the eyes. It is usually caused by liver disease, including sexually transmitted hepatitis infections.

The **hepatitis B** virus can be picked up by coitus or by anal or oral sex with an infected partner, as well as by contact with contaminated blood (by sharing needles, for example). The signs and symptoms of hepatitis B include **jaundice** (yellowing of the skin and mucous membranes—**Figure 15.16**), fever, general malaise, and tenderness and swelling of the liver. The majority of people with hepatitis B recover uneventfully and become noninfectious to others, but in about 6% of infected people (and a higher percentage of children) the infection progresses to a chronic state, which can lead to scarring (cirrhosis) of the liver, liver cancer, and fatal liver failure. Chronically infected people remain infectious to others. Several drugs are available for treatment of hepatitis B, but they need to be taken for many months and are more likely to suppress symptoms than to actually eliminate the virus from the body.

Routine vaccination of children against hepatitis B was implemented in the United States in 1991, and the incidence of the disease has dropped by about 90% since then. Nevertheless, about 1 million Americans are living with a chronic hepatitis B infection (National Prevention Information Network, 2011).

The **hepatitis A** virus is transmitted by the fecal-oral route; that is, viral particles in the feces of an infected person get into the mouth of another. It is often spread by food handlers, but it can also be spread sexually, especially by the practice of mouth-to-anus contact (anilingus) or by anal penetration. The symptoms are similar to those of hepatitis B but are usually milder. The disease does not progress to a chronic state, and no one remains infectious after recovery. There is no specific treatment.

Individual vaccines are available against hepatitis A and against hepatitis B, as well as a combined vaccine against both A and B (Twinrix). The combined vaccine is administered as three injections over 6 months.

The hepatitis C virus is another important cause of chronic liver disease. It is not commonly transmitted via sexual contact, however.

AIDS Is Caused by the Human Immunodeficiency Virus

Acquired immune deficiency syndrome (**AIDS**) is a relatively new disease: It was first described in 1981. Nearly uniformly fatal if untreated, the disease has spread as a devastating epidemic in the United States and worldwide (**Table 15.3**). It is caused by the **human immunodeficiency virus** (**HIV**) (**Figure 15.17**). This is a **retrovirus**, meaning that its genetic material, RNA, is transcribed into DNA once it enters the host cell. "Retro" refers to the fact that transcription runs backward in comparison with the usual DNA-to-RNA direction.

hepatitis viruses   Viruses that cause liver disease.

hepatitis B   Liver disease caused by the hepatitis B virus, a virus that is often transmitted sexually.

jaundice   Yellowing of the skin and mucous membranes, caused by liver disease.

hepatitis A   Liver disease caused by the hepatitis A virus. It is sometimes transmitted sexually.

acquired immune deficiency syndrome (AIDS)   The disease caused by the human immunodeficiency virus (HIV); its onset is defined by the occurrence of any of a number of opportunistic infections, or on the basis of blood tests.

human immunodeficiency virus (HIV)   The retrovirus that causes AIDS.

retrovirus   An RNA virus whose genome is copied into DNA within the host cell.

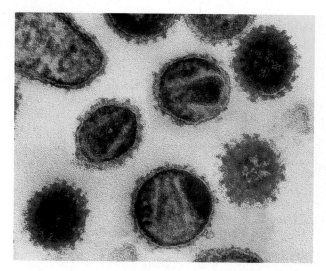

Figure 15.17 HIV particles in a colorized electron micrograph. Each viral particle is about 0.1 micrometers across.

TABLE 15.3
HIV/AIDS Statistics for the United States and Worldwide, 2012

	United States	Global
Cumulative AIDS deaths[a]	648,000	30 million
AIDS deaths per year[a]	14,000	1.7 million
Persons currently infected with HIV	1.2 million	34 million
New HIV infections per year	48,000	2.5 million

After AVERT, 2014a; Centers for Disease Control, 2014h.
[a]Deaths from any cause of persons diagnosed with AIDS.

HIV evolved from a very similar virus that infects chimpanzees in west-central Africa. The virus spread to humans quite recently—probably in the 1920s (Pepin, 2011). The first people to be infected may have been involved in the killing and butchering of chimpanzees for "bush meat." Although the first human cases must have been in Africa, the first outbreak to be recognized as a new disease struck gay men in San Francisco, Los Angeles, and New York in the mid-to-late 1970s. (See **Web Activity 15.1: Milestones in the Global HIV/AIDS Pandemic.**) HIV has since spread by other routes, including heterosexual sex, contaminated needles, blood transfusions, and perinatal transmission from mother to child, but more than 6 in 10 infections in the United States still result from sex between men (**Figure 15.18A**). Young gay and bisexual men and blacks of both sexes (**Figure 15.18B**) are particularly at risk of acquiring and passing on the virus. The prevalence of HIV infection is especially high among young men who are both black and gay or bisexual.

AIDS has spread around the world, but it has caused the worst humanitarian disaster on the continent where it originated—Africa. In at least nine sub-Saharan countries, 10% or more of the adult population carry HIV, and AIDS-related deaths have orphaned millions of children and devastated national economies.

There is increasingly good news, however: Worldwide, AIDS-related deaths fell by 35% between 2005 and 2013, and new infections fell by 35% just during the 3-year period from 2011 to 2014 (UNAIDS, 2014). In South Africa, overall life expectancy at birth increased by 9 years between 2005 and 2014—nearly recovering to its pre-AIDS peak of 62 years—thanks to the increasing availability of effective antiviral drugs

Figure 15.18 The demographics of HIV infections in the United States. (A) Mode of infection. (B) Racial/ethnic breakdown of infections. (Data from Centers for Disease Control, 2014l.)

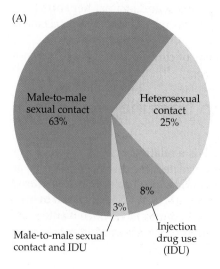
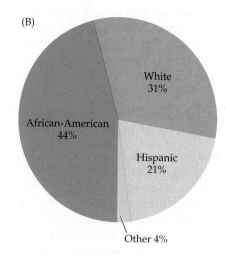

(BBC News, 2014). The AIDS pandemic is not spiraling out of control as some had feared a decade or so ago; in fact, the United Nations has optimistically described the present time as "the beginning of the end" of the pandemic (UNAIDS, 2014).

Sexual transmission is chiefly by coitus and anal sex

In this discussion, we are mainly interested in the sexual modes of HIV transmission; this is a sexuality textbook, after all. To evaluate the risks of transmission, it's important to understand that HIV exists in several body fluids of infected people—blood, semen, vaginal fluid, breast milk, tears, and saliva—but in very different concentrations. The levels of HIV in tears and saliva are too low for those fluids to be infectious. Kissing—even deep kissing—an HIV-infected person carries a very low risk of transmission. Because of the possibility that there might be blood or open sores in the infected person's mouth, however, the risk is not completely zero. For that reason, the CDC recommends against open-mouth kissing with an HIV-infected person.

HIV is present at high concentrations in semen and vaginal fluid. Thus, there is at least a theoretical risk of transmission by oral sex; that is, a person who takes the oral role in fellatio or cunnilingus with an HIV-infected partner has a chance of acquiring an infection. Transmission by fellatio has been documented by actual case studies (Public Health Agency of Canada, 2004), but the risk is lower than with vaginal or anal sex. The risk of transmission by cunnilingus is extremely low, but there have been a few cases where the virus was apparently transmitted by this route (Centers for Disease Control, 2009). Presumably, the likelihood of transmission in the reverse direction, from the mouth of an HIV-infected person to the penis or vagina of his or her partner, is also very low. There is one reported case of oral-to-anal transmission.

The sexual behaviors that carry a high risk of HIV transmission are unprotected (condomless) coitus and anal penetration. The very highest risk is associated with taking the receptive (insertee) role in anal sex with an HIV-positive partner: Each such act carries about a 1 in 200 chance of acquiring HIV (Varghese et al., 2002). In the case of receptive vaginal sex the risk is somewhat lower—about 1 in 1000. This difference is probably because the rectal mucosa possesses immune system cells that pick up the virus easily (Owen, 1998).

Taking the insertive role with an HIV-positive partner is not quite as risky—it's about half the risk for the receptive role in the case of vaginal sex and one-eighth the risk in the case of anal sex (Varghese et al., 2002). The risk to the insertor is about 60% lower if he is circumcised than if he is not, at least in the case of vaginal sex (World Health Organization, 2014).

The transmission risk also varies greatly depending on the stage of the infected partner's disease. According to one study conducted in Africa, the risk of transmission per sex act is more than 10 times higher soon after infection than during the latent phase of the disease (see below) but rises again after AIDS itself sets in (Wawer et al., 2005). Treatments that reduce viral loads to undetectable levels greatly reduce the risk of transmission, perhaps to near zero (Rodger et al., 2014).

The presence of preexisting STIs such as syphilis, gonorrhea, herpes, and chlamydia facilitates transmission in either direction. In fact, any condition that causes ulcers or other damage to the skin or mucosa increases the risk of transmission. Coitus during a woman's menstrual period increases the risk of woman-to-man transmission.

The risks cited above, such as 1 in 1000 in the case of receptive vaginal sex, may seem quite low, but bear in mind that they relate to single acts. A person might engage in a thousand such acts within the space of a few years (with either a single or multiple partners), thus dramatically increasing his or her likelihood of becoming infected.

CD4 lymphocyte A type of lymphocyte that carries the CD4 receptor; one of the major targets of HIV.

seroconversion The change from negative to positive on an antibody test, such as occurs a few weeks or months after HIV infection.

HIV-symptomatic disease Health problems caused by HIV, especially those that occur before the criteria for an AIDS diagnosis have been met.

antiretroviral drugs Drugs effective against retroviruses.

The risk of acquiring HIV by any kind of sexual contact between women is low, but occasional instances have been reported. Of course, bisexual and lesbian women can contract HIV infection from sex with men or from injection drug use.

HIV infection progresses in a characteristic way

Now let's look in more detail at the course of the disease following HIV infection. During the weeks after the initial infection, the virus multiplies inside cells in the person's blood and lymph nodes. Its main targets are the **CD4 lymphocytes**, which are white blood cells that make up an important part of the body's immune system. Other cell types may also be infected. During this initial period there are no symptoms, and the infected person's immune system has not yet produced significant levels of antibodies to the virus. Thus, the person is "HIV-negative," meaning that the usual HIV blood test, which detects the presence of antibodies to HIV, gives a negative response. Nevertheless, the virus itself is present at high levels and can be detected by a technique called the polymerase chain reaction (PCR). Thus, the person is capable of infecting other people. This is the reason why members of high-risk groups are not allowed to donate blood, even if they test HIV-negative.

At some point, usually between 6 weeks and 6 months after infection, the infected person's immune system does mount a response to the virus—antibodies appear in the blood, and the person tests HIV-positive. This change is called **seroconversion**. Seroconversion may be preceded or accompanied by an acute flu-like illness marked by fever, nausea, muscle pain, and sometimes a rash; however, some people experience no symptoms at all during this phase. Even those who do may mistake the symptoms for some other illness.

The body's immune response to the HIV greatly reduces the level of virus in the infected person's blood. The symptoms of acute illness subside, and the person now enters a prolonged asymptomatic period, or latent phase, that may last 7 to 10 years or even longer.

Some signs and symptoms may begin to appear several years before the diagnosis of AIDS. These signs include thrush (a fungal infection of the mouth and throat), shingles (a painful rash caused by reactivation of a latent chicken pox infection), unexplained fever, diarrhea, night sweats, and a generalized swelling of lymph nodes. To distinguish these disorders from full-blown AIDS, they are referred to collectively as **HIV-symptomatic disease**.

HIV-positive people are considered to have AIDS when their CD4 levels drop from the normal level of about 1000 cells per microliter (cells/μL) to below 200 cells/μL or when certain illnesses appear. These include opportunistic infections, such as unusual forms of pneumonia or meningitis, as well as certain cancers, extreme weight loss, or dementia. Without treatment, people diagnosed with AIDS (not just HIV infection) typically survive for less than a year before succumbing to one of the complications of the disease.

Antiretroviral drugs suppress but don't eliminate HIV

Antiretroviral drugs fall into four classes that target specific phases of the virus's replication cycle (**Figure 15.19**):

- Fusion inhibitors, or entry inhibitors, block the attachment of the virus to the host cell or the fusion of the viral and host cell membranes, thus preventing the virus from entering the cell.

- Reverse transcriptase inhibitors block the copying of the viral RNA into DNA.

- Integrase inhibitors block the insertion of this DNA into the host cell's own genome.

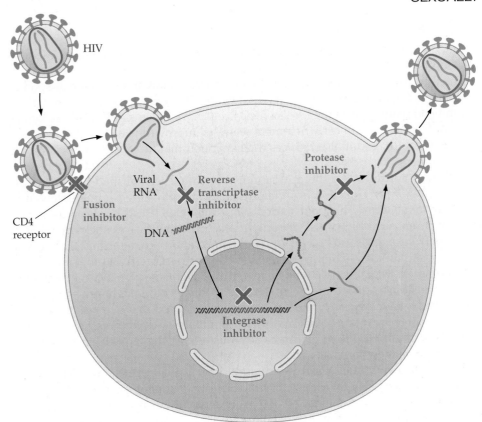

Figure 15.19 HIV replication cycle and the sites of action of antiretroviral drugs.

- Protease inhibitors block the cutting of newly synthesized viral proteins into the shorter lengths that are required for function.

Typically these drugs are administered in combinations of three or more different drugs, to attack the virus on several fronts and reduce its ability to develop resistance. The multiple drugs may be combined into a single pill.

Antiretroviral therapy has greatly reduced the death rate from AIDS in the United States and other countries (**Figure 15.20**). Still, current antiretroviral therapy has several shortcomings: It does not eradicate the virus from the body, so the drugs must

Figure 15.20 Living with HIV
(A) Basketball star and businessman Magic Johnson announced he had HIV in 1991. (B) Figure skater Rudy Galindo announced he was HIV-positive in 2000. (C) Safer-sex advocate Rebekka Armstrong (shown when she was a *Playboy* Playmate) has been HIV-positive since 1994.

(A)

(B)

(C)

post-exposure prophylaxis (PEP)   A drug treatment designed to prevent establishment of an infection after exposure to a disease agent such as HIV.

pre-exposure prophylaxis (PrEP)   A drug taken before exposure to a disease agent to prevent infection.

be taken indefinitely; drug resistance can develop; and the drugs may have serious side effects.

The U.S. government recommends that antiretroviral treatment begin as soon as a person is diagnosed as having HIV (AIDSinfo, 2014). Some other organizations recommend waiting until the levels of CD4 cells have fallen significantly or symptoms have appeared, but early treatment seems to improve an HIV-positive person's long-term health, and it also reduces the likelihood that he or she will pass on the virus to others.

Although antiretroviral therapy cannot eradicate an established HIV infection, it might prevent an infection from taking hold if administered immediately after exposure to the virus. This **post-exposure prophylaxis (PEP)** has been used with some apparent success in cases of occupational exposure (needlesticks by medical personnel), sexual assaults by HIV-positive men, and sexual encounters between sero-opposite couples—couples where one partner is infected and the other is not (McCarty et al., 2011). People who believe they have been exposed to HIV should get medical advice immediately—preferably within a couple of hours and no later than 72 hours after exposure. The most effective way to do this is to visit the nearest hospital emergency room. To reduce the risk of mother-to-child transmission, a brief course of antiretroviral therapy can be administered to the mother before delivery as well as to her newborn baby.

An exciting new strategy is **pre-exposure prophylaxis (PrEP)**, in which persons at risk of acquiring HIV take antiretroviral drugs on an ongoing basis. A once-daily pill named Truvada (a combination of two antiretroviral drugs) greatly reduced the risk of infection both in gay men (Centers for Disease Control, 2010a) and in heterosexual women and men (Family Health International, 2011). Compliance with the Truvada regimen is not always consistent. For that reason, an injectable form of Truvada, administered once every 4 months, has been developed and is currently entering clinical trials.

The U.S. Public Health Service has recommended PrEP for all HIV-negative members of high-risk groups, such as anyone who has an HIV-positive partner, or men who have multiple male partners and don't always use condoms (U.S. Public Health Service, 2014). Usage rates of PrEP within the gay community have so far been disappointing, in part because gay men don't wish to be identified as promiscuous "Truvada whores" (Murphy, 2013).

In spite of an enormous research effort over 25 years, no HIV vaccine has so far provided reliable protection in clinical trials (Cohen, 2013). The results of some of the trials have provided pointers toward the future development of an effective vaccine. Regardless of the success or failure of these efforts, epidemiologists are increasingly optimistic that the AIDS pandemic can be halted without a vaccine.

You Can Reduce Your STI Risks

In spite of the many medical advances documented in this chapter, STIs remain a major public health problem. Well-meaning people disagree on the best strategies for combating them, but there are several methods that are important to know. Here we consider the main options: sexual abstinence, choice of sex partners, choice of sex practices, and use of condoms.

Abstinence prevents STIs

Although it may seem too obvious to be worth saying, people who have no sexual contacts with others cannot acquire or transmit any disease by the sexual route. Complete abstinence from sexual contacts has other potential benefits besides disease prevention. It offers complete protection against unwanted pregnancy. It allows people to concentrate their time and energies on nonsexual relationships as well as on nonsexual goals. "Abstinence" is interpreted in different ways by different people, however. If it is interpreted to allow for sexual contacts other than coitus, it may not offer much protection against STIs (see below).

Sexually active people can reduce their risk of STIs

People who do not choose to be abstinent still have options for reducing their risk of acquiring STIs. One way they can do this is to reduce the total number of people with whom they have sexual contact and to select partners who are less likely to have STIs:

- A person who has had many previous sex partners is more likely to have an STI than someone who has had few or no partners.
- An injection drug user may have acquired an STI by nonsexual means.
- Someone with whom you can feel comfortable discussing STI issues is likely to be a safer partner than someone who avoids the topic.
- Someone you know well is more likely to tell you if they have an STI than someone you just met.

There are mobile phone apps, such as Healthvana, that make it easy to get tested for STIs and to communicate the results to potential sex partners. If you don't have that information, just looking at your partner's genitals offers some degree of protection: Sores, warts, herpes lesions, and genital discharges are obvious warning signs, if you just take a look.

Different individuals may have different likelihoods of acquiring an STI even when their total numbers of sex partners and their sexual behaviors are the same, on account of demographic variations in STI prevalence. For example, we mentioned above that HIV prevalence is much higher among gay and bisexual black men than among other groups. This is not because these men have more partners or use condoms less than gay or bisexual men of other races—in fact they have fewer partners and engage in less unprotected sex, according to a study by Michael Newcomb and Brian Mustanski of Northwestern University (Newcomb et al., 2014). However, this same study found that the sex partners of gay and bisexual black men are about 11 times more likely to be other black men than is true for members of other racial groups, so each sexual encounter is much more likely to be with an HIV-positive partner. In other words, gay and bisexual black men form an interconnected network within which HIV infection can readily spiral out of control, in spite of relatively cautious sexual behavior by individuals within the network.

Some sexual behaviors are riskier than others for STI transmission

As we've already discussed in the case of HIV, women and men who are sexually active can greatly influence their likelihood of acquiring or transmitting an STI by the choice of sexual behaviors they engage in (**Box 15.2**).

Coitus, anal sex, and anilingus (mouth-to-anus contact) are high-risk sexual behaviors, with anal sex being the riskiest with regard to HIV transmission. Anilingus has a low likelihood of transmitting HIV, but it is a risky practice because of the likelihood of transmission of hepatitis A or B (in the anus-to-mouth direction), as well as other STIs.

Oral sex (fellatio or cunnilingus) is a moderate-risk behavior. Although transmission of HIV by oral sex is far less common than by coitus or anal sex, this route readily transmits some other STIs, such as gonorrhea and syphilis. Other sexual behaviors, such as kissing, fondling, hand-genital contact, and general body contact, are low-risk

Box 15.2 Society, Values, and the Law

STIs and the Law

Would you agree to be infected with an STI for $900,000? No? How about $2.5 million? OK then, $6.7 million? Before you jump at this offer, though, be aware that certain restrictions apply, and your payout may vary.

The quoted amounts were awarded in civil suits brought by three West Coast women who contracted STIs from their male partners (Green, 2012; Murphy, 2013). But most people who get STIs have no hope of scoring at those levels, if at all. First, the STI has to be a lifelong infection, even if not an especially serious one. (Those three women contracted herpes.) Readily curable infections like gonorrhea are nonstarters, unless there are long-lasting complications. Second, the defendant has to actually have the STI: Singer Tony Bennett successfully defended a $90 million lawsuit by producing medical records showing that he didn't have the STI in question, and he filed a $100 million countersuit for defamation—not something that you'd want to deal with (ABC News, 2011b). Third, the defendant must have transmitted the STI intentionally (a tort legally defined as "battery"), or at least recklessly ("negligent injury") (Nolo, 2014). If you can't show that the defendant knew he or she had the STI, your chances of collecting are slim. Fourth, you should have a backstory that will resonate with a jury: In the case of the $2.5 million award, for example, the plaintiff was an innocent wife whose husband contracted herpes during an extramarital affair. Most important, the defendant must have deep pockets: No lawyer is going to take on a case where there is little chance of collecting.

Penniless perps can still get into trouble with the *criminal* justice system, however, especially if the STI in question is HIV. Many states have enacted statutes that compel people who are HIV-positive to inform their sex partners about their HIV status. In 2002 an HIV-positive student at Huron University in South Dakota was handed a 5-year suspended sentence for violating such a statute. (He eventually served 18 months for violating his probation.) At least two women who had sex with him tested positive for HIV (Simon, 2002).

No I'm not! Model Avril Nolan sued for damages because the photo implied that she was infected with HIV.

There are other ways to monetize STIs beyond suing the person who infected you. A 13-year-old boy collected over $700,000 from the Milton Hershey School in Hershey, Pennsylvania, after the school denied him admission on account of his positive HIV status (Advocate.com, 2012). In 2014 an HIV-positive man was awarded $532,000 in a disability discrimination lawsuit against his former employer, a New York City hotel (Schapiro, 2014).

In fact, you don't even have to have an STI to profit from it. A Massachusetts woman was awarded $2.5 million after she was wrongly diagnosed with AIDS and treated for it for almost 9 years (CBS News, 2007). And in 2014 an HIV-negative New York City model won the first round in a $450,000 lawsuit against a stock-photo agency: She alleges that she suffered emotional distress because her photo appeared in an HIV-related public service announcement with the caption "I am positive (+)" (see figure) (Marsh, 2014).

behaviors. They are certainly not free of risk—herpes and syphilis, for example, can both be transmitted by these behaviors—but they are so much safer than the high- and moderate-risk activities described above that they offer a sensible alternative for sexually active people when STI transmission is a concern.

The use of sex toys is risky if the toys are not kept scrupulously clean. Sex toys should not be shared.

Having sex while you or your partner is under the influence of alcohol or drugs increases the chances that you will ignore all the information in this chapter.

Condoms are the mainstay of STI prevention

The condom is the key to STI prevention for sexually active people, especially for those who are not in a long-term relationship. The proper use of condoms has already been described in the context of contraception (see Chapter 9). Two points are worth reemphasizing in the context of STI protection:

1. Natural-tissue condoms ("skins"), although possibly effective as contraceptives, do not provide adequate protection against STIs because they have pores through which viruses can pass. No disease agents can pass through an unbroken latex or polyurethane condom.

2. Anal sex places greater demands on a condom than does vaginal sex. For anal sex, extra-strength condoms are recommended. This is particularly important when the insertive partner is known to be HIV-positive.

Female condoms are probably at least as effective as male condoms for STI prevention.

The condom is—let's face it—a pretty medieval solution to a 21st-century health crisis. We look forward to the day when advances in prophylaxis, vaccines, and non-barrier contraception—combined with better sex education—will consign the condom to history. In the meantime, it's a lifesaver.

Condom distribution on a beach near Santiago, Chile.

Not Everything Is an STI

By this point, you quite likely have diagnosed several STIs in yourself, including a couple of fatal ones! If so, it's time for a reality check. HIV is uncommon in the college student population and very uncommon among heterosexual students. Hepatitis usually cures itself. Syphilis and gonorrhea can be easily cured with antibiotics. Herpes won't kill you.

Students often mistake other medical conditions, or even perfectly healthy traits, for STIs. **Figure 15.21** shows some examples of conditions that are not STIs but might be interpreted as such by people without medical training. Shaving the pubic area may cause a rash that is misinterpreted as herpes. Little bumps around the head of the penis, called "pearly penile papules," are natural and harmless growths, not genital warts caused by HPV. (Some women have similar skin tags on or near the clitoris.) A round swelling on the labia is more likely to be caused by a blocked mucus gland than any kind of STI. Canker sores within the mouth have many causes, but they are not the result of infections, sexual or otherwise.

We encourage you to take all reasonable steps to protect your own health and that of your sex partners. By all means get yourself checked out if you are in doubt about whether you have an STI or would like to be screened for HIV. But don't let fear of AIDS or other sexually transmitted infections so preoccupy you as to leave no room for emotional or physical intimacy.

FAQ

Is there any way to reduce STI risk during cunnilingus?

For oral stimulation of the vulva or the anus you can buy flat sheets of latex called "dams"—some are flavored. Ask at your campus health center, go to a website that sells condoms, or make your own by cutting a condom lengthwise. The effectiveness of plastic food wrap as an STI barrier has not been well studied, but it is certainly better than no barrier at all.

Figure 15.21 We're not STIs.
(A) Folliculitis, such as might be caused by shaving pubic hair. (B) "Pearly penile papules" are harmless little bumps that ring the glans of the penis in some men. (C) This cyst on the labia was caused by blockage of the duct of a mucous gland. (D) A canker sore in the mouth may result from accidental biting or other causes.

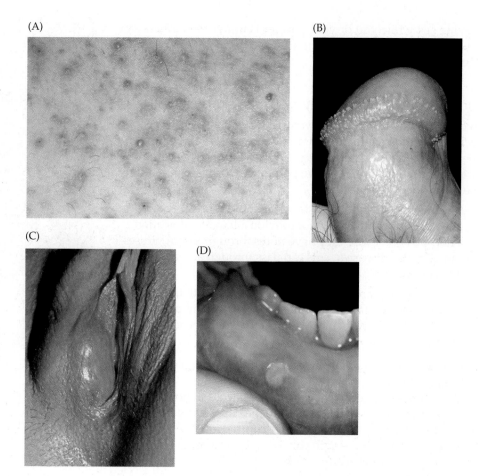

Go to the
**Discovering
Human Sexuality**
Companion Website at
**sites.sinauer.com/
discoveringhumansexuality3e**
for activities, study questions, quizzes, and other study aids.

Summary

- Nearly 20 million new cases of sexually transmitted infections (STIs) occur annually in the United States. STIs are caused by lice, mites, protozoans, bacteria, and viruses. In spite of medical advances, STIs remain a major public health problem. They also bolster common perceptions of sex as something dangerous or immoral.

- Skin infestations that can be transmitted sexually include pubic lice and scabies. Pubic lice attach themselves to hair shafts, especially in the pubic region. Scabies mites burrow under the surface of the skin. Both infestations can cause severe itching but do not otherwise threaten health. Pubic lice and scabies mites can be eliminated by use of insecticidal lotions or shampoos.

- Trichomoniasis is an infection of the vagina or urethra by a protozoan. In women it causes discomfort, a vaginal discharge, and the urge to urinate frequently. In men, the infection is usually asymptomatic. It is generally eliminated by a single oral dose of Flagyl.

- Syphilis is caused by infection with the bacterium *Treponema pallidum*. The disease has several stages. Primary syphilis is marked by a sore (chancre) at the site of infection. Some weeks later, a rash and fever occur (secondary syphilis). The infection then becomes latent, but it may eventually attack a variety of organ systems (tertiary syphilis) and cause death. The disease is readily curable with penicillin in its early stages.

- Gonorrhea is caused by infection with the bacterium *Neisseria gonorrhoeae*. In men it usually infects the urethra, causing painful urination. In women it can infect the cervix, causing a vaginal discharge. The infection in women is commonly asymptomatic, but it can spread to the internal reproductive tract, causing pelvic inflammatory disease (PID) and reduced fertility. Rectal and oral infections can occur in either sex. Gonorrhea can be treated with antibiotics, but antibiotic resistance is an increasing problem.

- Infection with the bacterium *Chlamydia trachomatis* is very common. It can cause a urethral or vaginal discharge and painful urination, but many infected men and women do not have symptoms. Anal and oral infections can occur. Chlamydia is readily treatable with antibiotics. In women, untreated chlamydia infections can lead to PID.

- Molluscum contagiosum is a common skin condition caused by a pox virus. It consists of small skin growths that usually disappear permanently after a few months. Although any kind of interpersonal contact can allow for transmission, molluscum in the genital area is usually the result of sexual transmission.

- Genital herpes is a very common condition caused by infection with the herpes simplex virus type 1 or 2 (HSV-1 or HSV-2). It causes an outbreak of sores at the site of infection, which is usually somewhere in the anogenital region but can also be in the mouth. The initial outbreak heals spontaneously, but it may be followed by further outbreaks at the same location that recur for the remainder of the person's life. Herpes infection is incurable, but outbreaks can be treated or prevented with antiviral drugs.

- Human papillomaviruses (HPVs) cause genital warts and other lesions of the genital skin and urogenital tract. Genital warts can be removed by a variety of treatments. Some HPV types (not those that cause bulky, raised genital warts) infect the cervix and are the principal cause of cervical cancer and anal cancer. HPV vaccines are available; they should be administered to a young person before he or she becomes sexually active.

- Hepatitis A and B are viral infections of the liver that can be acquired sexually as well as by other routes. Anal sex (especially oral-anal contacts) are the sexual behaviors most likely to transmit hepatitis A. Hepatitis B is transmitted by coitus or oral sex; in a minority of cases it leads to chronic liver disease and liver cancer. No cure exists for either form of hepatitis, but effective vaccines are available.

- Acquired immune deficiency syndrome (AIDS) is caused by infection with the human immunodeficiency virus (HIV). The virus originated in central Africa, but a worldwide pandemic began with outbreaks in gay male communities in the United States in the late 1970s. Transmission now occurs by both male-female and male-male sexual contacts (principally by coitus and anal penetration), as well as by exposure to contaminated blood. Female-to-female transmission is uncommon.

- HIV infection is marked by an acute illness followed by a several-year asymptomatic period. Eventually the infection impairs the person's immune system to the point that certain opportunistic infections and cancers may occur. Symptomatic AIDS is a life-threatening condition that cannot be cured, but it may be held in check with a combination of drugs that interfere with various stages of the virus's replication cycle. These drugs are slowing the global AIDS epidemic. There is no HIV vaccine, but high-risk populations can take antiviral drugs (Truvada) as prophylaxis against infection.

- Women and men can reduce their risk of acquiring STIs by a variety of means. Complete sexual abstinence offers complete protection. Sexually active people can reduce their risk by keeping the number of their sexual partners low (ideally, by forming a mutually monogamous relationship), by discussing STIs and sexual history with prospective partners, by getting tested for STIs, and by engaging in relatively low-risk sexual behaviors as an alternative to coitus or anal sex. Careful and consistent use of condoms is another key to lowering the risk of acquiring and transmitting STIs.

Discussion Questions

1. Can you think of any circumstances in which it would be acceptable for someone who has an STI not to inform his or her sex partner? If others in your class have a different opinion, discuss the reasons for your differing views and attempt to reach a consensus on the subject.

2. Do you think that there are any circumstances in which a person should be legally punished for transmitting a serious STI to a partner? Or do you think that such action is counterproductive? Should people simply be held responsible for protecting themselves from STIs?

3. Imagine you are embarking on a sexual relationship with your first partner or a new partner. How would you bring up the matter of STIs and what to do about them? Try to imagine the actual conversation you would have and what the difficulties might be.

4. Imagine you are returning to your high school to give a half-hour presentation about STIs. What age students would you choose to speak to? What would be the main goals you'd like to accomplish? Do you think any particular styles of communication would be most effective? Is there any way in which you think you could do a better job than an STI specialist from the local health department?

Web Resources

American Sexual Health Association
www.ashasexualhealth.org/stdsstis

Centers for Disease Control and Prevention. Sexually Transmitted Diseases www.cdc.gov/std

Centers for Disease Control and Prevention. HIV/AIDS www.cdc.gov/hiv

UNAIDS www.unaids.org

National Minority AIDS Council www.nmac.org

UNAIDS: Gap report (on AIDS pandemic)
tinyurl.com/nnbwqnx

University of California, San Francisco. HIV InSite
hivinsite.ucsf.edu/InSite

Recommended Reading

Barnett, T. & Whiteside, A. (2006). *AIDS in the twenty-first century: Disease and globalization* (2nd ed.). Palgrave Macmillan.

Holleran, A. (2008). *Chronicle of a plague, revisited: AIDS and its aftermath.* Da Capo.

Marr, L. (2007). *Sexually transmitted diseases: A physician tells you what you need to know* (2nd ed.). Johns Hopkins University Press.

Pepin, J. (2011). *The origins of AIDS.* Cambridge University Press.

Reverby, S. (2009). *Examining Tuskegee: The infamous syphilis study and its legacy.* University of North Carolina Press.

Stine, G. (2013). *AIDS update 2014.* McGraw-Hill.

Chapter 16

Everyone has the right to freedom from unwanted sexual contacts.

Sexual Assault, Harassment, and Partner Violence

This chapter deals with the dark side of sex. Sex is not limited to balanced, happy interactions between loving couples. It can be grossly one-sided, involving sexual desire on one person's part and disinterest, perhaps aversion, on the other's. It can involve physical assault. And intimate sexual relationships can be marred by cruelty and violence. We touched on these issues earlier: In Chapter 7 we discussed the difficult feelings resulting from unrequited love, as well as the breakup of relationships. In Chapter 13 we described paraphilic disorders such as exhibitionism that can lead to the victimization of others. Here we take a broader look at sex as a context for physical and psychological injury. We omit one important form of sexual victimization—that of children by adults—because we have covered this topic in Chapters 10 and 13.

What Is Rape?

rape Coitus (and sometimes other penetrative sex acts) accomplished by force or the threat of force.

sexual assault Coercive or nonconsensual sexual contact: a broader category of behaviors than rape.

statutory rape Penetrative sex when a partner is legally unable to give consent on account of young age, intellectual disability, or unconsciousness.

date rape Rape between dating or socially acquainted couples.

acquaintance rape Rape by a person known to the victim.

The terms that describe acts of sexual victimization have been given many different definitions. Here we use these terms in ways that correspond approximately to legal usage. **Rape** or "forcible rape" is used to mean penetration of the vagina, anus, or mouth by the penis when performed by force or the threat of force. (Legal definitions vary among states: Sometimes oral or anal penetration is not considered rape, and sometimes vaginal or anal penetration by a finger or an object *is* considered rape.) **Sexual assault** is a broader term that includes any sexual act performed by force or the threat of force. **Statutory rape** means coitus, anal penetration, or oral penetration performed without force, but also without the partner's consent; it is usually applied to cases in which the partner cannot legally give consent on account of young age or mental incapacity. When we use the term "rape" without qualification, we are excluding statutory rape.

Another frequently used term is **date rape**: This is not a legal term but an informal way of referring to rape that occurs in a situation where some kind of consensual sexual interaction is a possibility or is actually under way when the rape takes place. It is not restricted to occasions when the two people are on a traditional "date."

The term **acquaintance rape** is a broader term than "date rape": It includes date rape but also includes any rape where the perpetrator is a friend or social acquaintance of the victim. Most rapes are acquaintance rapes.

For a rape charge to stick, it must usually be shown that the victim made evident to the rapist her (or his) unwillingness to engage in sex. This unwillingness is often expressed by physical resistance, but not necessarily: A verbal refusal is sufficient. The courts are aware that physical resistance is sometimes impossible or unwise.

Rape law does not necessarily cover every sexual situation. There exists a rather broad "gray area" in which a woman isn't comfortable with having sex but hasn't said either "yes" or "no" and hasn't offered even token resistance to the man's advances. This is unlikely to be considered rape, legally speaking, even though the woman hasn't given explicit consent to sex, but it might be grounds for disciplinary action in a college setting. It's also important to be aware that the details of laws governing rape and sexual assault vary considerably from state to state.

Young women are the most frequent victims of rape

Many rapes are not reported to the police. We therefore rely on random-sample surveys of the U.S. population as the best available source for rape statistics. In the National Intimate Partner and Sexual Violence Survey (NISVS—a large-scale telephone survey of adults conducted by the CDC), 19% of women said that they had experienced at least one completed or attempted rape in their lifetime;* 79% of these women experienced rape (or their first rape) before they were 25 years old (Centers for Disease Control, 2014n). Some critics maintain that the CDC uses overly broad definitions of rape in coming up with these figures (Sommers, 2012).

The figures for men are much lower, but not insignificant: In the NISVS, 1.7% of men said that they had experienced a completed or attempted rape over their lifetime, nearly always at the hands of male perpetrators. Twenty-three percent of men had experienced some unwanted sexual event over their lifetime, most commonly at the hands of female perpetrators. As with women, victimization of males begins early: In one survey, over 40% of male high school students had experienced some kind of sexual coercion (French et al., 2014).

Thankfully, in the United States there has been a marked long-term decline in the reported incidence of rape, beginning around 1980, and this decline continues today

---

* Because "lifetime" meant "up until the interview," the overall lifetime experience would likely be higher.

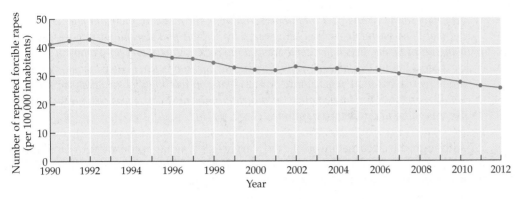

Figure 16.1   Declining U.S. rape rates, 1990 to 2012 This graph shows the number of reported forcible rapes per 100,000 inhabitants. (Data from Disaster Center, 2014.)

(**Figure 16.1**). The decrease in rapes roughly matches a decrease in the incidence of other violent crimes. The reasons for this overall decrease have been widely debated but are not well understood (Wilson, 2011).

Most rapes are not reported

According to the National Crime Victimization Survey (NCVS), only 28% of rapes and sexual assaults were reported to the police in 2012 (Bureau of Justice Statistics, 2013a). This is considerably lower than the 44% rate for violent crimes in general. Reporting rates are highest when the perpetrators are strangers and lowest when they are current or former spouses or partners. Victims who do not report rapes most frequently give one of the following reasons for not doing so (Utah Coalition Against Sexual Assault, 2006):

- It was a personal matter.
- They were afraid of reprisals.
- They wanted to protect the perpetrator.
- They believed the police were biased or would do nothing.

Most rape prevention organizations encourage a person who has been sexually assaulted to report the crime. They believe that doing so can help the victim regain a sense of control and can reduce the likelihood that the perpetrator will offend again. Even if he is not prosecuted, the fact that his name is on file with the university or police can facilitate his prosecution for a later offence. Still, the decision to report or not report any rape or sexual assault is a deeply personal one that only victims can make for themselves.

Most perpetrators are men known to the victims

Who are the people who commit rape or sexual assault? Contrary to a common perception, the majority of them are known to the victim, either as their intimate partners or as friends or acquaintances (U.S. Department of Justice, 2010) (**Figure 16.2**).

Nearly all rapes and the majority of sexual assaults are committed by men—usually young men. Nearly 1 in 3 rapes are committed by juveniles (Gannon et al., 2008). Of people incarcerated for sexual assault—typically the more serious offenders—nearly 100% are male (Texas Tribune, 2014). Still, aggressive sexual behavior by women, including sexual assault and even rape, does occur. Here's one account:

When I was at a student party, . . . a very drunk (and physically rather large) woman came on to me, very strongly indeed. I tried to escape with a tactical toilet break. She followed me, forced me up against the basin, pushed her tongue into my mouth and her hand into my jeans. I had to summon up quite a lot of physical strength to escape.

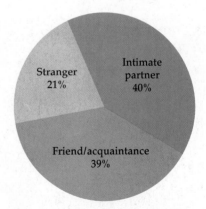

Figure 16.2   Most rapists are known to their victims. The graph shows the relationships of the perpetrators of rape and sexual assault to their female victims. (Data from U.S. Department of Justice, 2010.)

This may sound strange, but my understanding of the incident, then and now, was not that I had narrowly escaped being raped by her, but that she had narrowly escaped being raped by me. When her hand grasped my cock it reacted and for a moment I considered letting her have her wish. I refrained, partly because I knew I would regret it afterwards, but more importantly because I knew it was highly likely that she would regret it, if not immediately, then certainly the next day. I was also pretty sure she was going to throw up any minute. (Fogg, 2013)

Although the circumstances of rape vary greatly, what is common to most rapes is their severe effects on the raped woman or man. These effects are illustrated by first-person accounts of rape (**Box 16.1**).

College Rapes Are Becoming Less Common

According to NCVS data, about 0.4% of female college students experienced a rape or sexual assault in 2013 (Bureau of Justice Statistics, 2014c). This is considerably lower than the rates reported in some other studies, one of which estimated that a female student has a 20% to 25% chance of experiencing an attempted or completed rape in the course of a 5-year college career (Fisher et al., 2000). The difference has in part to do with the fact that the earlier survey inquired about a wider range of unwanted sexual behaviors; but in addition, the numbers of campus rapes and sexual assaults have fallen dramatically over the last 20 years—the current rate is about half of what it was in 1997, according to the NCVS data. Female college students are less likely to be raped than similar-age women who are not college students.

Most campus rapes occur after 6 PM in residences—most commonly the victim's own residence. Most victims know the perpetrator, who is usually a classmate, friend, ex-boyfriend, or acquaintance. Thus, many of these crimes could be described as "acquaintance rapes" or "date rapes," although the two persons may not have been dating in the traditional sense. About 1 in 5 campus rapes involve additional injuries, such as bruises and cuts.

A phenomenon that contributes to date rape in a college setting as much as elsewhere is what has been called the "cold-to-hot empathy gap." That means that as people become aroused (sexually, in this case), they become more strongly motivated to consummate their desire and pay less attention to moral issues such as consideration for the interests of a partner. This was strikingly demonstrated in a study by Dan Ariely of the Massachusetts Institute of Technology and George Loewenstein of Carnegie Mellon University (Ariely & Loewenstein, 2006). These researchers had male students answer questions about their likely sexual behavior in a range of situations. The questions were asked while the students were in two different states: while they were in a normal nonaroused state ("cold"), and while they were highly aroused sexually through masturbation and viewing of erotic images ("hot"). The men expressed a greater interest in a diverse range of sexual options, and a greater willingness to take morally questionable steps to obtain sex, when they were aroused than when they were not (**Figure 16.3**). Thus, it appears that people—college men at least—are not aware while "cold" of how much their decision making may change when they are "hot."

Members of collegiate (and high school) sports teams, especially football players, have an unenviable record as perpetrators of sexual violence. On one day in 2014 the *New York Times*

An acquaintance rape–prevention workshop at Hobart College, New York.

Box 16.1 Personal Points of View

It Happened to Me

Rape is a horrific experience for the victim, regardless of the exact circumstances of the rape or the level of violence involved. Here we present three accounts by rape survivors. The first account, by "Steph," describes the most common form of rape: male-on-female acquaintance rape that includes the involvement of alcohol or drugs:

The girl invited me to a party that her friends were having. So I went there with her. I met the girls having the party, and they seemed very nice. I started talking to a guy who seemed to be a few years older than me. He was very nice and polite. Maybe I should have seen it coming.

I had a boyfriend at the time, so I just talked to him with only intentions of friendship. To make this story shorter, I ended up in a room with him. I have no idea how. He ended up touching me and removing quite a bit of my clothing. I struggled and I cried the whole time. He took off his pants as well. Then he tried to go inside of me, which he succeeded at. But to be very blunt, it was only a few thrusts of going in and out. It was all so horrible and hurt so much. I ended up getting out from underneath of him. Not quite sure how. He apologized as I ran out of the room very quickly.

Since I was a virgin at the time, I think I lost my virginity to him. However, it might sound silly, but I do not consider that to be very true. I consider it to be the time with my boyfriend now. In my head I have a definition of losing virginity that involves love. What he did to me did not contain any love.

Male-on-male rape can happen in prison, as well as elsewhere. Here is an account by "Taz":

Two of the "homies" that I use to be tight with come by my building and ask me to take a walk. I didn't think nothing of it so I went and we landed up at one of their cells. One of the dudes leaves and blocks the door from the outside. The other one starts telling me to give him head and I tell him I don't get down that way. That just because I'm gay doesn't mean I'll have sex with everyone. So he gets mad and punches me in the stomach. I lose my wind and before I can catch my breath I'm laying face down on the bottom bunk with lotion and grease between my ass and I'm being sexually violated. I blackout from the pain and not wanting to feel anything. . . .

CDC did a mock investigation that lasted about 10 days. Then I went in front of the committee who basically said

University of California, Berkeley, student Sofie Karasek breaks down as she testifies in 2013 at the California State Legislature about her experience of campus sexual assault.

I was making things up just like all the gays do. We have sex with people then cry rape. I was so mad I wanted to strangle everyone in the room. I had to deal with nightmares and sleepless nights right after the incident. I even tried to commit suicide by overdose.

The third account is by a woman who was raped by three lesbians:

After a while one of them said it was now my turn to pleasure them. I said I didn't want to, & that's when the mood changed! Two of them dragged me onto the floor on my back & held me down while the other sat on my face & ground her pussy hard against my mouth. I struggled but they were too strong & too determined. they each took turns on my face, the others holding me down all the while, then one of them let go of me & moved away. I couldn't see what she was doing, but suddenly I felt my legs being forced apart & raised up. Then she was between my thighs & I felt something being pushed into my vagina. —to my horror, she was wearing a "strap on" dildo—quite a big one—and she was fucking me. . . . The more they raped me, the more I struggled. Eventually I passed out, and when I came to sometime later, I was alone on the floor, naked. They had gone to bed. . . . That was 15 years ago, and to this day I can't bring myself to tell my husband or anyone else about it. Sometimes I feel it was entirely my fault for leading them on.

Sources: Survive-UK, 2001; Just Detention International, 2014; Experience Project, 2014.

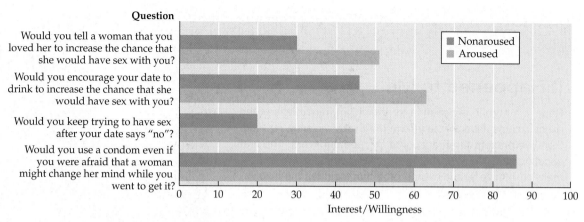

Question

Would you tell a woman that you loved her to increase the chance that she would have sex with you?

Would you encourage your date to drink to increase the chance that she would have sex with you?

Would you keep trying to have sex after your date says "no"?

Would you use a condom even if you were afraid that a woman might change her mind while you went to get it?

Interest/Willingness

Figure 16.3 In the heat of the night This bar graph shows the averaged responses of 35 male (presumably heterosexual) college students to a series of computer-generated questions, while they were nonaroused and again while they were highly sexually aroused. For each question the subject could place a cursor anywhere from 0 (no) through 100 (yes). These are four examples from a larger set of questions. (Data from Ariely & Loewenstein, 2006.)

FAQ

Don't women sometimes provoke rape by the way they dress or act?

Women's clothing or actions may increase or decrease their risk of being raped, but nothing they do or fail to do changes the culpability of the rapist.

reported on two such cases. In one story, football players at Florida State University were reported to have engaged in numerous acts of sexual assault, rape, and intimate partner violence; according to the *Times* they were treated lightly by law enforcement on account of their status as star athletes (McIntire & Bogdanich, 2014). The other story reported the arrest of seven members of the football team at a high school in New Jersey for a series of sexual assaults that were said to have been committed as part of a hazing ritual (Southall, 2014). In the same week, news stories reported on similar cases of alleged or proven rapes or sexual assaults by football players at Vanderbilt University, the University of Kentucky, Brown University, and Penn State.

According to one review of studies, collegiate athletes perpetrate sexual victimization at higher rates than other students on account of higher alcohol consumption, socialization to the "jock" culture (i.e., peer group pressure), and selection for aggressive personalities (Sonderland et al., 2014). After a series of sexual assaults were committed by University of Montana footballers, a member of the university's board of regents said, "The university has recruited thugs for its football team, and this thuggery has got to stop." Yet in spite of the well-documented association between college athletics and sexual violence, most college athletes—including footballers—have not committed sexual assaults and will not do so in the future.

Colleges have become very conscious of the problem of sexual violence on campus. Many have introduced policies that are more restrictive than state laws, especially after the Obama administration forcefully reminded colleges of their obligation to protect students from sexual violence under Title IX, the federal law that prohibits gender discrimination in schools receiving federal funding (Campus Safety, 2011; White House, 2014). The new policies have not gone unchallenged, however. In 2014, for example, Harvard administrators introduced a new policy intended to be Title IX compliant, but 28 Harvard Law School professors demanded that the policy be rescinded, claiming that the new procedures were overwhelmingly stacked against the accused (Bartholet, 2014).

In 2014 the state of California enacted a law that requires colleges and universities to set an "affirmed consent" standard for campus sex. This means that both parties must express their voluntary agreement throughout the course of a sexual interaction. Silence, or lack of protest or resistance, does not count as consent. Nevertheless the consent does not have to be expressed verbally; it can be communicated by smiling, taking an active role in sex, and the like. Does your institution have an affirmed consent standard, and if not, would you support the enactment of such a standard?

Colleges also have to ensure fair treatment for students accused of sexual assault. If they don't, they open themselves to Title IX actions by men who claim that they were disciplined for sexual offenses without due process—several such cases have made the news recently (Watanabe, 2014). One case illustrating the difficulty of achieving fair adjudication involved two gay men at Brandeis University (Anderson, 2014). The men dated for nearly 2 years and then broke up. Six months later one man filed a sexual misconduct complaint against the other, saying that during the time they had been dating, the other man had awoken him on more than one occasion with aggressive and unwanted sexual activity, had forced him to engage in oral sex, and had failed to respect his privacy in the bathroom. The university temporarily suspended the accused man and then gave him a disciplinary warning and ordered him to undergo training in sexual assault prevention. The accuser then organized demonstrations protesting the leniency of the punishment, while the accused man protested his innocence and tried to have his record cleared. "Why someone would be found responsible for nonconsensual behavior for a kiss from a boyfriend in the morning was beyond me," he told the *Washington Post*. The federal Department of Education's Office for Civil Rights is investigating whether he was denied a fair hearing. Very often, sexual misconduct cases like this one involve a "he says, she says" (or "he says, he says") situation that college personnel are poorly trained to adjudicate.

College hookups are inherently risky situations in which date rape can readily occur. In fact, it is not always easy to distinguish between a consensual hookup and a rape, because in real-world hookups, "consent" is often expressed not verbally but by a sequence of actions and inactions whose meanings may be difficult to interpret, especially if alcohol is involved. Without wishing to minimize the responsibility of rape perpetrators, we emphasize that women (and men) can best protect themselves from date rape by avoiding situations in which sexual interactions can get out of control—which often means situations in which one or both parties have been drinking heavily. We also urge both women and men to express in words their desire or unwillingness to engage in specific sexual acts, rather than rely on ambiguous body language. Far from spoiling the atmosphere, a quick "Would you like to go down on me?" or "Yes, I'd like to have sex with you—if you use a condom" builds trust and intimacy.

An important question is whether students accused of sexual assaults should be dealt with by college disciplinary procedures—in which case, suspension or expulsion is the most severe punishment they are likely to experience—or whether they should be turned over to law enforcement officials and processed through the regular judicial system. The National Organization for Women (NOW) has taken the view that colleges are too protective of men accused of sexual assault and rarely fulfill their legal obligation to report criminal offenders to law enforcement agencies (National Organization for Women, 2014). The reality, however, is that even if they are reported, campus date and acquaintance rapes stand only a small chance of leading to prosecution or conviction, so college disciplinary procedures may offer a more effective deterrent (Kingkade, 2014).

The number one "date rape drug" is alcohol

In recent years, a lot of attention has been paid to the use of drugs that can facilitate date rape (Office on Women's Health, 2013a). The most notorious of these is Rohypnol (flunitrazepam), a Valium-type drug popularly known as roofies. However, the use of Rohypnol as a "date rape drug" was never very common and now is rarely if ever

(A)

(B)

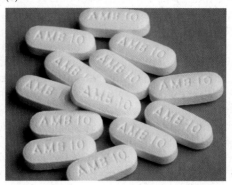

Figure 16.4 Alcohol (A) is a far more widely used date rape drug than Ambien (B) or other chemicals.

detected in drinks analyzed after suspected drug-facilitated rapes. Other drugs occasionally used for date rape include the central nervous system depressant gamma-hydroxybutyrate (GHB) and the veterinary anesthetic ketamine.

The sleep aid zolpidem (Ambien) is said to have largely replaced those drugs on account of its ready availability. This misuse of Ambien came to public attention in 2014 when former New Orleans Saints safety Darren Sharper faced five rape or sexual assault charges in California, Louisiana, and Arizona: Sharper was alleged to have used Ambien to facilitate at least some of these rapes. Sharper maintained his innocence and the cases had not yet come to trial by early 2015.

In contrast to the relatively infrequent use of the above-mentioned drugs to facilitate rape, alcohol is very widely used for that purpose (Bliss, 2013) (**Figure 16.4**). In one analysis, nearly 3 million women in the United States have been victims of substance- (mostly alcohol-) facilitated rape. These are rapes in which the rapists gave their victims alcohol or other drugs in order to facilitate the rape.

Another 3 million women drank heavily of their own accord and men took advantage of their incapacitated state to rape them (Kilpatrick & Resnick, 2013). These "incapacitated rapes" constitute more than half of all college rapes (Testa & Livingston, 2009). The very fact that a woman is drinking is sometimes interpreted as a signal that she wants sex, according to an experimental study of college men and women (Maurer & Robinson, 2008). In reality, however, the more alcohol a woman has consumed, the less a man is entitled to take anything she says or fails to say as conveying her consent to sex.

Of course, alcohol also promotes rape when consumed by the rapist—by reducing his inhibitions. In one survey of college women, two-thirds of the women who had experienced a sexual assault said that the perpetrator was drinking at the time of the attack (Frintner & Rubinson, 1993). It's not just that men who happen to be drinking are more likely to rape: Rather, men often drink with the conscious intent of facilitating sexual behaviors that they would not engage in otherwise (Cowley, 2014). All in all, alcohol is certainly the number one "date rape drug," whether consumed by the rapist or the victim. The fact that alcohol is so often involved should not cause us to excuse rapists or blame victims: It is simply a fact that everyone needs to be aware of.

Rape Can Have Severe Effects on the Victim

Women can take many steps to reduce the likelihood that they will be raped (**Box 16.2**). If a woman is raped, however, many options and services are available to help her, aid her recovery, and reduce the long-lasting psychological harm that rape may cause.

Rape crisis centers provide education, advocacy, and support to victims.

Box 16.2 Sexual Health

Reducing the Risk of Rape

Rape and sexual assault are never the fault of the victim. Nevertheless, you can take precautions to reduce the risk of being raped. Rape crisis centers and rape prevention organizations offer the following advice:

General

- A man who has sexual contact with you against your will is committing a serious crime, no matter what his relationship to you and no matter what the circumstances. By reporting the crime, you can help prevent someone else from becoming a victim.

- Prepare yourself for "fight or flight": Take self-defense and fitness classes (see figure).

Preventing acquaintance rape

- Until you know a man well, meet him in a group environment in which there are other women present, or in a public place.

- Pay for some of the expenses of the date.

- Avoid drugs and excessive alcohol use, and take the man's use of either, or his attempts to persuade you to use them, as a warning sign. Be explicit if you don't want to have intercourse (or any kind of sex). Be assertive, not coy.

- If the man commences an assault, protest vehemently, threaten to call the police, escape from the situation if possible, or create a loud disturbance.

Preventing stranger rape

- Make your home secure. If you are a woman living alone, do not make that fact obvious. Do not open the door to strangers.

- Keep your car doors locked whether you are inside or outside of the car. Park where it will be safe for you to return—think about what the environment will be like after dark. Avoid deserted or ill-lit places. Jog with friends or at times and places where other people jog.

- Never hitchhike or pick up hitchhikers.

Learning to resist sexual assault.

- If you find yourself in a threatening situation, run away. If that's not possible, resist forcefully. Fighting or creating a loud disturbance is more effective than pleading or offering no resistance.

- Carry an alarm device such as an air horn. If you carry any kind of weapon, be sure you know how to use it and what the law is. Generally, a person who is in imminent danger of rape may inflict whatever injury is necessary to prevent it, but no more than that.

If you become a victim of a sexual assault

- Whether or not there was a completed rape, call the police or go to an emergency room immediately or call 1-800-656-HOPE.

- Do not shower, wash, douche, change your clothes, urinate, eat, drink, or clean up the location of the assault before you go—you may be destroying evidence. Take spare clothes with you.

- If the assailant was a stranger, try to remember his appearance and clothes and any details, such as a car license plate number or any part of it.

- If you do not report the assault right after it happens, do so later. Consider contacting a rape crisis center, where you can get expert advice and understanding in a confidential environment.

Services are available for rape victims

The first and foremost step toward recovery is getting medical attention. The best place for this is an emergency room or a specialized forensic clinic, in which the staff are trained in the appropriate medical and reporting procedures. A victim can also go to her own doctor, but that option may involve a delay, and the doctor might not have adequate expertise. Many colleges and rape crisis centers will provide a rape advocate—a volunteer who will accompany the victim to the hospital and provide various kinds of practical and emotional support.

All health care providers are required to report rapes and other sexual assaults to the police, but this does not mean that the victim herself is obliged to cooperate or to press charges. In many communities, a woman can have a full, evidence-collecting examination and still not press charges. Thus, she can keep her options open until she is sure whether or not she wants to pursue the matter legally. (Even if she doesn't press charges, the record of her victimization may be of assistance in the prosecution of the perpetrator if he subsequently assaults another woman.) The desire not to report the crime should not prevent a woman from getting medical attention.

Providers who examine rape victims must assess and treat the physical and psychological injuries that the victims have sustained. Careful assessment is important because there may be injuries of which the victim is unaware—particularly if, as is likely, she is in a state of emotional shock. Providers can assess the likelihood of pregnancy or disease transmission and suggest steps to prevent either eventuality. As described in Chapter 9, emergency contraception can be used within 5 days after coitus to reduce the likelihood of pregnancy. Prophylaxis against STIs may include antibiotics. If there seems to be a substantial risk of HIV transmission, a short course of antiretroviral medications (post-exposure prophylaxis) might be advised.

Samples collected from the victim's body or clothing can be analyzed for DNA that might identify the perpetrator. Many of these "rape kits" are never analyzed, however—either on account of the cost (over $1000 per test) or because the case can be successfully prosecuted or resolved without DNA evidence (Eckholm, 2014). Even in the latter case DNA analysis is desirable, however, because the results may be used to identify other victims of the perpetrator. In 2014 the U.S. Congress allocated funds to help reduce the backlog of untested kits.

Counseling, both in the immediate aftermath of the rape and in the longer term, plays a vital role in helping "victims" of rape become "survivors." Many schools and colleges, rape crisis centers, and governmental agencies offer such counseling, which may be conducted on either an individual or a group basis.

Several organizations, including Men Can Stop Rape (see Web Resources at the end of this chapter), work to reduce rape by encouraging men to act responsibly toward women and to speak up in the face of attitudes and actions that encourage sexual aggression (**Box 16.3**).

FAQ

I didn't fight back—will people blame me?

People understand that rape victims' main concern is to survive. Rapists can be successfully prosecuted without evidence that the victim fought back, even when no weapon was involved.

rape trauma syndrome A cluster of persistent physical and psychological symptoms seen in rape victims; comparable to post-traumatic stress disorder.

Rape can inflict long-lasting harm

The effect of rape is likely to extend far beyond the immediate shock or any physical injury that the victim may sustain. Rape is an assault on a person's autonomy in the most intimate aspect of personal life. Different people react to the immediate experience of rape in different ways—some with an emotional outpouring, some with tightly controlled feelings—but all are at risk of developing a collection of long-term symptoms akin to the post-traumatic stress disorder (PTSD) experienced by survivors of other horrific events. In the context of rape or attempted rape, these symptoms have been called **rape trauma syndrome**. In fact, rape trauma syndrome is PTSD caused by a rape. Some experts prefer to use the term PTSD because, unlike rape trauma syndrome, PTSD is a diagnostic category in the *Diagnostic and Statistical Manual of Mental Disorders*, 5th edition (*DSM-5*).

The symptoms of rape trauma syndrome may include feelings of numbness or disconnection, alternating with flashbacks and preoccupation with the rape; irrational self-blame; anxiety, depression, or anger; sleeplessness; inability to concentrate; and physical symptoms such as headaches and digestive disturbances. In the first 2 weeks after being raped, 94% of women have symptoms of rape trauma syndrome,

Box 16.3 Sexual Health

Ten Ways Men Can Prevent Sexual Violence

The following action agenda, compiled by Men Can Stop Rape, is reproduced here by permission.

Be Bold

- *Define your own manhood.* Consider how common messages such as "don't take no for an answer" play a role in creating unhealthy and unsafe relationships. Choose what kind of man you want to be.

- *Understand from a female's perspective.* Ask a woman you know how often and in what situations she has feared being sexually assaulted. How has this affected her daily life? Does she know someone who has been assaulted? How has it affected her? Listen and learn.

- *Get a guy's perspective.* Ask a friend—how would it feel to be viewed as a potential rapist? How would he react if a woman or girl in his life—his mother, a sister, a girlfriend, or a friend—was sexually assaulted?

- *Take note of pop culture's messages.* Daily, we're surrounded by movies, TV shows, magazines, and video games that sometimes communicate harmful messages about masculinity and relationships. Don't let images in popular culture dictate your behavior.

- *Pledge to be a man of strength.* Don't ever have sex with anyone against their will. Pledge to be a man whose strength is used for respect, and not for hurting others.

Be Strong

- *Talk it over first.* Create a space to speak honestly about sex: Listen to your partner, state your desires openly, and ask questions if a situation seems unclear.

- *If drunk or high, wait for consent.* If your partner is drunk or high and can't give consent, back off and wait until you both are ready to enthusiastically say yes.

Poster created by Men Can Stop Rape.

Take Action

- *Choose your words carefully.* When you put down women, you support the belief that they are less than human. It is easier to ignore a woman's decisions or well-being if she is seen as inferior. Choose respectful language.

- *Stand up.* You will probably never see a rape in progress, but you will hear attitudes and see behaviors that degrade women and promote a culture of violence. When your friend tells a rape joke, let him know it's not funny.

- *Get involved.* Contact Men Can Stop Rape to start a high school Men of Strength Club or a Campus Strength affiliate at your college.

---

and 46% still exhibit symptoms at 3 months after the event. Even several years later, women who have been raped are at increased risk of depression, anxiety, and substance dependency. The long-term ill effects are particularly severe for people who belong to ethnic groups in which rape victims are stigmatized.

Not surprisingly, rape trauma syndrome can be marked by severe sexual problems. In a 1979 study, 40% of female rape victims said that they did not engage in any sexual contacts for several months after the rape, and almost 75% of the women, when they were interviewed 4 to 6 years after the rape, said their frequency of sexual activity was still reduced (Burgess & Holmstrom, 1979). The reasons given for the

exposure therapy A form of psychotherapy for victims of rape or abuse in which they are encouraged to recall the traumatic event in a safe environment.

low sexual activity included a loss of interest in sex, difficulty with arousal, painful intercourse, vaginismus, and difficulty experiencing orgasm.

A much more recent study focused on women who had been raped during adolescence and diagnosed with rape trauma syndrome. Three years later these women also reported sexual problems such as pain and failure of lubrication, but they were just as sexually active as a control group of women who had not been raped (Postma et al., 2013). The reason for the better outcome could include improvements in treatment since the 1970s, as well as the relatively young age of the women, which may have given them more ability to adapt to the trauma.

Many forms of help can facilitate a rape victim's psychological recovery. Partners, family, and friends can offer practical and emotional support by such steps as the following:

- Offer a place to stay.
- Be willing to listen in a loving and nonjudgmental fashion.
- Accept the victim's account of what happened.
- Emphasize that the rape was not the victim's fault.
- Give the rape survivor time and space to make her own decisions about how to deal with the situation.

In a more general way, we all help people who have been raped when we do our part to create a culture that rejects rape, both as an actual deed and as the subject of humor, boasting, wishful thinking, and the like.

Various forms of therapy can be used to prevent or treat rape trauma syndrome (Vickerman & Margolin, 2009). Rather than general supportive counseling, cognitive methods show the best results. An example is **exposure therapy**. In this approach, the person recalls the traumatic event in a safe and supportive environment, usually in combination with relaxation techniques, such as breathing exercises, to counteract negative emotions. The procedure for recall entails not just remembering the event but describing it aloud to the therapist in as vivid detail as possible, and this is done repeatedly over a series of sessions, as well as in the form of "homework" between sessions. In general, cognitive treatments such as this one benefit about two-thirds of the people who undergo them.

It's useful to bear two points in mind: First, recovery from rape, as from other traumatic events, does not occur overnight—whatever therapeutic measures are undertaken. Second, most people who have experienced rape or sexual assault are eventually able to recover, think of themselves as survivors rather than victims, and get on with their lives. A notable example is that of Elizabeth Smart (now Smart-Gilmour), who at the age of 14 was abducted from her bedroom in her family home in Utah, held captive, tied up, and raped daily for 9 months. Smart recovered sufficiently from this horrific experience to successfully attend Brigham Young University, go abroad on her Mormon mission, testify in the trial of the perpetrator (who received two life terms), take up work as a commentator for ABC News, and start a foundation whose mission is to reduce predatory crimes against children. Smart and her boyfriend married in 2012.

Male victims have special concerns

According to some studies, men are sexually victimized at roughly the same rate as women, and these acts are perpetrated about equally often by other men and by women (Weiss, 2010; Stemple & Meyer, 2014). Regarding female-on-male victimization, narrowly defined rape (physically forced coitus) is uncommon, but it does sometimes occur when the man already has an erection and the women forces him to penetrate her, or when the man develops an erection in the course of a sexual assault (Centers for Disease Control, 2011a). The fact that a man develops an erection does not mean that he wants to have sex, but it may cause him to feel an irrational guilt about the event. More commonly, a woman may engage in coitus or other forms of sexual contact with a man without violence but without his consent—as, for example, when he is under the influence of alcohol or drugs or is underage.

There are many similarities between men's and women's experiences of sexual victimization, but there are also some differences (Walker et al., 2005; Rosin, 2014). Men (or male youths) who have been sexually assaulted by women may experience little support or understanding from their peers, who may treat the matter as a joke. Male victims may believe that rape crisis centers, medical staff, therapists, and the legal system are all geared toward seeing males as perpetrators, and thus are not likely to be sympathetic or helpful to male victims. Oftentimes this belief is false, because professionals who deal with sexual assault are familiar with the fact that men can be victimized. Even if false, however, this belief tends to inhibit male victims from obtaining the help they need. In addition, men may feel guilty about being sexually assaulted because they feel they have violated an ethic of masculinity.

Rapes of males in prisons are something of a special case, not only because they are mostly committed by other males, but because they involve considerations of power as well as sex. Historically, prison authorities have not taken effective steps to prevent prison rape or to punish offenders. This has changed somewhat with the passage in 2003 of the Prison Rape Elimination Act, which authorized funds for programs to study the problem and reduce its prevalence.

There is some controversy about how widespread prison rape actually is. According to a 2008 federal study, up to 16% of male prisoners say they have been raped (U.S. Department of Justice, 2008). A study by Mark Fleisher of Kent State University and Jessie Krienert of Illinois State University came to rather different conclusions (Fleisher & Krienert, 2009). Basing their findings on interviews with hundreds of prisoners, these researchers concluded that many reports of rape are fictitious, that inmates do not live in fear of rape, and that correctional staffers try to keep prisoners safe from rape. In 2011 there were only 224 substantiated incidents of nonconsensual prisoner-on-prisoner sexual acts in all adult correctional facilities in the United States (Bureau of Justice Statistics, 2014b). Of course the actual number of such incidents must have been higher, but how much higher is a matter of speculation.

LGBT people are at high risk

Non-heterosexual men and women experience more sexual victimization than those who are straight. In the NISVS, bisexual women and men reported the highest rates of sexual victimization; gay men were also victimized more often than heterosexual men (Centers for Disease Control, 2014n) (**Figure 16.5**). The difference between reported victimization rates for lesbian and heterosexual women was not significant in the NISVS data, but another survey, which compared heterosexual and non-heterosexual siblings, did find that the lesbian siblings experienced more sexual victimization than their straight sisters (Balsam et al., 2005). For the heterosexual men, nearly all the perpetrators were women; for the other groups, the majority of perpetrators were men, but significant minorities were women. What reasons can you think of for why bisexuality is associated with especially high rates of sexual victimization?

According to several self-report studies, 50% or more of transgender women and men have been sexually assaulted (Stolzer, 2009). Trans women are at greater risk than trans men (Kenagy, 2005). Most victims report that homophobia or trans-

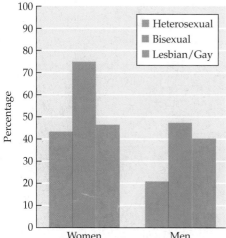

Figure 16.5 Sexual assault and sexual orientation These bar graphs show the percentages of heterosexual, bisexual, and gay or lesbian adults who reported having experienced sexual violence at least once in their lifetime. "Violence" included noncontact events such as nonconsensual exposure to a person's genitals. (Data from Centers for Disease Control, 2013h.)

rape shield laws Laws that protect rape victims, for example, by limiting the introduction of evidence about their prior sexual behavior.

phobia were the motivation for the assaults. "In my neighborhood, either they want to beat you up or they want a free blow job," said one interviewee (Bockting, 1998).

Rape Laws Have Become More Protective of Victims

As recently as the 18th century, women in Western societies were considered the property of men, and rape of women was considered an offense against men—against the woman's father if she was unmarried or against her husband if she was married (Geddes & Lueck, 2000). A woman who was raped lost value, was shamed, and brought shame on her family. Thus, her kinsfolk might reject her, in addition to seeking vengeance on the rapist. These ideas still persist in some traditional patriarchal societies.

U.S. law inherited from English law the concept of a "marital exemption" to rape, meaning that it was not rape for a man to force sex on his wife. The thinking was that the wife had given consent to sex by virtue of her marriage vows and could not retract it. Marital rape did not become a crime in all U.S. states until 1993. Even today, many states allow a man to have sex with his wife in circumstances that would constitute *statutory* rape if it took place between unmarried persons, such as when the wife is unconscious, mentally impaired, or underage. (In some states, youths can marry below the age of consent—usually with parental or court permission.)

As an informal extension of the marital exemption, the legal system used to be quite forgiving of rapes that occurred between cohabiting or socially acquainted couples, rapes of dates or pickups, or rapes of prostitutes. The women in these circumstances were viewed as having voluntarily placed themselves at the man's disposal. Simply demonstrating that the victim was of "unchaste character" was often enough to get the rape charges reduced or to secure an acquittal. Evidence that the victim used contraceptives even though unmarried, that she frequented bars, or that she had a reputation as a promiscuous woman might be introduced for this purpose. In other words, rape laws were used primarily to protect "women of virtue"—women who either were virgins or were married to someone other than the perpetrator.

Reforms began in the 1970s

The women's movement brought about many significant changes in the ways in which the legal system and the general public view rape. Beginning in the 1970s, **rape shield laws** were introduced. These laws protect rape victims in a number of ways, most notably by preventing the alleged perpetrator from introducing evidence about the victim's prior sexual history. In other words, the defendant can no longer escape from legal penalty by painting the victim as a "slut."

Laws have also been modified to introduce a range of sexual offenses in addition to rape, as traditionally defined. These offenses are called "sexual battery," "sexual assault," "forcible or aggravated sodomy," and the like. The definitions of such offenses vary considerably from state to state. The key point is that it is no longer necessary to prove that coitus occurred, which makes it easier to obtain convictions in many cases—although the sentences are often much lighter than for a rape conviction. In addition, it is no longer necessary in many states to prove that the victim physically resisted the rape or assault, nor is it necessary to provide corroborating evidence from third parties.

What happens to men who rape?

Since the majority of rapes are not reported to law enforcement officials, we can assume that the majority of rapists go unpunished. Nevertheless, about 20,000 adults

---

FAQ

I was raped 7 years ago—can I still file charges?

The statute of limitations varies from state to state, and it varies according to exactly which charge is brought against the perpetrator. In California, for example, the statute of limitations is 6 years for rape in most circumstances but could be longer if DNA evidence is involved. Prosecuting old cases can be difficult unless the evidence is very strong.

or juveniles are arrested for forcible rape in the United States each year; 99% of these are males (Bureau of Justice Statistics, 2012).

Some rape reports, of course, are judged by law enforcement officials or by independent researchers to be false. In seven studies directed at this issue, estimates of the prevalence of false reports ranged between 2.1% and 10.9% (Lisak et al., 2010). It's obviously not possible to be sure of the true prevalence, which could even be outside this range. Still, these studies suggest that false rape allegations are neither common nor especially rare. When one considers the devastating consequences a rape conviction can have for the accused person, the need for caution in accepting rape allegations should be clear.

This issue seized the headlines in 2011, when the then director of the International Monetary Fund, Dominique Strauss-Kahn, was charged with sexually assaulting a maid in a New York hotel. The case fell apart when it emerged that the maid had lied about several matters and had previously made a fictitious rape allegation (Eligon, 2011). Another much-publicized case involved three male lacrosse players at Duke University who in 2006 were accused of rape by an exotic dancer. They were expelled from the university and charged with first-degree forcible rape. It later emerged that the allegations were fabricated; the university apologized and reached settlements with the men for undisclosed sums said to be in the multimillion-dollar range. The prosecutor in the case was convicted of criminal contempt and disbarred, and the men's accuser was more recently convicted of murdering her boyfriend (Karlamangla, 2013).

About half of all men arrested for rape are convicted (usually of felony rape)—most, after a guilty plea (Greenfeld, 1997). Over two-thirds of convicted defendants receive a prison sentence; the average term is 14 years. Others are sentenced to terms in local jails or placed on probation. Convicted rapists typically serve about half of their prison terms before release. At any one time, about 65,000 men and 500 women are in state prisons for rape, and another 92,000 men and 1300 women are in prison for other sexual assaults (Bureau of Justice Statistics, 2010).

Repeat offending is common

Only 3.2% of imprisoned rapists are convicted of any new sex offense within 3 years of their release (Bureau of Justice Statistics, 2003). This recidivism rate is lower than for all other violent crimes except homicide. By itself, this statistic suggests that rape is a sporadic crime that perpetrators are not especially likely to repeat. As with other crimes, however, many convicted rapists have committed more rapes than those for which they were arrested or convicted (Weinrott & Saylor, 1991). This raises the possibility that a significant fraction of all rapes are committed by serial offenders.

An illustrative case at the college level is that of Elton Yarborough, a 23-year-old economics major at Texas A&M University who was convicted and sentenced to 18 years in prison for a single offense: raping a female British exchange student while she was intoxicated. At his trial, however, four other women testified that he had raped them under similar circumstances (Diaz, 2010). To study whether this kind of repeat offending is common, psychologists David Lisak and Paul Miller surveyed 1882 male college students. In total, these students admitted to having committed 483 acts that met the definition of rape or attempted rape, but 91% of these rapes were committed by just 76 men—a median of 3 rapes per man—and these men also committed many other acts of interpersonal violence (Lisak & Miller, 2002).

These findings mean that it would be valuable to identify individuals who are especially prone to committing sexual violence. They also offer reassurance that most men—students or otherwise—are unlikely to do so. Men in general are not potential rapists.

Why Do Men Rape?

Understanding the reasons why some men rape seems like an important first step toward developing effective strategies for preventing rape. This question has been approached from a variety of different perspectives, and there is no consensus on what are the most important causal factors.

Rape may have evolutionary roots

Gang rape? Five male mallard ducks attempt to copulate with one (barely visible) female.

Forced copulation is quite common among nonhuman animals, including some of our close primate relatives such as orangutans (Knott et al., 2010). (Bonobos, on the other hand, rarely if ever engage in such behavior.) In some species in which forced copulation occurs, it is clearly an evolutionary adaptation; that is, the behavior has evolved because it increases the animals' reproductive success. Whether the human capacity for rape is an evolutionary adaptation has been the subject of much debate. It could have evolved simply as a by-product of selection for adaptive traits such as sexual desire and aggressiveness, which have evolved for reasons that have no direct connection with the benefits or costs of rape (Thornhill & Palmer, 2000; Dadlez et al., 2009).

Evolutionary theory is less useful to our understanding of why particular individuals commit rape and others do not. However, it has been observed in several species that males turn to rape as a secondary strategy when regular courtship is unsuccessful, which could be relevant to human rape (see below).

Some characteristics distinguish rapists from nonrapists

Researchers have focused a great deal of attention on men who commit rape. The hope is that through such study it might be possible to identify personality traits, early experiences, or other factors that predispose these men to commit their crimes.

Some extremely violent rapists have severe personality disorders or are driven by sadistic impulses (see Chapter 13). The majority of rapists, especially those who commit acquaintance or date rape, are fairly unremarkable people, but in a statistical sense, at least, they do differ from nonrapists. For one thing, they tend to be of lower socioeconomic status and to have had less education; this could hamper their ability to acquire voluntary sex partners and thus make rape a more attractive option, in accordance with evolutionary theory (Miller, 2014). As one rapist put it, "I figure if you're not going to give it to me, then it's my right to take it" (Sussman & Bordwell, 1981).

Rapists tend to have worse relationships with their parents, to have more self-centered personalities, and to have less capacity for **empathy**, compared with nonrapists (Chantry & Craig, 1994; Gannon et al., 2008). These attributes are common in other criminal offenders, so they do not by themselves account for a proclivity to rape.

Neil Malamuth of UCLA and his colleagues have done extensive studies of male college students to investigate factors associated with an inclination to rape. They reported that male college students who grew up in violent home environments, were abused as children, became involved in juvenile delinquency, had large numbers of sex partners, were interested in impersonal sex, or had dominating or hostile attitudes toward women all expressed a greater willingness to engage in coercive sex than did other men. Over a 10-year follow-up period, such men were more likely than other men to actually engage in aggressive sexual or nonsexual behavior toward

empathy The ability to share or understand other people's feelings.

women (Malamuth et al., 1995). The researchers also found, however, that men who were capable of empathy were less likely to be aggressive toward women, even when all other factors predisposed them to be so (Dean & Malamuth, 1997).

It has often been claimed, especially by feminists, that male-on-female rape is motivated by hatred of women or the desire to control them, rather than by sexual desire. The truth seems to be that either factor, or a combination of both, may trigger rape. Here are two statements by rapists about their victims that illustrate contrasting motivations, both from a period when rape was much more prevalent than it is today:

> I couldn't stand [my teacher]. I used to humiliate her. I used to hit her in the ass with paperclips because I hated her, man. (Sussman & Bordwell, 1981)

> She stood there in her nightgown, and you could see right through it—you could see her nipples and breasts, and, you know, they were just waiting for me. (Groth, 1979)

Social forces influence the likelihood of rape

Social scientists and feminists have generally taken the view that rape is a learned behavior. Here is an expression of this point of view by Diana Russell, professor emeritus of sociology at Mills College in Oakland, California:

> Males are trained from childhood to separate sexual desire from caring, respecting, liking or loving. One of the consequences of this training is that many men regard women as sexual objects, rather than as full human beings. . . . [This view] predisposes men to rape. Even if women were physically stronger than men, it is doubtful that there would be many instances of female rapes of males: Female sexual socialization encourages females to integrate sex, affection, and love, and to be sensitive to what their partners want. (Russell, 1984)

Here is a specific example that seems to illustrate a "culture of rape" in at least one sector of U.S. society. After the 2000 Puerto Rican Day parade in New York, a mob of men assaulted, stripped, groped, or sexually abused 50 women in Central Park. There was no intervention by police or bystanders. Some bystanders did provide videotapes to the police, but these videotapes were broadcast repeatedly on local TV stations, further traumatizing the victims. To some cultural critics, the media reaction to the event focused inappropriately on "mob psychology" and ignored the culture of sexism that permitted it to occur (Katz & Jhally, 2000).

In the United States, social forces work not only to encourage rape but also to restrain it. One social institution, the criminal justice system, presents a major deterrence to would-be rapists. In the 2000 Puerto Rican Day case just mentioned, for example, 30 men were charged and 18 were convicted for their roles in the incident and given sentences of up to 5 years of imprisonment (Finkelstein, 2001). In many parts of the world there would have been no prosecutions in connection with an incident of this kind. The power of social controls is illustrated by what happens when they collapse, as may happen during wartime (**Box 16.4**).

Intervention Programs Are of Uncertain Value

Treatment programs aimed at reducing rapists' likelihood of reoffending typically employ cognitive behavioral therapy in a group setting. These programs do seem to reduce recidivism, but the effect is small: In one meta-analysis, treatment reduced recidivism by only about 6% compared with nontreated controls (Lösel & Schmucker, 2005).

Partly because of the disappointing results with men who have already raped, efforts to prevent rape by changing attitudes and behaviors in young people have

Box 16.4 Personal Points of View

Rape and War

Among the horrors of war, rape has long held a preeminent place. Rape serves to terrorize and humiliate the enemy, to reward victorious troops, and to propagate the victors' genes.

Among the most notorious users of wartime rape were the Mongols, who swept across Asia in the 13th century. After killing most of the men in the conquered cities, they systematically raped the women, either immediately or after enslavement. The Mongol leaders—Genghis Khan and his male relatives—always had first choice among the captured women. Thanks to this behavior, at least 16 million contemporary Asian men possess a Y chromosome inherited from Genghis Khan's family, meaning that they are descended from the Khans in an unbroken male line (Zerjal et al., 2003).

Wartime rape was banned by the 1949 Geneva Conventions, and the systematic use of rape, as employed by the Mongols, was more recently declared an instrument of genocide (United Nations, 1994). Yet it continues. During the recent warfare in Syria and Iraq, for example, ISIS jihadists have committed thousands of rapes—either immediately against captured women or after enslaving them. This is official policy according to the ISIS propaganda magazine *Dabiq*: "One should remember," it stated, "that enslaving the families of the unbelievers and taking their women as concubines is a firmly established aspect of the Sharia that if one were to deny or mock, he would be denying or mocking the verses of the Quran and the narrations of the Prophet" (McLaughlin, 2014). (Although there are passages in the Quran that appear to legitimize rape of captured/enslaved women, few present-day Muslims would condone either rape or enslavement.)

The Democratic Republic of Congo (DRC), especially its eastern region, has been in a near-continuous state of conflict since the mid-1990s. In 2008 alone 16,000 rapes were reported to authorities, but this figure is thought to greatly underestimate the true numbers (Human Rights Watch, 2010). In 2009 an estimated 9000 rapes occurred in the course of a single government offensive against a militia group. Many rapes are committed by armed men who waylay women foraging for firewood (UN News Centre, 2013). The following account concerns a 13-year-old Congolese girl interviewed by a reporter for the *Times* of London at a clinic for rape victims (McConnell, 2010):

"I had bought bananas in the morning and was coming back from the market when I met four armed men," she

These Korean women were forced to work as sex slaves by the Japanese during World War II. Here they demand redress from the Japanese government.

said. "Two of them took my bananas and started to eat them, the others grabbed me from behind and took me in to the bushes. All four raped me. They put a banana in my mouth to stop me crying and they raped me until I was bleeding."

The gang of rapists was arrested and then released after bribing the authorities, an all too common scenario in a country with a dysfunctional and easily corruptible judiciary. . . . Her attackers' release left the young girl hopeless. "I have been raped by four men so I'm not a girl anymore, anyone can have me," she said.

At the end of the interview the girl's counselor who had been acting as translator whispered in English so that her patient would not understand: "How are we supposed to tell her that she has HIV?"

In one survey, 40% of women and 24% of men in the eastern DRC reported having experienced sexual violence (Johnson et al., 2010).

been widespread. Programs designed to increase male college students' empathy toward rape victims do reduce the men's self-assessed likelihood of committing rape (Foubert & Newberry, 2006). Whether they reduce the frequency of actual rapes is less clear.

Given that sexual violence begins early, some rape prevention programs aim at adolescents who are beginning to date. A team led by Vangie Foshee of the University of North Carolina tested the effectiveness of one such program, which they call the Families for Safe Dates Program. The program consists of mailed booklets containing information and activities that teens and their parents or caregivers are asked to go through together (Foshee et al., 2012). Followed up 3 months later, the teens who went through the program had engaged in less physical dating victimization and the parents/caregivers were more involved in the prevention of dating abuse, compared with control families. It is not known whether these benefits persist over longer periods.

It has been forcefully argued that a key step in preventing violence by adults is promoting the development of empathy in young children (Swick, 2005). Empathy is a necessary precondition for loving relationships and interpersonal respect. Although all children have a natural capacity for empathy, this capacity needs to be fostered, or it will wither and die. This seems to be especially true for boys, who typically grow up in a highly competitive culture that rewards aggressive, self-promoting behaviors. Whether programs to foster the early development of empathy and respect for others could actually reduce sexual violence, however, is a question that remains to be studied.

Intimate Partner Violence Is a Crime with Many Names

The terms have changed over the years—from "wife beating" to "battering" to "spousal abuse" to "domestic violence" to **intimate partner violence**. The ugly reality remains the same: violent acts committed within what are supposed to be loving or at least caring sexual relationships.

Fifteen percent of all acts of violent victimization in the United States occur between intimate partners (Bureau of Justice Statistics, 2014a). In the United States and many different countries, women and men are about equally likely to commit violence against their partners, but women are more likely than men to suffer injury as a result of these incidents (Straus, 2012).

According to the NISVS, 36% of U.S. women and 29% of men have experienced some kind of violence (sexual or nonsexual) or stalking (see below) at the hands of an intimate partner over their lifetime (Centers for Disease Control, 2011a). Thankfully, the rate of intimate partner violence has dropped very dramatically in recent years. According to the National Crime Victimization Survey, the total intimate partner victimization rate for women fell by a remarkable 71% between 1994 and 2011, and that for men fell by 50% (Bureau of Justice Statistics, 2013b) (**Figure 16.6**). The decrease affected both simple and severe assaults. As with rape and sexual assault, the reason for this decline is not well understood. One part of the reason could be the decline in the marriage rate at the low-income end of the socioeconomic spectrum, where domestic violence is most common (see below): Unmarried sex partners may find it easier to split up before their relationships become abusive.

Of the violent acts committed by intimate partners, the majority are simple assaults, meaning assaults that are carried out without a weapon and that cause no injury or only minor injury (Bureau of Justice Statistics, 2013b) (**Figure 16.7**). About one-third are aggravated assaults, sexual assaults, robberies, or murders. About 50% of the crimes are reported to the police.

intimate partner violence
Violence within a sexual or romantic relationship.

In 2010 actor Charlie Sheen was convicted of assaulting his then wife Brooke Mueller.

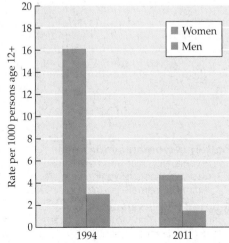

Figure 16.6 Decline in intimate partner violence The bar graph shows the overall rates of partner violence against women and against men, for 1994 and 2011. (After Bureau of Justice Statistics, 2013b.)

Figure 16.7 **Violent crimes against intimate partners** These pie charts show that simple assaults are the most common violent offenses against both women and men. Sexual violence against male intimate partners is very uncommon. Although these two pie charts are the same size, bear in mind that the total victimization of female intimate partners is much greater than perpetrated against male partners, as shown in Figure 16.6. (After Bureau of Justice Statistics, 2013b.)

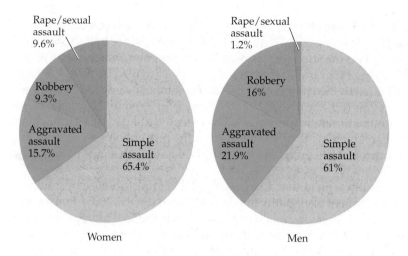

Women

Men

Risk factors for intimate partner violence include being divorced or separated, African-American, or young, or living in a city or having a low income. The association with poverty is particularly marked: Women living in the lowest-income households experience intimate partner violence at seven times the rate of women in affluent households. (It is possible that this difference is exaggerated if affluent people are less willing to report violence.)

Intimate partner violence is a particular problem on college campuses. To get the broadest possible overview of this problem, Murray Straus of the University of New Hampshire analyzed survey data obtained at 31 universities in 16 countries (Straus, 2004). At the average university, 29% of the students admitted having physically assaulted an intimate partner within the previous 12 months. Most of these assaults involved such things as slapping, shoving, or arm-twisting and did not cause injuries, but 9.4% of students had committed severe assaults involving use of a knife or gun, slamming against a wall, and the like, and 2% of students admitted having caused a severe injury. Surprisingly, there was little difference between the rates of assault committed by male and female students. There were, however, major differences between institutions. Universities in Louisiana (United States) and Juarez (Mexico) topped the list with 45% and 42% of students, respectively, admitting to having assaulted their partners, while universities in Utah (United States) and Braga (Portugal) ranked at the bottom with only 18% and 17% of students, respectively, having committed assaults.

These wide differences show that dating violence is by no means an inevitable concomitant of the college experience; thus, there should be opportunities to reduce its prevalence at the worst-affected institutions. Measures to reduce heavy drinking are leading candidates because intimate partner violence, like rape, is strongly associated with alcohol use on campus. Among male and female students who are heavy drinkers, over half have committed some kind of aggression (including psychological aggression) against an intimate partner in the previous 12 months (Fossos et al., 2007).

More significant than the physical injuries in most cases are the psychological effects of intimate partner violence: depression, suicidal thoughts and suicide attempts, lowered self-esteem, substance abuse, and post-traumatic stress disorder (National Research Council, 1996). The specific type of post-traumatic stress disorder that occurs in these circumstances is called **battered-woman syndrome** (Walker, 2009), or "battered person syndrome" in acknowledgment of the fact that men can also be the victims. This syndrome is often characterized by **learned helplessness**— a depressive condition following multiple experiences in which attempts to escape aversive events have not succeeded.

battered-woman syndrome A version of post-traumatic stress disorder affecting women who are victims of intimate partner violence.

learned helplessness Depression associated with failure to escape intimate partner violence.

Those who physically abuse their intimate partners may also do so online. **Cyber dating abuse** can include abusive texts or cell phone calls, emailed threats, use of social media sites to post or solicit hateful statements about the partner, and the distribution of sexually explicit images of the partner without consent. Obviously it's not possible to physically assault someone online, but in one study of teenagers, 34% of those students who said they had perpetrated cyber dating abuse also admitted to physically assaulting their dating partners, whereas only 2% of nonperpetrators did so (Zweig et al., 2013).

Young children are present in 38% of the households where a woman is subjected to intimate partner violence (Bureau of Justice Statistics, 2011). These children very often witness the violence directly, and they are at risk of being assaulted themselves. The violent atmosphere may profoundly affect the children's social development, increasing the likelihood that they, too, will commit intimate partner violence, abuse children, and exhibit other behavioral problems in adolescence and adulthood.

cyber dating abuse Abusive online behavior between dating or other sex partners.

Intimate partner violence follows an escalating cycle

Domestic violence typically occurs as one phase of a three-phase cycle (Walker, 2009) (**Figure 16.8**):

1. *The tension-building phase.* In this phase, the longest of the three, the abuser may be increasingly moody, nitpicky, or sullen. He may threaten the victim or commit minor assaults or property damage. The victim may attempt to stop the progression of the cycle by trying to calm him, by avoiding confrontation, or by satisfying his demands—by keeping the children quiet, having food ready on time, and so on. (Although we use "he" and "she" for the abuser and victim respectively, bear in mind that not all intimate partner violence is perpetrated by males on females.)

2. *The violent phase.* The actual violent behavior constitutes the shortest phase, typically lasting no more than a day. As many as 9 out of 10 perpetrators are under the influence of alcohol or drugs during the assault, which is often carried out in the presence of children. The victim tries to protect herself (and her children if she has them), fights back, kicks the abuser out, or flees. The victim, other family members, or neighbors may call the police, who have usually been to this address several times before.

3. *The reconciliation phase.* In this phase, the perpetrator is apologetic and tries to make amends by declarations of love. He promises to cease the abusive behavior, to stop drinking, or to seek treatment. He showers the victim with gifts and attention. The victim is relieved and happy, forgives the abuser, and returns to him (or allows him back, if he has been kicked out). The victim may retract statements made to the police, with the hope of stopping legal proceedings, or may lie to doctors about the cause of her injuries.

Often, the severity of the violence escalates from cycle to cycle, so it may be more descriptive to refer to an "upward spiral of violence" rather than a cycle. In the worst cases, relationships degenerate into a condition of nonstop violence; in a study of cases in which police were called to scenes of domestic violence, 35% of the victims said that they were assaulted every day (Brookoff et al., 1997).

Breaking up is hard to do

Sympathetic outsiders who see a victim—usually a woman—sticking with her abusive mate through escalating cycles of violence often ask, "Why on earth does she stay with that awful man?!" Some of the answers to this question are

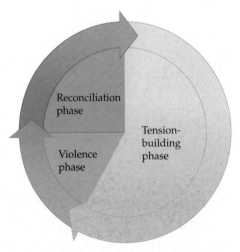

Figure 16.8 The cycle of intimate partner violence

sexual harassment Unwanted sexual advances or other intimidating sexual behavior, usually in the workplace.

apparent from narratives written by the victims themselves (Weiss, 2004). Information also comes from research studies (Walker, 2009).

Victims of intimate partner violence may stay with their partners because they are socially isolated, are economically dependent, lack self-esteem, or believe that separation and divorce are wrong. They may irrationally believe that the battering is their own fault. In addition, victims may fear that breaking up will bring shame on them and that the perpetrators will pursue and punish them—a fear that is frequently justified. Victims may also fear that their children will suffer in a breakup. Perpetrators may sense and reinforce all these traits; in particular, they often keep the victims socially isolated and punish them for reaching out to any potential sources of help. Nevertheless, many victims do eventually break free from their abusive relationships and are able to start new lives (Weiss, 2004).

Help is available

Services are available to help battered women, whether or not they remain in an abusive relationship (RAINN, 2014):

- Emergency room staff are trained to treat domestic violence injuries and to recognize their cause. When a victim has multiple head and neck injuries at different stages of healing and there is no other predisposing factor, such as a neurological disorder, domestic violence is likely to be the cause.
- Law enforcement officers and lawyers can assist a domestic violence victim who decides to leave an abusive relationship by arresting the abuser or by helping the victim obtain a restraining order. In some states, such as California, prosecutors will continue domestic violence cases even when the victims retract their accusations (the "no-drop policy"). Legal assistance is often available to low-income victims.
- Hotlines, battered women's shelters, women's crisis centers, and city social services can provide practical assistance for women who leave abusive relationships temporarily or permanently.
- Psychotherapists and support groups can help abused women understand the process of victimization and regain the strength and motivation to end it.

Services for male victims and for victims of same-sex abuse are less well developed than those for women who are abused by men. Still, most public services for abuse victims are gender neutral, and the gay and lesbian organizations in many metropolitan areas have domestic violence services. The Los Angeles LGBT Center, for example, provides survivors' groups, a batterers' treatment program, crisis counseling, shelter referrals, and educational programs (Los Angeles LGBT Center, 2014).

Sexual Harassment Occurs in Many Environments

Sexual harassment is unwelcome sexual behavior in the workplace or in other structured environments. Most sexual harassment is perpetrated by men on women, but men are sometimes sexually harassed, either by women or by men (**Figure 16.9**). Women are occasionally sexually harassed by other women.

Besides being motivated by sexual desire, sexual harassment may also be an expression of a wish by men to control women. This idea is supported by some experimental studies. For example, Jennifer Berdahl of the University of Toronto reasoned that if sexual harassment is motivated by sexual desire, women who meet feminine ideals will be most harassed, but if it is motivated by a desire to control women, then women who *violate* feminine ideals will be most harassed. She found, in both college and work environments, that it was indeed the gender violators who were most harassed—that is, the women who showed stereotypically "masculine" traits such as assertiveness,

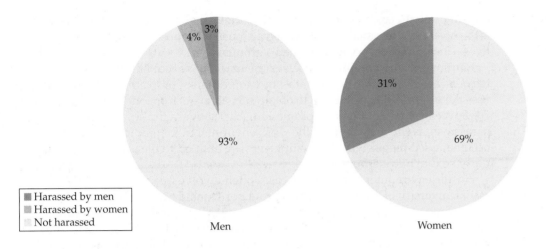

dominance, and independence (Berdahl, 2007). This supported the idea that an important motivation for sexual harassment is to "keep women in line."

Unwelcome sexual behavior can arise in faculty-student relationships at colleges and in relationships between doctors, therapists, lawyers, ministers, and other professionals and their patients or clients. Such behaviors are not always illegal, but they are widely prohibited by college administrations, professional governing bodies, and the like.

quid pro quo harassment
Unwelcome sexual advances, usually made to a worker in a subordinate position, accompanied by promises or threats.

hostile environment harassment
Sexual harassment involving a pattern of conduct that creates an intimidating work environment.

There are two kinds of workplace sexual harassment

Sexual harassment in the workplace takes two different forms. The first involves an explicit or implicit "deal": "If you go out with me, I'll see that you get a merit raise," or "If you don't have sex with me, you can kiss your job goodbye." This kind of sexual harassment is called **quid pro quo** (literally "what for what?") **harassment**. It is generally considered the more reprehensible kind—if the facts are not in dispute, there can be little doubt about its illegal and damaging nature.

Unfortunately the facts often *are* in dispute. As with sexual assault allegations, quid pro quo harassment allegations quite often come down to the credibility of the accuser and the accused. An example came up in 2014 in the form of an unusual "she says, she says" case. A female Yahoo employee accused a female executive of coercing her into sex. Allegedly, after the employee refused further sex, the executive responded by giving her a poor performance review and removing her as project leader. Yahoo sided with the executive, saying that the employee had provided no evidence to support her allegations, and the executive countersued the employee for defamation (Soper, 2014). Given the glacial pace at which these cases proceed, it's unlikely that this one will have been resolved by the time you read this.

The second kind of sexual harassment, called **hostile environment harassment**, involves a pattern of unwelcome sexual attention or advances that make life difficult for the victim. This kind of harassment causes a great deal of suffering, but it is not so easy to characterize and document. For one thing, it depends on the victim's reactions to the perpetrator's actions. Men are less likely to be upset by sexual advances from women than women are by sexual advances from men. Even among women, some will feel more harmed than others. Also, in many cases, it's not obvious how effectively the victim has communicated the unwelcomeness of the behavior to the harasser. Thus, it's not always

A woman often experiences touching by a man to be unwelcome sexual contact, but the man may be unaware of this unless the woman tells him.

third-party sexual harassment
Indirect negative effects of sexual harassment on other employees, or sexual harassment by non-employees.

easy to draw the line between acceptable social behavior and sexual harassment. It is the hostile environment cases that have aroused the most criticism from conservatives—including conservative women's groups.

Employees who are not themselves the object of sexual harassment may suffer harm as a consequence of the harassment of others. For example, if an employer uses the promise of a promotion to obtain sexual favors from one employee, another employee may lose out on that promotion. Alternatively, the knowledge that sexual harassment is rife may degrade the work environment for employees who have not been harassed themselves. Such employees are entitled to file a suit claiming **third-party sexual harassment**.*

Hostile environment harassment cases often involve free speech issues. In a 1994 case, University of New Hampshire professor Donald Silva got himself into trouble during a technical writing class. In attempting to explain the meaning of the word "simile," Silva quoted the words of belly dancer Little Egypt: "Belly dancing is like Jell-O on a plate with a vibrator under the plate." Seven women in the class complained of sexual harassment, and Silva was ordered to apologize and undergo counseling. He refused and sued the school, whereupon the school suspended him without pay. Two years later, a federal court ordered Silva reinstated, saying that the school had violated his First Amendment free speech rights (Honan, 1994). The school had to pay Silva substantial damages. In general, sexual harassment means a pattern of behavior, not a one-time incident such as in the Silva case.

In 2011 the federal Department of Education initiated a sexual harassment investigation of Yale University under Title IX. This was in response to a formal complaint by a group of students that the university had failed to eliminate a hostile sexual environment on campus. The students cited a number of events, including one in which members of the Delta Kappa Epsilon fraternity allegedly gathered near a female students' residence and chanted "No means yes! Yes means anal!" (Yale Herald, 2011). The university promised to cooperate with the investigation and banned the DKE chapter for 5 years. In 2012, a settlement was reached in which the university agreed to change its policies and to provide Title IX compliance reports for 2 years (Ariosto & Remizowski, 2012).

Sexual harassment often begins early

For many children, sexual harassment begins as soon as they enter puberty—if not before. In a study conducted by the American Association of University Women, 48% of students in grades 7 to 12 said that they had suffered some form of sexual harassment during the school year, and most said that the harassment had a negative effect on them (American Association of University Women, 2013) (Table 16.1).

It is possible that many sexually colored incidents in schools are of no great significance. A school in Lexington, North Carolina, for example, earned national ridicule in 1996 when it suspended a 6-year-old boy for kissing a female classmate (Nossiter, 1996). But sexual harassment in school can be persistent and traumatic, as was made clear by the 4000 letters received by *Seventeen* magazine in response to an article and poll on the subject (Stein, 1999). Here is one typical letter, from a 12-year-old Mexican American student in Michigan:

> In my case there were 2 or 3 boys touching me, and trust me they were big boys. And I'd tell them to stop but they wouldn't. This went on for about 6 months until finally I was in one of my classes in the back of the room minding my own business when all of them came back and backed me into a corner and started touching me all over. So

"If I turn him down, will I lose my A?"

It's never okay.

If it feels like harassment, it probably is. But how do you know for sure? And what are your rights? Visit www.state.il.us/dhr/ to learn what constitutes harassment, and what you can do about it. For immediate help call 312-814-6200 or 217-785-5100.

Because sexual harassment in higher education is against the law.

State of Illinois
Department of Human Rights

ILLINOIS DEPARTMENT OF
Human Rights

A sexual harassment awareness poster.

---

* This term also refers to sexual harassment by outsiders, such as delivery persons or company clients.

TABLE 16.1

Types of Sexual Harassment Experienced in School by Students in Grades 7 to 12

	Girls (%)	Boys (%)
Unwelcome sexual comments, jokes, or gestures	46	22
Called gay or lesbian in a negative way	18	19
Being shown sexual pictures against your will	16	10
Unwelcome sexual touch	13	3
Physically intimidated in a sexual way	9	2
Someone exposed themselves to you	7	7
Forced to do something sexual	4	0.2
Unwanted sexual material sent to you or posted about you	26	13

Source: American Association of University Women, 2013.

I went running out of the room and the teacher yelled at me and I had to stay in my seat for the rest of the class.

A common theme of the letters, as in this one, was the lack of concern shown by teachers and school officials; often the harassed students felt that they were treated as offenders rather than victims.

Schools are beginning to take sexual harassment more seriously, partly as a result of successful legal actions by students who have been harassed. The key case was that of LaShonda Davis, a 5th-grade student in Forsyth, Georgia. A male classmate sexually taunted Davis for months, but the school authorities failed to stop the abuse. With the help of the ACLU, LaShonda's mother sued the school board, and the case went all the way to the U.S. Supreme Court. In 1999 the court ruled in her favor, stating that federally funded schools that are willfully indifferent to student-on-student sexual harassment can be held liable. Since then schools have made greater efforts to prevent harassment and to respond appropriately to harassment allegations.

Sexual harassment harms its victims

Although adults are better able to resist sexual harassment than are schoolchildren, the harmful effects of harassment in adulthood are still considerable (Willness et al., 2007). The effects on harassed workers include decreased job satisfaction, lower organizational commitment, withdrawing from work, physical and mental ill health, and even symptoms of post-traumatic stress disorder. Employers also suffer in terms of lost productivity and the costs of insurance premiums or claim settlements.

College policies on sexual relationships vary in their restrictiveness. Some schools, such as Yale University, ban sexual relationships between faculty members and those students for whom they have some academic responsibility. The University of California, Berkeley, bans sexual *or romantic* relationships between faculty members and their own students. A few schools, such as the College of William & Mary, ban sexual or romantic relationships between faculty members and *any* undergraduate students. Brigham Young University's honor code prohibits sexual activity between all unmarried persons, including between unmarried students.

Victims of sexual harassment can take steps to end it

Many organizations, such as the AFL-CIO, the National Partnership for Women & Families, and Feminist Majority, have formulated recommendations for dealing with sexual harassment:

stalking Obsessive pursuit of a previous, current, or desired sex partner in such a way as to put that person in a state of fear.

cyberstalking Stalking via the Internet.

intimate partner stalking Stalking of a current or former spouse or other intimate partner.

- Know your rights. Consult your organization's written policies concerning sexual harassment.

- Tell your harasser that he or she is harassing you. Recount what he or she is doing, explain how it affects you, and demand that it stop. Be sure your tone of voice, facial expression, and body language match the seriousness of your message. Don't accept any excuses the harasser may offer or be sidetracked by diversionary topics. If the harassment is especially severe, so that you might anticipate a violent response to your complaint, do not confront the harasser directly but go to a supervisor.

- Keep a journal documenting every incident of harassment as it happens, how it affected you, and how you responded. Keep photographs or the originals of any offensive messages or images you receive. Don't erase offensive text messages or emails.

- Tell other people, such as trusted coworkers, about the harassment as it occurs. Ask whether others have experienced sexual harassment from the same person, whether they have witnessed the harassment that you have experienced, and whether they will support you if you take action.

- If the harasser does not stop the offensive behavior or responds with any vindictive action, complain to your supervisor, your supervisor's boss, your union steward, your personnel department, your principal, or your student advisor, or file an official complaint via the channels established by your organization. Keep records of these actions and their results.

- If you do not get satisfaction through these channels, consider obtaining a lawyer and filing a complaint with the federal Equal Employment Opportunity Commission (EEOC), your state's Fair Employment Practice Agency, or the federal Department of Education's Office for Civil Rights. Such complaints must be filed within a certain deadline (within 6 months of the most recent incident of harassment, in the case of the EEOC). These agencies may help you settle the case, or they may give you a "right-to-sue" letter that will facilitate a private lawsuit. If criminal behavior such as sexual assault is involved, you should go directly to the police.

Most large companies provide training programs that cover sexual harassment issues. In fact, such programs may be required by state employment laws. Contracting companies typically provide the training, and it is probably quite effective in increasing awareness of sexual harassment and the harm that it causes.

There Are Three Kinds of Stalkers

If rape is the dark side of sex, then **stalking** is the dark side of love. A stalker is emotionally obsessed with a particular victim, and that obsession usually has, or once had, a romantic element. Stalkers put their victims in fear by repeatedly following them, harassing them, lying in wait for them, making phone calls or sending messages to them, vandalizing their property, and the like. In the NISVS, 16% of U.S. women, as well as 5% of men, said that they had been the victim of some kind of stalking behavior over their lifetime (Centers for Disease Control, 2011a). Stalking via the Internet, called **cyberstalking**, is an increasing problem. When workplace romances go sour, one party sometimes harasses or stalks the other online (Mainiero & Jones, 2013).

There are three distinct kinds of stalking. The most common is **intimate partner stalking**, in which the victim is stalked by a current or former spouse, cohabitational partner, boyfriend, girlfriend, or date. In the NISVS, 9% of women reported that they had been stalked by an intimate partner at least once in their lifetime, as did 2.5% of men (Centers for Disease Control, 2014n).

Actor Mila Kunis was repeatedly stalked by a man, Stuart Dunn, who also tried to break into her home. In 2013 Dunn was convicted of felony stalking and ordered to spend 6 months in a rehab center and to stay away from Kunis for 10 years.

Figure 16.10 When does stalking occur? The graph shows the timing of stalking of women by intimate partners. (Data from Tjaden & Thoennes, 2006.)

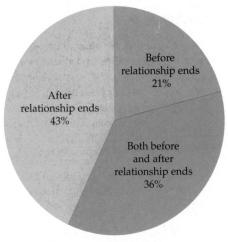

Before relationship ends 21%

After relationship ends 43%

Both before and after relationship ends 36%

It is often assumed that intimate partner stalkers do their stalking after the relationship has broken up, but in actuality stalking can take place while a relationship is still intact (National Institute of Justice, 2012) (**Figure 16.10**). Intimate partner stalkers often show a controlling or suspicious attitude toward the victims even before the stalking behavior begins. Anger is a major motivational factor in intimate partner stalking. These stalkers often have a prior psychiatric or criminal history (Meloy et al., 2000), and over half are alcohol or drug abusers (Macfarlane et al., 1999).

According to Brian Spitzberg of San Diego State University and William Cupach of Illinois State University, intimate partner stalking is an extreme example of a common behavior pattern that they call **obsessive relational intrusion** (Spitzberg & Cupach, 2014). A rejected lover will frequently make attempts to continue a relationship, perhaps in an attempt to see whether the rejection is wholehearted or not. Most women and men have experienced this kind of unwanted attention at some time or another, as described in Chapter 7. Certain personality traits in the pursuer, such as a tendency toward exploitation, coerciveness, or obsessive thinking, may help turn this behavior into persistent stalking.

In the second kind of stalking, **delusional stalking**, the stalker has the fixed belief that the victim is in love with him or could easily be made to fall in love with him, even though there has never been an intimate relationship between the two of them. This kind of delusional thinking is sometimes called **erotomania**. Anyone may be stalked, but celebrities are at particular risk (Meloy et al., 2008). Halle Berry, David Letterman, Miley Cyrus, Usher, Mel Gibson, and countless others have been plagued by stalkers, some of whom have broken into the celebrities' homes. Occasionally a stalker insists that he or she is married to the celebrity.

The most notorious delusional stalker was John Hinckley, Jr., who stalked actress Jodie Foster. In 1981, after countless rebuffs, Hinckley attempted to assassinate President Reagan as a means to draw Foster's attention. In doing so, he was mimicking the plot of the film *Taxi Driver*, in which Foster played a child prostitute. At trial, Hinckley was found not guilty by reason of insanity and was institutionalized. In a letter to the *New York Times*, Hinckley described his assassination attempt as "the greatest love offering in the history of the world" (Taylor, 1982). Over the ensuing years Hinckley is reported to have recovered from his mental illness, and he is allowed extended periods of leave from confinement.

The third type of stalking is **grudge stalking**, in which the stalker pursues the victim to seek revenge for some actual or imagined injury. This kind of stalking is not usually sexual; common targets are coworkers, employers, administrators, and the like.

Being stalked is an extremely traumatic and stressful experience and one that may go on for years. Besides having to deal with the constant harassment, the victim is often in fear that the stalking will escalate to violence—and with good reason. According to a national survey of violence against women, 81% of women who were stalked by a current or former intimate partner were also physically assaulted by the stalker, and 31% were also sexually assaulted (U.S. Department of Justice, 1998). Actress Rebecca Schaeffer was shot dead by a stalker in 1989.

Stalking is illegal in all 50 states, and stalking across state lines is a federal offense. In many states, however, first-offense stalking is only a misdemeanor, in which case the penalties may be minor. Furthermore, it may not be enough just to prove that you were put in fear by the stalker—in some jurisdictions, the stalker must make "credible threats" against you in order to be convicted of a crime.

obsessive relational intrusion Obsessive pursuit of a person by a rejected lover.

delusional stalking Stalking motivated by the delusional belief that the victim is in love with, or could be persuaded to fall in love with, the stalker.

erotomania The delusional belief that a sexually desired but unattainable person is actually in love with oneself.

grudge stalking Nonsexual revenge stalking.

Go to the
**Discovering
Human Sexuality**
Companion Website at
**sites.sinauer.com/
discoveringhumansexuality3e**
for activities, study questions, quizzes, and other study aids.

Summary

- "Rape" means coitus or other penetrative sex acts accomplished without consent by force or the threat of force. "Sexual assault" covers a wider range of coercive sex acts. Although both men and women of all ages may experience rape, young women in the 16 to 19 age range are at the highest risk. The great majority of perpetrators are male.

- The rape rate has decreased markedly over the past 30 years. The majority of rapes and sexual assaults are committed by people known to the victim (acquaintances, relatives, or intimate partners).

- According to one study, a college campus with 10,000 female students will experience 350 rapes or attempted rapes per year, although this figure includes many incidents that the victims do not consider to have been rape. Most campus rapes are perpetrated by acquaintances or current or former boyfriends. About 20% of campus rapes involve additional injuries.

- Drugs such as Ambien may be used in the perpetration of rape, but alcohol (consumed by the perpetrator or the victim) is much more commonly associated with rape, including rapes on college campuses.

- Besides physical injuries, victims of sexual assaults may suffer a variety of ill effects, including post-traumatic stress disorder. These effects may be countered by counseling and by survivors' groups, which help victims regain a sense of control.

- The law has become increasingly protective of rape victims, but many victims of rape and sexual assault do not report the crimes, perhaps because of a fear of retribution, shame, or a sense that they share the blame for what happened. Men who are convicted of rape are typically sentenced to lengthy prison terms, but only a small minority of rapes are reported and prosecuted.

- Conflicting theories attempt to explain rape. Evolutionary psychologists have raised the possibility that it evolved because it increased the reproductive success of men who committed it.

- Individual men may be predisposed to rape on account of childhood abuse, personality disorders, or a lack of empathy and respect for others. Social forces may encourage a "culture of rape." Conversely, they may discourage rape, as, for example, through the criminal justice system. Rape is often used as an instrument of war or genocide.

- Rape prevention programs teach teenagers rape awareness and avoidance, attempt to overcome gender stereotypes, and promote conflict management skills. Many teens are never exposed to these programs, and their effectiveness is uncertain. It is possible that efforts to help foster empathy development in young children would be a more effective long-term strategy.

- Violence between intimate partners causes both physical and psychological injuries. Battered women may come to see the violence as inevitable and therefore do little to escape it. The rate of intimate partner violence has dropped substantially over the past 30 years.

- Intimate partner violence typically follows a three-phase cycle that includes tension building, violence, and reconciliation. As the cycle repeats, the violent phase tends to intensify and may eventually occur without interruption.

- Victims of intimate partner violence often stay with their partners. The reasons for this may include social isolation, economic dependence, low self-esteem, shame, and fear of retribution. Many services are now available to help victims of intimate partner abuse, whether or not they remain in their abusive relationships.

- Unwelcome sexual attention in the workplace (sexual harassment) is a form of illegal sex discrimination. It can take the form of quid pro quo harassment, in which a demand for sex is accompanied by some inducement or threat, or the form of hostile environment harassment, in which the sexual attention makes life difficult for the victim. Harassment can also occur in other structured environments, such as schools and colleges.

- Sexual harassment causes psychological and practical problems for its victims and reduces workplace productivity. Victims can take steps to end sexual harassment by confronting their harassers or by reporting the harassment.

- Stalking is obsessive following, calling, lying in wait, sending mail or messages, and the like, all directed at a specific victim. In intimate partner stalking, the stalker is a current or former spouse or romantic partner, and the stalking is motivated by sexual jealousy and anger. In delusional stalking, the stalker is mentally disturbed and believes that the victim (often an acquaintance, teacher, therapist, or celebrity) is in love with him or could be made to fall in love with him. In grudge stalking, the stalker is not motivated by sexual interest. Whatever the type of stalking, it can progress to violence. Stalking is illegal, but legal remedies are of limited effectiveness.

Discussion Questions

1. "On this campus, men still get away with a lot of sexist talk, sexual harassment, and even date rape." "On this campus, political correctness has got to the point that men are scared to show normal friendly behavior to women." Which of these two statements corresponds more closely to your opinion, and why? Do you think your sex influences your opinion?

2. If you had to establish your college's policy regarding faculty-student sex, what considerations would be most important to you in setting the policy? What would the policy be, and how would it compare with your college's actual policy? (If you don't know what your college's actual faculty-student sex policy is, find out.)

3. How would you advise a female friend who tells you she is being stalked by her former boyfriend? Would your advice be different if it were a male friend being stalked by his former girlfriend?

4. Both men and women may sometimes give unclear signals about whether they are willing to engage in sexual contact when they are in a potentially sexual situation. How can a man or woman best make sure that the other person is really willing to engage in sex? What if you or your companion has had a few drinks?

5. Not uncommonly, victims recant accusations that their partners beat them. Would you support a "no-drop policy" in your community (i.e., a policy to continue a prosecution in these circumstances)? What kind of evidence could be used to get a conviction if the victim recants?

Web Resources

Advocates for Human Rights: Sexual Harassment www.stopvaw.org/sexual_harassment

A Voice for Male Students: What to do if you are wrongly accused of sexual misconduct http://tinyurl.com/sexmisc

Just Detention International (formerly Stop Prisoner Rape) www.justdetention.org

Men Can Stop Rape www.mencanstoprape.org

National Coalition Against Domestic Violence (hotline: 1-800-799-7233) www.ncadv.org

National Sexual Violence Resource Center www.nsvrc.org

Not Alone (U.S. government site focusing on sexual assault) www.notalone.gov

Rape, Abuse, and Incest National Network (hotline: 1-800-656-4673) www.rainn.org

Recommended Reading

Baker, C. N. (2007). *The women's movement against sexual harassment.* Cambridge University Press.

Carpenter, E. (2013). *Life, reinvented: A guide to healing from sexual trauma for survivors and loved ones.* Quantum.

Fisher, B. S., Daigle, L. E. & Cullen, F. T. (2009). *Unsafe in the ivory tower: The sexual victimization of college women.* Sage.

Hicks, G. L. (1995). *The comfort women: Japan's brutal regime of enforced prostitution in the Second World War.* Norton.

Howard, L. G. (2007). *The sexual harassment handbook.* Career.

Lalumiere, M., Harris, G. T., Quinsey, V. L. & Rice, M. E. (Eds.). (2005). *The causes of rape: Understanding individual differences in male propensity for sexual aggression.* American Psychological Association.

Schewe, P. A. (Ed.). (2002). *Preventing violence in relationships: Interventions across the lifespan.* American Psychological Association.

Spitzberg, B. H., & Cupach, W. R. (2014). *The dark side of relationship pursuit: From attraction to obsession and stalking* (2nd ed.). Routledge.

Thornhill, R. & Palmer, C. T. (2000). *A natural history of rape: Biological bases of sexual coercion.* MIT Press.

Walker, L. E. A. (2009). *The battered woman syndrome* (3rd ed.). Springer.

Weiss, E. (2004). *Surviving domestic violence: Voices of women who broke free.* Volcano.

Chapter 17

Sex itself can be used as an asset, as illustrated by these "window prostitutes" in Amsterdam.

Sex as a Commodity

Like anything that people want, sex has a cash value. Indeed, in one way or another, sex fuels a significant part of the U.S. economy. In this chapter, we focus primarily on the selling of sex itself (prostitution) and the commercial production of sexually arousing materials (pornography). The selling of sex raises a variety of practical and ethical concerns, and few aspects of sexuality so sharply divide conservatives and liberals.

prostitution   The practice of engaging in sex for pay.

hustler   A male prostitute.

sex trader   A person who exchanges sex for money, drugs, or other benefits; a broader term than "prostitute."

sex worker   A person who engages in prostitution, pornography, or another sex-related occupation.

Can Money Buy You Love?

A great deal of wealth is transferred between sexual and romantic partners, the bulk of it flowing from men to women. From this perspective, prostitution is merely an unvarnished and extreme expression of something that goes on in many or most sexual relationships. What is morally offensive to many people about prostitution is not simply that money is involved, for many women (and some men) receive their entire financial support from their sex partners. Rather it is that the relationship between prostitute and client is brief and loveless and that the payment is for sex only, not as part of the complex web of commitments, attachments, and dependencies that characterize more lasting relationships. Prostitution violates many people's belief that sexual behavior is morally justified only in the context of a loving, committed relationship.

There is some inconsistency in the use of terms that refer to prostitution and related activities. Here is how we use them. A **prostitute** is a person (of either sex) who engages in sex for money. Old slang or abusive terms for prostitutes, such as "hooker" and "whore," have to some extent been reclaimed by present-day prostitutes and the organizations that represent them (as, for example, in the name of San Francisco's Hookers' Ball). Male prostitutes are often called **hustlers**. The term **sex trader** is broader, referring to anyone who exchanges sex for money, drugs, or some other material incentive. Even broader is the term **sex worker**: This includes sex traders as well as people who work in related occupations, such as phone sex operators, exotic dancers, and the like.

Historically, prostitution was viewed as a necessary evil

Prostitution is often called "the oldest profession," and with good reason. For millennia, prostitution was just about the only way in which unattached women could support themselves. Jewish and Christian scriptures include frequent references to prostitutes (or "harlots"), and Christian tradition holds that one of Jesus's followers, Mary Magdalene, was a reformed prostitute (**Figure 17.1**).

Prostitution, like all sex between unmarried people, has been condemned as "fornication" throughout the Christian era. Still, moralists such as St. Augustine and St. Thomas Aquinas condoned the social structure of prostitution because they saw it as providing a necessary "safety valve" for the release of male sexual energy. Although most prostitutes were despised and downtrodden, a few mingled with the rich and famous (**Box 17.1**).

The heyday of prostitution was probably the late-18th and 19th centuries, when large numbers of men migrated to cities where women were in short supply. In response to the terrible conditions experienced by prostitutes in London, William Booth founded the Salvation Army in 1865; its first shelter for prostitutes and vagrant girls opened 3 years later.

In the latter part of the 19th century, most U.S. cities saw the development of "red-light districts," in which prostitution was tolerated or, in a few locations, even legal. In the early 20th century, however, a coalition of reformers, early feminists, and health authorities forced most of these districts out of existence. Epidemics of gonorrhea and other diseases during World War I triggered a major campaign against prostitution, and the profession went underground.

Prostitution is on the decline

Over the course of the 20th century prostitution became much less prevalent in the United States and other developed nations. Kinsey estimated that men's usage of female prostitutes had dropped by nearly 50% over the few

Figure 17.1   St. Mary Magdalene has often been portrayed with immodestly long red hair—a reference to her supposed earlier life as a prostitute.

Box 17.1 Sex in History

Courtesans

Throughout history, most prostitutes have led lives of degradation and danger. Yet there have also been women at the very top levels of society whose job descriptions included, but went far beyond, the provision of sexual services. These were **courtesans**—women at the courts of kings, emperors, and other rulers whose wit, beauty, and loose morals secured them a life of privilege and luxury.

Courtesans often came from aristocratic families. Unlike most women of their time they were well educated, so they were able to discuss politics and other matters of interest to men. They were familiar with courtly manners, and sometimes they were skilled musicians or poets. The 16th-century Venetian courtesan Veronica Franco (1546–1591) is a good example (see figure). Franco was prominent in literary circles; she published several books, including two volumes of poetry, founded a charity, and was an outspoken feminist. She also found time to have sex with numerous Venetian nobles as well as with distinguished visitors, including the king of France. Unfortunately she was charged with witchcraft, and though she was acquitted, she lost favor and eventually died in poverty.

Wherever there were courts, there were courtesans. During the imperial eras in Japan and China, for example, courtesans were trained in such arts as calligraphy, flower arrangement, and the tea ceremony.

When women acquired power, male courtesans appeared, such as the Italian cicisbei, who served aristocratic ladies. Queen Elizabeth I of England famously doted on Robert Devereux, Earl of Essex (1565–1601), who was 32 years her junior. Elizabeth eventually soured on her boy toy, and this cost

A Venetian courtesan—probably Veronica Franco—painted by Jacopo Tintoretto.

him dearly: Devereux was the last man to be beheaded in the Tower of London.

In recent usage, the term "courtesan" has come to be used as a euphemism for any prostitute, especially one who caters to the rich and famous.

courtesan Historically, a woman of refined manners who provided sexual services at royal courts.

decades prior to the time of his survey in the 1940s. Still, Kinsey's survey showed that the average unmarried man in his 30s visited a prostitute once every 3 weeks (Kinsey et al., 1948).

A further major decline in prostitution accompanied the sexual revolution of the 1960s and its aftermath. Thanks to oral contraceptives and a sea change in sexual morality, unmarried women became much more willing to have sex with their boyfriends, so the main incentive for men to visit prostitutes lost much of its force. Whereas 7% of men born between 1933 and 1937 lost their virginity to a prostitute, only 1.5% of men born between 1968 and 1974 did so, according to National Health and Social Life Survey (NHSLS) data. During this same period, employment opportunities for many women expanded greatly, so the main incentive for women to work as prostitutes lessened.

Statistics on the prevalence of prostitution today are hard to come by. One of the best studies of prostitution was conducted in Chicago by the Center for Impact Research (O'Leary & Howard, 2001). According to this study, an estimated mini-

Figure 17.2 At a "school for johns," attendees learn about the negative aspects of prostitution.

mum of 1800 to 4000 women and girls work as prostitutes in the Chicago metropolitan area at any one time, which is less than 0.1% of the female population. Other sources have estimated (very roughly) that 1 in 100 U.S. women has worked as a prostitute at some point in her life (ProCon.org, 2013).

Although most prostitutes are female, the proportion of prostitutes who are male or transgender is significant in some large cities. In San Francisco, for example, an estimated 20% to 30% of prostitutes are male, and 25% are trans women (Prostitutes Education Network, 2011). Most of the trans women have not undergone genital surgery, but they may have breast implants and/or be taking estrogens.

All forms of prostitution are illegal everywhere in the United States except for 11 nonurban counties of Nevada, in which brothel prostitution is legal. Engaging in prostitution is usually a misdemeanor. Enforcement varies greatly, however. Prostitution that is publicly visible is much more likely to run afoul of the law than are other types of prostitution. Some jurisdictions have instructed their police forces to make the enforcement of prostitution laws a low priority. Other cities have set up "diversion programs" that spare prostitutes jail time and help them move on to other occupations without the stigma of a criminal record. Men who use prostitutes are also breaking the law; if convicted, they may have to attend a "school for johns" (**Figure 17.2**), and in some jurisdictions they are publicly shamed by having their names and photos posted online.

The United States is something of an exception in banning all forms of prostitution. In Canada, Mexico, and most countries in Western Europe and Central and South America, some form of prostitution is legal. Usually this is off-street prostitution. Public solicitation for prostitution, and living off the earnings of prostitutes (pimping), is often illegal.

There Is a Hierarchy of Prostitution

Prostitution is difficult to characterize because it takes many different forms. In general there is a hierarchy, ranging from forms that are street-based, cheap, and dangerous, to less visible forms involving larger sums of money and greater security for the prostitutes and the prostitutes' clients.

Street prostitution has many risks

In the Chicago study just described, 30% to 35% of the prostitutes worked on the streets. Street prostitution (or "streetwalking") is the most visible and familiar part of the industry. Streetwalkers are usually picked up by clients ("johns") driving automobiles, but they may also be picked up in bars located near recognized streetwalking zones. After agreement between prostitute and client about the kind of sex to be engaged in and the fee, sex takes place in the automobile, in a pay-by-the-hour motel, or at some other location.

Street prostitutes (in the United States and worldwide) occupy the lowest rank of the prostitution hierarchy. Their income from prostitution is low, but higher than they could expect to earn in "straight" work (**Box 17.2**). Some street prostitutes experience a lifetime of social degradation, beginning with a violence-ridden childhood and

Box 17.2 Research Highlights

The Economics of Prostitution

Because prostitution involves cash transactions, it lends itself readily to economic analysis. Steven Levitt (an economics professor at the University of Chicago and author of the bestseller *Freakonomics*) and Sudhir Venkatesh carried out a study of streetwalking and brothel prostitution by women in Chicago (Levitt & Venkatesh, 2007; Levitt, 2009). They hired "trackers" (usually ex-prostitutes) who befriended and followed streetwalkers, getting information from them after each trick about what transpired and how much was paid. Their data were based on over 2200 tricks turned by about 160 prostitutes in 2006–2007. They also got information from pimps and from police records.

Unlike most criminal activities, prostitution involves no obvious victims; instead, the researchers noted, it is a marketplace in which prostitutes and johns engage in mutually beneficial transactions (beneficial in economic theory at least). Because prostitutes and johns have to find each other, the marketplace has to be highly localized—about half of all prostitution arrests in Chicago took place on less than 0.3% of all city blocks.

The women in the study earned an average of $50 for each trick ($58 in 2014 dollars). They had less than one customer per hour, making the average hourly pay only $27. Because they worked as prostitutes for limited hours, their annual income from prostitution was less than $20,000, even if they worked year-round. When they worked at other jobs, however, they earned much less—an average of $7 per hour. The fourfold higher pay for prostitution compensated the women (in economic terms) for the unpleasantness and stigma associated with prostitution as well as for the risks of arrest, injury, and disease. The women experienced an estimated 12 incidents of violence and 300 acts of unprotected sex annually, and those prostitutes who worked the streets were arrested about once every 300 tricks.

Prices charged by the prostitutes varied according to the type of sex act: Manual sex cost about $25, oral sex $30 to $45, vaginal sex $60 to $90, and anal sex $85 to $100 (see figure). Several other factors affected the prices, however. White men paid more than black or Hispanic men, even for the same sex act, and they also had more money stolen from them. Customers under 25 or over 40 paid more than those age 25 to 40. Repeat customers usually got a discount. Sex was cheaper on Mondays than any other day of the week, and it was more expensive during high-demand periods such as the 4th of July week. Surprisingly, sex without a condom added only about $2 to the price.

Prostitutes working for pimps earned more per week compared with free agents, even after paying the pimps a 25% cut of their takings, and they usually worked indoors, worked fewer

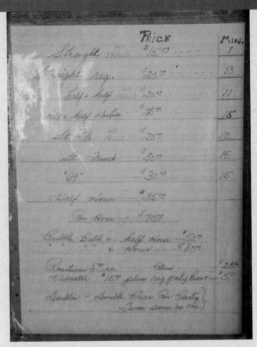

Price list at the Oasis Bordello in Wallace, Idaho, in 1988, its last year of operation. The price for 8 minutes of "straight no frills" sex—$15—equals $29 after adjustment for inflation.

hours, experienced less violence, and were rarely arrested. Most of their tricks were arranged by their pimps. Thus the image you might have of pimps as controlling parasites may not be accurate.

About 1 in 20 tricks turned by the prostitutes in the study were "freebies" given either to police officers (to avoid arrest) or to gang leaders (for protection). Prostitutes were much more likely to have sex with on-duty police officers than to be arrested by them. Vice division officers are occasionally convicted of extorting sex from prostitutes (Branson-Potts, 2014).

The price of prostitution services, like any other commodity, is influenced by supply and demand. According to one analysis, the supply of prostitutes has increased in recent years, due to the shortage of other work and the increasing safety and efficiency afforded by web-based prostitution. Simultaneously the demand for prostitution has declined, both because of a drop in disposable income caused by the recession and because of the increasing availability of nonpaid sexual outlets for men. Thus prostitutes are having to charge less: Web-based escort prostitutes—whose services are always much more expensive than those of streetwalkers—charged an average of $340 per hour in 2006, but by 2014 this dropped to $260 per hour (The Economist, 2014c).

pimp A man who manages prostitutes in exchange for part of their earnings.

continuing into homelessness, alcoholism, and drug use (Raphael, 2004). The risk of being beaten or raped exists every time a streetwalker steps into a stranger's car. One study conducted in Colorado concluded that active street prostitutes are nearly 18 times more likely to fall victim to homicide than other women (Potterat et al., 2004).

Street prostitutes are less able or likely to insist on condom use than are other prostitutes, so they face a greater risk of acquiring sexually transmitted infections and becoming pregnant. A British study of street-based prostitutes found that every one of them was drug or alcohol dependent; for most, their days were a nonstop cycle of selling sex, buying and using drugs, and then returning to work (Jeal & Salisbury, 2004; Jeal et al., 2008). In another study, which focused on young men who exchanged sex for money (or drugs) in Harlem, New York, 41% of the men tested HIV-positive (El-Bassel et al., 2000). Some U.S. states have passed "aggravated prostitution" laws, which make it a felony for anyone to engage in prostitution while HIV-positive. In Tennessee, conviction for aggravated prostitution results in lifelong registration as a violent sex offender (Galletly et al., 2014).

The majority of female street prostitutes are mothers (Dalla, 2000). The fathers are not usually the women's customers; however, the fathers are very often unavailable to support the children. The prostitutes themselves may give up or lose their parental rights. Street prostitutes who retain custody of their children experience considerable shame and anxiety about their own and their children's safety and may be reluctant to avail themselves of social services in case they should be deemed unfit mothers and lose custody of their children (Sloss & Harper, 2004).

Female, male, and transgender streetwalkers have different experiences

Although female, male, and transgender streetwalkers all service male clients and all receive about the same payment per client, their experiences are otherwise quite different, according to a study led by sociologist Martin Weinberg of Indiana University (Weinberg et al., 1999). Female and transgender prostitutes tend to be in their late 20s, while male prostitutes are younger. Prostitution is more of a full-time occupation for women: They service more clients and earn a larger weekly income from prostitution than do either men or trans women. Men spend about twice as much time with each client as do either natal women or trans women, so their pay per hour is less.

The nonfinancial aspects of prostitution work out better for men, however. Most significantly, male and transgender prostitutes are much less likely to be beaten or raped by a client than are women (but see below). They cannot become pregnant and for the most part do not have children to worry about. Also, men in general have more interest in casual sex and in having multiple sex partners than do women. Accordingly, male prostitutes get more sexual enjoyment and experience orgasm more often in the course of their work than do women, according to the Weinberg study.

Another difference that traditionally worked to the advantage of male prostitutes was that they tended to be independent agents working only for themselves, whereas women often worked for **pimps**. The women gave the pimps part or all of their earnings. In return, the pimps set up the women's living and working arrangements, protected their turf, provided drugs, and paid off mobsters and the police (or, if that didn't work, bailed the women out of jail).

In spite of the glorification of the pimp lifestyle in hip-hop culture, pimps have become less common in recent years. In Weinberg's San Francisco study, only 4% of the women prostitutes worked for pimps, and the Chicago study quoted law enforcement officials as saying there were few remaining pimps in that area. In some cities, the pimps' role has been taken over by gang members who control the street economy.

A good deal of deception occurs in street prostitution. Prostitutes often con their clients: At least half the prostitutes in the Weinberg study said they had failed to provide promised services or they had demanded more money than initially agreed to. Transgender prostitutes frequently deceive their clients about their anatomical sex. They may tape back their penis and refuse to remove their panties, saying that they are having their period. Alternatively, they may use their anus or even their hands to fake coitus.

Transgender prostitutes do not always need to deceive, however, because plenty of men are specifically attracted to trans women, who they call "shemales." According to the transgender prostitutes interviewed in the Weinberg study, it happened about 13 times a year that a client initially thought that the transgender prostitute was a natal woman but discovered the truth during the course of the encounter. About 15% of these clients responded violently; of the remainder, about half broke off the encounter, but the others simply carried on, suggesting that the discovery did not affect their enjoyment in a substantial way.

Some prostitutes work out of massage parlors and strip clubs

Higher up the hierarchy are prostitutes who work at or out of a fixed commercial location such as a **massage parlor** or an exotic dance venue (strip club). Massage parlors are often the most readily available locations for prostitution in suburban areas, but because they have become so associated with prostitution, they have become a frequent target for police raids. In 2011 more than 30 people associated with "Goddess Temples" in Phoenix and Sedona, Arizona, were arrested on prostitution-related charges (ABC News, 2011a). At the "temples," prosecutors alleged, johns were called "seekers" and coitus was called "sacred union."

Services at these kinds of locations vary, but hand-genital contact is the most common. At strip clubs, exotic dancers may provide sex by rubbing their body against the customer's genitals during a "lap dance." Alternatively, sex may take place in a "VIP room" or off-site after the show. Not all masseuses and exotic dancers are prostitutes, of course, but ads or word of mouth usually make it clear what services are available at a particular establishment.

The one kind of locale for prostitution that is hard to find in the United States today is an old-fashioned **brothel**, or whorehouse, whose traditional red lantern placed in the doorway gave red-light districts their name. Today, legal working brothels can be found only in some rural counties of Nevada (**Figure 17.3**). Brothels also function under the radar in some remote mining and logging communities. A handful of the countless brothels that once flourished in the United States have been preserved for their historical value. The best known of these is the Dumas Brothel in Butte, Montana, which was designated a National Historic Landmark in 1973—while it was still operating.

Legal brothels are found in several European countries. The city of Zurich, Switzerland, has built a municipal "drive-in brothel" as part of an effort to reduce street prostitution. The brothel has a series of carwash-style booths

Figure 17.3 Sex in the sticks Nevada's legal brothels are far from the bright lights of Las Vegas.

massage parlor An establishment for massage that may also offer the services of prostitutes.
brothel A house of prostitution.

Drive-in brothel in Zurich. The posters promote condom use.

where the action takes place, as well as a café, shower facilities, and a laundry, and security staff are on-site. Although the prostitutes have to pay a nightly fee, the city has been losing money on the enterprise (Agence France-Presse, 2014).

Escort services are the main form of prostitution in the United States

The most prevalent form of prostitution in the United States is **escort service** prostitution. This is off-street prostitution that is not tied to a specific service location. **Escorts** (or **call girls**) may promote their services by a variety of means, including ads in newspapers and adult entertainment magazines, but the Internet is now their principal advertising medium. Escorts may have their own websites, they may work for an agency that has a site, or they may advertise on general purpose sites such as Craigslist or Facebook. (Under pressure from state prosecutors Craigslist eliminated its "adult services" section in 2010, but there are still plenty of escort ads in other sections.)

In addition to these channels, special purpose websites are becoming increasingly important as an advertising medium in the escort business. Examples are Roomservice2000.com (female) and Rentboy.com (male). Some of these sites offer customers "verification membership," which means that the site verifies who the customer is, and the customer can then use his verification to contact escorts. This is a benefit both to the customer, who can avoid giving the escort personal information such as credit card numbers, and to the escort, who can use the verification to be sure of the customer's identity and to avoid police stings. Because prostitution is illegal almost everywhere, code terms are widely used in prostitutes' advertising and communications (**Table 17.1**). The sites themselves often state that their advertisers are not selling sex and that any sex that happens has nothing to do with the contracted services.

Another advantage of these sites is that they may allow for customers to review escorts in the same way that they might review restaurants or hotels. Another site, TheEroticReview.com, is wholly dedicated to reviews of escorts by self-described "hobbyists"; it reports receiving about 250,000 unique visitors daily. Such sites provide valuable information not only for other customers but also for researchers. In one study of escort service prostitution in the United States and other Westernized countries, researchers matched customers' descriptions of prostitutes with the prices they charged per hour, thus coming up with an estimate of the monetary value of various physical attributes (The Economist, 2014b). The woman's build ("very fat" to "athletic") was the most important variable, but hair length, hair color, and bust size all influenced prices (**Figure 17.4**). Based on these figures, a woman who spends $3700 on plastic surgery to go from flat-chested to D-cup earns about $40 more per hour, so she will recoup her outlay after about 90 hours' work.

None of this is very surprising, given that the objectification of women (and sometimes of men) lies at the very core of prostitution. You might be surprised, however, to learn that having a college degree also increases a prostitute's value, and by a hefty 31%, which is a similar premium to that which college graduates enjoy in other fields

escort service   A service that provides prostitutes, generally contacted by telephone.

escort   Euphemism for a prostitute who advertises by print, word of mouth, or the Internet.

call girl   An escort service prostitute, especially one who is relatively upscale in terms of clientele and price.

(Cunningham & Kendall, 2010). This is not because they earn more per hour or have more clients, but because they have much longer sessions with their clients, who tend to be older men wanting a "girlfriend experience." These "talk and cuddle" sessions take more time and require a higher level of education than regular assignments.

Escort service prostitution is much safer for the escorts than street work: Escorts face a lower risk of violence or arrest, and they are more able to require the use of condoms. It is also safer for the client—he is less likely to be robbed or arrested. Compared with "straight" work, however, escort service prostitution is still a risky business.

Although much of an escort's work is anonymous and loveless, some escorts see the same clients over and over again, and their relationships with these "regulars" can become quite intimate and pleasurable to both parties. Regulars are also desirable because they are predictable and therefore safer for the prostitute.

At the top of the prostitution hierarchy are the premier escorts—beautiful and well-presented young women or men that a client can take to dinner or a show without embarrassment. Such a prostitute might stay with a visiting businessperson or politician for an entire weekend or even travel abroad to spend time with a well-heeled oil sheikh. These top-end escort service prostitutes often work for **madams** who have some access to affluent society. Alternatively, they may work for prostitution rings. One such ring, named the Emperors Club, charged $1000 to $5000 per hour for its escorts' services; it was shut down in a 2008 scandal that cost the job of the then governor of New York, Eliot Spitzer.

TABLE 17.1
Some Coded Terms and Slang Used in Prostitution

Provider	Escort prostitute
Generous (or gen)	Willing to pay for sex
Incall	At escort's place
Outcall	At customer's place
Girlfriend experience	Longer session with romantic flavor
Massage rates	Manual stimulation
Full companionship (or full service)	Coitus
Half-and-half	Fellatio and coitus
Interpreter	Condom
Bareback	Without a condom
Fully functional (in reference to trans prostitute)	Has a penis
420 friendly	Into sex under influence of marijuana
Party'n'play (PNP)	Into sex on drugs (usually methamphetamine)
Versatile (in male ads)	Into insertive or receptive anal sex
Donation	Price
Roses	Dollars

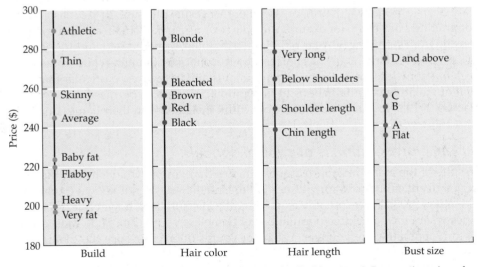

Figure 17.4 Looks matter. This figure shows how physical features influence the price of one hour with a female prostitute, based on data from several countries. (After The Economist, 2014b.)

madam A woman who manages a brothel or an escort service.

Only a minority of men use prostitutes

It has often been claimed, especially in the popular media, that men who use prostitutes are very ordinary men—the "johns next door," as *Newsweek* put it (Bennetts, 2011). This may have been true in the distant past, when prostitution was far more prevalent than it is today and most men had used prostitutes at some time in their lives. Now, however, only 14% of men have ever had sex with a prostitute, and only about 1% have done so during the previous 12 months, according to a study of data from the General Social Survey and other sources by Martin Monto and Christine Milrod of the University of Portland (Monto & Milrod, 2013). This raises the possibility that users of prostitutes have special characteristics that distinguish them from the general male population.

Monto and Milrod found this to be true, at least for the "hobbyists" who are frequent users of Internet-based escort-style prostitutes. These men were more highly educated and had higher incomes than the general male population, and they had far more liberal attitudes on sexual matters: Only 6% thought that gay sex was wrong, for example, versus 55% in the control sample. Most of them believed that prostitutes enjoy their work and said that they would be willing to marry a prostitute. Not surprisingly, nearly all of the hobbyists believed that prostitution should be legalized, and they rarely if ever ran into trouble with the law. Thus the users of escort prostitutes are very different from non-users of prostitutes, but not in pathological ways. Rather, they seem to be freethinking enthusiasts. Men arrested for seeking to hire street-based prostitutes, on the other hand, tend to be younger, unmarried men who have little experience with prostitution and are therefore more likely to be caught in police sting operations.

Some women use male prostitutes

Male escorts are the only kind of prostitute that women use in any significant numbers. Male escorts who are paid by women are called **gigolos**. Gigolos are usually very presentable young men who are able to interact socially with their clients in addition to providing sexual services. There are some websites, such as cowboys4angels.com, that provide gigolos, but this kind of service forms only a minute portion of the escort industry in the United States.

Rather than hire expensive gigolos, some older white women travel to Africa, the Caribbean (especially Jamaica), or elsewhere for sexual pleasure. In the coastal resort communities of Kenya, for example, female sex tourists can obtain sex and companionship from strapping 20-year-old Masai tribesmen, sometimes for as little as a pair of sunglasses (Clarke, 2007). It's not just about economics, though: White women who seek out nonwhite men in exotic environments are driven by a particular fantasy—that of violating colonial taboos to find intimacy with a hypermasculine "native" (Jacobs, 2010). No amount of money can fulfill this fantasy in their home countries.

Juvenile prostitution is of special concern

In spite of the many unfounded guesstimates that you may have heard, the number of juvenile (under 18) prostitutes in the United States is not known (Stransky & Finkelhor, 2008). They certainly exist in significant numbers, however, especially in cities where there are large populations of homeless youth (**Box 17.3**). Most are age 14 to 17, but a few are younger. The older youths often have false IDs that identify them as adults.

Not all juvenile prostitutes are homeless, but many are. These youths have often fled abusive home environments. Some are mentally ill. They have little of mar-

gigolo A male prostitute who caters to women.

Box 17.3 Society, Values, and the Law

Juvenile Prostitutes in Portland, Oregon

As any visitor to Portland knows, this vibrant city has a large population of street-based youths, some of whom survive through prostitution. One of them, "Kendall," told her story to the *Portland Mercury* (Marcus, 2009). At the age of 16, Kendall left home to live with DJ, the homeless, abusive, and alcoholic boyfriend with whom she had fallen in love. Within days he had persuaded her to sell herself on the street—sometimes as often as 25 times in a day. DJ took most of her earnings and also beat her. Although Kendall continued to attend school, she sometimes had to wear sunglasses to conceal a black eye or invent an explanation for visible bruises. As soon as school let out each afternoon, she began turning tricks.

This continued for a year. Eventually she told DJ she was leaving him, and she returned to her parents' home, but DJ came to visit while her parents were out. "In 2 hours your dad is going to come home and find your dead body on the basement floor," he said, and he attacked her and tried to strangle her. Luckily, Kendall was able to dial 911. As the police battered on the door, DJ begged Kendall to say they had just been having sex, but the welt around her neck, and several broken ribs, told the true story. DJ was arrested; he was eventually sentenced to 8 years in prison for assault and for pimping.

Kendall's experience was not unusual. "Most of the teens I meet with have suffered repeated, horrific abuse at the hands of both pimps and johns," said Esther Nelson of Portland's Sexual Assault Resource Center. "Many have been burned, stabbed, shot, strangled, thrown from moving cars, tied up, branded, and starved."

Girls from Seattle and Portland are often trafficked by their pimps down the Interstate 5 corridor to Los Angeles and Las Vegas. In the latter city, over 100 underage girls are picked up by the police for on-street prostitution every year (see figure). For her master's thesis in criminal justice at the University of Nevada, Las Vegas, Alanna Robinson studied 52 of these girls, along with a control group of girls detained for other offenses (Robinson, 2010). Most came from dysfunctional homes where at least one family member had served time in prison. Most had been physically, sexually, or emotionally abused in their home environment. Many had been removed at least once from an abusive family environment by child welfare authorities.

In 2011 actors Ashton Kutcher and Demi Moore began a campaign against juvenile prostitution, in the course of which

Underage prostitutes are more victims than criminals.

they claimed that between 100,000 and 300,000 children are lost to prostitution and sex trafficking in the United States every year (McLaughlin, 2011). This figure (which has been cited frequently in the media, including the *New York Times*) is based on a misinterpretation of a 2002 study by social scientists Richard Estes and Neil Weiner of the University of Pennsylvania (Estes & Weiner, 2002). Those researchers actually gave these figures as the number of children who were *at risk* of commercial sexual exploitation, not those who actually fell victim to it. Researchers at the University of New Hampshire have estimated the total yearly arrests for juvenile prostitution in the United States at 1450 (Mitchell et al., 2010), but this does not account for juveniles who engage in prostitution without being arrested.

Kendall's history was actually an unusual one in that she had run away from a stable, loving home environment, and this may have been her ultimate salvation. After recovering from DJ's assault, she completed high school, enrolled in a community college, and now has aspirations for a career in law enforcement.

sex trafficking Transportation of a person for the purpose of prostitution.

ketable value aside from their youthful bodies, so prostitution is often a necessity ("survival sex") rather than the best-paid option out of many. They are vulnerable to further abuse, violence, exploitation, and disease.

Drug use is very common, and withdrawal symptoms are often the immediate reason for turning a trick. "When I was on junk [heroin] I'd get so sick without it that I'd have to be working," said a young woman who entered prostitution at age 14. "I'd have to have money for drugs to be OK" (Downe & "Ashley-Mika," 2003).

Male youths usually work independently. Females may work independently or, more commonly, are controlled by a third party such as a pimp (K. J. Mitchell et al., 2013a). The independent operators nearly always work on the streets, and they typically earn less than $50 per trick. If they are caught in prostitution by the police, they are often charged with some form of delinquency.

Those juvenile prostitutes who are controlled by third parties also mostly work on the streets, but some are marketed by escort services or via the Internet. Some have been brought from out of state (trafficked—see below). When they are caught by the police, they are usually treated as victims, and the criminal focus is on the pimps or the johns. Sometimes they are charged with offenses and detained simply in order that they can be provided with needed services.

There is another group of juvenile prostitutes—nearly all female—who still live with their parents, attend school, and have not been abused. They engage in prostitution not to survive but to obtain money for luxuries such as expensive clothes. This phenomenon was brought to public attention by a 2003 article in *Newsweek* (Smalley, 2003), but little is known about the numbers of youths involved. In 2014 a 17-year-old female high school student in Venice, Florida, was charged with running an underage prostitution ring—according to police, she pimped high school students as young as 15 for $40 to $200 a trick (Womack, 2014).

Sex trafficking is a global business

The term **sex trafficking** has acquired a variety of meanings. We use the term to mean the transportation of a person from one place to another for the purpose of prostitution. This purpose is in the mind of the person who does the trafficking; the person who is trafficked may or may not know of this purpose or consent to it. Elsewhere you may see the term "sex trafficking" used in a more general sense, referring to any form of prostitution instigated by a third party such as a pimp, or to any juvenile prostitution, or even to any form of prostitution or sex trading—usually with the implication that all prostitutes should be viewed as victims.*

In Box 17.3 we described how juveniles are trafficked from Portland, Oregon, to Las Vegas. This practice has the main objective of satisfying the high demand in "Sin City," but it has the additional benefit (to the trafficker) of isolating the juveniles from their home environment, thus making them easier to control, and it may make the juveniles harder to trace by law enforcement. If state lines are crossed, however, there will be a violation of federal law: In 2012, for example, three Somali gang members were convicted by a federal court of trafficking Somali women from Minnesota to Ohio, where they engaged in sex for money, liquor, or drugs (Shah, 2012).

Transnational trafficking means the transportation of individuals—usually women or girls—from one country to another to supply the demand for prostitutes. The direction of transport is usually from poorer to richer countries (**Figure 17.5**). For example, many women are transported from Bangladesh to Pakistan and India, from Myanmar (Burma) to Thailand, from Vietnam to China, and from the Philippines and Thailand to Japan. Women are trafficked to the United States from places all over the

---

* The various possible meanings result from the ambiguity of the verb "to traffic," which can mean either to transport something or to trade in something, in either case with nefarious intent.

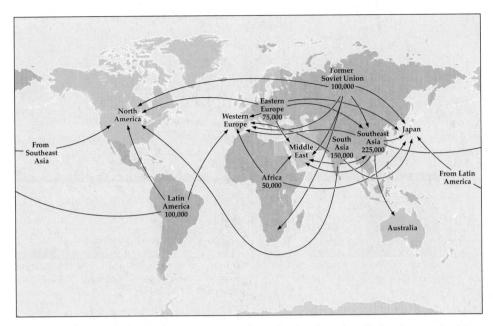

Figure 17.5 Traffic in women and girls for prostitution flows largely from poorer to richer countries. (After Terrorism Research Center.)

world, including Latin America, Southeast Asia, Eastern Europe, and Russia. Western Europe is also a major destination for trafficked prostitutes.

There is a lot of variation in how willingly women participate in sex trafficking. Some women know what they are letting themselves in for and see it as a chance for economic betterment. At the other extreme, some women are deceived, enslaved, held prisoner in the host country, and forced to engage in prostitution against their will. Most cases fall into a gray area: The women travel voluntarily and know that they will be working in the sex industry, but they experience some degree of deception or coercion. For example, they may have to work longer as prostitutes in the host country to "pay back" their traffickers than they were initially led to believe.

The Coalition Against Trafficking in Women (CATW) takes an unreservedly negative view of this trade. "To say that these women are voluntarily allowing themselves to be trafficked is to ignore the powerful social conditions that push women and girls into that kind of life," says Dorchen Leidholdt, one of CATW's founders. "The valuation of women as commodities in the global marketplace is devastating to the rights of all women." Whereas CATW opposes all forms of prostitution, another organization, the Global Alliance Against Traffic in Women (GAATW), takes a different stance: While also opposing trafficking as exploitation, GAATW affirms the right of women to migrate and to choose their own occupations, including sex work.

The converse of transnational trafficking is **sex tourism**. In this case, instead of the prostitute being brought to the more affluent consumer's country, the consumer travels to the home country of the prostitute. We already mentioned sex tourism by women in the context of gigolos, but the great majority of sex tourists are men. Popular destinations include the Dominican Republic, the Netherlands, Thailand, and Indonesia. The reason for travel may

sex tourism   Traveling to a foreign country to find sex partners (usually prostitutes).

Juvenile prostitutes are highly visible in some cities around the world, such as here in Bangkok, Thailand.

Figure 17.6   Should prostitution be legalized? (A) The percentage of Americans who support or oppose legalization. (B) Among those who oppose legalization, their main reasons for doing so. (After YouGov, 2012.)

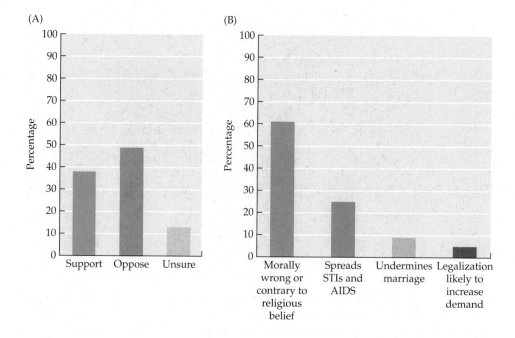

include the legality of prostitution in the countries visited (or the lax enforcement of whatever anti-prostitution laws exist), the low prices sex tourists expect to pay in Third World countries, and the availability of very young prostitutes.

Some men actually relocate to foreign countries on account of the availability and low price of sex. In 1998, for example, Britain's *Sunday Mirror* alleged that the science fiction writer Arthur C. Clarke (1917–2008) was a pedophile who lived in Sri Lanka in order to have sex with underage Sri Lankan boys (Popham, 1998). Clarke denied the allegation but did not sue the newspaper.

There Are Conflicting Views on Prostitution

In 2008 the residents of San Francisco rejected a ballot measure that would have legalized prostitution by adults in that city (SFGate, 2008). Their vote was representative of American attitudes in general: More people oppose legalization than support it, according to a poll by the market research firm YouGov (YouGov, 2012) (**Figure 17.6A**). Women are more likely to oppose legalization than men. Among those who oppose legalization, the majority do so for moral or religious reasons rather than because of the potential negative effects of prostitution such as the spread of STIs (**Figure 17.6B**).

Moral opposition to prostitution is probably rooted in the belief that casual sex itself is morally wrong. Younger people are much more likely than their elders to believe that casual or recreational sex is acceptable, and in the YouGov poll younger respondents were more likely to support legalization of prostitution. Those young people who opposed it were more likely than their elders to cite practical rather than moral reasons for their opinions.

Some feminists see men's use of prostitutes as misogynistic. A well-known proponent of this view was anti-prostitution and anti-pornography crusader Andrea Dworkin (1946–2005). "When men use women in prostitution, they are expressing a pure hatred for the female body," she wrote. Prostitution, according to Dworkin, is "gang rape punctuated by money exchange" (Dworkin, 1994). Contemporary feminists seldom take such an extreme stance, but many believe that prostitution is fundamentally exploitative because it depends on an unequal power balance between prostitutes and their customers. Prostitution, in this view, represents "the last bastion of men's dominance over women" (Bindel, 2006).

Some clients of prostitutes do maltreat them; in fact, some serial murderers have focused their attacks on prostitutes. Yet there are also men who take a great deal of interest in the women they pay and take pains to please them. "I have found that escorts are some of the finest and most interesting women you'll ever meet and it's a real treat to get to know them," writes Marc Perkel, author of an online guide to escort service prostitution. "I recommend that you prepare for your escort's arrival the same way you would for a date. After all, escorts offer more than just sex. Often you can get good conversation and personal companionship as well. And you get these other services by being as nice to them as to any other woman you date" (Perkel, n.d.). Similar ideas are expressed by numerous "hobbyists" on review sites like TheEroticReview.com (Milrod & Weitzer, 2012). "Yes, it's a paid friendship," wrote one reviewer, "but it's still a friendship."

There is a legitimate question as to whether harms suffered by prostitutes are inherent to prostitution, or whether they result from the way society views and treats the practice (Moen, 2014). The concept of occupational health and safety, for example, which has greatly improved working conditions in many fields, is difficult or impossible to apply to an occupation that is illegal. It has therefore been argued that legalization would greatly reduce the harms associated with prostitution (Ross et al., 2012). In the legal brothels of Nevada, for example, prostitutes seldom experience violence or acquire STIs—and of course they are not arrested in connection with their work (Brents & Hausbeck, 2005). These beneficial effects associated with legalization have been noted in many other countries.

There is also a libertarian point of view. This is the idea that, even if prostitution is intrinsically harmful, governments should allow adults to make choices about their lives, including bad choices, if any resulting harm is to the choosers rather than to others. In the case of prostitution, the prostitute and her client voluntarily make a deal that is unlikely to harm anyone beyond those two people. And to the extent that there is any potential harm to others, such as the spread of STIs, these harms characterize casual sex in general rather than being specific to sex that is paid for. Thus the Libertarian Party includes prostitution in an extensive list of activities that it believes government has no business concerning itself with (OnTheIssues.org, 2014). Quite a few feminists and activists, especially those who have had personal experience with prostitution, share this point of view. They may be primarily concerned with prostitutes' welfare and rights rather than with their status.

There are several options for legal reform

If Americans ever come to believe that prostitution—or some forms of prostitution—should no longer be a crime, they will have at least three options. The first is **decriminalization**—that is, the laws banning prostitution would simply be eliminated. Although this avenue is favored by prostitutes' rights organizations (Prostitutes Education Network, 2014), simple decriminalization is so unlikely to happen in the United States that we don't consider it further here.

The second alternative is **legalization with regulation**. This corresponds roughly to the conditions under which Nevada's legal brothels operate. Prostitutes would be allowed to work in prescribed locations and under defined conditions. They might be required to be licensed, to take safe-sex classes, or to have periodic medical examinations for STIs. Proponents argue that this system would reduce the harmful side effects of prostitution, such as disease, unwanted pregnancy, violence, and organized crime (Fuchs, 2013).

In the European experience, there has been a negative relationship between the strictness of regulations governing prostitution and the extent to which prostitutes follow them. In the Netherlands, for example, prostitutes are not individually licensed or compelled to have medical tests; thus, most Dutch prostitutes are happy to operate

decriminalization Removal of laws that criminalize activities such as prostitution.

legalization with regulation Conversion of an activity such as prostitution from a crime to a governmentally regulated occupation.

within the legal structure, although underage girls and nonresident aliens do still operate illegally. In Germany, where individual registration and occasional health examinations are required, only an estimated 25% of prostitutes operate within the law. In Greece, where prostitutes must register individually and receive mandatory health inspections twice a week, it has been estimated that less than 5% of prostitutes operate legally; for the remaining 95%, health and social services are largely inaccessible (U.S. Department of State, 2008). And in Nevada, the 300 or so prostitutes who work at the legal brothels and are subject to health checks are greatly outnumbered by those who work illegally as escorts in Las Vegas and elsewhere in the state. (Of course the remoteness of the locations of the brothels makes it difficult for them to compete for clients.)

Anyone concerned with legal reform of prostitution in the United States needs to bear in mind the reality of this trade-off. It might not be an easy matter to reinvent America's freewheeling system of prostitution as a state-regulated industry. The prostitutes' rights organizations oppose this kind of reform altogether, demanding instead that prostitutes be free to conduct their business how and where they choose (Prostitutes Education Network, 2014).

A third avenue is to decriminalize the *selling* of sex but to maintain or strengthen penalties for the *buying* of sex; that is, to transfer the entire legal culpability for prostitution from prostitutes to their customers. It may seem an odd idea for one side of a transaction to be legal and the other side illegal, but this is currently the situation in Norway, Sweden, and Iceland. (Legislation to establish the same system in France failed to gain passage in 2014.) This so-called "Nordic model" is supported by feminists who see prostitutes as victims rather than free agents (Bien-Aime, 2014).

If this model were enacted, prostitutes might be less exposed to extortion and more willing to seek medical care. Prostitution would remain a crime, however, and the stigma associated with it would remain; thus prostitutes would not be able to function as sex workers with rights and obligations comparable to those of workers in "straight" occupations.

The question of what (if anything) to do about the legal status of prostitution in the United States is a difficult one, and there are merits to diverse views. We hope that you will take advantage of this class to develop your own opinion based on your background, your readings, and discussions inside and out of the classroom.

There Is More to Sex Work than Prostitution

Prostitution—the selling of actual sexual contact—is the most controversial form of commercial sex work, but there are plenty of other forms, such as exotic dancing or stripping, as well as phone sex and its many spin-offs. These activities straddle the boundary between prostitution and pornography.

Stripping is going mainstream

Striptease artists, more commonly known as strippers, may be female or male. They usually perform in strip clubs, but there are also agencies that provide strippers for private parties and other events. Some male strippers ("gogo boys") work in gay bars.

Laws governing what can happen in strip clubs—and whether they can exist at all—vary greatly from place to place. Mostly, strip clubs are legal but are restricted to certain parts of a city. Full nudity may or may not be allowed—most commonly it is. In some places no contact between dancer and customer is permitted, but in others the dancer may grind against the customer's crotch in a "lap dance." Many strip clubs have private areas where there is little oversight over what transpires.

The trend, however, is toward greater restraint, because strip clubs are becoming more popular with a mainstream audience than previously. Some strip clubs are popular with businesspeople—men and sometimes women too—who visit to have a drink and conduct business or entertain clients. (To some, this practice is just another way in which career advancement is made more difficult for women.) In these establishments the dancers are likely to avoid direct contact with customers and focus mostly on pole dancing and the like. Pole dancing itself has gone mainstream: Middle-aged suburbanites now take pole dancing classes as a form of fitness workout.

Phone sex has diversified

In traditional **phone sex** the customer calls an operator who engages him in erotic conversation while he masturbates or fantasizes. The customer is charged around $4 per minute. Billing via premium-rate telephone numbers ("900 numbers") has largely given way to the use of credit cards.

Phone sex companies like to create the impression that their operators are motivated by sex, not money, of course. "Missy is a diagnosed nymphomaniac and phone sex is her therapy," announces one website. "Most operators will orgasm with the caller," says another. Anyone who believes this might want to read an amusing account of the "unsexy realities" of the job posted by a retired phone sex operator (Mannen, 2014). Still, she does acknowledge that phone sex serves a purpose for some operators beyond the financial rewards. "They don't like the way they look," she writes, "and pretending to be what the client wants them to be allows them to feel desirable. . . . There are more grandmothers than you'd care to know about in this industry." Phone sex spares the operators most of the risks associated with prostitution, so long as they resist the numerous requests to meet customers in person. In addition, most operators now work from home, so they can fit the work into their daily schedules.

A more recent variant on phone sex is **sexual webcamming** (**Figure 17.7**). Webcammers perform online and customers can request specific acts, for which they tip with "tokens" purchased ahead of time or with Bitcoin. Webcammers have to be more presentable than regular phone sex operators, and they may need to show more authentic signs of sexual engagement, but the potential rewards are greater because the webcammer can service more than one customer simultaneously.

Underage webcamming is a serious problem. The most notorious case involved a Californian boy named Justin Berry, who at the age of 13 began performing in his bedroom at his family home, without his parents' knowledge. He went on to recruit other juveniles. Over the space of a few years Berry received hundreds of thousands of dollars in goods and cash from his male customers. He became a national celebrity after the *New York Times* published a story about him (Eichenwald, 2005); he appeared on national talk shows, and he testified before Congress about how he had been victimized online and in the real world.

Pornography Has Always Been Part of Human Culture

The word **pornography** (often abbreviated as "porn") refers to depictions of people or behaviors that are intended to be sexually arousing. The depictions can be in any medium, but the most common ones are photography, video/film, written text, and drawing/painting. Sometimes the term "pornography" is restricted to the more down-market products, or products of which the speaker disapproves. More expensive works, or those that are considered to have literary or artistic merit,

phone sex   Erotic telephone conversations, usually carried out for pay.

sexual webcamming   Live sexual performances or nudity supplied over the Internet for pay.

pornography   Material (such as art, writing, photographic images, and film) that is intended to be sexually arousing. Also called *porn*.

Figure 17.7   **Melissa Gira Grant,** webcamming pioneer and writer on the sex industry.

erotica Sexually themed works, such as books or sculpture, deemed to have literary or artistic merit.

sexually explicit materials A nonjudgmental phrase denoting pornography.

obscene Related to sexually themed publications, art, films, performances, or behavior that is deemed offensive to public morals or that violates legal standards of acceptability.

may be called **erotica**. This distinction is very subjective, of course. One catchall, nonjudgmental term that is popular with academics and policy makers is **sexually explicit materials**.

Pornographic works survive from many ancient cultures. Often, as with the sexually themed ceramics created by pre-Incan and Incan cultures, the intent of the artist remains mysterious. However, some ancient works, such as the sculptures and wall paintings that decorated the brothels of the ancient Roman city of Pompeii, are clearly intended to be sexually arousing.

Pornography has battled censorship

During the 19th century, almost anything that was potentially arousing was considered **obscene**—that is, sexually offensive or threatening to public morality. In the United States, the federal Comstock Act of 1873 and comparable state laws criminalized the sale or possession of obscene materials. Some writings were banned as obscene even though they had no content that would be considered pornographic today. These included writings about contraception and homosexuality. The legal suppression of such materials continued well into the 20th century.

At present, the law regarding pornography in the United States is governed by the Supreme Court's decision in the 1973 case *Miller v. California*. According to *Miller*, there is no broad, First Amendment protection for pornography, but states may restrict a pornographic work only under certain conditions:

- The average person, applying contemporary community standards, must find that the work, taken as a whole, appeals to the prurient interest (i.e., is intended to be sexually arousing).
- The work depicts or describes, in a patently offensive way, sexual conduct or excretory functions.
- The work, taken as a whole, lacks serious literary, artistic, political, or scientific merit.

In recent years *Miller* has become difficult to interpret and apply. The reason is the increasing globalization of pornography, facilitated by the Internet, which has made it harder to establish which "community's" standards should be used to judge any particular work. In addition, the use of the term "contemporary" has ensured that legal standards must shift with changing public opinion, which has gradually become more tolerant of pornography: Two out of three Americans now believe that pornography should be legally available to adults (National Opinion Research Center, 2013). The practical result has been a general lessening or even abandonment of efforts to restrict print- and Internet-based pornography.

The main exception to this liberalizing trend concerns pornography involving minors. The law prohibits the manufacture, distribution, and possession of images or videos portraying minors in sexual situations. Moreover, this "child porn" doesn't have to be real, so long as it is believable. Thus materials in which adult actors are made to look like minors, or minors are made to look as if they are engaged in sexual activity, or videos showing believable computer-generated simulations of minors engaged in sexual activity are all illegal in U.S. law. Even unrealistic images such as cartoons may be illegal if they portray minors engaged in acts that are "obscene" by *Miller* criteria. As these criteria are poorly defined, the only safe strategy is to stay well clear of anything vaguely pornographic involving minors.

New technologies mean new kinds of pornography

Developments in communication technologies have always affected pornography in important ways. The invention of printed books, photography, cinematography, glossy magazines, videocassettes, DVDs, the Internet, smartphones, and virtual real-

FAQ

I know downloading child porn is illegal, but is it OK if I simply view it online?

No, viewing counts as downloading, and it will probably leave images on your hard drive.

ity each spurred a new, more explicit, and more accessible genre of pornography. Here are some historical highlights:

- The magazine *Playboy* was founded by Hugh Hefner in 1953; by 1971 it was selling 7 million copies a month. *Playboy* was **soft-core** pornography—it included no images of actual penetrative sex. It was followed by magazines that ventured into **hard-core** pornography, such as *Hustler*, founded by Larry Flynt in 1974.

- The pornographic film *Deep Throat* (starring Linda Lovelace) appeared in 1972. Because this film and others that followed it incorporated humor, they helped dissipate the shame and secretiveness that had been associated with the genre (**Figure 17.8**), and they won a degree of middle-class acceptance.

- The introduction of videocassettes in the late 1970s, followed by DVDs in the 1990s, made the production and distribution of porn movies much easier, and a great diversity of movies catering to every taste appeared. Because videos could be rented and watched at home, they put most porno theaters out of business.

- Broadband Internet connections, which became widespread during the first decade of this century, enabled the viewing of streaming porn online.

The pornographic video industry was long based in the San Fernando Valley area of Los Angeles: An estimated 5000 videos were shot there in 2011. In 2012, however, Los Angeles County enacted an ordinance mandating condom use during production, with the aim of safeguarding the actors' health (Verrier, 2014). As a result, most production moved to other California counties, Nevada, or even eastern Europe, where there is little regulation and production costs are lower. A few companies, such as Falcon Studios, continue filming in Los Angeles but digitally remove the condoms during editing (Woollaston, 2014). Only one major company, Wicked Pictures, uses and shows condoms in all its videos (Morris, 2013).

The sexual content of porn videos doesn't change much over the years, but there are stylistic changes driven in part by technological advances. The introduction of lightweight film cameras, for example, has allowed for "point-of-view" (POV) videos, in which the actors themselves do the filming (**Figure 17.9**). This is intended to make the viewer feel like a participant in the action rather than a passive onlooker. In

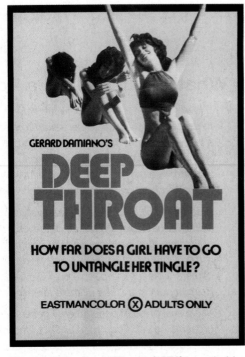

Figure 17.8 Deep Throat (1972) is probably the most famous pornographic film of all time. It featured a woman (played by Linda Lovelace) whose sex life was unexciting until a doctor discovered that her clitoris was located in her throat—a finding that triggered a bonanza of oral sex.

soft-core Related to relatively nonexplicit pornography.

hard-core Related to explicit pornography, such as images of penetrative sex and ejaculation.

Figure 17.9 **Point-of-view pornography** shows the action as filmed by one of the participants.

Box 17.4 Personal Points of View

What's It Like to Be a Porn Star?

"I love sex, I get to have sex all the time. . . . As lame as it is to say, it's quasi-artistic. There is art to what we do, there's a vision, a performance. It's like acting but you get to come. At the end of the day porn is fun because you get to have awesome sex every day with beautiful women and travel around and get paid." James Deen

"I definitely think you need to be a very sexual person, because that's just the nature of the job. . . . I do love sex, but for me, that's not the point of doing porn. Porn, for me, is the ultimate fantasy. I like being on display, I like being on camera, I like turning people on, I like being a sex object. Being a porn star is the ultimate fantasy, to me." Asa Akira

"If it's anal or deep penetration, I generally have two orgasms on set. For me it's all about the intensity. I want hardcore. In real life, you have passion and intimacy, and it's gentler, but overall on camera, I just expect and want a rougher sexual experience. If it's regular sex, I come less often. Maybe once per scene." Courtney Cummz

"Deep throating is not always awesome. If a girl's going down on you for a scene, she's going to be at it for a long time. So she gets tired, and eventually you start feeling molars on the head of your dick. Getting paid to receive oral sex is basically like getting your dick chewed on for an hour." Lance Hart

"I cannot film more than 1 boy/girl scene in a week, because the sex is so intense and usually with a much-larger-than-average sized penis. My vagina needs a few days to recuperate." Siri (not the iPhone Siri)

"All that bouncing around can really hurt, especially if one of those silicone pumpkins whacks you in the head." Anonymous

Sources: Clark-Flory, 2011; Dickson, 2014; Cummz, 2014; Evans, 2014; Quora, 2014; Harrison, 2014.

2013 MiKandi released the first two-way POV porn video filmed with Google Glass—it was viewed over 1 million times within the first 24 hours of its release (Rodriguez, 2013). Porn actors have to adapt to the rapid changes in the industry (**Box 17.4**).

Another way for consumers to immerse themselves in porn is through virtual reality. The online virtual reality game Second Life, for example, has its own red-light district called Amsterdam, where players take the roles of prostitutes and their customers. Like the real-life Amsterdam, however, this site features less action now than it did a few years ago (Resident, 2013). More recently, the Oculus Rift virtual reality headset has been used to deliver 3-D erotic games, sometimes in conjunction with a computer-controlled masturbatory device (Sebastian, 2014). Virtual porn will only catch on, however, when the virtual actors are as convincing as real-life ones.

Assuming that actual humans continue to perform in porno videos, the question arises about how an increasingly aging population will affect the industry. The answer comes from Japan, where "elder porn" now constitutes nearly 20% of the market (Glionna, 2011). In these videos, however, it's only the male actors who are old—one 76-year-old gave up a desk job to work full-time as a porn actor. The female actors remain as young as ever, if not younger. Presumably the older male actors provide characters with whom aging male consumers can identify.

Figure 17.10 Lesbian pornography "Fierce femmes, bashful bois, fisting, wrestling, squirting, and squealing, *The Crash Pad* (Pink and White Productions, 2007) is one fictional apartment that any voyeur would love to call neighbor" (Schadewald, 2011). (A "boi" is a young tomboyish lesbian.)

The collapse of the DVD market and the increasing availability of free porn on the Internet—free teasers, pirated videos, and amateur-produced material—have undercut the profitability of the U.S. porn industry. The actors' earnings have dropped, and production values are generally lower than in the past. The porn business is still a multibillion-dollar industry—estimated figures vary wildly—but it is not as big as it was before the 2007–2009 recession.

There is some pornography for women

Most pornography is produced by men and marketed to men. That doesn't necessarily mean that it's unappealing to women—some women love it, especially those who like to watch porn in male company. But there are also porn videos made by women with women in mind. Companies such as Sssh.com produce videos that differ from regular porn in having romantic story lines in addition to sex scenes. They also feature more attractive men. (Some famous male porn actors, such as longtime star Ron Jeremy, have been average looking at best.) Some heterosexual women enjoy gay male porn—in which looks and physique are valued—in the same way that many straight men enjoy "lesbian" sex scenes.

We put "lesbian" in quotation marks because those scenes don't feature lesbians and are not very likely to appeal to lesbian consumers. Much more to lesbians' taste are videos such as the *Crash Pad* series (produced by Pink and White Productions), which feature women—often tattooed and sporting unconventional hairstyles—who are highly diverse in their skin colors, body shapes, and personalities (Urquhart, 2014) **(Figure 17.10)**. Their approach to sex is athletic and involves liberal use of sex toys such as strap-on dildos.

A woman-oriented genre that has no close male equivalent is the romance novel. The ubiquitous Harlequin Romance novels belong to this category. Many of these novels would hardly be considered pornographic, because their main emphasis is on relationships rather than on sex acts. There are also romance novels that include steamy sex scenes, but even those typically end with a "happily ever after" emotional union—quite different from the "happy endings" (orgasms) that wrap up most male-oriented pornography (Ogas & Gaddam, 2011).

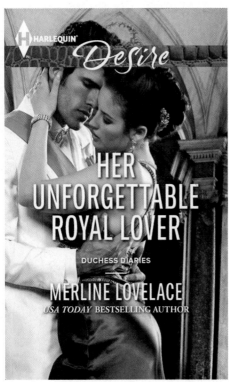

Feminism hasn't had much impact on the Harlequin Desire series.

Figure 17.11 **Anti-porn march** through the Times Square area of New York City in 1979. Feminists including Susan Brownmiller, Andrea Dworkin, Gloria Steinem, and Bella Abzug led the march. Dworkin's speech at the closing rally is available online (Dworkin, 1979).

There Are Conflicting Perspectives on the Value or Harm of Pornography

Although pornographers have basically won their battle with the censors, debate continues about the effects of pornography on society. On the one hand, it can be argued that pornography is victimless: The people who create it do so voluntarily and get paid, and the people who consume it also do so voluntarily and get sexual pleasure. On the other hand, it can be argued that the production and consumption of pornography have deleterious social consequences beyond its effects on the producers and consumers and should therefore be banned or regulated by society in some way.

What might these harmful social consequences be? According to *religious conservatives*, pornography promotes general moral decay and undermines traditional social institutions such as the family. Such allegations are very hard to prove or disprove.

More focused allegations come from the *radical feminist* perspective. The possibility that has provoked the most discussion is that pornography promotes physical or sexual violence or other forms of harm against women (**Figure 17.11**). In fact, radical feminist writer Diana Russell defined pornography in a way that incorporates this alleged effect. Heterosexual pornography, she wrote, is "material created for heterosexual males that combines sex and/or the exposure of genitals with the abuse or degradation of females in a manner that appears to endorse, condone, or encourage such behavior" (Russell, 1994). It has also been claimed that female porn actors are the most direct victims of this alleged abuse, especially with the increasing popularity of videos that feature rough sex or BDSM scenes (Dines, 2008).

The *liberal* perspective generally downplays any harmful effects of pornography and even sees beneficial effects, in terms of encouraging sexual exploration or providing a harmless outlet for fantasies that could be dangerous in real life. Liberals also argue that pornography is protected by the First Amendment and that exceptions to First Amendment protection cover only forms of expression that put people in immediate danger. Some feminists, such as Shine Louise Houston (owner of Pink and White Productions, mentioned above), themselves produce porn videos, some of which contain rough sex or BDSM-type elements, and feminist porn is recognized at the Feminist Porn Awards held annually in Toronto (Good For Her, 2014).

Research has not resolved the question of pornography's effects

A great deal of research has been done on the question of whether the consumption of pornography by men causes them to harm women. Some studies have been done on "regular" men with no special history of sexual violence. Male college students, for example, may be asked to provide information about their use of pornography and to answer questions that assess their attitudes on the topic of violence toward women. According to a meta-analysis of such studies, there is indeed a positive correlation between men's pornography consumption and their acceptance of violence (Hald et al., 2010). Not surprisingly, the association is especially strong for consumption of pornographic materials that actually portray sexual violence. This could be a matter of concern, because there has been a marked trend toward increasing amounts of violent content, such as slapping, spanking, and gagging, in pornography. In one study of several hundred scenes from recent videos, nearly 90% included these behaviors (Bridges et al., 2010).

In experimental studies, men are exposed to various kinds of pornographic and nonpornographic materials in a laboratory setting. Then they may be given the opportunity to "harm" a woman by, say, giving her an electric shock (that is not actually delivered to her). In these studies, only a minority of men—about 7% or so—become more likely to "harm" women after exposure to pornography (Hald & Malamuth, 2014). These are men with a preexisting hostility toward women or a violence-prone personality, perhaps as a result of childhood experiences.

There is some question about the relevance of these findings to the problem of real-world violence against women. For that reason, studies have been done on men who have been convicted of actual violent crimes against women (along with control groups of men who have not committed such crimes). These studies have basically come up negative: Perpetrators of violent crimes against women do not report a greater exposure to pornography—or only a slightly greater exposure—compared with men in the control groups (Allen et al., 2000).

Cross-cultural studies also cast doubt on the idea that pornography consumption promotes violence against women. In Japan, for example, pornography—including violent pornography—is produced and consumed in very large quantities, yet sex crimes against women are relatively infrequent. During the period from 1972 to 1995, when the availability and consumption of pornography exploded, the annual number of reported rapes in Japan fell from 4677 per year to 1500 per year (Diamond & Uchiyama, 1999). In fact, a broad analysis of pornography availability and sex crime rates in numerous countries, including the United States, suggests that the Japanese experience is typical: When pornography consumption increases, sex crime rates decrease or stay the same, but do not rise (Diamond, 2009; Ferguson & Hartley, 2009). This may be because pornography gives potential sex criminals an alternative channel for their sexual desires (Diamond & Uchiyama, 1999), or it may be that some underlying social process, such as sexual liberation, causes both an increase in pornography and a decrease in sex crimes.

In spite of the wealth of research in this area, it is still not clear whether pornography increases violence, decreases it, or has no effect, according to one recent review (Fisher et al., 2013).

Figure 17.12 Backhanded compliment? The CW channel used a comment from the Parents Television Council to promote the 2008 season of its teen sex drama, *Gossip Girl*.

Sex Is Part of the Mass Media

Sexually themed content on broadcast television and in advertising is rarely as explicit as it is in pornographic videos and the like. However, television and advertising reach a much wider audience, including children and people who may not have chosen to see erotic material. Thus, even mildly provocative sexual material can elicit a great deal of protest.

Images of genitalia, female nipples, anuses, and hard-core sex, as well as the use of sexual slang words such as "fuck," are all off-limits on network TV, and if they do occur, the broadcasters may be penalized by the Federal Communications Commission (FCC). One test case involved the 2002 and 2003 Billboard Music Awards, in which the presenters uttered vulgarities. In the 2003 incident, for example, Nicole Richie said in reference to her city-girls-on-a-farm TV series, "Why do they even call it *The Simple Life*? Have you ever tried to get cow shit out of a Prada purse? It's not so fucking simple." The Fox network, joined by the other networks, argued that the FCC acted arbitrarily in penalizing fleeting obscenities such as these. After a long-running legal battle the Supreme Court sided with Fox on narrow grounds, but it did not reject the FCC's right to penalize even brief obscenities (Liptak, 2012).

Although explicit sexual vulgarities are uncommon on broadcast TV, television programs in general are rife with sexual content—most of it verbal references to sex. A study by the Parents Television Council (PTC)—a conservative group that works to reduce the amount of sex, violence, and foul language on television—reported that the number of sexual references and profanities on prime-time TV increased by nearly 70% between 2005 and 2010 (Parents Television Council, 2010). Whether the PTC's campaign against sex on television is having any effect is open to question because it spreads its condemnation so widely. During the most recent week of ratings that we examined, PTC could not identify a single prime-time show to honor with its green light ("Family-friendly show promoting responsible themes and traditional values"). Sometimes it seems as if a damning critique from the PTC actually helps *increase* a show's viewership (**Figure 17.12**).

In 1996 the U.S. television industry was ordered by Congress to introduce a "voluntary" ratings system that indicates the presence and intensity of sexual content (along with violence and foul language) in individual programs. In combination with the V-chip—a device built into all new television sets—this system allows parents to filter out entire categories of programs they deem unsuitable for their children. The ACLU opposed the system, saying that it amounted to government censorship. In any case, few parents use the V-chip, and if they do, it can easily be overridden by any child literate enough to read the TV manual.

Sex sells, sometimes

Sex has been used in advertising for as long as advertising has existed, and roughly one-fifth of all contemporary advertising has overt sexual content (Reichert & Lambiase, 2003; Reichert, 2007). People often pay attention to and recall sexy ads better than ads containing nonsexual imagery (G & R Research and Consulting, 2008).

A problem with the use of sexual content in advertising is that it may distract the viewer from attending to or remembering the name of the product or the advertising message. Thus, sexual content is most effective when the product itself is related to sex—as perfume is, for example. Sex doesn't sell lawn mowers so well.

Another problem has to do with the different responses of men and women to sexually themed advertising. An informative study on this topic was performed by an international group led by Darren Dahl of the University of British Columbia (Dahl et al., 2011). They found, first, that men respond favorably to sexually themed advertising that is devoid of any relationship context, whereas women respond negatively to such material; they only respond favorably when the sexual content is clearly embedded in a committed relationship. So much we might have guessed. For women to react most favorably, however, there must be an indication that the commitment is a resource that is being transferred from the man to the woman. (Think beribboned new car in driveway.) Unfortunately for advertisers, this kind of content is perceived negatively by men—apparently because it reminds them how "high-maintenance" a sexual relationship can be. So advertisers have to figure out which partner is likely to be the decision maker for any particular purchase before they create their ads.

Female nudity in advertisements is something that women say they dislike. When market researchers interviewed women about an ad for Calvin Klein's Obsession perfume, for example (**Figure 17.13A**), most women's responses were strongly negative. One woman described it as "obscene—nothing about love—purely physical pornography. Absolutely useless for selling perfume" (G & R Research and Consulting, 2008). Obsession was a blockbuster success in the marketplace, however—either because men were doing the buying or because women's unconscious responses didn't correspond with what they told interviewers.

Advertisers are constantly trying to extend the limits of acceptability. For their spring 2007 campaign, Dolce & Gabbana used an ad in which a woman was pinned to the ground by a kneeling, bare-chested man while four other men looked on. It provoked a storm of criticism. NOW, for example, accused Dolce & Gabbana of glorifying gang rape (National Organization for Women, 2007), and in Italy the ad was banned outright. Stefano Gabbana defended the ad by claiming that it was intended to represent an "erotic dream." (Women may indeed have rape fantasies, as we discussed in Chapter 5.) The company pulled the ad from publications worldwide but has since come out with ads in which men are represented as sexual victims (**Figure 17.13B**).

(A)   (B)

Figure 17.13 Sex in advertising (A) Women reacted negatively to this ad for Calvin Klein's Obsession perfume. (B) This Dolce & Gabbana ad appears to represent a gay BDSM scene.

Summary

- Many relationships involve an exchange of resources for sex. Prostitution—paid sex—is the extreme version of this phenomenon. Prostitutes can be female, male, or transgender, but nearly all users of prostitutes are male. Prostitution is illegal almost everywhere in the United States, but enforcement varies.

- Historically, prostitution has been condemned as wrong but also tolerated as necessary. Concern about STI transmission has been a major factor in anti-prostitution campaigns. Prostitution declined greatly during the 20th century in the United States, probably because unmarried women became more willing to engage in sexual relations with men.

- Streetwalkers are the lowest-paid prostitutes. They face a relatively high risk of violence and STIs, and many use drugs. Street prostitutes who are minors may be runaways or homeless; these prostitutes face a heightened risk of violence and exploitation. Among street prostitutes, women do better economically than men, but men enjoy their work more. Female street prostitutes traditionally worked for pimps, but increasing numbers are independent operators or are controlled by gangs.

- Some prostitutes work at commercial locations such as massage parlors or exotic dance venues. Brothels—establishments that have the sole purpose of prostitution—are rare today and, in the United States, are legal only in some rural counties of Nevada.

- Escorts are off-street prostitutes who obtain clients by advertising or by word of mouth. They may go to the client's location or receive clients at a fixed location. Many work for escort services, which arrange their appointments. Escorts are more numerous than street prostitutes; they charge more, and they work in somewhat safer conditions.

- Women and men prostitute themselves principally because they can earn much more from prostitution than from other occupations available to them, but sexual pleasure plays some role for high-end escorts and for some male prostitutes. Men use prostitutes for a wide variety of reasons, including difficulty in obtaining unpaid partners, the quest for sexual variety, or the excitement of illicit sex. According to some feminists, men use prostitutes to express their hatred of women, but some accounts by men suggest otherwise.

- Feminists have campaigned successfully for increased prosecution and punishment of men who use prostitutes. There is some support for regulated legalization of prostitution, as has happened in some European countries.

- Prostitutes in developing countries work in risky conditions, but the occupation does offer them an above-average income. Some international agencies believe that prostitution should be recognized, governed by fair labor codes, and integrated into regional economies. Some international women's groups believe that activities associated with prostitution, but not prostitutes themselves, should be criminalized.

- Many women are trafficked between countries for purposes of prostitution. Some women participate in this traffic voluntarily in search of economic betterment; others are enslaved and prostituted against their will. In sex tourism, men or women travel to foreign countries where prostitution is legal or cheap. Going overseas to have sex with minors is a crime under U.S. and Canadian laws.

- Pornography consists of depictions of people or behaviors that are intended to be sexually arousing. Censorship of pornography increased greatly in Victorian times but eased after World War II. In 1973, the U.S. Supreme Court ruled that the legality of sexually explicit work must be judged by "contemporary community standards."

- Developments in communication technologies—the printing press, photography, film, and computers—have all affected pornography in important ways. Feature-length pornographic movies became popular in the 1970s. The introduction of the videocassette format made production and consumption easier and allowed for greater diversity of content. Thanks to the Internet, consumers can now access a diverse range of pornography—often for free—and they can create their own pornography for sale or exchange. Virtual reality sites allow for the enactment of sexual fantasies with like-minded others.

- Pornography designed for women tends to be less sexually graphic than male-oriented pornography—emphasizing intimacy and romance more than sex alone. Still, there is a trend toward more sexually explicit material for women. Some lesbians have pioneered a more hard-core approach to pornography.

- There is debate about the potential harmful effects of pornography. Research studies suggest that pornography does not cause most normal men to harm women, but pornography that includes violence may make a few men more likely to do so. Studies of convicted sex offenders indicate that they have not had greater exposure to pornography than other men. Countries with high rates of pornography consumption do not have unusually high rates of violence against women.

- Pornography featuring real sexual activity by minors, as well as believable simulations of such activity, is illegal in the United States.

- Sexual content on television has increased greatly. Responding to public and congressional concern, the television industry introduced a rating system that warns of sexual (and violent) content. In combination with the V-chip, it allows parents to filter out material they don't want their children to see, but the system is little used.

- Sexually themed advertising can sell products, but women and men react to such advertising in different ways. Advertisers are constantly pushing the boundaries of what's acceptable in terms of nudity or the kinds of sexual activity shown or suggested by advertisements.

Discussion Questions

1. Do you think that prostitution should be decriminalized, legalized with regulation, or illegal? Give your reasons.

2. If prostitution remains illegal, should the emphasis be on prosecuting prostitutes or on prosecuting their customers ("johns")? Should law enforcement devote equal resources to reducing street prostitution and escort service prostitution?

3. Should all depictions of sex involving underage people (whether real or simulated) be illegal? Why or why not?

4. Female college students have sometimes been hired as high-priced call girls. What do you think would be the pros and cons of this occupation? If your best friend considered this as a way to pay a tuition bill that was overdue, what would you advise her?

5. Parents are often very upset to find their young sons viewing pornographic material. How would you advise parents to respond in that situation?

6. Do you think children should be protected from seeing pornographic material on the Internet? If you do, how would you accomplish this?

Web Resources

Association of Sites Advocating Child Protection (porn industry association) www.asacp.org

Coalition Against Trafficking in Women www.catwinternational.org

End Child Prostitution (ECPAT) www.ecpat.net

International Sex Worker Foundation for Art, Culture and Education www.iswface.org

Parents Television Council www.parentstv.org

ProCon.org: Should prostitution be legal? www.prostitution.procon.org

Prostitutes' Education Network www.bayswan.org/penet.html

Recommended Reading

Boyle, K. (Ed.). (2010). *Everyday pornography*. Routledge.

Brown, C. (2011). *Paying for it: A comic-strip memoir about being a john*. Drawn & Quarterly.

Delacoste, F. & Alexander, P. (Eds.). (1998). *Sex work: Writings by women in the sex industry* (2nd ed.). Cleis.

Dworkin, A. (1981). *Pornography: Men possessing women*. Putnam.

Lane, F. S., III. (2000). *Obscene profits: The entrepreneurs of pornography in the cyber age*. Routledge.

McNair, B. (2013). *Porno? Chic!: How pornography changed the world and made it a better place*. Routledge.

Mulholland, M. (2013). *Young people and pornography: Negotiating pornfication*. Palgrave Macmillan.

Ogas, O. & Gaddam, S. (2011). *A billion wicked thoughts: What the world's largest experiment reveals about human desire*. Dutton. (Mines Internet porn usage and other sources to probe male and female sexuality.)

Raphael, J. (2004). *Listening to Olivia: Violence, poverty, and prostitution*. Northeastern University Press.

Reichert, T. & Lambiase, J. (Eds.). (2003). *Sex in advertising: Perspectives on the erotic appeal*. Lawrence Erlbaum.

Strossen, N. (2000). *Defending pornography: Free speech, sex, and the fight for women's rights*. NYU Press.

Tolman, D. L. & Diamond, L. M. (Eds.). (2014). *APA handbook of sexuality and psychology, Vol. 2*. American Psychological Association.

Whisnant, J. & Stark, C. (2005). *Not for sale: Feminists resisting prostitution and pornography*. Spinifex.

Appendix A
Sex and Evolution

Our sexuality evolved from the sex lives of nonhuman creatures that preceded us in the long history of life on Earth. By studying this evolutionary process, we can hope to find clues to some very basic "why" questions about ourselves: Why are we sexual beings? Why are there two sexes? Why are the numbers of men and women approximately equal? Why do we find some people more attractive than others? Why don't all sex acts lead to pregnancy? Why are men more interested in casual sex than women are? Why do some of us cheat on our partners? And why do some of us remain faithful? The study of evolution does not provide complete answers to these questions, but it does remind us that answers are needed. Without the evolutionary perspective, it is too easy to view our own sexuality as the natural order of things, requiring no explanation.

Most of the examples and research studies described here feature nonhuman animals. This may seem odd for a textbook on human sexuality. What we are discussing here, however, are general evolutionary principles; in the main text of the book we consider how relevant these principles may be to our own sex lives.

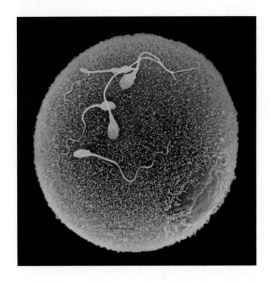

Figure A.1   Gametes A human ovum and several sperm. Note the difference in size: The sperm contributes nothing to the zygote except its genes.

asexual reproduction
Reproduction in which all the offspring's genes are inherited from a single parent.

genome An organism's entire complement of DNA, including all its genes. In some viruses, such as HIV, the genome is composed of RNA.

sexual reproduction Reproduction in which the offspring inherit genes from two parents.

gamete A germ cell (ovum or sperm) that fuses with another to form a new organism.

ovum (pl. ova) A mature female gamete, prior to or immediately after fertilization.

sperm or spermatozoon (pl. spermatozoa) A male gamete, produced in the testis.

meiosis A pair of cell divisions that produces haploid gametes.

zygote A cell formed by the fusion of gametes; a fertilized ovum.

adaptive Helping the propagation of an organism's genes.

Rival Theories Offer Explanations for Sexual Reproduction

Living organisms produce offspring by two alternative methods: asexual and sexual reproduction. The key feature of **asexual reproduction** is that each individual organism receives its **genome**—the entirety of its genetic endowment—from just one parent. One example that you may be familiar with is the reproduction of hydras and other microscopic animals by a simple budding process; another example is the propagation of plants from cuttings.

In **sexual reproduction**, on the other hand, an organism receives its genome from two parents. Each parent produces specialized reproductive cells known as **gametes**: **ova** in females and **spermatozoa** (or sperm) in males (**Figure A.1**). What's special about gametes is that they possess half the number of chromosomes that is typical for that species. (This halving takes place by means of a two-step process known as **meiosis**; see **Web Activities A.1 Mitosis; A.2 Mitosis Time-Lapse Video; A.3 Meiosis;** and **A.4 Differences and Similarities between Meiosis and Mitosis**). Thus, when ovum and sperm unite to form a **zygote**, the full genome is restored, but it's a mixed genome, half coming from the mother and half from the father.

Nearly all multicellular organisms are capable of sexual reproduction, and most vertebrates (including all mammals) rely on it as their only means of reproduction. This tells us that the capacity for sexual reproduction must be **adaptive**; that is, it must help the organism to perpetuate its genes in future generations. How does it do so?

Surprisingly, the answer to this very basic question is a bit of a mystery. On the face of it, asexual reproduction is more adaptive than sexual reproduction. This is because an animal that reproduces asexually devotes all its resources to passing on its own genes, and those genes are perpetuated in all of its descendants (**Figure A.2**). An animal that reproduces sexually, however, dilutes its genes with those of another animal, thus reducing the representation of its own genes in future generations. This seems like a pointless self-sacrifice.

The paradox is particularly striking in species in which one sex—usually the female—invests far more in reproduction than the other sex. In such species, it would

Figure A.2   The paradox of sexual reproduction An asexually reproducing female's genes (red) are propagated without loss into future generations, but a sexually reproducing female's genes are mixed with the genes of unrelated males (white) and thus are reduced by half in each ensuing generation.

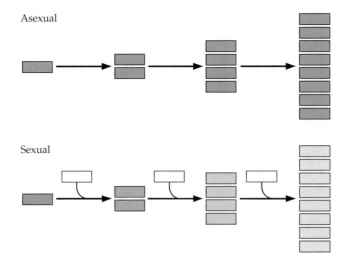

seem that females would do better to give birth **parthenogenetically** (by asexual "virgin birth") rather than to give some male's genes a free ride into the next generation. If a single parthenogenetically reproducing female arose in a population of a million sexually reproducing individuals, then—other things being equal—it would take less than 50 generations for her clonal descendants to replace the entire population. Yet, except for a few unusual species, females engage in sexual reproduction all or some of the time. So other things must not be equal—but in what way, exactly?

parthenogenesis Asexual reproduction from an unfertilized ovum; "virgin birth."

mutation A change in an organism's genome.

Sexual reproduction may remove harmful mutations

One hypothesis suggests that sexual reproduction is adaptive because it helps organisms cope with the problem of harmful **mutations**. Mutations are random changes in an organism's genome caused by errors in the copying of DNA or by damaging chemicals, sunlight, or radiation. Many mutations are neutral—they have no effect on an organism's ability to survive and reproduce—but of those that are not neutral, far more are harmful than beneficial, just as random changes in computer software are far more likely to degrade its performance than to improve it.

When organisms reproduce asexually, harmful mutations accumulate over the generations. Because all the descendants of a given animal possess exact copies of that animal's genes, there is no way to get rid of a harmful mutation short of eliminating that entire lineage. When organisms reproduce sexually, however, harmful mutations *can* be eliminated. That's because offspring receive a randomly selected half of their mother's genes and half of their father's genes. If one parent carries a particular damaged gene, about half of that parent's offspring will not inherit it—they will inherit the normal version of the gene from the other parent instead.

In reality, most organisms carry numerous harmful mutations. Thus, each offspring is likely to inherit some harmful mutations from each parent. But because of the lottery-like nature of sexual reproduction, some offspring will receive a greater total load of harmful mutations, and other offspring will receive fewer (**Figure A.3**). Natural selection will favor the survival and reproduction of the offspring that have fewer harmful mutations. Thus, sexual reproduction may help maintain an equilibrium state in a population of organisms, in which the appearance of new harmful mutations is balanced by the gradual elimination of old ones.

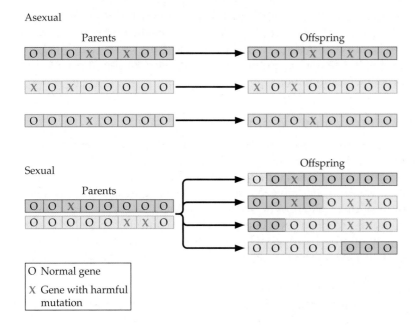

Figure A.3 Reproduction and harmful mutations In this diagram, each organism is represented as a genome with eight genes, some of which have harmful mutations (each marked with an X). In asexual reproduction (top), each offspring inherits the entire genome of its parent, along with any harmful mutations. In sexual reproduction (bottom), each offspring inherits random chunks of its father's (purple) and mother's (orange) genomes. Thus, some offspring, such as the lowermost one in the diagram, may inherit few or no harmful mutations. If this lucky offspring enjoys great reproductive success and its unlucky siblings die out, the harmful mutations will be eliminated from the population.

Some experimental evidence favors this hypothesis. For example, Susanne Paland and Michael Lynch of Indiana University measured the rate at which harmful mutations accumulated in two lineages of the water flea *Daphnia*. One of the lineages reproduced sexually, the other asexually. In conformity with the hypothesis, the sexual lineage accumulated harmful mutations at a much lower rate than the asexual lineage (Paland & Lynch, 2006). Still, it is not yet clear whether this advantage to sexually reproducing organisms is a universal phenomenon.

Sexual reproduction may generate beneficial gene combinations

Another hypothesis ignores the matter of harmful mutations and attributes the value of sexual reproduction to the novel combinations of genes that it produces. Having offspring with different combinations of genes might be useful because those offspring would have different ways of utilizing the resources available in the environment (eating different foods, for example). In this case, the offspring would compete less with one another for available resources, so their parents could have more surviving offspring than would otherwise be possible.

Alternatively, the mixing of genes might be useful in dealing with environmental changes. Evidence in support of this idea came from British researchers who compared the growth rates of yeast cells from two different strains—a natural strain that was capable of sexual reproduction and a genetically engineered strain that could reproduce only asexually (Goddard et al., 2005). In a normal, benign environment the cells of both strains reproduced at an equal rate. When the yeast cells were stressed by being placed in a high-temperature environment, however, the sexually reproducing cells reproduced faster than those that reproduced asexually. Presumably, new gene combinations arose in the offspring of some of the sexually reproducing yeast cells that favored growth in high-temperature conditions. Supporting the idea that sexual reproduction exists to help organisms cope with changes in the environment is the observation that in species that can reproduce either sexually or asexually, the sexual route is often adopted when environmental conditions become stressful, and the offspring generated by the sexual route are fitter (survive and reproduce better) than those generated asexually (Becks & Agrawal, 2012).

Many species engage in an endless war with parasites, in which the parasites are constantly evolving new ways to outwit the host's defenses. Gene mixing may be an effective way for the host species to rapidly deploy new defenses against these ever-changing attacks (Ridley, 2003; Lively, 2010). In this conception, the genetic variations among individuals in a sexually reproducing species are like the numbers in combination locks: When a parasite develops the ability to "pick" a common combination, many individuals die, but sexual reproduction quickly reestablishes a population with novel, "unpickable" combinations.

Future research may solve the puzzle

We don't know which of these two sexual reproduction hypotheses is correct—perhaps *both* are. Several avenues of research may help clarify the issue. One avenue involves the observation of host-parasite interactions in natural, isolated environments such as lakes. These studies have lent some support to the idea that resistance to parasites is an important function of sexual reproduction (Wolinska & Spaak, 2009). Another avenue is "in silico" evolution, in which a computer models the evolutionary process. This approach can test whether theories—however good they may sound at first—actually have the logical structure required to cause sexual reproduction to persist.

Finally, it is worth studying the few species that never engage in sexual reproduction. By analyzing how these species survive without sex, we may better understand why sex is so essential for the rest of us. A group of microscopic animals called bdelloid rotifers, for example, haven't reproduced sexually for tens of millions of years (Flot et al., 2013), but they seem to be none the worse for it, because they are found in large numbers in most freshwater environments (**Figure A.4**). Bdelloid rotifers have the unusual ability to take up genes from their surroundings—genes that have leaked out of dying organisms in their environment—and patch them into their own genomes (Gladyshev et al., 2008). It is possible that this process, though a random one, leads in time to the selection of organisms in which mutated genes have been replaced by "clean copies." This could support the idea that an important function of sex is the removal of harmful mutations, and that bdelloid rotifers have simply hit on an alternative means to the same end.

Why Are There Two Sexes?

The hypotheses previously discussed offer possible explanations for sexual reproduction, but they don't explain the existence of males and females. Across the biological realm, "male" is the name given to individuals with small gametes (sperm, in the case of humans), and "female" is the name given to individuals with large gametes (ova). But why should these two kinds of individuals exist? Why shouldn't a sexually reproducing species consist of individuals that are all alike, any two of which could pair off and fuse their gametes ("sex without sexes," as it were)?

Actually, sex without sexes might well be an ideal arrangement for a species. But because natural selection operates at the individual level and not at the species level, it does not necessarily produce arrangements that are ideal for the species as a whole. Rather, it produces compromises—states in which the conflicting interests of countless individuals are in dynamic equilibrium. Sex without sexes is not generally an equilibrium state, and here's why: Reproduction requires an **investment**—a commitment of resources. For many organisms, that investment is the time and energy required to produce a gamete. That gamete must be endowed with enough nutrient material so that, once it has fused with the other parent's gamete, it can develop into a new organism. How much nutrient material is required? That depends, in part, on how much nutrient material the *other* parent contributes.

Let's consider a hypothetical sex-without-sexes species, in which the gametes of all individuals are roughly similar in size and nutrient content (**Figure A.5**). Even in this situation, there will be some natural variation, so some individuals will produce slightly larger gametes and some will produce slightly smaller ones. Over time, natural selection will favor individuals that produce larger gametes (containing more nutrients) because those gametes stand a better chance of developing into offspring. But individuals that produce smaller gametes will also be favored because such gametes require a smaller investment and are therefore easier to produce. And as long as there are some larger gametes available to fuse with, those smaller gametes can still develop into offspring. The only individuals that are not especially favored are those that produce middle-sized gametes, because middle-sized gametes are suboptimal in terms of both nutrient content and ease of production. Thus, the individu-

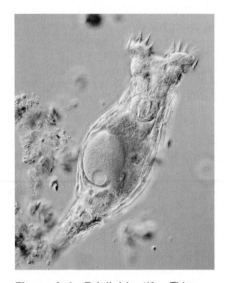

Figure A.4 Bdelloid rotifer This freshwater animal and those in other Bdelloidea species haven't reproduced sexually for millions of years.

investment The commitment or expenditure of resources for a goal, such as reproductive success.

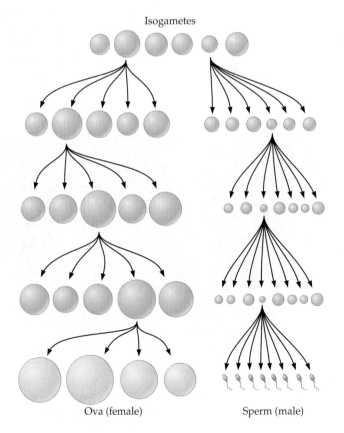

Isogametes

Ova (female)   Sperm (male)

Figure A.5 Disruptive selection splits a single population of similar-sized gametes (isogametes) into large (female) and small (male) types.

hermaphrodite   An organism
that combines male and female
reproductive functions.

sex determination   The biological
mechanism that determines whether
an organism will develop as a male
or a female.

als producing middle-sized gametes tend to die out, and the population gradually
diverges into two groups pursuing different strategies. One group produces large,
nutrient-loaded gametes (ova); the other produces small, nutrient-poor gametes
(sperm). The two groups that result are females and males, respectively (Scharer et
al., 2012).

Several other factors come into play. For one, there is the question of mobility. To
fuse, gametes need to come together, which usually means that at least one of the
gametes has to be motile. It is much easier for small gametes to move than large ones,
so gametes produced by males are usually the motile ones. There is also the matter of
numbers. Because a small gamete requires so little investment to produce, males can
produce many more gametes than females. In fact, some factors that we'll consider
below often make it essential for males to produce large numbers of gametes. Thus,
the total investment in gamete production may end up being similar in the two sexes.

Hermaphrodites combine male and female reproductive functions

Although we usually think of males and females as being two different kinds of
individuals within a species, it is not uncommon for individuals to combine male
and female reproductive functions within a single body. Such individuals are called
hermaphrodites. In some species, including most flowering plants and trees as well
as some invertebrate animals such as worms and snails, all the individuals are hermaphrodites; there are no pure males or females.

One might imagine that hermaphrodites would fertilize themselves. Such self-
fertilization, however, would nullify much of the genetic advantage that sexual reproduction is thought to confer. Thus, in hermaphroditic species there generally exist
mechanisms to reduce the likelihood of self-fertilization. Male and female gametes
may be generated at different times, or at distant locations on the organism. In the
corn plant, for example, the male flower (the *tassel*) is at the top of the plant and
develops early, while the female flower (the *ear silk*) is lower on the plant and develops somewhat later. As a result, less than 3% of all corn kernels are the result of
self-pollination. In other species of plants, such as the potato, self-fertilization is prevented by molecular tricks that make male and female gam-
etes from the same plant incompatible. In hermaphroditic
animals, behavioral mechanisms often prevent self-fertilization: The animals simply don't inseminate themselves, even
though they are physically capable of doing so (**Figure A.6**).
Some hermaphroditic mollusks engage in a bizarre behavior
called "penis fencing" (for a video clip, see Web Resources
at the end of this appendix): Each of the two mating animals
acts as if it is trying to inseminate the other while at the same
time avoiding being inseminated itself. They behave in this
way because each animal is advantaged if the other takes on
the task of producing their offspring.

Evolution Has Led to Diverse Methods of Sex Determination

Seeing that so many species throughout the animal kingdom
have settled on sexual reproduction, one might expect that the
mechanisms of **sex determination**—controlling whether an
embryo becomes male or female—would also have become
fixed early in evolution, and would now be universal. In fact,
however, a variety of sex-determining mechanisms have

Figure A.6   Nudibranchs (marine mollusks related to slugs
and snails) are simultaneous hermaphrodites: They produce both
sperm and ova at the same time. They do not fertilize themselves,
however; instead, they pass sperm from one individual to another.

evolved (Bachtrog et al., 2014). For example, in many reptiles the offspring's sex is determined by the temperature at which the fertilized eggs are incubated, but the details vary from species to species: among lizards and alligators, eggs incubated at low temperatures develop into females and those incubated at high temperatures produce males, while among some turtles it's the other way around.

In mammals, sex is determined by chromosomes

In humans—and in most mammals—an embryo's sex is determined by the chromosomes it possesses. Forty-four of our 46 chromosomes are known as **autosomes**; they come in 22 homologous (corresponding) pairs, regardless of a person's sex. With the remaining two chromosomes, the **sex chromosomes**, the situation is more complicated. Females possess a homologous pair of sex chromosomes, termed **X chromosomes**, but males possess one X chromosome and one much smaller chromosome, called a **Y chromosome**. (The human chromosomes are shown in Figure 4.1, page 88.)

   As mentioned above, gametes are produced by meiosis, a process of cell division in which the number of chromosomes is halved. Human ova receive 22 autosomes and one X chromosome. Sperm, however, receive 22 autosomes and either one X or one Y. Thus, when the ovum and sperm fuse at fertilization, the resulting zygote receives an X from the ovum and either an X or a Y from the sperm. If an X chromosome is received from the sperm, the zygote will develop as a female (XX); conversely, if a Y chromosome is received, the zygote will develop as a male (XY). Since there are roughly equal numbers of X-bearing and Y-bearing sperm, the chances of an offspring being female or male are approximately equal. The details of human sex determination and sexual development are discussed in Chapter 4.

Sexual Selection Produces Anatomical and Behavioral Differences between Males and Females

In many respects, natural selection acts similarly on females and males. It ensures that women and men are both adapted to life on land, for example, and that female and male fish are both adapted to life in water. Yet marked differences can develop between males and females of a single species. Think of peacocks and peahens, for example: The males strut to and fro and shake their gorgeous tail feathers, while the plainer females watch silently, evaluate their prospective mates, and decide which male to mate with. Such differences in the appearance and behavior of males and females result from competition for mates. Charles Darwin called this process **sexual selection**.

Males and females follow different reproductive strategies

Two common, though not universal, features of sexual selection among nonhuman animals are competition among males and choice by females. These features result from the differing strategies adopted by males and females early in the evolution of the two sexes. Females committed themselves to a "nurturing" strategy by virtue of their investment in large, nutrient-rich ova, while males committed themselves to an "exploitative" strategy by virtue of their production of sperm—cells so small and nutrient poor that they contribute little to the zygote beyond a set of genes. In some animals, the evolution of these strategies has led to very marked differences in the roles played by the two sexes in reproduction.

   Female mammals, for example, carry the burden of **internal fertilization** followed by a prolonged period of **gestation** (pregnancy), which may last from 2 or 3 weeks

autosome   Any chromosome other than a sex chromosome.

sex chromosome   Either of a pair of chromosomes (X or Y in mammals) that differ between the sexes.

X chromosome   A sex chromosome that is present as two copies in females and one copy in males.

Y chromosome   A sex chromosome that is present only in males.

sexual selection   The evolution of traits under the pressure of competition for mates or of choice by mates.

internal fertilization   Fertilization within the body.

gestation   Bearing young in the uterus; pregnancy.

lactation   The production of milk in the mammary glands.

semen   The fluid, containing sperm and a variety of chemical compounds, that is discharged from the penis (ejaculated) at the male sexual climax.

(in rodents) to 22 months (in elephants). Following delivery of their young, female mammals continue to nourish them through milk production (**lactation**) and nursing and usually provide most or all of the care and protection that mammalian infants require. This prolonged investment results in offspring that have a far greater chance of surviving to adulthood than the young of other vertebrates, but it also greatly limits the total number of offspring that female mammals can produce in a lifetime. A female frog can produce hundreds or thousands of tadpoles; it's unusual for a woman to produce more than a dozen children.

Males, however, can often get away with a very small investment in reproduction—a few drops of **semen** containing sperm. In theory, a male mammal could father as many offspring as a female frog produces tadpoles, simply by inseminating female after female and walking away from each. But that is reckoning without two practical constraints: competition from other males, and the ability of females to choose whom they mate with, as we'll see below.

Females and males are exposed to different reproductive risks

Female and male animals typically experience different kinds of risks in their reproductive lives. For a female, the maximum number of potential offspring is rather low, but her chances of having close to this number are quite good, since there will usually be plenty of males willing to mate with her. The risk for a female is not so much that she will produce few offspring, but that her offspring will fail to survive and reproduce in their turn. To maximize the likelihood that her offspring will survive, she needs not only to invest her own resources in them, but also to ensure that they are fathered by the best available male. (What "best" means, we'll discuss in a moment.)

While the variation in the number of offspring that females produce is quite limited, males can father numerous offspring or they can easily end up having none. In some species, for example langur monkeys and elks, dominant males control large harems of females, leaving subordinate males without mates. A dominant male fathers many offspring every year, at least as long as he can maintain his dominant position. Subordinate males will have no offspring unless they can displace a dominant male or evade his surveillance. Although there are wide differences among species, males typically face the real possibility of having few or no offspring. In other words, the variation in reproductive success is greater for males than for females of most species, including humans (Betzig, 2012) (**Figure A.7**), and this encourages the evolution of "risky" sexual strategies by males.

Males often compete for access to females

Because of this difference in reproductive risks experienced by males and females, males often compete with one another for access to females, while females often choose among males. We should emphasize, though, that words such as "compete" and "choose" are really figures of speech. We don't mean to imply that animals consciously try to achieve certain goals—we don't know enough about the basis of animal behavior to make such assertions. All we are saying is that animals behave as *if* they are goal driven.

What traits are influenced by sexual selection? Competition among males naturally leads to selection for traits that confer success in that competition. The most obvious traits are large size and physical strength; males are commonly larger and stronger than females, sometimes markedly so, especially among mammals (**Figure A.8**). Along with these physical traits goes the behavioral trait of aggressiveness—the willingness to engage in the interminable bouts of roaring, head butting, biting, and general mayhem that establish a male animal's position in the dominance hierarchy and thus influence his ability to mate with females.

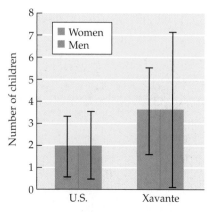

Figure A.7   Reproduction is a riskier game for men. These bar graphs show the number of children born to women and men in the United States, a monogamous culture (left), and among the Xavante people of Brazil, where men may have multiple wives (right). Each data set is plotted as a mean and a standard deviation (a measure of the dispersion of the data around the mean, shown by the vertical lines). In both cultures, the standard deviation is greater for men than for women, but this difference is more marked for the polygamous Xavante. (Data from Brown et al., 2009.)

Figure A.8 Intermale aggression
Male elephant seals compete for access to females, so aggressiveness and large size are assets.

Competition among males also favors traits that assist males in locating receptive females before other males do. Such traits may include well-developed sensory skills that aid them in finding females, such as the ability to detect sexually attractive odors (**pheromones**) and to home in on their source. Another trait that helps males get to females quickly is early sexual maturation—early in life or early in the breeding season.

Females often choose among males

What about female choice? One advantageous choice females can make is to mate with healthy, genetically favored males (Clutton-Brock & McAuliffe, 2009). How can they identify such males? Just the fact that a male has battered other males into submission speaks volumes about his health and fitness, of course. Not all species engage in such male-male contests, however. In these cases, females may choose among males on the basis of their physical appearance or behavior.

CHOICE BASED ON APPEARANCE One aspect of males' appearance to which females often pay attention is their bodily symmetry. Vertebrates are roughly bilaterally symmetrical, at least in outward appearance. The developmental reason for this symmetry is that, aside from obviously asymmetrical structures such as the heart, a single set of genetic instructions directs the development of both sides of the body. Good genes operating in a good environment will therefore produce a highly symmetrical organism. Poor genes, or a poor environment, will disturb this process, leading to asymmetries. This kind of perturbation, in which the direction of asymmetry is random, is called **fluctuating asymmetry** (Graham et al., 2010). A high degree of fluctuating asymmetry has been correlated with a number of disadvantageous characteristics or experiences, such as chromosomal defects, infections, exposure to toxins, and environmental stress (Breno et al., 2013). Low fluctuating asymmetry, however, has been correlated with a number of advantageous characteristics, such as high sprinting speed in humans (Trivers et al., 2013).

It turns out that animals are very good at assessing the symmetry of other individuals of the same species, and they prefer to mate with highly symmetrical individuals. For example, manipulating the tail feathers of male barn swallows to make them less symmetrical renders those males less attractive to females (Møller, 1992).

pheromone A volatile compound that is released by one organism and that triggers a specific behavior in another member of the same species.

fluctuating asymmetry A difference between the left and right sides of the body that results from random perturbations of development.

Figure A.9 The ornate tail feather **display** of a male peacock shows females his general health and the quality of his genes.

Thus, there is sexual selection for symmetry, especially in males. In addition, females are selected for the cognitive skills that are required to evaluate symmetry and the motivation to do so.

Besides symmetry, females often look for other anatomical characteristics in males. Female barn swallows, for example, prefer those males whose outermost tail feathers are not only symmetrical, but also longer than those of other males. Female deer prefer the males with the largest antlers, female fish often prefer the most brightly colored males, and so on. Generally, the rule is: The bigger and brighter, the better—especially with regard to features that are obviously related to sexual displays (**Figure A.9**).

This preference for "bigger and brighter" seems to be open-ended. If one exaggerates the features that females pay attention to—giving a male barn swallow an artificial tail longer than *any* male normally possesses, for example—such males will be preferred over any "natural" males. Because of this open-ended quality, sexual selection can lead to a runaway process in which the display characteristics of males become highly exaggerated, as has happened with the peacock.

Nevertheless, something holds this process in check. The tails of male barn swallows are not getting longer, for example, even though a male with a superlong tail would attract a lot of females. The most plausible reason why the runaway process comes to a halt is that these displays have a *cost* for males. It takes an investment of food to grow long tail feathers. Large antlers hamper a stag's ability to move through the forest. Bright coloration attracts predators. At some point, the cost of these displays balances their reproductive advantage, and an equilibrium situation is reached.

It is precisely the fact that these attractive features have a cost that makes them attractive (Zahavi & Zahavi, 1997). Only a peacock that is genetically well endowed, is healthy, and has had ample access to food can sustain the cost of a tail ornate enough to attract peahens. What these displays say is, "I have been able to take on the incredible burden of this tail (or antlers or coloration) and still survive—so I must be a superior animal." And indeed, there is some evidence that these displays are honest advertisements of reproductive superiority. One study, for example, found that male deer with large, complex antlers also had higher-quality sperm than other males (Malo et al., 2005).

CHOICE BASED ON BEHAVIOR   Besides choosing males on the basis of anatomical features, females also choose on the basis of **courtship behavior**. Sometimes this behavior is of practical use to the female in producing young. Female spiders, for example, often demand that their suitors provide some food prior to mating, such as a dead insect (failing which, the female may snack on the male himself). Some female birds demand that the male provide a nesting site or actually construct a nest.

Besides the direct value of such gifts to the female, there's another, more subtle benefit. Demanding that a male provide resources tests his genetic fitness in the same way that demanding anatomical features such as ornate tail feathers does. Thus, it may be beneficial to the female to make the male expend resources, even if that expenditure does not benefit her in any direct way.

In fact, in numerous instances courtship by males seems to involve useless "make-work." Male bowerbirds, for example, must construct elaborate thatched structures—bowers—and decorate them with hard-to-find items, such as colored shells, berries, and bottle tops, before females will pay attention to their advances (**Figure A.10**). The bowers have no direct value to the females—they are not nests—but they do have the indirect value of testing the male's fitness. Courtship song is another example: Singing for hours at a time offers no direct reproductive benefit, but by doing so, a male bird advertises the fact that he is not foraging—and if he can survive so long without foraging, he must be a well-endowed animal. Much courtship behavior has this flavor: Males inflict handicaps on themselves—the behavioral equivalent of peacock's tails—to prove that they are fit enough to withstand them.

So far, we've given the impression that females choose among males simply by assessing their courtship behavior. In fact, however, females often initiate courtship. If the caterwauling from your neighbor's cat has ever awakened you, for example, you know that female mammals advertise when they are sexually receptive. At around the time when they ovulate, when **copulation** (penile-vaginal sex) can result in fertilization, hormonal changes cause females to undergo **estrus**, or "heat." Besides complex internal processes connected with ovulation, estrus involves the production of auditory, olfactory, or visual signals intended to alert males to the female's receptive state.

Females also may approach individual males and show **proceptive behavior**—behavior designed to elicit reciprocal courtship. Estrous female mice and rats, for example, perform a hopping, darting, and ear-wiggling routine that may induce the

courtship behavior   Behavior that attracts a mate.

copulation   Sexual intercourse; coitus.

estrus   The restricted period within the ovarian cycle when females of some species are sexually receptive; "heat."

proceptive behavior   Behavior by females that may elicit sexual advances by males.

Figure A.10   The male satin bowerbird (dark blue) is not as eye-catching as a peacock, but he makes up for it by building an elaborate bower and decorating its entrances with blue-colored objects, such as shells, berries, bottle tops, or feathers. If a female approves of his work, she will mate with him within the avenue of the bower.

male to attempt a mount. During the remainder of their ovarian cycle (when fertilization is not possible), females do not make these displays or approach males, and they forcefully reject male courtship.

Sometimes males make significant investments in reproduction

Insofar as females induce males to make an investment in reproduction, they may restore some balance between female and male reproductive strategies. The more resources males invest, the more interest they will have in ensuring their investment is not wasted. If a male has to spend days or weeks courting a female, or if he has to provide "expensive" nuptial gifts or accomplish burdensome tasks, he may become as committed as the female to seeing that the offspring of their union survive. Otherwise, he will have to start all over again with another female. His life, or the mating season, may simply not be long enough to allow that.

Thus, while males of many species make little or no contribution to the care of their offspring, in other species, males make contributions as great as those made by females. This kind of cooperative investment can allow for the evolution of lifestyles that would otherwise be impossible. Pairs of seagulls, for example, take alternating shifts at the nest (incubating eggs or protecting hatchlings) and away from the nest (finding food for themselves and the chicks). A single bird cannot accomplish both tasks, so male investment has been essential to the evolution of seagulls, as well as many other species of birds.

In a few species, males take on the entire responsibility of caring for eggs or young. A male stickleback fish, for example, constructs an underwater nest in which females lay eggs; after fertilizing them, the male spends about 2 weeks guarding the eggs and the newly hatched fry. Some male waterbirds, such as phalaropes and jacanas, also take on the entire responsibility for incubating eggs and feeding the hatchlings.

If males invest, sexual selection may work differently

If males and females invest about equally in reproduction, sexual selection may not lead to any marked anatomical or behavioral differences between the sexes. Male and female seagulls, for example, are nearly the same size, and neither one has any special display feathers or other sexually distinct characteristics. In fact, the only reliable way to tell the sex of a seagull is to examine its internal anatomy.

If males invest *more* than females in reproduction, and thus are limited in how many offspring they can produce, the effects of sexual selection on the two sexes can actually be reversed. Among phalaropes and jacanas, for example, females compete for the sexual favors of males, and males choose among females. Consistent with this pattern, female phalaropes and jacanas are larger, more brightly colored, and more aggressive than males.

Sometimes males choose among females because individual females vary in how much they can invest in reproduction. This variation is most obvious in species in which individuals continue to grow after reaching reproductive maturity. Whereas humans stop growing soon after the end of puberty, some animals, such as tortoises, grow throughout their lives. In such species, the oldest and largest females are capable of laying the largest clutches of eggs, so males mate preferentially with the oldest females.

Among some primate species, males invest considerably in reproduction, even if not to the same degree as females. For that reason, there may be competition and choosing by both sexes. Take baboons, for example. Male baboons are larger than females and compete intensely for mates, as is true in so many other species. In addition, however, female baboons compete for the sexual attention of dominant

Figure A.11   Sexual swellings of female baboons appear at the time of ovulation and attract a great deal of attention from males.

males. They do this by means of "sexual swellings"—patches of pigmented genital and perianal skin that swell around the time of ovulation (**Figure A.11**). The females with the largest swellings seem to be genetically favored: They have more offspring than other females, and their offspring are more likely to survive. Thus, males try to copulate with the females with the largest swellings (Domb & Pagel, 2001).

It turns out, in fact, that competition among females is much more common than has been thought in the past. Whereas males may compete simply for access to females, females more commonly compete for resources, such as social rank, that enhance their offspring's prospects for survival (Clutton-Brock, 2007).

Diverse Relationship Styles Have Evolved

Evolution has led to a bewildering variety of sexual relationships, from sexual free-for-alls to lifelong, sexually exclusive pairings. Understanding the basis for this diversity can be quite a challenge. Still, we can start with the basic assumption that evolution is always at work. In other words, animals' genes are likely to promote sexual behaviors and relationships that offer the best prospects for leaving copies of those genes in future generations.

Social and sexual arrangements are not necessarily the same

In looking at animal liaisons, we need to distinguish carefully between two phenomena: *social arrangements* and *sexual reality*. In the past, people (including biologists) have tended to take animals' social arrangements at face value—as if these arrangements tell us unambiguously who is having sex with whom. Sometimes they do. It turns out, however, that humans are not the only species in which social and sexual arrangements are imperfectly aligned.

In many species, individuals are essentially solitary or belong to same-sex groups, and they reproduce by mating with strangers (either one or many) whom they never see again. This is the pattern seen in the majority of invertebrates, fishes, amphibians, and reptiles. Among mammals, there is considerable diversity in relationship styles, even between related species. For example, montane voles (*Microtus montanus*) mate with strangers and immediately go their separate ways, whereas their prairie cousins (*Microtus ochrogaster*) form stable pair bonds (Carter & Getz, 1993) (see Chapter 7).

monogamy   1. Marriage limited to two persons. 2. A sexual relationship in which neither partner has sexual contact with a third party.

pair bond   A durable sexual relationship between two individuals.

polygamy   Marriage to or (mostly in animals) mating with more than one partner.

polygyny   The marriage or mating of one male with more than one female.

polyandry   The marriage or mating of one female with more than one male.

sexual monogamy   Pair bonding that is sexually exclusive.

social monogamy   Pair bonding that is not sexually exclusive.

promiscuity   Engaging in numerous casual or short-lived sexual relationships.

When reproduction does involve lasting relationships, we see two basic patterns: monogamy and polygamy. In **monogamous** relationships, two animals (usually of different sexes) form a **pair bond** for the duration of the breeding season or even for their entire lifetimes. Many birds, such as the seagulls described earlier, pair up for a season. Swans are famous for forming lifelong pair bonds. In **polygamous** relationships, one animal forms stable bonds with several individuals of the other sex. In most polygamous species, single males form relationships with multiple females. This "harem" arrangement is technically called **polygyny** ("many females"). The opposite arrangement—a single female with a harem of males—is called **polyandry** ("many males"). It is a rare arrangement, but one animal that does adopt it is the jacana, the waterbird we have already described on account of its unusual "females compete, males choose" behavior. In southern Texas one may come across a pond occupied by a single female jacana and several males in a loose social group.

That polygyny is more common than polyandry is consistent with the greater investment in reproduction by females. It simply would not be possible for females of most species to mate with multiple males and have offspring with all of them. Only when the balance of reproduction investment is reversed, as with jacanas, does polyandry crop up.

The terms "monogamy" and "polygamy," as just described, refer to bonding relationships, not to sexual behavior as such. Some pair-bonding species mate only within the pair bond and are therefore called **sexually monogamous**. More commonly, pair-bonded individuals will mate not only with their partners but also, on some occasions, with strangers. Species in which this occurs are called **socially monogamous**. Individuals of polygamous species may also mate with strangers. A male lion will readily mate with a female from outside his pride, for example, if he can get to her before the female members of his pride drive her off. We'll call the willingness to engage in sex outside of an animal's established relationship or relationships **promiscuity**—without the negative connotation this word may carry when applied to humans.

Male promiscuity offers obvious evolutionary benefits

From an evolutionary standpoint, male promiscuity is more or less to be expected: The investment in mating outside the pair bond ("extra-pair sex") is usually so slight that it is "worth it" for the male, even if the chances that the mating will lead to viable offspring are not very great. Thus, one has to wonder: Why are males of some species less disposed to promiscuity than are males of other species?

In some species, females may impose sexual monogamy on males: Females may simply refuse to engage in extra-pair sex. This is true for some species of birds. Sometimes males mate with only one female simply because they mate only once—period. Deep-sea anglerfishes offer an extreme example (**Figure A.12**). In these species, a male homes in on a female and partially fuses with her. His eyes degenerate, and he remains permanently attached to the female, providing her with sperm whenever required. Once attached to his mate in this manner, he is ill-equipped to embark on extramarital affairs!

Why are females promiscuous?

Male promiscuity makes evolutionary sense, but what about female promiscuity? At first glance, it seems there is no reason for it, since females can usually produce all the offspring they are capable of pro-

Figure A.12   Deep-sea threesome Two small males have attached themselves permanently to the lower surface of this female anglerfish.

ducing with the aid of a single male. But in fact, female promiscuity is fairly common, even in species that have long been considered sexually monogamous.

The best evidence for female promiscuity comes from DNA analysis. Individuals of the same species have numerous differences in their DNA; these differences can be detected with simple enzymatic tests. Offspring inherit their particular DNA sequences from their parents, so by comparing the sequences from the offspring and the individuals who are candidates to be its parents, the true parents can be identified. Since it is usually the identity of the father that is in doubt, the procedure is generally called **paternity testing**.

Paternity testing has now been done on a wide variety of species, with a wide variety of results. In some socially monogamous birds, up to three-fourths of a female's offspring are fathered by males other than her social mate (Birkhead, 1998). Among chimpanzees, as many as half of all offspring are fathered by males from outside the group to which the mother belongs. In the hamadryas baboon, on the other hand, females seem never to cheat on their male partners, even if their partners are sterile, in which case there are no offspring (Birkhead, 2000).

Female promiscuity may be adaptive for a number of reasons, which may differ among species. In species in which males provide resources such as food or protection, obtaining these resources from multiple mates may make promiscuity worthwhile. Another possibility is that socially monogamous females are promiscuous in order to obtain sperm from higher-quality males than their social partners. After all, if males vary in quality, most females will not be partnered with the very best males, so they may seek a higher-quality male to mate with. To test this idea, Susan Smith observed the mating behavior of black-capped chickadees (Smith, 1988). She found that when a female chickadee engages in extra-pair sex, she usually does so with a male who was dominant over her social mate during the previous winter. This finding suggests that promiscuous females are indeed shopping for better genes than their regular mates can provide. In another study of songbirds, the offspring of a female's promiscuous matings were found to be fitter (had more lifetime offspring of their own) than her offspring by her regular mate (Gerlach et al., 2012). This suggests that shopping for better genes really is an adaptive behavior.

Female promiscuity leads to adaptive responses by males

While female promiscuity benefits females, it harms the reproductive success of the males who are their social mates. As a result, males of many species have developed behavioral strategies to prevent their mates from engaging in sex with other males. A common behavior of this type is **mate guarding**: A male remains close to a female throughout the period when she is fertile and attempts to keep other males away from her. To evaluate the effectiveness of this behavior in a songbird, Dutch researchers observed how closely male birds guarded their mates; later, they determined the paternity of the pair's nestlings by DNA analysis (Komdeur et al., 2007). As one might expect, the more closely a female was guarded by her mate, the fewer of her nestlings were fathered by outside males. Thus, mate-guarding behavior really does serve an adaptive function—for males. Do you think that human males ever engage in this kind of behavior?

Another way that males may respond to female promiscuity is by producing large numbers of sperm. By sheer force of numbers these sperm compete with the sperm of other males within the females' reproductive tracts. If we compare our close relatives, the chimpanzee and the gorilla, for example, we find that a female chimpanzee mates many times with many different males for every time that she becomes pregnant, whereas female gorillas mate with only one or two males per pregnancy. Correspondingly, the testes of chimpanzees are far larger (in relation to overall body

paternity test A test to identify an individual's father by DNA analysis.

mate guarding A behavior in which a male animal prevents sexual contact between his mate and other males.

vulva The female external genitalia.

size) than those of gorillas, and this allows chimpanzee males to produce ejaculates that contain far more sperm and to ejaculate more frequently. In humans, testis size is intermediate between that of chimpanzees and gorillas, suggesting that female promiscuity and sperm competition have played a role in human evolution, but not an unusually large one.

No primate can compare with the pig, however, in terms of sperm statistics. Pigs mate promiscuously, so sperm competition is probably very strong. Correspondingly, each ejaculate of a male pig (boar) measures a pint or more in volume and contains an average of 750 billion sperm (compared with a mere 350 *million* in men). Furthermore, the boar's penis is long enough to deposit the ejaculate directly into the sow's uterus, rather than into the vagina as in humans—another trait that has been driven by sperm competition.

Males may copulate with females by force

Forced copulation is seen in a wide variety of animals, from insects to primates. In some of these animals it is clearly an adaptive behavior; that is, it persists because those animals who engage in it have more offspring than they would have otherwise.

Perhaps the most detailed study of forced copulation has been done on scorpionflies by evolutionary psychologist Randy Thornhill of the University of New Mexico (Thornhill & Palmer, 2000). In these insects, a male is able to mate with a female by one of two strategies. In one strategy, he offers the female a nuptial gift, such as a dead insect; the female approaches the gift-bearing male, and they mate. If a male approaches a female without a gift, the female attempts to flee. In this case, however, the male may grasp the female and hold her immobile with a special appendage called a notal organ, which enables him to force copulation. Because the notal organ has no use other than for forced copulation (it is not required for unforced sex), Thornhill concluded that forced copulation is not a random by-product of scorpionfly evolution, but an adaptive behavior resulting from countless generations of sexual selection.

Only a couple of other species (also insects) have anatomical adaptations that facilitate forced copulation. In fact, quite a few species have the opposite—arrangements of the female anatomy that make copulation impossible without her active collaboration. For example, a female rat's **vulva** is situated on the underside of her rump and is inaccessible to males unless she exposes it by arching her rump upward—a behavior called lordosis. It is likely that arrangements of this kind are adaptations to prevent forced copulation.

Most animals do not have anatomical specializations that either facilitate or prevent this behavior, but attempts at forced copulation by males, and resistance by females, have been observed in numerous species, including primates (Muller & Wrangham, 2009) (**Figure A.13**). Orangutans are notorious in this respect (Knott et al., 2010). Male orangutans exist in two anatomically distinct forms, one larger than the other. (These are not simply different maturational stages of a single form.) During the portion of her menstrual cycle when she is not fertile, a female orangutan will mate cooperatively with any male. During the fertile portion of her cycle, however, she will only mate cooperatively with the larger type of male. To impregnate a female during the fertile portion of her cycle, a smaller male must overcome violent resistance on her part. This rape-like behavior may leave one or both parties with significant injuries, but it results in pregnancy often enough to make the behavior adaptive for the smaller type of male. A key factor here is that orangutans lead widely dispersed, solitary lifestyles, so males are not able to monitor or control the sexual behavior of other males. The smaller type of male, with its violent mating strategy, has apparently evolved to take advantage of this fact (Harrison & Chivers, 2007).

(A)

(B)

Figure A.13 Unforced sex and coercive sex in the beetle *Tegrodera aloga*. (A) The male (right) courts the female by drawing her antennae into grooves on his head. The female may or may not respond by copulating with him. (B) In an alternative strategy, the male (below) runs up to the female, throws her on her side, and inserts his genitalia as she struggles to free herself from his grasp.

Sometimes, Helping Relatives Reproduce Is a Good Strategy

Genes act within the individual who possesses them. At first thought, therefore, it would seem that genes should cause their owners to focus 100% of their efforts on reproducing themselves. And there is indeed a lot of selfish sexual behavior in this world: The topic we have just discussed—forced copulation—is an extreme example. But selfless, altruistic behavior is also quite common.

One kind of altruistic behavior with an obvious adaptive value is parental care. In evolutionary terms, it's no use having offspring if those offspring don't have offspring in their turn, so it may pay to help one's offspring survive and become sexually mature, even if that limits the number of offspring one can produce. Genes promoting parental care (or at least maternal care) are evidently widespread.

Genes promoting altruistic behavior toward one's offspring survive because the offspring have a good chance of possessing those same genes. (Specifically, any gene in a parent has a 50% chance of being handed down to each offspring.) Therefore, genes for altruism toward one's offspring are helping *themselves* get handed on to the third and future generations. But parents and offspring are not the only kinds of relatives who inherit the same genes. Siblings also co-inherit one half of their genes, on average. First cousins co-inherit about one-eighth of their genes, and so on. Thus, if you happen to possess genes that cause you to help a relative reproduce, those same genes may exist in that relative too. If so, your "altruism" helps propagate those genes into the next generation.

In the 1960s the British evolutionary theorist W. D. Hamilton laid out the logic behind this theory, which is known as **kin selection** (Dugatkin, 2007). Hamilton proposed that natural selection causes individuals to devote resources to helping their relatives reproduce, to an extent determined by the degree of relatedness. For example, an individual might be willing to give up having one offspring herself if by doing so she enables her sister to have *two* offspring beyond what she would otherwise produce. In terms of genes, it's a toss-up: either a single 50% copy (a child) or two 25% copies (nephews or nieces). To help a cousin reproduce, however, an individual should sacrifice one offspring's worth of resources only if that sacrifice helps that cousin have *eight* extra offspring—not a likely situation.

kin selection The theory that it can be advantageous, in evolutionary terms, to support the reproductive success of close relatives.

Kin selection theory does seem to explain quite a lot of social and sexual behavior in the animal kingdom. For example, subordinate males in lion prides and other groups may have few or no offspring of their own, at least as long as they are subordinate. If the dominant male is their brother or other close relative, however, it may still be worth it for them to remain in the group and help him reproduce, for by doing so, they are propagating copies of some of their own genes. Kin selection also favors the development of "aunting" behavior in primates—the tendency of females to share maternal duties—because the females who share these duties are likely to be sisters or other close relatives.

Avoiding Incest Is an Evolved Behavior

Most people believe that incest—sex with a close relative such as a sibling—is morally wrong. And in fact sexual relationships between adult siblings are very uncommon. This is a good thing because any children resulting from sex between siblings stand a higher than usual likelihood of suffering from certain inherited disorders. But it is not just our moral judgments or our knowledge of genetics that cause us to avoid incestuous relationships: Rather, evolution has provided us with a psychological mechanism that makes siblings sexually unattractive to each other.

This mechanism depends on the close and prolonged contact that usually exists between siblings during childhood. Thus, adopted children are just as unattractive to their siblings as biological siblings, even though there is no rational reason for adoptive siblings to avoid having children together. Conversely, biological siblings who *don't* live together during childhood may find each other sexually attractive when they meet in adulthood, and most cases of sibling incest involve siblings who were brought up apart.

A similar mechanism operates in nonhuman animals. Infant mice, for example, learn the smell of their littermates (which carries information about a set of variable genes called MHC markers). After puberty, they avoid sex with animals carrying similar MHC markers—animals who might be their close relatives. Whether incest avoidance in humans depends on the sense of smell is not known: Most likely, it depends on a broader array of cues including visual appearance, behavior, and so on. Whatever these cues may be, they operate below the level of consciousness—we're not sexually attracted to our siblings, but we don't know why.

Sex Has Acquired Other Functions beyond Reproduction

In evolutionary terms, reproduction was doubtless the original function of sexual behavior. In many species, however, sex has acquired other functions that are not directly connected with establishing pregnancy. We know this because individuals of many species engage in sexual behaviors that cannot produce offspring, such as sex between two males or between two females. Why do they do so?

In part, animals may be motivated to engage in sexual behaviors simply by the physical pleasure that sexual activity brings (Vasey, 2006). Engaging in nonreproductive sex for pleasure alone would not be adaptive in an evolutionary sense. But some species have found functions for nonreproductive sex that are truly adaptive. Notable among these species is our close relative, the bonobo (*Pan paniscus*), which lives along the Congo River in Central Africa.

Female and male bonobos engage in nonreproductive sex

Like most female mammals, female bonobos advertise when they are willing to copulate (estrus). Bonobos, like baboons, do so by means of their genital swellings. In striking contrast to mammals such as mice, however, the estrus of a bonobo extends over almost two-thirds of her entire ovarian cycle, which lasts about 2 months. In fact, the female bonobo is out of estrus only for a few days around the time of menstruation (the periodic shedding of the lining of the uterus). Although the bonobo ovulates at some point during her estrus, the ovum is viable for only a day or two; sperm do not survive in her reproductive tract for more than a day or two, either. In other words, for most of the time when the female bonobo is willing to have sex, there is no chance that sex will result in pregnancy. From your knowledge of human sexuality, this may not strike you as particularly remarkable, but in evolutionary terms it is a real novelty.

Not only are female bonobos sexually receptive for most of the ovarian cycle, but they are also receptive when they are not cycling at all. Bonobo mothers breast-feed their young for several years after they are born, and lactation suppresses ovulation. Thus, bonobos cannot become pregnant while they are still nursing previous offspring. Even so, they are sexually receptive throughout this period.

Further accentuating the nonreproductive nature of much bonobo sex, both female and male bonobos engage in frequent homosexual encounters (**Figure A.14**). When two females have sex, they embrace face to face, and each rubs her swollen **clitoris** (the erectile component of the external female genitalia that mediates sexual pleasure) sideways against the other's. This behavior, called genito-genital rubbing, is unique to female-female encounters—it's quite different from the behavior shown by females during sexual encounters with males.

Sexual encounters between males occur in one of two ways. In one kind, the males face away from each other, and one male rubs his **scrotum** (the sac containing the testes) against the other male's buttocks. In the other, the two males rub their penises together while hanging from a tree branch.

Bonobos use sex for conflict resolution and alliance formation

All this nonreproductive sexual activity raises an obvious question—why? Close observation of bonobo colonies in captivity (Parish & de Waal, 2000) and in the wild (Kano, 1992) indicates that bonobos use sex for the prevention and resolution of conflicts. Two bonobos who are faced with a conflict in food allocation, for example, will engage in sex and then divide the food peacefully. This happens regardless of the sex or age of the two animals. Alternatively, one animal may take food from another and "pay" with the currency of sex. When an entire troop of bonobos comes upon a food source—a situation that triggers wild fighting in other species such as chimpanzees—the bonobos engage in extensive bouts of sex with one another before dividing up the food. The bonobos' motto seems to be "make love, not war." And bonobos make love amicably—forced copulation is virtually unknown in this species (Paoli, 2009).

A related function of sex in bonobos is the cementing of social relationships and the formation of alliances. This function is particularly important for females. Bonobo females leave their natal (birth) groups and join new ones, whereas males stay in their natal groups. Females joining a group are initially unwelcome, but they solidify their position by forming close alliances with high-ranking females. The activity that bonds females in these alliances is genito–genital rubbing. So effective are these sex-mediated alliances that female

Figure A.14   Two female bonobos engage in sexual behavior known as genito-genital rubbing

clitoris   The erectile organ in females, whose external portion is located at the junction of the labia minora, just in front of the vestibule.

scrotum   The sac behind the penis that contains the testicles.

bonobos have largely taken the control of bonobo society away from males. In fact, a male's rank depends in large part on the rank of his mother.

Because bonobos, like many humans, see much more to sex than making babies, we might imagine that we have inherited this aspect of our sexuality from bonobos. But such an assumption would be risky, for chimpanzees—who are about equally closely related to us—are far more restricted in their use of nonreproductive sex. What is remarkable about the Hominoidea—the superfamily that includes gibbons, orangutans, gorillas, chimpanzees, bonobos, and humans—is the diversity of their sexual and social arrangements. Gibbons are monogamous; orangutans are solitary; gorillas are polygynous; chimpanzees are polygamous and male dominated; bonobos are polygamous and female dominated. Human culture may cause people to adopt any of these arrangements, but evolutionary forces are still at work in human sexuality, as is discussed in several chapters of this book.

Summary

- The original function of sex—and its only function in many species—is reproduction. The reasons why many species rely on sexual rather than asexual reproduction are disputed. Two general theories have been presented. First, sexual reproduction may promote the elimination of harmful mutations. Second, by mixing genes from different individuals, sexual reproduction may foster the selection of advantageous traits.

- Natural selection has caused gametes to diverge into female and male forms. Female gametes are large and contain nutrients; male gametes are small and motile. Natural selection also acts to keep the ratio of the sexes near equality in most species, because any imbalance favors animals that have offspring of the minority sex.

- Sex may be determined by chromosomal mechanisms, as in mammals, or by the temperature at which eggs are incubated, as in many reptiles.

- Sexual selection, driven by competition for mates, has led to different morphological and behavioral traits in males and females. Because females generally invest more than males in reproduction, males often compete among themselves for access to females. This competition may select for large, aggressive individuals.

- Females often choose among males. Their choices may be based on morphological features such as symmetry, display feathers, or antlers, or on behavioral traits such as the provision of food. Some female choice seems aimed at forcing males to make a greater investment in reproduction than they otherwise would. In species in which males do make significant investments, males become choosier, and females become more competitive.

- A wide variety of relationship styles exist. Animals may engage in sex without establishing any social bond, or they may bond in socially monogamous or polygamous relationships. Polygamy usually involves one male and several females (polygyny); the reverse arrangement (polyandry) is rare.

- In many socially monogamous or polygynous species, both males and females engage in sex outside these social structures. Promiscuity has obvious benefits for males in terms of increased numbers of offspring. For a female, promiscuity may offer a range of benefits: It may help her gain resources from males, it may give her access to high-quality genes, or it may favorably influence the behavior of males toward her or her offspring.

- Forced copulation has been observed in many species. In a few species, this behavior is clearly adaptive, increasing the male's likelihood of having offspring.

- Because close relatives share many genes, evolution has led to altruistic behavior among relatives, including behavior in the reproductive domain.

- Sexual behavior has developed other functions besides reproduction. Bonobos offer a striking example: In this species, much sex takes place when the female is incapable of becoming pregnant, or between individuals of the same sex. Bonobo sex is directed not only toward reproduction, but also toward the avoidance or resolution of conflicts and the establishment of social bonds.

Recommended Reading

Beukeboom, L. & Perrin, N. (2014). *The evolution of sex determination.* Oxford University Press.

Birkhead, T. (2000). *Promiscuity: An evolutionary history of sperm competition.* Harvard University Press.

Buss, D. M. (2003). *The evolution of desire: Strategies of human mating* (4th ed.). Basic Books.

Dawkins, R. (2006). *The selfish gene* (3rd ed.). Oxford University Press.

Geary, D. C. (2009). *Male, female: The evolution of human sex differences.* American Psychological Association.

Ridley, M. (2003). *The red queen: Sex and the evolution of human nature.* Harper Perennial.

Ryan, C. & Jetha, C. (2010). *Sex at dawn: The prehistoric origins of modern sexuality.* Harper.

Sommer, V. & Vasey, P. L. (2006). *Homosexual behaviour in animals: An evolutionary perspective.* Cambridge University Press.

Web Resources

Colby, C. The TalkOrigins Archive: Introduction to evolutionary biology tinyurl.com/60qt

Lively, C. M. Evolution of sex and recombination tinyurl.com/kyzdmbv

Newman, L. Penis fencing in a marine mollusk (video) tinyurl.com/kz2eqf7

PBS: Evolution—Show #5: Why Sex? tinyurl.com/587f2

University of California Museum of Paleontology: Evolution 101 tinyurl.com/23e8y6

Appendix B
Sex and the Nervous System

*Sexual behavior is under the control of two of the body's three major communication networks: the nervous system and the endocrine system. (The third—the immune system—plays little role in sex.) Here we consider the role of the nervous system, focusing on very basic functions such as penile and clitoral erection. **Box B.1** offers a brief refresher course on the organization of the nervous system, emphasizing elements that are referred to in this textbook.*

Box B.1 Biology of Sex

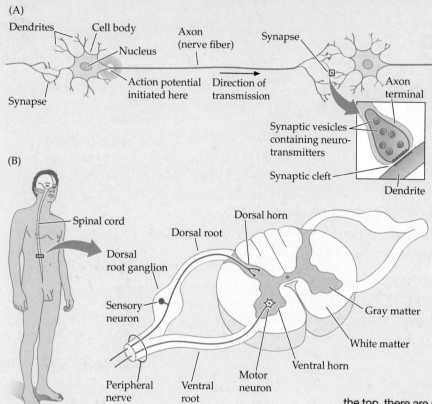

(A) Dendrites, Cell body, Nucleus, Synapse, Action potential initiated here, Direction of transmission, Axon (nerve fiber), Synapse, Axon terminal, Synaptic vesicles containing neurotransmitters, Synaptic cleft, Dendrite

(B) Spinal cord, Dorsal root, Dorsal horn, Dorsal root ganglion, Sensory neuron, Peripheral nerve, Ventral root, Motor neuron, Ventral horn, White matter, Gray matter

The nervous system is divided into three subsystems: the central nervous system, the peripheral nervous system, and the autonomic nervous system. (There is also an enteric nervous system that controls the gut, which will not concern us here.) The **central nervous system (CNS)** comprises the spinal cord and the brain. Most regions of the CNS consist of gray matter and white matter. The **gray matter** is where the CNS carries out its all-important computations; it contains a mix of neuronal cell bodies, dendrites, synapses, and supporting nonneuronal cells, and it is organized into sheets (**cortex**) or clumps (**nuclei**). The **white matter** contains only axons interconnecting various parts of the CNS, along with supporting cells.

The **spinal cord**, although it is a continuous structure, is conventionally divided into segments; these segments are defined by the vertebrae through which the bundles of nerve fibers enter and leave the spinal cord. Counting down from the top, there are eight cervical, twelve thoracic, five lumbar, and five sacral segments. The gray matter of the spinal cord can be divided into two **dorsal horns** and two **ventral horns**, one on either side of the cord. Axons enter and leave these areas through the **dorsal** and **ventral roots**, respectively (**Figure B**).

The brain (**Figure C**) is divided into two general regions: the forebrain and the brainstem. The main elements of the fore-

The Nervous System

The elementary units of the nervous system are nerve cells, or **neurons** (**Figure A**; see also Figure D). A typical neuron has a **cell body**, in which its nucleus and part of its cytoplasm are located, plus two kinds of cytoplasmic extensions: **dendrites**, which receive and integrate numerous input signals from other neurons or from sensory receptors, and an **axon**, or nerve fiber, which transmits the neuron's output signals in the form of electrochemical **action potentials** or nerve impulses. The axon may span many centimeters (e.g., from the spinal cord to the foot), or it may end in the same region as the cell body. (In the latter case, the neuron is called an **interneuron**.) The terminals of the axon form **synapses** with the dendrites of other neurons or with muscle fibers. (In the latter case, the neurons are called **motor neurons** and the synapses are called **neuromuscular junctions**.)

When action potentials reach synapses, they cause the release of chemical **neurotransmitters**, which are small molecules such as amino acids (e.g., glutamate), catecholamines (e.g., norepinephrine), or acetylcholine. Neurotransmitters diffuse rapidly across the narrow **synaptic cleft** and raise or decrease the excitability of the postsynaptic neuron or muscle fiber.

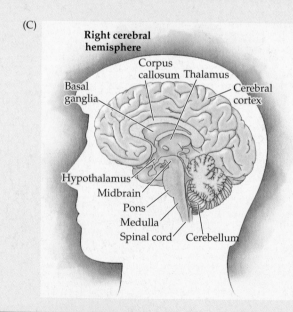

(C) Right cerebral hemisphere, Corpus callosum, Thalamus, Basal ganglia, Cerebral cortex, Hypothalamus, Midbrain, Pons, Medulla, Spinal cord, Cerebellum

(D)
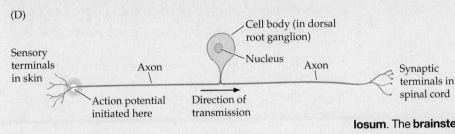

(E)
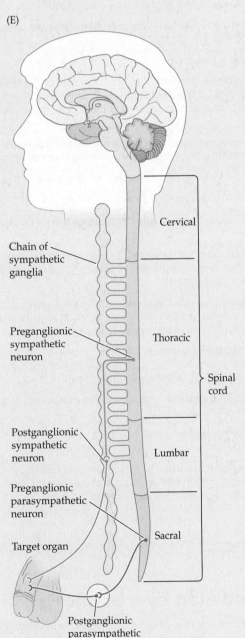

brain are the left and right **cerebral hemispheres**, each of which consists of several lobes of **cerebral cortex** and underlying white matter, along with deeper structures known as the **basal ganglia**. The two hemispheres are interconnected via the **corpus callosum**. The **brainstem** includes several subregions: starting from the lower end, these regions are the **medulla**, the **pons** with the attached cerebellum, the **midbrain**, and the **thalamus** with the underlying **hypothalamus**. Several of these regions contain cell groups involved in sexual functions.

The **peripheral nervous system** is the set of motor axons that leaves the CNS to innervate striated (voluntary) muscles, plus the sensory axons that bring information into the CNS. These two kinds of axons are also called **efferent** (i.e., carrying signals away from the CNS) and **afferent** (bringing signals into the CNS), respectively. The motor axons belong to motor neurons whose cell bodies are located in the ventral horn of the spinal cord. The sensory axons belong to neurons whose cell bodies are located in **ganglia** within the dorsal roots. Sensory neurons are unusual in that they have no dendrites; rather, a T-shaped axon conveys impulses from the body into the dorsal horn of the spinal cord (**Figure D**).

The **autonomic nervous system** (**Figure E**) controls—largely without our volition—the activity of smooth muscles, heart muscle, and glands throughout the body. Within the autonomic nervous system are two further subsystems: the **sympathetic** and **parasympathetic nervous systems**, which often act in opposition to each other. (For example, activity in the sympathetic nerves of the heart causes the heartbeat to speed up, while activity in the parasympathetic nerves causes it to slow down.) Both subsystems consist of two sets of neurons: a set of **preganglionic neurons** that reside in the spinal cord and send their axons to **autonomic ganglia** outside the spinal cord, and a set of **postganglionic neurons** that reside in the ganglia and send their axons to peripheral targets, such as smooth muscle and glands. The ganglia for the sympathetic nervous system lie in a chain next to the spinal cord as well as in other locations, while those for the parasympathetic nervous system are near the target organs that they innervate.

neuron   A single nerve cell with all its extensions.

cell body   The part of a neuron where the nucleus is located.

dendrites   The extensions of a neuron that receive incoming signals from other neurons.

axon   The extension of a neuron that conveys impulses, usually in a direction away from the cell body. Also called nerve fiber.

(continued on next page)

Box B.1 Biology of Sex (continued)

action potential   An electrochemical signal that travels rapidly along an axon.

interneuron   A neuron whose connections are local.

synapse   A junction where signals are transmitted between neurons or from neurons to muscle fibers.

motor neuron   A neuron that triggers the contraction of muscle fibers.

neuromuscular junction   A synapse between an axon and a muscle fiber.

neurotransmitter   A compound released at a synapse that increases or decreases the excitability of an adjacent neuron.

synaptic cleft   The narrow space between two neurons at a synapse.

central nervous system (CNS)   The brain and spinal cord.

gray matter   A region of the central nervous system containing the cell bodies of neurons.

cortex   The outer portion of an anatomical structure, as of the cerebral hemispheres or the adrenal gland.

nucleus (pl. nuclei)   In neuroanatomy, a recognizable cluster of neurons in the central nervous system.

white matter   A region of the central nervous system that contains bundles of axons but no neuronal cell bodies.

spinal cord   The portion of the central nervous system within the vertebral column.

dorsal horn   The rear portion of the gray matter of the spinal cord; it has a sensory function.

ventral horn   The portion of the gray matter of the spinal cord nearer to the front of the body, where motor neurons are located.

dorsal root   A bundle of sensory axons that enters a dorsal horn of the spinal cord.

ventral root   A bundle of motor axons that leaves a ventral horn of the spinal cord.

forebrain   The cerebral hemispheres and basal ganglia.

cerebral hemispheres   The uppermost and largest portion of the brain, divided into left and right halves.

cerebral cortex   Convoluted, layered gray matter that covers most of the brain.

basal ganglia   Deep noncortical structures of the forebrain.

corpus callosum   A band of axons interconnecting the left and right cerebral hemispheres.

brainstem   The region of the brain between the forebrain and the spinal cord.

medulla   The portion of the brainstem closest to the spinal cord.

pons   A region of the brain above the medulla.

midbrain   The region of the brainstem between the pons and the thalamus.

thalamus   The uppermost region of the brainstem.

hypothalamus   A small region at the base of the brain on either side of the third ventricle; it contains cell groups involved in sexual responses and other basic functions.

peripheral nervous system   The motor and sensory connections between the central nervous system and peripheral structures such as muscles and sense organs.

efferent   Carrying signals away from the CNS.

afferent   Carrying signals toward the CNS.

ganglia   Collections of neurons outside the central nervous system.

autonomic nervous system   The portion of the nervous system that controls smooth muscles and glands without our conscious involvement.

sympathetic nervous system   A division of the autonomic nervous system; among other functions, its activity inhibits penile erection but helps trigger ejaculation.

parasympathetic nervous system   A division of the autonomic nervous system; among other functions, its activity promotes erection of the penis and clitoris.

preganglionic neuron   An autonomic motor neuron in the spinal cord.

autonomic ganglion   A cluster of autonomic neurons outside the CNS.

postganglionic neuron   A neuron with its cell body in an autonomic ganglion and an axon that innervates glands or smooth muscles in a peripheral organ such as the genitalia.

Erection Can Be Mediated by a Spinal Reflex

One simple behavior that illustrates the role of the nervous system in sex is the erection of the penis or clitoris in response to tactile stimulation of the genital area. This behavior requires five elements that collectively form a reflex loop running from the genitals to the spinal cord and back:

1. Sensory nerve endings detect the stimulation.
2. Nerves convey the sensory information to the spinal cord.
3. Information is processed in the spinal cord.
4. Nerves carry an output signal to the penis or clitoris.
5. Vascular elements are responsible for the actual erection.

Although the brain also plays a significant role in promoting or inhibiting erection, this role is not essential. People who have suffered spinal injuries that prevent communication between the brain and the lower portion of the spinal cord are usually still capable of having erections in response to genital stimulation. In women with such injuries, vaginal lubrication may still occur, though it is often reduced in amount (Spinal Cord Injury Information Network, 2007).

Sensory innervation of the genitalia

The penis and clitoris possess a unique class of sensory nerve endings termed **genital end-bulbs**, which we describe and illustrate in Chapter 3 (Figure 3.4, page 69). These are thought to sense the kind of tactile stimulation that occurs during sexual behavior.

The pudendal and pelvic nerves

If we trace the sensory nerve fibers from the penis or clitoris, we find that they travel toward the spinal cord in the left and right **pudendal nerves** (**Figure B.1**). The sensory fibers enter the sacral segments (labeled S2–S4 in the figure) of the spinal cord by passing through the dorsal roots. The cell bodies of the sensory fibers are located within the dorsal roots, but no synaptic connections occur there—signals go directly into the spinal cord.

The central endings of the sensory nerve fibers form synaptic connections with interneurons (local circuit cells) in the gray matter of the spinal cord. These interneurons in turn form synaptic connections with output neurons, which in this case are preganglionic neurons of the parasympathetic nervous system (see Box B.1, Figure E). The cell bodies of these neurons are located in the sacral segments of the spinal cord, and their efferent axons leave the cord in the ventral roots and travel toward the genitals in the **pelvic nerves**. On reaching ganglia near the bladder, they form synapses with postganglionic parasympathetic neurons, whose axons in turn travel to the erectile tissues in the penis and clitoris.

Before considering how erection occurs, we need to mention another set of nerve fibers that also innervate the erectile tissues. These fibers are components of the sympathetic nervous system.

genital end-bulbs Specialized nerve endings, found in the genital area, that probably detect the tactile stimulation associated with sexual activity.

pudendal nerves Peripheral nerves supplying the external genitalia.

pelvic nerves Nerves that convey parasympathetic signals from the lower spinal cord to the genitalia and other organs.

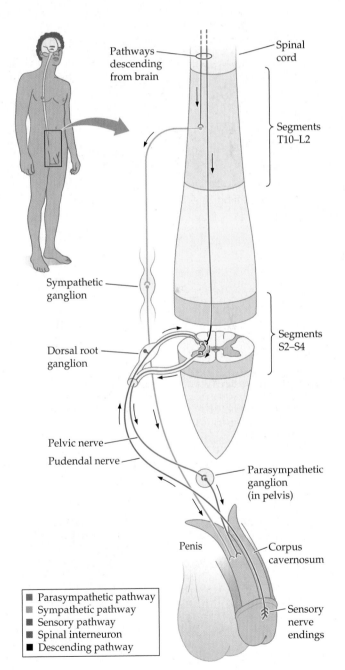

Parasympathetic pathway
Sympathetic pathway
Sensory pathway
Spinal interneuron
Descending pathway

Figure B.1 Nerve pathways involved in erection Erection depends on the balance of activity in the sympathetic and parasympathetic fibers innervating the erectile tissue of the penis or clitoris. Parasympathetic activity (promoting erection) is triggered by tactile stimulation of the genital skin (a spinal reflex). Descending inputs from the brain modulate the activity of both the parasympathetic fibers and the countervailing sympathetic fibers, whose activity prevents erection.

sinusoids A vascular space, such as within erectile tissue, capable of being expanded by filling with blood.

trabeculae Connective tissue partitions separating the sinusoids of erectile tissue.

This system also originates in preganglionic neurons in the spinal cord, but its neurons are situated at higher levels of the cord—in the lower thoracic and upper lumbar segments. The axons of these neurons pass out of the cord and travel to sympathetic ganglia, where they form synaptic connections with postganglionic neurons. The postganglionic neurons send their axons to the erectile tissues of the penis and clitoris. The parasympathetic and sympathetic nerve fibers work in opposition to each other in controlling the state of the erectile tissue.

Erectile Tissue Forms a Hydraulic System

The erectile tissue within the corpora cavernosa consists of irregular vascular spaces called **sinusoids**, which are separated by walls of connective tissue called **trabeculae** (Figure B.2A). Blood enters the sinusoids via arterioles and exits via veins. The trabeculae contain smooth muscle

Figure B.2 The mechanism of penile or clitoral erection (A) Erectile tissue of a corpus cavernosum, showing sinusoids (some with red blood cells) and trabeculae (the cellular walls between the sinusoids). (B) Diagram of the erectile mechanism. Note that for simplicity, the illustration shows the penis as if it contains a single, large sinusoid. In reality, thousands of microscopic sinusoids make up the erectile tissue of the corpora cavernosa and the corpus spongiosum.

(A)

Red blood cells

Sinusoids

Trabeculae

80 μm

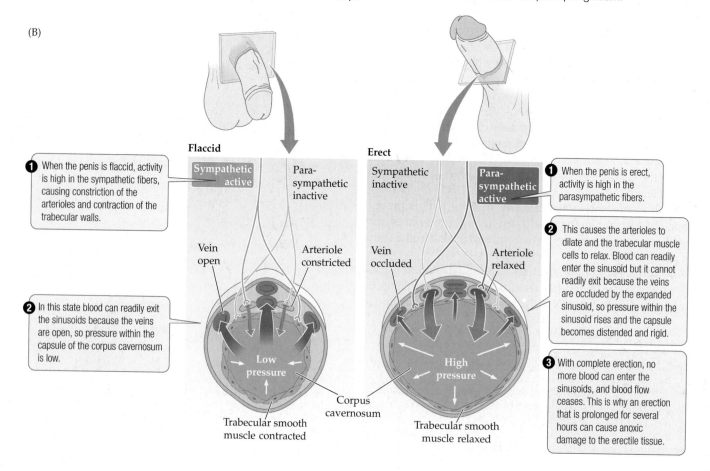

(B)

Flaccid

❶ When the penis is flaccid, activity is high in the sympathetic fibers, causing constriction of the arterioles and contraction of the trabecular walls.

Sympathetic active

Parasympathetic inactive

Vein open

Arteriole constricted

❷ In this state blood can readily exit the sinusoids because the veins are open, so pressure within the capsule of the corpus cavernosum is low.

Low pressure

Trabecular smooth muscle contracted

Corpus cavernosum

Erect

Sympathetic inactive

Parasympathetic active

❶ When the penis is erect, activity is high in the parasympathetic fibers.

Vein occluded

Arteriole relaxed

❷ This causes the arterioles to dilate and the trabecular muscle cells to relax. Blood can readily enter the sinusoid but it cannot readily exit because the veins are occluded by the expanded sinusoid, so pressure within the sinusoid rises and the capsule becomes distended and rigid.

High pressure

Trabecular smooth muscle relaxed

❸ With complete erection, no more blood can enter the sinusoids, and blood flow ceases. This is why an erection that is prolonged for several hours can cause anoxic damage to the erectile tissue.

cells, and contraction of these cells shrinks the spaces, thus diminishing the volume of the erectile tissue as a whole. The other major control element consists of smooth muscle cells in the walls of the arterioles. Contraction of these cells constricts the arterioles, diminishing the flow of blood into the sinusoids.

The flaccid state of the penis and clitoris is not simply an inactive condition in which the erectile tissue receives no input from the nervous system. Rather, it is actively maintained by a continuous flow of impulses in the sympathetic nerve fibers. These impulses, on reaching the nerve terminals in the erectile tissue, cause the release of the sympathetic neurotransmitter norepinephrine. This transmitter in turn causes an ongoing contraction of the smooth muscle of the arterioles (thus narrowing the arterioles and restricting the flow of blood into the sinusoids) and of the trabecular walls (thus keeping the volume of the sinusoids low).

Erection results from a *decrease* in this activity of the sympathetic fibers and a reciprocal *increase* in the activity of the parasympathetic fibers. The parasympathetic fibers release three different neurotransmitters from their nerve terminals in the erectile tissue. The most important of these is nitric oxide (chemical formula NO), which is a dissolved gas. Nitric oxide causes the relaxation of the smooth muscle cells of the arterioles and the trabecular walls. As a result, more blood flows into the sinusoids, and the erectile tissue expands. This expansion compresses and closes the veins that receive the outflow from the sinusoids, causing the volume of the erectile tissue to increase further (**Figure B.2B**).

With complete erection, no more blood can enter the sinusoids, and blood flow ceases. The pooled blood gradually loses its oxygen, taking on the purplish color of venous blood. This color change can be observed in the glans, which has only a thin, translucent capsule.

Muscles Are Also Involved in Erection

Several striated (voluntary) muscles of the pelvic floor are also involved in erection of the penis and clitoris (**Figure B.3**). The most important of these are the ischiocavernosus and bulbospongiosus muscles. The action of these muscles is most obvious in the case of the penis. If a man's penis is already erect but hanging down from the

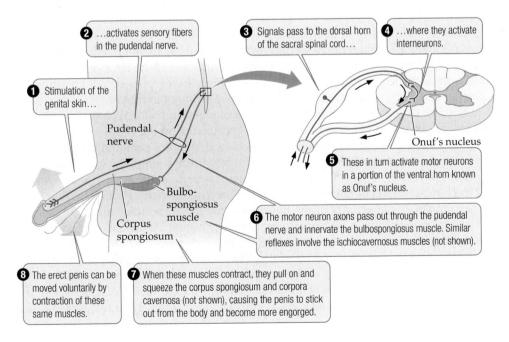

2 ...activates sensory fibers in the pudendal nerve.

3 Signals pass to the dorsal horn of the sacral spinal cord...

4 ...where they activate interneurons.

1 Stimulation of the genital skin...

Pudendal nerve

Onuf's nucleus

5 These in turn activate motor neurons in a portion of the ventral horn known as Onuf's nucleus.

Bulbo-spongiosus muscle

Corpus spongiosum

6 The motor neuron axons pass out through the pudendal nerve and innervate the bulbospongiosus muscle. Similar reflexes involve the ischiocavernosus muscles (not shown).

8 The erect penis can be moved voluntarily by contraction of these same muscles.

7 When these muscles contract, they pull on and squeeze the corpus spongiosum and corpora cavernosa (not shown), causing the penis to stick out from the body and become more engorged.

Figure B.3 **The bulbospongiosus muscle** and the ischiocavernosus muscle are involved in erectile reflexes.

Onuf's nucleus A sexually dimorphic group of motor neurons in the sacral segments of the spinal cord that innervates striated muscles associated with the penis and clitoris.

sexual dimorphisms An anatomical difference between the sexes.

locus coeruleus A nerve center in the pons that helps regulate the state of consciousness.

body, a light touch on the sensitive areas of the penis, or even on nearby skin, will cause the penis to jump up and project directly forward or upward. At the same time, the glans of the penis will become more enlarged. This involuntary reflex response is caused by contraction of the ischiocavernosus and bulbospongiosus muscles, which pull on and squeeze the corpora cavernosa and corpus spongiosum in the root of the penis. (It is also possible to produce the same movement voluntarily, without any stimulation of the genitals.)

This reflex has the same afferent pathway we described earlier—the sensory fibers running to the spinal cord through the pudendal nerve—but the efferent pathway is different, and it does not involve the autonomic nervous system. Instead, the terminals of the sensory fibers in the sacral segments of the spinal cord activate a set of interneurons, which in turn connect with a set of motor neurons in the ventral horn of the cord. These motor neurons form a cell group known as **Onuf's nucleus**. Onuf's nucleus is significantly larger—and contains more motor neurons—in men than in women. This difference is one of many **sexual dimorphisms**, or anatomical differences between the sexes, in the human central nervous system (CNS); other differences are described elsewhere in this book.

The axons of the motor neurons of Onuf's nucleus run back down the pudendal nerves to the genitalia, where some of them innervate the ischiocavernosus and bulbospongiosus muscles. (Other axons innervate the anal sphincter, the bladder, and other muscles of the pelvic floor.) When impulses reach the endings of the nerves in the muscles (the neuromuscular junctions), they cause the release of the neurotransmitter acetylcholine, which causes the muscles to contract.

The Brain Influences Erection and Ejaculation

So far, we have discussed erection as if it were only a spinal reflex triggered by genital stimulation. In fact, however, erection can occur without any tactile stimulation. The stimulus may consist of erotically arousing sights or sounds, or erotic fantasies.

These influences on erection are mediated by higher levels of the CNS (see Box B.1, Figure C). One brain region that is particularly important for the regulation of sexual excitation (and other drives such as hunger and thirst) is the hypothalamus, which is located at the base of the brain. Descending pathways from the hypothalamus activate lower centers in the brain stem, specifically in the pons and medulla, which in turn send control signals to the sympathetic and parasympathetic neurons in the spinal cord, increasing or decreasing their activity levels. This higher-level control ensures that the spinal reflexes mediating genital arousal are not fixed and constant, but are responsive to circumstances: Tactile stimulation of the penis or clitoris may elicit physiological arousal in some circumstances (in the presence of an attractive partner or during sexual fantasies, for example)—but not in others.

Another example of higher-level control of erection concerns erections during sleep. As described in Chapter 3, erections occur during the rapid eye movement (REM) phases of sleep. These erections are controlled from a center in the pons called the **locus coeruleus**. Here's how it works: Most of the time, the locus coeruleus neurons are active; their activity then stimulates activity in the sympathetic neurons of the lumbar region of the spinal cord, thus keeping the penis flaccid. During REM sleep, however, the activity of the neurons in the locus coeruleus drops; this leads to a corresponding drop in sympathetic activity, shifting the balance in favor of the parasympathetic neurons, so an erection occurs.

Seminal emission—the loading of the semen into the urethra just before ejaculation—is triggered by activity in the sympathetic innervation of the prostate gland, seminal vesicles, and vasa deferentia. Ejaculation—the expulsion of semen from the urethra—results from the combined activity of sympathetic neurons, which cause

Figure B.4   The pons controls ejaculation and orgasm. (A) The pons receives inputs from the hypothalamus and sends its output to the spinal cord. The horizontal line indicates the level of the slices shown in B. (B) Activity in the pons of men while ejaculating (left) and women while experiencing orgasm (right), using positron emission tomography (PET). The front of the head is at the top of the scans. Note that the region labeled "POSC" is active only on the left side, whereas the region labeled "PFSC" is active only on the right side. (PET scans courtesy of Gert Holstege.)

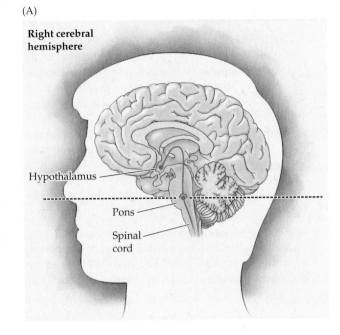

(A)

Right cerebral hemisphere

Hypothalamus

Pons

Spinal cord

contraction of the walls of the urethra, and of the motor neurons of Onuf's nucleus, which trigger a sequence of contractions of muscles of the pelvic floor that forcefully squeeze the urethra.

Most paraplegic men, whose spinal cords have been damaged or severed, are unable to ejaculate. This indicates that a descending pathway from the brain to Onuf's nucleus in the spinal cord is important for ejaculation. This pathway originates in the hypothalamus, but a crucial way station is located in the region of the brain stem known as the pons (Facchinetti et al., 2014) (**Figure B.4A**).

In a functional imaging study in men and women, two regions within the pons, named the pelvic organ stimulating center (POSC) and the pelvic floor stimulating center (PFSC), were active during ejaculation (in men) and orgasm (in women) (Huynh et al., 2013) (**Figure B.4B**). However, the POSC was only active on the left side of the pons, while the PFSC was only active on the right side. This illustrates the fact that the brain stem, like the cerebral cortex, is not functionally symmetrical but assigns different tasks to the left and right sides. (In the case of the POSC, the right side is concerned with another task in which fluid is ejected from the body—urination.) Both the POSC and PFSC were more active in men than in women, perhaps because Onuf's nucleus is larger in men and innervates a greater mass of muscle.

The PFSC was not active in women during faked orgasms, suggesting that this brain region controls the vaginal and pelvic contractions that women cannot consciously control.

There is much more to the brain's role in sexuality than these "low-level" functions, of course:

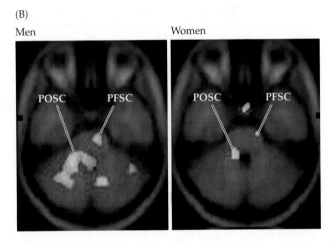

(B)

Men

Women

POSC   PFSC

POSC   PFSC

- The brain helps regulate sex hormone levels, the menstrual cycle in women, and spermatogenesis in men.
- Neurotransmitters such as serotonin and dopamine are involved in sexual desire and sexual pleasure.
- Differences in brain structure and function between women and men help create sex differences in cognitive functions and personality.
- Interactions between sex hormones and the brain play a role in the development of a person's sexual orientation.
- Falling in love requires the activation of specific brain regions.
- The brain-derived hormones oxytocin and vasopressin are involved in orgasm, lactation, and possibly falling in love.

In the main text of this book we touch on these and other ways in which the brain plays a central role in human sexuality.

Summary

- Sexual functions are regulated by the nervous and endocrine systems. In the absence of sexual stimulation, erection of the penis or clitoris is prevented by ongoing activity in the sympathetic axons that innervate the genitals. This activity causes constriction of the arterioles supplying the erectile tissue. Erection involves a spinal reflex that begins with stimulation of nerve endings in the genital skin, followed by processing in the spinal cord and outgoing activity in the parasympathetic axons that innervate the genitals. This activity dilates the arterioles, so more blood enters the sinusoids within the erectile tissue.

- In males, seminal emission (loading of the urethra with semen) involves the coordinated action of sympathetic inputs to the prostate gland, seminal vesicles, and vasa deferentia. Ejaculation is brought about by activity in spinal motor neurons that innervate the muscles of the pelvic floor, causing them to contract in a pulsatile fashion and eject semen from the urethral opening.

- The brain influences these processes in various ways. The hypothalamus influences genital reflexes so that they are modulated by circumstances and erotic images and thoughts. Activity in the locus coeruleus increases the activity of sympathetic neurons in the spinal cord: A decrease in activity in the locus coeruleus during REM sleep leads to a decrease in sympathetic input to the genitals and thus to a nocturnal erection. Regions called the pelvic organ stimulating center (POSC) and the pelvic floor stimulating center (PFSC) trigger the pulsatile muscle contractions associated with male ejaculation and female orgasm.

Glossary

Numbers in brackets refer to the chapter(s) where the term is defined.

5α-dihydrotestosterone (DHT) An andro-gen derived from testosterone that plays an important role in the development of the male external genitalia. [3]

A

abstinence-only program A sex-ed pro-gram that teaches abstinence and omits mention of safer-sex practices, homosexu-ality, etc. [10]

acquaintance rape Rape by a person known to the victim. [16]

acquired immune deficiency syndrome (AIDS) The disease caused by the hu-man immunodeficiency virus (HIV); its onset is defined by the occurrence of any of a number of opportunistic infections, or on the basis of blood tests. [15]

acrosome A structure capping the head of a sperm that contains enzymes necessary for fertilization. [3]

action potential An electrochemical signal that travels rapidly along an axon. [App. B]

adaptive Helping the propagation of an organism's genes. [App. A]

adolescence The period of psychosexual and social maturation that accompanies and follows puberty. [10]

adult baby An adult who obtains sexual satisfaction from acting as a baby or tod-dler. [13]

afferent Carrying signals toward the CNS. [App. B]

afterbirth The placenta, whose delivery constitutes the final stage of labor. [8]

afterplay Sexual behavior engaged in after coitus or orgasm, or at the end of a sexual encounter. [6]

alveolus (pl. alveoli) Microscopic cavity, such as one of those in the breast where milk is produced. [2]

amenorrhea Absence of menstruation. [2]

amniocentesis The sampling of the amni-otic fluid for purposes of prenatal diagno-sis. [8]

anal fold The posterior portion of the ure-thral fold, which gives rise to the anus. [4]

anal sex Penetration of the anus by the pe-nis, or any sexual behavior involving the anus. [6]

androgen insensitivity syndrome (AIS) The congenital absence of a functional an-drogen receptor, making the body unable to respond to androgens. [4]

androgens Any of a class of steroids—the most important being testosterone—that promote male sexual development and that have a variety of other functions in both sexes. [2]

andropause In men, the gradual decline of fertility with age; a hypothetical male equivalent of menopause. [11]

androphilic Sexually attracted to men. [12]

aneuploidy A nonstandard set of chro-mosomes, as in Down syndrome or Klinefelter syndrome [8]

anilingus Sexual contact between the mouth or tongue of one person and the anus of another. [6]

anorgasmia Difficulty experiencing or in-ability to experience orgasm. In women, also called *female orgasmic disorder*. [14]

anti-Müllerian hormone (AMH) A hormone secreted by the testes that prevents the development of the female reproductive tract. [4]

antiretroviral drugs Drugs effective against retroviruses. [15]

anus The opening from which feces are released. [2]

aphrodisiac A substance believed to im-prove sexual performance, enhance sexual pleasure, or stimulate desire or love. [5]

areola The circular patch of darker skin that surrounds the nipple. [2]

artificial insemination by donor (AID) Artificial insemination using sperm from a man who is not the woman's partner. [8]

artificial insemination An assisted repro-duction technique that involves the place-ment of semen in the vagina or uterus with the aid of a syringe or small tube. [8]

asexual reproduction Reproduction in which all the offspring's genes are inher-ited from a single parent. [App. A]

asexual Describes a person who does not experience sexual attraction. [5]

assisted reproductive technology (ART) In vitro fertilization and related technolo-gies. [8]

asymptomatic carrier Someone who is in-fected with a disease organism but is not experiencing symptoms. [15]

attachment theory The idea that relation-ship styles are influenced by the quality of the early parent-child bond. [7]

autoerotic asphyxia Self-strangulation for purposes of sexual arousal. [13]

autoerotic Providing sexual stimulation to oneself or being aroused sexually by oneself. [6]

autogynephilia A form of male-to-female transexuality characterized by a man's sexual arousal at the thought of being or becoming a woman. [4, 13]

autonomic ganglion A cluster of autonom-ic neurons outside the CNS. [App. B]

autonomic nervous system The portion of the nervous system that controls smooth muscles and glands without our conscious involvement. [3, App. B]

autosome Any chromosome other than a sex chromosome. [App. A]

aversion therapy A form of behavior ther-apy that attempts to eliminate unwanted desires or behaviors by associating them with some unpleasant experience, such as a noxious smell. [13]

axon The extension of a neuron that con-veys impulses, usually in a direction away from the cell body. Also called nerve fiber. [App. B]

B

bacterial vaginosis A condition in which the normal microorganisms of the vagina are replaced by other species, causing discomfort and a foul-smelling discharge. [15]

balanitis Inflammation of the glans of the penis. [3]

bar mitzvah Jewish coming-of-age ceremo-ny for boys. [10]

barrier method Any contraceptive tech-nique in which a physical barrier, such as a condom or diaphragm, prevents sperm from reaching the ovum. [9]

basal ganglia Deep noncortical structures of the forebrain. [App. B]

bat mitzvah Jewish coming-of-age ceremo-ny for girls. [10]

bathhouse A facility, usually in the form of a private club, used for casual sex be-tween men. [12]

battered-woman syndrome A version of post-traumatic stress disorder affecting women who are victims of intimate part-ner violence. [16]

BDSM An all-inclusive term for forms of sexual expression that involve inflicting and receiving physical pain, restraint, or humiliation. [13]

bear In gay slang, a burly gay man with plenty of body hair; more generally, a member of a gay male subculture that re-jects many of the prevailing standards of gay male attractiveness and behavior. [12]

behavior therapy Treatment of mental dis-orders by training of behavior. [13]

behavioral couples therapy (BCT) Therapy focused on improving styles of communication between partners in relationships. [7]

benign prostatic hyperplasia Noncancerous enlargement of the prostate gland. [3]

bestiality Obsolete term for sexual contact between a person and an animal. [13]

bi Colloquial term for bisexual. [12]

bigamy In law, the crime of marrying someone while being already married to another spouse. [11]

biphobia Prejudice against bisexuals. [12]

birth canal The canal formed by the uterus, cervix, and vagina, through which the fetus passes during the birth process. [2, 8]

birthing center A facility specializing in childbirth care. [8]

bisexual erasure Ignoring or denying the existence of bisexual people. [12]

bisexuality Sexual attraction to persons of both sexes. [12]

bondage The use of physical restraint for purposes of sexual arousal. [13]

Bradley method A method of childbirth instruction that stresses the partner's role as birth coach and that seeks to avoid medical interventions. [8]

brainstem The region of the brain between the forebrain and the spinal cord. [App. B]

Braxton Hicks contractions Irregular uterine contractions that occur during the third trimester of pregnancy. Also called *false labor*. [8]

breast bud The first stage of breast development at puberty. [10]

breast ironing In Cameroon, a traumatic procedure to delay breast development in girls. [10]

brothel A house of prostitution. [17]

bulbourethral glands (or Cowper's glands) Two small glands near the root of the penis whose secretions ("pre-cum") may appear at the urethral opening during sexual arousal prior to ejaculation. [3]

butch Masculine-acting, often used to describe certain lesbians. [12]

C

calendar rhythm method A fertility awareness method of contraception that takes account of variability in the length of a woman's menstrual cycles. [9]

call girl An escort service prostitute, especially one who is relatively upscale in terms of clientele and price. [17]

candidiasis A fungal infection of the vagina. Also called thrush or a yeast infection. [2]

castration Removal of the gonads. (In males, may include removal of the penis.) [1, 11]

casual sex Sexual encounters that do not take place within a lasting sexual relationship. [7]

CD4 lymphocyte A type of lymphocyte that carries the CD4 receptor; one of the major targets of HIV. [15]

cell body The part of a neuron where the nucleus is located. [App. B]

cell-free fetal DNA analysis The diagnosis of fetal disorders by sequencing fetal DNA that leaks into the maternal circulation. [8]

central nervous system (CNS) The brain and spinal cord. [App. B]

cerebral cortex Convoluted, layered gray matter that covers most of the brain. [App. B]

cerebral hemispheres The uppermost and largest portion of the brain, divided into left and right halves. [App. B]

cervical cap A small rubber or plastic cap that adheres by suction to the cervix, used as a contraceptive. [9]

cervical mucus method A fertility awareness method of contraception that depends on observing changes in the cervical mucus. [9]

cervix The lowermost, narrow portion of the uterus that connects with the vagina. [2]

cesarean section (C-section) The delivery of a baby through an incision in the abdominal wall and the uterus. [8]

chancre A primary sore on the skin or a mucous membrane in a person infected with syphilis. (Pronounced SHANK-er.) [15]

child molester An adult who has sexual contact with a prepubescent child. [13]

chlamydia A sexually transmitted infection caused by infection with the bacterium *Chlamydia trachomatis*. [15]

chorionic villus sampling The sampling of tissue from the placenta for purposes of prenatal diagnosis. [8]

chronic pelvic pain syndrome An alternative, more-inclusive term for chronic prostatitis. [3]

cilia Microscopic, hairlike extensions of cells, often capable of coordinated beating motions. [2]

Circles of Support and Accountability (COSA) A program of community support for released sex offenders. [13]

circumcision The removal of the male foreskin. In women, an alternative term for genital cutting. [3]

cisgender Having a conventional gender—masculine if anatomically male, feminine if anatomically female. "Cis" is the opposite of "trans." [4]

civil union A legal arrangement that confers most or all of the rights and obligations of marriage except the name. [11]

classical (or Pavlovian) conditioning A form of behavioral learning in which a novel stimulus is tied to a preexisting reflex. [5]

climacteric The transition to infertility at the end of a woman's reproductive life, lasting for several years and culminating in menopause. [11]

clitoral hood A loose fold of skin that covers the clitoris. [2]

clitoridectomy Removal of the entire external portion of the clitoris (glans, shaft, and hood). [2]

clitoris The erectile organ in females, whose external portion is located at the junction of the inner labia, just in front of the vestibule. [2, App. A]

cloaca The common exit of the gastrointestinal and urogenital systems; in humans it is present only in embryonic life. [4]

cognitive psychology The study of the information-processing systems of the mind. [1]

cognitive therapy Therapy based on changing a person's beliefs and thought processes. [13]

cognitive Related to the aspects of the mind that process knowledge or information. [4]

cohabitation A live-in sexual relationship between individuals who are not married to each other. [1, 11]

coital alignment technique (CAT) A variation of the man-above position for coitus that increases clitoral stimulation. [14]

coitus Penetration of the vagina by the penis. [1, 2, 6]

colostrum The milk produced during the first few days after birth; it is relatively low in fat but rich in immunoglobulins. [8]

colposcopy The examination of the cervix with the aid of an operating microscope. [2]

come out of the closet (or come out) Reveal a previously concealed identity, such as being gay. [12]

commitment The cognitive component of love: the decision to maintain a relationship. [7]

companionate marriage A form of marriage in which the husband and wife are expected to be emotionally intimate and to engage in social activities together. [11]

comprehensive sex-education programs Sex-ed programs that discuss abstinence as well as safer-sex practices, sexual and gender diversity, etc. [10]

compulsive sexual behavior Sexual behavior perceived subjectively as involuntary and diagnosed as a symptom of a compulsive disorder. Also called *obsessive-compulsive sexual disorder*. [14]

concubine A woman who cohabits with a man but is not his wife, usually in a polygamous culture. [11]

conditioning The modification of behavior by learning through association and/or reinforcement. [13]

congenital adrenal hyperplasia (CAH) A congenital defect of hormonal metabolism in the adrenal gland, causing the gland to secrete excessive levels of androgens. [4]

constant-dose combination pill An oral contraceptive regimen in which all pills (except any dummy pills) contain the same drug dosage. [9]

contraceptive implant   A device implanted in the body that slowly releases a hormonal contraceptive. [9]

contraction   In childbirth, a periodic coordinated tightening of the uterine musculature, felt as a cramp. [8]

control group   A group of subjects included in a study for comparison purposes. [1]

Coolidge effect   The revival of sexual arousal caused by the presence of a novel partner. [5]

copulation   Sexual intercourse; coitus. [App. A]

corona   The rim of the glans of the penis. [3]

corpus callosum   A band of axons interconnecting the left and right cerebral hemispheres. [App. B]

corpus cavernosum (pl., corpora cavernosa)   Either of two elongated erectile structures within the clitoris or penis that also extend backward into the pelvic floor. [2, 3]

corpus luteum   A secretory structure in the ovary derived from an ovarian follicle after ovulation. [2]

corpus spongiosum   A single midline erectile structure. In both sexes it fills the glans; in males it extends backward along the underside of the penis, surrounding the urethra. [2, 3]

cortex   The outer portion of an anatomical structure, as of the cerebral hemispheres or the adrenal gland. [App. B]

courtship behavior   Behavior that attracts a mate. [App. A]

courtship disorder   A paraphilia or cluster of paraphilias seen as a disorder of normal courtship behavior. [13]

couvade   Pregnancy-like symptoms in the male partner of a pregnant woman. [8]

covenant marriage   A form of marriage that requires a stronger vow of commitment than a regular marriage and that makes divorce harder to obtain. [11]

cremaster muscle   A sheetlike muscle that wraps around the spermatic cord and the testicle. [3]

cross-dressing   Wearing the clothing of the other sex, for any of a variety of reasons. [13]

crowning   The appearance of the fetal scalp at the vaginal opening. [8]

cruising   Looking for casual sex partners in public spaces. [7]

crura (sing. crus)   The two internal extensions of the corpora cavernosa of the clitoris or penis. [2, 3]

crush   A short-lived, intense, unreciprocated love, often experienced during adolescence. [7]

cryptorchidism   Failure of one or both testicles to descend into the scrotum by 3 months of postnatal age. [4]

cultural anthropology   The study of cultural variations across the human race. [1]

cunnilingus   Sexual contact between the tongue or mouth of one person and the vulva of another. [6]

cyber dating abuse   Abusive online behavior between dating or other sex partners. [16]

cyberstalking   Stalking via the Internet. [16]

cycle of abuse   The cycle in which some abused children grow up to perform similar forms of abuse on others. Also called *victim-perpetrator cycle*. [13]

D

date rape   Rape between dating or socially acquainted couples. [16]

decriminalization   Removal of laws that criminalize activities such as prostitution. [17]

deep kissing   Kissing, with entry of the tongue into the partner's mouth. [6]

delayed ejaculation   Difficulty achieving or inability to achieve orgasm and/or ejaculation. Also called *male orgasmic disorder*. [14]

delayed labor   Labor that occurs more than 3 weeks after a woman's due date. [8]

delayed puberty   Puberty that begins later than normal. [10]

delusional jealousy   Persistent false belief that one's partner is involved with another person. [7]

delusional stalking   Stalking motivated by the delusional belief that the victim is in love with, or could be persuaded to fall in love with, the stalker. [16]

demisexual   Experiencing sexual attraction only in the context of a strong emotional bond. [5]

dendrites   The extensions of a neuron that receive incoming signals from other neurons. [App. B]

Depo-Provera   An injectable form of medroxyprogesterone acetate, used as a contraceptive in women or to decrease the sex drive in male sex offenders. [9]

Depo-SubQ Provera   A form of Depo-Provera designed for subcutaneous injection. [9]

designer steroids   Synthetic steroids intended to evade detection in drug tests. [3]

diaphragm   A barrier placed over the cervix as a contraceptive. [9]

dilation and evacuation (D&E)   A procedure involving the opening of the cervix and the scraping out of the contents of the uterus with a curette (spoonlike instrument). D&E may be done as an abortion procedure or for other purposes. [9]

dilation   In childbirth, the expansion of the cervical canal. Also called *dilatation*. [8]

dildo   A sex toy, often shaped like a penis, used to penetrate the vagina or anus. [6]

discrepant sexual desire   The situation in which one partner in a relationship has much more interest in sex than the other. [14]

disorders of sex development   Medical conditions producing anomalous sexual differentiation or intersexuality. [4]

dissociation   The distancing of oneself from the emotions evoked by some traumatic experience or memory. [10]

domestic partnership   A legal arrangement that confers some or most of the rights and obligations of marriage. [11]

dominance   The use of humiliation or subservience for purposes of sexual arousal. [13]

dominatrix   A woman who acts the role of the dominant partner in a BDSM setting. [13]

dorsal horn   The rear portion of the gray matter of the spinal cord; it has a sensory function. [App. B]

dorsal root   A bundle of sensory axons that enters a dorsal horn of the spinal cord. [App. B]

double standard   The application of different moral standards to the behavior of males and females. [1, 4]

douche   To rinse the vagina out with a fluid; the fluid so used. [2]

Down syndrome   A collection of birth defects caused by the presence of an extra copy of chromosome 21. [8]

drag   The wearing of exaggeratedly feminine clothing by a man, or male clothing by a woman, often for entertainment purposes. [13]

dysmenorrhea   Menstrual pain severe enough to interfere with a woman's activities. [2]

dyspareunia   Pain during coitus. [14]

E

ectopic pregnancy   Implantation and resulting pregnancy at any site other than the uterus. [8]

effacement   Thinning of the cervix in preparation for childbirth. [8]

efferent   Carrying signals away from the CNS. [App. B]

ejaculatory duct   Either of the two bilateral ducts formed by the junction of the vas deferens and the duct of the seminal vesicle. The ejaculatory ducts empty into the urethra within the prostate. [3]

elective abortion   An abortion performed in circumstances when the woman's health is not at risk. [9]

ella   A form of emergency contraception that is effective for 5 days after sex. [9]

emergency contraception   Use of high-dose contraceptives to prevent pregnancy after unprotected sex. [9]

emission   The loading of the constituents of semen into the posterior portion of the urethra immediately before ejaculation. [3]

emotional jealousy   Fear that one's partner is becoming emotionally committed to another person. [7]

empathy   The ability to share or understand other people's feelings. [16]

endocrine disruptors   Substances that interfere with development by mimicking sex hormones. [10]

endometrial cancer   Cancer of the endometrium of the uterus. [2]

endometriosis The growth of endometrial tissue at abnormal locations such as the oviducts. [2]

endometrium The internal lining of the uterus. [2]

engagement The sinking of a fetus's head into a lower position in the pelvis in preparation for birth. Also called *lightening*. [8]

epididymis A structure, attached to each testicle, where sperm mature and are stored before entering the vas deferens. [3]

epididymitis Inflammation of the epididymis. [3, 15]

epidural anesthesia Anesthesia administered just outside the membrane that surrounds the spinal cord. [8]

epiphyseal plates The growth zones in limb bones, which cease to function after puberty. [10]

episiotomy A cut extending the opening of the vagina backward into the perineum, performed by an obstetrician with the intention of facilitating childbirth or reducing the risk of a perineal tear. [8]

erectile disorder (ED) A persistent inability to achieve or maintain an erection sufficient to accomplish a desired sexual behavior such as coitus to orgasm. Also called *erectile dysfunction*. [14]

erotica Sexually themed works, such as books or sculpture, deemed to have literary or artistic merit. [17]

erotomania The delusional belief that a sexually desired but unattainable person is actually in love with oneself. [16]

escort service A service that provides prostitutes, generally contacted by telephone. [17]

escort Euphemism for a prostitute who advertises by print, word of mouth, or the Internet. [17]

Essure A method of tubal sterilization that blocks the oviducts by use of metal coils. [9]

estradiol The principal estrogen, secreted by ovarian follicles. [2]

estrogens Any of a class of steroids—the most important being estradiol—that promote the development of female secondary sexual characteristics at puberty and that have many other functions in both sexes. [2]

estrus The restricted period within the ovarian cycle when females of some species are sexually receptive; "heat." [App. A]

ethnography The study of a cultural group, often by means of extended individual fieldwork. [1]

eunuch A man who has been castrated. [1, 11]

evolutionary psychology The study of the influence of evolution on mental processes or behavior. [1]

excitement phase The beginning phase of the sexual response cycle. [5]

exhibitionism Sexual arousal by exposure of the genitals to strangers. [13]

exposure therapy A form of psychotherapy for victims of rape or abuse in which they are encouraged to recall the traumatic event in a safe environment. [16]

extended-use regimen A regimen of contraceptive pills that allows for fewer or no menstrual periods. [9]

external genitalia The sexual structures on the outside of the body. [2]

extra-pair relationship A sexual relationship in which at least one of the partners is already married to or partnered with someone else. [7]

extrafamilial child molester A person who has had sexual contact with children outside his immediate family. [13]

F

fantasy An imagined experience, sexual or otherwise. [5]

fellatio Sexual contact between the mouth of one person and the penis of another. [6]

female circumcision Any of several forms of ritual cutting or excision of parts of the female genitalia. [2]

female condom A nitrile rubber pouch inserted into the vagina as a contraceptive and/or to prevent disease transmission. [9]

female sexual arousal disorder Lack or insufficiency of physiological sexual arousal in women. [14]

FemCap A type of cervical cap that has a raised brim. [9]

feminism The movement to secure equality for women; the study of social and psychological issues from women's perspectives. [1]

femiphobia Prejudice against femininity, especially in males. [12]

femme Feminine-acting, often used to describe certain lesbians or bisexual women. [12]

fertility awareness methods Contraceptive techniques that rely on avoiding coitus during the woman's fertile window. Also called *rhythm methods* or *periodic abstinence methods*. [9]

fetal alcohol syndrome A collection of physical and behavioral symptoms in a child who was exposed to high levels of alcohol as a fetus. [8]

fetish Sexual fixation on an inanimate object, material, or part of the body. [13]

fibroid A noncancerous tumor arising from muscle cells of the uterus. [2]

fimbria The fringe at the end of the oviduct, composed of fingerlike extensions. [2]

flagellum A whiplike cellular structure, such as the tail of a sperm. [3]

fluctuating asymmetry A difference between the left and right sides of the body that results from random perturbations of development. [App. A]

follicle A fluid-filled sac that contains an egg (ovum), with its supporting cells, within the ovary. [2]

follicle-stimulating hormone (FSH) One of the two major gonadotropins secreted by the pituitary gland; it promotes maturation of ova (or sperm in males). [2]

follicular phase An alternative term for preovulatory phase. [2]

fondling Any kind of sexual touching of the partner's body. [6]

forebrain The cerebral hemispheres and basal ganglia. [App. B]

foreplay Sexual behavior engaged in during the early part of a sexual encounter, with the aim of increasing sexual arousal. [6]

foreskin (or prepuce) The loose skin that partially or completely covers the glans in males who have not been circumcised. [3]

formicophilia Sexual arousal from having ants crawling on the body. [13]

frenulum A strip of loose skin on the underside of the penis, running between the glans and the shaft. [3]

frotteurism Sexual arousal from touching or rubbing the genitals against strangers without their consent or without their knowledge, as in a crowded public place. [13]

G

gamete A germ cell (ovum or sperm) that fuses with another to form a new organism. [App. A]

ganglia Collections of neurons outside the central nervous system. [App. B]

gay Colloquial term for homosexual. [12]

gay bashing Hate crimes against gay people. Sometimes includes verbal abuse as well as physical violence. [12]

gaydar The ability to recognize gay people on the basis of unconscious behaviors, voice quality, gait, and so on. [12]

gender The collection of psychological traits that differ between males and females. [1, 4]

gender dysphoria The unhappiness caused by discordance between a person's anatomical sex and gender identity. [4]

gender identity A person's subjective sense of being male or female. [4]

gender role The expression of gender identity in social behavior. [4]

gender-variant Atypical in gender characteristics. [12]

General Social Survey (GSS) A long-running periodic survey of the U.S. population run by the National Opinion Research Center. [1]

genital end-bulbs Specialized nerve endings found in the genital area that probably detect the tactile stimulation associated with sexual activity. [3, App. B]

genital herpes An infection of the genital area caused by HSV-2 or (less commonly) HSV-1. [15]

genital swelling Regions of the genitalia in the embryo that give rise to the outer labia (in females) or the scrotum (in males). [4]

genital tubercle A midline swelling in front of the cloaca, which gives rise to the glans of the clitoris (in females) or penis (in males). [4]

genital warts Wart-like growths on or near the genitalia or anus, caused by infection with human papillomavirus. [15]

genome An organism's entire complement of DNA, including all its genes. In some viruses, such as HIV, the genome is composed of RNA. [App. A]

gestation Bearing young in the uterus; pregnancy. [App. A]

gestational age A fetus's age timed from the onset of the mother's last menstrual period. [8]

gigolo A male prostitute who caters to women. [17]

glans The terminal knob of the clitoris or penis. [2, 3]

glycogen A polymer of glucose used for energy storage. [8]

gonad An organ that produces ova or sperm and secretes sex hormones. [2]

gonadal intersexuality The possession of both testicular and ovarian tissue in the same individual. [4]

gonadotropin-releasing hormone (GnRH) A hormone secreted by the hypothalamus that stimulates the release of gonadotropins from the anterior pituitary gland. [2]

gonadotropins Hormones that regulate the function of the gonads. [2]

gonorrhea A sexually transmitted infection caused by the bacterium *Neisseria gonorrhoeae*. [15]

Good Lives model A form of therapy for sex offenders that focuses on improving the subject's ability to achieve a broad range of life goals. [13]

Gräfenberg spot (G-spot) A possible area of increased erotic sensitivity on or deep within the front wall of the vagina. [2]

gray matter A region of the central nervous system containing the cell bodies of neurons. [App. B]

group marriage Three or more people living together in a marriage-like relationship. Also called *polyfidelity*. [11]

grudge stalking Nonsexual revenge stalking. [16]

gynecomastia The development of breasts in males. [10]

gynephilic Sexually attracted to women. [12]

H

habituation A psychological or physiological process that reduces a person's response to a stimulus or drug after repeated or prolonged exposure. [5, 11]

hard-core Related to explicit pornography, such as images of penetrative sex and ejaculation. [17]

harem The quarters for wives and children in a polygamous Muslim household. [11]

heavy petting Sexually touching the partner's genitalia or breasts. [6]

hebephile An adult whose sexual attraction is directed mainly toward pubescent children. [13]

hepatitis A Liver disease caused by the hepatitis A virus. It is sometimes transmitted sexually. [15]

hepatitis B Liver disease caused by the hepatitis B virus, a virus that is often transmitted sexually. [15]

hepatitis viruses Viruses that cause liver disease. [15]

hermaphrodite An organism that combines male and female reproductive functions. [App. A]

heteroflexible Mostly straight but having some interest in same-sex contacts or relationships. [7]

heterosexism The cultural establishment of heterosexuality as the normal and preferred form of sexual expression. [12]

heterosexuality Sexual attraction to, or behavior with, persons of the opposite sex. [1, 12]

hijra A member of a class of male-to-female transexuals in northern India and Pakistan. [4]

HIV-symptomatic disease Health problems caused by HIV, especially those that occur before the criteria for an AIDS diagnosis have been met. [15]

homogamy The tendency of sexually partnered couples, or married couples, to resemble each other in a variety of respects. [7]

homophobia Prejudice against homosexuality or gay people. [12]

homosexuality Sexual attraction to, or behavior with, persons of the same sex. [1, 12]

hooking up Uncommitted sex with an acquaintance. [7]

hostile environment harassment Sexual harassment involving a pattern of conduct that creates an intimidating work environment. [16]

hot flashes (or hot flushes) Episodes of reddening and warmth of the skin associated with menopause. [11]

human immunodeficiency virus (HIV) The retrovirus that causes AIDS. [15]

human papillomavirus (HPV) Any of a group of viruses that can be sexually transmitted and that cause genital warts or other lesions; some types predispose infected persons to cancer of the cervix or anus. [15]

hustler A male prostitute. [17]

hydrocele A collection of fluid around a testicle. [3]

hymen A membrane, usually perforated or incomplete, that covers the opening of the vagina. It may be torn by first coitus or by other means. [2]

hypersexuality Excessive sexual desire or behavior. [13, 14]

hypoactive sexual desire disorder Low or absent interest in sex, when this condition causes distress. [14]

hypogonadal Producing insufficient levels of sex hormones. [5]

hypospadias An abnormal location of the male urethral opening on the underside of the penis or elsewhere. [4]

hypothalamus A small region at the base of the brain on either side of the third ventricle; it contains cell groups involved in sexual responses and other basic functions. [2, App. B]

hysterectomy Surgical removal of the uterus. [2]

hysterotomy An abortion performed via a surgical incision in the abdominal wall and the uterus. [9]

I

illegitimacy An obsolete term referring to children born to unmarried parents. [11]

imperforate hymen A hymen that completely closes the introitus. [2]

implantation The attachment of the embryo to the endometrium. [8]

implicit association test A psychological test that is intended to reveal unconscious or unstated preferences. [11, 12]

in vitro fertilization (IVF) Any of a variety of assisted reproduction techniques in which fertilization takes place outside the body. [8]

INAH3 Third interstitial nucleus of the anterior hypothalamus—a neuronal cell group in the hypothalamus that differs in size between men and women and between gay and straight men. [12]

incompetent cervix A weakening and partial opening of the cervix caused by a previous traumatic delivery, surgery, or other factors. [8]

indecent exposure The crime of exposing the genitals or female breasts in public—exact legal definitions vary. [13]

induced abortion An abortion performed intentionally by medical or surgical means. [9]

induced labor Labor induced artificially by drugs. [8]

infant formula Manufactured breast milk substitute. [8]

infantilism Sexual satisfaction from acting as an infant. [13]

infertility Inability (of a man, woman, or couple) to achieve pregnancy. [8]

infibulation The most invasive form of female genital cutting; involves removal of the clitoris, inner labia, and parts of the outer labia, plus the sewing together of the outer labia over the vestibule. [2]

inguinal canal A short canal passing through the abdominal wall in the region of the groin in males. [3]

inner labia (or labia minora) Thin, hairless folds of skin located between the outer labia and immediately flanking the vestibule. [2]

internal fertilization Fertilization within the body. [App. A]

interneuron A neuron whose connections are local. [App. B]

interpersonal scripts Patterns of behavior that develop between couples. [7]

intersex Having a biologically ambiguous or intermediate sex. [4]

interstitial cells Cells located between the seminiferous tubules in the testicle that secrete hormones. [3]

intimacy The sense of connectedness in an established relationship. [7]

intimate partner stalking Stalking of a current or former spouse or other intimate partner. [16]

intimate partner violence Violence within a sexual or romantic relationship. [16]

intracytoplasmic sperm injection (ICSI) Fertilization of an ovum by injection of a single sperm into it. [8]

intrafamilial child molester A person who has had sexual contact with his own children or stepchildren. Also called *incest offender*. [13]

intrauterine device (IUD) A device placed in the uterus as a contraceptive. Also called intrauterine contraceptive (IUC). [9]

introitus The entrance to the vagina, usually covered early in life by the hymen. [2]

investment The commitment or expenditure of resources for a goal, such as reproductive success. [App. A]

isoflavones Estrogen-like compounds of plant origin. [11]

J

jaundice Yellowing of the skin and mucous membranes, caused by liver disease. [15]

jealousy Fear that a partner may be sexually or emotionally unfaithful. [7]

K

kathoey Trans women in Thailand. [4]

Kegel exercises Exercises to strengthen pelvic floor muscles, with the aim of improving sexual function or alleviating urinary leakage. [14]

kin selection The theory that it can be advantageous, in evolutionary terms, to support the reproductive success of close relatives. [App. A]

kink Colloquial term for an unusual sexual desire or behavior; a paraphilia. [13]

Kinsey scale A 7-point scale of sexual orientation devised by Alfred Kinsey. [12]

kisspeptin A signaling molecule in the hypothalamus that promotes the onset of puberty. [10]

Klinefelter syndrome A collection of traits caused by the possession of one or more extra X chromosomes in a male (XXY, XXXY). [4]

L

labia Two pairs of skin folds that form the sides of the vulva. [2]

labor The process of childbirth. [8]

lactation The production of milk in the mammary glands. [8, App. A]

Lamaze method A method of childbirth instruction that focuses on techniques of relaxation and other natural means of pain reduction. [8]

laparoscopy Abdominal surgery, such as tubal sterilization, performed through a small incision with the aid of a laparoscope (a fiber-optic viewing instrument). [9]

latent phase An asymptomatic phase of syphilis or other infectious disease. [15]

learned helplessness Depression associated with failure to escape intimate partner violence. [16]

legalization with regulation Conversion of an activity such as prostitution from a crime to a governmentally regulated occupation. [17]

leptin A hormone secreted by fat cells that acts on the hypothalamus. [10]

lesbian Homosexual—applied to women only. [12]

lobe A subdivision of a gland or other organ. [2]

lochia A bloody vaginal discharge that may continue for a few weeks after childbirth. [8]

locus coeruleus A nerve center in the pons that helps regulate the state of consciousness. [App. B]

lubrication The natural appearance of slippery secretions in the vagina during sexual arousal, or the use of artificial lubricants to facilitate sexual activity. [2]

luteal phase An alternative term for post-ovulatory phase. [2]

luteinizing hormone (LH) One of the two major gonadotropins secreted by the pituitary gland; it triggers ovulation and promotes the secretion of sex steroids by the ovaries (or testicles). [2]

Lybrel A contraceptive pill designed for complete elimination of menstrual periods. [9]

M

madam A woman who manages a brothel or an escort service. [17]

mahu A man who took a female gender role in Polynesian society and performed ritual dances. [4]

male condom A sheath placed over the penis as a contraceptive and/or to prevent disease transmission. [9]

mammary glands The milk-producing glands within the breasts. [2]

mammography Radiographic inspection of the breasts. [2]

masochism Sexual arousal from being subjected to pain, bondage, or humiliation. [13]

massage parlor An establishment for massage that may also offer the services of prostitutes. [17]

mastectomy Surgical removal of a breast. [2]

mastitis Inflammation of the breast. [8]

masturbation Sexual self-stimulation. Sometimes also used to refer to manual stimulation of another person's genitalia. [6]

masturbatory reconditioning The attempt to change a person's sexual attractions by control of fantasy content during masturbation. [13]

mate guarding A behavior in which a male animal prevents sexual contact between his mate and other males. [App. A]

media fetishism Sexual attraction to materials such as rubber or silk. Also called *material fetishism*. [13]

medial preoptic area A region of the hypothalamus involved in the regulation of sexual behaviors typically shown by males. [12]

medical abortion An abortion induced with drugs. Also called *medication abortion*. [9]

medulla The portion of the brainstem closest to the spinal cord. [App. B]

meiosis A pair of cell divisions that produces haploid gametes. [App. A]

menarche (Pronunciations vary; MEN-ar-kee is most common.) The onset of menstruation at puberty. [2, 10]

menopausal hormone therapy Use of hormones to treat symptoms occurring during or soon after menopause. [11]

menopause The final cessation of menstruation at the end of a woman's reproductive years. [11]

menstrual cramps Sharp pelvic pains that may accompany or precede menstruation. [2]

menstrual cup A cup placed within the vagina that collects the menstrual flow. [2]

menstrual phase The days of the menstrual cycle on which menstrual bleeding occurs. [2]

menstrual toxic shock syndrome A rare but life-threatening illness caused by a staphylococcal infection and associated with tampon use. [2]

menstruation The breakdown of the endometrium at approximately monthly intervals, with consequent loss of tissue and blood from the vagina. [2]

methotrexate A drug used in some medical abortions. [9]

metoidioplasty Surgical contruction of a small penis from a clitoris. [4]

midbrain The region of the brainstem between the pons and the thalamus. [App. B]

midpiece The portion of the tail of a sperm closest to the head, containing mitochondria. [3]

mifepristone An anti-progesterone drug used to induce abortion. Also known as *RU-486*. [9]

milk letdown reflex The ejection of milk into the milk ducts in response to suckling. Also called *milk ejection reflex*. [8]

mini-laparotomy Abdominal surgery, such as tubal sterilization, performed through a short incision. [9]

Mirena A hormone-releasing IUD that is effective for 5 years. [9]

misoprostol A prostaglandin used in medical abortions. [9]

molluscum contagiosum A skin condition marked by small raised growths; it is caused by a pox virus. [15]

monogamy 1. Marriage limited to two persons. 2. A sexual relationship in which neither partner has sexual contact with a third party. [App. A]

mons (or mons veneris) The frontmost component of the vulva: a mound of fatty tissue covering the pubic bone. [2]

motor neuron   A neuron that triggers the contraction of muscle fibers. [App. B]

mucosa   A surface layer of cells that is lubricated by the secretions of mucous glands. [2]

mucus   A thick or slippery secretion. [2]

Müllerian duct   Either of two bilateral ducts in the embryo that give rise to the female reproductive tract. [4]

multiple orgasms   Two or more orgasms, between which the person descends only to the plateau level of arousal. [5]

mut'a   In Shia Islam, a contract to marry for a fixed period of time. [11]

mutation   A change in an organism's genome. [App. A]

mutual masturbation   Reciprocal, simultaneous manual stimulation of a partner's genitals. [6]

mycoplasmas   A group of very small cellular organisms that may cause urethritis. [15]

myometrium   The muscular layers of the wall of the uterus. [2]

myotonia   A general increase in muscle tension. [5]

N

Naegele's rule   A traditional rule for the calculation of a pregnant woman's due date: 9 calendar months plus 1 week after the onset of the last menstrual period. [8]

natal   Describing a person's condition at birth. [4]

National Health and Social Life Survey (NHSLS)   A national survey of sexual behavior, relationships, and attitudes in the United States, conducted in the early 1990s. [1]

National Survey of Sexual Attitudes and Lifestyles (NSSAL)   A periodic British survey of sexual behavior, relationships, and attitudes, most recently conducted in 2013. [1]

National Survey of Sexual Health and Behavior (NSSHB)   A national survey of sexual behavior in the United States, based at Indiana University and published in 2010. [1]

necking   Kissing or caressing of the head and neck. [6]

necrophilia   A paraphilia involving sexual arousal from viewing or having contact with dead bodies. [13]

neuromuscular junction   A synapse between an axon and a muscle fiber. [App. B]

neuron   A single nerve cell with all its extensions. [App. B]

neuroses   Mental disorders such as depression that, in Freudian theory, are strategies for coping with repressed sexual conflicts. [1]

neurotransmitter   A compound released at a synapse that increases or decreases the excitability of an adjacent neuron. [App. B]

Nexplanon   An implanted hormonal contraceptive. [9]

Next Choice One-Dose   A progestin used for emergency contraception. [9]

nitric oxide   A dissolved gas that functions as a neurotransmitter in erectile tissue. [3]

no-fault divorce   Divorce without proof of wrongdoing by either party. [11]

nocturnal emission   Ejaculation during sleep. [3]

nocturnal orgasm   Orgasm during sleep. [3]

non-cohabiting relationship   An ongoing sexual relationship between two people who do not live together. [7]

nongonococcal urethritis (NGU)   Urethritis not caused by gonorrhea. [15]

nucleus (pl. nuclei)   In neuroanatomy, a recognizable cluster of neurons in the central nervous system. [App. B]

nucleus accumbens   A nucleus within the basal ganglia that is part of the brain's reward system. [5]

NuvaRing   A contraceptive ring placed in the vagina. [9]

O

object fetishism (or objectophilia or objectum sexuality)   Sexual arousal by objects that are not associated with bodies. [13]

obscene   Related to sexually themed publications, art, films, performances, or behavior that is deemed offensive to public morals or that violates legal standards of acceptability. [17]

obsessive relational intrusion   Obsessive pursuit of a person by a rejected lover. [7, 16]

obsessive relational intrusion   Obsessive pursuit of a person by a rejected lover. [16]

obsessive-compulsive disorder (OCD)   A mental disorder marked by anxiety, repetitive thoughts or urges, and behaviors that temporarily relieve those urges. [13]

Onuf's nucleus   A sexually dimorphic group of motor neurons in the sacral segments of the spinal cord that innervates striated muscles associated with the penis and clitoris. [App. B]

oral herpes   Herpes infection of the mouth, caused by HSV-1 or (less commonly) HSV-2. [15]

orchitis   Inflammation of a testicle. [3]

orgasm   The intense, pleasurable sensations at sexual climax, and the physiological processes that accompany them. [5]

orgasmic platform   The outer portion of the vagina and surrounding tissues, which thickens and tenses during sexual arousal. [5]

Ortho Evra   A contraceptive patch. [9]

os   The opening in the cervix that connects the vagina with the cervical canal. [2]

osteoporosis   Reduction in the mineral content of bone, predisposing an individual to fractures. [11]

outer labia (or labia majora)   Fleshy skin folds, partially covered in pubic hair, that extend from the mons. [2]

outercourse   Sexual activities other than coitus, promoted as a means for preventing unwanted pregnancy and reducing the risk of STI transmission. [6, 9]

ovarian cysts   Cysts within the ovary that can arise from a number of different causes. [2]

ovary   The female gonad; the organ that produces ova and secretes sex hormones. [2]

oviduct   Either of two bilateral tubes that lead from the uterus toward the ovaries, the usual site of fertilization. Also called a fallopian tube. [2]

ovulation   Release of an ovum from an ovary. [2]

ovum (pl. ova)   A mature female gamete, or egg, prior to or immediately after fertilization. [2, App. A]

oxytocin   A hormone secreted by the pituitary gland that stimulates uterine contractions and the secretion of milk. [5]

P

pair bond   A durable sexual relationship between two individuals. [App. A]

pansexuality   Sexual attraction to persons of any sex or gender. [12]

Pap test   The microscopic examination of a sample of cells taken from the cervix or (less commonly) the anus. [2]

Paragard   A copper-containing IUD. [9]

paraphilia   A persistent, intense sexual desire or behavior that is uncommon or unusual. [13]

paraphilic disorder   A paraphilia that causes distress or harms others. [13]

paraphimosis   Entrapment of the retracted foreskin behind the corona. [3]

paraplegia   Paralysis affecting the lower half of the body. [6]

parasympathetic nervous system   A division of the autonomic nervous system; among other functions, its activity promotes erection of the penis and clitoris. [App. B]

paraurethral glands   Glands situated next to the female urethra, thought to be equivalent to the prostate gland in males. Also known as Skene's glands. [2]

parthenogenesis   Asexual reproduction from an unfertilized ovum; "virgin birth." [App. A]

partialism   A fetishistic attraction to a specific part of the body. [13]

partible paternity   The belief that two or more men may be fathers of the same child. [1]

parturition   Delivery of offspring; childbirth. [8]

passion   The overwhelming feeling of attraction typical of the early stage of a loving relationship. [7]

paternity test   A test to identify an individual's father by DNA analysis. [App. A]

pedophile   A person whose sexual feelings are directed mainly toward prepubescent children. [13]

pedophilic disorder   Pedophilia that causes distress or that is expressed in sexual contacts with children. [13]

pelvic examination A visual and digital examination of the vulva and pelvic organs. [2]

pelvic floor muscles A muscular sling that underlies and supports the pelvic organs. [2]

pelvic inflammatory disease (PID) An infection of the female reproductive tract, often caused by sexually transmitted organisms. [2, 8, 15]

pelvic nerves Nerves that convey parasympathetic signals from the lower spinal cord to the genitalia and other organs. [App. B]

penile bulb An expansion of the corpus spongiosum at the root of the penis. [3]

penile implant An implanted device for treatment of erectile disorder. [14]

penis The erectile, erotically sensitive genital organ in males. [3]

perfect-use failure rate The percentage of women using a contraceptive technique correctly who will become pregnant in the course of one year. [9]

perimenopause The phase prior to menopause that is marked by irregular menstrual cycles. [11]

perimetrium The outer covering of the uterus. [2]

perineal massage Manual stretching of the perineum in preparation for childbirth. [8]

perineum The region of skin between the anus and the vulva or scrotum. [2]

peripheral nervous system The motor and sensory connections between the central nervous system and peripheral structures such as muscles and sense organs. [App. B]

persistent genital arousal disorder Long-lasting physiological arousal in women, unaccompanied by subjective arousal or pleasure. [14]

personality The collection of mental and behavioral traits, especially those related to emotions and attitudes, which characterizes an individual. [4]

perversion An obsolete term for atypical sexual desire or behavior, viewed as a mental disorder. [1]

petting Sexually touching the partner's body (often taken to exclude the breasts or genitalia). [6]

Peyronie's disease Pathological curvature of the penis. [3]

pheromone A volatile compound that is released by one organism and that triggers a specific behavior in another member of the same species. [App. A]

phimosis A tightening of the foreskin, preventing its retraction from the glans. [3]

phone sex Erotic telephone conversations, usually carried out for pay. [17]

pimp A man who manages prostitutes in exchange for part of their earnings. [17]

pituitary gland A gland under the control of and situated below the hypothalamus; its anterior lobe secretes gonadotropins and other hormones. [2]

placenta previa An abnormally low position of the placenta, such that it partially or completely covers the internal opening of the cervix. [8]

placenta The vascular organ, formed during pregnancy, that allows for the supply of oxygen and nutrients to the fetus and the removal of waste products. [8]

Plan B One-Step A progestin used for emergency contraception. [9]

plateau phase The phase of the sexual response cycle during which arousal is maintained at a high level. [5]

polyamory The formation of nontransient sexual relationships in groups of three or more. [11]

polyandry The marriage or mating of one female with more than one male. [11, App. A]

polycystic ovary syndrome (PCOS) A condition marked by excessive secretion of androgens by the ovaries. [2]

polygamy Marriage to or (mostly in animals) mating with more than one partner. [1, 11, App. A]

polygyny The marriage or mating of one male with more than one female. [11, App. A]

pons A region of the brain above the medulla. [App. B]

pornography Material (such as art, writing, photographic images, and film) that is intended to be sexually arousing. Also called *porn*. [17]

post-exposure prophylaxis (PEP) A drug treatment designed to prevent establishment of an infection after exposure to a disease agent such as HIV. [15]

post-traumatic stress disorder (PTSD) A cluster of physical and psychological symptoms that can affect persons who have experienced severe trauma. [10]

postganglionic neuron A neuron with its cell body in an autonomic ganglion and an axon that innervates glands or smooth muscles in a peripheral organ such as the genitalia. [App. B]

postmenopausal hormone therapy Hormone treatment extending for a long time after menopause. [11]

postnuptial agreement A financial agreement between spouses. [11]

postovulatory phase The phase of the menstrual cycle between ovulation and the beginning of menstruation. [2]

postpartum depression Depression in a mother during the postpartum phase. [8]

postpartum depressive psychosis Postpartum depression accompanied by seriously disordered thinking. [8]

postpartum period The period after birth. [8]

pre-exposure prophylaxis (PrEP) A drug taken before exposure to a disease agent to prevent infection. [15]

preadolescence The age range including the beginning of puberty, from approximately age 8 to 12 or 13 years. [10]

precocious puberty Puberty that begins earlier than normal. [10]

preconception care Medical care and counseling provided to women before they become pregnant. [8]

preganglionic neuron An autonomic motor neuron in the spinal cord. [App. B]

preimplantation genetic screening (PGS) Testing of in vitro fertilization embryos for genetic defects prior to implantation. [8]

premature birth (or preterm birth) Birth that occurs more than 3 weeks before a woman's due date. [8]

premature ejaculation Ejaculation before the man wishes, often immediately on commencement of coitus. Also called *rapid ejaculation*. [6, 14]

premenstrual dysphoric disorder PMS-associated mood changes that are severe enough to interfere with relationships [2]

premenstrual syndrome (PMS) A collection of physical and/or psychological symptoms that may start a few days before the menstrual period begins and continue into the period. [2]

prenatal care Medical care and counseling provided to pregnant women. [8]

prenuptial agreement A contract signed before marriage, spelling out the disposition of wealth in the event of divorce. [11]

preovulatory phase The phase of the menstrual cycle during which follicles are developing in the ovaries. [2]

priapism A persistent penile erection in the absence of sexual arousal. [3]

primary amenorrhea The failure to begin menstruating at puberty. [2, 10]

primary disorder A disorder that is not preceded by any period of healthy function. [14]

primary dysmenorrhea Painful menstruation that begins at puberty and has no clear cause. [2]

primary syphilis The first phase of syphilis, marked by the occurrence of a chancre. [15]

pro-choice Believing that abortion should be legal under some or all circumstances. [9]

pro-life Opposed to abortion; believing that abortion should be illegal under most or all circumstances. [9]

proceptive behavior Behavior by females that may elicit sexual advances by males. [App. A]

progesterone A steroid hormone secreted by the ovary and the placenta; it is necessary for the establishment and maintenance of pregnancy. [2]

progestin-only pill An oral contraceptive that contains progestin but no estrogen. Also called the "mini-pill." [9]

progestins Any of a class of steroids, the most important being progesterone, that cause the endometrium to proliferate and help maintain pregnancy. [2]

prolactin A protein hormone, secreted by the anterior lobe of the pituitary gland, that promotes breast development, among other effects. [8]

prolapse The slipping out of place of an organ, such as the uterus. [2]

promiscuity Engaging in numerous casual or short-lived sexual relationships. [App. A]

prostaglandin E1 A hormone that is injected into the penis to produce an erection. [14]

prostate cancer Cancer of the prostate gland. [3]

prostate gland A single gland located at the base of the bladder that surrounds the urethra; its secretions are a component of semen. [3]

prostate-specific antigen (PSA) An enzyme secreted by the prostate gland; its presence at high levels in the blood is suggestive of, but not diagnostic of, prostate cancer. [3]

prostatitis Inflammation of the prostate gland; may be acute or chronic. [3]

prosthesis An artificial replacement for a body part. [2]

prostitution The practice of engaging in sex for pay. [17]

psychology The study of mental processes and behavior. [1]

puberty The biological transition that confers the capacity to be a parent. [10]

pubic hair Hair that appears on portions of the external genitalia in both sexes at puberty. [2]

pubic lice Insects (*Phthirus pubis*) that preferentially infest the pubic region. [15]

pubococcygeus muscle A muscle of the pelvic floor that runs from the pubic bone to the coccyx (tailbone). In women it forms a sling around the vagina. [2]

pudendal nerves Peripheral nerves supplying the external genitalia. [App. B]

pulmonary surfactant A compound produced in the fetal lung that reduces surface tension and thus facilitates inflation of the lungs with air at birth. [8]

Q

quadriplegia Paralysis affecting almost the entire body below the neck. [6]

quickening The onset of movements by the fetus that can be felt by the mother. [8]

quid pro quo harassment Unwelcome sexual advances, usually made to a worker in a subordinate position, accompanied by promises or threats. [16]

quinceañera Hispanic coming-of-age ceremony for girls. [10]

R

radical prostatectomy Surgical removal of the entire prostate gland and local lymph nodes. [3]

rape shield laws Laws that protect rape victims, for example, by limiting the introduction of evidence about their prior sexual behavior. [16]

rape trauma syndrome A cluster of persistent physical and psychological symptoms seen in rape victims; comparable to post-traumatic stress disorder. [16]

rape Coitus (and sometimes other penetrative sex acts) accomplished by force or the threat of force. [16]

real-life experience A period of living in the role of the other sex as a prelude to sex reassignment. [4]

recidivism The tendency of convicted offenders to reoffend. [13]

rectum The final, straight portion of the large bowel. It connects to the exterior via the anus. [2, 6]

refractory period In males, a period of reduced or absent sexual arousability after orgasm. [5]

relapse prevention therapy Therapy aimed at training a person to avoid or cope with situations that trigger the undesirable behavior. [13]

reportable disease A disease, cases of which must by law be reported to health authorities. [15]

reproductive tract The internal anatomical structures in either sex that form the pathway taken by ova, sperm, or the conceptus. [2]

resolution phase The phase of the sexual response cycle during which physiological arousal subsides. [5]

retrovirus An RNA virus whose genome is copied into DNA within the host cell. [15]

Rh factor An antigen on the surface of red blood cells that, when present in a fetus but not in its mother, may trigger an immune response by the mother, resulting in life-threatening anemia of the fetus or newborn. [8]

rubella German measles, a viral infection that can cause developmental defects in fetuses whose mothers contract the disease during pregnancy. [8]

S

sadism Sexual arousal by the infliction of pain, bondage, or humiliation on others, or by witnessing the recipient's suffering. [13]

sadomasochism (S/M) The infliction and acceptance of pain or humiliation as a means of sexual arousal. [13]

saline-induced abortion An abortion induced by use of a strong salt solution. [9]

scabies Infestation with a mite (*Sarcoptes scabiei*) that burrows within the skin. [15]

script theory The analysis of sexual and other behaviors as the enactment of socially instilled roles. [1]

scrotum The sac behind the penis that contains the testicles. [3, App. A]

Seasonale An extended-use contraceptive pill. [9]

Seasonique An extended-use contraceptive pill. [9]

secondary amenorrhea The cessation of menstruation at some time after menarche. [10]

secondary disorder A disorder that follows some period of healthy function. [14]

secondary dysmenorrhea Painful menstruation that begins during adult life, usually as a consequence of a pelvic disorder. [2]

secondary sexual characteristics Anatomical characteristics, such as breasts and facial hair, that generally differ between the sexes but are not used to define an individual's sex. [2]

secondary syphilis The second phase of syphilis, marked by a rash and fever. [15]

selection effect An effect caused by preexisting differences between subject groups. [11]

selective serotonin reuptake inhibitors (SSRIs) A class of drugs, including antidepressants such as Prozac and Lexapro, that depress sexual function. [13]

semen The fluid, containing sperm and a variety of chemical compounds, that is discharged from the penis (ejaculated) at the male sexual climax. [3, App. A]

seminal nurture The belief that fetuses require repeated infusions of semen to grow. [6]

seminal vesicles Two glands situated to either side of the prostate; their secretions are a component of semen. [3]

seminiferous tubules Convoluted microscopic tubes within the testicle; the site of sperm production. [3]

sensate focus A form of sex therapy that involves graduated touching exercises. [14]

serial monogamy Engagement in a series of monogamous relationships. [7 10]

serial orgasms Two or more orgasms with no more than a few seconds between them. [5]

seroconversion The change from negative to positive on an antibody test, such as occurs a few weeks or months after HIV infection. [15]

sex addiction The idea that a person may be addicted to sexual behavior by a mechanism similar to that of substance addiction. [14]

sex chromosome Either of a pair of chromosomes (X or Y in mammals) that differ between the sexes. [4, App. A]

sex determination The biological mechanism that determines whether an organism will develop as a male or a female. [App. A]

sex pheromones Chemical signals released by an animal that influence the sexual behavior or physiological state of other individuals of the same species. [5]

sex play A variety of playful activities that add pleasure to sexual interactions. [6]

sex steroid Any of the steroid hormones that are active in sexual and reproductive processes. [2]

sex therapist A person who treats sexual disorders, usually by means of psychotherapy and sexual exercises. [14]

sex tourism Traveling to a foreign country to find sex partners (usually prostitutes). [17]

sex trader A person who exchanges sex for money, drugs, or other benefits; a broader term than "prostitute." [17]

sex trafficking Transportation of a person for the purpose of prostitution. [17]

sex worker A person who engages in prostitution, pornography, or another sex-related occupation. [17]

sex-reassignment surgery Surgery to change a person's genitals or other sexual characteristics. [4]

sex A person's identity as female or male, or sexual behavior. [1]

sexology The scientific study of sex and sexual disorders. [1]

sexting Sending sexually explicit text or images via mobile phone. [3]

sexual assault Coercive or nonconsensual sexual contact: a broader category of behaviors than rape. [16]

sexual dimorphisms An anatomical difference between the sexes. [App. B]

sexual harassment Unwanted sexual advances or other intimidating sexual behavior, usually in the workplace. [16]

sexual intercourse Sexual contact, usually understood to involve coitus. [2]

sexual interest/arousal disorder Lack of interest in sex or insufficient sexual arousal, when it causes distress. [14]

sexual jealousy Fear that one's partner is engaging in sexual contacts with another person. [7]

sexual monogamy The formation of pair-bonds or marriages that are sexually exclusive. [7, App. A]

sexual orientation The direction of an individual's sexual feelings: sexual attraction toward persons of the opposite sex (heterosexual), the same sex (homosexual), or both sexes (bisexual). [1, 4, 12]

sexual reproduction Reproduction in which the offspring inherit genes from two parents. [App. A]

sexual response cycle The sequence of physiological processes that accompany sexual behavior. [5]

sexual sadism disorder Sexual arousal by the suffering of others, viewed as a paraphilic disorder. [13]

sexual script A socially negotiated role that guides sexual behavior. [4]

sexual selection The evolution of traits under the pressure of competition for mates or of choice by mates. [App. A]

sexual webcamming Live sexual performances or nudity supplied over the Internet for pay. [17]

sexuality The feelings, behaviors, and identities associated with sex. [1]

sexually explicit materials A nonjudgmental phrase denoting pornography. [17]

sinusoid A vascular space, such as within erectile tissue, capable of being expanded by filling with blood. [3, App. B]

situational disorder A disorder that appears only in certain circumstances. [14]

Skyla A hormone-releasing IUD that is effective for 3 years. [9]

smegma A whitish, greasy secretion that builds up under the foreskin of the penis or the clitoral hood. [2, 3]

social monogamy The formation of pair-bonds, or marriages between two persons, that may or may not be sexually exclusive. [7, App. A]

social psychology The study of one's relationship to others. [1]

sociology The scientific study of society. [1]

sociosexuality Interest or engagement in sex without commitment. [4, 7]

soft-core Related to relatively nonexplicit pornography. [17]

softening The elimination of connective tissue from the cervix, allowing it to thin out and dilate during labor. Also called *ripening*. [8]

sperm (or spermatozoon; pl. spermatozoa) The male gamete, produced in the testicles. [App. A, 3]

sperm bank A facility that collects, stores, and provides semen for artificial insemination. [8]

spermatic cord Either of two bilateral bundles of structures, including the vas deferens, blood vessels, and the cremaster muscle, that pass through the inguinal canal to a testicle. [3]

spermatogenesis The production of sperm. [3]

spermicide A chemical that kills sperm, available as a contraceptive in a variety of forms, such as foams, creams, and suppositories. [9]

sphincter A circular muscle around a tube or orifice whose contraction closes it. [2, 6]

spina bifida A congenital malformation caused by incomplete closure of the neural tube. [8]

spinal cord The portion of the central nervous system within the vertebral column. [App. B]

spirochete Any of a class of corkscrew-shaped bacteria, including the agent that causes syphilis. [15]

SRY A gene located on the Y chromosome (*Sex-determining Region of the Y* chromosome) that causes the embryo to develop as a male. [4]

stalking Obsessive pursuit of a previous, current, or desired sex partner in such a way as to put that person in a state of fear. [7, 16]

standard days method A simplified fertility awareness calendar method of contraception usable by women with regular cycles. [9]

statutory rape Penetrative sex when a partner is legally unable to give consent on account of young age, intellectual disability, or unconsciousness. [16]

stereotype A common opinion about a class of people that is false or overgeneralized. [4]

sterilization A surgical procedure to eliminate fertility in either sex. [9]

stillbirth The delivery of a dead fetus late in pregnancy. [9]

stop-start method A sex therapy technique for the treatment of premature ejaculation that involves alternating between stimulating and not stimulating the penis. [14]

straight Colloquial term for heterosexual. [12]

subfertility Difficulty in establishing a pregnancy; arbitrarily defined as the absence of pregnancy after a couple has had frequent unprotected sex for 12 months. [8]

submission Taking the subservient role in BDSM activity. [13]

suitor A person who is seeking to establish a romantic relationship with another. [7]

sunnah Female genital cutting limited to incision or removal of the clitoral hood. [2]

super peer theory The idea that teens learn from glamorous teen role models in the media. [10]

surgical abortion An abortion induced by a surgical procedure. [9]

surrogate mother A woman who carries a pregnancy on behalf of another woman or couple. [8]

swingers Couples who agree to engage in casual sexual contacts with others. [11]

sympathetic nervous system A division of the autonomic nervous system; among other functions, its activity inhibits penile erection but helps trigger ejaculation. [App. B]

sympto-thermal method A fertility awareness method of contraception that depends on the measurement of basal body temperature and the testing of cervical mucus. [9]

synapse A junction where signals are transmitted between neurons or from neurons to muscle fibers. [App. B]

synaptic cleft The narrow space between two neurons at a synapse. [App. B]

syphilis A sexually transmitted infection caused by a spirochete, *Treponema pallidum*. [15]

T

telephone scatalogia Sexual arousal from making obscene telephone calls. [13]

tertiary syphilis The third phase of syphilis, marked by multiple organ damage. [15]

testicle (or testis; pl. testes) The male gonad: one of the two glands within the scrotum that produce sperm and secrete sex hormones. [3]

testicular torsion Twisting of a testicle that cuts off its blood supply. [3]

testosterone The principal androgen, synthesized in the testes and, in lesser amounts, in the ovaries and adrenal glands. [2, 3]

thalamus The uppermost region of the brainstem. [App. B]

therapeutic abortion An abortion performed to safeguard a woman's life or health. [9]

third-party sexual harassment   Indirect negative effects of sexual harassment on other employees, or sexual harassment by non-employees. [16]

trabeculae   Connective tissue partitions separating the sinusoids of erectile tissue. [App. B]

transexual (or transsexual)   A person who identifies with the other sex and who seeks to transition to the other sex by means of hormone treatment and sex-reassignment surgery. [4]

transgender (or trans)   Having a gender identity that is not fully congruent with one's birth sex. Identifying with the other sex or rejecting gender norms. [1, 4]

transition   The final phase of dilation of the cervix during labor. [8]

transitioning   Changing one's physical sex and social gender. [4]

transphobia   Hatred of transgender people. [4]

transvestism   Wearing clothes of the other sex for purposes of sexual arousal. The term is sometimes applied to cross-dressing for any reason. [4, 13]

tribadism   Sexual behavior between two women, who lie front to front and stimulate each other's vulvas with thrusting motions. [6]

trichomoniasis (or "trich")   Infection with the protozoan *Trichomonas vaginalis*. [15]

trimester   One of three 3-month divisions of pregnancy. [8]

triphasic combination pill   An oral contraceptive regimen that varies the doses of estrogens and progestins around the menstrual cycle. [9]

triple-X syndrome   A collection of traits caused by the possession, in a female, of three X chromosomes rather than two. [4]

tubal ligation   A procedure in which the oviducts are blocked by tying them off. [9]

tubal sterilization   Any procedure that prevents sperm transport in the oviducts. [9]

Turner syndrome   A collection of traits caused by the possession of one X and no Y chromosome. [4]

two-spirit person   In Native American cultures, a person with the spirit of both a man and a woman; a transgender person. Also called *berdache*. [4]

typical-use failure rate   The percentage of women using a contraceptive technique with a typical degree of care who will become pregnant in the course of one year. [9]

U

ultrasound scan   An imaging procedure that depends on the reflection of ultrasonic waves from density boundaries within the body. Also called *ultrasonographic scan*. [8]

unrequited love   Love that is not reciprocated. [7]

urethra   The canal that conveys urine from the bladder to the urethral opening. [2]

urethral folds   Folds of ectodermal tissue in the embryo that give rise to the inner labia (in females) or the shaft of the penis (in males). [4]

urethritis   Inflammation of the urethra, usually caused by an infection. [15]

urogenital sinus   The common opening of the urinary and genital systems in the embryo. [4]

uterus   The womb; a pear-shaped region of the female reproductive tract through which sperm pass and where the conceptus implants and develops. [2]

V

vacuum aspiration   An abortion procedure in which the conceptus is destroyed and removed by suction. [9]

vacuum constriction system   A device for treating erectile disorder that creates a partial vacuum around the penis, thus drawing blood into the erectile tissue. [14]

vagina   A muscular tube extending 3 to 4 inches (8 to 10 cm) from the vestibule to the uterine cervix. [2]

vaginal dilator   A plastic cylinder used to enlarge the vagina or to counteract vaginismus. [14]

vaginismus   Inability to experience coitus due to spasm of the muscles surrounding the outer vagina combined with pain, or fear of pain. [14]

varicocele   Enlargement of the veins that drain the testicle. [3]

vas deferens (pl. vasa deferentia)   Either of the two bilateral ducts that convey sperm from the epididymis to the ejaculatory duct. [3]

vasectomy   A male sterilization technique that involves cutting or tying off the vas deferens from each testicle. [9]

vasocongestion   The swelling of tissue caused by an influx of blood to local blood vessels. [2, 5]

vasomotor control   The physiological regulation of peripheral blood flow. [11]

vasovasostomy   Surgery to reverse a vasectomy. [9]

venereal disease   Obsolete term for a sexually transmitted infection. [15]

ventral horn   The portion of the gray matter of the spinal cord nearer to the front of the body, where motor neurons are located. [App. B]

ventral root   A bundle of motor axons that leaves a ventral horn of the spinal cord. [App. B]

vestibular bulbs   Erectile structures beneath the inner labia, on either side of the vestibule. [2]

vestibule   The potential space between the left and right inner labia. [2]

vibrator   An electrically powered vibrating device used to provide sexual stimulation. [6]

virginity-pledge programs   Programs in which teens take formal pledges not to have sex before marriage. [10]

virus   An extremely small infectious agent. When not inside a host cell, viruses are metabolically inert but infectious. [15]

vomeronasal organ (VNO)   A special sense organ within the nose that many mammals possess, which is specialized for the detection of pheromones. [5]

voyeurism   Sexual arousal by watching persons while they are undressing, naked, or engaged in sex. [13]

vulva   The female external genitalia. [2, App. A]

vulvodynia   Painful sensitivity of the vulva to touch. [14]

W

waist-to-hip ratio (WHR)   The ratio of the circumference of the body at the waist to the circumference at the hip. [5]

wet nurse   A woman who breast-feeds someone else's infant. [8]

white matter   A region of the central nervous system that contains bundles of axons but no neuronal cell bodies. [App. B]

withdrawal method   A method of contraception in which the man withdraws his penis from the vagina prior to ejaculation. [9]

Wolffian duct   Either of two bilateral ducts in the embryo that give rise to the male reproductive tract. [4]

X

X chromosome   A sex chromosome that is present as two copies in females and one copy in males. [4, App. A]

XYY syndrome   A collection of traits caused by the possession, in a male, of an extra Y chromosome. [4]

Y

Y chromosome   A sex chromosome that is present only in males. [4, App. A]

Z

zoophilia   A persistent preference for sexual contacts with animals. [13]

zygote   A cell formed by the fusion of gametes; a fertilized ovum. [App. A]

Photo Credits

of Women's Capital Corporation. **9.22:** © David Kadlubowski/ Corbis. **Box 9.1:** © Rolex Dela Pena/epa/Corbis. **Box 9.4:** Courtesy of Dave Fayram/Flickr. **Box 9.5:** © Associated Press. **p. 268:** David McIntyre. **p. 279:** © Norbert Bieberstein/istock. **p. 280:** David McIntyre. **p. 285:** © Thomas Pullicino/istock. **p. 288:** © Ingram Publishing (Superstock Limited)/Alamy. **p. 299:** © Associated Press.

CHAPTER 10 *Opener:* © moodboard/Corbis. **10.1:** © Owen Franken/Corbis. **10.2:** Courtesy of Devadarshan Gurumayum. **10.4–10.6:** From van Wieringen et al., 1971. **10.7:** © Medical-on-Line/Alamy. **10.8:** © UKraft/Alamy. **Box 10.1:** © Tomas Abad/ Alamy. **Box 10.2A:** © Bettmann/Corbis. **Box 10.2B:** © Jodi Hilton/ Pool/Reuters/Corbis. **Box 10.3:** Courtesy of Kathy Pickus, Dot Girl Products. **p. 306:** © Paz Ruiz Luque/istock. **p. 307** *bottom:* © YouraPechkin/Shutterstock. **p. 322:** © Siphiwe Sibeko/Reuters/ Corbis. **p. 324:** © Asaf Hanuka. **p. 329:** © Ammentorp Photography/Alamy. **p. 330:** © Karen Kasmauski/Corbis.

CHAPTER 11 *Opener:* © MBI/Alamy. **11.4** *left:* © Interfoto/Alamy. **11.4** *right:* © RubberBall/Alamy. **11.6A:** © Tracy Kahn/Corbis. **11.10A:** © Science VU/Visuals Unlimited, Inc. **11.10B:** Courtesy of Dr. Geoffrey Higgs/Advanced Orthopaedic Centers. **11.13B:** © Darren Modricker/Corbis. **Box 11.1:** © Associated Press. **Box 11.3:** © AP Photo/Mike Wintroath. **Box 11.4:** © Ron McGinnis. **Box 11.5:** © LWA-Dann Tardif/Corbis. **p. 336:** © Radius Images/Alamy. **p. 338:** © Splash News/Corbis. **p. 340:** © China Photos/Getty Images. **p. 351** *top:* © Hill Street Studios/Blend Images/Corbis. **p. 351** *bottom:* © Denise Truscello/WireImage/Getty Images. **p. 353:** © Ariel Skelley/Blend Images/Corbis. **p. 357:** © Radius Images/ Alamy.

CHAPTER 12 *Opener:* © Viviane Moos/Corbis. **12.2:** © Fox Photos/ Stringer/Getty Images. **12.5B:** Courtesy of Simon LeVay. **12.6:** Courtesy of Ivanka Savic. **12.7:** © Globe Photos/Zuma Press. **12.8:** © Bettmann/Corbis. **12.11:** © Pablo Martinez Monsivais/AP/ Corbis. **12.12** *left:* Courtesy of the U.S. Senate. **12.12** *right:* © USA Today Sports/Reuters/Corbis. **12.13:** © OFF WHITE PRODUC-TIONS/Ronald Grant Archive/Alamy. **12.14:** © 2001, Amabear Publishing, Inc. All Rights Reserved. Used with permission. **12.15:** © Associated Press. **Box 12.2:** © Heritage Image Partnership Ltd/ Alamy. **Box 12.3A:** © Roger Ressmeyer/Corbis. **Box 12.3B:** From *Call Me Kuchu*, 2012, Wright Film Company. © AF archive/Alamy. **Box 12.4:** © Qwaves, LLC. **Box 12.5:** © David Pierini/Chicago Tribune/Zuma Press. **p. 382:** Courtesy of the Human Rights Campaign. **p. 394:** © Andrew Snook/Corbis. **p. 395:** © Zuma Press, Inc./Alamy.

CHAPTER 13 *Opener:* © Roy Botterell/Corbis. **13.1:** © 2005 Katharine Gates/deviantdesires.com. **13.3:** © Barry Bland/Fame Pictures, Inc. **13.4:** © Interfoto/Alamy. **13.5:** © Jack Picone/Alamy. **13.7:** From *The Hours of Louis XII.* **13.11:** From www.meganslaw. ca.gov. **13.14:** © UPPA/Zuma Press. **13.15:** © Associated Press. **13.16:** © Associated Press. **Box 13.1:** © Christian Charisius/ Reuters/Corbis. **Box 13.2:** © Eddie Gerald/Alamy. **Box 13.3:** Courtesy of the Massachusetts Bay Transportation Authority. **Box 13.4:** © Sunshine/Zuma Press. **p. 402:** © Mark Peterson/Corbis. **p. 406:** © PYMCA/Alamy. **p. 407:** Courtesy of the Society for the Second Self, Inc. **p. 417:** © Associated Press. **p. 418:** © David Jennings/ Alamy. **p. 420** *bottom:* © Elaine Thompson/Pool/Reuters/Corbis.

CHAPTER 14 *Opener:* © Agencja FREE/Alamy. **14.6A:** Courtesy of Endocare, Inc. **14.8:** Courtesy of UroMetrics, Inc. **14.9B:** Photo

by Judy Summers, courtesy of Intelligence Engineering, LLC, all rights reserved. **Box 14.4:** © Image Source/Corbis. **p. 433:** © Ned Frisk/Blend/Photolibrary. **p. 438:** © [apply pictures]/Alamy. **p. 443:** David McIntyre. **p. 450:** © RazoomGame/Shutterstock. **p. 452** *top:* © Lori Moffett/Bloomberg, pool/Retna Ltd./Corbis. **p. 452** *bottom:* © Suzanne Plunkett/Reuters/Corbis.

CHAPTER 15 *Opener:* © Jeffrey Markowitz/Sygma/Corbis. **15.1:** © Oliver Meckes/Science Source. **15.2** *left:* © Eye of Science/Science Source. **15.2** *right:* © Dr. P. Marazzi/Science Source. **15.3:** © Dr. David M. Phillips/Visuals Unlimited, Inc. **15.4:** © Kallista Images/ SuperStock/Corbis. **15.5:** © SPL/Science Source. **15.6:** © Martin M. Rotker/Science Source. **15.7:** © Lester V. Bergman/Corbis. **15.9:** © Biomedical Imaging Unit, Southampton General Hospital/Science Source. **15.10A:** Courtesy of the Geneva Foundation for Medical Education and Research, www.gfmer.ch. **15.10B:** Courtesy the Seattle STD/HIV Prevention Training Center and the University of Washington. **15.11:** © Medical-on-Line/Alamy. **15.12:** Dr. Fred Murphy; Sylvia Whitfield/CDC. **15.13A:** © Biophoto Associates/ Science Source. **15.13B:** © Lester V. Bergman/Corbis. **15.14:** © Dr. P. Marazzi/Science Source. **15.15:** Courtesy of the Geneva Foundation for Medical Education and Research, www.gfmer.ch. **15.16:** © Medical-on-Line/Alamy. **15.17:** © Eye of Science/Science Source. **15.20A:** © Jeff Greenberg/Alamy. **15.20B:** Photo by Jason Moore/ ZUMA Press/Alamy. © Copyright 2006 by Jason Moore. **15.20C:** © Getty Images/Handout. **15.21A:** © Dr. P. Marazzi/Science Source. **15.21B:** Courtesy of Kissekatt/Wikipedia. **15.21C:** © Dr. Daniel Logen/Visuals Unlimited, Inc. **15.21D:** David McIntyre. **Box 15.1:** Courtesy of the Department of Health, Education, and Welfare/ Centers for Disease Control. **p. 462:** Courtesy the National Library of Medicine. **p. 487:** © Eliseo Fernandez/Reuters/Corbis.

CHAPTER 16 *Opener:* © Jack Carey/Alamy. **16.4A:** © Loop Images Ltd/Alamy. **16.4B:** © Rick Friedman/Corbis. **Box 16.1:** © Max Whittaker/Prime Collective. **Box 16.2:** © Frances Roberts/Alamy. **Box 16.3:** Courtesy of Men Can Stop Rape. **Box 16.4:** © Reuters/ Corbis. **p. 496:** © Bob Mahoney/Time Life Pictures/Getty Images. **p. 500** *bottom:* © SCPhotos/Alamy. **p. 508:** © blickwinkel/Alamy. **p. 511:** © Mike Stotts/Zuma Press/Corbis. **p. 515:** © Sven Hagolani/Corbis. **p. 516:** Courtesy of the Illinois Department of Human Rights. **p. 518:** © Beth Herzhaft/Corbis.

CHAPTER 17 *Opener:* © Graham Prentice/Alamy. **17.1:** © Arte & Immagini srl/Corbis. **17.2:** © ZUMA Press, Inc/Alamy. **17.3:** © Ximena Griscti/Alamy. **17.7:** © Christina Koci Hernandez/San Francisco Chronicle/Corbis. **17.8:** Reproduced with permission of Arrow Productions. **17.10:** Courtesy Pink & White Productions (pinkwhite.biz). **17.11:** © Bettmann/Corbis. **Box 17.2:** © Jürgen Horn/for91days.com. **Box 17.3:** © Chris Matula/Palm Beach Post/Zuma Press. **Box 17.4:** © George Steinmetz/Corbis. **p. 530:** © Arnd Wiegmann/Reuters/Corbis. **p. 535:** © Jack Fields/Corbis.

APPENDIX A **A.1:** © Dr. David Phillips/Visuals Unlimited, Inc. **A.4:** © blickwinkel/Alamy. **A.6:** © Roger Munns/Alamy. **A.8:** © National Geographic Image Collection/Alamy. **A.9:** © Henri Faure/istock. **A.10:** © Dave Watts/Alamy. **A.11:** © Jochen Tack/ imageBROKER/AGE Fotostock. **A.12:** © Peter David/Getty Images. **A.13:** Courtesy of John Alcock. **A.14:** © Mint/Frans Lanting/AGE Fotostock.

APPENDIX B **B.2A:** © Biophoto Associates/Science Source.

References

Numbers in brackets refer to the chapter(s) where the reference is cited.

AAHCC. (2014). *The Bradley method.* (www.bradleybirth.com) [8]

AAP Task Force on Circumcision. (2012). Circumcision policy statement. *Pediatrics, 130,* 585–586. [3]

Abbott, E. (2011). *A history of marriage.* Seven Stories. [1]

ABC News. (2004). *Primetime live poll: The American Sex Survey.* (abcnews.go.com/images/Politics/959a1AmericanSexSurvey.pdf) [7]

ABC News. (2005). *Tables: Births and deaths by month, 1995–2002.* (abcnews.go.com/Health/Science/story?id=990641) [6]

ABC News. (2011a). *Phoenix Goddess Temple raided as alleged brothel.* (abcnews.go.com/US/phoenix-goddess-temple-raided-alleged-brothel/story?id=14481945) [17]

ABC News. (2011b). *Woman gets $6.7 million in herpes lawsuit.* (abcnews.go.com/US/california-court-upholds-67-million-award-herpes-lawsuit/story?id=13159756) [15]

ABC News. (2012). *Straight single men, wanting kids, turn to surrogacy.* (abcnews.go.com/US/straight-single-men-wanting-kids-turn-surrogacy/story?id=16520916) [8]

Abel, G. G. & Osborn, C. A. (2000). The paraphilias. In: Gelder, M. G., et al. (Eds.), *New Oxford textbook of psychiatry.* Oxford University Press. [13]

Abell, A., Ernst, E. & Bonde, J. P. (2000). Semen quality and sexual hormones in greenhouse workers. *Scandinavian Journal of Work and Environmental Health, 26,* 492–500. [8]

Abramson, P. R. & Pinkerton, S. D. (2002). *With pleasure: Thoughts on the nature of human sexuality* (rev. ed.). Oxford University Press. [2]

ACLU. (2005). *ACLU and former 911 dispatcher file lawsuit challenging North Carolina anti-cohabitation law.* (www.aclu.org/womens-rights/aclu-and-former-911-dispatcher-file-lawsuit-challenging-north-carolina-anti-cohabitati) [11]

Adams Hillard, P. J. (2003). *Imperforate hymen.* (www.emedicine.com/med/topic3329.htm) [2]

Adams, H. E., Wright, L. W., Jr. & Lohr, B. A. (1996). Is homophobia associated with homosexual arousal? *Journal of Abnormal Psychology, 105,* 440–445. [12]

Advocate.com. (2012). *Pa. school settles AIDS discrimination lawsuit for $700K.* (www.advocate.com/society/education/2012/09/12/school-pay-700k-denying-hiv-student-admission) [15]

Agence France-Presse (2014). "Sex drive-in" hailed as success after year-long experiment in Zurich. *Guardian (London),* August 26. [17]

Agency for Healthcare Research and Quality. (2005). *Management of menopause-related symptoms.* (www.ahrq.gov/clinic/epcsums/menosum.htm) [11]

AIDSinfo. (2014). Guidelines for the use of antiretroviral agents in HIV-1-infected adults and adolescents. (aidsinfo.nih.gov/contentfiles/lvguidelines/adultandadolescentgl.pdf) [15]

Akkus, D. E. (2011). Orgasm treatment in migraine: A native and costless choice? A clinical observation. *Archives of Neuropsychiatry, 48,* 268–269. [6]

AL.com. (2013). *Christian Adamek case: Streaking does not lead to sex offender registry, prosecutor says.* (blog.al.com/breaking/2013/10/christian_adamek_case_streakin.html) [13]

Alarie, M. & Gaudet, S. (2013). "I don't know if she is bisexual or if she just wants to get attention": Analyzing the various mechanisms through which emerging adults invisibilize bisexuality. *Journal of Bisexuality, 13,* 191–214. [12]

Alexander, B. M., Skinner, D. C. & Roselli, C. E. (2011). Wired on steroids: Sexual differentiation of the brain and its role in the expression of sexual partner preferences. *Frontiers in Endocrinology (Lausanne), 2,* 42. [12]

Alexander, G. M. & Hines, M. (2002). Sex differences in response to children's toys in nonhuman primates (*Cercopithecus aethiops sabaeus*). *Evolution and Human Behavior, 23,* 467–479. [4]

Alexander, G. M. & Saenz, J. (2012). Early androgens, activity levels and toy choices of children in the second year of life. *Hormones and Behavior, 62,* 500–504. [4]

Alexander, G. M., Wilcox, T. & Woods, R. (2009). Sex differences in infants' visual interest in toys. *Archives of Sexual Behavior, 38,* 427–433. [4]

Alexander, M. G. & Fisher, T. D. (2003). Truth and consequences: Using the bogus pipeline to examine sex differences in self-reported sexuality. *Journal of Sex Research, 40,* 27–35. [4]

Ali, L. & Kelley, R. (2008). The curious lives of surrogates. *Newsweek,* April 7. [8]

Allen, M., D'Alessio, D. & Emmers-Sommer, T. M. (2000). Reactions of criminal sexual offenders to pornography: A meta-analytic summary. In: Roloff, M. (Ed.), *Communication yearbook 22.* Sage. [17]

Allison, R. & Risman, B. J. (2013). A double standard for "hooking up": How far have we come toward gender equality? *Social Science Research, 42,* 1191–1206. [7]

Alpizar, K., Islas-Alvarado, R., Warren, C. R. & Fiebert, M. S. (2012). Gender, sexuality and impression management on Facebook. *International Review of Social Sciences and Humanities, 4,* 121–125. [10]

Althof, S. E. (2007). Treatment of rapid ejaculation: Psychotherapy, pharmacotherapy, and combined therapy. In: Leiblum, S. R. (Ed.), *Principles and practice of sex therapy.* Guilford. [14]

Althof, S. E. & Schreiner-Engel, P. (2001). The sexual dysfunctions. In: Gelder, M. G., et al. (Eds.), *New Oxford textbook of psychiatry.* Oxford University Press. [14]

Amato, P. R. (2010). Research on divorce: Continuing trends and new developments. *Journal of Marriage and Family, 72,* 650–666. [11]

Amberson, J. I. & Hoon, P. W. (1985). Hemodynamics of sequential orgasm. *Archives of Sexual Behavior, 14,* 351–360. [5]

American Academy of Dermatology. (2014). *iPledge.* (www.aad.org/members/practice-and-advocacy-resource-center/compliance-and-legal-issues/ipledge) [8]

American Academy of Ophthalmology. (2013). *Long-term oral contraceptive users are twice as likely to have serious eye disease.* (www.aao.org/newsroom/release/oral-contraceptives-increase-glaucoma-risk.cfm) [9]

American Academy of Pediatrics. (2006). Menstruation in girls and adolescents: Using the menstrual cycle as a vital sign. *Pediatrics, 118,* 2245–2250. [2]

American Academy of Pediatrics. (2010). *Should we have our son circumcised?* (www.healthychildren.org/english/ages-stages/prenatal/decisions-to-make/pages/Circumcision.aspx) [3]

American Academy of Pediatrics. (2012). *AAP reaffirms breastfeeding guidelines.* (www.aap.org/en-us/about-the-aap/aap-press-room/pages/AAP-Reaffirms-Breastfeeding-Guidelines.aspx) [8]

American Academy of Pediatrics. (2013). Planned home birth. *Pediatrics, 131,* 1016–1020. [8]

American Academy of Pediatrics. (2014). Contraception for adolescents. (pediatrics.aappublications.org/content/134/4/e1244.full) [9]

American Association for Marriage and Family Therapy. (2014). *Sexual addiction.* (www.aamft.org/imis15/aamft/Content/Consumer_Updates/Sexual_Addiction.aspx) [14]

American Association of Retired Persons. (2010). *Sex, romance, and relationships: AARP Survey of Midlife and Older Adults.* (assets.aarp.org/rgcenter/general/srr_09.pdf) [11]

American Association of University Women. (2013). *Crossing the line: Sexual harassment at school.* (www.aauw.org/files/2013/02/crossing-the-line-sexual-harassment-at-school-executive-summary.pdf) [16]

American Cancer Society. (2010). *American Cancer Society guidelines for the early detection of cancer.* (www.cancer.org/Healthy/FindCancerEarly/CancerScreeningGuidelines/american-cancer-society-guidelines-for-the-early-detection-of-cancer) [2]

American Cancer Society. (2013a). *What are the key statistics about prostate cancer?* (www.cancer.org/cancer/prostatecancer/detailedguide/prostate-cancer-key-statistics) [3]

American Cancer Society. (2013b). *Breast awareness and self-exam.* (www.cancer.org/cancer/breastcancer/moreinformation/breastcancerearlydetection/breast-cancer-early-detection-acs-recs-bse) [2]

American Cancer Society. (2013c). *Survival rates for endometrial cancer.* (www.cancer.org/cancer/endometrialcancer/overviewguide/endometrial--uterine--cancer-overview-survival-rates) [2]

American Cancer Society. (2014a). *What are the key statistics about anal cancer?* (www.cancer.org/cancer/analcancer/detailedguide/anal-cancer-what-is-key-statistics) [15]

American Cancer Society. (2014b). *What are the key statistics about testicular cancer?* (www.cancer.org/cancer/testicularcancer/detailedguide/testicular-cancer-key-statistics) [3]

American Cancer Society. (2014c). *Breast reconstruction after mastectomy.* (www.cancer.org/cancer/breastcancer/moreinformation/breastreconstructionaftermastectomy/index) [2]

American Cancer Society. (2014d). *Sexuality after breast cancer.* (www.cancer.org/cancer/breastcancer/detailedguide/breast-cancer-after-sexuality) [2]

American College of Nurse-Midwives. (2005). *Perineal massage in pregnancy.* (www.midwife.org/ACNM/files/ccLibraryFiles/Filename/000000000656/Perineal%20Massage%20in%20Pregnancy.pdf) [8]

American College of Obstetricians and Gynecologists. (2011). *Annual mammograms now recommended for women beginning at age 40.* (www.acog.org/About-ACOG/News-Room/News-Releases/2011/Annual-Mammograms-Now-Recommended-for-Women-Beginning-at-Age-40) [2]

American College of Obstetricians and Gynecologists. (2013). *The Rh factor: How it can affect your pregnancy.* (www.acog.org/~/media/For%20Patients/faq027.pdf?dmc=1&ts=20140429T1619291285) [8]

American College of Obstetricians and Gynecologists. (2014). Medical management of first-trimester abortion. *Obstetrics and Gynecology, 123,* 676–692. [9]

American Congress of Obstetricians and Gynecologists. (2007). *New recommendations for Down syndrome: Screening should be offered to all pregnant women.* (www.acog.org/About-ACOG/News-Room/News-Releases/2006/New-Recommendations-for-Down-Syndrome) [8]

American Congress of Obstetricians and Gynecologists. (2011). *The American College of Obstetricians and Gynecologists issues opinion on planned home births.* (www.acog.org/About-ACOG/News-Room/News-Releases/2011/The-American-College-of-Obstetricians-and-Gynecologists-Issues-Opinion-on-Planned-Home-Births) [8]

American Council on Science and Health. (2014). *Merck's new nine-valent HPV vaccine.* (acsh.org/2014/02/mercks-new-nine-valent-hpv-vaccine) [15]

American Institute of Bisexuality. (2014). *What is the difference between bisexual and terms like pansexual, polysexual, omnisexual, ambisexual, and fluid?* (bisexual.org/qna/what-is-the-difference-between-bisexual-and-terms-like-pansexual-polysexual-omnisexual-ambisexual-and-fluid) [12]

American Pregnancy Association. (2014). *Epidural anesthesia.* (www.americanpregnancy.org/labornbirth/epidural.html) [8]

American Psychiatric Association. (2008). *Report of the APA Task Force on the Sexualization of Girls.* (www.apa.org/pi/women/programs/girls/report.aspx) [10]

American Psychological Association. (2004). *Sexual orientation, parents, and children.* (www.apa.org/pi/lgbc/policy/parents.html) [14]

American Psychological Association. (2011). *Guidelines for psychotherapy with lesbian, gay, and bisexual clients.* (www.apa.org/pi/lgbc/publications/guidelines.html) [12]

American Sexual Health Association. (2014). *Statistics on sexually transmitted infections.* (www.ashasexualhealth.org/stdsstis/statistics/) [15]

American Society for Reproductive Medicine. (2013). Criteria for number of embryos to transfer: A committee opinion. *Fertility and Sterility, 99,* 44–46. [8]

American Urological Association. (2013). *Penile augmentation surgery.* (www.auanet.org/about/policy-statements/penile-augmentation-surgery.cfm) [3]

Amstey, M. S. (1994). The political history of syphilis and its application to the AIDS epidemic. *Womens Health Issues, 4,* 16–19. [15]

Anapol, D. (2010). *Polyamory in the 21st century: Love and intimacy with multiple partners.* Rowman & Littlefield. [11]

Andersen, A. G., Jensen, T. K., Carlsen, E., Jorgensen, N., Andersson, A. M., Krarup, et al. (2000). High frequency of sub-optimal semen quality in an unselected population of young men. *Human Reproduction, 15,* 366–372. [8]

Andersen, A. M., Andersen, P. K., Olsen, J., Gronbaek, M. & Strandberg-Larsen, K. (2012). Moderate alcohol intake during pregnancy and risk of fetal death. *International Journal of Epidemiology, 41,* 405–413. [8]

Anderson, E., Adams, A. & Rivers, I. (2012). "I kiss them because I love them": The emergence of heterosexual men kissing in British institutes of education. *Archives of Sexual Behavior, 41,* 421–430. [6]

Anderson, N. (2014). Behind a sexual misconduct case at Brandeis University: Questions on all sides. *Washington Post,* August 20. [16]

Anderson, T. A., Schick, V., Herbenick, D., Dodge, B. & Fortenberry, J. D. (2014). A study of human papillomavirus on vaginally inserted sex toys, before and after cleaning, among women who have sex with women and men. *Sexually Transmitted Infections,* published online April 16. [6]

Andrews, L. R. (2002). Letter to the editor. *New York Times,* July 5. [13]

Angulo, J. C., Garcia-Diez, M. & Martinez, M. (2011). Phallic decoration in paleolithic art: Genital scarification, piercing and tattoos. *Journal of Urology, 186,* 2498–2503. [3]

Anonymous. (1999). Confessions of a LUG. *Cincinnati CityBeat,* August 26. [7]

Anonymous. (2012). *I am a woman with a complete uterine didelphys…which means I have two vaginas.* (tinyurl.com/9crskxl) [3]

Anonymous. (2014a). *Can anyone else orgasm just from nipple stimulation?* (www.reddit.com/r/sex/comments/1yinb5/can_anyone_else_orgasm_just_from_nipple) [5]

Anonymous. (2014b). *I am the guy with two penises.* (www.tinyurl.com/lydahk2) [3]

Anonymous. (2014c). *The Cosmo sex challenge: 77 positions in 77 days.* (www.cosmopolitan.com/sex-love/great-sex-ideas/77-positions-introduction) [6]

Apicella, C. L., Feinberg, D. R. & Marlowe, F. W. (2007). Voice pitch predicts reproductive success in male hunter-gatherers. *Biology Letters, 3,* 682–684. [5]

Archer, J. (2004). Sex differences in aggression in real-world settings: A meta-analytic review. *Review of General Psychology, 8,* 291–322. [4]

Arden, M. A. & Dye, L. (1998). The assessment of menstrual synchrony: Comment on Weller and Weller (1997). *Journal of Comparative Psychology, 112,* 323–324; discussion 325–326. [2]

Ariely, D. & Loewenstein, G. (2006). The heat of the moment: The effect of sexual arousal on sexual decision making. *Journal of Behavioral Decision Making, 19,* 87–98. [16]

Ariosto, D. & Remizowski, L. (2012). *Yale settles sexual harassment complaint.* (www.cnn.com/2012/06/15/justice/connecticut-yale-settlement) [16]

Armstrong, E. A., England, P. & Fogarty, A. C. K. (2009). Orgasm in college hookups and relationships. In: Risman, B. J. (Ed.), *Families as they really are.* Norton. [7]

Arnold, A. P. (2009). The organizational-activational hypothesis as the foundation for a unified theory of sexual differentiation of all mammalian tissues. *Hormones and Behavior, 55,* 570–578. [4]

Associated Press. (1996). *Husband seeks divorce over on-line affair.* (www.lectlaw.com/files/fam22.htm) [7]

Associated Press. (2004). *Sprinter banned from Olympics.* (www.cbsnews.com/stories/2004/06/16/national/main623465.shtml) [3]

Associated Press. (2007). *Track star admitted to doping, will return prize money.* (sportsillustrated.cnn.com/2007/more/11/23/jones.annulled.ap/index.html) [3]

Associated Press. (2008). Feds outline steroids case vs. cyclist. *New York Times,* March 6. [3]

Associated Press. (2011a). Texas: Polygamist leader gets life sentence. *New York Times,* August 10. [11]

Associated Press. (2011b). *UN group backs gay rights for the first time ever.* (www.southfloridagaynews.com/news/world-news/3902-un-group-backs-gay-rights-for-the-1st-time-ever.html) [12]

Association of Gay and Lesbian Psychiatrists. (2008). *AGLP online referral system.* (aglp. memberclicks.net/aglp-referral) [14]

Auger, J., Kunstmann, J. M., Czyglik, F. & Jouannet, P. (1995). Decline in semen quality among fertile men in Paris during the past 20 years. *New England Journal of Medicine, 332,* 281–285. [8]

Austoni, E., Guarneri, A. & Cazzaniga, A. (2002). A new technique for augmentation phalloplasty: Albugineal surgery with bilateral saphenous grafts—three years of experience. *European Urology, 42,* 245–253; discussion 252–243. [3]

Auvert, B., Taljaard, D., Lagarde, E., Sobngwi-Tambekou, J., Sitta, R. & Puren, A. (2005). Randomized, controlled intervention trial of male circumcision for reduction of HIV infection risk: The ANRS 1265 Trial. *PLOS Medicine, 2,* e298. [3]

Averett, P., Yoon, I. & Jenkins, C. L. (2012). Older lesbian sexuality: Identity, sexual behavior, and the impact of aging. *Journal of Sex Research, 49,* 495–507. [14]

AVERT. (2014a). *Global HIV and AIDS epidemic.* (www.avert.org/global-hiv-aids-epidemic. htm) [15]

AVERT. (2014b). *Stories.* (www.avert.org/stories) [12]

Avis, N. E., Zhao, X., Johannes, C. B., Ory, M., Brockwell, S. & Greendale, G. A. (2005). Correlates of sexual function among multi-ethnic middle-aged women: Results from the Study of Women's Health Across the Nation (SWAN). *Menopause, 12,* 385–398. [11]

Ayuda, T. (2011). *An Asian American perspective: How to address the stigma surrounding sex.* (www.mochimag.com/2010/12/talking-about-sex-safe-stigma-asian-american-culture) [7]

B4U-ACT. (2011). *The B4U-ACT Survey.* (www. b4uact.org/science/survey/01.htm) [13]

B4U-ACT. (2014). B4U-ACT: Living in truth and dignity. (www.b4uact.org) [13]

Bachtrog, D., Mank, J. E., Peichel, C. L., Kirkpatrick, M., Otto, S. P., Ashman, T. L., et al. (2014). Sex determination: Why so many ways of doing it? *PLOS Biology, 12,* e1001899. [App. A]

Bagby, D. (2008). Proud "mama's boys." *Southern Voice,* May 9. [12]

Bailey, A. A. & Hurd, P. L. (2005). Finger length ratio (2D:4D) correlates with physical aggression in men but not in women. *Biological Psychology, 68,* 215–222. [4]

Bailey, J. M. (2003). *The man who would be queen: The science of gender-bending and transsexualism.* Joseph Henry. [4, 13]

Bailey, J. M. & Oberschneider, M. (1997). Sexual orientation and professional dance. *Archives of Sexual Behavior, 26,* 433–444. [12]

Bailey, J. M. & Zucker, K. J. (1995). Childhood sex-typed behavior and sexual orientation: A conceptual analysis and quantitative review. *Developmental Psychology, 31,* 43–55. [12]

Bailey, J. M., Kim, P. Y., Hills, A. & Linsenmeier, J. A. (1997). Butch, femme, or straight acting? Partner preferences of gay men and lesbians. *Journal of Personality and Social Psychology, 73,* 960–973. [12]

Baldwin, J. & Baldwin, J. (2001). *Behavior principles in everyday life* (4th ed.). Prentice Hall. [4]

Balsam, K. F., Rothblum, E. D. & Beauchaine, T. P. (2005). Victimization over the life span: A comparison of lesbian, gay, bisexual, and heterosexual siblings. *Journal of Consulting and Clinical Psychology, 73,* 477–487. [16]

Bamberg, C., Scheuermann, S., Slowinski, T., Duckelmann, A. M., Vogt, M., Nguyen-Dobinsky, et al. (2011). Relationship between fetal head station established using an open magnetic resonance imaging scanner and the angle of progression determined by transperineal ultrasound. *Ultrasound in Obstetrics and Gynecology, 37,* 712–716. [8]

Bancroft, J. & Graham, C. A. (2011). The varied nature of women's sexuality: Unresolved issues and a theoretical approach. *Hormones and Behavior, 59,* 717–729. [10]

Bancroft, J., Herbenick, D. L. & Reynolds, M. A. (2003a). Masturbation as a marker of sexual development. In: Bancroft, J. (Ed.), *Sexual development in childhood.* Indiana University Press. [10]

Bancroft, J., Loftus, J. & Long, J. S. (2003b). Distress about sex: A national survey of women in heterosexual relationships. *Archives of Sexual Behavior, 32,* 193–208. [14]

Baptist Press. (2012). *Cohabitation harms marriage, expert says.* (www.bpnews.net/38776) [11]

Barber, N. (2000). On the relationship between country sex ratios and teen pregnancy rates: A replication. *Cross-Cultural Research, 34,* 26–37. [1]

Barker, R. (1987). *The green-eyed marriage: Surviving jealous relationships.* Free Press. [7]

Barnhart, K., Furman, I. & Devoto, L. (1995). Attitudes and practice of couples regarding sexual relations during the menses and spotting. *Contraception, 51,* 93–98. [2]

Baron-Cohen, S. (2003). *The essential difference: Men, women, and the extreme male brain.* Penguin. [4]

Barriger, M. & Velez-Blasini, C. J. (2013). Descriptive and injunctive social norm overestimation in hooking up and their role as predictors of hook-up activity in a college student sample. *Journal of Sex Research, 50,* 84–94. [10]

Barry, D. (2008). Trading vows in Montana, no couple required. *New York Times,* March 10. [11]

Bartels, A. & Zeki, S. (2000). The neural basis of romantic love. *Neuroreport, 11,* 3829–3834. [7]

Bartels, A. & Zeki, S. (2004). The neural correlates of maternal and romantic love. *Neuroimage, 21,* 1155–1166. [5]

Barth, J., Bermetz, L., Heim, E., Trelle, S. & Tonia, T. (2013). The current prevalence of child sexual abuse worldwide: A systematic review and meta-analysis. *International Journal of Public Health, 58,* 469–483. [10]

Bartholet, E. (2014). Rethink Harvard's sexual harassment policy. *Boston Globe,* October 15. [16]

Bartoli, A. M. & Clark, M. D. (2006). The dating game: Similarities and differences in dating scripts among college students. *Sexuality and Culture, 10,* 54–60. [1]

Bartz, D. & Greenberg, J. A. (2008). Sterilization in the United States. *Reviews in Obstetrics and Gynecology, 1,* 23–32. [9]

Basaria, S., Davda, M. N., Travison, T. G., Ulloor, J., Singh, R. & Bhasin, S. (2013). Risk factors associated with cardiovascular events during testosterone administration in older men with mobility limitation. *Journals of Gerontology Series A, Biological Sciences and Medical Sciences, 68,* 153–160. [11]

Baseman, J. G. & Koutsky, L. A. (2005). The epidemiology of human papillomavirus infections. *Journal of Clinical Virology, 32*(Suppl. 1), S16–24. [15]

Basson, R. (2000). The female sexual response: A different model. *Journal of Sex and Marital Therapy, 26,* 51–65. [5]

Basson, R. (2001). Human sex-response cycles. *Journal of Sex and Marital Therapy, 27,* 33–43. [5, 14]

Basson, R. (2007). Sexual desire/arousal disorders in women. In: Leiblum, S. R. (Ed.), *Principles and practice of sex therapy* (4th ed.). Guilford. [14]

Basson, R. (2012). The recurrent pain and sexual sequelae of provoked vestibulodynia: A perpetuating cycle. *Journal of Sexual Medicine, 9,* 2077–2092. [14]

Basson, R., McInnes, R., Smith, M. D., Hodgson, G. & Koppiker, N. (2002). Efficacy and safety of sildenafil citrate in women with sexual dysfunction associated with female sexual arousal disorder. *Journal of Women's Health and Gender-Based Medicine, 11,* 367–377. [14]

Bauermeister, J. A., Johns, M. M. & Zimmerman, M. (2011). Measuring love: Sexual minority male youths' ideal romantic characteristics. *Journal of LGBT Issues in Counseling, 5,* 102–121. [7]

Baumeister, R. F. & Dhavale, D. (2001). The two sides of romantic rejection. In: Leary, M. R. (Ed.), *Interpersonal rejection.* Oxford University Press. [7]

Baumeister, R. F. & Vohs, K. D. (2004). Sexual economics: Sex as female resource for social exchange in heterosexual interactions. *Personality and Social Psychology Review, 8,* 339–363. [1]

Baumeister, R. F., Catanese, K. R. & Vohs, K. D. (2001). Is there a gender difference in strength of sex drive? Theoretical views, conceptual distinctions, and a review of relevant evidence. *Personality and Social Psychology Review, 5,* 242–273. [4]

Baumeister, R. F., Wotman, S. R. & Stillwell, A. M. (1993). Unrequited love: On heartbreak, anger, guilt, scriptlessness, and humiliation. *Journal of Personality and Social Psychology, 64,* 377–394. [7]

BBC News. (2014). *HIV drugs "boost South African life expectancy."* (www.bbc.co.uk/news/world-africa-28592255) [15]

Beaver, K. M., Vaughn, M. G., Delisi, M. & Wright, J. P. (2008). Anabolic-androgenic steroid use and involvement in violent behavior in a nationally representative sample of young adult males in the United States. *American Journal of Public Health, 98,* 2185–2187. [3]

Beckerman, S. & Valentine, P. (Eds.) (2002). Cultures of multiple fathers: The theory and practice of partible paternity in lowland

South America. University of Florida Press. [1]

Becks, L. & Agrawal, A. F. (2012). The evolution of sex is favoured during adaptation to new environments. *PLOS Biology, 10,* e1001317. [App. A]

Beckstead, L. (2001). Cures versus choices: Agendas in sexual reorientation therapy. *Journal of Gay and Lesbian Psychotherapy, 5,* 87–115. [12]

Bedford, J. M. (1991). Effects of elevated temperature on the epididymis and testis: Experimental studies. *Advances in Experimental Medicine and Biology, 286,* 19–32. [3]

Been, J. V., Nurmatov, U. B., Cox, B., Nawrot, T. S., van Schayck, C. P. & Sheikh, A. (2014). Effect of smoke-free legislation on perinatal and child health: A systematic review and meta-analysis. *Lancet, 383,* 1549–1560. [8]

Belizan, J. M., Althabe, F. & Cafferata, M. L. (2007). Health consequences of the increasing caesarean section rates. *Epidemiology, 18,* 485–486. [8]

Beltz, A. M., Swanson, J. L. & Berenbaum, S. A. (2011). Gendered occupational interests: Prenatal androgen effects on psychological orientation to Things versus People. *Hormones and Behavior, 60,* 313–317. [4]

Belzer, E., Whipple, B. & Moger, W. (1984). A female ejaculation. *Journal of Sex Research, 20,* 403–406. [5]

Bennett, J. (2009). Only you. And you. And you. *Newsweek,* July 25. [11]

Bennett, J. (2014). The big chill: Why egg freezing may be our generation's Pill. *Time,* October 27. [8]

Bennetts, L. (2011). The john next door. *Newsweek,* July 25. [17]

Bentlage, B. & Eich, T. (2007). *Hymen repair on the Arab Internet.* (openaccess.leidenuniv.nl/handle/1887/17113) [2]

Berdahl, J. L. (2007). The sexual harassment of uppity women. *Journal of Applied Psychology, 92,* 425–437. [16]

Berenbaum, S. A. & Snyder, E. (1995). Early hormonal influences on childhood sex-typed activity and playmate preferences: Implications for the development of sexual orientation. *Developmental Psychology, 31,* 31–42. [4]

Berenbaum, S. A., Bryk, K. K., Nowak, N., Quigley, C. A. & Moffat, S. (2009). Fingers as a marker of prenatal androgen exposure. *Endocrinology, 150,* 5019–5124. [4]

Berenbaum, S. A., Bryk, K. L. & Beltz, A. M. (2012). Early androgen effects on spatial and mechanical abilities: Evidence from congenital adrenal hyperplasia. *Behavioral Neuroscience, 126,* 86–96. [4]

Berglund, H., Lindstrom, P. & Savic, I. (2006). Brain response to putative pheromones in lesbian women. *Proceedings of the National Academy of Sciences of the United States of America, 103,* 8269–8274. [12]

Bergstrand, C. & Blevins Williams, J. (2000). Today's alternative marriage styles: The case of swingers. *Electronic Journal of Human Sexuality,* online publication at www.ejhs.org/volume3/swing/body.htm. [11]

Bertone-Johnson, E. R., Hankinson, S. E., Bendich, A., Johnson, S. R., Willett, W. C. & Manson, J. E. (2005). Calcium and vitamin D intake and risk of incident premenstrual syndrome. *Archives of Internal Medicine, 165,* 1246–1252. [2]

Bettcher, T. M. (2014). Trapped in the wrong theory: Rethinking trans oppression and resistance. *Signs, 39,* 383–406. [4]

Betzig, L. (2012). Means, variances, and ranges in reproductive success: Comparative evidence. *Evolution and Human Behavior, 33,* 309–317. [App. A]

Bianchi, D. W. & Wilkins-Haug, L. (2014). Integration of noninvasive DNA testing for aneuploidy into prenatal care: What has happened since the rubber met the road? *Clinical Chemistry, 60,* 78–87. [8]

Bien-Aime, T. (2014). *France takes first steps towards abolition of prostitution.* (www.huffingtonpost.com/taina-bienaime/france-prostitution-laws_b_4775608.html) [17]

Bigner, J. & Wetchler, J. L. (2004). *Relationship therapy with same-sex couples.* Routledge. [14]

Billy, J. O. G., Brewster, K. L. & Grady, W. R. (1994). Contextual effects on the sexual behavior of adolescent women. *Journal of Marriage and the Family, 56,* 387–404. [10]

Bindel, J. (2006). Eradicate the oldest oppression. *Guardian (London),* January 18. [17]

Binik, Y. M., Bergeron, S. & Khalife, S. (2007). Dyspareunia and vaginismus. In: Leiblum, S. R. (Ed.), *Principles and practice of sex therapy.* Guilford. [14]

Bird, B. S., Schweitzer, R. D. & Strassberg, D. S. (2011). The prevalence and correlates of postcoital dysphoria in women. *International Journal of Sexual Health, 23,* 14–25. [6]

Birkhead, T. R. (1998). Sperm competition in birds: Mechanisms and functions. In: Birkhead, T. R. & Møller, A. P. (Eds.), *Sperm competition and sexual selection.* Academic. [App. A]

Birkhead, T. R. (2000). *Promiscuity: An evolutionary history of sperm competition.* Harvard University Press. [7, App. A]

Biro, F. M., Galvez, M. P., Greenspan, L. C., Succop, P. A., Vangeepuram, N., Pinney, S. M., et al. (2010). Pubertal assessment method and baseline characteristics in a mixed longitudinal study of girls. *Pediatrics, 126,* e583–590. [10]

Biro, F. M., Greenspan, L. C., Galvez, M. P., Pinney, S. M., Teitelbaum, S., Windham, G. C., et al. (2013). Onset of breast development in a longitudinal cohort. *Pediatrics, 132,* 1019–1027. [10]

BishopAccountability. (2014). *Documenting the abuse crisis in the Roman Catholic Church.* (www.bishop-accountability.org) [13]

Bivona, J. & Critelli, J. (2009). The nature of women's rape fantasies: An analysis of prevalence, frequency, and contents. *Journal of Sex Research, 46,* 33–45. [5]

Bivona, J. M., Critelli, J. W. & Clark, M. J. (2012). Women's rape fantasies: An empirical evaluation of the major explanations. *Archives of Sexual Behavior, 41,* 1107–1119. [5]

Black, D. L. & Lichter, D. T. (2004). Homogamy among dating, cohabiting, and married couples. *Sociological Review, 45,* 719–737. [7]

Blanchard, R. (1993). Varieties of autogynephilia and their relationship to gender dysphoria. *Archives of Sexual Behavior, 22,* 241–251. [13]

Blanchard, R. (2005). Early history of the concept of autogynephilia. *Archives of Sexual Behavior, 34,* 439–446. [4]

Blanchard, R. & Hucker, S. J. (1991). Age, transvestism, bondage, and concurrent paraphilic activities in 117 fatal cases of autoerotic asphyxia. *British Journal of Psychiatry, 159,* 371–377. [13]

Blanchard, R., Barbaree, H. E., Bogaert, A. F., Dickey, R., Klassen, P., Kuban, M. E. & Zucker, K. J. (2000). Fraternal birth order and sexual orientation in pedophiles. *Archives of Sexual Behavior, 29,* 463–478. [13]

Blanchard, R., Kuban, M. E., Blak, T., Cantor, J. M., Klassen, P. & Dickey, R. (2006). Phallometric comparison of pedophilic interest in nonadmitting sexual offenders against stepdaughters, biological daughters, other biologically related girls, and unrelated girls. *Sexual Abuse, 18,* 1–14. [13]

Blanchard, V. L., Hawkins, A. J., Baldwin, S. A. & Fawcett, E. B. (2009). Investigating the effects of marriage and relationship education on couples' communication skills. *Journal of Family Psychology, 23,* 203–214. [7]

Blanchflower, D. G. & Oswald, A. J. (2004). Money, sex and happiness: An empirical study. *Scandinavian Journal of Economics, 106,* 393–415. [6]

Bleyer, A. & Welch, H. G. (2012). Effect of three decades of screening mammography on breast-cancer incidence. *New England Journal of Medicine, 367,* 1998–2005. [2]

Bliss, J. (2013). *Police, experts: Alcohol most common drug in sexual assaults.* (www.usatoday.com/story/news/nation/2013/10/28/alcohol-most-common-drug-in-sexual-assaults/3285139/?sf18825604=1) [16]

Bobrow, D. & Bailey, J. M. (2001). Is male homosexuality maintained via kin selection? *Evolution and Human Behavior, 22,* 361–368. [12]

Bockting, W. (1998). Transgender HIV prevention: A qualitative needs assessment. *AIDS Care, 10,* 505–526. [16]

Bogaert, A. F. & Skorska, M. (2011). Sexual orientation, fraternal birth order, and the maternal immune hypothesis: A review. *Frontiers in Neuroendocrinology, 32,* 247–254. [12]

Bogle, K. A. (2008). *Hooking up: Sex, dating, and relationships on campus.* NYU Press. [7]

Bohannon, C. (2014). When arousal is agony. *Scientific American Mind,* July 1. [14]

Bohlen, D., Hugonnet, C. L., Mills, R. D., Weise, E. S. & Schmid, H. P. (2000). Five meters of H(2)O: The pressure at the urinary bladder neck during human ejaculation. *Prostate, 44,* 339–341. [3]

Borini, A., Suriano, R., Barberi, M., Dal Prato, L. & Bulletti, C. (2011). Oocyte donation programs: Strategy for improving results. *Annals of the New York Academy of Sciences, 1221,* 27–31. [8]

Bornstein, K. (1994). *Gender outlaw: On men, women, and the rest of us.* Routledge. [4]

Boroditsky, L. (2011). How language shapes thought. *Scientific American,* February. [4]

Boswell, J. (1980). *Christianity, social tolerance, and homosexuality.* University of Chicago Press. [12]

Both, S., Spiering, M., Laan, E., Belcome, S., van den Heuvel, B. & Everaerd, W. (2008).

Unconscious classical conditioning of sexual arousal: Evidence for the conditioning of female genital arousal to subliminally presented sexual stimuli. *Journal of Sexual Medicine, 5,* 100–109. [5]

Bowlby, J. (1988). *A secure base: Parent-child attachment and healthy human development.* Basic Books. [7]

Brakefield, T. A., Mednick, S. C., Wilson, H. W., De Neve, J. E., Christakis, N. A. & Fowler, J. H. (2014). Same-sex sexual attraction does not spread in adolescent social networks. *Archives of Sexual Behavior, 43,* 335–344. [12]

Branson-Potts, H. (2014). Former officer gets 25 years in assaults. *Los Angeles Times,* October 28. [17]

Bratter, J. L. & King, R. B. (2008). "But will it last?": Marital instability among interracial and same-race couples. *Family Relations, 57,* 160–171. [11]

Bratton, E. (2014). *Pier life: The kids* (documentary film). (www.pierkidsthelife.com) [12]

Braun, C., Gründl, M., Marberger, C. & Scherber, C. (2001). *Beautycheck: Babyfaceness.* (www.uni-regensburg.de/Fakultaeten/phil_Fak_II/Psychologie/Psy_II/beautycheck/english/kindchenschema/kindchenschema.htm) [5]

Bray, J. H. (1999). From marriage to remarriage and beyond: Finding from the Developmental Issues in Stepfamilies research project. In: Hetherington, E. M. (Ed.), *Coping with divorce, single parenting, and remarriage.* Lawrence Erlbaum Associates. [11]

Breedlove, S. M. (2010). Organizational hypothesis: Instances of the fingerpost. *Endocrinology, 151,* 4116–4122. [4]

Brennan, R. (2010). *OMG Lady Gaga gives herself mental orgasms!* (www.glamour.com/sex-love-life/blogs/smitten/2010/03/omg-lady-gaga-gives-herself-me.html) [6]

Breno, M., Bots, J., De Schaepdrijver, L. & Van Dongen, S. (2013). Fluctuating asymmetry as risk marker for stress and structural defects in a toxicologic experiment. *Birth Defects Research Part B: Developmental and Reproductive Toxicology, 98,* 310–317. [App. A]

Brents, B. G. & Hausbeck, K. (2005). Violence and legalized brothel prostitution in Nevada. *Journal of Interpersonal Violence, 20,* 270–295. [17]

Bressler, E. & Balshine, S. (2006). The influence of humor on desirability. *Evolution and Human Behavior, 27,* 29–39. [5]

Bressler, E., Martin, R. & Balshine, S. (2006). Production and appreciation of humor as sexually selected traits. *Evolution and Human Behavior, 27,* 121–130. [5]

Brewster, P. W., Mullin, C. R., Dobrin, R. A. & Steeves, J. K. (2011). Sex differences in face processing are mediated by handedness and sexual orientation. *Laterality, 16,* 188–200. [5]

Bridgeman, B. & Roberts, S. G. (2010). The 4-3-2 method for Kegel exercises. *American Journal of Men's Health, 4,* 75–76. [14]

Bridges, A. J., Wosnitzer, R., Scharrer, E., Sun, C. & Liberman, R. (2010). Aggression and sexual behavior in best-selling pornography videos: A content analysis update. *Violence Against Women, 16,* 1065–1085. [17]

Briggs, N. (2014). Subway rider: I helped take perv down after being sexually assaulted on train. *New York Daily News,* June 23. [13]

Briken, P., Habermann, N., Berner, W. & Hill, A. (2006). XYY chromosome abnormality in sexual homicide perpetrators. *American Journal of Medical Genetics. Part B, Neuropsychiatric Genetics, 141,* 198–200. [4]

Bringle, R. G., Winnick, T. & Rydell, R. J. (2013). The prevalence and nature of unrequited love. *SAGE Open, 3* (June 13). [7]

British Broadcasting Corporation. (2002). *Human instinct: Deepest desires.* (www.bbc.co.uk/science/humanbody/tv/humaninstinct/programme2.shtml) [7]

Brody, J. E. (2013). Questioning the pelvic exam. *New York Times,* April 29. [2]

Brookoff, D., O'Brien, K. K., Cook, C. S., Thompson, T. D. & Williams, C. (1997). Characteristics of participants in domestic violence: Assessment at the scene of domestic assault. *JAMA, 277,* 1369–1373. [16]

Brotman, R. M., Klebanoff, M. A., Nansel, T. R., Andrews, W. W., Schwebke, J. R., Zhang, J., et al. (2008). A longitudinal study of vaginal douching and bacterial vaginosis--a marginal structural modeling analysis. *American Journal of Epidemiology, 168,* 188–196. [15]

Brotto, L. A. & Basson, R. (2014). Group mindfulness-based therapy significantly improves sexual desire in women. *Behaviour Research and Therapy, 57,* 43–54. [14]

Brown, G. R., Laland, K. N. & Mulder, M. B. (2009). Bateman's principles and human sex roles. *Trends in Ecology and Evolution, 24,* 297–304. [App. A]

Brown, J. D., Halpern, C. T. & L'Engle, K. L. (2005). Mass media as a sexual super peer for early maturing girls. *Journal of Adolescent Health, 36,* 420–427. [10]

Brown, J. M., Hess, K. L., Brown, S., Murphy, C., Waldman, A. L. & Hezareh, M. (2013). Intravaginal practices and risk of bacterial vaginosis and candidiasis infection among a cohort of women in the United States. *Obstetrics and Gynecology, 121,* 773–780. [15]

Brown, W. M., Price, M. E., Kang, J., Pound, N., Zhao, Y. & Yu, H. (2008). Fluctuating asymmetry and preferences for sex-typical bodily characteristics. *Proceedings of the National Academy of Sciences of the United States of America, 105,* 12938–12943. [5]

Bryant, D. M., Hoeft, F., Lai, S., Lackey, J., Roeltgen, D., Ross, J. & Reiss, A. L. (2012). Sex chromosomes and the brain: A study of neuroanatomy in XYY syndrome. *Developmental Medicine and Child Neurology, 54,* 1149–1156. [4]

Bucar, B. (2014). *Klinefelter syndrome.* (www.measurection.com/fbbuploads/1040765274-klinefelters1.pdf) [4]

Buck Louis, G. M., Sundaram, R., Sweeney, A. M., Schisterman, E. F., Maisog, J. & Kannan, K. (2014). Urinary bisphenol A, phthalates, and couple fecundity: The Longitudinal Investigation of Fertility and the Environment (LIFE) Study. *Fertility and Sterility. 101,* 1359–1366. [8]

Buisson, O. & Jannini, E. A. (2013). Pilot echographic study of the differences in clitoral involvement following clitoral or vaginal sexual stimulation. *Journal of Sexual Medicine, 10,* 2734–2740. [5]

Bull, S. S., Levine, D. K., Black, S. R., Schmiege, S. J. & Santelli, J. (2012). Social media-delivered sexual health intervention: A cluster randomized controlled trial. *American Journal of Preventive Medicine, 43,* 467–474. [10]

Bureau of Justice Statistics. (2003). *Recidivism of sex offenders released from prison in 1994.* (www.bjs.gov/content/pub/pdf/rsorp94.pdf) [16]

Bureau of Justice Statistics. (2010). *Prisoners in 2009.* (bjs.ojp.usdoj.gov/content/pub/pdf/p09.pdf) [16]

Bureau of Justice Statistics. (2011). *Intimate partner violence.* (bjs.ojp.usdoj.gov/index.cfm?ty=tp&tid=971) [16]

Bureau of Justice Statistics. (2012). *Arrest in the United States, 1990–2010.* (www.bjs.gov/content/pub/pdf/aus9010.pdf) [16]

Bureau of Justice Statistics. (2013a). *Criminal victimization, 2012.* (www.bjs.gov/content/pub/pdf/cv12.pdf) [16]

Bureau of Justice Statistics. (2013b). *Intimate partner violence: Attributes of victimization, 1993–2011.* (www.bjs.gov/content/pub/pdf/ipvav9311.pdf) [16]

Bureau of Justice Statistics. (2014a). *Nonfatal domestic violence, 2003–2012.* (www.bjs.gov/content/pub/pdf/ndv0312.pdf) [16]

Bureau of Justice Statistics. (2014b). *Sexual victimization reported by adult correctional authorities, 2009–2011.* (www.bjs.gov/content/pub/pdf/svraca0911.pdf) [16]

Bureau of Justice Statistics. (2014c). *Rape and sexual assault victimization among college-age females, 1995-2013.* (www.bjs.gov/content/pub/pdf/rsavcaf9513.pdf) [16]

Burgess, A. W. & Holmstrom, L. L. (1979). Rape: Sexual disruption and recovery. *American Journal of Orthopsychiatry, 49,* 648–657. [16]

Burke, A. E. (2011). The state of hormonal contraception today: Benefits and risks of hormonal contraceptives: Progestin-only contraceptives. *American Journal of Obstetrics and Gynecology, 205,* S14–17. [9]

Burnham, T. C., Chapman, J. F., Gray, P. B., McIntyre, M. H., Lipson, S. F. & Ellison, P. T. (2003). Men in committed, romantic relationships have lower testosterone. *Hormones and Behavior, 44,* 119–122. [3]

Burns, E. E., Boulton, M. G., Cluett, E., Cornelius, V. R. & Smith, L. A. (2012). Characteristics, interventions, and outcomes of women who used a birthing pool: A prospective observational study. *Birth, 39,* 192–202. [8]

Buss, D. M. (2000). *The dangerous passion: Why jealousy is as necessary as love and sex.* Free Press. [7]

Buss, D. M. (2011). *Evolutionary psychology: The new science of the mind* (4th ed.). Pearson. [4, 5, 7]

Buss, D. M. (2013). Sexual jealousy. *Psychological Topics, 22,* 155–182. [4]

Bussey, K. & Bandura, A. (1984). Influence of gender constancy and social power on sex-linked modeling. *Journal of Personality and Social Psychology, 47,* 1292–1302. [4]

Buster, J. E., Kingsberg, S. A., Aguirre, O., Brown, C., Breaux, J. G., Buch, A., et al. (2005). Testosterone patch for low sexual desire in surgically menopausal women: A randomized trial. *Obstetrics and Gynecology, 105*, 944–952. [14]

Byne, W., Tobet, S., Mattiace, L. A., Lasco, M. S., Kemether, E., Edgar, M. A., et al. (2001). The interstitial nuclei of the human anterior hypothalamus: An investigation of variation with sex, sexual orientation, and HIV status. *Hormones and Behavior, 40*, 86–92. [12]

Byrd, J. E., Hyde, J. S., DeLamater, J. D. & Plant, E. A. (1998). Sexuality during pregnancy and the year postpartum. *Journal of Family Practice, 47*, 305–308. [8]

Cahill, L. (2014). *Equal is not the same: Sex differences in the human brain.* (www.dana.org/Cerebrum/2014/Equal_%E2%89%A0_The_Same__Sex_Differences_in_the_Human_Brain) [4]

Camilleri, J. A. & Quinsey, V. L. (2008). Pedophilia: Assessment and treatment. In: Laws, D. R. & O'Donohue, W. T. (Eds.), *Sexual deviance: Theory, assessment, and treatment.* Guilford. [13]

Campbell, D. W. & Eaton, W. O. (1999). Sex differences in the activity level of infants. *Infant and Child Development, 8*, 1–17. [4]

Camperio Ciani, A., Cermelli, P. & Zanzotto, G. (2008). Sexually antagonistic selection in human male homosexuality. *PLOS ONE, 3*, e2282. [12]

Campus Safety. (2011). *Obama administration warns schools to follow sex crime protocol.* (www.campussafetymagazine.com/article/Obama-Administration-Kicks-Off-Sexual-Violence-Awareness-Effort) [16]

Candib, L. M. (2002). A new view of women's sexual problems: A family physician's response. In: Kaschak, E. & Tiefer, L. (Eds.), *A new view of women's sexual problems.* Haworth. [14]

Canli, T., Desmond, J. E., Zhao, Z. & Gabrieli, J. D. (2002). Sex differences in the neural basis of emotional memories. *Proceedings of the National Academy of Sciences of the United States of America, 99*, 10789–10794. [4]

Carel, J. C., Lahlou, N., Roger, M. & Chaussain, J. L. (2004). Precocious puberty and statural growth. *Human Reproduction Update, 10*, 135–147. [10]

Carey, B. (2005). Straight, gay or lying? Bisexuality revisited. *New York Times*, July 5. [12]

Carlsen, E., Giwercman, A., Keiding, N. & Skakkebaek, N. E. (1992). Evidence for decreasing quality of semen during past 50 years. *BMJ, 305*, 609–613. [8]

Carmichael, M. S., Warburton, V. L., Dixen, J. & Davidson, J. M. (1994). Relationships among cardiovascular, muscular, and oxytocin responses during human sexual activity. *Archives of Sexual Behavior, 23*, 59–79. [5]

Carnes, P. (2001). Out of the shadows: Understanding sexual addiction (3rd ed.). Hazelden. [14]

Carpenter, C. L., Ross, R. K., Paganini-Hill, A. & Bernstein, L. (2003). Effect of family history, obesity and exercise on breast cancer risk among postmenopausal women. *International Journal of Cancer, 106*, 96–102. [2]

Carpenter, L. M. (2005). Virginity lost: An intimate portrait of first sexual experiences. New York University Press. [10]

Carroli, G. & Mignini, L. (2009). Episiotomy for vaginal birth. *Cochrane Database of Systematic Reviews*, CD000081. [8]

Carroll, J. S. & Doherty, W. J. (2003). Evaluating the effectiveness of premarital prevention programs: A meta-analytic review of outcome research. *Family Relations, 52*, 105–118. [7]

Carter, C. S. & Getz, L. L. (1993). Monogamy and the prairie vole. *Scientific American, 268*, 100–106. [App. A]

Carter, D. (2004). *Stonewall: The riots that sparked the gay revolution.* St. Martin's. [12]

Carter, D. (2012). Comprehensive sex education for teens is more effective than abstinence. *American Journal of Nursing, 112*, 15. [10]

Caruso, S., Agnello, C., Malandrino, C., Lo Presti, L., Cicero, C. & Cianci, S. (2014). Do hormones influence women's sex? Sexual activity over the menstrual cycle. *Journal of Sexual Medicine, 11*, 211–221. [5]

Catholic Online. (2014). What Pope Francis said about married men and the Catholic priesthood on that plane. (www.catholic.org/news/national/story.php?id=55618) [13]

Catlin, D. H., Sekera, M. H., Ahrens, B. D., Starcevic, B., Chang, Y. C. & Hatton, C. K. (2004). Tetrahydrogestrinone: Discovery, synthesis, and detection in urine. *Rapid Communications in Mass Spectrometry, 18*, 1245–1249. [3]

CBS News. (2007). *Woman misdiagnosed with HIV awarded $2.5M.* (www.cbsnews.com/news/woman-misdiagnosed-with-hiv-awarded-25m) [15]

Center for Sexual Health Promotion. (2010). *National Survey of Sexual Health and Behavior.* (www.nationalsexstudy.indiana.edu) [10]

Centers for Disease Control. (1989). *First 100,000 cases of acquired immunodeficiency syndrome—United States.* (www.cdc.gov/mmwr/preview/mmwrhtml/00001442.htm) [12]

Centers for Disease Control. (2004). *Cohabitation, marriage, divorce, and remarriage in the United States.* (www.cdc.gov/nchs/data/series/sr_23/sr23_022.pdf) [11]

Centers for Disease Control. (2004). *Genital candidiasis.* (www.cdc.gov/fungal/diseases/candidiasis/genital/index.html) [2]

Centers for Disease Control. (2007). *Drug use and sexual behaviors reported by adults: United States, 1999–2002.* (www.cdc.gov/nchs/data/ad/ad384.pdf) [10]

Centers for Disease Control. (2009). *Oral sex and HIV risk.* (www.cdc.gov/hiv/resources/factsheets/pdf/oralsex.pdf) [15]

Centers for Disease Control. (2010a). *CDC statement on results of iPrEx trial examining pre-exposure prophylaxis (PrEP) for HIV prevention among men who have sex with men.* (www.cdc.gov/nchhstp/newsroom/iPrExMediaStatement.html) [15]

Centers for Disease Control. (2010b). *Deaths: Final Data for 2007.* (www.cdc.gov/nchs/data/nvsr/nvsr58/nvsr58_19.pdf) [2]

Centers for Disease Control. (2010c). *Estimated number of male newborn infants, and percent circumcised during birth hospitalization, by race: United States, 1979–2008.* (www.cdc.gov/nchs/data/nhds/9circumcision/2007circ9_regionracetrend.pdf) [3]

Centers for Disease Control. (2010d). *Use of contraception in the United States: 1982–2008.* (www.cdc.gov/nchs/data/series/sr_23/sr23_029.pdf) [9]

Centers for Disease Control. (2010e). *Youth risk behavior surveillance—2009.* (www.cdc.gov/mmwr/pdf/ss/ss5905.pdf) [10]

Centers for Disease Control. (2011a). *National Intimate Partner and Sexual Violence Survey.* (www.cdc.gov/ViolencePrevention/pdf/NISVS_Report2010-a.pdf) [16]

Centers for Disease Control. (2011b). *Sexual behavior, sexual attraction, and sexual identity in the United States: Data from the 2006–2008 National Survey of Family Growth.* (www.cdc.gov/nchs/data/nhsr/nhsr036.pdf) [11, 12]

Centers for Disease Control. (2012a). *First marriages in the United States: Data from the 2006–2010 National Survey of Family Growth.* (www.cdc.gov/nchs/data/nhsr/nhsr049.pdf) [11]

Centers for Disease Control. (2012b). *Home births in the United States, 1990–2009.* (www.cdc.gov/nchs/data/databriefs/db84.htm) [8]

Centers for Disease Control. (2013a). *Births: Final data for 2012.* (www.cdc.gov/nchs/data/nvsr/nvsr62/nvsr62_09.pdf#table01) [8]

Centers for Disease Control. (2013b). *First premarital cohabitation in the United States: 2006–2010 National Survey of Family Growth.* (www.cdc.gov/nchs/data/nhsr/nhsr064.pdf) [11]

Centers for Disease Control. (2013c). *Gay and bisexual men's health: Substance abuse.* (www.cdc.gov/msmhealth/substance-abuse.htm) [12]

Centers for Disease Control. (2013d). *Incidence, prevalence, and cost of sexually transmitted infections in the United States.* (www.cdc.gov/std/stats/STI-Estimates-Fact-Sheet-Feb-2013.pdf) [15]

Centers for Disease Control. (2013e). *National marriage and divorce rate trends.* (www.cdc.gov/nchs/nvss/marriage_divorce_tables.htm) [11]

Centers for Disease Control. (2013f). *Planning for pregnancy.* (www.cdc.gov/preconception/planning.html) [8]

Centers for Disease Control. (2013g). *Pregnancy mortality surveillance system.* (www.cdc.gov/reproductivehealth/MaternalInfantHealth/PMSS.html) [8]

Centers for Disease Control. (2013h). *The National Intimate Partner and Sexual Violence Survey (NISVS): 2010 findings on victimization by sexual orientation.* (www.cdc.gov/violenceprevention/pdf/nisvs_sofindings.pdf) [16]

Centers for Disease Control. (2013i). *What is HPV?* (www.cdc.gov/hpv/whatishpv.html) [15]

Centers for Disease Control. (2014a). *2010 STD treatment guidelines.* (www.cdc.gov/std/treatment/2010/default.htm) [15]

Centers for Disease Control. (2014b). *2012 sexually transmitted disease surveillance: Gonorrhea.* (www.cdc.gov/std/stats12/gonorrhea.htm) [15]

Centers for Disease Control. (2014c). *Assisted reproductive technology (ART).* (www.cdc.gov/art) [8]

Centers for Disease Control. (2014d). *Bacterial vaginosis: CDC fact sheet.* (www.cdc.gov/std/bv/STDFact-Bacterial-Vaginosis.htm) [15]

Centers for Disease Control, (2014e). *Draft CDC recommendations for providers counseling male patients and parents regarding male circumcision and the prevention of HIV infection, STIs, and other health outcomes.* (www.cdc.gov/nchhstp/newsroom/docs/MC-factsheet-508.pdf) [3]

Centers for Disease Control. (2014f). *Fetal alcohol spectrum disorders.* (www.cdc.gov/ncbddd/fasd/facts.html) [8]

Centers for Disease Control. (2014g). *Gonorrhea statistics.* (www.cdc.gov/std/Gonorrhea/stats.htm) [15]

Centers for Disease Control. (2014h). *HIV in the United States: At a glance.* (www.cdc.gov/hiv/statistics/basics/ataglance.html) [15]

Centers for Disease Control. (2014i). *HPV-associated anal cancer rates by race and ethnicity.* (www.cdc.gov/cancer/hpv/statistics/anal.htm) [15]

Centers for Disease Control. (2014j). *Human papillomavirus (HPV) infection.* (www.cdc.gov/std/treatment/2010/hpv.htm) [2]

Centers for Disease Control. (2014k). *Infertility service use in the United States: Data from the National Survey of Family Growth, 1982–2010.* (www.cdc.gov/nchs/data/nhsr/nhsr073.pdf) [8]

Centers for Disease Control. (2014l). *Infographic resources.* (www.cdc.gov/hiv/library/infographics.html) [15]

Centers for Disease Control. (2014m). *National overview of sexually transmitted diseases (STDs), 2012.* (www.cdc.gov/std/stats12/natoverview.htm) [15]

Centers for Disease Control. (2014n). *Prevalence and characteristics of sexual violence, stalking, and intimate partner violence victimization: National Intimate Partner and Sexual Violence Survey, United States, 2011.* (www.cdc.gov/mmwr/preview/mmwrhtml/ss6308a1.htm?s_cid=ss6308a1_e) [16]

Centers for Disease Control. (2014o). *Primary and secondary syphilis—United States, 2005–2013.* (www.cdc.gov/mmwr/preview/mmwrhtml/mm6318a4.htm?s_cid=mm6318a4_w) [15]

Centers for Disease Control. (2014p). *Smoking during pregnancy.* (www.cdc.gov/tobacco/basic_information/health_effects/pregnancy) [8]

Centers for Disease Control. (2014q). *Youth Risk Behavior Survey—United States, 2013.* (www.cdc.gov/mmwr/pdf/ss/ss6304.pdf) [10]

Chalett, J. M. & Nerenberg, L. T. (2000). "Blue balls": A diagnostic consideration in testiculoscrotal pain in young adults: A case report and discussion. *Pediatrics, 106,* 843. [5]

Chalmers, K. (2004). Sad end to boy/girl life. *Winnipeg Sun,* May 10. [4]

Chantry, K. & Craig, R. J. (1994). Psychological screening of sexually violent offenders with the MCMI. *Journal of Clinical Psychology, 50,* 430–435. [16]

Chen, L. P., Murad, M. H., Paras, M. L., Colbenson, K. M., Sattler, A. L., Goranson, E. N., et al. (2010). Sexual abuse and lifetime diagnosis of psychiatric disorders: Systematic review and meta-analysis. *Mayo Clinic Proceedings, 85,* 618–629. [10]

Cherlin, A. J. (2009). Married with bankruptcy. *New York Times,* May 28. [11]

Cheyney, M., Bovbjerg, M., Everson, C., Gordon, W., Hannibal, D. & Vedam, S. (2014). Outcomes of care for 16,924 planned home births in the United States: The midwives alliance of North America statistics project, 2004 to 2009. *Journal of Midwifery and Women's Health, 59,* 17–27. [8]

Chida, Y. & Mao, X. (2009). Does psychosocial stress predict symptomatic herpes simplex virus recurrence? A meta-analytic investigation on prospective studies. *Brain, Behavior, and Immunity, 23,* 917–925. [15]

Children's Bureau. (2013). *The AFCARS Report.* (www.acf.hhs.gov/sites/default/files/cb/afcarsreport20.pdf) [8]

Chiu, R. W., Akolekar, R., Zheng, Y. W., Leung, T. Y., Sun, H., Chan, K. C., et al. (2011). Non-invasive prenatal assessment of trisomy 21 by multiplexed maternal plasma DNA sequencing: Large scale validity study. *BMJ, 342,* c7401. [8]

Chivers, M. L., Rieger, G., Latty, E. & Michael Bailey, J. (2004). A sex difference in the specificity of sexual arousal. *Psychological Science, 15,* 736–744. [12]

Chivers, M. L., Seto, M. C. & Blanchard, R. (2007). Gender and sexual orientation differences in sexual response to sexual activities versus gender of actors in sexual films. *Journal of Personality and Social Psychology, 93,* 1108–1121. [5]

Chivers, M. L., Seto, M. C., Lalumière, M. L., Laan, E. & Grimbos, T. (2010). Agreement of self-reported and genital measures of sexual arousal in men and women: A meta-analysis. *Archives of Sexual Behavior, 39,* 5–56. [5]

Chun, A. B., Rose, S., Mitrani, C., Silvestre, A. J. & Wald, A. (1997). Anal sphincter structure and function in homosexual males engaging in anoreceptive intercourse. *American Journal of Gastroenterology, 92,* 465–468. [6]

Ciftcioglu, S. & Erci, B. (2009). Coitus interruptus as a contraceptive method: Turkish women's perceptions and experiences. *Journal of Advanced Nursing, 65,* 1686–1694. [9]

Circles UK. (2014). Linking circles of support and accountability. (www.circles-uk.org.uk) [13]

Clark-Flory, T. (2011). *A male porn star speaks.* (www.salon.com/2011/07/28/porn_13) [17]

Clark, R. D. & Hatfield, E. (1989). Gender differences in receptivity to sexual offers. *Journal of Psychology and Human Sexuality, 2,* 39–55. [7]

Clark, R. D., III & Hatfield, E. (2003). Love in the afternoon. *Psychological Inquiry, 14,* 227–231. [7]

Clark, S. K., Jeglic, E. L., Calkins, C. & Tatar, J. R. (2014). More than a nuisance: The prevalence and consequences of frotteurism and exhibitionism. *Sexual Abuse,* published online March 4. [13]

Clarke, D. L., Buccimazza, I., Anderson, F. A. & Thomson, S. R. (2005). Colorectal foreign bodies. *Colorectal Disease, 7,* 98–103. [6]

Clarke, J. (2007). *Older white women join Kenya's sex tourists.* (www.reuters.com/article/newsOne/idUSL1434216920071126) [17]

Clarridge, C. (2010). Man who ran animal-sex operation sentenced for probation violation. *Seattle Times,* July 16. [13]

Claxton, S. E. & van Dulmen, M. H. M. (2013). Casual sexual relationships and experiences in emerging adulthood. *Emerging Adulthood, 1,* 138–150. [7]

Clement, K., Vaisse, C., Lahlou, N., Cabrol, S., Pelloux, V., Cassuto, D., et al. (1998). A mutation in the human leptin receptor gene causes obesity and pituitary dysfunction. *Nature, 392,* 398–401. [10]

Clutton-Brock, T. (2007). Sexual selection in males and females. *Science, 318,* 1882–1885. [App. A]

Clutton-Brock, T. & McAuliffe, K. (2009). Female mate choice in mammals. *Quarterly Review of Biology, 84,* 3–27. [App. A]

CNN World. (2013). *International adoptions in decline as number of orphans grows.* (www.cnn.com/2013/09/16/world/international-adoption-main-story-decline) [8]

CNN. (2006). *Evangelical confesses to "sexual immorality" in letter.* (articles.cnn.com/2006-11-05/us/haggard.allegations_1_gayle-haggard-pastor-ross-sexual-immorality?_s=PM:US) [12]

CNN. (2014). *Hopkins to pay $190 million after doctor secretly photographed patients.* (www.cnn.com/2014/07/21/us/hopkins-doctor-settlement/index.html?hpt=hp_t2) [13]

Cochrane Collaboration. (2009). *Antenatal perineal massage for reducing perineal trauma.* (www.elastolabo.com/pdf/1.%20Beckmann%20Cochrane%20Database%20Syst%20Rev%202009.pdf) [8]

Coffman, K. B., Coffman, L. C. & Marzilli Ericson, K. M. (2013). *The size of the LGBT population and the magnitude of anti-gay sentiment are substantially underestimated.* (www.nber.org/papers/w19508.pdf) [12]

Cohen, C. E., Giles, A. & Nelson, M. (2004). Sexual trauma associated with fisting and recreational drugs. *Sexually Transmitted Infections, 80,* 469–470. [6]

Cohen, C. R., Lingappa, J. R., Baeten, J. M., Ngayo, M. O., Spiegel, C. A., Hong, T., et al. (2012). Bacterial vaginosis associated with increased risk of female-to-male HIV-1 transmission: A prospective cohort analysis among African couples. *PLOS Medicine, 9,* e1001251. [15]

Cohen, J. (2013). AIDS research. More woes for struggling HIV vaccine field. *Science, 340,* 667. [15]

Colapinto, J. (2000). *As nature made him: The boy who was raised as a girl.* HarperCollins. [4]

Cole, L. A. (2011). The utility of six over-the-counter (home) pregnancy tests. *Clinical Chemistry and Laboratory Medicine, 49,* 1317–1322. [8]

Cole, L. A. (2012). The hCG assay or pregnancy test. *Clinical Chemistry and Laboratory Medicine, 50,* 617–630. [8]

Coleman, M., Ganong, L. & Fine, M. (2000). Reinvestigating marriage: Another decade of progress. *Journal of Marriage and the Family, 62,* 1288–1307. [11]

Coleman, P. K., Coyle, C. T., Shuping, M. & Rue, V. M. (2009). Induced abortion and anxiety, mood, and substance abuse disorders: Isolating the effects of abortion in the National Comorbidity Survey. *Journal of Psychiatric Research, 43*, 770–776. [9]

Collaborative Group on Hormonal Factors in Breast Cancer. (1996). Breast cancer and hormonal contraceptives: Collaborative reanalysis of individual data on 53 297 women with breast cancer and 100 239 women without breast cancer from 54 epidemiological studies. *Lancet, 347*, 1713–1727. [2]

College Confidential. (2014). *Would you go to prom without a date?* (talk.collegeconfidential.com/high-school-life/1241797-would-you-go-to-prom-without-a-date.html) [10]

Collier, K. L., Horn, S. S., Bos, H. M. & Sandfort, T. G. (2014). Attitudes toward lesbians and gays among American and Dutch adolescents. *Journal of Sex Research*, published online February 10. [12]

Collins, G. (2014). This is what 80 looks like. *New York Times*, March 22. [11]

Collins, R. L. (2011). Content analysis of gender roles in media: Where are we now and where should we go? *Sex Roles, 64*, 290–298. [4]

Columbia Health. (2013). *Blue balls, blue ovaries?* (goaskalice.columbia.edu/blue-balls-blue-ovaries) [5]

Confer, J. C. & Cloud, M. D. (2011). Sex differences in response to imagining a partner's heterosexual or homosexual affair. *Personality and Individual Differences, 50*, 129–134. [7]

Conley, T. D., Ziegler, A. & Moors, A. C. (2012). Backlash from the bedroom: Stigma mediates gender differences in acceptance of casual sex offers. *Psychology of Women Quarterly, 37*, 392–407. [7]

Conley, T. D., Ziegler, A., Moors, A. C., Matsick, J. L. & Valentine, B. (2013). A critical examination of popular assumptions about the benefits and outcomes of monogamous relationships. *Personality and Social Psychology Review, 17*, 124–141. [11]

Conrad, R. (Ed.). (2014). *Against equality: Queer revolution, not mere inclusion.* AK Press. [12]

Conway, L. (2013). *How many of us are there? An investigative report.* (www.gendercentre.org.au/resources/polare-archive/archived-articles/how-many-of-us-are-there.htm) [4]

Cooper, A. (Ed.) (2002). *Sex and the Internet: A guidebook for clinicians.* Brunner-Routledge. [7]

Cooper, E. B., Fenigstein, A. & Fauber, R. L. (2014). The faking orgasm scale for women: Psychometric properties. *Archives of Sexual Behavior, 43*, 423–435. [14]

Cordier, S. (2008). Evidence for a role of paternal exposures in developmental toxicity. *Basic and Clinical Pharmacology and Toxicology, 102*, 176–181. [8]

Cosgrove, K. P., Mazure, C. M. & Staley, J. K. (2007). Evolving knowledge of sex differences in brain structure, function, and chemistry. *Biological Psychiatry, 62*, 847–855. [4]

Costa, E. M., Domenice, S., Sircili, M. H., Inacio, M. & Mendonca, B. B. (2012). DSD due to 5alpha-reductase 2 deficiency—from

diagnosis to long term outcome. *Seminars in Reproductive Medicine, 30*, 427–431. [4]

Costa, P. T., Jr., Terracciano, A. & McCrae, R. R. (2001). Gender differences in personality traits across cultures: Robust and surprising findings. *Journal of Personality and Social Psychology, 81*, 322–331. [4]

Council on Contemporary Families. (2009). *Are babies bad for marriage?* (contemporaryfamilies.org/news-can-use-babies-bad-marriage) [8]

Courtiol, A., Raymond, M., Godelle, B. & Ferdy, J. B. (2010). Mate choice and human stature: Homogamy as a unified framework for understanding mating preferences. *Evolution, 64*, 2189–2203. [7]

Cowley, A. D. (2014). "Let's get drunk and have sex": The complex relationship of alcohol, gender, and sexual victimization. *Journal of Interpersonal Violence, 29*, 1258–1278. [16]

Coyle, K. K., Franks, H. M., Glassman, J. R. & Stanoff, N. M. (2012). Condom use: Slippage, breakage, and steps for proper use among adolescents in alternative school settings. *Journal of School Health, 82*, 345–352. [9]

Crimes Against Children Research Center. (2014). *Trends in unwanted online experiences and sexting.* (www.unh.edu/ccrc/pdf/Full%20Trends%20Report%20Feb%202014%20with%20tables.pdf) [10]

Crocker, W. H. & Crocker, J. G. (2003). *The Canela: Kinship, ritual and sex in an Amazonian tribe* (2nd. ed.). Wadsworth. [1]

Cui, M. & Donnellan, M. B. (2009). Trajectories of conflict over raising adolescent children and marital satisfaction. *Journal of Marriage and Family, 71*, 479–494. [11]

Cumming-Bruce, N. (2014). U.N. panel assails Vatican over sexual abuse by priests. *New York Times*, February 5. [13]

Cummz, C. (2014). *What it's really like to be a porn star.* (www.cosmopolitan.com/sex-love/advice/a6170/courtney-cummz-porn-star) [17]

Cunningham, S. & Kendall, T. D. (2010). *Moonlighting: Skill premia in commercialized sex markets.* (papers.ssrn.com/sol3/papers.cfm?abstract_id=1583510) [17]

Curran, D. (2011). *Introduction to menopause.* (emedicine.medscape.com/article/264088-overview) [11]

Cuzick, J., Sestak, I., Forbes, J. F., Dowsett, M., Knox, J., Cawthorn, S., Saunders, C., Roche, N., Mansel, R. E., von Minckwitz, G., Bonanni, B., Palva, T. & Howell, A. (2013). Anastrozole for prevention of breast cancer in high-risk postmenopausal women (IBIS-II): An international, double-blind, randomised placebo-controlled trial. *Lancet, 384*, 1041–1048. [2]

D'Onofrio, B. M., Rickert, M. E., Frans, E., Kuja-Halkola, R., Almqvist, C., Sjolander, A., et al. (2014). Paternal age at childbearing and offspring psychiatric and academic morbidity. *JAMA Psychiatry*, published online February 26. [8]

Dadlez, E. M., Andrews, W. L., Lewis, C. & Stroud, M. (2009). Rape, evolution, and pseudoscience: Natural selection in the academy. *Journal of Social Philosophy, 40*, 75–96. [16]

Dahabreh, I. J. & Paulus, J. K. (2011). Association of episodic physical and sexual activity with triggering of acute cardiac events: Systematic review and meta-analysis. *JAMA, 305*, 1225–1233. [6]

Dahl, D. W., Vohs, K. D. & Sengupta, J. (2011). Sex in advertising: Only on Mars and not on Venus? *GfK Marketing Intelligence Review, 3*, 54–57. [17]

Dahlburg, J.-T. (1994). Where killing baby girls is "no big sin." *Toronto Star*, February 28. [8]

Dalke, K. A., Fein, L., Jenkins, L. C., Caso, J. R. & Salgado, C. J. (2013). *Complications of genital piercings.* (omicsonline.org/complications-of-genital-piercings-2161-1173-2-122.pdf) [2]

Dalla, R. L. (2000). Exposing the "Pretty Woman" myth: A qualitative examination of the lives of female streetwalking prostitutes. *Journal of Sex Research, 37*, 344–353. [17]

Darling, C. A., Davidson, J. K., Sr. & Conway-Welch, C. (1990). Female ejaculation: Perceived origins, the Grafenberg spot/area, and sexual responsiveness. *Archives of Sexual Behavior, 19*, 29–47. [5]

Darling, C. A., Davidson, J. K., Sr. & Jennings, D. A. (1991). The female sexual response revisited: Understanding the multiorgasmic experience in women. *Archives of Sexual Behavior, 20*, 527–540. [5]

Davies, L. (2014). Pope Francis encourages mothers to breastfeed—even in the Sistine Chapel. *Guardian (London)*, January 12. [3]

Davies, S. L., Glaser, D. & Kossoff, R. (2000). Children's sexual play and behavior in preschool settings: Staff's perceptions, reports, and responses. *Child Abuse and Neglect, 24*, 1329–1343. [10]

Davis, M. K. & Gidycz, C. A. (2000). Child sexual abuse prevention programs: A meta-analysis. *Journal of Clinical Child Psychology, 29*, 257–265. [10]

Davis, S. R. & Davison, S. L. (2012). Current perspectives on testosterone therapy for women. *Menopausal Medicine, 20*, S1–S4. [10]

Dawson, S. J. & Chivers, M. L. (2014). Gender-specificity of solitary and dyadic sexual desire among gynephilic and androphilic women and men. *Journal of Sexual Medicine, 11*, 980–994. [12]

Dawson, S. J., Suschinsky, K. D. & Lalumiere, M. L. (2012). Sexual fantasies and viewing times across the menstrual cycle: A diary study. *Archives of Sexual Behavior, 41*, 173–183. [5]

de Andrade, E., de Mesquita, A. A., Claro Jde, A., de Andrade, P. M., Ortiz, V., Paranhos, M. & Srougi, M. (2007). Study of the efficacy of Korean Red Ginseng in the treatment of erectile dysfunction. *Asian Journal of Andrology, 9*, 241–244. [5]

de Graaf, H. & Rademakers, J. (2011). The psychological measurement of childhood sexual development in Western societies: Methodological challenges. *Journal of Sex Research, 48*, 118–129. [10]

de Graaf, P. M. & Kalmijn, M. (2006). Divorce motives in a period of rising divorce: Evidence from a Dutch life-history survey. *Journal of Family Issues, 27*, 483–505. [11]

de Magalhaes, P. (1576/1922). *The histories of Brazil.* Cortes Society. [4]

De Smet, D., Van Speybroeck, L. & Verplaetse, J. (2014). The Westermarck effect revisited: A psychophysiological study of sibling incest aversion in young female adults. *Evolution and Human Behavior, 35,* 34–42. [5]

Dean, K. E. & Malamuth, N. M. (1997). Characteristics of men who aggress sexually and of men who imagine aggressing: Risk and moderating variables. *Journal of Personality and Social Psychology, 72,* 449–455. [16]

Dehlin, J. P., Galliher, R. V., Bradshaw, W. S., Hyde, D. C. & Crowell, K. A. (2014). Sexual orientation change efforts among current or former LDS Church members. *Journal of Counseling Psychology,* published online March 14. [12]

Del Giudice, M., Booth, T. & Irwing, P. (2012). The distance between Mars and Venus: Measuring global sex differences in personality. *PLOS ONE, 7,* e29265. [4]

DeLamater, J. (1987). A sociological approach. In: Geer, J. H. & O'Donohue, W. T. (Eds.), *Theories of human sexuality.* Plenum. [7]

DeMaris, A. (2013). Burning the candle at both ends: Extramarital sex as a precursor of marital disruption. *Journal of Family Issues, 34,* 1474–1499. [11]

DeMaris, A., Sanchez, L. A. & Krivickas, K. (2012). Developmental patterns in marital satisfaction: Another look at covenant marriage. *Journal of Marriage and Family, 74,* 989–1004. [11]

Deng, J. M., Satoh, K., Wang, H., Chang, H., Zhang, Z., Stewart, M. D., et al. (2011). Generation of viable male and female mice from two fathers. *Biology of Reproduction, 84,* 613–618. [12]

Denizet-Lewis, B. (2004). Friends, friends with benefits and the benefits of the local mall. *New York Times,* May 30. [10]

Dennis, M. & Grix, J. (2012). *Sport under communism: Behind the East German 'miracle.'* Palgrave Macmillan. [3]

Denny, K. E. (2011). Gender in context, content, and approach: Comparing gender messages in Girl Scout and Boy Scout handbooks. *Gender and Society, 25,* 27–47. [4]

Deonandan, R., Green, S. & van Beinum, A. (2012). Ethical concerns for maternal surrogacy and reproductive tourism. *Journal of Medical Ethics, 38,* 742–745. [8]

Dettori, J. R., Koepsell, T. D., Cummings, P. & Corman, J. M. (2004). Erectile dysfunction after a long-distance cycling event: Associations with bicycle characteristics. *Journal of Urology, 172,* 637–641. [14]

Dettwyler, K. A. (1994). Dancing skeletons: Life and death in West Africa. Waveland. [5]

Dewaraja, R. & Money, J. (1986). Transcultural sexology: Formicophilia, a newly named paraphilia in a young Buddhist male. *Journal of Sex and Marital Therapy, 12,* 139–145. [13]

Dhejne, C., Lichtenstein, P., Boman, M., Johansson, A. L., Langstrom, N. & Landen, M. (2011). Long-term follow-up of transsexual persons undergoing sex reassignment surgery: Cohort study in sweden. *PLOS ONE, 6,* e16885. [4]

Diamond, L. M. (2008a). Female bisexuality from adolescence to adulthood: Results from a 10-year longitudinal study. *Developmental Psychology, 44,* 5–14. [12]

Diamond, L. M. (2008b). *Sexual fluidity: Understanding women's love and desire.* Harvard University Press. [12]

Diamond, M. (2009). Pornography, public acceptance and sex related crime: A review. *International Journal of Law and Psychiatry, 32,* 304–314. [17]

Diamond, M. (2013). Transsexuality among twins: Identity concordance, transition, rearing, and orientation. *International Journal of Transgenderism, 14,* 24–38. [4]

Diamond, M. & Sigmundson, H. K. (1997). Sex reassignment at birth. Long-term review and clinical implications. *Archives of Pediatrics and Adolescent Medicine, 151,* 298–304. [4]

Diamond, M. & Uchiyama, A. (1999). Pornography, rape, and sex crimes in Japan. *International Journal of Law and Psychiatry, 22,* 1–22. [17]

Diaz, F. (2010). *The problem of the undetected rapist: A Texas A&M case study.* (www.huffingtonpost.com/2010/02/26/the-problem-of-the-undete_n_478679.html) [16]

Dibble, J. L. & Drouin, M. (2014). Using modern technology to keep in touch with back burners: An investment model analysis. *Computers in Human Behavior, 34,* 96–100. [7]

Dickson, E. J. (2014). *The "insatiable" life of porn star Asa Akira.* (www.dailydot.com/lifestyle/asa-akira-memoir-qanda) [17]

Dines, G. (2008). *Penn, porn and me.* (www.counterpunch.org/2008/06/23/penn-porn-and-me) [17]

Dirie, W. (1998). *Desert flower: The extraordinary journey of a desert nomad.* William Morrow. [2]

Disaster Center. (2014). *United States crime rates 1960–2012.* (www.disastercenter.com/crime/uscrime.htm) [16]

Dixson, A. F. (2009). *Sexual selection and the origins of human mating systems.* Oxford University Press. [6]

Dixson, B. J., Grimshaw, G. M., Linklater, W. L. & Dixson, A. F. (2011). Eye-tracking of men's preferences for waist-to-hip ratio and breast size of women. *Archives of Sexual Behavior, 40,* 43–50. [5]

Domb, L. G. & Pagel, M. (2001). Sexual swellings advertise female quality in wild baboons. *Nature, 410,* 204–206. [App. A]

Dominguez, R. C., Nelke, C. F. & Perry, B. D. (2002). Child sexual abuse. In: Levinson, D. (Ed.), *Encyclopedia of crime and punishment.* Sage. [12]

Doorbar, J., Quint, W., Banks, L., Bravo, I. G., Stoler, M., Broker, T. R. & Stanley, M. A. (2012). The biology and life-cycle of human papillomaviruses. *Vaccine, 30*(Suppl. 5), F55–70. [15]

Dorn, L. D. (2007). Psychological and social problems in children with premature adrenarche and precocious puberty. In: Pescovitz, O. H. & Walvoord, E. C. (Eds.), *When puberty is precocious: Scientific and clinical aspects.* Humana. [10]

Dose, R. (2014). *Magnus Hirschfeld: The origins of the gay liberation movement.* Monthly Review. [12]

Dowbiggin, I. R. (2003). Keeping America sane: Psychiatry and eugenics in the United States and Canada, 1880–1940. Cornell University Press. [13]

Downe, P. & "Ashley-Mika." (2003). "The people we think we are": The social identities of girls involved in prostitution. In: Gorkoff, K. & Runner, J. (Eds.), *Being heard: The experiences of young women in prostitution.* Fernwood. [17]

Downer, E. J. & Campbell, V. A. (2010). Phytocannabinoids, CNS cells and development: A dead issue? *Drug and Alcohol Review, 29,* 91–98. [8]

Drabant, E. M., Kiefer, A. K., Eriksson, N., Mountain, J. L., Francke, U., Tung, J. Y., et al. (2012). *Sexual orientation in a large, Web-based cohort.* (blog.23andme.com/wp-content/uploads/2012/11/Drabant-Poster-v7.pdf) [12]

Dreger, A., Feder, E. K. & Tamar-Mattis, A. (2012). Prenatal dexamethasone for congenital adrenal hyperplasia: An ethics canary in the modern medical mine. *Journal of Bioethical Inquiry, 9,* 277–294. [8]

Dreifus, C. (2005). Declaring with clarity, when gender is ambiguous. *New York Times,* May 31. [4]

Drummond, K. D., Bradley, S. J., Peterson-Badali, M. & Zucker, K. J. (2008). A follow-up study of girls with gender identity disorder. *Developmental Psychology, 44,* 34–45. [4]

Dryden, W. (1999). *Overcoming jealousy.* Sheldon. [7]

Dugatkin, L. A. (2007). Inclusive fitness theory from Darwin to Hamilton. *Genetics, 176,* 1375–1380. [App. A]

Dukers-Muijrers, N. H., Niekamp, A. M., Brouwers, E. E. & Hoebe, C. J. (2010). Older and swinging: Need to identify hidden and emerging risk groups at STI clinics. *Sexually Transmitted Infections, 86,* 315–317. [11]

Dunn, M. E. & Trost, J. E. (1989). Male multiple orgasms: A descriptive study. *Archives of Sexual Behavior, 18,* 377–387. [5]

Dworkin, A. (1979). *The lie.* (www.nostatusquo.com/ACLU/dworkin/WarZoneChaptIa.html) [17]

Dworkin, A. (1994). *Prostitution and male supremacy.* (www.nostatusquo.com/ACLU/dworkin/MichLawJourI.html) [17]

Earls, C. M. & Lalumière, M. L. (2002). A case study of preferential bestiality (zoophilia). *Sexual Abuse, 14,* 83–88. [13]

Earls, C. M. & Lalumière, M. L. (2009). A case study of preferential bestiality. *Archives of Sexual Behavior, 38,* 605–609. [13]

Eastwick, P. W. & Finkel, E. J. (2008). Sex differences in mate preferences revisited: Do people know what they initially desire in a romantic partner? *Journal of Personality and Social Psychology, 94,* 245–264. [5]

Eastwick, P. W. & Hunt, L. L. (2014). Relational mate value: Consensus and uniqueness in romantic evaluations. *Journal of Personality and Social Psychology, 106,* 728–751. [5]

Eaton, A. A. & Rose, S. (2011). Has dating become more egalitarian? A 35 year review using *Sex Roles. Sex Roles, 64,* 843–862. [7]

Eaton, N. R., Keyes, K. M., Krueger, R. F., Balsis, S., Skodol, A. E., Markon, K. E., et al. (2012). An invariant dimensional liability model of gender differences in mental disorder prevalence: Evidence from a national sample. *Journal of Abnormal Psychology, 121,* 282–288. [10]

Eckholm, E. (2007). Boys cast out by polygamists find help. *New York Times,* September 9. [11]

Eckholm, E. (2014). No longer ignored, evidence solves rape cases years later. *New York Times,* August 2. [16]

Eddleman, K. A., Malone, F. D., Sullivan, L., Dukes, K., Berkowitz, R. L., Kharbutli, Y., et al. (2006). Pregnancy loss rates after midtrimester amniocentesis. *Obstetrics and Gynecology, 108,* 1067–1072. [8]

Eibl-Eibesfeldt, I. (2007). *Human ethology.* Aldine. [7]

Eichel, E. W., Eichel, J. D. & Kule, S. (1988). The technique of coital alignment and its relation to female orgasmic response and simultaneous orgasm. *Journal of Sex and Marital Therapy, 14,* 129–141. [14]

Eichenwald, K. (2005). Through his webcam, a boy joins a sordid online world. *New York Times,* December 19. [17]

Einstein, M. H., Baron, M., Levin, M. J., Chatterjee, A., Edwards, R. P., Zepp, F., et al. (2009). Comparison of the immunogenicity and safety of Cervarix and Gardasil human papillomavirus (HPV) cervical cancer vaccines in healthy women aged 18-45 years. *Human Vaccines, 5,* 705–719. [15]

Eisenberg, M. E., Ackard, D. M., Resnick, M. D. & Neumark-Sztainer, D. (2009). Casual sex and psychological health among young adults: Is having "friends with benefits" emotionally damaging? *Perspectives on Sexual and Reproductive Health, 41,* 231–237. [7]

Eisner, S. (2013). *Bi: Notes for a bisexual revolution.* Seal. [12]

Ejegard, H., Ryding, E. L. & Sjogren, B. (2008). Sexuality after delivery with episiotomy: A long-term follow-up. *Gynecologic and Obstetric Investigation, 66,* 1–7. [8]

El-Bassel, N., Schilling, R. F., Gilbert, L., Faruque, S., Irwin, K. L. & Edlin, B. R. (2000). Sex trading and psychological distress in a street-based sample of low-income urban men. *Journal of Psychoactive Drugs, 32,* 259–267. [17]

Eligon, J. (2011). Strauss-Kahn drama ends with short final scene. *New York Times,* August 23. [16]

Elliott, A. J. & Niesta, D. (2008). Romantic red: Red enhances men's attraction to women. *Journal of Personality and Social Psychology, 95,* 1150–1164. [5]

Elliott, S. (2009). Sexuality after spinal cord injury. In: Field-Fote, E. C. (Ed.), Spinal cord injury rehabilitation. F.A. Davis. [6]

Ellis, B. J. & Malamuth, N. M. (2000). Love and anger in romantic relationships: A discrete systems model. *Journal of Personality, 68,* 525–556. [7]

Ellison, C. R. (2000). *Women's sexualities: Generations of women share intimate secrets of sexual self-acceptance.* New Harbinger. [6]

Emmelot-Vonk, M. H., Verhaar, H. J., Nakhai-Pour, H. R., Aleman, A., Lock, T. M., Bosch, J. L., et al. (2008). Effect of testosterone supplementation on functional mobility, cognition, and other parameters in older men: A randomized controlled trial. *JAMA, 299,* 39–52. [14]

Emmelot-Vonk, M. H., Verhaar, H. J., Nakhai-Pour, H. R., Grobbee, D. E. & van der Schouw, Y. T. (2011). Low testosterone concentrations and the symptoms of testosterone deficiency according to the Androgen Deficiency in Ageing Males (ADAM) and Ageing Males' Symptoms rating scale (AMS) questionnaires. *Clinical Endocrinology, 74,* 488–494. [14]

Emmers-Sommer, T. (2014). Adversarial sexual attitudes towards women: The relationships with gender and traditionalism. *Sexuality & Culture,* published online February 4, 1–14. [7]

Endsjo, D. O. (2011). *Sex and religion: Teachings and taboos in the history of world faiths.* Reaktion. [1]

Engman, M., Wijma, K. & Wijma, B. (2010). Long-term coital behaviour in women treated with cognitive behaviour therapy for superficial coital pain and vaginismus. *Cognitive Behavioral Therapy, 39,* 193–202. [14]

Epperson, C. N., Steiner, M., Hartlage, S. A., Eriksson, E., Schmidt, P. J., Jones, I. & Yonkers, K. A. (2012). Premenstrual dysphoric disorder: Evidence for a new category for DSM-5. *American Journal of Psychiatry, 169,* 465–475. [2]

Erikson, E. H. (1968). *Identity: Youth and crisis.* Norton. [10]

Esquire. (2007). *The state of sex.* (www.esquire.com/features/ESQ0207stateofsex) [4, 6]

Esquire. (2012). *Sex and the American man: A preview.* (www.esquire.com/women/sex/sex-survey-2012–0412) [1]

Estes, R. J. & Weiner, N. A. (2002). *The commercial sexual exploitation of children in the U.S., Canada and Mexico* (rev. ed.). (www.hawaii.edu/hivandaids/Commercial%20Sexual%20Exploitation%20of%20Children%20in%20the%20US,%20Canada%20and%20Mexico.pdf) [17]

Evans, R. (2014). *5 reasons being a male porn star is less fun than it looks.* (www.cracked.com/article_21339_5-reasons-being-male-porn-star-less-fun-than-it-looks.html) [17]

Evans, R. W. & Couch, R. (2001). Orgasm and migraine. *Headache, 41,* 512–514. [6]

Evenhouse, E. & Reilly, S. (2004). A sibling study of stepchild well-being. *Journal of Human Resources, 34,* 248–276. [11]

Experience Project. (2014). *I have been raped.* (www.experienceproject.com/stories/Have-Been-Raped/1979934) [16]

Fabes, R. A., Martin, C. L. & Hanish, L. D. (2003). Young children's play qualities in same-, other-, and mixed-sex peer groups. *Child Development, 74,* 921–932. [4]

Facchinetti, P., Giuliano, F., Laurin, M., Bernabe, J. & Clement, P. (2014). Direct brain projections onto the spinal generator of ejaculation in the rat. *Neuroscience, 272,* 207–216. [App. B]

Facelle, T. M., Sadeghi-Nejad, H. & Goldmeier, D. (2013). Persistent genital arousal disorder: Characterization, etiology, and management. *Journal of Sexual Medicine, 10,* 439–450. [14]

Faderman, L. (1981). *Surpassing the love of men: Romantic friendship and love between women from the Renaissance to the present.* William Morrow. [7]

Fagot, B. I., Leinbach, M. D. & O'Boyle, C. (1992). Gender labeling, gender stereotyping, and parenting behaviors. *Developmental Psychology, 28,* 440–443. [4]

Family Health International. (2011). *Partners PrEP and TDF2 pre-exposure prophylaxis trials both demonstrate effectiveness in preventing HIV infection among heterosexuals.* (www.fhi360.org/en/AboutFHI/Media/Releases/res_PrEP.htm) [15]

Fausto-Sterling, A. (2000). *Sexing the body: Gender politics and the construction of sexuality.* Basic Books. [4]

FDA. (2009). *Depo-Provera (medroxyprogesterone acetate injectable suspension).* (www.fda.gov/Safety/MedWatch/SafetyInformation/SafetyAlertsforHumanMedicalProducts/ucm154784.htm) [9]

Feinberg, D. R., DeBruine, L. M., Jones, B. C. & Perrett, D. I. (2008). The role of femininity and averageness of voice pitch in aesthetic judgments of women's voices. *Perception, 37,* 615–623. [5]

Ferguson, C. J. & Hartley, R. D. (2009). The pleasure is momentary. . . the expense damnable?: The influence of pornography on rape and sexual assault. *Aggression and Violent Behavior, 14,* 323–329. [17]

Fine, P., Mathe, H., Ginde, S., Cullins, V., Morfesis, J. & Gainer, E. (2010). Ulipristal acetate taken 48–120 hours after intercourse for emergency contraception. *Obstetrics and Gynecology, 115,* 257–263. [9]

Finer, L. B. & Henshaw, S. K. (2006). Disparities in rates of unintended pregnancy in the United States, 1994 and 2001. *Perspectives on Sexual and Reproductive Health, 38,* 90–96. [9]

Finer, L. B. & Philbin, J. M. (2013). Sexual initiation, contraceptive use, and pregnancy among young adolescents. *Pediatrics, 131,* 886–891. [10]

Finer, L. B. & Zolna, M. R. (2014). Shifts in intended and unintended pregnancies in the United States, 2001–2008. *American Journal of Public Health, 104*(Suppl. 1), S43–48. [9]

Finer, L. B., Frohwirth, L. F., Dauphinee, L. A., Singh, S. & Moore, A. M. (2005). Reasons U.S. women have abortions: Quantitative and qualitative perspectives. *Perspectives on Sexual and Reproductive Health, 37,* 110–118. [9]

Fink, B., Neave, N., Manning, J. T. & Grammer, K. (2006). Facial symmetry and judgements of attractiveness, health and personality. *Personality and Individual Differences, 41,* 491–499. [5]

Finkelstein, J. W., Susman, E. J., Chinchilli, V. M., D'Arcangelo, M. R., Kunselman, S. J., Schwab, J., et al. (1998). Effects of estrogen or testosterone on self-reported sexual responses and behaviors in hypogonadal adolescents. *Journal of Clinical Endocrinology and Metabolism, 83,* 2281–2285. [5]

Finkelstein, K. E. (2001). Man is sentenced to 5 years in attacks in Central Park. *New York Times,* May 19. [16]

Fisher, B. S., Cullen, F. T. & Turner, M. G. (2000). *The sexual victimization of college women.* (www.ncjrs.gov/pdffiles1/nij/182369.pdf) [16]

Fisher, H. E. (1989). Evolution of human sexual pair-bonding. *American Journal of Physical Anthropology, 78,* 331–354. [11]

Fisher, H. E. (2006). Broken hearts: The nature and risks of romantic rejection. In: Crouter, A. C. & Booth, A. (Eds.), *Romance and sex in adolescence and emerging adulthood: Risks and opportunities.* Lawrence Erlbaum. [7]

Fisher, H. E., Aron, A. & Brown, L. L. (2006). Romantic love: A mammalian brain system for mate choice. *Philosophical Transactions of the Royal Society of London Series B: Biological Sciences, 361,* 2173–2186. [7]

Fisher, M. M. & Eugster, E. A. (2014). What is in our environment that effects puberty? *Reproductive Toxicology, 44,* 7–14. [10]

Fisher, T. D. (2013). Gender roles and pressure to be truthful: The bogus pipeline modifies gender differences in sexual but not nonsexual behavior. *Sex Roles, 68,* 401–414. [4]

Fisher, W. A., Kohut, T., Di Gioacchino, L. A. & Fedoroff, P. (2013). Pornography, sex crime, and paraphilia. *Current Psychiatry Report, 15,* 362. [17]

Fisher, W. A., Rosen, R. C., Eardley, I., Sand, M. & Goldstein, I. (2005). Sexual experience of female partners of men with erectile dysfunction: The female experience of men's attitudes to life events and sexuality (FEMALES) study. *Journal of Sexual Medicine, 2,* 675–684. [14]

Fleischman, A. R., Oinuma, M. & Clark, S. L. (2010). Rethinking the definition of "term pregnancy." *Obstetrics and Gynecology, 116,* 136–139. [8]

Fleisher, M. S. & Krienert, J. L. (2009). *The myth of prison rape: Sexual culture in American prisons.* Rowman & Littlefield. [16]

Flot, J. F., Hespeels, B., Li, X., Noel, B., Arkhipova, I., Danchin, E. G., et al. (2013). Genomic evidence for ameiotic evolution in the bdelloid rotifer *Adineta vaga. Nature, 500,* 453–457. [App. A]

Fogg, A. (2013). *The startling facts on female sexual aggression.* (freethoughtblogs.com/hetpat/2013/09/04/the-startling-facts-on-female-sexual-aggression) [16]

Fooladi, E., Bell, R. J., Jane, F., Robinson, P. J., Kulkarni, J. & Davis, S. R. (2014). Testosterone improves antidepressant-emergent loss of libido in women: Findings from a randomized, double-blind, placebo-controlled trial. *Journal of Sexual Medicine, 11,* 831–839. [14]

Ford, C. S. & Beach, F. A. (1951). *Patterns of sexual behavior.* Harper. [3, 5, 6, 10]

Forum on Child and Family Statistics. (2013). *Sexual activity.* (www.childstats.gov/americaschildren/tables/beh4a.asp) [10]

Foshee, V. A., McNaughton Reyes, H. L., Ennett, S. T., Cance, J. D., Bauman, K. E. & Bowling, J. M. (2012). Assessing the effects of Families for Safe Dates, a family-based teen dating abuse prevention program. *Journal of Adolescent Health, 51,* 349–356. [16]

Fossos, N., Neighbors, C., Kaysen, D. & Hove, M. C. (2007). Intimate partner violence perpetration and problem drinking among college students: The roles of expectancies and subjective evaluations of alcohol aggression. *Journal of Studies on Alcohol and Drugs, 68,* 706–713. [16]

Foubert, J. D. & Newberry, J. T. (2006). Effects of two versions of an empathy-based rape prevention program on fraternity men's survivor empathy, attitudes, and behavioral intent to commit rape or sexual assault. *Journal of College Student Development, 47,* 133–148. [16]

Fowler, G. A. (2012). When the most personal secrets get outed on Facebook. *Wall Street Journal,* October 15. [10]

Fraley, C. (2010). *A brief overview of adult attachment theory and research.* (internal.psychology.illinois.edu/~rcfraley/attachment.htm) [7]

Francouer, R. T., & Noonan, R. J. (2004). *The Compendium complete international encyclopedia of sexuality.* (kinseyinstitute.org/ccies) [6]

Franke, W. W. & Berendonk, B. (1997). Hormonal doping and androgenization of athletes: A secret program of the German Democratic Republic government. *Clinical Chemistry, 43,* 1262–1279. [3]

Frayser, S. G. (1994). Defining normal childhood sexuality: An anthropological approach. *Annual Review of Sex Research, 4,* 173–217. [10]

Frazer, J. G. (1922). *The golden bough: A study of magic and religion* (abridged ed.). Macmillan. [5]

Freakonomics. (2013). *Are gay men really rich?* (freakonomics.com/2013/12/12/are-gay-men-really-rich-full-transcript) [12]

Frederick, D. A., Peplau, A. & Lever, J. (2008). The Barbie mystique: Satisfaction with breast size and shape across the lifespan. *International Journal of Sexual Health, 20,* 200–211. [5]

Freeman, E. W., Halberstadt, S. M., Rickels, K., Legler, J. M., Lin, H. & Sammel, M. D. (2011). Core symptoms that discriminate premenstrual syndrome. *Journal of Womens Health (Larchmont), 20,* 29–35. [2]

Freeman, E. W., Halbreich, U., Grubb, G. S., Rapkin, A. J., Skouby, S. O., Smith, L., et al. (2012). An overview of four studies of a continuous oral contraceptive (levonorgestrel 90 mcg/ethinyl estradiol 20 mcg) on premenstrual dysphoric disorder and premenstrual syndrome. *Contraception, 85,* 437–445. [2]

French, B. H., Tilghman, J. D. & Malebranche, D. A. (2014). Sexual coercion context and psychosocial correlates among diverse males. *Psychology of Men and Masculinity,* published online March 17. [16]

Freud, S. (1905/1975). *Three essays on the theory of sexuality.* Basic Books. [12]

Freund, K. & Blanchard, R. (1986). The concept of courtship disorder. *Journal of Sex and Marital Therapy, 12,* 79–92. [13]

Freund, K. W. (1974). Male homosexuality: An analysis of the pattern. In: Lorraine, J. A. (Ed.), *Understanding homosexuality: Its biological and psychological bases.* Elsevier. [12]

Freund, K., Watson, R. & Rienzo, D. (1989). Heterosexuality, homosexuality, and erotic age preference. *Journal of Sex Research, 26,* 107–117. [13]

Freunscht, I. & Feldmann, R. (2011). Young adults with Fetal Alcohol Syndrome (FAS): Social, emotional and occupational development. *Klinische Padiatrie, 223,* 33–37. [8]

Fricker, J. & Moore, S. (2008). Internet infidelity and its correlates. *Australian Journal of Counselling Psychology, 9,* 15–22. [7]

Friedrich, W. N., Fisher, J., Broughton, D., Houston, M. & Shafran, C. R. (1998). Normative sexual behavior in children: A contemporary sample. *Pediatrics, 101,* E9. [10]

Friedrich, W. N., Sandfort, T. G. M., Oostveen, J. & Cohen-Kettenis, P. T. (2000). Cultural differences in sexual behavior: 2–6 year old Dutch and American children. *Journal of Psychology and Human Sexuality, 12,* 117–129. [10]

Frintner, M. P. & Rubinson, L. (1993). Acquaintance rape: The influence of alcohol, fraternity membership, and sports team membership. *Journal of Sex Education and Therapy, 19,* 272–284. [16]

Frisch, M., Aigrain, Y., Barauskas, V., Bjarnason, R., Boddy, S. A., Czauderna, P., et al. (2013). Cultural bias in the AAP's 2012 Technical Report and Policy Statement on male circumcision. *Pediatrics, 131,* 796–800. [3]

Frith, H. (2009). Sexual scripts, sexual refusals, and rape. In: Horvath, M. & Brown, J. (Eds.), *Rape: Challenging contemporary thinking.* Willan. [1]

Fruhauf, S., Gerger, H., Schmidt, H. M., Munder, T. & Barth, J. (2013). Efficacy of psychological interventions for sexual dysfunction: A systematic review and meta-analysis. *Archives of Sexual Behavior, 42,* 915–933. [14]

Fuchs, E. (2013). *7 reasons why America should legalize prostitution.* (www.businessinsider.com/why-america-should-legalize-prostitution-2013-11) [17]

Furtbauer, I., Mundry, R., Heistermann, M., Schulke, O. & Ostner, J. (2011). You mate, I mate: Macaque females synchronize sex not cycles. *PLOS ONE, 6,* e26144. [2]

G & R Research and Consulting. (2008). *Sex in advertising.* (gandrllc.com/tableofcontents.html) [17]

Galenson, E. (1990). Observation of early infantile sexual and erotic development. In: Perry, M. E. (Ed.), *Handbook of sexology. Vol. 7: Childhood and adolescent sexology.* Elsevier. [10]

Galletly, C., Lazzarini, Z., Sanders, C. & Pinkerton, S. D. (2014). Criminal HIV exposure laws: Moving forward. *AIDS and Behavior, 18,* 1011–1013. [17]

Gallup, A. M. & Newport, F. (2008). *The Gallup Poll: Public opinion 2007.* Rowman & Littlefield. [11]

Gallup. (1997). *Family values differ sharply around the world.* (www.gallup.com/poll/9871/1997-Global-Study-Family-Values.aspx) [8]

Gallup. (2000). *Americans are overwhelmingly happy and optimistic about the future of the United States.* (www.gallup.com/poll/2434/Americans-Overwhelmingly-Happy-Optimistic-About-Future.aspx) [11]

Gallup. (2001). *Over half of Americans believe in love at first sight.* (www.gallup.com/poll/2017/over-half-americans-believe-love-first-sight.aspx) [7]

Gallup. (2006). *Americans at odds over gay rights.* (www.gallup.com/poll/23140/Americans-Odds-Over-Gay-Rights.aspx) [12]

Gallup. (2011). *Americans still split along "pro-choice," "pro-life" lines.* (www.gallup.com/poll/147734/Americans-Split-Along-Pro-Choice-Pro-Life-Lines.aspx) [9]

Gangestad, S. W. & Thornhill, R. (1997). The evolutionary psychology of extrapair sex: The role of fluctuating asymmetry. *Evolution and Human Behavior, 18*, 69–88. [7]

Gannon, T. A., Collie, R. M., Ward, T. & Thakker, K. (2008). Rape: Psychopathology, theory, and treatment. *Clinical Psychology Review, 28*, 982–1008. [16]

Ganong, L. H. & Coleman, M. (2003). *Stepfamily relationships: Development, dynamics, and interventions.* Springer. [11]

Garcia-Falgueras, A. & Swaab, D. F. (2008). A sex difference in the hypothalamic uncinate nucleus: Relationship to gender identity. *Brain, 131*, 3132–3146. [4, 12]

Garcia, J. R. & Reiber, C. (2008). Hook-up behavior: A biopsychosocial perspective. *Journal of Social, Evolutionary, and Cultural Psychology, 2*, 192–208. [7]

Garcia, J. R., Reiber, C., Massey, S. G. & Merriwether, A. M. (2012). Sexual hookup culture: A review. *Review of General Psychology, 16*, 161–176. [7]

Gaskins, A. J., Mendiola, J., Afeiche, M., Jorgensen, N., Swan, S. H. & Chavarro, J. E. (2013). Physical activity and television watching in relation to semen quality in young men. *British Journal of Sports Medicine, Online First*, February 14. [8]

Gates, G. J. (2011). *How many people are lesbian, gay, bisexual and transgender?* (escholarship.org/uc/item/09h684x2#) [4, 12]

Gates, G. J. (2013). *LGBT parenting in the United States.* (williamsinstitute.law.ucla.edu/research/census-lgbt-demographics-studies/lgbt-parenting-in-the-united-states) [12]

Gay, N. (2004). Four Raiders avoid '03 punishment. *San Francisco Chronicle*, November 21. [3]

Geddes, R. & Lueck, D. (2000). *The gains from self-ownership and the expansion of women's rights.* (www.sfu.ca/~allen/LueckGeddes.PDF) [16]

Georgiadis, J. R., Kortekaas, R., Kuipers, R., Nieuwenburg, A., Pruim, J., Reinders, A. A. & Holstege, G. (2006). Regional cerebral blood flow changes associated with clitorally induced orgasm in healthy women. *European Journal of Neuroscience, 24*, 3305–3316. [5]

Gerlach, N. M., McGlothlin, J. W., Parker, P. G. & Ketterson, E. D. (2012). Promiscuous mating produces offspring with higher lifetime fitness. *Proceedings of the Royal Society B: Biological Sciences, 279*, 860–866. [App. A]

Gerressu, M., Mercer, C. H., Graham, C. A., Wellings, K. & Johnson, A. M. (2008). Prevalence of masturbation and associated factors in a British national probability survey. *Archives of Sexual Behavior, 37*, 266–278. [4, 6]

Gettleman, J. (2010). Americans' role seen in Uganda anti-gay push. *New York Times*, January 3. [12]

Gibson, L. E. & Leitenberg, H. (2000). Child sexual abuse prevention programs: Do they decrease the occurrence of child sexual abuse? *Child Abuse and Neglect, 24*, 1115–1125. [10]

Gilbert, R. M. (2006). *The eight concepts of Bowen theory: A new way of thinking about the individual and the group.* Leading Systems Press. [8]

Gilfoyle, N. F. P. (2010). *Brief of the American Psychological Association, the California Psychological Association, the American Psychiatric Association, and the American Association for Marriage and Family Therapy as amici curiae in support of plaintiff-appellees.* (cdn.ca9.uscourts.gov/datastore/general/2010/10/27/amicus29.pdf) [12]

Gillison, M. L., Broutian, T., Pickard, R. K. L., Tong, Z., Xiao, W., Kahle, L., et al. (2012). Prevalence of oral HPV infection in the United States, 2009–2010. *JAMA*, (published online, Jan 26). [15]

Gladyshev, E. A., Meselson, M. & Arkhipova, I. R. (2008). Massive horizontal gene transfer in bdelloid rotifers. *Science, 320*, 1210–1213. [App. A]

Glina, S., Sharlip, I. D. & Hellstrom, W. J. (2013). Modifying risk factors to prevent and treat erectile dysfunction. *Journal of Sexual Medicine, 10*, 115–119. [14]

Glionna, J. M. (2011). A Japanese porn star at 76. *Los Angeles Times*, March 6. [17]

Goddard, M. R., Godfray, H. C. J. & Burt, A. (2005). Sex increases the efficacy of natural selection in experimental yeast populations. *Nature, 434*, 636–640. [App. A]

Goldberg, A. B. & Grimes, D. A. (2007). Injectable contraceptives. In: Hatcher, R. A., et al. (Eds.), *Contraceptive technology* (19th ed.). Ardent Media. [9]

Goldenberg, R. L., McClure, E. M., Bhattacharya, A., Groat, T. D. & Stahl, P. J. (2009). Women's perceptions regarding the safety of births at various gestational ages. *Obstetrics and Gynecology, 114*, 1254–1258. [8]

Goldey, K. L. & van Anders, S. M. (2011). Sexy thoughts: Effects of sexual cognitions on testosterone, cortisol, and arousal in women. *Hormones and Behavior, 59*, 754–764. [5]

Goldey, K. L. & van Anders, S. M. (2012). Sexual thoughts: Links to testosterone and cortisol in men. *Archives of Sexual Behavior, 41*, 1461–1470. [5]

Goldman, R. & Goldman, J. (1982). Children's sexual thinking: A comparative study of children aged 5 to 15 years in Australia, North America, Britain and Sweden. Routledge & Kegan Paul. [10]

Goldstein, I. (2000). The mutually reinforcing triad of depressive symptoms, cardiovascular disease, and erectile dysfunction. *American Journal of Cardiology, 86*, 41F–45F. [14]

Goldstein, I. & Berman, J. R. (1998). Vasculogenic female sexual dysfunction: Vaginal engorgement and clitoral erectile insufficiency syndromes. *International Journal of Impotence Research, 10*(Suppl. 2), S84–90; discussion S98–101. [14]

Good For Her. (2014). *Feminist Porn Awards: 2014 winners.* (www.goodforher.com/2014-fpa-winners) [17]

Good Lives Model. (2014). *The Good Lives Model of offender rehabilitation.* (www.goodlivesmodel.com) [13]

Goode, E. (2012). Researchers see decline in child sex abuse rate. *New York Times*, June 28. [10]

Gordon, S. (2008). Symptoms plus blood test boost ovarian cancer detection. *Washington Post*, June 23. [2]

Gottlieb, L. (2014). Does a more equal marriage mean less sex? *New York Times*, February 6. [11]

Gottman, J. M. & Krokoff, L. J. (1989). Marital interaction and satisfaction: A longitudinal view. *Journal of Consulting and Clinical Psychology, 57*, 47–52. [7]

Gottman, J. M. & Levenson, R. W. (1999). What predicts change in marital interaction over time? A study of alternative models. *Family Process, 38*, 143–158. [7]

Gottman, J. M. & Notarius, C. I. (2000). Decade review: Observing marital interaction. *Journal of Marriage and the Family, 62*, 927–947. [8]

Gottman, J. M., Levenson, R. W., Gross, J., Frederickson, B. L., McCoy, K., Rosenthal, L., et al. (2003). Correlates of gay and lesbian couples' relationship satisfaction and relationship dissolution. *Journal of Homosexuality, 45*, 23–43. [7, 14]

Goy, R. W., Bercovitch, F. B. & McBrair, M. C. (1988). Behavioral masculinization is independent of genital masculinization in prenatally androgenized female rhesus macaques. *Hormones and Behavior, 22*, 552–571. [4]

Grace, D. M., David, B. J. & Ryan, M. K. (2008). Investigating preschoolers' categorical thinking about gender through imitation, attention, and the use of self-categories. *Child Development, 79*, 1928–1941. [4]

Graham, C. A., Crosby, R., Yarber, W. L., Sanders, S. A., McBride, K., Milhausen, R. R. & Arno, J. N. (2006). Erection loss in association with condom use among young men attending a public STI clinic: Potential correlates and implications for risk behaviour. *Sexual Health, 3*, 255–260. [9]

Graham, J. H., Raz, S., Hel-Or, H. & Nevo, E. (2010). Fluctuating asymmetry: Methods, theory, and applications. *Symmetry, 2*, 466–540. [App. A]

Grant, J. E., Pinto, A., Gunnip, M., Mancebo, M. C., Eisen, J. L. & Rasmussen, S. A. (2006). Sexual obsessions and clinical correlates in adults with obsessive-compulsive disorder. *Comprehensive Psychiatry, 47*, 325–329. [14]

Gray, R. H., Kigozi, G., Serwadda, D., Makumbi, F., Watya, S., Nalugoda, F., et al. (2007). Male circumcision for HIV prevention in men in Rakai, Uganda: A randomised trial. *Lancet, 369*, 657–666. [3]

Green, J. (2012). Herpes verdict in Portland: Woman wins $900,000 after getting disease from date. *Oregonian*, June 4. [15]

Green, R. (1987). *The "sissy-boy syndrome" and the development of homosexuality.* Yale University Press. [12]

Green, R. (2009). Keep the river flowing: An exploratory study to assess the effect of daily ejaculation for 7 days on semen parameters and sperm DNA damage. (humrep.oxfordjournals.org/content/24/suppl_1/i56.full.pdf) [6]

Green, R., Polotsky, A. J., Wildman, R. P., McGinn, A. P., Lin, J., Derby, C., et al. (2010).

Menopausal symptoms within a Hispanic cohort: SWAN, the Study of Women's Health Across the Nation. *Climacteric, 13,* 376–384. [11]

Greene, S. (2008). *Regina McKnight released from prison.* (www.carolinalive.com/news/story.aspx?id=149364) [9]

Greenfeld, L. A. (1997). *Sex offenses and offenders: An analysis of data on rape and sexual assault.* (www.mincava.umn.edu/documents/sexoff/sexoff.pdf) [16]

Greenwood, D. C., Alwan, N., Boylan, S., Cade, J. E., Charvill, J., Chipps, K. C., et al. (2010). Caffeine intake during pregnancy, late miscarriage and stillbirth. *European Journal of Epidemiology, 25,* 275–280. [8]

Grimes, D. A. & Schulz, K. F. (2011). Nonspecific side effects of oral contraceptives: Nocebo or noise? *Contraception, 83,* 5–9. [9]

Gronich, N., Lavi, I. & Rennert, G. (2011). Higher risk of venous thrombosis associated with drospirenone-containing oral contraceptives: A population-based cohort study. *Canadian Medical Association Journal, 183,* E1319–1325. [9]

Grossman, K. (2008). *Penis piercing.* (menshealth.about.com/cs/teenhealth/a/penis_piercing.htm) [3]

Grossman, M. (2007). *Unprotected: A campus psychiatrist reveals how political correctness in her profession endangers every student.* Sentinel. [7]

Grote, N. K., Bridge, J. A., Gavin, A. R., Melville, J. L., Iyengar, S. & Katon, W. J. (2010). A meta-analysis of depression during pregnancy and the risk of preterm birth, low birth weight, and intrauterine growth restriction. *Archives of General Psychiatry, 67,* 1012–1024. [8]

Groth, A. N. (1979). *Men who rape: The psychology of the offender.* Plenum. [16]

Grunbaum, J. A., Lowry, R., Kann, L. & Pateman, B. (2000). Prevalence of health risk behaviors among Asian American/Pacific Islander high school students. *Journal of Adolescent Health, 27,* 322–330. [10]

Guay, A. T. (2001). Decreased testosterone in regularly menstruating women with decreased libido: A clinical observation. *Journal of Sex and Marital Therapy, 27,* 513–519. [14]

Guéguen, N. (2012). Gait and menstrual cycle: Ovulating women use sexier gaits and walk slowly ahead of men. *Gait and Posture, 35,* 621–624. [5]

Guerrero, L. K., Andersen, P. A. & Afifi, W. A. (2013). *Close encounters: Communication in relationships* (4th ed.). Sage. [7]

Guiora, A. Z., Beit-Hallahmi, B., Fried, R. & Yoder, C. (1982). Language environment and gender identity attainment. *Language Learning, 32,* 289–304. [4]

Guttmacher Institute. (2014a). *Induced abortion in the United States.* (www.guttmacher.org/pubs/fb_induced_abortion.html) [9]

Guttmacher Institute. (2014b). *American teens' sexual and reproductive health.* (www.guttmacher.org/pubs/FB-ATSRH.html) [10]

Guttmacher Institute. (2014c). *State policies in brief: Sex and HIV education.* (www.guttmacher.org/statecenter/spibs/spib_SE.pdf) [10]

Guzick, D. S., Overstreet, J. W., Factor-Litvak, P., Brazil, C. K., Nakajima, S. T., Coutifaris, C., et al. (2001). Sperm morphology, motility, and concentration in fertile and infertile men. *New England Journal of Medicine, 345,* 1388–1393. [8]

Halata, Z. & Munger, B. L. (1986). The neuroanatomical basis for the protopathic sensibility of the human glans penis. *Brain Research, 371,* 205–230. [3]

Hald, G. M. & Malamuth, N. N. (2014). Experimental effects of exposure to pornography: The moderating effect of personality and mediating effect of sexual arousal. *Archives of Sexual Behavior,* published online April 12. [17]

Hald, G. M., Malamuth, N. M. & Yuen, C. (2010). Pornography and attitudes supporting violence against women: Revisiting the relationship in nonexperimental studies. *Aggressive Behavior, 36,* 14–20. [1, 17]

Hall, E. & Steiner, M. (2013). Serotonin and female psychopathology. *Womens Health (London England), 9,* 85–97. [4]

Hall, J. A., Carter, S., Cody, M. J. & Albright, J. M. (2010). Individual differences in the communication of romantic interest: Development of the Flirting Styles Inventory. *Communication Quarterly, 58,* 365–393. [7]

Halperin, D. M. (1990). *One hundred years of homosexuality and other essays on Greek love.* Routledge. [12]

Halpern, C. J. T., Udry, J. R., Suchindran, C. & Campbell, B. (2000a). Adolescent males' willingness to report masturbation. *Journal of Sex Research, 37,* 327–232. [10]

Halpern, C. T., Joyner, K., Udry, J. R. & Suchindran, C. (2000b). Smart teens don't have sex (or kiss much either). *Journal of Adolescent Health, 26,* 213–225. [10]

Halpern, C. T., Kaestle, C. E. & Hallfors, D. D. (2007). Perceived physical maturity, age of romantic partner, and adolescent risk behavior. *Prevention Science, 8,* 1–10. [10]

Halpern, C. T., Udry, J. R. & Suchindran, C. (1997). Testosterone predicts initiation of coitus in adolescent females. *Psychosomatic Medicine, 59,* 161–171. [10]

Halpern, C. T., Udry, J. R. & Suchindran, C. (1998). Monthly measures of salivary testosterone predict sexual activity in adolescent males. *Archives of Sexual Behavior, 27,* 445–465. [10]

Hamer, D. & Wilson, J. (2014). *Kumu Hina* (documentary film). (kumuhina.tumblr.com) [12]

Hamer, D. H. (2002). Genetics of sexual behavior. In: Benjamin, J., et al. (Eds.), *Molecular genetics and human personality.* American Psychiatric Publishing. [12]

Hamer, D. H., Hu, S., Magnuson, V. L., Hu, N. & Pattatucci, A. M. (1993). A linkage between DNA markers on the X chromosome and male sexual orientation. *Science, 261,* 321–327. [12]

Hanson, R. K., Harris, A. J., Helmus, L. & Thornton, D. (2014). High-risk sex offenders may not be high risk forever. *Journal of Interpersonal Violence. 29,* 2792–2813. [13]

Hantsoo, L., Ward-O'Brien, D., Czarkowski, K. A., Gueorguieva, R., Price, L. H. & Epperson, C. N. (2014). A randomized, placebo-controlled, double-blind trial of sertraline for postpartum depression. *Psychopharmacology, 231,* 939–948. [8]

Hardeman, J. & Weiss, B. D. (2014). Intrauterine devices: An update. *American Family Physician, 89,* 445–450. [9]

Hare, E. H. (1962). Masturbatory insanity: The history of an idea. *Journal of Mental Science, 108,* 1–25. [6]

Hare, L., Bernard, P., Sanchez, F. J., Baird, P. N., Vilain, E., Kennedy, T. & Harley, V. R. (2009). Androgen receptor repeat length polymorphism associated with male-to-female transsexualism. *Biological Psychiatry, 65,* 93–96. [4]

Harel, Z., Riggs, S., Vaz, R., Flanagan, P., Harel, D. & Machan, J. T. (2010). Bone accretion in adolescents using the combined estrogen and progestin transdermal contraceptive method Ortho Evra: A pilot study. *Journal of Pediatric and Adolescent Gynecology, 23,* 23–31. [9]

Harper, J. C. & Sengupta, S. B. (2012). Preimplantation genetic diagnosis: State of the art 2011. *Human Genetics, 131,* 175–186. [8]

Harper, J., Coonen, E., De Rycke, M., Fiorentino, F., Geraedts, J., Goossens, V., et al. (2010). What next for preimplantation genetic screening (PGS)? A position statement from the ESHRE PGD Consortium Steering Committee. *Human Reproduction, 25,* 821–823. [8]

Harper, K. N., Zuckerman, M. K., Harper, M. L., Kingston, J. D. & Armelagos, G. J. (2011). The origin and antiquity of syphilis revisited: An appraisal of Old World pre-Columbian evidence for treponemal infection. *American Journal of Physical Anthropology, 146*(Suppl. 53), 99–133. [15]

Harrison, M. E. & Chivers, D. J. (2007). The orang-utan mating system and the unflanged male: A product of increased food stress during the late Miocene and Pliocene? *Journal of Human Evolution, 52,* 275–293. [App. A]

Harrison, S. (2014). *The hard life of the male porn star.* (www.yourtango.com/20086446/the-hard-life-of-the-male-porn-star) [17]

Harte, C. B. & Meston, C. M. (2012). Recreational use of erectile dysfunction medications and its adverse effects on erectile function in young healthy men: The mediating role of confidence in erectile ability. *Journal of Sexual Medicine, 9,* 1852–1859. [14]

Hartmann, U. & Waldinger, M. D. (2007). Treatment of delayed ejaculation. In: Leiblum, S. R. (Ed.), *Principles and practice of sex therapy* (4th ed.). Guilford. [14]

Hartocollis, A. (2006). Women have seen it all on subway, unwillingly. *New York Times,* June 24. [13]

Haselton, M. G., Mortezaie, M., Pillsworth, E. G., Bleske-Rechek, A. & Frederick, D. A. (2007). Ovulatory shifts in human female ornamentation: Near ovulation, women dress to impress. *Hormones and Behavior, 51,* 40–45. [5]

Hassett, J. M., Siebert, E. R. & Wallen, K. (2008). Sex differences in rhesus monkey toy preferences parallel those of children. *Hormones and Behavior, 54,* 359–364. [4]

Hatcher, R. A., Trussell, J., Nelson, A. L., Cates, W., Kowal, D. & Policar, M. S. (2011).

Contraceptive technology (20th ed.). Ardent Media. [9]

Hatfield, E. & Rapson, R. L. (1993). *Love, sex, and intimacy: Their psychology, biology, and history.* HarperCollins [7]

Hatfield, E. & Rapson, R. L. (2005). *Love and sex: Cross-cultural perspectives.* University Press of America. [7]

Hatfield, E. & Rapson, R. L. (2011). Equity theory in close relationships. In: Van Lange, P. A. M., et al. (Eds.), *Handbook of theories of social psychology: Volume Two.* Sage. [7]

Hatfield, E., Forbes, M. & Rapson, R. L. (2012). Marketing love and sex. *Society, 49,* 506–511. [5]

Hatfield, E., Rapson, R. L. & Martel, L. D. (2007). Passionate love and sexual desire. In: Kitayama, S. & Cohen, D. (Eds.), *Handbook of cultural psychology.* Guildford. [7]

Hatzenbuehler, M. L., Bellatorre, A., Lee, Y., Finch, B. K., Muennig, P. & Fiscella, K. (2014). Structural stigma and all-cause mortality in sexual minority populations. *Social Science and Medicine, 103,* 33–41. [12]

Hawkes, K. & Coxworth, J. E. (2013). Grandmothers and the evolution of human longevity: A review of findings and future directions. *Evolutionary Anthropology, 22,* 294–302. [11]

Haydon, A. A., Cheng, M. M., Herring, A. H., McRee, A. L. & Halpern, C. T. (2014). Prevalence and predictors of sexual inexperience in adulthood. *Archives of Sexual Behavior, 43,* 221–230. [11]

Hayes, R. D., Dennerstein, L., Bennett, C. M., Sidat, M., Gurrin, L. C. & Fairley, C. K. (2008). Risk factors for female sexual dysfunction in the general population: Exploring factors associated with low sexual function and sexual distress. *Journal of Sexual Medicine, 5,* 1681–1693. [11]

Hayes, S. L. & Carpenter, B. J. (2010). *Absence of malice: Constructing the female sex offender.* (eprints.qut.edu.au/41899/2/41899.pdf) [13]

Hazan, C. & Shaver, P. (1987). Romantic love conceptualized as an attachment process. *Journal of Personality and Social Psychology, 52,* 511–524. [7]

Heiman, J. R. (2007). Orgasmic disorders in women. In: Leiblum, S. R. (Ed.), *Principles and practice of sex therapy* (4th ed.). Guilford. [14]

Heisz, J. J., Pottruff, M. M. & Shore, D. I. (2013). Females scan more than males: A potential mechanism for sex differences in recognition memory. *Psychological Science, 24,* 1157–1163. [4]

Helmus, L., Hanson, R. K., Thornton, D., Babchishin, K. M. & Harris, A. J. R. (2012). Absolute recidivism rates predicted by Static-99R and Static-2002R sex offender risk assessment tools vary across samples: A meta-analysis. *Criminal Justice and Behavior, 39,* 1148–1171. [13]

Hens, K., Dondorp, W., Handyside, A. H., Harper, J., Newson, A. J., Pennings, G., et al. (2013). Dynamics and ethics of comprehensive preimplantation genetic testing: A review of the challenges. *Human Reproduction Update, 19,* 366–375. [8]

Henton, C. L. (1976). Nocturnal orgasm in college women: Its relation to dreams and anxiety associated with sexual factors. *Journal of Genetic Psychology, 129,* 245–251. [3]

Herbenick, D., Reece, M., Sanders, S. A., Dodge, B., Ghassemi, A. & Fortenberry, J. D. (2009). Prevalence and characteristics of vibrator use by women in the United States: Results from a nationally representative study. *Journal of Sexual Medicine, 6,* 1857–1866. [6]

Herbenick, D., Reece, M., Sanders, S. A., Dodge, B., Ghassemi, A. & Fortenberry, J. D. (2010a). Women's vibrator use in sexual partnerships: Results from a nationally representative survey in the United States. *Journal of Sex and Marital Therapy, 36,* 49–65. [6]

Herbenick, D., Reece, M., Schick, V. & Sanders, S. A. (2014). Erect penile length and circumference dimensions of 1,661 sexually active men in the United States. *Journal of Sexual Medicine, 11,* 93–101. [3]

Herbenick, D., Reece, M., Schick, V., Sanders, S. A., Dodge, B. & Fortenberry, J. D. (2010b). Sexual behavior in the United States: Results from a national probability sample of men and women ages 14–94. *Journal of Sexual Medicine, 7*(Suppl. 5), 255–265. [6, 10]

Herbenick, D., Reece, M., Schick, V., Sanders, S. A., Dodge, B. & Fortenberry, J. D. (2010c). Sexual behaviors, relationships, and perceived health status among adult women in the United States: Results from a national probability sample. *Journal of Sexual Medicine, 7*(Suppl. 5), 277–290. [6]

Herbenick, D., Schick, V., Reece, M., Sanders, S. & Fortenberry, J. D. (2010d). Pubic hair removal among women in the United States: Prevalence, methods, and characteristics. *Journal of Sexual Medicine, 7,* 3322–3330. [2]

Herdt, G. (2005). The Sambia: *Ritual, sexuality, and change in Papua New Guinea.* Wadsworth. [6, 10]

Herek, G. M., Norton, A. T., Allen, T. J. & Sims, C. L. (2010). Demographic, psychological, and social characteristics of self-identified lesbian, gay, and bisexual adults in a US probability sample. *Sexuality Research and Social Policy, 7,* 176–200. [12]

Herman-Giddens, M. E., Steffes, J., Harris, D., Slora, E., Hussey, M., Dowshen, S. A., et al. (2012). Secondary sexual characteristics in boys: Data from the Pediatric Research in Office Settings Network. *Pediatrics, 130,* e1058–1068. [10]

Hertlein, K. M. & Weeks, G. R. (2007). Two roads diverging in a wood. *Journal of Couple and Relationship Therapy, 6,* 95–107. [7]

Hess, N. H. & Hagen, E. H. (2006). Sex differences in indirect aggression: Psychological evidence from young adults. *Evolution and Human Behavior, 27,* 231–245. [4]

Hewlett, B. S. & Hewlett, B. L. (2010). Sex and searching for children among Aka foragers and Ngandu farmers of Central Africa. *African Study Monographs, 31,* 107–125. [6]

Hines, M. (2006). Prenatal testosterone and gender-related behaviour. *European Journal of Endocrinology, 155,* S115–S121. [4]

Hines, M. (2011). Gender development and the human brain. *Annual Review of Neuroscience, 34,* 69–88. [4]

Hines, T. & Kilchevsky, A. (2014). The G-spot discovered? Comments on Ostreenski's article. *Journal of Sexual Medicine, 10,* 887–888. [2]

Hiraishi, K., Sasaki, S., Shikishima, C. & Ando, J. (2012). The second to fourth digit ratio (2D:4D) in a Japanese twin sample: Heritability, prenatal hormone transfer, and association with sexual orientation. *Archives of Sexual Behavior, 41,* 711–724. [12]

Hite, S. (2003). *The Hite report: A nationwide study of female sexuality.* Seven Stories. [6]

Hodges-Simeon, C. R., Gaulin, S. J. & Puts, D. A. (2010). Different vocal parameters predict perceptions of dominance and attractiveness. *Human Nature, 21,* 406–427. [5]

Holman, A. & Sillars, A. (2012). Talk about "hooking up": The influence of college student social networks on nonrelationship sex. *Health Communication, 27,* 205–216. [10]

Holmes, R. M. (2012). The outdoor recess activities of children at an urban school: Longitudinal and intraperiod patterns. *American Journal of Play, 4,* 327–351. [4]

Holstege, G., Georgiadis, J. R., Paans, A. M., Meiners, L. C., van der Graaf, F. H. & Reinders, A. A. (2003). Brain activation during human male ejaculation. *Journal of Neuroscience, 23,* 9185–9193. [5]

Honan, W. H. (1994). Professor ousted for lecture gets job back. *New York Times,* September 17. [16]

Hook, E. B. & Warburton, D. (2014). Turner syndrome revisited: Review of new data supports the hypothesis that all viable 45,X cases are cryptic mosaics with a rescue cell line, implying an origin by mitotic loss. *Human Genetics, 133,* 417–424. [4]

Howard, B. D. (2010). *Postpartum depression.* (goop.com/journal/be/93/postpartum-depression) [8]

Hubacher, D. & Grimes, D. A. (2002). Noncontraceptive health benefits of intrauterine devices: A systematic review. *Obstetrical and Gynecological Survey, 57,* 120–128. [9]

Hucker, S. J. (2011). Hypoxyphilia. *Archives of Sexual Behavior, 40,* 1323–1326. [13]

Huffington Post Canada. (2014). Dale Decker, man with persistent genital arousal syndrome, has 100 orgasms a day. (www.huffingtonpost.ca/2014/09/23/dale-decker-100-orgasms_n_5869262.html) [14]

Huffstutter, P. J. & Frammolino, R. (2001). Lights! Camera! Viagra! When the show must go on, sometimes a little chemistry helps. *Los Angeles Times,* July 6. [14]

Hughes, C. M., Damon, I. K. & Reynolds, M. G. (2013). Understanding U.S. healthcare providers' practices and experiences with molluscum contagiosum. *PLOS ONE, 8,* e76948. [15]

Hughes, S. M., Harrison, M. A. & Gallup, G. G. J. (2007). Sex differences in romantic kissing among college students: An evolutionary perspective. *Evolutionary Psychology, 5,* 612–631. [6]

Hultman, C. M., Sandin, S., Levine, S. Z., Lichtenstein, P. & Reichenberg, A. (2011). Advancing paternal age and risk of autism: New evidence from a population-based study and a meta-analysis of epidemiological studies. *Molecular Psychiatry, 16,* 1203–1212. [8]

Human Rights Campaign. (2014). *Maps of state laws and policies.* (www.hrc.org/resources/entry/maps-of-state-laws-policies) [12]

Human Rights Watch. (2010). *Sexual violence in Congo.* (www.hrw.org/en/node/84366/section/7) [16]

Humbach, J. A. (2010). "Sexting" and the First Amendment. *Hastings Constitutional Law Quarterly, 37,* 433–485. [10]

Hunter, D. J., Colditz, G. A., Hankinson, S. E., Malspeis, S., Spiegelman, D., Chen, W., et al. (2010). Oral contraceptive use and breast cancer: A prospective study of young women. *Cancer Epidemiology, Biomarkers and Prevention, 19,* 2496–2502. [2]

Hurley, D. (2005). Divorce rate: It's not as high as you think. *New York Times,* April 19. [11]

Huynh, H. K., Willemsen, A. T., Lovick, T. A. & Holstege, G. (2013). Pontine control of ejaculation and female orgasm. *Journal of Sexual Medicine, 10,* 3038–3048. [App. B]

Hyde, J. S. (2005). The gender similarities hypothesis. *American Psychologist, 60,* 581–592. [4]

IJzerman, H., Blanken, I., Brandt, M. J., Oerlemans, J. M., Van den Hoogenhof, M. M. W., Franken, S. J. M. & Oerlemans, M. W. G. (2014). Sex differences in distress from infidelity in early adulthood and in later life: A replication and meta-analysis. *Social Psychology, 45,* 202–208. [4]

ILGA. (2013). *Lesbian and gay rights in the world.* (old.ilga.org/Statehomophobia/ILGA_map_2013_A4.pdf) [12]

Ilias, I., Spanoudi, F., Koukkou, E., Adamopoulos, D. A. & Nikopoulou, S. C. (2013). Do lunar phases influence menstruation? A year-long retrospective study. *Endocrine Regulations, 47,* 121–122. [2]

Im, E., Lee, B., Chee, W., Brown, A. & Dormire, S. (2010). Menopausal symptoms among four major ethnic groups in the U.S. *Western Journal of Nursing Research, 32,* 540–565. [11]

Imperato-McGinley, J., Guerrero, L., Gautier, T. & Peterson, R. E. (1974). Steroid 5α-reductase deficiency in man: An inherited form of male pseudohermaphroditism. *Science, 186,* 1213–1215. [4]

Imperato-McGinley, J., Miller, M., Wilson, J. D., Peterson, R. E., Shackleton, C. & Gajdusek, D. C. (1991). A cluster of male pseudohermaphrodites with 5 alpha-reductase deficiency in Papua New Guinea. *Clinical Endocrinology, 34,* 293–298. [4]

Imperato-McGinley, J., Peterson, R. E., Gautier, T. & Sturla, E. (1979). Androgens and the evolution of male-gender identity among male pseudohermaphrodites with 5α-reductase deficiency. *New England Journal of Medicine, 300,* 1233–1237. [4]

Independent (London). (2010). *Till [my] death do us part.* (www.independent.co.uk/lifestyle/health-and-families/til-my-death-do-us-part-object-love-1927732.html?) [13]

Ingalhalikar, M., Smith, A., Parker, D., Satterthwaite, T. D., Elliott, M. A., Ruparel, K., Hakonarson, H., Gur, R. E., Gur, R. C. & Verma, R. (2014). Sex differences in the structural connectome of the human brain. *Proceedings of the National Academy of Sciences of the United States of America, 111,* 823–828. [4]

Inhorn, M. C. (1996). *Infertility and patriarchy: The cultural politics of gender and family life in Egypt.* University of Pennsylvania Press. [11]

Institute for Reproductive Health. (2008). *Research to practice: The TwoDay Method.* (archive.irh.org/RTP-TDM.htm) [9]

Institute of Marriage and Family Canada. (2009). *Cohabitation statistics.* (www.imfcanada.org/fact-sheet/canadian-cohabitation) [11]

International Male Contraception Coalition. (2014). *Male contraceptives.* (www.malecontraceptives.org) [9]

International Professional Surrogates Association. (2014). *About IPSA.* (www.surrogatetherapy.org) [14]

International Society for Sexual Medicine. (2010). Guidelines for the diagnosis and treatment of premature ejaculation. *Journal of Sexual Medicine, 7,* 2947–2969. [14]

Irwig, M. S. & Kolukula, S. (2011). Persistent sexual side effects of finasteride for male pattern hair loss. *Journal of Sexual Medicine, 8,* 1747–1753. [5]

Ishak, W. W., Berman, D. S. & Peters, A. (2008). Male anorgasmia treated with oxytocin. *Journal of Sexual Medicine, 5,* 1022–1024. [5]

Jackson, J. B., Miller, R. B., Oka, M. & Henry, R. G. (2014). Gender differences in marital satisfaction: A meta-analysis. *Journal of Marriage and Family, 76,* 105–129. [11]

Jacobs, J. (2010). *Sex, tourism, and the postcolonial encounter.* Ashgate. [17]

James, A. (2004). *"Autogynephilia": A disputed diagnosis.* (www.tsroadmap.com/info/autogynephilia.html) [4]

Jankowiak, W. R. & Fischer, E. F. (1992). A cross-cultural perspective on romantic love. *Ethnology, 31,* 149–155. [7]

Jannini, E. A., Whipple, B., Kingsberg, S. A., Buisson, O., Foldes, P. & Vardi, Y. (2010). Who's afraid of the G-spot? *Journal of Sexual Medicine, 7,* 25–34. [2]

Jannini, E., McMahon, C. G. & Waldinger, M. D. (Eds.) (2012). *Premature ejaculation: From etiology to diagnosis and treatment.* Springer. [14]

Janssen, E., Carpenter, D. & Graham, C. A. (2003). Selecting films for sex research: Gender differences in erotic film preference. *Archives of Sexual Behavior, 32,* 243–251. [4]

Jayson, S. (2005). Cohabitation is replacing dating. *USA Today,* July 17. [11]

Jeal, N. & Salisbury, C. (2004). A health needs assessment of street-based prostitutes: cross-sectional survey. *Journal of Public Health (Oxford), 26,* 147–151. [17]

Jeal, N., Salisbury, C. & Turner, K. (2008). The multiplicity and interdependency of factors influencing the health of street-based sex workers: a qualitative study. *Sexually Transmitted Infections, 84,* 381–385. [17]

Jeltsen, M. (2014). *Why this transgender teen's big victory matters.* (www.huffingtonpost.com/2014/02/03/transgender-rights_n_4705613.html) [4]

Jennings, V. H. & Arevalo, M. (2007). Fertility awareness-based methods. In: Hatcher, R. A., et al. (Eds.), *Contraceptive technology* (19th ed.). Ardent Media. [9]

Jerse, A. E., Bash, M. C. & Russell, M. W. (2014). Vaccines against gonorrhea: Current status and future challenges. *Vaccine, 32,* 1579–1587. [15]

Jezebel. (2010). *College girl's PowerPoint "fuck list" goes viral.* (jezebel.com/5652114/college-girls-power-point-fuck-list-goes-viral-gallery) [7]

Jick, S. S., Hagberg, K. W., Hernandez, R. K. & Kaye, J. A. (2010). Postmarketing study of ORTHO EVRA and levonorgestrel oral contraceptives containing hormonal contraceptives with 30 mcg of ethinyl estradiol in relation to nonfatal venous thromboembolism. *Contraception, 81,* 16–21. [9]

Joachim, D. S. (2014). Supreme Court declines case contesting ban on gay "conversion therapy." *New York Times,* June 30. [12]

Jobe, A. H., Kallapur, S. G. & Kramer, B. W. (2012). Perinatal events and their influence on lung development and function. In: Bancalari, E. (Ed.), *The newborn lung: Neonatology questions and controversies.* Elsevier. [8]

Johansson, P., Hall, L., Sikstrom, S. & Olsson, A. (2005). Failure to detect mismatches between intention and outcome in a simple decision task. *Science, 310,* 116–119. [5]

Johnson, A. A., Hatcher, B. J., El-Khorazaty, M. N., Milligan, R. A., Bhaskar, B., Rodan, M. F., et al. (2007). Determinants of inadequate prenatal care utilization by African American women. *Journal of Health Care for the Poor and Underserved, 18,* 620–636. [8]

Johnson, K. L., Gill, S., Reichman, V. & Tassinary, L. G. (2007). Swagger, sway, and sexuality: Judging sexual orientation from body motion and morphology. *Journal of Personality and Social Psychology, 93,* 321–334. [12]

Johnson, K., Scott, J., Rughita, B., Kisielewski, M., Asher, J., Ong, R. & Lawry, L. (2010). Association of sexual violence and human rights violations with physical and mental health in territories of the Eastern Democratic Republic of the Congo. *JAMA, 304,* 553–562. [16]

Johnson, M. A. (2007). *Essential reproduction* (6th ed.). Blackwell. [8]

Johnson, S. D., Phelps, D. L. & Cottler, L. B. (2004). The association of sexual dysfunction and substance use among a community epidemiological sample. *Archives of Sexual Behavior, 33,* 55–63. [5]

Johnston, V. S., Hagel, R., Franklin, M., Fink, B. & Grammer, K. (2001). Male facial attractiveness: Evidence for hormone mediated adaptive design. *Evolution and Human Behavior, 22,* 251–267. [5]

Jolie, A. (2013). My medical choice. *New York Times,* May 14. [2]

Jonason, P. K., Li, N. P. & Richardson, J. (2010). Positioning the booty-call relationship on the spectrum of relationships: Sexual but more emotional than one-night stands. *Journal of Sex Research,* 1–10. [7]

Jones, B. C., Debruine, L. M., Little, A. C., Conway, C. A. & Feinberg, D. R. (2006). Integrating gaze direction and expression in preferences for attractive faces. *Psychological Science, 17,* 588–591. [5]

Jones, C., Chan, C. & Farine, D. (2011). Sex in pregnancy. *Canadian Medical Association Journal, 183,* 815–818. [8]

Jordan-Young, R. M. (2011). *Brain storm: The flaws in the science of sex differences.* Harvard University Press. [4]

Joshi, S., Khandwe, R., Bapat, D. & Deshmukh, U. (2011). Effect of yoga on menopausal symptoms. *Menopause International, 17,* 78–81. [11]

Joyal, C. C., Cossette, A. & Lapierre, V. (2014). What exactly is an unusual sexual fantasy? *Journal of Sexual Medicine.* Published online October 30. [5]

Jozwiak, G. (2014). Breast ironing in Cameroon: Empowering girls to speak out. *Guardian* (London), January 17. [10]

Ju, H., Jones, M. & Mishra, G. (2014). The prevalence and risk factors of dysmenorrhea. *Epidemiologic Reviews, 36,* 104–113. [2]

Jurewicz, J., Radwan, M., Sobala, W., Ligocka, D., Radwan, P., Bochenek, M., et al. (2013). Human urinary phthalate metabolites level and main semen parameters, sperm chromatin structure, sperm aneuploidy and reproductive hormones. *Reproductive Toxicology, 42,* 232–241. [8]

Just Detention International. (2014). *Survivor stories.* (spr.igc.org/en/survivorstories/taz-ca.html) [16]

Kafka, M. P. (2008). Neurobiological processes and comorbidity. In: Laws, D. R. & O'Donohue, W. T. (Eds.), *Sexual deviance: Theory, assessment, and treatment.* Guilford. [13]

Kahlenberg, S. M. & Wrangham, R. W. (2010). Sex differences in chimpanzees' use of sticks as play objects resemble those of children. *Current Biology, 20,* R1067–1068. [4]

Kanazawa, S. (2011). Intelligence and physical attractiveness. *Intelligence, 39,* 7–14. [5]

Kane, P. (2014). *Queer flight: Does the success of gay rights mean the end of gay culture?* (www.sfweekly.com/2014-06-04/news/lgbt-castro-gay-bars) [12]

Kano, T. (1992). *The last ape: Pygmy chimpanzee behavior and ecology.* Stanford University Press. [App. A]

Kaplan, C. (2006). Caring for women with disabilities: Specific disability considerations. *Journal of Midwifery and Women's Health, 51,* 450–456. [9]

Kaplan, H. S. (1979). *Disorders of sexual desire.* Simon & Schuster. [5]

Kaplan, H. S. (1992). Does the CAT technique enhance female orgasm? *Journal of Sex and Marital Therapy, 18,* 285–291. [14]

Kaplan, M. S. & Krueger, R. B. (2010). Diagnosis, assessment, and treatment of hypersexuality. *Journal of Sex Research, 47,* 181–198. [14]

Kaplowitz, P. B. & Oberfield, S. E. (1999). Reexamination of the age limit for defining when puberty is precocious in girls in the United States: Implications for evaluation and treatment. *Pediatrics, 104,* 936–941. [10]

Karlamangla, S. (2013). Former Duke lacrosse accuser convicted of murder. *Los Angeles Times,* November 23. [16]

Katz, G. (2006). Not standing still for subway gropers. *New York Times,* July 5. [13]

Katz, J. & Jhally, S. (2000). Put the blame where it belongs: On men. *Los Angeles Times,* June 25. [16]

Kawahara, M., Obata, Y., Sotomaru, Y., Shimozawa, N., Bao, S., Tsukadaira, T., et al. (2008). Protocol for the production of viable bimaternal mouse embryos. *Nature Protocols, 3,* 197–209. [12]

Keesling, B. (2006). Sexual healing: The completest guide to overcoming common sexual problems (3rd ed.). Hunter House. [14]

Kelly, K. (2014). The spread of "Post Abortion Syndrome" as social diagnosis. *Social Science and Medicine, 102,* 18–25. [9]

Kenagy, G. P. (2005). Transgender health: Findings from two needs assessment studies in Philadelphia. *Health and Social Work, 30,* 19–26. [16]

Kennedy, E. L. & Davis, M. D. (1983). *Boots of leather, slippers of gold: The history of a lesbian community.* Routledge. [12]

Kennedy, S. & Ruggles, S. (2014). Breaking up is hard to count: The rise of divorce in the United States, 1980–2010. *Demography, 51,* 587–598. [11]

Kessel, B. (2000). Premenstrual syndrome: Advances in diagnosis and treatment. *Obstretrical and Gynecological Clinics of North America, 27,* 625–639. [2]

Khera, M., Bhattacharya, R. K., Blick, G., Kushner, H., Nguyen, D. & Miner, M. M. (2011). Improved sexual function with testosterone replacement therapy in hypogonadal men: Real-world data from the Testim Registry in the United States (TRiUS). *Journal of Sexual Medicine, 8,* 3204–3213. [5]

Kilchevsky, A., Vardi, Y., Lowenstein, L. & Gruenwald, I. (2012). Is the female G-spot truly a distinct anatomic entity? *Journal of Sexual Medicine, 9,* 719–726. [2]

Killingsworth, M.A. & Gilbert, D. T. (2010). A Wandering Mind Is an Unhappy Mind. *Science, 330,* 932. [6]

Kilpatrick, D. G. & Resnick, H. S. (2013). *Drug-facilitated, incapacitated, and forcible rape: A national study.* BiblioGov. [16]

Kimball, M. M. (1986). Television and sex-role attitudes. In: Williams, T. M. (Ed.), *The impact of television: A natural experiment in three communities.* Academic. [4]

Kimura, D. (1999). *Sex and cognition.* MIT Press. [4]

King, M. C., Marks, J. H. & Mandell, J. B. (2003). Breast and ovarian cancer risks due to inherited mutations in *BRCA1* and *BRCA2. Science, 302,* 643–646. [2]

King, M., Green, J., Osborn, D. P., Arkell, J., Hetherton, J. & Pereira, E. (2005). Family size in white gay and heterosexual men. *Archives of Sexual Behavior, 34,* 117–122. [12]

King, M., Semlyen, J., Tai, S. S., Killaspy, H., Osborn, D., Popelyuk, D. & Nazareth, I. (2008). A systematic review of mental disorder, suicide, and deliberate self harm in lesbian, gay and bisexual people. *BMC Psychiatry, 8,* 70. [12]

King, R. & Belsky, J. (2012). A typological approach to testing the evolutionary functions of human female orgasm. *Archives of Sexual Behavior, 41,* 1145–1160. [5]

King, R., Belsky, J., Mah, K. & Binik, Y. (2011). Are there different types of female orgasm? *Archives of Sexual Behavior, 40,* 865–875. [5]

Kingkade, T. (2014). *Prosecutors rarely bring charges in college rape cases.* (www.huffingtonpost.com/2014/06/17/college-rape-prosecutors-press-charges_n_5500432.html) [16]

Kinsey, A. C., Pomeroy, W. B. & Martin, C. E. (1948). *Sexual behavior in the human male.* Saunders. [3, 6, 10, 17]

Kinsey, A. C., Pomeroy, W. B., Martin, C. E. & Gebhard, P. H. (1953). *Sexual behavior in the human female.* Saunders. [6, 10]

Kippen, R., Chapman, B., Yu, P. & Lounkaew, K. (2013). What's love got to do with it? Homogamy and dyadic approaches to understanding marital instability. *Journal of Population Research, 30,* 213–247. [7]

Kirkey, S. (2013). *Canada's pediatricians set to reveal new policy on circumcision.* (o.canada.com/news/canadas-pediatricians-set-to-reveal-new-policy-on-circumcision) [3]

Klatt, J. D. & Goodson, J. L. (2013). Oxytocin-like receptors mediate pair bonding in a socially monogamous songbird. *Proceedings of the Royal Society B, 280,* 2012–2396. [7]

Klein, R. (1999). *Penile augmentation surgery.* (www.ejhs.org/volume2/klein/penis10.htm) [3]

Kleinplatz, P. J., Menard, A. D., Paquet, M. P., Paradis, N., Campbell, M., Zuccarino, D. & Mehak, L. (2009). The components of optimal sexuality: A portrait of "great sex." *Canadian Journal of Human Sexuality, 18,* 1–13. [6, 11]

Kluger, J. (2014). A preemie revolution. *Time,* June 2. [8]

Klusmann, D. (2002). Sexual motivation and the duration of partnership. *Archives of Sexual Behavior, 31,* 275–287. [5]

Knickmeyer, R. & Baron-Cohen, S. (2006). Fetal testosterone and sex differences. *Early Human Development, 82,* 755–760. [4]

Knott, C. D., Emery Thompson, M., Stumpf, R. M. & McIntyre, M. H. (2010). Female reproductive strategies in orangutans, evidence for female choice and counterstrategies to infanticide in a species with frequent sexual coercion. *Proceedings of the Royal Society B: Biological Sciences, 277,* 105–113. [1, 16, App. A]

Knox, D., Zusman, M. & McNeely, A. (2008). University students' beliefs about sex: Men vs. women. *College Student Journal, 42,* 181–185. [14]

Kolata, G. (2007). Training through pregnancy to be marathon's fastest mom. *New York Times,* November 3. [8]

Kolata, G. (2014). Vast study casts doubt on value of mammograms. *New York Times,* February 12. [2]

Komdeur, J., Burke, T. & Richardson, D. S. (2007). Explicit experimental evidence for the effectiveness of proximity as mate-guarding behaviour in reducing extra-pair fertilization in the Seychelles warbler. *Molecular Ecology, 16,* 3679–3688. [App. A]

Komisaruk, B. R., Beyer-Flores, C. & Whipple, B. (2006). *The science of orgasm.* Johns Hopkins University Press. [5]

Komisaruk, B. R., Whipple, B., Crawford, A., Liu, W. C., Kalnin, A. & Mosier, K. (2004). Brain activation during vaginocervical self-stimulation and orgasm in women with complete spinal cord injury: fMRI evidence of mediation by the vagus nerves. *Brain Research, 1024,* 77–88. [6]

Komisaruk, B. R., Wise, N., Frangos, E., Liu, W. C., Allen, K. & Brody, S. (2011). Women's clitoris, vagina, and cervix mapped on the sensory cortex: fMRI evidence. *Journal of Sexual Medicine, 8,* 2822–2830. [3]

Kornrich, S., Brines, J. & Leupp, K. (2012). Egalitarianism, housework, and sexual frequency in marriage. *American Sociological Review, 78,* 26–50. [11]

Koskela, P., Anttila, T., Bjorge, T., Brunsvig, A., Dillner, J., Hakama, M., et al. (2000). *Chlamydia trachomatis* infection as a risk factor for invasive cervical cancer. *International Journal of Cancer, 85,* 35–39. [2]

Kost, K., Singh, S., Vaughan, B., Trussell, J. & Bankole, A. (2008). Estimates of contraceptive failure from the 2002 National Survey of Family Growth. *Contraception, 77,* 10–21. [9]

Kosters, J. P. & Goetzsche, P. C. (2008). *Regular self-examination or clinical examination for early detection of breast cancer.* (www.cochrane.org/reviews/en/ab003373.html) [2]

Kotz, D. (2008). A risky rise in C-sections. *US News and World Report,* April 7. [8]

Kowal, D. (2007). Coitus interruptus (withdrawal). In: Hatcher, R. A., et al. (Eds.), *Contraceptive technology* (19th ed.). Ardent Media. [9]

Kozhimannil, K. B., Macheras, M. & Lorch, S. A. (2014). Trends in childbirth before 39 weeks' gestation without medical indication. *Medical Care, 52,* 649–657. [8]

Krahe, B., Bieneck, S. & Scheinberger-Olwig, R. (2007). The role of sexual scripts in sexual aggression and victimization. *Archives of Sexual Behavior, 36,* 687–701. [4]

Kramer, M. S., Aboud, F., Mironova, E., Vanilovich, I., Platt, R. W., Matush, L., et al. (2008). Breastfeeding and child cognitive development: New evidence from a large randomized trial. *Archives of General Psychiatry, 65,* 578–584. [8]

Kraut-Becher, J., Eisenberg, M., Voytek, C., Brown, T., Metzger, D. S. & Aral, S. (2008). Examining racial disparities in HIV: lessons from sexually transmitted infections research. *Journal of Acquired Immune Deficiency Syndromes, 47*(Suppl. 1), S20–27. [15]

Kremer, W. (2013). *The return of the female condom?* (www.bbc.com/news/magazine-25348410) [9]

Kroeger, R. A. & Smock, P. J. (2014). Cohabitation: Recent research and implications. In: Treas, J., et al. (Eds.), *The Wiley-Blackwell Companion to the Sociology of Families.* Wiley. [11]

Kross, E., Berman, M. G., Mischel, W., Smith, E. E. & Wager, T. D. (2011). Social rejection shares somatosensory representations with physical pain. *Proceedings of the National Academy of Sciences of the United States of America, 108,* 6270–6275. [7]

Kundal, V. K., Gajdhar, M., Shukla, A. K. & Kundal, R. (2013). A rare case of isolated complete diphallia and review of the literature. *BMJ Case Reports, 2013.* [3]

Kuperberg, A. (2014). Age at coresidence, premarital cohabitation, and marriage dissolution: 1985–2009. *Journal of Marriage and Family, 76,* 352–369. [11]

La Leche League. (2014). *LLLI updates breastfeeding counsellor criteria.* (www.llli.org/llli_updates_breastfeeding_counsellor_eligibility_criteria_21_april_2014) [4]

Labelle, A., Bourget, D., Bradford, J. M., Alda, M. & Tessier, P. (2012). Familial paraphilia: A pilot study with the construction of genograms. *ISRN Psychiatry,* published online January 1, 692813. [13]

LaBrie, J. W., Hummer, J. F., Ghaidarov, T. M., Lac, A. & Kenney, S. R. (2014). Hooking up in the college context: The event-level effects of alcohol use and partner familiarity on hookup behaviors and contentment. *Journal of Sex Research, 51,* 62–73. [7]

LaCour, M. J. & Green, D. P. (2014). When contact changes minds: An experiment on transmission of support for gay equality. *Science, 346,* 1366–1369. [12]

Ladas, A. K., Whipple, B. & Perry, J. D. (2004). *The G spot and other recent discoveries about human sexuality.* Holt. [2, 5]

Lahdenpera, M., Lummaa, V., Helle, S., Tremblay, M. & Russell, A. F. (2004). Fitness benefits of prolonged post-reproductive lifespan in women. *Nature, 428,* 178–181. [11]

Lakehomer, H., Kaplan, P. F., Wozniak, D. G. & Minson, C. T. (2013). Characteristics of scheduled bleeding manipulation with combined hormonal contraception in university students. *Contraception, 88,* 426–430. [2]

Lamaze International. (2014). *Lamaze for parents.* (www.lamaze.org) [8]

Lancaster, R. N. (2011). *Sex panic and the punitive state.* University of California Press. [10]

Landor, J. M. & Simons, L. G. (2013). Why virginity pledges succeed or fail: The moderating effect of religious commitment versus religious participation. *Journal of Child and Family Studies,* published online June 13. [10]

Landovitz, R. J., Tseng, C. H., Weissman, M., Haymer, M., Mendenhall, B., Rogers, K., et al. (2013). Epidemiology, sexual risk behavior, and HIV prevention practices of men who have sex with men using Grindr in Los Angeles, California. *Journal of Urban Health, 90,* 729–739. [7]

Langlois, J. H. & Roggman, L. A. (1990). Attractive faces are only average. *Psychological Science, 1,* 115–121. [5]

Långstrom, N. & Zucker, K. J. (2005). Transvestic fetishism in the general population: Prevalence and correlates. *Journal of Sex and Marital Therapy, 31,* 87–95. [13]

Långstrom, N., Enebrink, P., Lauren, E. M., Lindblom, J., Werko, S. & Hanson, R. K. (2013). Preventing sexual abusers of children from reoffending: Systematic review of medical and psychological interventions. *BMJ, 347,* f4630. [13]

Långström, N., Rahman, Q., Carlström, E. & Lichtenstein, P. (2010). Genetic and environmental effects on same-sex sexual behavior: A population study of twins in Sweden. *Archives of Sexual Behavior, 39,* 75–80. [12]

Larsson, I. & Svedin, C. G. (2002a). Sexual experiences in childhood: Young adults' recollections. *Archives of Sexual Behavior, 31,* 263–273. [10]

Larsson, I. & Svedin, C. G. (2002b). Teachers' and parents' reports on 3- to 6-year-old children's sexual behavior: A comparison. *Child Abuse and Neglect, 26,* 247–266. [10]

Larsson, I., Svedin, C. G. & Friedrich, W. N. (2000). Differences and similarities in sexual behavior among pre-schoolers in Sweden and USA. *Nordic Journal of Psychiatry, 54,* 151–157. [10]

Laumann, E. O. & Michael, R. T. (Eds.). (2000). *Sex, love, and health in America: Private choices and public policies.* University of Chicago Press. [10]

Laumann, E. O., Gagnon, J. H., Michael, R. T. & Michaels, S. (1994). *The social organization of sexuality: Sexual practices in the United States.* University of Chicago Press. [1, 5, 10, 11]

Laumann, E. O., Glasser, D. B., Neves, R. C. & Moreira, E. D., Jr. (2009). A population-based survey of sexual activity, sexual problems and associated help-seeking behavior patterns in mature adults in the United States of America. *International Journal of Impotence Research, 21,* 171–178. [14]

Laumann, E. O., Masi, C. M. & Zuckerman, E. W. (1997). Circumcision in the United States. Prevalence, prophylactic effects, and sexual practice. *JAMA, 277,* 1052–1057. [3]

Laumann, E. O., Paik, A. & Rosen, R. C. (2000). Sexual dysfunction in the United States: Prevalence and predictors. In: Laumann, E. O. & Michael, R. T. (Eds.), *Sex, love, and health in America: Private choices and public policies.* University of Chicago Press. [14]

Lavin, M. (2008). Voyeurism: Psychopathology and theory. In: Laws, D. R. & O'Donohue, W. T. (Eds.), *Sexual deviance: Theory, assessment, and treatment* (2nd ed). Guilford. [13]

Lavner, J. A., Karney, B. R. & Bradbury, T. N. (2013). Newlyweds' optimistic forecasts of their marriage: For better or for worse? *Journal of Family Psychology, 27,* 531–540. [11]

Lawrence, A. A. (2003). Factors associated with satisfaction or regret following male-to-female sex reassignment surgery. *Archives of Sexual Behavior, 32,* 299–315. [4]

Lawrence, A. A. (2011). Autogynephilia: An underappreciated paraphilia. *Advances in Psychosomatic Medicine, 31,* 135–148. [4]

Lawrence, A. A. (2013). *Men trapped in men's bodies: Narratives of autogynephilic transsexualism.* Springer. [4]

Lawrence, A. A. (2014). *Practice information.* (www.annelawrence.com/practice/index.html) [14]

Lawrence, E., Rothman, A. D., Cobb, R. J. & Bradbury, M. T. (2008). Marital satisfaction across the transition to parenthood. *Journal of Family Psychology, 22,* 41–50. [11]

Laws, D. R. & O'Donohue, W. T. (2008). *Sexual deviance: Theory, assessment, and treatment* (2nd ed.). Guilford. [13]

Leiblum, S. R. (2007). Sex therapy today: Current issues and future perspectives. In: Leiblum, S. R. (Ed.), *Principles and practice of sex therapy* (4th ed.). Guilford. [14]

Lemieux, R. & Hale, J. L. (1999). Intimacy, passion, and commitment in young romantic relationships: Successfully measuring the triangular theory of love. *Psychological Reports, 85,* 497–503. [7]

Lemieux, R. & Hale, J. L. (2000). Intimacy, passion, and commitment among married individuals: Further testing of the triangular theory of love. *Psychological Reports, 87,* 941–948. [7]

Leone, P. & Corey, L. (2005). *Genital herpes: Prevalence, transmission, and prevention.* (www.medscape.com/viewarticle/502718_1) [15]

Lepage, J. F., Hong, D. S., Raman, M., Marzelli, M., Roeltgen, D. P., Lai, S., Ross, J. & Reiss, A. L. (2014). Brain morphology in children with 47,XYY syndrome: A voxel- and surface-based morphometric study. *Genes, Brain and Behavior, 13,* 127–134. [4]

Lester, L. J. & Agarwal, S. K. (2011). Hepatitis viruses as sexually transmitted diseases. In: Gross, G. & Tyring, S. K. (Eds.), *Sexually transmitted infections and sexually transmitted diseases.* Springer. [15]

LeVay, S. (1991). A difference in hypothalamic structure between heterosexual and homosexual men. *Science, 253,* 1034–1037. [1, 12]

LeVay, S. (2006). *Same sex—different rules.* (www.simonlevay.com/essay) [6]

LeVay, S. (2008). When science goes wrong: Twelve tales from the dark side of discovery. Plume. [15]

LeVay, S. (2011). *Gay, straight, and the reason why: The science of sexual orientation.* Oxford University Press. [1, 12]

LeVay, S. & Nonas, E. (1995). *City of friends: A portrait of the gay and lesbian community in America.* MIT Press. [12]

Levenson, J. S. & Macgowan, M. J. (2004). Engagement, denial, and treatment progress among sex offenders in group therapy. *Sexual Abuse, 16,* 49–63. [13]

Lever, J. (1995). Lesbian sex survey. *The Advocate,* August 22, 21–30. [6]

Lever, J., Frederick, D. A. & Peplau, L. A. (2006). Does size matter? Men's and women's views on penis size across the lifespan. *Psychology of Men and Masculinity, 7,* 129–143. [3]

Levin, R. J. & Wagner, G. (1985). Orgasm in women in the laboratory—quantitative studies on duration, intensity, latency, and vaginal blood flow. *Archives of Sexual Behavior, 14,* 439–449. [5]

Levine, S. B. (2010). What is sexual addiction? *Journal of Sex and Marital Therapy, 36,* 261–275. [14]

Levis, S., Strickman-Stein, N., Ganjei-Azar, P., Xu, P., Doerge, D. R. & Krischer, J. (2011). Soy isoflavones in the prevention of menopausal bone loss and menopausal symptoms: A randomized, double-blind trial. *Archives of Internal Medicine, 171,* 1363–1369. [11]

Levitt, S. D. (2009). *Trading tricks: The economics of prostitution.* (www.chicagobooth.edu/capideas/apr09/4.aspx) [17]

Levitt, S. D. & Venkatesh, S. A. (2007). *An empirical analysis of street-level prostitution.* (economics.uchicago.edu/pdf/Prostitution%205.pdf) [17]

Lewin, T. (2014). A surrogacy agency that delivered heartache. *New York Times,* July 27. [8]

Lewis, M. A., Granato, H., Blayney, J. A., Lostutter, T. W. & Kilmer, J. R. (2012). Predictors of hooking up sexual behaviors and emotional reactions among U.S. college students. *Archives of Sexual Behavior, 41,* 1219–1229. [7]

Lewis, R. J. & Janda, L. H. (1988). The relationship between adult sexual adjustment and childhood experiences regarding exposure to nudity, sleeping in the parental bed, and parental attitudes toward sexuality. *Archives of Sexual Behavior, 17,* 349–362. [10]

Ley, D. (2012). *The myth of sex addiction.* Rowman & Littlefield. [14]

Ley, D., Prause, N. & Finn, P. (2014). The emperor has no clothes: A review of the "pornography addiction" model. *Current Sexual Health Reports, 6,* 94-105. [14]

Li, C. Y., Kayes, O., Kell, P. D., Christopher, N., Minhas, S. & Ralph, D. J. (2006). Penile suspensory ligament division for penile augmentation: Indications and results. *European Urology, 49,* 729–733. [3]

Li, N. P., Valentine, K. A. & Patel, L. (2011). Mate preferences in the US and Singapore: A cross-cultural test of the mate preference priority model. *Personality and Individual Differences, 50,* 291–294. [5]

Li, P., Griskevicius, V., Durante, K. M., Jonason, P. K., Pasisz, D. J. & Aumer, K. (2009). An evolutionary perspective on humor: Sexual selection or interest indication? *Personality and Social Psychology Bulletin, 35,* 923–936. [5]

Liberles, S. D. (2014). Mammalian pheromones. *Annual Review of Physiology, 76,* 151–175. [5]

Liew, Z., Ritz, B., Rebordosa, C., Lee, P. C. & Olsen, J. (2014). Acetaminophen use during pregnancy, behavioral problems, and hyperkinetic disorders. *JAMA Pediatrics, 168,* 313–320. [8]

Lifelong Adoptions. (2014). *LGBT adoption laws.* (www.lifelongadoptions.com/lgbt-adoption-resources/lgbt-adoption-laws) [8]

Lillard, L. A., Brien, M. J. & Waite, L. J. (1995). Premarital cohabitation and subsequent marital dissolution: A matter of self-selection? *Demography, 32,* 437–457. [11]

Lim, M. M., Wang, Z., Olazabal, D. E., Ren, X., Terwilliger, E. F. & Young, L. J. (2004). Enhanced partner preference in a promiscuous species by manipulating the expression of a single gene. *Nature, 429,* 754–757. [7]

Lindau, S. T., Schumm, L. P., Laumann, E. O., Levinson, W., O'Muircheartaigh, C. A. & Waite, L. J. (2007). A study of sexuality and health among older adults in the United States. *New England Journal of Medicine, 357,* 762–774. [11]

Linderman, J. (2014). New president: Southern Baptist won't change its stance on gay marriage, transgender identity. *Star Tribune,* June 11. [11]

Lindh, I., Ellstrom, A. A. & Milsom, I. (2011). The long-term influence of combined oral contraceptives on body weight. *Human Reproduction, 26,* 1917–1924. [9]

Ling, L. (2010). *The positive side of divorce.* (www.oprah.com/relationships/The-Positive-Side-of-Divorce-Lisa-Ling) [11]

Linz, D., Blumenthal, E., Donnerstein, E., Kunkel, D., Shafer, B. J. & Lichtenstein, A. (2000). Testing legal assumptions regarding the effects of dancer nudity and proximity to patron on erotic expression. *Law and Human Behavior, 24,* 507–533. [3]

Lippa, R. A. (2005). *Gender, nature, and nurture* (2nd. ed.). Erlbaum. [4]

Lippa, R. A. (2006). The gender reality hypothesis. *American Psychologist, 61,* 639–640; discussion 641–642. [4]

Lippa, R. A. (2008). Sex differences and sexual orientation differences in personality: Findings from the BBC Internet survey. *Archives of Sexual Behavior, 37,* 173–187. [4, 12]

Lippa, R. A. (2009). Sex differences in sex drive, sociosexuality, and height across 53 nations: Testing evolutionary and social structural theories. *Archives of Sexual Behavior, 38,* 631–651. [4]

Liptak, A. (2012). Supreme Court rejects F.C.C. fines for indecency. *New York Times,* June 21. [17]

Lisak, D. & Miller, P. M. (2002). Repeat rape and multiple offending among undetected rapists. *Violence and Victims, 17,* 75–83. [16]

Lisak, D., Gardenier, L., Nicksa, S. C. & Cote, A. M. (2010). False allegations of sexual assault: An analysis of ten years of reported cases. *Violence Against Women, 16,* 1318–1334. [16]

Little AB. (2014). *Little AB's babyland.* (www.littleab.com) [13]

Little, A. C., Apicella, C. L. & Marlowe, F. W. (2007). Preferences for symmetry in human faces in two cultures: Eata from the UK and the Hadza, an isolated group of hunter-gatherers. *Proceedings of the Royal Society B: Biological Sciences, 274,* 3113–3117. [5]

Little, A. C., Debruine, L. M. & Jones, B. C. (2013). Sex differences in attraction to familiar and unfamiliar opposite-sex faces: Men prefer novelty and women prefer familiarity. *Archives of Sexual Behavior, 43,* 973–981. [5]

Little, A. C., Jones, B. C. & DeBruine, L. M. (2011). Facial attractiveness: Evolutionary based research. *Philosophical Transactions of the Royal Society of London Series B: Biological Sciences, 366,* 1638–1659. [5]

Lively, C. M. (2010). An epidemiological model of host-parasite coevolution and sex. *Journal of Evolutionary Biology, 23,* 1490–1497. [App. A]

Loftus, E. F. & Davis, D. (2006). Recovered memories. *Annual Review of Clinical Psychology, 2,* 469–498. [10]

Lönnerdal, B. (2003). Nutritional and physiological significance of human milk proteins. *American Society for Clinical Nutrition, 77,* 1537S–1543S. [8]

López Bernal, A. & TambyRaja, R. L. (2000). Preterm labour. *Best Practice & Research Clinical Obstetrics & Gynecology, 14,* 133–153. [8]

Lopez, B. (2013). Sliver of sky: Confronting the trauma of sexual abuse. *Harper's,* January. [10]

Los Angeles LGBT Center. (2014). *Domestic violence services.* (www.lalgbtcenter.org/domestic_violence_services) [16]

Los Angeles Times. (1994). *Polls finds widespread claims of sexual harassment in workplace.* (articles.latimes.com/1994-03-28/business/fi-39362_1_sexual-harassment) [16]

Lösel, F. & Schmucker, M. (2005). The effectiveness of treatment for sexual offenders: A comprehensive meta-analysis. *Journal of Experimental Criminology, 1,* 117–146. [16]

Lovett, I. (2013). After 37 years of trying to change people's sexual orientation, group is to disband. *New York Times,* June 20. [12]

Lu, M. C., Jones, L., Bond, M. J., Wright, K., Pumpuang, M., Maidenberg, M., et al. (2010). Where is the F in MCH? Father involvement in African American families. *Ethnicity and Disease, 20*(Suppl. 2), 49–61. [11]

Luhn, R. (2013). Russian anti-gay law prompts rise in homophobic violence. *Guardian (London)*, September 1. [12]

Lumley, V. A. & Scotti, J. R. (2001). Supporting the sexuality of adults with mental retardation. *Journal of Positive Behavior Interventions, 3*, 109–119. [6]

Luo, T., Yan, H. M., He, P., Luo, Y., Yang, Y. F. & Zheng, W. (2012). Aspirin use and breast cancer risk: A meta-analysis. *Breast Cancer Research and Treatment, 131*, 581–587. [2]

Lussier, P. & Piché, L. (2008). Frotteurism: Psychopathology and theory. In: Laws, D. R. & O'Donohue, W. T. (Eds.), *Sexual deviance: Theory, assessment, and treatment* (2nd ed.). Guilford. [13]

Lyden, M. (2007). Assessment of sexual consent capacity. *Sexuality and Disability, 25*, 3–20. [6]

Lykins, A. D., Meana, M. & Strauss, G. P. (2008). Sex differences in visual attention to erotic and non-erotic stimuli. *Archives of Sexual Behavior, 37*, 219–228. [5]

Maccoby, E. E. (1998). *The two sexes: Growing up apart, coming together.* Harvard University Press. [4]

MacDonald, H. (2008). *The campus rape myth.* (www.city-journal.org/2008/18_1_campus_rape.html) [16]

Magga, G. (2010). *Female circumcision and Ugandan politics.* (www.afrik-news.com/article18458.html) [2]

Mail Online. (2013). *World's oldest mother, 74, says giving birth to her daughter, now five, has kept her living longer because she's determined to live to see her marry.* (www.dailymail.co.uk/news/article-2369218/Worlds-oldest-mother-Rajo-Devi-Lohan-74-says-giving-birth-daughter-kept-living-longer.html) [8]

Mainiero, L. A. & Jones, K. J. (2013). Workplace romance 2.0: Developing a communication ethics model to address potential sexual harassment from inappropriate social media contacts between coworkers. *Journal of Business Ethics, 114*, 367–379. [16]

Malamuth, N. M., Addison, T. & Koss, M. (2000). Pornography and sexual aggression: Are there reliable effects and can we understand them? *Annual Review of Sex Research, 11*, 26–91. [1]

Malamuth, N. M., Linz, D., Heavey, C. L., Barnes, G. & Acker, M. (1995). Using the confluence model of sexual aggression to predict men's conflict with women: A 10-year follow-up study. *Journal of Personality and Social Psychology, 69*, 353–369. [16]

Malo, A. F., Roldan, E. R., Garde, J., Soler, A. J. & Gomendio, M. (2005). Antlers honestly advertise sperm production and quality. *Proceedings of the Royal Society of London B: Biological Sciences, 272*, 149–157. [App. A]

Mamo, L. (2007). *Queering reproduction: Achieving pregnancy in the age of technoscience.* Duke University Press. [12]

Maniglio, R. (2013). Child sexual abuse in the etiology of anxiety disorders. *Trauma, Violence, & Abuse, 14*, 96–112. [10]

Manktelow, B. N., Seaton, S. E., Field, D. J. & Draper, E. S. (2013). Population-based estimates of in-unit survival for very preterm infants. *Pediatrics, 131*, e425–432. [8]

Mannen, A. (2014). *6 unsexy realities of being a phone sex operator.* (www.cracked.com/article_21357_6-unsexy-realities-being-phone-sex-operator.html) [17]

Manning, J. T., Churchill, A. J. & Peters, M. (2007). The effects of sex, ethnicity, and sexual orientation on self-measured digit ratio (2D:4D). *Archives of Sexual Behavior, 36*, 223–233. [12]

Manning, J., Kilduff, L., Cook, C., Crewther, B. & Fink, B. (2014). Digit ratio (2D:4D): A biomarker for prenatal sex steroids and adult sex steroids in challenge situations. *Frontiers in Endocrinology (Lausanne), 5*, 9. [4]

Manning, W. D. & Cohen, J. A. (2012). Premarital cohabitation and marital dissolution: An examination of recent marriages. *Journal of Marriage and the Family, 74*, 377–387. [11]

Manning, W. D. & Smock, P. (2007). Measuring and modeling cohabitation: New perspectives from qualitative data. *Journal of Marriage and the Family, 67*, 989–1002. [11]

Marazzini, D., Di Nasso, E., Masala, I., Baroni, S., Abelli, M., Mengali, F., Mungai, F. & Rucci, P. (2003). Normal and obsessional jealousy: A study of a population of young adults. *European Psychiatry, 18*, 106–111. [7]

Marazziti, D., Torri, P., Baroni, S., Catena Dell'Osso, M., Consoli, G. & Boncinelli, V. (2011). Is androstadienone a putative human pheromone? *Current Medicinal Chemistry, 18*, 1213–1219. [5]

Marchbanks, P. A., Curtis, K. M., Mandel, M. G., Wilson, H. G., Jeng, G., Folger, S. G., et al. (2012). Oral contraceptive formulation and risk of breast cancer. *Contraception, 85*, 342–350. [9]

Marchbanks, P. A., McDonald, J. A., Wilson, H. G., Folger, S. G., Mandel, M. G., Daling, J. R., et al. (2002). Oral contraceptives and the risk of breast cancer. *New England Journal of Medicine, 346*, 2025–2032. [2]

Marcus, R. (2009). Confessions of a teenage prostitute. *Portland Mercury*, September 3. [17]

Markey, P. M. & Markey, C. N. (2013). Seasonal variation in Internet keyword searches: A proxy assessment of sex mating behaviors. *Archives of Sexual Behavior, 42*, 515–521. [6]

Markman, H. J. (1981). Prediction of marital distress: A 5-year follow-up. *Journal of Consulting and Clinical Psychology, 49*, 760–762. [7]

Markman, H. J., Stanley, S. M. & Blumberg, S. L. (2010). *Fighting for your marriage* (3rd. ed.). Jossey-Bass. [7]

Marques, J. K., Wiederanders, M., Day, D. M., Nelson, C. & van Ommeren, A. (2005). Effects of a relapse prevention program on sexual recidivism: Final results from California's Sex Offender Treatment and Evaluation Project (SOTEP). *Sexual Abuse, 17*, 79–107. [13]

Marrazzo, J. M., Thomas, K. K., Agnew, K. & Ringwood, K. (2010). Prevalence and risks for bacterial vaginosis in women who have sex with women. *Sexually Transmitted Diseases, 37*, 335–339.

Marsh, J. (2014). Model wins round in HIV-ad lawsuit. *New York Post*, March 10. [15]

Marshall, D. S. (1971). Sexual behavior on Mangaia. In: Marshall, D. S. & Suggs, D. N. (Eds.), *Human sexual behavior.* Basic Books. [10]

Marshall, R. (2012). *The British army's fight against venereal disease in the "heroic age of prostitution."* (ww1centenary.oucs.ox.ac.uk/body-and-mind/the-british-army%E2%80%99s-fight-against-venereal-disease-in-the-%E2%80%98heroic-age-of-prostitution%E2%80%99) [15]

Marshall, T. C., Bejanyan, K., Di Castro, G. & Lee, R. A. (2013). Attachment styles as predictors of Facebook-related jealousy and surveillance in romantic relationships. *Personal Relationships, 20*, 1–22. [7]

Marshall, W. L. & Fernandez, Y. M. (2003). *Phallometric testing with sexual offenders.* Safer Society. [13]

Martin, C. L. & Ruble, D. N. (2010). Patterns of gender development. *Annual Review of Psychology, 61*, 353–381. [4]

Martin, D. (2008). Mildred Loving, who fought marriage ban, dies. *New York Times*, May 6. [7]

Martin, J. A., Hamilton, B. E., Ventura, S. J., Osterman, M. H. S. & Mathews, T. J. (2013). *Births: Final data for 2011.* (www.cdc.gov/nchs/data/nvsr/nvsr62/nvsr62_01.pdf) [1]

Martin, J. T. & Nguyen, D. H. (2004). Anthropometric analysis of homosexuals and heterosexuals: Implications for early hormone exposure. *Hormones and Behavior, 45*, 31–39. [12]

Martinez, C. S., Ferreira, F. V., Castro, A. A. & Gomide, L. B. (2014). Women with greater pelvic floor muscle strength have better sexual function. *Acta Obstetricia et Gynecologica Scandinavica, 93*, 497–502. [14]

Martinson, F. M. (1976). Eroticism in infancy and childhood. *Journal of Sex Research, 2*, 251–262. [10]

Maruthupandian, J. & Marimuthu, G. (2013). Cunnilingus apparently increases duration of copulation in the Indian flying fox, *Pteropus giganteus*. *PLOS ONE, 8*, e59743. [6]

Masters, W. H. & Johnson, V. (1970). *Human sexual inadequacy.* Little, Brown. [14]

Masters, W. H. & Johnson, V. (1979). *Homosexuality in perspective.* Little, Brown. [12]

Masters, W. H. & Johnson, V. E. (1966). *Human sexual response.* Little, Brown. [5, 6]

Masters, W. H., Johnson, V. E. & Kolodny, R. C. (1982). *Human sexuality.* Little, Brown. [10]

Matteson, D. (1991). Bisexual feminist man. In: Hutchins, L. & Kaahumanu, L. (Eds.), *Bi any other name: Bisexual people speak out.* Alyson. [12]

Matthews, M. (1994). *Horseman: Obsessions of a zoophile.* Prometheus. [13]

Maurer, T. W. & Robinson, D. W. (2008). Effects of attire, alcohol, and gender on perceptions of date rape. *Sex Roles, 58*, 423–434. [16]

Mayo Clinic. (2014a). *Hypospadias.* (www.mayoclinic.org/diseases-conditions/hypospadias/basics/definition/con-20031354) [4]

Mayo Clinic. (2014b). *Kegel exercises: A how-to guide for women.* (www.mayoclinic.org/healthy-living/womens-health/in-depth/kegel-exercises/art-20045283) [14]

Mayo Clinic. (2014c). *Toxic shock syndrome.* (www.mayoclinic.org/diseases-conditions/toxic-shock-syndrome/basics/definition/con-20021326) [2]

Mayo Clinic. (2014d). *Ectopic pregnancy.* (www.mayoclinic.org/diseases-conditions/ectopic-pregnancy/basics/definition/con-20024262) [8]

Mayo Clinic. (2014e). *Pregnancy weight gain: What's healthy?* (www.mayoclinic.org/healthy-living/pregnancy-week-by-week/in-depth/pregnancy-weight-gain/art-20044360) [8]

McCabe, M. P. & Goldhammer, D. L. (2013). Prevalence of women's sexual desire problems: What criteria do we use? *Archives of Sexual Behavior, 42*, 1073–1078. [14]

McCarthy, M. M. & Arnold, A. P. (2011). Reframing sexual differentiation of the brain. *Nature Neuroscience, 14*, 677–683. [4]

McCarty, E. J., Quah, S., Maw, R., Dinsmore, W. W. & Emerson, C. R. (2011). Post-exposure prophylaxis following sexual exposure to HIV: a seven-year retrospective analysis in a regional centre. *International Journal of STD and AIDS, 22*, 407–408. [15]

McClintock, M. K. (1971). Menstrual synchrony and suppression. *Nature, 229*, 244–245. [2]

McClintock, M. K. (1999). Reproductive biology: Pheromones and regulation of ovulation. *Nature, 401*, 232–233. [2]

McConaghy, N. (2005). Sexual dysfunction and disorders. In: Maddux, J. E. & Winstead, B. A. (Eds.), *Psychopathology: Foundations for a contemporary understanding.* Erlbaum. [13]

McConnell, T. (2010). Sexual violence "becoming normal" in Congo. *Times (London)*, April 16. [16]

McCormack, M. & Anderson, R. E. (2014). The influence of declining homophobia on men's gender in the United States: An argument for the study of homohysteria. *Sex Roles*, published online March 4. [12]

McFadden, D. & Pasanen, E. G. (1999). Spontaneous otoacoustic emissions in heterosexuals, homosexuals, and bisexuals. *Journal of the Acoustical Society of America, 105*, 2403–2413. [12]

McFarlane, J. M., Campbell, J. C., Wilt, S., Sachs, C., Ulrich, Y. & Xu, X. (1999). Stalking and intimate partner femicide. *Homicide Studies, 3*, 300–317. [16]

McGraw, L. A. & Young, L. J. (2010). The prairie vole: An emerging model organism for understanding the social brain. *Trends in Neurosciences, 33*, 103–109. [7]

McIntire, M. & Bogdanich, W. (2014). At Florida State, football clouds justice. *New York Times*, October 10. [16]

McLaughlin, J. (2014). *ISIS magazine promotes slavery, rape, and murder of civilians in God's name.* (www.motherjones.com/politics/2014/10/isis-propaganda-magazine-rape-slavery-murder-allah-dabiq) [16]

McLaughlin, K. (2011). *Moore, Kutcher: Join our crusade to end child sex trafficking.* (articles.cnn.com/2011-04-14/world/kutcher.moore.piers.morgan_1_human-trafficking-child-prostitution-end-child?_s=PM:WORLD) [17]

McMahon, C. G., Althof, S. E., Kaufman, J. M., Buvat, J., Levine, S. B., Aquilina, J. W., et al. (2011). Efficacy and safety of dapoxetine for the treatment of premature ejaculation: Integrated analysis of results from five phase 3 trials. *Journal of Sexual Medicine, 8*, 524–539. [14]

McNeil, D. G. (2007). Circumcision's anti-AIDS effect found greater than first thought. *New York Times*, February 23. [3]

McNeil, D. G. (2013a). Cancer vaccines get a price cut in poor nations. *New York Times*, November 23. [15]

McNeil, D. G. (2013b). Circumcision device approved by World Health Organization. *New York Times*, May 31. [3]

McNulty, J. K., Olson, M. A., Meltzer, A. L. & Shaffer, M. J. (2013). Though they may be unaware, newlyweds implicitly know whether their marriage will be satisfying. *Science, 342*, 1119–1120. [11]

McRobbie, L. R. (2014). *The real victims of satanic ritual abuse.* (www.slate.com/articles/health_and_science/medical_examiner/2014/01/fran_and_dan_keller_freed_two_of_the_last_victims_of_satanic_ritual_abuse.single.html) [10]

McShane, L. (2009). David Carradine a fan of "potentially deadly" deviant sex acts, ex-wife said in court papers. *New York Daily News*, June 5. [13]

Mehta, D., Newport, D. J., Frishman, G., Kraus, L., Rex-Haffner, M., Ritchie, J. C., et al. (2014). Early predictive biomarkers for postpartum depression point to a role for estrogen receptor signaling. *Psychological Medicine, 44*, 1–14. [8]

Meloy, J. R., Rivers, L., Siegel, L., Gothard, S., Naimark, D. & Nicolini, J. R. (2000). A replication study of obsessional followers and offenders with mental disorders. *Journal of Forensic Sciences, 45*, 147–152. [16]

Meloy, J. R., Sheridan, L. & Hoffmann, J. (Eds.). (2008). *Stalking, threatening, and attacking public figures: A psychological and behavioral analysis.* Oxford University Press. [16]

Meltzer, A. L., McNulty, J. K., Jackson, G. L. & Karney, B. R. (2014). Sex differences in the implications of partner physical attractiveness for the trajectory of marital satisfaction. *Journal of Personality and Social Psychology, 106*, 418–428. [11]

Meltzer, M. (2014). Below the bikini line, a growing trend. *New York Times*, January 30. [2]

Memorial Sloan Kettering Cancer Center. (2013). *How do I decide whether I should bank cord blood from my newborn?* (www.mskcc.org/blog/how-do-i-decide-whether-i-should-bank-cord-blood-my-newborn) [8]

Meneses, L. M., Orrell-Valente, J. K., Guendelman, S. R., Oman, D. & Irwin, C. E., Jr. (2006). Racial/ethnic differences in mother-daughter communication about sex. *Journal of Adolescent Health, 39*, 128–131. [10]

Mercer, C. H., Tanton, C., Prah, P., Erens, B., Sonnenberg, P., Clifton, S., et al. (2013). Changes in sexual attitudes and lifestyles in Britain through the life course and over time: Findings from the National Surveys of Sexual Attitudes and Lifestyles (Natsal). *Lancet, 382*, 1781–1794. [1]

Mertz, G. J. (2008). Asymptomatic shedding of herpes simplex virus 1 and 2: implications for prevention of transmission. *Journal of Infectious Diseases, 198*, 1098–1100. [15]

Messe, M. R. & Geer, J. H. (1985). Voluntary vaginal musculature contractions as an enhancer of sexual arousal. *Archives of Sexual Behavior, 14*, 13–28. [14]

Meston, C. M. & Bradford, A. (2007). Sexual dysfunctions in women. *Annual Review of Clinical Psychology, 3*, 233–256. [14]

Meston, C. M. & Buss, D. M. (2007). Why humans have sex. *Archives of Sexual Behavior, 36*, 477–507. [5]

Meston, C. M. & Buss, D. M. (2009). *Why women have sex: The psychology of sex in women's own voices.* Times Books. [14]

Meyer-Bahlburg, H. F., Dolezal, C., Baker, S. W. & New, M. I. (2008). Sexual orientation in women with classical or non-classical congenital adrenal hyperplasia as a function of degree of prenatal androgen excess. *Archives of Sexual Behavior, 37*, 85–99. [12]

Michigan Womyn's Music Festival. (2014). *Michigan Womyn's Music Festival.* (www.michfest.com/festival/index.htm) [12]

MicroSort. (2012). *Purity and results.* (www.microsort.com/?page_id=453) [8]

Miller, A. B., Wall, C., Baines, C. J., Sun, P., To, T. & Narod, S. A. (2014). Twenty five year follow-up for breast cancer incidence and mortality of the Canadian National Breast Screening Study: Randomised screening trial. *BMJ, 348*, February 11. [2]

Miller, B., Messias, E., Miettunen, J., Alaraisanen, A., Jarvelin, M. R., Koponen, H., et al. (2011). Meta-analysis of paternal age and schizophrenia risk in male versus female offspring. *Schizophrenia Bulletin, 37*, 1039–1047. [8]

Miller, D. I. & Halpern, D. F. (2014). The new science of cognitive sex differences. *Trends in Cognitive Sciences, 18*, 37–45. [4]

Miller, G., Tybur, J. M. & Jordan, B. D. (2007). Ovulatory cycle effects on tip earnings by lap dancers: Economic evidence for human estrus? *Evolution and Human Behavior, 28*, 375–381. [5]

Miller, L. (2014). Rape: Sex crime, act of violence, or naturalistic adaptation? *Aggression and Violent Behavior, 19*, 67–81. [16]

Miller, S. A. & Byers, E. S. (2004). Actual and desired duration of foreplay and intercourse: Discordance and misperceptions within heterosexual couples. *Journal of Sex Research, 41*, 301–309. [6]

Milrod, C. & Weitzer, R. (2012). The intimacy prism: Emotional management among the clients of escorts. *Men and Masculinities, 15*, 447–467. [17]

Mimiaga, M. J., Mayer, K. H., Reisner, S. L., Gonzalez, A., Dumas, B., Vanderwarker, R., et al. (2008). Asymptomatic gonorrhea and chlamydial infections detected by nucleic acid amplification tests among Boston area men who have sex with men. *Sexually Transmitted Diseases, 35*, 495–498. [15]

Min, K. J., Lee, C. K. & Park, H. N. (2012). The lifespan of Korean eunuchs. *Current Biology, 22*, R792–793. [14]

Miner, M. M., Bhattacharya, R. K., Blick, G., Kushner, H. & Khera, M. (2013). 12-month observation of testosterone replacement effectiveness in a general population of men. *Postgraduate Medicine, 125*, 8–18. [5]

Mitchell, K. J., Finkelhor, D. & Wolak, J. (2010). Conceptualizing juvenile prostitution as child maltreatment: Findings from the National Juvenile Prostitution Study. *Child Maltreatment, 15*, 18–36. [17]

Mitchell, K. J., Finkelhor, D. & Wolak, J. (2013a). *Sex trafficking cases involving minors.* (www.unh.edu/ccrc/pdf/CV313_Final_Sex_Trafficking_Minors_Nov_2013_rev.pdf) [17]

Mitchell, K. J., Jones, L. M., Finkelhor, D. & Wolak, J. (2013b). Understanding the decline in unwanted online sexual solicitations for U.S. youth 2000–2010: Findings from three Youth Internet Safety Surveys. *Child Abuse and Neglect, 37*, 1225–1236. [10]

Mitchell, K. R., Mercer, C. H., Ploubidis, G. B., Jones, K. G., Datta, J., Field, N., et al. (2013). Sexual function in Britain: Findings from the third National Survey of Sexual Attitudes and Lifestyles (Natsal-3). *Lancet, 382*, 1817–1829. [7]

Moen, O. M. (2014). Is prostitution harmful? *Journal of Medical Ethics, 40*, 73–81. [17]

Møller, A. P. (1992). Female swallow preference for symmetrical male sexual ornaments. *Nature, 357*, 238–240. [App. A]

Molnar, B. E., Buka, S. L. & Kessler, R. C. (2001). Child sexual abuse and subsequent psychopathology: Results from the National Comorbidity Survey. *American Journal of Public Health, 91*, 753–760. [10]

Mondaini, N., Ponchietti, R., Muir, G. H., Montorsi, F., Di Loro, F., Lombardi, G. & Rizzo, M. (2003). Sildenafil does not improve sexual function in men without erectile dysfunction but does reduce the postorgasmic refractory time. *International Journal of Impotence Research, 15*, 225–228. [14]

Money, J. & Ehrhardt, A. E. (1971). *Man and woman, boy and girl: The differentiation and dimorphism of gender identity from conception to maturity.* Johns Hopkins University Press. [4]

Montgomery, M. J. & Sorell, G. T. (1998). Love and dating experience in early and middle adolescence: Grade and gender comparisons. *Journal of Adolescence, 21*, 677–689. [7]

Monti-Bloch, L., Jennings-White, C. & Berliner, D. L. (1998). The human vomeronasal system: A review. *Annals of the New York Academy of Sciences, 855*, 373–389. [5]

Monto, M. A. & Milrod, C. (2013). Ordinary or peculiar men? Comparing the customers of prostitutes with a nationally representative sample of men. *International Journal of Offender Therapy and Comparative Criminology, 20*, 1–19. [17]

Moore, M. M. (2010). Human nonverbal courtship behavior—a brief historical review. *Journal of Sex Research, 47*, 171–180. [7]

Morin, J. W. & Levenson, J. S. (2008). Exhibitionism: Assessment and treatment. In: Laws, D. R. & O'Donohue, W. T. (Eds.), *Sexual deviance: Theory, assessment, and treatment* (2nd ed.). Guilford. [13]

Morris, C. (2013). *Condoms in porn? Just another day at Wicked Pictures.* (www.cnbc.com/id/100359796#) [17]

Morris, D. H., Jones, M. E., Schoemaker, M. J., McFadden, E., Ashworth, A. & Swerdlow, A. J. (2012). Body mass index, exercise, and other lifestyle factors in relation to age at natural menopause: Analyses from the breakthrough generations study. *American Journal of Epidemiology, 175*, 998–1005. [11]

Morris, P. H., White, J., Morrison, E. R. & Fisher, K. (2013). High heels as supernormal stimuli: How wearing high heels affects judgements of female attractiveness. *Evolution and Human Behavior, 34*, 176–181. [5]

Morris, T., Greer, H. S. & White, P. (1977). Psychological and social adjustment to mastectomy: A two-year follow-up study. *Cancer, 40*, 2381–2387. [2]

Moskowitz, D. A. & Hart, T. A. (2011). The influence of physical body traits and masculinity on anal sex roles in gay and bisexual men. *Archives of Sexual Behavior, 40*, 835–841. [12]

Moskowitz, D. A., Rieger, G. & Roloff, M. E. (2008). Tops, bottoms and versatiles. *Sexual and Relationship Therapy, 23*, 191–202. [12]

Moskowitz, D. A., Turrubiates, J., Lozano, H. & Hajek, C. (2013). Physical, behavioral, and psychological traits of gay men identifying as bears. *Archives of Sexual Behavior, 42*, 775–784. [12]

Mroz, J. (2011). From one sperm donor, 150 children. *New York Times*, September 5. [8]

Muehlenhard, C. L. & Shippee, S. K. (2010). Men's and women's reports of pretending orgasm. *Journal of Sex Research, 47*, 552–567. [14]

Muir, A. (2006). Precocious puberty. *Pediatrics in Review, 27*, 373–381. [10]

Muise, A., Christofides, E. & Desmarais, S. (2009). More information than you ever wanted: Does Facebook bring out the green-eyed monster of jealousy? *CyberPsychology & Behavior, 12*, 441–444. [7]

Muller, M. N. & Wrangham, R. W. (Eds.). (2009). *Sexual coercion in primates and humans: An evolutionary perspective on male aggression against females.* Harvard University Press. [App. A]

Munarriz, R., Maitland, S., Garcia, S. P., Talakoub, L. & Goldstein, I. (2003). A prospective duplex Doppler ultrasonographic study in women with sexual arousal disorder to objectively assess genital engorgement induced by EROS therapy. *Journal of Sex and Marital Therapy, 29*(Suppl. 1), 85–94. [14]

Munk-Olsen, T., Laursen, T. M., Pedersen, C. B., Lidegaard, O. & Mortensen, P. B. (2011). Induced first-trimester abortion and risk of mental disorder. *New England Journal of Medicine, 364*, 332–339 [9]

Munk-Olsen, T., Laursen, T. M., Pedersen, C. B., Mors, O. & Mortensen, P. B. (2006). New parents and mental disorders: A population-based register study. *JAMA, 296*, 2582–2589. [8]

Munson, M. & Stelbourn, J. P. (Eds.). (2013). *The lesbian polyamory reader: Open relationships, non-monogamy, and casual sex.* Harrington Park. [7]

Murad, M. H., Elamin, M. B., Garcia, M. Z., Mullan, R. J., Murad, A., Erwin, P. J. & Montori, V. M. (2010). Hormonal therapy and sex reassignment: A systematic review and meta-analysis of quality of life and psychosocial outcomes. *Clinical Endocrinology, 72*, 214–231. [4]

Murphy, L. L., Cadena, R. S., Chavez, D. & Ferraro, J. S. (1998). Effect of American ginseng (*Panax quinquefolium*) on male copulatory behavior in the rat. *Physiology and Behavior, 64*, 445–450. [5]

Murphy, M. R., Checkley, S. A., Seckl, J. R. & Lightman, S. L. (1990). Naloxone inhibits oxytocin release at orgasm in man. *Journal of Clinical Endocrinology and Metabolism, 71*, 1056–1058. [5]

Murphy, T. (2013). *Is this the new condom?* (www.out.com/news-opinion/2013/09/09/hiv-prevention-new-condom-truvada-pill-prep?page=full) [15]

Murphy, W. D. & Page, I. J. (2008). Exhibitionism: Psychopathology and theory. In: Laws, D. R. & O'Donohue, W. T. (Eds.), *Sexual deviance: Theory, assessment, and treatment* (2nd ed). Guilford. [13]

Musick, K. & Bumpass, L. (2006). *Cohabitation, marriage, and trajectories in well-being and relationships.* (escholarship.org/uc/item/34f1h2nt) [11]

Mustanski, B. S., Dupree, M. G., Nievergelt, C. M., Bocklandt, S., Schork, N. J. & Hamer, D. H. (2005). A genomewide scan of male sexual orientation. *Human Genetics, 116*, 272–278. [12]

Nagrath, A. & Singh, M. (2012). Sex during pregnancy. In: Nagrath, A., et al. (Eds.), *Progress in Obstetrics & Gynecology—3.* Jaypee Brothers. (Available at tinyurl.com/sexduringpregnancy.) [8]

Nair, H. P. & Young, L. J. (2006). Vasopressin and pair-bond formation: Genes to brain to behavior. *Physiology (Bethesda), 21*, 146–152. [7]

Najman, J. M., Dunne, M. P. & Boyle, F. M. (2007). Childhood sexual abuse and adult sexual dysfunction: Response to commentary by Rind and Tromovitch. *Archives of Sexual Behavior, 36*, 107–109. [10]

Najman, J. M., Dunne, M. P., Purdie, D. M., Boyle, F. M. & Coxeter, P. D. (2005). Sexual abuse in childhood and sexual dysfunction in adulthood: An Australian population-based study. *Archives of Sexual Behavior, 34*, 517–526. [10]

Nanda, S. (1998). *Neither man nor woman: The hijras of India* (2nd ed.). Cengage Learning. [1]

NARTH. (2014). Home page. (www.narth.com) [12]

Nath, J. K. & Nayar, V. R. (1997). India. In: Francoeur, R. T. (Ed.), *The international encyclopedia of sexuality*. Continuum. [1, 6]

National Bureau of Economic Research. (2006). *An economic history of fertility in the U.S., 1826–1960.* (www.nber.org/papers/w12796) [8]

National Campaign to Prevent Teen and Unplanned Pregnancy. (2012). *Teen birth rates: How does the United States compare?* (thenationalcampaign.org/sites/default/files/resource-primary-download/fast-facts_internationalcomparisons.pdf) [10]

National Campaign to Prevent Teen and Unplanned Pregnancy. (2014). *Teen pregnancy: Why it matters.* (thenationalcampaign.org/why-it-matters/teen-pregnancy) [10]

National Cancer Institute. (2008). *Prostate cancer screening.* (www.cancer.gov/cancertopics/pdq/screening/prostate/HealthProfessional/page1) [3]

National Cancer Institute. (2010). *Tamoxifen: Questions and answers.* (www.cancer.gov/cancertopics/factsheet/Therapy/tamoxifen) [2]

National Cancer Institute. (2011). *Human papillomavirus vaccines.* (www.cancer.gov/cancertopics/factsheet/prevention/HPV-vaccine) [15]

National Center for Family and Marriage Research. (2013). *Age variation in the remarriage rate, 1990–2011.* (www.bgsu.edu/content/dam/BGSU/college-of-arts-and-sciences/NCFMR/documents/FP/FP-13-17.pdf) [11]

National Center for Family and Marriage Research. (2014). *Marital status in the U.S., 2012.* (www.bgsu.edu/content/dam/BGSU/college-of-arts-and-sciences/NCFMR/documents/FP/FP-14-07-marital-status.pdf) [11]

National Center for Health Statistics. (2014a). *Sexual orientation and health among U.S. adults: National Health Interview Survey, 2013.* (www.cdc.gov/nchs/data/nhsr/nhsr077.pdf) [12]

National Center for Health Statistics. (2014b). *Trends in out-of-hospital births in the United States, 1990–2012.* (www.cdc.gov/nchs/data/databriefs/db144.htm) [8]

National Conference of State Legislatures. (2014). *State policies on sex education in schools.* (www.ncsl.org/research/health/state-policies-on-sex-education-in-schools.aspx) [1]

National Down Syndrome Society. (2012). *What is Down syndrome?* (www.ndss.org/Down-Syndrome/What-Is-Down-Syndrome) [8]

National Gay and Lesbian Task Force. (2013). *Hate crime laws in the U.S.* (www.thetaskforce.org/downloads/reports/issue_maps/hate_crimes_06_13_color.pdf) [12]

National Gay and Lesbian Task Force. (2014). *State nondiscrimination laws in the U.S.* (www.thetaskforce.org/downloads/reports/issue_maps/non_discrimination_5_14_color.pdf) [12]

National Healthy Marriage Resource Center. (2010). *Covenant marriage: A fact sheet.* (www.healthymarriageinfo.org/download.aspx?id=329) [11]

National Institute of Justice. (2012). *Intimate partner stalking: Duration and trajectory.* (www.nij.gov/topics/crime/intimate-partner-violence/stalking/pages/duration.aspx) [16]

National Library of Medicine. (2001). *Kegel exercises.* (www.nlm.nih.gov/medlineplus/ency/article/003975.htm) [14]

National Marriage Project. (2010). *The state of our unions.* (nationalmarriageproject.org/wp-content/uploads/2012/06/Union_11_12_10.pdf) [11]

National Opinion Research Center. (2013). *Trends in public attitudes about sexual morality.* (www.norc.org/PDFs/sexmoral-final_06-21_FINAL.PDF) [7, 12, 17]

National Organization for Women, (2007). *Sexy or sadistic? Sexist, actually.* (www.now.org/issues/media/070319advertising.html) [17]

National Organization for Women. (2014). *Campus sexual assault bill provides support for college women.* (now.org/blog/campus-sexual-assault-bill-provides-support-for-college-women) [16]

National Prevention Information Network. (2014). *STDs today.* (www.cdcnpin.org/scripts/std/std.asp#who) [15]

National Research Council. (1996). *Understanding violence against women.* National Academies Press. [16]

National Scientific Council on the Developing Child. (2009). *Maternal depression can undermine the development of young children.* (developingchild.harvard.edu/index.php/download_file/-/view/582) [8]

National Vital Statistics Reports. (2010). *Births: Preliminary data for 2009.* (www.cdc.gov/nchs/data/nvsr/nvsr59/nvsr59_03.pdf) [8]

National Vital Statistics Reports. (2012). *Estimated pregnancy rates and rates of pregnancy outcomes for the United States, 1990–2008.* (www.cdc.gov/nchs/data/nvsr/nvsr60/nvsr60_07.pdf) [8]

National Vital Statistics Reports. (2013). *Births: Final data for 2012.* (www.cdc.gov/nchs/data/nvsr/nvsr62/nvsr62_09.pdf#table01) [8]

National Vital Statistics Reports. (2014). *Births: Preliminary data for 2013.* (www.cdc.gov/nchs/data/nvsr/nvsr63/nvsr63_02.pdf) [10]

Naturist Education Foundation. (2009). *NEF California poll 2009.* (www.naturisteducation.org/nef.ca.poll.2009/#note 01) [3]

NBC Bay Area. (2014). *Several people arrested during San Francisco's "Body Freedom" nudity ban protest and parade.* (www.nbcbayarea.com/news/local/Police-Arrest-Several-People-During-San-Franciscos-Nudity-Ban-Protest-243142861.html) [3]

NBC News. (2013). *5 million babies born through IVF in past 35 years, researchers say.* (www.nbcnews.com/health/kids-health/5-million-babies-born-through-ivf-past-35-years-researchers-f8C11390532) [8]

Nedelec, J. L. & Beaver, K. M. (2014). Physical attractiveness as a phenotypic marker of health: An assessment using a nationally representative sample of American adults. *Evolution and Human Behavior,* published online June 16. [5]

Newcomb, M. E., Ryan, D. T., Garofalo, R. & Mustanski, B. (2014). The effects of sexual partnership and relationship characteristics on three sexual risk variables in young men who have sex with men. *Archives of Sexual Behavior, 43,* 61–72. [15]

Newmahr, S. (2011). *Playing on the edge: Sadomasochism, risk, and intimacy.* Indiana University Press. [1, 13]

Ngun, T. C., Ghahramani, N., Sanchez, F. J., Bocklandt, S. & Vilain, E. (2011). The genetics of sex differences in brain and behavior. *Frontiers in Neuroendocrinology, 32,* 227–246. [4]

Nichols, M. & Shernoff, M. (2007). Therapy with sexual minorities. In: Leiblum, S. R. (Ed.), *Principles and practice of sex therapy* (4th ed.). Guilford. [14]

Nielsen, J. & Pernice, K. (2008). *Eyetracking Web usability.* New Riders. [5]

Nishizawa, S., Benkelfat, C., Young, S. N., Leyton, M., Mzengeza, S., de Montigny, C., Blier, P. & Diksic, M. (1997). Differences between males and females in rates of serotonin synthesis in human brain. *Proceedings of the National Academy of Sciences of the United States of America, 94,* 5308–5313. [4]

Noffsinger, O. (2014). *Teen mom—minus the MTV.* (sexetc.org/info-center/post/teen-mom-minus-the-mtv) [10]

Nojo, S., Tamura, S. & Ihara, Y. (2012). Human homogamy in facial characteristics: Does a sexual-imprinting-like mechanism play a role? *Human Nature, 23,* 323–340. [7]

Nolo. (2014). *Sexually transmitted diseases (STDs) and lawsuits.* (www.nolo.com/legal-encyclopedia/sexually-transmitted-diseases-stds-lawsuits.html) [15]

Noonan, A. & Taylor Gomez, A. (2010). Who's missing: Awareness of gay, lesbian, bisexual and transgender people with intellectual disability. *Sexuality and Disability, 29,* 175–180. [6]

Nosek, B., Banaji, M. & Greenwald, A. (2004). *Implicit association test.* (implicit.harvard.edu/implicit/demo/selectatest.html) [12]

Nosek, M. A., Howland, C. A., Rintala, D. H., Young, M. E. & Chanpong, G. F. (1997). *National study of women with physical disabilities: Final report.* (www.bcm.edu/research/centers/research-on-women-with-disabilities/national_study/national_study.html) [6]

Nossiter, A. (1996). 6-year-old's sex crime: Innocent peck on cheek. *New York Times,* September 27. [16]

Nunes, K. L., Hermann, C. A., Renee Malcom, J. & Lavoie, K. (2013). Childhood sexual victimization, pedophilic interest, and sexual recidivism. *Child Abuse and Neglect, 37,* 703–711. [13]

Nurnberg, H. G., Hensley, P. L., Heiman, J. R., Croft, H. A., Debattista, C. & Paine, S. (2008). Sildenafil treatment of women with antidepressant-associated sexual dysfunction: A randomized controlled trial. *JAMA, 300,* 395–404. [14]

Nussbaum, M. C. (2010). A right to marry? *California Law Review, 98,* 667. [11]

O'Brien, M. (1990). *On seeing a sex surrogate.* (thesunmagazine.org/issues/174/on_seeing_a_sex_surrogate) [6]

O'Connell, H. E., Hutson, J. M., Anderson, C. R. & Plenter, R. J. (1998). Anatomical relationship between urethra and clitoris. *Journal of Urology, 159,* 1892–1897. [2]

O'Connor, D. B., Lee, D. M., Corona, G., Forti, G., Tajar, A., O'Neill, T. W., et al. (2011). The relationships between sex hormones and sexual function in middle-aged and older European men. *Journal of Clinical Endocrinology and Metabolism, 96,* E1577–1587. [11]

O'Crowley, P. (2004). Student orientation: More teenage girls are testing gender boundaries. *Star-Ledger,* May 26. [7]

O'Hara, M. W. & McCabe, J. E. (2013). Postpartum depression: Current status and future directions. *Annual Review of Clinical Psychology, 9,* 379–407. [8]

O'Leary, C. & Howard, O. (2001). *The prostitution of women and girls in metropolitan Chicago: A preliminary prevalence report.* (www.impactresearch.org/documents/prostitutionreport.pdf) [17]

Oakley, S. H., Vaccaro, C. M., Crisp, C. C., Estanol, M. V., Fellner, A. N., Kleeman, S. D. & Pauls, R. N. (2014). Clitoral size and location in relation to sexual function using pelvic MRI. *Journal of Sexual Medicine*, published online February 13. [14]

Objectum-Sexuality Internationale. (2013). *Welcome to Objectum-Sexuality Internationale.* (www.objectum-sexuality.org) [13]

Ocean, F. (2012). *Whoever you are, wherever you are. I'm starting to think we're a lot alike.* (liveweb.archive.org/web/20140530082404/25.media.tumblr.com/tumblr_m6me6uSdO81q-drz3yo1_1280.png) [12]

Office of Population Research. (2014). *Are emergency contraceptive pills effective for overweight or obese women?* (ec.princeton.edu/questions/ecobesity.html) [9]

Office on Women's Health. (2009). *Menstruation and the menstrual cycle.* (womenshealth.gov/publications/our-publications/fact-sheet/menstruation.pdf) [2]

Office on Women's Health. (2013a). *Date rape drugs fact sheet.* (womenshealth.gov/publications/our-publications/fact-sheet/date-rape-drugs.html) [16]

Office on Women's Health. (2013b). *Infertility fact sheet.* (www.womenshealth.gov/publications/our-publications/fact-sheet/infertility.html#c) [8]

Ogas, O. & Gaddam, S. (2011). *A billion wicked thoughts: What the world's largest experiment reveals about human desire.* Dutton. [17]

Oh, K. J., Chae, M. J., Lee, H. S., Hong, H. D. & Park, K. (2010). Effects of Korean red ginseng on sexual arousal in menopausal women: Placebo-controlled, double-blind crossover clinical study. *Journal of Sexual Medicine*, 7, 1469–1477. [5]

Okami, P., Olmstead, R. & Abramson, P. R. (1997). Sexual experiences in early childhood: 18-year longitudinal data from the UCLA Family Lifestyles Project. *Journal of Sex Research*, 34, 339–347. [10]

Okami, P., Olmstead, R., Abramson, P. R. & Pendleton, L. (1998). Early childhood exposure to parental nudity and scenes of parental sexuality ("primal scenes"): An 18-year longitudinal study of outcome. *Archives of Sexual Behavior*, 27, 361–384. [10]

OKtrends. (2010). *The big lies people tell in online dating.* (blog.okcupid.com/index.php/the-biggest-lies-in-online-dating) [12]

Ono, M. & Harley, V. R. (2013). Disorders of sex development: New genes, new concepts. *National Review of Endocrinology*, 9, 79–91. [4]

OnTheIssues.org. (2014). *Libertarian Party on crime.* (www.ontheissues.org/Celeb/Libertarian_Party_Crime.htm) [17]

Oswalt, S. B. & Wyatt, T. J. (2013). Sexual health behaviors and sexual orientation in a U.S. national sample of college students. *Archives of Sexual Behavior*, 42, 1561–1572. [7, 11]

Overby, L. M. (2014). Etiology and attitudes: Beliefs about the origins of homosexuality and their implications for public policy. *Journal of Homosexuality*, 61, 568–587. [12]

Owen, J. & Fincham, F. D. (2011). Young adults' emotional reactions after hooking up encounters. *Archives of Sexual Behavior*, 40, 321–330. [7]

Owen, R. L. (1998). M cells as portals of entry for HIV. *Pathobiology*, 66, 141–144. [15]

Pachankis, J. E. (2004). Clinical issues in working with lesbian, gay, and bisexual clients. *Psychotherapy: Theory, Research, Practice, Training*, 41, 227–246. [14]

Pachankis, J. E. & Hatzenbuehler, M. L. (2013). The social development of contingent self-worth in sexual minority young men: An empirical investigation of the "best little boy in the world" hypothesis. *Basic and Applied Psychology*, 35, 176–190. [12]

Pachankis, J. E., Hatzenbuehler, M. L. & Starks, T. J. (2014). The influence of structural stigma and rejection sensitivity on young sexual minority men's daily tobacco and alcohol use. *Social Science and Medicine*, 103, 67–75. [12]

Paechter, C. & Clark, S. (2007). Learning gender in primary school playgrounds: Findings from the Tomboy Identities Study. *Pedagogy, Culture and Society*, 15, 317–331. [4]

Paik, A. (2010). "Hookups," dating, and relationship quality: Does the type of sexual involvement matter? *Social Science Research*, 39, 739–753. [7]

Palacios, S., Henderson, V. W., Siseles, N., Tan, D. & Villaseca, P. (2010). Age of menopause and impact of climacteric symptoms by geographical region. *Climacteric*, 13, 419–428. [11]

Paland, S. & Lynch, M. (2006). Transitions to asexuality result in excess amino acid substitutions. *Science*, 311, 990–992. [App. A]

Panfilov, D. E. (2006). Augmentative phalloplasty. *Aesthetic Plastic Surgery*, 30, 183–197. [3]

Paoli, T. (2009). The absence of sexual coercion in bonobos. In: Muller, M. N. & Wrangham, R. W. (Eds.), *Sexual coercion in primates and humans: An evolutionary perspective on male aggression against females.* Harvard University Press. [App. A]

Pappas, K. B., Wisniewski, A. B. & Migeon, C. J. (2008). Gender role across development in adults with 46,XY disorders of sex development including perineoscrotal hypospadias and small phallus raised male or female. *Journal of Pediatric Endocrinology and Metabolism*, 21, 625–630. [4]

Parents Television Council. (2010). *Habitat for profanity: Broadcast TV's sharp increase in foul language.* (w2.parentstv.org/main/MediaFiles/PDF/Studies/2010_HabitatforProfanity.pdf) [17]

Parish, A. R. & de Waal, F. B. (2000). The other "closest living relative." How bonobos (*Pan paniscus*) challenge traditional assumptions about females, dominance, intra- and intersexual interactions, and hominid evolution. *Annals of the New York Academy of Sciences*, 907, 97–113. [1, App. A]

Parsonnet, J., Hansmann, M. A., Delaney, M. L., Modern, P. A., Dubois, A. M., Wieland-Alter, W., et al. (2005). Prevalence of toxic shock syndrome toxin 1–producing *Staphylococcus aureus* and the presence of antibodies to this superantigen in menstruating women. *Journal of Clinical Microbiology*, 43, 4628–4634. [2]

Patel, R., Alderson, S., Geretti, A., Nilsen, A., Foley, E., Lautenschlager, S., et al. (2011). European guideline for the management of genital herpes, 2010. *International Journal of STD and AIDS*, 22, 1–10. [15]

Paul, E. L. & Hayes, K. A. (2002). The casualties of 'casual' sex: A qualitative exploration of the phenomenology of college students' hookups. *Journal of Social and Personal Relationships*, 19, 639–661. [7]

Paul, M. & Stewart, F. H. (2007). Abortion. In: Hatcher, R. A., et al. (Eds.), *Contraceptive technology* (19th ed.). Ardent Media. [9]

Pawlowski, M., Atwal, R. & Dunbar, R. I. M. (2008). Sex differences in everyday risk-taking behavior in humans. *Evolutionary Psychology*, 6, 29–42. [1]

Peltason, R. (2008). *I am not my breast cancer: Women talk openly about love and sex, hair loss and weight gain, mothers and daughters, and being a woman with breast cancer.* William Morrow. [2]

Pennsylvania Catholic Conference. (2009). *Living together without commitment harms marriage.* (www.pacatholic.org/living-together-without-commitment-harms-marriage) [11]

Penton-Voak, I. S. & Perrett, D. I. (2000). Female preference for male faces changes cyclically: Further evidence. *Evolution and Human Behavior*, 21, 39–48. [5]

Penton-Voak, I. S., Perrett, D. I. & Pierce, J. (1999). Computer graphic studies of the role of facial similarity in judgements of attractiveness. *Current Psychology*, 18, 104–117. [5]

People's Daily Online. (2010). *China sees sex ratio at birth slightly down.* (english.peopledaily.com.cn/90001/90776/90882/7011709.html) [8]

Pepin, J. (2011). *The origins of AIDS.* Cambridge University Press. [15]

Peplau, L. A. & Garnets, L. D. (2000). A new paradigm for understanding women's sexuality and sexual orientation. *Journal of Social Issues*, 56, 329–350. [12]

Peplau, L. A., Spalding, L. R., Conley, T. D. & Veniegas, R. C. (1999). The development of sexual orientation in women. *Annual Review of Sex Research*, 10, 70–99. [7]

Perel, E. (2006). *Mating in captivity: Reconciling the erotic and the domestic.* HarperCollins. [11]

Perelman, M. A. (2013). Delayed ejaculation. *Journal of Sexual Medicine*, 10, 1189–1190. [14]

Perez-Fuentes, G., Olfson, M., Villegas, L., Morcillo, C., Wang, S. & Blanco, C. (2013). Prevalence and correlates of child sexual abuse: A national study. *Comprehensive Psychiatry*, 54, 16–27. [10]

Perkel, M. (n.d.). *How to use escort services: A men's guide.* (sex.perkel.com/escort/index.htm) [17]

Perovic, S. V. & Djordjevic, M. L. (2003). Metoidioplasty: A variant of phalloplasty in female transsexuals. *BJUI*, 92, 981–985. [4]

Perrett, D. (2010). *In your face: The new science of human attraction.* Palgrave Macmillan. [5]

Perrett, D. I., Burt, D. M., Penton-Voak, I. S., Lee, K. J., Rowland, D. A. & Edwards, R. (1999). Symmetry and human facial attractiveness. *Evolution and Human Behavior*, 20, 295–307. [5]

Perrett, D. I., Lee, K. J., Penton-Voak, I., Rowland, D., Yoshikawa, S., Burt, D. M., et al. (1998). Effects of sexual dimorphism on facial attractiveness. *Nature*, 394, 884–887. [5]

Perrett, D. I., May, K. A. & Yoshikawa, S. (1994). Facial shape and judgements of female attractiveness. *Nature*, 368, 239–242. [5]

Perry, D., Walder, K., Hendler, T. & Shamay-Tsoory, S. G. (2013). The gender you are and the gender you like: Sexual preference and empathic neural responses. *Brain Research, 1534,* 66–75. [1]

Peskin, M. & Newell, F. N. (2004). Familiarity breeds attraction: Effects of exposure on the attractiveness of typical and distinctive faces. *Perception, 33,* 147–157. [5]

Pew Research Center. (2013). *In gay marriage debate, both supporters and opponents see legal recognition as "inevitable."* (www.people-press.org/2013/06/06/in-gay-marriage-debate-both-supporters-and-opponents-see-legal-recognition-as-inevitable) [12]

Phillips, D. M., Sudol, K. M., Taylor, C. L., Guichard, L., Elsen, R. & Maguire, R. A. (2004). Lubricants containing N-9 may enhance rectal transmission of HIV and other STIs. *Contraception, 70,* 107–110. [6]

Pierce, A. P. (2000). The coital alignment technique (CAT): An overview of studies. *Journal of Sex and Marital Therapy, 26,* 257–268. [14]

Pierrehumbert, J. B., Bent, T., Munson, B., Bradlow, A. R. & Bailey, J. M. (2004). The influence of sexual orientation on vowel production. *Journal of the Acoustical Society of America, 116,* 1905–1908. [12]

Pilkington, E. (2014). Indiana woman charged with feticide after unborn child's death. *Guardian (London),* August 26. [9]

Pincus, J. H. (2001). Base instincts: What makes killers kill? Norton. [13]

Pines, A. M. (2005). *Falling in love: Why we choose the lovers we choose* (2nd ed.). Routledge. [7]

Planned Parenthood. (2014a). *Cervical mucus method.* (www.plannedparenthood.org/health-topics/birth-control/fam-cervical-mucus-method-22140.htm) [9]

Planned Parenthood. (2014b). *Crisis pregnancy centers.* (www.plannedparenthood.org/health-topics/pregnancy/standard-21507.htm) [9]

Planned Parenthood. (2014c). *Spermicide.* (www.plannedparenthood.org/health-topics/birth-control/spermicide-4225.htm) [9]

Plaud, J. J. & Martini, J. R. (1999). The respondent conditioning of male sexual arousal. *Behavior Modification, 23,* 254–268. [13]

Plaud, J., Gaither, G. A., Amato Henderson, S. & Devitt, M. K. (1997). The long-term habituation of sexual arousal in human males: A crossover design. *Psychological Record, 47,* 385–398. [5]

Plöderl, M., Wagenmakers, E. J., Tremblay, P., Ramsay, R., Kralovec, K., Fartacek, C. & Fartacek, R. (2013). Suicide risk and sexual orientation: A critical review. *Archives of Sexual Behavior, 42,* 715–727. [12]

Poeppl, T. B., Nitschke, J., Santtila, P., Schecklmann, M., Langguth, B., Greenlee, M. W., et al. (2013). Association between brain structure and phenotypic characteristics in pedophilia. *Journal of Psychiatric Research, 47,* 678–685. [13]

Pollack, A. E., Thomas, L. J. & Barone, M. A. (2007). Female and male sterilization. In: Hatcher, R. A., et al. (Eds.), *Contraceptive technology* (19th ed.). Ardent Media. [9]

PollingReport.com. (2014). *Abortion and birth control.* (www.pollingreport.com/abortion.htm) [9]

Pontari, M. & Giusto, L. (2013). New developments in the diagnosis and treatment of chronic prostatitis/chronic pelvic pain syndrome. *Current Opinions in Urology, 23,* 565–569. [3]

Poole, S. M. & Boone, C. (2011). Eddie Long case officially dismissed. *Atlanta Journal-Constitution,* May 11. [12]

Popham, P. (1998). The mysterious Sri Lankan world of Arthus C. Clarke. *Independent (London),* February 3. [17]

Portman, D. J., Edelson, J., Jordan, R., Clayton, A. & Krychman, M. L. (2014). Bremelanotide for hypoactive sexual desire disorder: Analyses from a Phase 2B dose-ranging study. *Obstetrics and Gynecology, 123*(Suppl. 1), 31S. [14]

Postma, R., Bicanic, I., van der Vaart, H. & Laan, E. (2013). Pelvic floor muscle problems mediate sexual problems in young adult rape victims. *Journal of Sexual Medicine, 10,* 1978–1987. [16]

Potterat, J. J., Brewer, D. D., Muth, S. Q., Rothenberg, R. B., Woodhouse, D. E., Muth, J. B., et al. (2004). Mortality in a long-term open cohort of prostitute women. *American Journal of Epidemiology, 159,* 778–785. [17]

Pound, N., Lawson, D. W., Toma, A. M., Richmond, S., Zhurov, A. I. & Penton-Voak, I. S. (2014). Facial fluctuating asymmetry is not associated with childhood ill-health in a large British cohort study. *Proceedings of the Royal Society B,* Published online August 13. [5]

Powdermaker, H. (1933). *Life in Lesu: The study of a Melanesian society in New Ireland.* Norton. [6]

Prause, N. & Graham, C. A. (2007). Asexuality: Classification and characterization. *Archives of Sexual Behavior, 36,* 341–356. [5]

PREP Inc. (2011). *PREP - Successful relationships, successful lives.* (www.prepinc.com) [7]

Priest, R. J. (2001). Missionary positions: Christian, modernist, postmodernist. *Current Anthropology, 42,* 29–68. [6]

ProCon.org. (2013). *How many prostitutes are in the United States and the rest of the world?* (prostitution.procon.org/view.answers.php?questionID=000095#answer-id-000225) [17]

Prostitutes Education Network. (2011). *Prostitution in the United States: The statistics.* (www.bayswan.org/stats.html) [17]

Prostitutes Education Network. (2014). *About BAYSWAN and PENET.* (www.bayswan.org) [17]

Public Health Agency of Canada. (2004). *Oral sex and the risk of HIV transmission.* (www.phac-aspc.gc.ca/publicat/epiu-aepi/epi_update_may_04/13_e.html) [15]

Puppo, V. (2012). The Grafenberg spot (G-spot) does not exist—a rebuttal of Dwyer PL: Skene's gland revisited: Function, dysfunction and the G spot. *International Urogynecology Journal, 23,* 247; author reply 249. [2]

Putnam, R. D. (2007). E pluribus unum: *Diversity and community in the twenty-first century.* (onlinelibrary.wiley.com/doi/10.1111/j.1467-9477.2007.00176.x/full) [12]

Puts, D. A., Bailey, D. H., Cardenas, R. A., Burriss, R. P., Welling, L. L., Wheatley, J. R. & Dawood, K. (2013). Women's attractiveness changes with estradiol and progesterone across the ovulatory cycle. *Hormones and Behavior, 63,* 13–19. [5]

Puts, D. A., McDaniel, M. A., Jordan, C. L. & Breedlove, S. M. (2008). Spatial ability and prenatal androgens: Meta-analyses of congenital adrenal hyperplasia and digit ratio (2D:4D) studies. *Archives of Sexual Behavior, 37,* 100–111. [4]

Pytynia, K. B., Dahlstrom, K. R. & Sturgis, E. M. (2014). Epidemiology of HPV-associated oropharyngeal cancer. *Oral Oncology, 50,* 380–386. [15]

Quart, A. (2008). When girls will be boys. *New York Times,* March 16. [4]

Queen, C. (1998). Bend over boyfriend: A couple's guide to male anal pleasure. Fatale Video. [6]

Quinn, A. & Koopman, P. (2012). The molecular genetics of sex determination and sex reversal in mammals. *Seminars in Reproductive Medicine, 30,* 351–363. [4]

Quittner, J. (2001). Death of a two spirit: A Colorado town searches for answers in the senseless death of a transgendered Navajo teenager. *The Advocate,* August 28, 24–26. [4]

Quora. (2014). *What is a day in the life of a porn star like?* (www.quora.com/What-is-a-day-in-the-life-of-a-porn-star-like) [17]

Rabin, R. C. (2010). Steep drop seen in circumcisions in U.S. *New York Times,* August 16. [3]

Radical Faeries. (2014). *A web site for radical faeries.* (www.radfae.org) [12]

Rahman, Q. & Hull, M. S. (2005). An empirical test of the kin selection hypothesis for male homosexuality. *Archives of Sexual Behavior, 34,* 461–467. [12]

Rahman, Q., Abrahams, S. & Wilson, G. D. (2003a). Sexual-orientation-related differences in verbal fluency. *Neuropsychology, 17,* 240–246. [4]

Rahman, Q., Abrahams, S. & Wilson, G. D. (2003b). Sexual-orientation-related differences in verbal fluency. *Neuropsychology, 17,* 240–246. [12]

Rahman, Q., Kumari, V. & Wilson, G. D. (2003c). Sexual orientation-related differences in prepulse inhibition of the human startle response. *Behavioral Neuroscience, 117,* 1096–1102. [12]

RAINN. (2014). *Get help now.* (www.rainn.org/get-help) [16]

Ralph, D., Eardley, I., Kell, P., Dean, J., Hackett, G., Collins, O. & Edwards, D. (2007). Improvement in erectile function on vardenafil treatment correlates with treatment satisfaction in both patients and their partners. *BJUI, 100,* 130–136. [14]

Ramachandran, V. S. & Blakeslee, S. (1999). Phantoms in the brain: Probing the mysteries of the human mind. William Morrow. [5]

Rametti, G., Carrillo, B., Gomez-Gil, E., Junque, C., Segovia, S., Gomez, A. & Guillamon, A. (2011a). White matter microstructure in female to male transsexuals before cross-sex hormonal treatment: A diffusion tensor imaging study. *Journal of Psychiatric Research, 45,* 199–204. [4]

Rametti, G., Carrillo, B., Gomez-Gil, E., Junque, C., Zubiarre-Elorza, L., Segovia, S., Gomez, A. & Guillamon, A. (2011b). The microstructure of white matter in male to female transsexuals before cross-sex hormonal treatment: A DTI study. *Journal of Psychiatric Research, 45,* 949–954. [4]

Randall, T. (2006). Letter to the editor. *New York Times,* July 5. [13]

Ranganath, R., Jurafsky, D. & McFarland, D. (2009). It's not you, it's me: Detecting flirting and its misperception in speed-dates. *Proceedings of the 2009 Conference on Empirical Methods in Natural Language Processing.* Association for Computational Linguistics. [7]

Ranke-Heinemann, U. (1990). *Eunuchs for the kingdom of heaven: Women, sexuality, and the Catholic church.* Doubleday. [1]

Raphael, J. (2004). *Listening to Olivia: Violence, poverty, and prostitution.* Routledge. [17]

Rasberry, C. N. & Goodson, P. (2009). Predictors of secondary abstinence in U.S. college undergraduates. *Archives of Sexual Behavior, 38,* 74–86. [11]

Raya-Rivera, A. M., Esquiliano, D., Fierro-Pastrana, R., Lopez-Bayghen, E., Valencia, P., Ordorica-Flores, R., Soker, S., Yoo, J. J. & Atala, A. (2014). Tissue-engineered autologous vaginal organs in patients: A pilot cohort study. *Lancet, April 11 (online ahead of print).* [4]

Raymond, E. G. (2007). Progestin-only pills. In: Hatcher, R. A., et al. (Eds.), *Contraceptive technology* (19th ed.). Ardent Media. [9]

Raznahan, A., Lee, Y., Stidd, R., Long, R., Greenstein, D., Clasen, L., et al. (2010). Longitudinally mapping the influence of sex and androgen signaling on the dynamics of human cortical maturation in adolescence. *Proceedings of the National Academy of Sciences of the United States of America, 107,* 16988–16993. [10]

Raznahan, A., Shaw, P. W., Lerch, J. P., Clasen, L. S., Greenstein, D., Berman, R., et al. (2014). Longitudinal four-dimensional mapping of subcortical anatomy in human development. *Proceedings of the National Academy of Sciences of the United States of America, 111,* 1592–1597. [10]

Reece, M., Herbenick, D., Dodge, B., Sanders, S. A., Ghassemi, A. & Fortenberry, J. D. (2010a). Vibrator use among heterosexual men varies by partnership status: Results from a nationally representative study in the United States. *Journal of Sex and Marital Therapy, 36,* 389–407. [6]

Reece, M., Herbenick, D., Fortenberry, J. D., Dodge, B., Sanders, S. A. & Schick, V. (2010b). *National Survey of Sexual Health and Behavior.* (www.nationalsexstudy.indiana.edu) [1, 4]

Regan, P. C., Levin, L., Sprecher, S., Christopher, F. S. & Cate, R. (2000). Partner preferences: What characteristics do men and women desire in their short-term sexual and long-term romantic partners. *Journal of Psychology and Human Sexuality, 12,* 1–21. [5]

Regnerus, M. & Uecker, J. (2011). *Premarital sex in America: How young Americans meet, mate, and think about marrying.* Oxford University Press. [7, 11]

Rehman, J. & Melman, A. (2001). Normal anatomy and physiology. In: Mulcahy, J. J. (Ed.), *Male sexual function: A guide to clinical management.* Humana. [6]

Reichert, T. (Ed.). (2007). *Investigating the use of sex in media promotion and advertising.* Haworth. [17]

Reichert, T. & Lambiase, J. (Eds.). (2003). *Sex in advertising: Perspectives on the erotic appeal.* Lawrence Erlbaum. [17]

Reiner, W. G. (2004). Psychosexual development in genetic males assigned female: The cloacal exstrophy experience. *Child and Adolescent Psychiatric Clinics of North America, 13,* 657–674. [4]

Reis, H. T., Maniaci, M. R., Caprariello, P. A., Eastwick, P. W. & Finkel, E. J. (2011). Familiarity does indeed promote attraction in live interaction. *Journal of Personality and Social Psychology, 101,* 557–570. [5]

Reiss, I. L. (1986). *Journey into sexuality: An exploratory voyage.* Prentice-Hall. [1]

Reiss, I. L. & Miller, B. C. (1979). Heterosexual permissiveness: A theoretical analysis. *Journal of Marriage and the Family, 42,* 395–410. [7]

Religious Tolerance.org. (2012). *Bisexuality: Part 1: Quotations.* (www.religioustolerance.org/bisexuality0.htm#don) [12]

ReligiousTolerance.org. (2005). *Public opinion polls on abortion: Overview.* (www.religious-tolerance.org/abopollover.htm) [9]

Rellini, A. H. & Clifton, J. (2011). Female orgasmic disorder. *Advances in Psychosomatic Medicine, 31,* 35–56. [14]

Resident, C. (2013). *The Amsterdam red light district in Second Life.* (www.second-life-adventures.com/the-amsterdam-red-light-district-in-second-life) [17]

Reverby, S. M. (2000). *Tuskegee's truths: Rethinking the Tuskegee syphilis study.* University of North Carolina Press. [15]

Reverby, S. M. (2011). "Normal exposure" and inoculation syphilis: A PHS "Tuskegee" doctor in Guatamala, 1946–48. *Journal of Policy History, 23,* 6–28. [15]

Reynolds, M. (2002). Kandahar's lightly veiled homosexual habits. *Los Angeles Times,* April 3. [12]

Reynolds, M. A., Herbenick, D. L. & Bancroft, J. (2003). The nature of childhood sexual experiences. In: Bancroft, J. (Ed.), *Sexual development in childhood.* Indiana University Press. [10]

Rice, M. E. & Harris, G. T. (2002). Men who molest their sexually immature daughters: Is a special explanation required? *Journal of Abnormal Psychology, 111,* 329–339. [13]

Richard-Davis, G. & Wellons, M. (2013). Racial and ethnic differences in the physiology and clinical symptoms of menopause. *Seminars in Reproductive Medicine, 31,* 380–386. [11]

Ridley, M. (2003). *The Red Queen: Sex and the evolution of human nature.* Harper Perennial. [App. A]

Rieger, G. & Savin-Williams, R. C. (2012). Gender nonconformity, sexual orientation, and psychological well-being. *Archives of Sexual Behavior, 41,* 611–621. [12]

Rieger, G., Chivers, M. L. & Bailey, J. M. (2005). Sexual arousal patterns of bisexual men. *Psychological Science, 16,* 579–584. [12]

Rieger, G., Linsenmeier, J. A., Gygax, L. & Bailey, J. M. (2008). Sexual orientation and childhood gender nonconformity:

Evidence from home videos. *Developmental Psychology, 44,* 46–58. [12]

Rieger, G., Linsenmeier, J. A., Gygax, L., Garcia, S. & Bailey, J. M. (2010). Dissecting "gaydar": Accuracy and the role of masculinity-femininity. *Archives of Sexual Behavior, 39,* 124–140. [12]

Rieger, G., Rosenthal, A. M., Cash, B. M., Linsenmeier, J. A., Bailey, J. M. & Savin-Williams, R. C. (2013). Male bisexual arousal: A matter of curiosity? *Biological Psychology, 94,* 479–489. [12]

Riela, S., Rodriguez, G., Aron, A., Xu, X. & Acevedo, B. P. (2010). Experiences of falling in love: Investigating culture, ethnicity, gender, and speed. *Journal of Social and Personal Relationships, 27,* 473–493. [7]

Rifkin-Graboi, A., Bai, J., Chen, H., Hameed, W. B., Sim, L. W., Tint, M. T., et al. (2013). Prenatal maternal depression associates with microstructure of right amygdala in neonates at birth. *Biological Psychiatry, 74,* 837–844. [8]

Rijksen, H. D. (1978). *A field study on Sumatran orang utans* (Pongo pygmaeus abelli *Lesson 1827*). Wageningen Academic. [6]

Riley, J. (2013). *Maryland's gay wunderkind.* (www.metroweekly.com/2013/08/marylands-gay-wunderkind) [12]

Rind, B. (2001). Gay and bisexual adolescent boys' sexual experiences with men: An empirical examination of psychological correlates in a nonclinical sample. *Archives of Sexual Behavior, 30,* 345–368. [10]

Rind, B. & Tromovitch, P. (2007). National samples, sexual abuse in childhood, and adjustment in adulthood: A commentary on Najman, Dunne, Purdie, Boyle, and Coxeter (2005). *Archives of Sexual Behavior, 36,* 101–106; discussion 107–109. [10]

Rind, B., Tromovitch, P. & Bauserman, R. (1998). A meta-analytic examination of assumed properties of child sexual abuse using college samples. *Psychological Bulletin, 124,* 22–53. [10]

Robaire, B., Oakes, C. C. & Zubkova, E. V. (2007). Effects of aging on spermatogenesis and sperm function. In: Kandeel, F. R. (Ed.), *Male reproductive function: Pathophysiology and treatment.* Informa Healthcare. [8]

Robbins, L. (2012). Baby's death renews debate over a circumcision ritual. *New York Times,* May 7. [3]

Robinson, A. (2010). *Characteristics of adolescent females sexually exploited through prostitution.* (digitalscholarship.unlv.edu/thesesdissertations/323) [17]

Rodger, A., Bruun, T., Cambiano, V., Vernazza, P., Estrada, V., Van Lunzen, J., et al. (2014). *HIV transmission risk through condomless sex if HIV+ partner on suppressive ART: PARTNER study.* Paper presented at Conference on Retroviruses and Opportunistic Infections 2014, Abstract 153LB. [15]

Rodriguez, A. (2013). *First Google Glass porn hits 1 million views, BTS released.* (www.xbiz.com/news/166593) [17]

Roenneberg, T. & Aschoff, J. (1990a). Annual rhythm of human reproduction: I. Biology, sociology, or both? *Journal of Biological Rhythms, 5,* 195–216. [6]

Roenneberg, T. & Aschoff, J. (1990b). Annual rhythm of human reproduction: II. Environmental correlations. *Journal of Biological Rhythms, 5,* 217–239. [6]

Rogge, R. D. & Bradbury, T. N. (1999). Till violence does us part: The differing roles of communication and aggression in predicting adverse marital outcomes. *Journal of Consulting and Clinical Psychology, 67,* 340–351. [7]

Rolland, M., Le Moal, J., Wagner, V., Royere, D. & De Mouzon, J. (2013). Decline in semen concentration and morphology in a sample of 26,609 men close to general population between 1989 and 2005 in France. *Human Reproduction, 28,* 462–470. [8]

Roovers, J. P., van der Bom, J. G., van der Vaart, C. H. & Heintz, A. P. (2003). Hysterectomy and sexual wellbeing: Prospective observational study of vaginal hysterectomy, subtotal abdominal hysterectomy, and total abdominal hysterectomy. *BMJ, 327,* 774–778. [2]

Rosario, I. J., Kasabwala, K. & Sadeghi-Nejad, H. (2013). Circumcision as a strategy to minimize HIV transmission. *Current Urology Reports, 14,* 285–290. [3]

Rosario, M., Schrimshaw, E. W. & Hunter, J. (2011). Different patterns of sexual identity development over time: Implications for the psychological adjustment of lesbian, gay, and bisexual youths. *Journal of Sex Research, 48,* 3–15. [12]

Rosario, M., Schrimshaw, E. W., Hunter, J. & Braun, L. (2006). Sexual identity development among gay, lesbian, and bisexual youths: Consistency and change over time. *Journal of Sex Research, 43,* 46–58. [12]

Rosario, M., Schrimshaw, E. W., Hunter, J. & Levy-Warren, A. (2009). The coming-out process of young lesbian and bisexual women: Are there butch/femme differences in sexual identity development? *Archives of Sexual Behavior, 38,* 34–49. [12]

Roselli, C. E. & Stormshak, F. (2009). The neurobiology of sexual partner preferences in rams. *Hormones and Behavior, 55,* 611–620. [12]

Rosen, R. C. (2007). Erectile dysfunction: Integration of medical and psychological approaches. In: Leiblum, S. L. (Ed.), *Principles and practice of sex therapy* (4th ed.). Guilford. [14]

Rosenbaum, J. E. (2009). Patient teenagers? A comparison of the sexual behavior of virginity pledgers and matched nonpledgers. *Pediatrics, 123,* e110–120. [10]

Rosenthal, A. M., Sylva, D., Safron, A. & Bailey, J. M. (2011). Sexual arousal patterns of bisexual men revisited. *Biological Psychology, 88, 112–115.* [12]

Rosin, H. (2014). *When men are raped.* (www.slate.com/articles/double_x/doublex/2014/04/male_rape_in_america_a_new_study_reveals_that_men_are_sexually_assaulted.html) [16]

Rosman, J. P. & Resnick, P. J. (1989). Sexual attraction to corpses: A psychiatric review of necrophilia. *Bulletin of the American Academy of Psychiatry and the Law, 17,* 153–163. [13]

Ross, J., Zinn, A. & McCauley, E. (2000). Neurodevelopmental and psychosocial aspects of Turner syndrome. *Mental Retardation and Developmental Disabilities Research Reviews, 6,* 135–141. [4]

Ross, M. W., Crisp, B. R., Mansson, S. A. & Hawkes, S. (2012). Occupational health and safety among commercial sex workers. *Scandinavian Journal of Work and Environmental Health, 38,* 105–119. [17]

Rothaus, S. (2010). *Rekers: I am not gay and never have been.* (miamiherald.typepad.com/gay-southflorida/2010/05/rekers-i-am-not-gay-and-never-have-been.html) [12]

Rothschild, B. M., Calderon, F. L., Coppa, A. & Rothschild, C. (2000). First European exposure to syphilis: The Dominican Republic at the time of Columbian contact. *Clinical Infectious Diseases, 31,* 936–941. [1]

Rowland, D., Crisler, L. & Cox, D. (1982). Flirting between college students and faculty. *Journal of Sex Research, 18,* 346–359. [7]

Rowland, D., McMahon, C. G., Abdo, C., Chen, J., Jannini, E., Waldinger, M. D. & Ahn, T. Y. (2010). Disorders of orgasm and ejaculation in men. *Journal of Sexual Medicine, 7,* 1668–1686. [14]

Rozenberg, S., Vandromme, J. & Antoine, C. (2013). Postmenopausal hormone therapy: Risks and benefits. *Nature Reviews Endocrinology, 9,* 216–227. [11]

Rubin, A. J. (2000). Public more accepting of gays, poll finds. *Los Angeles Times,* June 18. [12]

Rudder, C. (2010). *The case for an older woman.* (blog.okcupid.com/index.php/the-case-for-an-older-woman) [5]

Rue, V. M. (1997). *The psychological safety of abortion: The need for reconsideration.* (afterabortion.org/1997/the-psychological-safety-of-abortion-the-need-for-reconsideration) [9]

Ruigrok, A. N., Salimi-Khorshidi, G., Lai, M. C., Baron-Cohen, S., Lombardo, M. V., Tait, R. J. & Suckling, J. (2013). A meta-analysis of sex differences in human brain structure. *Neuroscience and Biobehavioral Reviews, 39,* 34–50. [4]

Russell, D. E. H. (1984). *Sexual exploitation: Rape, child sexual abuse, and workplace harassment.* Sage. [16]

Russell, D. E. H. (1994). *Against pornography: The evidence of harm.* Russell Publications. [17]

Rust, J., Golombok, S., Hines, M., Johnston, K. & Golding, J. (2000). The role of brothers and sisters in the gender development of preschool children. *Journal of Experimental Child Psychology, 77,* 292–303. [4]

Rutter, P. S. (2012). Sex therapy with gay male couples using affirmative therapy. *Sexual and Relationship Therapy, 27,* 35–45. [14]

Ryan, M. J. (1998). Sexual selection, receiver biases, and the evolution of sex differences. *Science, 281,* 1999–2003. [5]

Sacher-Masoch, L. v. (1870/2000). *Venus in furs.* Viking Penguin. [13]

Saidi, J. A., Chang, D. T., Goluboff, E. T., Bagiella, E., Olsen, G. & Fisch, H. (1999). Declining sperm counts in the United States? A critical review. *Journal of Urology, 161,* 460–462. [8]

Saincome, M. (2013). *Meet the man who had sex with a dolphin (and wrote a book about it).* (www.sfweekly.com/exhibitionist/2013/01/07/meet-the-man-who-had-sex-with-a-dolphin-and-wrote-a-book-about-it) [13]

Salazar, L. F., DiClemente, R. J., Wingood, G. M., Crosby, R. A., Harrington, K., Davies, S., et al. (2004). Self-concept and adolescents' refusal of unprotected sex: A test of mediating mechanisms among African American girls. *Prevention Science, 5,* 137–149. [10]

Samal, P. K., Farber, C., Farooque, N. A. & Rawat, D. S. (1997). Polyandry in a central Himalayan community: An eco-cultural analysis. *Man in India, 76,* 51–56. [11]

San Francisco Human Rights Commission. (2011). *Bisexual invisibility: Impacts and recommendations.* (sf-hrc.org/sites/sf-hrc.org/files/migrated/FileCenter/Documents/HRC_Publications/Articles/Bisexual_Invisiblity_Impacts_and_Recommendations_March_2011.pdf) [12]

Sanchez-Garrido, M. A. & Tena-Sempere, M. (2013). Metabolic control of puberty: Roles of leptin and kisspeptins. *Hormones and Behavior, 64,* 187–194. [10]

Sanchez, F. J. & Vilain, E. (2012). "Straight-acting gays": The relationship between masculine consciousness, anti-effeminacy, and negative gay identity. *Archives of Sexual Behavior, 41,* 111–119. [12]

Sand, M. & Fisher, W. A. (2007). Women's endorsement of models of female sexual response: The Nurses' Sexuality Study. *Journal of Sexual Medicine, 4,* 708–719. [14]

Sandberg-Thoma, S. E. & Kamp Dush, C. M. (2014). Casual sexual relationships and mental health in adolescence and emerging adulthood. *Journal of Sex Research, 51,* 121–130. [7]

Sanders, A. R., Dawood, K., Rieger, G., Badner, J. A., Gershon, E. S., Krishnappa, R. S., et al. (2012). *Genome-wide linkage scan of male sexual orientation.* (www.ashg.org/2012meeting/abstracts/fulltext/f120122263.htm) [12]

Sanders, A. R., Martin, E. R., Beecham, G. W., Guo, S., Dawood, K., Rieger, et al. (2014). Genome-wide scan demonstrates significant linkage for male sexual orientation. *Psychological Medicine, 1–10.* [12]

Sanders, S. A. & Reinisch, J. M. (1999). Would you say you "had sex" if…? *JAMA, 281,* 275–277. [6]

Santelli, J. S., Kaiser, J., Hirsch, L., Radosh, A., Simkin, L. & Middlestadt, S. (2004). Initiation of sexual intercourse among middle school adolescents: The influence of psychosocial factors. *Journal of Adolescent Health, 34,* 200–208. [10]

Santelli, J. S., Lindberg, L. D., Finer, L. B. & Singh, S. (2007). Explaining recent declines in adolescent pregnancy in the United States: The contribution of abstinence and improved contraceptive use. *American Journal of Public Health, 97,* 150–156. [10]

Santoro, N. (2005). The menopausal transition. *American Journal of Medicine, 118*(Suppl. 12B), 8–13. [11]

Santos-Iglesias, P., Sierra, J. C. & Vallejo-Medina, P. (2013). Predictors of sexual assertiveness: The role of sexual desire, arousal, attitudes, and partner abuse. *Archives of Sexual Behavior, 42,* 1043–1052. [5]

Saslow, D., Solomon, D., Lawson, H. W., Killackey, M., Kulasingam, S. L., Cain, J., et al. (2012). American Cancer Society, American Society for Colposcopy and Cervical Pathology, and American Society for Clinical Pathology screening guidelines for the prevention and early detection of cervical cancer. *CA: A Cancer Journal for Clinicians, 62,* 147–172. [2]

Sauvageau, A. & Geberth, V. J. (2009). Elderly victim: An unusual autoerotic fatality involving an 87-year-old male. *Forensic Science, Medicine, and Pathology, 5,* 233–235. [13]

Sauvageau, A. & Racette, S. (2006). Autoerotic deaths in the literature from 1954 to 2004: A review. *Journal of Forensic Sciences, 51,* 140–146. [13]

Savic, I. & Lindstrom, P. (2008). PET and MRI show differences in cerebral asymmetry and functional connectivity between homo- and heterosexual subjects. *Proceedings of the National Academy of Sciences of the United States of America, 105,* 9403–9408. [12]

Savic, I., Berglund, H. & Lindstrom, P. (2005). Brain response to putative pheromones in homosexual men. *Proceedings of the National Academy of Sciences of the United States of America, 102,* 7356–7361. [5, 12]

Savin-Williams, R. C. (2005). *The new gay teenager.* Harvard University Press. [12]

Savin-Williams, R. C. & Diamond, L. M. (2004). Sex. In: Lerner, R. M. & Steinberg, L. (Eds.), *Handbook of adolescent psychology* (2nd ed.). Wiley. [10]

Savin-Williams, R. C. & Joyner, K. (2013). The dubious assessment of gay, lesbian, and bisexual adolescents of Add Health. *Archives of Sexual Behavior, 43,* 413–422. [1]

Savin-Williams, R. C., Joyner, K. & Rieger, G. (2012). Prevalence and stability of self-reported sexual orientation identity during young adulthood. *Archives of Sexual Behavior, 41,* 103–110. [12]

Sayle, A. E., Savitz, D. A., Thorp, J. M., Jr., Hertz-Picciotto, I. & Wilcox, A. J. (2001). Sexual activity during late pregnancy and risk of preterm delivery. *Obstetrics and Gynecology, 97,* 283–289. [8]

Schadewald, A. (2011). *The Crash Pad series celebrates episode 100 with a list of San Francisco pleasures.* (www.sfbg.com/sexsf/2011/07/29/crash-pad-series-celebrates-episode-100-list-san-francisco-pleasures) [17]

Schapiro, R. (2014). Man with HIV wrongly fired from Manhattan hotel job awarded more than $500G. *New York Daily News,* March 17. [15]

Scharer, L., Rowe, L. & Arnqvist, G. (2012). Anisogamy, chance and the evolution of sex roles. *Trends in Ecology and Evolution, 27,* 260–264. [App. A]

Schewe, P. A. (2002). Preventing violence in relationships: Interventions across the lifespan. American Psychological Association. [14]

Schiavi, R. C., Theilgaard, A., Owen, D. R. & White, D. (1988). Sex chromosome anomalies, hormones, and sexuality. *Archives of General Psychiatry, 45,* 19–24. [4]

Schiffer, B., Peschel, T., Paul, T., Gizewski, E., Forsting, M., Leygraf, et al. (2007). Structural brain abnormalities in the frontostriatal system and cerebellum in pedophilia. *Journal of Psychiatric Research, 41,* 753–762. [13]

Schmid, D. M., Schurch, B. & Hauri, D. (2000). Sildenafil in the treatment of sexual dysfunction in spinal cord-injured male patients. *European Urology, 38,* 184–193. [6]

Schmid, T. E., Eskenazi, B., Baumgartner, A., Marchetti, F., Young, S., Weldon, R., et al. (2007). The effects of male age on sperm DNA damage in healthy non-smokers. *Human Reproduction, 22,* 180–187. [8]

Schmidt, G. (Ed.). (2000). *Kinder der sexuellen Revolution.* Psychosozial-Verlag. [6]

Schmidt, H. M., Munder, T., Gerger, H., Fruhauf, S. & Barth, J. (2014). Combination of psychological intervention and phosphodiesterase-5 inhibitors for erectile dysfunction: A narrative review and meta-analysis. *Journal of Sexual Medicine, 11,* 1376–1391. [14]

Schmidt, M. S. (2009). Rodriguez said to test positive in 2003. *New York Times,* February 7. [3]

Schmidt, P. J., Nieman, L. K., Danaceau, M. A., Adams, L. F. & Rubinow, D. R. (1998). Differential behavioral effects of gonadal steroids in women with and in those without premenstrual syndrome. *New England Journal of Medicine, 338,* 209–216. [2]

Schmitt, D. P. (2004). Patterns and universals of mate poaching across 53 nations: The effects of sex, culture, and personality on romantically attracting another person's partner. *Journal of Personality and Social Psychology, 86,* 560–584. [7]

Schneider, H. J., Pickel, J. & Stalla, G. K. (2006). Typical female 2nd-4th finger length (2D:4D) ratios in male-to-female transsexuals—possible implications for prenatal androgen exposure. *Psychoneuroendocrinology, 31,* 265–269. [4]

Schneider, J. P., Weiss, R. & Samenow, C. (2012). Is it really cheating? Understanding the emotional reactions of spouses and partners affected by cybersex infidelity. *Sexual Addiction and Compulsivity, 19,* 123–139. [7]

Schneider, S., Peters, J., Bromberg, U., Brassen, S., Menz, M. M., Miedl, S. F., et al. (2011). Boys do it the right way: Sex-dependent amygdala lateralization during face processing in adolescents. *Neuroimage, 56,* 1847–1853. [4]

Schnyder, U., Schnyder-Luthi, C., Ballinari, P. & Blaser, A. (1998). Therapy for vaginismus: In vivo versus in vitro desensitization. *Canadian Journal of Psychiatry / Revue Canadienne de Psychiatrie, 43,* 941–944. [14]

Schubach, G. (2001). Urethral expulsions during sensual arousal and bladder catheterization in seven human females. *Electronic Journal of Human Sexuality,* online publication at www.ejhs.org/volume4/Schubach/Intro.html. [5]

Schultz, W. W., van Andel, P., Sabelis, I. & Mooyaart, E. (1999). Magnetic resonance imaging of male and female genitals during coitus and female sexual arousal. *BMJ, 319,* 1596–1600. [6]

Schuster, M. A., Bell, R. M., Nakajima, G. A. & Kanouse, D. E. (1998). The sexual practices of Asian and Pacific Islander high school students. *Journal of Adolescent Health, 23,* 221–231. [10]

Schwartz, C. R. & Graf, N. L. (2009). Assortative matching among same-sex and different-sex couples in the United States, 1990–2000. *Demographic Research, 21,* 843–878. [7]

Schwartz, M. F. (2008). Developmental psycho-pathological perspectives on sexually compulsive behavior. *Psychiatric Clinics of North America, 31,* 567–586. [14]

Science Daily. (2007). *Alcohol amount, not type—wine, beer, liquor—triggers breast cancer.* (www.sciencedaily.com/releases/2007/09/070927083251.htm) [2]

Scorolli, C., Ghirlanda, S., Enquist, M., Zattoni, S. & Jannini, E. A. (2007). Relative prevalence of different fetishes. *International Journal of Impotence Research, 19,* 432-437. [13]

Seattle Times. (2004). *Green River killings.* (seattletimes.com/html/greenriverkillings) [13]

Sebastian, A. (2014). *Virtual reality and the future of sex.* (www.extremetech.com/extreme/181436-virtual-reality-and-the-future-of-sex) [17]

Seelye, K. Q. & Robbins, L. (2010). Duke winces as a private joke slips out of control. *New York Times,* October 7. [7]

Segal, N. L. & Diamond, M. (2014). Identical reared apart twins concordant for transsexuality. *Journal of Experimental and Clinical Medicine, 6,* 74. [4]

Serrano, B., Alemany, L., Tous, S., Bruni, L., Clifford, G. M., Weiss, T., et al. (2012). Potential impact of a nine-valent vaccine in human papillomavirus related cervical disease. *Infectious Agents and Cancer, 7,* 38. [15]

Service, R. N. (2013). *Conservatives say Utah polygamy ruling confirms their worst fears.* (www.religionnews.com/2013/12/14/federal-judge-utah-polygamy-law-unconstitutional-sister-wives) [11]

Servin, A., Bohlin, G. & Berlin, L. (1999). Sex differences in 1-, 3-, and 5-year-olds' toy-choice in a structured play-session. *Scandinavian Journal of Psychology, 40,* 43–48. [4]

Setchell, J. M., Kendal, J. & Tyniec, P. (2011). Do non-human primates synchronise their menstrual cycles? A test in mandrills. *Psychoneuroendocrinology, 36,* 51–59. [2]

Seto, M. C. (2008). Pedophilia: Psychopathology and theory. In: Laws, D. R. & O'Donohue, W. T. (Eds.), *Sexual deviance: Theory, assessment, and treatment.* Guilford. [13]

SexualityandU. (2012). *Birth control.* (www.sexualityandu.ca/birth-control) [9]

SFGate. (2008). *Election results for San Francisco propositions.* (www.sfgate.com/politics/article/Election-results-for-San-Francisco-propositions-3187007.php) [17]

Shacham, E., Godlonton, S. & Thornton, R. L. (2013). Perceptions of male circumcision among married couples in rural Malawi. *Journal of the International Association of Providers of AIDS Care.* [3]

Shackelford, T. K. & Mouzos, J. (2005). Partner killing by men in cohabiting and marital relationships: A comparative, cross-national analysis of data from Australia and the United States. *Journal of Interpersonal Violence, 20,* 1310–1324. [11]

Shackelford, T. K., Schmitt, D. P. & Buss, D. M. (2005). Universal dimensions of human mate preference. *Personality and Individual Differences, 35,* 447–458. [5]

Shah, A. (2012). Three Twin Cities Somalis guilty of sex trafficking. *Star-Tribune,* May 4. [17]

Shah, J. & Christopher, N. (2002). Can shoe size predict penile length? *British Journal of Urology International*, 90, 586–587. [3]

Shamloul, R. & Ghanem, H. (2013). Erectile dysfunction. *Lancet*, 381, 153–165. [14]

Sharma, B. (2011). *For young women, a horrifying consequence of Mubarak's overthrow.* (www.newrepublic.com/article/world/96555/egypt-genital-mutilation-fgm-muslim-brotherhood) [2]

Sharpe, R. M. (1997). Do males rely on female hormones? *Nature*, 390, 447–448. [10]

Sharpe, R. M. (2012). Sperm counts and fertility in men: A rocky road ahead. *EMBO Reports*, 13, 398–403. [8]

Shell-Duncan, B. & Hernlund, Y. (Eds.). (2000). *Female "circumcision" in Africa: Culture, controversy, and change.* Lynne Rienner. [2]

Sheppard, L. A. (2008). Breast cancer and sexuality. *Breast Journal*, 14, 176–181. [2]

Sheppard, M. & Mayo, J. B. (2013). The social construction of gender and sexuality: Learning from two-spirit traditions. *The Social Studies*, 104, 259–270. [1]

Sheridan, M. (2010). California elects nation's first openly transgender judge, Victoria Kolakowski. *New York Daily News*, November 17. [4]

Sherwin, B. B. & Gelfand, M. M. (1987). The role of androgen in the maintenance of sexual functioning in oophorectomized women. *Psychosomatic Medicine*, 49, 397–409. [2]

Shifren, J. L., Monz, B. U., Russo, P. A., Segreti, A. & Johannes, C. B. (2008). Sexual problems and distress in United States women: Prevalence and correlates. *Obstetrics and Gynecology*, 112, 970–978. [14]

Shilts, R. (1982). *The mayor of Castro Street: The life and times of Harvey Milk.* St. Martin's. [12]

Shilts, R. (1987). *And the band played on: Politics, people, and the AIDS epidemic.* St. Martin's. [12]

Shores, M. M., Smith, N. L., Forsberg, C. W., Anawalt, B. D. & Matsumoto, A. M. (2012). Testosterone treatment and mortality in men with low testosterone levels. *Journal of Clinical Endocrinology and Metabolism*, 97, 2050–2058. [11]

Shostak, M. (2000). *Nisa: The life and words of a !Kung woman.* Harvard University Press. [7]

Showstack, J., Lin, F., Learman, L. A., Vittinghoff, E., Kuppermann, M., Varner, R. E., et al. (2006). Randomized trial of medical treatment versus hysterectomy for abnormal uterine bleeding: Resource use in the Medicine or Surgery (Ms) trial. *American Journal of Obstetrics and Gynecology*, 194, 332–338. [2]

Shumaker, S. A., Legault, C., Rapp, S. R., Thal, L., Wallace, R. B., Ockene, J. K., et al. (2003). Estrogen plus progestin and the incidence of dementia and mild cognitive impairment in postmenopausal women: The Women's Health Initiative Memory Study: A randomized controlled trial. *JAMA*, 289, 2651–2662. [11]

Shweder, R. A. (2013). The goose and the gander: The genital wars. *Global Discourse*, 3, 348–366. [2, 3]

Siciliano, C. (2012). *Denied shelter beds, many of NYC's homeless youth turn to prostitution.* (www.huffingtonpost.com/carl-siciliano/denied-shelter-beds-many-of-nycs-homeless-youth-turn-to-prostitution_b_1949526.html) [12]

Siegel, R., Ma, J., Zou, Z. & Jemal, A. (2014). Cancer statistics, 2014. *CA: A Cancer Journal for Clinicians*, 64, 9–29. [2]

Silver, N. (2010). *Divorce rates higher in states with gay marriage bans.* (fivethirtyeight.com/features/divorce-rates-appear-higher-in-states) [11]

Silverberg, C. (2008). *How to achieve male multiple orgasms.* (sexuality.about.com/od/orgasms/ht/htmalemultiples.htm) [5]

Silverthorne, Z. A. & Quinsey, V. L. (2000). Sexual partner age preferences of homosexual and heterosexual men and women. *Archives of Sexual Behavior*, 29, 67–76. [5]

Simon, S. (2002). AIDS scare at tiny college shakes town. *Los Angeles Times*, April 30. [15]

Simon, W. & Gagnon, J. H. (1986). Sexual scripts: Permanence and change. *Archives of Sexual Behavior*, 15, 97–120. [1, 4]

Simpson, J. A., Collins, W. A., Tran, S. & Haydon, K. C. (2007). Attachment and the experience and expression of emotions in romantic relationships: A developmental perspective. *Journal of Personality and Social Psychology*, 92, 355–367. [7]

Sinclair, H. C. & Frieze, I. H. (2001). Initial courtship behavior and stalking: How should we draw the line? In: Davis, K. E., et al. (Eds.), *Stalking: Perspectives on victims and perpetrators.* Springer. [7]

Sine, R. (2014). *Sex drive: How do men and women compare?* (www.webmd.com/sex/features/sex-drive-how-do-men-women-compare) [4]

Singh, D. (2002). Female mate value at a glance: Relationship of waist-to-hip ratio to health, fecundity and attractiveness. *Neuroendocrinology Letters*, 23 (Suppl. 4), 81–91. [5]

Sionean, C., DiClemente, R. J., Wingood, G. M., Crosby, R., Cobb, B. K., Harrington, K., et al. (2002). Psychosocial and behavioral correlates of refusing unwanted sex among African-American adolescent females. *Journal of Adolescent Health*, 30, 55–63. [10]

Sipski, M. L., Alexander, C. J. & Rosen, R. (2001). Sexual arousal and orgasm in women: Effects of spinal cord injury. *Annals of Neurology*, 49, 35–44. [6]

Sivalingam, V. N., Duncan, W. C., Kirk, E., Shephard, L. A. & Horne, A. W. (2011). Diagnosis and management of ectopic pregnancy. *Journal of Family Planning and Reproductive Health Care*, 37, 231–240. [9]

Skjaerven, R., Wilcox, A. J. & Lie, R. T. (1999). A population-based study of survival and childbearing among female subjects with birth defects and the risk of recurrence in their children. *New England Journal of Medicine*, 340, 1057–1062. [8]

Skorupskaite, K., George, J. T. & Anderson, R. A. (2014). The kisspeptin-GnRH pathway in human reproductive health and disease. *Human Reproduction Update*, 20, 485–500. [10]

Sloss, C. M. & Harper, G. W. (2004). When street sex workers are mothers. *Archives of Sexual Behavior*, 33, 329–341. [17]

Smalley, S. (2003). Law-enforcement officials note marked nationwide increase in teen prostitution: Trends show kids getting younger, more from middle-class homes. *Newsweek*, August 18. [17]

Smith, D. K. (2014). South African traditional leaders attack graphic male circumcision website. *Guardian (London)*, January 29. [3]

Smith, S. M. (1988). Extra-pair copulation in black-capped chickadees: The role of the female. *Behaviour*, 107, 15–23. [App. A]

SmithBattle, L. (2007). "I wanna have a good future": Teen mothers' rise in educational aspirations, competing demands, and limited school support. *Youth and Society*, 38, 348–371. [10]

Solomon, T. M., Halkilis, P. N., Moeller, R. M., Siconolfi, D. E., Kiang, M. V. & Barton, S. C. (2011). Sex parties among young gay, bisexual, and other men who have sex with men in New York City: Attendance and behavior. *Journal of Urban Health*, 88, 1063–1075. [7]

Sommer, F., Goldstein, I. & Korda, J. B. (2010). Bicycle riding and erectile dysfunction: A review. *Journal of Sexual Medicine*, 7, 2346–2358. [14]

Sommers, C. H. (2012). How the CDC is overstating sexual violence in the U.S. *Washington Post*, January 27. [16]

Sonderland, A. L., O'Brien, K., Kremer, P., Rowland, B., De Groot, F., Staiger, et al. (2014). The association between sports participation, alcohol use and aggression and violence: A systematic review. *Journal of Science and Medicine in Sport*, 17, 2–7. [16]

Soper, T. (2014). *Yahoo exec countersues for defamation in sexual harassment case.* (www.geekwire.com/2014/yahoo-exec-former-seattle-startup-ceo-files-counter-claim-sexual-harassment-case) [16]

Sorensen, K., Mouritsen, A., Aksglaede, L., Hagen, C. P., Mogensen, S. S. & Juul, A. (2012). Recent secular trends in pubertal timing: Implications for evaluation and diagnosis of precocious puberty. *Hormone Research in Paediatrics*, 77, 137–145. [10]

Southall, A. (2014). High school football players charged in N.J. hazing case. *New York Times*, October 11. [16]

Southern Poverty Law Center. (2007). *Bishop Eddie Long.* (www.splcenter.org/get-informed/intelligence-report/browse-all-issues/2007/spring/face-right/bishop-eddie-long) [12]

Spalding, L. R. & Peplau, L. A. (1997). The unfaithful lover: Heterosexuals' stereotypes of bisexuals and their relationships. *Psychology of Women Quarterly*, 21, 611–625. [12]

Spencer, R. (2014). Libidos, vibrators and men, oh my! This is what your ageing sex drive looks like. *Guardian (London)*, March 25. [11]

Spinal Cord Injury Model System Information Network. (2007). *Sexuality for women with spinal cord injury.* (tinyurl.com/l28pouk) [App. B]

Spitzberg, B. H. & Cupach, W. R. (2014). *The dark side of relationship pursuit: From attraction to obsession and stalking* (2nd ed.). Routledge. [16]

Sprecher, S. (2014). Evidence of change in men's versus women's emotional reactions to first sexual intercourse: A 23-year study in a human sexuality course at a midwestern university. *Journal of Sex Research, 51,* 466–472. [10]

Sprecher, S. & Hendrick, S. (2004). Self-disclosure in intimate relationships: Associations with individual and relationship characteristics over time. *Journal of Social and Clinical Psychology, 23,* 836–856. [7]

Sprecher, S. & Regan, P. C. (2002). Liking some things (in some people) more than others: Partner preferences in romantic relationships and friendships. *Journal of Social and Personal Relationships, 19,* 463–481. [5]

Sprecher, S., Treger, S. & Sakaluk, J. K. (2013). Premarital sexual standards and socio-sexuality: Gender, ethnicity, and cohort differences. *Archives of Sexual Behavior, 42,* 1395–1405. [4]

Stanger-Hall, K. F. & Hall, D. W. (2011). Abstinence-only education and teen pregnancy rates: Why we need comprehensive sex education in the U.S. *PLOS ONE, 6,* e24658. [10]

Starkweather, K. E. & Hames, R. (2012). A survey of non-classical polyandry. *Human Nature, 23,* 149–172. [11]

Steensma, T. D., McGuire, J. K., Kreukels, B. P. C., Beekman, A. J. & Cohen-Kettenis, P. T. (2013a). Factors associated with desistence and persistence of childhood gender dysphoria: A quantitative follow-up study. *Journal of the American Academy of Child and Adolescent Psychiatry, 52,* 582–590. [4]

Steensma, T. D., van der Ende, J., Verhulst, F. C. & Cohen-Kettenis, P. T. (2013b). Gender variance in childhood and sexual orientation in adulthood: A prospective study. *Journal of Sexual Medicine, 10,* 2723–2733. [12]

Stein, N. (1999). *Incidence and implications of sexual harassment in K-12 schools.* (www. hawaii.edu/hivandaids/Sexual%20 Harassment%20and%20Sexual%20 Violence%20in%20K-12%20Schools.pdf) [16]

Steinberg, J. R. & Finer, L. B. (2011). Examining the association of abortion history and current mental health: A reanalysis of the National Comorbidity Survey using a common-risk-factors model. *Social Science and Medicine, 72,* 72–82. [9]

Steinberg, L. (2013). *Adolescence* (10th ed.). McGraw-Hill. [10]

Stemple, L. & Meyer, I. H. (2014). The sexual victimization of men in America: New data challenge old assumptions. *American Journal of Public Health, 104,* e19–26. [16]

Stepp, L. S. (2007). *Unhooked: How young women pursue sex, delay love, and lose at both.* Riverhead. [7]

Stern, S. R. & Willis, T. J. (2007). What are teenagers up to online? In: Mazarella, S. R. (Ed.), *20 questions about youth and the media.* Peter Lang. [7]

Sternberg, R. J. (1986). A triangular theory of love. *Psychological Review, 93,* 119–135. [7]

Sternberg, R. J. (1998). *Love is a story: A new theory of relationships.* Oxford University Press. [7]

Sternberg, R. J. & Barnes, M. (1985). Real and ideal others in romantic relationships: Is

four a crowd? *Journal of Personality and Social Psychology, 47,* 1586–1608. [7]

Stief, M. C., Rieger, G. & Savin-Williams, R. C. (2014). Bisexuality is associated with elevated sexual sensation seeking, sexual curiosity, and sexual excitability. *Personality and Individual Differences, 66,* 193–198. [12]

Stinson, R. D. (2010). Hooking up in young adulthood: A review of factors influencing the sexual behavior of college students. *Journal of College Student Psychotherapy, 24,* 98–115. [7]

Stochholm, K., Bojesen, A., Jensen, A. S., Juul, S. & Gravholt, C. H. (2012). Criminality in men with Klinefelter's syndrome and XYY syndrome: A cohort study. *BMJ Open, 2,* e000650. [4]

Stokes, J. P., Damon, W. & McKirnan, D. J. (1997). Predictors of movement toward homosexuality: A longitudinal study of bisexual men. *Journal of Sex Research, 34,* 304–312. [12]

Stoleru, S., Fonteille, V., Cornelis, C., Joyal, C. & Moulier, V. (2012). Functional neuroimaging studies of sexual arousal and orgasm in healthy men and women: A review and meta-analysis. *Neuroscience and Biobehavioral Reviews, 36,* 1481–1509. [5]

Stolk, L., Perry, J. R., Chasman, D. I., He, C., Mangino, N., Sulem, P., et al. (2012). Meta-analyses identify 13 loci associated with age at menopause and highlight DNA repair and immune pathways. *Nature Genetics, 44,* 260–268. [11]

Stolzer, R. L. (2009). Violence against transgender people: A review of United States data. *Aggression and Violent Behavior, 14,* 170–179. [16]

Stop Street Harassment. (2014). *Harassed in public spaces: A national street harassment report.* (www.stopstreetharassment.org/wp-content/uploads/2012/08/2014-National-SSH-Street-Harassment-Report.pdf) [13]

Stowers, L., Holy, T. E., Meister, M., Dulac, C. & Koentges, G. (2002). Loss of sex discrimination and male-male aggression in mice deficient for TRP2. *Science, 295,* 1493–1500. [5]

Strano, M. M. (2008). User descriptions and interpretations of self-presentation through Facebook profile images. *Cyberpsychology, 2*(2), article 1. [10]

Stransky, M. & Finkelhor, D. (2008). *How many juveniles are involved in prostitution in the U.S.?* (www.unh.edu/ccrc/prostitution/Juvenile_Prostitution_factsheet.pdf) [17]

Strassberg, D. S., McKinnon, R. K., Sustaita, M. A. & Rullo, J. (2013). Sexting by high school students: An exploratory and descriptive study. *Archives of Sexual Behavior, 42,* 15–21. [3]

Strassmann, B. I. (1992). The function of menstrual taboos among the Dogon: Defense against cuckoldry? *Human Nature, 3,* 89–131. [2]

Strassmann, B. I. (1996). Menstrual hut visits by Dogon women: A hormonal test distinguishes deceit from honest signaling. *Behavioral Ecology, 7,* 304–315. [2]

Strassmann, B. I. (1997). The biology of menstruation in *Homo sapiens*: Total lifetime menses, fecundity, and nonsynchrony in a natural fertility population. *Current Anthropology, 38,* 123–129. [2]

Strassmann, B. I. (1999). Menstrual synchrony pheromones: Cause for doubt. *Human Reproduction, 14,* 579–580. [2]

Straus, M. A. (2004). Prevalence of violence against dating partners by male and female university students worldwide. *Violence Against Women, 10,* 790–811. [16]

Straus, M. A. (2012). *Assaults by women on male partners in male dominant nations: Preliminary tests of an explanatory theory.* (pubpages.unh.edu/~mas2/ID71doc30%20 Violence%20By%20Women%20in%20Male-Dominant%20Nations.pdf) [16]

Streissguth, A. P., Barr, H. M. & Sampson, P. D. (1990). Moderate prenatal alcohol exposure: Effects on child IQ and learning problems at age 7 1/2 years. *Alcoholism, Clinical and Experimental Research, 14,* 662–669. [8]

Stuart, H. (2013). *Not all pedophiles have mental disorder, American Psychiatric Association says in new DSM.* (www.huffingtonpost.com/2013/11/01/dsm-pedophilia-mental-disorder-paraphilia_n_4184878.html) [13]

Suh, D. D., Yang, C. C., Cao, Y., Heiman, J. R., Garland, P. A. & Maravilla, K. R. (2004). MRI of female genital and pelvic organs during sexual arousal. *Journal of Psychosomatic Obstetrics and Gynaecology, 25,* 153–162. [2]

Sullivan, A. (2014). *The dish: Biased and balanced.* (dish.andrewsullivan.com) [12]

Sumter, S. R., Valkenburg, P. M. & Peter, J. (2013). Perceptions of love across the lifespan: Differences in passion, intimacy, and commitment. *International Journal of Behavioral Development, 37,* 417–427. [7]

Sunil, T. S., Spears, W. D., Hook, L., Castillo, J. & Torres, C. (2010). Initiation of and barriers to prenatal care use among low-income women in San Antonio, Texas. *Maternal and Child Health Journal, 14,* 133–140. [8]

Survive-UK. (2001). *It happened to me.* (survive.org.uk/stories.html) [16]

Suschinsky, K. D., Elias, L. J. & Krupp, D. B. (2007). Looking for Ms. Right: Allocating attention to facilitate mate choice. *Evolutionary Psychology, 5,* 428–441. [5]

Suschinsky, K. D., Lalumiere, M. L. & Chivers, M. L. (2009). Sex differences in patterns of genital sexual arousal: Measurement artifacts or true phenomena? *Archives of Sexual Behavior, 38,* 559–573. [5]

Sussman, L. & Bordwell, S. (1981). *The rapist file: Interviews with convicted rapists.* Chelsea House. [16]

Sutton, M., Sternberg, M., Koumans, E. H., McQuillan, G., Berman, S. & Markowitz, L. (2007). The prevalence of *Trichomonas vaginalis* infection among reproductive-age women in the United States, 2001–2004. *Clinical Infectious Diseases, 45,* 1319–1326. [15]

Swaab, D. F. & Garcia-Falgueras, A. (2009). Sexual differentiation of the human brain in relation to gender identity and sexual orientation. *Functional Neurology, 24,* 17–28. [4]

Swamy, G. K., Ostbye, T. & Skjaerven, R. (2008). Association of preterm birth with long-term survival, reproduction, and next-generation preterm birth. *JAMA, 299,* 1429–1436. [8]

Swick, K. (2005). Preventing violence through empathy development in families. *Early Childhood Education Journal, 33,* 53–59. [16]

Tafoya, B. (2012). *UIC study examines toward college students who "hook up."* (chicago.cbslocal.com/2012/08/17/uic-study-examines-views-toward-college-students-who-hook-up) [7]

Talley, A. E. & Bettencourt, B. A. (2008). Evaluations and aggression directed at a gay male target: The role of threat and antigay prejudice. *Journal of Applied Social Psychology, 38*, 647–683. [12]

Tan, M., Jones, G., Zhu, G., Ye, J., Hong, T., Zhou, S., et al. (2009). Fellatio by fruit bats prolongs copulation time. *PLOS ONE, 4*, e7595. [6]

Tanfer, K. & Aral, S. O. (1996). Sexual intercourse during menstruation and self-reported sexually transmitted disease history among women. *Sexually Transmitted Diseases, 23*, 395–401. [2]

Tarin, J. J. & Gomez-Piquer, V. (2002). Do women have a hidden heat period? *Human Reproduction, 17*, 2243–2248. [2]

Taylor, K. (2013). Sex on campus: She can play that game, too. *New York Times*, July 12. [7]

Taylor, R. D. (2010). Risk and resilience in low-income African American families: Moderating effects of kinship social support. *Cultural Diversity and Ethnic Minority Psychology, 16*, 344–351. [11]

Taylor, S. (1982). Hinckley hails "historical" shooting to win love. *New York Times*, July 9. [16]

Teachman, J. D. (2003). Premarital sex, premarital cohabitation, and the risk of subsequent marital dissolution among women. *Journal of Marriage and the Family, 65*, 444–455. [11]

Testa, M. & Livingston, J. A. (2009). Alcohol consumption and women's vulnerability to sexual victimization: Can reducing women's drinking prevent rape? *Substance Use and Misuse, 44*, 1349–1376. [16]

Texas Tribune. (2014). *Texas prison inmates.* (www.texastribune.org/library/data/texas-prisons) [16]

The Economist. (2014a). *A new condominium.* (www.economist.com/news/asia/21600749-ruling-suggests-roman-catholic-church-no-longer-all-powerful-new-condominium) [9]

The Economist. (2014b). *More bang for your buck: How new technology is shaking up the oldest business.* (www.economist.com/news/briefing/21611074-how-new-technology-shaking-up-oldest-business-more-bang-your-buck) [17]

The Economist. (2014c). *Why the price of commercial sex is falling.* (www.economist.com/blogs/economist-explains/2014/08/economist-explains-7) [17]

TheGuardian.com. (2014). *Lesbian, gay, bisexual and transgender rights around the world.* (www.theguardian.com/world/ng-interactive/2014/may/-sp-gay-rights-world-lesbian-bisexual-transgender) [12]

Thibaut, F., De La Barra, F., Gordon, H., Cosyns, P. & Bradford, J. M. (2010). The World Federation of Societies of Biological Psychiatry (WFSBP) guidelines for the biological treatment of paraphilias. *World Journal of Biological Psychiatry, 11*, 604–655. [13]

Thigpen, J. W. (2009). Early sexual behavior in a sample of low-income, African American children. *Journal of Sex Research, 46*, 67–79. [10]

Thigpen, J. W. & Fortenberry, J. D. (2009). Understanding variation in normative childhood sexual behavior: The significance of family context. *Social Service Review, 83*, 611–631. [10]

Thomsen, R. (2000). *Sperm competition and the function of masturbation in Japanese macaques* (Macaca fuscata*). Dissertation, Ludwig-Maximilians-Universität München. (edoc.ub.uni-muenchen.de/105/1/Thomsen_Ruth.pdf) [6]

Thornhill, R. & Palmer, C. T. (2000). *A natural history of rape: Biological bases of sexual coercion.* MIT Press. [16, App. A]

Tiefer, L. (2002). Sexual behaviour and its medicalisation. Many (especially economic) forces promote medicalisation. *BMJ, 325*, 45. [14]

Tirtayasa, P. M., Prasetyo, R. B. & Rodjani, A. (2013). Diphallia with associated anomalies: A case report and literature review. *Case Reports in Urology, 2013*, 192960. [3]

Tjaden, P. & Thoennes, N. (2006). *Extent, nature, and consequences of rape victimization: Findings from the National Violence Against Women Survey.* (www.ncjrs.gov/pdffiles1/nij/210346.pdf) [16]

Tobian, A. A., Serwadda, D., Quinn, T. C., Kigozi, G., Gravitt, P. E., Laeyendecker, O., et al. (2009). Male circumcision for the prevention of HSV-2 and HPV infections and syphilis. *New England Journal of Medicine, 360*, 1298–1309. [3]

Tong, Y. (2013). Acculturation, gender disparity, and the sexual behavior of Asian American youth. *Journal of Sex Research, 50*, 560–573. [10]

Toro-Morn, M. & Sprecher, S. (2003). A cross-cultural comparison of mate preferences among university students: The United States vs. the People's Republic of China (PRC). *Journal of Comparative Family Studies, 34*, 151–174. [4]

Tovee, M. J., Swami, V., Furnham, A. & Mangalparsad, R. (2006). Changing perceptions of attractiveness as observers are exposed to a different culture. *Evolution and Human Behavior, 27*, 443–456. [5]

Townsend, L. (2007). *Leatherman's handbook II.* Booksurge. [7]

Traish, A. M., Hassani, J., Guay, A. T., Zitzmann, M. & Hansen, M. L. (2011). Adverse side effects of 5α-reductase inhibitors therapy: Persistent diminished libido and erectile dysfunction and depression in a subset of patients. *Journal of Sexual Medicine, 8*, 872–884. [14]

Trenholm, C., Devaney, B., Fortson, K., Quay, L., Wheeler, J. & Clark, M. (2007). *Impacts of four Title V, Section 510 abstinence education programs.* (www.mathematica-mpr.com/publications/pdfs/impactabstinence.pdf) [10]

Trevathan, W. R., Burleson, M. H. & Gregory, W. L. (1993). No evidence for menstrual synchrony in lesbian couples. *Psychoneuroendocrinology, 18*, 425–435. [2]

Trivers, R., Palestis, B. G. & Manning, J. T. (2013). The symmetry of children's knees is linked to their adult sprinting speed and their willingness to sprint in a long-term Jamaican study. *PLOS ONE, 8*, e72244. [App. A]

Tronstein, E., Johnston, C., Huang, M. L., Selke, S., Magaret, A., Warren, T., et al. (2011). Genital shedding of herpes simplex virus among symptomatic and asymptomatic persons with HSV-2 infection. *JAMA, 305*, 1441–1449. [15]

Trotier, D. (2011). Vomeronasal organ and human pheromones. *European Annals of Otorhinolaryngology, Head and Neck Diseases, 128*, 184–190. [5]

Trussell, J., Schwartz, E. B. & Guthrie, K. (2009). Obesity and oral contraceptive pill failure. *Contraception, 79*, 334–338. [9]

Tschudin, S., Bertea, P. C. & Zemp, E. (2010). Prevalence and predictors of premenstrual syndrome and premenstrual dysphoric disorder in a population-based sample. *Archives of Women's Mental Health, 13*, 485–494. [2]

Tulviste, T. & Koor, M. (2005). "Hands off the car, it's mine!" and "The teacher will be angry if we don't play nicely": Gender-related preferences in the use of moral rules and social conventions in preschoolers' dyadic play. *Sex Roles, 53*, 57–66. [4]

Tuteur, A. (2009). *What's the right C-section rate? Higher than you think.* (www.sciencebasedmedicine.org/whats-the-right-c-section-rate-higher-than-you-think) [8]

Twain, M. (1879). *Some thoughts on the science of onanism.* (www.textfiles.com/etext/AUTHORS/TWAIN/onanism.txt) [6]

U.S. Census Bureau. (2006). *Remarriage in the United States.* (www.census.gov/hhes/socdemo/marriage/data/sipp/us-remarriage-poster.pdf) [11]

U.S. Census Bureau. (2010). *America's families and living arrangements: 2010.* (www.census.gov/population/www/socdemo/hh-fam/cps2010.html) [11]

U.S. Census Bureau. (2011a). *America's families and living arrangements: 2011.* (www.census.gov/population/www/socdemo/hh-fam/cps2011.html) [11]

U.S. Census Bureau. (2011b). *Census Bureau releases estimates of same-sex married couples.* (www.census.gov/newsroom/releases/archives/2010_census/cb11-cn181.html) [11]

U.S. Census Bureau. (2013). *American Community Survey data on same sex couples.* (www.census.gov/hhes/samesex/data/acs.html) [12]

U.S. Census Bureau. (2014). *Estimated median age at first marriage.* (www.census.gov/hhes/families/files/ms2.csv) [11]

U.S. Department of Justice. (1998). *Stalking in America: Findings from the National Violence Against Women Survey.* (www.ncjrs.gov/pdffiles/169592.pdf) [16]

U.S. Department of Justice. (2008). *Report on rape in federal and state prisons.* (nicic.gov/Library/023323) [16]

U.S. Department of Justice. (2010). *Criminal victimization, 2009.* (bjs.ojp.usdoj.gov/content/pub/pdf/cv09.pdf) [16]

U.S. Department of State. (2008). *2008 human rights report: Greece.* (www.state.gov/j/drl/rls/hrrpt/2008/eur/119082.htm) [17]

U.S. Food and Drug Administration. (2009). *Questions and answers for estrogen and estrogen with progestin therapies for postmenopausal women (updated).* (www.fda.gov/drugs/drugsafety/informationbydrugclass/ucm135339.htm) [11]

U.S. Public Health Service. (2011). *The Surgeon General's call to action to support breastfeeding.* (www.surgeongeneral.gov/library/calls/breastfeeding/index.html) [8]

U.S. Public Health Service. (2014). *Preexposure prophylaxis for the prevention of HIV infection in the United States.* (www.cdc.gov/hiv/pdf/PrEPguidelines2014.pdf) [15]

Ueno, K., Roach, T. & Peña-Talamantes, A. E. (2013). Sexual orientation and gender typicality of the occupation in young adulthood. *Social Forces, 92,* 81–108. [12]

Ulrich, H., Randolph, M. & Acheson, S. (2005/6). Child sexual abuse. *Scientific Review of Mental Health Practice, 4,* 37–51. [10]

UN News Centre. (2013). *New UN statistics show alarming rise in rapes in strife-torn eastern DR Congo.* (www.un.org/apps/news/story.asp?NewsID=45529) [16]

UNAIDS. (2007). *Male circumcision: Global trends and determinants of prevalence, safety, and acceptability.* (whqlibdoc.who.int/publications/2007/9789241596169_eng.pdf) [3]

UNAIDS. (2014). *The Gap report.* (www.unaids.org/en/media/unaids/contentassets/documents/unaidspublication/2014/UNAIDS_Gap_report_en.pdf) [15]

United Nations Human Rights Committee. (2008). *Report of the Human Rights Committee, Volume 1.* (www.ccprcentre.org/wp-content/uploads/2012/11/A_63_40_Vol.I_E.pdf) [11]

United Nations. (1994). *Security Council Resolution 955, 8 November 1994.* (daccess-dds-ny.un.org/doc/UNDOC/GEN/N95/140/97/PDF/N9514097.pdf?OpenElement) [16]

United States Preventive Services Taskforce. (2009). *Screening for breast cancer.* (www.uspreventiveservicestaskforce.org/uspstf/uspsbrca.htm) [2]

Urology Care Foundation. (2014). *Undescended testicles (cryptorchidism).* (www.urologyhealth.org/urology/index.cfm?article=64) [4]

Urquhart, V. V. (2014). *Straight porn is full of "lesbians." So why is lesbian porn so boring?* (www.slate.com/blogs/outward/2014/04/07/pornography_for_lesbians_why_is_it_so_uninspiring.html) [17]

Utah Coalition Against Sexual Assault. (2006). *Rape and sexual violence research report.* (www.ucasa.org/2006ResearchReport.pdf) [16]

Utian, W. H. & Woods, N. F. (2013). Impact of hormone therapy on quality of life after menopause. *Menopause, 20,* 1098–1105. [11]

Van Dijk, J. W., Anderko, L. & Stetzer, F. (2011). The impact of Prenatal Care Coordination on birth outcomes. *Journal of Obstetric, Gynecologic, and Neonatal Nursing, 40,* 98–108. [8]

Van Vliet, H. A., Grimes, D. A., Lopez, L. M., Schulz, K. F. & Helmerhorst, F. M. (2011). Triphasic versus monophasic oral contraceptives for contraception. *Cochrane Database of Systematic Reviews,* CD003553. [9]

van Wieringen, J. C., Wafelbakker, F., Verbrugge, H. P. & de Haas, J. H. (1971). *Growth diagrams 1965 Netherlands: Second National Survey on 0–24-year-olds.* Netherlands Institute for Preventative Medicine TNO, Leiden and Wolters Noordhoff. [10]

Vance, E. B. & Wagner, N. N. (1976). Written descriptions of orgasms: A study of sex differences. *Archives of Sexual Behavior, 5,* 87–98. [5]

Vander Ven, T. & Beck, J. (2009). Getting drunk and hooking up: An exploratory study of the relationship between alcohol intoxication and casual coupling in a university sample. *Sociological Spectrum, 29,* 626–648. [7]

VanderLaan, D. P., Forrester, D. L., Petterson, L. J. & Vasey, P. L. (2012). Offspring production among the extended relatives of Samoan men and *fa'afafine. PLOS ONE, 7,* e36088. [12]

Vanita, R. (2001). *Same-sex love in India: Readings from literature and history.* Palgrave Macmillan. [6]

VanOss Marin, B., Coyle, K. K., Gómez, C. A., Carvajal, S. C. & Kirby, D. B. (2000). Older boyfriends and girlfriends increase risk of sexual initiation in young adolescents. *Journal of Adolescent Health, 27,* 409–418. [10]

Vardi, Y., Har-Shai, Y., Gil, T. & Gruenwald, I. (2008). A critical analysis of penile enhancement procedures for patients with normal penile size: Surgical techniques, success, and complications. *European Urology, 54,* 1042–1050. [3]

Varghese, B., Maher, J. E., Peterman, T. A., Branson, B. M. & Steketee, R. W. (2002). Reducing the risk of sexual HIV transmission: Quantifying the per-act risk for HIV on the basis of choice of partner, sex act, and condom use. *Sexually Transmitted Diseases, 29,* 38–43. [15]

Vasey, P. L. (2006). The pursuit of pleasure: An evolutionary history of female homosexual behaviour in Japanese macaques. In: Sommer, V. & Vasey, P. L. (Eds.), *Homosexual behaviour in animals.* Cambridge University Press. [App. A]

Vasey, P. L. & Bartlett, N. H. (2007). What can the Samoan "Fa'afafine" teach us about the Western concept of gender identity disorder in childhood? *Perspectives in Biology and Medicine, 50,* 481–490. [4]

Vasey, P. L. & VanderLaan, D. P. (2009). Kin selection and the evolution of male androphilia. *Archives of Sexual Behavior, 38,* 170–171. [12]

Vatsyayana (1991). *The Kama Sutra of Vatsyayana* (R. F. Burton, Trans.). Arkana. [1]

Veale, J. F., Clarke, D. E. & Lomax, T. C. (2008). Sexuality of male-to-female transsexuals. *Archives of Sexual Behavior, 37,* 586–597. [4]

Vennemann, B. & Pollak, S. (2006). Death by hanging while watching violent pornographic videos on the Internet: Suicide or accidental autoerotic death? *International Journal of Legal Medicine, 120,* 110–114. [13]

Verrier, R. (2014). Porn production in Los Angeles plummets. *Los Angeles Times,* August 6. [17]

Vicinus, M. (1989). Distance and desire: English boarding school friendships, 1870–1920. In: Duberman, L., et al. (Eds.), *Hidden from*

history: Reclaiming the gay and lesbian past. New American Library. [7]

Vickerman, K. A. & Margolin, G. (2009). Rape treatment outcome research: Empirical findings and state of the literature. *Clinical Psychology Review, 29,* 431–448. [16]

Villarosa, L. (2013). *Chirlane McCrae: From gay trailblazer to politician's wife.* (www.essence.com/2013/05/09/politicians-wife-chirlane-mccray) [12]

Vingilis-Jaremko, L. & Maurer, D. (2013). The influence of symmetry on children's judgments of facial attractiveness. *Perception, 42,* 302–320. [5]

Virk, J., Zhang, J. & Olsen, J. (2007). Medical abortion and the risk of subsequent adverse pregnancy outcomes. *New England Journal of Medicine, 357,* 648–653. [9]

Virtuous Pedophiles. (2014). *Welcome to our website.* (www.virped.org) [13]

Voracek, M., Hofhansl, A. & Fisher, M. L. (2005). Clark and Hatfield's evidence of women's low receptivity to male strangers' sexual offers revisited. *Psychological Reports, 97,* 11–20. [7]

Voyer, D. (2011). Time limits and gender differences on paper-and-pencil tests of mental rotation: A meta-analysis. *Psychonomic Bulletin and Review, 18,* 267–277. [4]

Vrangalova, Z. (2014). *The Casual Sex Project.* (www.thecasualsexproject.com) [7]

Vrangalova, Z. & Savin-Williams, R. C. (2011). Adolescent sexuality and positive well-being: A group-norms approach. *Journal of Youth and Adolescence, 40,* 931–944. [10]

Waite, L. J. & Joyner, K. (2001). Emotional and physical satisfaction with sex in married, cohabiting, and dating sexual unions: Do men and women differ? In: Laumann, E. O. & Michael, R. T. (Eds.), *Sex, love, and health in America: Private choices and public policies.* University of Chicago Press. [11]

Waite, L. J., Laumann, E. O., Das, A. & Schumm, L. P. (2009). Sexuality: Measures of partnerships, practices, attitudes, and problems in the National Social Life, Health, and Aging Study. *Journal of Gerontology: Social Sciences, 64B,* i56–i66. [11]

Wald, A. (2006). Genital HSV-1 infections. *Sexually Transmitted Infections, 82,* 189–190. [15]

Waldinger, M. D. (2004). Lifelong premature ejaculation: From authority-based to evidence-based medicine. *BJUI, 93,* 201–207. [14]

Waldinger, M. D. & Olivier, B. (2004). Utility of selective serotonin reuptake inhibitors in premature ejaculation. *Current Opinion in Investigational Drugs, 5,* 743–747. [14]

Waldinger, M. D., de Lint, G. J., van Gils, A. P., Masir, F., Lakke, E., van Coevorden, R. S. & Schweitzer, D. H. (2013). Foot orgasm syndrome: A case report in a woman. *Journal of Sexual Medicine, 10,* 1926–1934. [5]

Waldinger, M. D., Venema, P. L., van Gils, A. P. & Schweitzer, D. H. (2009). New insights into restless genital syndrome: Static mechanical hyperesthesia and neuropathy of the nervus dorsalis clitoridis. *Journal of Sexual Medicine, 6,* 2778–2787. [14]

Waldinger, M. D., Venema, P. L., van Gils, A. P., de Lint, G. J. & Schweitzer, D. H. (2011). Stronger evidence for small fiber sensory neuropathy in restless genital syndrome: Two case reports in males. *Journal of Sexual Medicine, 8,* 325–330. [14]

Waldinger, M. D., Zwinderman, A. H. & Olivier, B. (2001). Antidepressants and ejaculation: A double-blind, randomized, placebo- controlled, fixed-dose study with paroxetine, sertraline, and nefazodone. *Journal of Clinical Psychopharmacology, 21,* 293–297. [14]

Walker, J., Archer, J. & Davies, M. (2005). Effects of rape on men: A descriptive analysis. *Archives of Sexual Behavior, 34,* 69–80. [16]

Walker, L. E. A. (2009). *The battered woman syndrome* (3rd ed.). Springer. [16]

Walker, R. S., Flinn, M. V. & Hill, K. R. (2010). Evolutionary history of partible paternity in lowland South America. *Proceedings of the National Academy of Sciences of the United States of America, 107,* 19195–19200. [1]

Wallen, K. (2000). The development of hypothalamic control of sexual behavior. In: Bourguignon, J.-P. & Plant, T. M. (Eds.), *The onset of puberty in perspective.* Elsevier. [10]

Wallen, K. & Lloyd, E. A. (2011). Female sexual arousal: Genital anatomy and orgasm in intercourse. *Hormones and Behavior, 59,* 780–792. [14]

Waller, K. L. & MacDonald, T. K. (2010). Trait self-esteem moderates the effect of initiator status on emotional and cognitive responses to romantic relationship dissolution. *Journal of Personality, 78,* 1271–1299. [7]

Wallien, M. S. & Cohen-Kettenis, P. T. (2008). Psychosexual outcome of gender-dysphoric children. *Journal of the American Academy of Child and Adolescent Psychiatry, 47,* 1413–1423. [4]

Wallin, D. J. (2007). *Attachment in psychotherapy.* Guilford. [7]

Wang, H., Yuan, J., Hu, X., Tao, K., Liu, J. & Hu, D. (2014). The effectiveness and safety of avanafil for erectile dysfunction: A systematic review and meta-analysis. *Current Medical Research and Opinion, 30,* 1565–1571. [14]

Ward, T. & Beech, A. R. (2008). An integrated theory of sexual offending. In: Laws, D. R. & O'Donohue, W. T. (Eds.), *Sexual deviance: Theory, assessment, and treatment.* Guilford. [13]

Warner, L. & Steiner, M. J. (2007). Male condoms. In: Hatcher, R. A., et al. (Eds.), *Contraceptive technology* (19th ed.). Ardent Media. [9]

Warner, P. & Bancroft, J. (1987). A regional clinical service for sexual problems: A three-year survey. *Sexual and Marital Therapy, 2,* 115–126. [14]

Warren, J. T., Harvey, S. M. & Henderson, J. T. (2010). Do depression and low self-esteem follow abortion among adolescents? Evidence from a national study. *Perspectives on Sexual and Reproductive Health, 42,* 230–235. [9]

Washington, H. A. (2007). Medical apartheid: The dark history of medical experimentation on black Americans from colonial times to the present. Doubleday. [15]

Wassersug, R., Walker, L. & Robinson, J. (2014). *Androgen deprivation therapy: An essential guide for prostate cancer patients and their loved ones.* Demos Health. [1]

Watanabe, T. (2014). More college men are fighting back against sexual misconduct cases. *Los Angeles Times,* June 7. [16]

Waterman, J. M. (2010). The adaptive function of masturbation in a promiscuous African ground squirrel. *PLOS ONE, 5,* e13060. doi:10.1371/journal.pone.0013060. [6]

Wawer, M. J., Gray, R. H., Sewankambo, N. K., Serwadda, D., Li, X., Laeyendecker, O., Kiwanuka, N., et al. (2005). Rates of HIV-1 transmission per coital act, by stage of HIV-1 infection, in Rakai, Uganda. *Journal of Infectious Diseases, 191,* 1403–1409. [15]

Wax, J. R., Cartin, A., Pinette, M. G. & Blackstone, J. (2004). Patient choice cesarean: An evidence-based review. *Obstetrical and Gynecological Survey, 59,* 601–616. [8]

Weinberg, M. S., Shaver, F. M. & Williams, C. J. (1999). Gendered sex work in the San Francisco tenderloin. *Archives of Sexual Behavior, 28,* 503–521. [17]

Weinberger, L. E., Sreenivasan, S., Garrick, T. & Osran, H. (2005). The impact of surgical castration on sexual recidivism risk among sexually violent predatory offenders. *Journal of the American Academy of Psychiatry and the Law, 33,* 16–36. [13]

Weiner, L. & Avery-Clark, C. (2014). Sensate focus: Clarifying the Masters and Johnson's model. *Sexual and Relationship Therapy, 29,* 307–319. [14]

Weinrott, M. R. & Saylor, M. (1991). Self-report of crimes committed by sex offenders. *Journal of Interpersonal Violence, 6,* 286–300. [16]

Weisfeld, G. E., Czilli, T., Phillips, K. A., Gall, J. A. & Lichtman, C. M. (2003). Possible olfaction-based mechanisms in human kin recognition and inbreeding avoidance. *Journal of Experimental Child Psychology, 85,* 279–295. [5]

Weiss, E. (2004). *Surviving domestic violence: Voices of women who broke free.* Volcano. [16]

Weiss, K. G. (2010). Male sexual victimization: Examining men's experiences of rape and sexual assault. *Men and Masculinities, 12,* 275–298. [16]

Weiss, R. (2013). Cruise control: Understanding sex addiction in gay men (2nd ed.). Gentle Path. [14]

Weller, A. & Weller, L. (1997). Menstrual synchrony under optimal conditions: Bedouin families. *Journal of Comparative Psychology, 111,* 143–151. [2]

Weller, A. & Weller, L. (1998). Prolonged and very intensive contact may not be conducive to menstrual synchrony. *Psychoneuroendocrinology, 23,* 19–32. [2]

Weller, L., Weller, A. & Avinir, O. (1995). Menstrual synchrony: Only in roommates who are close friends? *Physiology and Behavior, 58,* 883–889. [2]

Wellings, K., Field, J., Johnson, A. M. & Wadsworth, J. (1994). *Sexual behavior in Britain: The National Survey of Sexual Attitudes and Lifestyles.* Penguin . [12]

Wellings, K., Field, J., Johnson, A. M. & Wadsworth, J. (1994). *Sexual behavior in Britain: The National Survey of Sexual Attitudes and Lifestyles.* Penguin. [1, 5]

Wellings, K., Macdowall, W., Catchpole, M. & Goodrich, J. (1999). Seasonal variations in sexual activity and their implications for sexual health promotion. *Journal of the Royal Society of Medicine, 92,* 60–64. [6]

Wellman, J. D. & McCoy, S. K. (2014). Walking the straight and narrow: Examining the role of traditional gender norms in sexual prejudice. *Psychology of Men and Masculinity, 15,* 181–190. [12]

Weng, X., Odouli, R. & Li, D. K. (2008). Maternal caffeine consumption during pregnancy and the risk of miscarriage: A prospective cohort study. *American Journal of Obstetrics and Gynecology, 198,* 279. [8]

Werner, M. A., Ford, T., Pacik, P. T., Ferrara, M. & Marcus, B. S. (2014). Botox for the treatment of vaginismus: A case report. *Journal of Women's Health Care, 3,* published online February 26. [14]

Wessells, H., Lue, T. F. & McAninch, J. W. (1996). Complications of penile lengthening and augmentation seen at 1 referral center. *Journal of Urology, 155,* 1617–1620. [3]

Whipple, B., Myers, B. & Komisaruk, B. R. (1998). Male multiple ejaculatory orgasms: A case study. *Journal of Sex Education and Therapy, 23,* 157–162. [5]

Whipple, B., Ogden, G. & Komisaruk, B. R. (1992). Physiological correlates of imagery-induced orgasm in women. *Archives of Sexual Behavior, 21,* 121–133. [6]

Whisman, M. A. & Snyder, D. K. (2007). Sexual infidelity in a national sample of American women: Differences in prevalence and correlates as a function of method of assessment. *Journal of Family Psychology, 21,* 147–154. [7]

White House. (2011). *Statement by the President on the killing of David Kato.* (www.whitehouse.gov/the-press-office/2011/01/27/statement-president-killing-david-kato) [12]

White House. (2014). *Not alone: Protecting students from sexual assault.* (www.whitehouse.gov/the-press-office/2014/04/29/fact-sheet-not-alone-protecting-students-sexual-assault) [16]

White, N. D., Hill, D. M. & Bodemeier, S. (2008). Male condoms that break in use do so mostly by a "blunt puncture" mechanism. *Contraception, 77,* 360–365. [9]

Whitehead, B. D. & Popenoe, D. (2000). *Changes in teen attitudes toward marriage, cohabitation and children: 1975–1995.* National Marriage Project. [11]

Wiedemann, K. (2009). *Guilty verdict in SW Wisconsin grave digging case.* (www.kcrg.com/news/local/51327922.html) [13]

Wilcox, A. J., Day Baird, D., Dunson, D. B., McConnaughey, D. R., Kesner, J. S. & Weinberg, C. R. (2004). On the frequency of intercourse around ovulation: Evidence for biological influences. *Human Reproduction, 19,* 1539–1543. [2]

Wilcox, A. J., Dunson, D. & Baird, D. D. (2000). The timing of the "fertile window" in the menstrual cycle: Day specific estimates from a prospective study. *British Medical Journal, 321,* 1259–1262. [9]

Wilcox, A. J., Weinberg, C. R. & Baird, D. D. (1995). Timing of sexual intercourse in relation to ovulation: Effects on the probability of conception, survival of the pregnancy, and sex of the baby. *New England Journal of Medicine, 333,* 1517–1521. [8]

Wilcox, W. B. & Marquardt, E. (2011). *When marriage disappears: The new Middle America.* Broadway. [1]

Williams Institute. (2012). *Serving our youth: Findings from a national survey of services providers working with lesbian, gay, bisexual and transgender youth who are homeless or at risk of becoming homeless.* (williamsinstitute. law.ucla.edu/wp-content/uploads/Durso-Gates-LGBT-Homeless-Youth-Survey-July-2012.pdf) [12]

Williams, C. J. & Weinberg, M. S. (2003). Zoophilia in men: A study of sexual interest in animals. *Archives of Sexual Behavior, 32,* 523–535. [13]

Williams, P. T. (2013). Breast cancer mortality vs. exercise and breast size in runners and walkers. *PLOS ONE, 8,* e80616. [2]

Williams, T. J., Pepitone, M. E., Christensen, S. E., Cooke, B. M., Huberman, A. D., Breedlove, N. J., et al. (2000). Finger-length ratios and sexual orientation. *Nature, 404,* 455–456. [12]

Williams, W. L. (1986). *The spirit and the flesh: Sexual diversity in American Indian culture.* Beacon. [1, 4, 12]

Willness, C. R., Steel, P. & Lee, K. (2007). A meta-analysis of the antecedents and consequences of workplace sexual harassment. *Personnel Psychology, 60,* 127–162. [16]

Wilson, C. A. & Davies, D. C. (2007). The control of sexual differentiation of the reproductive system and brain. *Reproduction, 133,* 331–359. [4]

Wilson, J. Q. (2011). Hard times, fewer crimes. *Wall Street Journal,* May 28. [16]

Wilson, R. J. (2014). *Circles of Support and Accountability.* (www.robinjwilson.com/circles.shtml) [13]

Wilson, R. J., Cortoni, F. & McWhinnie, A. J. (2009). Circles of Support and Accountability: A Canadian national replication of outcome findings. *Sexual Abuse, 21,* 412–430. [13]

Wilson, S. K., Delk, J. R., II & Billups, K. L. (2001). Treating symptoms of female sexual arousal disorder with the Eros-Clitoral Therapy Device. *Journal of Gender Specific Medicine, 4,* 54–58. [14]

Wimpissinger, F., Tscherney, R. & Stackl, W. (2009). Magnetic resonance imaging of female prostate pathology. *Journal of Sexual Medicine, 6,* 1704–1711. [5]

Wincze, J. P. (2009). Enhancing sexuality: A problem-solving approach to treating dysfunction (2nd ed.). Oxford University Press. [14]

Wisner, K. L., Sit, D. K., McShea, M. C., Rizzo, D. M., Zoretich, R. A., Hughes, C. L., et al. (2013). Onset timing, thoughts of self-harm, and diagnoses in postpartum women with screen-positive depression findings. *JAMA Psychiatry, 70,* 490–498. [8]

Wlodarski, R. & Dunbar, R. I. M. (2014). What's in a kiss? The effect of romantic kissing on mate desirability. *Evolutionary Psychology, 12,* 178–199. [6]

Wolfram, S. (2013). *Data science of the Facebook world.* (blog.stephenwolfram.com/2013/04/data-science-of-the-facebook-world) [7]

Wolinska, J. & Spaak, P. (2009). The cost of being common: Evidence from natural *Daphnia* populations. *Evolution, 63,* 1893–1901. [App. A]

Wollan, M. (2012). San Francisco officials approve a ban on public nudity. *New York Times,* November 20. [3]

Womack, C. (2014). Police: Sarasota High School student led prostitution ring. *Sarasota Herald-Tribune,* November 24. [17]

Women's Health Initiative. (2002). Risks and benefits of estrogen plus progestin in healthy postmenopausal women: Principal results from the Women's Health Initiative randomized controlled trial. *JAMA, 288,* 321–333. [11]

Wong, W. I., Pasterski, V., Hindmarsh, P. C., Geffner, M. E. & Hines, M. (2013). Are there parental socialization effects on the sex-typed behavior of individuals with congenital adrenal hyperplasia? *Archives of Sexual Behavior, 42,* 381–391. [4]

Wood, J. M., Koch, P. B. & Mansfield, P. K. (2006). Women's sexual desire: A feminist critique. *Journal of Sex Research, 43,* 236–244. [14]

Woods, L. N. & Emery, R. E. (2002). The cohabitation effect on divorce: Causation or selection? *Journal of Divorce and Remarriage, 37,* 101–122. [11]

Woollaston, V. (2014). *California pornographers turn to CGI airbrushing to make compulsory condoms disappear.* (www.dailymail.co.uk/sciencetech/article-2561982/How-CGI-keeping-porn-sexy-Digital-penises-airbrushing-help-hide-actors-condoms.html) [17]

Working Group for a New View of Women's Sexual Problems (2002). A new view of women's sexual problems. In: Kaschak, E. & Tiefer, L. (Eds.), *A new view of women's sexual problems.* Haworth. [14]

World Association for Sexual Health. (2007). *Sexual health for the millennium: A declaration and technical document.* (176.32.230.27/worldsexology.org/wp-content/uploads/2013/08/millennium-declaration-english.pdf) [1]

World Health Organization. (2010). *Female genital mutilation.* (www.who.int/mediacentre/factsheets/fs241/en) [2]

World Health Organization. (2014). *Male circumcision for HIV prevention.* (www.who.int/hiv/topics/malecircumcision/en) [15]

World Professional Association for Transgender Health. (2008). *Standards of care for the health of transsexual, transgender, and gender-nonconforming people, Version 7.* (www.wpath.org/uploaded_files/140/files/IJT%20SOC,%20V7.pdf) [4]

Wright, J. D., Ananth, C. V., Lewin, S. N., Burke, W. M., Lu, Y. S., Neugut, A. I., et al. (2013a). Robotically assisted vs laparoscopic hysterectomy among women with benign gynecologic disease. *JAMA, 309,* 689–698. [2]

Wright, J. D., Herzog, T. J., Tsui, J., Ananth, C. V., Lewin, S. N., Lu, Y. S., et al. (2013b). Nationwide trends in the performance of inpatient hysterectomy in the United States. *Obstetrics and Gynecology, 122,* 233–241. [2]

Wright, J. L., Lin, D. W. & Stanford, J. L. (2012). Circumcision and the risk of prostate cancer. *Cancer, 118,* 4437–4443. [3]

Wright, L. (2001). *The bear book II: Further readings in the history and evolution of a gay male subculture.* Routledge. [12]

Wroblewski, P., Gustafsson, J. & Selvaggi, G. (2013). Sex reassignment surgery for transsexuals. *Current Opinion in Endocrinology, Diabetes, and Obesity, 20,* 570–574. [4]

Wu, F. C., Tajar, A., Beynon, J. M., Pye, S. R., Silman, A. J., Finn, J. D., et al. (2010). Identification of late-onset hypogonadism in middle-aged and elderly men. *New England Journal of Medicine, 363,* 123–135. [11]

Wurtele, S. K., Simons, D. & Moreno, T. (2013). Sexual interest in children among an online sample of men and women: Prevalence and correlates. *Sexual Abuse,* published online November 11. [13]

Wylie, K. R. & Eardley, I. (2007). Penile size and the "small penis syndrome." *BJUI, 99,* 1449–1455. [3]

Xie, R. H., He, G., Liu, A., Bradwejn, J., Walker, M. & Wen, S. W. (2007). Fetal gender and postpartum depression in a cohort of Chinese women. *Social Science and Medicine, 65,* 680–684. [8]

Xu, X., Aron, A., Brown, L., Cao, G., Feng, T. & Weng, X. (2011). Reward and motivation systems: A brain mapping study of early-stage intense romantic love in Chinese participants. *Human Brain Mapping, 32,* 249–257. [7]

Yale Herald. (2011). *Title IX complaint press release.* (yaleherald.com/uncategorized/title-ix-complaint-press-release) [16]

Yang, Z. & Schank, J. C. (2006). Women do not synchronize their menstrual cycles. *Human Nature, 17,* 433–447. [2]

Yarab, P. E., Sensibaugh, C. C. & Allgeier, E. R. (1998). More than just sex: Gender differences in the incidence of self-defined unfaithful behavior in heterosexual dating relationships. *Journal of Psychology and Human Sexuality, 10,* 45–57. [7]

Yardley, J. (2014). Pope asks forgiveness from victims of sex abuse. *New York Times,* July 7. [13]

Yonkers, K. A., O'Brien, P. M. & Eriksson, E. (2008). Premenstrual syndrome. *Lancet, 371,* 1200–1210. [2]

Yonkers, K. A., Pearlstein, T. B. & Gotman, N. (2013). A pilot study to compare fluoxetine, calcium, and placebo in the treatment of premenstrual syndrome. *Journal of Clinical Psychopharmacology, 33,* 614–620. [2]

YouGov. (2012). *Polling the political debate on the legalization of prostitution.* (today.yougov.com/news/2012/03/23/legalization-of-prostitution) [17]

Young-Bruehl, E. (1996). *The anatomy of prejudices.* Harvard University Press. [12]

Young, L. J. & Wang, Z. (2004). The neurobiology of pair bonding. *Nature Neuroscience, 7,* 1048–1054. [7]

Yule, M. A., Brotto, L. A. & Gorzalka, B. B. (2014). Biological markers of asexuality: Handedness, birth order, and finger length ratios in self-identified asexual men and women. *Archives of Sexual Behavior, 43,* 299–310. [5]

Yupanqui, T. (1999). *Becoming woman: Apache female puberty sunrise ceremony.* (www.

webwinds.com/yupanqui/apachesunrise.htm#Introduction) [10]

Zahavi, A. & Zahavi, A. (1997). *The handicap principle: A missing piece of Darwin's puzzle.* Oxford University Press. [App. A]

Zaviacic, M. & Whipple, B. (1993). Update on the female prostate and the phenomenon of female ejaculation. *Journal of Sex Research, 30,* 148–151. [2]

Zeki, S. (2007). The neurobiology of love. *FEBS Letters, 581,* 2575–2579. [7]

Zerjal, T., Xue, Y., Bertorelle, G., Wells, R. S., Bao, W., Zhu, S., et al. (2003). The genetic legacy of the Mongols. *American Journal of Human Genetics, 72,* 717–721. [16]

Zhang, J., Troendle, J., Reddy, U. M., Laughon, S. K., Branch, D. W., Burkman, R., et al. (2010). Contemporary cesarean delivery practice in the United States. *American Journal of Obstetrics and Gynecology, 203,* 326 e321–326 e310. [8]

Zhou, W., Yang, X., Chen, K., Cai, P., He, S. & Jiang, Y. (2014). Chemosensory communication of gender through two human steroids in a sexually dimorphic manner. *Current Biology, 24,* 1091–1095. [5]

Zhu, B., Kong, A., Sun, Z. & Zhu, R. (2011a). Transition from paroxysmal disorder in infancy to the masturbatory orgasm in childhood. *International Journal of Sexual Health, 23,* 278–281. [10]

Zhu, W., Chen, C. J., Thomas, C. E., Anderson, J. E., Jerse, A. E. & Sparling, P. F. (2011b). Vaccines for gonorrhea: Can we rise to the challenge? *Frontiers in Microbiology, 2,* 124. [15]

Zivony, A. & Lobel, T. (2014). The invisible stereotypes of bisexual men. *Archives of Sexual Behavior, 43,* 1165–1176. [12]

Zollner, U. & Dietl, J. (2012). Perinatal risks after IVF and ICSI. *Journal of Perinatal Medicine, 41,* 17–22. [8]

Zucker, K. J. (2005). Gender identity disorder in children and adolescents. *Annual Review of Clinical Psychology, 1,* 467–492. [4]

Zverina, J., Hampl, R., Sulocava, J. & Starka, L. (1990). Hormonal status and sexual behaviour of 16 men after surgical castration. *Archivio Italiano di Urologia, Nefrologia, Andrologia, 62,* 55–58. [13]

Zweig, J. M., Dank, M., Yahner, J. & Lachman, P. (2013). The rate of cyber dating abuse among teens and how it relates to other forms of teen dating violence. *Journal of Youth and Adolescence, 42,* 1063–1077. [16]

Author Index

Subject Index

Entries with an italic *f* next to the page number indicate that the information will be found in a figure. Entries with an italic *b* next to the page number indicate that the information will be found in a box. Entries with an italic *t* next to the page number indicate that the information will be found in a table.

National Organization for Women (NOW), 375, 499
National Partnership for Women & Families, 517
National Survey of Family Growth, 2011, 336
National Survey of Sexual Attitudes and Lifestyles (NSSAL), 15, 164
National Survey of Sexual Health and Behavior (NSSHB), 15
Native American populations
STI rates, 463
"two-spirit" people within, 14–15
navigating skills, 103
necking, 163
necrophilia, 419–420, 420*f*
Neisseria gonorrhoeae, 464*t*
Nelson, Esther, 533*b*
neonates
adaptation by, 255
circumcision of, 63*f*
nervous system
components of, 574*b*–575*b*
sex and, 573–582
neuromuscular junctions, 574*b*, 576*b*
neurons, 574*b*, 575*b*
neuroses, 11
neuroticism, 99
neurotransmitters, 426–427, 574*b*, 576*b*
New Life Church, Colorado Springs, 391
newborns
adaptation by, 255
circumcision, 63*f*
Newcomb, Michael, 485
Newmahr, Staci, 16, 409*b*
Nexplanon, 298, 298*f*
Next Choice One Dose, 289–290
Nickles, Don, 396
nitric oxide, 69
no-fault divorces, 344*b*
nocturnal emissions, 70
nocturnal orgasms, 70
Nolan, Avril, 486*b*
non-cohabiting relationships, 203, 205
noncoital sex, 328–328
nongonococcal urethritis (NGU), 473
nonmarital sex, 6, 195–196
norbolethone, 80*b*
norethindrone, 281
Notel experiment, 106–107
nuclei, CNS, 574*b*, 576*b*
nucleus accumbens, 148
nudibranchs, 556*f*
nudity
children and, 307*f*
cultural regulation of, 81–83
impact of society on, 6
nutrition, during pregnancy, 242–243
NuvaRing, 284, 284*f*

O

Oasis Bordello, 527*b*
obesity
attraction to, 402
breast cancer and, 53
object fetishism, 404, 404*f*

objectophilia, 404
objectum sexuality, 404
O'Brien, Mark, 182*b*
obscene, definition of, 540
obscene telephone calls, 413
obsessive-compulsive disorder, 424
obsessive relational intrusion, 212, 519
obstetric ultrasound, 234*b*
occupations, choice of, 383–384
Ocean, Frank, 397
Oculus Rift, 542
OKCupid, 129
older adults
partner gaps, 358*f*
sex drive in, 358*f*
sex lives of, 357–361
omnisexuality, 395
Online College Social Life Survey, 198
Onuf's nucleus, 580, 581
openness, gender and, 99
opiates, sexual arousal and, 142*b*
oral cancer, 477
oral herpes, 474
oral sex, 165*f*, 166*f*, 485–486
orangutans, 175, 566
orchitis, 75*b*
organism, phantom, 184
orgasmic platform, 145
orgasms
brain activity during, 13*f*, 147–149
fake, 450, 581
foot-related, 148*b*
gender gap in, 15
male, 79*f*
multiple, 150–151
nocturnal, 70
sexual response cycle, 145–147
orgies, sculpture of, 179*f*
The Origin of the World (Courbet), 23
Ortho Evra patches, 283–284, 283*f*
Ortho Micronor, 281
Ortho-Novum 7/7/7, 278
os, 32
osteoporosis, 355, 355*f*
Oswald, Andrew, 157*b*
outer labia (labia majora), 23
outercourse, 163, 288
ova, 552
depletion of, 354
description of, 37
ovarian cancer, 40, 279
ovarian cysts, 40
ovaries, 37–40, 37*f*
oviducts, 36–37
ovulation, 37, 236
oxytocin, 148
action of, 39*t*
pair bond formation and, 207–208
production of, 39*t*

P

pair bonds, 207, 564
pansexuality, 395
Pap tests, 34, 34*f*, 477
ParaGard IUD, 276, 290
paraphilias, 410–412
prevalence of, 412*f*
paraphilic disorders, 411

biological factors, 422–423
courtship disorders, 423–424
cycle of abuse, 424
escape route, 424
hypersexuality and, 424
learning process, 423
obsessive-compulsive disorder and, 424
theories of causation, 424–427
paraphimosis, 66
paraplegia, 184
parasympathetic nervous system, 575*b*, 576*b*
paraurethral glands, 31, 146*b*
Parents, Families and Friends of Lesbians and Gays (PFLAG), 383
Parents Television Council (PTC), 546
parthenogenesis, 553
partialism, 402
partible paternity, 6*b*
partner gaps, 358*f*
partner status, masturbation and, 159*f*
passion, definition of, 208
Patand, Susan, 554
Patel, Purvi, 300*b*
paternity tests, 565
Pavlovian conditioning, 141
peacocks, 560*f*
pearly penile papules, 488*f*
pedophilia, 415–417
age of onset, 416
child molestation and, 416*f*
familial, 422*f*
pedophilic disorders, 416
pelvic examinations, 34, 35
pelvic floor muscles, 29, 70
pelvic floor stimulating center (PFSC), 581
pelvic inflammatory disease (PID), 236, 240, 469
chlamydia and, 472
description of, 37
IUDs and, 277
pelvic nerves, 577–578
pelvic organ stimulating center (POSC), 581
penile bulb, 65
penile cancer, 66–67
penile implants, 442
penile strain gauge, 134*f*
penis
description of, 63
development of, 316*f*
erection of, 68–71, 69*f*, 578–579, 578*f*
functions of, 63–68
internal structure of, 65*f*
medical problems, 66
sensory innervation of, 69*f*
size of, 67*b*
Perel, Esther, 347, 348
perfect-use failure rates, 268
perimenopause, 354
perimetrium, 33
perineal massage, 250
perineum, 22*f*, 29
periodic abstinence methods, 285–286
peripheral nervous system, 575*b*, 576*b*

permethrin, 465
permissiveness, attitudes toward, 99
Perry, Katy, 197*f*
persistent genital arousal disorder, 444
personality
definition of, 98
sexual attractiveness and, 130–133
personhood, gender and, 97–99
perversions, 11
pesticides, sperm counts and, 231*b*
petting, 163
Peyronie's disease, 66
phalaropes, 562
phalloplasty, 114
pheromones, 131*b*, 372, 559
phimosis, 66
phone sex, 539
photocells, 31*f*
phthalates, 231*b*
physical strength, gender and, 102
piercings
clitoral hood, 25*f*
Prince Albert, 66*f*
pimps, 527*b*, 528
Pitt, Brad, 237, 338*f*
pituitary gland
hormone levels and, 80–81
hormone production and, 38*b*
oxytocin synthesis, 148
placenta
expulsion of, 255–256
function of, 239
placenta previa, 247
Plan B One-Step, 289–290
Planned Parenthood Federation, 267*b*
plateau phase, 144–145
play
gender differences, 101–102
hormones and, 104*f*
primate, 103*b*
sex toys, 176–177
Playboy, 541
Pliny the Elder, 45*b*
point-of-view pornography, 541f
pollution, sperm counts and, 231b
polyamory, 342–343, 342*f*
polyandry, 341–342, 564
polycystic ovary syndrome (PCOS), 40
polygamy, 564
definition of, 7, 340
Mormon, 341*b*
societies permitting, 340–342
polygyny, 340, 564
polyisoprene condoms, 271
polyurethane condoms, 271
pons, 576*b*, 581
population density, STIs and, 8
porn stars, 542*b*
pornography
effects of, 544–547
gender differences, 100
hard core, 541
history of, 539–543
lesbian, 534*f*
personal point of view, 542*b*
soft core, 541
technology and, 540–543

S

sadism, 407
sadomasochism (S/M), 407–410
salicylic acid, 318
saline-induced abortion, 296
Salvation Army, 524
Sam, Michael, 384, 384f
same-sex couples, scripts of, 205
Sanger, Margaret, 9, 266, 267b
satin bowerbirds, 561, 561f
scabies (*Sarcoptes scabiei*), 464t, 466–467, 466f
Schaeffer, Rebecca, 519
"school for johns," 526
Schubach, Gary, 146b
Schultz, Willibrord, 169b
Schwartz, Pepper, 348
Scientific-Humanitarian Committee, 375
"scissoring," 163
scorpionfly, 566
script theory, 16
scrotoplasty, 114
scrotum, 569
  anatomy, 71f
  temperature regulation by, 70–71
seagulls, 562
Seasonale, 280
seasonality, sex, 171b
Seasonique, 280
Second Life game, 542
secondary amenorrhea, 321
secondary disorders, 433
secondary dysmenorrhea, 48
secondary sexual characteristics, 50
secondary syphilis, 468
selection, disruptive, 555f
selection effects, 339
selective serotonin reuptake inhibitors (SSRIs), 426–427, 451–452
self-examination
  breast, 54, 55b
  genital, 33b, 33f
  testicular, 75f
semen, 558
  description of, 72, 74–77
  glandular contributions to, 77f
  pH of, 77
seminal emission, 78f, 580
seminal nurture, 181
seminal vesicles, 73
seminiferous tubules, 72, 73f
seniors. *see* older adults
sensate focus, 433, 434b
senses of humor, 132
serial monogamy, 205, 330
serial orgasms, 150–151
seroconversion, 482
serotonin, 92, 435
sex
  in advertising, 544–547, 547f
  biology of, 80b, 574b–576b
  definition, 4
  development, 88–93
  economical approach to, 16–18
  evolution and, 541–571
  forced, 567f
  functions of, 8, 568
  in groups, 177–179

happiness and, 157b
interest in, 442
justification for, 208
the media and, 546–547
negotiation of, 201–203
nervous system and, 573–582
noncoital, 288, 288f
during pregnancy, 247, 247f
quality of, 178b
sales value of, 546–547
seasonality, 171b
social discussions on, 9–10
study of mechanisms in, 12
suggestibility and, 313b
talking with children about, 308b
unforced, 567f
sex addition, 451
sex-change surgery, 113–115
sex chromosomes, 88, 557
sex determination, 556
sex drive
  androgens and, 79
  gender differences, 99
sex education, 10
sex hormones, gender differences and, 103–104
Sex Offender Treatment and Evaluation Project (SOTEP), 426
sex offenders
  density of, 422f
  repeat offenses, 422
sex pheromones, 131b
sex play, toys in, 176–177
sex ratios, sexual negotiations and, 17
sex-reassignment surgery, 114, 114f, 115f
sex selection, child, 234b
sex steroids. *see also* Specific steroids
  actions of, 50
  description of, 38, 39t, 40
sex surrogates, 182b, 433
sex therapists, 433
sex therapy, 454–455
sex tourism, 535–536
sex toys, 175–177
sex traders, 524
sex trafficking, 534–536, 535f
sex work, 538–539
sex workers, 524
sexology, 17
sexting, 82
sexual activity
  consent in, 408–409
  early, 314–315, 314f
sexual arousal, 455–456
  brain regions and, 140
  date rape and, 498f
  fantasies and, 138
  hormones and, 140–141
  response cycle for, 143–152
  response to partners, 139–140
  roots of, 137–142
sexual arrangements, 563–564
Sexual Assault Resource Center, 533b
sexual assaults
  definition of, 494
  steps after, 501b

sexual attitudes
  changes over time, 195–196, 195f
  demographic factors in, 192–195, 193f
sexual attraction, 124. *see also* attractiveness
sexual behavior, 155–188
  children's, 309
  cultural variations, 179–181
  diversity of, 156
  female couples, 385
  gender differences, 101
  male couples, 385
  overview, 156f
  social influences, 323–325
  STI risk reduction and, 485–487
  variety in, 402–410
sexual coercion, 100
sexual desire, 151
  lack of, 452–454
  menopause and, 354–355
sexual dimorphism, 580
sexual disorders, 431–458, 432
sexual exploration, adolescent, 322–329
sexual expression
  in children, 306–311
  gender differences, 100
  of young adults, 336–343
sexual harassment, 514
  ending, 517–518
  harm caused by, 517
  onset of, 516–517, 517t
  workplace, 515–516
sexual intercourse, 29
sexual interest/arousal disorder, 443–444
sexual jealousy
  description of, 218
  gender differences, 100
sexual maturation, puberty and, 92
sexual minorities, sexual disorders and, 453b. *see also* Specific minorities
sexual monogamy, 220, 564
sexual orientation, 365–399
  brain structure and, 373, 373f
  changing of, 388–389
  definition of, 12, 97, 366
  distribution of, 366f
  empathy gaps and, 14
  gender differences, 100
  global perspectives on, 380b
  hypothalamus and, 372f
  Magnus Hirschfeld's theory of, 11b
  masturbation and, 161f
  prenatal hormone theory of, 371–374, 371f
  sexual assault and, 505–506, 505f
  Sigmund Freud's theory on, 11b
  socialization and, 370–371
  traits and, 367–368
sexual relationships, 191–224
  cost-benefits analysis of, 16
  life experiences and, 213–214
  love and, 207–210
  moral judgments about, 192–195, 192f
  motivations for, 192
sexual reproduction, 552
  genetic benefits of, 554

paradox of, 552f
research goals, 554–555
theories of, 552–555
sexual response cycles, 143–152
  aging and, 359
  gender differences, 100
  genital changes in men, 144f
  genital changes in women, 143f
  patterns within, 149–150, 149f
  refractory periods, 151
  resolution phase, 149
  satisfaction with, 150
sexual revolution, 10
sexual sadism disorders, 411
sexual scripts, 108
sexual selection, 557
sexual violence. *see also* rape
  criminal justice system and, 110f
  as paraphilia, 420–421
  pornography and, 545
  prevention of, 503b
  study of, 13
sexual webcamming, 539
sexuality
  during adulthood, 335–362
  atypical, 400–429
  benefits of study of, 4
  changes over time, 4–11
  childhood, 306–311
  definition, 4
  deviant, 403f
  impact of childbirth on, 258–259
  impact of parenthood, 258–259
  impact of society on, 5–8
  menstrual cycle and, 44
  of older adults, 359–360
  psychological approaches to, 13–16
  sex differences in, 99–102
  social movements affecting, 10
  study of, 12–18
sexually explicit materials, 540
sexually-transmitted infections (STIs), 461–490
  basic facts, 464t
  cultural influences on, 8
  legal aspects of, 486b
  partner notification, 466–467
  prostitution and, 524
  protection against, 270–271
  risk reduction, 484–487
  U.S incidence, 461–465, 462t
Sheen, Charlie, 511f
"shemales," 529
Shiite Islam, temporary marriages, 339–343
Shimizu, Jenny, 384
Shippee, Sheena, 450
siblings, influence of, 105–106, 105f
side-by-side position, 170f
sildenafil (Viagra), 271
Silver Ring Thing, 324
Simon, William, 108
sinusoids, 69, 69f, 578
Siri, 542b
situational disorders, 433
"69," 166f
16 and Pregnant, 324
Skyla, 276
sleep problems, menopausal, 355
slimness-fatness continuum, 127–128